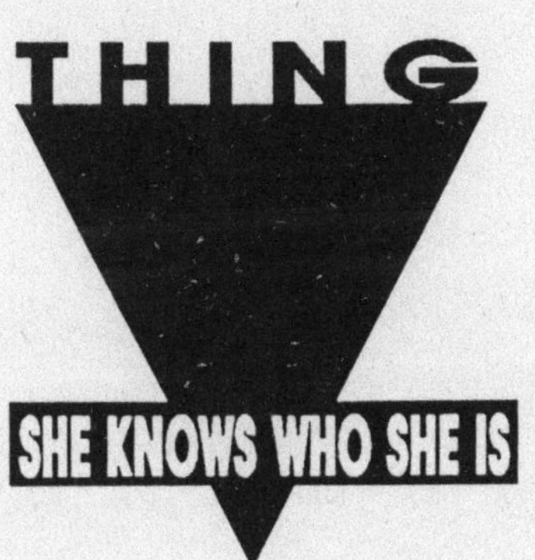

Primary Information

THING

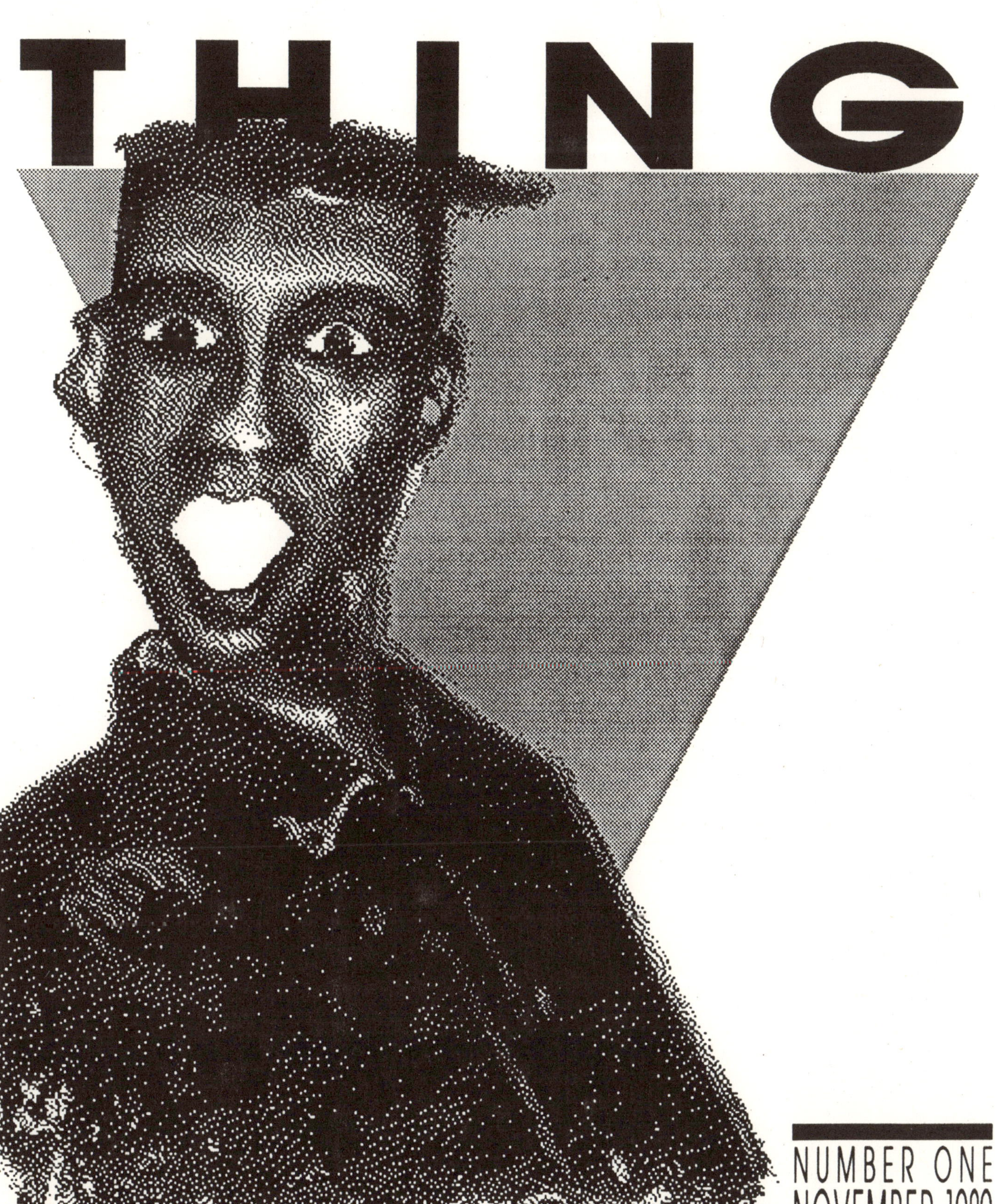

NUMBER ONE
NOVEMBER 1989

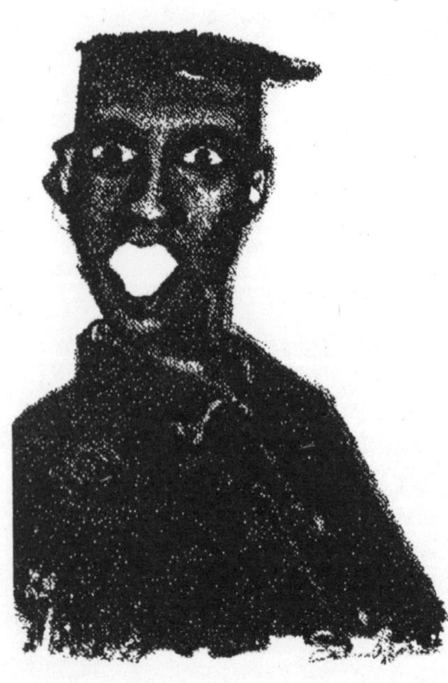

ON THE COVER:
From "My Husband the Thing"
Oil pastels on paper of Ken Hare by
Simone Bouyer

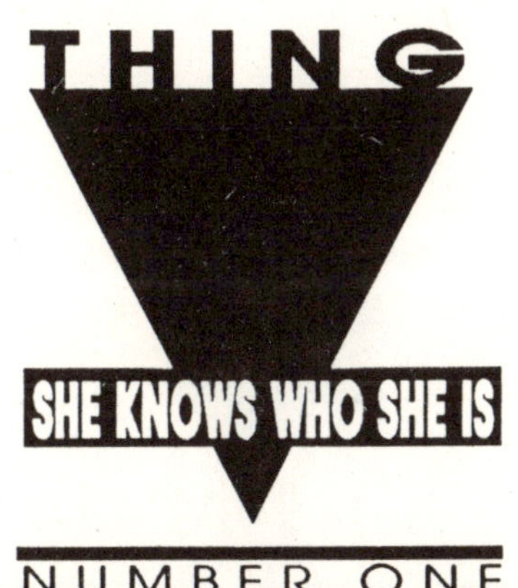

C O N T E N T S

THING EDITORIAL

4

WHO THING
Coverboy Hare, All About Ce Ce, Reading Steve

5

LIFE THING
Remembrances: LDW on Sylvester; Isaia

6

STYLE THING
Don't Worry, Be Nappy!

7

MEDIA THING
R. Ford on the media on gay sex

FICTION

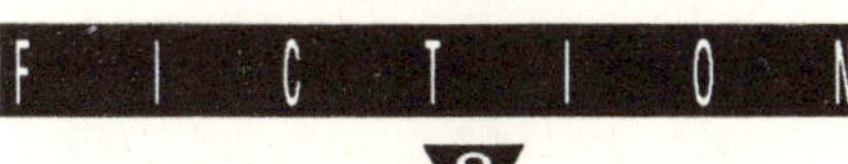

8

The sexual act with Rita Mae Black

9

"Did you see Oprah ?"

12

Bunny and Pussy : ribald recipes

FEATURES

14

THINGS : a random listing

16

TEE Time with T.A.

18

TEE terminology

poetry and photography insert follows page 10

PUBLISHER/EDITOR
Robert Ford
CO-EDITORS
Trent Adkins
Lawrence D. Warren
LAYOUT/ART DIRECTION
Robert Ford
GRAPHIC SERVICES
Simone Bouyer

CONTRIBUTORS
Rita Mae Black, Meikil Berry, Simone Bouyer, Bunny and Pussy, Stephanie Coleman, Juan Colón, the Darva, Tor Dettwiler, Sherman Malone, Terry Martin, j.s. savage, David Sedaris, Bob Toledo, Bernie White

THANKS TO
Chas. Brack, Pedro Caraballo, Gerry Fisher, the Fords, Kathryn Hixson, Steve LaFreniere, Penny, Planet Roc, Wendy Quinn, John Savage, Simone and Stephanie, Nick, Phyllis Swan, Pete Victor

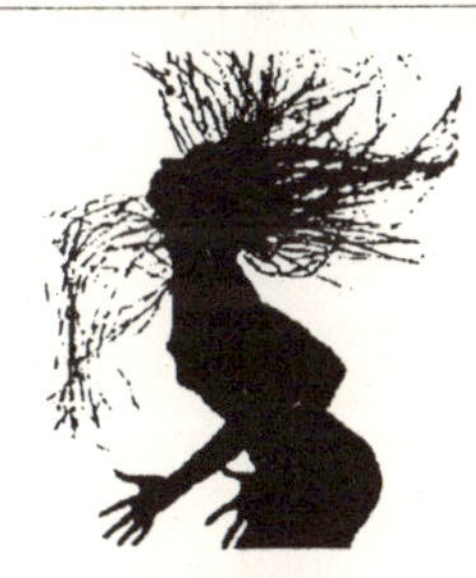
6

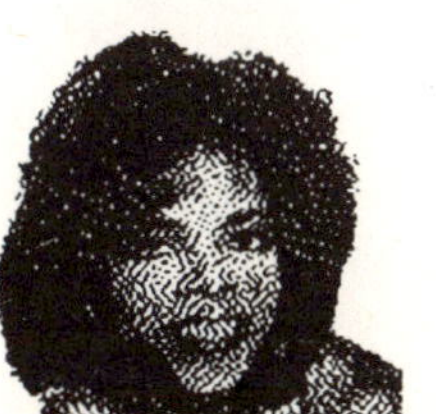

9

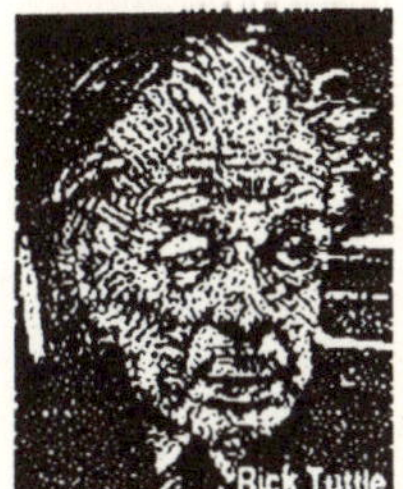

16

THING is published capriciously. Subscriptions: five dollars for three issues postpaid, free per issue with a self addressed stamped envelope. Donations encouraged! Make checks payable to publisher Robert Ford. THING encourages unsolicited submissions of any printable matter. Only those with self addressed stamped envelopes will be returned. Artists' payment is the satisfaction of contribution. Editorial inclusion casts no aspersions on one's racial or sexual categorization (Things know who they are). Opinions expressed are those of individual contributors, and do not always reflect those of THING. ▼ ©1989 THING (Call your lawyer)

DIRECT COMMUNICATION TO: THING 1516 Sedgwick, Chicago, Illinois 60610-1223 (312) 944-5850

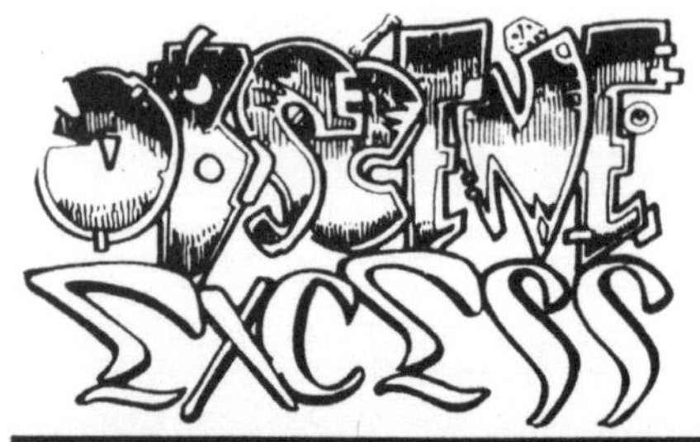

OBSCENE EXCESS

When is a title like Obscene Excess an understatement? When it comes from OE designer, Cecilia Hunt. The daughter of famed sculptor Richard Hunt, she's also a Psychotronic Film Society member, and a die-hard Fredricks of Hollywood follower. Not surprisingly, many art and cultural references populate her line of handcrafted accessories.

From the sublime to the outright kooky, wearable art as earrings, braclets, belts, scarves, and gloves,— heavily influenced by celluloid, old Hollywood glamour, Sci-Fi, Horror, and Comics, as well as the high and low ends of other cultures: African, Asian, Indian, etc. Beads, beads, and more beads! Ce Ce's been an avid collector of jewelry, beads, and period clothing since early childhood and has a workroom that more closely resembles a pirate's treasure; the space is brimming with every manner of bauble, bangle, and glitz imaginable. OE extravagantly appoints exotic and unique materials with a serious respect for good craftsmanship. Ce Ce unexpectedly mixes antique plastic or glass with African, Dutch, and Italian trade beads with semiprecious stones such as amber. The line even includes some separate hand knitted pieces that are based on sportswear shapes: narrow, multi textured and beaded pull-on skirts that all but glow in the dark! Plus a really funky pair of miniature baby dolls set in dayglo high-chairs! Rather like a 'multi-cultist', if she keeps this up, Ce Ce's likely to develop a cult following all her own.

— T.A

who THING

On Steve LaFreniere's mailing list? Well, you'd want to be. That's the only way to get his occasional guerrilla publications. He does it all from his own personal budget; it's not a business but a personal investment in free speech. The latest mailed a couple of months ago. Artfully Kinko-ed and boasting of REAL typesetting, it's a collection of fiction, reviews, "reprints", and other provocative visuals. Its editorial stance is very (though not exclusively) gay lit. Gary Indiana and Dennis Cooper are among the contributors. The few copies that have made it to New York are being re-constructed and circulated among the literati who aren't fortunate enough to live in Chicago. Taking full advantage of the "Copy This" disclaimer, we've reprinted David Sedaris' piece in this issue of Thing (see pg. 9) Thanks, guys !

JOKER *shoulda been a drag queen !*

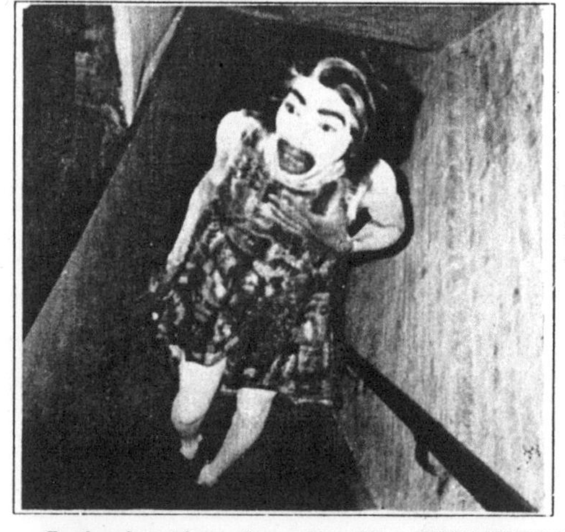

PHOTOS Stephanie Coleman

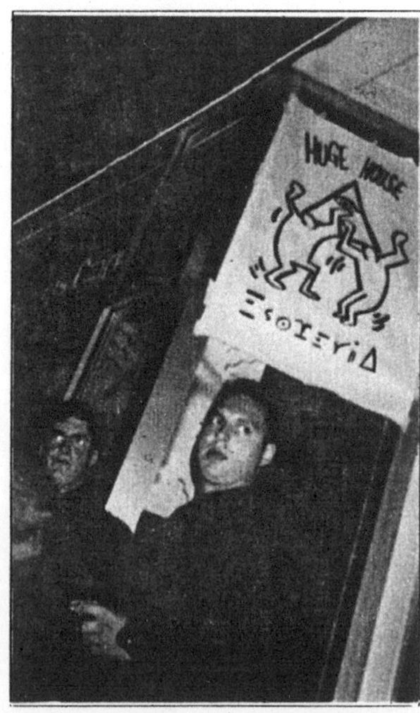

Professional bon vivant **Ken Hare (NEW YORK/LONDON/CHICAGO) changes his look as often as his name (Ylon, Booswana, King Faruk, etc.). And his looks are often calculated scene stealers; outrageous, but in an "other worldly" spacey sort of way.**

Well, one night MONTHS before Halloween, "Daddy" decided to let Esoteria have it!

Posing as an anatomically correct Queen Helene's Mint Julep Mask doll, (covered head to toe in the stuff) he tipped out of Wholesome Roc (above) to wreak havoc on Esoteria's Huge House party.

This is not New York or London., as Ylon soon found out. Instead of Julie Jewels or the like greeting him with open arms, the reception is best summed up by the expression of the door person in the photo on the right. He did not get in the club. Her Greeness made her way home, presumably to stew, crack, and peel. (THIS TOWN NEEDS AN ENEMA !)

—R.F.

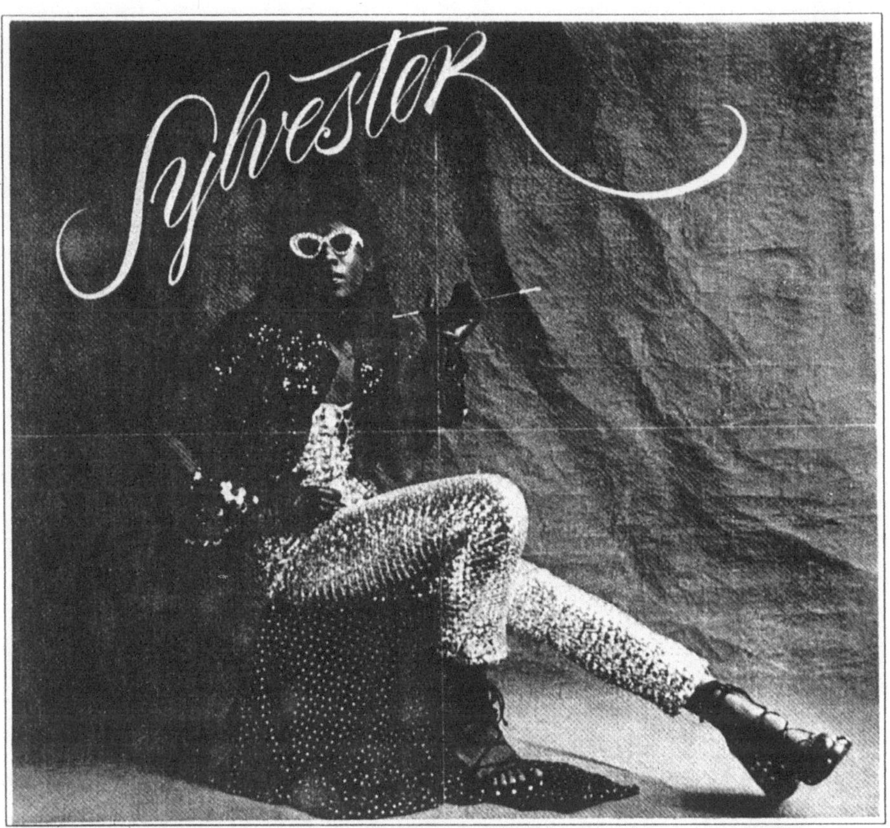

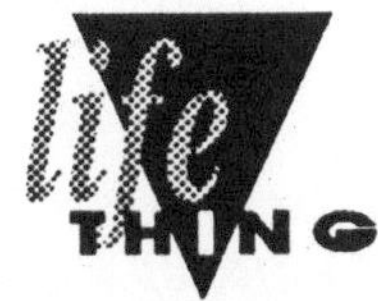

My Dearest Sylvester—

It's hard to believe that it has already been a decade since I was introduced to you through the powerful medium of television.

How can I forget sprawling in front of the TV — and you, my dear sister, splashing into my family room real as ice water and twice as cold—screamin' and hollerin' and shoutin' and irreversibly disrupting the tedium and boredom of my conservative, God-fearing, middle-class styleless life? Too late, my sainted mother rushed to snap you off-commanding me to go to my room and pray; instead I went to my room and worshipped - you in all your glitzy, glamourous, gaudy Gospel glory. You beckoned me to a promised land that was only a dance (partner) away.

It's hard to believe that is has already been five years since I was introduced to you at the PowerPlant, the dance party of the mid-eighties.

How can I forget being overwhelmed as you, my dear sister, kissed me and thanked me for being your faithful fan, inquiring about all the little details of my comparatively dull life, and encouraging me to be proudful of my rich faggot heritage and unashamed of my flamboyant sissyhood ("As long as you mind your manners and always say Miss Thing!)? Awestruck, you rushed me to the dance floor and straightaways to ecstasy via your piercing high notes, imparting blessings of excitement and visions of heaven.

It's hard to believe that just as that long-gone club had to end, even you, a good (Miss) thing, had to end.

How can I forget crying as you, my dear sister, fought the good fight for your life — and lost? Where went the promises that we would never stop dancing?

I shall always remember the verve, the fun and the panache you brought to a world that didn't want you here. It is amazing the way you wrung every drop of respect out of a life determined to give you none. It is nothing short of a miracle that you could find joy in an existence constructed to despise and hate you. It is comforting to know that you had already blazed this trail, demanding acceptance and inspiring me to believe that even Big Legged Coloured Girls could be, like you — a star.

I mean, you made me feel mighty real.

— LDW

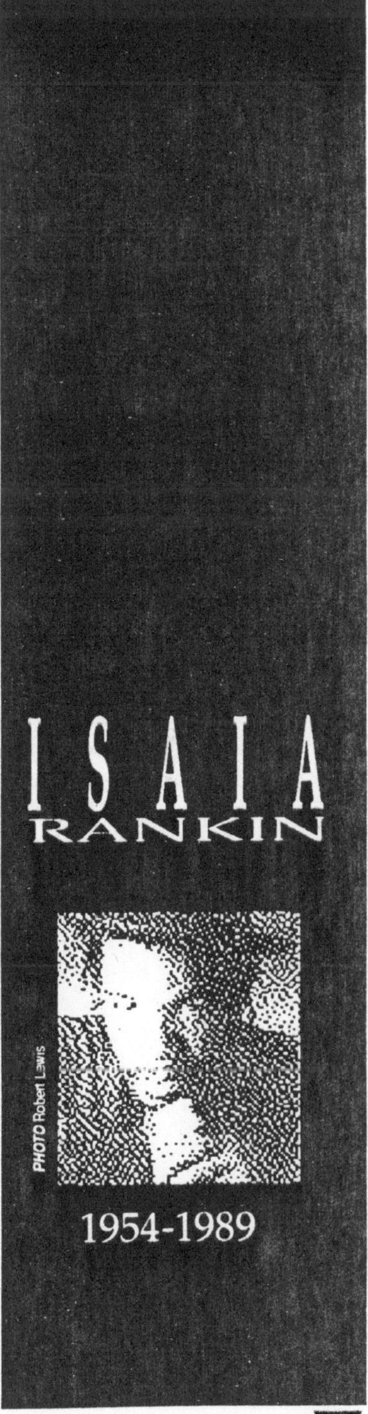

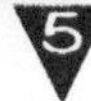

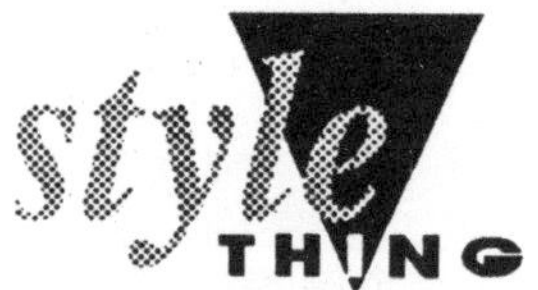

how's the hair ?

BY TRENT ADKINS

style THING

● **TRY NATURAL CRIMPS:** *Braid clean, damp hair, spritzing with water to keep moist while braiding. Air dry. Finger comb. Braided or unbraided, the style can last for weeks without heat from curling irons or blow dryers. With some imagination (pinned-up, pulled-back, or loose), the knotty silhouette can work for day or night.*

● **TO PREVENT MOISTURE LOSS,** *Ken Hare of Vidal Sassoon in Chicago recommends, "After shampooing, leave in a little conditioner. It helps to keep the hair from dehydrating, and you get better texture and body." To avoid conditioner 'build-up', Hare suggests this only after shampoos. Ones to try:*

- *Estrg Hair Food adds luster and body as it locks in moisture.*
- *Australian Formula Hair Salad Re-moisturizer with fruit and vegetable extracts noticibly protects hair from the drying and damaging effects of the sun, water, and air.*
- *African Formula SuperGrow Botanical Moisturizing Creme Rinse prevents hair loss and stimulates hair growth by moisturizing the hair and scalp. The list of ingredients reads good enough to eat: West African Palm Nuts, Camomile, Hops, Nettle, African Shea Butter, Basil, Sage, and Rosemary.*

Black is back. Not that African-Americans had ever really gone anywhere. Hopefully, Black Power was, is, and always will be. But now it's much nearer the forefront of American and world popular conscience. Some may argue that African-Americans really haven't progressed too far from the earlier days of our history in this country when we hadn't the right to vote and segregation was the law. Maybe the idea of 'Black nationalism' hasn't reached the level it did in the sixties or effected real social change, but it's apparent that Black people are increasingly realizing the importance of being true to their cultural roots and ancestry. In the late sixties and seventies, a popular manifestation of Black consciousness was 'Black is Beautiful', and the round, fluffy picked 'Afro' was the hair of choice. It was perhaps the first time in American history that African-Americans collectively began asserting pride in their African heritage. Now as then, hair makes a statement. Black people are thinking before they *image* their hair with chemicals, curling irons, straightening combs and blow dryers. "Who am I trying to be? Am I trying to be 'white' ?" Black folks have *always* had this thing about hair. Good hair vs. Bad hair. Straight hair vs. nappy hair, the long and short of it. That mess is old hat nowadays. "Good hair" is hair that you take good care of. Good hair isn't necessarily long and silky straight. The post-modern image of Black beauty celebrates the diversity of color, rhythm, broad noses, full lips, round asses, *and* kinky hair.

"Dreaded hair is not a hair style, it's a hair culture."

— Hiddekel Burk
Braiders' Network *founder/director*
and proprietor of Hyde Park's Starchild and Braiders Corner

Ironically, here at the end of the eighties, there are a lot of Caucasian kids in the trendier quarters of several American cities emulating sixties and seventies hip , especially *Black* sixties and seventies hip. Items like 'diamond-in-the-back', Huggy Bear styled bell bottoms and platform shoes, Barry White, Rudy Ray Moore, coconut pimp oil, Isaac Hayes, and "Shaft", are all being rediscovered by the kids of boomers who missed out on the real thing. African-Americans themselves, however, continue to assert their right and freedom to be different and look different; regardless of the white American standard. (Did you notice that as soon as they were IN, colored contact lenses became OUT?)

What used to be known as the 'Afro' has evolved, like a great many things since the the late sixties, into something sleeker, more sharply defined. In the sixties and seventies, the term 'natural' meant no perms, no color. Maybe the most chemical you ever got with a natural then was with a 'blowout' relaxer for a bigger 'fro. Now natural is redefined so that even chemically treated or colored hair is processed to *complement* the hair's natural texture and curl. Gentler and kinder hair for the Nineties with less use of harmful styling tools. Less straining for a bone straight effect.

● **A PROFUSION OF NATTY DREDLOCKS,** *sculpted "fades", "Gumbies", and other variations on kinky textures can be seen on the street — and on media figures like* **Guy, Neneh Cherry, Bobby Brown, Living Colour, The Boys, Lenny Kravitz, Soul II Soul, Tracy Chapman, Lisa Bonet, Yannick Noah, De La Soul, Whoopi Goldberg, Alice Walker , Cassandra Wilson, Angela Davis, Joie Lee, and Milli Vanilli.**

—T.A.

Soulful Silhouettes: **Jazzie B** *(left)* and **Wumni** *(above)* from **Soul II Soul,** the definitive *Funki Dreds.*

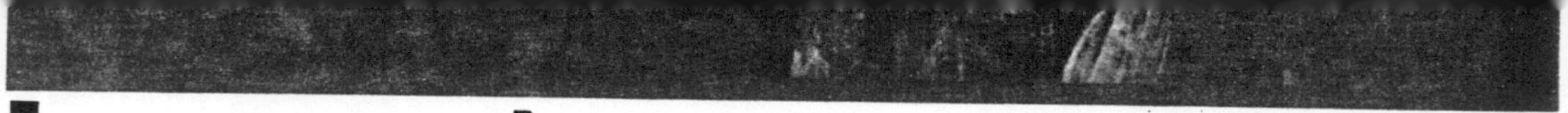

Tor Dettwiler

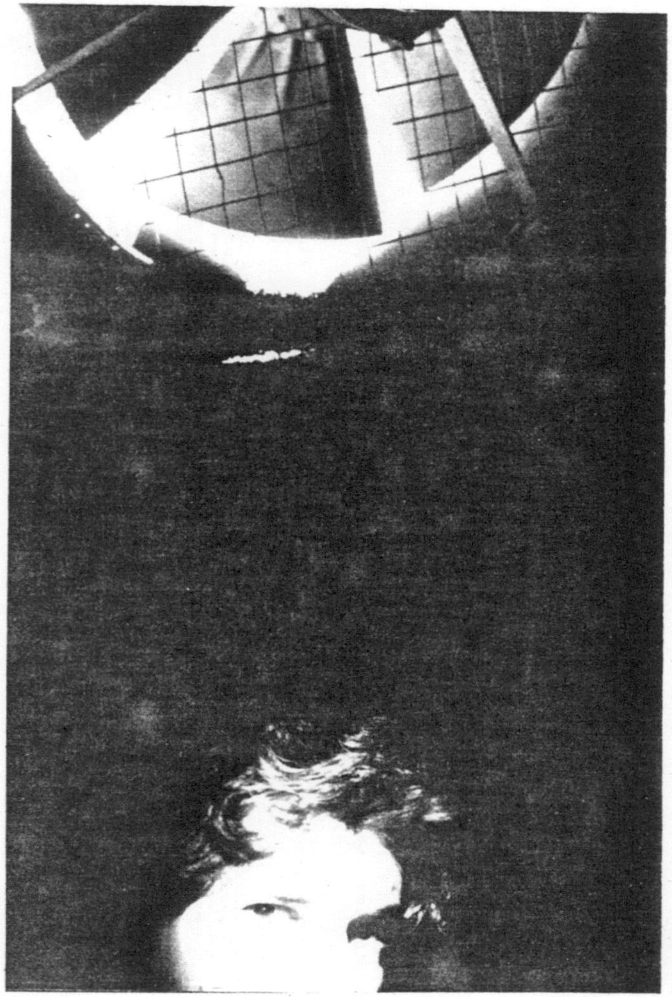

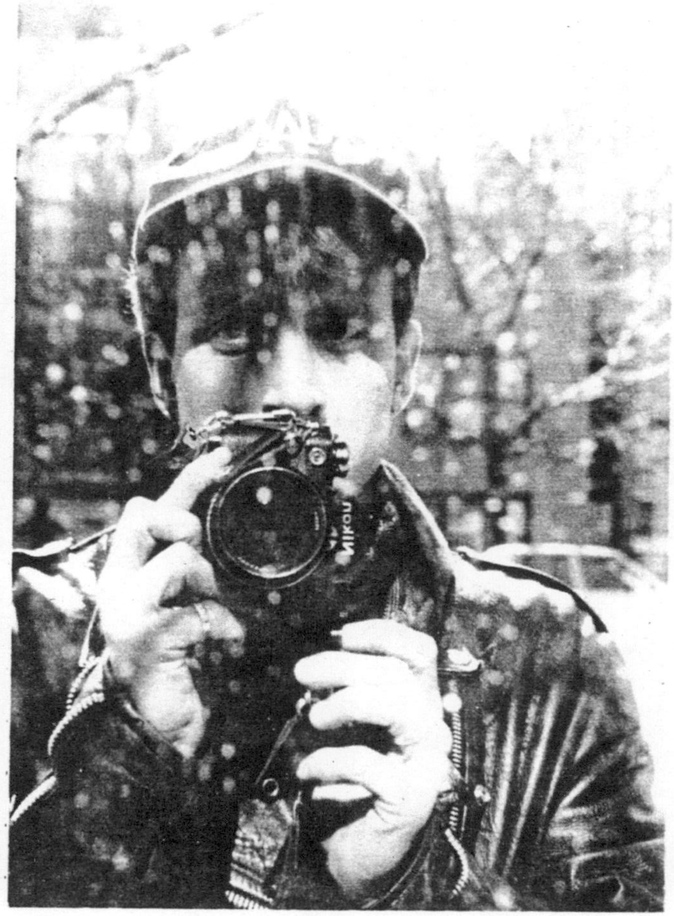

Terry Martin

CALLING MR. TELEPHONE

BY ROBERT FORD

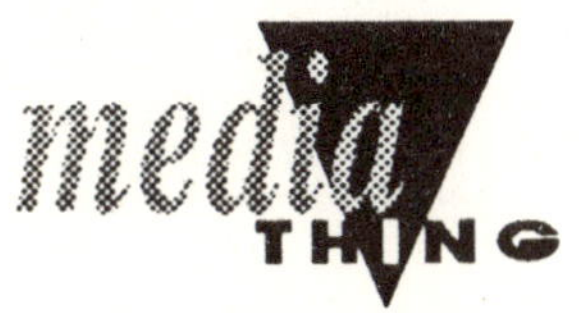

Coming out at the end of the seventies was like being thrust forward into a world where sexuality was limited only by one's own stamina. Outside of the specter of heterosexual disapproval (they thought us either sick or chic anyway) and without the heterosexual sex burden of pregnancy, we could "do it" as often as we wished, and lots of us did. The Village People were on American Bandstand and poppers were everywhere. *Burn baby, burn.*

Here at the close of the Eighties with its new disease and subsequent sex guidelines, I've watched things change a lot. Actual physical contact can seem like an out-of-body experience, and imagination often replaces bodily fluids.

Remarkably, this all happened during the Eighties, where hi-tech is the advanced opiate of the people. The telephone, once a passive instrument of simple voice communication, is now a mini-computer hooked into a database of your every desire. You can check your bank balance, have your tarot cards read, and buy South African gold from the Home Shopping Network over the phone. You can also tap into a number of "party lines" and order sex (or some facsimile thereof) like a pizza.

There is no precedent that compares to the modern phone sex community. The 1-900 party lines have opened up a network of local and national electronic pen pals. In many ways, it has become a new niche within the gay community. (It's too bad it's all in the hands of the telephone line owners, whose prices are outrageous. Their "free lines" are overworked and usually jammed.)

Unlike the bar scene, where there is often no talk, the phone is all talk. And it makes for amazing listening late at night. Guys who can't give out their phone numbers because they're married; who want to "try it." Guys looking for geographical proximity and real sex. Guys into phone sex. Men into cross-dressing and other kinky scenes. Lonely guys looking to talk. Gabby queens chatting and camping across state lines.

And there's a variety of lines, too. The newest is "The Buddy System," a super techno one-on-one line that gives you sales pitches for itself while it hooks you up with other callers. There are primitive "party lines" where ten voices shout into the darkness, having darting, fragmented conversation and exchanging phone numbers. Of course there's a leather line, complete with the verbal versions of the whole "Drummer" thing, lots of attitude. The pre-recorded "voice mailbox" ads are the strangest; people pitching themselves with "spoken personals" ads. Mr. Right in thirty seconds or less.

And since we don't have Jetson-type picture phones, there's the whole dynamic of the imagination. There's a shorthand for self-description: height, weight, body hair, endowment, preference (top or bottom), and age. Lots of well-built super-hunks; without the threat of meeting face to face it's an easy claim. Race is assumed white, and often questioned if the voice has an ethnic accent. (The wrong answers can leave you talking to a dial tone — disconnecting is as easy and faceless as connecting.) There's certainly a lot of talk about modern day no-nos — fisting, rimming, sex without condoms, etc. Though probably not a complete substitute for sex for many of the men who do it, talk has replaced at least some of its activities.

The phenomenon of this is fascinating, for it illustrates approaches to redefining our own sexualities and ideas of relationships. We've learned to talk to strangers, long a taboo in the aloof state of cruising. It's a campaign for reaching out and touching someone that AT&T would never run.

UNDER THE WEAR?...*There's a vaguely homoerotic undercurrent in Hanes' new campaign to sell kiddy underwear. This spot sells "feeling," the only thing left to sell in the mass produced blandness that is kids' underwear. The spot stars the son of some NFL hunk. The little boy's voiceover has him talking about how good his Hanes make him "feel," and how his humpy dad (shown roughhousing with the undie-clad cherub in slow motion) tells him that "After a big game nothing 'feels' as good as Hanes." It's all fairly tame, but seems like the roots of an underwear fetish to me.*

OH, BROTHER!...*WPWR-TV is currently running the sitcom "Brothers." The "situation" of this alleged comedy is a group of three brothers: one an ex-football star who owns a bar, one an overdrawn blue-collar bigot., and one is a GAY MAN. What follows is a series of scripts that often tries to be liberal and fair, but usually comes off as mawkish and condescending. Of course, en route to the humanistic moral are scores of "queer jokes," and there is a recurring character, Donald, who is our worst pre-Stonewall stereotype incarnate with his swishing, dishing, and limp wrists. Pull the plug on this one.*

WHO'S THAT GIRL?...*Have you noticed how usually invisible lesbians are enjoying a modicum of media chic? First Madonna and Sandra Bernhard encouraged tongues to wag, then there are the unsinkable Whitney Houston rumors. WEA has Phranc and k.d. lang under contract; the former frank and the latter silent. This is the most refreshing trend since the Elton John/David Bowie heyday of the '70's.*

— R.F.

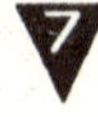

He sauntered up to the mahogany bar and tossed his head in the direction of the bartendress. She bought him a J&B after first serving a couple of double brandies to some love bugs at the other end of the bar. He glanced around disappointed that the place wasn't packed with people to look at.

"Slow," the bartendress murmured.

He tapped out a cigarette. A dull cross-over hit droned from the box and he considered quartering for some tunes, but remembered the dull selection.

Later.

He opened his magazine to the interview. The famous star was recounting how a particular role had liberated him from a dull marriage to experiment in the lifestyles of the night—homosexuals, transvestites, wildness.

The second drink relaxed him. He looked at his reflection in the mirror behind the bar. He smoothed his hair.

He wasn't really depressed, just tired. Maybe that guy last night wasn't so self-centered after all. Well, it was too late for that. He was probably back in Montreal by now.

The interviewee had had a great success and was considering directing. He had a script that "delved into the oblivion of despair" while maintaining "a resurgent optimism of enlightened experience."

The television flashed images of beautiful bodies with things.

He played some of the last good r&b tunes still on the box, in an effort to console himself. He swayed on his stool to the back beat.

One More.

The love bugs were rubbing limbs, obviously an affair.

Some old guys were downing shots, the regular.

He walked into the men's room, locked the door, and masturbated.

RITA MAE BLACK

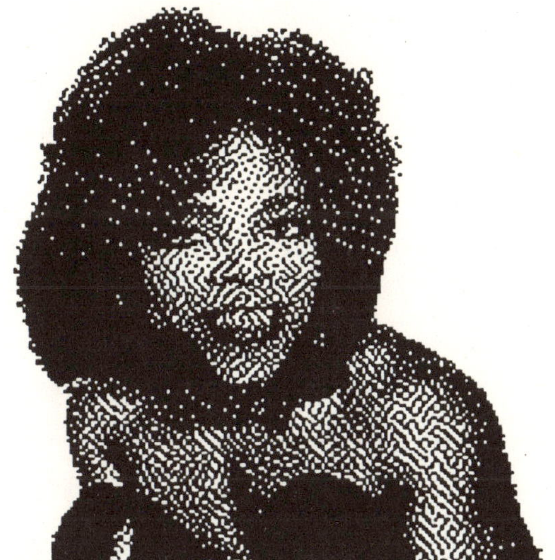

I was on Oprah a while ago, talking about how I used to love too much. Did you see it? The other guests were men who continued to love too much. Those men were in a place I used to be and I felt sorry for them. I was the guest who went from loving too much to being loved too much. Everybody loves me. I'm the most important person in the lives of almost everyone I know and a good number of people I've never even met. I don't say that casually, I'm just pointing out my qualifications. Because I know the issues from both sides, I am constantly asked for advice. People want to know how I did it. They want to know if I can recommend a therapist, how much will it cost, how long may it take to recover. When asked, I tell them like I'm telling you, that I have never visited a therapist in my life. I worked things out on my own. I don't see it as any great feat, I just looked at the pattern of my life, decided I didn't like it, and changed it. The only reason I agreed to appear on Oprah's panel was because I thought her show could use some sprucing up. Oprah is a fun girl, but you'd never know it from watching that show of hers, that parade of drunks and one-armed welfare cheats. And of course I did it to help people. I try and make an effort whenever I can.

Growing up, my parents were so very into themselves that I got very little love and attention. As a result I would squeeze the life out of everyone I came into contact with. I would scare away my dates on the first night by telling them that this was IT, the love experience I'd been waiting for. I would plan our futures together. Everything we did held meaning for me and would remain bright in my memory. By the second date I would arrive at the boyfriend's apartment carrying a suitcase and and a few small pieces of furniture so that when I moved in completely I wouldn't have to hire a crew of movers. When they became frightened and backed away I would hire detectives to follow those boyfriends. I needed to know that they weren't cheating on me. I would love my dates so much that I would become obsessed. I would dress like them, think like them, listen to the records they enjoyed. I would forget about me!

To make a long story short, I finally confronted my parents who told me that they were only into themselves because they were afraid that I would reject them if they loved me as hard as they pretended to love themselves. They were hurting too, and very vulnerable. They always knew how special I was, that I had something extra, that I would eventually become a very big celebrity who would belong to the entire world and not just to them. And they were right. I can't hate them for being right. I turned my life around and got on with it.

Did you see the show? Chuck Connors and Governor Bill Clinton were, in my opinion, just making an appearance in order to bolster their sagging careers, but not Jesse Helms. Man, I used to think that I had it bad! Jesse Helms has chased away every boyfriend he's ever had, he's still doing it. Jesse is a big crier. He somehow latched onto me and he's been calling and crying ever since the show. That's his trademark, crying and threatening suicide if you don't listen. That guy is a mess, but the other panel members didn't seem fit to speak on the subject. E.G. Marshall, for example, would talk about driving past his ex-boyfriend's house or calling him in the middle of the night just to hear his voice. Bill Clinton said he used to shower his boyfriends with gifts; he tried to buy their love. He wouldn't recognize love if it was his own hand, and E.G. Marshall if it was both his hands, one down there and the other careful on his throat.

CONTINUED ON NEXT PAGE

I am in this week's People magazine, but not on the cover. Bruce Springsteen is on the cover with what's her name, that flat faced new girlfriend of his, Patty Scholastica...Scholiosis — something like that. In the article she refers to Bruce as "The Boss" and discusses what she calls his "private side."

If she's calling Bruce "The Boss" then I can tell you she knows absolutely nothing about his private side.

I was the boss when Bruce and I were together. I should give this Patty person a call and tell her how Bruce needs to have it, give her a few pointers and clear up this Boss issue. Tell her about how Bruce begged me for a commitment, how he behaved when I turned him down. I'd said, "What's the use of being a rock star if you're going to run around like a second shift welder at U.S. Pipe and Boiler?"

Bruce took it hard and picked up the women on the rebound. I remember running into that last wife of his, this model, at a party. It was her, me, Morley Safer, and Waylon Jennings. We were waiting for the elevator and she was saying to Waylon that Bruce had just donated seven figures to charity, and I said, "No matter how much Bruce gives to charity, I still say he's one of the tightest men I've ever known." It went right over her head, but Morley knew what I was talking about, and we shared a smile.

I am in this week's People magazine celebrating my love with Charlton Heston. There are pictures of me tossing a pillow into his face, pretending to be caught up in a playful spat. You know that we can be real with one another because on the next page there I am standing on tip-toe and planting a big kiss on his neck while Burgess Meredith, Malcolm Forbes, and some other old queens are standing in the background applauding. Then I'm in the kitchen flipping pancakes to show I'm capable. I'm walking down the street with Charlton Heston and then I'm staring into the sea, digging my bare toes deep into the sand in this week's People magazine.

The press is having a field day over the news of my relationship with Mike Tyson. We tried to keep it a secret but between Mike and me there can be no privacy. Number one, we're good copy, and number two-we just look so damned good together, so perfect, that everyone wants pictures.

Charlton Heston and I are finished and he's hurt. I can understand that , but to tell you the truth, I can't feel sorry for him. He had started getting on my nerves a long time ago, before the People story, before our television special, even before that March of Dimes telethon. Charlton can be very manipulative, very possessive. It seems to have taken me a long time to realize that, all along, I was in love with the old Charlton Heston, the Charlton who stood before the Primate Court of Justice in "Planet of the Apes". The Charlton who had his loin cloth stripped off by Dr. Zaus and stood there naked but unafraid. What a terrific ass Charlton Heston used to have, but, like everything else about him, it's nothing like it used to be.

In the papers he is whining about our relationship and how I've supposedly hurt him. I'm afraid that unless Charlton learns to keep his mouth shut he's going to learn the true meaning of the word hurt. Mike is very angry at Charlton right now—very, very angry.

Let me say for the record that Mike Tyson, although he showers me with gifts, is not paying for my company. I resent the rumors to the contrary. Mike and I are each very wealthy, very popular men. The public loves us and we love one another. I don't need Mike Tyson's money any more than he needs mine. This is a difficult concept for a lot of people to grasp, people who are perhaps envious of what Mike and I share. This is the case with Charlton Heston who has lost most of his money on a series of bad investments. It's sad. The man is a big star who makes a fortune delivering the Ten Commandments one day, and then loses it all as a silent partner in Sambo's restaurants the next.

Mike and I would gladly give everything we've got in exchange for a little privacy. We would be happy living in a tent, cooking franks over an open fire on that plot of land we bought just outside of Reno.

Mike and I are that much in love. It is unfortunate that our celebrity status does not allow us to celebrate that love in public. Since we were spotted holding hands at a Lakers game all hell has broken loose and the "just good friends" line has stopped working. None of this is helping Mike's divorce case or my breakup with Charlton, who I might add, is demanding some kind of a settlement. For the time being, Mike Tyson and I are lying low. It is killing us, but we've had to put our relationship on the back burner.

I accidentally swallowed Mike Tyson's false teeth. I can't believe it! They were gold, but the money isn't the issue. Between the two of us we could buy gold teeth for every man, woman and child with the gums to harbor them. It's not the money that bothers me.

It was late and Mike had taken his teeth out for the evening. He'd set them in a tumbler of water we keep next to our bed. Mike could sleep with his teeth in but, believe me, it's better with them out. We had just finished making very strenuous, very complete love and I reached for that glass of water and drank it down, the teeth too. It was unsettling. The

A SEED FELL

a seed fell
        into a pond
and was eaten by a fish.
then it rained.

a worm
who had been sleeping
was awakened by the rain.
it decided to go for a swim.

a man
        carrying a grey metal box
filled with pink and plastic furry things
with steel snakelike tongues
        saw a worm
        and picked it up.
it died easily.

the rain stopped.

he flung the worm
        who was no longer a worm
        but a pink j
into the pond.

it was eaten by the fish.
        the fish that ate the seed.

he
  opened the fish
  like junk mail.
poured its innards onto the ground.
        worms would later eat this
        except for the seed.
the fish made a good meal.

the man was killed by a bear
as he began to leave.

then it rained
in not too many summers
her cubs will sleep
        in the shade
            of a new tree.

—j.s. savage

LET HIM BE

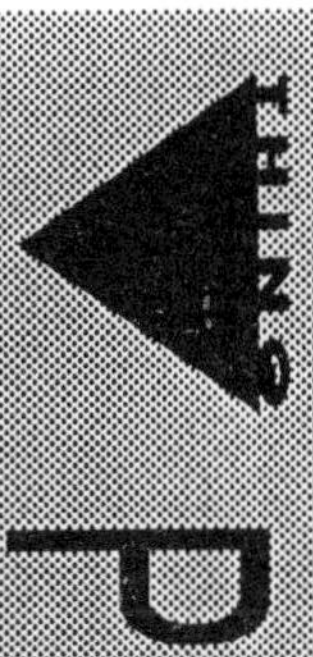

He has to be special
for i want to love him in that way

his love should be like sunshine
to warm and nourish me

let him be a dancer
who takes me in his strong arms
and romances me with rhythm
and a love song

let fire be his substance
and candlelight his soul

i wish him to be a flower budding
spewing forth his brilliant colors
and his fresh scent

let it be an aroma to my desires

let his life be of found peace
from journeys through low and high roads

let love mean something precious to him
and let him show it so

let us be contrasting
still let us blend as one
a fortress to all others

that we may be what love is

two unified as one

—Sherman Malone

edited by
Lawrence
D. Warren

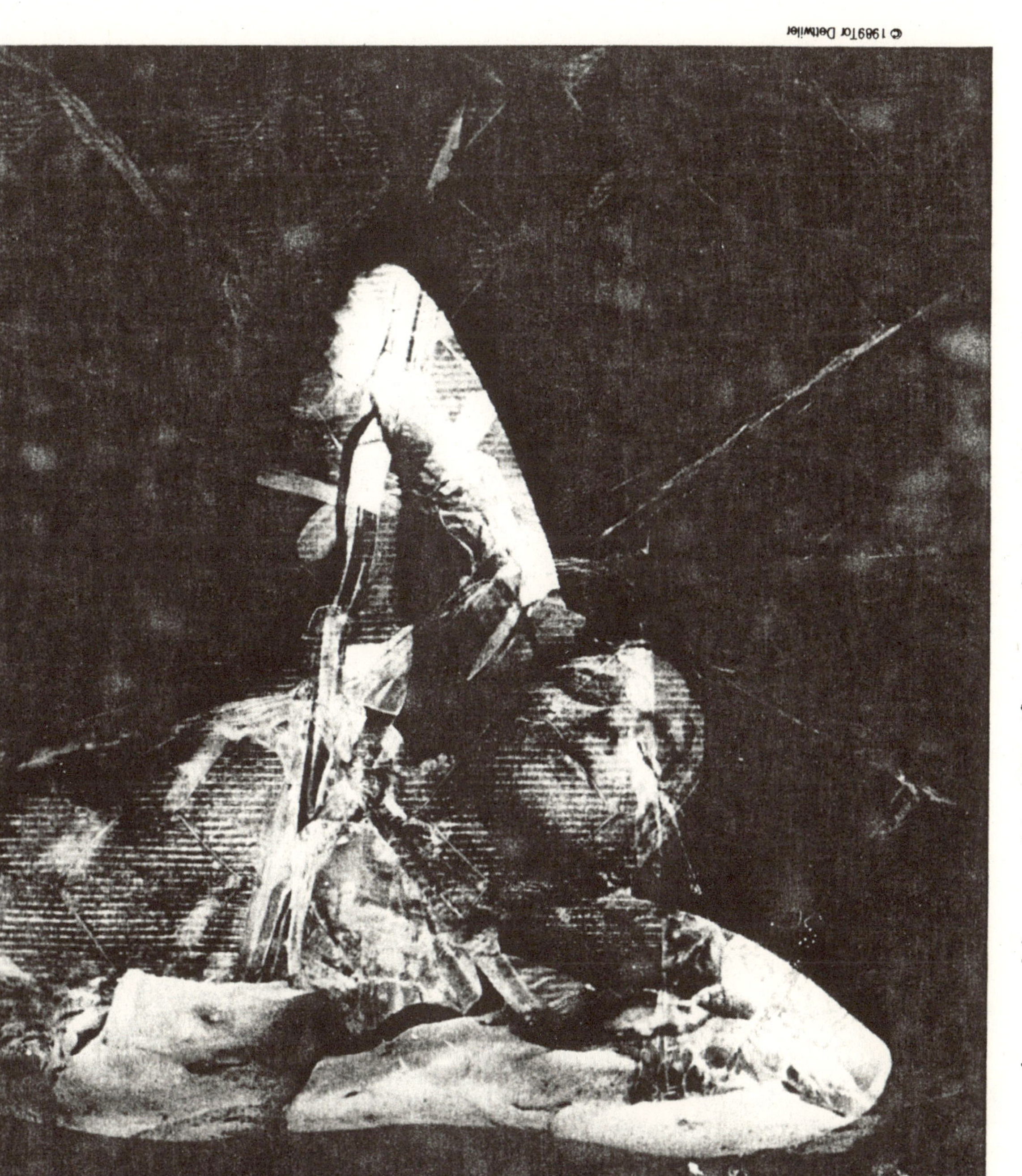

PHOTOGRAPHY

A D A N C E R

you're a sly little thing
trying to test me
with your feminine wiles
and sexy ways

girl,don't you know
what you keep doing to me
when you brush your small yellow frame
against my hot, aching sex

i wanna touch you all over on the inside;
your heart, soul, and mind
by way of your mounds of fleshly desires'
form the auburn strands of your herbal-scented mane
to your delectable, delightful, taste-like-vanilla toes

then you've got this exotic dance
you do in front of me
you call it "just walking"
womyn, whatcha trying to do?

i'm thinking about
changing my life to suit yours
with your warm golden brown eyes and hot tongue
just watching you breathe makes my head spin

you're a magical, playful nymph
and i've met your kind before
going through you is like
a jet soaring through clouds
giving sudden jolts of new surprises

god,chile, you gotta stop making me
wanna snuggle in your love nest
and play house forever
dream the impossible dream

when your palms gently explore
my stratosphere they send waves
of hot and cold flashes through my being
i see lightning and feel thunder in my core

so, let's travel in our world once more
let's go south of the border
and lie naked on the beaches of the big o
where warm crested waters are filled with our love

— Meikil Berry

O W E D T O B R O T H E R S

he is the kind
of man who can entertain
with the slightest word, gesture, or look
his unique thinking
vision
and tantalizing little smile
takes your breath away
he has a deceptive intelligence that
makes you quiver with its thunder

all fire and brimstone
wrapped in black silk and pointed feet
part vixen
part 'b' girl.
a spark beyond years
my earth mother
soul mate
companion, we walk through life together.

TANTRUM "I'm not going to be your friend
    I'm gonna scream
        yell
        accuse
        abuse
    and do everything short of banging my
    head on the ground...
    (oh yeah, I did that already)
    just to get
    my way.
    I'm not your friend anymore..."

in a battle of wits, few if any, will stand triumphant
in the battle of the bulge the gauntlet has fallen
in the battle of the sexes, (s)he is both
    and stands victorious

my 3 am friend
my Boo-Boo (no relation to Yogi Bear)
my pupa
my God...
    it's the larva!

— The Darva

problem is that Mike had planned on having those teeth set for me in a medallion of commitment. He was very gracious and forgiving and said it was no problem, that he'd just have some others made. But those teeth were special, his first real good teeth. Those were the teeth that had torn into all of the exotic meals I had introduced him to. Those were the teeth I polished with my tongue on our first few dates, the teeth that hypnotized me across a candlelit table, the teeth that reflected the love light shining in my eyes. I swallowed Mike Tyson's teeth and have let him down. I've been waiting for days but still they haven't passed. They have to come out sooner or later, don't they? Even if I do find them I can't expect Mike to put them back into his mouth. That was a big part of our commitment ceremony. I was supposed to reach into my mouth and pull out a rather expensive diamond-studded ID bracelet I had made and Mike was going to reach into his and withdraw the medallion. Mike says what the hell, it's not like his teeth haven't been up my ass before, but it's the principle of the thing and it's got me down.

Mike and I were arguing over what to name the kitten we'd bought. I would have just as soon taken one of the many kittens that have been offered to us. Everyone wants to give Mike and me kittens. I thought we might just take one of those but Mike said no. He wanted the kitten that had captured his heart in a pet shop window last week, a white Persian/Himalayan female. I don't care for puffy cats in the first place and this one, with her flat face, reminded me of what's-her-name, Bruce's new girlfriend, Patty. "All right, Mike," I said, "if you want this Persian/Himalayan mix, then that's what we'll get." I can love just about anything on all fours so I said, "Fine, whatever." Let me say that a long-haired cat is one thing, but a white Persian/Himalayan blend named

Pitty Ting is something else altogether.

I'd wanted to name the kitten Sabrina 2. I'd had another cat, my Sabrina, for years before she died. I was used to the name and the connotations it carried in my mind. Mike, though, was very adamant about the name Pitty Ting which was unfair seeing as I hadn't wanted a puffy cat in the first place, especially a white one. White would be so hard to keep clean. Besides, this is a relationship where compromise is supposed to be the name of the game. I gave a little, so why couldn't he?

Driving home from the pet store we started to argue. Mike said some pretty rough things and I responded tit for tat. Well, you know Mike "mister-jab-and-duck-all-over-the-place" Tyson. I thought he was rolling up the window so that the kitten wouldn't climb out. I saw his hand raised and then again I guess I didn't see it.

After he hit me I got out of the car and walked. I've had some physical fights with boyfriends before, Norman Mailer and Peter Jennings to name just a few, so I'm no stranger to a flaring temper. This time, though, I just walked away. Mike followed me. He drove his car up onto the sidewalk, but I kept on walking, pretending not to notice. Then Mike got out of his car and started begging, begging on his knees and whimpering. I put my hand up to my eye, pretending to wipe away some of the blood, and then, boy, did I clip him!

While he was unconscious, I let the kitten out of the car and sort of kicked her on her way, no problem. A puffy cat like that will have no problem finding someone to love. When he came to, Mike had forgotten the entire incident. That happens all the time, he forgets. He didn't even ask why we were spattered with blood. He said "What happened?" and I said, "Don't you remember? You said you wanted to buy me a pony." So now we have a beautiful Shetland pony named Sabrina 2. Now we have

forgotten about kittens, about naming things, about anything but our relationship. We round the block on our pony who groans beneath the collected weight of our rich and overwhelming capacity for love and understanding.

Mike Tyson is making an ugly face in the Newsmakers section of this week's Newsweek magazine, an ugly face directed toward me. I'm not frightened so much as shamed and concerned. In the picture Mike's skin looks sallow and blotchy. He looks like he's been rolling around in an ashtray. Our breakup was hard on him, but, whining to the press won't help. I left as soon as Pat Buckley moved in. I guess Mike thought I would change my mind and welcome her into our lives. I guess Mike was wrong.

Pat Buckley didn't stay long. She was dating Lauren Bacall and stayed only three weeks before taking off to Cannes or Rio, someplace. Looking back on it, I can't put all the blame on her. Mike and I had problems before she came along, big problems that we would have been forced to deal with sooner or later. I don't want to go into any of the details of our relationship but I would like to set the record straight and say that there is no truth to the rumors about me and Morley Safer. I resent Mike's accusation that Morley and I are anything more than friends.

I resent Mike Tyson's self-pitying ploys for attention. I resent his suggestion that I was in any way false or insincere. Unlike him, I don't care to dwell on the unpleasant aspects of our relationship. I prefer to remember a time when Mike and I, having finished a simple game of cards, were sitting side by side in comfortable reclining chairs. Mike took my hand in his and began, very gently, to pet my fingers, kissing them and addressing them as individuals.

— David Sedaris

DOIN' LUNCH

DINING AL FRESCO

PUSSY: After spending a whole month on the wagon in **New Orleans,** imbibing nothing stronger than Peychaud Bitters and soda, it seemed apropos to bid the town adieu with a sleazy barcrawl accompanied by my friend Brad, owner of Clancy's, a fashionable Uptown eatery, and his waitstaff.

After popping in and out of several different boites, my entourage steered me to Benny's—an all-nite joint what makes the Checkerboard look like the Ritz bar—where I drank Southern Comfort from a go-cup and where, on an innocent trip to the loo, I managed to topple a commode and arouse concern among *mes amis.*

Buddy, a chivalrous young bartender, rose to the occasion, offering to chariot me home in his mother's Country Squire. No sooner had I settled into the passenger seat when I felt the irrepressible urge to show my gratitude by performing that most miraculous act. I dove to the occasion and the ride commenced with me happily installed beneath the dashboard.

Sudden sirens and flashing lights caught me in mid-mouthful and Buddy in mid-moan. "Shit, ma'am," he gasped, "I don't have a driver's license." Peering out the back window, I saw one lone Black cop alight from his Plymouth. "Honeychile," I cooed, hastily wiping the lipstick from my chin, "I'll handle this one." I flagged the officer over to my side and poked my head from the window. "I know what this looks like," said I, my speech slightly slurred from excess drink and strenuous exercise, "but I'm a successful writer with a college degree."

Nonplussed, he demanded my IDs *and* Buddy's. I pleaded for clemency. "For thirty days my lips have touched nothing stronger than Peychaud Bitters. This being my last night in this lair of lust, I figured on getting drunk and *laid.* The boy to my left is very willing and I swear on my life if you detain us so long that his ardor cools, you'll have hell to pay with every Republican judge in this goddamned parish."

The cop stood resolute—lewd conduct notwithstanding, there had been a serious traffic infraction. Our dear Buddy had been traveling at a high speed in the wrong direction down a one way street.

"I don't doubt that he was," I replied. "After all, he was getting a blowjob—which can wreak havoc on a boy's equilibrium even if he isn't driving. And, if you yourself haven't had the honor of receiving that most cherished of gifts while piloting any craft small or large, you are really in no position to quibble."

The young officer rolled his eyes skyward and exhaled wistfully and I knew that victory was mine. "There, there darlin'," I said, placing my hand on his arm, ever so gently, "You're young. There's time. Someday you'll meet a wonderful girl. In the meantime, please be a honey and hop back into your car'n escort Buddy and me back to the Best Western so we can finish what we started." Which is exactly what he did— but not before I kissed him on the cheek and proclaimed him both an Officer and a Gentleman.

Back at the mo-tel, both of our ardors had waned, but that still didn't stop me from blabbing the tale to half of New Orleans before daybreak. The result: the highest honor of all New Orleans cafe society—a drink named after me at Clancy's restaurant: **The MOVING VIOLATION,** of course! **(Pour a tumbler of Southern Comfort over crushed ice; serve with a sidecar of Peychaud Bitters and soda).**

BUNNY: Pre-plague, I took a certain flamboyant female friend (not PUSSY) on a nuit d'amour nature tour of Lincoln Park. She dressed for the bush. donning an Ace bandage for camouflage and hiding her locks under a turban, Sabu style. The friend-ette fit right in, scampering gingerly through rats and refuse, stalking her prey like a real man—until the moment of truth when a frisky fellah reached down her pantaloons, forcing the fabulous fake to flee for her life...or risk exposure in more ways than one!

▼

PUSSY: This birthday found me considering suicide, quaffing martinis alone in an artsy bar. Somewhere between drink 4 and 11, I was joined by a handsome stranger in shorts who knew Proust as well as prost. Next thing I knew, we were both on a fire escape, poised to dive——but not to the pavement below. My angel of the evening wasn't named Clarence. I called him Mike Nelson, Because he didn't come up 'til he'd touched bottom and found the buried treasure. just like in SEA HUNT. Yes, IT'S A WONDERFUL LIFE!

EAVESDROPPINGS

At a recent party, we heard a young man waxing rhapsodic about his favorite rolls. "Are you a baker?" we queried conjuring pictures of bialys and brioche. "I am an *actor*!" he spewed, feathers ruffled. We've decided we don't approve of including actors in any social setting (unless they're on the catering staff; even then they should be closely monitored). On the other hand we're all in favor of revamping the old rule about not hobnobbing with one's coiffeur. After all, most of us would rather hear about styling than Strindberg any day.

▼

Somewhere we ran into someone—we can't remember who—who suggested a fabulous TV show: each day a different socialite would be the sole guest, appearing on camera with her head hidden from view by a Bloomie's bag. Thus obscured she would tell *all*: Why certain top execs have glass-topped conference tables...whose deb daughters are dykes...talkshow title? **COVERED DISHES** of course!

POLITE SOCIETY

BUNNY: I hate being involved in other peoples' social lives. Once, I was emotionally blackmailed into accompanying a friend (I use that term loosely) to a men's encounter group. I planned on being a sullen spectator; the host had other ideas. After the intros, he asked me to tell the group a little bit about myself. Preferring to talk a little bit about other people, I chose, instead, to recount an amusing tale my companion had just told me *en route* about a bizarre sex act he'd observed in a Water Tower tea room. The room grew strangely still. The host grew redfaced and began squirming in his seat but not because of the risqué subject matter. *Au contraire*—he was the washroom-wonder whose tea party had been witnessed.

LET THEM EAT CHALK

...the teacher who described a date with a guy who called his weenie a truncheon, and then gleefully admitted she had no idea what the hell a truncheon was.

...the forensics coach who thought "The Killing of Sister George" was comedy. "Aren't the roommates a hoot," she said of Childie and her lover George, "And they're so much funnier than the Odd Couple."

...the high school band director with an M.A. in music ed. who's hard pressed to name five Romantic symphonists.

with bunny and pussy

...or the scores of teachers whose paper-grading leaves them too exhausted to read daily papers, Time, Newsweek, or anything in print except their contracts...

SPLITTING JEANS

PUSSY: *(speculates)* Now that fertilization can be done *in vitro*, the penis—having been rendered unnecessary for procreative purposes—will become a recessive trait. Gay men—connoisseurs of phallic *grandeur*—will be forced to mate with females to ensure survival of the biggest. Leading to a race of no-dicked straight guys who jerk off into Petrie dishes and big-pricked faggots who don't.

DIVAN D'AMOUR

BUNNY: A friend of mine was dating a young Mexican. Eager to make it a foursome, the *muchacho* suggested fixing me up with an *amigo* of his—a Catholic priest. I agreed, figuring that, since I found the idea so amusing, my anti-clerical feelings could be kept under control.

Imagine my astonishment when my date showed up in uniform and asked me to give him a lurid description of all my mortal and venial sins—while holding the key to my salvation in the palm of his hand. *HOLY MOLE!:* **Perk up the standard** mixture with brown sugar instead of white. Reduce to desired consistency and whip with reverence.

KIDDIE MENU

PUSSY: I invited a 25-year-old to dinner and, ahem, dessert. As a prologue to the poke, I served a meal from the Arabian Nights: curried lamb, felafel, cous cous, hot sauce, and fresh figs—he was only mildly enthused and mildly aroused. When I served a repeat repast to a 40-year old, WE were *in flagrant delicto* before we finished the felafel. **Moral: when feeding a child, McDonalds will suffice.**

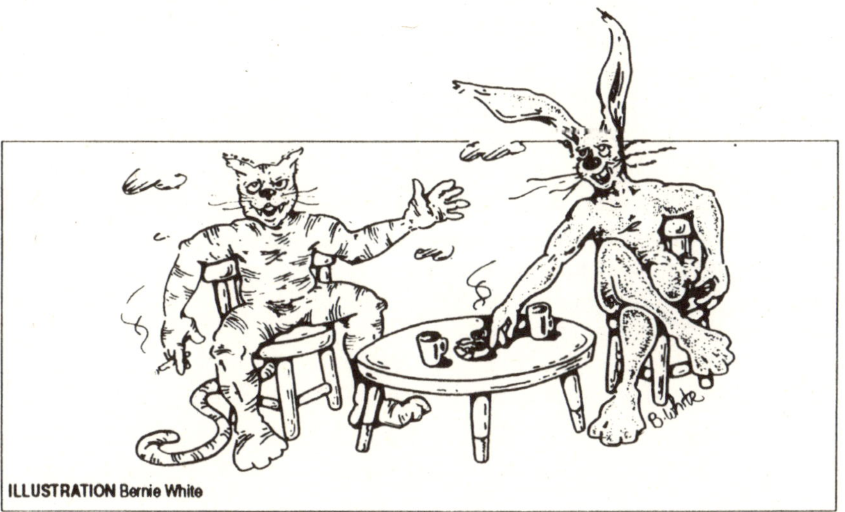

ILLUSTRATION Bernie White

Unlikely singer/producers we'd love to hear
    Liza Minnelli and the Pet Shop Boys (whoops, that's happened already)
    Petula Clark and Guns 'N' Roses
    Peggy Lee and Inner City
    Luther Vandross and Ten City (really)
    NOBODY ELSE and Narada Michael Walden
    John Cougar Mellencamp and Teddy Riley

Homophobes who make you question the validity of the First Amendment
    Eddie Murphy
    Sam Kinison
    Andrew Dice Clay
    Spike Lee
    Axl Rose
    Zsa Zsa Gabor
    Donna Summer
    Jesse Helms

Trent's favorite inside jokes
    how's the hair?
    braid my hair
    call your lawyer
    house hayride
    "that lady"
    "Do I know you?"
    Rachel Cain's hat trick
    "is she hot?"

Most annoying pop songs of the late '80s
    "I'll Always Love You" by Taylor Dayne
    "Pump Up The Volume" by M/A/R/R/S
    "Knocked Out" by Paula Abdul
    "The Way That You Love Me" by Paula Abdul
    "Straight Up" by Paula Abdul
    "Forever Your Girl" by Paula Abdul
    "Cold Hearted Snake" by Paula Abdul (especially the rap)
    "Hanging Tough" by The New Kids On The Block
    "So Emotional" by Whitney Houston
    "She Drives Me Crazy" by Fine Young Cannibals
    "Monkey" by George Michael
    "Keep Feeling (Fascination)" by the Human League
    "I Want To Have Some Fun" by Samantha Fox
    "Electric Youth" by Debbie Gibson
    Anything by Milli Vanilli

Perfect casting
    "I, Tina (Turner)" starring Neneh Cherry
    "West Side Story" with Sa-Fire as Anita, Sweet Sensation and the Cover Girls as the Sharks'
    girls, New Kids on the Block as the Jets, and Rick Astley as Tony
    "Flashdance" with Paula Abdul (who, if nothing else, could do her own dancing)
    "Jailhouse Rock" with James Brown
    "Sweet Dreams" with k.d. lang
    " The Roy Orbison Story" with k.d. lang
    "Tom Jones" with Tom Jones and the Art of Noise
    "The Josephine Baker" Story with Naomi Campbell
    "Slaves of New York" with Patty Ryan as Eleanor
    "The Swinger" with Belinda Carlisle as Ann-Margaret
    "The Flinstone Movie" with Belinda Quarrylisle as Ann-Margrock

LDW's THING/ NO THING LIST

THING	NO THING
James Baldwin	Tom Wolfe
Branford Marsalis	Wynton Marsalis
Ty Jones	Jeff Stryker
Cosmetology	Astrology
Michael Kilian	Bob Greene
Roger Ebert	Rex Reed
Suzy Funtown	Suzy Chapstick
Chaka Khan	Donna Summer
Joseph Beam	Jim Beam
"The Boss" Diana Ross	"The Boss" Bruce Springsteen
Dorothy Tillman	Kathy Osterman
DuSable Museum	Terra Museum
WilliWear	Polo
BLK	EM

A decade and still spinning
    "Rappers Delight" by The Sugarhill Gang
    "Life During Wartime" by the Talking Heads
    "There But For The Grace of God Go I" by Machine
    "Dance (Disco Heat)" by Sylvester
    "Ring My Bell" by Anita Ward
    "Le Freak" by Chic

Most embarassing comeback efforts
    "Time Waits for No One" by Mavis Staples
    "Workin' Overtime" by Diana Ross
    "My First Night Without You" by Cyndi Lauper
    "Stronger Than Pride" by Sade
    Pia and Phil
    "Back in the S___" by Millie Jackson

Essential Miles Davis recordings
    Tutu
    Kind of Blue
    Amandla
    Porgy and Bess
    The Man With the Horn

House records we'd like to put in a time capsule (for a LONG time)
    "Let No Man Put Asunder" by First Choice
    "Can You Handle It" by Sharon Redd
    "You've Got That Something" by Logg
    "Love Hangover" by Diana Ross
    "Love Is The Message" by M.F.S.B.
    "Heavy Vibes" by Montana Sextet
    "Let's Do It" by Conversion
    "Mainline" by Black Ivory

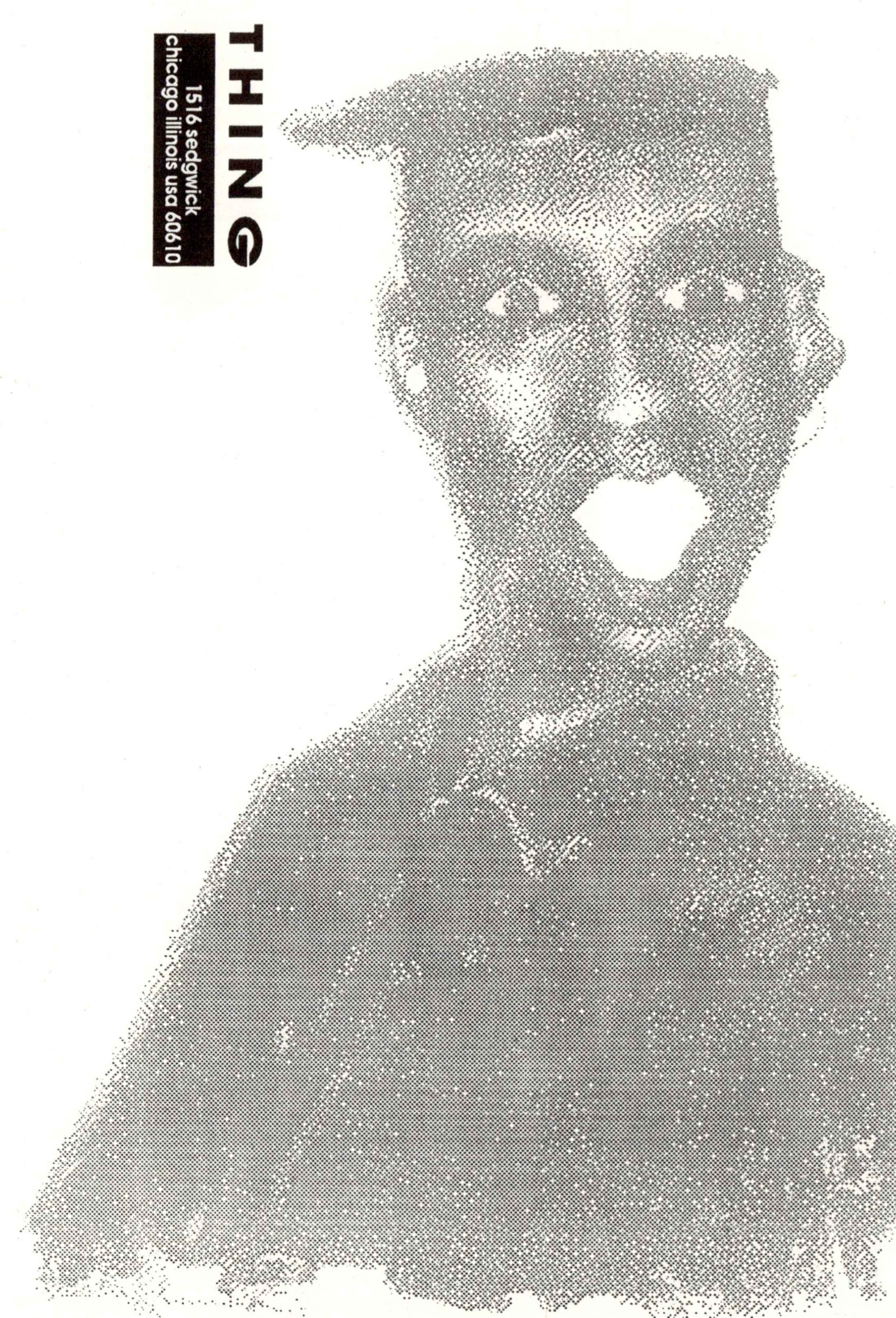

THING
1516 sedgwick
chicago illinois usa 60610

The club tarts' all time panty rippers
"Don't Go Lose It Baby" by Hugh Masekela
"On The Floor" byTony Cook
"Spank" by Jimmy "Bo" Horne
"Tee's Happy" by North End featuring Michelle Wallace
"Just a Touch Of Love" by Slave
"Billy Who" by Billy Frazier
"Ye Ye De Smell" by Fela
"Can't Take It" by Keith Thompson
"Throw 'em The Chicken" by Crowd Control
"Standing In Line" by ESG

If Jean-Paul Gaultier can make a disco record, why not...
an aerobics record by Cheryl Tiegs
a vogueing record by Patrick Kelly
Bobby Short and Gloria Vanderbilt
a tango record by Christian La Croix

Kids who sing along
Effie Mae
Chas.
Gentle
Darryl Pandy
Karen McCormick
Henry White aka Henri Blanc
April Pughsley
Wardell Ford
Tony Wilkins
Toy (I Don't Play) Patton

Club Shirley
Shirley Bassey
Shirley Horn
Sheryl Lee Ralph
Cheryl "Pepsii" Riley
Sherri Riley
Shari James
Cheryl Lynn
Saralynn Crittendon
Terri Lyne Carrington
Siedah Garrett

Bob Toledo's Top Ten Things To Do This Winter
1. Feign disinterest in sex and money
2. Eschew major studio movies
3. Write a science fiction book and make a quick $5,000
4. Listen to *Virgin Beauty* by Ornette Coleman
5. Buy American whenever convenient
6. Discuss Tibet with your friends
7. Take your enemies to White Castle
8. Compare and contrast Telemann with Schœnberg
9. Politely decline to reproduce
10. Re-examine the hype

Some girls that gay men are stereotyped to love and emulate

The Black Girls
Whitney Houston
Diana Ross
Dorothy Dandridge
Patti LaBelle
Zora Neale Hurston
Eartha Kitt
Dionne Warwick
Josephine Baker
Pam Grier
Pearl Bailey
Butterfly McQueen
Aretha Franklin
Melba Moore
Stephanie Mills
Phyllis Hyman
Nancy Wilson
Billie Holiday
Grace Jones
Lena Horne

The White Girls
Judy Garland
Bette Davis
Joan Crawford
Marilyn Monroe
Divine
Debbie Harry
Jean Harlow
Doris Day
Cher
Tallulah Bankhead
Madonna
Gloria Swanson
Barbra Striesand
Marlene Dietrich
Elizabeth Taylor
DV
Joan Collins
Connie Francis
Greta Garbo

Love (Disco Style)
Love Hangover
Love Sensation
Love Break
Love to Love You Baby
I Feel Love
Love Masterpiece
Love and Happiness
Let Love Shine
Love Has Come Around
No Frills Love
I Need Your Lovin'
Loving is Really My Game
You Can't Hide (Your Love From Me)
I Love It
Don't Take Your Love Away
Falling In Love
This Is Not A Love Song
I Love Music
Love and Music
Too Hot for Love
Love Thang
Burning Love Breakdown
I'm in Love
Down to Love Town
Love Pains
Love Train
My Love Is Free
Your Love
Your Love (Is a Lifesaver)
Love Fever

Interviews LDW would like to read in Thing
Ron Pruitt interviewed by Harold Cherry
Derrick May interviewed by Leonard Murphy
Keith Kendall interviewed by Reginald Thomas
André Walker interviewed by Wardell Ford
Marshall Jefferson interviewed by Marshall Titus
Ernest Collins interviewed by Paul Mainor
Walter Whitman interviewed by Shelby Webb Jr.
André Hatchett by André Halmon
Randson Boydkin by Arnold Rice

15

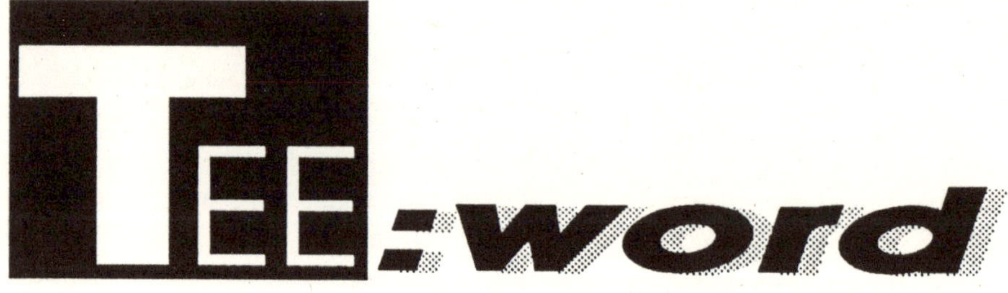

KIND OF BLUE

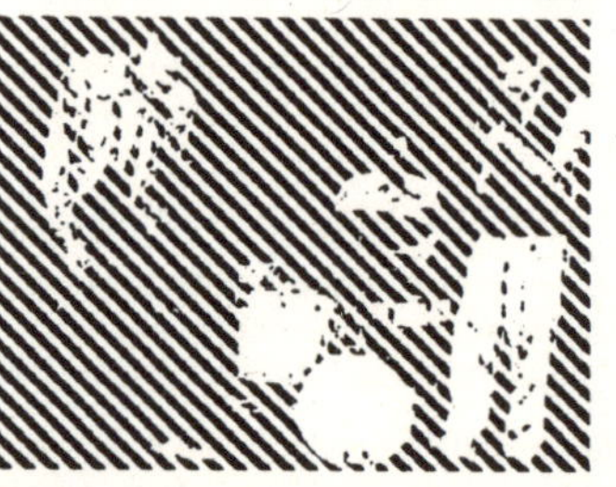

For those of you who don't know, **Robert Ford** is most decidedly a jazz buff. Having an impressive collection of jazz recordings isn't enough; now he's a Jazz Institute of Chicago member and even writes for their newsletter, *Jazzgram*. So, when photographer/DJ/promoter **Terry Martin** approached him about doing a party at **Medusa's**, he, of course, had the brilliant idea of doing a jazz party. (He also had a year old draft for a Blue themed jazz party and *Think Ink's* not-for-profit status, allowing them to get a one-day beer and wine license.) Something Up but low keyed. Conversational. Schmoozey. Cool and ambient classic jazz. Miles of **Miles Davis; Spike Lee's** "Tutu" video, and some real early footage of Miles in the studio. The "Celebrating Bird" video and other jazz visuals. These images ran all night on the third floor of the club. Downstairs were the kids who normally come to Medusa's. And *some* of them did the right thing to stroll upstairs. Medusa's club manager, **Blue**, and his friends were parked at the bar, enjoying the novelty of beer there. Meanwhile, people like **LDW, Kim Davis, Dr. Smith, Gerry Fisher, Wendy Quinn, Michael Alroy** (holy Toledo!), **Simone** and **Stephanie, Ken Hare, Jason Jarques**, and others were in the outer rooms checking out vocalist **Sherri Riley** or into the photo display of **Eduardo Sciammarella.** A good turnout. By the way, **Riqué Green** is *the* person you'd want to work your party. Where does he get all those one liners? He helped make pumping those kegs like madmen every bit as hilarious as you'd expect. All night, back and forth, between the bar and the DJ booth-- keeping the tapes going, the beer flowing, and an eye on *everything* . Sometime late into the party, two white girls stagger up to the DJ booth, drunkenly whining for

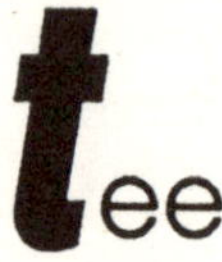

can dance to!" Riqué and I both set out to explain that the theme of the party was Jazz. And that there was a strict format we were adhering to that unfortunately didn't include "something really funky with a beat you can dance to," and that if she really had a complaint to take it up with Robert. Well, *she* told *us* that she ought to just come back there and play something herself since she knew everybody important and that we were just a couple of "AIDS carriers" anyway! I had the urge to give her a kind of blue eye. In a loud and stern voice and not a moment too soon, Riqué screamed, "Do you know her? *I didn't think so!* She's givin' *me* the Blues!" WHAM! And the booth was made BLUE VIP ONLY!

"Something really funky with a beat you

NAKED AT THE FEAST

You already know this is the title for **Josephine Baker's** biography, right? Well, in honor of *La Baker* and all the glamorous jig-a-booing she inspired, LDW and Robert Ford co-hosted a cook out of the same name July 1. There really is no describing the party's location, Catalpa Flats. Just west of Old Town (new Old Town?), it's probably safe to say it's one of the last architectural expressions of the glorious beatnik/hippie days when Old Town was the happenin' place. Very rustic. Look for such structural oddities as salt and pepper shakers and butter dishes lodged into brick walls, mismatched tiling, bric-a-brac moldings, and a spiked wrought iron railing so treacherous and menacing we've dubbed it "The Vincent Price School of Architecture and Design."

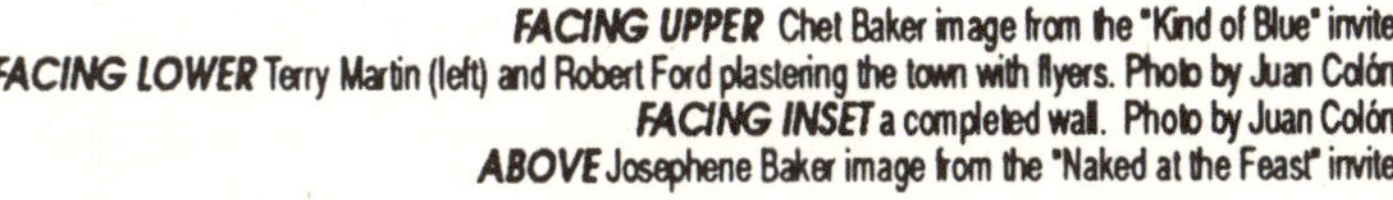

Things were in high gear when I arrived sometime around 7pm. Can you believe this bunch started carrying on as early as 3p ! And that the invite specified 1p! Although the temperature outside was way up there, no one went as far as showing up naked. As for the feast: everything from ribs to chops to bratwurst to chicken to shrimp on the barbie. The music was fun. Robert climbed off of his jazz high horse to spin from his awesome collection of 12" dance singles and bumpier CD's. Riqué and **Donald Redrick** even took turns at the box. I didn't buy the portion of stopping the music for the privilege of watching "Mildred Pierce" and "What ever Happened to Baby Jane" IN STEREO! Plus videos by **Grace Jones, Jody Watley, Madonna, and Diana Ross** (who was the running joke of the party for "Workin' Overtime" . I've never seen so many good impersonations of her being so bad!) **Shelby Webb, Leroy Grant, Ephraim Walls, Judd, Franda, Evil, Penny** (playing Polaroid papparazzi), **Tony Wilkins, Tim Neufville, Larry J.**, and other people. Oh, and writer **Nick Smith** feasting his eyes on the entire twelve page "Baker Mania" piece in the debut issue of *Mirabella* — text and all!

FACING UPPER Chet Baker image from the "Kind of Blue" invite.
FACING LOWER Terry Martin (left) and Robert Ford plastering the town with flyers. Photo by Juan Colón.
FACING INSET a completed wall. Photo by Juan Colón.
ABOVE Josephene Baker image from the "Naked at the Feast" invite.

BAD KATZ

Remember the **Men Of Katz** ? Well, now they're **Bad Boys** (not to be confused with the North Broadway clothiers?). I wondered what else would be new other than the name change. **Johnny Washington** and **Steve Boykin** are still the heads that wear the crowns, but gone is the DJ **Rodney "Quick Mixin'" Slick(?)** who lately had begun to wear the kids thin with too predictable and repetitious a mix of old dance tunes. **Mike Isabuku** has now been installed as the resident DJ, dashing in from around the corner after spinning at the Rialto. After hosting parties at spaces like Wholesome Roc, etc., Bad Boys are back in the Wabash loft where the parties first began a couple of years back as Men Of Katz. On this night, I was reminded of times in Manhattan and early morning hours at 206. My friend **John Pierre** and I bounced in there sometime after 6a to find a cute bunch of kids still winding up/down from the July 4th fireworks at Grant Park and the last night of Taste Of Chicago. **Marsha Burnette** was sitting on the floor behind the desk lounging with friends; standing just at the beginning of the hall was **Mia La Ville** sporting the darkest tan. She said it was a result of working the Taste at the V103 booth. Thank goodness for the soft blue lighting and cool climate in the middle room. We did nothing but chill out in there. The only thing missing was wait service.

EFFIE MAE'S XMAS LIGHT LOUNGE ?

Deciding on one party rather than two parties, I opted to stay on the southside and brazenly strolled down East 51st Street to Ephraim Walls' party at "Effie Mae's Christmas Light Lounge," (just south of the Harlem House,) And though the lounge is safely ensconced within the confines of Walls' spacious, newly purchased condo, getting there proved a challenge; East 51st Street is no pedestrian paradise. I was indeed fortunate to make a safe and early arrival at 11p. This affair was in honor of the departure of Walls' friend **Richard Brown**, who introduced himself to me as "The Party Boy". (It wasn't until I got to the "Goodbye Richard!" banners in the back that the introduction made more sense. I thought he was just being flip.) I wondered about the southside location; too perilous or too out of the way? But a good number of northsiders were there. Walls manages a strict guest list and "invite only" policy, and it works because all the right people get there. (I may have been a crasher but LDW and Robert asked me.) But, a good age mix, a few out-of-towners, a handful of gorgeous women. And Franda, **Greg Mimms**, Evil, **Daryl Hunt**, Penny, **Kim Davis, Rotie**, Nick Smith, and a slew of **Michaels** and **Kevins** and a rare assemblage of young southside cuties. Robert, ever the promoter, was there with "Kind Of Blue" invites and *Thing* submission flyers in tow. Another Walls chum, **Roland Jackson**, provided the sounds and although it got too rhythm-tracky at times and the breaks needed less interruptions, for the most part, the sound and selection were fabulous. Other amenities like a bartender, bus staff, and coat check were a smart addition. The only thing missing was valet parking. That and a couple of copies of "Standing In Line".

CONTINUED ON NEXT PAGE

...MORE **T**EE

MEANWHILE, BACK AT THE RANCH...

One hot and sunny Sunday afternoon, following the very first *Thing* editorial meeting, we moseyed over to the Ponderosa Picnic in Wicker Park hosted by **Bob Caskey,** Terry Martin, the **Glasscocks**, **Mike Kular**, **Bob** and **Tina Painter**, **Keith Callen**, and **Jan Sullivan.** Amazingly, these people have apartments and houses that share the same giant lot as a backyard. The whole enchilada is referred to as "The Compound." It was like a big block party. A House Hayride Americana. Properly displayed U.S. flags all over the place. (We were half expecting a ceremonial burning of at least one before the end of the party). There was volley ball, frisbee, and horseshoes; dogs, cats, and kiddies. The true highlight, however, was the food: a cornucopia of fresh salads (especially the three star Grecian salad!) and every manner of grilled meat. After pigging out in the sun, we decided to hole up in the lively climbs of Terry's coachhouse. We had the chance to meet Symbols and Instruments' **Mark Farina,** **Chris Nazuka** and **Derrick** (Importes, Etc.) **Carter.** We even got the chance to hear their tee fresh demo of techno house hip hop jack swing sounds. (Jeeze!) They're supposedly in production with Detroit's fabulous **Kevin (Inner City) Saunderson** and **Derrick May.** Later, there was more mixing it up when designer and Compound neighbor, **Patty Ryan,** biked over, serving up juicy, bitchy dish, and hitting it right off with **Juan Colón.**

THE GOODBYE GIRL

On a Thursday evening, just as the air had begun to gain its fall crispness, Robert, **Cecilia Hunt,** and myself decided on O'Rourke's for a cocktail in honor of CeCe's birthday (nearly a week before) mainly be-cause of its low key old bohemian flavor and its close proximity to Robert's apartment. Well, it takes Robert to inform us that , as we're drinking, we are enjoying one of the last nights in the place. It turns out that O'Rourke's is going the way of all flesh and shutting its doors once and for all sometime very soon. Some developers have gotten a hold of the joint and a total makeover (read gentrification) is being planned. As we drank and chatted and looked over the aged posters and the colorful gathering of poets, writers, painters, and such, we could only sigh and shake our heads in dismay. And order another round. Funny, too, that I was with CeCe at the closing of Chicago's historic hillbilly heaven, The Ranch.

VAGUELY REMINISCENT

The night of Simone's group opening at the Gallery Off The Alley, (which really isn't *off* any

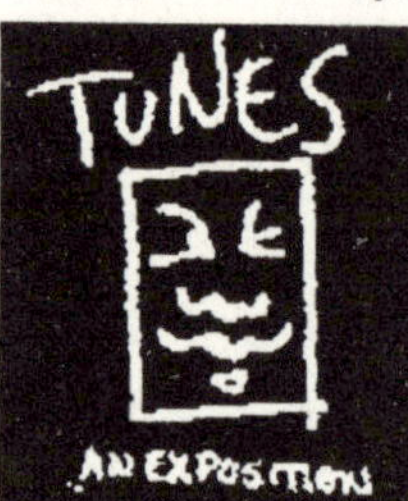

alley), Simone, Stephanie and I dropped off Robert and headed for Damen Avenue to **Rick Tuttle's** opening at the Buckin 'A' Cafe, in Bucktown, of course. It's really a nice place, however. Clean and comfortable without being too sterile or showy. Good coffee. Simple menu. And friendly service. On display were about a dozen of Rick's pieces from his collection of jazz paintings entitled "Tunes". The subject matter and style of the paintings, (real and imagined scenes of figures in jazz and literature rendered in an expressionist mode), went well with the retro-Forties **Rickie Lee Jones** feel of the place. It's good to see Rick continuing to find showcases for these very impressive works. The conversation turned from a discussion of **Spike Lee**'s "Do The Right Thing" to Rick's sixteen-year-old son being a huge **Public Enemy** fan; from Buckin 'A' s cups and saucers being the same pattern as Rick's grandmother's to other remembrances of things past. *Holsum Roc Revisited.*

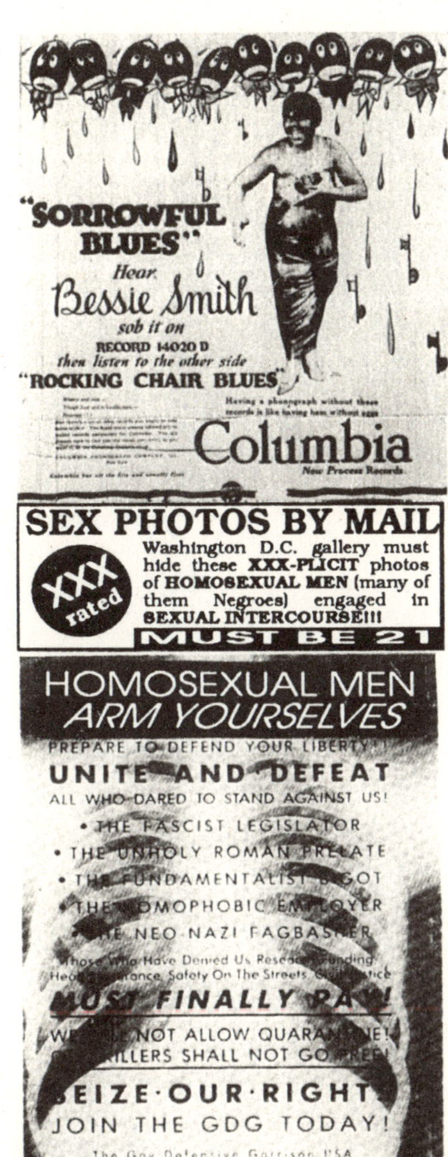

SEX PHOTOS BY MAIL

XXX rated

Washington D.C. gallery must hide these **XXX-PLICIT** photos of **HOMOSEXUAL MEN** (many of them Negroes) engaged in **SEXUAL INTERCOURSE!!!**

MUST BE 21

HOMOSEXUAL MEN
ARM YOURSELVES

PREPARE TO DEFEND YOUR LIBERTY!

UNITE AND DEFEAT

ALL WHO DARED TO STAND AGAINST US!

- THE FASCIST LEGISLATOR
- THE UNHOLY ROMAN PRELATE
- THE FUNDAMENTALIST BIGOT
- THE HOMOPHOBIC EMPLOYER
- THE NEO-NAZI FAGBASHER

Those Who Have Denied Us Research Funding, Health Insurance, Safety On The Streets, Our Justice

MUST FINALLY PAY!

WE WILL NOT ALLOW QUARANTINE! OUR KILLERS SHALL NOT GO FREE!

SEIZE OUR RIGHT

JOIN THE GDG TODAY!

The Gay Defensive Garrison USA

DRAW ANY PERSON
in one minute!
NO LESSONS! NO TALENT!

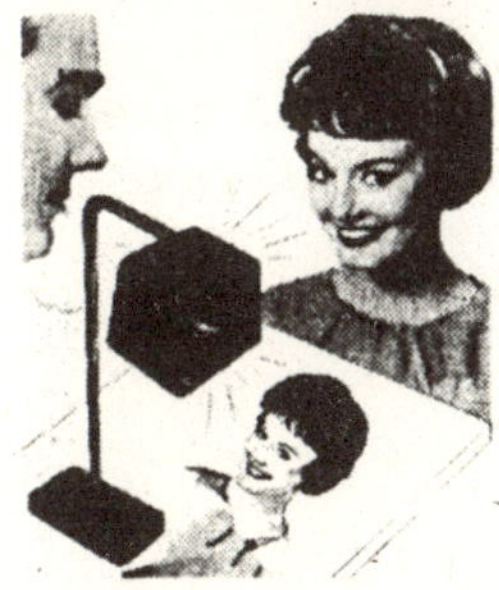

New Amazing Invention —"Magic Art Reproducer." You can draw Your Family, Friends, animals, landscapes, buildings, vases, bowls of fruit, copy photos, comics, designs, maps, anything — Like An Artist Even if You CAN'T DRAW A Straight Line! Anything you want to draw is automatically seen on any sheet of paper thru the "Magic Art Reproducer." Then easily follow the lines of the "Picture Image" with a pencil for an original "professional looking" drawing. Also reduces or enlarges.

Artist's Conception

EARN MONEY AT HOME

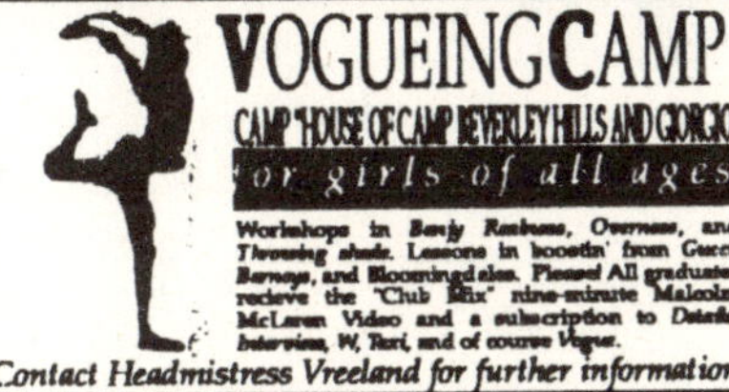

S U P P O R T
THING

Subscribe to alternitive media
(if you don't who will?)

```
NAME_______________________
ADDRESS____________________
CITY____________ ST____ ZIP______
☐ Here's FIVE DOLLARS. Send me the next 3 issues!
☐ Here's MORE I really like what you're doing!
☐ Here's a SASE, because I'm broke. Send me the next one.
```

The next THING will be out before you know it — look for it!

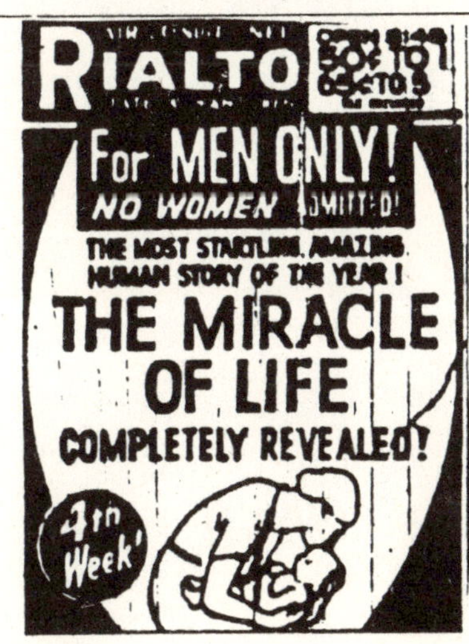

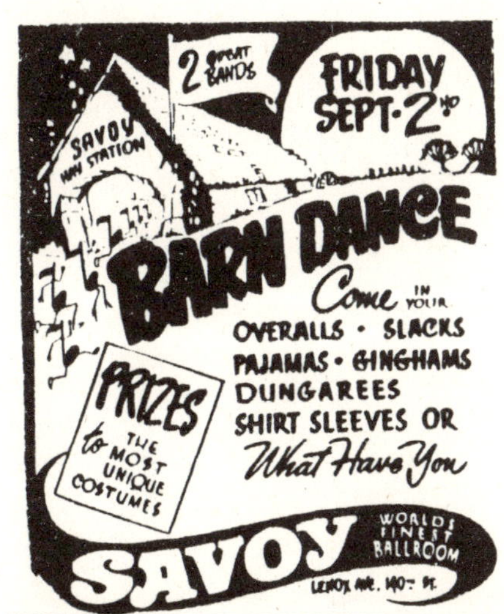

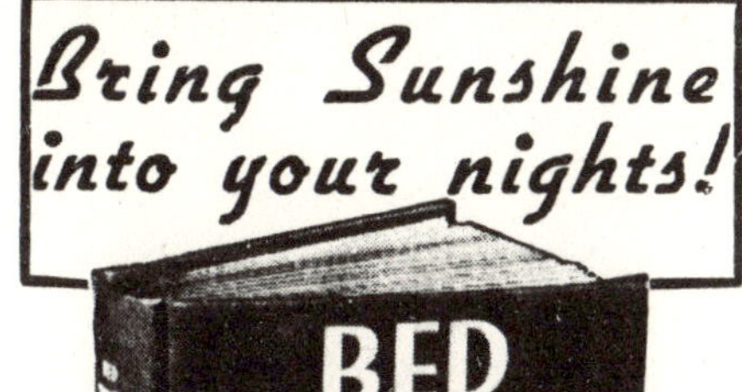

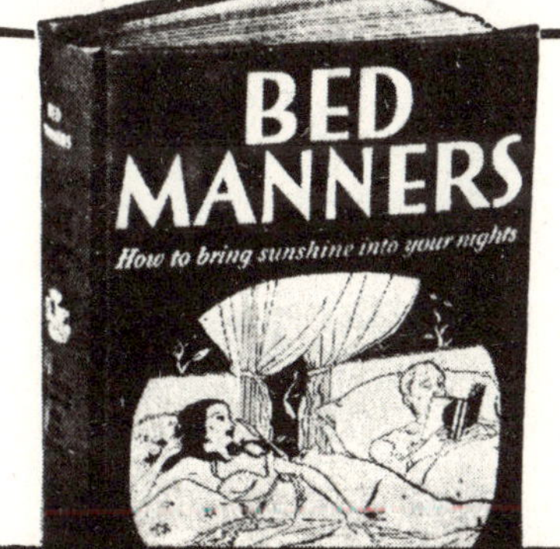

BED MANNERS

Now presenting in one volume:
BED MANNERS and BETTER BED MANNERS
247 bedlam pages—37 enthusiastic chapters!

Ideal GIFT—only $1.98 Postpaid

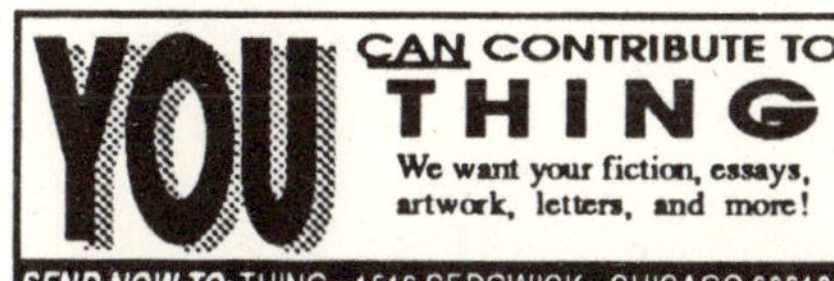

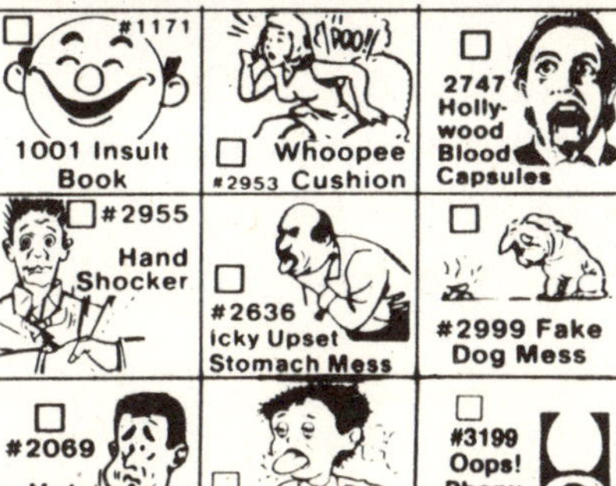

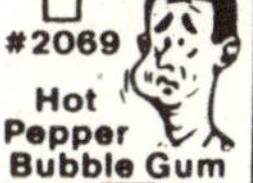

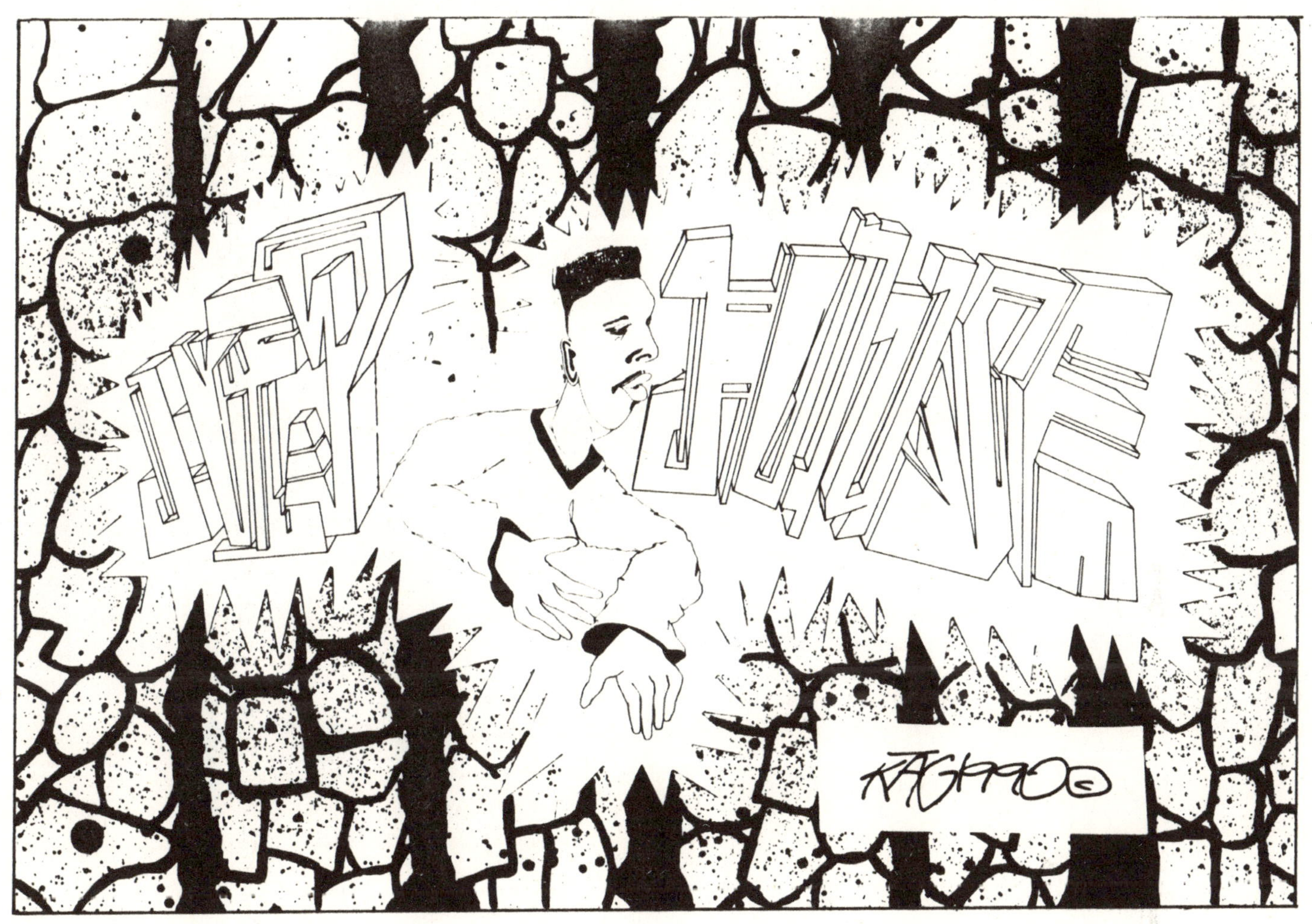

There has always been rap in the house, now there's a name for it. Earliest hip-house includes the seminal T.S.O.B. (1980), "To the Beat Y'all" by Lady B. (1983) and of course the king of funky rap, Kurtis Blow.

The end of the eighties found the whole rap scene integrating different musical influences along the way, including an increasing infusion of house. The Wee Papa Girl's "Heat it Up", Tyree Cooper's D.J. International L.P. "Nation of Hip-House", Farley "Jackmaster" Funk's new "Real Hip-House" compilation, and the "house mix" of any M.C. Lyte 12" are prime examples of the genre.

The Nineties started with the first crossover hip house hit: "Pump up the Jam" by Technotronic featuring Felly. A little Euro, very house-acid, phonetic New Yawk rap. Yo, pump it!

THING

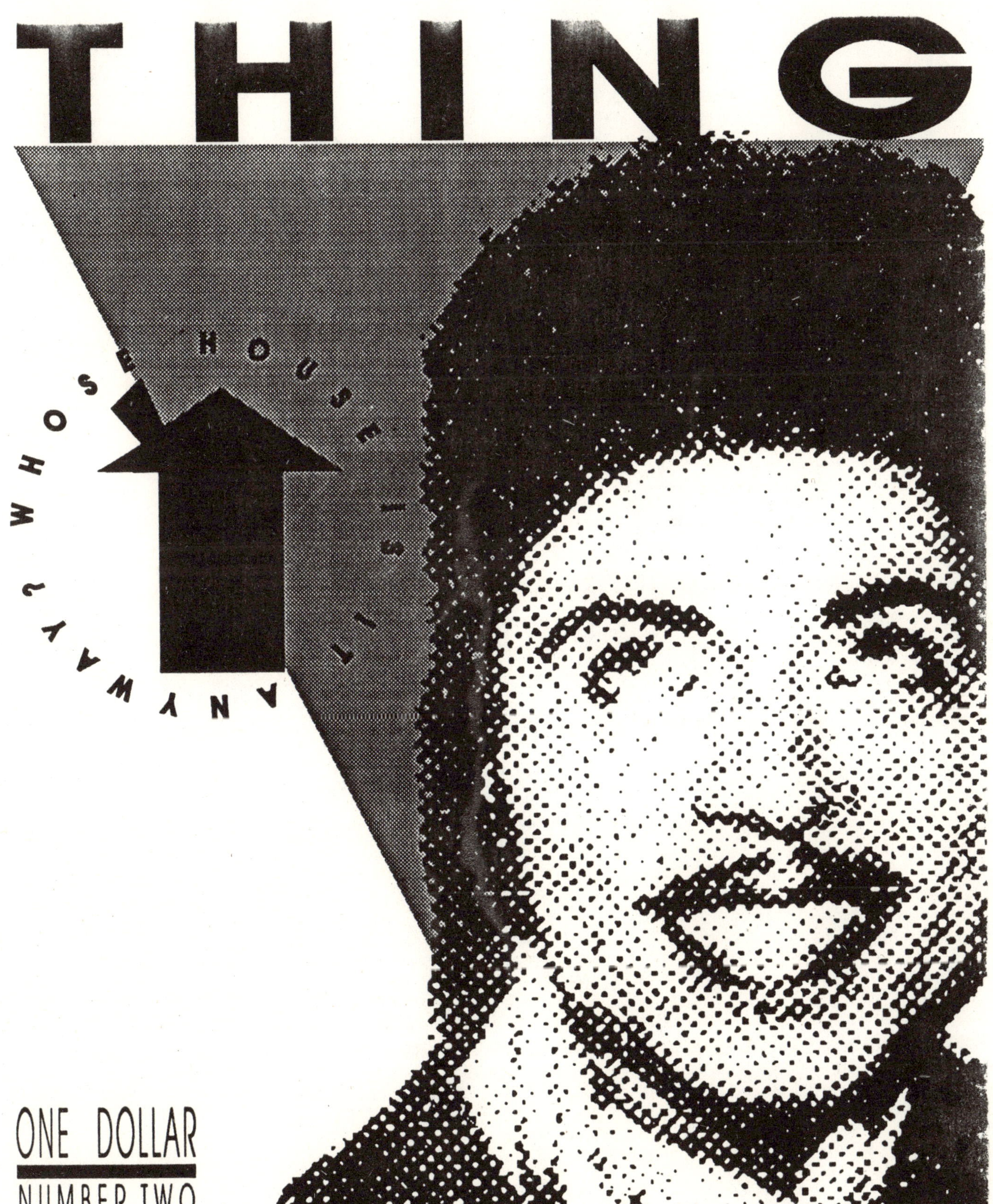

ONE DOLLAR

NUMBER TWO

Can you send me 5-10 more November issues of *Thing*? What w/ all the coming cavortin' around the cornacopia I'd kinda like to have sompin to show the relatives (Yeah right).

Well, I've enclosed a check for $12.50 = alls I kin spare till I find myself a new job.

Thanks again for the exposure (I liked the artlcle on dreaded hair).

TOR DETWILLER
CHICAGO, IL

Hey, I love your *Thing*! Picked up your premiere issue at Different Light in L.A. Too fab, as Bill Coleman would say - speaking of Bill Coleman, send him a comp issue. He's the singles reviewer at *Billboard* and also writes their dance column. Never know if you'll warrant a mention. He's definitely a thing. Me, I'd like a subscription: here's $5.

The blackness of your *Thing* is the best! Your cover to #1 is a little like pointilism. Maybe I'll think up a contribution. Meanwhile you can publish this letter with my address so things can write me.

— P.S. Send a copy to my friend Tom Jennings at Homocore zine and he'll send you a copy of his and maybe give you a review. Tell him Gary sent ya!

— P.P.S. OK, so I just sent him a review myself. He'll probably publish it in issue #6 coming out in early 1990.

GARY REYNOLDS
112 A. CEDAR STREET
SANTA CRUZ, CA 95060

It was real. Thanks very much for your participation (Horizon's 12th Annual Fall Conference) and for *Thing*! Keep up the good stuff!

NATALIE HUTCHISON
HORIZONS COMMUNITY SERVICES
CHICAGO, IL

Congratulations on your first issue. It displays spirit, good humor, and a healthy attitude of self acceptance, and it is attractively laid out. You are certainly off to a good start, and you undoubtedly have a good future as a publication in front of you, because you are doing necessary, spirited, and accessible work.

ALAN E. MILLER
OAKLAND, CA

Thing magazine's November 1989 issue #1 was a delight to read and re-read.

It inspired me to write something from my own experience. Whether it is right for your next issue is for you to decide. I'd like to circulate it to a couple of different publishers to see who publishes it first and to be able present my ideas to as many people as possible.

MAX SMITH
CHICAGO, IL

Please send us *Thing* number one which I, for one, missed entirely. (Spend enough time working, and it's remarkable how much you can miss.) So I'm quite curious as to what you're up to.

I look forward to seeing *Thing*.

JACK HAFFERKAMP
CO-PUBLISHER, *LIBIDO*
CHICAGO, IL

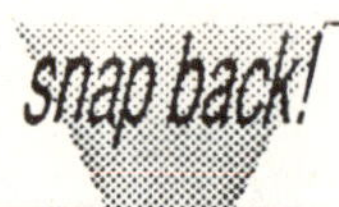

The piece from "Gentlewomen" in the first issue of *Thing* (inside back cover) was originally from a work I exhibited at N. A. M. E. last year. I'm sending two shots. Thought its origins might interest you. I was working as Stuart Japheth then.

I'm also sending the text from a performance piece I did in January that you might find interesting. I'm working on a visual language xerox book of these, but it's not on the front burner.

Thing looks great. This kind of graphic look for a photocopy format is overdue. Good luck. Hope to meet you one of these days

KERMIT BERG
CHICAGO, IL

I picked up the first issue and I loved it from cover to cover. Thank you for providing a media just for girls like us!

So here's a little donation to keep "things" going.

TONY GREENE
PASEDENA, CA

YOU CAN WRITE TO US, TOO!

THING
1516 N. SEDGWICK
CHICAGO, ILLINOIS USA 60610-1223

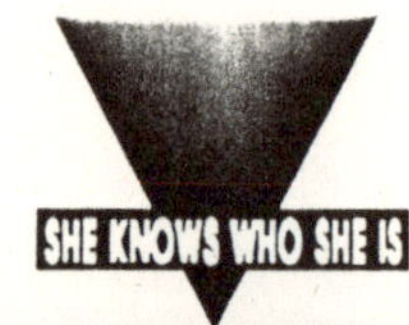

NUMBER TWO

PUBLISHER/EDITOR
Robert Ford
CO-EDITORS
Trent Adkins
Lawrence D. Warren
LAYOUT/ART DIRECTION
Robert Ford
GRAPHIC SERVICES
Simone Bouyer

CONTRIBUTORS

Bunny and Pussy, Dennis Cooper, Marcelino Y. Fahd, André Halmon, KAG, Iris Kit, Terry A. Martin, Alan Miller, Marc Pentecoste, Wendy Quinn, Max Smith, Louis Walker, Tony Wilkins

NUMBER TWO · APRIL 1990

Thing is published capriciously. Subscriptions: Five dollars for the next three issues published postpaid, one dollar per issue with a self-addressed stamped envelope. Donations encouraged! Make checks payable to publisher Robert Ford. *Thing* encourages unsolicited submissions of any printable matter; only those with self-addressed stamped envelopes will be returned. Artists' payment is the satisfaction of contribution. Editorial inclusion casts no aspersions on one's racial or sexual categorization (Things know who they are). Opinions expressed are those of individual contributors, and do not always reflect those of *Thing*.
©1990 *Thing*

DIRECT COMMUNICATION TO
Thing, 1516 N. Sedgwick, Chicago, Illinois USA 60610-1223
1.312.944.5850

ABOUT THE CONTRIBUTORS

ALAN E. MILLER

IS A BLACK GAY POET WHO LIVES IN OAKLAND, CALIFORNIA. A NATIVE OF CHICAGO AND A GRADUATE OF AMHERST COLLEGE, HIS POEMS HAVE APPEARED IN MAWA REVIEW, THE AMHERST REVIEW, BLACK AMERICAN LITERATURE FORUM, AND THE BERKLEY REVIEW.

ANDRÉ HALMON

DANCE MUSIC PRODUCER SLASH PROMOTER SLASH DISTRIBUTOR SLASH PUBLICIST ANDRÉ HALMON STARTED OUT DOING RECORD RETAIL AND DEE JAYING AT A FEW OF THE CLUBS AND PRIVATE PARTIES ABOUT TOWN. NOW WITH IMPACT DISTRIBUTORS, HE HANDLES RADIO PROMOTIONS AND 12" SALES. ANDRÉ NEEDS A CLUB TO SPIN AT; CALL HIM IF YOU CAN HELP!

DENNIS COOPER

NEW YORK WRITER DENNIS COOPER IS ENJOYING THE GOOD RECEPTION OF HIS NOVEL "CLOSER" (GROVE PRESS), IS AN ART CRITIC WITH SEVERAL NEW YORK PUBLICATIONS, AND IS AN INDISPENSABLE FIXTURE ON THE UNDERGROUND GAY PRESS CIRCUIT.

TONY WILKINS

FREELANCE WRITER TONY WILKINS IS DIRECTOR OF HIS OWN TELEMARKETING CONSULTING FIRM, TELECORP. HE ALSO CO-PRODUCES AND CO-WRITES FOR "THE TEN PERCENT SHOW" ON CHANNEL 19 (PUBLIC ACCESS CABLE).

CONTENTS

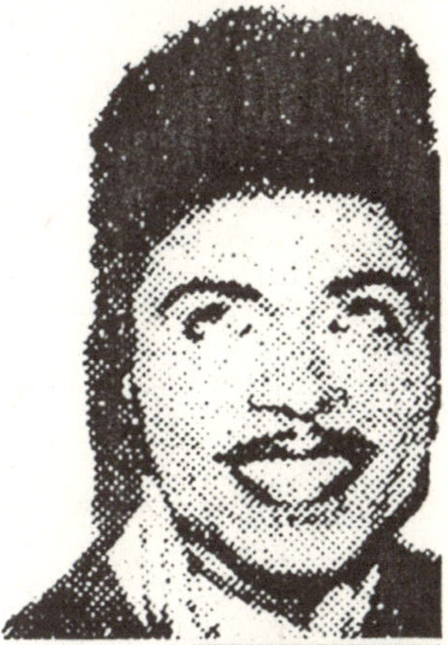

ON THE COVER

No, Little Richard was not a d.j., or a house musician, but he was the first real thing who got over *bigtime* (before Sylvester, Liberace, et.al.) His image says a lot about house, and it's exploitation by the crossover hungry music industry.

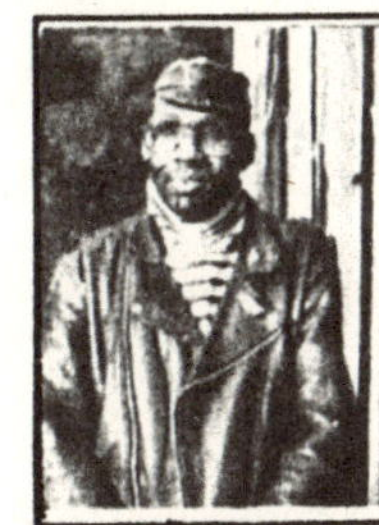

FEATURE INTERVIEW

house musician Riley Evans

FEATURES

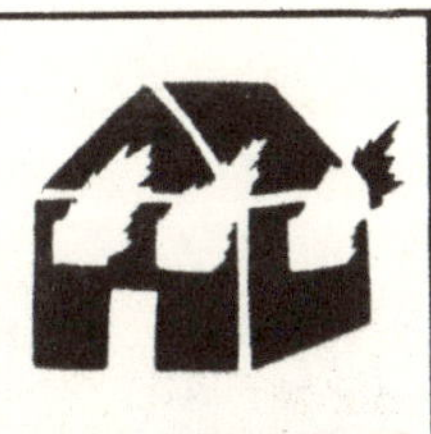

BURNING HOUSE

1979 stencil/spray paint by David Wojnarowicz.
p. 19

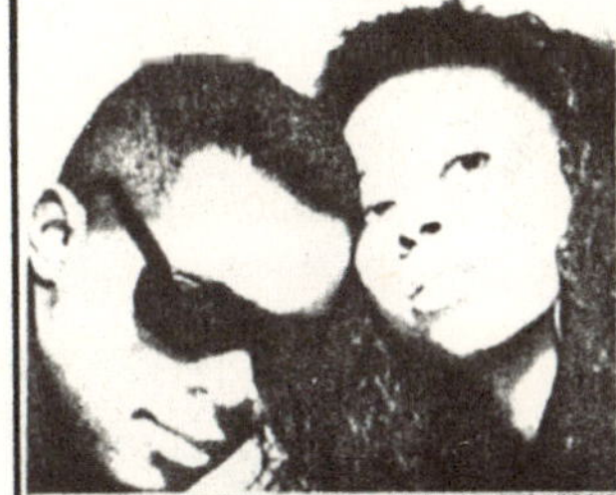

SPRINGTIME IN PARIS

The Paris/ London Connection. T.A. reminisces about the big break of "Big Fun" for Detroit's Inner City.
p.6

KEITH HARING

and his last visit to Chicago
p.18

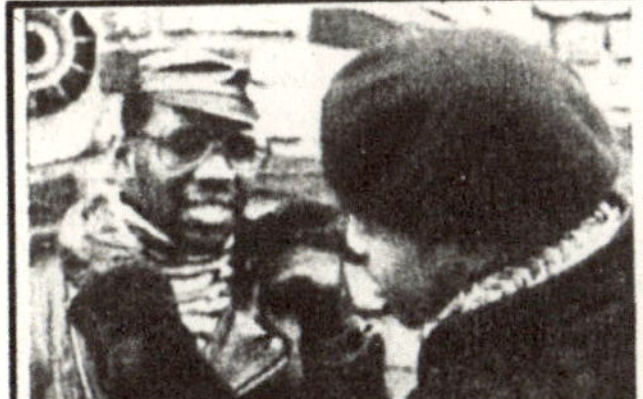

HOUSE THE HAIR?

Stylist Trent Adkins caught off guard and hard at work by Terry Martin at the Riley Evans portrait shoot for this issue.
p.8

ACID

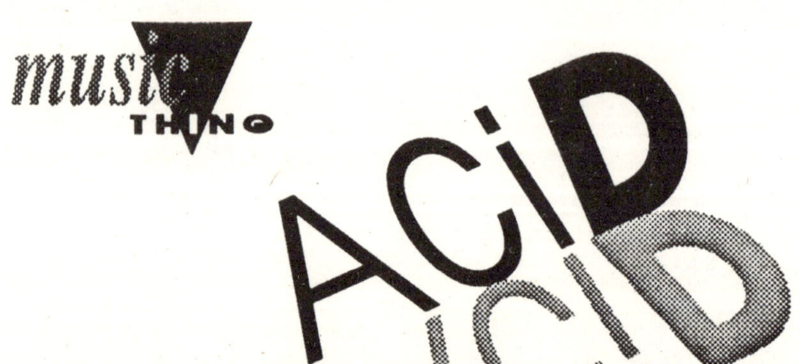

Mark Farina, Derrick "the Maestro" Carter, and Chris Nazuka are *Symbols and Instruments*, arguably Chicago's hippest acid trio. Derrick is a vinyl junkie with the definitive disco library. Mark provides the visual energy in images on cards, posters, and other promotional items. Chris plays piano and other keyboards. And they <u>all</u> play records, and take turns spinning.

Their use of various live digital effects with traditional dj wizardry makes their sets incredible aural journeys, which takes acid from song to experience. Their cuts "Mood" "Science of Numbers" and "Teardrops of Yesterday" are just out on KMS, Kevin Saunderson's Detroit techno label and have been licensed for U.K. release on Big Life records (Cold Cut, Yazz, etc.)

CHRIS BY CHRIS • Computer video self portrait of Chris Nazuka

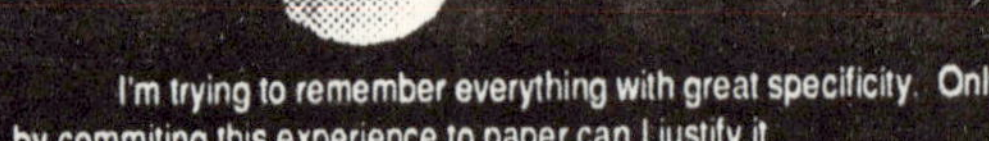

I'm trying to remember everything with great specificity. Only by commiting this experience to paper can I justify it.

It had been years since I'd done acid. I can still remember first experiencing it. I'd read about it in "Go Ask Alice", but that white hippie thing seemed light years away from any thing I knew of life. My first time was at the Warehouse; when I first saw the end of a party. Hadn't done it in years, but what the fuck.

I felt the fibers of the tiny, rough paper crumble in my saliva. I knew it was far too soon to feel anything, but I wanted to be aware of the first twinge; articulate the point of departure. But my mind is filled with how annoying this cacaphony is. This is real acid house, alright. Baselines and echoes and nothing like a melody! The only resemblance to the New York funk that was the house of my youth was an occasional sample.

The acid kids seem to be stuck on the abstraction of the experience: just at that point where you're *too* full. They've made it its own cult; connected acid to house like heroin to be-bop or ganja to reggae. Except that *this* music is only about the intoxication; the trip is the destination.

I think briefly that I hope this isn't just the speed and strychnaine stuff that I hear these kids think is the real thing. Then I think that I used to think that years ago, when I thought we had missed that really good, hallucenogenic stuff, like in 'Hair'.

I'm aware of my thought processes. Is that the blotter starting? Or am I just bored?

It's been a long time. The guy I got this from looked younger than I was when I did *my* first hit. The blotter was at least familiar: the same Tweety Bird from the 206 days.

I remember how strange and modern this kind of music used to sound to me, how every Saturday was devoted to more, without question. What else was there to do? (I did acid every Saturday for a while, too, but luckily stopped before I became one of those mad queens stealing Louis Vuitton and Gucci bags from Field's.)

Still nothing in my head. Mabye I should dance. I remembered that dancing always seemed to unleash it. I actually recognize this record, and I dance despite the choking chemical fog which adds to the visual intrigue. I'm noticing the lights and their movement. I think this is it.

An echo over matched beats take us to the next record, which is that record that I don't know the name of that's like just the first three seconds of "Time Warp" over and over until you want to pull your hair out.

Oh, shit. What a baseline. I know this language, and have already memorized all the words. Movement in the strobe amuses me; each gesture seems profound and beautiful. I watch the trails that my hand makes as it moves across the brick wall that I hold onto. The melody bounces off the aftertraces, and I swear it's even LOUDER! My brain is like soup, this makes me laugh so hard I want to piss.

I sweat a while ago and took off my shirt. Now I call myself not dancing, standing against a wall near a door that lots in some air. I want to stand but the bounce of the beat keeps me moving. I couldn't stop moving if I wanted to. But I don't want to. I'm waiting for a keyboard or something to pierce this rhythm track, to make me dance more.

I exchange a look with my friend here, and we lock into a shared highness in our pupils. We grin at each other like idiots; smug in sharing this unsharable thing.

The last record was "Back to Life"; the only "song" all night. The poetically banal lyrics suddenly are clear and meaningful. The speakers go silent and the worklights on and there's a buzz I know are my battered eardrums. Soul II Soul won't leave my head. I whisper "...back to reality, "all the way home. Turn off the phone and start the bathwater.

BIG 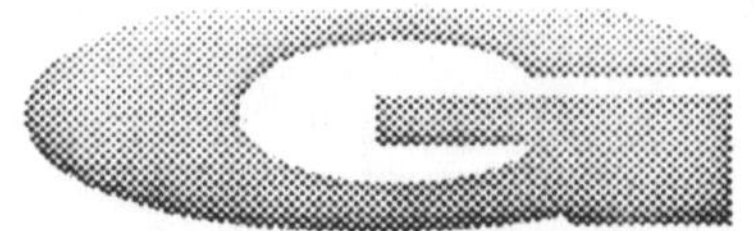fun?

IT ALL STARTED ONE EVENING in August of '88 after I'd finally received a call from **André Halmon** of Real Estate fame. At the time, Halmon was busy producing **Howard, Sanders, and Turner** and working with names like **Keith Alexis, Adonis,** and practically everybody else into house music here. He was also doing a stint at Rose Records' North State Parkway store as the 12" dance specialist, and editting a music column called "Real Estate" for Think Ink magazine. I was desperate to talk to him about this, about that, but mostly about the names of a few new records: one in particular that was getting fierce club play (and good response) with a woman singing 'We-don't-really-need-a-crowd-to-have-a-party!' André was undoubtedly too busy to be bothered. After many messages left on his answering machine, I'd given up any hopes of a returned call. I was truly worn out with all the tele-tagging. Anyway, <u>he</u> was phoning <u>me</u> looking for a photographer and stylist for a woman named **Paris Gray** who was signing with Virgin Records in London. A big deal since Virgin already had acts like Soul II Soul, Boy George, and Paula Abdul. The name of the group was Inner City. Paris wrote lyrics and did vocals and **Kevin Saunderson** produced the music.

Virgin was late in getting photos of her to the press and needed pix taken right away. Fine. No problem. "Expect a call from London in a couple of days," André was saying. "Sure," I said, "but you still haven't told me who's the girl that does, 'We- don't- really-need-a-crowd-to-have-a-party! Just-a-funky-beat...We're-having-big-fun!'" "That's her! Paris Gray!", he answered. " It's called 'Big Fun' and she's signing with Virgin. They asked me who did I know to do pictures so I said you." Knowing how *everybody* wants to get paid, he added, "They'll pay you the rate and everything." I'm like, "Oh. I see!"

★★★★

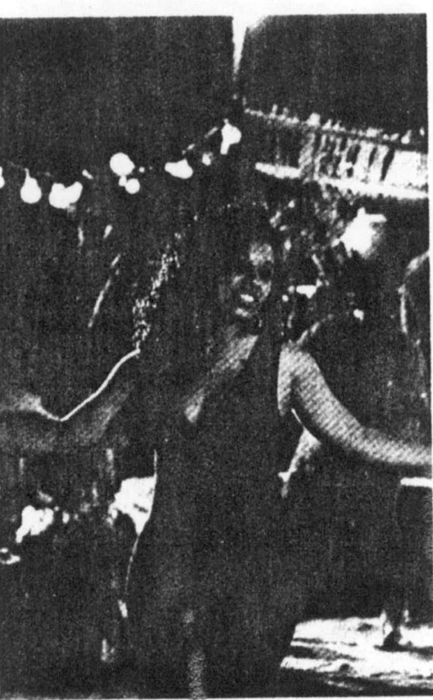

PARIS IN LONDON? We grabbed this from London's MixMag. Mabye it's a still from one of her videos.

TWO DAYS LATER, I received a call from **Sam Russell**, then at the London Press offices of Virgin. She gave me Paris' phone number in Chicago and took Brad's information. I found this amusing and ironic 'cause here's this girl calling me from London to give me a woman's number who lives and works right here in Chicago! That same evening, I called Brad with the news. The next day Sam called Brad about the details of how much film to shoot and where to courier the film. Telephone tag? Later that same day, after speaking with Brad, I'm on the phone with Paris Gray, putting together a meeting among the three of us. She wanted to plan it out before we'd set a date and she had to get her hair done. Fine.

Meanwhile, "Big Fun" is all over the place. Everybody's buying it. It's on the hot mix dance parties on all the radio stations in Chicago (even on B 96) and all over Europe. It's in the clubs in town, in London, New York, Detroit. It's on the top of the charts. In no time at all, kids on Soul Train, Club MTV, and American Bandstand, are havin' big fun, too. And, of course, *everybody* saw and/or heard the the Old Style Dry commercial that used "Big Fun" as the background music: all the young trendy kids, black clad and Haircut One Hundred-ed at Medusa's or someplace *drying themselves off* and 'Havin'-big-fun!'

★★★★

WHEN I FINALLY DID GET TO MEET PARIS in person, I couldn't have imagined her to be more unaffected by all the hype. This may have been due to the fact that nobody knew what she looked like or had been even vaguely familiar with her voice until "Big Fun" broke and became a mega hit. There'd been "Don't Leave Me", (an underground hit tune she'd recorded with **Terry Baldwin** and Kevin Saunderson), but Paris was using a different name then. At any rate, very few people knew Paris Gray by face and/or name and she was still

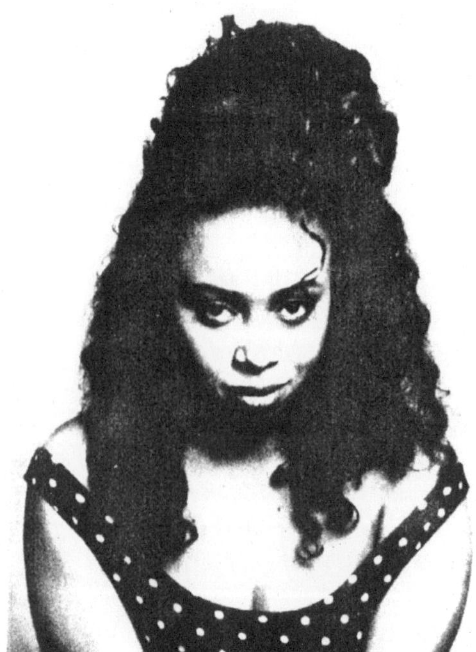

GOOD LIFE: Paris photographed by Bradley Starks. One seven-month-old paycheck and two remixes later, the above glossy finally arrived in the mail.

able to enjoy the kind of anonymity that let her keep her day job at the hosiery counter at a certain chi-chi department store out in Oak Brook.

By now, it seemed as if Sam Russell was calling every day with, "Are they done yet?" As soon as Paris got her hair done. Finally, the day she <u>did</u> get her hair done, Paris enters the studio with her longtime friend **Diedra** and we begin the make-up and clothes act. She pops some rough mixes of "Big Fun" and "Don't Leave Me" into the tape player and Brad's like, "<u>This</u> is your record ?! Great!" Paris was an extremely easy and pleasant person to work with.

★★★★

THE LAST TIME I SAW PARIS, she was in the Loop running around with her brother, picking up her passport, etc. She hugged me and I told her how thrilled I was that the record was doing so well and to keep up the good work. She was leaving for London that evening and had also been booked in Detroit. Originally, she had been scheduled in London for a show but it had been cancelled. Then it was put back on. Then cancelled again. Just the day or so before she was totally unaware of it being on again. Suddenly, a former shop girl is rushing to make gigs in Germany, London, Detroit, Amsterdam, New York. It was all too fairy-tale-over-night-success for me.

She finally did spend a few mad days in London. "We didn't really get to go anywhere, they ran me around so," she later told me. "We shot the "Big Fun' video, but I didn't do a show there. I had on a *tight* yellow dress and basically it wasn't much of a place. It was this really huge warehouse. It was very dark. I guess that's why the yellow dress ... so you could see me. But I didn't go anywhere. We were supposed to make this one club with Kevin (Saunderson), but that fell through. I barely had time to rest." *We're-havin'-big-fun!*

★★★★

WEEKS AND WEEKS LATER, I caught up with her at home and she told me briefly about the warm reception every-- where. She said that the management at the different clubs such as Todd's in Detroit and The World in NYC were really together. She even talked about some girl in Detroit or someplace who had been busy impersonating her. Someone had illegally aquired some master tapes and got a cute girl to pose as Paris and lip sync "Big Fun." Boy, she really was becoming obscenely famous. I told her I heard her record almost everywhere and that **Frankie Knuckles** mixed "Big Fun" when he was in Chicago at the Riviera for a Thanksgiving party. "So the Knuckles is playin' 'Big Fun' huh?" She seemed genuinely surprised. But, would anybody be that surprised when a year or so later Virgin would release an Inner City cover version of the Stephanie Mills hit "What Cha Gonna Do With My Loving" mixed by non other than Frankie Knuckles and **David Morales** for DEF Productions? No one was a bit surprised.

—TRENTON D. ADKINS

For all of you wondering where to send the get-well roses for Next Plateau recording artist **Sybil**, wonder no longer. Sources say that she's signed out of the "Three Faces of Eve Home for Wayward Girls" and is taking medication to combat schizophrenia. It all started when I sang "My Love Is Guaranteed" over **M'A R R S** ("Pump Up the Volume" not the planet.) Next thing I knew, I'd been possessed with the souls of Dionne Warwicke and Jazzie B. Sybil (no relation to the more famous schizoid of the same name) confides the worst part is the Warwicke overbite, which adds tension headaches to her list of maladies. Though gratified by the results (both "Walk on By" and "Don't Make Me Over" are mega hits), Sybil worries about the fight that will come when Jazzie B wants to dred and Dionne wants a press and curl. As soon as she's recuperated, she'll be entering into the studio with "Do You Know the Way Back to Life in San Jose, Allie?". Not to be outdone by **Janet Jackson's** stab at a concept album. **Jody Watley** is preparing her next effort, *Jody Watley's Fashion Nation Chanel No. 5.* Look for her campaign of epigrams soon: Shoulder pads: NO! Culottes: NO! Polyester NO! And the new **Knuckles** project, *Frankie Knuckles' Booty Nation 1015-206* is set to ship soon. EMI's entrant in the **Whitney** race, **D'atra Hicks**, failed to ignite sales of great proportion with her debut album. Look for her to push cosmetics to help keep her profile up: *"D'atra Skin Tone Cream"* Bitch On The Block? Many **Quincy Jones** fans have noticed a name often associated with the Q missing from the all star lineup of "Back on the Block": **Patti** (Cakes) **Austin**. Wasn't good girlfriend Patti Quincy's "discovery" on his last solo album, "The Dude"? What happened in those last eight years that Patti won't chirp a note for him now? Rumor has it that it was all that pie. Sources say he's fed up. Quincy was reported to say "When she couldn't even shop at Lane Bryant anymore, I knew she'd gotten too fat offa me!". That a very chicken New Kid and a just-post-pubescent former lead singer of New Edition were extras in the all male video "Sex Bazaar" is being vehemetly denied by both parties. Singin in the rain? Is it true that that's really **Evelyn King** singing for **Lisa Stansfield** (a lá Lena Lamont) in the "All Around the World" video? Or is she really a grad of the "**Teena Marie** School for White Girls"? Bonofied bull! **Cher** says she's fed up with the tabloids. They got it all wrong about her daughter's "coming out." Cher first knew when she bumped into Chastity in the 'jane' at New York's famed lesbian haunt the Cubbyhole. When asked if she saw any irony in naming her daughter Chastity, Cher replied, "What's in a name?"

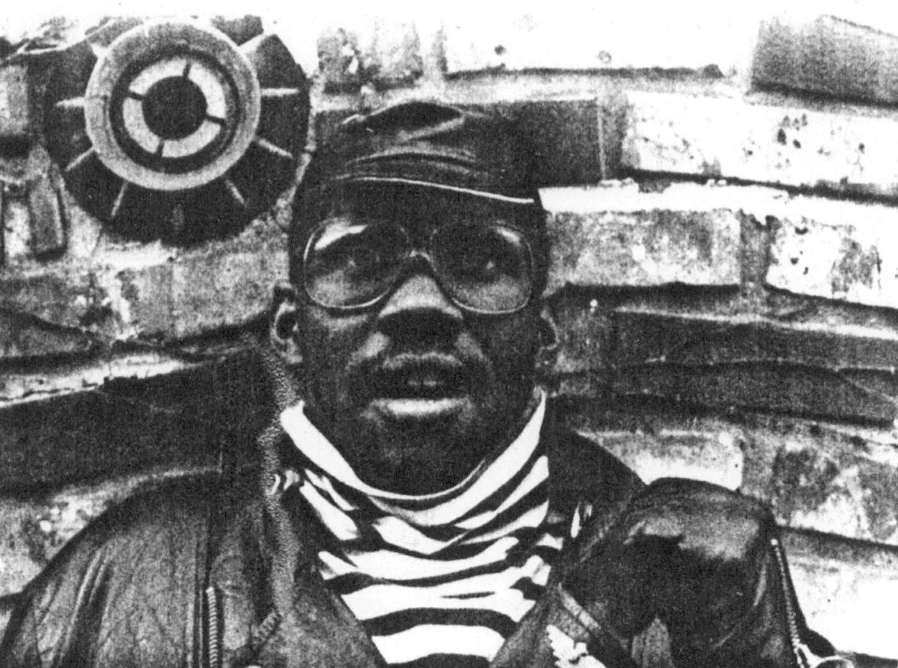

The Life of RILEY

Riley Evans is not the most famous of Chicago's house music exports, but is certainly one of the most real. His style has been dubbed "deep house", but his sound is a complex mix of his roots in gospel music and training in classical music. Steeped in the black gay disco sound at the Warehouse and Powerplant, Riley makes dance music that is musical. Low piano lines, soaring strings, and of course what Riley calls "…that sickening break that goes into a minor key!" He's done various amounts of work on records too numerous to mention, from uncredited keyboards to full production and writing credits. But his hasn't been a Cinderella house success story, either. Trauma with fly-by-night disco labels pushed him to start his own label to keep artistic control.

Riley came by our office for the interview, with an entourage of vocalist Sonya Grant and her sister Lisa Jones, who was girl friday over Riley's Filofax. Oh, yes and they brought much pie. Coconut Creme from Bakers Square, and Riley's homemade cheesecake. So with a 90 minute cassette in the recorder, there was more than enough dish.

INTERVIEWED BY TRENT ADKINS, ROBERT FORD, AND LAWRENCE WARREN

ROBERT FORD: Actually I must say you were right on the button this evening. "Seven-thirty, I'll be there." You were here at seven-twenty nine.

RILEY EVANS: Well since Total Spectrum records has opened I've been on it!

LAWRENCE D. WARREN: Yeah, 'cause that's what made me take the slow route because I said, 'Riley is never on time! I needn't worry!'

RE: Oh, honey now for business functions, I'm on time.

RF: The dog stopped eating his homework.

LDW: How did you get introduced to the whole "house music" scene? Before that, wasn't your background mainly classical?

RE: That was kind of sudden, wasn't it? I came from the VanderCook College of Music. What was called "Summer Music Recreation Camp". In the summer, instead of us going off to camp to just play, we went off to camp to learn to play classical music. Study theory, conducting, and stuff like that. We had recreation time between two in the afternoon and seven pm, then it was back to theory class, and a final band rehearsal every night. And this went on for a week each summer.

RF: ...then you were part of the whole Warehouse thing ?

RE: Yeah, at first I'd just kinda, you know, used to just fall up in there. I'd be too full to really dance. I'd just stand on the wall and listen to the music. I couldn't understand where all these kids were coming from. It just wasn't logical to me. I liked a lot of the arrangements, the string and horn arrangements, and the music in general. That's what got me there. At that time I was formulating my own style.

RF: If you could name five records that were your influences...

RE: I'd have to say "Romeo and Juliet" by Alex Constantinos ...Love and Kisses "You're the Most Precious Thing In My Life"; "Love in C Minor" by Cerrone; "Supernature" by Cerrone. "Disco Circus" by Martin Circus...what fascinated me were these fifteen minute songs with constantly changing themes and motifs, with different themes interwoven and recapitulated throughout...

RF: "Too Hot For Love"...the concerto!

RE: OKAY?! Then, all of a sudden, this "New House" era came about: with this one bassline...

in the old days I was intrigued by the way they gave you melody after melody and the song was never boring. It took you somewhere, it made you forget that you had a horrible week. That's what music should do. Music shouldn't just be the same thing over and over and not really say much of anything, it should take the person somewhere else.

LDW: OK, at the point that you went from the Powerplant as a mere observer to participant to part of the "in" group... How did you get to the point where your music started getting played on the turntables? How did that first big break happen?

RE: There were countless sessions that I'd sat in on with Frankie just observing , watching , taking notes from the background. A lot of the times I would be in the studio with Frankie all night long and leave directly from the studio at six-thirty, seven o'clock in the morning and go to work and then pass out later on in the evening. And then meet Frankie again that night.

No one was going to come right out and say "Look, this is how it is done". It was the relationship we had had. From the Powerplant days through those rough days thereafter...you remember Lawrence. I recall those days of us putting what change we had together, until the unemployment checks came to get hamburger and hamburger helper over at Frankie's. The wonders that Frankie could cook up out of very little at all — the infamous breaded pork chops and Frankie's special macaroni and cheese supreme!

Then, just before "Let the Music Use You" came out on Danica (Walter Pass' label) I met Brett Wilcotts, who worked for Walter at the time. I had seen Brett at parties at the Powerplant before that.

Brett and Jim actually saved me... they came to my rescue ! I had gone knocking on everyone's door... EVERYONE...Brett told me down at Danica when I last saw him that he and a friend were getting ready to start a record label. You hear that so many times.... But Brett *did* start a label and started putting out tunes on Gherkin. I finally begged a project out of Brett and Jim Stivers over

at Gherkin, and they arranged for Larry Heard and me to produce and mix "Don't Walk Out on Love" for Gallifre' featuring Mondee Oliver .

I hadn't worked with Larry since "Distant Planet". I've always admired Larry's music because it's so what I've always thought real new house music should be. He took it to that next phase, he gave us what it used to be. He had his own style... it was almost new age like.

There was some vocals already tracked by

another vocalist from Ohio on the track and for some reason Gherkin wasn't really pleased with the way the new production went with the old vocals so Jimmy, Brett's roommate, suggested we get Mondee Oliver, who used to sing with Roy Ayers! So Brett and Jim decided to contact Mondee. She came to Chicago and did it.

The strange thing about the project is that I kicked up a fuss about a bell solo that I failed to use in any of my mixes but when Frankie did the European mix he added it and it sounds real nice.

When "Don't Walk Out on Love" came out, the reviews floored me! On my mixing, my production...

And then there was "Let the Music Use You" with the Knight Riders. It was licensed to Europe from Danica. The girls overseas were bumping and kicking up their heels and had made this song a damn house music anthem! If the party was dead, the DJ's would stop the music, turn off the lights, and start "Let the Music Use You" from the beginning. And the kids just rushed to the dance floor! I mean, honey, artists like Reggie Hall, Darryl Pandy, and Adonis would return from Europe and tell me "we don't know what you did to that song, but when they hear it, everybody puts their hands up in the air like in the old days, when we did that to one of those tunes that really *did* us! Everybody was sweating, shirts were off, girls were just full..." OKAY! I heard that's how they carry on to my song. It was never that kind of song to me. It was just something to try to make some money to keep from starving!

So, I just decided to pull my resources together and I got enough songs put together, a catalog of maybe nine songs... and I would push those nine songs on everybody! Having already had "Let the Music Use You" out and press clippings on that helped. It was like, this is what I've done, this is where I've come from.

In the meantime, I was frantically running around to everybody I knew in the house music business who had a keyboard, a drum machine, or something, barely getting enough time in to finish a tune. I had to learn how to come in with my percussion line memorized. Keep the percussion

simple, when you go into the studio you can add all the fluff and glitter. Whip out the basslines, know where they're coming, know how many measures.

Whenever I went to visit someone in the back of my mind I had this tune lurking. I had to chit-chat with them for a while to make it look like I didn't just come over here to use the equipment and hit it.

CONTINUED ON NEXT PAGE

> **"Music shouldn't just be the same thing over and over and not really say much of anything; it should take the person somewhere else."**

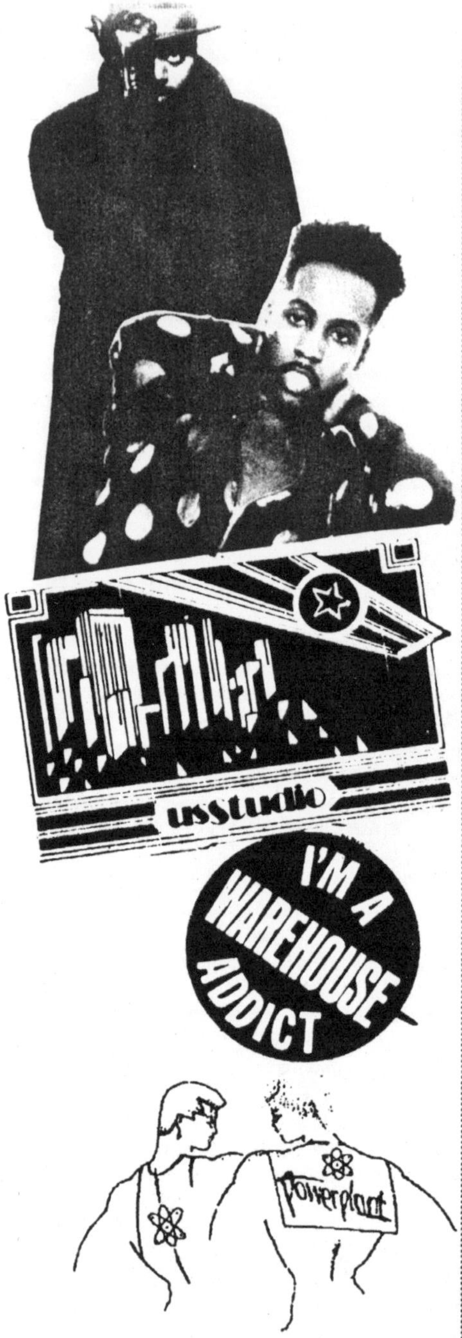

TOP TO BOTTOM

• Frankie Knuckles

• Lil Louis photographed by Hubert Von Stephens

• original US Studios Warehouse membership card

• *"say it loud! I'm house and I'm proud!"*

• Frankie's Antonio Lopez inspired illustrations, from a Powerplant poster

---

TRENT ADKINS: I hate to eat and run... in fact, I hate to bump out a mix and run but I've got to dash.

RE: ...a lot of times I would end up having to use the bass sounds they already had in their keyboards. A lot of times I had to use Candy's drums on my demo and when people like Larry Heard would listen to them they could tell I had been over so-and-so's house. Everyone was starting to tell where I had been working on my demos at. Candy has a drum pattern and a sound that is so her no matter what the song is you know it's a Candy J tune. It's like her trade mark.

RF: Some things they never change!

RE: HELLO! I would have to use the sounds she could pull up for me. Sometimes I would ask her "do you have something that sounds like this..." and then she'd find something that maybe she wasn't using. I would have to make my demos real sparse because, they only had three or four tracks I could use to create a tune, and usually she would erase it. I always had a tape with me to record what I had done.

But Candy's my very good girlfriend. We turned San Francisco out! Miss Candy dragged me into some bar named the Black Rose. It was run by these hard looking drag queens, and every drag who came through the door had stiletto pumps like *that!* And she was walking like *this!* Candy and I come swirling in: I'm in my suede jacket and the jeans with the leather across the ass and things, and Candy serving up these flats and titties just hanging everywhere! They were like, "are you real fish? And she's like (deep and masculine) "girl, *stop!*"

I got kind of tired of all the rush demos, you see. I started feeling like I was inconveniencing Jere McAllister's mother because I would come over there full and just lay out in the floor, and hum off bass lines and parts to Jere and he'd play it into the keyboard and sequencer. So I thought "maybe I should learn to do this for myself". I bought a cheap Casio. One of those rinky-dink numbers. I paid five dollars a week ... I was hurting, though because I wasn't working so to cough up twenty dollars a month was a major feat! I finally got one and did about five tapes of demos and they all sounded the same because I only had six sounds to work with and I had all this pre-programmed percussion what CASIO thought was disco, what THEY thought was pop and what THEY thought was rap and none of it sounded like any of those styles of music at all!

But I was just tired of waiting, and I knew the European public was waiting for another Knight Riders, unless I was going to go the same way as Brooklyn Dreams or other groups like Love and Kisses ...

RE: ...Trussel...

LDW: ...the Peech Boys...

RE: HELLO! Where she came out with like one or two tunes and then nothing !

RF: Visual!

RE: OKAY! Then it's like "Whatever happened to them?" Sarah Dash!

RF: Don Kirschner's rock concert!

RE: I just didn't want to go that route. So I just that I decided to stop taking the bullshit, and do my own label, Total Spectrum, with Brett. My reason for going with Gherkin was the fact that "Big Fun" by Inner City originally came out as a Gherkin subsidiary on KMS Records. Kevin M. Saunderson. That's who KMS Records was and no one had any faith in "Big Fun" except Brett. After that came Lil Louis and "French Kiss".

RF: That was on KMS?

RE: No that was on Diamond Records. A subsidiary of Gherkin records. See, Brett lets you put out your own label but they take care of manufacturing and distributing for you.

What I eventually want to do is license my newest Gherkin tune "I Don't Feel Nothin' for You Now" to a major independent, and then continue putting songs out on Total Spectrum. I prefer being my own boss. I work in a timely way; the budget for "I Don't Feel Nothin' for You Now" was less than a thousand dollars. Brett picked up the p&d (pressing and distribution) part of it for me. And that's the only way this song is out. I owe it all to Brett Wilcotts.

Brett said "if you're going to put it out on Total Spectrum it should be the Knight Riders coming out with a new tune. Riley Evans presents the Knight Riders. You've got to start associating your name with the Knight Riders."

So now on the "Nice and Slo" track with Lil Louis for Epic/CBS it appears: Riley Evans. On this Total Spectrum record: Riley Evans. On the Knight Riders album it's going to be: Riley Evans. On the Hot Mix Five "Rush" it's going to be: Riley Evans. I'm starting to associate MY name with MY work.

But I also have a a Mr. Strings EP coming out!

RF: Now who is Strings?

RE: That's me! The reason why I'm going under Mr. Strings is because Larry Heard is Mr. Fingers. And Larry and I are basically the creative force behind Gherkin. Our subsidiaries being Alleviated Music, Larry Heard's division, and Total Spectrum being my division. Why not? Mr. Fingers and Mr.

Strings. Because everything I touch I have to put strings in it. I very rarely do a tune without strings because strings give it that....basically that's what the music we work together on sounds like.

And then the Lil Louis project happened. I co-wrote the tune "Nyce and Slo" on his CBS album and it will be used as a single! I'm happy to report that the L'il Louis album went gold! Every ad you see is "Nyce and Slo" and "French Kiss"! That Lil Louis album is so versatile! That album should be like THE album! He's got classical-like new age music on there, there's a pseudo-religious song called "Blackout" where he does quotes from the Bible basically trying to tell kids to get their act together–tomorrow is not promised! And if it comes, will you be ready? I think it is so ingenious of him to do that! Everybody feels that you have to go to church. Well honey, the girls in church already know about God...what about these girls out here kicking up their heels? Somebody's got to bring them the Word! That's why when the kids were dishing Miss Tramaine Hawkins and the Clark Sisters, I said "look, honey, somebody's got to do it!"

RF: What kind of setup do you have at home now?

RE: I have three keyboards, a drum machine, a mixer, a four-track, a mike and an effects box. That's all I can afford right now.

LDW: Quite a difference from when you were my piano teacher and we had to hunt up a piano!

RE: Now when ever I feel creative I get up and work. Sometimes at three o'clock in the morning.

LDW: You know, I always wondered what happed to you the night of the benefit concert for the Clubhouse in D.C. ?

RE: I got sick. *That* was during the time of SRO records... and also the mess that was going on with Rockin' House records. They were dickin' me around left and right.

LDW: no grease...

RE: ...not even a little bit of spit! So I ended up ripping and running in the streets in the dead of winter with very few logical clothing... getting up in the morning, taking a shower, and rushing out to try and make a meeting, and try to find some money to eat on. I wasn't eating well because I didn't have any money... it was microwave pop-corn and water. That was basically it for six to seven months...I guess that microwave popcorn and water ain't gonna do it as far as vitamins and nutrition and shit . So I came down with pneumonia...and then all the girls started screaming she's got the package! Sister's got AIDS! So there I sat wondering whether I got the package or what? So

my pastor announced on the radio that I had AIDS and that I was ready to kick off. Needless to say, now everybody's wondering why I'm still here now! "Why is she so fat?" "What's wrong, she should be dead by now!"

Today I went through my telephone book and I whited out so many names , it's really sad! Everytime you turn around, someone else has died. It's so frightening, all the kids who've fallen by the wayside.

RF: Have you seen the Chicago music industry start to pull together around AIDS?

RE: There was the benefit that Frank Sells and I did down at Carol's, "Let's Get It Together", Me and Frank pulled that whole benefit off! Candy J came down, Darryl Pandy, Ten City, Kym Mazelle , North and Clybourn, and other little groups all came down. Even the big groups like Ten City, (their album was on its way out) did it for free. They said "whatever you would have given us give to the or-ganization." I thought that was so nice.

RF: How do you see the whole AIDS cri-sis affecting the dance community?

RE: In a negative way, it's taken away some of the better dance mu-sicians. Like Sylvester, which was a terrible loss, a terrible tragedy from which we as a community may never recover ! People are now trying to be more socially correct... with their lyrical content , they don't want to imply that you can go run and do it like we did in 1975 ! With a bag on our heads!

TA: ...put the bag somewhere else!

RE: OKAY!

RF: Down , further!

RE: Exactly ! One of the songs I did for the Knight Riders album with Ricky Dillard is called "I've

Been Good, Girl" and it's a song that says a rea-sonable alternative to promiscuity IS settling down with one partner — you don't have to have a differ-ent person every night. In other words, being good is not bad, if you know what I mean! Basi-cally, that's the message behind the song.

RF: Do you see AIDS affecting the way the community works together? Has it created more divisiveness between people or do you think it has brought people together?

RE: I think it has brought them together.

LDW: Since so much of the current dance music product is made by young boys,have you seen a reluctance on their part to be associated with anyone gay, don't want to work with anyone gay...

RE: No. You don't get any of that. Most of the new groups that are out now are pretty open-minded. They're really about the music.

RF: I think that to some degree the young dance commu-nity has been given a bum rap. I think a lot of them do real-ize the roots of house music (the foundation, if you will) is of black and gay origin and though they are

outsiders, they are real respectful of what has come before them and are willing to work with those people.

RE: Yes. It's not like they're trying to take over, it's like they're trying to add to... a tradition.

TA: Thank you for talking with us!

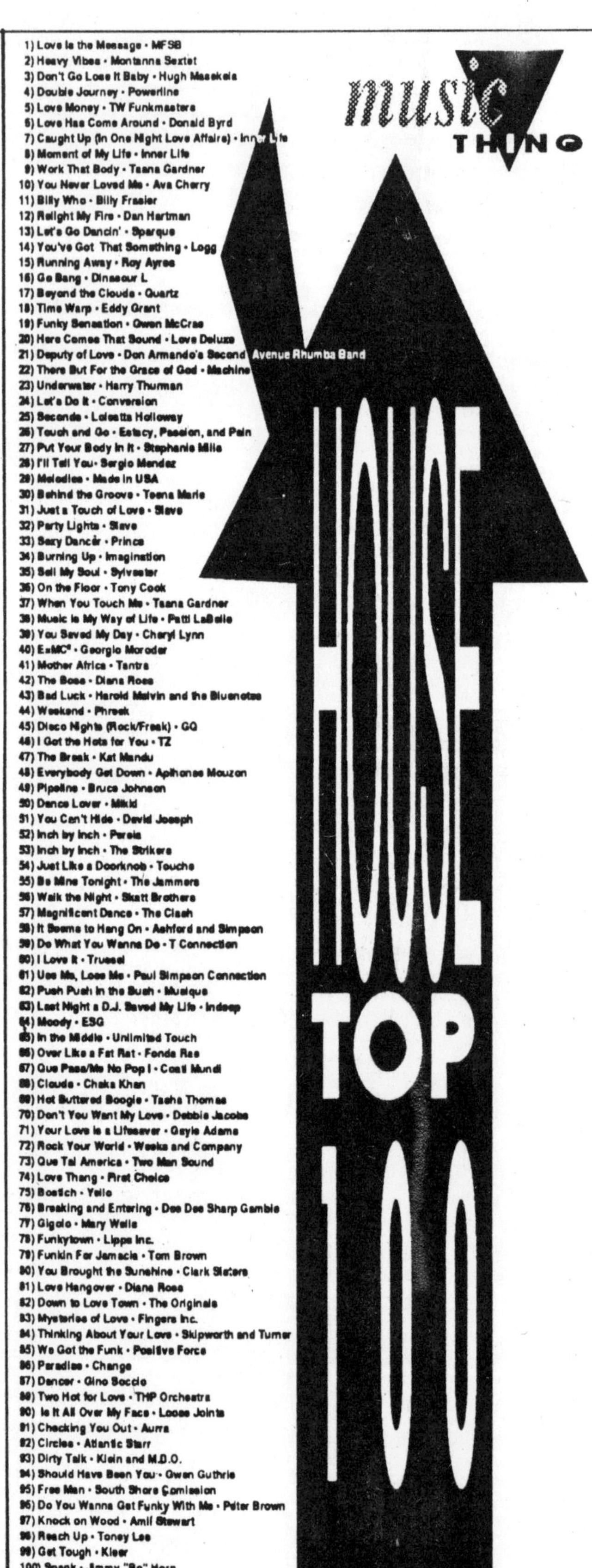

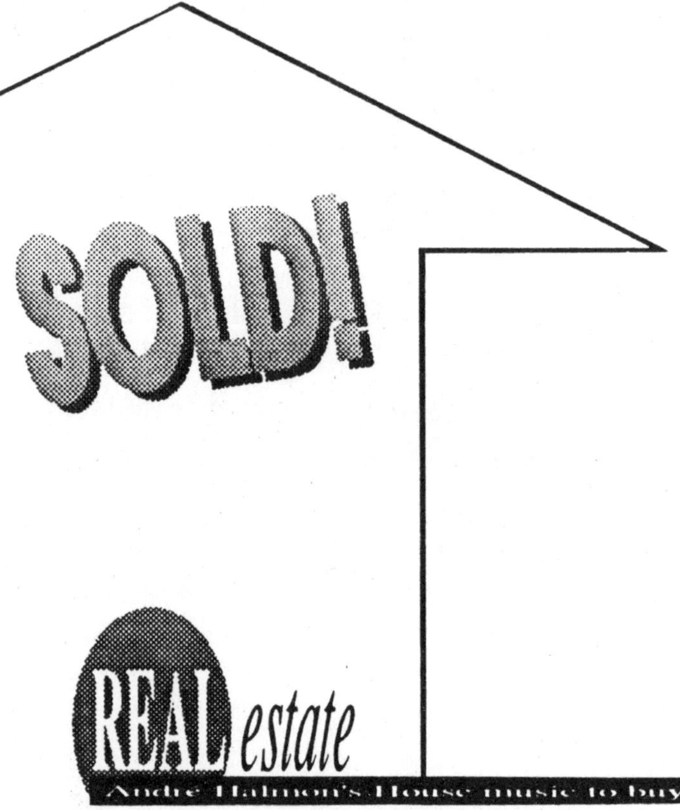

1. **No Time to Waste** *Jarvic 7* (Play it Again Sam U.K.)
2. **Pacific State** (Remix) *808 State* (Tommy Boy)
3. **Space Shuttle** (Deep Dub) *Gil Scott Heron* (Castle U.K.)
4. **In Full Effect** *Big Audio Dynamite* (CBS U.K.)
5. **From The Mind Of Lil Louis** (LP) *Lil Louis* (Epic)
6. **Best Part of Me** (Remix) *Cynthia Abrams* (Republic U.K.)
7. **Rejoice** (LP) *Joe Smooth* (DJ International)
8. **Come Together As One** *Will Downing* (Island)
9. **Keepin My Faith In Love** *Sharon Dee Clark* (Rumor U.K.)
10. **Affection** (LP) *Lisa Stansfield* (Arista)
11. **Most Wanted** (Remix) *Fast Eddie* (DJ International)
12. **Hazme Sonar** *Morenas* (BCM Germany)
13. **Feel the Melody** (Remix) *Underground Crew* (Club House)
14. **We're All InThis Together** *David Peaston* (Geffen)
15. **Searchin' Hard** (Remix) *Da Posse* (Dancemania)
16. **The Rains** *MK* (KMS)
17. *FX/Eyes Of Sorrow* *A Guy Called Gerald* (CBS U.K.)
18. **Der Erdbeermund** *Culture Beat* (CBS Germany)
19. **O BAN 1** *North and Clybourn* (Gherkin)
20. **Unity** *On Top* (Bigbeat)
21. **Come Fly With Me** *D.J. Pierre* (Jive)
22. **Mantra For A State Of Mind** (B.F. Mix) *S-Express* (Rhythm King U.K.)
23. **Gettin Crazy** (LP) *Doug Lazy* (Atlantic)
24. **Appreciate** *Mr. Monday* (Greedy B U.K.)
25. **Put Your Hands Together** (Brixton Mix) *D Mob* (FFRR U.K.)

at the club
poems by alan miller

the dance floor crowded
with divas mouthing the words:
everyone's a star!

like their cigarettes
alive only at the tips
these lovely fireflies

quickly recognizing
who spends all night preparing
for grand entrances

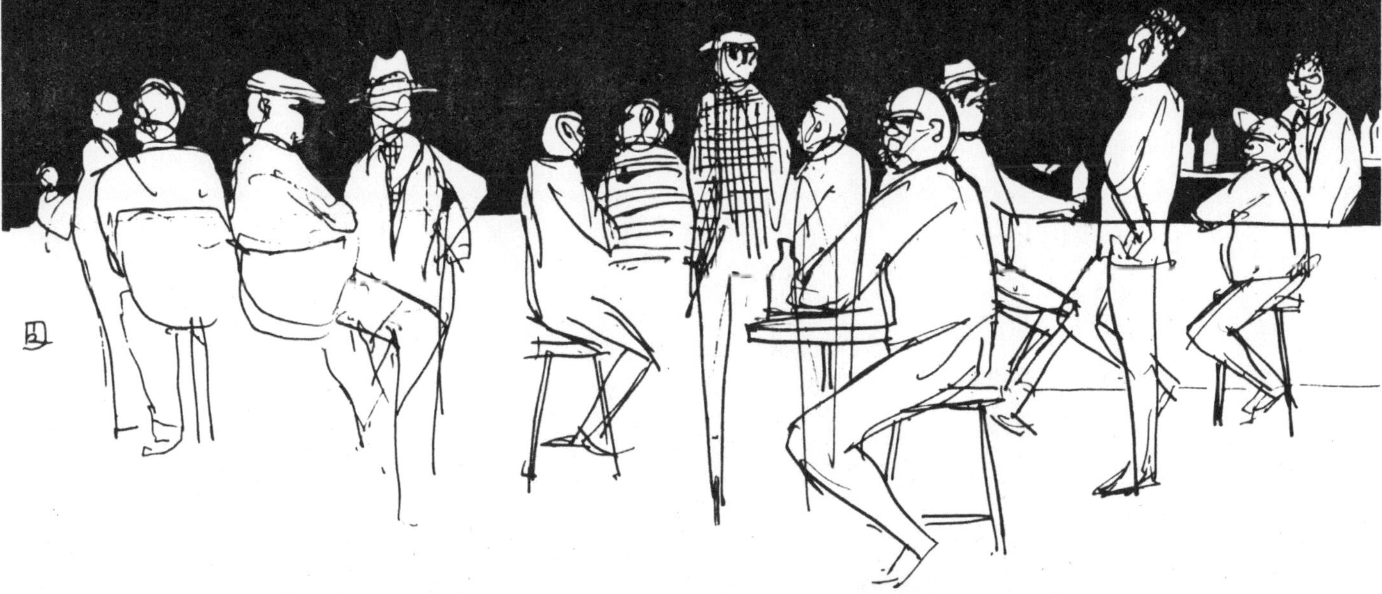

These are selected haikus from Alan Miller's chapbook "at the club".
It is available at People Like Us and Unabridged Books for $6.00, or by mail (with an additional $1.50 for postage).
Write: Grand Entrances Press, box 20624, Oakland, California 94620.

START
HERE

Go to Smart Bar, and have your worst fears realized listening to New Order and The Cure all night.
BACK 1

Learn to sing, put out a record, license it overseas make $
AHEAD 1

Go to Lo...
have you...
realized lis...
Stanley ar...
all night.

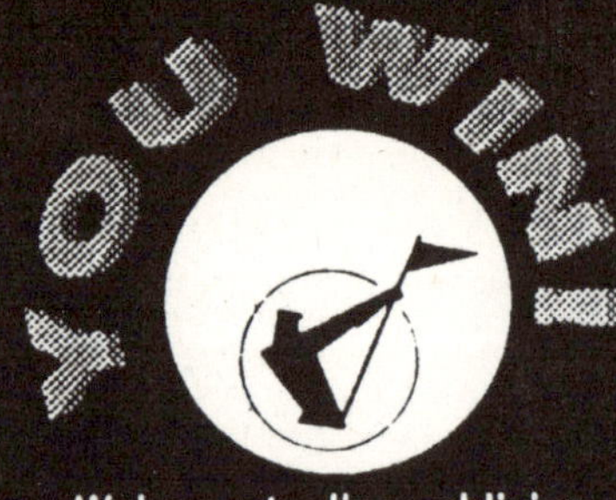

YOU WIN!
Welcome to disco oblivion.

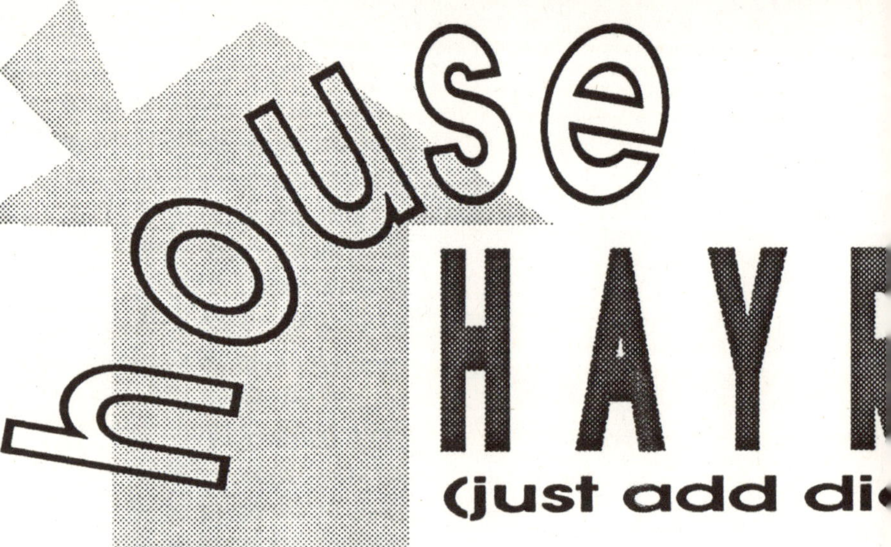

house
HAYR...
(just add di...

Lose your $50.00
Fiorucci
sunglasses on the dance floor when Frankie plays #60 on the House top 100.
AHEAD 1

Valley of the Dolls
aka Betty Ford Clinic
LOSE A TURN

HAVE
Steve "Silk" Hurley
remix your album track into a Billboard #1 Disco record
AHEAD 3

Whoops!
you're NOT on the guest list!
BACK 3

CL...
RA...
GO

Dock, and
rst fears
to Pamela
ck Cowley

bad acid.

GO TO
VALLEY OF THE DOLLS

BACK
3

Buy the Soul II Soul c.d.
at 16.00, only to find
that "Back to Life" *is*
not *really* on there!

BACK
3

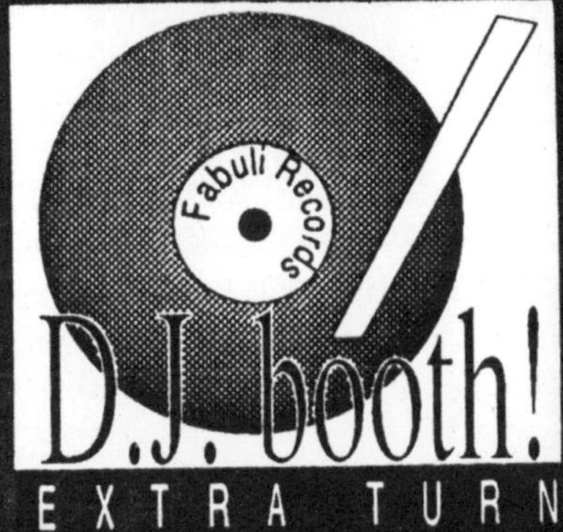

B O O S T

fabulous Claude
Montanna leather jacket to
true the whores at the club!

AHEAD
1

D A M N!

Claude Montanna leather
jacket boosted by those
shady bitches in coatcheck!

BACK
1

I D E !

(and spin!)

RULES

1) THERE ARE NO RULES

2) MAKE UP RULES AS YOU GO ALONG

3) CHEAT AS OFTEN AS YOU CAN

4) STEAL WHEN NECESSARY

5) DON'T GET CAUGHT

6) CALL YOUR LAWYER IF CAUGHT

UB
D!

JAIL

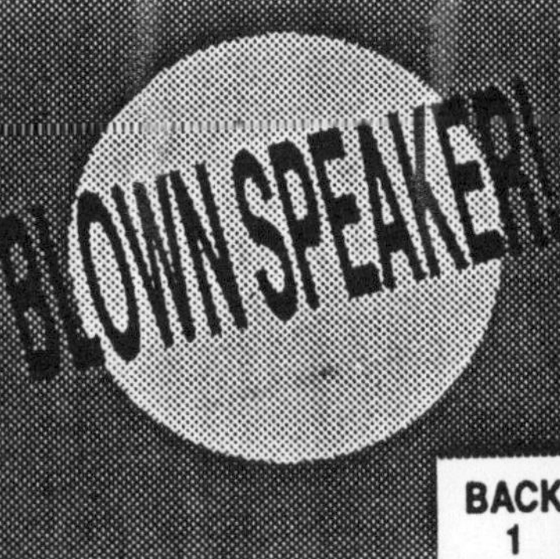

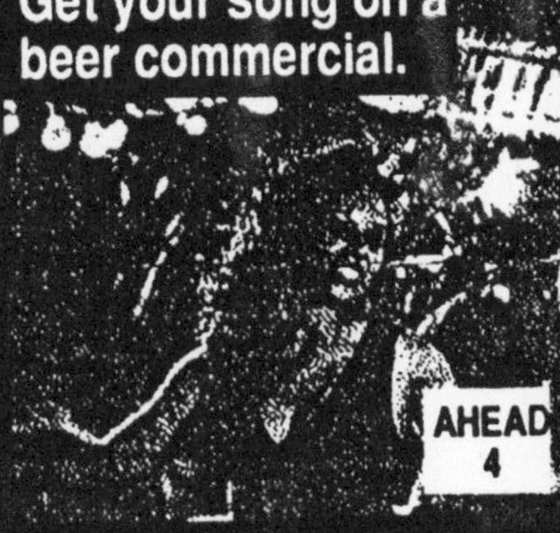

FRIENDLY BISEXUAL MEN

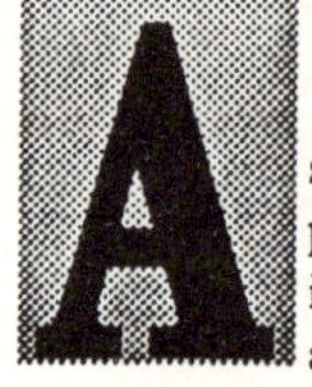

As far as Tyrone is concerned, the Stonewall revolt of 1969 against gay oppression may as well never have happened. You see, Tyrone isn't a particular individual, but for simplicity in writing, his thoughts, attitudes and actions are typical of many so-called straight men.

Tyrone is Black and lives near 65th St. and S. Laflin Ave. or 86th and S. Rhodes or near 3300 W. Fulton St. or, in any of the thousands of closets scattered throughout the Black community. You would really like him as a friend because he features a strong 9 to 5 work ethic, he's trustworthy, loyal, helpful, friendly, courteous, kind, obedient, cheerful, thrifty, brave, clean, and sincere in his Baptist faith. He was probably a Cub Scout, Boy Scout and Explorer when he was growing up. Tyrone retains the athletic strength, vigor and agility gained on his school's track, football or basketball teams years ago.

But, Tyrone didn't come out at Gay Horizons. He had a girlfriend when he started to deal with dudes. He believes support groups are for sissies and he's no sissy. In fact, he's a real man: very naturally masculine, Mr. Straight Arrow to his family and to the people on his job. Besides, he has always thought that someone's love life is private.

When he comes over to visit me he may glance at Chicago Outlines or other lesbian and gay community magazines and newspapers, but he just scans the headlines of the news stories and is amused by the arts and entertainment section articles. Not until he gets to the personal classified ads does he do any really serious reading. I've told him all about the National Coalition for Black Lesbians and Gays and he responded by showing up at the Belmont Rocks beach after the gay pride parade every year since 1986 to enjoy the picnic food, dance to the disco beat, and to cruise the bronze hued beefcakes.

Unwittingly, I gave him the rationale for not joining NCBLG: I told him that since November 1979, when it was organized in Chicago, most of the members have been women and men who moved here from other cities and states and feel free to come out because we don't have parents and close relatives on West Fulton Street or somewhere on the south side who might find out if we lobbied the alderman or did a radio talk show.

Sometimes, when Tyrone is feeling particularly closeted and horny, he'll show up at my door at one or two o'clock in the morning and say through the intercom that he's cold and wants in. Once inside he says he came over because he thought I was having a Black Jacks party. Then he gets that look of lust in his eyes. Instead of saying that we have been seeing each other around for several months and like each other's company and that he wants to develop a sexual and emotional relationship with me, he says: I brought you a Phillip Morris menthol light 100. We laugh. After all, Phillip Morris doesn't sell cigarettes one at a time, wrapped in E-Z Wider rolling papers!

Tyrone is unable to have man to man sex without first drinking a cocktail or a couple beers or smoking a Phillip Morris menthol light 100. He rationalizes away being gay every step of the way. The next morning he can say something like: man, we got so high last night that freak movie you put on your VCR got me turned on and before I knew it we were really into it.

Over breakfast, Tyrone may speak of his girlfriend or a daughter or Michael Jordan's 42 points in the Bulls-Hornets game. Talk of love and emotional depth to match our sexual intensity doesn't happen. The possibility of that kind of talk is slim to remote because of Tyrone's absolute refusal to identify himself with a lesbian and gay community which loves and embraces sissies.

BY MAX SMITH

NOTES FROM AN INTERRACIAL MARRIAGE

First, let me say that I love this man like no other in my history. At this writing, we have known each other for a year and a half, and for almost the last year of it romantically linked. Being married to a "white man" isn't much different from being married to a Black man. But don't be fooled; there *are* differences!

For example, many of my black friends have no problem eating or dealing with the awful stench that comes with feasting on a pot of chitterlings. Needless to say, we won't be having any more chitterlings anytime soon in our house.

You must understand, however, that I'm not your typical Black person. I mean, I can take or leave watermelon and I don't eat fried chicken every chance I get. (Though he is amazed at the things I can do with a chicken).

Our beliefs are not very different, but then again, there are differences. Especially when it comes to family background. And we don't even discuss politics (too much of a variation).

Craig comes from a very stable, traditional nuclear family that doesn't believe in divorce or infidelity. My family is anything but traditional, and I don't think I even heard this word "conservative" until I entered the corporate world. Prejudice occasionally rears its ugly head, usually because I'm the outspoken of the two: I'll tell someone to go to hell if need be! We try not to let these differences interfere with the main point: to take care of each other.

There are, of course, similarities in our somewhat tenacious relationship. For instance, we both love soap operas, spaghetti, german chocolate cake, and oh yes, salsa and chips! We both love to entertain at home, but find going out occasionally and supporting our community to be fulfilling.

Craig also has this need for togetherness that I've never really needed, having been a loner most of my life. He does, however, (finally) understand the need for me to have time and space to myself (without *him*) I We are taking our first separate vacations for Christmas this year. (My choice.)

The main point is: no matter where you come from or who you are, if you love someone and they in turn love you back, the relationship can (and should) work. It's not important *who* you love, just that you remember that the big picture is love.

INSET: The Black & White Men Together logo.

BY TONY WILKINS

" H E L P ! "

In Steven King's novel It, the subject matter is a constantly self-reinventing nonentity whose lack of physical focus is exactly the narrative's "problem" and point. King wrote it as his final word on the subject of horror, and the book contains just about every effect of which a so-so genre writer could be capable. It is also the least satisfying of his tomes— flabby, overwrought, and everything but scary. I may be stretching a little when I compare a popular novelist's yarn to something as honestly spooky as government policy on, say, "The Drug War," but the two share the same fatal flaw— an unbelievable enemy. You can't just confer the old fashioned status of demon onto something as inexplicable as drug use and expect your audience to feel like it's witnessing a bonified night of the living dead, any more than you can expect to instigate the ultimate horrific effect by one—the recent history of literary.

Both it and the drug policy are part and parcel of the fallacy of the spectacle, that lumberingly prevalent, weirdly christianesque notion that there exists a single communal cloth from which relevant contemporary ideas need to be cut. The cult of the fanzine (a magazine scaled to and organized around an editor's particular obsession) is one of the most interesting phenomenons to emerge from this culture of the devalued. " Zines," as these publications are generally called, are the Phlebital matter coarsing through the veins of the corpse of capitalism, to use an imprecise, emotional image just because I fucking feel like it. They have names like Muck Zine, Useless Youth, The Kansas Intelligencer, and Stranger Fanzeen. Expressive phrases positively lumpen with amateurism. They spring from no collective, spectacle-like ideology, per se. They tend to look like shit, and they're about as hard to follow as the rantings of people who know they're on to something without knowing what it is.

Despite the best intentions of a couple of theorists, critics, et. al., reality's still pretty much unreadably crude. To examine, then represent it in the art world's clean, centralized, programmatic way is tantamount to... what? Well, five, six years ago that modus operandi contrasted interestingly with the premise that art was a hyper-personal, soul-wrenched doodling. Against that historical backdrop, seeing artists' brains as small businesses was kind of sexily fresh. At this point however, at least to me anyway, the homemade, the expressive, the xeroxed, et cetera, are starting to look pretty auricular in context.

Example: When you fall in love, as I have fallen of late, you'd rather bore your friends and correspondents with a detailed account of your feelings than suppress all that importance in fear of losing one or two of their ears forever. Right? Maybe it's weird to compare a public acknowledgement of intense, unknowable emotion to the need to speak out against and/or through a benumbed art world. But why should the needs be dissimilar? Maybe the main thing is not to become so sophisticated and comfortably surrounded by like-minded sophisticates that you can't bring yourself to put a pencil (or whatever) to a piece of paper (or whatever) and scribble something on the order of, "Help!"

B Y   D E N N I S   C O O P E R

FERTILE LA TOYAH JACKSON MAGAZINE

MY COMRADE

PANSY BEAT

My Comrade

The biggest, glossiest, and best known of the gay 'zines, this one is made by kids who can get into ALL the New York hip clubs! It comes back-to-back with Sister, for post-modern lesbians. It's rough and tumble cut-and-paste; humurous and affirming.
WRITE: My Comrade, 326 E. 13th Street #15, New York NY 10013

Fertile La Toyah Jackson Magazine

Certainly the most iconoclastic of the rags, Ms. Jackson is editor, magazine, and media goddess extrodinaire. It claims a circulation of 40,000 readers (oh, please!) but seems like it's written for about twenty of them. Published without a timetable, in the words of Fertile: "Fertile La Toyah Jackson, the living, breathing, TV movie, rock video, woman and magazine is published whenever Fertile becomes so indignant, so frustrated with the goings on of our critical times of which we live that she feels it's time for her to make comment."
WRITE: Fertile La Toyah Jackson Magazine, 7850 Sunset Boulevard #110, West Hollywood CA 90046

Pansy Beat

It's big black and white graphics and small size give it a certain preciousness. Very New York based, it celebrates camp while operating in the present tense. Their editorial focus is (in their words), their "own peculiar brand of offbeat obsessive humor..."
WRITE: Pansy Beat ,236 W. 10th Street # 1FE, New York NY 10011

MORE ZINES

ANDROZINE c/o B. Peuportier, B.P. 192 75623 Parism Cedex, 13 France
AQUA, p.o. box 1251 Canal Street Station, New York, NY 10013
BOYSVILLE, U.S.A., Jeffery Kennedy, 12 1/2 N. Central, #4, Olympia, Washington 98506
DR. SMITH, 2nd Fl. 383 Markham St.. Toronto, Ontario,Canada M6G 2KB
FACTSHEET FIVE, c/o Mike Gunderloy, 6 Arizona Ave., Resselaer, New York 12144
FAGS AND FAGGOTRY, M. Neiderman, 48 Craig Street, London,Ontario, Canada,N6C 1E8
HELIUM RAVINGS, 239 E. College, Kent, Ohio 44240
J.D.'s,Box 110, Adealaide Street Station,Toronto, Canada MC5 ZK5
HOMOCORE, box 77731, San Fransisco, California 94107
NOTES FROM THE FLOORBOARDS, c/o Dead Dog Press, box 1949, Warren, Ohio 44482-1949
PLANET ROC, c/o Simone Bouyer, 1030 N. Winchester #1R, Chicago, Illinois 60622
RAGING HORMONES, box 1944, Boulder, Colorado 80306
SALMON HUT, box 612, Station A, Toronto, Ontario, Canada M5W 1G2

REMEMBERING HARING

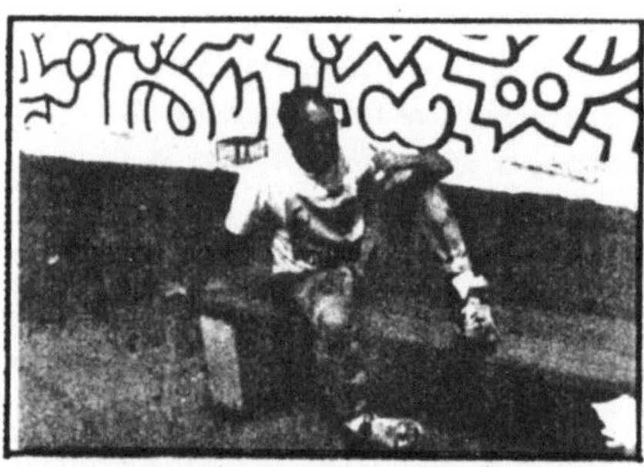

A computer scan of an unfinished mural detail

As this issue of Thing raced to press (well, xerox machine), the flurry of editorial activity came to a quieting halt with what was first an unfounded report: Keith Haring had just lost his valiant battle with AIDS. I met Keith briefly when he was here in the spring of 1989 to do the Board of Education mural project. A big party was held for him at Cabaret Metro, and we were formally introduced by my friend Irving Zucker, who organized the project. Actually, Irving had tried to get me to do a full-fledged interview with Keith for publication during that visit, but I put it off. I said I was busy; in reality I was paralyzed by my awe of his talent and fame. I also wanted to believe that I could do it "later" — Irving had also told me the then confidential news: that Keith had Kaposi's Sarcoma. My most passionate hope was that somehow he'd beat the odds, that his constant efforts to make the planet better for us all would transcend biology and keep him alive. His death was personally affecting though I never really knew him. A little of my inspiration died with him.

I often think that the inevitable swoop of the vultures is harder to watch than the death of artists like Keith, and there is sure to be a morbid increase in prices for his original art. But since he was such a populist artist, putting his images on shirts, watches, record covers (among the last, ironically, was Sylvester's last 12" "Someone Like You"), and a myriad of other artifacts, millions of people own his art.

His work also tried to educate people and address issues: AIDS, crack, apartheid, etc. The positive thrust of this work will still be felt posthumously. Shortly before his death, he tapped Irving Zucker to be president and director of the Keith Haring Art Foundation, set up to give scholarships to Chicago Public High School art students who are in financial need, as well as provide funding for other special projects. The initial funding for the foundation will come from the sale of several panels of the mural that Keith completed here last spring.

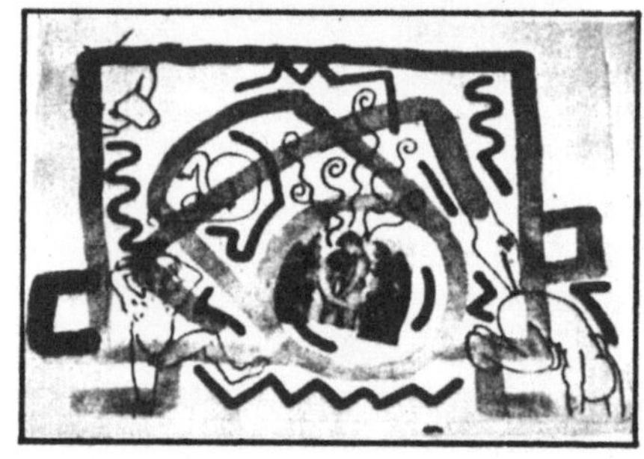

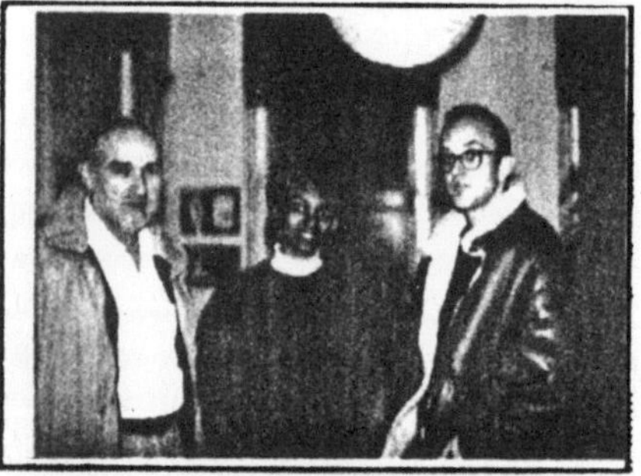

TOP: Keith taking a break at the mural site
CENTER: untitled; from Irving Zucker's collection
BOTTOM: (L to R) Irving Zucker, Simone Bouyer, and Keith Haring at Wholesome Roc Gallery and Café during a brief visit before the mural project
all photos by Marcelino Y. Fahd

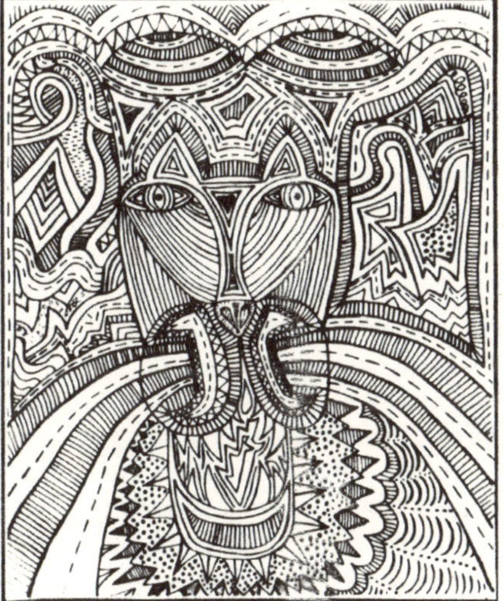

"The Cat's Meow" by Louis Walker

Louis Walker is an artist outside of the art community. His drawings present the urgency of his embattled childhood and a distinctly African—American urban perspective. His work sometimes suggests the doodles of black kids; people with skinny bodies and big 'Fros, colorful animals and fantasy creatures.

Their detail, boldness, and clarity have begun to win notice of other artists and collectors. His work is scheduled to be part of an outsider show at Yolanda Gallery.

ANGER IN THE AGE OF AIDS

David Wojnarowicz is the next in a string of gay male artists who have been 'cultified' as AIDS artists that have emerged recently. Keith Haring brought us consummerist icons, and Mapplethorpe looked unflinchingly at lust and desire and stirred up a media tempest. But the ascent of David Wojnarowicz to that level of media awareness is not because of the titilation or accesibility of his work. His articulation of the rage with which many gay men live in the age of AIDS has demanded attention.

His pointedly political prose in the Artists Space catalogue tested the NEA's new guidelines and made headlines. "Tongues of Flame", the major retrospective of a decade of David Wojnarowicz's

Chicago's upstart <u>New City</u> beat the <u>Village Voice</u> to putting him on the cover, though the <u>Voice's</u> biography and review was many pages longer. Art critic Kathryn Hixson, writing for <u>Arts,</u> describes his work as "...within the self-critical post-pop deconstructive dialogue developed in the eighties art world, manipulating the aesthetic to reflect the contradictions inherent in contemporary society, but fuses his negative outsider's critique with a yearning for a lost spirituality and a connection to the natural, testing artmaking's possibility to trancend, diverting aggression (rage) into positive personal catharsis and societal interaction."

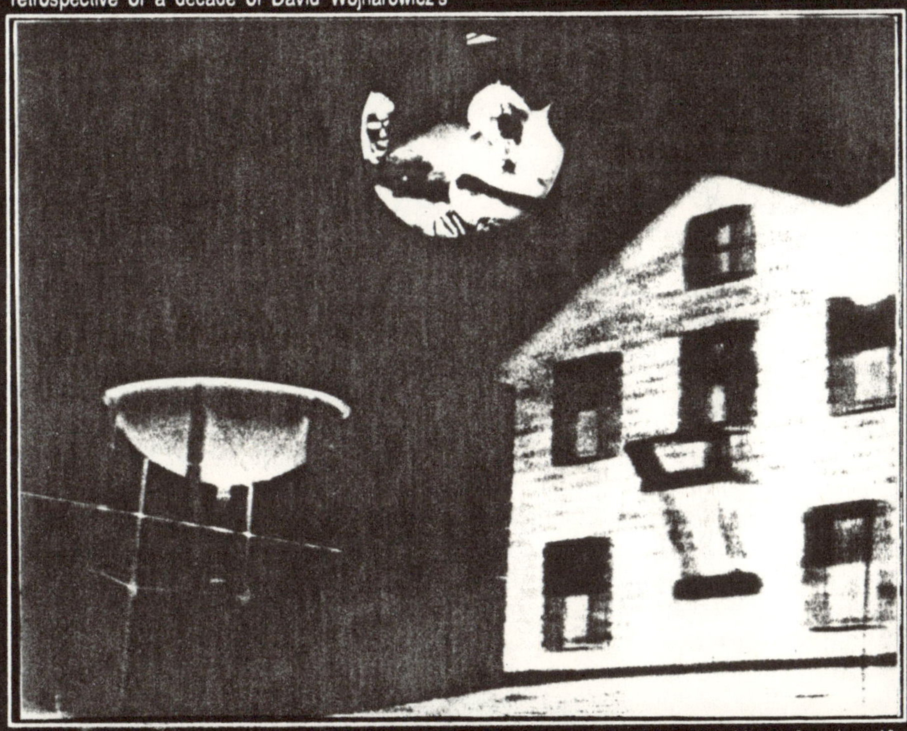

David Wojnarowicz Untitled, 1989, black and white photograph. From "Sex Series" (for Marion Scemama)"

works curated by Barry Blenderman at the University Galleries at Illinois State, (in Normal Illinois, of all places) continued to keep him in ink. it caused its own quiet controversey by circumstance: "Tongues of Flame" was partially funded by the NEA also.

The opening was packed: 300 people jammed the space, mesmerized by the specific and honest words that David spoke about class, politics, homosexuality within a heterosexual culture, and a plethora of other topics. His voice moved from whisper to roar, silenced only by pauses to gulp some water. He read in darkness from his stream of consciousness writings, with video images of sex, suburbs, and snakes running out-of-synch.

"Tongues of Flame" did not cause the headlines that Mapplethorpe at the Museum of Contemporary Art did. Perhaps he has been able to gain media attention without hysteria because of the ultimate clarity of his work. He is as much a writer as a visual artist, and while his dreamlike juxtapositions leave room for dream-like (mis)interpretations, the careful reader will find the message of his prose absoloutley clear and unmistakable.

A catalogue of the "Tounges of Flame" show featuring color prints and writings is availible: write University Galleries, Illinois State University, Normal, Illinois 61761.

D O I N '

WE were so anxious to see our nomes-de-dirt in print, we couldn't wait for our mailed comp-copies of THING, so we scoured the town looking in the most logical places where our readership might hang out.(We eschewed Cook County Jail and Hospital, figuring we'd hit them on our regularly scheduled visits.) Alas, this marvelous mag was nowhere to be found. Nonetheless, we made loads of new best friends, all of whom had fabulous stories to tell. Here's a sample :

WE WERE PRACTICALLY bowled over by Brenda, who'd just breezed in from New York. "Girlfriends," she shrieked, "am I glad to see you. I was in a bookstore in Brooklyn and this MAN tried to fuck me with the LARGEST DICK I'd ever laid eyes on. He kept ramming and ramming but there was just NOWHERE for it all to GO. Until he said 'I guess it's just too big for you to handle' Well, that was all I needed to hear. I opened up like the Red Sea and took the whole goddamned thing. He banged me for about 45 minutes and when he came, I SWORE the come was going to SHOOT out of my PORES! I walked out of that place dragging my cooch like a Galapagos tortoise—and I STILL had a plane to catch!"

Later, we spied Sphincterina, whom we hadn't seen in just ages. She suggested a get-together. "Monday lunch would be fine," said she. "A policeman is coming over to ravish me, but that will be in the morning."

▼

MISS GIGI, an amateur realtor, told us he recently showed an apartment to a couple of young fellows. As he led them through the floor plan, they chatted like magpies, exchanging decorating tips. Gigi was sure he heard them call each other LARRY and EARL. But at lease-signing time, they provided names like Frank Neilbasa and Wayne Whitetrash. Gigi was totally confounded— but not for long. The duo, ecstatic that the apartment was theirs for the having, embraced, exclaiming, " Oh, MARY, I'm so happy!" "Me, too, GIRL!"

▼

A VICE COP we'd like to get to know better, had this amusing tale to tell. A call came in about a sexual assault in progess. A search of the premises— a vacant house— turned up a victim, hiding in a closet, and a suspect, crouching in the gangway with pants around his knees. The victim, too distraught to make a positive ID, was taken, by ambulance, to a nearby hospital. The suspect was hauled off to jail, where he was grilled, to no avail. Finally, an ambitious detective hit upon a plan. He inked up the alleged criminal's weenie, pressed it to a sheet of notebook paper, and left the suspect to wipe down and cool off. Several hours later, Officer Friendly returned and announced that the jig was up. Seems the culprit's "print" matched several left being at the scene.. and on the victim. And as everyone knows, dickprints, like fingerprints, are one-of-a-kind. The suspect broke down and confessed to the rape in question, as well as several other unsolved cases. Pussy wonders if lips leave traces, too...not THOSE lips.

▼

THEN THERE'S THE FABULOUS Puerto Rican boxer who, while butch in every sense of the word, wasn't afraid to take it like a woman, every now and again. Until the fateful day when a little afternoon delight almost done him in. Seems his honey purchased a new vibrator—simulated black leather with a gleaming chrome tip. After tethering him to the bedposts and attaching the gag, she loaded the dildo with long-life Duracells and revved up. José bucked and thrashed like a woman possessed, his eyes pleading for mercy. But his ladyfriend thrust onward, refusing to relent, leading him to what she thought was the climax of a lifetime... until she smelled smoke. CAUTION: Unless you want a seared sphinctre, stick to man-made materials.

▼

WE HEARD THIS THIRD-HAND and it made us weep. A gal met a nice prospect in a local bar and they began to date. HE insisted on weeknites, always dashing off before the stroke of 12. Suspecting she was being two-timed, Our Gal Wednesday demanded a Friday slot and a slumber party. The beau complied, suggesting an entire fun-filled weekend for 2. Saturday AM began with chocolate chip pancakes a la mode—and two forks. The trip to the zoo was delish. After dinner, a double-feature (with double helpings of Snowcaps and Sprite). Later, lovemaking fueled to a frenzy by a snack of choco-covered strawberries he'd brought along. The next morning his ardor had cooled... literally. Reaching over to stroke his arm, she found it icy-cold and bent in an odd position. Later as the paramedics hunted through his backpack for clues to his untimely demise, they found a hypodermic needle and bottle of insulin. Boy, was SHE shocked...but not as much as the PREGNANT WIFE, who called her three days later!

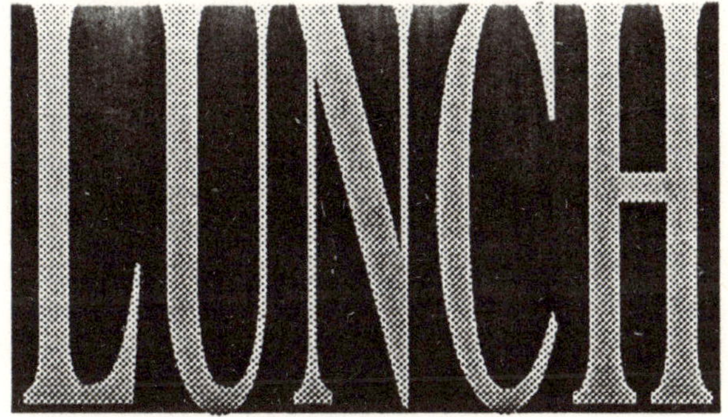

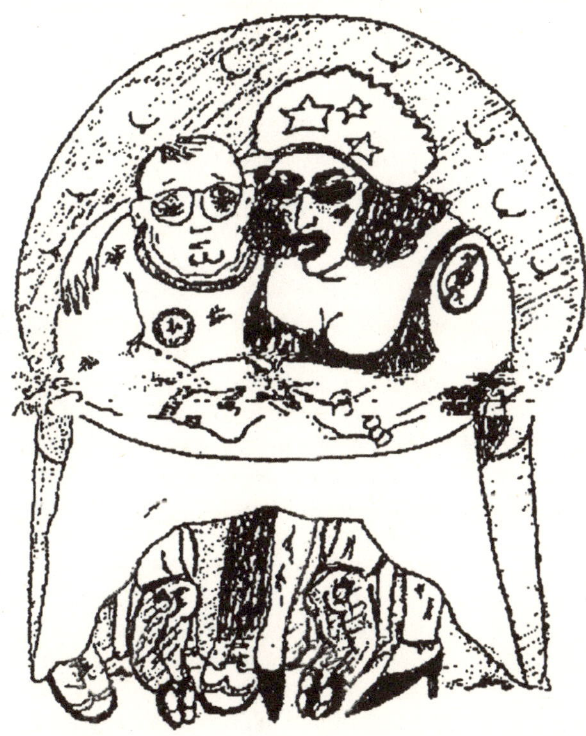

LUNCH

WITH BUNNY & PUSSY

DPDQ...

While we're soooo excited that Barneys New York is finally opening in Chicago, their plans to build on the present site of the Oak Tree will leave countless DQs without a late-nite place to dish. We propose an environmental impact statement, or asking Barney's corporate for enuf scratch to open a shelter of some sort where Queens and their consorts can thaw out their mascara over a Pattie-melt and (Diet) Cherry-Coke.

CODE CORDON BLEU...

Speaking of food and death, a musician we know (we do admit to knowing several, though we NEVER lend them money) was paid to fiddle for a foreign function (diplomatic of course) at the State-of-Illinois Rotunda. Alas, the guest of honor was stricken by a massive coronary halfway through a stuffed mushroom. While the paramedics worked feverishly to revive him, from behind a screen, the guests continued to graze the buffet. And the band played on.

CRITICS NOTEBOOK...

Before we found out Walter Netsch designed Circle Campus, we were sure it had been done by a homo. The washrooms are mini-labyrinths that would have made the Minotaur see red. (All the better for thwarting casual perusal by the uninitiated.) We've heard tales of undergrads forced to leave toilet paper trails, to find their way out. Though whenever we visit, we remove them...

HOLIDAY LEFTOVERS...

A pederast we know, celebrated this X-mas season by seducing a young neighbor boy.. The supposedly straight stud had taken to spending an inordinate amount of time over at Monsieur's Poulet's where he'd jabber incessantly about his desire to be hypnotized. Mr. Chicken cautioned that people under hypnotic suggestion sometimes do things they regret later, but the boy pressed on. Daddy Drumstick rose to the occasion. Lacking watch and fob, he seized the nearest golden object—an ornament of Rudoph—which he dangled in front of the young fellow's eyes, from a strand of dental floss. The kid went under faster than Campeau and Bloomie's while Friar Fryer hummed "he came upon a midnight clear." And, from what we heard, he did...

GOD SAVE THE QUEENS...

Everyone we know just abhors the Brits. Their bad blood, unintelligble humor, prissy men, horsey women, and rheumy eyes notwithstanding, their irrepressible lack of flair... ugly PM, uglier royalty and their tacky tendency to empire-build at the drop of a crumpet gives us the willies. Why, a Brit we met, once blew a bloke in the basement of a Bloomsbury Bookshop. Ex pucker facto, the lad looked up, expecting a compliment, or at least a word of thanks. What he got was a tip.. of the hat, that is. Figures.

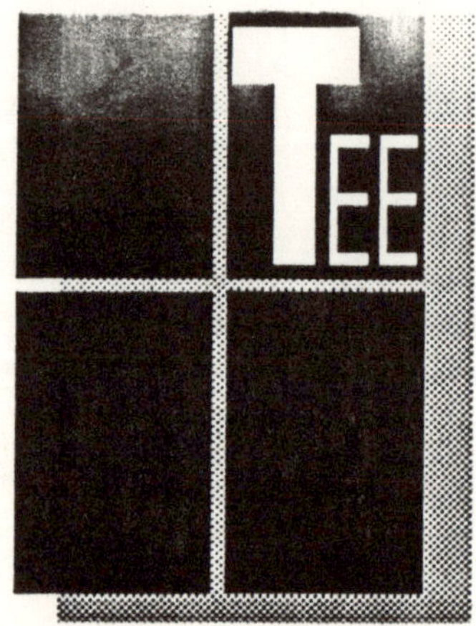

> *The perfect attitude at a dance is a mixture of gaiety and decorum: gay hosts who are still mindful of their guests' well-being; gay guests who, while enjoying themselves, are still aware of their responsibilities as guests. Granted this attitude as the ideal, the rest of good behavior at a dance is a matter of technique."*
> *— The Vogue Book Of Etiquette, 1948*

WENDY QUINN'S XMAS LIGHT LOUNGE ?

I can't be sure about *Effie Mae's Xmas Light Lounge*, but it's a sure thing that musicologist, hostess with the mostess, and Elizabeth Taylor devotee **Wendy Quinn** has her Xmas effect *permanently* installed in the dining room of the Sheridan Park apartment she shares with her sister **Janet Quinn** (in what's now called Sheridan Park). How appropriate that we could enjoy the lights this Xmas eve! Do we smell a trend? String a few lights and you too can play host/hostess, maybe the closest some of us will ever get to seeing our name in lights. Wendy's is a tradition that dates back to a few years ago when she was store manager at Rose Records State Street. Some of the people working at the store then were Robert Ford, **Gerry Fisher, André Halmon, Paula Harris**, and **Howard Kaplan**. Fortunately, it takes more than a few artfully installed Xmas lights and Rose Records State Street Alumni to make a good party. In the back, she had a cute buffet of sweets and crunchies befitting the holiday season. (Mysteriously missing eggnog?) However enough beer, wine, and spirits to satisfy even the heartiest of holiday appetites. The dining room also featured the Xmas Light Lounge: Xmas lights making big electric wave-like on three of the walls. Jagged shapes like bolts of electricity.   Good music, of course : Patsy Cline, Elvis, Hank Williams, even an entry of tapes mixed by **Steve** ("I-didn't-know-he-was-a-dee-jay!") **LaFreniere**. Also Quinn chums, artist/performer **John Smith**, the merry **Gerald Paoli** (doin' a long red flannel "Macho" night shirt and black leather biker boots!), **Michael Thompson, James** (Andy) **Warren, Chuck Gonzalez**, Gerry Fisher, Robert and **Cynthia P. Caster**. Everybody but Janet, who was off in Geneva (Illinois). Asked what she thought it was that helped to make a good party, Wendy replied, " I think that lighting is crucial. If it's well lit, everything else sort of falls into place. People feel comfortable." She's quite right.

T 's XMAS/KWANZAA THING

The funny thing about this party is that it got written up in Wholesome Roc's newsletter, *Planet Roc* (January 1990, *Past* pg. 3) as "an informal Ujima (Collective Work and Responsibility) celebration at Terry's home." It didn't matter in the least that clubby music promoter **Terry Martin** and his coachouse mate **Steve Collier** are not at all of African or African American decent. But guess what? You don't have to be African American to celebrate Kwanzaa! Though it's of African American origin, Kwanzaa is based on universally valued principles like Unity, Self Determination, and Community. So what there was a big Xmas tree. And candles, a fire, hot cider and rum. We snacked on crackers, bread, assorted-cheeses, stuffed mushrooms, light and flavorful vegetable patés.   **Stepanie** and **Simone**, Symbols and Instruments' **Derrick Carrter, Mark Farina** and company, photograher **Rich Renaldi**, and **Paul Glasier** (who's now in the Florida Keys doing a new club... more to follow), **Evan Coleman**, Robert, new kid on the block **Eric Johnson**, and a really cute Oriental girl named **June** who was in the SI entourage. Though he could have been there, writer **Pete Victor** was not in attendance as the *Roc*'s article had mistakenly reported.

:word

ANOTHER NEW YEAR'S EVE KABASH

You know its going to be a good party when you drive and you drive and you still can't find the damn place. Or at least you pray it will be. We, (myself, **Ricque Green**, and Robert Ford) were in a taxi (a miracle in and of itself since 99.9% of the cabbies in this town refuse to stop for young black men) circling and circling this westside neighborhood looking for **Larry Steger's** loft party celebrating New Year's Eve. All I could think of was how we'd have to ring in the New Year in a cab and the thought just made me so nervous. I was tempted to hop out and search on foot. A maze of one way streets. The Alizé we'd consumed earlier had long since lost its quieting effect. I was quickly returning from fabulousness to an unwanted "Maybe-I-should-have-stayed-in?" kind of anxiety. Then we found it! There is a God! Or something. It was kind of what we'd expected. But younger than expected. A lot of artsy kids mostly white kids dressed in black, doing...? I don't know. Dancing and things? Ricque and me made a bee line for the dj's booth (Larry's bedroom) to find personality Steve (Not a Dee-jay/ Not a writer) LaFreniere at the turntables and a very up and sexy **Burle Avant** perched on the bed anxiously waiting his turn to spin. What can I say about Steve's set? An eclectic mix to say the least! Parliament, Elvis, Sonny and Cher, Talking Heads, Ofra Haza, Doctor Buzzard's Original Savannah Band, and the ubiquitous Lil Louis "French Kiss". When we weren't dancing, we were gagging. Then Burle *dived* in mixing House with the Butthole Surfers and Damanda Galas, and scratching to beat the band! Needless to say, we hung out between the bedroom/booth and the dancefloor for most of the evening. We spent our time there dancing and chatting and trying to guard a special bottle of champagne for Larry, with little luck. John Smith, Wendy and Janet Quinn, Psychotronic Film Society's **Michael Flores** and **Pam Smith**, photographer **Jenny Knolton**, and Michael Thompson. And many other timely people.

parties
and
other

*t*ee

by

t.adkins

PARTY AT PENNY'S PALMER'S SQUARE PARK

Marc Pentecoste (a.k.a. The Penny) has also come to be lovingly known as *Miss Chip And Dip*, a name bestowed upon him by none other than **LDW**; who comes to your party and first looks at your guest talley then at your food, and, who has been quick to criticize Penny for too often taking the easy way out, trying to provide sustenance for the post- party gang. For many years, after the clubs would close, kids would head over to Penny's for a breakfast of Aunt Jemima and Brown & Serve sausages. Well, what would *you* do? Still, Jays and Lipton Onion Soup Dip Mix ranks with cheese balls, nut logs, Ritz Crackers, and Carlo Rossi at the top of the Forever OUT Party Food List. Imagine our surprise when Penny decided to do a Thanksgiving dinner and went all-out, *all-out,* to prepare a spread fit for a queen. He asked **Darryl Hunt**, **Rick Smith**, and **LDW** (who'd asked me). A fabulously browned and juicy turkey, scrumptious corn bread dressing, super rich macaroni and cheese casserole, homemade dinner rolls, butter laden sweet potatoes, crisp string beans and potatoes, *and* a jello mold. We th'ew down! Penny put his foot in it. The only cop-out may have been the sweet potatoe and pumpkin pies courtesy of Let Them Eat Cake. After dinner it was a few more champagne cocktails, some fireside chit chat, some videos, record and cd playing, and dancing. Then we took off for Club Flamingo for the Gay Night party hosted by Deception (designers OJ White, Klee, and Kevin). Saw some of everybody there including **Reginald Thomas** (sporting a black baseball cap wighat with detachable hair?), RT Design assistant **Victor Evans**, and Bad Boys' **Johnny Washington** and **Steve Boykin**.

CONTINUED ON NEXT PAGE

One afternoon, in the middle of transcribing the **Riley Evans** Interview in this issue, this reporter suddenly got a craving for Jerry's Kitchen and entered the restauraunt to meet (by total surprise) **Maia LaVille**, **Miisha du Part**, and **Djuna Baker** who make up Dekko productions. The question is, is Dekko on its way to being the next *Seduction*? The girls were lunching and promoting their *Secret Garden* party at Club Flamingo planned for the following Saturday. Maia hadn't seen a copy of the Thing debut issue including her at the Bad Boys party, so I said come on over, we're right around the corner. Just then, this guy had this rather large duffle bag in the aisle and that older waitress they have there went sailing over the bag with a full order of chicken and dressing right into her customer's lap. Later, they show up at the offices with the guy with the bag at the restauraunt. Turns out he's this British photographer named **Chris** in from London to take pictures of producer **Larry Heard**, (who, coincidentally, is mentioned in the aforementioned Riley Evans piece). That explained the bag from hell. He was scouting locations and wanted to shoot in front of the office. We loved Maia's idea of success. On their way out she said, "Just remember whoever gets there first reaches back to lend a helping hand!" *How 'bout a big hand?!*

3 Girls 3: Miisha duPart, Maia LaVille and Djuna Baker are Dekko Productions. The next Exposé ?

What's goin' on at the offices of THING magazine? Actually located at Robert Ford's tiny studio apartment, in Old Town, we're fixed with everything but xerox and fax machines. Still, we carry on. One Saturday found the crew busy updating THING's database (compliments of Marc Pentecoste who also played polaroid paparazzi), editing and proofing copy, brainstorming. Later, Simone and Stephanie made it over to enter and layout Planet Roc (top right). Though he usually does Oscar's barbershop, LDW talked me into giving him a trim, (bottom left).

TEE : *know what I'm sayin' ?*

STRAIGHT Don't ask how mostly black straight people got to circulating this term to mean 'I'm cool' or 'I'm OK'. There's a connection in there somewhere. Nearly every home boy and girl have heard 'straight.' Everytime I here some dude in the street say, "Yeah, I'm straight," I'm reminded of the same kind of brothers you hear proudly proclaiming, "I like pussy!" But catch it turning it around, as they are wont to do, the gay brothers and lesbian sisters can be heard saying, "I'm straight."

IT'S GOIN' ON What's Goin' On? Somewhere around the summer of 1989 one began hearing kids in the city saying "It's goin' on! to describe people, places and/or events that were hot, poppin', happenin', and def. Variations come as "It will be goin' on," "We will be goin on," "He (she, they, we) got it goin' on," and "It ain't goin' on!" See It's A Black Thing; You Wouldn't Understand. To "Get it goin' on" to get with the program.

BUT GUESS WHAT? During the most recent Thanksgiving holiday, Chicago was visited by none other than thespian, bon vivant, happy camper, Lavender Light founder/ director, recent BLK cover guy and Associate Video Producer for New York City's Commission on Human Rights' AIDS Discrimination Division, Chas. B. Brack, a k a King Booty. Yeah, he's real fab. Among some of the madness that was his visit came a phrase that Mr. Brack would turn frequently. 'But guess what?' A kind of question that could answer any and everything! By the time of the king's parting only a few days later, it had become a fixture in the vocabulary of all the girls. "I know we shouldn't be bashing Zsa Zsa Gabor... but, guess what?" or "I know you got a big bird...but, guess what?"!!

Excuse me, but what's up with this 'Gay Night' thing? Something strange and peculiar's goin' on since a few straight bars in the city got busy doin' so-called 'Gay Nights.' And you were thinking that gay was a fulltime life-long thing. Pick a day, any day. If it's Monday, this must be USA Rainbo. Is this trend nothing more than opportunism, buck hungry-ness and cheap schmoozing in the guise of a good time? Maybe. Will this special scheduling do anything to change the climate of homophobia that's the standard at these clubs on any other night of the week? And finally, will this do anything like undermine the gay/lesbian community's economic base by seeing gay/lesbian dollars spent at bars owned and operated outside the community? I don't know. Heroes? Union? Club Flamingo? These places don't really welcome gays the other nights they're open and by the time you're invited it's like you're stigmatized: beware gay bashers. What's next? Black Night at FX or Gatz? Better yet, why not really act up and have the gay bars do Straight Nights? And places like the Taste and Mr. Ricky's could do White Nights. Anybody for Boy Night at Paris Dance or Augie/CK's ?

— T.A.

Bob Toledo's Essential Miles Cut-Outs

On the Corner
Agharta
Get Up With It
Pangaea
We Want Miles

Black and Read All Over

Jet
Ebony
Sepia
BlacTress
Bronze Thrills
Tan
N'digo

Wendy Quinn's Bedside Reading List

A Voice Through A Cloud — *Denton Welch*
Among The Believers: An Islamic Journey — *V. S. Naipaul*
Anna Karenina — *Leo Tolstoy*
Betrayed By Rita Hayworth — *Manuel Puig*
Boss — *Mike Royko*
Brando — *Christopher Nickens*
Cleopatra — *Carlo Maria Franzonera*
Critiques of Contemporary Rhetoric — *Karlyn K. Campbell*
The Decay of the Angel — *Yukio Mishima*
The Dialectic of Sex — *Shulamith Firestone*
Diet For A New America — *John Robbins*
Duluth — *Gore Vidal*
Elizabeth Taylor — *Ruth Waterbury*
Existentialism and Human Emotions — *Jean Paul Sartre*
Extraordinary Popular Delusions & the Madness of Crowds — *Charles Mackay*
The Fifth Child — *Doris Lessing*
Granta — *Various*
Great Britain — *Baedaker's*
Great Expectations — *Charles Dickens*
I Know Why The Caged Bird Sings — *Maya Angelou*
In Search of Excellence — *Peters/Waterman*
Irish Folk Tales — *Henry Glassie*
Journal Of A Solitude — *May Sarton*
The Late Mrs. Dorothy Parker — *Leslie Frewin*
Les Liasons Dangereuses — *Choderlos de Laclos*
Losing Battles — *Eudora Welty*
Louise Brooks — *Barry Paris*
The Louvre — *Pierre Quoniam*
Midddlemarch — *George Eliot*
The Mimic Men — *V. S. Naipaul*
Native Son — *Richard Wright*
One Day At A Time In Al-Anon — *Al-Anon*
Oscar Wilde — *Frank Harris*
Overcoming Procrastination — *Albert Ellis, PhD*
Paris In My pocket — *Barron's*
The Road Less Traveled — *M. Scott Peck, M D*
The Satyricon — *Petronius*
Seventeenth Century Painting — *Raymond Cogniat*
Shikasta — *Doris Lessing*
The Temple of the Golden Pavilion — *Yukio Mishima*
Thomas Paine: Selections from His Writing — *Thomas Paine*
Three Continents — *Ruth Prawer Jhabvala*
The Unbearable Lightness Of Being — *Milan Kundera*
The Wicked Ways of Malcom McLaren — *Craig Bromberg*
William Styroh's Nat Turner: Ten Black Writers Respond — *John H. Clarke*
The Wretched of the Earth — *Frantz Fanon*

TA's Thing/No Thing

Sensuous Black Woman — Karen Finley
Fashionation — Facism
Our World — Your World
Linda Evangilista — Evangeiine Bruce
Michael Musto — Michael Kilian
Pat Stevens — Pat Buckley
Gangsta lean — Gang banging

Looney Tunes

Betty Boop
Jessica Rabbit
Natasha Fatalé
Bugs Bunny
Aunt Fritzl
Little Lulu
Krazy Kat
Smurfette

House To Do That

Housekeeping
House Dressing
It's My House
Welcome Home
House Boy
Haus Frau
House Nigger
Speaker of the House
Doll House
Bathhouse
Outhouse
Gin House
Crack House
Full House
Ambient House
Deep House
Acid House
Hip House
House coat
House shoes
House Dress
Birdhouse
Play House
House and Garden
House Dick
Brick House
This Old House
It's House
House Call
House Fly
House Doctor
Haunted House
House of Games
Green House
House Rules
Road House
House of 7 Gables
Housequake

Club Shirley

Shirley Bassey
Shirley Horn
Cheryl Lynn
Cherly Lynn Bruce
Sheryl Lee Ralph
Sheryl Lutz-Brown
MertieLynnTina
Terri Lyne Carrington
Saralynne Crittenden
MertieLynnTina
Phyllis Lynne Swan
Pepsi and Shirley
Cheryl "Pepsii" Riley
Sherri Riley
Shari James
Siedah Garrett

Another piece of pie?

Sonya Grant
Patti Austin
Luther Vandross
Aretha Franklin
Sybil
Chaka Khan
David Peaston
Heavy D.
Oprah Winfrey
Delta Burke
Roseanne Barr

LDW's Thing/No Thing

Shelly Winters — Donna Summer
"Welcome Home" — Welcome Mat
Bobby Short — Harry Connick Jr.
Fuck Me — Fuck You
Michael Evans — Mike Sneed
One Nation Under a Groove — Rhythm Nation
One World — Third World

Sinema

Git Out of Africa
When Harry Met Larry
Stellllaaaaaaall
Glitzy Gaudy Glamourous Gospel Glory
The Fabulous Baker Boys
Men Don't Leave
Buttfucked In The Park
Extremities
Three Men And A Baby
Dangerous Lesions
Breakfast At Gladys'
The White Boy
Prick Up Your Ears
They Shoot Wads Don't They?

Feelin' Free

Free Noriega
Set Me Free
Freedom's Just Another Word (For Nothin'Left To Lose)
Fat Free
Cholesterol Free
Sugar Free
Free Nelson Mandela
Free Fred Hampton
Free Angela Davis
Free Leona
Free James Brown
Free Scot Tyler
Scot Free
Free butter with your popcorn
Free (for a limited time only)
Free to be you and me
Free yo' mind — yo' ass will follow
Free Za Za, dalink!
Butterflies are free
Freelance
Free at last
Freedom is the key (To lovin' me)
Get out of jail free
Free Me From My Freedom
Born Free
That's When We'll Be Free
Freehand
Free-for-all
Stay Free
Stay Free Maxipads
Pussy Ain't Free (Gotta Give Up the Money)
Don't Cost You Nothin'

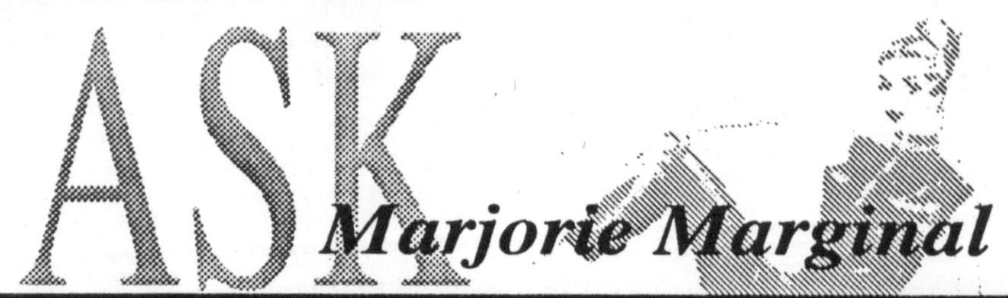

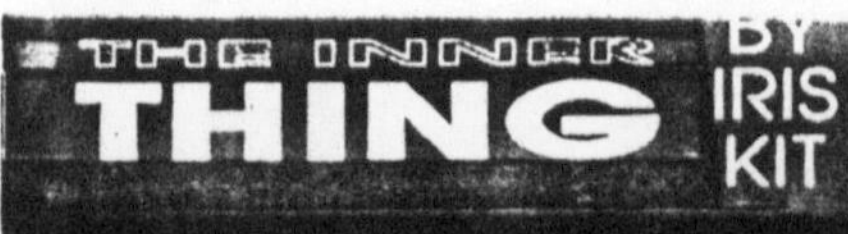

Dear Marjorie,

Having given up on cruising and its indecipherable rules, I've decided to try the personal ads to find a (ahem) "mate". However, I've encountered a line that seems to exclude me from answering all but the most repulsive ads: "No fats, fems, or drugs". Now, I'm no Dawn Davenport clone injecting liquid eyeliner or anything, but I do sport a spare tire, love to camp occasionally, and smoke a doobie now and again. What am I to do?,

—Fat Fem Druggie

Dear FFD,
Lose weight, butch up, kick the habit. Do you honestly think that ANYONE would want to date a flabby, addicted sissy like you? The whole point of personals is to find human perfection. If you're NOT human perfection, don't come crying to Miss Marjorie. She's looking for a drug free, butch hunk of a stud herself, and will accept nothing less. Write back after a few courses with Jenny Craig, Betty Ford, and Sly Stallone. Maybe we can do lunch.

Dear Marjorie,

I keep seeing the phrase "safe sex" bandied about like a mantra these days. And granted, it makes lots of sense for the "uninfected" among us to stay that way. But being HIV positive, I'd like to know just what "safe sex" keeps me safe from? The Boogeyman? Jesse Helms? What? It seems like all the information is going to the uninfected or the dying. What about those of us who live with an impending diagnosis of fatal illness? Are we to "play safe" to avoid the demon that already lurks within? Or masturbate alone until the full-blown "big 'A'" sets in?

—Just Curious

Dear Curious,
You are not to bother the sick or uninfected among us with your sniveling and whining. Find some anonymous bozo who will let you dump up his rump like it was 1975. They're out there; if they don't know why they shouldn't, they deserve every drop. We've got enough problems without dealing with folks like you. Get a life!

Dear Marjorie,

I hate to whine and complain, but I have a slight problem that I'm hoping you can be of some help in solving. You see, I'm tired of my friends and other gay bretheren referring to me as girl, girlfriend, she, and Miss Thing. I'm a gay man, not a woman. I am very proud to be who I am and feel very confident and secure in my manhood and sexuality. But I feel really slighted when people just naturally assume that 'gay' means cross dressing or opposite gender indentification. By the way, I do enjoy camping it up as much as the next fag. I do not, however, live my life longing to be a 'woman'.

—Michael Mujere

Dear Mujere,
Girl, you need a change of mind! What do you think the title 'Miss' Macho implies? Assuming that you are indeed secure with your sexuality and 'proper gender identification', what's the problem? What's with all the 'man' mess? Catch it: Being a queen has everything and nothing to do with being a man and being a man has everything and nothing to do with being a queen. Get it? Got it? Good.

Dear Marjorie,

Could you please give us your honest opinion on oat bran? First we were told it was the best thing since sliced bread, now researchers are saying it's no more fabulous than any other bran product. What's goin' on? I'm so...

—Fed Up

Dear Fed Up,
What, are you constipated? Miss Marjorie also hopes you don't mean to imply that Miss Marjorie has nothing better to do than to sit around and contemplate the correctness (?) of oat bran? She does however realize that in these times of information overload and hype as high fiber fodder, some poor child may be sitting in a pickle just plucked over what to eat and how much of it. Miss Marjorie offers that you: 1) please perceive media antics and all manner of hype to be what it is, (DON'T BUY ANY OF IT) 2) do your own research, and 3) take oat (or any other) bran(d) advisably remembering that we are, after all, intelligent, cultured ladies ... not cattle!

★★★★★

Confidential to "Will You Marry Me?": *NO!*
Confidential to "Call Your Lawyer": *Let her take the damned snotnosed brat, keep the condo, BMW, and stocks and bonds. What are you, stupid?*
Confidential to "Cum-Guzzling Slut": *Spit dear, don't swallow. And don't forget the Listerine!*
Confidential to "Beaten and Bruised": *Give me your beau's number, honey!*

MARJORIE WILL READ YOU, TOO!
Send your earthshattering question to:
MISS MARJORIE MARGINAL
C/O THING
1516 N. SEDGWICK AVENUE
CHICAGO, ILLINOIS 60610-1223
All replies kept confidential (ASK ANYONE!)

HOW TO ANNOY YOUR CLOSEST FRIENDS

AQUARIUS: Stand too close to them and get intimate and personal. Tell them they're too conformist. Insist that they check in with you 17 times a day.

PISCES: Tell them they're self-pitying martyrs. Drag them to overly bright bars.

ARIES: Tell them you don't like them. Cut in front of them in lines. Show no passion.

TAURUS: Vascillate. Be non-committal. Tell them they have poor taste. Don't return what you've borrowed from them.

GEMINI: Talk for hours in detail about your feelings. Tell them they think too much. Don't answer any of their questions.

CANCER: Tell them their home lacks warmth. Constantly remind them that they're too sensitive.

LEO: Forget their birthday. Act like you know more than they do. Tell them they need to do something with their hair.

VIRGO: Wear dirty, unpressed clothing. Spill things in their home. Spill things on them. Fold their laundry into little crumpled balls.

LIBRA: Insist that they make the final decision. Pick your nose in public in front of them.

SCORPIO: Pry into their personal affairs. Be friendly to their enemies. Tell them you can see right through them. Tell them they have no sex appeal.

SAGITARIUS: Invite them to stupid, tacky parties. Criticize their philosophies. Tell them they need to be more responsible. Don't laugh at their jokes....but laugh at them.

CAPRICORN: Make fun of their reputation. Tell them they look foolish. Question their competence.

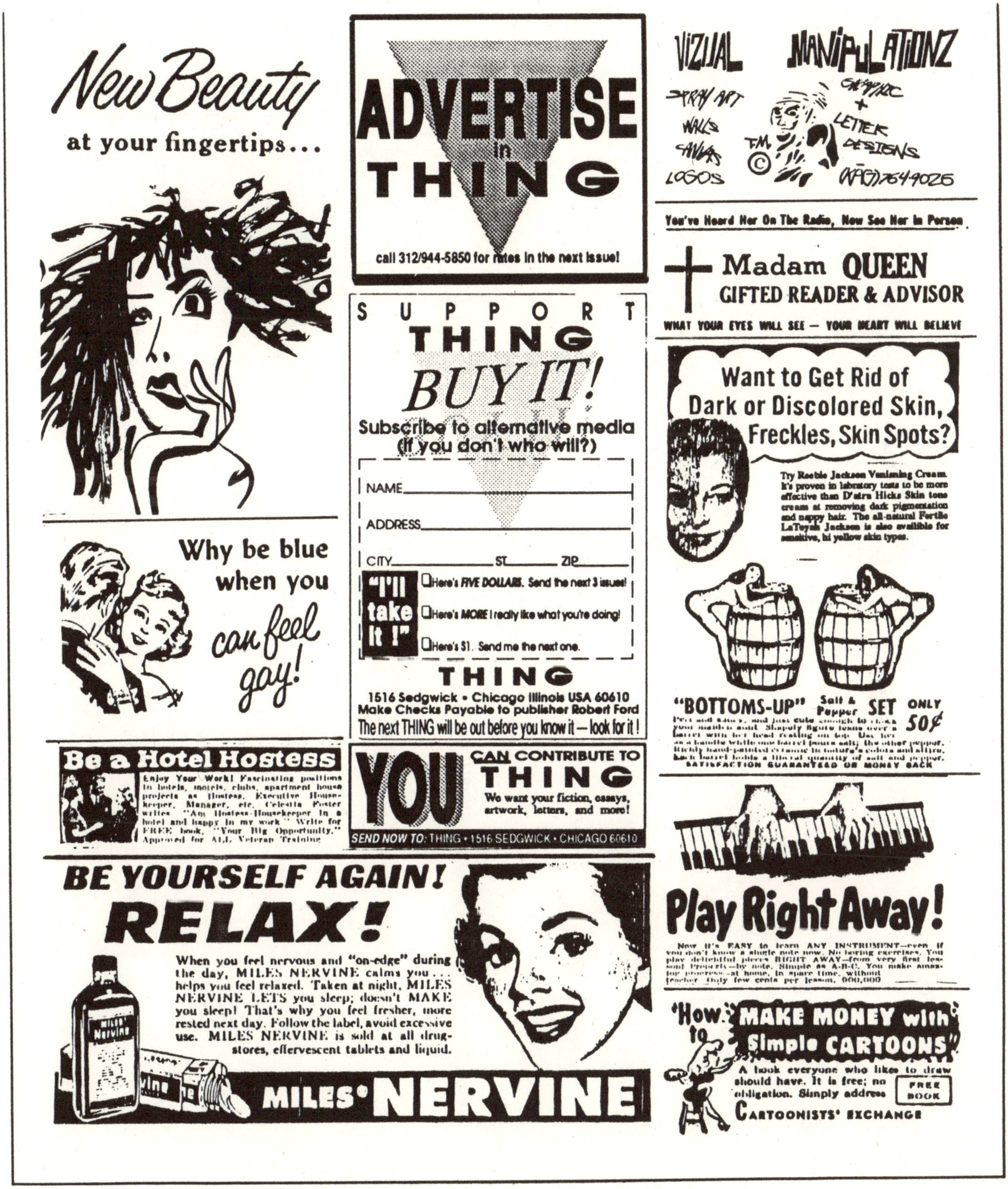

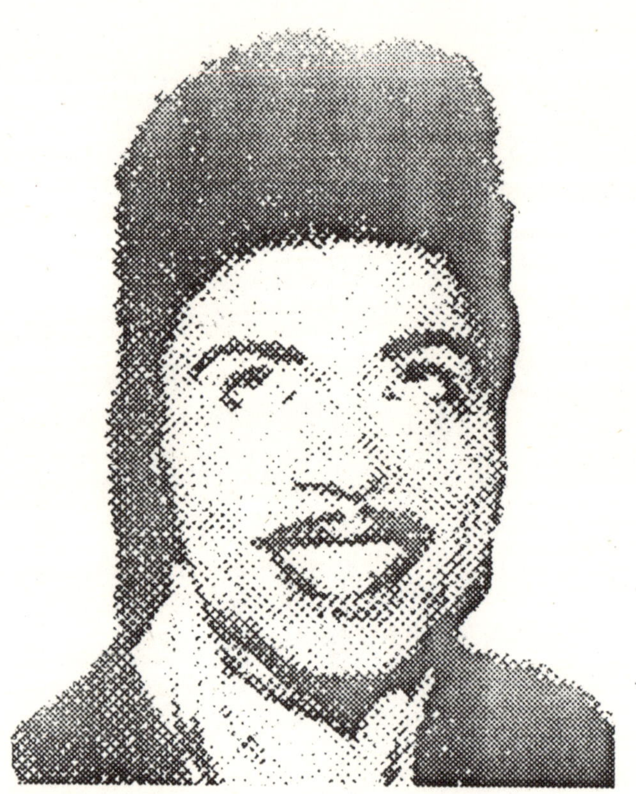

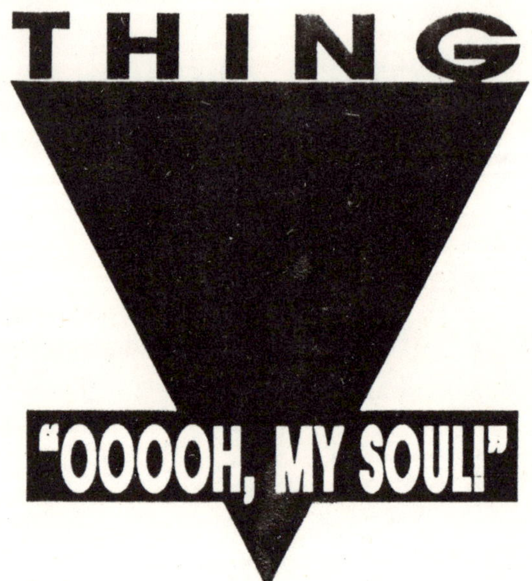

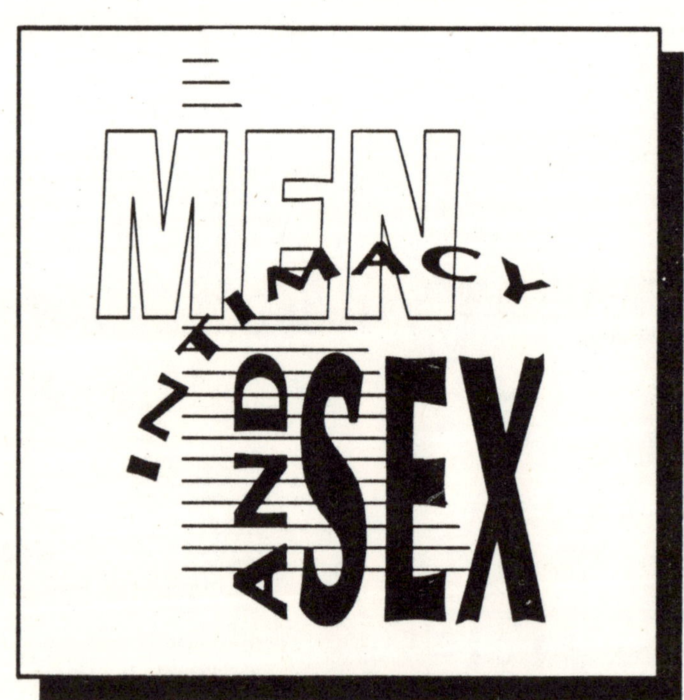

An innovative
approach
to enhancing
your lifestyle.

For more information call
(312) 472-6469

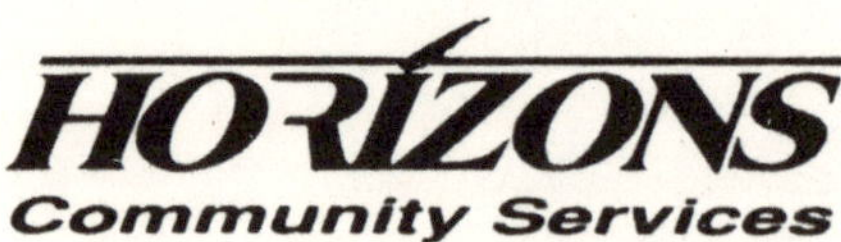

THING

SUMMER CAMP !

**Number Three
Two Dollars**

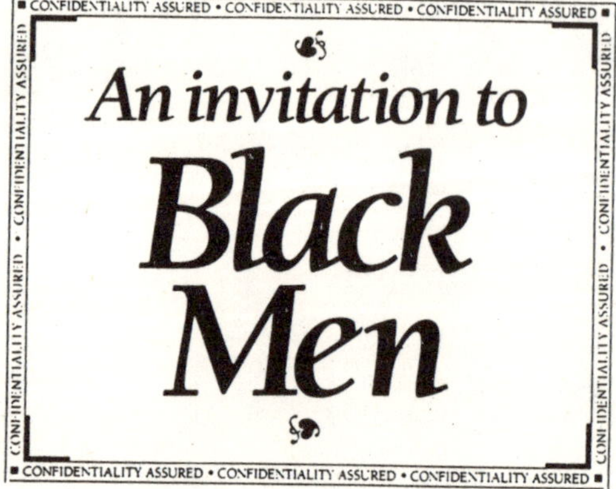

R E C E I V E :

- ❧ Travel Reimbursement
- ❧ Free Blood Work
- ❧ Free Personal Health information and/or counseling

If you have had sex with another man in the past six months you may participate in this program…

FOR INFORMATION CALL:
NIH PROJECT COORDINATOR

871-5777

Unfriendly Bisexual Response

Your article, "Friendly Bisexual Men", was 100% polyester.

In all truth, reality, and honesty, you should have entitled it singularly— "A Friendly Bisexual Man". Your fantasized (the side-effects of somebody's medication?) 'Tyrone' is only one (singular) type of bisexual brother. There are a great many other types of bisexual men; also, there are men who regard themselves as "non-gay homosexuals" engaging in loving, honest, serious (long-term as opposed to 'snap'), productive, healthy relationships that are financially, politically, spiritually, and otherwise contributing to and supportive of this and the larger community.

I can understand why you don't personally know any of us. You should. Stop Black on Black grime!

B. NIA NGULU
NEW YORK, NY

P.S.:Richard Penniman presented positively on the cover of your magazine...do you know what he says about homosexuality in his current autobiography? Take some time to read something other than each other! What next, Donna Summer?!?

Our reasons for choosing Little Richard as cover image were fully explained on the contents page of the "offending" issue. Yes, he is a repressed, born again, closeted, homophobe. But you, I, and he all know that he is still a flaming queen. No matter how backwards his own politics and self image are.

— editors

Reading Miss Marjorie

The Number 2, April 1990, edition of Thing carried a very disturbing response to an inquiry regarding the issue of "safe sex" in the Ask Marjorie Marginal column (p.26).

There is no question that safe sex should be practiced by all individuals, regardless of antibody status. Furthermore, it is of utmost importance that a person already testing positive for HIV practice safe sex to avoid re-infection. Studies have indicated that repeated exposure to HIV can, in fact, hasten the destruction of the immune system.

The writer, "Just Curious" seems to believe that the "uninfected" segment of the gay population is practicing all kinds of unprotected, unsafe sex. If that were the case, why is the rate of new HIV infection among gay men less than 1% per year. Clearly, most uninfected gay men are practicing safe sex.

Those who "live with an impending diagnosis of fatal illness" should seek out professional counseling, if need be, not exacerbate their problems by having indiscriminate unsafe sex. Miss Marginal's response of "finding some anonymous bozo who will let you dump up in his rump" is a prime example of poor judgment and irresponsible journalism.

Anyone having questions regarding HIV/AIDS would be well-advised to consult with an agency like Howard Brown Memorial Clinic or the State of Illinois AIDS Hotline for correct information.

LARRY WOLF
EDUCATION COORDINATOR, HBMC

"Ask Marjorie Marginal" is intended strictly as satire. Thank you for a much more practical and thoughtful response to this issue.

— editors

CORRECTION FROM ISSUE TWO

Louis Walker is not represented by the Yolanda Gallery; we regret any inconvenience this may have caused.

THING

SHE KNOWS WHO SHE IS

**Number Three
August 1990**

PUBLISHER/EDITOR
Robert Ford

CONTRIBUTING EDITORS
Trent Adkins
Stephen Freshwaater
W. Delon Strode
Lawrence D. Warren

ART DIRECTION/LAYOUT
Robert Ford

ADVERTISING SALES
Stephen Freshwater

GRAPHIC SERVICES
Simone Bouyer

CONTRIBUTORS
Simone Bouyer, Tim Brennan, Bunny & Pussy, Stephanie Coleman, Riley Evans, Evil, Tyrone Fields, Tony Greene, André Halmon, Jeffrey Kennedy, Iris Kit, Steve Lafreniere, Terry Martin, Steve Marton, Wendy Quinn, Stephen Winter, Rob Wittig

Thing is published capriciously. Subscriptions are five dollars for the next three issues published postpaid. Single issues available at your favorite gay bookseller. Wholesale inquiries invited. Donations encouraged! *Thing* preferrs all checks made payable to publisher Robert Ford. *Thing* encourages unsolicited submissions of any printed matter; only those with self-addressed stamped envelopes will be returned. Artists' payment is the satisfaction of contribution. Editotial inclusion casts no aspersions on one's racial or sexual categorization (Things know who they are.) Opinions expressed are those of individual contributors and do not always reflect those of *Thing*.
Thing does not sell or rent its mailing list.
©1990 *Thing*

DIRECT COMMUNICATION TO
Thing, 2151 W. Division, Chicago, Illinois 60622-3056
☎ 1.312.276.0398

please note this is a new address

CONTENTS

a special bonus edition follows page 16 in all newsstand and subscriber copies
see its table of contents for additional credits

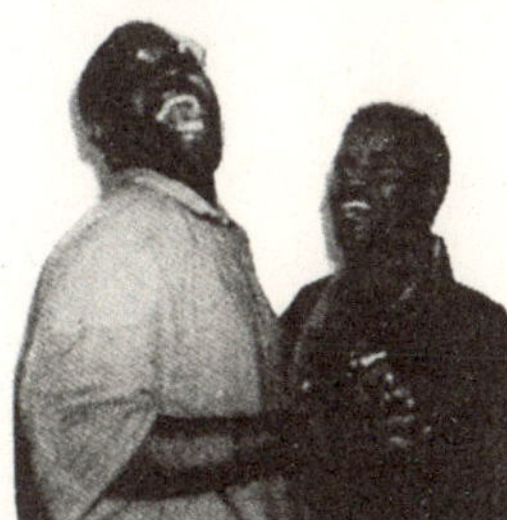

ON THE COVER:
a detail of Trent and daHoover kee-keeing at the old Wholesome Roc Gallery.
Photo: Stephanie Coleman

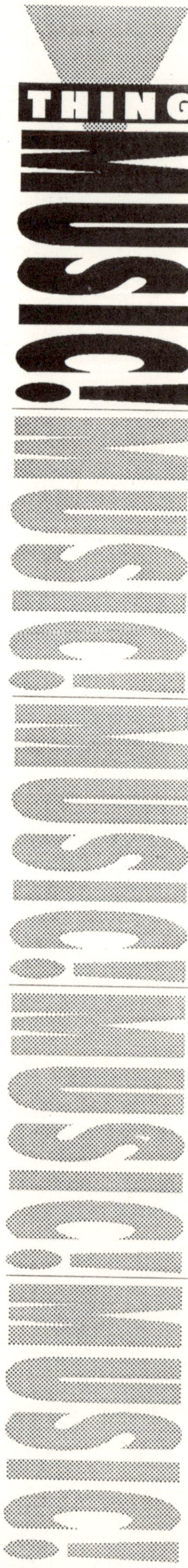

Tony Greene

For what it's worth, here is my contribution to the "Summer Camp" issue. This was really hard for me to think about because I like so many tunes. But from the latest tunes played on 92.3 KKBT, Los Angeles, I picked these. There are some older tunes that I like better but I believe myself to be a fashionable and modern thing so my music should reflect that.

Tony-Toni-Toné *The Blues*
What's mine is mine, what's yours is mine.
Babyface *Whip Appeal*
Whip it On Me!
By All Means *I Wanna Be Rich*
Madonna *Vogue*
Rita Hayworth gave good face?? (so do I!)
Regina Belle *What Goes Around Comes Around*
You'd better watch your back boy!
Quincy Jones *The Secret Garden*
"I'll take good care of you, that's what a man is supposed to do... and I'll be there for you always."
M.C. Hammer *You Can't Touch This*
Ring the bell-school is in!
Keith Sweat *Make You Sweat*
I bet I can make you sweat!
Bell Biv Devoe *Poison*
Never trust a big butt and a smile
Patti LaBelle *Yo, Mister*
Hey Mr., where's your daughter?

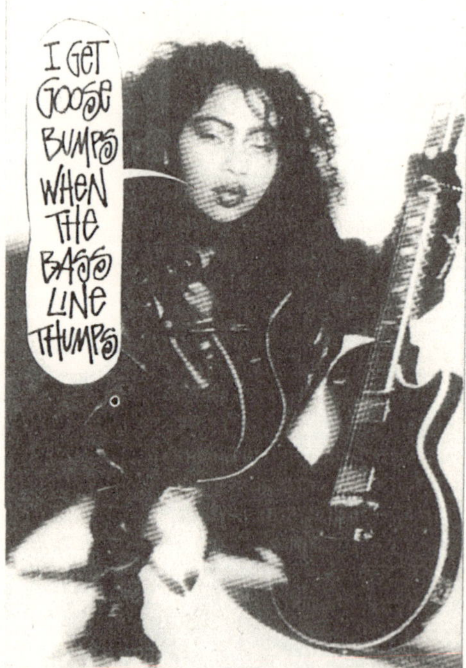

Robert Ford

All Time Classic Downtempo Summer Disco (112 BPM or less)
Deee-Lite *What Is Love*
Soul II Soul (almost anything by them)
Gwen Guthrie (almost anything by her, notably the *Padlock* EP)
Rufus With Chaka Khan *Ain't Nobody*
Gwen McRae *Funky Sensation*
Heartbeat *Tanna Gardner* (NOT *Seduction* !)
Innocence *Natural Thing*
Jody Watley *Still A Thrill*
The Chimes *Underestimate (remix)*
En Vogue *Hold On*
Family Stand *Ghetto Heaven*
Gaz Nevada *I.C. Love Connection*
The Whatnuts *Help Is On The Way*
Lil Louis *Nyce and Slo (remix)*
Girls Can't Help It *Baby Doll*
Grace Jones *Feel Up (remix)*
Rolling Stones *Miss You*
Bob James *Rotation*
Imagination *Just An Illusion*
Donna Summer *Love to Love You Baby*

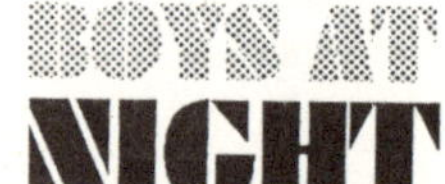

808 State *Cubik (remix)*
Deee-Lite *Groove Is In the Heart*
Wop Bop Torledo *Jungle Fever (Extra III Fever Mix)*
Vision *Robert Owens*
E&J *Easy Listening*
Kid Creole *The Sex of It (Dub Mix)*
Maxi Priest *BonaFide (LP)*
The Time *Pandemonium (LP)*
Raul Orellana *Guitarra (LP)*
Soul II Soul *Volume II 1990 (LP)*
Black Box *Dreamland (LP)*
A Guy Called Gerald *Automatikk (LP)*
The Grid *Flotation*
JT and the Big Family *Moments In Soul*
EZEE Posse featuring Dr. Mouthquake *Love on Love*

Jeffery Kennedy

Jeffery's Ten Favorite Songs of the Summer (so far!)
Beat Happening *Nancy Sin*
Courtney Love
The Second Most Beautiful Girl in the World
Madonna *Vogue*
Brenda Lee *All the Way*
Betty Boo *Doin' the Do*
808 State with MC Tunes *The Only Rhyme that Bites*
Soho *Hippychick*
Kitchens of Distinction *Quick as Rainbows*
Shonen Knife Flying *Jelly Attack*
Dionne Warwick *Trains and Boats and Planes*

graphic

by

Simone

Bouyer

Andre Halmon

Black Box *Everybody, Everbody* (RCA)
Lil Louis *Nyce & Slo — remix* (Epic)
Ron Trent *Altered States* (Warehouse)
Blaze *We All Must Live Together* (Motown)
Ram Jam *Black Betty — remix* (Epic)
King Amazin *Double Asunder— remix* (House Jam)
Dee-Lite *What Is Love* (Elektra)
Johanna Law *The First Time Ever I Saw Your Face* (Easy Street)
Richard Rodgers *Can't Stop Loving You— remix* (Sam)
Liz Torrez *If You Keep It Up —Bootleg Dub* (Jive)
Freestyle Orchestra *Keep On Pumpin' It Up* (SBK)
Vision *Other Side of Life* (Interface)
Da Da Na Da *Deep Love— remix* (One Voice)
A Jersey Artist *Drink On Me* (Express)
Cooltempo Orchestra *K-Jee* (Cooltempo/UK)
A Way of Life *Trippin On Your Love — remix* (Eternal/UK)
Nayobe *I Love The Way You Love Me* (WTG)
Darryl Pandy *I Love Music* (Eternal/WB)
Shawn Christopher *Another Sleepless Night* (Arista/UK)
K.T.E. *House of Calypso — remix* (Irma-Italy)
Homeboy *'m Gonna Get You— remix* (C.T./UK)
Mondee Oliver *Newsy Neighbors* (Gherkin)
Satoshi Tomiie *And I Loved You* (FFRR)
Soft House Company *What You Need* (Irma-Italy)
Pressure Drop *Feeling Good* (BCM-Germany)

Trent Adkins

I can dance to this
Soul II Soul *Time (Untitled)/People (do-it-yourself remix)*
Ultra Naté *It's Over Now*
Talking With Myself *Electribe 101*
808 State *Pacific (Break)/ Quadra State (UK LP)*
Black Box *Everybody, Everybody*
Masterplan *Diana Brown & Barrie K. Sharpe*
Deee-Lite *Groove Is In the Heart*
Adeva *Respect*
Kid Creole and the Coconuts *The Sex of It*
Public Enemy *911 Is A Joke (remix)*

Crispy Queen

Bad Ideas
CD singles
Cassette singles
no more vinyl 12" singles
DJs that can't count BPMs
Loleatta Holloway samples
First Choice samples
James Brown samples
Paula Abdul *Shut Up and Dance*
Janet Jackson *Rhythm Nation 1814*
Madonna *I'm Breathless*
New Kids On the Block *(anything)*
Milli Vanilli *(anything)*
use of water in music videos
use of girls in tight black dresses in music videos

Old Queen

Best reissues
The Best of Cerrone (HOT records)
Billboard top R&B Hits 1970-74 (Rhino)
The Disco Series Vol I-II (Rhino)
Club Epic (Epic)
Club Columbia (Columbia)
Nippers Greatest Hits of the 70's (RCA)

Jazz Queen

Best New Jazz
Branford Marsalis *Crazy People Music*
Cassandra Wilson *Jumpworld*
Vernell Brown Jr. *A Total Eclipse*
Soundtrack *Mo' Better Blues*
John Zorn *Naked City*
Courtney Pine *The Visions Tale*
Chet Baker *The Last Great Concert*

sex, lies, and audiotape

Video pop superstation VH1's "24 hour Superstar" days have proven really popular, featuring non-stop programming by such prolific pop icons as **Gloria Estefan, Rod Stewart,** and **Phil Collins.** So popular in fact, that the pool of artists with 24 hours worth of material is dangerously dwindling. Just announced: 24 hours with **Pebbles.** Sure it's only fifteen minutes worth of material, but by the 9th hour, such delirium has set in with most viewers that they hardly notice...Not to be outdone by the rampant success of **David Lynch**'s *Twin Peaks* series, another network has gotten the idea to combine the post-modern serial concept with the reunion show. The resulting return of *The Dick Van Dyke Show* stars **Richard Moll** as a pie-eating comedy writer for Alan Brady (**Herve Villachez**). Written and directed by **Edward Albee** under the working title *Who's Afraid of Jerry and Millie Helper,* the show revolves around the enigmatic question "Who Killed Laura Petrie?". Meanwhile a cable system has hooked up with **Peter Sellars** to do an update of the *Patty Duke Show* starring **Drew Barrymore.** This time there's only one of her; she's just a split personality (*While Cathy adores a line of coke/a hit of speed/ to smoke some dope/Our Patti's only seen the sights a girl can see from Bellvue Heights/What a crazy pair*)... **Ed McMahon**'s latest spin-off from *Star Search* is *Comeback*, where faded stars compete each week for the most disgusting display of professional embarrassment. Hosted by **Sam Harris,** the first show features **Barry White, Sarah Dash,** and **Hall and Oates** competing in the music category, with **Rula Lenska** and **Suzanne Sommers** battling it out for celebrity spokesmodel...Was **Marvin Gaye**?...we hear **Harvey Feirstein** is crushed that **Linda Lavin** beat him out as **Tyne Daly**'s replacement as Mama Rose in *Gypsy* (she and **Sandra Bernhard** are working on a tv miniseries based on *The Children's Hour*), but it's left him open to pursue the plumb role in the forthcoming **Divine** biopic...Is it true that **Loleatta Holler-way,** fed up with the disco scene, is auditioning for the Met? We've heard of "Bubbles", but this smells more like Champale...it's whispered that downtown diva **Wendy Quinn** is being tapped as a lighting stand-in for the next **Liz Taylor** "Passion" spot...Have you heard **Dionne Warwick**'s new **Cole Porter** songbook album? What's next, *Michel'le sings Rogers and Hart*?...Maybe with the *Dick Tracy* craze, **Diana Ross** will finally get that *Friday Foster* project off the ground...still gone left over the fact that **Madonna**'s sanitized vogueing became the American pop phenemenon and not his *Waltz Darling* project , **Malcolm Mc Laren** has decided to take on **Maurice Starr** full-force with his new act —five effeminate young men who vogue like crazy and are aimed at the mass market. Their name? **The New Things on the Block,** what else?

THING MUSIC!

NMS Mess

- Dance panel featuring **Marshall Jefferson** and **Derrick May** in which members of **Happy Mondays** told the audience that they take ecstasy to be like the black man — it makes them feel funky. Without it they would have no rhythm. (Derrick walked out!)
- A fight broke out between west coast rappers in which the Marriott Marquis switched all escalators to down only, sending New Music Seminar patrons out of the hotel for about an hour.
- The drag queens at the Quick club. The front lounge area featured one of them playing some *fierce* classic tunes.
- Taking the Pathway trains to the Club Zanzibar in Newark, New Jersey, and hearing all the diva singers that performed that night.
- On the eighth floor at the bar-in-the-round a man walked in looking like a human version of the Rocky cartoon character. He was wearing a long trench coat, avaitor's cap, black tights and boots. (Gag!)
- The tired manager at the Kilmanjaro Club (Tuesdays with David De Pino) not honoring New Music Seminar badges for admission. Nevertheless, everyone had a great time partying with some very "real" folks.

— André Halmon

R.I.P

Gone into a "record store" lately and noticed the lack of "records"? The major labels are in love with the higher profit margins of compact discs and are out to wipe vinyl off the globe by the year 2000. Did you know the average cd costs only a couple of bucks to manufacture? Yet because of its super sound and sleek appearance they can get away with charging Joe Consumer sixteen bucks a crack. (To say nothing of the environmental incorrectness of most discs, outerwraping the tiny disc in layers of disposable and un-recyclable cardboard.) And cassette and cd singles satisfy everyone but the at-home DJ market. Even if you can afford a mixable cd player, it just ain't the same.

The positive outcome of all of this is that the 12" dance industry will go back underground, the majors content with multiplatinum Anita Baker cd sales.

— RF

Total Spectrum records is putting the final touches on the first 12", by composer/producer/keyboardist Riley Evans, entitled "Such As I Have" featuring **TJ Slaughter** on vocals and co-produced by **Ralphi Rosario**; and the **Knight Writers'** new 12" entitled "Trust" featuring TJ Slaughter and co-produced by **Carl Bias**. Due in stores in September — for more info call (312)994-4356.

Alleviated records is completing its next two 12" releases: "Shine" featuring **Chris Coleman** and "Prove It To Me" by **Ron Wilson**. Due in stores in September. For additional information contact Gherkin Records Distributors at (312)880-5580.

Composer/producer/keyboardist **Larry Heard** recently completed production on the new **The It** LP, *State of the World.*, due out any day now on MCA here in the states and on Big Life Records overseas. Vocals are by **Harry Dennis** and Chris Coleman. The long awaited "Brazilian Love Dance" and "Screams of Pain" are also included. Lee A. Pearson Jr. co-wrote the lyrics with Erwin McEwen on "Screams of Pain". The first 12" will be "Rain Forest".

Sound Development records has slated its first release —"Bart's Bounce", written, performed and produced by Riley Evans with additional production by **Rick Lenoir, Gary Wallace** and **Larry Thompson**. Due out in late August or early September. For more info call Gherkin Record Distributors at (312)880-5580.

Subsonic records, which gave you "Higher" by **Transient** featuring **Sherman Benton,** is about to release their second tune. A fresh hip-hop song titled "Posse in Effect" by **Hard Core** and written, produced and performed by **Scott Free**. For more information contact Scott Free at (312)664-5525.

Velvet City records has just completed production on their first release — "Passion" by the group **Mys-tique**. Written and produced by Carl Bias. Due out in late August or early September. For more info contact (312)477-7460.

Epic records recently released the next 12" from the *Lil' Louis* and the World LP, entiled "Nyce and Slo" which was co-written by Riley Evans and

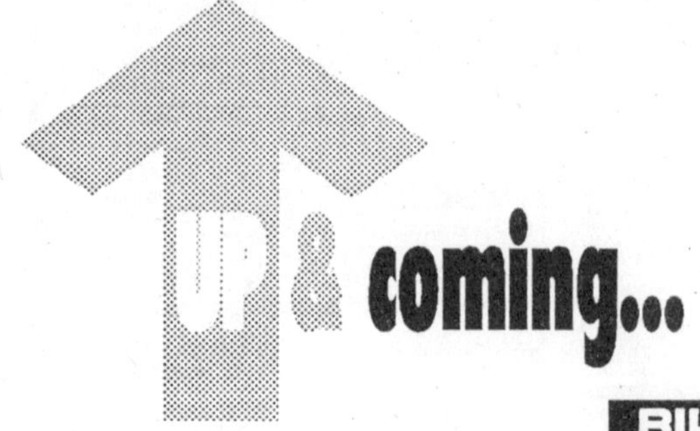

remixed by **Tony Humphries**. With the new import version currently available on FFRR. 'Tis a pity the co-writer never received a copy of either the LP or the 12"! Talk about a tight budget!

Atlantic records is putting the finishing touches on the new **Ten City** LP and the first 12", entitled "Whatever Makes You Happy." A definite must have for any one who has a turntable! Mixes were done by Ralphi Rosario and Rick Lenoir as well as Ten City. Due out early October!

Gherkin records recently released their first LP, *The Best Of Gherkin Volume 1*, which contains remixes of some of their best hits over the years and also contains two previously unreleased cuts. The first is "I See Visions" by Riley Evans featuring **Sonya Grant** and "Set Your Mind to It" by **Gallifré** featuring **Jimmy Lee**. Also due out on Gherkin in August is the new cut by **Dezz** entitled "Don't Go". *The Best Of Gherkin Volume 1* is available on CD cassette and LP. The new Mondee' Oliver cut "Newsy Neighbors" is also available - catch it!

Chicago Trax records recently released the new Ralphi Rosario 12" titled "Running Away" with vocals by Lindell and produced and written by Ralphi Rosario and **George Andros**. Catch it! It's HOT!

Powerhouse records recently released Volume 2 of their DJ only subscription service which contains remixed versions of such hits as "You Used To Hold Me" mixed by **Jimmy Drossos**; "Turn the Beat Around" mixed by Ralphi Rosario and "Rub You The Wrong Way" mixed by **Edward Crosby**. Volume 1 contained such hits as Janet Jackson's "Alright"; Rob Base's "If You Really Want to Party" and Jaya's "If You Leave Me Now". For more info call (708) 614-9600.

Ms. J records is currently enjoying tremendous club and radio play with the fantastic cover version of the classic "Let's Get Together" by **Ms. Candy J** — also available on the extended cassette are her new cuts "Night and Day","Find A Way" and "You Can Live Your Life". Candy recently completed her mini tour with **Gwen Guthrie** and **Loletta Holloway** - talk about a DIVA FEST! For more info call (312)248-0750.

That's all for now - which is more than enough! Take care and remember — "Love somebody today!"

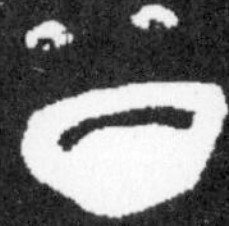

Evil SPEAKS !

Many an issue have crossed mine eyes to move me to speak; none, however, quite as fatuous as this: TO BURN or NOT TO BURN (THE FLAG)?

The question is, at best, laughable.

I would never burn the flag. Not because I am a patriot, or because I believe in all the hypocritical bullshit the flag represents; no, because the thought of paying $20 for a flag to fly, or to burn, just doesn't sit well with me.

LAND OF THE FREE, HOME OF THE BRAVE, EQUAL RIGHTS FOR EVERYONE SO LONG AS YOU'RE THE RIGHT COLOR!

OPPRESSION, HUNGER, HOMELESS-NESS, DRUGS,etc...

Sound familiar? This is what comes to mind when I think of the flag.

The country our flag represents was once (I guess) something to be proud of . But now the country is little more than a once beautiful whore who has been RAPED,SOLD, and EXPLOITED for the glory of man.

The country our flag represents is dying of cancer—you have but to open an eye to see that she has cancer of the colon; Nuclear bombs and waste have been shoved up her ass to the point that if she farts, to hell we all will go.

Cancer of the stomach also plagues this country. Homeless children starve daily! (Some-body, please ask Sally Struthers where the 70 cents a day is for these children?!?)

I'm expected to look to this great flag with respect... GET REAL!!!

As previously mentioned, I would never burn the flag. If a person wants to burn the flag, however, I feel they have that right. After all, this great country (for which the flag stands) has been burning the CROSS for years; no amend-ment to stop this behavior has been proposed. (IN GOD WE TRUST, INDEED!)

Most people who burn the flag do it out of some sort of protest. Personally, I feel this is in-effective, as I'm sure most politicians don't give a shit, except to look good telling the country that they're against "flag burning".Translation: VOTES.

SO, with that in mind, I've come up with a viable alternative to get the respective (not re-spectable) politicians where they live. You must wait 'til election time, then whip out your check-book and make out a good-sized contribution; burn the half of your check with your signature, then send the remaining portion and ashes to the politician with a little note saying how pleased you are with his labor.

I know not what's next for old glory—how about a comic strip? That's the extent of the flag's usefulness...

AND I AM NOT LU PALMER!!!

COOKIN WITH GAS

Look out, Child(s)...Miss Julia has true competition nowadays from two (count 'em) cut-ups on WTTW-11 (Chicago's PBS station.) *Cookin' Cheap* (Saturdays at 9:30 AM) is the new culinary class of choice. Featuring the campy clownings of Larry Bly and Leban Johnson, these girls school you in the fine art of burnin' while dishin' the audience-submitted recip-ies. Catch it...it's hot!

—LDW

MEN ON VIDEOTAPE

By now, I would imagine most readers have seen FOX TV's new black comedy revue *In Living Color*, and the returning segment "Men on Film". If you haven't, it's an *At the Movies* parody as done by two old school black queens. It's sparked quite a number of varied responses from black gay men. Some find it uproariously funny, and have adopted "two snaps up in 'Z' formation" into their vocabularies. Others have taken offense, feeling that these fey, pre-Stonewall stereotypes are insulting and derrogatory. The show lambasts all types on *Color*; black homosexuals are but one of the groups that are parodied. But I couldn't help but feel that two real queens reading the movies wouldn't be a lot funnier. These guys have the cadence, inflection, and gestures all wrong; seem-ingly modeled more from *Norman, Is That You?* or *The Boys In the Band* than any real life gay "types". Still, in light of our invisibility on TV 99.9 percent of the time, this left-handed compliment is better than nothing.

— RF

ZINE SCENE QUIZ

BY R. FORD

Since the publication of the last issue of our zine, we've been innundated with more zines than we can shake a stick at. The gay print underground network is growing by leaps and bounds.

HomoTure/Piss Elegant

Elegant to look at (though just a bit crispy crunchy in tone) are the zines of the *HomoTure* empire. *HomoTure* itself is a small zine of gay artists writings from the San Francisco bay area. Very art directed, with deft use of color, stickers, overlays, etc. Sister publication *Piss Elegant* is just that; a two-sheet big glossy thing with Greg Louganis on the cover. They promise the next issue will be in a smaller, less piss elegant size. Pretentious, but quite good. Both worth a look.

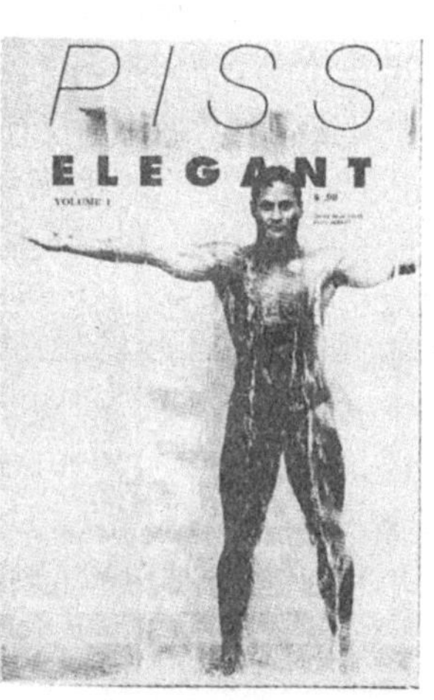

The new *HomoTure* is out in August, the next *Piss Elegant* in September. Probably $2 per copy, write for current rates.

Box 191781/San Francisco, California 94199-1781

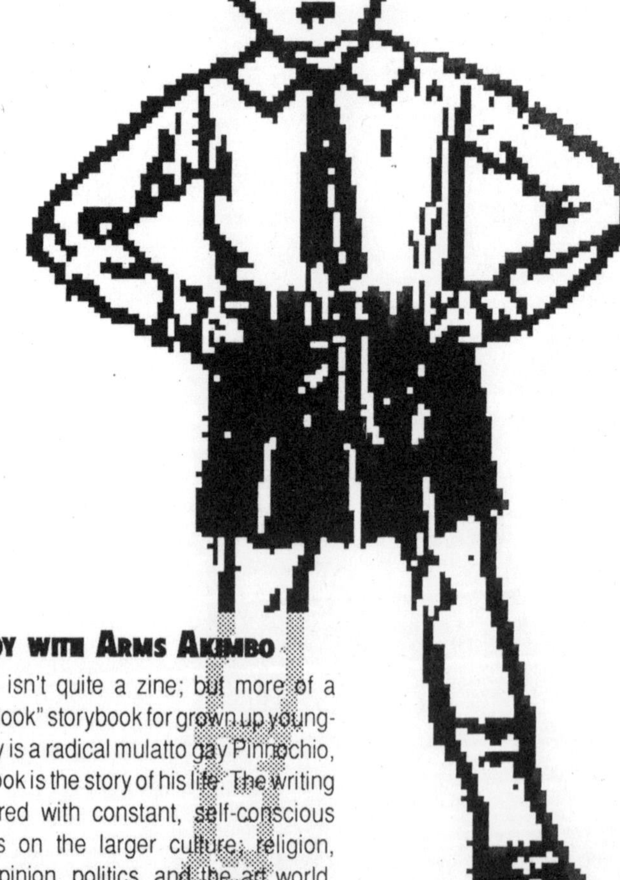

Boy with Arms Akimbo

Well, this isn't quite a zine; but more of a "Golden Book" storybook for grown up youngsters. Boy is a radical mulatto gay Pinnochio, and the book is the story of his life. The writing is structured with constant, self-conscious comments on the larger culture; religion, popular opinion, politics, and the art world. $1.69 Well worth reading.

Healing Tales
Box 77271/San Francisco, California 94107

HOLY TITCLAMPS

Small, chapbook-like format and quietly punky demeanor. This is from Minneapolis, and the minds of their gay artsy community. Editor/Publisher Larry-Bob's goal is to publish "anything and everything that is sent to me."

Boxholder/Box 3054/Minneapolis, Minnesota 55403

GAWK

GAWK stands for Gay Artists and Writers Kollective. A totally Macintoshed, open and friendly zine from San Francisco. Publisher Tom Shearer weaves together works of varying quality with his own personal, sardonic, slightly hippie-ish sensibility. The result is likeable and fresh; one of the warmest zines around. They are also publishers of the yet-to-debut zine *Diseased Pariah News*, a "cranky and irreverent alternative magazine for people who are HIV+." Various subscription rates start at $1 for four issues.

Box 31431/San Francisco, California 94117

BIMBOX

A real thick, homemade looking 8"x14" xerox from Canada. Very rough and rude. Free to those who deserve it, and they dare you to ask how they can afford to do it. An amusing balance of rant and camp, of the Dusty Springfield/Ann Margaret variety. Lots of cut-and paste weenies. The pop-ups in number two would be worth the price alone, if they'd let you pay for it. And "Jo Jo Price-Morgan's Clone Watch" column is a much needed, if acerbic, critique of the mainstream gay press.

262 Parliament St #68/Toronto M5A 3A4

MILQUETOAST

A tiny little folded one sheet from Jeffery Kennedy in San Francisco. Intriguing post-pop pastiches of gay icons. Subtext and juxtaposition is all; there is no text to compete. Real funny.

3491 17th Street/San Francisco, California 94110

THE DRACHIR NOTSHURT NEWSLETTER

Drachir was one of the early *Think Ink*-ers, full of opinion and enthusiasm. An outspoken young pro-gay African-American writer, he's now putting out his own aptly-titled newsletter. A one sheet, it's full of typos and unbridled positivity. It's sort of a farmers' almanac of trivia about the ecology and black history, with lots of his opinion on the way of the world.

Box 369105/Chicago Illinois 60636-9998

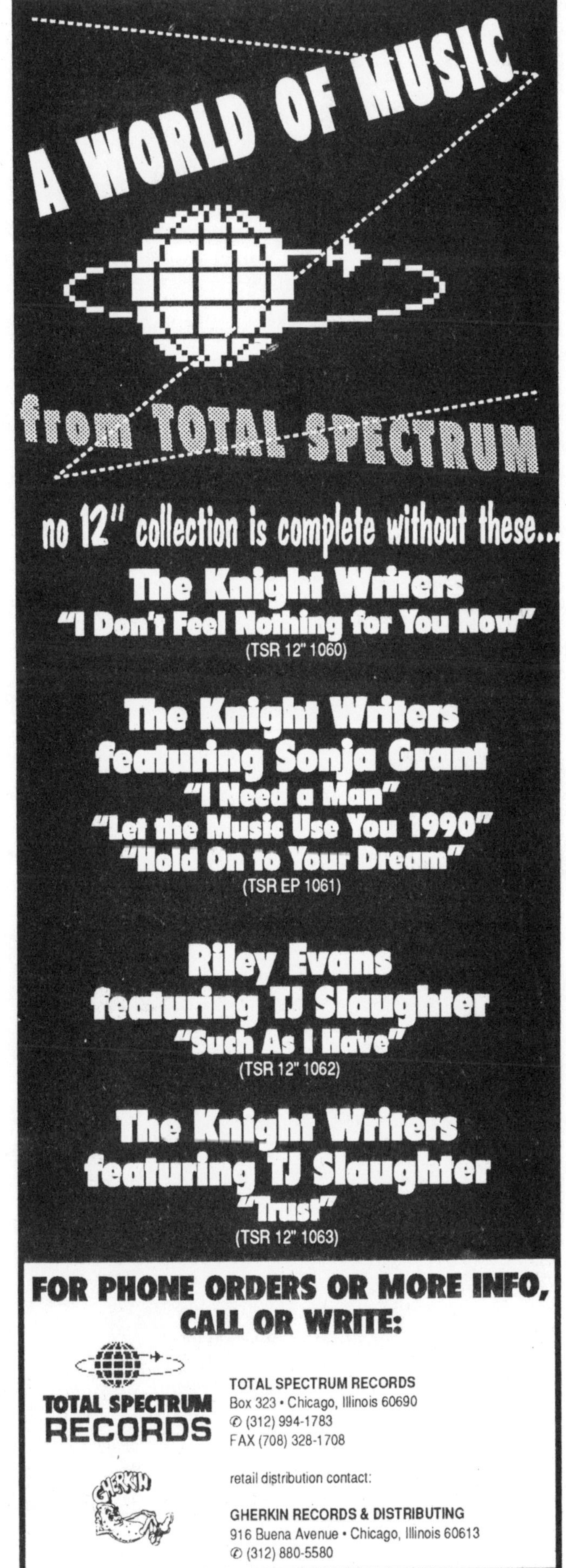

T H I N G Lists.

Now We Know Our ABC's...

AID
AIDS
AZT
PCP
CDC
THC
TAC
LSD
HIV
XTC
ADC
NIH
PWA
PLWA
AC/DC
IOU
IRS
ACT UP
AEIOU

Lies

The check is in the mail.
I'll fax it to you first thing in the morning.
I've never been tested, but I'm sure I'm negative.
Just this once; I'll pull out before I come.
Be gentle, I'm not on the bottom very often.
I'm his manager.
The administration has thrown everything into AIDS research.
I'm straight.
Just say no.
That remark was taken out of context.

Steve Lafreniere's bedside reading list

And Even Now **Max Beerbohm**
Storming Heaven-LSD and the American Dream **Jay Stevens**
In the Life anthology (edited by **Joseph Beam**)
Up on Madison, Down on 75th **J. F. Rice**
The Tears of Eros **George Bataille**
The Sadeian Woman **Angela Carter**
Saints and Strangers **Angela Carter**
The White Nile: Northeast Africa in the 19th Century **Alan Moorehead**
The Sinking of the Odradek Stadium **Harry Mathews**
Idols **Dennis Cooper** (re-issue)
A Very Easy Death **Simone de Beauvoir**
Fertile Latoyah Jackson Magazine (Paris Issue)
The Wig *Charles Wright*
Horse and Other Stories *Bo Houston*
Raymond Roussel anthology

Livin' Large Part 1

Franda B. Goodcookie
Nick Smith
Kevin Smith
da Hoover
Kevin Clady
Lady Ashley
DuAne Baskins
Louis Johnson
LDW
Chas. Brack
André Halmon
Frankie Knuckles
fat Brian

Livin' Large Part C

Cock
Clothes
Coins
Career
Car
College
Companionship
Condo(m)

Thermonuclear Sweat

The Powerplant
The Powerhouse
The Factory
The Reactor
The Shelter
The Underground
N-R-G

Gone but not forgotten

Benny Winfield Jr.
Victor Flynn
Jay Paul Thompson
Isaia Rankin
Patrick Kelly
Willi Smith
Keith Haring
Antonio Lopez
Eric Singleton
Clois Hughes

KITTY KITTY BANG BANG

Sheena Easton
Vanity
Kat Glover
Xaviera Gold
Pebbles
Madonna
Ava Cherry
Neneh Cherry
Tina Turner
Seduction
Mariah Carey
Downtown Julie Brown
The Ikettes
The Coconuts
Tyler Collins
En Vogue
Lita Ford

SINEMA

Bird on a Wire
Boys From Brazil
Kids On The Verge of a Nervous Breakdown
Honey, I Shrunk the Tits
Tie Me Up, Tie Me Down
The Cook, The Thief, His Wife, and Her Trade
Look Who's Sucking
How To Make Love To A Negro Without Getting Tired
Dick Tracy
Die Hard-on
Without You I'm Fine
Teenage Mutant Ninja Turtle Soup
Nightmare on Oak Street
Less Worse Blues

I Love A Man In A Uniform

Manuel Noriega
Fidel Castro
Minister Louis Farrakan
Sgt. Glenn Swann
Gomer Pyle
General Malaise
Colonel Bellows
Major Nelson
Captain America
Sargent Shriver
Private Benjamin
Corporal Punishment
Boogie Woogie Bugle Boy of Company B
Navy Seals

'I Ain't Buying It!' II

Marlboro cigarettes
Miller beer
Coors beer
Coca-Cola
the Chicago Transit Authority
meat
Interview's new art director
Vanity Fair
Donna Summer
the House Ways and Means Committee
Shelter
Clybourn Corridor
900 N. Michigan Avenue
strip malls
Neon (even if they *did* subscribe to *Thing*)
the programmer(s) at VH-1

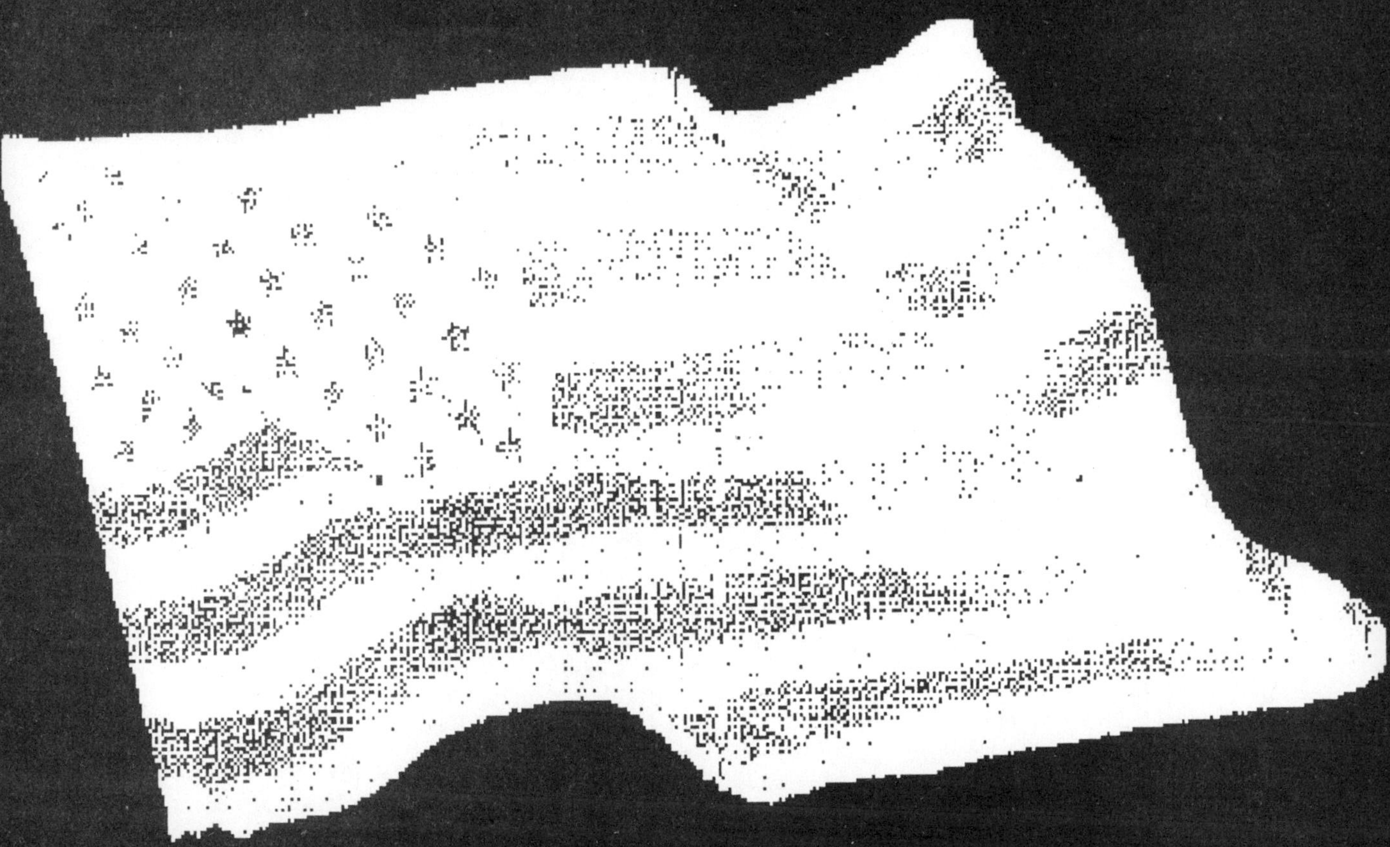

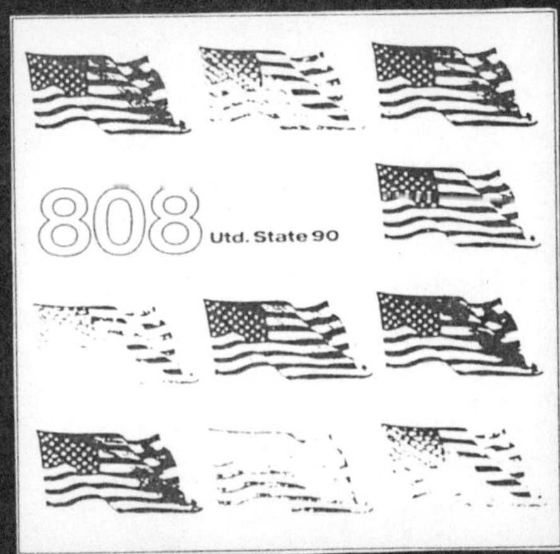

Utd. STATE 90 (United State 90), the debut album from **808 STATE**, the newest export from Manchester, England, home of the most intoxicating new music scene in the world. **808 STATE** are techno, industrial, jazz, new beat, new age, disco, psychedelic...estasy for the mind and body. On **Tommy Boy**. Includes the singles **PACIFIC** (also availible on 12"/12" cassette) and **CUBIK** (remix) (also availible on 12", 12" cassette & CD-5)

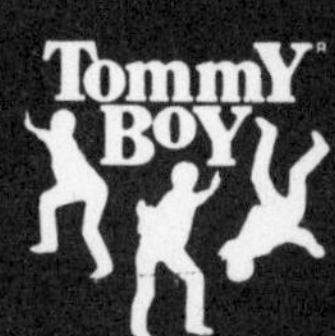

performance review by Rob Wittig

Steve Lafreniere refuses to be bored. The price of staying interested is energy, and Lafreniere is tireless in his pursuit of the extraordinary.

Steve Lafreniere refuses to be detached. In *Bend It*, the benefit for ACT UP he co-hosted with Wendy Quinn at Club Lower Links May 31st, a thread of political steel wound through a cabaret evening that was by turns hilarious, terrifying, and full of bounce and body, but was never less than defiant.

What makes Steve Lafreniere the premiere producer of the exploding Chicago cabaret-format art event scene? A veteran of cutting edge music productions and collaborations with performance artist/gallery owner/voyant Hudson, he teamed up with David Sedaris for 1988's legendary, month-long *Puffy vs. Puffy* series of shows. *Puffy vs. Puffy* sent a jolt of pure, cushiony-soft electricity through Lower Links' fledgling performance/reading schedule and helped build it into one of the city's busiest avant garde venues. Ah, Lower Links, the darkest little club in the world, where you could stand next to your best friend for an hour before recognizing her, a basement retreat from blizzard and heat, home to the scruffy chinese lantern and the dilapidated card table. Lower Links is the punk-black 80's womb out of which Lafreniere and what is now known as the *Puffy* crowd have delivered a creative style that is colorful, smart, and new.

Bend It was a night of tilt-a-whirl emotion, a series of carefully planned "surprise cancellations" and "substitutions."

Lafreniere juggled the line-up like the young Casey Stengal and the audience was left gasping in admiration. He is a true experimenter in a scene that prides itself on being experimental but generally manages to offer only the tried and true. He is an alchemist who trusts his own wide-ranging enthusiasms enough to put astonishing contrasts onto the same bill. He genuinely loves the moment when he can sit back and judge the unexpected results of his mix.

Typical of his format is the cold start. No fumbling with a microphone, none of the "I guess we're ready to start now" heard at so many other Lower Links events. Here, the lights go down, the video rolls, the music comes (way) up. Lafreniere does the hard, behind-the-scenes work that lets the audience and the individual acts relax and play with the ideas.

The cold start to this show was an astonishing sound/video concatenation that dreamily intercut slow scenes of siren fascination from the black and white film *I Walked With a Zombie* with footage from the April 23,1990 ACT UP Chicago demonstrations. The easy, insidious pace of the alternation gradually accelerated under the electrifying rumble of Lafreniere's voice as he loomed on the stage, reading Angela Carter's step-by-step build up to Lizzie Borden's axe attack on her parents— a careful, furiously reasoned political and psychological justification of Lizzie's inevitable actions.

Once the opening concluded, the crowd was plunged into momentary despair by the announcement that Linda St. Saéns (Director of Performance at Santa Monica Contemporary Exhibitions, and a Lower Links favorite) would not be able to attend in person. Then it was buoyed by the revelation that Linda had prepared a few choice interventions on videotape. But there would be more surprises. What did Lafreniere have up his sleeve? Suddenly, Liz Taylor was there. As simply as that. As sudden and as "aw!"-inspiring. What had been an event was now an occasion. Off of her recovery-bed for her friends Linda and Steve, Liz (Wendy Quinn) imprisoned the audience for nearly seven-minutes with her gosling-like generosity and eyes that seemed a sublime weave of *Velvets*, *National* and *Blue*.

The matinee idol of the Chicago cabaret literary scene, David Sedaris, proved once again (as though the Links crowd needed to be convinced) that he is one of the best writers in America 1990. We have our "we used to see David Sedaris read in person all the time, yeah, 89-90" stories all ready for posterity, do you? This was a brilliant short story (a bitchy, sweet, pathetic, narcissistic, ironpumping narrator strains to understand the world of his AIDS activist roommate) delivered with all of Sedaris' understated showmanship.

What could have been better for the music fan than the autoharp wizardy of Darlene!, served on a bed of her patented homespun country formality? Only one thing: Darlene! introduced by her friend and mentor elegantissima Sassy Fitzpatrick, whose participation live by satellite from the seat of ACT UP

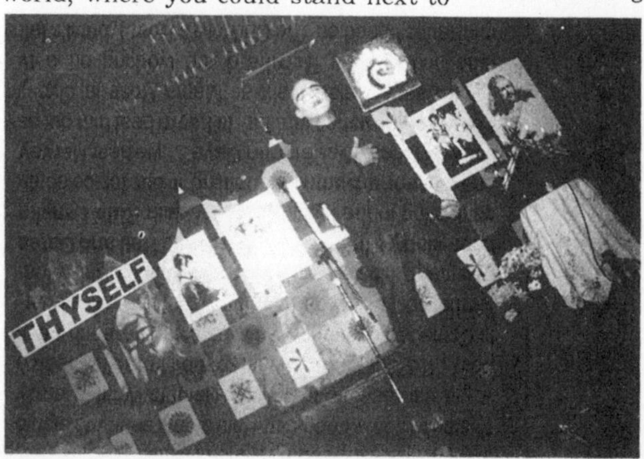

Andy Soma: dramatic at this angle.

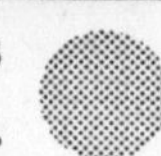

Monte Carlo included vintage Darlene!-in-the-old-days gossip not even the most shameless biographers have been able to uncover.

A newcomer to the scene who seems like she's belonged here among the bricks and broken glass all her life, writer/performer Cheryl Trykv was unable to upstage her own entrancing, memorized, slices of sociosexual life by her shy opening announcement that she was feeling especially reticent this evening, followed by the quick removal of her dress to reveal the ruby red crushed velvet hot pants beneath!

The inclusion of the piece by the remarkable Kay Rosen not only reaffirms her influence on Chicago artists and her importance on the national map, but is another tribute to Lafreniere's wide-ranging intelligence. Much of the Chicago cabaret performance scene is based around a romantic ideology of the breath, the voice, "writing like you speak," and the "authenticity" of live words opposed to the "artificiality" of writing. Mixing Rosen's work, which is so visual and so flagrantly "written", into this context is just the kind of cultural chemistry he relishes. Under the guise of an evening's entertainment, an alternative to fly-by-the-seat-of-your-guts, individualistic Romanticism was being proposed. In this slide-and loudspeaker piece, called *Rock N' Roll*, Rosen flogged us with misspelling after misspelling — all phonetically correct — of the name of that perpetual Greek toiler Sisyphus, against a maddening loop of a Led Zeppelin drum intro that kept building but never reached orgasm.

Not the bright colors of the 60's, but the eerie offset dots of a seed catalog... the cone of the slide-projector's light painting the flowers on the back of the stage... a Bertoia chair containing the lovely Fonderella, another containing the dextrous Fontana Fallopia... a fog machine that must have been borrowed from the Yankee Stadium production of *Phantom*, so completely did it engorge tiny Lower Links with sweet smoke — this was Wessonality Crisis! The girls lip-synched a conversation made up of snippets from 60's & 70's pop vinyl, while, adjointly, two hermossimas maidens with cardboard houses over their heads (the House Dancers) behaved like the suburban id on a spending spree.

The other turns, too luminous not to mention, included: the most excellent Richard House, who read an erotic vision of religious severity likely to make a Baptist cry for mercy; acclaimed actor

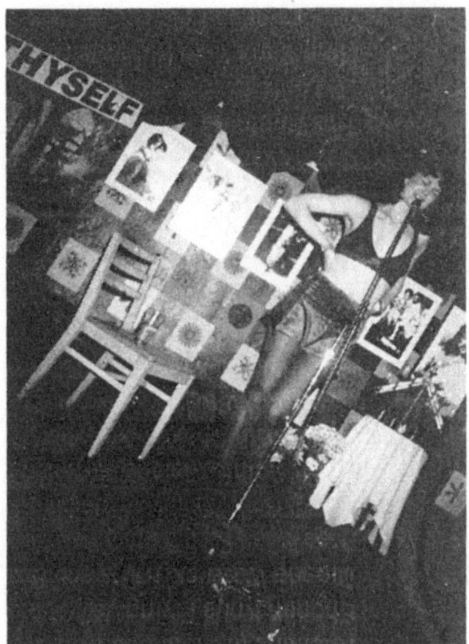

Cheryl Trykv: "He really sucks the butt!"

Harry Althaus who read the bare events of Diana Ross' Central Park concert in a manner that set a new high-water mark of archness, and performances by Andy Soma (emotionally crucified between two spiralling video screens while he did a heart wrenching enactment of Roy Orbison's "Pantomine"), and Lawrence Steger, whose stark decanting of the loudest liquid ever poured was framed by the projected names of *Bend It*'s participants.

The video montage edited by Luv Corporation that anchored *Bend It*'s second half (including scenes from Wigstock, Sassy Fitzpatrick's French hit video of " Night Fever", Reno's "Rage and Rehab", and rappers Queen Latifah and Ms. Melodie) is emblematic of Lafreniere and his projects. He is pointedly political; for him the overwhelming importance of *Bend It* was that it raised money for ACT UP. He possesses unprejudiced curiosity, an encyclopedic mind, and a gentle impatience with anything that is less than smart. These qualities are combined with postmodern creative habits (collaboration, sampling, collage, graphic design) that come with years of event production, publications, and tape editing. Lafreniere consistently and modestly refuses to let anyone call him an artist. Whatever his activity comes to be called (editor, anthologist, producer/director, master sampler, alchemist) it will be the chief artistic activity of the 1990s, and he sets the standard for it.

DANGEROUS PLEASURES
LOWER LINKS, MAY 23

When Paula Killan plunged onto Lower Links' concrete stage May 23rd, a little shiver ran over me. Earlier in the evening, I'd been impressed by Jenny Magnus' arch spew of anecdotal contradictions — she'd been to a funeral that day, you see. And I'd sat straight up at Marcia Wilke's goofy, wrenching monologue about a lover who talks her into moving out to Winnetka, of all places. As usual, Marcia Wilke had me in her fist. But then BOOM and Paula Killan was on, acting out a bull-run nightmare of infernal "celebrity" parties presided over by a murderous Anti-Modonna, garish faux po-mo Bucktown condos with trick doors, and a harrowing flight from a mob of midget Pentecostals being egged on by the ghostly remains of her first abortion. The room was hers.

Paula Killan is a big woman, tall-wise, with a lot of juice. She inhabits herself like no local performer I've seen since Jimmy Skafish, a freakish, gorgeosity that makes her audience feel...safe, actually. Oddly, this plays off what she is telling you — itchy, cruel, black dried-up peach pit things. It's a cliche'd contradiction she punctures without looking like a jerk. Admirable.

Look forward to seeing her in Live Bait Theater's *Girls, Girls, Girls!*, a theatrical piece about strippers she's developed with fellow sometimes-actresses Catherine and Sharon Evans.

The Lower Links event was part of a month-long series of performances by women. "Dangerous Pleasures" was curated and hosted by Susie Silver and Iris Moore, two of the more contentious, forward-looking persons in town. More from them, please.

— Steve Lafreniere

LONGTIME COMPANION
review by Stephen Winter

Being a gay student filmmaker, I was happy to learn that *Longtime Companion*, a Hollywood feature film that directly and compassionately dealt with gays and AIDS had been produced. Simultaneoulsy, as a black man I was apprehensive as to the possible omission or derogatory portrayal of people of color and women in the film, given Hollywood and the gay community's notorious history of discrimination towards these groups. Unfortunately, my concern was justified. Upon viewing *Longtime Companion*, I found it to be nothing more than a racist, sexist, elitist second-rate soap opera which catered exclusively to white, upper middle-class fantasies of reality.

Longtime Companion follows a clique of nine gay men from 1981 to the present and chronicles how they deal with AIDS. The men in this film are all white, successful and "straight-acting", (to quote the personals). They all have "macho" or "acceptably gay" jobs like body-builder, lawyer, writer or actor in a soap opera. This presents a confined and constricted view of gay life representative of only a few.

Which would be fine with me if the film's characterizations of people of color and women weren't so atrocious. The only black character (also the only fey one) is Henry, the servant of David, an older, wealthy gay man who hires Henry to clean up after him and his dying lover, Sean. Although Henry's social status is never explicitly stated, David orders him about in very curt, business-like tones, never the kind, loving terms he reserves for his studly, white friends. David even has the nerve to say after Sean's death, "I'm sure gonna miss Henry coming around to clean up after me and Sean." A statement which further reduces Henry's character to a disposable, ineffectual servant whose only concern is to oblige the needs of white guys.

The only Latino character gets even worse treatment. He is never directly referred to by name so I'll call him "the Latino Man". "The Latino Man" lives in a 'bad' section of town. This is made perfectly clear when Willy, the body-builder volunteering to deliver "the Latino man"'s laundry, registers shock and dismay to find little black kids running out of his apartment building (I wonder if the place has been sprayed?). He reaches "the Latino man's" apartment and begins to lecture him. Willy finds him to be surly, lazy, uncooperative, and ungrateful. Willy proceeds to scold "the Latino man" like one would a child and berate him him for "letting himself wither away." Wealthy, white Willy just can't understand this Latino man's belligerence! Why, all of Willy's friends have died serenely and graciously of AIDS in penthouse apartments and private hospitals rooms. And everybody knows that "Randy" is dying of AIDS in a beachhouse on Fire Island exactly the same way that "Ramos" is dying of AIDS in Hell's Kitchen, exactly! "The Latino man" rightfully becomes enraged and tells Willy to leave and give back his key; "you're fired," he says. "You can't fire me," declares big, brave, upper-middle class Willy, "I'm volunteering!" In this way *Longtime Companion* dares to infer that white people know exactly what people of color with AIDS need and feel. Willy's gestures are presented as noble and just, while "the Latino Man's" response is asinine and infantile. This is condescension to people of color on an epic scale.

But I haven't even gotten to *Longtime Companion*'s token IV drug abuser. This nameless, hapless fellow happens to be in the same hospital room the day the soap opera star, Howard, visits his lover who's newly diagnosed as HIV positive. The drug abuser suddenly throws an irrational yelling fit, rips out his IV, and tries to run out of the room. How horrible that this awful man should do that, reacts Howard, the stunned soap opera stud. Here I am trying to visit my angelic boyfriend who is quietly living with AIDS while this maniac drug abuser is ripping out his IV and getting blood all over the floor. Even the drug abuser's girlfriend proves useless in the situation and it's up to Howard to gallantly yell, "Nurse, we need help over here...there's blood everywhere!" One of the most misunderstood and politically invisible groups in the AIDS crisis are IV drug abusers. For *Longtime Companion* to characterize IV drug users as schizoid lunatics only furthers negative public misconceptions.

The film's only prominent female character is a wise-cracking straight woman who loves hanging out with her gay friends. She is the only woman shown helping with the AIDS crisis, which leaves the massive lesbian contribution to the AIDS war completely invisible. The injustice of this omission is heinous when one considers how quickly lesbians jumped to the forefront of the cause during the early 1980's, the years *Longtime Companion* claims to be portraying.

Regardless of any dramatic or educational worth *Longtime Companion* might have, these offensive and contemptuous characterizations of people of color and IV drug abusers, plus the veritable absence of lesbians or women and children with AIDS, are inexcusable infractions.

Also, for a film that claims to want to educate folks about AIDS it features a major health discrepancy. During the 1985 sequence Willy cryptically complains how "you can even get AIDS from saliva." Yes, in 1985 health officials stated that, but in 1990 the information is the opposite. You cannot get AIDS from dry kissing and deep kissing is not considered a major risk. *Longtime Companion* does not bother to update the information and thus perpetuates one of the biggest myths abour AIDS transmission and sets safe sex back five years. Pathetic in a film heralded as "Hollywood's breakthrough film on AIDS and gays."

Still, I'm reluctantly pleased that *Longtime Companion* was made. The fact that a Hollywood feature film dealing directly with homosexuality and AIDS has received prominent backing and production is heartening. *Longtime Companion* may open the door for more feature films about gays and AIDS to be produced. And hopefully these later films will include, if not focus on, people of color, IV drug abusers, and women in a realistic and truly compassionate way. For at the center of *Longtime Companion* is the burning need to tell the stories of the AIDS crisis and the people affected by it. People who are black, white, red, yellow, male, female, gay, straight, alive, dead, and scattered in the middle. All of us.

Tongues Untied
review by Trent Adkins

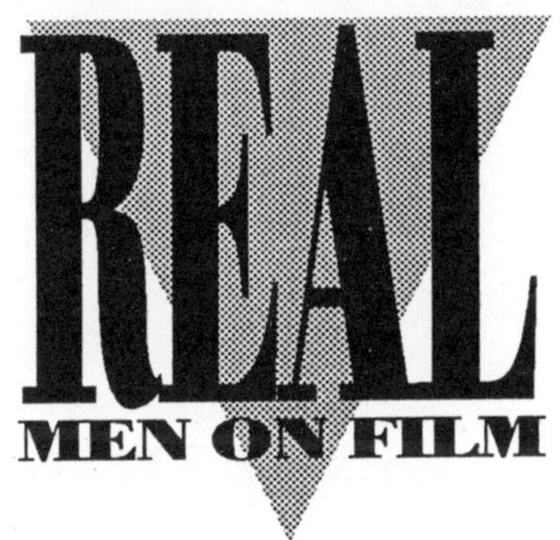

Fear and loathing have kept many of us in the black gay community silent so that it becomes an easy thing for myths and stereotypes to be perpetuated and respect and understanding to remain elusive.

I was reminded of the need to end this silence while viewing a brilliant video entitled *Tongues Untied*, which was produced and directed by black gay videographer Marlon Riggs.

It contains a scene where a young man is listening to a preacher ("It's an abomination!"), a revolutionary activist ("What kind of a role model is a punk, anyway?"), a contemporary ("Spreadin' disease to women and babies!") while a voice-over is introduced urging the gay brother to no longer be silent, to stand up, and set the record straight (as it were).

The entire video is a masterpiece, deftly mixing poetry, humor, and interesting visuals. The film affirms for countless people that the experience of the black gay male is real and very valid. We are a unique lot in having to deal with racism and homophobia. We are afforded neither a place to be valued in the society at large, the black community, or even the white gay community.

Without mincing any words, this film embraces and explores practically every aspect of the black gay experience including the often misunderstood world of cross-dressers, black men who are attracted to white men, and even subcultural practices such as the way we snap our fingers for dramatic effect and emphasis (done in a segment entitled The School of Snapthology, which very humorously displays our penchant for self-parody).

In the end, any black gay person can come away from viewing this film feeling a lot better about themselves and their perceptions, feelings of alienation, fear, and frustration, perhaps coming a lot closer to finding a real place to call home and real self-acceptance. Trust me, *Tongues Untied* is long overdue. It is a vivid reminder that silence=death.

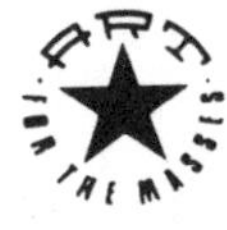

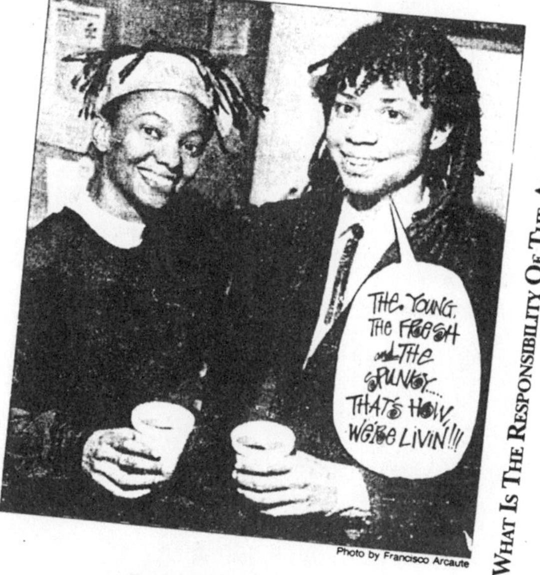

Photo by Francisco Arcaute

THE *GRAND OPENING* OF THE *NEW*

Wholesome Roc

Gallery, Museum & Café

1444 N. Greenview Chicago, Il 60622

(ONE BLOCK SOUTH OF NORTH AVENUE, 2 BLOCKS EAST OF ASHLAND)

(312) 252•1905

Open Tuesday through Saturday 7pm to Midnight

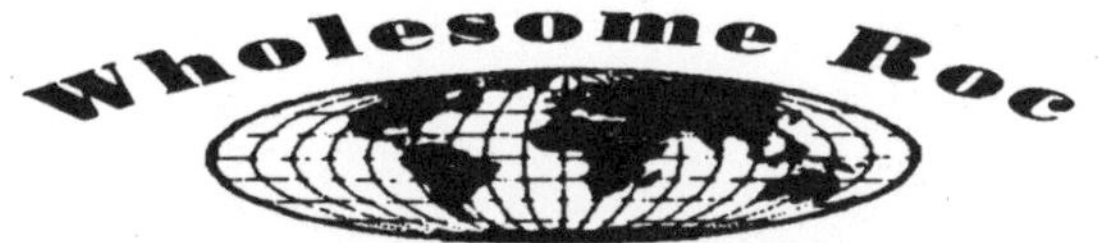

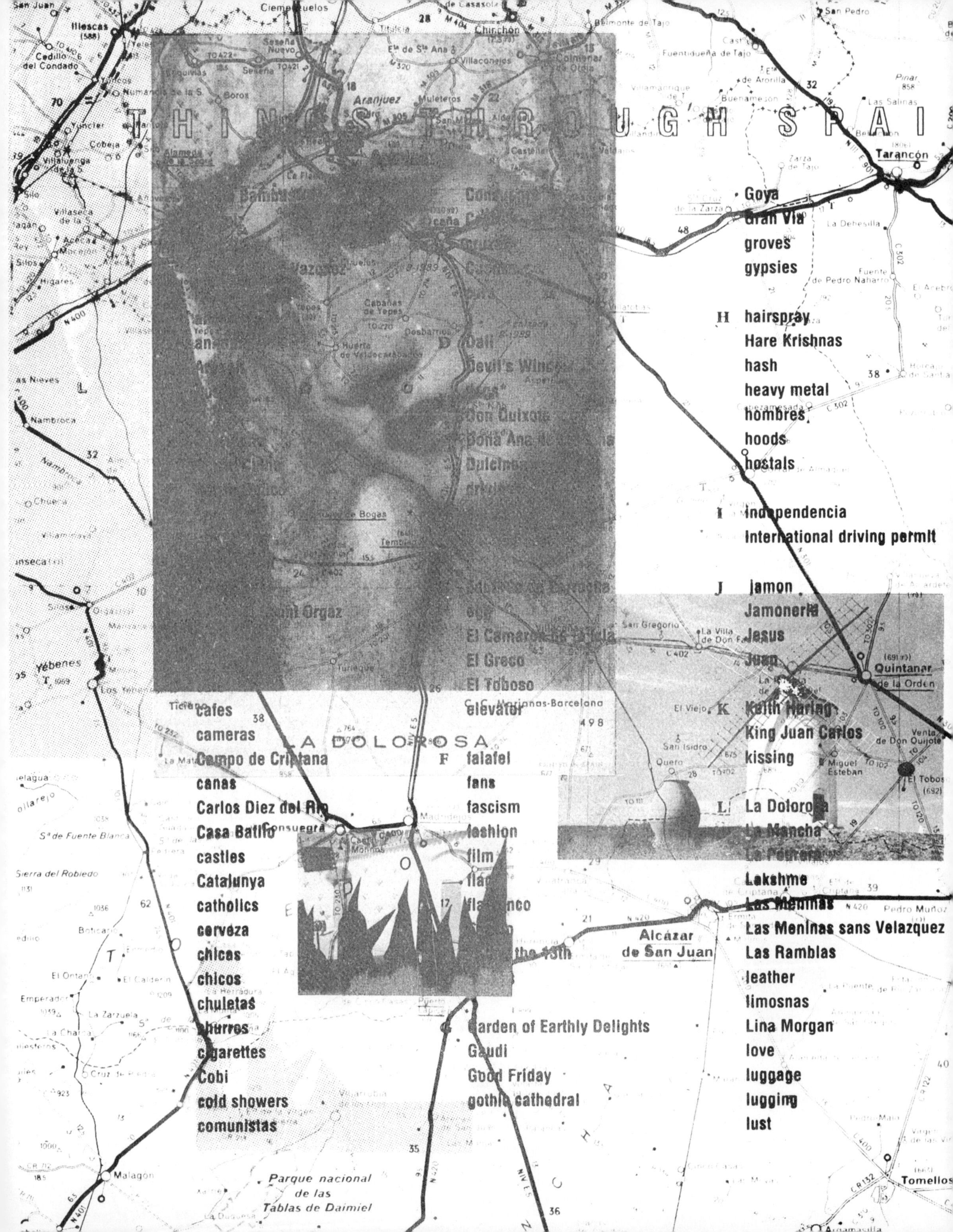
THINGS THROUGH SPAIN

cafes
cameras
Campo de Criptana
canas
Carlos Diez del Rio
Casa Batllo
castles
Catalunya
catholics
cerveza
chicas
chicos
chuletas
churros
cigarettes
Cobi
cold showers
comunistas

Dali
Devil's Window
Diego
Don Quixote
Doña Ana de la Mancha
Dulcinea

El Orgaz
ego
El Camaron de la Isla
El Greco
El Toboso
elevator

falafel
fans
fascism
fashion
film
flag
Flamenco

Garden of Earthly Delights
Gaudi
Good Friday
gothic cathedral

Goya
Gran Via
groves
gypsies

hairspray
Hare Krishnas
hash
heavy metal
hombres
hoods
hostals

independencia
International driving permit

jamon
Jamoneria
Jesus
Juan

Keith Haring
King Juan Carlos
kissing

La Dolorosa
La Mancha
La Pedrera
Lakshmi
Las Meninas
Las Meninas sans Velazquez
Las Ramblas
leather
limosnas
Lina Morgan
love
luggage
lugging
lust

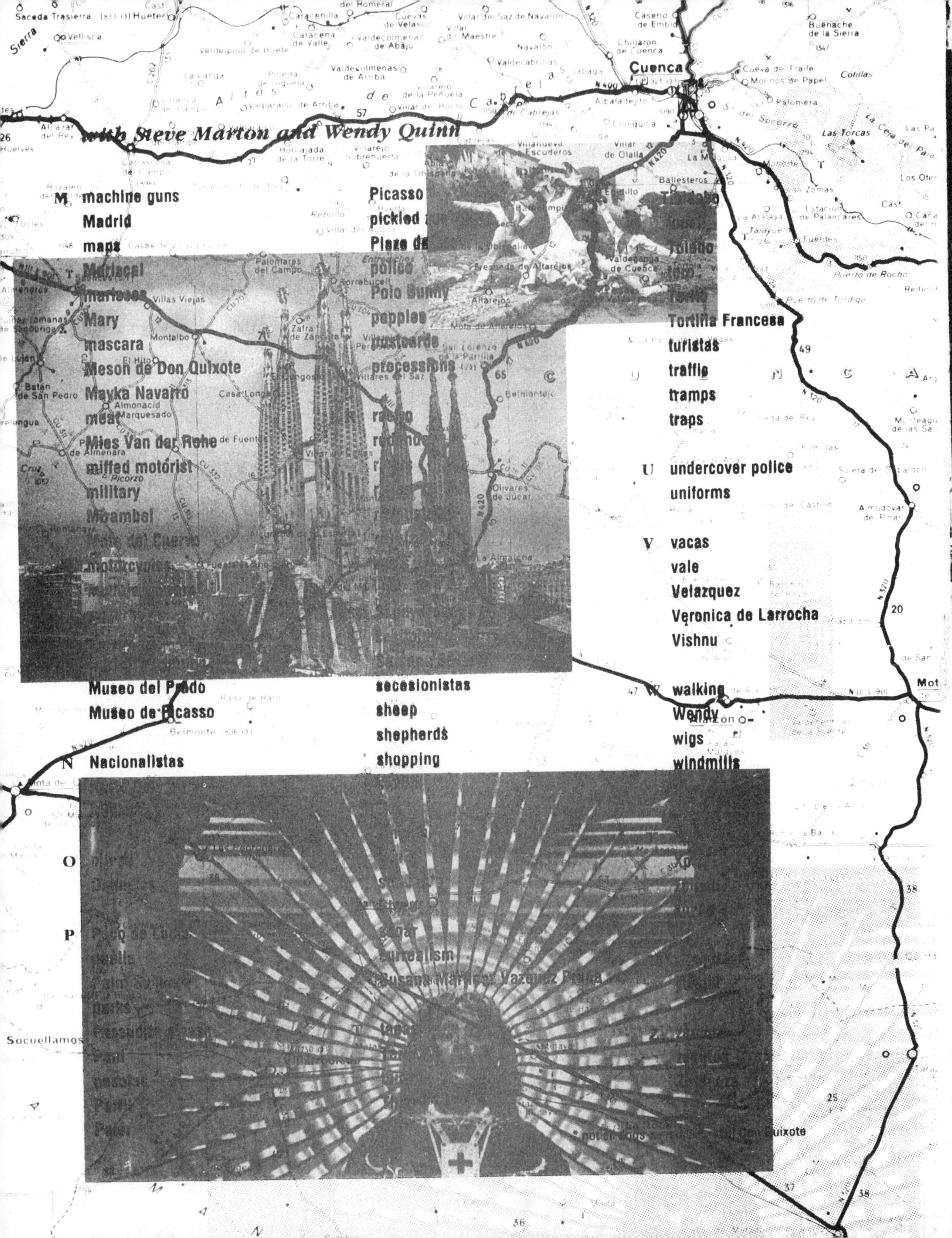

with Steve Marton and Wendy Quinn

M machine guns
Madrid
maps
Mariscal
mariscos
Mary
mascara
Meson de Don Quixote
Mayka Navarro
meat
Mies Van der Rohe
miffed motorist
military
Mirambel
motorcycles

Museo del Prado
Museo de Picasso

N Nacionalistas

Picasso
pickled
Plaza de
police
Polo Bunny
poppies
postcards
processions
radio

secesionistas
sheep
shepherds
shopping
surrealism
Susana Marquez Vazquez

Toledo
Toledo 1980

Tortilla Francesa
turistas
traffic
tramps
traps

U undercover police
uniforms

V vacas
vale
Velazquez
Veronica de Larrocha
Vishnu

W walking
Wendy
wigs
windmills

DOIN' LUNCH WITH bunny & pussy

When in Doubt,
Reach For the Throat

PUSSY: According to a recent blotter item in the Near North News, a gaggle of Cat-lick school girls pounced on a passing damsel, tugged her coiffeur 'til her scalp burned, shrieking, "You ain't no woman— you're a man!" And I knew just how she felt...

Many moons ago, I joined a foppish friend on a visit to his hometown, somewhere below Highway 30. One night we sat and dished over pizza at the local mall. After the waitress delivered the check, she lingered at our table, coughing nervously, shifting from foot to foot. Finally, gathering her courage, she popped a most unusual question. The owner, having espied our entrance, was curious to know if I was indeed, the genuine item... or a he-she. Astounded, I placed her hand on my ample hips. "Come now, I demanded, how many boys are built this way?" The sweet young thing blushed and commenced wailing for her boss—who came, ambling sheepishly, from the kitchen. Apologizing profusely, he explained that his wife had just returned from a visit to the Mardi Gras and that, after looking at all her snapshots, he thought he saw something familiar in my gestures...Or was it the makeup... the voice.. the June Pointer padded shoulders? I showed him picture IDs stopping short of baring the bush, but nothing I said or did could convince him of the (awful) truth. Until I produced an appointment card for a pap smear at the local women's clinic. He threw down the gauntlet and picked up the tab. But that wasn't the last time I've been queried on this issue...

Like the sweet Venezuelan teener who sat beside me on an Amtrack train from here to there. I pretended to sleep, letting my hand 'bounce' perilously close to his crotch with every bump until I hit the jackpot. As my Lee Press-On-Nails danced the fandango up and down his zipper, he planted a kiss on my mouth and a hand on my breast. "Ay carumba!" I exclaimed, smashing my cheek against his, breathing fire into his ear. He jerked his face away, as if stung, and ran the back of his hand against my chin— which, I admit, does sport a bit of a five o'clock shadow in between trips to Carol Block. His other hand made a frantic ascent from my nipple to my adam's apple, as he groped for the telltale sign. Indeed, he seemed confounded, yet comforted, when he could barely find it— it is, after all, the most petite appendage on this otherwise pulchritudinous gal. But wait, there's more...

Like the (now) well-known local theatrical producer who is, himself, a bit of a fence-straddler in the gender department. During a *nuit d'amour* fueled by my fierce desire (to have an original musical produced) he let down his guard and confessed his wish to be, well, roughed up a bit. In mere moments, I saw my name in lights...and he saw stars. "God, yes!" he brayed from behind the gag, "No woman has ever touched me like this!" And suddenly his voice trailed.. and he looked stricken. He begged me to untie him and, after a few rounds of "Who's Your Daddy?" I relented. No sooner were his hands unfettered, then they moved, quickly toward my throat. As they so often do.

South American Bandstand

A mild mannered, semi-reclusive opera buff we know recently met a handsome South American boy and found himself with a growing interest in native arts from below the equator. Feigning an interest in the Spanish language, he invited the *muchacho* over for a night of conjugation. Somewhere between subject and predicate, he slipped on a salsa disc. Pepito, roused by the throbbing drums of his homeland, shed his chinos and began undulating wildly. Caught up in the primitive passions the music inspired, our normally reserved friend, stripped down to skivvies and joined in. The *pas d'amour* whirled and twirled around the apartment, until there came an ominous rapping on the door—*a lá* Three Cornered Hat. Our friend, hastily wiping the sweat from his-er-brow, managed a modicum of composure. He opened the door a wee crack to find his landlord, packing a pistol and a menacing leer—which quickly melted. "Oh, you're home," said the landlord, surprised. "I heard this loud Latin music and presumed someone had broken in.. I never dreamed you were only entertaining."

A Room With a Few

Like Sebastian in *Suddenly Last Summer*, another, elderly, friend found himself "tired of the light ones, famished for the dark ones." Faster than he could say *huevos rancheros* he hastened himself to a sleepy little Spanish town way, way, South of the border. There, he rented a room in a quaint hotel— with a balcony overlooking the old colonial square. Day and night our friend perched on his porch, peeking from behind his fan, perusing the local talent down below, while swilling gimlets and the like. Ever the gentleman, he eschewd "yoo hoos" and "heys", preferring instead to make eye contact with the juicy ones and signal a discreet *uno momento*. But, alas, the hotel's creaky elevator was exceptionally slow—and by the time he reached ground level, his "finds" had already blended into the crowd. Necessity prompted him to return to a wonderful tradition from his genteel Southern youth—the calling card (in reality his business card, hotel room number scrawled on the back, weighted with a swizzle stick and, often, a leftover cocktail onion). These he flung form his window in such abundance that townsfolk came to expect nightly flurries which they fondly referred to as "*puta nieve*" or "fairy snow."

Big Man On Campus

Long, long ago, during the summer of love, a handsome hippie we knew manned a campus drug counseling line. Late one night, he received a call from a man with a pressing problem. After several false starts, the conversation finally came to a head. "My dick is too big," Joe College lamented. "I can't find anyone to fuck. And I've left a trail of sprained jaws from the student union to the football field." Our friend, undaunted by the size of the crisis, invited the forlorn fratboy in for a face to face consultation. And before he knew it, he'd gotten pinned.

How To Mount Olympus

PUSSY: Back before the A-word had entered the *argot*, I was a serious slut with a weak spot for the swarthy shepherd-type. Late one night I found myself stranded in a singles bar with a huge picture window facing on to a busy street. Suddnley a Checker taxi pulled up and deposited five low-budget Balkis on the curb—each garbed in identical black trousers and white starched shirts. "Yummy," I said to myself, "waiters! Greek waiters!" As luck would have it, they stood right behind me.

I writhed in my seat to get their attention, but to no avail. They were deep in conversation, badmouthing females in their ancient tongue, never guessing gutter Athenian is my second language. Locking my eyes on a Tom Selleck look-alike, I dove into the conversation. "*Parakalo*," I said, lowering my eyes, faking a blush, "I'm not used to such filthy expressions, being a good Greek girl from a good Greek family." (Great grandpa was a rabbi in Kiev, but we all know the Mediterranean is a hotbed of anti-Semitism.) Trembling, he asked how he could show his respect. "Easy," I replied, "take me home and eat my pussy."

★★★★

We wandered off into the dawn, to his four-plus-one on immigrant alley. The furnishings were truly Spartan—only a bed and a very large dresser. As we began fondling, my personal Apollo switched out the lights—but only for a moment. As our tongues were making their own introductions, he switched them on again. "Wait. Please, I must show you something," he mumbled, while rummaging under the bed. I presumed he was hunting for the usual (handcuffs, restraints, olive oil, filo dough). He produced, instead, a faded snapshot of a child in a tutu. "My niece in Corfu," he beamed. "Such a pretty ballerina," said *moi* whilst stepping out of my panties, "let's talk about your spongediving uncles..." I pushed his head south toward the Aegean, but Poseidon wouldn't even go wading. And before I could say "You missed the calamari!", the lights were blazing once again. The archaelogical dig had moved to his dresser drawer, where, I surmised, he was excavating for a condom. Ulysses returned with a whole armload...of V-necked sweaters, in all the colors of the rainbow. "Ralph Lauren," he whispered reverently, as if repeating the name of Zeus himself. I managed a weak smile and a nod, which was all the encouragement he needed. The studio apartment became his runway, as he paraded about in an endless progression of garments all bearing the Polo emblem. "Preppy! The preppy look! I love the preppy look!" he shrieked like a man possessed. I made my exit somewhere between the lounging pyjamas and the parka and went hunting for a pay phone—to call Bunny... and a cab home (in that order). The tale left both of us salivating for souvlaki. Next evening we hied ourselves to the Parthenon for a Grecian Feast. As the waiter approached our table, I couldn't get a fix on his features in the darkened restaurant, but I could make out a

CONTINUED ON NEXT PAGE

CONTINUED FROM LAST PAGE

little man on horseback right above the breast pocket on his crisp white shirt.

For a Fistful of Deustchmarks

Overheard on Alexanderplatz, on the eve of reunification: "I've waited a lifetime to get my hands on Blue Money! Now, I can buy little Gretschen her first Klaus Barbie doll!"

6969 Closet Cul de Sac

Miss Gigi offered this delightful vignette: It seems that somewhere in the suburbs, there exists a coven of married men who bite the bullet every now and again. The same ones who, according to one of our stringers, commute to the foliage at Foster Beach, where every third car sports a "baby-on board" sticker and an (empty) infant seat. *Bye, bye, bunting... Daddy's gone a hunting!*

Gigi, also known as Miss Lunchbreak Lips, usually services these kind of clients during normal business hours...But, on this occasion, she was asked to pay an evening house call to a babysitting dad, which inspired this nursery tale:

While the rugrat was nestled all snug in his bed,
Mr. Mom was receiving (and giving) some head...

When out in the yard Gigi heard such a clatter
(four unturned cylinders), she screeched "What's the matter?"

Daddy went limp and arose in a flash
jumped in his robe and tightened the sash

Suddenly a big haired brunette did appear
She shouted inside "Duh, Honey, I'm here!"

As she headed upstairs, the two men headed down
Dad said, "Ted here's my manager, he's new in town"

Wife said "Wanna cold drink?", Gigi cooed "I just ate"
Dad growled "Talk about business and act like you're straight"

The next several minutes were quite an ordeal
As dad prattled on about ordering steel

Poor Gigi was rattled, her poor head was reeling...
She picked fuzz from the uphlolstery and stared up at the cieiing

"Fuck this" she thought, "I'm through being pensive
I want out of this tract home" and went on the offensive

She bellowed, "Thanks, Dick, I think I've heard enough
Tomorrow we'll review the rest of the stuff."

Gigi turned to the wife and said "Dick is sure great.
We'd be lost without him. Will you let him work late?"

"Gosh, do I need to?" Dick whined way too loudly
But wifey said "sure" as she eyed hubby proudly

She shook Gigi's hand and turned on the porch light
and said "Thank you for coming. Drive safely. Goodnight."

Later, dreams of promotions danced in her head,
'til she rolled onto something and sat up in bed

And cried "Honey wake up! What the hell is this thing?
This small studded bracelet? This big metal ring?"

"It's all full of spikes, snaps, and chainmail and junk,
Oh dear, do you think little Dickie's turned...punk?"

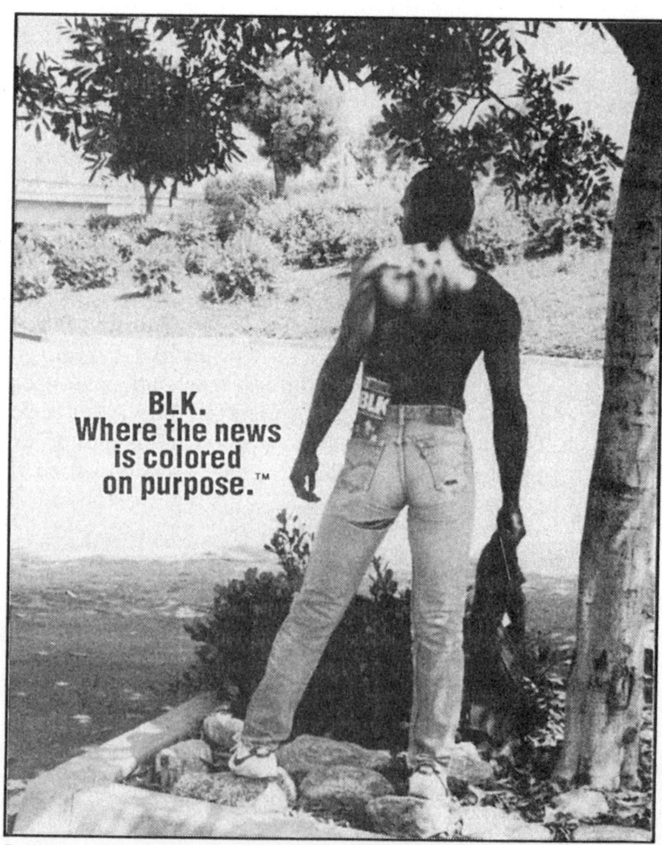

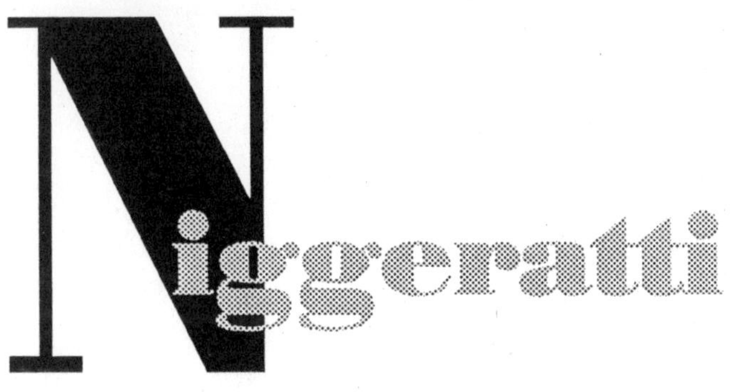

by Lawrence D. Warren

MAHUSHANFEST, PART II

Socially and politically correct newswriter **Nick Smith** recently threw a birthday bash for himself at his new Chicago digs and though I normally eschew such obvious self-aggrandizing promo parties, I was fully aware of his past performances, so I gladly rushed!

Boy (and I should say, Boyzz) was it great! From start to finish, Nick was the supreme hostess: greeting guests individually, chatting up friends, turning strangers into friends, seeing to everyone's comfort and needs.

What's a New Wave Nationalist to do for decor? Why, what other than an Afrocentric Temple of Emenge (pronounced M-N-G), featuring collectibles and antiquities from her overly Egyptological studies. The only bow to modernity were the state-of-the-art music system (from which we grooved to the freshest combination of 206 House tapes with the newest acid hip-house cds around) and her large-screen television/VCR ensemble (from which we viewed an advance copy of *In Living Color*...friends in the business, don't you know!)

Mind boggling was the display wall of degrees (not just those of Nick (who has three) but those of his mother, who after she pushed Miss Nicky out of the nest, returned to college to pursue her degree). Talk about HIS-STORY!

Delicious salads and delectable finger foods (with, of course, fried chicken) were served to round out the downhome flavor to the affair.

Nick's guest list always shows great diversities and surprises: the most gorgeous black hunks, artists, political activists, several doctors (including **Kevin Smith, Art Brewer, John Davis**), fellow newsies (especially **Babs Allen** and **Larry Griffin**), and consummate club tarts **da Hoover, Evil Lady Caldonia** (aka **Calvin Holmes**), **Mike Evans**, and **Henry Hill.**

Stunning was chanteuse **Felicia Williams** who did not grace us with a song, but entertained us with witty repartee.

Upon departure, we were, of course, admonished to write Fox Broadcasting to ensure the optioning of *In Living Color*... Must Miss Nicky *always* do the right thing?

BACK ON THE BLOCK

I know **Larvetta Larvon.** I've known her since her days growing up on the SouthSide of Chicago, where all she had were her dreams of overcoming her tawdry past, where all she had were her dreams of making it into high society, where all she had was a tremendous fortune to fuel her climb.

I knew her when her ambitions took her to enroll in the Lucy Baines Fine Finishing School for Wayward Women and the ensuing scandal regarding her dalliance with headmistress **E. Randall van Buren.** I've known for years how her father had to bail her out of that one (causing Lucy Baines' closure and Ms. van Buren's career change to manager of a south side Xmas Light Lounge).

I've known her through all her many triumphs and failures (and I've known her father to bail her out of those, too). I've known her through her many marriages and subsequent divorces.

I even knew her during her bittersweet third marriage, the one that seemed like her dreams fulfilled: marriage to the **Vicomte de Larva** (social standing and a title, to boot!). I've known her through the embarrassing period when she lost it all: the money, the homes, the cars, the jewels, the husband, and even dear, faithful **Cosette**, her French maid.

I've known her when all she could cling to was shadowy memories, dim hope and her dusty, minor aristocratic title. I've known her as she climbed out of her pit of financial despair and social ruin to repair her life(style).

So when she recently was vindicated in her court decision against both the IRS and her ex, I knew a major social occasion was in the making!

What better way to express her immense gratitude (not to speak of relief) than by hosting a reception in honor of lead counsel, Mr. **David Cumberbatch**,Esq.,who triumphantly journeyed from the courtrooms of Washington, DC to pick up his check personally.

Need I say, la Vicomtesse went way out: she had her recovered North Shore villa redone from top to bottom, she even unearthed the stolen art treasures she'd been hiding (just in case, dear) for years! Her family silver and other heirlooms were in evident display and, of course, floral bouquets by M. Laurent were everywhere! Discrete, soft pink lighting and candle, candles, candles set the correct mood for subtlety and relaxation. Sensuous aromas from the more than abundant food, including a banana pudding (a passing nod to her humble beginnings), and the slow wailing of cool jazz from her exquisite sound system wafted through the air, further punctuating the mood.

Spirited conversation was enjoyed by all: **Trenton**, talk show personality **Tony Wilkins**, da Hoover, **Marvin Earl**, yummy **Chuck Gonzales, David Sedaris**, the **Penny**, Kevin Smith, **Allyson Bouldon** (with her new love, handsome **Art**), torch songstress **Berta Carta** (whom no one could even coax to render a number) and ever dynamic **Larry Hawthorne.**

Nick Smith phoned to express his regrets (he had to work on a late-breaking story). **Carlton Robinson** arrove with the ever dapper **Mike Evans** (the hospital administrator who oversaw Larvetta's brief stay during a particularly trying period). The showstopper came when E. Randall van Buren showed up to finally present la Vicomtesse with an honorary degree from the now defunct Lucy Baines, prompting Larvetta to squeal in tear-stained delight: *Quel Supris!* I knew she would.

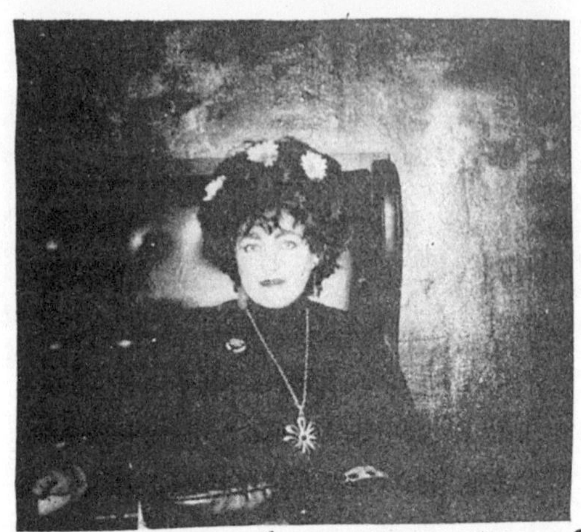

What's up Liz, er, Wendy?: Wendy Quinn dead rings Elizabeth Taylor at Bend It.

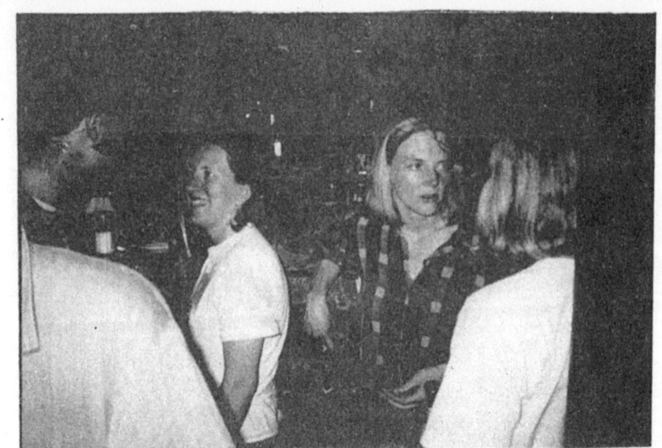

Dynamic Duo: Suzy Silver smiles w/ Richard House while Iris Moore chats it up w/...Jeanne Dunning? @ Bend It.

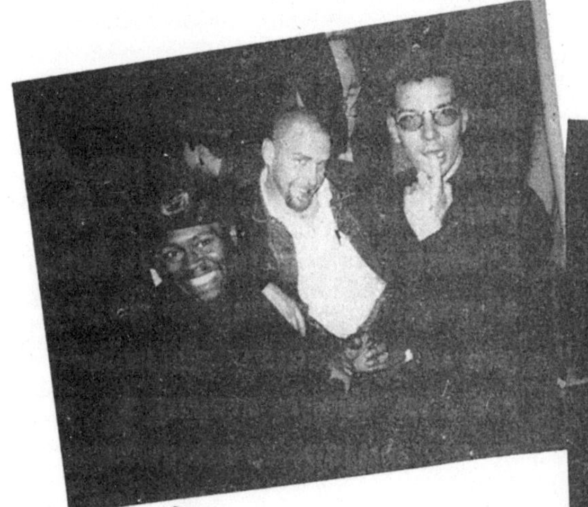

King Booty & Co.: L to R Chas. Brack, Arnold April, and Lawrence Steger at Bend It.

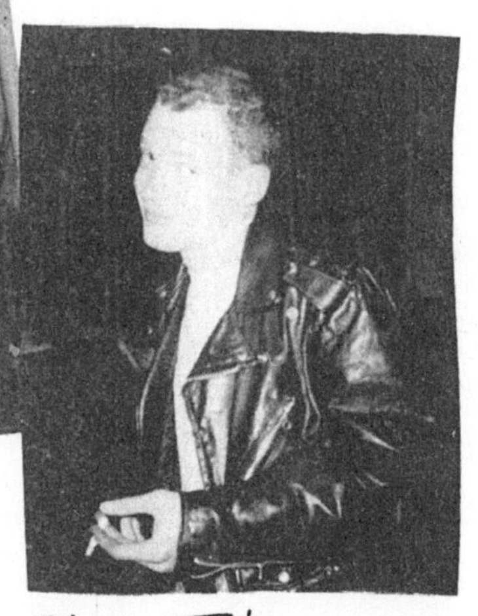

Club Tart cum Activist Tim Miller

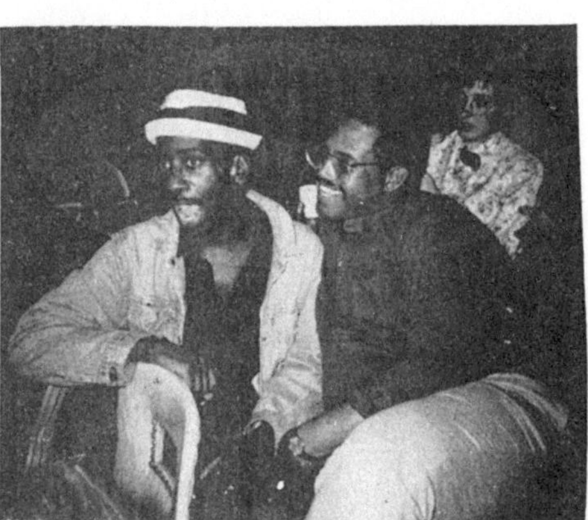

Kee-Kee: Ricqué Greene and CDW at LL's Bend It.

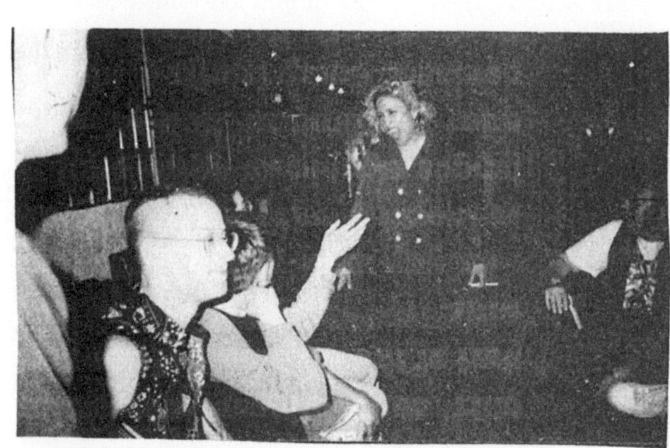

Funny Lady: Reno holding court @ Zanies.

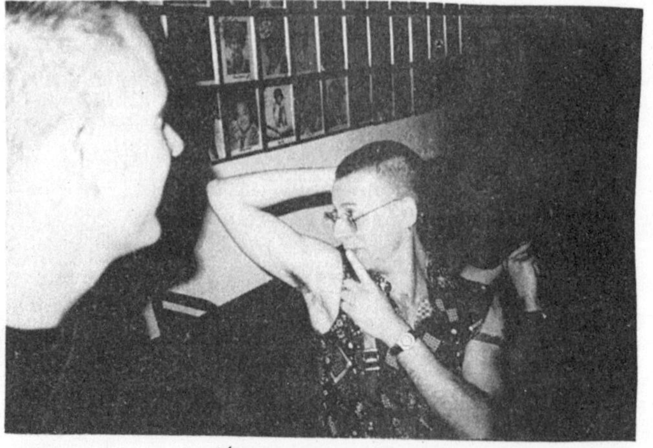

A guy called Gerald: the ever amusing Gerald Paoli clowning @ Zanies post Reno.

All Photos: T. Adkins

T t e e

by T. Adkins

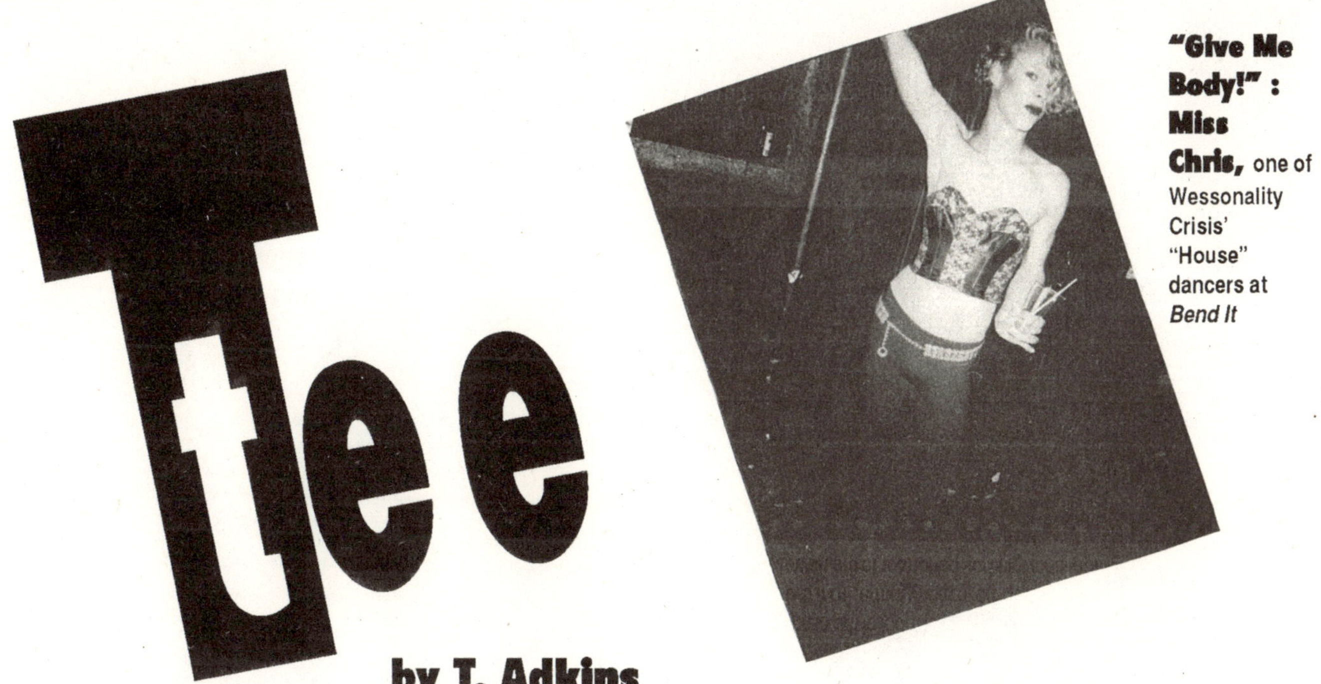

"Give Me Body!": **Miss Chris,** one of Wessonality Crisis' "House" dancers at *Bend It*

Cum To Where The Flavor Is

DON'T SMOKE MARLBORO CIGARETTES! Ultra-conservative and religious homophobe Senator **Jesse Helms** (R-North Carolina) is the real Marlboro Man, recieving political contributuions from the Phillip Morris Tabacco Company to the tune of $200,000. The funds are said to be earmarked for a Jesse Helms Museum. Can you imagine! And, recently, we're being asked to halt purchases of Miller beer, too. Miller, don't you know, is a subsidiary of Phillip Morris.

Marlboro is the company's number one selling brand of cigarrettes and we all know that not everybody who smokes them are in support of Senator Helms and his oppressive agenda. Not anything that would include or support art censorship, mandatory HIV testing, insurance redlining, the dismantling of the National Endowment for the Arts, and reduced government spending for AIDS research. The lesbian/ gay community, (via Washington D.C.'s ACT UP and local ACT UP affiliates, and GLAAD) is being advised to boycott these fags in particular. The argument being that the company needs only a demonstration of what buying and mobilizing power the gay/lesbian community yeilds, to learn that we are not invisible. It wouldn't hurt if the boycott yielded losses far out numbering $200,000. Then again, I suppose if we're really about doing the right thing, we'll seize the opportunity and quit smoking altogether. Puff-puff.

Reno At Zanies

Boy, did we have fun this night. After the show, everybody kept saying how rejuvenated they felt. This woman really is like a good shot in the arm, the medicine of hearty laughter for these ill'n, plagued times. Not only is she funny as hell— cracking on racial and sexual predjudices stereotypes, sharply referencing gallery hopping, conservative Republican politics, cops, dinining out, orgasms, condoms, "power bows," etc., her material is pointedly political and fringe targeted. She performs with lunatic levels of energy, bounding all over the stage making wild and manic gestures that are hilarious and amazingly appropos. We sat near the front row and laughed the loudest while the rest of the audience (a mostly white Old Town yuppie/tourist crowd) either kind of laughed along, were offended, or just didn't understand the humor. After the show we had a chance to chat with her and snap pix. She was fun, immediate, approachable. She's a really warm and friendly person. The word gracious comes to mind. "Where's the party?" she asked a few times. "Where do you guys hang out?" And since the first thing she said to me was how handsome I was, I think I've fallen in love with her.

If It's Straight...

This review of *Bend It*, the benefit for ACT UP Chicago held at Lower Links, ain't about much more than who was there, what they had on and what they said. For a more, um, descriptive or comprehensive review of the line-up see **Rob Wittig**'s piece in this issue (page 12). Sometimes you can go to LL and it's nice, it's OK, people seem to be having an OK time. But, let's face it, even LL, one of the city's more foward perfromance places can be off sometimes. Like, boring performances and/or a boring crowd. This night was special: the room was filled with folks who all knew each other or wanted to know each other. Iknow that's a terribly cliquish thing to say but this night it clicked. Besides, most of the acts were wickedly fun. My picks of the evening would have to be: **Gerald**'s and **John**'s goofy and sexy "strip" set to **Adeva**'s "Respect"; anytime surprise co-host **Elizabeth Taylor** got up to say anything; **Cheryl Trykv**'s funny, funky monologues; **David Sedaris**' reading that cut the too cute gay boys to shreds; **Darlene!** (in a vintage black chiffon cocktail dress replete with a pair of black, truly wicked come-fuck-me-pumps); **Darlene!** again, tipsily and mistakenly making a stink to ringleader **Steve Lafreniere** at the show's closing for not mentioning David's credit; **Linda St. Saéns'** reading about dreams which posed the question; "What does it mean when **Madonna** says '**Dietrich** and **DiMaggio!**' on her record Vogue?"; and, of course, the **Wessonality Crisis** dream sequence. Plus, **Chas. Brack**, in town just in time to see coucin **Denise Cox** (still my favorite coffee mate) and ex-roomate **Lawrence Steger**. "Yeah, that was when me and Charles had the only gay bar on campus," Steger said, referring to their days at Antioch (Anticock) College. Plus, (don't blink): **John Smith, Chandelle North, Andy Soma, Tim Mille, Fontana Fallopia** and **Fonderella, Craig Sigele, Ricque Green, Nick Smith, Kevin Smith, Scout, Brian Funk, Jeff Abell, Harry Althaus, Iris Moore, Suzy Silver, Michael Thompson, the Larva, Kathryn Hixson, Burle Avant,** and **Richard House**. I understand artist **Jeanne Dunning** was there (probably with Kathryn) but we've never met and at some point I'm sure I was looking dead at the back of her head and didn't know it. As fate would have it, **Destiny** of the **Talent Family** failed to show because she was busy moving. She's been talking of possibly moving to London for a yearsometime next summe. Let's hope we get to see more of her between now and then. One more thing; Steve Lafreniere does not always have a *"gentle* impatience with anything that is less than smart." There was the time recently, out at the bar, when he nearly beheaded a couple of less than smart guys for not only <u>not</u> boycotting Marlboro but for asking "Who's Jesse Helms?"

CONTINUED ON NEXT PAGE

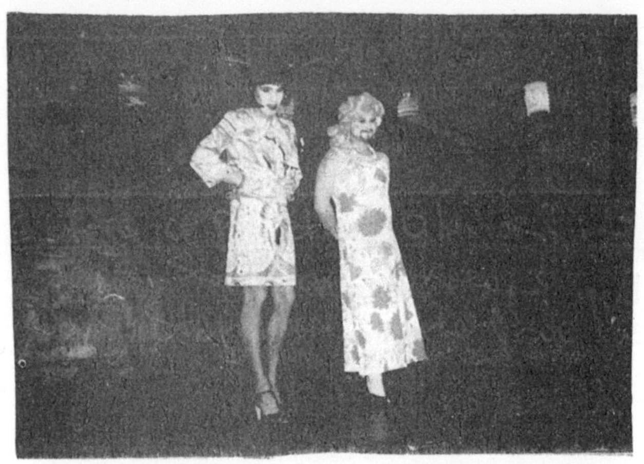

Girline & Girlette co-host their Rodeo Review @ Lower Links 'Hit it Girls!' Photo: Tim Brennan

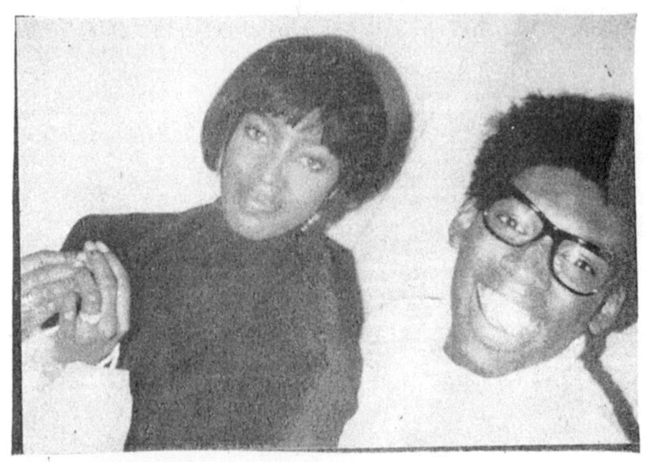

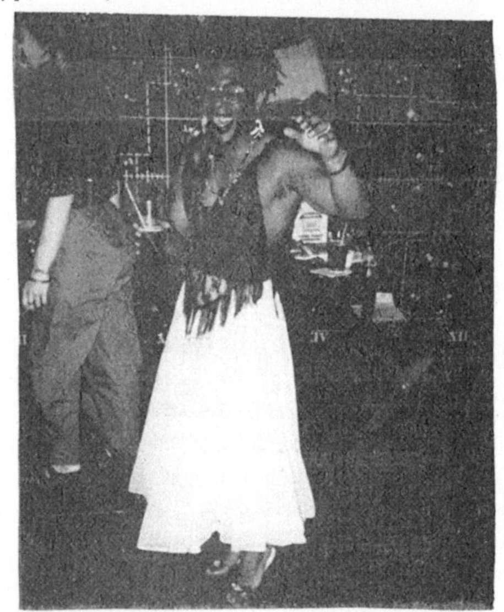

Blackk Enough For Ya?: Joan Jett Blackk AKA Terrence Smith @ Girline & Girlette's Rodeo Review. Photo: T. Brennan

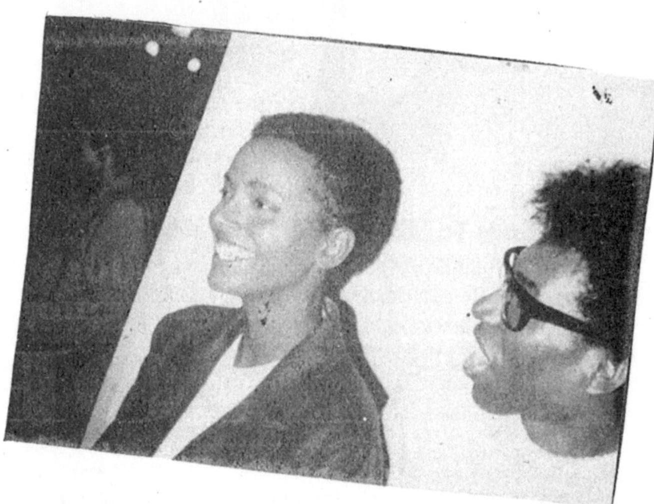

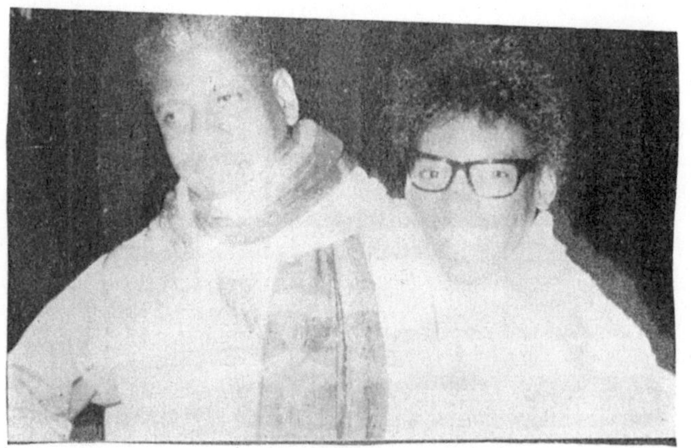

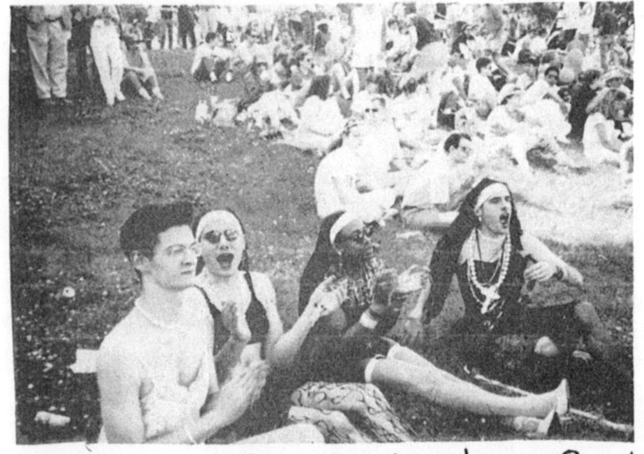

Sisters of Perpetual Glamor?: L to R D. Travers Scott, David Eckard, & Doug Stapelton @ the Pride Day Rally.

How's The Hare?: Camera Hog Ken Hare in N.Y.C. w/ (T to B) Naomi Campbell, Louise Vyent, and Andre Leon Talley @ Gordon Henderson's Spring/Summer show. Photos: Tyrone Fields

A

afro puffs
Debbie Allen
Ann Margret

B

Kathleen Battle
beans and rice
Josephine Baker
Jimmy Baldwin
Joseph Beam
blue
batt & balls
beauty school

C

Cleopatra Jones
Carmen Jones
Ava Cherry
Neneh Cherry
carrying the fuck on
cheap
chi-chi
champange

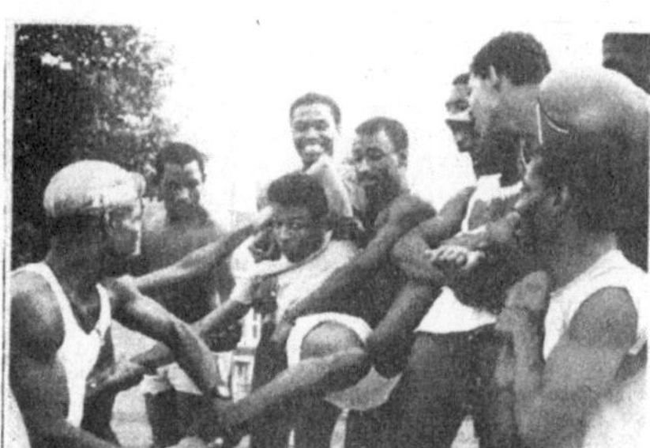

carrying the fuck on

D

disco
Tamara Dobson
Katherine Dunham
Dorothy Dandridge
Divine
double dutch

E

Eunice
"EEK! A wilderbeast!"
Erté

F

'retha Franklin
funk
felafil
Lola Falana
Fellini
Fat Brian
Fat Larry's Band
First Choice
Franda B. Goodcookie
Suzy Funtown

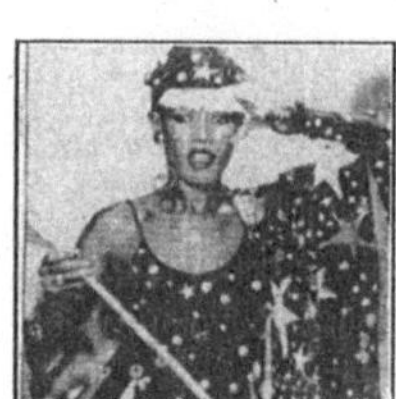

Grace Jones

G

Teresa Graves
Geraldine
girlfriend
gal
gospel

H

heels
hair
Hairspray
Billie Holiday
Phyllis Hyman
Hedda Hopper
Harlow
Langston Hughes
HELLO!

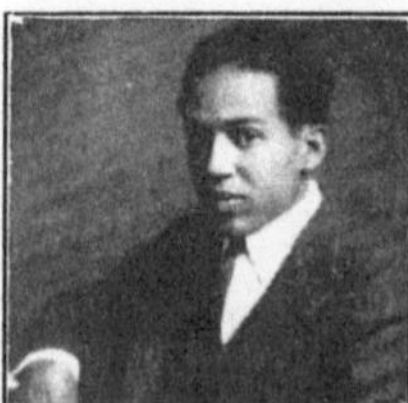

Langston Hughes

I

Iman
I'm so sure
In a Gadda Da Vida

J

Grace Jones
Beverly Johnson
Sheila Johnson
Fertile Latoyah Jackson

K

Chaka Kahn
Patrick Kelly
Eartha Kitt
Kid Creole and the Coconuts

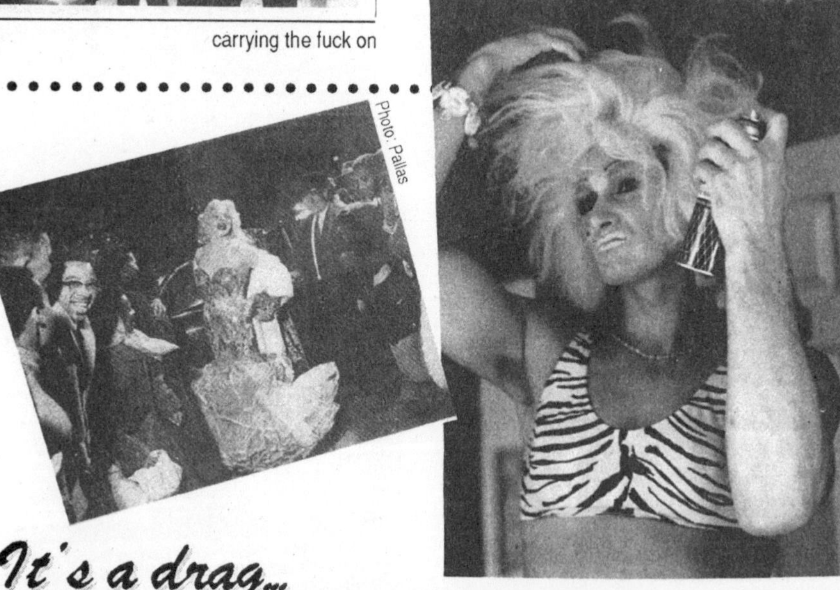

It's a drag...

Drag queens are probably the most visible symbol of the camp aesthetic. Men taking submergence in female artifice to its most (il)logical conclusion. DQs come in many forms: from the closeted suburban crossdresser to the hardened she-male streetwalker to the glittery showgirl-boy performer to the newest incarnation of crossdressing — as political provocation.

L

la la (see disco)
lisp
Labelle
La Boheme

M

Miss Thing
Marilyn
Bob Mackie

N

nada
niecey

O

OK!
Oprah
opera

P

Freda Payne
really pink

Q

quit!
quiche
queen

R

Diana Ross
Revlon
really red

S

snap
stilletos
Sylvester
Sun Ra
see there!

T

Tillie
Thing
That Girl
Torch Song Trilogy
the tee

U

Felix Unger
Under the Cherry Moon
Uvula Ovula

V

Vera Tate (see Tillie)
vogueing

W

Way Back!
Andy Warhol
wigs
Mae West

X

Xavier Gold
Xavier Hollander
X rated
X Ray specs

Y

Yullanda McCullough
your doll

Z

ga-Zillion lire
Za Za

Diana Ross

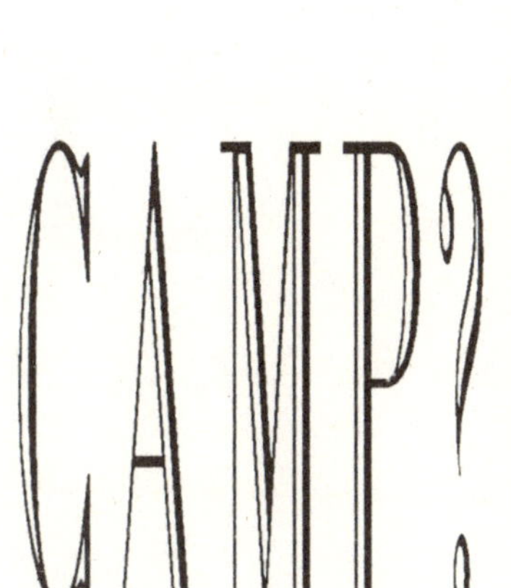

Camp is, by nature, an indescribable aesthetic. Much like kitsch and trash, camp is a method for transcribing the effects of our modern postmodern society on us. It is arguable, eclectic, and personal; born of the free spirited gay intelligentsia as a reaction to the constricting mass culture we exist within. It is a language that is known unspeakably among its followers. An injoke of cultural proportions, it's the nudge and wink at the pervasiveness of the gay sensibility on modern life. Glamor and glitz and silliness revered as part of the lifeblood of our persons.

As gay men, it's a flirtatious connection with all that challenges machismo as the status-quo for human beings with penises. Camp is often identification with the exaggerated female as expression of the female side of the male gender.

Some say that we have the power to stop homophobia by curtailing our "outrageousness"; by suppressing any hint of a sissified camp sensibility we can easily assimilate into the mainstream. Be more inconspicuous, invisible. But what reward is conditional freedom? Don't believe the hype. There's nothing wrong with being a queen.

HOMELESS IN CHICAGO

by W. Delon Strode

"Statistics show that over a period of one year, at least 40,000 men, women, children, and youth in Chicago go homeless. 40% are under the age of thirty-five; 40% are families, usually single women with children; nearly 40% are women; and African-Americans are disproportionately represented, accounting for more than 60%."
– "Homelessness in Chicago" fact sheet,
Chicago Coalition for the Homeless

"It matters not to relate how or when I became a denizen of Dreamthorpe [Chicago]; it will be sufficient to say that I am not a born native, but that I came to reside in it [several months ago]. The several towns and villages in which, in my time, I have pitched a tent did not please, for one obscure reason or another: this one was too large, t'other too small; but when, on a summer evening, I first beheld Dreamthorpe...I felt instinctively that my knapsack might be taken off my shoulders, that my tired feet might wander no more, that at last, on the planet, I had found a home. From that evening I have dwelt here, and the only journey I am likely now to make, is the very inconsiderable one, so far at least as distance is concerned, from the house in which I live to the graveyard..."

This quote from Alexander Smith's *Dreamthorpe* creatively and vividly describes how I feel, to date, about my arrival in Chicago. As morbid as the ending of the quote sounds, it is really a statement saying that I am happy and content for the first time in a long time. I have witnessed and experienced homelessness first hand since coming to this city, and have found that the numbers of gay/bisexual persons in this predicament to be quite staggering.

There are many different reasons and circumstances to create a situation of homelessness, but who would choose to voluntarily become homeless? No one, right? Wrong — for in a sense, that is exactly what I did.

I was completely over, underneath, beside, and through with life as I knew it in Nashville, Tennessee. There was no opportunity for growth for me as a black gay male...no way in which to enjoy even the simplest of an existence. For me, being in a non-creative, environment with limited freedom was detrimental to my attitude. By the time I decided to "break camp," I had enough bad attitude to serve everyone with whom I might possibly come in contact.

With impulses controlling a great portion of the decision-making part of my brain, I left a completely furnished apartment, full-time job, friends, and family to come to Chicago — a city in which I had never been before nor did I know anyone. I just knew that somehow, someway, everything would be taken care of.

Stepping off that Greyhound into this city was one of the most exhilarating and breathtaking moments of my life. I felt as one of the Israelites who had made it to the Promised Land! There were no more chains to shackle and hold me where I wished not to belong; I felt that I could pick, choose, or refuse all things that affected me. I was in such a state of relief to be away from Nashville that I spent all night and all the next day riding trains and buses in an attempt to orient myself with as much of the city as possible.

But alas — it took all of two days for me to begin to feel the effects of no sleep, thus forcing me to face the fact that acting on impulse had put me in a position that I had previously given very little thought...I was homeless.

The first two or three nights after that Mother Nature smiled upon me and blessed me with weather beautiful enough for me to sleep outside in Grant Park. I was using the showers at Union Station to keep clean as well as using the lockers at Greyhound and Union Station to store my clothes.

But, "into every life a little rain must fall," and I had begun to get rained on. My clothes were stolen from the locker at Union Station (or confiscated by security); I was running out of money for food; nor did I have an address to complete job applications. It did not take me long to realize that I couldn't make it very long just hanging out in the streets. I was in desperate need of shelter.

I finally began asking around as to where I might be able to find shelter and was referred to the Pacific Garden Mission on State Street. I have never been so dissappointed with an agency or establishment in all my life. For a Christian agency, Pacific Garden Mission shows very little compassion for their fellow man. "Unshackled" my eye! You are coerced into listening to their hypocritical sermons for their radio show, *Unshackled!*, in exchange for a frozen sandwich and old donut. After services (when the radio audience has gone home), the preacher takes on a totally different persona; he becomes a figure robed with criticism that is nowhere close to being constructive; he becomes a person with a loathing for the homeless people who supposedly give meaning to his work.

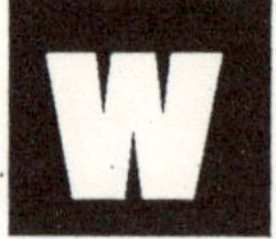

While staying at the mission I did, however, obtain information from other homeless people about numerous other agencies where I could receive assistance. Cooper's Place and Futures Employment Agency (with Transitional Living Programs, TLP) were the only ones to receive positive feedback on their efforts to do something about homelessness. And this was feedback from ones who know...the homeless themselves!

Needless to say, I checked out Cooper's Place and Futures and considered them much closer to being heavenly than what I had begun to refer to as the "Pacific Weed Garden Mission." For starters, at Cooper's I was served hot, fresh meals daily; given opportunity to launder clothes on a weekly basis; given an address to use to receive mail and public assistance; and assessed for placement in Future's job program.

With successful results from Cooper's and Futures, I was referred to yet another shelter — Unity. Unity had an even closer-to-home-type environment than the other agencies I had come in contact with. Among the many things that I needed at that point, Unity provided me with a stable schedule in which to productively seek employment. There was no being put out on the streets at 5 a.m. with all your possessions in hand while trying to look for a job.

In a little over a month's time, I had obtained employment with a loop based health food store. It wasn't exactly the job I was looking for so I continued looking as well as working daily. Not long afterwards, a more favorable position with another company was brought to my attention. I applied and got the position. Things were really beginning to look up for me and an introduction to Community Supportive Living Systems (CSLS) helped even more! CSLS has done more than any other agency with which I've been involved, yet I could not have begun to qualify for their services had it not been for my involvement with the previously mentioned agencies. With CSLS I quickly regained stability to the point where I eventually worked my life back to a state of independence. I was placed in an environnment that allowed me to upgrade my employment, living conditions, and a great many other areas in which a homeless person needs assistance.

The road has not been a smooth one, but thanks to the people and agencies I've come in contact with in the past year, things have gone extraordinarily well with no signs of progress ceasing.

"On many a day in every year does a man remember what took place on that self-same day in some former year, and chews the sweet or bitter herb of memory, as the case may be."

July 4, 1990 marked one year that I have been in Chicago and I know that the overall view of my experiences is going to be more sweet than bitter when I stop to consider the sources from which the Lord blesses me.

There is just enough here for someone who has never been in this type of situation to be able to relate; yet I have gone further into detail in order to give proper credit to those agencies and people who have helped me since "resting my knapsack and tired feet" in Chicago. I realize that not everyone will feel the emotions of the experience. I can't help but hope at least one person understands and attempts to give another what has been given to me and others by such a small group of individuals. I also want other gay, homelesss, young, black men to know there is help available in the city of Chicago.

CSLS is located at 10918 S. Western, Suite 6, Chicago, IL 60643. Inquires should be addressed to Mr. Herscel Gamble, Executive Director, phone (312) 239-0501.

While on my way to Sherwyn's, a health and herbal super store, I found myself thinking about (and pissed off at) the escapade that the recent Village Voice I read was reporting on. The article told of the events at the AIDS conference in San Francisco. What was most disturbing was how AIDS activists had bought into the American Medical Association's circus. When I refer to it as a "circus" I mean that the government as a whole is not the ones with the blood on their hands — it is the AMA.

Before the AIDS crisis even started, the AMA was practicing genocide. The philosophy of our medical system is, at best, maintaining the health of the already healthy.

With my background in the medical field (education that involved the practice of medicine) I learned just how the AMA works.

You see, the AMA and the Food and Drug Administration are capitalists. Their main objective is to make a profit. With the development of chemicals and artficial substances these two organizations work together to expose people to substances that later cause another illness or disease. They can then claim the malady "new" and then release a "cure."

You see, it's a sick cycle: creating the condition to create the market.

With the AIDS crisis, the AMA has created a market of scared, sick, and angry people who turn to them for answers. And yes, they have the answer all right. AZT — a poison that toxifies your blood so that nothing,not even red blood cells,can live in it. And its counterpart DDI is no better.

I guess what angered me was the fact that activists are spending too much time and energy protesting the ineffectiveness of the AMA and FDA. I feel they should be spending their energies seeking out alternative health care.

The FDA is working with the AMA to supress another form of health care that is beginning to find credibility among the people, though its practice and philosophy date back to 700 B.C.: homeopathic medicine.

Homeopathic medicine has several approches to the cure of a illness or a disease. Unlike their AMA counterparts, homeopatic practioners belieive an illness is both spiritual and biological. Homeopathic and holistic health care practitioners believe in a combination of herbal treatments, dietary supplements, and treating the disease, not the symptom. The practitioner will choose a prescription that contains a certain strength of either a herb or plant extraction in either a tablet form or in an alcohol based tincture. Then as prescribed, you place the medicine under your tougue or mix in water and drink. The practioner may perscribe more than one medicine depending on the illness.

It sounds more complicated than it really is. And there is plenty of literature that is written in easy to understand language so that even a layman can begin a path to good health.

On a visit to a health food store, when you don't know what you are looking for, you could get lost. I began my research in holistic health by reading two books, which I recommend to anyone looking to learn more about holistic health.

One was *Back to Eden* by Jethro Kloss. Written in the late 1950s, it has been revised in each of its printings . "Revolutionize the common manner of living, eating, and drinking, and you will have a happier and healthier people." This is Kloss' statement throughout the book. Kloss will take you step by step through the practie of healing herbs, home remedies, and diet and health. Most of the treatments recommended I have successfully tried myself. There is also a *Back to Eden Part Two*. If you can look past the author's dogmatic references to his supreme being, the book will give you a wealth of knowledge.

The second book I read is *SuperImmunity* by Paul Pearsall,PhD. Master your emotions and improve your health, this is the message of *SuperImmunity*. Pearsall postulates a great system within your body, capable of recognizing and repairing damage. Pearsall's stories from his experience as a doctor, clinic supervisor, and therapist, give examples of how the mind, spirit, and body work as one. Pearsall gives us great insight into the philosophy that we are all our own doctor through a series of tests and self-help procedures. The book will take you step by step towards better health and state of being. Pearsall uses a wealth of references to support his theories.

Making a decision to seek out alternative health care is a personal one. And I feel that making the decision doesn't mean to abandon Western medicine altogether. I suggest talking with your doctor before starting any new program.

A word of caution: some doctors are not open to the idea of homeopathic care. But remember the decision is up to you. It is *your* body! Many people are finding out that their doctors are willing to work with a homeopathic practitioner.

I have found a balance between the two that has been very effective for myself and my lover. I plan to discuss this in more detail in future columns. If you have any questions or would like more information, write to me c/o *Thing* magazine,2151 W. Division, Chicago, IL 60622.

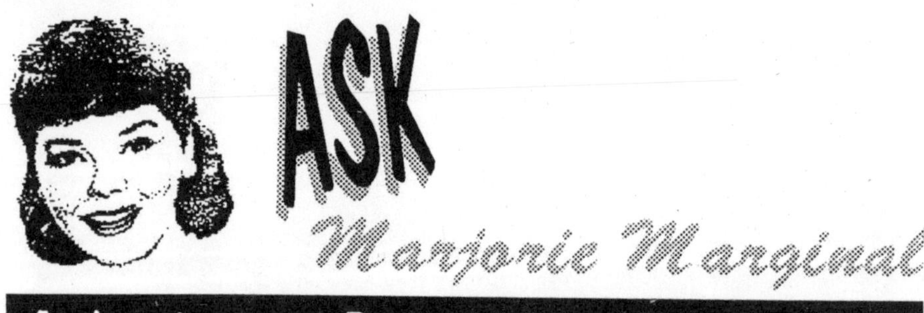

Dear Marjorie,

I have this black gay friend whom I have known for some ten years, who does not seem to understand that it is potentially politically and certainly personally incorrect to isolate himself in an interracial relationship that is not supportive of people of color, or more specifically his black gay friends. I don't think he knows how hurtful and dissappointing it is to watch him miss the whole point of having a black and gay identity, especially during this AIDS epidemic. I feel that if anything HIV related happens to him or his partner he will no longer solicit or welcome the love and support of his friends in his community (and isn't this what black gay pride is all about?).

But even more hurtful, disappointing and painful is the now blank space in my phone book where my friend's name used to be. I just don't need a collection of friends that aren't really friends. What if I get sick? I can't call him and expect him to be there for me. I can't even seem to get through his lover's very effective telephone screening process.

I understand that both men are from nuclear families, but the black family style is traditionally extended and inclusive of family and friends. This is the model that the black gay/lesbian community is built on. As a black gay man who has been in a number of interracial relationships, I know that no matter what, you need your family. How do we as black gay men keep our brothers from cutting themselves off from among their people?

– A Brother

Dear Brother,

Miss Marjorie wonders why are you telling her all of this? If you're feeling so snubbed by this friend, it is a probably a matter between you and him. Miss Marjorie doesn't know either of you well enough to agree willy-nilly with perceptions like "not supportive", "isolated", and "lover's very effective telephone screening process". (Miss Marjorie has no lover, but quite an effective telephone screening process nonetheless.) Your tone suggests to Miss Marjorie some deep-seated conclusion jumping and huffiness that she wishes not to tackle. (Has this lover of his burned a cross on your lawn lately?) Surely you can get a letter, telegram, carrier pigeon, or fax to your friend and pout to <u>him</u>. (And don't forget to check your ego at the door, too!)

Dear Marjorie,

My bestest girlfriend insists on being called by her parents-given (not God-given) name and referred to in the masculine gender.

Being so effeminate, she is as fishy as Queen of the Sea Tuna!!

I mean, she sucks cock better than *moi* (and I can DO a mean dick!). She is so real that I find it difficult to swallow her self-deluding, posing, closeted macho bullcrap—what's a socially and politically correct Thing (who KNOWS who SHE is) to do?

— A Good Girlfriend

Dear Good Girlfriend,
Please, don't you kids READ magazines, or what? I did this last issue, but to answer your question, unattentive reader: *Being a queen has everything and nothing to do with being a man and being a man has everything and nothing to do with being a queen. Don't ask me again.*

Dear Marjorie,

I have been in a relationship for two years, with a wonderful man that I have known for about five years. Before we actually made our relationship official (you know, a monogamous, live-in situation), I had a little privacy.

I have a penpal and our relationship is strictly platonic...HONESTLY! It is also personal. I feel that it isn't any of my lover's business. I don't write to my penpal about my lover and I don't talk to my lover about my penpal.

(If you were wondering if my penpal is gay, the answer is no. He's a black, muscular 5'7, 177 lbs. good-looking, hopelessly straight man!)

I keep a copy of the letters I send him on our computer, and recently my lover has read all of them, and even had the nerve to question me about some of the content. Mind you, there was nothing incriminating, or suggestive of anything other than a platonic relationship.

My lover has also searched through my briefcase on occasion. He always has a semi-valid reason for these intrusions, so I don't say anything about it. He also says that his life is an open book and I can read it anytime I want. Well, I don't want to search through his things—I might find something I don't need to know.

When you enter into a relationship, do you give up your right to privacy? Are these incidents real intrusions? Should I learn to live with it?

— Private I

Dear Private I,
You should 1) give Miss Marjorie your penpal's address, 2) invest in security password software, and 3) buy a briefcase with a lock. In that order.

Dear Marjorie,

I need help! My lover and I are in a major showdown! My lover wants to keep on going to this bar where all his black gay girlfriends hang out, even though the bar does not employ very many blacks or gays nor do they spend their dollars supporting other black businesses.

I, on the other hand, would rather spend our money on establishments that give something back to the community.

Please help, it could be our relationship...

— A.M. Chicago

Dear A.M. Chicago,
Politics are one thing, but parties are quite another. Miss Marjorie will herself go where the best party is no matter who's throwing it. But if it upsets you so much, why don't you alternate, or better yet, go out alone once in a while. Or stay home alone and send your bar money as a contribution to the NCBLG!

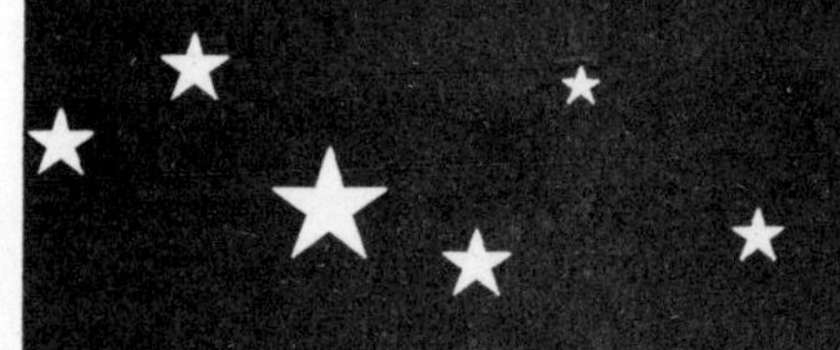

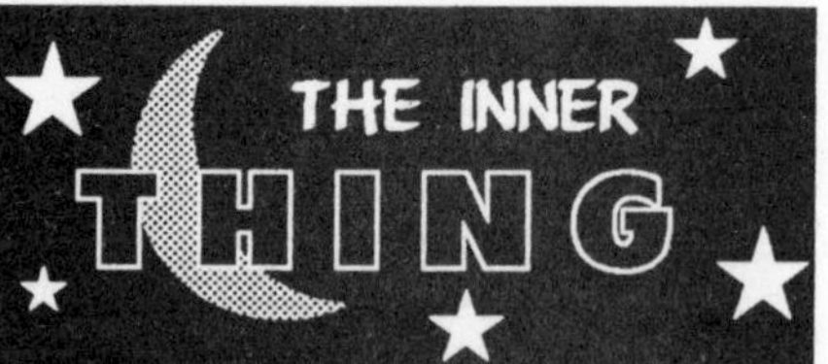

QUICK GUIDE FOR THE SEXUALLY DORMANT
(which buttons to push in bed)

ARIES: Do *anything* that appeals to the head (the upper one). Massage their scalp, kiss their forehead, and most importantly, say something that will go to their head (either one).

TAURUS: The bull likes attention on the throat and neck. And the Taurus neck is *beautiful*. Especially from the back.

GEMINI: Rare is the Gemini who enjoys having his/her arms restrained. They're a vital element of communication- especially when you communicate at *all* times, as Geminis do.

CANCER: As soft and squishy as you can get, is where the Crabs are happiest. The stomach and breasts are a good start, and *my* but the maternal instinct is strong.

LEO: The natural "ruler" of the zodiac, of course, claims the ruler of the human body. The Leo heart is the center of action. And of course, the Leo ego (right next to the heart...) can be reached through unabashed admiration of the Lion's mane.

VIRGO: How close can you get to the crotch and *still* behave "properly"? Yep. Just below the belly button.

LIBRA: The favorite here is the small of the back. Who knows? Maybe they know something we don't.

SCORPIO: The Scorpions get the goods. Virtually the powerhouse of sexuality, Scorpio can go right for your happiest spot- knowing exactly where it is; and derive their own pleasure from that. But *their* happiest spot is between the legs.

SAGITTARIUS: The Archer's libido starts in the hips and spreads to the thighs (including the ass...those lovely mounds of flesh that so often become target-practice for the archer's poised tongue).

CAPRICORN: The queen goat of dignity rules over the knees and bone structure in general. Perhaps tasteful appreciation of these fine lines would garner approval from Ms. Highcheekbones.

AQUARIUS: The calves get all the attention here, but don't be offended if their attention drifts. These people are out of their bodies half the time, anyway.

PISCES : *The* most sensitive spot on a Piscean body is the feet (don't ever make fun of them). Interesting, considering how sensual every other body part is on a Pisces. Especially the dramatic part.

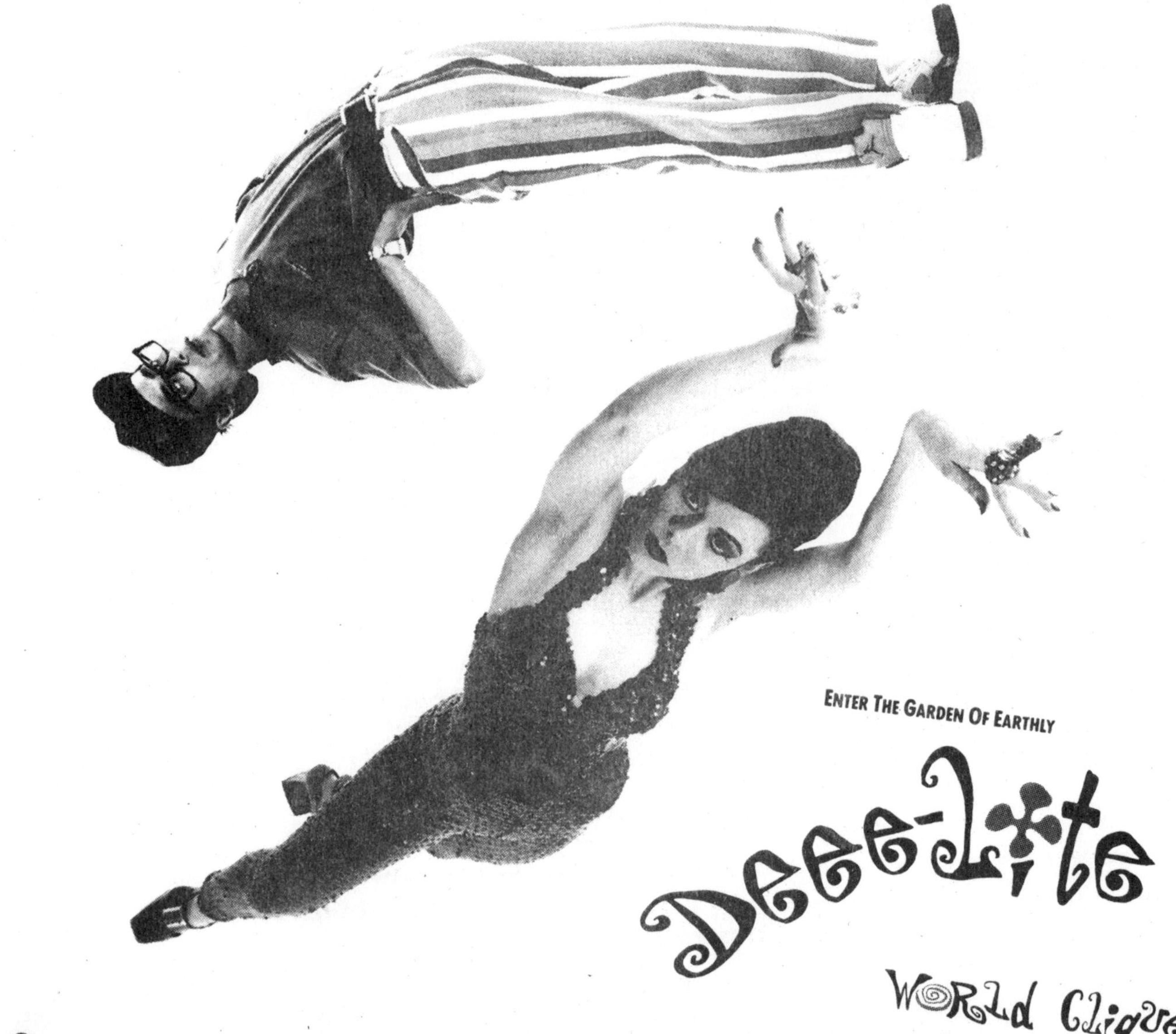

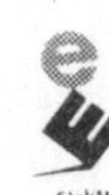

ENTER THE GARDEN OF EARTHLY

Deee-Lite

WORLD Clique

THE DEBUT ALBUM

DEEE-LITE SCRATCH THE UNIVERSAL ITCH

WITH A HOLOGRAPHIC HOUSE GROOVE.

Elektra

FUNKIFYING THE SCENE...ON ELEKTRA CASSETTES, COMPACT DISCS AND RECORDS.

©1990 Elektra Entertainment, a Division of Warner Communications Inc., ⊚

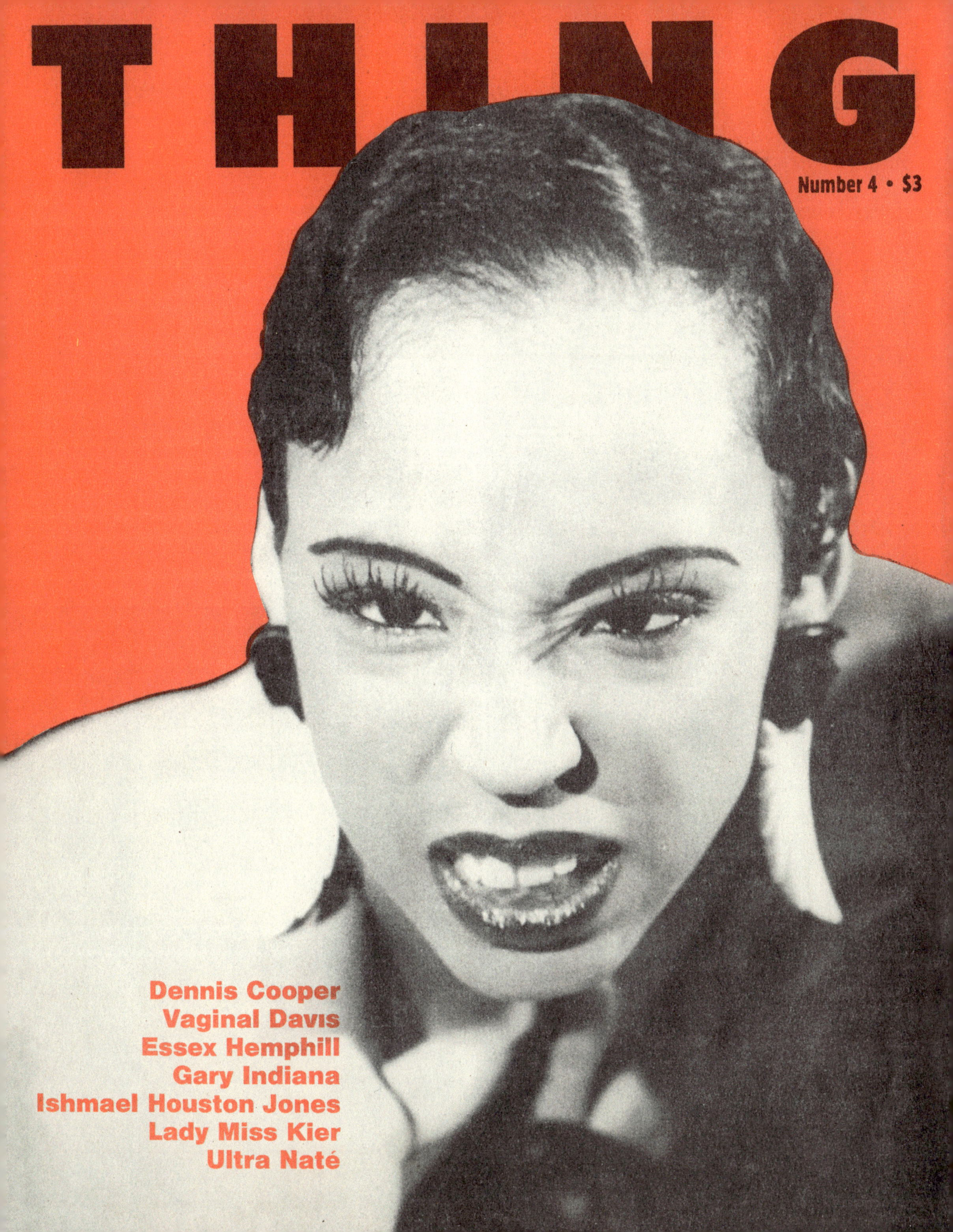

THING
Number 4 • $3
Dennis Cooper
Vaginal Davis
Essex Hemphill
Gary Indiana
Ishmael Houston Jones
Lady Miss Kier
Ultra Naté

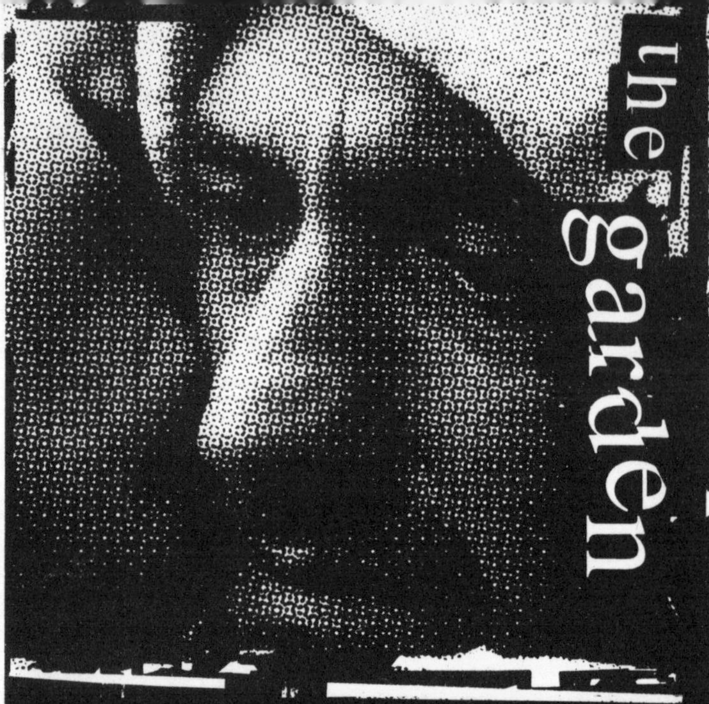

Original soundtrack on
Mute cassettes and compact discs.
Music by Simon Fisher Turner.
Directed by Derek Jarman.

"The Garden" will screen in Philadelphia, Boston, Cleveland,
St. Louis, Houston, San Francisco, Los Angeles, Pittsburgh
and Washington. Watch local listings for details.

© 1990 Mute Records Ltd. Manufactured & distributed by Elektra Entertainment, a division of Warner Communications Inc.

THING

She Knows Who She Is

Number Four • Spring 1991

PUBLISHER/EDITOR Robert Ford
EDITORS Trent Adkins, Stephen Freshwater, W. Delon Strode, Lawrence D. Warren
ART DIRECTION/LAYOUT Robert Ford
OPERATIONS MANAGER Stephen Freshwater
ADVERTISING SALES Sylvia Michaels, Stephen Freshwater
GRAPHIC SERVICES Simone Bouyer

CONTRIBUTORS Bunny & Pussy, Lee Collins, Edward Crosby, Scott Free, André Halmon, Larry Heard, Essex Hemphill, Kathryn Hixson, John Bernard-Jones, Iris Kit, Steve Lafreniere, Joe Lindsay, Roger Noel, Kevin Thaddeus Paulson, Todd Roulette, Lawrence Steger, Vincent Webster, Kurt Weston, Stephen Winter

THANKS Steve Lafreniere, Michael Thompson, Brett and Carrie at PLU, Ralph and Karen, Nick, John and Francisco at Pulp

Thing is published capriciously. Subscriptions are seven dollars for the next three issues published postpaid. Single issues available at your favorite gay bookseller. Wholesale inquiries invited. Donations encouraged! *Thing* encourages unsolicited submissions of any printed matter; only those with self-addressed stamped envelopes will be returned. Artists' payment is the satisfaction of contribution. Editorial inclusion casts no aspersions on one's racial or sexual categorization (Things know who they are.) Opinions expressed are those of individual contributors and do not always reflect those of *Thing*. *Thing* does not sell or rent its mailing list. © 1991 *Thing*

Thing, 2151 W. Division, Chicago, Illinois USA 60622-3056 ✆ 1.312.276.0398

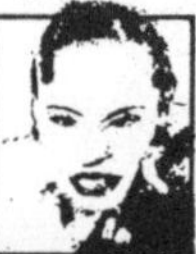

COVER Give us an homage to Josephine and we'll take it any time! Photo and styling by Stephen Winter, Hair/Makeup by Colin Josephs, Earrings by Window to Africa. Model, Pam Johnson.

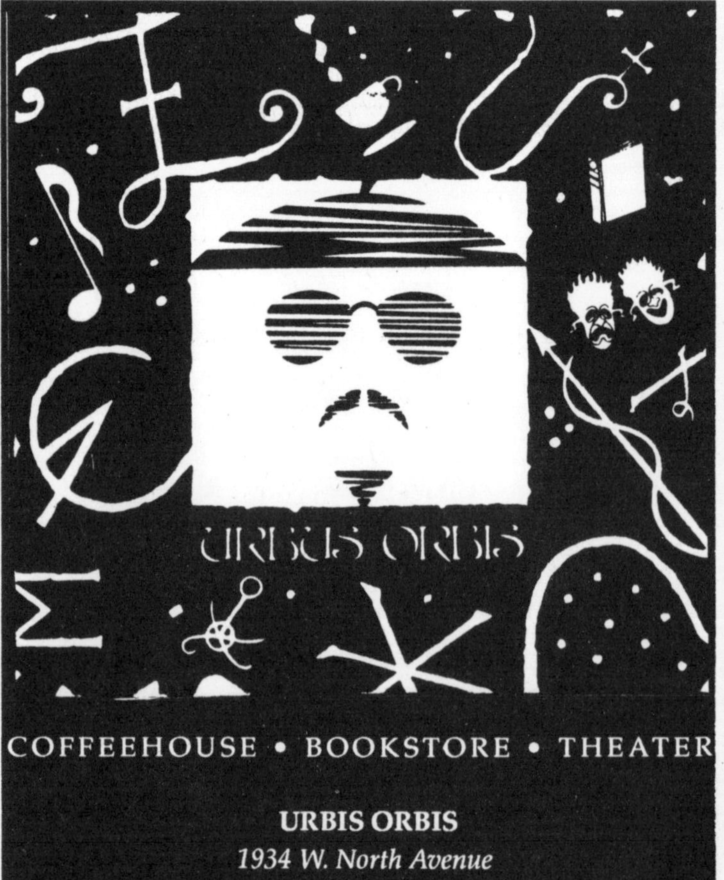

COFFEEHOUSE • BOOKSTORE • THEATER

URBIS ORBIS
1934 W. North Avenue
Chicago
312.252.4446

contents

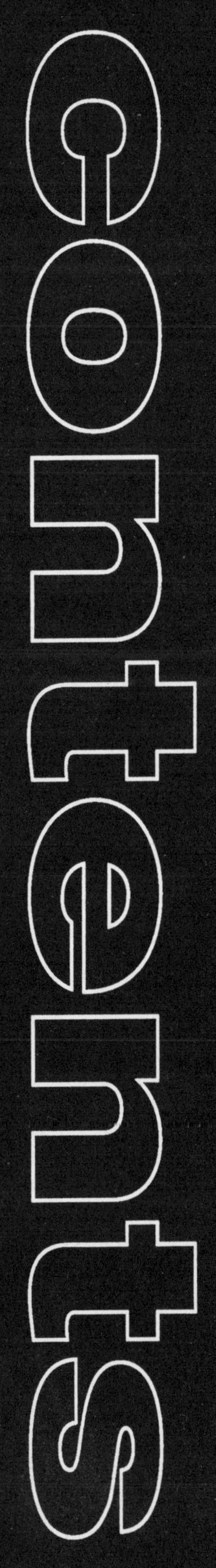

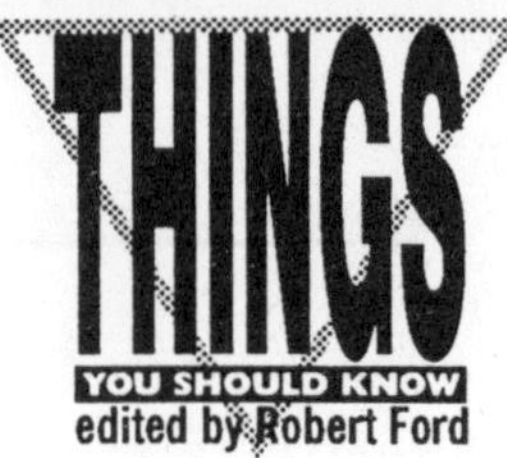

Sacred Sex

art enacts controversy

Homo-political communication and activism have largely relied upon visual and graphic propaganda to get the message across. The "SILENCE=DEATH" logo has become as instantly recognizable as that of GUESS? jeans, to those within and outside the community. Gran Fury monopolized the Chicago media when they used Madison Avenue's Bennetonesque warm fuzzies to challenge the invisibility of gay affection.

Denver artist and activist Joe Lindsay has created a visual which has pushed the envelope of activism beyond politics and visibility to directly address spirituality and sexuality. The "I Praise God" image graces a t-shirt sold to raise funds for Queer Nation Denver. The shirts immeadietly sparked a debate; they were the subject of numerous editorials and letters-to-the-editors in the Colorado gay press. Many were offended by the combination of eroticism and deity. The design has also come under criticism for it's allusion to promiscuity; with the arguement that this would only reinforce notions of gay men as obsessive "perverts". But the design also has a very spiritual feeling: the praise that celebrates sex is earnest and un-mocking.

Lindsay, who is active with ACT UP and Queer Nation in Denver, is no stranger to politically provocative works: His "cartoons" depicting homosexual persecution in Iran and Romania graced the last *Thing* sex issue, and his other drawings, paintings, and graphic assemblages explore issues of sexuality, spirituality, politics, and self-image. (Joe's work appears in this issue of *Thing* as well; in a rare turn as art critic on page 32) In his official response to the shirt controversy, he states that he sees "a time

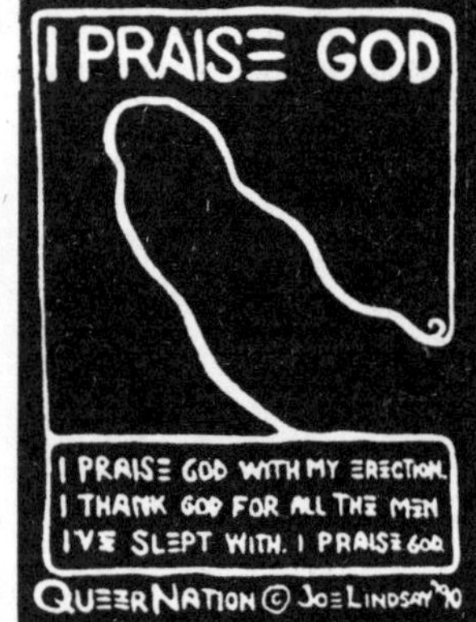

when spirituality and sexuality are accepted as one".

A similar women's shirt ("I Praise Life") has gone through a recent re-design (with lesbian input) and is due to go in production soon. The subtle change in wording addresses the issues of life-bearing as well.

Many more people than have protested are buying the shirt; you can too. They are $12 each t-shirt; $18 each sweatshirt. Sizes M, L, XL. Specify design. Write (and make checks payable to) Joe Lindsay, box 46201, Denver, CO 80201.

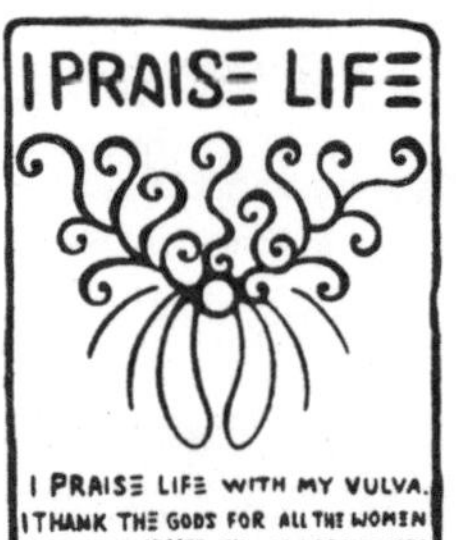

above: The two t-shirt images. below: One of Lindsay's political works.

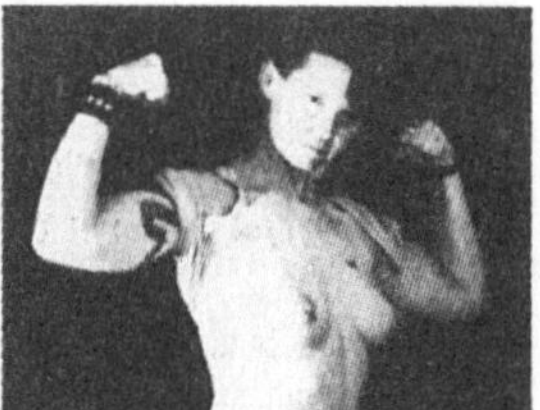

May I Help You?: "Pagan S/M Dyke" Raven, employee ADL Los Angeles

For the literary lesbian in your life, a great late gift is the A Different Light 1991 calendar. It features some of the women who work with ADL at their L.A., New York, San Francisco and West Hollywood locations. Good photography and thoughtful captions highlight the diversity of women who are part of ADL's succcess. The calendar doesn't observe patriarchal holidays (Christmas and Mothers day are missing, too), though your favorite lesbian or gay writer's birthday is probably here. Available by mail for $6.95. A Different Light, 4014 Santa Monica Boulevard, Los Angeles, CA 90029.

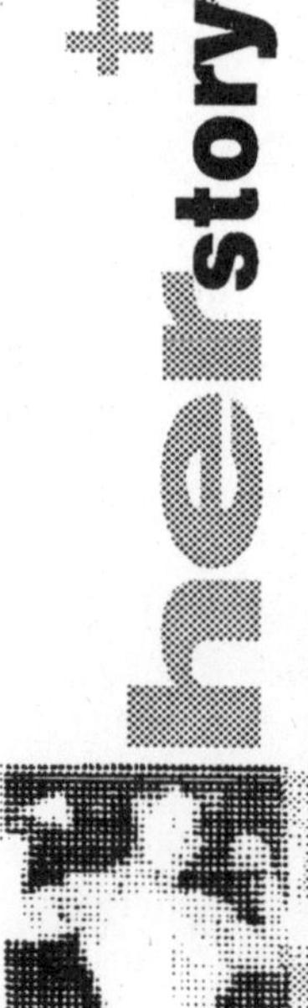

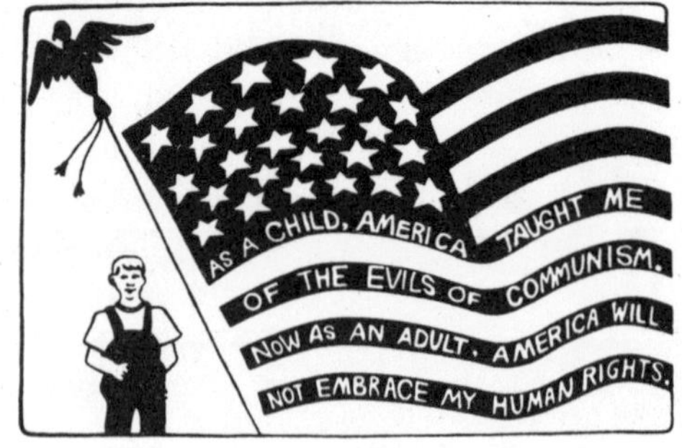

CONVERGENCE

XEROGRAPHIC XEROGRAPHIC XEROGRAPHIC XEROGRAPHIC XEROGRAPHIC XEROGRAPHIC XEROGRAPHIC XEROGRAPHIC XEROGRAPHIC

Suzie Silver, Susan Seizer, Steve Lafreniere, and "Suzette" Steger are staging a "Xerographic Convergence" here in Chicago on May 25. This promises to be to zines what Wigstock is to wigs. They've booked Randolph Street Gallery and snagged Dennis Cooper as a participant, and plan to bring in such farflung literati as Vaginal Creme Davis, and Johnny Noxzema. This special evening will kick off the second annual just-in-time-for-pride-week "In Through the Out Door" series. Drop a SASE to *Thing* for more info.

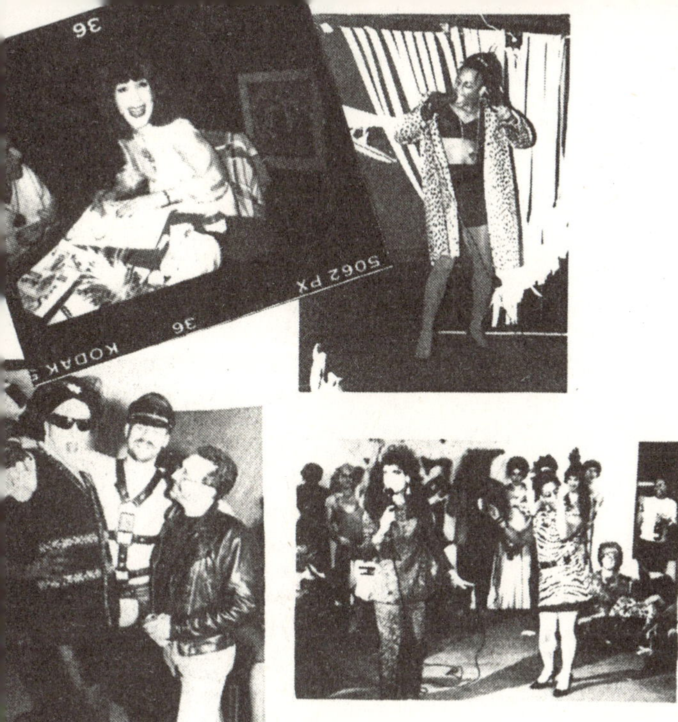

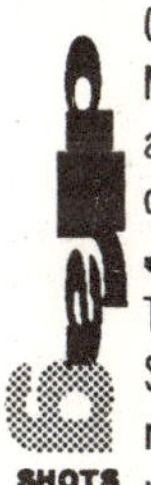

Clockwise from top left: **Hapi Phace** smiled into town March 6 with a cute show at Club Lower Links, with autographs afterwards. Photo by Trent Adkins.   Would you vote for this queen? Queer Nation's Chicago Mayoral Candidate **Joan Jett Blakk** in performance at "The National SCUM—A Tabloid Trash Fundraiser" for ACT UP Chicago, November 15 at Smart Bar. **Gurlene Hussey** and Joan Jett Blakk at a recent drag ball. Miss **Fraulein** mit leathermeister friend und **Kermit Berg**. Photos by Kurt Weston.

BROTHER TO BROTHER

Brother to Brother is the long awaited follow-up to the 1986 anthology **In the Life**, edited by the late Joseph Beam. This new anthology is 300-plus pages in length and contains poetry, essays, journal entries, and short fiction that, like it's forerunner, attempt to empower Black gay men. "The silences surrounding the lives and experiences of Black gay men have been aided and abetted by the tremendous amount of denial, homophobia, and heterosexism that exists in the African American community" says writer Essex Hemphill, a close friend of Beam's who completed editing **Brother to Brother** after his death in 1988. **In the Life** and **Brother to Brother** are both powerful and affirming works from which anyone can learn.

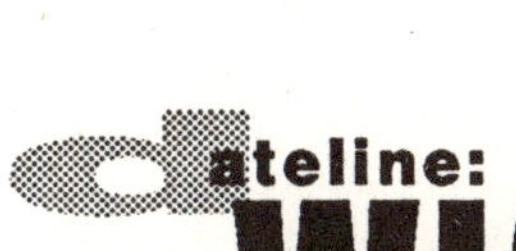

Brother to Brother: New Writings By Black Gay Men is available by mail for ten dollars from Alyson Publications, 40 Plympton Street, Boston, MA 02118.

Wigstock is like Woodstock, but with wigs-cum central theme. The be-all, end-all place to be Labor Day weekend in Manhattan, and this year was bigger and better than others, which didn't baffle the star and m.c., **Lady Bunny**, the ultimate in control and entertainment up on center stage. This event is one that brings everyone together to "oooh" and "aaah" in unison; not only are the queens and professional hams in heaven, but also them normal boys and girls, because this is the brightest spot in the universe on Labor Day. 1990's treat was **Deee-Lite**, those kids from down the block who we all know and love. I don't know much about the Asian boy, but I can add a spicy word or two about **Dimitri**'s past...

   RuPaul "this is the front, and this is the back" **Charles** served; she's very, very fierce on stage now. After all, she is the Queen of Manhattan, and that is no easy task. She was not the only one getting a life on stage, for there was **Jo-Jo** — who to me is like a God—giving us body and boy-girl drag. It just goes to show what so much drugs and dance floors can do, but there really were too many acts to mention, and besides, it is the real people who make the day. One queen sang "I did it my way"

dateline: WIGSTOCK

à la **Sammy Davis Jr.** while simultaneously peeling off polyester Sammy drag to reveal her falsies bra. Hari Bol **Lypsinka** did her phone number. **Flloyd** of the People Tree looked like a chicken and definitely cannot sing, so we were all sick of the dragon scene and happy when that little twinkle in our eyes, **Kier**, came out and put the Groove in our hearts!

   Leaving the park, the *cognoscenti* and yours truly, moved on to Silencio in order to get into the night thing and the real music. **Skinny Vinny** was there. I was happy to introduce **Jeffrey** to Ru. He had not heard of her in Philadelphia.

   Another soothing moment was Monday night out at the Pathmark in Jersey City of all places. This is the highest priced supermarket I've ever seen. I spend hours there comparison shopping. I was wheeling down the frozen food aisle at about eleven p.m. when I saw a large, beautiful girl who looked very much like **Queen Latifah**, but how? Not in a grocery store! Not in New Jersey! She did have on a real gold bracelet and one of those t-shirts you only get from record companies as promotion. The odds are stacking. Then a brother comes drooling up to me supplicating for a pen or pencil for her autograph, and yep, it is! Queen Latifah right here in Jersey! I ask her if she really is herself, and she says "yes." As bait, I say, "I know **Scott Gibson**," my friend who designed the jackets they wore on her album. She says, "Wow! Yes, I know Scott! He's a great designe!"

There is nothing better than actually having something to say to the famous.

   I must add that I'm glad to see a shift from the vogue of wearing gold chains to the wearing of wooden African beads instead. It's high time we stop feeding the sick black South African economy.

— **Vincent Webster**

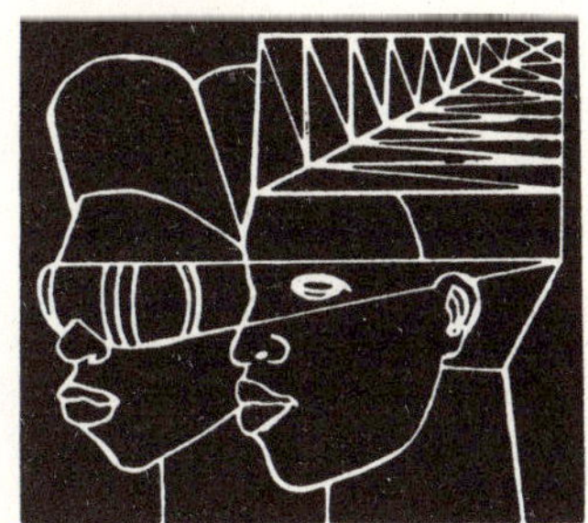

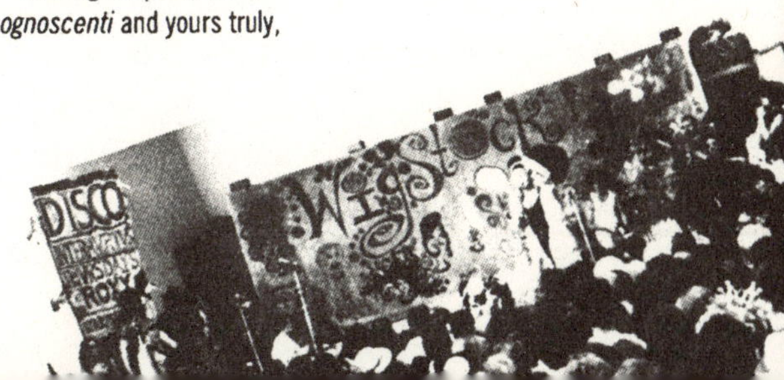

Ultra Naté

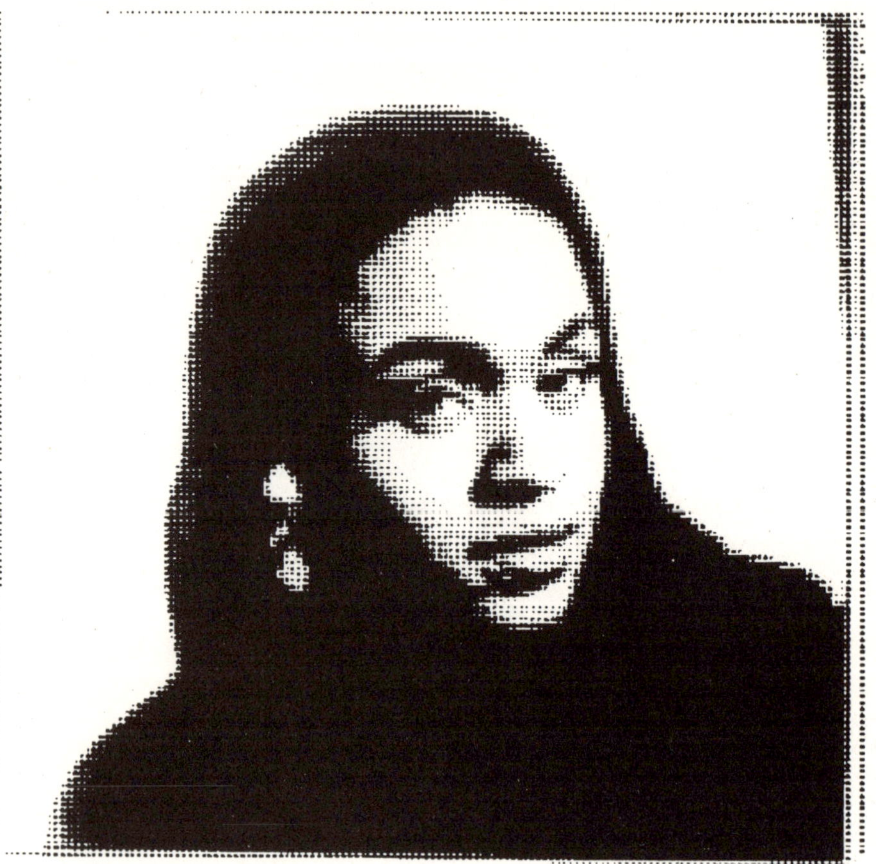

by Robert Ford

Another dance diva is born with Baltimore's Ultra Naté. Not a pseudo-operatic show-off like Mariah or Whitney, Ultra's strength is her ability to convey pure raw emotion with her voice. Hers is the classic disco-Cinderella tale; hooking up with local DJ/musicians the Basement Boys and snagging former Billboard writer Bill Coleman for management has suddenly found her on the brink of stardom. Her first single, "It's Over Now" has become a club anthem. Her newest double A-side single "Scandal/Is It Love" began to chart even before its release. Her first full length album, <u>Blue Notes In the Basement</u>, will be out by the time you read this. With a hectic schedule of club dates and remix sessions, Ultra took a few moments to do a "phoner," to talk about her new nand successful career.

Robert Ford: I s Ultra Naté your real name?

Ultra Naté: (laughs) Yes. Oh, gosh, that is always the first question I get! Yes, it's my real name.

RF: What's the underground scene like in Baltimore, is there a big underground dance music scene there?

UN: Not from the club perspective. There aren't really a lot of clubs to go to that play the real underground club music. But as far as the music goes, it's very good. We're pretty up on what's goin' on in the music world right now. And they stay pretty much on top of it. Most of the DJs that work at the clubs work in record stores, too; they order the music and they're pretty abreast of what's happening.

RF: How did you get hooked up with the Basement Boys?

UN: Well, it was quite a few years ago and I was at a point where I had been out of school for a year, and I was just trying to figure out what I was going to do with myself, exactly. I've always liked the artsy kind of things, though at the time I thought I was gonna persue medicine, that was my first love. But I used to do the artsy kind of stuff on the side. And one thing I wanted to try was doing some background vocals. I knew Tommy, Teddy, and Gerry through the club scene and through the record stores they worked at. So I knew them as friends. I knew they had put their own record out the year before, "Love Don't Live Here No More" on Jump Street. I went to Tommy and told him I was interested in doing some background vocals for him and he was like, "come on down and audition". I did, and they liked it, and we started working together. That's what I was doing for a couple of months, just working on different songs, background vocals. Until "It's Over Now" came into play.

RF: I saw in your bio where that was ad-libbed at two in the morning.

UN: Yeah (laughs) That was a very painful experience.

RF: I can only imagine. Did that get you started songwriting?

UN: It kind of snowballed after that. At first I really didn't believe that anything was gonna be done with it. I thought it was a cute little diddly that I did and

that was it. I didn't think they were gonna do anything with it. It wasn't until it started getting so much play and so much recognition and record deals and all that kind of stuff came that I thought about writing stuff. Just sit down and try it.

RF: "It's Over Now" first came out in the U.K., is that right?

UN: Right.

RF: Then it was liscenced back by Warner Brothers U.S. It's odd that so much house music goes through that, where it breaks in Europe first. Did you go overseas in support of it?

UN: By ending up on a U.K. label, everything was gonna happen first over there anyway. I went to the U.K. to shoot the video, to do pictures for the album cover. Everything was done in the U.K. The music is so widely accepted over there. It's not as underground as it is over here. A club performer can get more recognition faster overseas than they can here, which is sad but true.

RF: Do you have a feeling for which tracks are going to be the hits? Like with "Scandal"?

UN: Well, I told the record label way, way back when "Scandal" was even rawer than it is on the record that this was a big song. I wanted it to be the next release because it wasn't identical to "It's Over Now" but it was in the same vein. I felt it was good to use that to establish my sound. And then you go off and explore other avenues. But when you're a new artist, it's important first to establish some kind of sound that people can identify you with.

RF: When does the album ship?

UN: It's supposed to be released March 4th.

RF: And the "Scandal" 12" , is that out now?

UN: That will be out next Monday. "Scandal" is on the b-side, the a-side is "Is It Love."

RF: It seems like "Scandal" is already charting on all the music charts in this issue

UN: That's because it was gonna be released earlier. They decided to wait until the album was totally finished to have the album back it. Which is a good idea. But it had already leaked out, and people were already screamin' over it. ▼

DIVAFEST What becomes a legend most? The divas behind the credits.

Disco divas have always been big fish in little ponds. Before hers became the voice that launched a thousand hit singles, Martha Wash was a name known only to die hard club tarts as one of Two Tons of Fun aka Weathergirls. Now that she's wailed for everybody from Black Box to the C&C Music Company, she's *still* only known by true disco fans. It seems her hips are too wide to market on the cover of a cd. It also seems as if she'd rather just sing and get paid, and leave behind the video/tour/image side of it. A not unusual fate for the divas of the disco industry. A quick glance at other superstar session singers:

Sharon Redd
Sharon first burst upon the disco scene when multiple versions of "Can You Handle It" became disco sensations. "Beat the Streets" followed a few years later, the record that defined the New York sound with its crisp, simple syncopated synths and big throbbing bottom. She sustained a third Prelude album, which yielded the uninspired but serviceable "Activate" and hi-NRG surprise "You're a Winner." Sharon stumbled into obscurity after that, with only a couple of sporadically released, embarrassing singles out every few years since her mid 80's heyday.

Jocelyn Brown
She, too was a Harlette for a bit, though it was the retro swing of "Somebody Else's Guy" that was her breakthrough. The summer it hit number one, every independent New York label that had a vocal by her in the can released a "Jocelyn Brown" single. The major labels came courting after that, but superstardom was elusive. A handful of commercial releases have met with lukewarm success. But she still occasionally shows up on a New York indy, lending her golden voice to a more Garage-like setting.

Toni Smith
You'd have to be a disco sleuth to be a fan of this girl. She was the uncredited female vocal on Tom Browne's "Funkin For Jamacia." Later, she went on to do the underground classic "I Got the Hots For You" under the initials TZ. That song had more than a few clubgoers convinced that there was a new Chaka Khan record out. What else has she done? Beats me, I'm sure she sings on something.

Loleatta Holloway
The mother of the essence of big wailing diva house. The most sampled voice of the eighties and nineties. Hits include "Hit and Run," "Love Sensation"(recently reinvented as Black Box's "Ride on Time"), "Crash Goes Love," "Seconds," and "Runaway." Loleatta is also known for her over-the-top talkover breaks, in which she ad-libs like the oldest snap! diva around. "Girl, get up and put your stuff back on!"

And the list goes on. Dance floors around the world have benefited from the work of **Tina B., Corey Daye, Fonda Rae, Tanna Gardner, Valerie Simpson, Liz Torrez, Tina Fabrique, Mikki, Gayle Adams, Sharon Brown, Michelle Wallace, Linda Clifford, Norma Jean Wright, Xavier Gold, Thelma Houston, Jackie Moore, Shawn Christopher, Ava Cherry, Adeva, Gwen McCrae, Geraldine Hunt, Mary Wells, Jean Carne, Kym Mazelle, Dhar Braxton, Gwen Guthrie, Anita Ward, Paris Grey, O'Chi Brown, Sybil, Princess, Tia Monae, Melba Moore, Stephanie Mills, Karen Young, Edna Holt, Vickie Sue Robinson, Lori Eastside,** among countless other unsung singers of the disco dream.

— RF

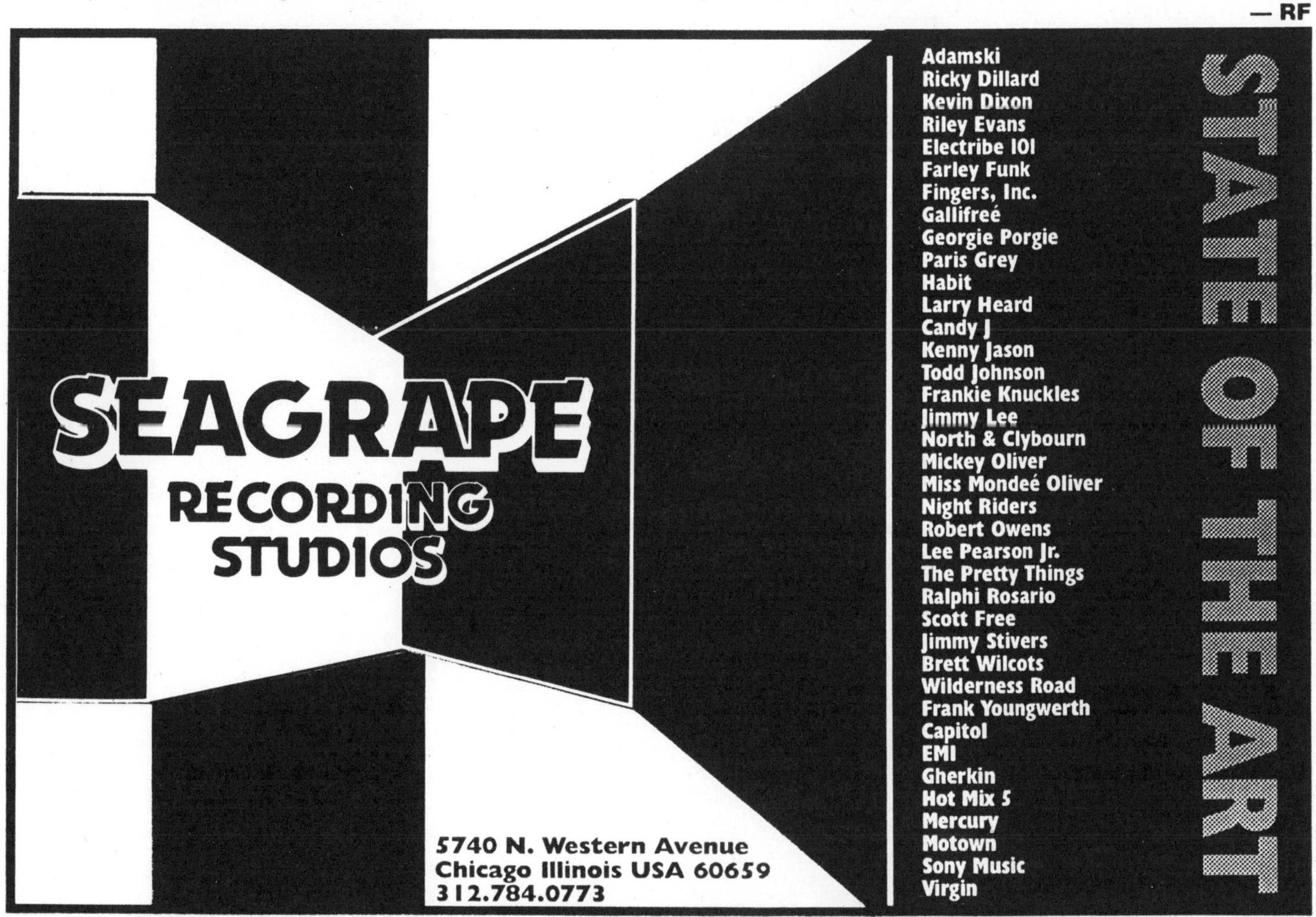

music reviews

UBQ Project
Into the Night
House N Effect Records 12"

This record has five mixes (please), although luckily, one of the mixes is so different, it could be another song. It's Aaron Smith's mix and it's the one that should really be called "Into the Night." It's a nice, downtempo blend of bass and echoed synths, with a trumpet break that is an instant classic. You've been hearing it in Edward "Get Down" Crosby's mixes.

Actually, both songs are very nice. Terry Hunter's instrumental mix glides along, built around a 4-chord solid piano line that has become synonymous with deep house. Then comes this synth line that sounds like "play along to the record." You know when you're in the middle of working on track and your friends stop by and say "cool- look at all that equipment. Hey, can I try it?" and soon their grubby little hands are adding mush to your perfecly produced track? OK, it's not that bad. It's more like you've been up for three nights straight because you're in the studio tomorrow, and you're putting down a synth line and you doze off and then before you know it, the track is over, and you wake up and say "great, it's done. Now I can got to bed." Actually, I'm being far too abusive. This is a really nice record.

Ron Trent's mix has the title of the song groaned out by an either frustrated of horny young man. Or both. I would have liked to have seen him perform it in the studio. The mix clips along at a nice pace, due to the incessant, high eq'd snare. The strange speed change sound effects at the end of the mix are nice too, unless that's my turntable.

— **Scott Free**

Barbara Tucker
Open Your Heart
Fourth Records 12"

In a word, beautiful. This piece is proof that dance music is on an up turn. The "R&B" mix is the mix. This mix makes it easy to forgive them for the other three mixes. At roughly 124 bpm, this song demonstrates great orchestration. Every instrument is played for maximum effect. If you like Mondee Oliver's "Stay Close", you'll love this.

So far I've talked about the mix and the music but what put the icing on the cake for me was Barbara. This girl sang this song like it was her last. I hope this is not the last time we hear her voice. This is a "10": in every category.

— **Lee Collins**

Sam Fan Thomas
African Typic
Virgin Earthworks CD/CS

What a concept. The baddest and the best. Francophone Africa by way of Paris. Polished pop with a techno-sheen. And the guitars, like two hot leads buzzing your brain. Mixes well with Salsoul or merengue, or just fine on its own. Catch them live if you can. Outstanding tracks: "Noa" and the title track.

— **Roger Noel**

Vincent Floyd
Cruising (Long ride)/Isolation/ Silent Noise
Resound Records 12"

All three of these are similar in feel. Lots of searing, soaring synths, shuffling beats and hypnotic bass lines. Unfortunately, the drum sounds are all pretty much the same. Silent noise has the best use of synths- very dense chords.

— **Scott Free**

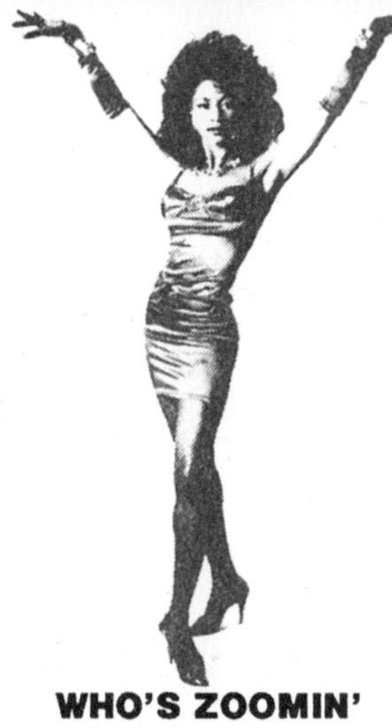

**WHO'S ZOOMIN'
WHO?:** C&C's Zelma Davis

Gonna Make You Sweat

Columbia CD/CS

Disco eats itself. This is high-powered corporate hit music, that has as much to do with contracts as collaboration; more boardroom than dance floor. But they've admittedly done their research — every disco hook and reference is here, from the Snap-meets-Bohannon hit title single, to the more-Blackbox-than-Blackbox "Just a Touch of Love (Everyday)'. "A Groove Of Love (What's This Word Called Love)" teams Suzanne Vega via DNA's "do-do-do's" with a similar alliteration of the melody of disco moldy "Mother Popcorn".

But who is the "C&C Music Factory"? That's where the contract part comes in. You can't tell the players without a scorecard, so hang on to your hats. The "C&C Music Factory" is the superstar disco production duo Robert Civillés and David Cole (responsible for Seduction,etc.) "featuring" Freedom Williams, a Latin rapper that adds "street credibility". And then there's Zelma Davis, who sings on some tracks. But not the big hit single "Gonna Make You Sweat (Everybody Dance Now)" —that's one of the "support" vocals provided by everyone's favorite ghost vocalist Martha Wash. But Miss Davis lip-synchs it in the video wearing a push-up bra. Got it? This is certianly a music factory, molding raw materials into a sale-able product. Destined for multi-platinum.

— Robert Ford

The Untouchables
Take A Chance/I'm For Real/Trippin'/ Yea C'mon'

Strictly Rythm Records 12"

"Take A Chance": the Todd Terry sound, again, in 1991. I hate to say it, but it still sounds great. I think they sampled the section with all the background noise. Why do you think Todd left that bare one out there? Actually including the crowd noise makes the record that much more intense. They even went after Todd's drum sound, which was equally important in the making of "that" record. There is a talent to stealing from other records. You have to know what to do with the samples. This one is well stolen.

"I'm For Real": this one sounds like it comes from somewhere East Of Africa. The dry drums are a little annoying, but the backwards snare sounds great, and I love the way the guy sample interrupts the girl sample.

"Trippin'": I'm not sure what drug they intended to go along with this song. Not to be played when you feel that slight headache coming on . It sounds like what the Gerkin Jerks were doing in 1990.

"Yea C'mon": I wanted to hear the 'I've fallen and I can't get up' sample in this one.

— Scott Free

Margareth Menezes
Elegibo

Mango CD/CS

The sister who stole the show on David Byrne's "Rei Momo" tour sets it out solo. From Bahia to Bob Marley via James Brown, this is real roots and up-to-date urban stylee with a difference. Sisters got the pipes and the spirit(s). Killer cuts: "Marmelada" and "Elegibo (a story of IFA)"

— Roger Noel

Armondo presents
Mike Dearborn
1991/ New Dimension/ Sexual X-perience

Muzique Records 12"

I feel sorry for Mike. On the label, the "presenter's" name, Armondo is in huge bold letters and then underneath, almost as an afterthought, is the artist's. Well Mike, maybe after this record you'll be qualified for "bold caps" status.

The record is solid (musically, that is) and fits in well with Muzique's last smash, "The After-life," by Ron Trent. It looks like Armondo is on his way to creating a "Muzique sound." The two songs on the the first side, "1991" and "New Dimension" are long and drawn out, but I wouldn't call it monotonous. The choice of sounds and and the simple, melodic lines make it very listenable. Person-ally, I took a shower to this record, but you could dance to it.

Side B has two versions of a song called Sexual X-perience. When a song is an instrumental, you can pretty much name it whatever you want. It has that Detroit techno feel to it, and the excellent drum programming keeps it interesting.

— Scott Free

Aster Aweke
Aster

Sony CD/CS

The ones to Aretha, Anita, and Janis even more so. From the land where womankind was born via chocolate city, Aster's a star. Take her on her own terms. You won't regret it.

— Roger Noel

Rythm Warfare
2 Notches

Strictly Rythm Records 12"

Unfortunately, a timely name for a group. The funk drums do have that scud feeling to them. A barrage of samples with attacking monophonic synths, and a bass line that slides in and out of enemy territory. Very intense, but I'm one of those peacenick types- I don't need four mixes of it.

— Scott Free

Smoove-Jam
Work The Rythm/ Syndromatic/ Tonight

Smoove-Jam Records 12"

The group and the label are the same name. Could cause some confusion if the group signed to another label. The first song, "Work The Rythm," mixes hip-house beats with samples of old chicago house records and dense, jazz-sounding female vocals. It also has a mini hip-house rap à la 2 In A Room. The dub mix has a de-mented violin part that makes the mix-actually it makes the record. The work of a truly disturbed man. Very mixable, very fun.

On the B-side is "Syndromatic," a wonderfully eerie techno track that is miles above anything com-ing out of wherever records come out of these days. Lots of incred-ible sounds floating out of the back of the mix. Very well produced. The kind of record I wish I had done.

Last is "Tonight," an oh-so-retrotrack that is just too, too disco. Deep rhodes piano, whis-pering female, violins, congas. One mirrored ball, please.

This record is very well thought out, constructed, and produced. It should make Eric Miller and Jere McAllister very famous. I don't know Eric, but I gave Jere a ride to the studio in my car once. I won't wash my car for a week.

— Scott Free

2nd Avenew
It's the New

Alleviated Records 12"

Don't you feel like you get to know someone bettter with each record they release? Well just when we were all getting concerned about Larry Heard's Moodiness (C'mon Lar-snap out of it), here comes 2nd Avenue, a fun escapade (have I resorted to quoting Janet Jackson?) into discoland, that is pure fun. Congas float in and out of the beat. Little synths drop in to say "hi." Then we get a spoken intro that means serious music ahead. We even get a retro rap-kinda Sugarhill. And a female vocalist that is a 'true delight." What more could you ask for? Ain't it funky, love?

— Scott Free

Dee Dee Brave
My My Lover

Movin' Records 12"

Another great product from Movin' records. After "Let the Rain Come Down", which headed my top 15 chart for many weeks, and Valerie Ingrams's "Are You Faith-ful", which also made it to number one and is still being heard around town,excellence still radiates from this small New Jersey label. This is a very strong track (hard drums and heavy bass—like most rec-ords with the "Jersey Sound"), the kind of track that demands to be danced to. On top of this track is a very melodious tune which is, in its own right, captivating.

This piece comes equipped with 4 mixes. My favorites are the "KOOS Again Mix" which consists of well done ad-libbing. David Camacho's mix is instrumental but more musical. This formula equates to yet another winner.

— Lee Collins

Music Lists

Larry Heard (Producer)

Top Ten
1. **Jump and Prance** Dreamhouse *White House*
2. **Into the Night** UBQ Project *House Effect*
3. **Drink on Me** Tuelé *Profile*
4. **Unification** E Culture *Strictly Rhythm*
5. **Jazz it Up** CFM Band *Underworld*
6. **Luv Dancin'** The Underground Solution *Strictly Rhythm*
7. **Moments in House** Essence *Strictly Rhythm*
8. **Across 110th St.** El Barrio *Fresh*
9. **Scandal** Ultra Naté *Eternal/Warner Brothers*
10. **It's Not Far Away** Scott Taylor *Beat*

Notables of 1990
1. **Koro Koro** No Smoke *Profile*
2. **You're Walking** Electribe 101 *Mercury*
3. **Transcendental Love** Project 1 *Tam Tam*
4. **Change** Baby Ford *Sire*
5. **What is Love** Deee-Lite *Elektra*
6. **Searchin'** 33 1/3 Queen *NuGroove*
7. **Love So Special** Cebil *Atlantic*

André Halmon (Dance Specialist)

Club America 25
1. **I'm Attracted To You** Anna Robinson *Smash*
2. **One Step At A Time** Jay Williams *Big Beat*
3. **Into The Night** UBQ Project *House N Effect*
4. **All True Man** Alexander O'Neal *Tabu*
5. **Love Come Down** Eve Gallagher *MP-U.K.*
6. **Keep It Up (Vocal)** L.U.P.O. *Yo Bro-U.K.*
7. **Don't Cha Want It** K-Alexi *Underground*
8. **Loose Flutes** Picture Perfect *Big Productions*
9. **Got A Love For You(Remix)** Jomanda *Big Beat*
10. **Let's Push It** Innocence *Chrysalis-U.K.*
11. **It's The New** 2nd Avenew *Alleviated*
12. **Dark Secret (RnB)** David Rudder *Sire*
13. **You+Me** Keytronics *Irma-Italy*
14. **Can't Give You Up** Life On Earth *Republic-U.K.*
15. **We Are Unity** Umosia *Otherside*
16. **Temple Of Love** Harriet *East West America*
17. **Fever** Way To Go *Tommy Boy*
18. **Drink On Me** Teulé *Profile*
19. **Scandal** Ultra Naté *Eternal/Warner Brothers*
20. **Jump and Prance** Dreamhouse *White House*
21. **Play Thing** Phoenix *Big Beat*
22. **Superficial People(Remix)** Ten City *Atlantic*
23. **Holding On(Remix)** Tikkle *House Jam*
24. **Missing You(Fabulous)** Soul II Soul *Virgin promo*
25. **Blood Vibes/Jump On It** Master At Work *Cutting*

Lee Collins (Rhythm)

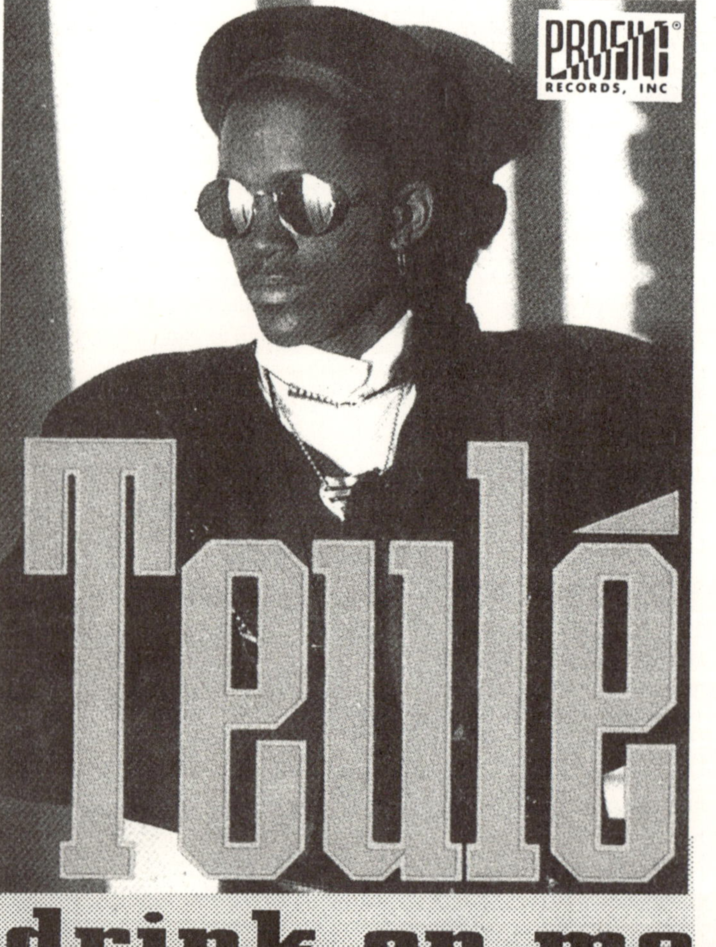

Section Productions
Top Fifteen
1. **Open Your Heart** Barbara Tucker *Fourth Floor*
2. **My My Lover** Dee Dee Brave *Movin'*
3. **Mummy I'm Sick Under Water** Electribe 101 *Mercury - import*
4. **Beaches** Mr. Stone Brothers Organization - import
5. **Passion** Mystique *Velvet City*
6. **Una Experience/ Whirlpool** The Deepest Area *Right Area*
7. **That's When It's Gold** Be Big *10 - import*
8. **That Moon** Paul Rutherford *Beat Farm Recordings - import*
9. **Guaraana** Love Bug Experience *Brothers Organisation - import*
10. **Where Love Lives** Allison Limmerick *Arista - import*
11. **Stay With You** Dubb Club *Sleeping Bag -import*
12. **It's a Jungle Out There** Julian Jonah *Cooltempo/Chrysalis - import*
13. **Imagination**

Shank *Sleeping Bag -import*
14. **That's Kickin' Me!** Underground Posse *Brothers Organisation - import*
15. **Electribal Memories** Electribe 101 *Mercury - import*
Scott Free Producer
Top Ten Jazz
1. **Impressions** Michael Camilo *Sony*
2. **Warm Valley** Paris All-Stars *A&M*
3. **No More** Music Revelation Ensemble
4. **Pannonica** Thelonious Monk
5. **Downstream** Trout/ Rodby *Columbia*
6. **Alone Together** Chet Baker
7. **On The Trail** Oscar Peterson
8. **Dance In the Morning** Dino Saluzzi *ECM*
9. **My Favorite Things** John Coltrane *Atlantic*
10. **You Won't Forget Me** Shirley Horn *Verve*
Steve Freshwater
Boys at Night

Top Fifteen
1. **I Feel Love** Fax Yourself *Sunshine*
2. **Crash (Emergency Landing Mix)** TKA *Tommy Boy*
3. **Power of Love** Deee-Lite *Elektra*
4. **Heading for the Night** Electribe 101 *Mercury - import*
5. **Unbelievable (BootLane Mix)** EMF *EMI*
6. **Scandal** Ultra Naté *Eternal/Warner Brothers*
7. **Drink On Me** Tuelé *Profile*
8. **Is it Love** Ultra Naté *Eternal/WarnerBrothers*
9. **Electribal Memories** Electribe 101 *Mercury - import*
10. **Passion** Mystique *Velvet City*
11. **What is Sadness** Device *Arista*
12. **One Nation (Zimba Mix)** Olu Rowe *Cardiac*
13. **Got a Love For You** Jomanda *Big Beat*
14. **Hold You Tight**

Tara Kemp *Giant*
15. **Ska Train (Tied To the Tracks Mix)** Beatmasters *Rhythm King*
Edward Crosby WGCI
Hot Music
1. **Just A Touch** Essence *Strictly Rythm*
2. **Scandal** Ultra Naté *Eternal/Warner Brothers*
3. **Get Into The Music** DJ's Rule *Hi-Bias*
4. **Night by Night** Alamda *ID*
5. **Spread A Little Love** Richard Rodgers *Sam*
6. **Don't Cha Want It** K-Alexi *DJ International*
7. **All True Man (Frankie Mix)** Alexander O'Neal *Tabu*
8. **Raw, Love/Party Time** Pal Joey *Loop D Loop*
9. **Don't Run Away (4 On the Floor Mix)** Denise M. *House Jam*
10. **Superficial People** Ten City *Atlantic*
11. **Feel It** Adonte *Republic - import*
12. **One Of My Moods/Pipe Dreams** DJ Delite *Jazzy Records*

13. **Drink On Me** Tuelé *Profile*
14. **More Love** Tamara Knight *About Music*
15. **My My Lover** Dee Dee Brave *Movin'*
16. **North on South Sreet (Bobby Konders Mix)** Herb Alpert *A&M*
17. **Code 1,2,3,4** Jazzy Document *NuGroove*
18. **One Step At a Time** Jay Williams *Big Beat*
19. **Anthem (Remix)** N-Joi *RCA*
20. **Nightlife** Al Mack Project *Strictly Rhythm*
21. **Do It To the Music** Street Side Boyz *Burnin' House*
22. **Till We Meet Again** Inner City *Virgin-import*
23. **Your Love Never Fails** Agape Sounds *Red Heat*
24. **Seasons of Love** Keith Nunnaly *Giant*
25. **Touch Me Baby** Static *Strictly Rhythm*

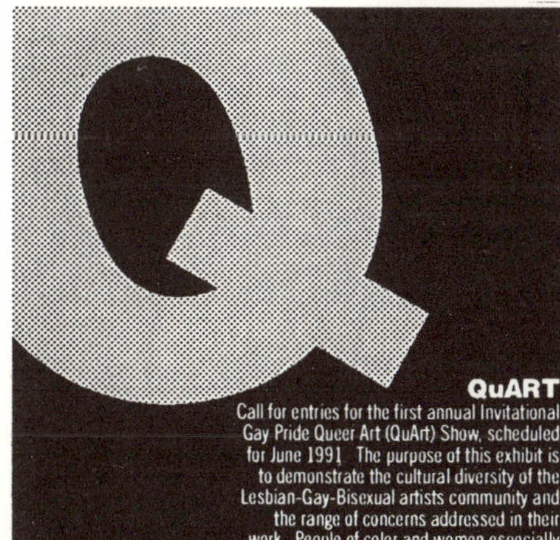

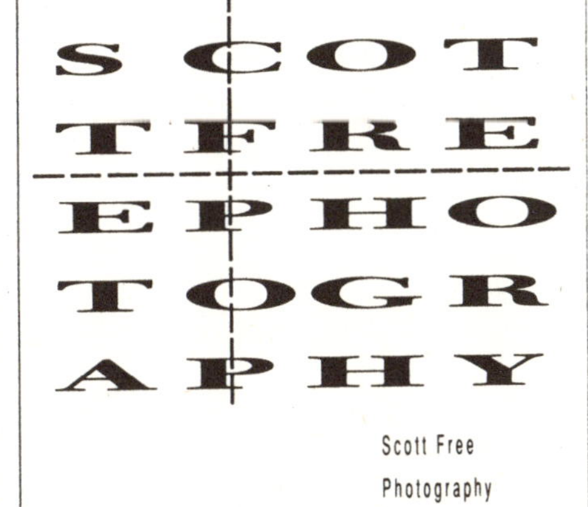

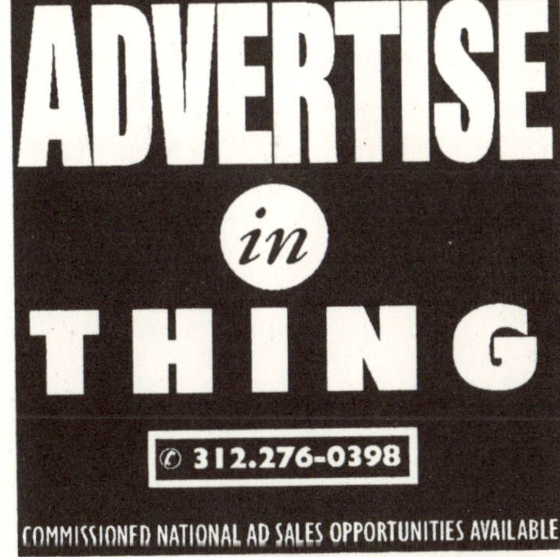

Cycles

Cycles hand-painted beads symbolize the duality of cycles of life. Some claim that they raise one's spirit.
Beads from $3
Necklaces from $15

Anne Raskin
2217 W. Belmont
Chicago, IL 60618
(312) 525-8495

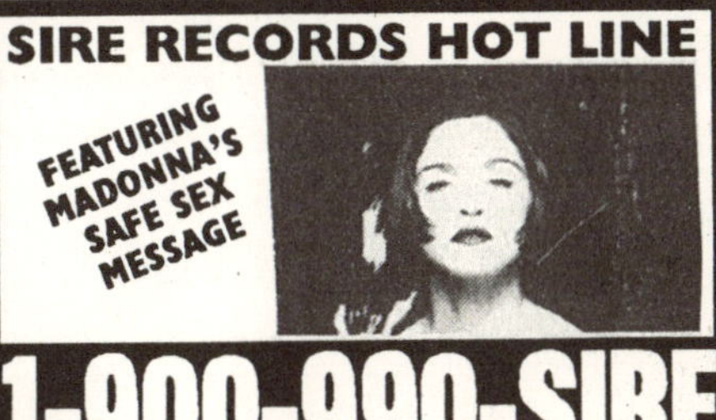

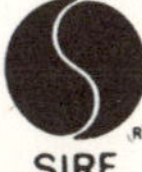

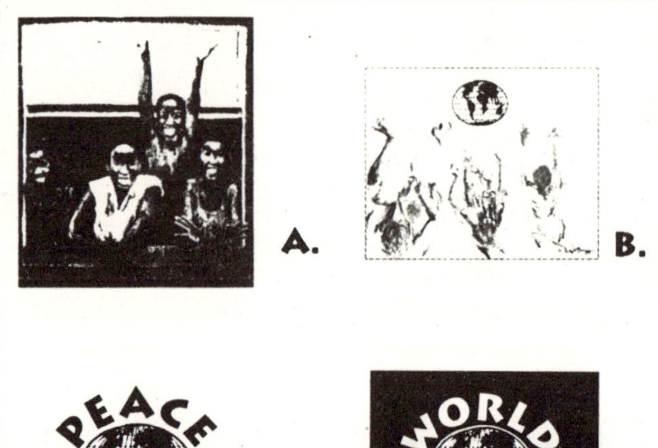

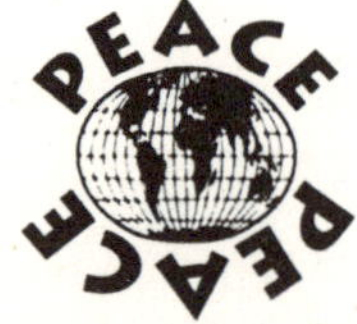

POSTERS AVAILABLE!
BLACK AND WHITE LIMITED EDITION PEACE POSTERS DESIGNED BY SIMONE BOUYER AND SHEREE A. SLAUGHTER. PRICE: $5. FOUR GRAPHIC DESIGNS TO CHOOSE FROM!

A NEW TREND IN GRAPHIC POETRY

A friend of yours feeling down, want to give them a lift?
Simone and Sheree have put together just the perfect gift.
It's a poster or a greeting card with a very special design.
There's a poem added to it so you can say what's on your mind.
Do you have a vision? Simone will draw it out.
Sheree can tell you in a poem what it will be about.
So drop us a line and don't delay,
It doesn't matter if you're straight or gay
We offer something unlike the rest,
And we promise it will be our best
Check us out and you will see,
a new trend in graphic poetry.

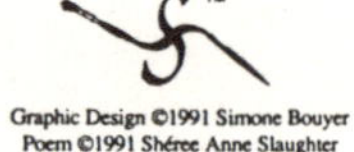

Graphic Design ©1991 Simone Bouyer
Poem ©1991 Shérée Anne Slaughter

Clip the coupon below and send all orders (Checks or money orders payable to Simone Bouyer) to:

PLANET ROC
P.O. BOX 476996
CHICAGO, IL 60647-6996

Name ___________________________________

Address _________________________________

City ____________________ State ___________

Zip ____________ Phone ___________________

I am ordering Poster Style (indicate letter) __________

____ **Special orders**, use a seperate sheet to describe.

sex, lies, & audiotape

Word has it that **Civillies and Cole** are looking for three humpy, multi-ethnic boys to form a singing trio à la **Seduction,** called **Erection**... **Candy J, Amanda Lear, Felly,** and **Katrin Quinol** are teaming up to cohost "Real Fish", where the world's leading gynecologists can win prizes by most correctly guessing the gender of todays music superstars... **Vanilla Ice** resents the rumours that have developed due to his stage name. He's been known to do light S&M occasionally... **Mariah Carey** has been pegged to star in the new remake of "Imitation of Life"...OUT IN THE WASH: Now it can be told; **Martha Wash** sang for everybody! She's talking with attourneys to receive compensation for her ghost vocals for **Aretha Franklin, Leontyne Price, Nana Mouskouri, Yma Sumac** and **Grace Jones**...Manhattan's **Amanda Lapore** has been approached to star in the "**Dianne Brill** Story," a mini-series for Fox...**Nancy Wilson's** daughter and **Esther Philip's** nieces have decided to do the black **Wilson Philips** act.

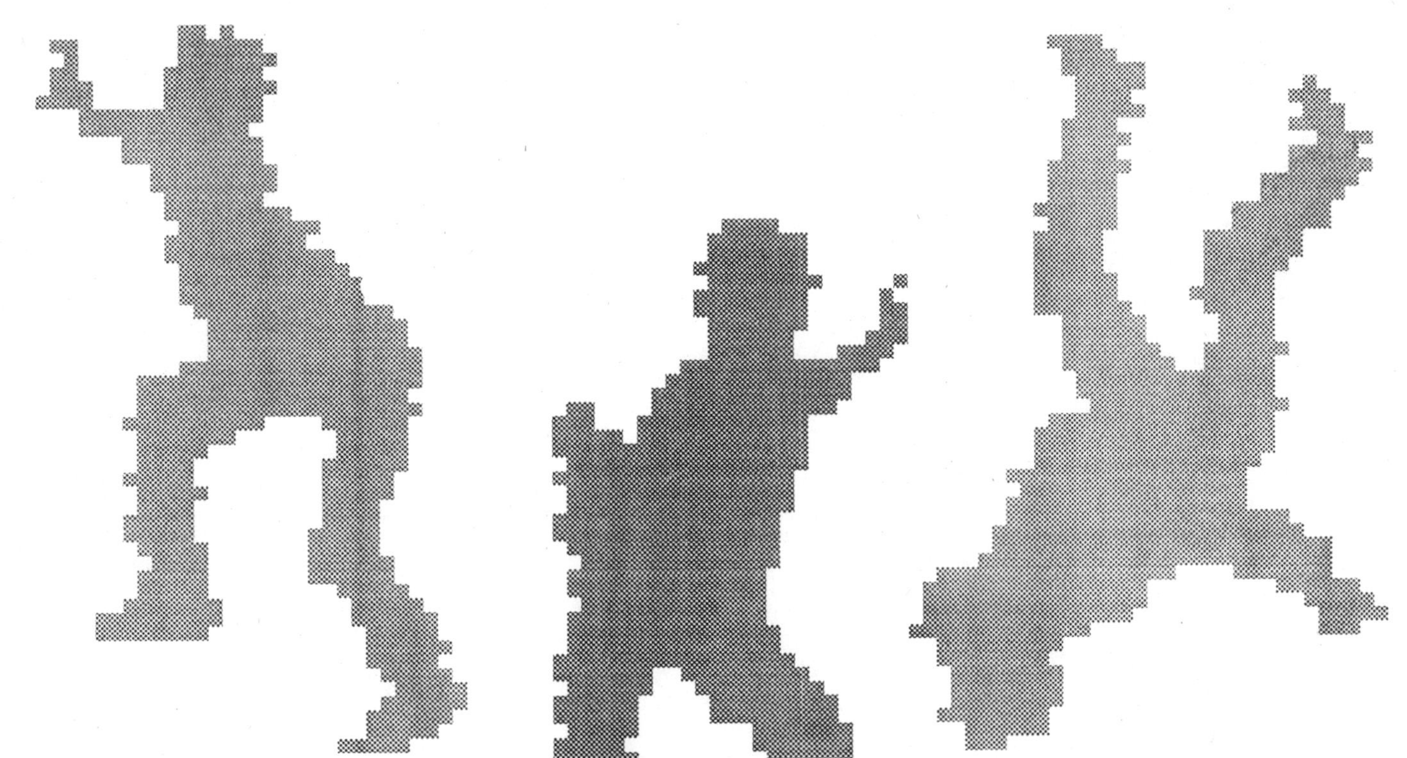

DON'T GIVE THIS STUFF A BAD RAP.

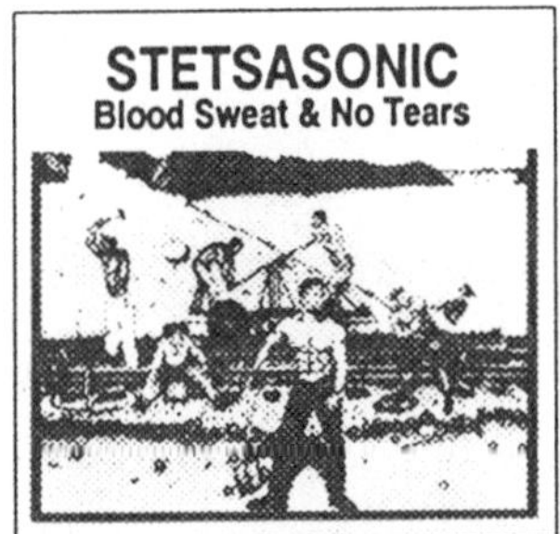

Electric and brutal, Stetsasonic is back, with seventeen killer cuts. New single and video: "No B.S. Allowed."

Do the humpty-hump. Those "Sex Packet" boys are back with fresh remixes, and four new songs. Featuring the new hit single "Same Song."

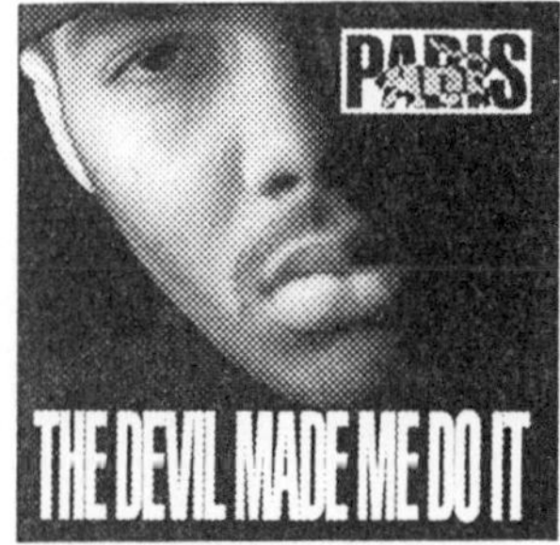

Paris — Black Nationalist, radical rap. Funk driven, low frequency rhythms, combining hard core hip hop, razor-edged rock, jazz and hypnotic funk.

ON TOMMY BOY CASSETTES, COMPACT DISCS AND RECORDS

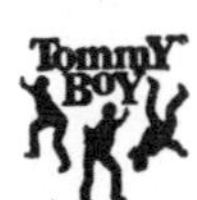

THING

lists.

Bad Press

"Chicago's coolest hip-hop paper"
— People Like Us

"Loose"
— Planet Roc

"...heavier on gossip than ideas"
— Frighten the Horses

"also from Oceanland"
— Lincoln Bulliten

"...to whom the more extreme acid house is punk"
— Dennis Cooper

"Lightweight"
— Bill Van Parys

"Kick It Girls"

Batgirl
Emma Peel
Two Tons O' Fun
Wilona Woods
Mary Wilson
Flo Ballard
Cindy Birdsong
Natasha Fatale
Super Girl
The Girl From U.N.C.L.E.
Jethrine
Miss Hathaway
Serena
Miss Moneypenny
Ethel Mertz
Betty Rubble
Millie Helper
Tara King

Po' Child

any Kennedy
any Sheen
any Barrymore
any Zappa
Liza Minnelli
Lorna Luft
Zowie Bowie
Chastity Bono
Kristy McNichol
CC Hunt
Tracie Spencer
Sinitta
Cheri
Mario Van Peebles
Shari Belafonte
Melanie Griffith
Another Bad Creation
New Kids On the Block
Isabella Rosellini
Todd Bridges
Paloma Picasso
Claude Picasso
Little Gloria, happy at last
Carter Cooper
Edie Sedgwick
LaToya Jackson
Rodney Allen Rippy
Christian Brando
Christina Crawford
Kadeem Hardison
Tawnee Welch
Tiffany
Debbie Gibson
Brooke Shields
Neneh Cherry
Jane Fonda
Peter Fonda
Carrie Fischer
Wilson Philips
Jade Jagger
Nancy Sinatra
Baby Jane Hudson
Blanche Hudson
Rhoda (the bad seed)
Little Orphan Annie
Tiny Tim
Sweet Pea
Emanuel Lewis
Veda Pierce
Princess Yasmin Aga Khan
Princess Caroline
Princess Stephanie
Richie Daley
Emilio Estevez
Macaulay Culkin
Brooke Shields
Rae Dawn Chong
Banig
Raven Simone
Dana Plato
Kitten

Famous Words

Fame costs, and right here is where you start payin'...in sweat
— *Debbie Allen*

I wanna live forever
— *Irene Cara*

In the future, everyone will be famous for fifteen minutes.
— *Andy Warhol*

I'm a star so love me, Goddamn it
— *Leslie Rejanee*

We'll call her "Vicki Vicki". That's "Vicki Vicki"
— *"A Star Is Born" (1937)*

The house of Extravaganza, the house of Dupree, who the hell are they? They're nobody, except when they're in that little ballroom.
— *Willie Ninja*

Don't give up your day job
— *Traditional*

Everybody Is a star
— *Sylvester Stewart*

Baby, I'm a star
— *Prince*

You're a superstar/that's what you are/you know it
— *Madonna*

I'm a winner, baby! They love me,Mahogany!
— *Diana Ross in "Mahogany"*

Look at all the fabulous people
— *Sylvester*

There's only one star in a Helen Lawson production and that's me, baby, Helen Lawson
— *Susan Hayward in "The Valley of the Dolls"*

...but I got a lot of publicity out of it.
— *Betty Boo*

Sing out, Louise!
— *"Gypsy"*

One Good Time For The Captain

Captain Nemo
Cap'N Crunch
Captain Kangaroo
Captain Queeg
Captain May I
Captains Courageous
Captain and Tenille
Captain Fantastic
O Captain, My Captain
Captain Kirk
Captain Picard
Captain America
Captain Bligh
Captain Hook
Captain Howdy
Mon Capitaine
Captain Morgan
Captain EO
Captain Stubing
Captain Ahab
Captain Long John Silver
the Skipper, too

Had the ticket but missed the boat

Phyllis Hyman
Nona Hendryx
Teena Marie
Angela Bofil
Nancy Wilson
Millie Jackson
Pia Zadora
Irene Cara
Cheryl Lynn
Freda Payne

Can We Talk?

Marsha Warfield
Michael Musto
Whoopi Goldberg
André Braugher
Grace Jones
Marlon Riggs
Naomi Campbell
Veronica Webb
Kim Webb
Spike Lee
Keenen Ivory Wayans
Nelson George
RuPaul
George Wayne

Cry Uncle

Uncle Festus
Uncle Martin
Uncle Henry
Uncle Ernie
Uncle Tom
Uncle Bill
Uncle Sam
Uncle Authur
Uncle Milty
Uncle Remus
Uncle Charlie
Uncle Buck
The Man From U.N.C.L.E.
Aunt Jemima

Call Your Lawyer

J.B. Ross
Dewayne A. Powell
Shelby Webb Jr.
Sammy Davis
Alyson Bouldon
A. Strode
Courtney B. Minor
David C. Cumberbatch

Litter-a-ture

I Know Why the Catty Queen Reads
Nightwood
Moby Dick
Tale of Two Titties
Myra Breckenridge
My Life As a Man
Querelle

John Bernard Jones' List of Un-Things

1. Poverty- Yours, mine, everyone else's.
2. Talk show topics- who invited this militant environmentalist ex-skinhead interracial adoptee to my party, anyway?
3. The Bold and the Beautiful- the soap opera and queens who think they are.
4. Gold- how many dead South Africans have you hung around your neck today?
5. EM Magazine- How many more is-sex-better-before-or-after-cum? articles can they write?
6. Convoluted geometric haircuts- If you didn't get it in school, having it cut in your head won't help now.
7. AIDS- the politically correct item to include, but I'm not wild about any disease to begin with.
8. Cigarettes, alcohol and drugs- Never tried them, never will. Three very real threats to Black men.
9. Dummies- If your trade thinks S&L crisis involves a shortage of whips, spank him and trade him in.
10. The Disney Corporation- And you thought you had to worry about the Japanese!

WHAT IS **CELEBRITY?**

When one asks who's who, what one really may be asking is why? Sometimes celebrity comes as a birth right, as is the case with certain royalty (or Tatum O'Neal, Mario Van Peebles, Shari Belefonte, Jenny Lumet, et al.). Are Claus Von Bulow or Bess Myerson `celebrated´? Never mind, Sukreet Gable is. Celebrated people, these days, happen to be any and everybody celebrating or being celebrated for anything. Imagine Mrs. Fletcher careening from the heavens, landing at just the right time and place even though she's ``…fallen and can't get up.´´ If there's room for a `galaxy´ of stars, we can safely assume that somewhere between Rachel Ward and ``Screamin´ ´´Rachel Cain lies a whole strata of, er, heavenly bodies all twinkling at varying intensities. Acts like Milli Vanilli and Black Box suggests that so-called talent is optional or at least of questionable merit. Take a hint from John Waters. Nowadays, if celebrity implies elitism it also happens as something self-created or homegrown. New media stars and personalities are manufactured as quickly as you can say Pia Zadora. Besides, with half a mind, a typewriter, and a xerox copier, one can create one's own media stars. Hell, *you* can be the star! Fortunately, persons within the marginal communities, like women and gays and lesbians, are empowering themselves, armed with camcorders and at-home presses — creating, collecting and dessiminating art and information that's crucial to their survival. The flow of ideas and real progress eventually define who gets to be noted or renowned for anything — be they infamously fraudulent or the famed real thing.

Vaginal Creme Davis

by Steve Lafreniere

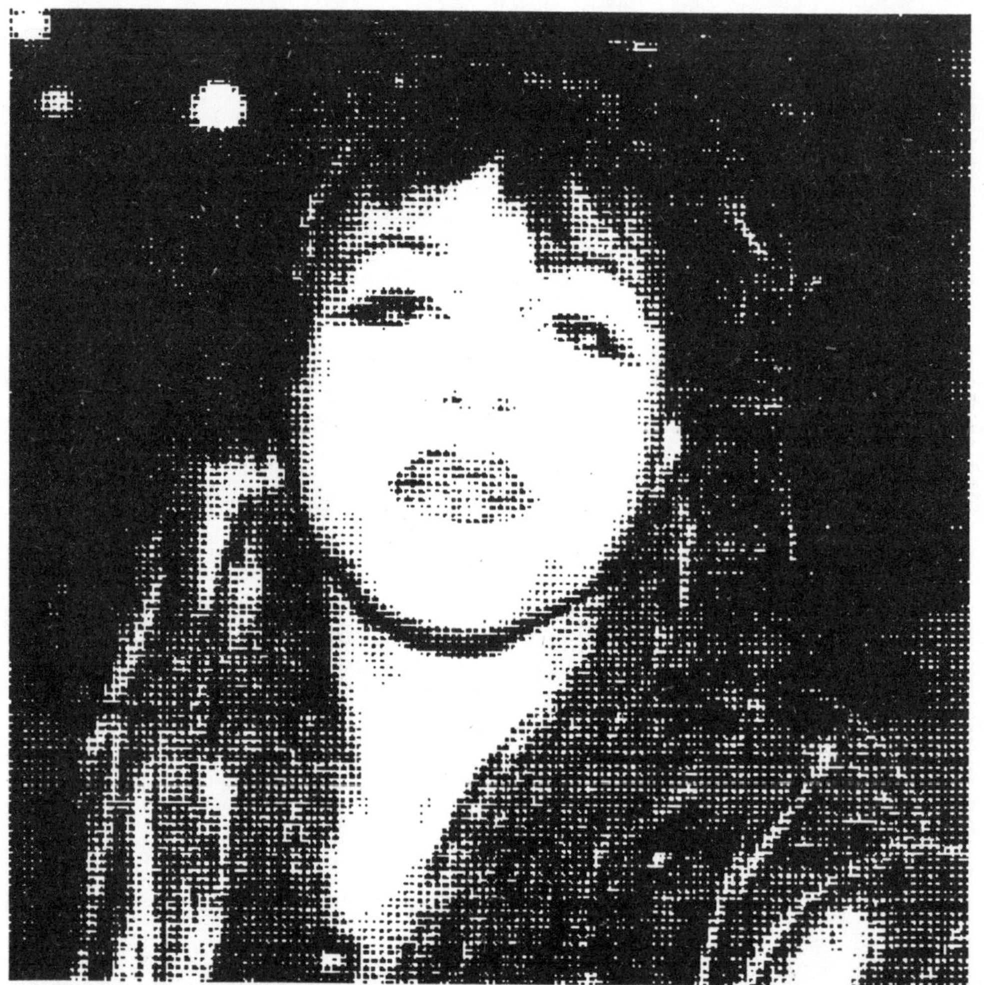

Blacktress **Vaginal Davis**, photographed by Bimbox publisher **Johnny Noxzema**, out lunching at Troy in L.A.

Steve Lafreniere: Would you consider the Afro Sisters a musical act?

Vaginal Davis: Well, the Afro Sisters sing *a capella*, original songs that I write, to a recorded musical backing track. When the Afro Sisters started, around...I don't know, '83, '84...we were purely *a capella*. And we'd go into a kind of rap banter, and then into me doing a little spiel telling everybody where I'm comin' from. Then I'd go into reading my poetry and whatnot.

SL: Oh you're a poet too? I've never seen any poetry in *Fertile La Toyah Jackson Maga-zine.*

VD: I do my poetry separately. I may print some of my poetry in the upcoming issue. It'll probably be our "Literary Issue." When we started off, it was me and two biological females. Vaginal Davis and the Afro Sisters, Urethra Franklin and Clitoris Turner. Clitoris Turner was going through some problems with a junkie boyfriend, the usual punk rock problems. She tried to commit suicide, and her family came out and got her. She was really a great Afro Sister, she had an amazing voice. When it came time to replace her I decided to use a boy instead of a girl. A white male. And then I used another white female, and made her Cherry Jefferson. When we got onstage no one could really tell which ones were drag queens, and which ones were the real girls. And I like that, I like keeping people guessing. I mean, I'd get on stage and people would even speculate as to whether I was a boy or a girl. Which I think is ludicrous, because first of all I'm 6-foot-6. I've been described as being part Harlem Globetrotter and part beautiful black Amazon. So, for someone to be in limbo as to whether I'm a boy or a girl, no matter how perfect my makeup looks, they're a little off. But I guess under the lights and stuff, any illusion is possible!

SL: Have you found happiness?

VD: Well, honey..there's no way....I don't consider myself an actor , and I don't consider myself a singer even though I sing, and I have acted in under-ground things and above-ground things. And I really don't consider myself a performance artist, although I'm lumped into the category. Perform-

What would the homocore movement of underground gay zines be without that wondrous bible of libel, *Fertile Latoyah Jackson Magazine?* Edited by Hollywood's famed performance queenpin/blacktress Vaginal Creme Davis, *Fertile Latoyah Jackson Magazine* is an hilarious account of the very hot days and nights of Vag and her cohorts the Afro Sisters, a multiracial, maxigenderal gang of "talented persons." The only way to describe *Fertile Latoyah Jackson Magazine* to someone is to show it to them. Ditto Miss Davis, who, as member of three musical acts (The Afro Sisters, Cholita, and Pedro Muriel and Esther) and sought-after mistress of ceremonies (Fuck Club, Café Hag, Sissy Club USA, Sit and Spin and sundry other Sin Bros. events) is one of the Los Angelenos currently slapping that city awake to a new decade. Let's all pray the goddess that a 6-foot-6, occasionally platinum-blonde, African-American drag queen becomes one of the archetypes of the '90s.

ance art...what is that? I mean, people want everything figured out for them.

SL: I read where you recently mc'd a big Sin Bros. event in L.A.

VD: Mmmmm-hmm, it was an event for ACT UP. We raised, oh God, about 17 or 18 thousand dollars, and it was like 1500 people. It was one of the first events that brought together the funky homos and the old school homos. All the really mainstream homos were there checking us out , like, "What is this with these homos with tattoos and piercings, and the shaved heads and the drag queens? What are these people that we never talk to ...what are they *doing?*" The monied homo crowd, the so-called politically correct crowd, the ones who have that showy display of their means. They're fascinated by the new breed. But they don't approve of us, and they wonder why we get so much attention! It's funny because I've been written up in so many magazines lately, like the *Advocate*. Years ago the *Advocate* would have never done anything on me. It hasn't come out yet, I just took the photo for it Saturday. They wanted to see the *FLJM* staff in their office.

SL: So would I.

VD: I went out to the UCLA campus, and found an office, and we just invaded. Used their computers and their whole office area. We brought two half-naked boys, stuck them on a desk and made them mock fuck. We were all dressed like secretaries, so while the drag queens are all busy at the typewriters and the computers and the fax machine, the naked, cute boys are on the desk fucking!

SL: Where do you put together *FLJM*? In your apartment?

VD: More or less. Wherever people donate space for me. Urethra Franklin, she owns a punk rock boutique on Melrose Avenue called Retail Slut. And she has a xerox machine. She bought herself a xerox machine to make her catalogue. Basically, the magazine was an offshoot of the Afro Sisters' performances, because whenever we do a performance I like to give something to my audience. To explain that better I have to go back in time a little. The boys and girls version of the Afro Sisters was about '85, '86, when *Interview* magazine did a piece about us.

SL: I think I remember that.

VD: It was when Andy Warhol was still alive. We were in the segment "New in Los Angeles." I'm in the string bikini. Later, when I played in New York at the Pyramid, all these queens said they cut that picture out and had it up in their dressing rooms. And that really makes a girl feel good.

SL: Have you ever at Wigstock?

VD: No, I've never performed there. I've talked to Lady Bunny about her doing a version of Wigstock on the west coast, though.

SL: At a speedway.

VD: I would like it to be kind of like a California Jam. In a park in Hollywood! But we want it to be huge. Bunny and I performed at a benefit in June in San Francisco at the AIDS conference. It was at a club called Collossus. They had drag queens from all over. They had DeAundra Peak from Atlanta, and me and Glen Meadmore and Chanda Lear and Jomala represented LA. The drag rock band Chastity from San Francisco. And Lady Bunny representing New York. And Lurleen, she came out from Atlanta. It was a benefit for ACT UP, and there were tons of people. I even got to see Lady Bunny not in drag. We both went to the Church of Phallic Worship. And honey, we went for communion! And we both had ourselves a really good time because, honeeeey, those San Francisco boys are frisky! And they enjoy us queens!

SL: You go to a lot of celebritiy parties that don't even make it to the magazine, right?

VD: Oh yeah. A lot I don't write about because they're so boring. People think that the entertainment industry here in Los Angeles , that it's all so glamorous and exciting, and in the long run people in the entertainment industry are very middle class. Their aspirations are real, y'know...having nice things. That's about it. They're quite boring. That's why the movies and music that you hear on the radio is so dull, because these people don't know anything about art, and they have not one creative bone in their bodies. They pay us weird people, like drag queens, to come to their dumb parties just to liven them up!

SL: Out of all those people, you have to have some favorites.

VD: The thing is, we ...the drag queens and whatnot who get invited to these things...we rate them according to the food spread, and the liquor. If it's a good food spread ...a lot of us girlies out here are vegetarians...if they have a large selection for vegetarians, that's how we rate a lot of the parties. And how good the liquor is, y'know, whether it's just beer and wine or mixed drinks. Things like that.

SL: In the last issue, there was a steamy encounter between you and Anthony of the Red Hot Chili Peppers. Did that actually, umm...occur?

VD: Honeeeeey, Anthony went to the same junior high school as my Afro Sister Fertile. They went to Bancroft Junior High School. And before Anthony was a Red Hot Chili Pepper, he was just a punk kid.

SL: Are you originally from Los Angeles?

VD: Honey! I was born in Watts. You know, the Watts riots?

SL: I know Watts.

VD: A lot of these people were more or less street kids. Like

Flea, he was in porno magazines posing, because he has a really big wiener. He was a male prostitute.

SL: But he's straight, right?

VD: Well, he's married now and he has a kid, but what does that mean? It doesn't mean very much. Before he was in the Red Hot Chili Peppers, he was in a band called Fear. With Lee Ving and Derf Scratch.

SL: Do you know Dennis Cooper?

VD: Oh yeah, Dennis Cooper just moved back here after living in New York. Miss Cooper is back in LA now. He just did a piece in *L.A. Weekly* talking about Fertile Latoyah Jackson. He loves Fertile. In L.A. there's a lot going on now. With my friend who's a fashion stylist, we did a club last week called Café Hag. It's a thing we do about once a month where we convert this little Czechoslovakian restaurant in Hollywood, we turn it into, like, Bricktop's, a little Paris speakeasy. You get a buffet dinner and then nonstop performers doing 1920s music. A lot of people that performed are out of the punk scene , and here they were singing songs from the 1920s. Somewhat cabaret style, but also New Orleans style. I was dressed real Louise Brooks and singing songs like "Muddy Water," and doing the Shimmy and the Black Bottom.

SL: It sounds a little like the Cockettes in the late '60s. That's sort of a constant with drag queens, that 1920s period. In the '70s it got all fucked up once middle America picked up on it, and started wearing polyester baggies and Cork-Eez. But even that was kind of hilarious. Are you familiar with the Cockettes and their version of home-grown fantasy and perversity, or...

VD: Well, Sylvester was a Cockette.

SL: But do your ideas, the magazine, performances , etc., come out of that homemade ethos?

VD: The Afro Sisters and Fertile Latoyah Jackson's performances and videos come out of the fact that there are a group of talented and creative people here in the city who create their OWN outlets; who have their own audience, their own support system. We can't just go into a studio and make a deal and make a movie...so we make our OWN movies. And we distribute them through an underground network so that people find out about us. And honey, the weird thing about it is that now, I go out and do my own films on little...video. And word gets out and...I just got offered to do a play! It was a stupid play and I turned it down because the part was really lame, but the reason I got offered this was not because I went knocking on doors and went on interviews. It was because of my magazine, because of the videos. I'd been seen on a cable show called "Decoupage," AND THEY CAME TO ME! You've got to make those things for yourself first, by doing it as cheaply as possible with whatever resources you've got. You've got to do it yourself. And not even THINK about what you're doing, just have a good time, have fun, and doing YOUR SHIT. And get it out there, and then those other stupid people, if they're interested...fine. But you don't even worry about that.

SL: Do you think this determined attitude of yours, which is currently paying off in at least the fame department, is that something that poor white and poor black queens share? From not ever having a lot, so your expectations aren't as easily... disappointed?

VD: I remember the first time we played in front of a really large audience. Since a majority of the Afro Sisters are white, in the guise of black people, they were saying, "Oh God, they're gonna lynch us! Here we are in afros, they're gonna think we're making fun of black people!" I said, "Don't worry about it, it'll be cool. They'll realize where we're coming from." And we went out there and we performed in front of all these black people, and, honey, they wanted my magazine...they were just saying, "That was hot!" And these were straight black people. At first they were like, "What is this?" They were, like, all angry. But once I got up there and started going into my thing, they could relate to it. Because it wasn't all stodgy and old school. It was quick and direct and to the point and it gave them a whole new look at a homosexual context. Of someone who's gay and black...and fearless in telling them, "Lookit, I'm gay, I'm black, I'm a drag queen, I'm dressed up and I'm shoutin' and yellin' and I'm a MILITANT!" You know? "I'll tell that white man!" And here I've got these white kids who are in my group, and they feel the same way too. They're feeling so strongly, they've taken on a black identity, not in jest, but because they identify with blackness. I would start the show off by walking up to the mike saying, "I'm black and I'm very, very proud." It always got a big laugh.

SL: I don't understand where Fertile comes in, though.

VD: Fertile came in a little bit down the line, later. Not until '87, early '88. Urethra Franklin every year would take her little European vacation. So one year she went on vacation, and I had a friend who is El Salvadoran take her place, and he became Urethra Franklin. He was so funny and original portraying her, I wanted him to stay in the group. So I had to create a new character for him, the character of Fertile Latoyah Jackson. Always pregnant, always giving birth, sort of a mother figure, icon. His character became the most popular character. That's why she's the perennial cover girl, she's on the cover of every issue of the magazine. Because ...you've seen the picture of her, look at that face! It says enough right there! What do you get when you see that face?

SL: What do you mean?

VD: Well, you have to admit, that's a different kind of face. Hooooooney, it's spelled out right there! The image of that face

and what it conjures up, all these maternal feelings, the madonna....A lot of people think Fertile is a real woman. But, then a lot of white people are so one-sided, when they see a bunch of white people dressed up in "black" clothes and what-not, they think they ARE black.

SL: The magazine is so well dreamt up. It's got this consistency, and what's great is how you can't even tell what's true and what's not. It's full of lies, but who cares?

VD: Well, yeah that's the point, y' know? But I do use a lot of pseudonyms in there because I'm always creating...I'm like Sybil, honey. I've got more faces than "The Three Faces of Eve." I've got all these personalities revolving through me.

SL: So you've been doing this your whole life?

"Lookit, I'm gay, I'm black, I'm a drag queen, I'm dressed up and I'm shoutin' and yellin' and I'm a MILITANT!"

VD: When I started school it was in the MGM program. For mentally gifted minors. The learning was very accelerated. But since I didn't fit the stereotype of a mentally gifted minor, a lot of the white teachers that I had saw me as a problem. I would question things that children didn't question. I was always argumentative, always challenging them, because I had this innate desire to learn. Because I think the education system in this country sucks! It really...sucks! And they were always calling my mother down, and they were saying that I was causing problems. You know? This was the rhetoric I got from grade one to high school.

SL: Plus it's a racist system.

VD: Oh definitely. Two of my Afro Sisters, Fertile, who is El Salvadoran, and Pussy Washington, who is Mexican, both are elementary school teachers. That's Fertile's day job! Both of them teach kindergarten and first grade. And the school board is so fucked it makes me and them very angry. They're so tied up in their fucking bureaucracy that they won't let good

teachers teach. In L.A. there's a lot of Spanish-speaking kids, but they want to rule out bi-lingualism, and that's the only thing that helps these kids learn. Both Fertile and Pussy work in the communities that they came out of, and they're giving back to their communities.

SL: Pussy Washington is a great name.

VD: Her real name is Alice Bag. She was in one of the seminal L.A. punk bands, the Bags. And she's also in my band Cholita, an offshoot of the Afro Sisters. We're like the female Menudo. We just played a new club here called Sissy Club USA, and she and I collaborated on some original material. Before, we just lip-synched obscure latin pop records. Our new songs in Spanish are really funny.

SL: Are you going to get all this stuff out on record?

VD: Well, my speed-metal thrash band *(Pedro Muriel & Esther -ed.)*, we're gonna do a record on America Records.

SL: Do you know the artist Mike Kelley?

VD: Oh, yeah, he's the one who does the little felt thing. He's so funny! He had a showing at a gallery here on gallery row, La Cienega Boulevard, and, like, it would be this piece of dirty felt, stuck with a thumb tack on the wall! And it'll be like $12,000! It's so funny!

SL: He's got a band with Raymond Pettibon.

VD: Oh I know Raymond Pettibon! I think the band is called Raymond Pettibon's Supersession. I think they just did a show.

SL: To end with, my friend Wendy wanted me to ask you this one. What does the phrase, "Fear of a Female Planet" mean to you?

VD: Well, I think the powers that be, the great white corporate structures, they're afraid of the feminine. But, honey, they should just relax and let loose, because there's a lot of power in femininity. The only way for this planet to survive is to not neglect the feminine portions of our personalities, but to revere them and to work with them. Empathy and love and trust. It sounds really simplistic doesn't it?

SL: No it doesn't. It sounds really difficult.

VD: Mmmmmmm——Hmmmmmm. ✪

Fertile LaToyah Jackson Magazine is available by mail. Write: 7850 Sunset Boulevard, penthouse suite 110, Los Angeles, CA 90046

Dennis Cooper & Gary Indiana

by Kathryn Hixson

On the occasion of the Grove Press 1989 publication of Gary Indiana's *Horse Crazy* and Dennis Cooper's *Closer*, the two intrepid auteurs scrambled around the country on what could ostensibly be considered a book tour. Alighting in lecture halls, performance spaces, and bookstores, the wearied duo gave provocative readings of excerpts from their fictive texts, and unabashedly exhorted audiences to join the swelling ranks of proud and enlightned owners of their significant tomes.

Though passed over by the plebian likes of Donahue and Oprah, Indiana and Cooper were besieged by a trickle of stampeding members of the press, eager to delve deep within the peculiar psyches of these formidable writers. After a stint at Randolph Street Gallery, one of Chicago's premiere not-for-profit performance venues, art critic Kathryn Hixson, employing a bribe of dinner at a modest Italian restauraunt, queried the writers on their new work in the context of a hot-house homosexual culture, and within a somewhat cooler mainstream literary society. Effectively exploiting their expertise, Hixson also grilled them on issues close to her heart: objectification of the body in sex and pornography, and the tenuous connections between pleasure and desire.

Kathryn Hixson: Is your work gay literature?

Dennis Cooper: Gay literature is a useless term. It's only useful marketing wise—the gay community supports its writers. There's these bookstores that stock the book, publications that review the book—which is great. Heterosexuals don't tend to get that. But my work is not about homosexuality at all, it's completely relative. It's useless in that sense. I mean Genet and Burroughs...are they gay writers? Is Bataille a heterosexual writer? Its not about that at all. It's not about homosexuality except that it's something that puts you outside of culture, which is where everyone should want to be anyway.

KH: It puts you on the outside of culture?

DC: It gives you a vantage point, so you don't have to participate in the same way, in the way society is set up. I mean the rules are set up for people who want to be happy and make a lot of money and have two kids and blah blah blah. If you don't want that-if you're gay or not gay, really, you don't have to play that game- you can observe it. Homosexuals, all minorities, are excluded from being involved in the process, so you work the margins where everything great always happens anyway.

KH: You're saying that you're marginal and taking the outsider stance, but the writing is saying that you're not.

DC: Well, our writing is not about gay society, gay ritual or thinking about what it means to be homosexual. Who cares?

Gary Indiana: It's not about coming out of the closet.

DC: It's about things that everybody's... fear of the Other, or obsession- things that everybody can relate to. People who are interested in our work are not just gay people. Most gay people are not interested in our work at all. There are some weirdo gay people who are interested. I've been publishing for a long time and I've gotten attacked all the time by the gay press, because they say my work is not politically correct: I shouldn't represent homosexual people as murderers, homosexuals should be represented as good upstanding people or this and that. That's bullshit! This is the first time I've gotten really good reviews in the gay press.

KH: Why do you think that is?

DC: There's a hunger out there for gay writing that isn't total dreck.

GI: There are plenty of self-defined gay novelists who write from the perspective of extreme, white, middle class privilege; who explore the very banal neuroticisms of people coming from that class, with the goals and ambitions of that class, which is assimilationist in a way I would never want to be. But that's not to say it has anything to do with being gay or not being gay, because if I had writrten a book about a man and a woman, people would be comparing it to *Lolita* or something. The

more conservative reviews in the trades say, "Despite the very specific sexual preferences of the main characters, this has universal appeal." It's ludicrous. It's just people, that's all.

DC: It's much more about being united with people that aren't officially sanctioned—blacks or women...

GI: You notice that we always have to define ourselves. Something that a woman does is always defined as something done by a woman, or a black or a gay. Heterosexual white males do not ever have to define themselves. They operate from a presumption of supreme cultural power where all else is the Other. But in fact, to me, they're the Other. I was told, and you can print this, that *Elle* magazine wasn't going to review my book, or Dennis' because they'd already reviewed David Leavitt's novel, which was the fag novel for the year— they weren't going to do any more— they'd done their part.

KH: But your work is still about homosexual culture.

DC: Mine isn't. It's about isolated individuals.

GI: Mine isn't, because my audience in New York for years was the audience for my theatre plays, which was basically the art world, which is very heterogenous. And my column (for the *Village Voice*) was not for a coterie audience, it was a mass audience. I don't feel like I'm specifically writing for other gay people, I'm writing for people like me. I know women that are like me, I know black people that are like me, gay people, and I know some straight guys that are like me.

DC: My concerns are much closer to, like, Sonic Youth. That's really where I come from. It's never been homosexual-specific. The characters are really isolated people. They talk about being gay occasionally , but it's not a central concern to them.

GI: I'm much more interested in defining the fact that writers like us are characterized by a sense of rebelliousness, and of telling unpleasant truths about thing, or just the truth about things, in the same way as an artist like Barbara Krueger - any number of other people do. The AIDS stuff, for instance, is another example of people's notion of politics. There is such a thing as realpolitik: things you have to do in the public sphere to get support for things or to make certain things happen which involves a certain amount of lying, or a certain amount of oversimplification.

But you're writing a piece of fiction and you're writing about real emotions, not the phony ones that people say to each other at funerals. You have to deal with your own fear of mortality, rather than pretending that you are this completely altruistic, idealistic person who suffers the loss of the other for their sake, rather than your own sake. I thought it was sort of important to get at certain issues that are not being dealt with in all of the AIDS literature. I'm not saying that I am trying to do anything extensive, but just to put it down the way that it happens, like during the time that I experienced it, and how the people I'm writing about feel about it, rather than the correct political sentiments they may say in public in a situation where

they're trying to raise money. The thing in Dennis' book about assholes, that complete objectification of something, how you were saying the other day, how much easier it is to look at an asshole than a face because you have to read so much information into a face and it's so complicated. But everybody, no matter what their orientation, goes through some process of objectification like that with their sexual partners at one time or another, or maybe all of the time.

KH: Is objectification a necessary part of sex?

DC: I think it should be fought, but I don't know- on the other hand, sex is much sexier when you are objectifying the other person.

KH: Why is that?

DC: I don't know! That's what is curious about it. I don't think people ever really connect in the way that you are led to believe people connect. I don't believe that souls intertwine, I don't believe it. I believe that we are totally isolated and that we desperately want to connect with each other and we do the best we can, but the idea that you merge with another human being is a lie. To me, it implies a belief in a higher god or something and I just don't believe that stuff.

GI: I believe that most people spend half their lives dumping the emotions that they think they should have, and dumping a lot of false consciousness. My book is about getting rid of a certain kind of obsessive fixé on another person, which is like total objectification, projection on a scrim, or what you want. You can take anybody and do it. There was a time in my life when I could look over there, see somebody, end up following them down the street, and spending a year of my life being insane about them. Everybody I know has done that, and those are false emotions, because you don't know that other person well enough to...

DC: When I was teenager, I was always suicidal and I would always put on Leonard Cohen's *Songs Of Love and Hate*. I would want it to give me the courage to kill myself, because it was all about that stuff. I think that is really common, and if not pop music, then something else - television.

GI: One area where gay culture does deserve some credit is like the demystification of Hollywood movies through the analysis of subtext, especially a camp subtext. In movies you can see much more how the machinery of sentiment is assembled. I feel that human beings all have essentially the same needs, and feelings and they are very simple feelings.

KH: What are they?

GI: The need to be nurtured, to be cared for...

DC: Security...

GI: Security. There's a classical range of feelings that everybody has. The trouble is that they are contradictory feelings because as children everyone has wishes. We are all creatures of wishes, and everybody does have a utopian longing. We want our parents to live forever, and at the same time we want them to be dead when we don't want them around. We are completely contradictory in our emotional life, because what we want are our wishes -which are utopian and unfulfillable- and so those get channelled into areas of culturally overdetermined plausibilities - you will fall in love with a suitable person, you will have children, you will do this, you will do that, you will have a happy life. There are all of these formulas that have to do with love and the correct channelling of negative feelings. Culture is a big factory for that use of emotions. There's also a state control of emotional life. You are always defined in a group, in a nation, in a country, you have these antagonists, these are your enemies -these are your allies . Then it breaks down into ethnic groups and special interest groups. You have to hate this one because they are not you- Everybody defines themselves in terms of the other, that's other I'm me. And the state makes use of it. For example television, the voice of the state, constant prescriptions of how to apply your emotions to everyday life. In the totally crude, barbaric TV culture, all resolution of conflict is through the model of the nuclear family. All social conflict is resolved by dividing social problems into criminals and the power of the state - the police and the criminal, and all social problems are resolved in the heart of the nuclear family. The family is the place where all conflicts between people can be resolved, and on the political level, conflicts can be resolved through the justice system and the punishment of criminals.

KH: Give me more.

DC: That's the way they want you to be, but you have to take an anarchical position. You have to really trust yourself. Trust what your eyes see. I mean you're constantly being told that people are not like you, the Russians, the blacks, straights and gays are different. The fact is that that we all have exactly the same needs. In *Closer*, George lets these things go on because he understands that Philipe is, like, fucked up and he needs to fuck some kid over, and he's like, "Ok, I understand this, I understand what's going on," and they all know that they're all fucked up and that's why it's like a sealed world and he's just like, "Yeah, ok. He needs to fuck somebody over."

KH: He'll be the victim

DC: Yeah, whatever... He doesn't care, or he feels this will fulfill his destiny. Or, I don't know why. You know, it's like a murderer, anybody can relate to a murderer. You don't do it, you don't have to do it to understand what it's about. It comes out of feelings that all of us possess. And fear. Its so important to understand that, but television, all those things are telling

us not to feel that way.

KH: The other thing...

DC: Yeah, they're isolating us in the wrong way. They are isolating us so much, making us believe that we are all so different from each other. It's so crazy! It's not just America. It's in every country, virtually.

KH: Why do you think there's this dictation of sentiment, or channeling of emotion? Is it merely to sustain the status quo?

GI: Traditionally, every state has the ambition to control everybody. It's the nature of the state. They do it through a moral code. They join forces with religion. If you see the kind of hatefulness that's manufactured in this country, phobias that people... incredible, fundamentalist hatred of sexuality, hatred of the body, hatred of the autonomy of individual human beings. When you look at that hatred objectively, you see that it's an hysterical denial of childhood wishes and impulses of polymorphous perversity. Hysterical denial of some pleasurable experience they may have had with a child of their own sex or another sex. It comes out of a puritan hysteria.

DC: What is so disgusting is that the answer to everything is religion, you can't argue with God. You can present this argument, "Well but, well but." Then they say, "Well, God tells us this is wrong," and you can't change their minds. They have this ridiculous excuse. This moral majority stuff is so manipulative and evil. How can you argue with that? It's a way of not thinking. They follow these supposedly humanist rules which aren't humanist at all.

KH: The questions abortion raises.

DC: Absolutely. Sex is a really powerful thing.

KH: Right. Why is that?

DC: Because other people are the only thing there is. It's the most intense contact you will ever have.

KH: Is it the best way to communicate?

DC: I don't know if it's the best but you have no choice. You are drawn to physically connect, to couple with other bodies that you are attracted to. It's an overwhelming, uncontrollable urge that has nothing to do with intellectualism or logic or anything. You shouldn't deny that, you should explore that because it's so powerful. What's that about? I don't know. Nobody knows what it's about. It's so incredibly important, it's the center for it's the beginnings of love.

KH: What about pornography?

DC: It's really interesting.

KH: Why?

DC: Well, for me, it's a way to study sex....

KH: What does it have to do with sex?

DC: It has the same relationship to sex as photography has to life. It's a thing by which you see something you wouldn't normally be able to see. It's like putting sex so you can study it, it's like a textbook to me.

KH: Isn't it too staged to have any relationship to reality?

DC: It depends on the sex. I've seen pornography that's so staged that it's absolutey without anything, and I've seen sex that is so full of intent and feeling and ideas that it's obviously something being done that enjoys having a camera on it. I study a lot of pornography, and it's obviously different from each other.

GI: There are lots of different kinds of pornography. I'm completely fascinated with pornography. Partly because it's become another cause that the right wing wants to stamp out, and to say that leads to all sorts of horrible things. I believe the classic old liberal line that it —pornography—makes sex more normal in a lot of ways. People being exposed to it does demystify the fact that people do stick these things into holes in each others' bodies, and there's nothing so outrageously perverse or abnormal about it. Unlike Europe, where at least there's much greater sophistication about the fact that people do have sex. A lot of Americans are brought up believing that people have smooth plastic between their legs. I know that my parents spent their whole lives without ever openly discussing sexuality except in the most stunted and repressed and joking terms. Growing up in that kind of environment, I certainly had a reaction against it. Robert Mapplethorpe was a great pornographer. He just worked from the aesthetic of how can you make pornography look better.

DC: For me, the stuff I've learned the most from is art or literature dealing with sex. Like deSade, everything you want to know about human nature is in his work. His entrance into that is through sex. It's like religion — ecstatic — the most ecstatic you'll ever be is having sex. What else is there?

KH: Why is it so ecstatic?

DC: Because you are connecting with other people and other people are the only interesting thing in the world — other people to be intimate and alone and to be the complete focus of another person and to have them as your focus is fantastic! There's nothing to compare to it.

KH: I'm trying to figure out this objectification thing.

DC: It's a toughie!

KH: Maybe I'm even obsessed with it.

DC: No, I don't care. It's an interesting issue. Some of it's just beyond our understanding.

KH: That's a cop-out.

DC: I don't think so at all. Do you think that intellectualism is the answer? I don't believe that's true. I don't believe that someone who has read all the books knows more than people that haven't read the books.

KH: Absolutely.

DC: There is instinct. There are all kinds of things that have nothing to do with ... you end up giving answers to things that aren't really answers, you're just willing to take an answer to have an answer.

KH: Just to get to the next minute?

DC: Right, we can never answer this question about objectification. Why do people do it? Who knows? We've been wondering ever since time began, or am I being ridiculous?

KH: That makes a lot of sense, but it's still problematic. It might be that I just have a...

DC: Bee in your bonnet. (*Laughter*) Well, are you straight?

KH: Yeah.

DC: Well, maybe it's a whole different thing because women are the victims of objectification in a whole different way than male homosexuals. Males, it's not the same thing.

KH: Really?

DC: Well, in my work, let's say if in *Closer* George were a girl, this would be a completely different book than it is now. Then, it would be about this woman who was a victim of a patriarchal system.

> "I believe the classic old liberal line that it — pornography — makes sex more normal in a lot of ways. People being exposed to it does demystify the fact that people do stick these things into holes in each others' bodies, and there's nothing so outrageously perverse or abnormal about it." —Gary Indiana

KH: Well, maybe that's why it works.

DC: You mean that it isn't a woman? Absolutely, that's one of the tricks of the work.

KH: I don't want to be a victim of patriarchal systems, I'd much rather be a male homosexual. (*Laughter*)

DC: Yeah, that's one of the great things about it. And lesbianism, too, although I guess...

KH: It's different, it's much different.

DC: It's different? Yeah, I guess that's right.

KH: Being in the majority and being a minority at the same time, so you can be inside and outside at the same time. Be critical but still have the power.

DC: Women are the majority aren't they? It's not who's in the majority but who has the power. You may be the majority in South Africa but that doesn't mean you have power. When you are objectifying another man you are objectifying yourself, you're sleeping with someone who's like you. You probably have more of a sense of what they're going to feel when they come. It's a whole different kind of thing. So when you objectify another guy it's partially about yourself. Our work would be very different if it were about women. If Gregory and George were women, it would be very different, I would never have written this book.

KH: That's pretty weird.

DC: It is weird.

KH: I wonder if a book like this could be written by a woman.

DC: A woman? Has anything like that happened?

KH: Not to my knowledge.

DC: Somebody ought to do that. There's a market there! Have you seen Dancenoise?

KH: No.

DC: Oh, they're really good. They deal with this subject - how women are represented in patriarchal society - but also they are just hysterically funny and I am a major fan of theirs. They're two heterosexual women.

KH: I'd heard differently.

DC: No, they are definitely. I just did a piece with Annie, and they are definitely heterosexual.

GI: You do so many things, Dennis.

DC: You do them too, you just do different things than I do.

GI: I just get more and more envious every day.

DC: Don't be envious of me, I suffer so terribly! (*Laughs*) You don't want to live in my head. Read my book- you don't want to live in that head!

GI: You're so industrious.

DC: Yeah, I'm so industrious, so I won't have to feel anything. It's true, it's really true!

KH: Indifference and repression, what's the difference?

GI: Well, I've gotten to an age where I am extremely indifferent to more things than I ever dreamed possible.

KH: Is that good?

GI: Yeah, I think so - it's good to get rid of bad ways of feeling about things, or being overreactive to things. When you're young, you can't let go of anything. As you get a little older, you realize in 30 years you are going to be dead, you might as well get rid of as much crap as you can. I *would* love to be able to fall for somebody in a big way.

KH: You still want that, right?

GI: No, not really.

KH: Yeah you do.

GI: But it would probably generate some more material. I'm burned out on a million and one different kinds of people, it would be impossible for me to get rivetted.

DC: I'm always interested in the same kind of person, always have been —— the George kind of character —— really passive and unable to express himself and relying on other people. I feel so sympathetic, I get really moved by them. I want to give them all power, they have no power, and they want power so badly. The thing is that they don't know what to do with power. I have a history of being involved with people like that, because I get involved with them and I give them all power and I become this horrible mushy nothing and then they don't know what to do with it so they treat me like shit. It's not because they're mean, it's because they don't know what to do. If you give them all power, they've been fucked over so many times that they don't trust, can't possibly trust that you are giving this power to them. It's the kind of thing that just fascinates me. And they're usually very interesting people. A lot of it is in the gay world. Gay men are so terrible towards pretty boys, they just think they're idiots. Very similar to the way men are about women —— beautiful women —— they can't possibly think. Gay men do that a lot. That whole Edmund White generation of writers - which is really that way about people who are beautiful, people who are young. They can be exploited.

GI: Predatory.

DC: Being predatory. That's a problem with homosexuals.

GI: The problem in my book was to try to give it up to Gregory, and to try to give some equality and try to find some equilibrium between them so that nobody would be exploiting anybody. But, of course, the problem is that Gregory has problems that can't be solved within this relationship so it all gets screwed up.

DC: But you get snagged in these things and you can't loosen yourself. It's so hard to free yourself from these situations, because you take on this responsibility, and if you were to drop this person, he'll have nothing because I've given him this power and he needs me, and if I take away that power he's just going to become more fucked up than before. It's a terrible thing.

KH: If desire and pleasure are so different, why do we spend so much time with desire?

GI: Because we are repressed and there isn't much opportunity for pleasure. We don't express it in a direct way. Culturally, it's so different from one place to another. Most places in America, if you make eye contact, they turn away immediately.

DC: In America, pleasure is a term that is usually applied to sex. When I hear the word pleasure I think immediately of floating around a swimming pool in a raft with suntan lotion on. I think of pleasure as being dull, like giving up and closing off your mind. People don't use the word leisure about sex. It's, like, leisure and pleasure.

GI: It's interesting that these things are so monadic in a way, with a family or with a couple or whatever. So much of what's cultural pleasure has been privatized with home video and so people don't go to the movie theatre anymore, sharing something with a whole room full of other people. They're doing something very private when they consume something. The way that these package tours and ocean liner cruises are advertised. I saw one with Bill Cosby the other day holding up pictues of his vacation and sort of sneering at his next door neighbor, "See what I'm doing while you're stuck back there!" And, "If your friends could see you now!" It's all about us vs. them. God forbid we should have anything in common.

DC: The good ol' competitive American spirit.

GI: We are smarter than you are so we get to go on this vacation or buy this car. I suppose that's the way that sexuality is transmorgrified into advertising and consumption in the same way. It's about rub this special crap on yourself and you will be more alluring than the other person and on and on and on. We don't connect just sitting around having a conversation with pleasure, people don't connect in this culture—— it's mediated through consumption.

DC: It's different in Europe. The bar thing; it's terrible because it's associated with alcohol, but people really meet after work in these pubs and talk and talk and talk and talk. It's too bad that it has to be lubricated by alcohol but...

GI: I'll have a beer.

DC: But they do that even in New York. Europe is oriented around communcation much more than we are here.

KH: You have to go further.

DC: Excuse me?

KH: We have to go further.

DC: Than what?

KH: Than just critiquing American culture like that.

DC: I don't do it on purpose. I critique American culture because I don't think about it when I write. The critics write about it, these are products of America, blah blah blah. It's true, but it's not something I do on purpose.

KH: Are you writing from experience?

DC: My own ideas- the fact that the characters in my book use things like pornography and Disneyland and splatter films to mediate things that are painful to them could be seen as a critique of American culture, but it's not something I think about. I was fascinated by Disneyland when I was a kid and I really wanted to live in Disneyland, like George does, and I really thought that was the way the world was supposed to be. So it's really just a personal thing, my own disappointments, and my own anger. But I'm not like Gary, I'm not being a social critic when I'm writing these books.

GI: There are several passages in my book, maybe because I write for the *Village Voice*, they are interpreted as social commentary but what I really wanted to do is to get at what this character was like, that if he is not obsessed with Gregory, he's obsessed with writing, he's obsessed with how stupid everything is. I thought of it as a function of the character.

DC: I'd be a theorist if I knew why I did things. To me, it's about the lack of feeling emotions, physical feelings, about trying not to turn off to things. It's about trying to wake myself up or trying to make myself feel something. That's what it's about and in some sense that emotions are the truth, I don't know. More than a critique of American culture.

KH: But you are American culture.

DC: That's funny, somebody else just told me that the other day. So are you.

KH: I know.

GI: We are sort of in a producer relationship at this point.

DC: What was that William Carlos Williams line, the pure products of American culture go crazy? I do it because I want to support things and attack things, that's all. ✪

Lady Miss Kier

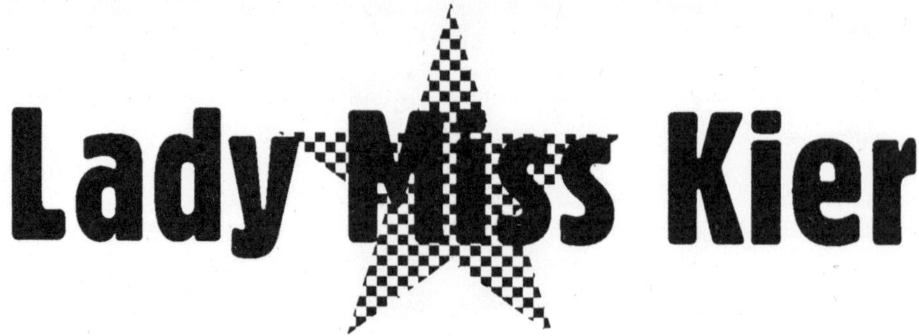

by Trent Adkins

The self-proclaimed "Mother of the Garden of Earthly Deee-Lite", Lady Miss Kier Kirby, was phoning from the East Village digs she shared with fellow band members Super DJ Dmitry and Jungle DJ Towa Towa. Since then, however, they've relocated to some other locale in New York City whilst whirling about on a World Tour. So far, they've played just about every major city here and abroad, the whole while managing to entertain and intrigue real party people because of the way they sound, look, and politic. Their subsequent visit to Chicago on November 1 at Shelter was both fabulous and a mess. The sound was pumpin' and what turned out to be a little crew on stage (Funkateers Latasha Natasha and Ronald, girlfriend on percussion) gave a marvelously "up" and too brief show. Very live. Alas, it was at Shelter. And, speaking of things famous for things and what constitutes celebrity, rumours were widely circulating that Miss Kier had overdosed on drugs à la Neely O'Hara and Edie Sedgwick. She was definitely too fabulous! Wasn't this the put down trend familiar with anything striving to be so positive or progressive? Should a musician and personality like Kier Kirby have to endure rumours of plastic surgery and dangerous liasons? Quit! This is <u>not</u> the Judy Garland story. In the midst of continuing live dates and promotional appearances, Deee-Lite's close friends and management maintain that Miss Kier Kirby is just fine.

Trent Adkins: It's great to be talking to you. You mentioned that you were trying to schedule press and everything, has that been the downside of all of this attention recently?

Lady Miss Kier: Not really. I think the downside is turning stuff down. I mean there's just so many things that two years ago I would have done anything to do that I've had to turn down 'cause I don't have time now.

TA : It's been said that you seem more interested in talking to gay underground press or even the national gay press and not as excited about more mainstream press coverage.

LMK: Well, I'd rather read your magazine than *People* any day! I know you had a thing on the zines... and there's *Pansy Beat*. You know about that?

TA: Yeah, sure. We had copies of *Pansy Beat* around here thanks to a friend who's a subscriber. Actually, we've been in touch with them to do an exchange. I see Pansy Beat Editor, Michael Economy, is doing your illustrations for the album. I know a lot of people have really negative attitudes towards drag queens, seeing them as being difficult and catty many times. *Pansy Beat* sure is helping to dispel that image. I saw the Wigstock

footage and La Homa, Lady Bunny, and Ru-Paul seemed so sweet. I couldn't believe how nice and laid back they seemed, however glamorous. Will Deee-Lite keep playing Wigstock?

LMK: Yeah, definitely keep doin' Wigstock. Oh, RuPaul is the sweetest person in the whole world! Nobody nicer. Basically that's what Wigstock is all about... it's a day for love. Michael Economy basically is *Pansy Beat*. He does just about all the graphics for it.

TA: As well as most of the editing and stuff.

LMK: Yeah.

TA: They're really fun!

LMK: The guy on the cover has two horns. Do you have that one?

TA: don't think so. We had one with Lady Bunny on the cover and another one, like a Christmas Issue.

LMK: Oh right! I had an illustration in that issue, too.

TA: Did you really? I'll have to go and research that one. I probably saw it already and just

didn't pay much attention to it. I didn't know you then and probably thought it was just another drag queen; everybody's a Miss This and a Lady That. Have you been approached by *People*?

LMK: Yeah. Like we were in it two weeks ago. I can't really dish them, but it's not something I would put on my list to get in.

TA: Did you expect that they would contact you? I mean, pretty soon we should be seeing you in *Vogue* or....

LMK: We'll be in Vogue, the December issue of *Vogue*. I'm doing the cover of Italian *Vogue* with Steven Miesel. Yeah, that I'm excited about! Doing a fashion thing.

TA: Great! Congratulations!

LMK: I just had to turn down Thiery Mugler and Jean-Paul Gaultier to do their fashion shows...

TA: Because your schedule won't allow it?

LMK: Because we're starting this tour and they wanted to do it on Thursday and I have to leave on Saturday and it was just like too much. I don't want to be jet-lagged at the beginning of the tour.

Deee-Doodlebugging: (opposite) Doodlebug **Lady Miss Kier** by doodlebug **Michael Economy**.

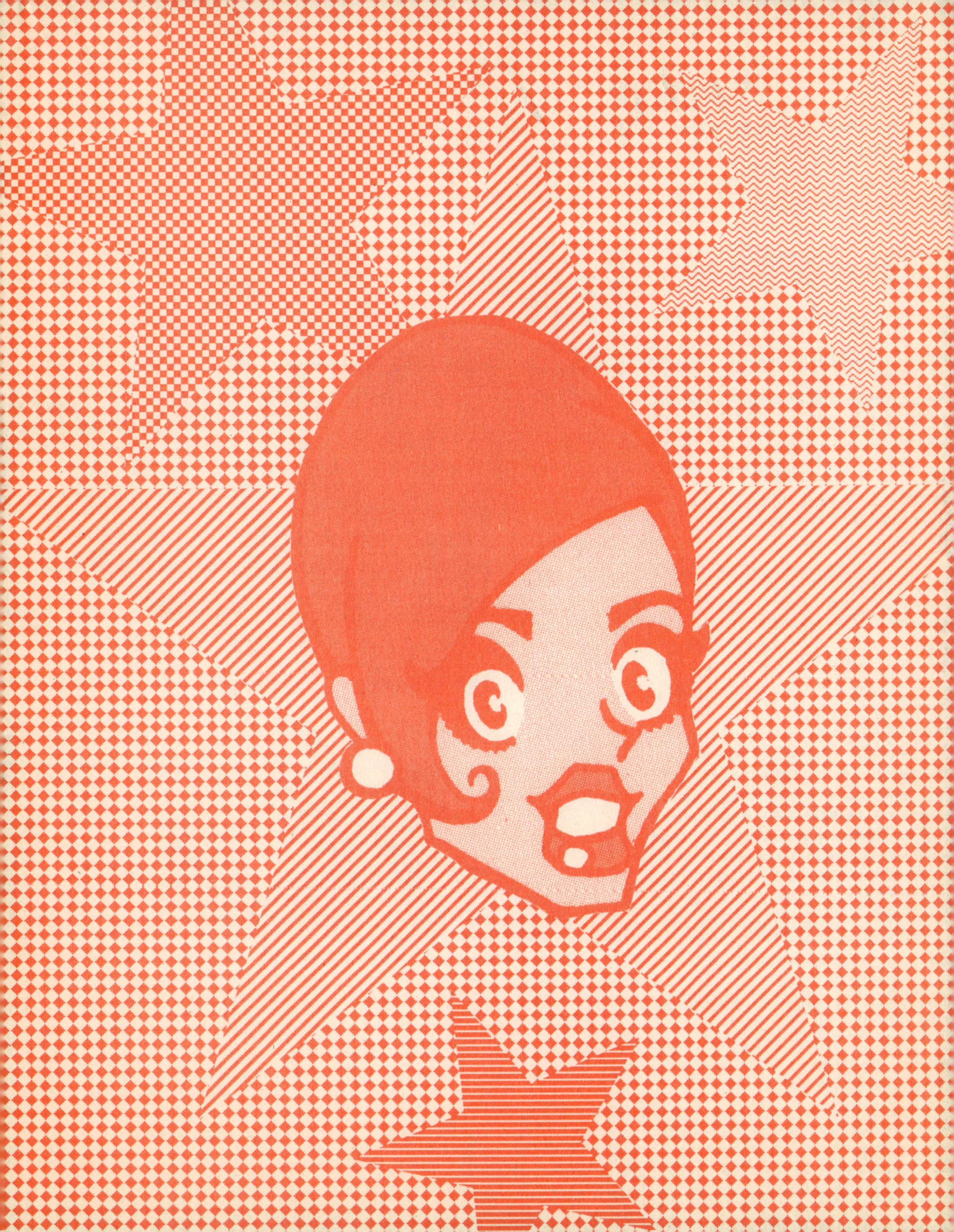

TA: I've read you're doing five European cities. Is that true?

LMK: Yeah. Well, we played England already.

TA: You got really good press there, too. Did you just do London or did you do other cities as well?

LMK: We did Manchester. This time we'll be doin' Amsterdam, four cities in Germany, and I think Italy.

TA: That sounds exciting. Will this be your first time in these cities?

LMK: Well, I'd never been to Europe before we went to London. Dmitry's been there because he's from there and Towa's never been there, so that's really one of the best parts about all of this. I'd never really been out of the states... and then all of a sudden it's like, Japan, London and the west coast... all in a month!

TA: So you've played Japan?

LMK: We didn't play but they flew me over there to kinda oversee the editing with the video because the guy who did it is Japanese.

TA: Is that Nakano?

LMK: Yeah. And he's amazing!

TA: I was really impressed with *World Clique* because it seemed that that was the way that a few groups were gonna go — psychedelic. You know, with the B 52's, with some of their releases and remixes, stuff that combines the best of funk, soul, and rock. People got excited when De La Soul came along because they brought together the '60s psychedelic and '70s funk with rap. And not just as a music thing but even stylistically with the fashion. Then here you kids come! I was impressed by your sampling. Is that a Sly Stone sample on "Try Me On"?

LMK: (singing) - That 'Na-na-na-na-na-naaa!'

TA: Yeah, that! It sounds like Sly. Where'd you get that?

LMK: Actually that's from a jazz record. A lot of the things we get are from the worst records!

TA: But you pull out some cute parts. Are there Led Zeppelin samples in there, too? I read where Dimitry was a big Zeppelin fan.

LMK: In "Try Me On"?

TA: Well, on the album?

LMK: No we didn't do Led Zeppelin either.

TA: I think my very favorite tune form the album is "The Power of Love." That song just

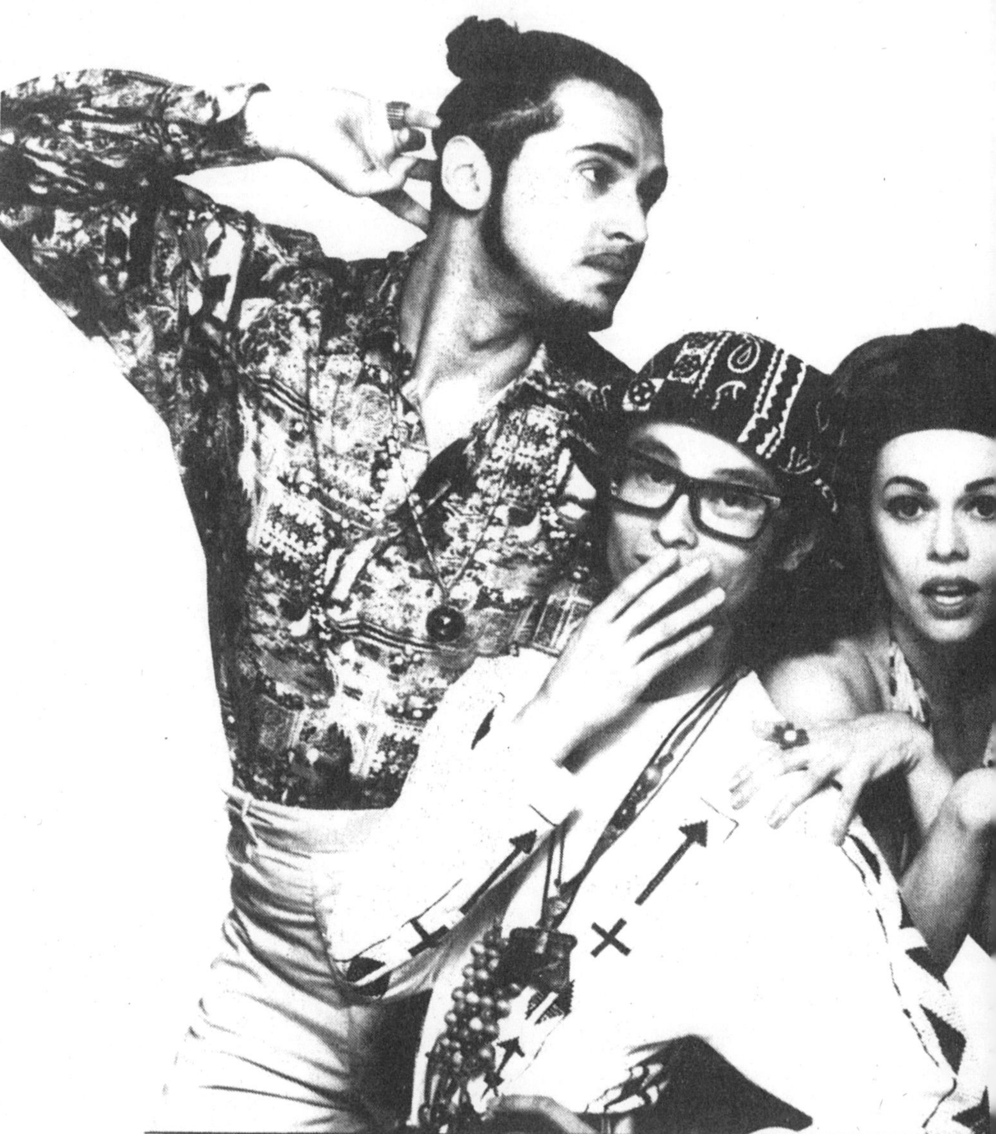

did it for me right away. It works! I've heard DJs remix it and it's awesome. I can imagine the single will be really hot.

LMK: We've totally changed it though. It's really like a whole new song.

TA: Well, I'm sure that in your hands it's bound to be fabulous.

LMK: We took the part at the end, 'ayee ayee ayee aaa,' and used that more as a hook. Instead of just something at the end, you get more of it.

TA: That's just what you hope most remixes would do because that's when you get crazy... at the end of the record. It's a dance sensibility, you think it's over and then it starts to jam. It's *not* over.

LMK: Yeah! It's so psychedelic! That's why it's so scary that they're trying to do away with vinyl. I don't mind that they're doing away with vinyl because the CD is... technologically it is much better, but, before they do away with vinyl, they better find a way to mix CDs. They, the record companies, didn't care. The record companies did not give a shit that it was going to hurt the DJs until the most ironic thing, and this is usually the way it works, the people they were trying to phase out started to break through and make them money. Once Technotronic broke through, they were like, 'Wait a minute! This band wouldn't have gotten here if it wasn't for the DJs playing them for months.' By then, it was almost too late to put stuff into motion. They didn't care. Basically they care about the money. But they still are trying to understand dance music.

TA: Where do you think that's going? Deee-Lite is obviously going to crossover into the mainstream. Where do you think all of this is going?

LMK: They all are looking for dance bands. No doubt about it, they're all trying to find dance groups. Groups that could write something that could be successful, yet, I hate that word crossover. What is crossover anyway? Crossover is just a matter of getting the music to the people. It's not really about people's choices.

TA: I agree. I think a lot of times people misinterpret and think that crossover implies that you have to overmarket to get a lot of people to buy your thing. I think some of the best efforts are where the product is what it is and people either buy it or they don't. And if what you're doing is good, it goes beyond just pure mass appeal. It's more than just the lowest common denominator. I think that's why a lot of people are excited about Deee-Lite because, you seem to have a strong sense of integrity that doesn't appear to be prone to "selling out," or doing any kind of great revising. I think people are excited about that because they think that you can retain that originality, you have real appeal.

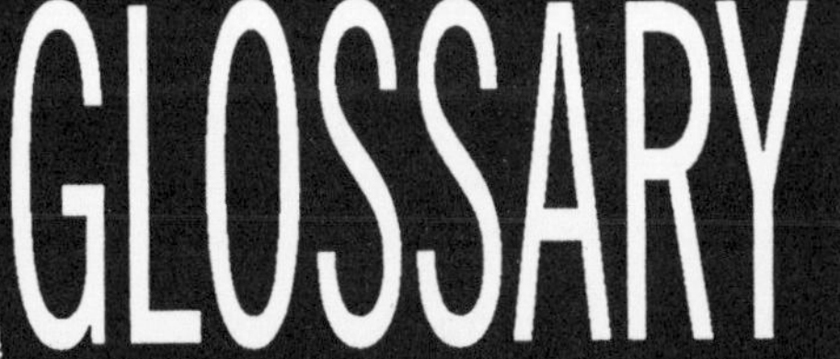

Deee-Lite, left to right: **Super DJ Dimitry, Jungle DJ Towa Towa, Lady Miss Kier.** Photo: Simon Fowler.

GLOSSARY

Deee- The prefix Deee put in front of anything the least bit groovy is taken to the nth degree. Deee-licious, it tastes so good. Deee-with it, it's the Shits. Get the picture of the Garden of Earthly Deee-Lite.

Doodlebug Groov-nick artists/ illustrators/designers.

Groov-nick Global Villager. Club Tart. Fabuli for the New Age.

Sampladelic Specialaudio effects that utilize digital sampling, computerized sound programming, and mixing, incorporating elements of House, Disco, Pop, Rock, etc. Also, Deee-Lite's production company, Sampledelic Prductions.

Global Village The place that is the Garden of Earthly Deee-Lite. New Ethnic.

Age Of Communication The global flow of ideas and information being the basis of the grooviness of things in the Garden Of Earthly Deee-Lite.

Holographic Groove Sound Deee-Lite's up-to-the-minute sound variation on the strong bass, hard drum and gospel influence in current dance music, better known as House. This stuff sounds like the real thing for a new age of hardcore dance club fans. Funky fresh multi-dimensional mix of 60s psychedelia, 70s funk sound, and 80's technology makes anything sound fun.

Groove O'clock When groov-nicks get busy; 'It's time to jam!' See the New Age Power Soul Wave.

Deee-Do Who'd a thought a headband on a flip, Pucci tights, and catsuits could become such the rage?

LMK: The English charts basically have all dance music right now. This can indicate to the major labels over here that it's not, I mean... First of all, the reason why there's so much more dance music, and there's so much that they can't ignore it, is because it was the dance community that embraced the technology. First. It wasn't like suburban, like college radio, you know. It wasn't like a rock crowd or whatever college radio is playing, you know. It was like the dance community in the urban areas, you know, the club scene. And they embraced the technology. That's why there's so much more music. That's why there's just a whole explosion of dance music. And the record companies have got to support it because they can't ignore it any longer.

TA: Right. Now, how do you see your development, the group's development over time in light of how the record companies might go? I saw something in your bio that said if you go mainstream that's fine, if they buy it, that's great, but we know who our audience is and we want to be true to our original following.

LMK: Well, we're gonna do our own thing. We'll just go where the music takes us. But, I think when we started we were a lot more cynical. Like we're really... Because in the mid- eighties there was like a lull in dance music coming out. You, know. So, when we started listening to classics and everything we started getting into the... Well, listening to classics musically. But I mean visually, all of a sudden we recognized (*chuckles*) like this whole thing that happened in the seventies with black exploitation movies, just how it kinda put a 'cap' on the Black Liberation movement. And so we were really cynical about that, progress. It was very... dressing and everything, that whole thing. Occasionally people would try to peg us. Like fashion magazines, "Oh y'all are a seventies revival band!" Like, wait a minute... *revive*? You know? They've got it all wrong! A lot of people say, "Oh, well nothing happened in the seventies." We were like, nobody wants to talk about what happened in the seventies and it was more like a punk thing. It was like, FUCK YOU! And then I think that happened to a lot of people in the eighties where it got very cynical. Towards the end of the eighties when it just seemed like it wasn't trendy to talk about certain issues or it wasn't like part of the thing to do. I hate to get something that's such a great issue down to something that's trendy. But I mean let's face it, in the sixties if it wasn't somewhat trendy to get a peace sign, we never would have ended the war. Not without putting the pressure on. Where like marching in front of the White House certain things might not have happened if it wasn't somewhat attractive to go to a peace march. It's just a whole kinda cynical thing that got a little bit more realistic. If anything's gonna change we've got to be more positive about it. So we got into more of a positive thing. It's not that we're all bubbling with positivity all the time, it's just that we realize, 'OK, you gotta work.' There's so much destruction facing us. I don't just mean Deee-Lite, I mean everybody.

TA: The world.

LMK: Yeah! I feel like Deee-Lite is just a reflection of the general feeling that's in the air. Obviously, that's got to be why people relate to us. They're buying the records. I mean, a lot of it's the music but it's also that there's the positive thing about us. 'OK, *we've* got to do something.' So, I think we'll probably stay in a positive direction. Unless, of course nothing gets done in the nineties. Like in the eighties nothing seemed to get done. I don't know, I mean, you can only guess about the future. If I don't see more people taking stands, it could easily get to be more of a cynical thing as far as change is concerned.

TA: Are there any things that Deee-Lite personally believes in or embraces spiritually to work on developing your own positive outlooks?

LMK: Well, I think dancing is one.

TA: Good answer.

LMK: Dancing and music. I guess that's the main thing. Music is really what takes me there. But also communicating with people. When you share information with someone, that to me is really uplifting, to learn something new. To learn about different organization doing different things. That's really positive.

TA: While you're mentioning organizations, have you done benefits with ACT UP there in New York? I think I saw a notice for a benefit you're scheduled to do with the Gay Men's Health Crisis in New York.

LMK: ACT UP...I don't think we did anything with them. We did do a benefit or two for Gay Men's Health Crisis and one with HEAL and one with Community Research..

TA: Are you pro ACT UP?

LMK: I have to know more. Certain things I love that they've done. Like when they went to this church here and they literally turned their backs. Basically the Cardinal turned his back on the gay community so they when in and they turned their back, literally. That was really beautiful, really amazing. I can't say that I've liked everything ACT UP's done. The outing thing is really fascist. I can't support that. If you're not together enough and you don't have the strength of character to say what you're about is who you are, then why should you be pointed out as a role model? You're twelve years old and you want to come out and it's pointed out that there's this coward who happens to be a celebrity yet they won't admit it, that's not going to help you. What I think would be more positive to do is to contact all the people that are afraid to come out who are celebrities and could be role models and give them information. Recommend some books....

TA: Try to help them develop some confidence so they can come out on their own.

LMK: Yeah. Contact them behind the scenes and say, "Look this is what I think would be helpful to the world if you were to take a stand on this." Leave it up to the individual because just pointing fingers.... that's not good. That's creating an hysteria, and this is not the time to be feeding any kind of hysteria. I think if you're together enough to say something that's gonna

be positive about your sexuality, then great! But if you have to denounce who you are then someone from your community should contact you and try to talk to you about how important it is to be more positive about it.

TA: I thought as much about your feelings towards outing when the *Advocate* asked if any of Deee-Lite's members were gay or bisexual and Dimitry answered that he really didn't think it was anyone's business or that it was important. Professionally it really shouldn't have anything to do with how good you are as musicians or whatever.

LMK: Right. As far as Deee-Lite is concerned, we're not gay straight or bisexual, we're open minded and sexually free. And beyond that it's nobody's business what we do unless you see it. (*Laughs*)

TA: Right! OK! Perfect. I know you sew and you've studied textile design in school. I think you'd be a fabulous designer, do you see yourself doing a line of clothing at some point in the future? Would you like to do a label?

LMK: I would. I mean, I wanted to be Pucci! I did! I was making costumes for this one band in New York which was Dimitry, Sister Dimension and Lady Bunny. I was go-go dancing, I started go-go dancing to support myself. Not stripping, but club dancing. And that's when I decided this , entertain-

ing, is better, it's so much more an in-depth expression of the joyous movement of dance that brings out your soul and everythin. s And so, I decided I'd go into music and dancing.

TA: Were you doing this at the Pyramid and Susanne Bartsch's Copa parties?

LMK: Yeah, Copa, I danced for her. I was the only one that wasn't a drag queen at the time. Actually, Deee-Lite played the opening night of the Copa. And I danced for her at Bentley's, because before Copa she had another club called Bentley's.

TA: The Wednesday night parties we heard so much about.

LMK: Oh, they were great. And then I did this club called Afrochine.

TA: Wasn't Dimitry spinning there?

LMK: Yeah, he was spinning there.

TA: Before you all went whole hog with the group, with performing and signing the record contract, did you have regular day jobs?

LMK: Well, let's see... Before Dimitry was DJ-ing he was a go-go dancer, too, at a place called Pizza A Go-Go. Then he managed a r restaurant and he was always DJ-ing but before he made a living with it he did these other things. But he's been DJ-ing for a while, something like four or five years. I was... God! I had every job in the book! I was a waitress, I worked as a bathroom attendant.

TA: In a restaurant or a club?

LMK: In a club. At Area.

TA: There's the story!

LMK: Yeah! (*Laughs*) Actually, I worked in the windows, too, at Area. I worked in a gallery doing errands and things. And then go-go dancing. I made furniture. I used to make, art furniture. 'I'm a jewelry designer! I'm a fashion designer! I make furniture!'

TA: (*Laughs*) OK! I guess you'll do whatever you have to do!

LMK: There's so many people in New York like that, that can do so many things.

TA: Right. Multi-talented. Speaking of which... do you co-write the songs and lyrics?

LMK: Basically, I write just about all of the lyrics. The ideas

As far as Deee-Lite is concerned, we're not gay straight or bisexual, we're open minded and sexually free. And beyond that it's nobody's business what we do unless you see it!

we all talk about. The they come from all of us. They aren't all mine. I write the words though and some of the music. We all write the music, that's pretty equally divided. Dimitry and Towa do more of the production. Like, Sampladelic Productions, which is also Deee-Lite, through which we do mixes . Dimitry and Towa do most of that. They just did a Jungle Brothers remix of "Black Woman" which is *gorgeous*!

TA: Where did you get your names? Were they given to you or did you adopt them yourselves?

LMK: Well, we were all born with them.

TA: Well, Kier Kirby.

LMK: But I used to be called Baby Kier but now I'm Lady Kier.

TA: All grown up. (*Laughs*)

LMK: Since I turned into a Lady they've dropped the Baby. I guess I was about four years old then. Let's see, Dimitry... Actually, you know they used to call him Daddy O. But then we thought people would confuse him with the other DJ, Big Daddy Kane. But some people still call him Daddy O. They call him different things from different clubs. Jungle DJ Towa Towa... I don't know, because he... well, that's his name Towa Towa, that's Korean. Towatae, and it means , it's ironic, it means peace from the east. His parents named him that not knowing that he would later moved to the west and bring a peaceful message. I think that's really sweet. That's the kind of thing that we've got to keep... destiny. It's a certain magic.

TA: There's a lot about karma and the mystical or psychic forces in your lyrics.

LMK: Were talking about the sort of magic that's in coincidences.

TA: It appears from all the many accounts of how you all came together that it was very karmic and not accidental. It was destiny and fate and it's obviously working out quite well.

LMK: I think so. I really think so. I don't believe in destiny to the point where, oh, with a Nazi victim and say that was his destiny. I don't believe in absolutes but I do believe to a certain extent you can make your own destiny which is making your own luck. Just by believing. For instance, we used to be really afraid of the music business; that's one of the reasons why we played for three years just doing it in clubs. It wasn't about trying to go to a record company and get signed. But at one point we just said, hey, if I believe in destiny then why can't I believe that there will be someone in the music industry that's gonna know and respect what we do? And once we started believing that, it wasn't so hard. We weren't surprised when we met Bill Coleman and Nancy Jeffries.

TA: How did you meet Bill and Nancy?

LMK: He came to one of the shows and then we talked to him afterwards and we gave him a tape, he asked for a demo tape. He was working at *Billboard* and that was it. That was the break we needed.

TA: Nancy is with Elektra?

LMK: Nancy is with Elektra. She's the Vice President over A&R (*Artist and Repertoire*). She's the only woman in that kind of position, a VP of A&R. And that was really like a blessing.

TA: Your destiny again.

LMK: Definitely!

TA: A lot of bands have that apprehension about the major labels because it is easy to be compromised or just overwhelmed by it all or just falling into the wrong hands because it is so money-grubbing.

LMK: Yeah, and you think that it's like us and them but actually it's a mistake to think that way because they need you and you need them and they're human. So, yeah, some people in the industry may have a money-grubbing attitude but you can say no. You don't have to do certain things that they may suggest.

TA: Was *World Clique* done when you signed the contract?

LMK: It wasn't recorded but we do most of it in our home so we gave them... well, most of the songs were already written, so then we signed the deal... we knew we were gonna get one of the companies, we were pretty sure it was going to be Elektra so we went in and started recording the album anyway. So we were half-way recorded by the time we signed the deal. We just had that much faith that it didn't matter, we were going to do this anyway.

TA: Have you already started work on the next album?

LMK: Well, we were together for three years before the album came out so we wrote enough material in those three years for about three albums.

TA: How will you pace their releases?

LMK: It really depends. Like, for the last five months we haven't had too much time to write new music so, we're really lucky that we had this stuff all ready. It's not produced but when we produce it, the production sound comes out differently every year. What we'll do as soon as this tour is over is stop everything and start writing again. But, like "Try Me On I'm Very You" that was totally spontaneous.

TA: You did that while you were recording the album?

LMK: Yeah, while we were doin' the album.

TA: That's really amazing because that's a really strong song.

LMK: That song's interesting because it's usually the least favorite song and then it grows on people. They like it a lot.

TA: I actually took to it right away. It's so funky. But it does grow on me more and more. It seems the more I listen to it, the more I hear different things going on in it. It's really danceable though. It's one of the funkiest ones on the album, maybe only second to "Who Was That" for that funky feeling. Your music is so refreshing because it is breaking through the lull that you spoke of earlier. It's not at all saying too much that Deee-Lite's music is boosting people's levels of hope, saying that we can still be happy and positive and feel good about things.

LMK: We've got to if we're going to survive in this day and age.

TA: I come in contact with quite a few ACT UP members and people in different activist organizations and there seems to be a new spiritualism emerging from these groups and individuals. People are learning or re-learning how to heal and nurture themselves and each other. A lot of people like to compare it to the sixties Love In thing because now there are all kinds of retreats and conferences and things. Are any of you involved personally in any organizations or AIDS activist movements? Where's Deee-Lite in all of this?

LMK: I think that positivity can change your life. There's no doubt about it. It's done it for me. I was basically kind of a cynical child and it wasn't until I got a little older and met a few people that were just so positive . I kind of studied them and I saw that it wasn't that everything went right for them but it was just that they appreciated each moment in life more. And as soon as I realized, 'What you mean every moment in your life matters!' Even when you think you're just killing time. There's really no such thing as 'killing time .' I think that positivity is great to enhance your life. I don't think it's curing AIDS. It will not. It can help you. It can help you enjoy what life you have left. There is evidence that a positive attitude can help in cases of terminal illness. But we need more money for AIDS and more education. I think we have to be positive to cure AIDS. We have to be positive that there will be a cure. There will be. We have to believe that. But we also can't just have 'blind faith,' we have to be ready to work to get the information out to the people who aren't aware of the facts. ✪

Ishmael Houston-Jones

by Lawrence Steger

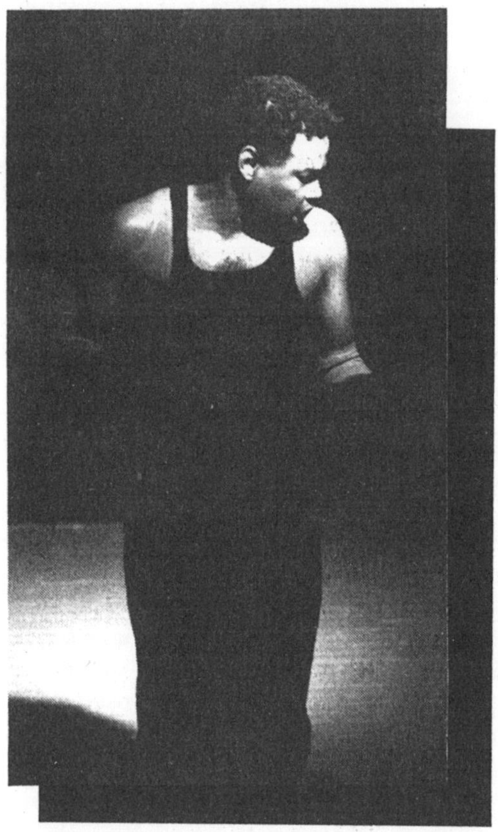

Ishmael Houston-Jones in his solo improvisation "Prelude To the End of Everything" at the School of the Art Institute of Chicago.

Photo: James Prinz.

Ishmael Houston-Jones, choreographer/dancer, has been living and performing in New York City since 1979. His work has been presented across the U.S., Canada, Europe, and in Nicaragua. He was in Chicago this past October as a visiting artist at the School of the Art Institute's Gallery 2. Ishmael conducted a week-long workshop at Gallery 2, culminating in an evening of group improv and solo performances. In 1990, The Undead, a collaboration with writer Dennis Cooper, premiered at the Los Angeles Festival of the Arts. He has also collaborated with photographer Robert Flynt, designers Huck Snyder and John DeFazio and composers Chris Cochrane, Fast Forward, and Guy Yarden, as well as appearing in the work of John Bernd, Ping Chong , Dancenoise, Yvonne Meier and John Sayles.

Lawrence Steger: The recent thing you did with Dennis Cooper, it was called...

Ishmael Houston-Jones: The Undead. It was developed last winter at the Mark Taper Forum in L.A. and was work-shopped for six weeks. Later it was accepted by LACE (Los Angeles Contemporary Exhibition) as their entry into the festival.

LS: Who was involved in the production?

IHJ: Robert Flynt did the visuals, he's a photographer. He photographed the cast underwater and we used those as projected images. Let's see. . Tom Recchione did the sound, Dennis wrote the text and I and Peter Brosius co-directed and choreographed.

LS: So you directed it together?

IHJ: Yeah, that was a decision that was made after the workshop just because of the working situation we found ourselves in. Even though he was basically a theatre director and I was basically a choreographer we found we were both doing things sort of equally. He was choreographing, I was staging. So it seemed sort of practical if we designated it that way.

LS: Where did you get the cast from?

IHJ: Well we auditioned about 80 people - all from L.A. I knew that I didn't want to work with all actors, so we called choreographers asked them to suggest people, we called performance people. In the end if you would like to categorize, we wound up with a cast of six: three who would call themselves actors, one person who was a dancer/choreographer and two people who would be called performance artists.

LS: And it was developed out of writings by Cooper?

IHJ: Actually, it was developed in tandem. The piece really started a year ago. There was no script at all, there was no writing. And we started with movement - Dennis interviewed the guys. I guess you could say the piece is about gay men, in their twenties now. I don't know how much more specific, . . .thread we have . . .

LS: He interviewed them?

IHJ: Yes about their lives, getting their language, their thoughts, ideas about music, sex, and he developed the writing while I started using movement ideas - just ideas I had . . .

LS: About what these people were talking about???

IHJ: Uhm, yeah, well, a lot of my movement seems to be a lot about relationships — physical relationships when people stand next to each other: having them do real tasks. Embracing, slapping, hugging, interrogating each other.

LS: Relationships?

IHJ: Yes.

So, then we started scripting things, creating monologues. We work well together and have a good repartee. It was a very curious thing, because when we set out, we knew we didn't want it to be actorly at all, or theatrical in a traditional way. Nothing stagey. I mean when Dennis writes it is in this real flat voice - I really love it - this complete flatness.

LS: Well, was it based on these interviews?

IHJ: No, not really, I guess that the interviews were more or less of a springboard. Kinda to see where these guys were: people if not a full generation, at least a half-generation removed from us just to see who they are, what it's like growing up gay.

LS: So do you feel like the writing or the performance of it reflected this distance between Cooper, yourself and these guys?

IHJ: Yeah. I think that the piece is a lot about disconnection. A lot of the movement ideas were things that never get fulfilled, things that almost, connections that almost get made but not. And the writing, most of the writing is done in monologue or even when it's dialogue it's actually two monologues hitting each other rather than real conversation.

LS: Would you say that what came out of the performance was about young gay-male sexuality?

IHJ: I don't know if it was so much focused on sexuality as a totality. More on young gay males in the age of AIDS not being able to connect.

LS: The title.

IHJ: Yes, it's the living but sort of the negative form of the living. That sort of unconnectedness of things is what Dennis and I have both been working on as a theme. A lot. Whether it's making love to a cinder block or Dennis' writings about brutality, cool brutality.

LS: Yes, a sort of slow brutality, to borrow a phrase. When did you start working with him?

IHJ: In 1985 - a piece called "Them". I went and saw him read

and I told him that he made me feel vulnerable. I guess that he had seen me perform but we got together and bantered around a lot of ideas and started working on this series called "Hole". Basically Dennis plays records and I respond to them. There's different themes. There was talk at one point as to doing them as a prelude to "The Undead" but we eventually thought it would be unnecessary.

LS: With "The Undead", do you feel like it's finished and that you can do it again like a theatrical piece?

IHJ: Yes, oh yeah, I mean it's a finished piece. There would be some changes if staged again and if the cast changes. I think even more than the choreography and the staging, the writing was really geared towards these six guys. They bonded as a group.

LS: So you would do it again with these guys?

IHJ: Yes. We did it again in San Diego and we had to make one cast change and it was very interesting — it was very fragile because I think that Dennis really has an ear for hearing voices and he had written all of these parts for these guys. When we replaced one cast member it sort of threw it a little bit — in an interesting way. We realized that if we had to change three guys then the writing itself would have to change.

LS: Don't you find that in the movement though - I mean you're working with people and their bodies?

IHJ: Yes, some people would be harder to replace in terms of the text and others for the movement. One person, the choreographer/dancer that was in the piece, Steven Craig, replacing him would be difficult since so much of his personality on stage was about giving him perimeters to work in and sort of framing his own movement.

LS: Is that a loosening up of what your role as a choreographer is or has that always been. . .

IHJ: That's always been. I've never liked giving people steps - giving people specific movement things. I've more or less looked at people, figure out what they're capable of and what they're comfortable with...It's sort of interesting because once the texts were written by Dennis, he allowed the same sort of changes. Kinda so they would fit their mouths and certain words, rhythms. I've never really wanted people to move like me in performances.

LS: What sort of imagery do you use in making new work?

IHJ: Strange question but I like working with violence, I'm not even sure why, and I think I've stopped trying to figure out why.

LS:Have other people stopped trying to figure out why?

IHJ: Yeah, right. No, people keep asking why. I mean it's a response, a possible response to the world. I like struggling. I mean this newest solo that I'm doing this weekend - I'm not sure how finished it is - but it's really a duet for me and a cinderblock. It's sort of about a story of a painting of Frida Kahlo and a death of a friend of mine. Wrestling imagery almost always shows up somewhere in my work - if it's not a cinderblock it's a dead goat, or my mother or . . .

LS: The floor?

IHJ: The floor. Or myself. Or other dancers. I mean, sort of wrestling imagery keeps recurring. An actual physical struggle.

LS: That's funny - I mean the title of the pieces don't refer to a struggle but more to a stoppage point - no more struggle. All of the work that I'm familiar with, either through writings or actually seeing it, is about this violence. Correct me if I'm making unwarranted generalizations, but all of the work that I'm familiar with has taken place in the eighties - the AIDS virus decade. And really, your career, as a dancer, choreographer, performer...

IHJ: Yes, I moved to NYC in 1979. I had made some work in Philadelphia. But I would think of that as more of an incubation period.

LS: Would you consider that your work is defined either through the violence or tragedy of what's happened in the eighties.

IHJ: I mean, I respond to what is going on around me and it's not just the AIDS crisis. I mean our political system, the incredible increase in homelessness. . .

LS: Well, I guess what I'm getting at is that there are others who are working with this violence. . .

IHJ: I think that we live in a particularly violent time where humanity is being threatened, if not by war, if not by disease, if not by, you know, being thrown out on the street by rampant real estate. I think it's sort of an insidious violence that it happening to people, to the environment. There is a lot of disconnectedness. I guess internalized violence - I feel that as a gay man. As much as I try not to, I feel like I have internalized a lot of it. As a gay black man - a double duty of internalized violence.

When I do these workshops, I try to work with who these people are, I try to get a sense of what they are. I like coming into a room full of people and getting them to reveal parts of themselves that they wouldn't reveal onstage or to a stranger - both in movement and in speaking words. Some guy in a review said that he found that I revealed onstage what most people wouldn't reveal in the privacy of their own home. ✪

Matt O'Neill

Every Roman was surrounded by slaves. The slave and his psychology flooded ancient Italy, and every Roman became inwardly, and of course unwittingly, a slave. Because living constantly in the atmosphere of slaves, he became infected through the unconscious with their psychology. No one can shield himself from such an influence.
— Contributions to Analytical Psychology, London, 1928
C. G Jung

Matt O'Neill's paintings are based in an academic European technique of underpainting and heavy glazing. Their rich time-consuming qualities convey a leisurely lifestyle where the aristocrats of Europe or of America's deep south could afford the days or weeks of sitting which were required to produce a single canvas — while crews of the less priviledged toiled to maintain their fields, cook their meals, or fight their battles.

In "Nude Portrait II," a black fighter is portrayed, not surrounded by accumulated material objects or perched upon a champion horse, but isolated, as an object in a dark void. The fighter seems caught in a time warp, as if the Civil War hadn't quite happened. He sits with a worn expression, waiting to be told what to do, who to fight, and whether to win or lose. At present he is told to sit and pose. Perhaps his owner wants to immortalize him as one more family holding, and — in his forefather's tradition — to guarantee his and his children's opportunities to parlor talk and to boast of family holdings, monies acquired, and battles won.

By contrast, in "Young Girl with House Pet," a fair-skinned, young girl sits on a wooden rocking horse, surrounded (hemmed in?) by material objects bought for her by the family. Both potraits seem painted from a patriarchal mandate, one to show privilege, the other to show possession. But the expression on the little girl's face is also drawn and bleak. Is she really privileged? Or will she grow up to be a sick, bedridden sister in a Tennessee Williams play, forever suffering from the unhealthy environment which surrounds her?

O'Neill successfully crosses the black/white border showing a sensitivity to the deficiencies of our aristocratic European based 20th century society. His images are timely and universal. As we await the slow revisionist process of our old paternalistic society, O'Neill gives us one more snapshot of these outdated conditions.

— Joe Lindsay

Matt O'Neill received a fellowship grant from the National Endowment for the Arts in 1990. The Denver Art Museum recently purchased two of his canvases for their permanent collection. He is represented by the Hassel/Haeseler Gallery, 1743 Wazee, Denver, CO, 80202, Phone (303) 295-6442.

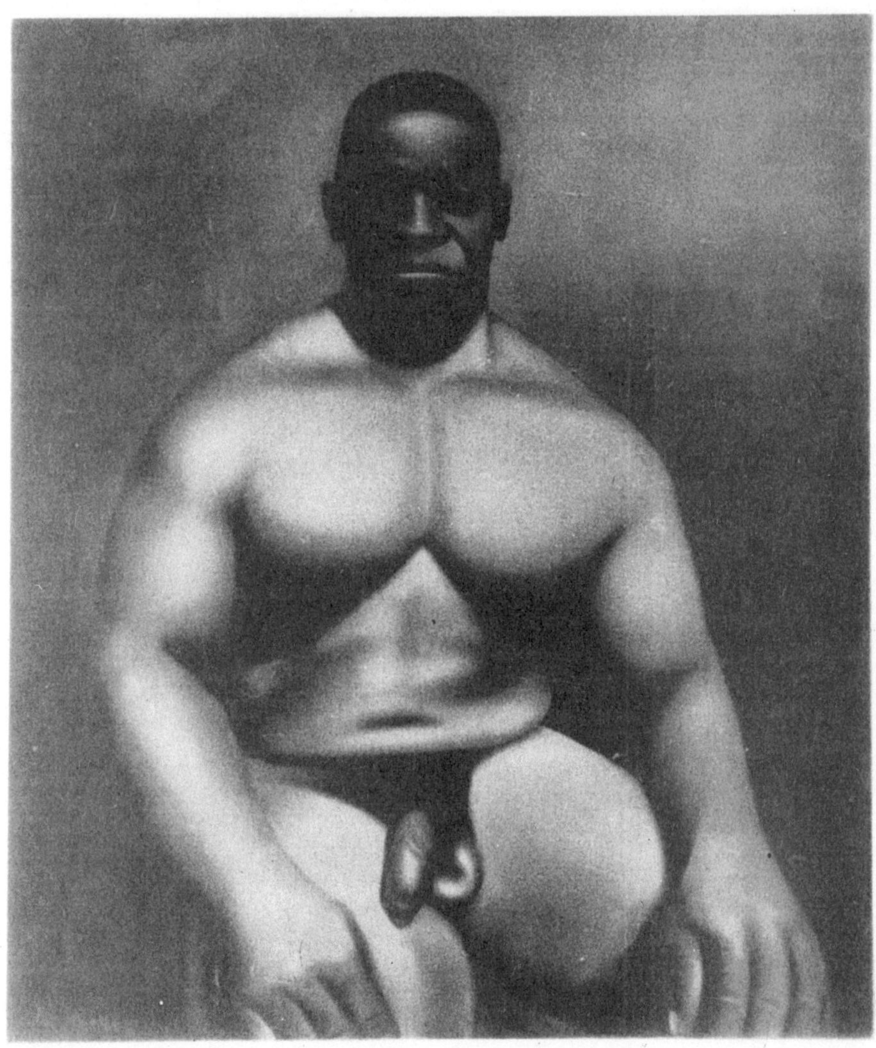

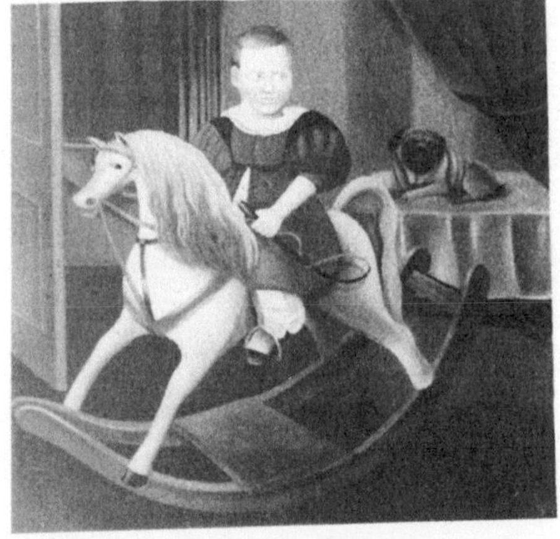

Above: Matt O'Neill, **Nude Portrait II**, 1990, oil on canvas
Left: Matt O'Neill, **Young Girl With House Pet**, 1990, oil on canvas

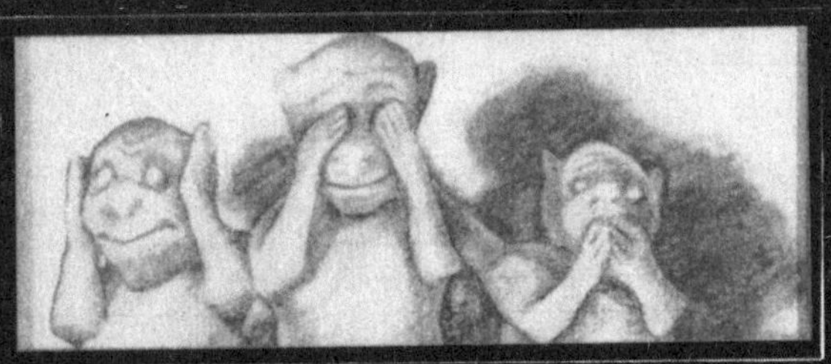

Adrian Piper, Pretend #3, 1990
4 enlarged photos, silkscreened text *(detail)*

ADRIAN PIPER

I felt a real sense of pride and strange relief when I walked into Adrian Piper's show at the John Weber gallery, N.Y.C. There I found large aesthetically pleasing and very commercial photographs of mostly black people in different settings. At the bottom of each photo were words which when presented in series read as phrases like "Pretend Not To Know What You Know" or single photos such as "Power" and "Knowledge". The single photographs of blacks I found moving read at the bottom "You are Safe", "We Are Among You" and one in particular featuring Africans read "We Are Within You". As I moved about the room taking in the images, I tried to specify and clarify my feelings.

I was initially shocked by the enlarged photographs of black men being attacked by police (circa 1960) juxtaposed with reassuring images of blacks seated around a dining table with the words "We Are Among You" I could not reconcile the two pictures and their messages. In short Piper's conceptual strategy was effective. It elicited an intellectual and gut reaction from me. I felt helpless — having initially thought "These are the black people I know, these are my people, my family" and then having my self assurance of place and identity shattered by viewing a white police attacking a black man cowering from

the blows. I realized that man could easily be myself.

Having been emotionally and intellectually jarred, I receptively and cautiously walked into the adjacent room containing the rest of Piper's work. There I found gallery goers waiting to go inside four large walk-in size black booths. Curious, I did also. Inside, again the faces of blacks confront me. The photographs this time

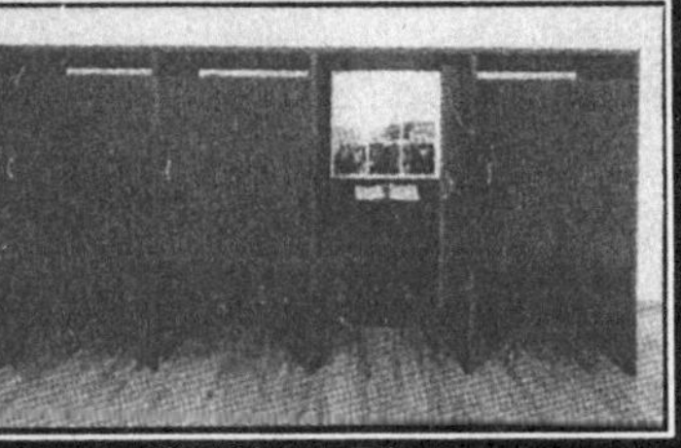

Adrian Piper
Vote/Emote
1990
mixed media installation

are lit from behind and encompass the entire upper half back of the booth. There is no way to avert one's gaze from the picture. The faces look disenchanted and tired (they are shots from the '63 civil rights march on Washington.) There was a thick three ring notebook and pen with the question probing what my deepest fears were that I was afraid of "we" knowing. Suspicious, I wrote. I went into the other three booths. The questions were similar. To 'what are you afraid we will do with the power once we gain it?' I wrote, feeling self-righteously exempt. Here anyway. Leaving the booths, continued to explore the room. Piper had piqued my own deep conflicts of identity and race in a way that no person has.

On the train back to Chicago I continued to relive my first impressions of Piper's photographs and texts and still have not reconciled my dual responses; the work was for me simultaneposly seductive, haunting and acutely relevant.

— Todd Roulette

I must say that you were **"Livin' Large"** (*as my friend Trent would say*) *at STUX gallery. And I'm not just talking about the deluxe private after party at* chez *McDonalds. (In N.Y.C.'s financial district no less). The work as a whole would qualify as* **"Livin' Large"**. *Every-* thing so **slick** *and custom — including that shocking* **PORNO-GRAPHIC** *calendar of* toi. *I saw children with those!* *Some of my favorites were the thought-provoking mini-baseball bats that read*

"I Want To Love U Butt I Don't No How"

and the Leibow-itz china serving set for six with various inscriptions beautifully packaged in gold boxes. Your tempting display of them, hundreds stacked one on top the other in the middle of the room made me want

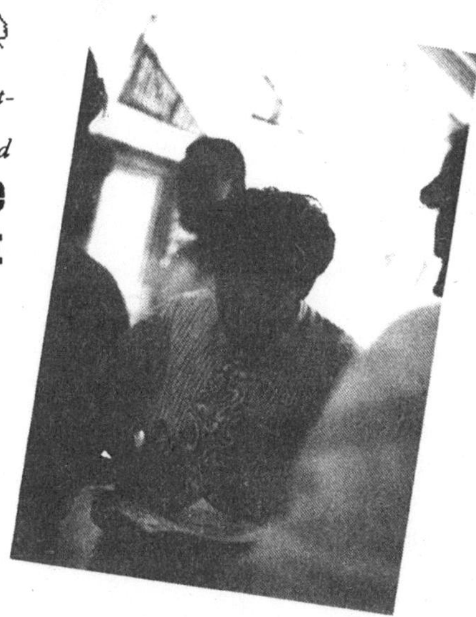

to charge enough for a wedding party of 500. *The hundreds of tiny teddy bears also, their yellow t-shirts that read* "Will Make a Cubist Painting Someday But Right Now It Is Not Important" *made me feel as though I was in an enlightened children's toy store. But, you really outdid yourself with the K-Mart size door mats reading* "Loser Line Forms Here" *and that* Romper-Room *colored rug with* "There Are 2 Things I Need To Watch 4 the Rest of My Life: My Weight and My Racism" *was too fantastic. Sentiments that I hope all guy men keep close to the ♥!*

The **in-your-face** *high school mascot banners (minus the mascots) with* "Don't Pretend 2 Like It" *and* "Expect Copying" *were nice. Is this a bit mocking of your audience? Oh well, you're the artist. Also, I had a time with those flat shipping boxes with the Whiney monologue. I knew it had to refer to something important — instability maybe?*

I am very proud of you. The after party was too much fun. *The Hampton crowd, too busy closing their summer places truly missed a treat by not attending.*

— TR

FICTION IS AUTOBIOGRAPHY, NOT LIFE AS IT IS, but life as we would like it to be. I create all sorts of literature that I can live in, but seldom share, even my tragedies.

But today, I would like to tell you a true story. Nothing happens in this tale, but it does tell you something of what I have learned about life.

The story begins at 2:45 A.M. Saturday morning, when I returned from having a drink with Tony at Mariee's Crisis Cafe. There was one message on the machine: "If Kevin Paulson lives here, this message is from his brother, Donald. Call me whenever you get in. I am leaving this message at eleven-thirty." *Beep*. So I took off my shoes and sat down on the window seat, staring at the copper green Statue of Liberty in the Harbor, wondering what new price I would pay for my freedom. I looked up Donald's number, then dialed.

"Donald, this is Kevin. Who died?"

"Grandma." For me there was no surprise, but Donald would have laughed if I told him what I had dreamt the night before. "She would have been ninety-five this week. She had a series of strokes and heart attacks. The doctors could have kept her alive with machines, but she refused to live that way. The funeral is Monday. In Johnstown."

"I'm sorry."

"We're leaving tomorrow. Let me give you Aunt Jane's number. That's where Mom is staying."

Elizabeth Kiniry was born, resided, ... and died in Johnstown , Pennsylvania , a coal smelting town in the northern Appalachian mountains. She had survived all

Tiny Tim

three of the great Johnstown floods. An Irish Catholic, she decided at eighteen to marry George Wise, a German Protestant. The rector at St. Andrews Roman Catholic Church allowed her to serve public penance for two months. Nevertheless, Elizabeth bore three Catholic daughters and three Catholic sons to George Wise. She bore to a travelling salesman one Catholic daughter, my mother, Vivian Ruth.

I had never known Grandma very well. My first memory of her was in the blue and orange year of 1964,

during her visit to the New York City World's Fair. I was five years old at the time. Grandma had taken the train out, and so my father drove us into Manhattan, which he hated to do, in the big red Chevrolet station wagon with fins. Dad and I waited in the car, eating lemon cookies and reading Justice League of America, number 43. Mom walked a white-haired, sagging woman in a floral dress to the car. At seventy, Grandma Wise was the oldest woman I had ever seen.

The next day, we went to the Flushing Meadows Fair Grounds. Grandma rode all the rides with me, because Dad had to work, and Mother was too faint. After the General Motors Exhibit, where I drove around in a real car, Grandma told Mother to get a driver's license. Mother was forty-three at the time.

Later, as Grandma and I waited for the Monorail, I asked, "Will Mother get to be as fun as you when she gets old?"

Mother overheard and said, "Only when I have done as many naughty things as Grandma. And then make you pay for them."

Grandma and I got on the monorail alone and she said, "Never stop having fun. Otherwise you'll pay your mother's price."

"And what's that?"

"Blaming your unhappiness on other people. It's very hard not to know whether or not you are happy." Sometimes when I am feeling numb, I think of that monorail ride with my grandma.

I saw Grandma only four or five times more in the years before I went to college. Then, when the trouble started with Mother, I did not see anyone in the family.

I had not seen Grandma for thirteen years before last October. Once more, Grandma took the train out, this time to stay with my parents in Yaphank, Long Island. She asked my mother to invite the three sons out to dinner, one at a time, with their wives.

Mother called Donald, the second son, and he brought over Christine and his children the next night. Early, the eldest son, was invited a week later and although Ginny had not lived with him for nine years, she came along.

Mother and I talked a few days after. Mother asked if I would like to bring someone to dinner with Grandma. I told her that Brian would be delighted to join us, the family.

"I meant a girl."

"I meant my lover. Or I don't come." Grandma would understand, I hoped.

So Brian and I rented a car on a Wednesday night and drove out to Yaphank. Mother was on edge, and was trying to cover. She served roast pork, baked potatoes, and her specialty: frozen stringbeans, baked in Campbell's Cream of Mushroom Soup, topped with Mrs. Paul's Onion Rings. I think that this was supposed to mean that she still loved me.

When the dishes were cleared away, Grandma said, "I think I'd like to sit a spell with my grandson." Brian and Dad took the hint and suggested to Mother that they go for a walk.

I poured tea into two large mugs and Grandma and I sat watching t.v. for a few minutes. Her mug read "World's Best Grandma." Mine read "Souvenir of Las Vegas."

Grandma said, "I'm going to die this year, but don't morn me. I've had a fun life. It's time to go."

"Oh grandma..."

"Now listen. That other boy, Brian, seems very nice. I'm glad I met him. Don't worry about your mother. She just goes around looking for excuses to be bitter. Now I haven't been the best mother either. Or the best grandmother. But I have enjoyed myself. Remember that I taught you life is getting

just send a mass card?"

"But, Mother I can..."

"I hear your father calling. I'll be back in New York next Sunday. Why don't you give me a call then?" *Click*.

Numb. Why did she always turn me off like that?

I watched the sunlight glisten on the river, and then I called Amanda, my best friend. "We were just about to call you! What are you doing tomorrow?" "Not going to my Grandma's funeral," I explained.

"Then you're going with us to Fire Island. Meet us in Penn Station at 9 a.m." As I hung up, the phone rang. Tim.

Tim is from East Millinoquit, Maine, and is my private hero. Tim told me once that he was named after the Dickens character, when he was adopted, which is sort of funny because Tim is anything but tiny. He is six-foot- one and weighs well over 200 pounds. He also told me that his nickname is Endora, but I have never heard anyone call him that.

Tim challenges and befuddles everyone. The first words I ever heard Tim say were not to me, but to Brian,

Grandma Wise &

what you can get out of life while you can get it."

"Yes, Grandma."

"And forgive your mother a little. She does not know what she has become."

I WOKE UP AT 7:31 THE MORNING after Donald called. I went to the gym, called the train station, called my buddy manager, Debbie, and told her that I would not be in. I cleaned the apartment, even though it had not gotten dirty in the seven months that Brian had been on tour.

At noon, I dialed the number which my brother Donald had given me.

"Hello?"

"Hello, this is Kevin Paulson." Pause. I gave her a moment to identify herself as my Aunt Jane, but she didn't say anything. Then I asked, "Is Vivian Paulson there?"

"Hold on," then away from the phone, "Vivian! It's him."

"Hello, " she said, as composed as ever.

"Hi, It's Kevin. I'm sorry to hear about Grandma."

"Thank you."

I'm taking the 8:01 train out of Newark tomorrow. Can someone pick me up at the station?"

"I don't think that will be necessary. Listen, we already have enough problems here. Why don't you

who at the time had been my boyfriend for seven hours. Tim threw open the door to the bedroom carrying a plate full of donuts and coffee and said, "I know that if you're dating someone as old and ugly as him that he must have money. So let's celebrate." Four weeks later , I moved in with both Brian and Tim, for four rocky years of cohabitation. As Lee, who also lived with us for a time, once said, "Tim is the best friend in the world to have as a former roomate."

Tim also challenges himself a lot, although these challenges usually backfire. Like when he cleans his bedroom, it is usually at the expense of the living room, the dining room, ... or when he started smoking to lose weight and got hooked on the after-dinner cigarette.

A year and a half ago, Tim was diagnosed as HIV positive. Two months ago he developed Esophageal Candidiasis, which means that he is officially a person with AIDS.

Tim moved out and moved into New York. I worry about Tim sometimes. He sweats constantly and is always tired. So I bicker with him when I see him about smoking, vitamins, drinking, and t-cell counts. It does neither of us any good.

But Tim has challenged himself to achieve some good out of a bad circumstance. His politics have changed from Reaganomic Republican to left wing. He is an integral member of ACT UP, the AIDS Coalition to Unleash Power.

Tim and I joined in March, 1988, and since then I

by

Kevin Thaddeus Paulson

have seen him blockade the FDA, attend the Civil Rights Commission in a clown mask, wrap the city's health commissioner in the bedsheets of the forgotten PWA's and , most recently, ignite the lesbian and gay community at this year's Stonewall Rally in Central Park. Tim has changed from bitchy queen to bitchy rebel.

'So whatcha doin'" he asked.

"Tim! Hi, how are you feeling?"

"Not so good. Wanna get together this weekend?"

"Can't. I'm going to Fire Island with the newlyweds. Unless you want to come."

"Sure, as long as you're paying. I've never been to Fire Island."

"Are you sure you're gay?"

"No, really, it's one of my few regrets in life. That and the fact I am the only person with AIDS who has not lost any weight."

I arrived at Penn Station the next morning at about ten minutes past nine, took more money out of the cash machine, and walked downstairs to the Long Island Railroad. Street people were sleeping in front of the closed shops, smelling of urine and sweat of Manhattan in July. I wanted to help them all and felt guilty that I could not.

I wanted coffee, extra light, extra sweet.

Tim was already there, in the beige shorts which he had bought for the gay pride march the year before ("Everyone wears shorts to the march, Kevin. Why do you think we started this revolution in June? So that we could get a tan.").

"What time is the train?" he asked. "Nine thirty-nine." "And which train will we take when Alice and Trixie show up two hours late?"

"They'll be here. And besides, this gives me the time to find coffee."

Amanda and Evelyn arrived at 9:36, and we jumped on to the Sayville train as the doors were closing. Amanda and Evelyn usually calculated their lateness pretty well, but this time they didn't allow enough time for coffee. So the four of us passed around my cup of extra light, extra sweet coffee like a communion cup, or a joint.

And I always knew where Evelyn had sipped from, by the imprint of candy apple lipstick.

Amanda and I have been daytrippers to Fire Island many times before. A daytripper is a person who spends usually one day at the beach because they cannot afford to rent or buy one of those clever cottages with backlit boardwalks whose rents are in excess of my student loan. Daytrippers are the scourge of the summer long residents, but a much needed source of tourist revenue. Especially if one can be convinced to stay in the Ice Palace for a night

or two at $100 a day, including all the benefits of cinder box luxury.

So, as daytrippers, we have learned to enjoy the little rituals: the diesel train through southern Long Island, the bus to the dock, and then the ferry ride over.

The ferry ride over is the best part. While we wait for the boat, we go to the refreshment stand/bar and play all the songs on the jukebox of our seven summers together. Then we hear the foghorn as the ferry docks, and we race to the top deck. This insures that we get a headstart on our tans, as well as the slap of the spray.

On the ride over, I pointed out to Tim the Hotel Belvedere, which I have always wanted to stay in, but have never been able to afford. Some night, Brian and I will come out here and take a room overlooking the bay.

The ferry docked just after noon. We walked through the town, past Michael's Restaurant, and Bloomin' Pail Florist and the Monster until we got to the beach. We took our shoes off and walked until we found the perfect spot.

The four of us lay down on Amanda's sheet, free of sand for the last time that day. Amanda lit a joint, and we passed it around in a circle, our second communion cup. Tim shrugged. "Oh well, what's another 50 t-cells?" and took a puff. Evelyn left her imprint of lipstick again.

"You know, now I know what they mean by lipstick lesbian."

"Let me tell you that I have worn lipstick a lot longer than I have been a lesbian."

Amanda and Evelyn took several long walks, as the young in love are prone to. Tim stared at the tanned men in Speedos. I napped in search of the perfect sunburn.

As we ate lunch in a restaurant overlooking the beach, I told them about my grandma and my mother. Evelyn and Amanda had met my mother the summer before. I had invited my mother and dad to see "The Music Man" at Westbury Music Fair, starring John Davidson. I had not told my mother that Brian was performing in it.

Amanda and Evelyn met my parents and I outside the theater. I introduced Amanda as my best friend. Mother was appalled that my friends were a lesbian couple, one member an Italian Jew and the other member a Black Baptist. Mother, having no other means of relating said, "You know we don't have any black friends, but while Harold and I were in Las Vegas, we did meet this American Indian. And he was just like regular people.'

I swear that my mother really said that.

So, as we sipped our ginger ale by the ocean, I told Amanda about the telephone call and she replied, "I'm not surprised. What can you expect from invertebrates?"

After lunch Tim and I decided to go swimming. I took out my contact lenses and the beach became a noisy blur. Tim took off his t-shirt and hustled me towards the water. God forbid anybody should see me without a shirt on. Especially Gregg Bordowitz." With that, he jumped into the cold, brown-green ocean. Knowing that a wet Tim was dangerous to a dry Kevin, I dove in also.

We stayed in the water for over an hour. Tim kept jumping, with his arms straight up, as each wave approached. "Maybe your mother didn't mean it. Maybe she was just trying to save you the trouble. If you don't forgive the idiots in your life for what they do to you, you'll end up with very few wise friends."

He did a somersault, then rose out on the surf, choking on the salt water. He vomited blood into the sea. I said, "Let's go back."

He said, "You go ahead; I want to remember this day as it is."

As I walked towards the sheet, I could not tell if the salt on my cheek was the spray of the ocean or my tears.

Evelyn asked if I would like to go to the grocery store with her. I nodded. We walked past the Ice Palace from where we could hear Kelly Marie singing, "*It feels like, It feels like I'm in love...*" Evelyn smiled and announced that it was time to party. She wanted to dance and to drink creamy piña coladas. We returned to the sheet, and Evelyn told Amanda. So we gathered our sneakers and suntan lotions and sheet. We woke up Tim. We checked everything (except Tim) at the coat check at the Ice Palace. Amanda and Evelyn went into the disco. I could hear a dance version of Bette Midler's "Wind Beneath My Wings." Tim said that he was tired, as he usually is nowadays, and he asked if I knew of someplace quiet. So we walked along a tree-shaded boardwalk that runs along the bay side. I told Tim my stories of Fire Island: sitting in hot tubs with glasses of cognac; swimming naked at 3 a.m. with the producer whom I had met at Tommy Tune's house; the fight with Jim Gibby about whether or not to have the menage with the pre-med student at the Carousel Guest House.

I told Tim about calling Amanda on Memorial Day weekend and making her join me here when a date had gone sour. A bleached blond twinkie had shown some proclivity for kinkier activities than I was interested in. I then jumped into a swimming pool with my contact lenses and jumped out with same. I was force to rely on my date, who thoroughly enjoyed my dependance. Amanda rescued me, her one comment: "This is truly a case of the blond leading the blind."

We spent many better days on the Island but the other time I talked about was when we came out for the Harmonic Convergence, the birth of a new age. And there was no room at the inn. At any of the inns. So we danced until four in the morning, then had breakfast at Michael's. We walked through the woods and the early fog until we reached the pines. We sat on the beach and waited. As the sky shifted from indigo to turquoise, hundreds joined us. We stood together in a ring as the sun, a bright red smear, crossed the horizon. And who cares whether or not that day brought about world peace? For one moment, I sang wordless tones with a score of others and I believed in something more than here and now.

Eventually, Tim had to pee, so we walked out to the little forest between the Grove and the Pines, a copse known in the seventies as the meat rack, where open gay sex lived an easier existence. "You know, Randy Shilts says that this is where it all began."

By the time we walked back, Amanda and Evelyn had already gone to dinner. I had twenty dollars left which would be enough for two drinks, a nice trip and the taxi fare back to Sayville Railroad Station. Tim and I had walked to Cherry's, a bar that I had not been in since the fateful menage with Jim Gibby. I ordered for Tim a strawberry daquiri and for myself a frozen mudslide. Tim only likes frothy drinks. I handed Tim the pink foam and took my own pale brown drink. We found a picnic bench overlooking the dock. We watched the sun slide into the bay and we talked about our sunburns and ACT UP and how Tim used to date Tony Rizzo. Tim likes to tell me the same stories over and over again. He never remembers telling me before.

It was cold by the time the 9:15 arrived. Unlike my wise, lesbian friends, I had not brought along a long sleeve shirt, and so I huddled under the beach towels. We still sat on the top deck because that is tradition. As the boat chopped back towards the harbor, Amanda tugged my sleeve. She smiled her secret smile and pointed out the first evening star. In silence, we made our wishes. I wished that, because I could not mourn for grandma, and would not mourn for Tim, that I would become, that I would choose to be a hero.

As the other three slept to the rumble of the train, I looked out the window and knew that life is a perfect Sunday afternoon on the beach with no clouds and few responsibilities. Life is knowing that you could die at any moment and sometimes choosing to do so. Even calling your mother.

Life is swimming alone in the Atlantic Ocean, sometimes with a friend. ▼

IF FREUD HAD BEEN A NEUROTIC COLORED WOMAN:

Reading Dr. Frances Cress Welsing by Essex Hemphill

In 1974, the year that Dr. Frances Cress Welsing wrote, "The Politics Behind Black Male Passivity, Effeminization, Bisexuality, and Homosexuality," I entered my final year of senior high school.

By that time, I had arrived at a very clear understanding of how dangerous it was to be a black homosexual in my black neighborhood and in society. I had no particular inclinations to slip on a dress like skin, wear loud lipstick, and wiggle my hips through the four a.m. shadows and streetlights of the tenderloin or the boulevards where erotic desire was claimed by the highest bidder or the loneliest man. Facing this then limited perception of homosexual life, I could only wonder where did I fit in? I had no particular inclination to want to chase down men while wearing platform pumps and mini-skirts. None of this behavior was the least bit appealing to me.

Conversely, I was perfecting my heterosexual disguise; I was practicing the necessary use of masks for survival; I was calculating the distance between the first day of class and graduation; the distance between graduation from high school and departure for college, and ultimately, awaiting the arrival of my freedom from home, community, and my immediate peers. I believed my imminent independence would allow me to explore what my hetero-disguise and my masks were preventing me from exploring.

It is fortunate that the essay by Dr. Welsing which I am citing here had not come to my attention during my adolescence. I can only imagine how little resistance the assault of her ideas would have been met with by me at that time. At 17, I wasn't coming out of nothin I couldn't get back into immediately, and that included closets. But in 1974, the concepts of "closets" had not come to my attention. I knew not to reveal my homosexual desires to my peers nor discuss them with my family or any school counselor.

During the course of the next 16 years I would articulate and politicize my sexuality. I would discover that homo-sex did not comprise a whole life nor did it negate my racial identity or constitute a substantive reason to be estranged from my family and black culture. I discovered, too, that the work ahead for me included all of my identities into a functioning self as opposed to accepting a dysfunctional existence as the consequence for my homosexual desires.

▼

In her "Black Male Passivity" essay, Dr. Welsing, a controversial, Washington, D.C.-based psychiatrist, cautions this:

Black psychiatrists must understand that whites may condone homosexuality for themselves, but we as Blacks, must see it as a strategy for destroying black people that must be countered. Homosexuals or bisexuals should neither be condemned nor degraded, as they did not decide that they would be so programmed in childhood. The racist system should be held responsible. Our task is to treat and prevent its continuing and increasing occurrence.

In other words, Dr. Welsing is suggesting, among other things, that black homosexuals are engaged in sexual-genocide, in treason against the race, and are programmed, by racism, to commit acts of self-destruction such as choosing to love and be loved by members of the same gender. If we dare follow Dr. Welsing's ideas to their illogical conclusions, then one could easily assign every black action that transgresses against or fails to conform to black society as being caused by racism. Such reasoning allows for the shirking of responsibility to the extent that a lack of responsibility for ourselves and a shifting of blame for our actions exacerbates the assault of racism and the subsequent crimes that occur. I am not suggesting that the victim be blamed for his victimization, I am only pointing that the addication of responsibility in the face of racism creates and reinforces the climate for the increased nihilism presently plaguing black communities. It is simply too easy to say, "the devil made me do it."

Dr. Welsing's questionable claim to fame is her controversial essay, "The Cress Theory of Color-Confrontation and Racism (White Supremacy): A Psychogenetic Theory and World Outlook (1970)." This essay appears with her "Black Male Passivity" essay in her recently released book, "The Isis Papers: The Keys to the Colors" (Third World Press, Chicago). Her "Theory of Color-Confrontation" essay is the basis for her examination of various issues confronting black Americans including sexuality. Her arguments about race and sexuality, based on her theory, are her sincerely held beliefs. Dr. Welsing contextualizes her sexuality arguments in a myopic analysis of black masculinity, an analysis constructed from the still very limited, very patriarchal, and culturally conservative view of what black liberation should be; a view which is woefully informed by heterosexism and homophobia which she attempts to make credible.

In her "Black Male Passivity" essay, she asserts her arguments at the willful exclusion of a logical analysis of sexuality, thus discrediting her theory by espousing black homophobia and heterosexism, imitations of the very oppressive forces she attempts to challenge — the hegemony of white male heterosexuality. She places herself in direct collusion with the forces that continually move against blacks, gays, lesbians, and all people of color. Thus, everytime a gay man or a lesbian woman is violently attacked, blood is figuratively on Dr. Welsing's hands as surely as blood is on the hands of the attackers. Her ideas reinforce the belief that gay and lesbian lives are expendable, and her views also provide a glimpse as to why the black community has failed to intelligently and coherently address critical, life-threatening issues such as AIDS.

Her reasoning flawed, out-dated, and totally hetero-reactionary, I am curiously reminded of the child who found himself faced with having to tell the emperor he's wearing one of the beautiful clothes that his court is leading him to believe he's wearing, or, as a more recent example, the discovery that Milli Vanilli really didn't sing a note of their hit song, "Girl You Know It's True."

Her Color-Confrontation theory is the justification for her homophobic and heterosexual assault. Her theory is very seductive, particularly for black people oppressed for so long. Her theory is very much like cocaine; a dose of her idea momentarily provides one with a rush of empowerment, but after the high is gone and one comes down, the harsh realities of racism still remain, and sexual diversity, as created by nature, still remains, irrevocably, uncontrollable, though she suggests that among black males, homosexuality and bisexuality are predictable behaviors by using her Color-Confrontation theory as a guide.

The basis of her theory, which is the basis for her puritanical assertions about black male sexuality and sexuality in general, is as follows:

[R]acism (white supremacy) is the dominant social system in today's world. It's fundamental dynamic is predicated upon the genetic recessive deficiency state of albinism, which is responsible for skin whiteness and thus the so-called "white race." This genetic recessive trait is dominated by the genetic capacity to produce any of the various degrees of skin melanation — whether black, brown, red, or yellow. In other words, it can be annihilated as a phenotypic condition. Control of this potential for genetic domination and annihilation throughout the world is absolutely essential if the condition of skin whiteness is to survive. "White survival is predicted upon aggressiveness and muscle mass in the form of technology directed against the "non-white" melaninated men on the planet Earth who constitute the numerical majority. Therefore, white survival and white power are dependent upon the various methodologies, tactics and strategies developed to control all "non-white" men, as well as bring them into cooperative submission. This is especially important in the case of Black men because they have the greatest capacity to produce melanin and, in turn, the greatest genetic potential for the annihilation of skin albinism or skin whiteness.

This theory comprises the primary basis of her perspective as she approaches black male sexuality. From this framework she then asserts that after 400 years of being forced into "passive and cooperative submission" to white males, the end result for black males is the occurrence of homosexuality and bisexuality — what she deems as dysfunctional behavioral responses to oppression. "Black male homosexuality and bisexuality are the only long-run by-products of males submitting in fear to other males." She concludes this argument by stating that:

> Black male bisexuallity and homosexuality has been used by the white collective in its effort to survive genetically in a world dominated by colored people, and Black acceptance of this imposition does not solve the major problem of our oppression but only further retards its ultimate solution.

In attempting to explain homosexuality among whites, she writes:

> [W]hite male and female homosexuality can be viewed as the final expression of their dislike of their genetic albinism in a world numerically dominated by colored people.This dislike of their appearance, though deeply repressed,causes a negation of the act of self-reproduction (sex), in various forms. This is the eventual origin of homosexuality...
> Unlike the white male, the Black male does not arrive at

the effeminate bisexual or homosexual stance from any deeply repressed sense of genetic weakness, inadequacy or disgust, which I refer to as primary effeminacy (effeminacy that is self-derived and not imposed forcibly by others). Instead, the Black male arrives at this position secondarily, as the result of the imposed power and cruelty of the white male and the totality of the white supremacy social and political apparatus that has forced 20 generations of Black males into submission.

Sexuality has been and will always be as variable as eye color, but this obviously eludes Dr. Welsing. Her concern for the plight of black males and the destruction of black homespace, and her efforts to conjure resistance and provide solutions are not admirable when placed alongside her personal, unscientific opinions about sexuality. Her opinions are puritanical dogma and imitative of the status quo. She might as well say, "God made Adam and Eve, not Adam for Steve," as justification for her heterosexism, then she could sit and suck post-plantation cocktails with others of her mindset, such as Rev. Jerry Falwell, who is also a rabid heterosexist and a staunch homophobe.

> Sex, having been granted as the one (though limited) area wherein Black males could express manhood, became the area of behavior where circular patterns of escape were acted out. Symbolically speaking, attempts were made to hide in the dark Black vaginal orifice. When that closed down, the white vaginal orifice was tried. When that also proved unsatisfactory as a hiding place or passage to freedom, Black and white male anuses were tried. Or one might say, these became the hoped for "undercover" railroads to freedom— the underground railroads as escape from the white man no longer being operative.

It is less than sophisticated reasoning to reduce such complexities as sexuality and its expression to the governing control and influence of white supremacy. To the extent that racism has aberrated the contexts and not the sexuality among people of color (and whites as well) is very much a legitimate examination of sexuality. However, her attempt to lead us to believe that passivity and submission in the context of racism causes homosexuality is to suggest that black liberation will somehow eradicate black homosexuality. And, if such eradication is to occur as a result of dismantling and destroying white supremacy, then what method(s) will be employed to achieve this? Does black liberation ultimately require the confinement or extermination of black homosexuals? Is there a heterosexual Similac that can be given to black infants to prevent them from growing up and choosing to love within their own gender? Will black liberation cancel out homosexual desire? The answer is surely a resounding NO! Will black liberation fail without the unqualified participation of black gays and lesbians? The answer is an equally resounding YES!

What is also disturbing about her essay is her lack of a feminist analysis when approaching black liberation struggle. Here she writes:

> All Black people are oppressed. I emphasize here that Black men are oppressed because ultimately, it is male muscle mass that oppresses a people, and only male muscle mass has the potential for achieving liberation. If the men of a people are oppressed., the women are brought under oppression — as they are dependent on their men for protection and defense. Women do not have the muscle mass to liberate a people and protect the young. Women develop the young, but their men must provide the protection and the security apparatus.

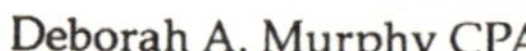

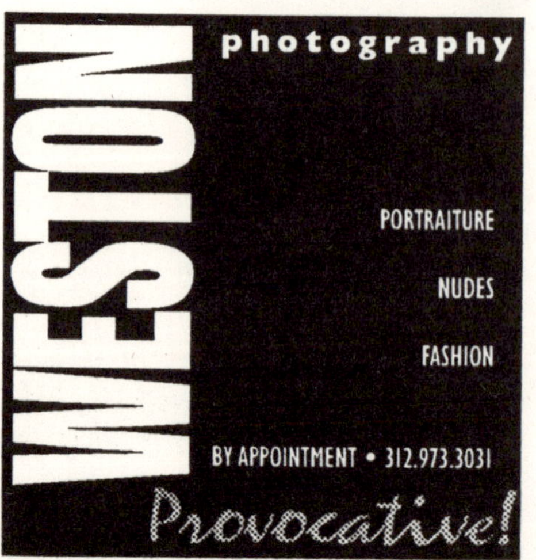

By making this assessment, in the glaring absence of a progressive feminist analysis, she expediently excludes recognizing the existence of and the continued effort to achieve a co-gendered liberation. Her contentions are the worn-out, heterosexist contentions of black nationalists regarding homosexuals and women. Black nationalists believe, as does Dr. Welsing, that racism causes homosexuality. Black nationalists have also traditionally treated women as objects and devalued their participation in black liberation struggles believing, essentially, that women are to be seen and not heard and that they best serve "the black man" and the "black struggle" in horizontal instead of vertical positions.

That racist oppression has tragically torn apart the black family is a given, and consequently, a critical site for serious, co-gendered resistance to avert continued destruction. But to the extent that sexual identity is a conscious, personal choice, and the sexuality practiced is the same, the most we can do is examine how sexuality is impacted upon and influenced by racism, in the same way that we can examine the impact of capitalism, religion, or patriarchy on sexuality.

Arguing that black men are alienated from their manhood by black women (their mothers in single-parent contexts) and society (white males), Dr. Welsing embarks upon the classic, homo-bashing tirade of black nationalist bullies who have consistently attacked homosexuals because they perceive us as simply being weak, irrelevant cock-suckers. She also buys into the patriarchal concept that the only legitimate family is one headed by a man with a submissive woman by his side. She blames black women who have been hurt by black men and left with raising children alone for also fostering the existence of black homosexuality,

because "the alienation, hate and disgust felt towards adult males are visited upon their sons subtly." This transference of "hate and disgust" supposedly alienates black male children from themselves and their manhood, "Black males soon learn that it is easier to be a female child than a male child, and more promising to be an adult Black female than an adult Black male." She additionally argues that this attitude is reinforced in black male children by the black women teachers they come into contact with who may also be "hurt and disgusted" with black men and again, transfer this to black males.

Arguing that the alienation between black men and women and the absence of male role models in the home and in the community promotes homosexuality, bisexuality, effeminization, and passivity, she writes:

> There is only one solution — that Black males collectively face the horrendous presence of white males and conquer the accompanying fear engendered by this act. After the white man is faced, he must be resisted steadfastedly and fought if he continues to wage war on Black people — as he has demonstrated historically that he intends to do. And it is Black males and not females who must do the fighting.

Finally, Dr. Welsing trots out the standard beliefs regarding prisons and the confinement of black men — that they, too, breed homosexuality as opposed to examining homosex in the context of the kinds of prison systems maintained in this country, and how homo-sex, more often than not, is essentially an act of domination and necessity within a prison context. These occurrences are exacerbated by an additional set of complex dynamics that cannot be excluded to simply revile homo-sex and homosexuality and construe

these occurrences to be caused by 20 generations of oppression and passive submission.

Dr. Welsing, speaking of an ex-prisoner patient whom she identifies as an example of 20 generations of racist abuse, confides in us that he said:

> "'It is easier to endure the life on the inside than to try to put up with the pressures of being a man, a husband and a father in the street.'" The intent of racist programming had been achieved: "Give up trying to be a Black man. Why not be a woman?" Many Black males have answered unconsciously, "Why not!" The braided and curled hair, the earrings and bracelets, the midriff tops, the cinch-waisted pants, the flowered underwear, the high-heeled shoes with platforms and the pocketbooks are all behavioral answers to the above. They say in loud and clear language, "White man, I will never come after you. I cannot run in my high-heels —you know that. And I may mess up my hair. "

I suspect, however, that if Freud had been a neurotic, Black nationalistic colored woman living in the noxious racism of America, out of desperation he might very well have formulated homophobic/heterosexist theories such as Dr. Welsing's. Her "Black Male Passivity" essay is left-over dogma and rhetoric that lacks the credibility of truth. It is simply an essay of manipulated conjectures that ultimately reveal themselves as bogus.

Even among the oppressed there is a disturbing need for a convenient "other" to vent anger against, to blame, to disparage, and to denigrate. Such behavior is surely as detrimental as any an oppressor can exercise against the oppressed. There is no excuse for such behavior just as there is no credibility for Dr. Welsing's theories regarding sexuality. At best, her theories reinforce the rampant heterosexism that has paralyzed the black liberation struggle. She widens the existing breach between black gays and lesbians and their heterosexual counterparts, offering no bridges for joining our differences. And throughout it all, she fosters, not an understanding of our differences as we would be led to believe, but instead she offers justifications for homophobia and heterosexism to continue.

Black gays and lesbians can take sustenance and inspiration from the words of Cheryl Clarke, who in her 1983 essay, "The Failure to Transform: Homophobia in the Black Community" firmly urges us to do this:

> [O]pen and proud black gay men and lesbians must take an assertive stand against the blatant homophobia expressed by members of the black intellectual and political community, who consider themselves custodians of the revolution. For if we will not tolerate the homophobia of the culture in general, we cannot tolerate it from black people, no matter what their positions in the black liberation movement. Homophobia is a measure of how far removed we are from the psychological transformation we so desperately need to engender. The expression of homophobic sentiments, the threatening political postures assumed by black radicals and progessives of the nationalist/communist ilk , and the seeming lack of any willingness to understand the politics of gay and lesbian liberation collude with the dominant white male culture to repress not only gay men and lesbians, but also to repress a natural part of all human beings, namely the bisexual potential in us all. Homophobia divides black people as political allies, it cuts off political growth, stifles revolution, and perpetuates patriarchal domination.

So, Dr. Welsing, you want to have a revolution, or are you just acting like you do? ▼

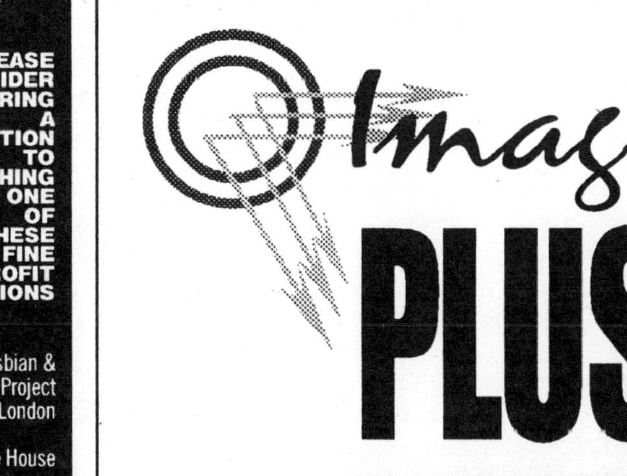

DOIN' LUNCH
with bunny & pussy

Shoes Don't Fail Me Now

PUSSY: Bunny, ever the arbiter of taste and fashion, keeps needling me about my spending habits in general, and my footwear in particular. He says as long as I can't walk in them anyway, and my feet are always in the dense shade of my hips, I could wear flip flops for the rest of my life and no one would notice. He just doesn't understand that shoes not only make the Girl, they must occasionally do double duty when the chauffeur doesn't show.

While shopping for *chapeaus* during the Mardi Gras (and wearing, incidentally, a pair of punky boots that cost three times Bunny's lifetime salary), I chanced into a vintage boutique run by a humpy Dago with a handlebar moustache and a bulge in his pants as big as the St. Charles streetcar.

Ever the *coquette*, I did my best Crawford, smearing Red Lust way up over my lipline and modeling everything from pegnoirs to Pendletons. I settled on a fabulous veiled *cloche* and a pair of the tallest "fuck me" pumps that set me back almost the price of my airfare.

Signor Shopboy asked if I was enjoying the sights and I said I could stand to see more of them... he dusted off a Borselino and a snazzy silk tie, and whisked me off to some really big balls. The next few days were a blur as we convulsed our way through Carnival, stopping only for an occasional pee and a re-touch. As the debacle reached its denouement, I had but one last request—a Mardi Gras morn viewing of the fearsome Black King Zula, atop his river barge. My obliging squire suggested that the final *fête* be an all-night spree, beginning with formal dinner in a fancy restaurant.

I was resplendent, if I say so, from the top of my head—crowned this night by an awesome Raymond Hudd original, replete with maribu and quail, to my Paige Mayberried shoulders, kissed by a sensuous *frappé* of *voile* and silk, to my dainty little toes, encased, as it were, in lovely little black velvet slippers with gilded metal heels, in the style of Charles Jourdan—but, in this instance, courtesy of K-Mart.

We dined and drank and danced and dined and drank some more until the wee hours when Guiseppe spirited me back to his shop for a spot of champagne, served on the floor in front of a quaint little wrought iron space heater. We sipped and giggled and groped by gaslight until quarter to Zulu, when my date sat bolt upright, adjusted his, ahem, tie and mumbled something about a previous engagement..a girl he'd been seeing...a Mardi Gras brunch...and parents from Kansas...

On another night they could have heard my shrieks all the way to Wichita as I demanded to know what, pray tell, he planned to do with me? The genius had it all worked out, or so he thought, suggesting I accompany him to this family affaire, where he'd pass me off as an old school chum. Fat chance, I rebutted, reminding him that, disheveled decolletage nonwithstanding, unless he went to beauty school or clown college, not even Auntie Em and Uncle Henry would fall for such crap. I stood up, tucked my titties, and with an ill-conceived theatrical flourish, stormed out the door...

★★★★

And now the humiliating *mise en scéne* unfolds. Picture an entire city paralyzed by pleasure, so much so that the buses can't run, and the cabbies are all in tights and masks, flinging dubloons from truckfloats in the parishes. Picture a neighborhood where no woman tread unescorted—ever—and where all the nasty boys have been drinking non-stop for three days in anticipation of this very morning. Picture a primitive street, semi-paved with bricks and stones and lined with open ditches, filled to an overflowing. Now picture Pussy.

Those fucking slippers didn't even last a block before one heel snapped right off, forcing me to limp down the street like a travelling production of Glass Menagerie. My audience—loaded locals *en route* to the parade—hoooted and cheered as the second heel broke and I collapsed in a heap in the gutter. I gave the pumps to a needy queen and trekked the ten blocks home in stocking feet.

On that day, I made a solemn vow:

> *If ever I find myself down on my luck*
> *Scouring for frocks in the dumps*
> *And getting my hair cut and blown at Bo-Rics*
> *I still will wear good pumps!*

An Open Apology To Our Readers

While neither of us can deny that we're powerhungry sluts, ever-eager to foist our *weltanschauung* on all those who cross our paths, we never dreamed it would happen like this. It seems the Piss Police have attacked the Circle Campus Fountain of Youths (Critics Notebook, *Thing* Number 2) reconfiguring the delightful spa of iniquity, removing the portals of pleasure and extending all possible sightlines for easy monitoring. While we truly feel for all those whose goings and comings have been disrupted, we can't help but wonder who the, ahem, whistleblower was and gloat that, perhaps, our manifesti have been read by poufs in powerful places.

Love Among the Ruins

The ever-intrepid Miss Gigi recalls a pre-AIDS interlude that began with the usual hunt and peck in a notorious sissy saloon and ended with an invitation to a *ménage-a-trois* extended by a soigne deuce from Tinley Park. In the process of getting from here to there, they acquired a large number of stragglers, prompting our Gal Gigi to wax ecstatic. "Surely in a group this size," she mused "there will be someone man enough to fuck me." Once ensconced in the suburban hometown, she acquitted herself in her usual grand style—suffering through the obligatory chips and dips and admiring the clown collection like the trooper she is, until finally, the host said, "Now."

Gigi beat a hasty path to the *boudoir*, where she dropped trow, bit the bedspread and braced herself for the onslaught. "Please God." she prayed, "let it hurt." And she waited and waited and waited for what seemed like eternity, till she opened her eyes, saw eight pairs of legs, soles facing skyward and sighed, "Shit! Another night in Stonehenge."

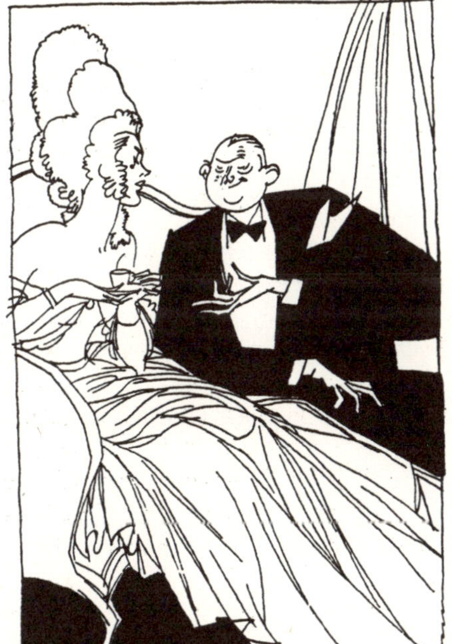

La Fanciulla Del West Hollywood

One of our far-hung correspondents sent this *communique* from La La Land:

...I was back up north again the first week of June for a retreat sponsored by the Body Electric school on the Russian River. It was a wonderful experience. I was re-birthed several times, gave and received a number of erotic massages and met many extraordinary people. I will give you more details when we next speak but this one-week retreat was worth years of therapy... I may start exploring the S&M scene, at least I have joined an S&M support group. Who knows, the next time I see you I might be wearing chains and chaps.

S&M support group? The more we think about it, we don't even want sex anymore...just disciples.

Louis Tiffany's Comfort

Entshudigen sie, bitte, ist das ihre Shvanz est in mein Tasche gefallen?
Excuse me, please, it seems your penis has fallen into my pocket.
— *A useful German Phrase*

One of our New Orleans cousins headed to the Big Apple to suck up some culture. Whilst at the Metropolitan Museum he made serious eye contact with a California surfer type who had no doubt journeyed East to suck up some of the same. Our friend snaked his way through the labyrinthine galleries, with Beach Buns in hot pursuit, dallying in front of several suggestive *oevres* and, finally, coming to rest in front of an imposing Tiffany triptych. The hushed reverence of the darkened alcove was suddenly ended by a hammerschlag zippppppppp—startling the lunchtime crowd and rousing our friend from his reveries, into the reality of a hot breath in his ear...and a hard cock in his hand. The impassioned art lovers scurried off to view the great porcelain throne—in whose chamber they spent well nigh the rest of the afternoon, recreating Michaelangelo's greatest hits as interpreted by Tom of Finland...until the moment of climax when the Sand Stud spurted a stunning homage to Jackson Pollack—on the wall of the stall. Ain't art grand.

A Moveable Feast

We could try and disguise the identity of the source for this sordid tale but, by now, you'd guess it was Gigi... and here's what she did this summer: It seems they were doing some roadwork near her home. For the convenience of the laborers, a porta-san was installed right by her expressway entrance. Ever the opportunist, she stopped her car on the median, feiggning engine trouble, and made a discrete dash into the loo, where she scribbled her number in indelible ink. As lust would have it, she received an inquiry that very day and was visited by a workingclass hero at the end of the night shift. *Apré tryst*, she promptly called in to file her report. When she got to the part about leaving her number in the "cute little outhouse" Bunny realized that the dear lamb had failed to grasp a fundamental concept about outdoor commodes. "You realize," he explained, patiently, "that the toilet is neither a permanent fixture nor a disposable one. It will be moved to another location as soon as the job is done. That's why it's called a Porta-Potty." Gigi was delighted by the news. "To think I've spent a fortune in petrol driving all around this confounded city, leaving my name in public restrooms, and, now the Highway Department will do it for me. I can't wait to taste my tax dollars at work."

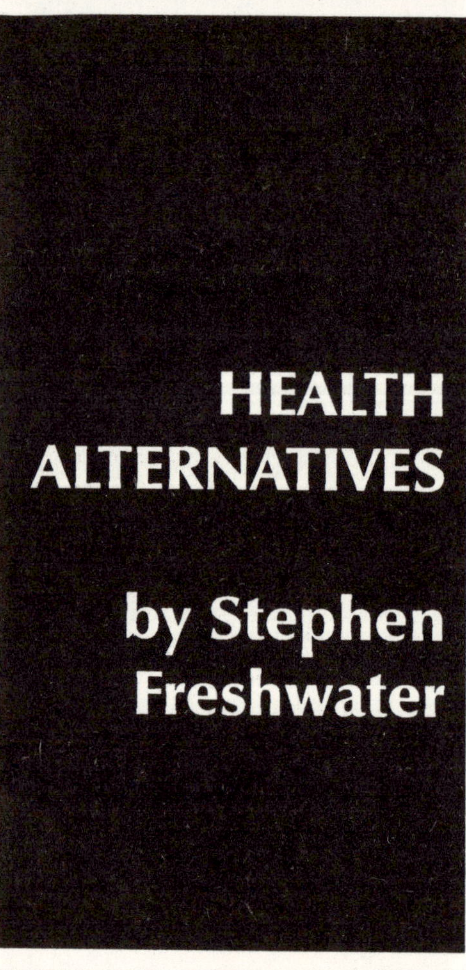

HEALTH ALTERNATIVES

by Stephen Freshwater

Since my words of frustration with ACT UP in the last issue of *Thing*, I was proven wrong by a small but growing minority of ACT UP members who *are* practicing alternative medicine and are dedicated to the release of information regarding alternative health care to individuals who have either HIV or AIDS.

From September 15-19 1990, ACT UP Kansas City (Missouri) hosted a "Health Fraud" conference protest along with ACT UP New York. The health confrence that was the target of protest was sponsored by the American Medical Association (AMA) and the Health Insurance Association with participation by the Food and Drug Administration (FDA).

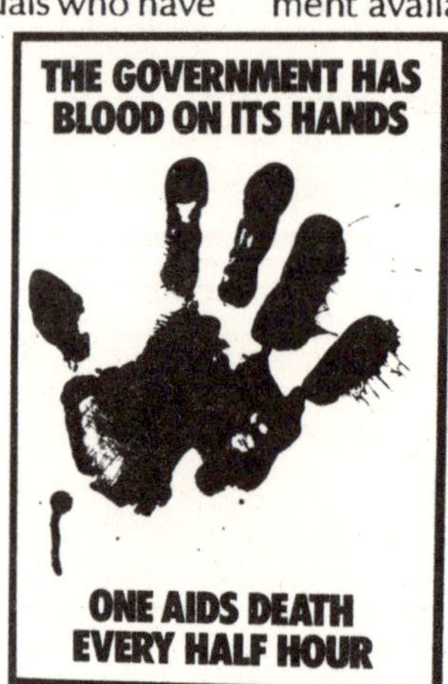

A Gran Fury graphic used by ACT UP New York. From Douglas Crimp's AIDS DEMO GRAPHICS (Bay Press).

The conference was designed to teach insurance, health and consumer officials techniques to discredit and suppress non-AMA, non-FDA approved treatments.

Twenty-three ACT UP members and supporters were arrested during this protest. Bob Lederer, member ACT UP New York, believes like many of us that "we don't need 'consumer protectors' to prevent people with HIV and AIDS from exercising informed choices of any treatment available, no matter from what system of healing." I'm glad to see their agenda go beyond free AZT, Pentab, and DDI.

There are actions to stop the supersession of alternative health care going on all over America, and in the rest of the world. If we don't succeed, there could be anti-fraud laws passed to outlaw selling, prescribing or even advising about such treatments. (Though there should be some legislation to keep an eye on this growing industry to watch for such things as over-pricing and fraudulent practioners.)

If you would like to help or want more information, write me c/o *Thing* and I will

DESIGN Haynes/Gomez Inc.

try to get it to you. Please enclose a SASE.

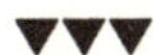

Reviewing the many news releases that we recieve here at Thing, I have to say that the Gay Men's Health Crisis (GMHC) in New York City has got it together. Craig G. Harris who is the Assistant Coordinator of the GMHC People of Color Prevention Program was quite pleased to note that GMHC has increased the number of people of color on their staff and volunteering, and has drastically increased the number of African-American gay men who have been served through GMHC's education program. Along with that, GMHC is beginning to form a tight union with the Gay Men of African Descent (GMAD). There are more programs, many which support alternative health care.

Here in Chicago, I am happy to see progress as well, with the opening of the Northside HIV Treatment Center (NHTC). Founded by accupuncturists Arthur Shattuck and Mary Kay Ryan, they've just opened their donation only clinic on Tuesdays and Thursdays at the new Rodde Center (4753 N. Broadway). They provide traditional Chinese medicine, massage and acupuncture for all people impacted by HIV. Future plans are to open a library of alternative health information. For appointments, to volunteer, or to make a much-needed donation contact Arthur Shattuck at (312) 472-9156.

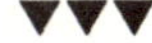

Many caregivers for HIV and AIDS patients frequently suffer from stress, burnout, and grief. I was glad to see a retreat sponsored in Chicago called "Building Bridges, Healing Ourselves" for AIDS caregivers, coordinated by Kermit Berg and friends. Reports are that it was quite energizing and successful, and another is being planned soon. For information or to make a donation write: Chicago Area AIDS Caregivers' Retreat c/o Kermit Berg, 321 Sangamon Street, Chicago, IL 60607.

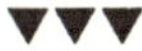

I would like to encourage all of you who are suffering from HIV or AIDS to look into Aloe Vera juice. There are many benefits to receive from this miracle plant. For HIV fatigue, a combination of Bee Pollen, Spirulina, Wheat Grass and Ginseng is highly recommended. I take a great product called Ultra Energy Plus. It gives you all of the above except the ginseng, so I supplement it with a ginseng capsule. Ultra Energy Plus contains bee pollen, spirulina, and wheat grass, as well as a number of other good energy supplying substances, including amino acids.

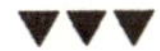

Finally, I would like for you to take a moment and ask yourself if you are at peace with yourself. Ask yourself "do I want to survive this Illness we call AIDS?" If you answered yes to these questions, then get control of your life and always picture yourself — in your mind and in the mirror— in good health. To learn more about a positive approach I suggest "The AIDS Book — Creating a Positive Approach" by Louise L. Hay (Hay House). She has help thousands of HIV and AIDS impacted people gain control of their illness. This book will also help anyone facing a life-threatening Illness.

May the Almighty bless you and and please stay healthy.

Ask Marjorie Marginal
Advice For Real Life

GO BALD

I'm wondering if I should braid my hair. Really. I mean, I'm one of those "hi yeller" types with good hair, and it just won't dread, no matter how hard I try. I'm looking to do a more Afrocentric kind of look, but I'm afraid that in braids it might be too Milli Vanilli. Please help.

— Fashion Dysfunctional

Dear Fashion,
Please don't braid Miss Marjorie's hair over whether you should braid your hair or not. Personal grooming decisions must be made, kept, and worn with a certain depth of conviction, or not at all. If you don't know if you want to braid your hair or not, Miss Marjorie certainly doesn't. Nor does anyone else. And braided hair, worn timidly or indecisively, will most certainly beg comparison to Milli Vanilli, Bo Derek, and Glodeen, to name a few. Do you seek advice on the color of your underpants and brand of mouthwash too? Miss Marjorie hopes not. As long as you eschew beads and don't pierce your nose, you won't look silly vanilli at all. Trust me.

SEARCHIN' TO FIND THE ONE

I'm having a hard time finding a lover. I've tried 900 numbers, dating services, cruising, volunteer work, etc. and I can't seem to reel one in. Oh sure, there are the quickies. The ones that want to "drop by" now and again. But I'm rapidly growing weary of this "That Girl" bachlorette life, and would like to settle down once and for all. Any advice?

— Lonely Reader

Dear Lonely,
Stop whining, honey. Miss Marjorie would like to see some of this trade that goes spinning through your revolving door. But seriously, the quest for l'amour is perilous at best, fraught with suffering and heartache. It ain't gonna change. Been that way for years. And once you do snag boyfriend, you'll find he leaves the cap off the toothpaste or some other little thing that makes you want to shoot him sometimes. That's how love is. My advice is to use condoms and stick to Barbara Cartland for the mushy stuff.

write to Marjorie...she cares about you!

★ THE INNER THING ★

Mundane astrology is the astrological study of countries, states and cities. Much can be discovered from the chart of the American people:

This chart of the American people originated from the creation of the oldest permanent European settlement in the country. Most of these planets are in mutable signs (Sagittarius, Gemini, Virgo, Pisces) and quite a few are air signs (Gemini, Libra). This mutable air (Gemini) quality points to the American love for novelty, movement and communication. Americans have a love of independence and freedom (Uranus on the Rising sign). In love with speed and always in a hurry, the American Sun is in Virgo. With the Sun and Jupiter at the midheaven, America will always occupy a position of prominence among the nations of the world. Americans have a great desire for achievement and success, and most rise above their "original station" in life (all a matter of perception, I suppose). Being an ambitious people with strong egos, Americans are more interested in foreign relations than in domestic relations. This is because six signs (in the chart) are in fire and air, the masculine and extrovertive signs. They stretch their hands (and their budgets) giving Americans the reputation of a universal Santa Claus. Our obsession with health and cleanliness may be traced to the Sun and Jupiter in Virgo. Mars in the seventh house points to the aggressive attitude Americans have taken towards foreign nations. While America has never openly provoked a war, they have stepped in other's. The danger in foreign alliances arises when America tries to dominate others, for they do not easily give in and compromise. They are a highly independent people preferring to go their own way instead of listening to the lessons of history.* The American Mars in Gemini seems to have profound meaning as our president is a Gemini with a Gemini rising. This is open ground for alot of Gemini adaptability, flexibility and cunning. Quite simply put, no one ever knows what face George Bush is really wearing...including George.

***Horoscopes of the Western Hemisphere,** Marc Heeren Penfield.

by iris kit

The Black Line

Where all men are welcome.

1-900-468-2522

1·900·HOT·BLACK

$1 Per Min • $2 1st Min • Must Be 18 Or Older • Prices Subject to Change Without Notice

THING

Number 5 • $3

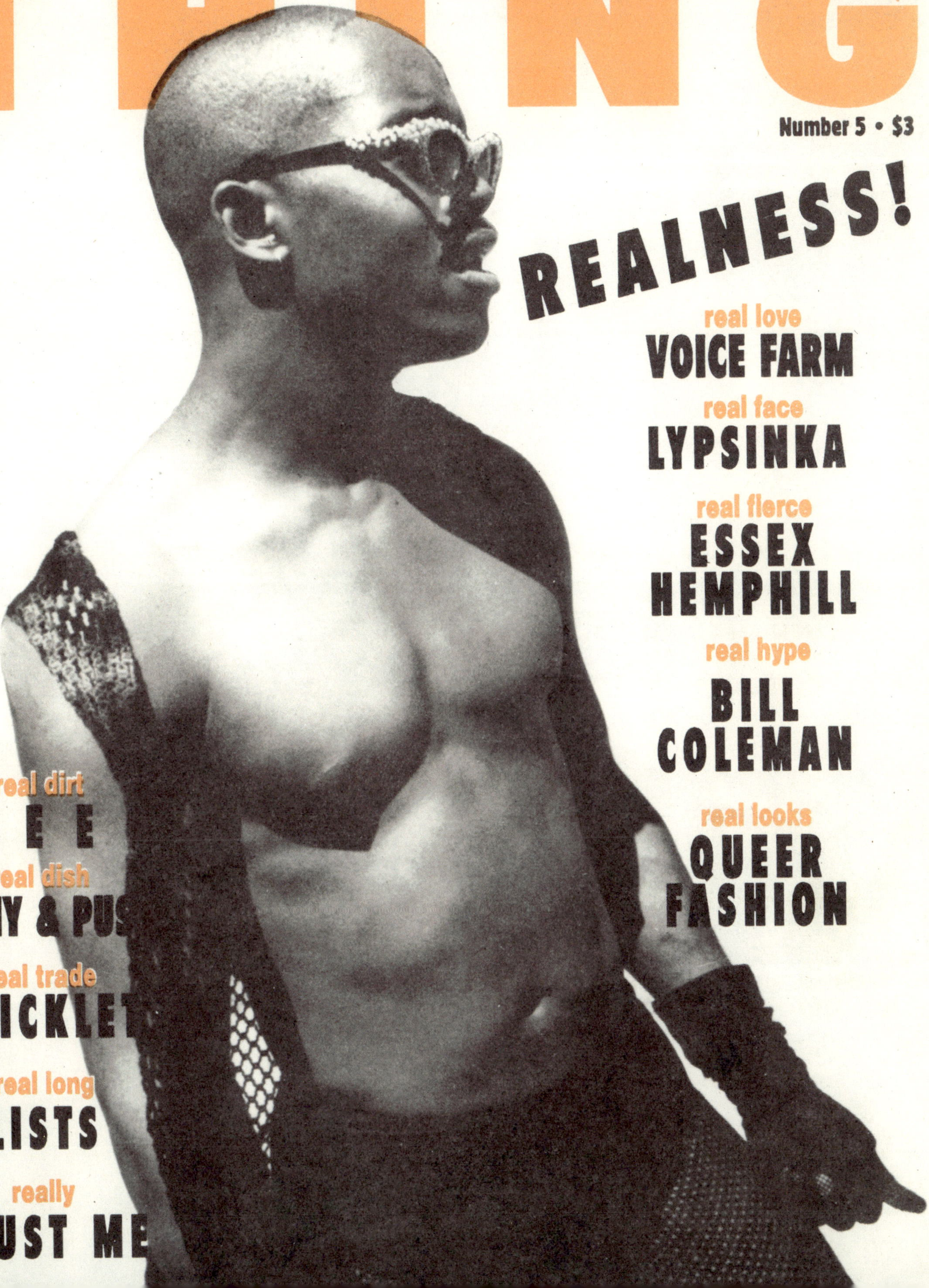

REALNESS!

real love
VOICE FARM

real face
LYPSINKA

real fierce
ESSEX HEMPHILL

real hype
BILL COLEMAN

real looks
QUEER FASHION

real dirt
T E E

real dish
BUNNY & PUS

real trade
CHICKLET

real long
LISTS

really
TRUST ME

contents

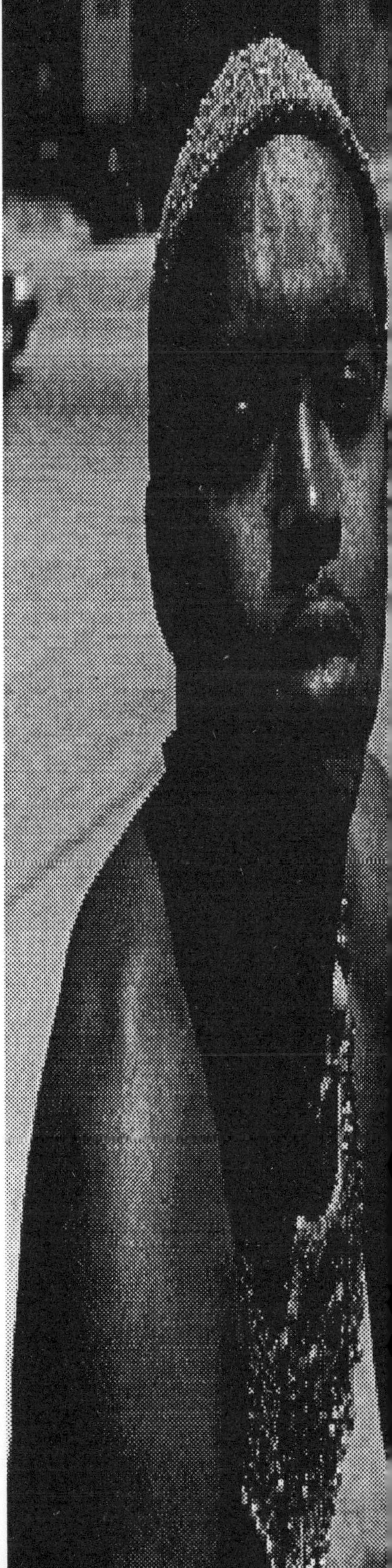

COVER AND THIS PAGE Photograph of Jeff Britton by
Stephen Winter. Styled by Paul Stura.

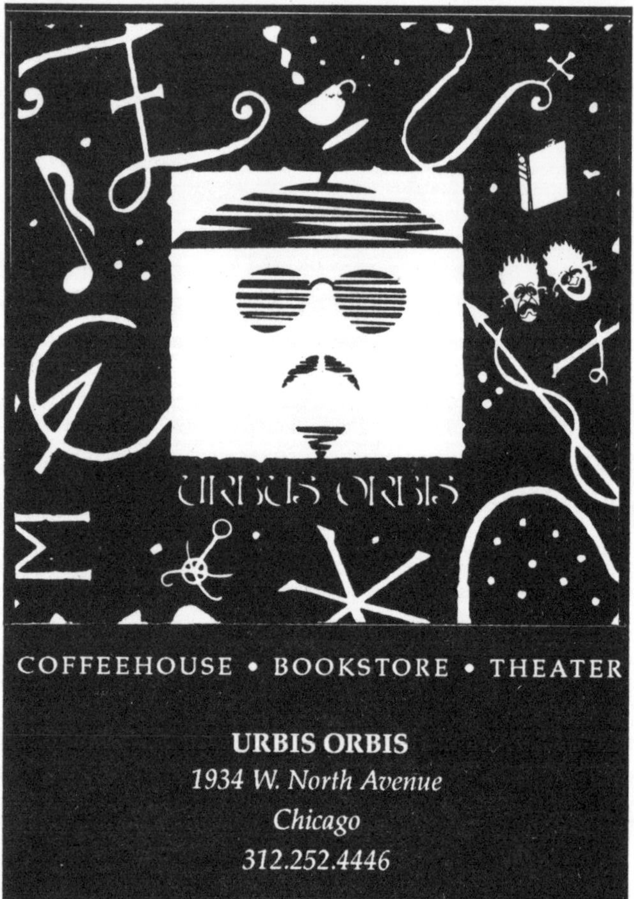

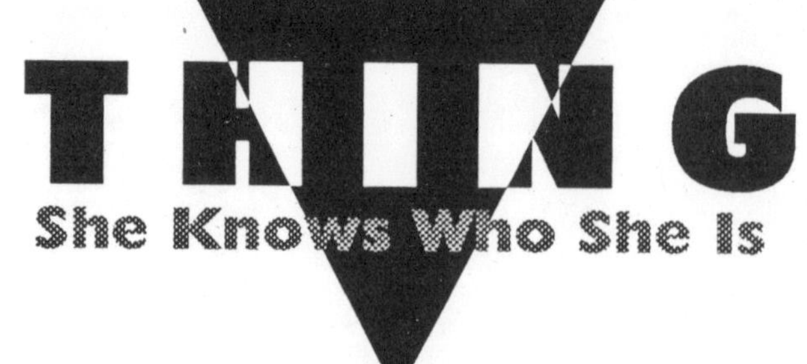

Number Five • Fall 1991

PUBLISHER/EDITOR Robert Ford
EDITORS Trent Adkins, W. Delon Strode, Lawrence D. Warren
ART DIRECTION/LAYOUT Robert Ford
ADVERTISING SALES Sylvia Michaels, Stephen Freshwater
GRAPHIC SERVICES Simone Bouyer
COMPUTER SERVICES International Media Associates
CONTRIBUTORS Fred Bain, Belasco, Simone Bouyer, Bunny & Pussy, Derrick Carter, Chicklet, Gregory Conerly, Robert Klein Engler, Scott Free, David Gandy, Spencer Kincy, Larvetta Larvon, Tod Roulette, Madrid St. Angelo, John Smith, Max Smith, Chip Wass, Stephen Winter
THANKS Ahndi Coffey, Stephanie Coleman, Steve Lafreniere, Savage Mann, John Preston, Chris Russell, Craig Siegel, Paul Stura, Michael Thompson, Shelby Webb, Jr., Walter Youngblood.

Thing is published capriciously. Subscriptions are seven dollars for the next three issues published postpaid. Single issues available at your favorite gay bookseller. Wholesale inquiries invited. Donations encouraged! *Thing* encourages unsolicited submissions of any printed matter; only those with self-addressed stamped envelopes will be returned. Artists' payment is the satisfaction of contribution. Editorial inclusion casts no aspersions on one's racial or sexual categorization (Things know who they are.) Opinions expressed are those of individual contributors and do not always reflect those of *Thing*. *Thing* does not sell or rent its mailing list. © 1991 *Thing*
Thing Publishing, 2151 W. Division, Chicago, Illinois USA 60622-3056
✆ 1.312.227.1780

Direct from San Francisco's Freethinker Movement — a fertile cultural breeding ground in the areas of music, art, film, fashion and design — Voice Farm has carved its niche by creating eclectic, sometimes demented mutant dance pop laced with many surprises.

So how did you guys come together? (Myke) Charly and I were working together around 1985 and we met Ken Weller. He plays guitar and bass and he actually started as our lighting tech. He was playing with another band and became frustrated with the other band. We said "well, just come on stage and do the encore with us." So he would do lights for the show and at the last number would come out with his guitar, spin around and do the encore. **That could be very hectic, huh?** Yes, actually it was very hectic. But it was fun and we started doing a lot of things together in the studio and then it evolved from there and he became a band member. **Who basically does the writing?** (Myke) Basically Charly Brown. (Charly) I write most of the lyrics. And sometimes I set the face part of a song or the basic rhythm. I tend to gravitate towards the mid-tempo/ballads and Mike picks up the higher tempos to disco. We change a lot of roles there, too. **What prompted the title of your latest album, <u>Bigger Cooler Weirder</u>? That's exactly what it is: bigger, cooler and definitely weirder.** (In unison) Thank you! (Myke) You know what? I remember how it evolved. We were working in the studio with Wally Brill, our manager and co-producer, and he would say, "How do you want this to sound?" He would refer to a drum sound or something and one of us would say, "Bigger." One of us would say, "Could we kinda make it cooler?" And one of us wanted it a lot weirder than it was before. That's the kind of references we would use towards the music . And so I think it kinda evolved out of that...it kind of came out of a joke. **I think it's so neat how things like that can happen. Living here in Chicago, the predominant music is house music. Has house influenced your music at all as far as your dance tracks, singles, and things like that?** Oh definitely. Yeah. **In what ways?** Well, I mean it's like in San Francisco there's a lot of dance clubs and we like to go dancing. You automatically get a hint of what's happening and you either incorporate it or you die. You either dig it or you don't...we dig it so I'm sure it shows up at some point. **Your bio mentions something called the Freethinking Movement. Could you enlighten those of us who don't know exactly what the Freethinking Movement is?** I guess what has been coined a "movement" didn't originate in San Francisco but is growing there. It's a culmination of all the previous sort of social groups like the hippies, the punks, the gay movement, the beatnik movement, that all culminate in San Francisco. All the people are freethinkers because they're living lifestyles that are outside the traditional cultural boundaries. It's pretty much self explanatory as it's literally people who think in a free form style: people who think for themselves. **Do you find that being from San Francisco, with your campy lyrics, people assume you're a gay group?** (Myke) I think we're pretty ambiguous. And the message is a positive ambiguity-if there's a message in it. We're not trying to tip the scales one way or another but as a part of that freethinking it's just being open

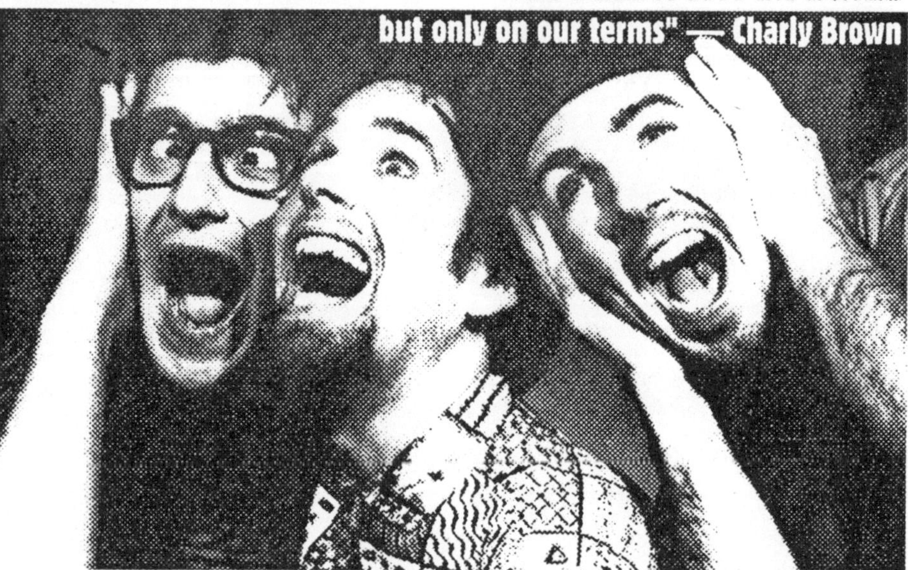

ALIVE WITH PLEASURE! (l to r) **Ken Weller, Charly Brown, & Myke Reilly.** Photo **Albert Sanchez.**

freethinking: VOICE FARM

interview by Delon Strode

to possibilities. **Has Voice Farm participated in any AIDS fundraisers in San Francisco?** About two weeks ago we had an event called Pink Saturday which was the Saturday night before the gay pride parade here in San Francisco. It was basically a benefit for Project Open Hand and other organizations. **Are any of you members of Queer Nation , ACT UP, or any other radical activist groups?** No, we're not members, but we support anything radical. **How do you deal with controversy?** So far we haven't. I don't think our profile is high enough to where we've had to deal with any controversy but I think we're ready to deal with the American Family Association. **Where do you find some of the weirder samples in your music?** A big source is television. We sometimes keep the tape deck going and record television. Then [at playback] you kind of listen to it in a new way. You listen for weird sounds. There are like all these atmospheric sounds, and just really stupid sounding effects on TV shows, people's voices, bad acting, porno movies. We've got some great stuff from porn movies on "Free Love". And occasionally we sample from other records. I use movies too. Any favorite part I remember, I'll just rent the movie and sample it. Like the intro to the "Free Love" video that says, "I have an immediate urge to pull off my bikini." That was from a funny movie called, "The Wild World of Jane Mansfield." **Are you all like a comedy dance group? Even the photo sent with your bio is hilarious.** That's our "Alive With Pleasure" look.

Ken, you remind me of Jerry Lewis in that picture with those glasses. (Ken) Why thank you. That's a good one and I love being compared to Jerry, in his prime, not his grouchier look I take it. **No, I don't mean the telethon look. More towards the younger Jerry Lewis and Dean Martin comedy movies.** (Ken) O.K. **Are you guys working on new music for the next album already? Or are your primary interest at this point promoting this album?** Right now we're doing both. We're putting a lot of energy into promoting the tour and working with a dancer. When we tour we'll probably take three male and female dancers. All that is being fine tuned and we're working on new material as well. **Is there anything else you guys would like to say? We've seemed to have covered quite a bit here. Ken, you've been kind of quiet.** (Ken) Well they've pretty much covered all the right stuff. ...I don't know if you can print this in your paper or not. **We can print anything you want.** Just a little message from San Francisco Beat: "Fuck freely comrades. Wear a rubber and do it with love!"

MUSIC

Sing Softly and Carry a Big Beat

Always a fan of slow, skanky, soulful, moody tunes, I'm too-too happy to have discovered **Massive Attack's** Blue Lines **(Virgin)**. At once urban and gritty yet soulful and mysterious. Vocalist **Shara Nelson** is reason enough to dash out and buy it. She's givin' voice very reminiscent of divas like **Randy Crawford, Cheryl Lynn**, even **Tanna Gardner**. On "Daydreaming", she pull's off the best intonations of **Aretha Franklin's** "Day Dreaming" (...and I'm thinking of you). In this era of over-sampling, Nelson's vocalizing á la the Queen of Soul work much better, sounding far more interesting than a plain old sample. "Lately" is truly wicked for continuing the skanky going's on put forth in **En Vogue's** "Hold On" or almost anything downtempo by **Caron Wheeler**. Massive Attack's first single, "Safe From Harm", is on 12" and it's quite the catchy tune. It's very downtempo so it's completely the other side of anything high energy or techno. Splendid chill pill sounds. More, Massive Attack, please.
— **TA**

Beyond the Hype

A funny thing happens when people become famous. Take DJ/producer **Frankie Knuckles** for instance. Suddenly, he's got all these newly-emerged, self-appointed critics complaining that his smash debut album, Beyond The Mix **(Virgin)** disappoints because it's not 'House-ier.' Here's yet another example of how some people misinterpret House. Certainly, if anybody could produce a well-rounded House album, it's Knuckles who's entertained many a club tart from New York to Chicago and back again. With *Beyond The Mix* he craftily creates a worthy homage to House's most humble beginnings (mainly Gospel, R&B and the Philly Sound) and a product that works for the radio. Merely making an effort to have mass appeal is not a sin. Under Knuckles' and DEF Mix Production's guidance, every track sounds of artistic integrity. They're all highly listenible and danceable. Wisely, Knuckles used the dance floor at New York City's Sound Factory to gauge crowd response. Favorite picks: "Work Out," "Sacrifice," "Party At My House," "Sold On Love." The very popular hit "The Whistle Song," is now the anthemic last song played at all the clubs. "Right Time" is catchy and bumpy and fully orchestrated without being heavyhanded and boasts beautiful vocals by **Lisa Michaelis**. There's also **Satoshi Tomiie** programming keyboards, **John Poppo's** sound engineering and **David Morales'** drum and percussion programming. Altogeher, *Beyond The Mix* perfectly sums up the many facets of Frankie Knuckles' musical genius: soulful, jazzy, smooth, sophisticated, matured and extremely marketable. — **TA**

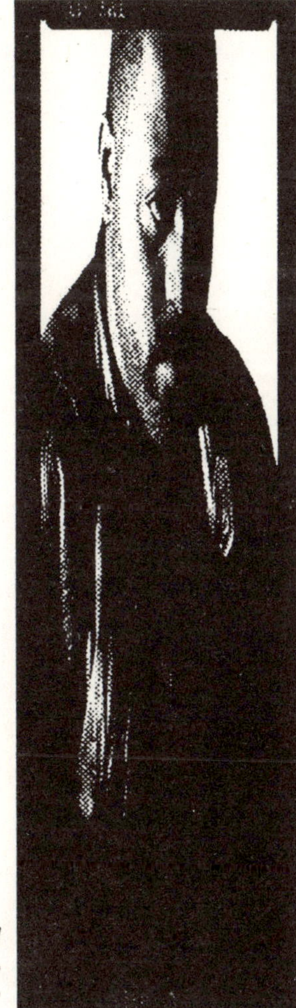

KNUCKLE SAMMICH: DJ/ Producer **Frankie Knuckles**. Photo **Alex Smith**.

Club Shirley Strikes Again!

Ceybil Jeffries' Let The Music Take Control **(Atlantic)** is *the* hot major-label underground house sound out of Chicago/New York. "Love So Special," the catchy club hit is included in both a new remix by **Steve Anderson** and the original fierce remix by **Tony Humphries**, best known for the "Zanzibar" sound. The disc also features collaborations with **Ten City** members (and labelmates) **Byron Stingily, Herb Lawson**, and **Byron Burke**. Chicago followers will also recognize the talents of **Yvonne** "Doin' It In a Haunted House" **Gage**. And there's even a collaboration with **Jennifer Holiday**. Ceybil (don't ask me how to pronounce it) has a strong, sanctified voice that rises above the mediocrity of some of the would-be divas on the block. Some tracks were produced in New York, others in Chicago, giving the project a balanced sound. — **RF**

REVIEWS

GHOST DAD? Are you buying the new **Natalie Cole** album, *Unforgettable*? She does a flawless duet on the title cut with her daddy **Nat King Cole**! They're walking out of the store! What's next, a new **Liza Minnelli** and **Judy Garland** CD? Or **Crystal Waters** sings with **Ethel Waters**? **RIMSHOTS** Q: When does Crystal Waters start to sound like **Muddy Waters**? A: Around the third or fourth track. Ah-hoohah! Q: What do you say when the last track of the **Ce Ce Peniston** CD single ends? A: FINALLY! **YOU HEARD IT HERE FIRST... Vaginal Creme Davis**, publisher of *Fertile Latoyah Jackson Magazine*, informed us on her recent visit to Chi-town that she'll soon began publishing a second zine. Named *Shrimp*, she says it's focus will be "feet and music coverage." We can't wait! Also, look for forward-thinking Tommy Boy to sign glamorous and leggy **Diahann Carroll** look-alike RuPaul **"Starr Booty."** And writer **Dennis Cooper** has reportedley nixed **Matt Dillon** as the star of the film version of his novel *Closer*. (Too long in the tooth, maybe?) **CHUBS "R" US** Who was bigger the last time you looked, **Oprah** or **Delta**? Are **Vesta Williams** and **Carnie Wilson** on the same diet? Or did they just trade tonnage with the now-svelte **Jennifer** "but-my-ego's-still-big-as-a-house" **Holiday**? And what about **Demi Moore** showing her pregnant privileged Hollywood fat white ass off on the cover of *Vanity Fair*! And then there's the **Paula Abdul** diet, where you eat anything you want and then have your video image sque-e-e-zed. Ooops! **GREASY KID STUFF** Now that "Pee-Wee's Playhouse" is off the air, Fox is prepping its **Blaine & Antoine** Saturday morning animated series. And can anyone believe that Paul was doing some hetero Debbie-does-Dallas styled porn? Right... Miss **Pee Wee Herman**, givin' you six year old sissy boy with a queenie genie and humpy, half-dressed Hispanic playmates? Maybe he stumbled into the wrong theater. **SUPERFREAK** More ridiculous scandalous celebrity news from Miss **Rick James**, who, along with girlfriend **Tanya Anne Hijazi**, was recently arrested on sexual assault charges. A story in *Entertainment Weekly* quotes Ms. **JoAnne Funderburg** of the **Mary Jane Girls**, "With all the things he's done over the years, this latest incident is just karma working its way around." Otay! **CHICKEN BREAST TO GO** Though its trendy to dis **Marky Mark**, the white boy is due his props for not only giving **Loleatta Holloway** credit and a video apperance on the otherwise dull "Good Vibrations", but for having much better pecs than his brother **Donnie**. **I WANT YOUR SEX** Lastly, what was super-straight pop idol **George Michael** doing playing pool at Ka-Boom! ...*on a Sunday (GAY) night?!*

EVERY THING to GO! TUN

David Gandy
Substance

1. **Put Your Hands Together (The Brixton Bass Mix)**
D-Mob *FFRR*
2. **Shine On (Joey Negro Mix)**
Sold Out featuring Sarah Warwick *Columbia*
3. **Give Me Your Love (Philly Mix)**
Be Noir *Irma*
4. **Musica De Amour**
A Man Called Adam *Ritmo*
5. **Everybody Have A Good Time**
Archie Bell and the Drells *CBS*
6. **Dream**
Insync featuring Dellroy *WAU*
7. **Can't Give You Up**
Life On Earth *Republic*
8. **I Desire You (Sample Version)**
A.B.T. *Nu Groove*
9. **Frenzy**
Transcendence *Strobe*
10. **Keep On Believing**
Jenifer Mickey *New Generation*

Derrick Carter
Shelter, Insanity, Substance

1. **Get Wize (Re-Mix)**
Rodeo Jones *A&M*
2. **Lift Every Voice**
Mass Order *White Label*
3. **Unique**
Danube Dance *Flying*
4. **Is It All Over My Face (Male Vocal)**
Loose Joints *West End*
5. **Everything's Goin'**
Dharma B *Acid Jazz*
6. **Plastica (Re-Mix)**
Pizzarro *Razz*
7. **Change**
Lisa Stansfield *Arista*
8. **If Only I Knew**
Paul Varney *White Label*
9. **The Saint**
Thompson Twins *Warner Brothers*
10. **The Pressure**
Sounds Of Blackness *A&M*

Spencer Kincy
Ka-Boom!, Shelter, Substance

1. **I'll Be Your Friend**
Robert Owens *Unknown*
2. **Feel**
Love Drops NYC *Warner Brothers*
3. **I'm Happy**
World Power (featuring Althea McQueen) *Cardiac*
4. **If I Only Knew**
Paul Varney *White Label*
5. **Tangled Thoughts**
Spencer Kincy *Unknown*
6. **Untamed World**
Bassic Tension Vol *Bassic*
7. **Feel My Soul**
UBO Project (featuring Kathy Summers) *House In Effect*
8. **Give Me Your Love**
Be Noir *Irma*
9. **Music Mental (Not Yet)**
Larry P. Rauson Jr. *New Generation*
10. **Don't Wanna Have To Ask You**
Temper Temper *Ten Records*

E S T H I N G S

Fred Bain
Cairo, Vortex, "Anywhere on the Underground Scene."

1. **I'm Not In Love**
Basscut *Charisma*
2. **Something Special**
Nomad *Capitol*
3. **The Pressure**
Sounds Of Blackness *A&M*
4. **Move To The Music**
Monica Deluxe *Meet*
5. **Get Wize (ReMix)**
Rodeo Jones *A&M*
6. **Deep Thoughts**
Paradise Inc. *4 On The Floor*
7. **Falling In Love**
Kelly Charles *Champion*
8. **Always There**
Incognito *Talking Loud*
9. **Tomorrow**
Tongue and Cheek
10. **Let's Get Together**
Candy J.

LIST YOUR TUNES

Thing magazine is looking for your personal best. Just jot down ten tunes — new, old, or in-between — and return this to us ASAP to be part of our next issue. We also have room for brief reviews; a paragraph or two on a fierce (or tired) new release DEADLINE: **YESTERDAY!**

NAME ___________________________

CLUB/AFFILIATION ___________________________

LIST TITLE (optional) ___________________________

TITLE	ARTIST	LABEL
1		
2		
3		
4		
5		
6		
7		
8		
9		
10		

2151 W. DIVISION STREET
CHICAGO ILLINOIS USA
60622-3056
(312) 227-1780

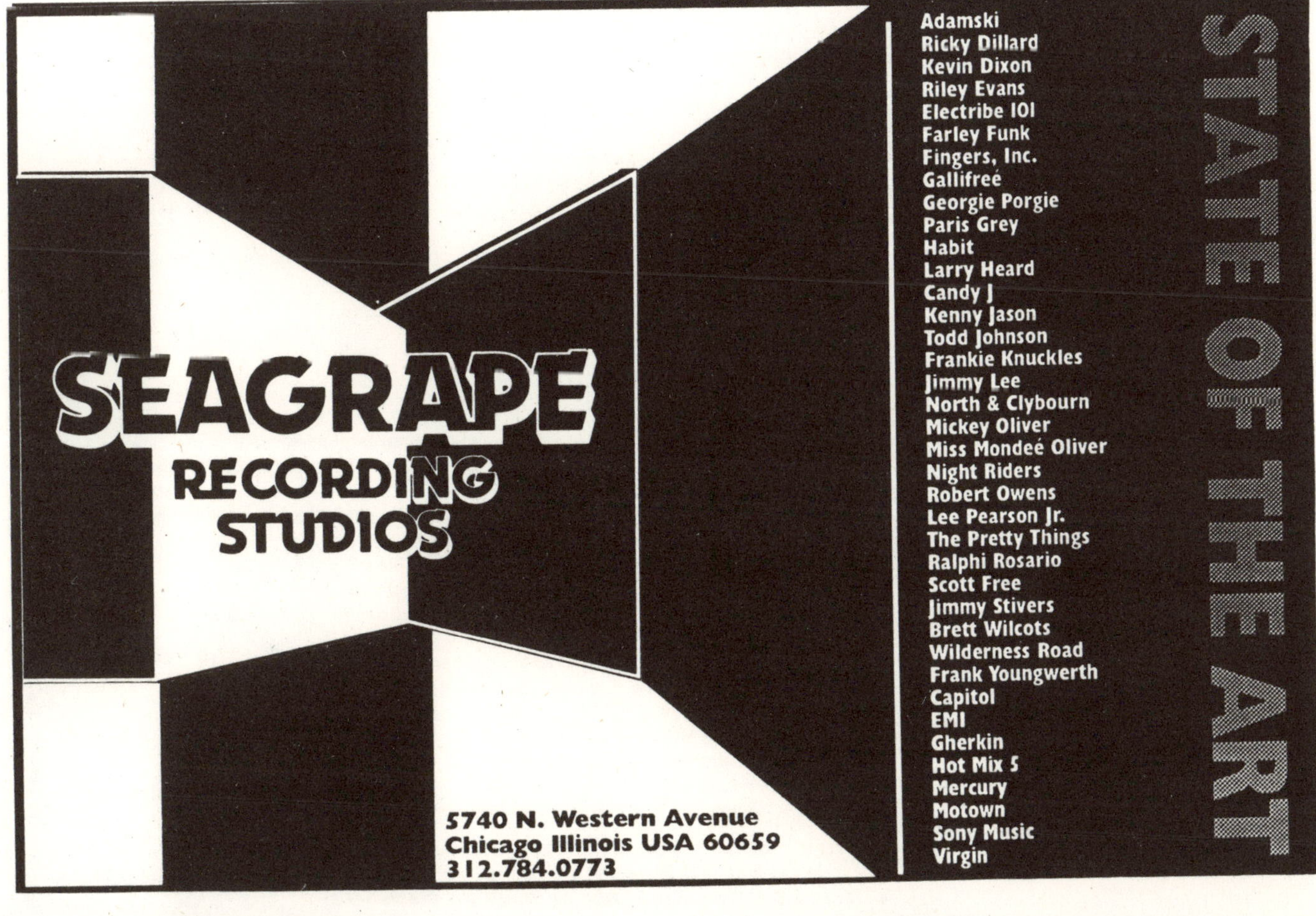

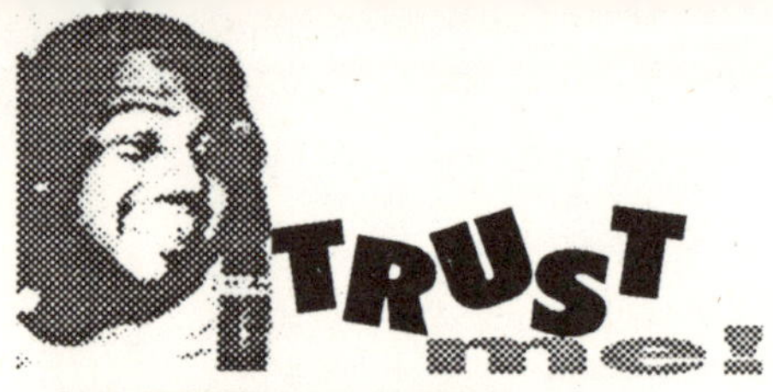

TRUST me!

CULTURE VULTURE... what racist rapist ad exec has been using Aframerican songs to sell images of white beauty? Boos to Revlon, Chic, et al.

SPEAKING OF BEAUTY, all the in-the-know booty boys go to **Oscar's**, where the interminable wait for a classic razor cut is made pleasant by all the scrumptious sights. Take along a copy of *Thing* so they'll know who you are!

READING RECONSTRUCTION is the mark of refinement; writing for *Reconstruction* is the mark of excellence. Under the superb editorship of **Randall Kenndey**, this new quarterly out of Harvard Law School is the journal of choice for anyone with a thought.

SO CLOSE AND YET SO FAR...
Peggy Noonan was a speechwriter for Reagan during his administrations, and is credited with giving us Bush's "thousand points of light"; now a columnist for *Mirabella*, she is witty, delightful, insightful, knowledge-able, and thought-provoking... too bad she's writing from the enemy camp; she's good.

DEFINITELY WRITING with *Thing* in mind is **Ms. Alice Walker**... her *Temple of My Familiar* has made the editorial rounds, and has sparked much healing and introspection...it's time to go to church.

HEAVENLY HOSTS... the missionary visionary, **Shelby "Selma Soul" Webb-jr.**, has finally realized his dream: a choral ensemble of trained voices that keep alive the vocal traditions of hymns and sacred, anthem, and gospel musics. Arduous research, rigorous training, and faithful renditionizin' make **Choral Thunder** a slice of heaven, here on earth. Let him who hath an ear...

FAYE BOLDEN, currently performing at the Pump Room, must have been giving Lounge Lizard lessons to up-and-coming chanteuse **Sherrilynn**...both of these ladies have class down to their gold lamé pumps, and their unique arrangements of jazz standards will leave you as bubbly as fine champagne...order heapin' platefuls of Sherrilynn at the Beat Kitchen (and do request an appetizer of "Stolen Moments").

AM I BLUE?...what could be better than a meal at **Mirador**? Admittedly nothing, but ranking up there has to be **The Blue Room**, Mirador's upstairs aperitif hang-out that has become a destination in and of itself. The Blue Room's bartender, ultra-fab boy-of-the-moment **David Ogden**, is gracious and becoming, delightful and seductive. Wednesday is the premiere night for mid-week relaxation and intimacies. If you spot LDW huddled in a candle-lit booth with songstress Sherrilynn, do send over a round of their famous blue margaritas. Perhaps she'll belt out a tune in gratitude...
— LDW

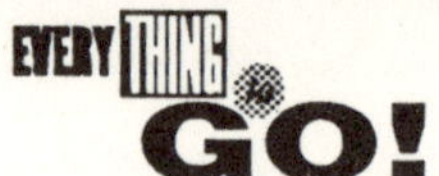

EVERY THING GO!

James Battle, like all great artists, is one of the biggest fools on the face of the planet.

Loyal, trusting, and frightfully forgiving, he was recently blessed with his first solo exhibit. Being solely dedicated to his art, he never found time or interest for mundane, common pursuits like management and making money, so wisely he thought to turn himself and his fate over to someone who had these skills. Unwisely, he chose a self-proclaimed artist, Berta Carta.

Berta Carta, better known for her culinary skills than her dubious and marginal vocal ones, seemed the natural choice: she was surprisingly proficient at organizing and mounting many an (unsuccessful) gathering to showcase her dismal and imagined talents; she had successfully garnered the time and abilities of far-more accomplished artists; and she even managed to position herself as the star in their august company (no mean feat, I assure you!)

Berta, who is no fool (proving once again she's no great artist), immediately did what she does best: turn to someone sincerely gifted to do the real work, someone who will slave uncomplainingly, someone who will let her hog the limelight. In one word: moi.

Moi, who can be quite a fool at times (a great artist, in her own right) gladly signed onto the project. Moi believed strongly in James' abilities; moi desired to see James as successful as he was so clearly deserving; and moi had long been a patron of struggling artists.

Berta, being the grand-standing, self-absorbed, insensitive lout that she is, dictated the date, time, and attendance of a fundraiser ostensibly for James Battle. After demanding it be held at her lushly appointed, shrine-to-herself villa, and seeing that the invites had been printed and mailed, she frivolously left town to perform her now infamous free-loading act (the only act she has perfected, I assure you!) of mooching off friends until they tire of her.

As the day of the affair dawned with still no word from Berta, we had not experienced such fear and dismay since the last time Berta attempted to disgrace a stage; we had no idea where she was or whether she would resurface in time for the gala or whether we would have to call the invitees and alert them to a change of address.

Scant hours before the appointed time, Berta breezed in with typically lame excuses and no apologies.

Not fresh from her East Coast tour, she was unconcerned about the lack of preparations of both her villa and and refreshments, but focused solely on her pressing need for ironed glad rags and for a hair trimming.

Thankfully, Trentarvicka was on hand to provide not only house-cleaning chores, but food preparation as well while madame busied herself with her futile and vain attempts at beauty.

Alas, karma is inescapable: she played to an empty room. NOT in attendance were some of the most notable names on the art patron scene: Carlton Robinson, S. Michael Evans, du Ane Baskins, David Carter, Dan Parker, Shelby Webb-jr., and Ephraim Walls-jr.

Sister Hoover was a no-show, too; she was smarting over a particularly painful and monstrous flop of her own (proving once again that karma is inescapable).

NIGGERATI
by Larvetta Larvon, la Vicomtesse deLarva

Sister Hoover invited the world to the warming of her new loft space; unfortunately, things got a little too hot even for her, when only the underworld showed: the Lindsey Duo, recently released Ray Dog Evans, Steve "Mrs. Marvin Lewis," and others of their ilk. True to her penny-pinching ways, she not only hired an inexperienced and clumsy DJ who should have been playing prison records for all the ne'er-do-wells there, but had the gall to have the surly, offensive, and incompetent Eric-What's-His-Name to tend (and I use this term loosely, I assure you) bar. Again, Ephraim Walls-jr was not in attendance.

After suffering through two such disasterous outings, I despaired that I would never be able go anywhere where the primary concern of the host was the comfort, security, and joy of his guests; where friends selflessly gave of their time, energy, and money in support of each other. I started to think that perhaps my expectations were too lofty and moi needed to keep my aristocratic black ass in my chateau being served flawlessly by faithful Cosette.

Languishing poolside, charming Lee Koonce phoned to offer insight. "Don't they realize how important this is?" he queried. Amidst the fog of disappointment, the true culprit emerged. Who had the skills and reputation for successful affairs? Who had the contacts, money,and experience? Who had even been headmistress of Lucy Baines' Fine Finishing School for Wayward Women? Who had been the manager of the X-mas Light Lounge? Who was missing from both affairs?

Effie Mae Randall van Buren knows who she is.

CLUB KMAs

Why should the editors and publisher of this magazine be dealt with so discourteously, rudely even, by *anybody* in the entertainment business? You'd think these people would be more than happy to get even bad press! Apparently, they presume they can dick us around because we haven't been on the map long. They think we're a flash in the pan. Grant Lukenville of the *now defunct Outweek* copped an attitude because we were competing for advertisers and he viewed us as a 'joke.' But the world treats you differently when it knows you can smear the hell out of them in print. It's true. Why, not more than a few months ago, people were just too happy to give us shit because they assumed that we were just some mindless black queens who thought they had it goin' on. Until, that is, they got wind of the **Lady Miss Kier** interview and associations with **Essex Hemphill, Alan Miller, Bill Coleman, Marlon Riggs, Ultra Naté,** etc. "Oh, you're *Thing* magazine!" they say. Yeah, and we can't wait to let your dumb asses have it! It ain't our style, nor is it necessary to good journalism to wear our contacts and achievements on our sleeves. We're about having fun and shedding light on things of interest to ourselves and our growing readership and hardly have time for any homophobic, racist, and egotistical forays in the process. So, to all the ultra-fab club owners, pretentious performers, petty promoters, deluded DJs, cheesy club kids, banal bouncers, backwards bartenders, mickey mouse managers, and generally uncooperative asswipes who wouldn't know opportunities for good business if they walked up and politely introduced themselves, thanks for nothing! Stay tuned for *Thing*'s KMA Hall of Fame list: kickin' ass and takin' names. Don't say we didn't warn you.

"A new club is opening up!" Michael Alig and DJ Keoki handily illustrate Club KMA. Reprinted from My Comrade. Photo by Michael Wakefield.

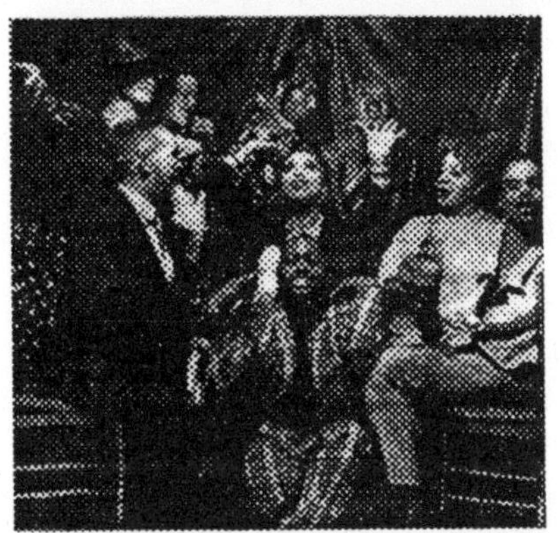

PARIS IS BURNING

<u>Paris is Burning</u> the new documentary film that explores the seminal drag balls of Harlem, is all humor, homegrown glamour, and pathos that exposes many of its subjects' burning desires for fame, fortune and fashionable living. Director Jennie Livingston was said to have come out as a lesbian during the process of completing the film. Not surprising when you view the movie and feel the unifying sense of family and security created by the various house members. It would be easy to come out with this bunch. Mostly black and gay, these children are the very fringe of the mainstream society. Through the houses and balls they communally share in one another's eccentricities, effectively sanctioning their own misfit-ness while subverting the fuck out of mass culture's and mass media's racist, sexist and homophobic assumptions. These kids aren't formally educated but they're as smart and perceptive a group as you'll ever find. Through sheer determination and wit, these kids manifest their fantasies to become self-created stars in their own right. This is a candid and fabulous glimpse into the now legendary houses of Extravaganza, Ninja, DuPree, Saint Laurent, and Labieja. In years to come, <u>Paris is Burning</u> should stand up as a major historic chronicle of the black gay culture that we currently see so much misunderstanding and exploitation of by the mainstream. A must see. — **TA**

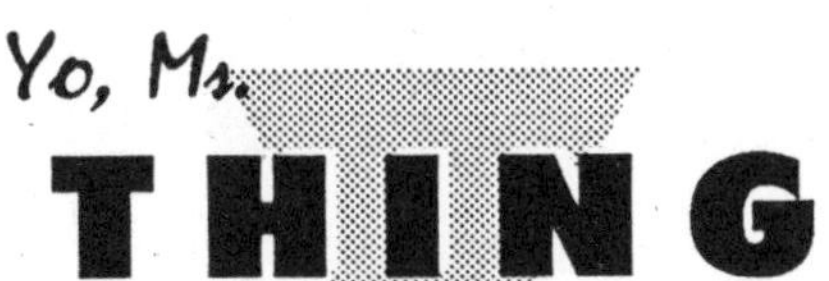

New York's black gay underground is getting much press due to Jennie Livingston's *Paris Is Burning*. Chicago's dynasty of fierce club queens was never quite as organized as NYC's "houses" and "balls". But that doesn't mean we don't have a celeb list of our own. Our gang: **Miss AARON** aka **MAGILLA GORILLA** Butch Queen Realness doin'! Fiercely muscular body, with a propensity for toe-jammed stiletto heels and high fashion cocktail dresses and gowns. Hot! (and we mean freshly mopped) Kansai, Gucci, and Louis Vuittion. **JOSE** and **LOUIS** These two hustled grooves into the dance floor. Local black fag lore has them pitching a brick through the window of Blums Vogue Furriers to let them have fur at the Warehouse. Notorious chain smokers, inspired the cry, "Phyllis, got another cigarette?" **WARDELL FORD** Designer to the stars. He turned out perfectly fitted diva garments given enough time, money and incentive. Wardell was possibly the first kid who had the nerve to dress the legendary party girl **Pamela DuPaty.** Along with **Aaron Pierre Brown,** Wardell is now co-founder of the Chicago-based House of Avant Garde. **CHIP** aka **MICHELLE** went under the scapel many times, going from that beautiful and fashionable boy at the Warehouse to a gorgeous married woman who now lives in the countryside. Soft, soft, soft, elegant and leggy. **FRANDA B. GOODCOOKIE** also known to the "old school" kids as **FRANDA PANDA** The mentor of Chicago's gay black club tarts, known for the quick read and timely barb. The official arbiter of Warehouse society (Grand Den Mother). Please, don't come for her!

SPEW

SPEW, the Homographic Convergence, held this past spring at Chicago's Randolph Street Gallery, was the first event of its kind and a landmark in the history of a burgeoning 'queer' culture. Organized by and for homo zine makers, it brought together folks from as far away as Toronto, Montreal, L.A., and San Francisco. Noticeably absent were editors from New York's *Pansy Beat* (publisher **Michael Economy** understandably just couldn't swing the travel expenses) and the groundbreaking zine *My Comrade*; everyone wanted to meet its publisher **Les/Linda Simpson**. However, many other independently produced homographic zines were represented by their publishers, editors and correspondents. Mainly a meeting of media manipulators, most were busy interviewing and/or photographing each other. Eyes are still smarting from all the camera flashes and glare of filming lights. Publisher of San Francisco's *Cunt* and former Chicagoan **Rachel Pepper** was there representing some of everybody from the West coast. She interviewed **Robert Ford** and **Trent Adkins** for *Outlines*; Ford interviewed everybody for *Thing*; **Larry Bob** interviewed and shot pix of everybody for *Holy Titclamps*. Ditto **Johnny Noxzema** and **Rex Boy** for *Bimbox* and **Fluffy Boy** for *Homoture*. *Maximum Rock and Roll's* **Mykel Board** was one of the free floating journalists on hand. **Nicolas Jenkins** (in from Montreal) seemed content to just sit and sell out of his sexy and smartly written zine, *Fuzz Box*. *Straight To Hell* editor **Billy Miller**, a far cry from his wilder days, sat calmly near the front, closing deals on *STH* back issues and t-shirts. Several people were videotaping everything. SPEW co-organizer and videophile **Steve Lafreniere** compiled a fierce program of queer videos and films including **Bruce La Bruce's** *No Skin Off My Ass*, **Summer Caprice**, **DeAundra Peek**, **Glen Meadmore**, *The RuPaul Film Festival*, and, of course, **John**

Canalli's footage from Wigstocks past. **Vaginal Creme Davis** came in from L.A. and managed a performance at RSG the day of the convergence, another performance at Hot House later that evening, and yet another performance/appearance at RSG the following Wednesday during an *In Through the Out Door* panel discussion. She won over many admirers and Fertile Latoyah Jackson converts. There were also readings by other underground faves like **Hudson** of New York's *Feature* Gallery and the literary zine *Farm*, bad boy genius **Dennis Cooper**, and Chicago's own **Jon-Henri Damski** who read from *Homocore*. Plus, performances by **Cheryl Trykv, Andy Soma, Sheree Slaughter, Joan Jett Blakk, Gurline** and **Gurlette Hussey, Mary Brogger, Bunny and Pussy, Iris Moore, A.K. Summers, D. Travers Scott, Kiwi, Fraulein, Thax Douglas,** and **David Eckard**. Very glamorous, too, with the likes of **Dora** of L.A.'s Sissy Club USA breezing about all day in chartreuse chiffon and gold stiletto mules. Later, the party at Hot House saw a nice crowd of folks and music by **Burle Avant**, Robert Ford and Trent Adkins. The dyke band **Fifth Column** performed, as did Vag. **Joan Jett Blakk** jumped in to play air guitar with the girls in Fifth Column. A few people are of the opinion that the event wasn't queer enough, was too expensive, blah-blah-blah. This was all done on a shoestring budget, with tables offered to zine editors for free and many of the out-of-towners able to enjoy free housing, I can't figure out what the hell these folks are talking about. A $6 cover? We all wish we had more money to make things free to more people. At SPEW, people enjoyed each other and planned for the future: Publishers and editors discussed an independent Canadian Queer Film Festival slated for next year and several individuals and groups left inspired to do their own zines and Cooper and Lafreniere are already conspiring for SPEW II, '92 to be held in L.A.

— **TA**

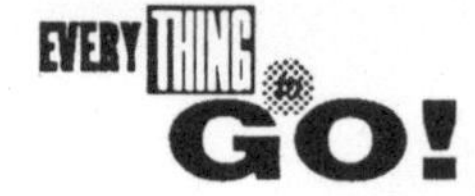

Top to bottom, photographer Stephen Winter. The Reverend Vaginal Creme Davis deliverin' at Hot House. Gloria (G.B.) Jones and Jena von Brucker at the Bitch Nation booth. Cheryl Trykv. Gurlene and Gurlette Hussey.

Clockwise, Fifth Column's Beverly Bevridge and filmaker Bruce La Bruce. Cheryl Bailey and Vaginal Creme Davis. Miss Scout with writer Walter Youngblood.

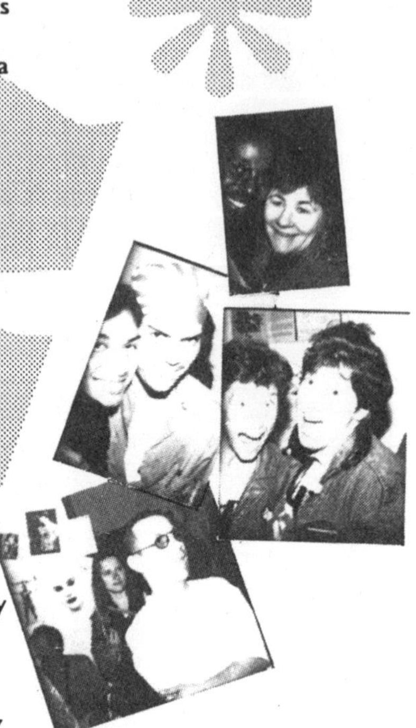

Clockwise from top, Michael Sheppard and Chandelle North. Women in the Director Chair's Jean Crocker and artist Mary Patton. Performer/ Gallery 2 curator Larry Steger. Bong and Juan.

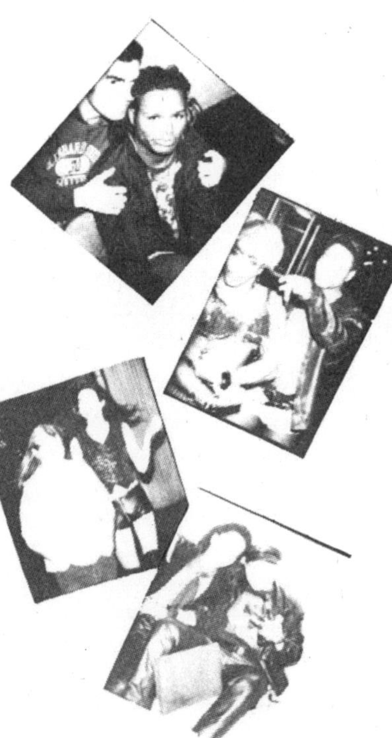

Top to bottom, desinger Darren Brown and writer Todd Roulette. TA and Joan Jett Blakk outside Hot House. Amoeba Record's Keith Holland and Miss Dora. Painter Simone Bouyer and poetess Sheree Slaughter. All photos Stephen Winter.

THING

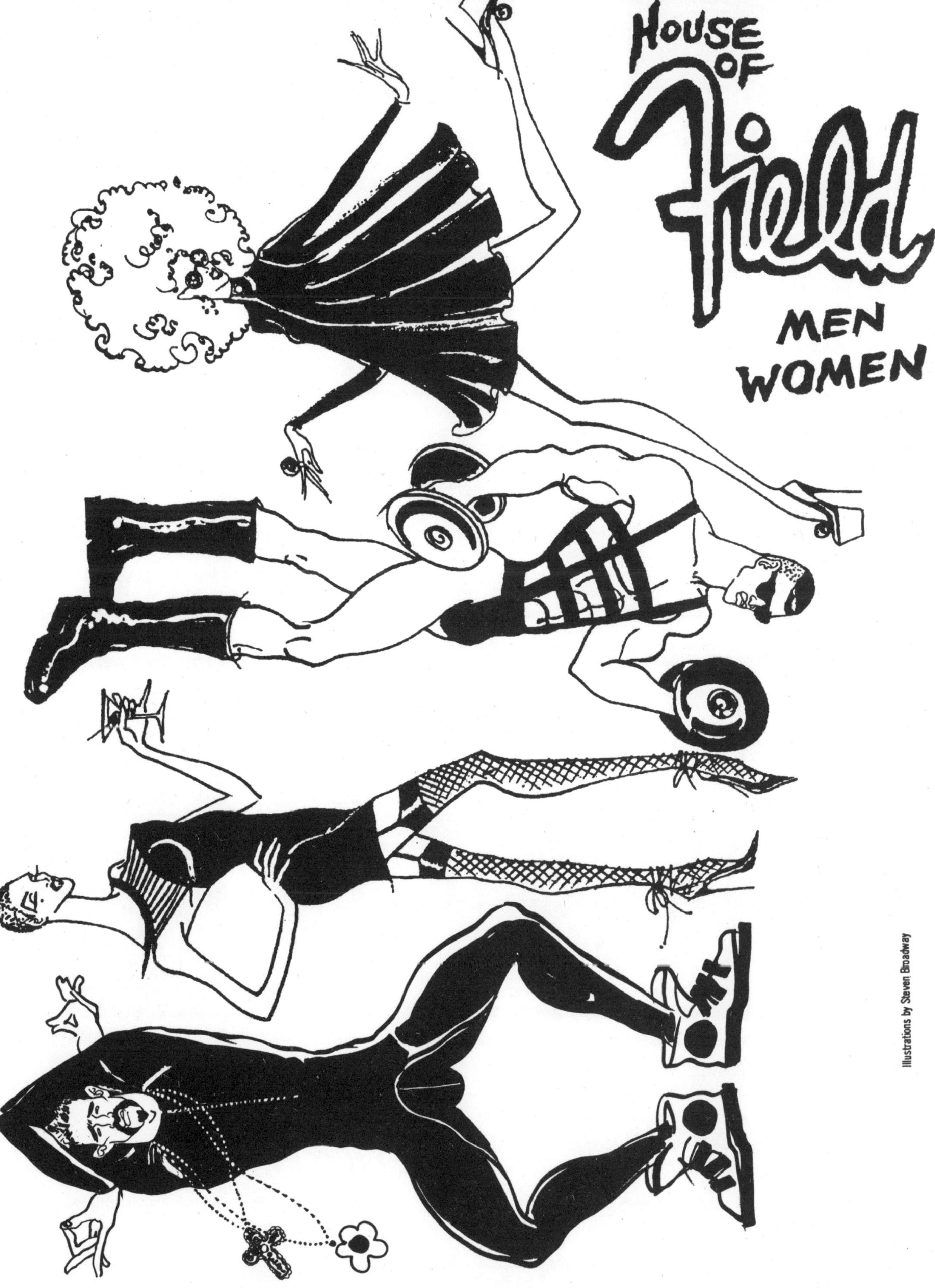

HOUSE OF
Field
MEN
WOMEN
Illustrations by Steven Broadway
AVAILABLE @ 99th FLOOR · 3406 N. HALSTED · CHICAGO 60657 · 312/348-7781

UNITED FAITH

A history of Chicago's black and gay church BY MAX SMITH

The book, *In The Life: A Black Gay Anthology* contains an article by the late Dr. James Tinney who was a Pentecostal Church minister. Entitled "Why a Black Gay Church?," Tinney's article explores the experience of three congregations, one of which continues to meet every Sunday at four P.M. in Chicago. Named United Faith Affinitas and located at 1448 E. 53rd Street, it is a group of Christian believers who see a need for a specific outreach.

As early as 1930 there was a black church in Chicago which opened its doors to people who were rejected by main-stream denominations. Over 60 years ago Reverend Clarence H. Cobbs saw street people, lesbians, gays, ex-offenders and other less popular children of God as needing a non-judgemental, spiritually uplifting worship service.

Over the years, week after week from his pulpit and over his radio broadcasts, Reverend Cobbs would repeat, "It does not matter what you think of me, but it does matter what I think of *you*. For I cannot allow hate, prejudice and deceit to keep me from knowing...that Jesus is the light of the world." So, long before the Stonewall revolt against gay oppression in 1969, the deeply spiritual nature of Black gay folks caused one to come forward from amongst our numbers, to meet our need to be ministered to just as we are.

There were limits to what privately gay ministers with pre-Stonewall ways of thinking could be expected to do. Reverend Cobbs mentored several other ministers, who by the 1960's had begun congregations of their own with high percentages of gay people in them. The words "lesbian" and "gay" would not be spoken from the pulpit in an affirming way at any of these churches: no acknowledgment of issues of importance to gay and bisexual communities was given. It was "known" that there was a gay presence in the congregation, choir, and pulpit, but it was not spoken.

In 1983, one of the ministers taught by Reverend Cobbs, was in a state of declining health, beset with AIDS-related conditions. He had been a bishop who was respected and adored, an excellent speaker with a ministry which met the needs of many people. But in the early 1980's few people understood AIDS and therefore the Bishop was treated coldly by many people.

One minister, Reverend Steven Handy, and a few members of his congregation became his caregivers when his illness became more than he could bear alone. The experience of being with the Bishop until the end of his life, when other ministers abandoned him, left a lasting impression on Reverend Handy. It caused him to see that the fear of AIDS in that situation was even greater than the love

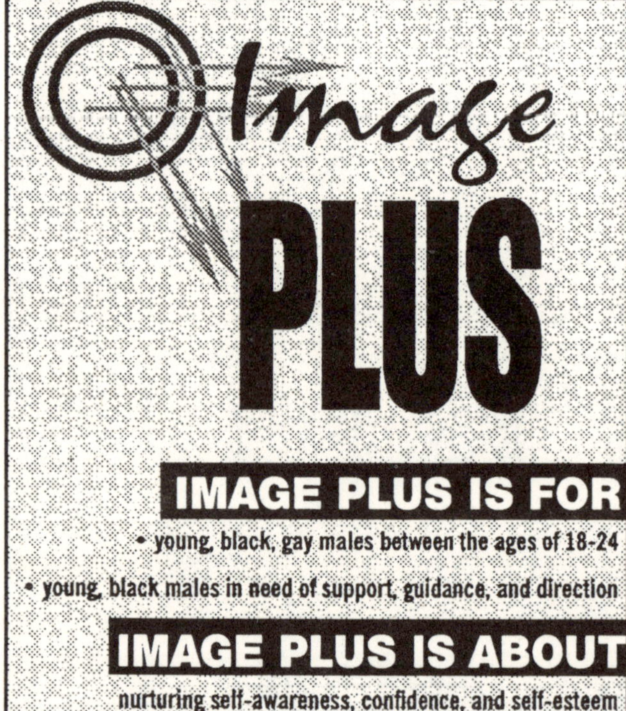

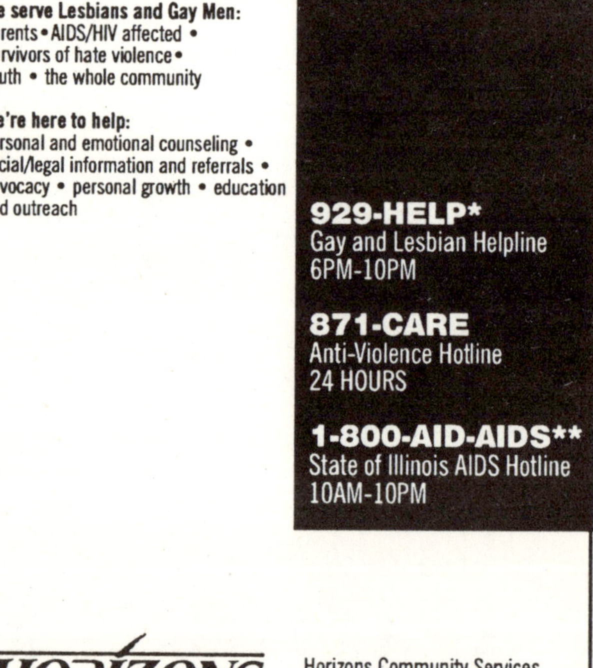

many people had for a person with AIDS. Given the disproportionately large number of people of color with AIDS, Reverend Handy saw a need for the religious community of color to face the issue of AIDS so that love ccould properly overcome fear.

I met Reverend Handy while he was struggling with that dynamic and pointed out to him how Reverend Tinney revealed the flip side of homophobia and AIDSphobia in *In The Life*. He asserted that when we become alienated from churches because people in them condemn our lifestyle, we lose our discipline to be committed to Christ, and begin to live in a tentative way, allowing impulses and instincts and passions to overrule our values. Without strong values there is a loss of willpower, self-control, and the ability to be dedicated to pursuits that require sacrifice for the sake of long-range plans and goals. Why must gay folks sacrifice the joyous blessings which result from accomplishing endeavors which take strength and tenacity to achieve? Of all the roles a church can serve, providing the spark of motivation we all need for successful living is certainly one of the most important.

Following the June 1990 Chicago Gay and Lesbian Pride Parade, Reverend Handy and several friends handed out hundreds of flyers at the Belmont Rocks beach picnic. The flyers read: "United Faith Affinitas Church. A church with a Black gay and lesbian ministry needs you!!! We meet each Sunday at four P.M. at Crittenhouse Chapel. This church has been designed to meet your spiritual needs and to positively affirm the development of your personhood. We ask that you share with us your talents to help create a ministry that will enhance your walk with God...We look forward to worshipping with you."

Since then we have met every Sunday and have established a positive relationship with the congregations who share our church building. In the tradition set over 60 years ago by Reverend Clarence Hobbs, all are welcome, just as you are. With an awareness of today, however, we have a progressive feeling of loving welcome for those who are HIV-impacted. While we started out to minister to a specific group of people with special needs, we do not limit our efforts to that area. All who believe in Jesus and God's gift of salvation will feel at home with us.

Reverend Steven Handy passed away on June 17, 1991.

It does not matter what you think of me, but it does matter what I think of you.

THING

15

HIV or AIDS CONCERNED?

Chicago Department of Health AIDS Prevention Program offers:

- **Free Counseling and Testing**
- **Confidential Counseling and Testing**
- **Anonomyous Counseling and Testing**

Schedule an appointment at one of eight convenient locations

LAKEVIEW 2861 N. Clark/348-8059

ENGELWOOD 641 W. 63rd/483-2443

NEAR SOUTH SIDE 1306 S. Michigan/435-5407

UPTOWN 845 W. Wilson/989-9070

WEST TOWN 2418 W. Division/292-6115

ROSELAND 200 E. 115th/995-2817/8

NEAR WEST SIDE 2160 W. Ogden/666-6965

LOWER WEST SIDE 1713 S. Ashland/942-2483

Health Educators and AIDS resources and education also available

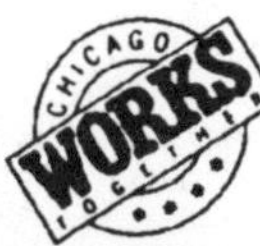

For further information contact:
Office of AIDS Prevention
Chicago Department of Public Health
Room 233, Daley Center, 50 W.Washington
Chicago Illinois 60602
(312) 744-4312

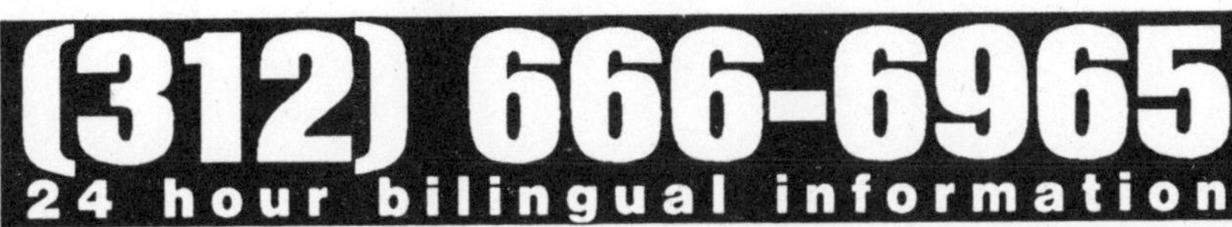

THING

16

I HEARD THAT!
notable quotes compiled by LDW

SNAP!...
"Our immediate task, as Black gay men creating our own literary tradition, is to work diligently and to utilize honesty and discipline as allies. If we commit ourselves to strive for excellence and nothing less, we will give way to the realization of just how fierce and necessary we really are!"
— *Essex Hemphill*
"Everyone should strive to offer, with his work, a service graced with elegance and style...blessed by great creativity and a touch of artistic inspiration, to add a spark of joy to people's lives." — *Pucci*

BORN TOO LATE...
"All these years I've been known just as an evil Black bitch;
we didn't know nothin' 'bout no PMS" — *Joanie*

LET'S BE FRIENDS...
"I don't need no mo' Judy Garland Girlfriends; I have so many, some of them I don't even know their names." —*Miss Nicky*

WHERE ARE THE BOYS?...
"Ain't no trade; only mistakes." — *more Miss Nicky, after yet another failed relationship*

YOU STEPPED IN IT...
"Do, by all means, exercise your 1st Amendment Rights to be a racist; then when I put my foot up your ass, I'll have a leg to stand on." — *TA*

CLEAN UP YOUR ACT...
"He don't know how to take constructive criticism. What he fails to realize is: ain't nobody ever gonna give nothin' to a dirty Black boy. EVER!" — *Delon*

ARE WE HAVING FUN, YET?...
"That's the nature of art — the odds are thousand to one against achieving great success, but that doesn't matter. The pleasure is in doing."
—*McKee*

TURN THE BEAT(LITERALLY) AROUND...
"Let 'em have it comin' and goin'... Sweetness and Light ain't never got nobody nothin'. I'm convinced that Bitterness is gonna change the world." —*Trentarvicka as Cruella de Vil*

YEAH, RIGHT...
"The more killing and homicides you have, the more havoc it prevents."
—*Richard M. Daley*

KEEP IT UNDER YOUR HAT...
"She oughta be glad I was raised right..."
— *Delon on his arch-nemesis, Michael*

WASTED...
"What a waste it is to lose one's mind, or not to have a mind is being very wasteful. How true that is." —*J. Danforth Quayle, at a United Negro College Fund luncheon trying to recall the UNCF's slogan, "A mind is a terrible thing to waste."*

YOU THINK YOU HAVE PROBLEMS...
"That the inadequate Danforth Quayle remains only a heartbeat away from the most powerful job on Earth is enough to give even America's staunchest allies the vapours." —*The Daily Mail, Great Britian*

BUT YOU ARE, BLANCHE...
"Why does everybody keep treating me like I'm the Bad Guy?!?" — *Adam Chandler, the Bad Guy*

WAKE UP CALL...
"The Pork Queen represents an industry that kills 92 million pigs a year to feed America's meat addiction. It's time she woke up to the cruelty that she represents." — *Robin Walker, after hitting the Pork Queen in the face with a pie.*

CUT TO THE QUICK...
"We call her Pig Dog 'cause Cunt Bitch Whore takes too long."— *Larry Griffin on his boyfriend's ex-wife.*

CLUTCH YOUR PEARLS...
"There are many, many people of great affluence who are suffering great spiritual angst as they step over prone bodies." — *Robert Hayes, counsel to the Coalition for the Homeless on the plight of the rich.*

KEEP IT SIMPLE...
"Considering the troubled times we are in, anything that is overdone is inappropriate." —*Lynn Wyatt, Houston socialite after spending $20,000 on a ball gown because its tartan plaid design "makes it less formal."*

LET THEM EAT CAKE...
"I want to live like Marie Antoinette, and I'm going to. If you don't like it, don't come over and don't eat my croissant." — *Joan Rivers*

THE (LAMP)SHADE ACT...
"It *was* a bit expensive, but you can't always throw a cheap party."— *Marvin Earl Lewis, the cheapskate*

588-2300

Tony Wilkins
Steve Freshwater
Haki Madhubuti
Margaret Burroughs
Stephanie Coleman
DeWayne A. Powell, Esq.
Oprah Winfrey
Eric Johnson
Joseph Kennedy
Johnnie Carson
Effie Mae Randall van
Buren
Don King
Don Cornelius
Spike Lee
Eddie Murphy
Donald Trump
Robert Williams
Stephen Boykin/Johnny
Washington
Nancy Reagan
Selma Soul

Git With It!

Get the Funk Out My Face
Get Happy
Get Lucky
Get the Blues
Got It Bad, and That Ain't
Good
Get You Some business

That's My Mama
I'll Always Love My
Momma
Mamma, I Want to Sing
Grandma's Hands
Come To Momma
Throw Momma From The
Train
Mommie Dearest
Mama's Got a Brand New
Bag
Mother Said (There'll Be
Days Like This)
My Momma Told Me (You
Better Shop Around)
Mama's Family
Mother of all Mothers
Mother of God
Mother Plumtree
Mother Nature
Mother Jefferson
Mother Stevens
Mother Wit
Mother's Milk
Mama Cass
The Mamas & Papas
Mother, Jugs, & Speed
Mother Jones
Mamie Eisenhower
Whistler's Mother
Mum's the Word!

St. Martin de Porres
(formerly Mendel)
The Bells of St. Mary's
Niki de Saint Phalle
St. Louis Blues

Blood Relations

My Sister's Circus
My Father's Glory
My Grandmother's
Funeral
My Mother's Castle
My Brother's Keeper
My Cousin's Boyfriend

Quite Contrary

Proud Mary
Mary Richards
Mary Tyler-Moore
Mother Mary
Mary Wilson
Mary Magdalene
Mary Steenbergen
Mary Steenberg
Mary Jane
Mary Jane Girls
Don't Try It, Mary!
Mary McFadden
Mary, Queen of Scots
Marilu Henner
Mary Lou Retton

Alicia Bridges
Vanity
Apolonia
Nancy Sinatra
Yoko Ono
Morrissey
Loose Joints
Samantha Fox
Jasmine Guy
Zelma Davis
Ultra Naté
Edrienne Jett
Rickie Lee Jones

There Goes the Neighborhood

Gladys Kravitz
Mr. Bentley
Mrs. Roper
Millie Helper
Mrs. Dr. Bellows
Lovey Howell
Clara/Aunt Bee
any of the Martins
Chuck Tyler
Wilona Woods
the Mertzs
the Rubbles
Mrs. Drysedale
Rhoda Morganstern
Miriam Radkin

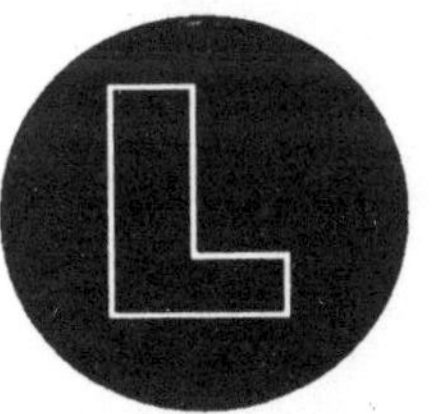
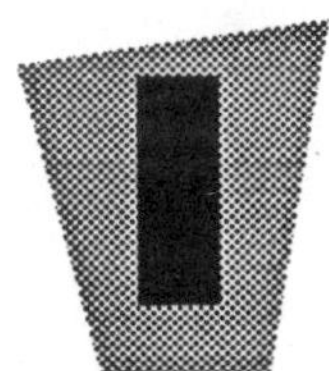
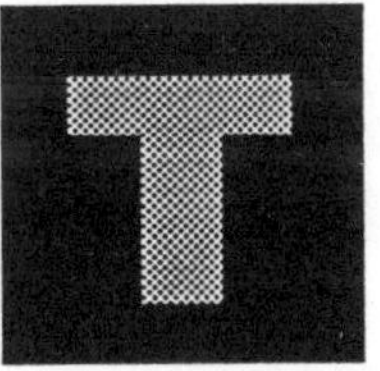
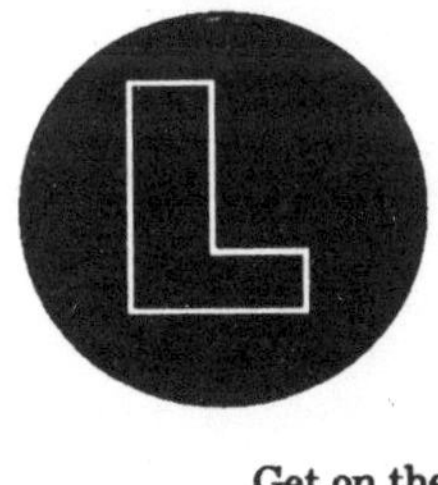

Get on the Good Foot
Get the Hell Out of Dodge
Get A Life
Get With It
Get Over It
Get Off
Get It Goin' On
Get Loose
Get Out
Get Real
Git out of Africa

Yo, Mamma!

Mama Gave Birth To The
Soul Children
Mama Said Knock You
Out
Mama Used to Say
Bad Mama Jama
Big Bad Momma
Mama Rose
Mother Theresa
Mother Popcorn
Old Mother Hubbard
Ma Rainey
Ma Barker
Ma Marton
Mom's Mabley
Medea
Mother Africa
Give Moms Some Sugar
I Love My Mama
Mama Don't
Mammy's little baby
Mother Hale
Mother may I?

Mama Tish
Mama Celeste
Mama Wouldn't Lie to You
Mama Told Me Not to
Come
Mothership Connection
Mother Lode
Bebe's Badass Kids

Saintcerely

Basil St. James
Linda St. Saëns
Saint-Saëns
Santa Claus
Simon Templar
Octavia Saint Laurent
Yves Saint Laurent
Lili St. Cyr
Buffy Saint Marie
Boofy Saint Marie
Giorgio di Saint Angelo
Jill Saint John
Eva Marie Saint
Susan Saint James
James St. James
Sterling St. Jaques
St. Christopher
St. Francis Of Assisi
St. Martin's Press
The Saint
St. Mark's Place
St. Elizabeth's
St. Sabina
St. Joan

Peter, Paul, & Mary
Bells of St. Mary's
Miss Mary Mack
Hail Mary

Lonely At the Top

Mahogany
Neely O'Hara
Norma Desmond
Donald Trump
Mildred Pierce
Scarlett O'Hara
Erica Kane
Adam Chandler
Frankie Knuckles
Michael Jackson
Helen Lawson
Eve Harrington
The Rose
LaVicomtesse de
Larvetta Larvon

Pass the Pitch Pipe

Crystal Waters
Billie
Paris Grey
Paula Abdul
Diana Ross
LaToya Jackson
Basia
Sade
Grace Jones
Screamin' Rachel
Cathy Dennis
Stevie Nicks

Off With Their Heads

Lypsinka
Gurlene & Gurlette
Joan Jett Blakk
Madonna

Rain for Days

When the Rain Falls
Rain
Walking In the Rain
Date With the Rain
Blame It On the Rain
Thunder and Lightning
Clouds
Cloudburst
Don't Rain On My Parade
Naked In the Rain
Go Outside In the Rain
It's Raining Men
Rainy Days & Mondays
Purple Rain
Someone left the cake out
in the rain
Acid rain
Raindrops Keep Fallin' On
My Head
Rain Maker
Rain Man
White Rain
Come Rain or Come Shine
Rainy Night in Georgia
Stormy Weather
Blame It On the Rain
I Can't Stand the Rain

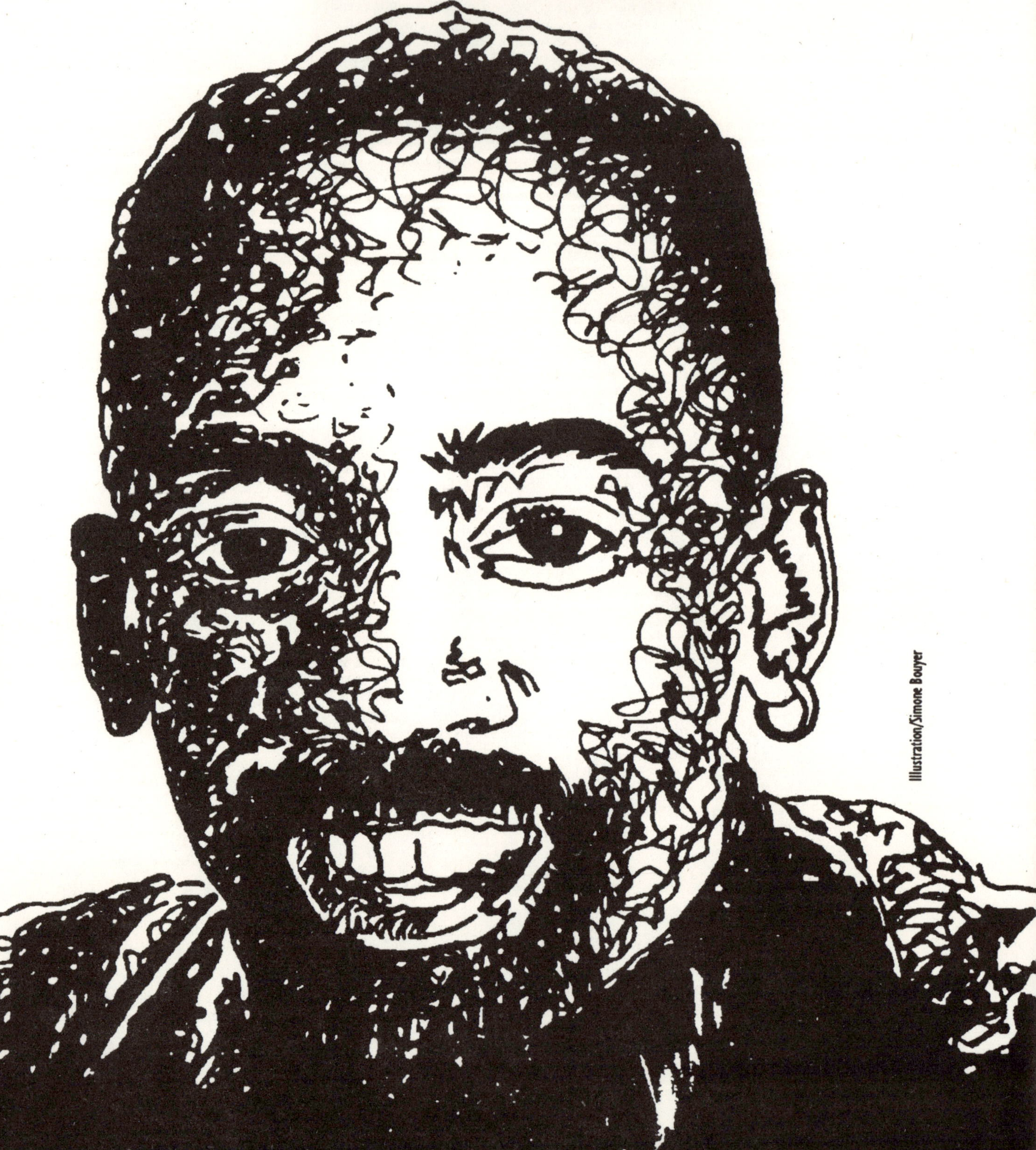

ESSEX HEMPHILL
by Tod Roulette

Tod Roulette: Earlier this week you addressed the Black gay vs. Gay black debate and said that it was a matter of semantics for you. Do you think a black gay identity is separate from a gay identity?

Essex Hemphill: They are separate identities, but I guess the trick of it all is that one hopes to meld those identities into one being. It is a semantical debate for me when one positions gay black vs. black gay. I can go anywhere in the country and I'm going to be dealt with as a black man— whether I'm flaunting my faggotry or being discreet. The first thing they see is a black male, and that is constant and on-going confrontation. Also, gay for me has always implied white and middle-class male, if you will, with a gay identity. I have found that I use 'gay' because it is expedient; because it is what popular culture uses to identify a homosexual. But, to the extent that I find affirmation for myself in that; affirmations for myself as a black man...that I don't see a lot of. And thus I wonder if there isn't another word that would more aptly affirm not only our sexual, but our racial identity and heritage. Maybe it is a word that we have to put into being.

TR: Where did all this activism and involvement in the black community come from?

EH: I come from a family that participates in the community on both sides. So it's natural that I would organize a fundraiser early on and participate in fundraisers for AIDS in the Washington area or gather artists together regardless of sexual identity to benefit a homeless shelter. An example of that would be me organizing some of my friends for a benefit in Washington. We raised $500 and turned in ten cases of canned food. None of us had $500 in our individual pockets to give. But, if I can use my art to empower or aid causes I believe in I've always been willing to do that. It just comes with the territory. But, there have been models for that. There's been a certain knowledge of giving back that's been instilled in me by family and by extension black images that I've been able to vicariously have empower me.

TR: Was there one significant event in your helping in the community while developing a sexual identity where you thought "Gee, it's great to be here, but where is everyone like me— where are the black gay men and lesbian women?"

EH: I guess early on I didn't think about sexual identity being affirmed through representation of our own history. I know that there was sexual turmoil in all that because I was dating girls as a way of protecting myself from being identified as a faggot around the school. I made sure I had me a girlfriend, o.k.! I had a succession of them. But, it wasn't until I become a young adult and living fully as a gay man with a lover and getting into my writing intensely that I began to come across transgressive sexual identities being speculated. Hughes was the first, then I discovered the Harlem Renaissance, Baldwin and now these times.

TR: How old were you?

EH: I was in my early 20's — 23,24. And mind you the other gay identities I was getting were coming out of my relationship because my lover was a year older. He was out with his family. As well I was out with my family. And he was welcome at family gatherings and various family moments as my 'friend,' never as my 'lover'! The other affirmations I was getting was by reading work by Audre Lourde, Adrienne Riche, Jean Genet, Cavafy, Walt Whitman, Pasolini, Sappho. And the Beat poets were affirming other parts of my personality—outrageousness, irreverence. But, in terms of getting first hand black gay affirmations, they didn't come fully until coming into an understanding of Baldwin's work. And then making the connection from Hughes to Baldwin, Alain Locke to Countee Cullen, etc. to speculation around members of the Harlem Renaissance and their sexual identities.

TR: So, this is where all this converges, the work you're doing now?

EH: I like to put out there what's not already out there. If I don't hear it and I'm waiting to and no one's saying it, then I'm going to have to say it o.k., If I can't see it then I'm going to have to figure out some way to make it be seen. That's how I started writing poems for twenty years now, in the beginning how important that would become for me. It is imperative for us to make up the evidence of us loving ourselves. So that that can be absorbed. We need to show ourselves loving ourselves fiercely, even if we think or believe or fear that it is perhaps lacking right now. Begin to make it up and put it out. It goes a long way to bringing that into actuality. Larry (Duckette) and I spoke this morning about some projects that we'd like to work on — the end result being an audio cassette the brothers could just pick up, because we're all hungry.

TR: That's what I find so powerful about your work. It speaks so directly to me as a black gay man. And your putting it out there and doing it is so encouraging.

EH: We need our own toys. It's nice to be able to play nice with other people's toys, but other people can be rude and say,"I don't want to play with you anymore. What did Billie Holliday say? "God Bless the Child"! We need publications like *Thing, BLK, Other Countries*, whatever it is. I published, produced and did all the work on *Earth Life and Conditions*. I've seen *Earth Life* go into two printings and both sell out. There is never a publisher that can do anything to me now because I now know whenever I want to put my work out there, you can't tell me it's not the right time. It frees you. You can walk with your head a little higher. My next book is being published by two black

lesbians in England who have a press called "Urban Fox". Their names are Maude Sulter and Lubaina Himid. They're not even thirty yet, fierce women! The thing I'm loving about witnessing the younger people coming up is you all are some fierce people! But, Maude and Lubaina said very pointedly they not only wanted to publish the work of women, but men also. Which I think is a very necessary step in some ways for us to begin working more closely together. When I hear people in the community say 'It's great that the men and women are finally coming together' maybe I've been on another zone of consciousness, and I'm trying not to be cynical by that. But, I have trouble adjusting when I hear that. It's just a simple matter of respect. It's not like my phone and address book is filled with only men's names or to pull gatherings together I invite only men.

TR: That's what I was going to ask. It seems that Craig Harris has a very conscious and theoretical approach to the inclusion of women-in terms of laying out practice, not being mysogynist or woman bashing. And it seemed to me that you didn't approach that. At least not in the formal way Craig Harris did and I didn't understand that.

EH: I guess it's just a matter of how one expresses profeminist theory definitely impacts, informs and continues to open my head. It's not like I know everything. I'm still learning and understanding and making connections as well. But, for me it's not that I have to theorize. I'm already living it, if you will.

TR: It seems to me of course, that all of this is a great undertaking in terms of consciousness. Do you think this calls for support groups for black males, sort of like the women's movement...consciousness raising?

EH: Yes. It's a necessary tool. And you have evidence of it around the country. You have GMAD (Gay Men of African Descent) in New York City. You have Black Gay Men United in Oakland. You have Unity and Adodi in Philadelphia. You have Black Men's Network in Delaware. There are rumblings in D.C. now that a black gay men's group is going to form. So I think now that we are witnessing perhaps largely in urban settings, but it's a realization among all of us of how desperately we need to talk to one another. And how important and critical it is to be there for one another.

TR: How do black gay men in predominately

"We need to show ourselves loving ourselves fiercely."

white organizations approach the issue of ethnic identity within a gay context?

EH: I think in the instance that you find yourself the sole black or one of very few blacks in a predominately white organization, you should be very clear about why you are working with a given organization. What are your objectives? Are you going to have to bring the sensitivity to race, etc., to the agenda of the organization? And are you willing to take the additional effort? The question that circulates in my mind is if these organizations are really failing to address and speak to our needs or even confronting issues, is it not time for us to start forming our own organizations? It's a question of how much educating do you feel like doing. And there may be some more critical issues that need to be dealt with and thus require you to find people of like mind to start your own organizations. I think it's a very valid thing to consider. And considering it in such a way that allows one to be free of criticism of separatism. That's a part of self-empowerment, self-affirmation.

TR: So what are some basic steps for groups to ensure they are all-inclusive of people of color?

EH: Well, one of the things is: what are the objectives of the organizations and how do those objectives impact on the various communities that you are striving to include. Then how do you engage members of those various communities in such a fashion that you are all able to give your best knowledge and energies to confronting the overall objectives. You can't outreach assuming that everyone's going to read or hear your message on this one frequency. I think you have to play on several frequencies. If you don't know those communities you need to have people from those communities engaged, respecting what they say will work. A part of me, admittedly has steered clear of any heavy group involvement. I've been a member of the National Coalition of Black Lesbians and Gays. I've been a member of various organizations in my life, but for the most part I guess my group experiences have occurred in the cultural context, the work that I do, performance arts. There are problems in our own communities that need to be addressed. Why can't we start our own groups and do our own addressing? There are ways we can work in tandem with other organizations on other issues that are on our agendas as well as theirs. As opposed to some of the frustration and anger that seems to swirl around trying to bend an organization that does not want to bend. There's nothing that says they absolutely have to. You have an option to start your own group, it would be different if those options weren't there. I mean I don't expect ACT UP and Queer Nation to march in the

neighborhoods that I know against the drugs that are in those communities. But, as a black gay man I feel like something needs to be done in those communities. So if I connect with other black people to address my community, then I'm all for that. And it's not as if they (ACT UP and Queer Nation) don't have my support as a gay man and that we can't work together when our goals are parallel, but I have to take care of home.

As an example, Charles Hart heads an AIDS care giving organization in Philadelphia which services largely black men and men of color. He said when they come to the center HIV-positive and/or AIDS complicative that's not the priority. Number one, he needs an education, he needs a job, he needs a place

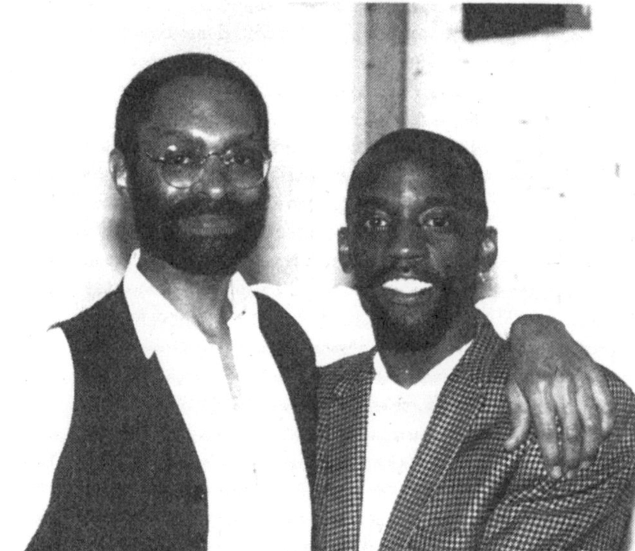

to live, he needs, he needs...It's not like you have men coming to the center who are well placed, well-educated. You've got men coming in from the edges of our society to begin with, so the work to do is not only saving lives or prolonging lives, but getting them some of the things that they need. Those are some of the issues you have to be sensitive to when you're talking about an organization that's going to be sensitive to different communities.

TR: What do you say to blacks who don't feel comfortable with your vision of coming home to the black community? Like your character in "A Tomb of Sorrow" who dreams about razor blades slicing away his dark skin? So when we talk about coming out, coming out is not a problem, but coming home is.

EH: *Well, if we don't come home where do we go?* That would be my question. And can we really sit back and let our communities go to hell; can we really allow our sexuality to create that much distance? For instance, some of my experiences in Washington D.C. I was going to rehearsal two summers ago. We walked into our rehearsal space in Northeast Washington in a black neighborhood. The minute we walked in the

door we heard 'pow, pow, pow'. I ran upstairs and looked out the window. Gunfire in the air and I'm looking out the window, o.k.! I told my friend 'I think somebody got shot." Then the neighborhood got quiet for like a second. Then you heard a woman scream. It started real low and sailed up over the roof tops and everything. You just heard this long scream. I said we have to go see what's wrong, there was no phone so we couldn't call the police. I ran out. By this point other people were coming out and running. I got up to the corner and what did I see...a car with both the front doors open. One black male is slumped over to the driver's side. The other black male in the driver's seat is slumped hanging out of the car. Blood is everywhere. This is my day to day reality. That's why I have a problem with people saying 'you can't say it like that'. Well then you make the life of my people something else so I won't have to write this. So for that reason I just can't sit back. That's what I mean about coming home. My sexuality isn't so big a thing that it's going to overwhelm my desire to see us live and survive.

TR: In ten years where would you like to find black gays and lesbians in terms of becoming part of the black community?

I would love to see us black gay men and black lesbians more openly and actively involved in programs that serve our community that raise our community to a consciousness of empowerment. Be that we are volunteers in literacy programs — I mean openly, be it that we start up programs to serve the community. I'd love to see us be able to some in and work as we are. And if they know it, fine but it isn't my gayness alone necessarily that is being brought to you. It's my intelligence, my love for black people, for the black community. That's what I bring. That's what I have to offer. I believe everybody has a little that they can offer. It's not only for people who are in the 'limelight'. That's one kind of work that's being done. But, it's that kind of unspoken work that black gays and lesbians find supporting our families. I'd like to see a consciousness about that. Not just a theoretical consciousness, but a consciousness that moves from being identified theoretically and developed, but to a state of action. Without being condescending toward our community and without accepting condescension of ourselves, but coming in as equal members of our community. Because the thing about it is, we have something to bring and to give to home. I think I can say for all of us our homes are important for us. It all begins at home. ▼

Larry Duckette and Essex Hemphill backstage at Randolph Street Gallery. Photo Tod Roulette.

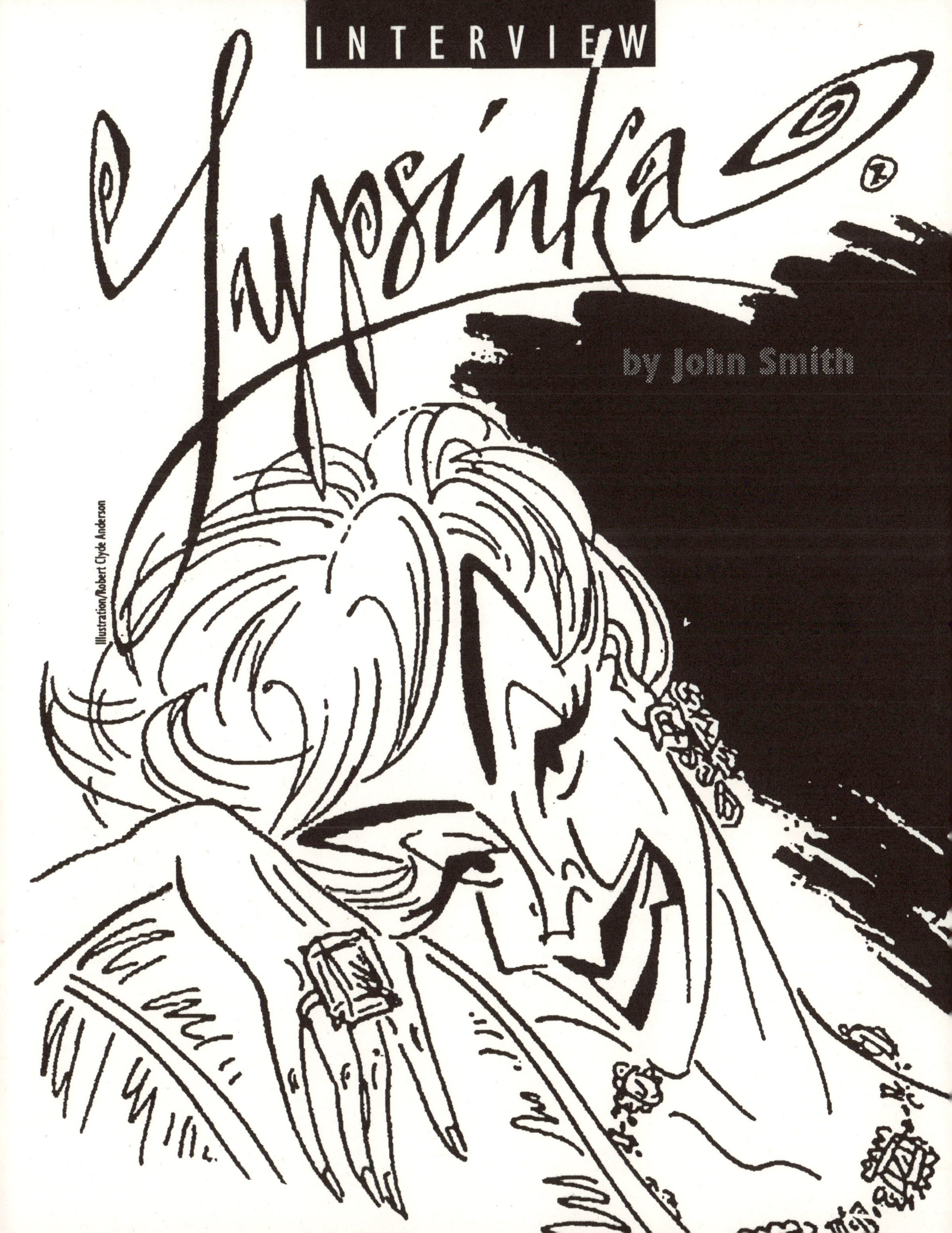

INTERVIEW
Yuppsinka
by John Smith
Illustration/Robert Clyde Anderson

John Smith: How long were you in Chicago?
Lypsinka: Only two nights, unfortunately.

JS: Did you have an opportunity to do anything?
L: I've been to Chicago many times, but only in February. I used to come with the American Ballet Theatre.

JS: You were their rehearsal pianist. Are you still doing that?
L: (emphatically) No!

JS: So you devote all your time to performing?
L: Yes, it's much more emotionally rewarding to perform and meet interesting people than to be the lowest person on the totem pole.

JS: I certainly imagine Lypsinka doesn't like being the lowest person on the totem pole. You bring an incredible intensity to your performance. Does it take you long to get into that character?
L: Oh no, I've never had any trouble. I just do it.

JS: How about coming out of the character?
L: I have no trouble with that either. I can't wait to get out of that stuff.

JS: I've read that you are from Jackson, Mississippi.
L: Actually I'm from Hazelhurst, Mississippi.

JS: Is Jackson the nearest hotspot?
L: Well, if there is one.

JS: Those drag queens you wrote about in *My Comrade* sound interesting.
L: That was the 1970's. I don't think they've progressed much...in fact, they've probably regressed.

JS: They remind me of drag queens I knew in the 70's from Paducah, Kentucky, who drove pick-up trucks with shotguns in the back window.
L: Like most all the rest of the entertainment history in the world, those Southern drag queens got stale. In the 70's everything was a lot more interesting. At the time, people were saying, "Oh, movies are over," but when you look back, they were a lot more interesting than what's going on now.

JS: I hate people who trash 70's culture. Do you consider that your formative period?
L: My formative period started the day I was born. But the 70's were a much more liberal era, looking back one can see what an exciting time it was.

JS: Do you refer to yourself as a drag queen, actor, female impersonator... How do you prefer to be characterized?
L: I consider myself an actor playing a female role.

JS: Do you feel you have a range that could go beyond Lypsinka?
L: Oh, yes. But this is what has caught on with the public.

JS: With good reason. Were the people you knew when you came to New York part of the drag/club scene?
L: No, I came to New York as green as they come.

JS: Had you been before?
L: I had been three years earlier with my mother when all I did was see Broadway show after Broadway show. In the summer of 1978, I finally said I'm ready to move.

JS: After that first trip, was every minute of your life devoted to finding a way to get there?
L: (Laughing) Yes. There actually was one other time I tried to move but I keep forgetting about it, it was really a bad scene. It didn't work out.

JS: But you got there?
L: For about six weeks. The second time it took. It was L.A. or New York and in Mississippi you have to drive a car and mine kept breaking down, so I decided that New York was the place. Plus theater is easier to break into than film.

JS: In the 70's were you aware of performers like Charles Ludlam and the Ridiculous Theatre Company? Did that intrigue you?
L: It definitely intrigued me. I didn't set out to become a drag performer by moving to New York, but it was always in the back of my mind that it was something I could try. I certainly was fascinated by him (Ludlam) and by Holly Woodlawn, Charles Pierce and Divine. But I had only read about these people. I had never seen them do anything. There used to be a magazine called *After Dark*, you couldn't even get it in Mississippi; you had to drive to New Orleans.

JS: Do you think growing up in that kind of isolation helped your personality ferment?
L: Well, when you can't get that kind of gratification, you become obsessive about it, and then obsession turns into a career.

JS: Are you obsessed with your career?
L: I don't know if I'm obsessed, but I spend most of my time dealing with it.

I've sacrificed a great deal of my personal life. I haven't seen my family in one and a half years.

JS: You've been performing Lypsinka for one and a half years?
L: I had a long stagnant period for about a year, but about nine months ago I came out here and had a huge success around Thanksgiving.

JS: Was that the club act or your play, "I Could Go On Lip-Synching?"
L: It was the show I'm doing now. It's called "The Fabulous Lypsinka Show," and it's a cabaret act. And then I went to L.A. with it and came back here immediately and had an even bigger success. And in the meantime, "I Could Go On Lip-Synching" had been in negotiations for about two years to open in L.A. and it finally did in March of this year. I did four months there which brings us up to the Chicago show and now I'm in California again.

JS: When do you go back to New York?
L: I'm going back mid-August and might be performing at the Ballroom in the last two weeks of August. The Ballroom is a high-profile cabaret where Peggy Lee, Eartha Kitt, Rosemary Clooney, Julie Wilson, and people like that perform.

JS: That's quite a legacy. Are those people you admire, cabaret performers, or are you drawn more to the larger-than-life Ethel Merman types?
L: I admire them all.

JS: Do you have any specific idols or influences?
L: Dolores Grey, who is really the emotional prototype of Lypsinka. She made a few films at MGM in the 50's, that can be rented. "The Opposite Sex," was one, "It's Always Fair Weather", was another, "Kismet," and "Designing Woman"

JS: What character is she in "Designing Woman?"
L: She's the television star that Gregory Peck leaves for Lauren Bacall.

JS: Who is another?
L: Kay Thompson. She was in the movie "Funny Face" with Audrey Hepburn and Fred Astaire. She does the number "Think Pink."

JS: That's a great production number. Have you ever done that?
L: No, not the whole things, but bits of it. She's still alive, but she doesn't do

"Yes, the face must be worked."

Lypsinka in performance at the Vortex in Chicago. Photo Scott Free.

anything. She wrote the "Eloise" books about the little girl who lives at the Plaza Hotel. She was also a great arranger and idea person at MGM. She was Judy Garland's vocal coach and she's Liza's godmother. She had quite an amazing career.

JS: Have you met her?

L: No, she's not meetable. She's a recluse. I do have her address and telephone number. Carol Burnett is also one of my idols.

JS: That I can really see in the physical quality of your performance. Have you had any professional dance training? Your body is so expressive.

L: I have had some. I started too late to be a real dancer, but that is really what I've become. As we're speaking I have ice on my knees, because they hurt so bad. So I guess I'm a dancer.

JS: I was watching you perform on a Wigstock video the other night. There were closeups of your face which were remarkable. Extremely expressive.

L: Yes, the face must be worked.

JS: Do you practice in front of a mirror?

L: Yes, but if you saw me off stage you wouldn't even know it was the same person.

JS: Do people treat you differently than they do when you are Lypsinka?

L: People naturally treat a man in a dress differently than they do when you're not in a dress. I'm also treated differently when someone meets me and they find out who I am.

JS: Do you find any resistance in the gay community to drag queens? It seems there has been a great rediscovery of the importance of drag.

L: There is definately something going on, enabling it to be accepted as a mainstream art form. It's been going on for quite awhile now and you would have thought it would have run its course.

JS: Do you see the opportunity to continue what you're doing for quite some time?

L: I certainly see the possibility. I don't know if the people who can help me maintain that do. I've had some interest from TV and film people. That would be the best test on whether or not this would go mainstream.

JS: Are you getting backing from Madonna?

L: I am getting backing from her, yes.

JS: How did this come about?

L: She came to see "The Fabulous Lypsinka Show," when I was doing it in L.A., around Christmas time. Sandra Bernhardt wanted to come because Isaac Mizrahi had been telling her about me, and she never had a chance. She was in town and so was I. A friend of mine who knows Alek Keshishian said he should go see the show, so between the two of them, it just fell into place that Madonna would come see it.

JS: Had you been a fan of Madonna?

L: Frankly, not really. The only thing she had done before "Vogue" that interested me was the "Material Girl" video because it was a clever take on the "Diamonds Are A Girl's Best Friend" number. When she came out with "Vogue," I thought, "Well vogueing has already had its day in the underground in New York," but when I saw the video I realized this was something; plus the song is really catchy. Last year when she did it on MTV Awards, that style of movement she was doing...I've seen dancers at the American Ballet Theatre try to do, but she had all the subtleties of the way people moved during the Marie Antoinette era. I was so impressed with her dancing, plus she was fun. I had never seen her be funny before. So there was some interest on my part. When she came to the show, I thought, "Oh, isn't this great? Here's Madonna." We met afterwards and she was very nice. A couple of days later, I got a phone call from our mutual friend telling me Madonna wanted me to perform at her Christmas party, which was the next day. I said that would be great and I would love to come to the party, but I can't perform unless she's going to pull it together. I need a stage, I need lights, I need sound. I can't just show up and do a show. So he said, "Well, if she still wants you, she'll call you herself," and she didn't call.

The people who were planning to produce "I Could Go On Lip-Synching," were coming to see the cabaret act every night bringing potential investors and they knew Madonna had been there. One of them worked for Propaganda Films which produced "Truth or Dare," and he got in touch with her and said we want to send a prospectus. About two weeks later I got a call in New York saying Madonna is an investor. She also did a photo session with me.

JS: Do you find that there's a difference between the crowd that comes to see you on the East and the West coasts, or the Midwest. Do they have different expectations?

L: Well, San Francisco and New York audiences are very much the same.

JS: In Chicago, I think you were an unknown quantity to many of the people at the Vortex, they weren't at all sure what to expect.

L: While I was onstage, looking at the audience I could see in many of the faces that they were thinking, "What is it?" It is always much more gratifying when they get obscure references, but, to their credit, that audience paid attention. They may not have understood everything, but they did pay attention, especially down front.

JS: I was in the back and you certainly had no problem projecting that far. Do you prefer a theater to working in a club like the Vortex?

L: Yes, when people are sitting down they have a longer and better attention span.

JS: You've said that drag, or playing a female role isn't all you can do. But do you think that lip-synching gives you a freedom you might not otherwise have?

L: Lip-synching gives me freedom to move more. That's the reason Madonna lip-synchs on stage. She's dancing her butt off. But I do plan to get away from lip-synching, but not give up the name Lypsinka... I have a whole, elaborate plan.

JS: I have no doubt about that. I want to know about the Temptations number you did at the Vortex. People were really thrown off by that.

L: (Laughing) Yes, but they started rocking out.

JS: That, and "The Telephone" piece. Did that just come to you one day when your own phone had been ringing off the hook?

L: Actually, I just realized that I had all these recordings about telephone stuff.

JS: It's a remarkable archive of material.

L: A lot of stuff you saw wasn't originally part of the"The Telephone" number. The stuff I originally did was like "Telephone Lover" that Connie Francis did, then I began to realize that you can just take anything and make a sample of it. The telephone is a universal thing that drives everyone crazy, everyone can relate to it.

JS: Does it continue to evolve?

L: I play around with it. It's what people remember most about me. What people always comment on first.

JS: What a trademark. I've always wanted to answer the phone saying, "Why don't you die?"

L: When I start to analyze why this character is so appealing to people it's because it's like early Bette Midler, who says things everyone wants to see but propriety and society keeps them from saying.

JS: Is Lypsinka that character for you? Do you do and say things as Lypsinka that John Epperson wouldn't say?

L: It's definitely a catharsis.

JS: Do you feel that it's revenge?

L: I've gotten a form of revenge. When I was growing up, I was a misfit in a small town when people made fun of me and I've taken my misfitness and turned it into a career and ended up in the pages of *People* magazine with the most famous woman in the world. How many people in my hometown got to do this?

JS: And the people in Hazlehurst knew that was you?

L: Oh they knew.

JS: That's a great kind of revenge. Does it bother you when someone like Sandra Bernhard capitalizes on the drag queeen tradition?

L: No, we're fellow postmodernists and iconographers.

JS: I love hearing you refer to yourself as a postmodernist, because that was one of my first impressions of you.

L: Well, it had to be explained to me. I always just called myself a nostalagia buff, but because people expect me to analyze myself more readily, I've learned what postmoderism is.

JS: You also said that you are very serious about not being serious.

L: Well, a lot of people think I'm boring because I don't go out every night, but I don't want to go to another smoky bar. After a show, I want to go soak in a hot tub somewhere. ▼

BILL COLEMAN

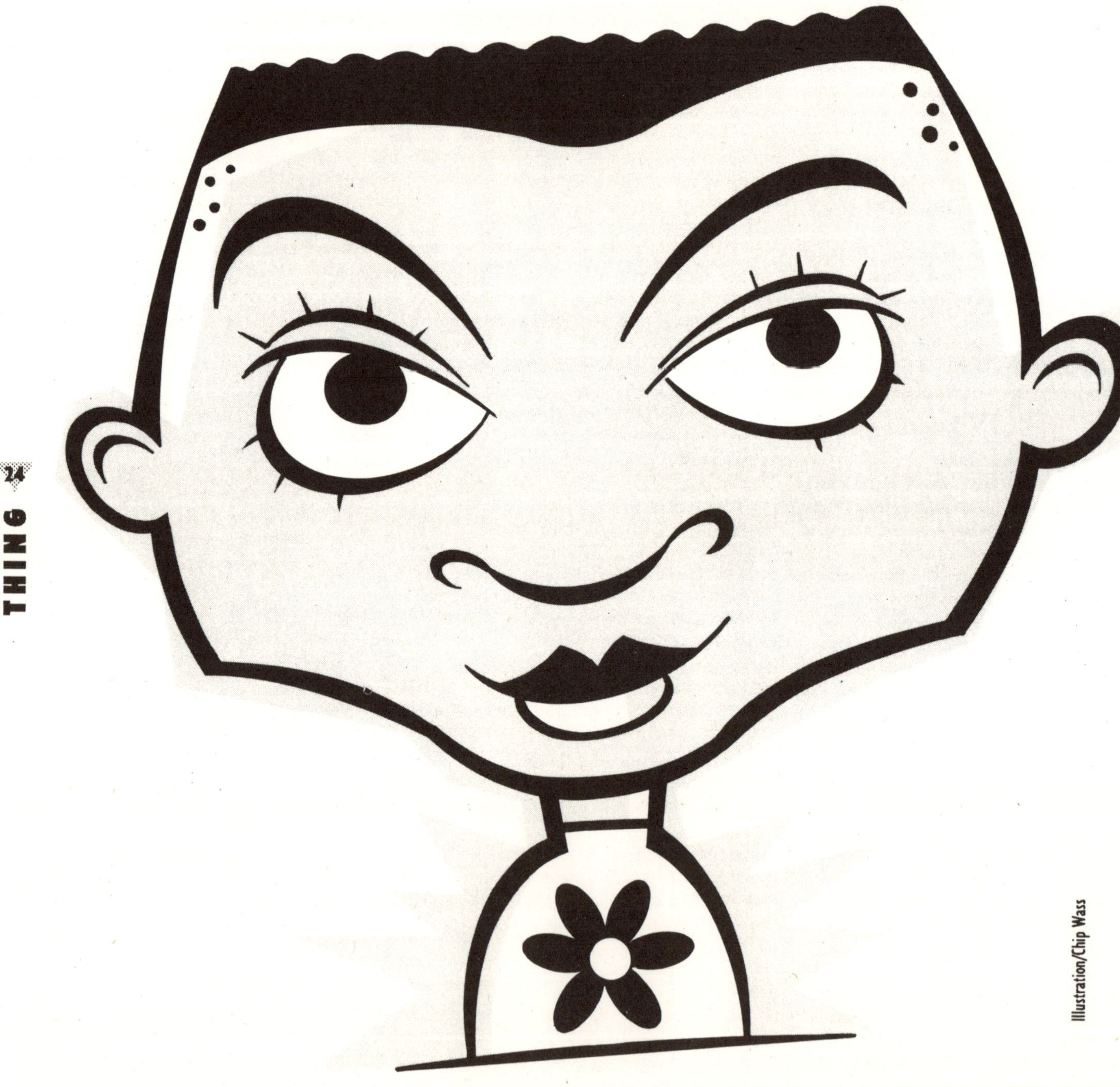

Illustration/Chip Wass

Musicians, singers, dancers, models, and lip-synchers are the visible members of the music community. Invisible to most are those behind the scenes responsible for everything else (besides the music) it takes to make a hit record. Promoters, producers, critics, publicisits, and a host of other "hooker-uppers" feed the pop music machine with their efforts. **Bill Coleman** is at the forefront of the dance music underground, managing and advising the careers of many talented artists. His Peace Bisquit Productions has had a hand in the successes of Deee-Lite, Ultra Naté, Basscut, and ESG. His column for Paper magazine is a lively run down of the best new music. And he's even got a few remixes under his belt. Bill Coleman is fierce, don't you understand?!

Robert Ford: Let's start with the basic stuff, like when and where were you born, and your zodiac sign and all that.

Bill Coleman: I'm a single Aries male, born in 1965 in Poughkeepsie, New York, which is in the Hudson Valley. I grew up in the Hudson Valley as well, and went to college there.

RF: What made you target the music industry? Were you always musical?

BC: Always. For as long as I can remember I've been entrenched in music. My mother has memories of me hoisting myself up onto the phonograph and watching the record go around. I was two or three. Ever since I was little, I've been fascinated by music. I would get really upset when they'd release the wrong singles off albums. I was like, "Why didn't they release that Chic song instead of what they did?" My parents used to forbid me from bringing records into the house. I used to work at a record store and spent all of my money on records. I had to leave them in the garage and sneak them in while they were asleep.

RF: Do you play any music at all?

BC: I fool around on keyboards and stuff. I've done four remixes so far in my lifetime.

RF: What's your DJ history?

BC: I started in high school, playing for school dances. Then when I went to college, there was a club called Bertie's which was basically a top 40 club, and I started what I considered an alternative night there. And to me, alternative meant anything the other DJs weren't playing. I would play anything from Dead Kennedys and Nina Hagen and Sex Pistols to go-go and the latest Liz Torres and house stuff...New Order and Propaganda and Grace Jones and Gwen Guthrie, a mix of a whole bunch of really eclectic things that I really liked and always loved to hear in a club. I really liked all different types of music. You could never go anywhere and hear a span of music. It was always like one type of music, and I hated that. That was back in '84. I DJ'd there until I moved to New York in '87. When I moved here I didn't really DJ regularly because, one: there wasn't a place I really wanted to do; and two: it was very difficult to get a DJ job here. So, I would just do parties for people, and lately I've been guest-spotting at the Pyramid in the downstairs lounge for Channel 69 night.

RF: How did you get hooked up with *Billboard* at such a tender age?

BC: Well, let's see...I graduated college in 86, and that fall I started at *Billboard*. During my college years I had done internships at Island Records and a local AOR station and was also DJing and also worked in a record store ordering stock and stuff. I had a lot of music-related things on my resume. I sent out resumes to all these record companies and got a couple of rejection letters and quite a few 'no replies'. And one day I was reading *Billboard* and I thought "I'm just gonna send my resume to everybody on the masthead and somebody's gotta call me back," and somebody did. They gave me this job as Territorial Rights Project

Coordinator. I started in November of '86, and by May of '87 I had started helping out the chart managers, and people saw that I knew a lot about different kinds of music, and they offered me the singles review position to review all the singles in the magazine. I had written a music column in college and in high school, so I had the writing experience. And it worked out pretty well. That summer, Brian Chin, who wrote the dance column, was leaving, and they wanted to keep it in-house which would also save them a salary. They were paying me beans at the time. So they offered me that job. By the end of October '87 I was a singles reviewer and dance music editor. I had only been there about a year. From '87 until last year I was doing that.

RF: What was behind you leaving *Billboard*?

BC: I was getting really bored. I'm the type of person where I'd just really rather leave when people still like the column and really enjoy what I am writing as opposed to waiting until how I was feeling started reflecting in my writing, and people would say "What is he talking about? His writing's gotten really stale." People said that as it was already.

RF: I always liked your *Billboard* column. It always had a good mix between dance stuff and more d.o.r. releases.

BC: Yeah, well, I really like those two types of music. I used to get, "You never write about hi-NRG." And I'm like, "Well, I write a little bit about it," but I admittedly say that I do not get hi-NRG music. I'm sorry, but Fun Fun is not really exciting. Basically, I got really, really bored writing every week, having that weekly deadline. Feeling so overwhelmed by the amount of records that were coming out that I wasn't really enjoying what I was listening to. And so, you know, for me it's not about just being in a powerful position, it's more about being happy with what I'm doing, and feeling I'm doing the best that I can.

RF: Did you get labels courting you for chart positions or good reviews while you were at *Billboard*?

BC: I basically built my reputation on no bullshit. Do not call me and hype me on a record if you know I'm not gonna like it, or if you know that it's bullshit. I did not cater to that kind of stuff. And luckily for me, a lot of times I would write about things that months later would become hits, and people really started to trust my ears. So they didn't feel the need to hype me on the new Debbie Gibson or Cher or whatever, because it would be a waste of time. I built my reputation on dealing with people on a very honest level. I'm very, very fair. One of the things I do miss about the job is the initial immediacy of seeing the reaction to what I

by Robert Ford

wrote a week or two later. To bring a record to peoples' attention that they wouldn't otherwise pay much attention to, stuff that was on independent labels. That I really do miss a lot, because I was

instrumental in a lot of records at least getting into view. When like, MC 900 Foot Jesus sends me a card saying, "Thanks for writing about my record," and Nettwerk picks them up because of the review, that's really cool. I get really excited about things like that. Cause that's what it's about. What's the point of being in a position of power or any kind of influence if you don't use it in a positive way, in a way that's gonna educate people. As far as what I'm doing now, I think it's been very difficult, and very often I have to keep reminding myself why I'm doing this and why I'm here. And it's to be influential in these people's careers, to help bring their music across. We all could use some positive reinforcement. And it's like the complete opposite of what I was doing before where I write about it and I get the reaction a week or two later. Now, I'm waiting a year for a project to come out. Or having to badger a record company to get the point. "Ultra Naté is fierce, don't you understand?!" You know, that kind of thing. It can be so draining. But at the same time, I'm in a position where people will listen to what I say for the most part. I can at least take someone like Ultra and bring her out of the level of "Wow, she's the girl with the cool 12" cover." That's kind of how I see where I fit into the puzzle of things. To help bridge things, being black, being gay, and tying all that stuff together, where as a lot of people either won't because they have no interest to or don't because they don't see it as necessary. To me, those things are really important. To tie everything all up. Because it's all connected. I don't know if that makes any sense.

RF: No, no, it makes perfect sense. About being out in what's still a very closeted industry, how do you see that personally. Of course it's politically correct to be out, but do you see it as a responsibility of yours?

BC: I don't really think in terms of being politically correct, I just think of things as how I feel and how things should be. Of course we should advertise in *Thing* and *Fertile Latoyah Jackson* because the people who read those magazines are the people who are gonna get the point. To me, it's just common sense. It's what we should be doing. You know, I'm just who I am, and luckily for me in a very short period of time I've gone from somebody that used to work in a record store to someone whom many people in the music industry respect for his opinion. Basically, when you're talking music business that cuts through anything. Bill can walk into the office or talk to the president of Charisma records and it has absolutely nothing to do with "He's got blonde hair this week," or "He talks with a lisp," or whatever. The point of the matter is that "I respect his opinion," and it's automatically just like "boom!..."

RF: ...knocks down the barriers.

BC: Completely. Because it's like, "this is someone whose opinion I respect."

**RF: Do you think your attitude about being out would be different if you weren't so "behind the

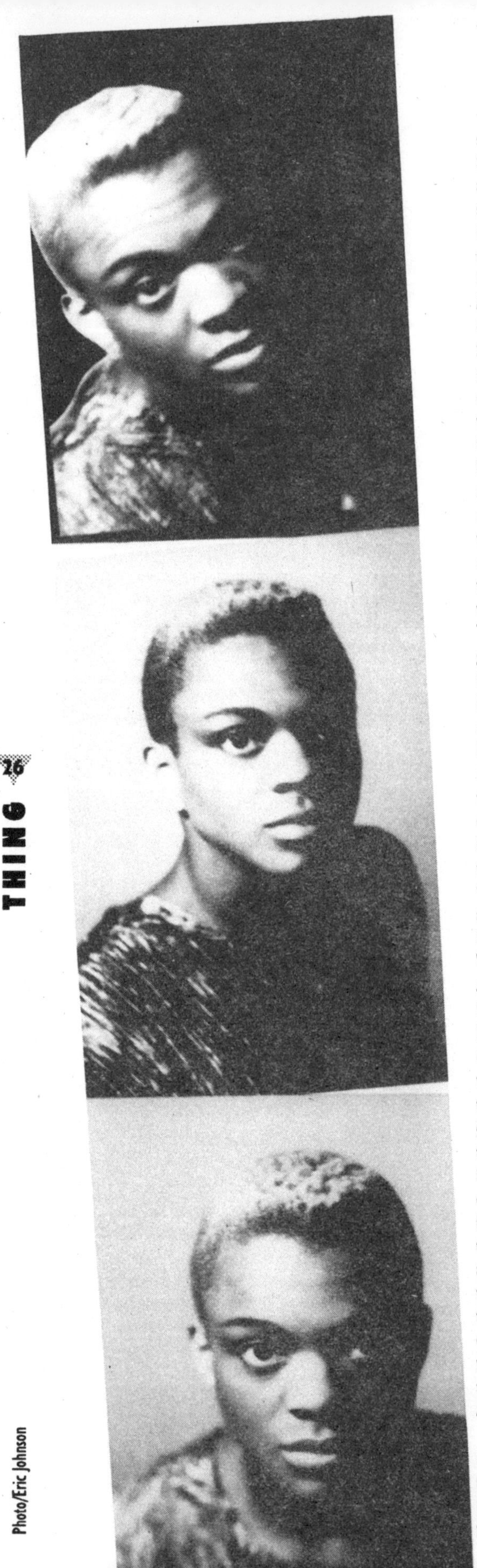

scenes?" I mean, except for Erasure and Jimmy Sommerville and a handful of others, we still aren't seeing performing artists who are out. It seems like David Geffen can do it because he's behind the scenes. If he was a recording artist rather than an executive producer, he might not have made the decision to blab it all to *Vanity Fair*.

BC: I think that a lot has to do with... That's a hard one. Someone like Jimmy Sommerville, Polygram just did not know how to market that record. I loved that record, and I thought it was a really good album, but why release "You Make Me Feel (Mighty Real)" as the first single? It doesn't make sense. It's like, "Alright, let's kill the project from the get go." Whose decision-making was that? With Erasure as well, there are some really bad marketing decisions. As far as trying to get them into the mainstream. Getting them in the mainstream wouldn't be a problem if people thought the project through. And it's not like, "Well, what are we doing here?"

There's so many people who, everybody knows they're gay anyway, that they might as well be open about it. I don't understand why they're not freer about it. It's basically a reflection on society. I see the world regressing at an alarming rate. America is really homophobic, very racist as well. I'm not surprised. It's 1991 and I still can't catch a cab, so I'm not surprised that someone's not screamin' on a video on MTV, "I'm queer!"

RF: Do you think that dance music has any power to eradicate that? Disco is still identified as "gay" music, yet it's gaining more mainstream acceptance.

BC: Dance music has the power to do a lot of things. Whether its gonna do it or not, I have my speculations. At the moment, I feel we're back where we were, as far as the industry repeating itself, in 1979. The term House might as well be Disco, the way people throw it around. I feel we're basically in the same position, where dance music makes record companies money, therefore they're willing to invest in it. But, whether or not the people who are making the music will use that music as a way of opening peoples' eyes to a lifestyle or correcting some wrong visions of the clubs or the scene, I don't see people doing that very often. Dance music now is a...I'm disappointed really. I think there's a lot of trash out there, there's a lot of fodder and there's a lot of money being spent on songs rather than on developing acts, which is the same problem that we had with disco ten years ago. No acts being developed, it's all about a track, or a song, and one-hit wonders. You'd think that it's only been ten years, that people would learn from the first time around. And it's just not happening.

It's great that the C+C Music Factory sold three million copies, but do I really think we're gonna be seeing Zelma Davis ten years from now? With all due respect to Robert (Civilliés) and David (Cole), I love them dearly, but it's like "C'mon guys!" That makes

me really, really upset. That million dollars... I could use a couple thousand of to get Ultra off the ground, someone who can sing and perform.

RF: Someone who wasn't put together by a corporate hit machine.

BC: The money's being spent for MTV-marketable acts. And MTV-marketable acts are probably not going to stand up and say "Hey, more power to the people who make the music, and respect us or whoever as they are. This is the deal." I don't see that happening.

RF: I'll be curious to see how Virgin markets Frankie Knuckles the recording artist, if they put him with a girl in the video.

BC: I hate that. That drives me up a wall. It's an insult to the intelligence. It's like, "Could we give the human race a little credit, please?" You'd think so, but it's, "We've got to appeal to this market, here in middle America. If we get them, we're home free!" And that's basically what it is. You work from the fringes to the middle of the country, and as soon as the middle of the country gets it...you need a hundred-thousand dollar video? You got it. You need promotion? You got it. You want a band and tour support?

RF: You got it.

BC: That's basically the way it works. And to me, being on this end of the business, I have learned so much about why I hate record company people. What it boils down to is someone sits behind a desk and says, "You can be a star...You can wait a minute...I don't get you...Maybe we'll try you out..." That's what it amounts to. To me, that gets so depressing cause it has nothing to do with the music. It's basically about marketability. Can you get that quick buck? It has nothing to do with developing acts. And if you find a record company that's willing to do that, you're lucky. We were really lucky with Elektra and Deee-Lite. They were willing to take a chance. They didn't believe it in the beginning, but they came around to it very well, and I take my hats off to them. Of course, they kind of lost the ball after the first single, but that's another story. But the fact that they took a chance, and were willing to listen to the band's ideas and translate that. They were like, "O.K. We'll give you the money for a good video, give you the money for promotion, give you the money for advertising, give you the money for tour support, and it paid off!

RF: I was really glad to see them make it as big as they did coming out of a real underground scene without diluting it for the MTV crowd. Selling MTV Deee-Lite's bill of goods.

BC: But see, that's the rare occurrence. What I've learned is you have to make it happen around the record company. Have people go to the record company and say "Hey, you've got this really cool record" and the company goes "Oh, we do?" And then they wake up. Maybe we do have something here. That's the approach I'm taking with Ultra Naté. I can't wait for all of Warner Brothers — not just the dance division — to get the point.

Everything ends up getting determined by chart numbers. If you have a top five dance record, then you're privy to being serviced to radio. Gee, thanks! The last (Ultra Naté) single, "Is It Love," I thought was a big top ten pop record. I'm still convinced that it's a hit pop record. Or a hit "mass appeal" record, cause I hate the term pop. "Is It Love" is so catchy, and her voice sounds great, and it's cool sounding, and the fact that it did not do well on the charts — made up of a hundred DJs in the entire country— shows it didn't get the attention it deserved. There's a video which no one has seen, very few people have seen it.

RF: I haven't seen it.

BC Exactly. Why did we waste forty thousand dollars to do the video if it's not gonna get serviced. I call the video guy at Warner Brothers and he's like, "Ultra Who?" Great!

That's the thing that fuels my fire for trying to make Ultra, or Deee-Lite or Basscut or whomever happen, that there are so many people in the positions of power who don't get the point. They don't get it. I'm very fortunate that I do, or at least I think I do. To help bring that out from the clouds, out to the people. There are a lot of people that would really get into this. That's how I see I fit into the whole thing.

RF: Were you on any of the New Music Seminar panels this year?

BC: I was on the management panel. I really don't participate too much —even when I was at *Billboard*, I'd go to the panels, write what I had to. But those situations' make me really nervous. Being around a bunch of people, and you're trying to have a conversation and someone taps you on the shoulder. It's not very productive. What's the point? I don't get real gung-ho about it. It ends up being a lot of opportunities missed. There are people I would love to have quality time with and you don't get to do it. I think they should scrap the panels, make it a big bar for six or seven hours a day. Drop the pretense that we're all learning something. It's all basically social.

RF: New Music Party.

BC: You'd probably get more done. At the panels they say the same stupid things every year. One of my frustrations when I used to moderate these panels was that people ask the same stupid questions. The same answers. They obviously didn't learn it the year before. And then, Farley gets up and tells us that house music started in Chicago. Thank you and have a nice day. So, I just stay in my office and then go out to the clubs and see people.

RF: I heard you participated in the Old Music Seminar...

BC: You guys keep tabs!

RF: We read a lot!

BC: I guess so! That was fun. That's Johnny Dynell and Chi-Chi Valenti. Their tribute to the New Music Seminar which was quite lovely.

RF: I'm sure it was more fun than the real thing.

BC: It was great! Aurthur Baker was there. The Basement Boys, and a bunch of drag queens.

RF: How do you compare doing business here and the U.K.?

BC: Well it depends on the label. Each one is different. I have grievances with all the labels I worked with, actually. And they probably have grievances with me. They're all run really differently.

RF: It seems that the UK labels understand US dance music better than we do?

BC: I think the UK is much more open to dance music in general. They're definitely more open to the artists. Dance music is revered there. But real soulful music still has a hard time getting on the charts there. A lot of the dance stuff that does happen is very techno, housey kind of thing. People like Ultra, or their own Mica Paris or Imagination or Loose Ends are usually mid-charting, kinda happening but not really exploding. The Black soul music over there doesn't really do well on the charts. I don't know why.

RF: It must do better than it does over here.

BC: Sometimes, but not necessarily. It depends on the artist, it depends on the label, there are so many different factors which play into it. It looks like I'm gonna be consulting this project for FFRR. Do you remember Carlton? He had a single out a year or two ago. He also released a single in the U.K. He's black, and he's gay. They're gonna release the project here. The label doesn't know what to do with him. His music is very cool. Very cool. Downtempo and moody. Almost reggae-ish but beyond that. He's a great songwriter and he didn't make it in his homeland. He's got this falsetto and deserved to be major over there and it didn't happen. So they don't always get it. But hopefully people will get it here and it will bounce back over there. But you never know. There are so many factors that play into a record being successful or not successful. I understand so much now why so many records that I love did not happen.

RF: Who's out there now that you wish was a Peace Bisquit artist?

BC: I'm really happy with the people that I have. I'm excited about the acts that I'm working with. I think Ultra's really fierce and Basscut comes from a completely different head, not really a dance band. They're a Eurythmics type act. It doesn't sound like anything that I've ever heard before.

RF: Those are the best releases.

BC: They're the best releases from an artistic standpoint, but at the same time trying to convince the record company that this is a really cool record can be one of the most frustrating things. I'm good friends with John Marsh from The Beloved and we've talked about working together on their next project. And there's a new group in the UK that are so fierce, D-Influence. They're signed to East/West records. They're a cross between Sade and The Chimes.

RF: Sounds like there's some great stuff to look forward to hearing.

BC: That's one of the things I really love about music. There's always something out there that you either never heard or that you're gonna hear. It amazes me at times. There's nothing like that rush when you hear something really cool and it makes you want to scream! There's not anything that can do that for me except for music. There's nothin' like hearing a fierce new song.

RF: What are your future plans?

BC: I want to test out my remixing and producing skills a little more. I basically take things a day at a time. I'm very committed to the projects I'm working on 'cause I think they have a lot to offer. I feel blessed to be able to pay my rent, do what I want to do, and be involved in a business in which I've always wanted to work in. I don't want to overextend my boundaries and take on too many acts. The Basement Boys asked me to manage Crystal Waters right when the record was about to happen and I was like "I'd love to, and I'm sure it's gonna be a hit," but I didn't want to. I was committed to Ultra, and I didn't want to overshadow her. I want to make Ultra the fiercest diva that I think she is. I'm not in it for the money. I'd rather do what I wanna do. I don't think too far ahead. If I started thinking about what I wanna do ten years from now, I'd lose it. I just like to chill out and have fun and not take this all too seriously. People tend to take this stuff much too seriously. For me, anyway, it's supposed to be about fun. I love being a fan of music, and I'm a fan of everyone I work with first and foremost. My goal is to be really happy, to have enough money to buy a house. I don't want to run Columbia Records in 15 years. No thank you. You can have that job; I do not want it.

RF: Happiness is the only goal that really matters.

BC: Ultimately. But a lot of people don't see it that way. Ultimately, for some people, power is the goal that they're looking for. I was in an A&R office at Warner Brothers and I shared the cab ride downtown with another manager (I'm not gonna say who). We were talking about the acts that he was working with, and he said to me, "I wanna be just like Russell Simmons. He has Cher's old apartment and he gets all the bitches." I know that the expression on my face when he said that could have just dropped to the ground. It was like "Oh. OK." And he's just one of many that think in those kind of terms. You can have all the bitches. Ultimate happiness isn't necessarily the first and foremost on peoples minds. It's really, really strange.

RF: It's a weird industry.

BC: Well, I guess it's like any other industry. I don't know what I would do if I was in any other industry. I don't know anything else. As Miss LaBelle said, "Music is my life." You take that away and I'm like nothing.

Bill Coleman can be reached at Peace Bisquit Productions, 225 W. 57th Street, 4th floor, New York, NY 10019. (212) 245-3445. ▼

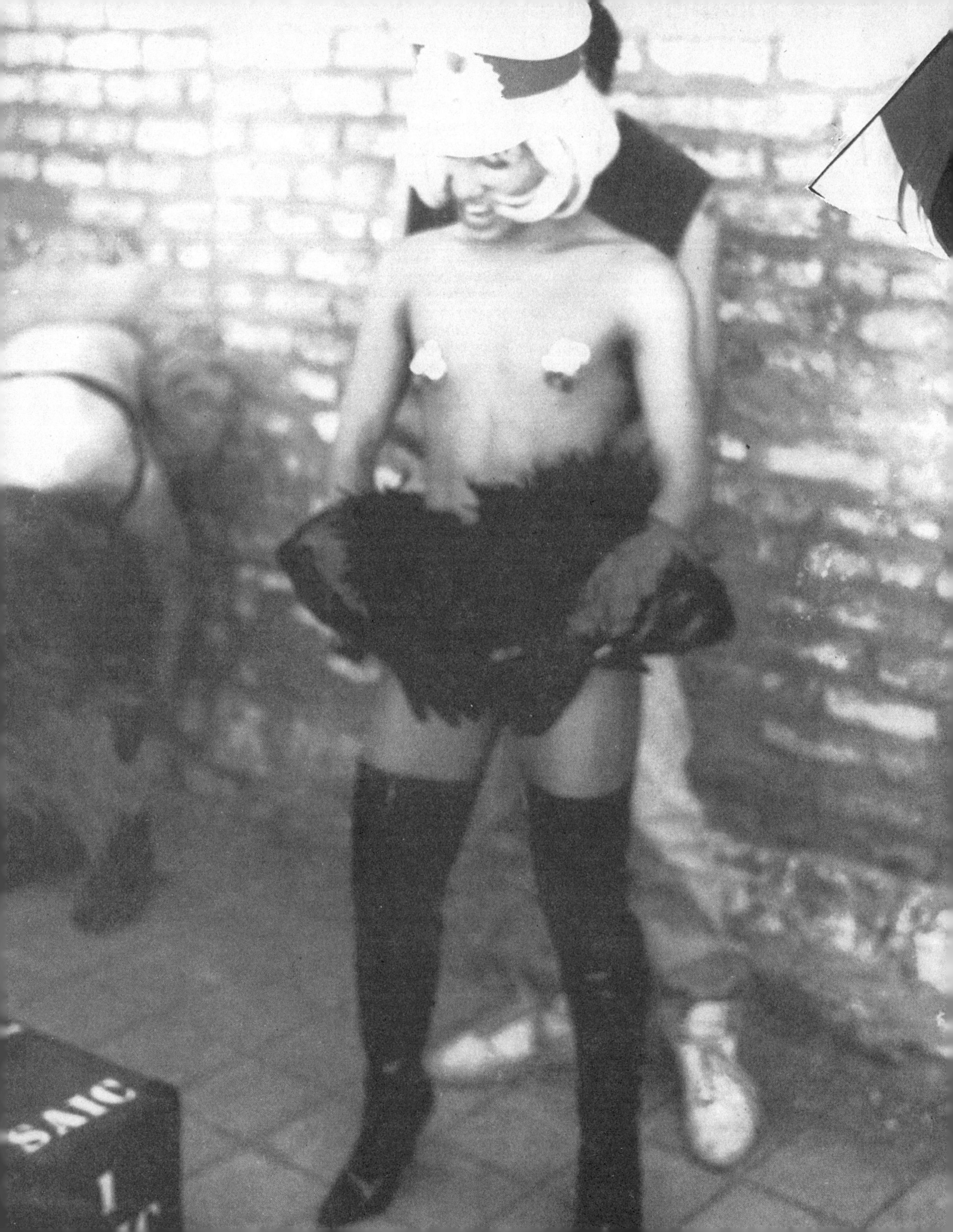
SAIC
1

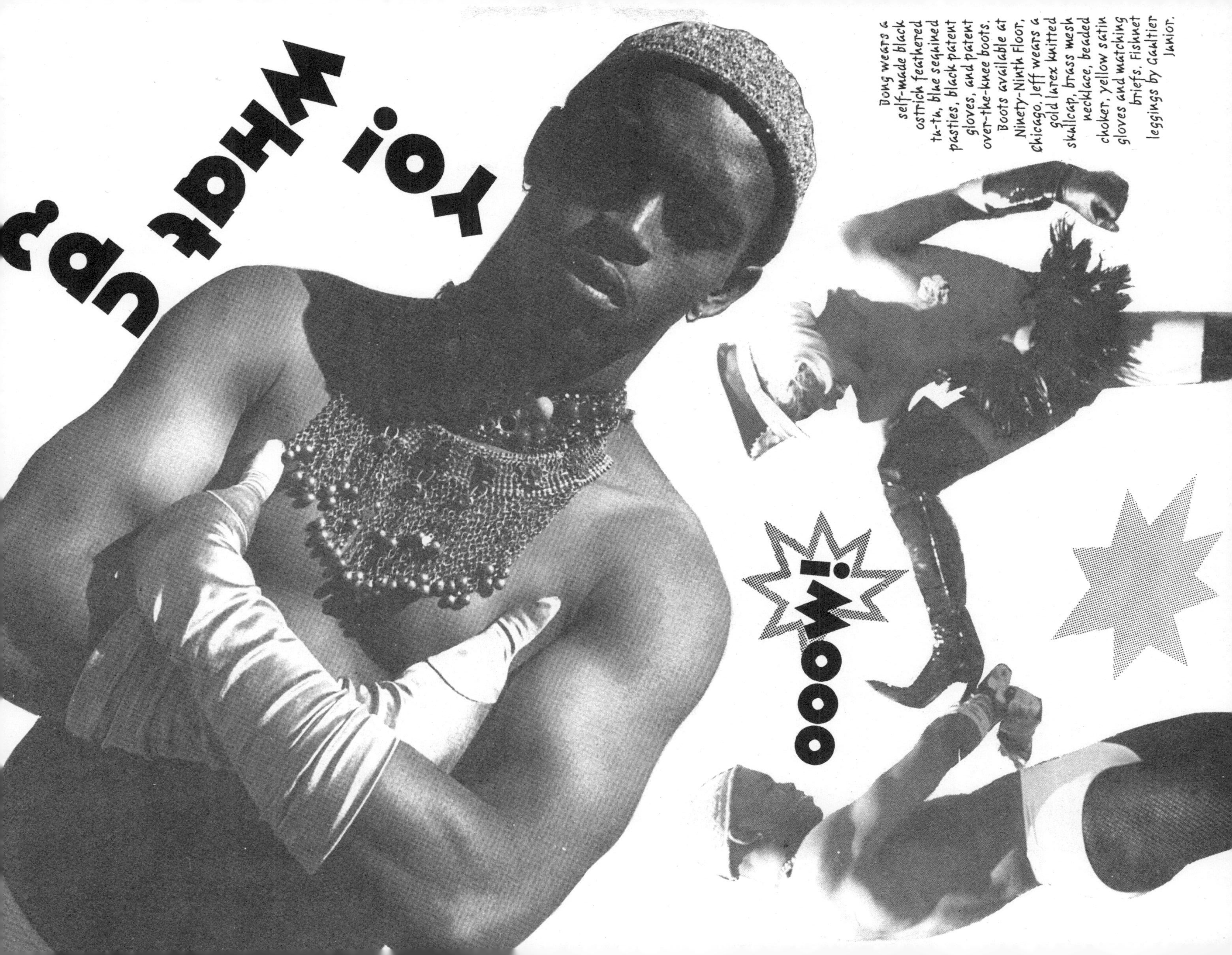

Yo! What Up?
OOOW!
Bong wears a self-made black ostrich feathered tu-tu, blue sequined pasties, black patent gloves, and patent over-the-knee boots. Boots available at Ninety-Ninth Floor, Chicago. Jeff wears a gold lurex knitted skullcap, brass mesh necklace, beaded choker, yellow satin gloves and matching briefs. Fishnet leggings by Gaultier Junior.

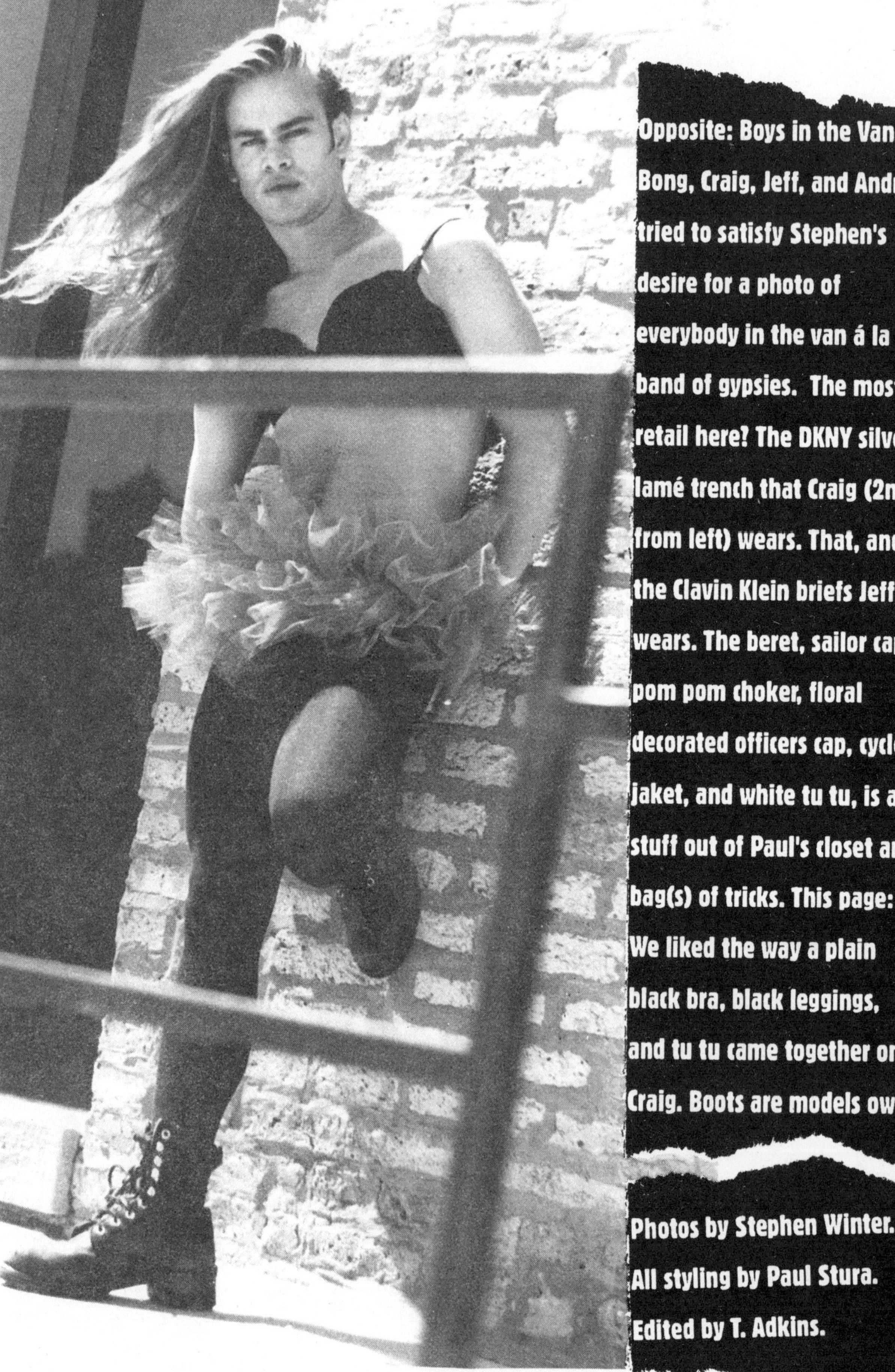

Opposite: Boys in the Van...
Bong, Craig, Jeff, and Andrew
tried to satisfy Stephen's
desire for a photo of
everybody in the van á la
band of gypsies. The most
retail here? The DKNY silver
lamé trench that Craig (2nd
from left) wears. That, and
the Clavin Klein briefs Jeff
wears. The beret, sailor cap,
pom pom choker, floral
decorated officers cap, cycle
jaket, and white tu tu, is all
stuff out of Paul's closet and
bag(s) of tricks. This page:
We liked the way a plain
black bra, black leggings,
and tu tu came together on
Craig. Boots are models own.

Photos by Stephen Winter.
All styling by Paul Stura.
Edited by T. Adkins.

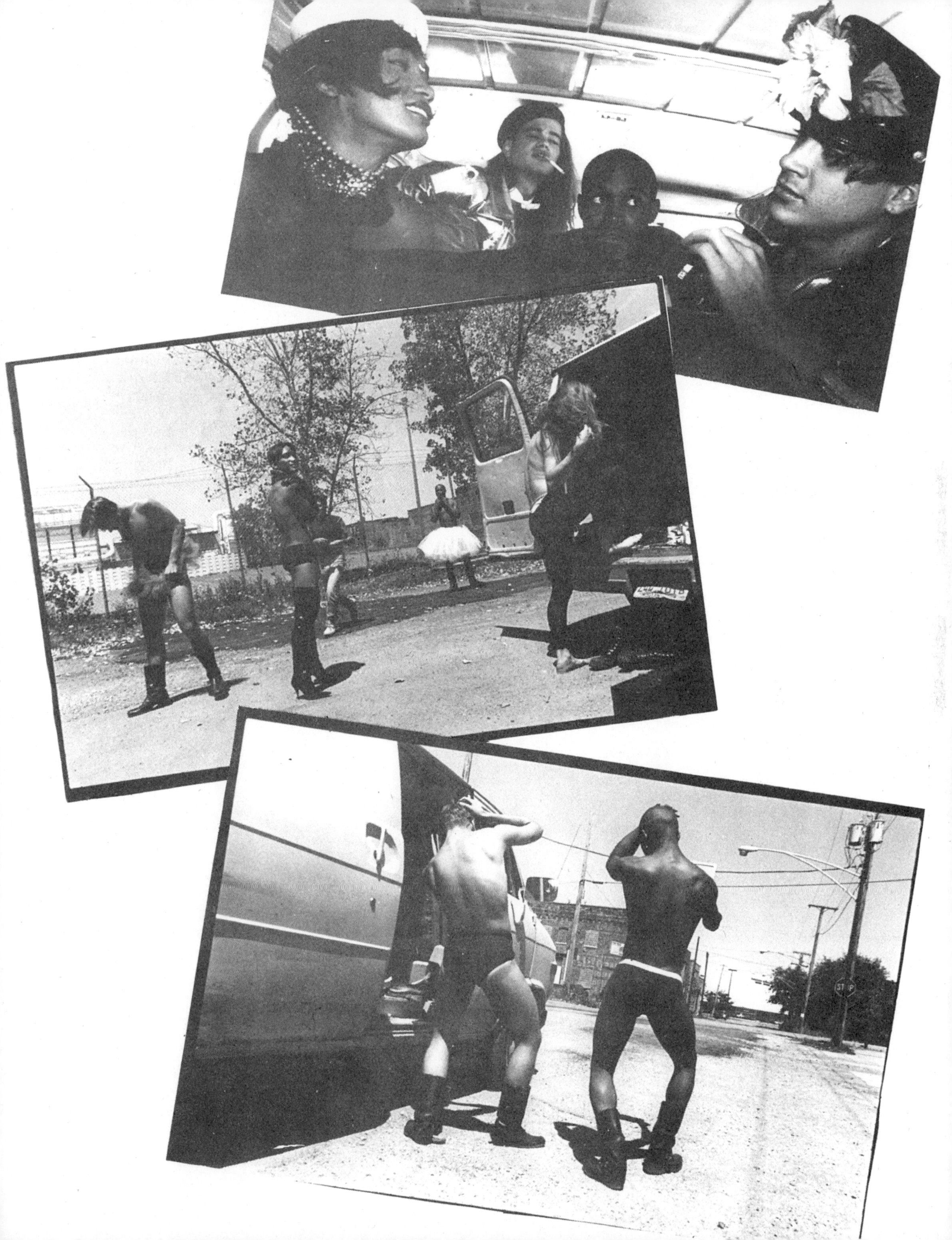

DEATH of a QUEEN

THING

"Rodney, Mr. Jackson would like to see you in his office."

Every eye in Mr. Martin's sixth grade Louisiana history class was on me. Mr. Goody-Two-Shoes being called to the vice-principal's office?

"Rodney..." Mr. Martin's voice was insistent.

I left my chair and began to follow the kid who'd brought the message to class.

"...and bring your books with you."

The eyes followed me as I went back to retrieve my books and followed the boy out the door. I couldn't look at anyone. And I tried to ignore the whispers and snickers. The door slammed shut behind me. I had difficulty swallowing as our footsteps echoed through the halls of Live Oak Middle School.

We reached his office. I was shown through the door and told to have a seat. Mr. Jackson would be with me in a minute. The tension was killing me; it was gettin' very hot in his office, and I had to fart real bad. But I was afraid that I would fart the second he walked in the door. And what kind of impression would that make?

I heard his heavy footsteps coming towards me. He told his secretary to hold his calls. He stepped

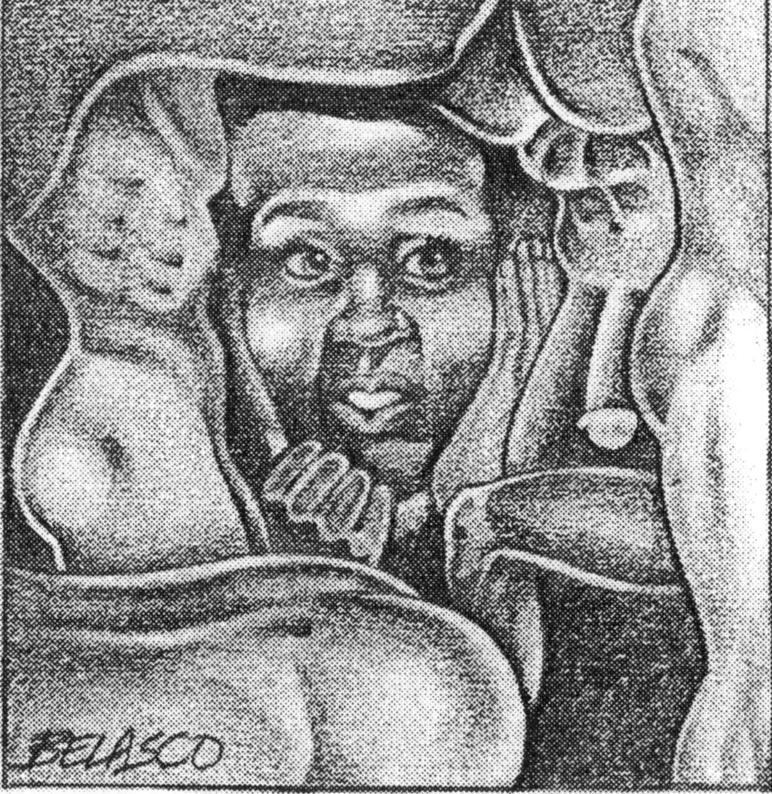

into his office, closed the door, and took a seat behind his desk. A very big, dark-skinned man sitting behind a very small desk in a very small office. Boy, was it getting hotter in that room.

"I called your mother in here earlier today," the bass voice boomed. "She was virtually in tears when we talked. Do you want to know what she was crying about?"

I couldn't speak, I couldn't do anything. Mom was here? I finally managed to shake my head.

"I've been watching you, son. We've all been watching you. And quite frankly, we haven't been pleased with your behavior. The way you walk. The way you carry your books. The way you talk. Do you realize how you look to other people?"

I shifted in my chair uneasily.

"You look like a damned sissy, that's what you look like. You don't act like the other boys do. I saw you in P.E. the other day. *You were playing with the girls.* I asked the coach why, and he said...he said you weren't *man* enough to play with the boys. Do you like sports, son?"

I couldn't believe this was happening. I stared vacantly.

by Gregory Conerly

The football sailed through the air. And it hit me in my ear. Chicken yelled "Tuesday," and realized he'd made a mistake. I wasn't the person he'd made a pact with to hit if he saw them before they saw him and recited the day of the week. It was a mistake he said. It was just a game, he said. He apologized. I tried to ignore the pain and continued to talk to my friend Lawrence in the school yard—even as the tears welled up in my eyes...

I was walking across the school yard toward Mr. Bannon, whom I had a big crush on. I'd wanted to congratulate him on the birth of his baby girl.

"Look at the way that dude walks, man."
"Yeah, he walks just like a fuckin' sissy."
Pointing. Laughter. As usual, I ignored it.

"Well?"

My voice cracked as I spoke. "I ran track a couple o' years back. And I like football."

"Uh huh," Silence. He shifted his formidable weight in his chair and rubbed his finger against his nose, as if in thought. He didn't buy it for a second. I hate sports and he knows it. I hated running track. And the only reason I like football is because I like to fantasize about the wide receivers with the tight ends, see the players tap each other on the ass in front of forty million people and not be self conscious about it, watch the quarterback and the center make passes at each other and engage in simulated doggie-style sex on the playing field, and see bodies clash into each other with violent grace and beauty. Football is the best gay porn on TV.

"What kind of relationship do you have with your father? I mean do you do things together, play ball?"

My father. So it's my father's fault he has a fag for a son. Did we play ball together like real fathers and sons did? No. Did we have father/son talks like the ones on TV did? No. And of course those fathers and sons, the ones you see on TV and read about in books, are the way real fathers and sons are supposed to be. Fathers aren't supposed to work all day, eat, then work at his second job and not come home 'til after his kids fall asleep. Fathers aren't supposed to go to the race track and watch ball games on TV on his days off instead of spending it with his kids. And fathers aren't supposed to beat the mother of his children in front of them. I live in a fantasy world. What's on TV is real.

"No. Not really."

"I thought so. Son, I don't mean to be harsh, but something has got to be done about you. When you carry your books, you clutch them to your chest instead of letting them hang to your sides. When you walk, you do so in short strides rather than long ones. And when you talk, good God, your voice is higher than most girls I know! Didn't your father show you the proper way for a young man like you to act?"

Silence.

"And you knew you weren't acting like the other boys. Why didn't you observe them and do as they did?"

I looked at the floor because I didn't want him to see the tears in my eyes. I still didn't say anything because I was afraid my voice would betray the emotional turmoil going on inside. Besides, I had nothing to say, no excuses to make. I was a twelve year old sissy, and that was that.

"Your mother said she didn't know what to do with you. But then in a situation like this, there isn't much a woman can do. I want to talk to your father. Obviously, he doesn't spend enough time with you, and you don't have any other male role model to compensate for it. What time does he usually get off from work?"

I told him the situation with my father.

"Well what days does he have off?"

"All day Sundays and Monday evenings."

"Ask your father if I can stop by next Monday evening to talk to him."

"Yes, Mr. Jackson."

"Now don't get me wrong. I think you're a very intelligent young man with a bright future ahead of you. Your awards for academic excellence and straight A report cards—well, except for P.E.— are evidence of that. But books aren't everything, boy. You need to learn more about life. It's a rough world out there, and you need to learn how to take care of yourself. You need to be more aggressive and competitive. And participating in sports will help you do that. Have the other kids picked on you because of your behavior?"

Reginald was mad. Our team lost the volleyball game because I failed to hit the ball over the net.

"If it wasn't f' yo' ol' 'maufadice-lookin' ass, we wouldna los' the fuckin' game," Reginald said, pushing me into the locker room.

"Let's drown his ass in the shower, " said one.

"I say we beat 'im up," said another.

Needless to say, I didn't want to take a shower. But if I didn't, five points would be taken off my final grade, and the coach, a super macho ex-New Orleans Saint, would force me to take one. I didn't seem to have a choice. Besides, I really didn't think they'd try to do what they said. I undressed and went into the shower with the other boys. Reginald and some of the others pushed me around several times, nearly causing me to lose my balance in the rising water.

"Look at this stupid-lookin' mothafucka."

Laughter.

"Go see if the coach is coming. We gonna drown his ass."

"Yeah." Nods of agreement.

The water was a half-a-foot deep and rising.

"There ain't nobody aroun'."

"Let's do it."

One foot.

One of the boys started singing "One Nation Under A Groove," a popular song on the radio. Others joined in as someone grabbed my arms from behind. Another locked my legs together.

The water was still rising.

"One nation under a groove. Gettin' down jus' for the funk of it."

I struggled wildly to break free. They tried to pick me up, but was dropped. Down in the water I went. I came up quickly and tried to stand. All the while, I was screaming, "Stop! Stop!"

"One nation, we're on the move. Nothin' can stop us now."

Hands tried to push my head back down.

"Coach!"

Naked brown bodies raced out of the shower at ninety miles per hour.

"What the hell's goin' on here?" It was the coach. He rushed to the shower entrance, ordered me out, roughly inspected my bruises, and shoved me aside.

"Get dressed." he said, and stormed into his office.

"One nation under a groove..." And laughter. Endless laughter. They tried to kill me in the shower. The coach didn't care. And now they're laughing about it.

"Yes." The incidents were numerous.

"I thought so. If you put a few pounds on that bony body, lifted some weights, and did all the other things I told you, you'd gain some respect. I'll have to ask your father about getting you a weight set and putting you on a diet when I talk to him. And what about girls? Have you been talking to any young ladies yet?"

Keith wanted to know if I was still a virgin. "Seriously, are you?"

Tyrone pointed at me and laughed. "I bet he is."

"I'm not going to deny it. Yes, I'm still a virgin. And I don't care what you say. I think you're still one too. You're too young to know anything about that."

"What's to know," said Keith. "All you do is wait 'til it get hard, make her get wet, slip it in, then you engage her in some pistol pumpin' action. Push an' pull, push an' pull."

"Yea." Tyrone shouted as Keith made pelvic thrusting motions.

"Then you rock her to the east."

Tyrone and Robert, the fourth person in the otherwise empty classroom, sang in unison, "Rock the body."

"Then you rock her to the west."

"Rock the body."

"Then you pump it harder and harder to make her scream."

"More. More. Harder. Harder."

"Then you come inside her."

"Ahhhhhhhhhhhhh."

"Oh Keith, you were so wonderful," said Tyrone in his best feminine voice.

"I think I have to go to the bathroom," said Keith.

We all laughed.

"I still don't believe you. You probably got that off TV. That's for older people."

Keith arched an eyebrow. "If you don't believe me, ask Hazel. I did it with her."

Tyrone laughed. "Everybody's done it but you." He looked at Robert. "Say you white boy, you ever did it with a girl?"

Robert grinned, exposing two rows of rotten black and green teeth. "Ya damn right I have."

"See that," Tyrone said. "Even that white boy done did it."

Keith made a face. "With them teeth, she musta had to put a paper bag over your head."

"No."

Mr. Jackson leaned forward in his chair. "You are interested in girls, aren't you? After all, you don't want to become one of those fag-, er, homosexuals you see prancing around in the French Quarter."

Sorry, Mr. Jackson. It's too late. I should stop this charade and tell him the truth. So that's what this was all about. He wanted to know if I was gay. Mom wouldn't have cried just because she thought I acted strange.

"Yes, I like girls." But I don't. My first wet dream was about Eric Estrada. I have crushes on Henry "The Fonz" Winkler and Mr. Bannon, my drama coach. And I fantasize about having sex with Stanley, the guy with the Billy Dee Williams smile, and Country, who has a beautifully shaped ass and a very lithe body. I never thought about girls sexually.

I wonder what would happen if I told him. Would I be sent to jail? To a mental institution? I mean, it's just a phase. I'll get over it. I even saw a book in the library called Overcoming Homosexuality. I'll get enough guts to check it out, follow it's instructions, and I'll be a normal person in no time. Just like those people on TV. No one will ever have to know. Please, God, I just want to be like everyone else. Please? I promise I won't lie or steal anymore. And I'll be good from now on. I'll even pay more attention in church and put more of my allowance in the basket. No, I won't tell Mr. Jackson. I'll do whatever he says, and I'll be a normal boy, just like he said. I know I will....I know I will.

"Good. Now, I hope you'll remember what we've talked about today. Your mother shouldn't have to worry about this."

Mama...

"And ask your father about my coming to visit. It's for your own good."

"Yes, sir."

He frowned. "Deeper."

"Your voice, make it deeper."

I spoke in a deeper voice.

"That's better. But keep working on it. I'm going to be checking up on you, so you'd better practice."

"I will."

"Now stand up....Hold your books....No, not that way. This way." He showed me the correct way to do it. "Okay. Now walk out the door. I'll be be right behind you...Go ahead. Walk back and forth along the hallway."

I obeyed.

"Longer strides, longer."

The bell rang for my next class. I was excused. For now. But I knew that from now on, I would be watched, frowned upon, and corrected. And I suspected this was going to be the start of a new kind of hell—one that was unlike the hell of being different I was already used to. The hell of trying to conform. ▼

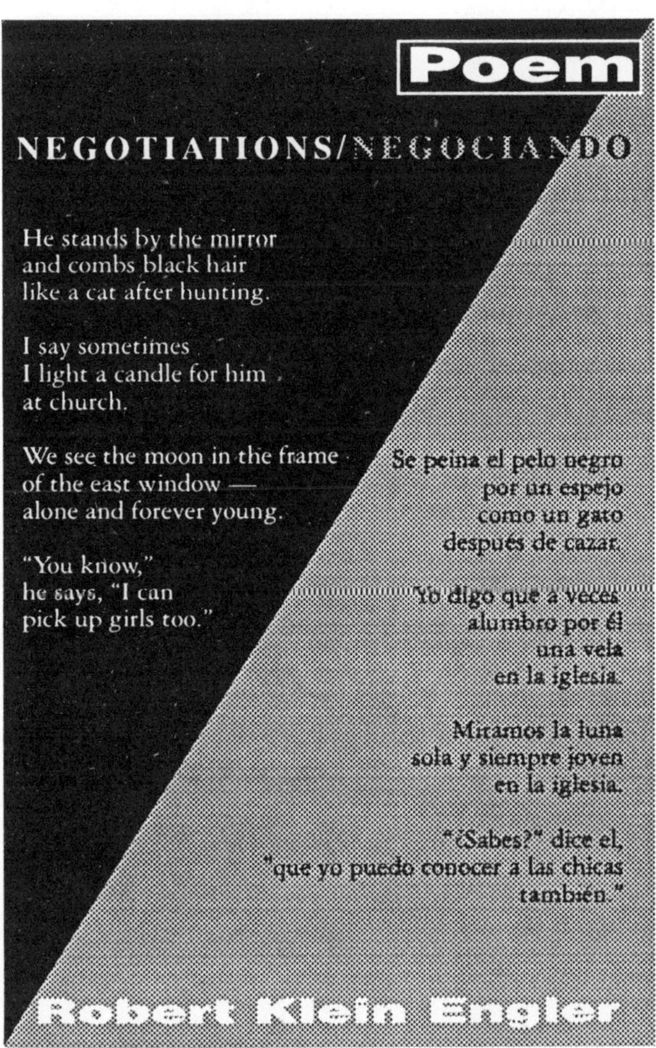

to live & WHORE in L.A.

Some queen once said to me, "L.A. is the only place in the world where you spend more money than you earn to impress people you don't even like." It is so true. From the hair weaved drag queens of Santa Monica Boulevard, to the pectoral implanted wanna-be's of Hollywood, everybody I've encountered during my current stay in LaLa land is hopelessly wraped up in illusion. Not ony does everyone claim to be good friends with Madonna, but apparently they've all slept with Rob Lowe, Scott Baio, and George Michael as well. Fabulous! Then why the hell are you sitting here asking me if I have an 'extra' cigarette? Buy your own, star-fucker.

This is not to say that everyone out here is a mess; I have made a few friends, and of course, have had my share of interesting sexcapades, including an encounter I recently had that left me (literally) breathless.

I met him one lovely afternoon while drunkenly cruising Griffith Park, which is a notorious meat rack in the Hollywood Hillls. The cruisy area, nestled deep into the woods, is actually quite pretty and relaxing, as long as you wear comfortable shoes and don't mind total strangers smilingly observing you while you relieve yourself behind a tree (I don't). So I happily marched into the wilderness, a song in my heart, and a six-pack in my belly. After warding off the advances of a few persistent old leather queens, I ended up 69'ing in the dirt with a FINE blonde mother-fucker. I was so drunk I only made a half-assed attempt to be the ferocious sex goddess that I usually am, but I must have been fierce enough, for he gave me his card and told me to call him.

Looking at the card later, after showering and a few hours of detox, it finally hit me: the delicious blonde snack I had earlier was none other than Leo Ford, porn star of many a queen's wet dream. I called him a week later (one musn't seem too eager) and we set up a time to meet.

He picked me up on his motorcycle, in front of Donut Time in Hollywood. I felt like the cat's meow as we tore up the Boulevard, my arms wrapped tightly around his waist, unbothered, nay, pleased by the jealous stares of the boy-toy street hustlers peddling their tired wares. We got to his apartment, and once inside, Leo turned on a slamming house tape and lit up a joint which we quickly smoked.

Now stoned out of our minds, we went after each other like mad bitches in heat. On the floor, rolling, groping, him making animalistic growling sounds, me his willing prey. I was lost in it, drowning in heat, slick with sweat and spit. Fuck the carpet burns on my back, this was FABULOUS!

In one sudden move, Leo lept over me and sat on my chest, and began spanking my lips with his fat cock. Shit, I hadn't realized just how big his dick was. And I had no time to think about it. In one swift move, he forced my mouth open, and his rod in. Surprise! His horse dick went so far down my throat it went past my collarbone! Jesus Christ, it was so fat that the pressure of it constricted the bloodflow in my throat. I was getting really fucking dizzy, but I wanted to swallow this dick! Not even swallow—I wanted to digest this motherfucker. "You can do it, Chicklet," I told myself. "Girl, just go on!" And honey, I went on! And on and on and on...

It was incredible. For one shining moment I lost consciousness. There was no time, no reality, nothing. Just my mouth and his cock. His masive, meaty, greedy fuckmonster. It was truly religious. He grabbed the back of my head and used my mouth as his warm, wet jack-off machine. In and out, deeper and deeper, I felt his cock grow stiffer, the head more thick and bulbous, and tasted the salty sheen of sweat on the shaft of his penis. Finally, urgently, he pulled out and shot his hot spurts of cum on my face as he put his balls in my mouth, which I hungrily, greedily sucked on. At this point, I shot my load, and Leo collapsed upon me, the both of us spent, sticky, and satisfied.

It was absolute heaven, but thinking about it later on, one thing concerned me — dick size. Now, I think there's something sexy about every man, mind you, but after having a thick, juicy, footlong slab of manhood rammed down your throat, you begin to wonder. Oh, okay, I'm a size queen, I confess. But even if a guy's dick was less than huge, somehow, someway, I'd have a good time anyway. Only now I'm afraid that the average penis will no longer do the trick. Honey, once you've tasted butter, margarine will never do.

Yes, I can see it now; I'll become insatiable, on a quest for even larger penises to fill my burning orifice, until one day I am found impaled on a fire hydrant, my face a mixture of shock and unbearable pleasure. Think of the pain! Think of the humiliation! Think of what it will cost to get my asshole sewn up! Ah, what the fuck. At least a fire hydrant won't expect me to cook breakfast the next morning.

by CHICKLET

PUSSY: A friend of ours who was dabbling in dominance found himself with so many hormones and so little time. Grabbing a willing stranger, he whisked into a cubicle, whipped out his cock and forced his new best friend to get his face fucked.

The poor sucker's throat was rammed raw and his head banged repeatedly against the doorjamb until our buddy shot his wad—upon which he withdrew and zippped up, wondering all the while if, perhaps he 'd been a touch too rough. As he turned to leave, the receptacle *d'amour* looked up and smiled, "That was wonderful," it gushed. "Just like it use to be in prison."

BUNNY: Speaking of drag queens, Pussy isn't the only gal I know who gets mistaken for a man on occasion. Miss Becky, a rather svelte, striking redhead I'm fond of, tells a tale of an encounter with a masher in a new wave bar. After getting rebuffed several times, he became quite hostile. "I bet you're really a transexual," he sneered. "Maybe," Becky shrugged, nonplussed and that enticed him even further. "Well," he leered, "Whatever the doctors did, it's making my dick hard!" "Mine too," the Beckster cooed..."It's at home in a jar of formaldehyde."

PUSSY: You know, on account of a queen, I will always believe the power of love—thanks to a miracle that happened one night, long ago...in Dago Rose's.

What I was doing in such a fetid, squalid dive remains unclear, but this is

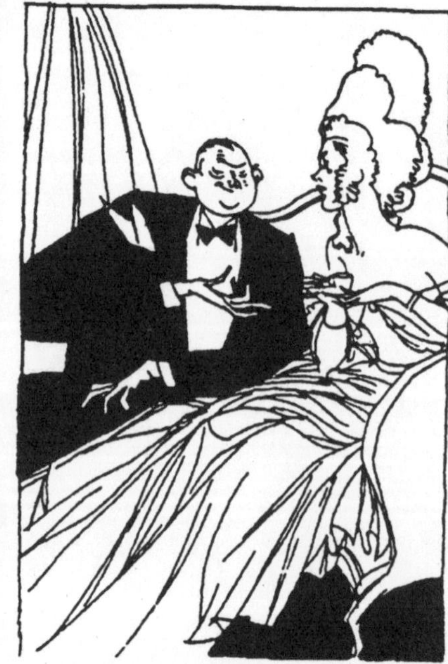

not deep analysis...just petty exhibition-ism. Anyway, there I was, way back in the rear of the bar, shooting the shit with some gentlemen friends when the door flew open up front and in came Dee Dee, the drugged out P.R. D.Q., shrieking at the top of her lungs! "*Carumba*, have I had a chitty day! I thin' I need to kill somebody."

She smashed an empty bottle on the edge of the bar and I looked up at the sound of the busting glass. Our eyed met. She waved her jagged scepter in the direction of my face and yelled, "She'll do!" At that very moment even religion seemed to make sense. "Dear God," I prayed. "Who and whatever you're suposed to be, please make her lose her train of thought before she gets from there to here."

Midway through the room she passed a pair of enormous forearms that stopped her dead in her tracks. "Mmm, Popeye!" she cooed, tracing her initials on a bicep. "Wanna pop my cherry?" And thus, my cheap misguided, miserable life was spared. God is love.

BUNNY:God may be love to you, but others have some more idiosyncratic interpretations. Here's a remarkable series of vignetttes I've curated that I call, "The Littlest Pederast"...or "Memoirs of Monsieur Poulet."

While he was still in his teens, passing mothers instinctively clutched their children to their breasts...as though his forehead sported a tattoo, "Bad News Babysitter." He was always moving in and out of town, for reasons soon to become clear. After one prodigal return, I agreed to wait for the telephone installer while Poulet sought work.

Armed with a freshly-minted key, I let myself into his new studio apartment, which I had not yet seen. I would classify the decor as early Bijou...into the tiny space he had managed to cram four couches (set up theater-style), one behind the other. Strewn about were vast quantities of Scandanavian kiddie porn including the complete edition of *Torrid Tots*. Lest the phone man phone the feds, I stacked them neatly in the corner under my own tattered copy of the *Nation*. That's what friends are for.

Poulet, ever questing for physical perfection, was quite the art aficionado—having photographed the bare backsides of some of the world's three dimensional masterpieces. Hence Poulet's Law:

Behind every great sculpture...is an amateur photographer.

In his search for eternal youth and beauty, Poulet prowled the playgrounds, camera at the ready. Like a most dedicated naturalist, the patient pedophile would wait for hours at a time to capture that one perfect shot of "Boy on a Swing."

Once he took a position in another state--as live-in nanny for the offspring of two alcoholic attorneys. Everything went fine until he confessed his predilections during a late night drinking bout, and then—realizing his potentially prosecutable *faux pas*—was forced to flee before dawn.

After his rude collision with reality, to quote Edmund Wilson—another famous bunny—Poulet had to lie low. Now he spends his days lost in reverie, poring over the pictures in his scrapbook, most of which seem to be decorative frieze which he insists contain pornographic images that elude all but he...

PUSSY: While the illustrious Poulet may have stumbled on something interesting—non-representational smut—not all of our friends photo document their exploits. Though she's not a shutterbug, Libidinous Letita understands the value of empirical verification. Too well-bred to whip out a ruler, the dear lamb—largely to appease us—has managed to record the size of her more substantial visitors by counting the squares on the plaid bedspread as the errant swains doze, *aprés la prod*.

Well at least she gets prodded. An aging divorcée I know alll too well, has had a rather unfulfilling relationship with an elderly escort for more years than she dares to think about—lest it lead to her suicide. In addition to his lackluster personality, Mr. Dullard is marriage shy and short on libido.

Recently my friend spent the night in her companion's apartment, and stayed over the next day while he went off to work...ostensibly to tidy up his bachelor digs and watch his cable TV.

Purely by chance (sure) she happened upon a box buried (deep) in the closet, containing (horrors) dozens of bondage magazines. That evening she confronted him, waiting til he was comfortable ensconced in his lazy-boy lounger, she dumped the offending box in his lap. "What is this trash!" she railed. Sheepish, he confessed to a long term adddiction to

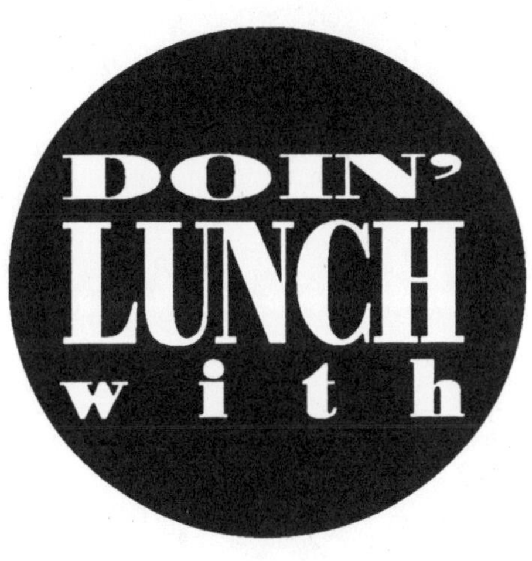

*bunny
&
pussy*

the S&M mystique. Which repulsed our friend who while lusty, is still rather bourgeois in her tastes. "How on Earth does a person get this way?" she demanded to know, and the tale unfolded: One day, as a boy, he'd traded his prize Green Hornet for a back issue of Superman. The lead story featured Lois Lane, bound and gagged, in the clutches of Lex Luther. One glance at the nubile beauty straining against her restraints was all it took. The die was cast...a pervert was born.

Paraphrasing Noel Coward in *Private Lives*: "How extraordinarily potent cheap comics are!"

BUNNY: And ditto for the zines...

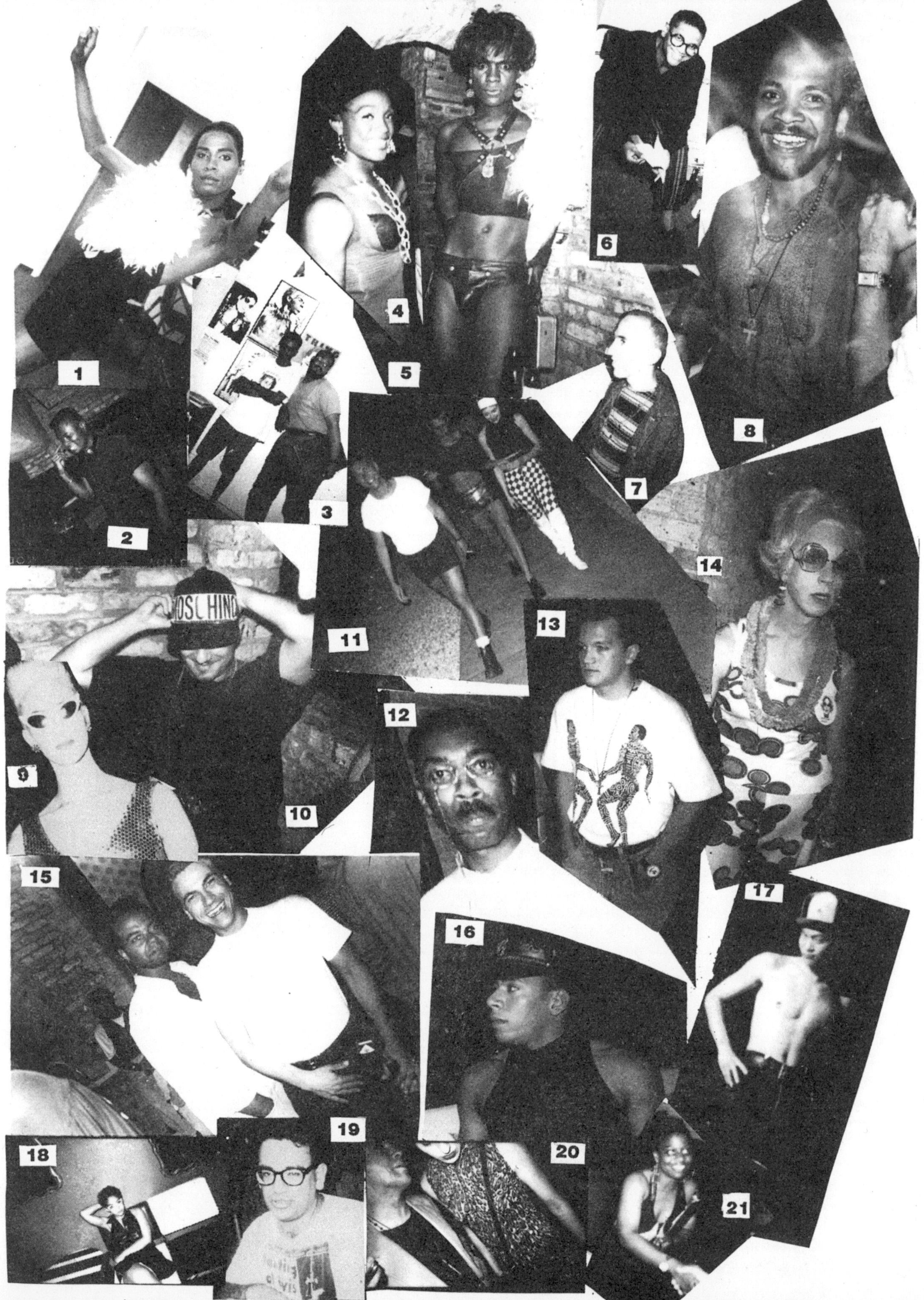

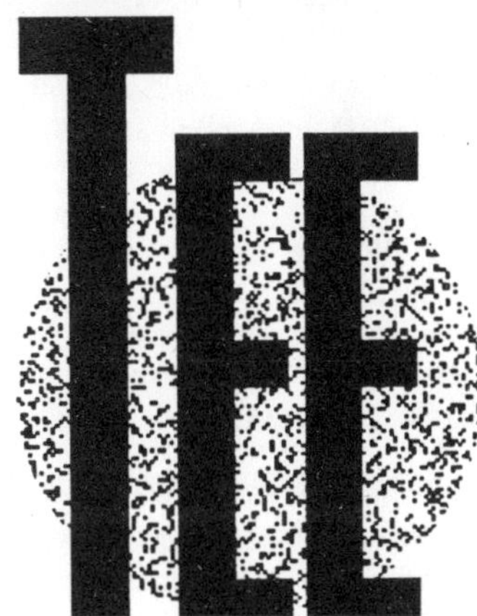

KER-PLUNK!

When publications like *Inside Chicago* begin ranting over how your club is "only the most fabulous place to see and be seen," well, I hope you favor lots of midwestern style Euro Trash and Tacky Wannabe Suburbanites because they will "come on down!" Ka-Boom!'s high rent location in a newly refurbished warehouse building at Chicago and Halsted, and the club's over-styled interiors suggest that a lot of money has gone into the place. Ka-Boom! is obligated to make lots of money to stay open and they seem determined to appeal to the lowest common denominator to attract as many patrons as possible. People like **Shanda Leer**, **Richard Knight**, **Michael Mangiaforte**, **Joe Lopresti**, **Paolo Pincinté**, and **Christasy** work at the club as promoters, hosts, and bartenders. They're bait and their work is cut out for them. This may only be partial protection against the illin' personnel one encounters at Shelter. As volatile as clublife is, by the time you read this, some of these people may no longer even work at the club. Let Ka-Boom! do whatever they want to bring in the spenders and filler people, but let's see how they are at running private parties or special events for the more seasoned urban clubgoers. I've never run a club, but the trick has to be providing a good atmosphere and a good mix of people as often as possible. Right now, Ka-Boom!'s crowd is pretty lightweight: posers and weekend suburbanites. And we've already seen clubs that get a bunch of trendy people to work for them, just to turn around and dick their employees and patrons by trying to second guess everybody. Take Slimelight for example. Limelight Chicago had some of the best kids in the city as staff. But, somehow, the club was still lacking. The opening night party at Ka-Boom! was true to Slimer: a big patriotic mess that over-capitalized on the then current Persian Gulf mania: every service employee dressed in some manner of red, white and blue, stars and stripes, and yellow ribbons! Flags everywhere! (This wasn't tongue-in-cheek, either. They were serious!) I'd only gotten as far as the t-shirt booth when I see **Steve Marton** and posse quickly on their way out. "You don't want it! It's sick. A total waste of time." And this after they got to see **Mary Irene** walk in the fashion show in red, white and blue, stars and stripes leather! (Courtesy of **Michael Hoban** for North Beach Leather, of course.) BMCS seems to lurk especially at the straight clubs that have "Gay Night(s)." Ka-Boom's opening gay night party F.U.C.K. (held on 6/9, oooh!) was B.O.R.I.N.G. And where were they hiding the members of Cirque Du Soliel for the circus' cast party there? That evening, the upstairs game room looked like a Gold Coast/Division Street circus: Mother's meets P.S. Chicago. Can people like Michael Mangiaforte get folks out for **Crystal Waters, RuPaul, Gina Tay, Ultra**, or whomever the children are following? We'll see. Advertisements for the club call it "Chicago's most explosive night club!" It's a dud sometimes, too!

MEN WITHOUT HATS

I knew it from the word go that anyplace having the nerve to name itself the Warehouse was doomed to be a drag. The original Warehouse was the end-all haven of jack for only the most fabulous black fags and it would appear that it met its demise due in large part to a door policy that became too lenient in allowing just any ol' body in. It had no sign out front or anything outwardly marking its location. You either knew where to find it or you didn't. Now *this* place is open, straight as the day is long, with a big red neon sign out front that says "The Warehouse". However, by the time sissies who are thinking of the original Warehouse *do* drop in, does the management have to be forced to remember its gay sensitivity training? A little more than a dozen of us were there for the House Hoedown, a house party by way of a country theme (not to be confused with **Christine Johnson**'s House Hayride of a similar bent). It was **John D'Armour** aka **Fraulein**, **Terence Smith** aka **Joan JettBlakk**, *J.D.s* publisher and filmmaker **Bruce La Bruce, videographers Stash Kybartas and Gabriel Gomez,** Steve Marton, **Craig Siegle, Brian Matthews, Brian Funk, Dave Williams**, SPEW organizers **Mary Jo Schnell, Suzie Silver** and **Steve Lafreniere, yummy Chuck Gonzales** and some others. We'd just left the "In Through The Out Door" series' *Approriation/Representation and the Subculture of Queer* panel at Randolph Street Gallery. One of the panelists, **Vaginal Creme Davis,** was going to meet us at the Warehouse. Much to her benefit, she missed the party. We can thank **Gina Love** and **Alan Louis** for ushering us in comp because we really didn't want the privilege of paying five bucks and having to re-do our looks, too. We were being denied entry because we were sporting baseball caps, a no-no in most straight clubs because gangs are represented by colors of caps. I overheard Miss Love explain to the manager (?) that she would eat the loss of the door cover but that the bar would still profit from our drinking if they'd allow us in. "Oh, ok." But think about it: gang members show up at the club, remove their hats and gain entry. So then you have hatless hoodlums in the club? OKAY! How 'bout a policy of "No Gang-Bangers!" Period. **Mark Farina** had the unenviable task of playing to a sparse crowd and was only spinning so-so. I've heard him in much better form which is why I couldn't understand **Lady Arlene** and **Gus Boy** getting so excited that Farina was dubbing the party for them to take home. I'd heard that the original owner of the place, **Ralphie Rosario**, had spent lots of money installing a fabulous sound system, but what I heard sounded rather average. A few kids danced for awhile on the overly lit dancefloor before we all finally settled in the upstairs lounge, continuing the weekend's SPEW induced gabfest.

BURNING DOWN THE HOUSE

The *Paris Is Burning* opening at the Fine Arts cinema proved fun because a good sized crowd turned out (mostly white kids) and everyone seemed 'up' and high spirited. It wasn't as glamorous as expected, even though we'd spotted a few queens on Halsted the day before shopping for outfits for the opening. However, the presence of super-hot **Lorraine Baskerville** more than made up for the conspicuously absent parade of glamor girls that usually accompanies events of this sort.

The party at Ka-Boom! directly following the screening was lacking. Don't get me wrong; the crowd and the music were probably the best it's ever going to get there, but it didn't fly. **Spencer Kincy** spun an eclectic and pared down mix of hot cuts that kept folks busy on the dance floor. But he's really a genius for not once resorting to playing **Madonna**'s "Vogue." (Thank You!) Lot's o' cosmotata in the crowd: **Robert Ford**, Steve Marton, **Michael Hyacinth, Jeff Britton, Andrew Sarver, celebrity hairdresser André Walker, Willie Crespo**, May Day, Alan Louis as **Azanda**, House of Avant Garde founders **Aaron Pierre Brown** and **Wardell Ford, Lady Arlene Casillas, Delon Strode**, Lorraine Baskerville, make-up man **Dwayne McKeever, Roderick Conrad**, Betsy Johnson's **Rebecca Hoffman**, stylist **Paul Stura**, and make-up wiz **Gina Sporacino.** Voguer extraordinaire, **Willie Ninja,** was scheduled for an appearance at the club but was a no-show. Hmmm? And don't try getting away with saying that Madonna was there. The cast and crew of *A League of Our Own* was on break for the weekend and Her Fabulousness was known to have left the area. Finally, *thank you, so very much!* whoever it was that sent us the tee kee fresh *Paris is Burning* full-color poster! ...It's goin' on and we love it!

THEY SHOOT CLUB KIDS, DON'T THEY?

When you say club kid you say *Project X.*, I think. It's supposed to be the club kid's Bible. But I don't know, club kids seem better covered by people like **Michael Musto** and **Stephen Saban** who come to the latest club scene more informed of clubdom's past incarnations. Club kids don't seem too interesting covering themselves, lacking in the pages of *Project X* is any amusing sense of tongue-in-cheek or self-parody. They seem to take themselves much too seriously. *Project X* likes hyping itself, going as far as to suggest filling the voids left by *Details* and *Egg*. The original *Details* mighn't ever be duplicated—they were able to assemble so impressive a stable of editors and contributors. Lots of clubby pix to look at but don't go mistaking Julie Jewels for the likes of Bill Cunningham. *Project X* is far from being another *Details*. I can remember, not long ago, when it didn't have the glossy cover or all the big name advertising. I wish them luck. The New York City styled club kid thing comes to Chicago via people like **Michael Mangiaforte**, **Gina Love**, **John Boy**, **GiGi**, who at times take to the dress and manner of people like **Mykl Tron**, **Ffloyd**, **James St. James**, **Zette**, **San D.**, and **Kenny Kenny** in NYC. Of course, the NYC originals are better. Sometimes. And sometimes the Chicago versions are rather inspired. Local club wars erupt when too many kids get too competitive between too few clubs and patrons. Like, what's so bloody holy about Sunday night as the night for gay parties? Not long ago, **Brian Kamp** and **Byron Dorsey** hosted an anniversary party for Brian in the Pyramid at Cairo. That same night, Michael Mangiaforte was hosting B.A.N.G. (Boys And Nasty Girls) at Ka-Boom! The Pyramid party was too loud, too crowded and too fast. Rumor had it that the party at Ka-Boom! was poorly attended and in retaliation for stealing the crowd, Mangiaforte reportedly had stink bombs set off at the party at Cairo. More recently, the same night that Mangiaforte planned a blow-out *Paris is Burning* party at Ka-Boom!, the *Project X* kids decide to import New Yorkers **Michael Alig**, **DJ Keoki**, **Ernie Glam**, **Sushi**, etc. for a party in the Catacombs at Cairo, promoting the new issue of the magazine. I could only get as far as handing Keoki a couple copies of *Thing* and snap his pic. He seemed nice enough because he was busy working and made time for me. Alig wasn't mean, but he wasn't helpful either. Too preoccupied. I was a basket case because the whole evening I was unable to score a copy of the magazine. (Note: the next week, on a regular Sunday night at the same club, they were all over the place and anyone's for the taking!) Keoki's sound quality was good, but the selection of music was too much on the techno/thrash side and, in my opinion, pitched way too fast to dance to, even considering the Ecstasy. You never saw so many camera hogs and so few cameras (just the two I had and **Al Carter** taking polaroids). It got real sad when we reached Josh's and Christasy's place later for an afterhours party and not one club kid had the vision to bring a camera or buy film. But, dearies, if I'm gonna play the photographer and columnist for you people, the least I could get out of it is some cooperation, namely a complimentary

APPLESAUCE

Out in New York City, in town for Wigstock, some club hopping and a much overdue visit with the illustrious **Charles (Chas) Bennet Brack**. It was both disturbing and comforting to see that not a whole lot has changed there. New Yorkers are still impatient and quick-tempered and some of the most fun-loving people anywhere. I arrived in town on the last day of a dreadful heatwave (way up in the 90's) and later found myself out at the comfortably air-conditioned After Five Plus with Chas, **Ricqué Green**, and Chas' friend **Leo.** We had a good ol' time. The people were very nice. The After Five Plus is a small bar in Brooklyn that attracts a pretty eclectic crowd of black, Puerto Rican, and white guys, a few women, and people of varied ages. Everyone insisted we were out on a good night and the music was crute, mostly tapes put together by one of the bartenders, a sexy Puerto Rican named **Jay**, who should have returned my calls. I figured if he posed for *Playguy*, he'd maybe pose for us. That was Friday night. Saturday night was the Sound Factory and finding the Chicago contingent and a whole bunch of city kids out for the Labor Day weekend in full force. Brian Mathews, Steve Marton, Craig Siegle, Montreal's **Nicolas Jenkins**, Lady Arlene, Christacy, Mangiaforte, Brian Funk, Byron Dorsey, Byrd Bardot, Sinisha, and N.Y.C.'s own **Bill Coleman** and Michael Hyacinth. DJ **Frankie Knuckles** is on top of the world, looking great, meeting and greeting only the sexiest guys and girls in the dj booth and enjoying huge success with his debut album *Beyond the Mix*. He graciously accepted our gift of a *Thing* T-shirt and bouquet of flowers before continuing to pound us to smithereens with sickening mixes of Basscut, Susan Clark, The Sounds of Blackness, and a yet-to-be-released tune from the album titled "Work Out." It's easy to see why the more serious dance kids flock to the Sound Factory week after week: the bass pumps and the place jacks 'til way past dawn.

Sunday night we were in Manhattan to attend a little party put together by Michael Hyacinth and painter **Darinka Navitovich** at the Flamingo East on 2nd Avenue. Everyone aforementioned at the Factory, plus, **Babs**, Homoture's **Fluffy Boy**, writer **Gary Indiana**, Steve Lafreniere, *STH* editor **Billy Miller**, **Gerald Paoli**, **John** Volkening, preferred promoter Bill Coleman, and writer **David Sedaris**. Graphic designer and ex-*Think Inker* **Arhlene Ayalin** and her friend, photographer **Tina Paul,** sat in the back with retailer **Pat Field** and several others being fashionable and true to the legend of the Flamingo. Later, we went over to Club Pyramid, quite lucky to run into **Hapi Phace** who remembered Steve Marton from her visit to Chicago and comped us in. The place was mobbed with pre-Wigstock folks just carrying on! It was fun even if a little too packed. As we were leaving, the fire marshals were checking out the scene and were unable to find any fire code violations. Whew! The day of the Wigstock extravaganza, I awoke feeling not quite up to the occassion and was mortified to find myself not on the press list for backstage access as promised by **Lady Bunny**, and too overwhelmed by the throng of ten thousand spectators to stick around and take in the show. So I left. Me and Ricqué headed out to Queens (Queen's Village to be exact) to join up with Chas and his friend **Tony Teal** who was hosting a cook-out and impromptu performance by a few members of Lavender Light, the Gay and Lesbian Black and People of All Colors Gospel Choir. We pigged out, sang and had a good ol' time.

The following week saw most of the Chicago kids heading home by Tuesday but Ricqué and myself continued our stay with Chas and Co. Wednesday night we got lost in Alphabet City en route to Pyramid for the Channel 69 taping. What a nightmare! Kids call it Crack Alley and the Badlands. It's a mess! Less jam-packed than the previous Sunday night, the Pyramid was worth our unfortunate detour. We saw everybody from RuPaul to **Page** to **Mona Foot** to **Codie Ravioli** to **Afro-Ditee** to **Linda Simpson** to *Thing* correspondent and former Chicagoan **Vincent Webster** to **Debbie Harry**. They were all really cute and friendly. We took lots of pix (except for Ms. Harry shaking her head back and forth, quietly indicating, "No photos, please.") Ms. Harry was very bubbly and seemed to be having a good time. Friday night, I ventured out alone and went to **Breeze's** loft party on Grand. It was right! Two floors and a rooftop in SoHo. Lots of fresh people and tee kee crute Margaritas! It was so goin' on that only a few hours into the festivities, the cops came in and kicked us all out. Something about a license... From there I split to Two Potato on Christopher St. Very black and Puerto Rican with "No Dancing!" It was packed. Hosted by a few drag queens, it was like a very well-attended cocktail party. I freaked running into fashion illustrator **Michael Ascendio** and designer **Stacey**, originally from Chicago, now both working for the **Oleg Cassini** label. I also met the delicious **Frankie Chillino**, who, among other

things, has a fetish for vintage **Pucci**, sixties lunch boxes and furnishings. We got to be fast friends. Saturday afternoon I ran around town feverishly playing beat the clock to complete a few interviews and stop at a few *Thing* distributors. Lady Bunny met me at Sha Sha Café in the West Village, "...it's close to my place." A lovely little spot where we enjoyed coffee, sinful desserts and dirt. Afterwards, we dashed over to the cozy Oscar Wilde bookshop and Wigstock co-sponsor MAC cosmetics. Then we popped by Bunny's friend and Wigstock co-organizer **Scott Lifshutz'** to get Wigstock programs. From there, we were off to Pat Field's, where I caught a glimpse of **Perfidia** and some of her very cute wigs. I browsed. Then I taxi'd over to Michael Musto's apartment where we gabfested and went through old photos together. (Full interviews with the genius Lady Bunny and the ultra-ovah Michael Musto to follow.) Saturday night, Ricqué and I did the Shampoo party at Limelight because Bunny invited us. It was cute. We ran directly into **Deaundra Peek** rushing out post-performance. "Hi Y'all!" We screamed and chatted for a moment, I snapped her and she was off. I could just eat her! Met **Johnny** (Hot-Man!) **Dynell** who was spinning and in fabulous form. He told me to look for his new release and that he and **Chi Chi**'s Jackie 60 was the club of the moment, that I should check it out Tuesday night. **Sister Dimension** was spinning in the big room. Bunny introduced us to **Miss Guy** who's as sweet as she is cute. And the guy named **Pearl** is a gem. We were off to the Building, accepting Linda Simpson and Page's invite, but just as we were about to leave, in walks Linda telling us that they closed up the bash around 3 AM. So, we hit it to the Sound Factory where we saw everybody we didn't see at Shampoo: **Larry Tee** and **Lahoma Van Zandt** (post Roxy) and **Ronald,** who dances with **Deee-Lite** who was very surprised to see me again (we'd first met when Deee-Lite played Shelter in Chicago last November.) I know just how he felt: I can't believe I ate the whole thing!

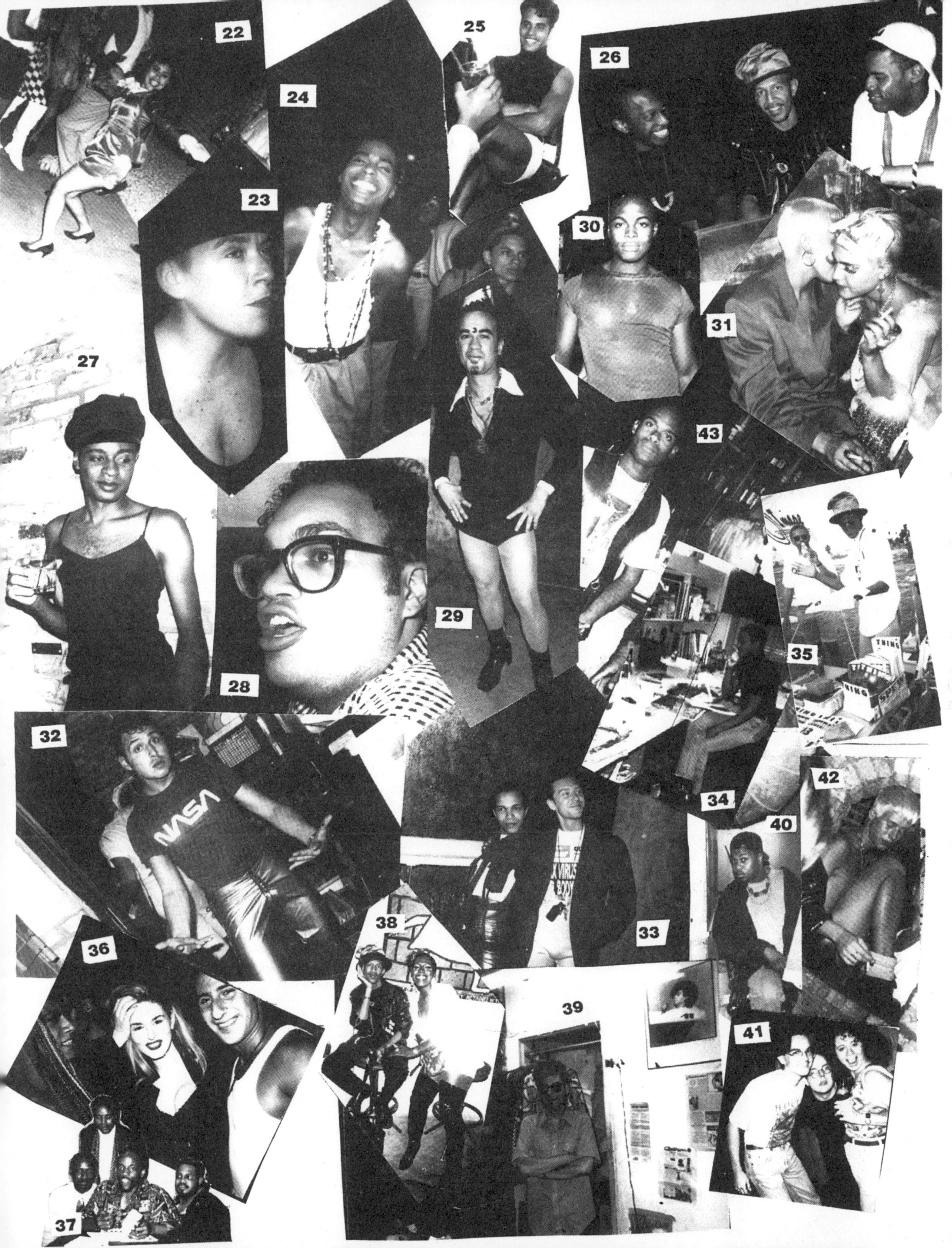

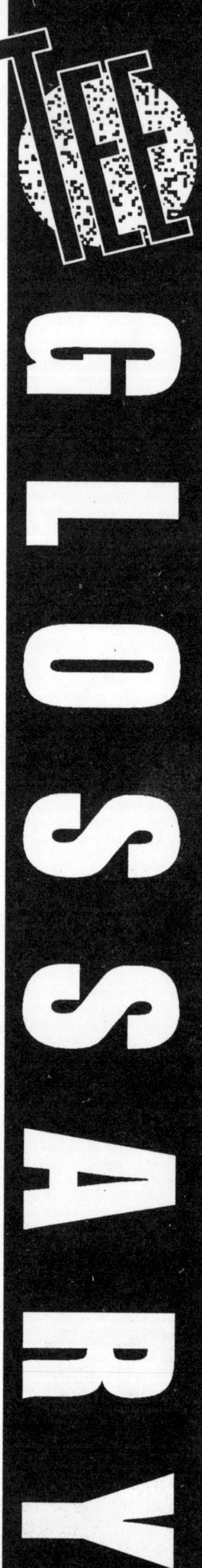

BAM NIEECIE: Bim Neecie's equally unfresh older sister. Even though she's old enough to enter the Club, we say no. "Quit ringin' it!" A.K.A. **Neecie, Skeezer.**

BEAT: Don't confuse this with the Beat in "Beat Generation." This is being so turned out, the girls gag. **Made. Painted. Done.** See **Bunta.**

BIM NIECEE: Part Bimbo, All Niecee. Synonymous with writer Drachir Notshurt's **Braid My Hair Girls.**

BMCS: CHRISTINE (Racy Beats, Inc.) JOHNSON dubbed it The B̲adly M̲anaged C̲lub S̲yndrome. Late-nite Murphy's Law. Struck by the bug to Boogie Down, eventually it's the reason you should have stayed home: Featuring Goonish Door Staff, Coatcheck by Booster's Galore, a DJ who should be reminded that it could be at least 10 more years before we hear those same old tunes again, and a menagerie of ne'er do wells and assorted Thugs and Skeezers. "Let's not and say we didn't!"

BOOF: Dammit! I hate it when that happens! '86ed" (Left "In the Lurch")

BOOSTERS: Den of Thieves or Twenty-One Robbers At My Door. Nail Everything Down! Also, to boost. To Mop. Those that boost. Thick as thieves.

BROKE FACE: Facial expression of shock, surprise or asstonishment. "Pick up your face." "Clutch your pearls." See **"In yo' face!"**

BUSSIN'!: It, The thing of the moment. Syns.: **SMOKIN', COLD, ICE,** or **HOT.** Happnin' The Answer. The Tee. The Real Thing. You want it. The One To Buy.

BUNTA: Pronounced Boonta. John Jordan Young's definitive Black Beauty esthetic: Beverly Johnson, Grace Jones, Iman, Kahdija, Pat Cleveland, Sheila Johnson, Sade, Pam Shields, Chevette, Gloria Shelby, Aisha Mays, Phyllis Swan, Mina Shaw, Liza Cruzat, Adrian Griffin, Alva Chin, Octavia Saint Laurent, Tookie Smith, etc. Beat or lookin' that-a-way. Black Diva.

BUYING IT: Popular goods: The Farm. Lunch. The Brooklyn Bridge. All That Glitters. Florida Swampland (sight unseen). Ant.: **Not having any of it.**

CLUB TART: Black Gay Party Animal, circa 1970-1989. Elite of the U.S. Studio Warehouse, D.C. Clubhouse, the original Powerplant, and the Paradise Garage N.Y.C. The fringe did Better Days and Melons in N.Y.C. and Rialto and the Ritz in Chicago. Kids who followed DJ's like, Larry Levan, Frankie Knuckles, Craig Cannon, Paul Simson, Tee Scott, Nicky Siano. Also **Party Tart.** Ant.: **Club Kid**

COME FOR ME: Attitude doin'. Every bit as challenging as it sounds, a ruling queen's way of asking for it in yo' face with ovahness. "Don't come for me, I'll let you have it!"

COSMOTATA: From LDW's Cosmetata (Cosmetic Kaflama) denoting all the models, photographers, hair dressers, stylists, designers and various persons in the fashion/beauty field. Fortunately, Cosmotata can be distinguished from Fabulashes since they actually work in the "Boodie Bid'niss" or at least read magazines (rather than just look at the pictures). Ant. **Model-Model.**

CRUSTY PASTEY: Bitchy Attitude. Crunchy and cross-tempered. Also Crispy Pastey, Pustey Ooozzy, Cheesey Ooozy, and Extra Crispy Cheesey. Smegma.

CRUTE: Did Evil or Toy say this first? No matter, everybody says it now. CUTE with an R...CRUTE. Crute Hair Crute Face Crute Attitude Crute Stuff.

DOLLS: Girlfriends. Especially of the DQ Variety. Darva: "You know how dolls carry on at Miss Delay!" "Your Doll," refering to oneself. Ant: **Toy (I'm Not Your Plaything) Patton.**

DON'T EVEN TRY IT: To put a notion out of one's mind; "CHILE, PLEASE!" Also, **D.E.T.I.O.M.T.** (Don't EVEN try it on my time!) and **D.Y.T.I.** (Snap! Don't you try it!)

FABULASHES: Posers. Font Font Fake Fashion Victims. 'Fluffy' Glamabugs. "Quit ringin' it!"

FABULI: From the Cult of the DJ, The Fabulous Ones. Stars in this category usually manage entourages made up of Cosmotata, fabulous Queens and Divas.

FULL: Buzzed, Lightheaded, Bubbly, Tipsy, Giddy. To get full. As in "I'm Full Out My Trees!" (more like smashed) Ant.: **SAY NO** and **DON'T DRIVE DRUNK.**

GOOD LUCK: Okay! "See there!" "Told you so!"

KAFLAMA: The word Ken Hare made famous. Much "To-do," brouhaha, hoopla, or major phenomenon of either good or bad quality. Also **Flama,. Kaflamala** (mess).

KEE KEE: 1) Giggle or mull over something funny. 2) Smile sheepishly and play dumb: "Oh."

MODEL-MODEL: It takes Pam Shields to talk about vain and totally self-centered Cosmotatas who literally let all the styling mousse go to their heads; "I'm the stuff!" Strike a pose!

NIEECIE: Home Girl. Or LaShondra Maleeka Johnson (Tyrone's girlfriend). Also **Pookie.**

NOT USING IT: "Not Buying It" or "Not Having Any Of It." You don't want it!

OH, PLEASE!: Responding to Kaflama. "Yeah, right!"

OKAY?!: Not the California surfer-girl variety. The sarcastic affirmation as in "See!" or "See there!" Interchanges with "I'm sayin'" and "Don't you know!" Also **"OTAY?!"**

POOCHED: Prissy and persnickety. Seditty. Too Crute. "Pooched that-a-way." Posey. Also **POOCHI.**

PUNISHMENT: Dressed to kill. The Darva. "You should have seen her! She was Punishin' those Dolls!"

READ: From "Read the Riot Act," which the dictionary defines as "to insist that disobedience, etc. must cease." The kids say "Wasn't that a Read!" (Mess. Kaflama) "Don't you ever try it, I'll read you!" Giving them the what-for. Read Your Beads and to 'Read For Points, cut-up and keep score.

RIP YO' PANTIES: Dancing in the spirit of "Damn-the-torpedoes-never-mind-the-duds-break-a-leg-shake-a-tailfeather-baby-jig-and-cut-a-rug!" Also **Jiggin'** and **Jackin'** or **PUNKIN'.**

SICKENING! : Overwhelmingly fresh! More than you can stomach. "Tee crute, sickenin' ol' pumps!"

THING: A person or Thing of incorrigible and unbearable Fabulousness. As in the salutation, "Miss Thing!" or "Thing's not buying it!" She knows who she is!

WOOGIES: The male counterpart to **BIM** and **BAM NIEECIES.** Banjy Realness.

WOPS: From the term 'DOO WOP' describing the 60's black street music. "We Real Cool!" Near woogie state of mo' macho.

ZUBA: The latest term for those children of the chitlin circuit: Too Black for ya!

The Black Line
Where all men are welcome.
1-900-468-2522
Call Now!
1-900-HOT-BLACK
$1 Per Min • $2 Connection Charge • Must Be 18 Or Older • Prices Subject To Change Without Notice

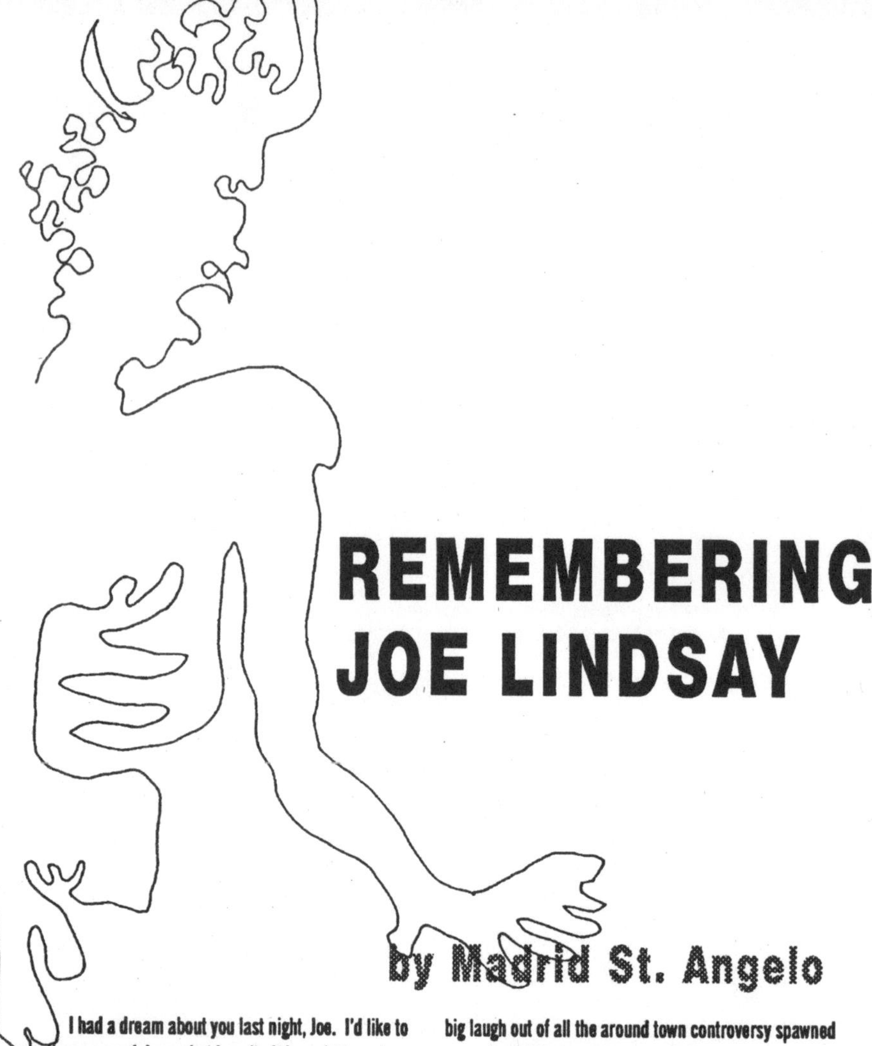

REMEMBERING JOE LINDSAY

by Madrid St. Angelo

I had a dream about you last night, Joe. I'd like to say it was a good dream but I can't. It brought tears to my eyes. Maybe that ain't so bad. You're definitely worth crying over. When you passed I couldn't cry then—but I was with you right up until your last breath. I was your friend holding your hand, whispering in your ear—telling you it's okay baby, it's just a dream. Let go.

That afternoon they called and said that someone should be with him because he was probably on his way out. I was in the shower when I received the call. I quickly dried off, dressed, and caught a cab over to St. John's Hospice where Joe had been staying nearly a month.

Although Joe hadn't been doing too well for a long time, I thought back to our late nights just hanging out, drinking a few beers and our delving into every facet of pop-political culture. Joe and I were comrades in ACT UP. We were pioneers for Queer Nation/Denver. We fed each other's ego — mine from my New York upbringing, his being Chicago-styled — expounding upon one another's knowledge of our respective downtown art scenes involvements. Joe Lindsay was a diverse man. His art ranged from political graffiti-styled cartoons to large oil and acrylic paintings promoting social change to self-portrait photographs.

This last year he had spent time working on his t-shirts. One he designed for ACT UP which bore his "I'M OUT" logo and the other he designed for Queer Nation — his controversial (Denver is so lame) and now infamous "I Praise God" with my erection and vagina t-shirts. Joe got a big laugh out of all the around town controversy spawned over a t-shirt that never even made it to press.

I remember one night spent with Joe listening to Karen Finley, Debbie Harry and the Velvet Underground while chatting away about Haring, Basquiat and Mapplethorpe- the night seemed endless. Joe prepared a fillet of sole dish with cajun rice and seasonings extraordinaire. And me being too tired to go back to my place—just crashed with him in his bed.

Yeah, that night we talked about the disease but neither of us offered up a godamned solution- thinking that the government had already established a platform for the disease that solicits little change for the better. We decided to remain ACTing UP. We both wished George Bush and Jessie Helms an HIV positive diagnosis.

That night holding Joe I felt good about my ability to love and encourage physically someone closer to the grave than myself. I've been so lucky, I thought. Asymptomatic for 6 years now. Poor Joe.

That's why I couldn't cry for Joe when he passed. I was too proud. For me it was a great honor to be by the side of a man I not only cared for, but respected and loved as well. There were few people Joe wanted by his side those last weeks, only three to be exact. I was one of them. And there was Alan. And there was Wendell.

Joe, from this side of life I still dream about you. And now at this writing my eyes swell. I have only my heart and my mind full of memories to thank you with and for. You're so missed.

Line drawing from Joe Lindsay's Illuminations (1990)

LOSS

You don't have to face it alone.

The death of someone you love is always difficult...Howard Brown Memorial Clinic bereavement groups can help you deal with loss from any cause, including cancer, suicide, accidents, and AIDS.

- **12 week program @ $20 per session**
- **Facilitated by mental-health professionals**
- **Gay/Lesbian oriented**

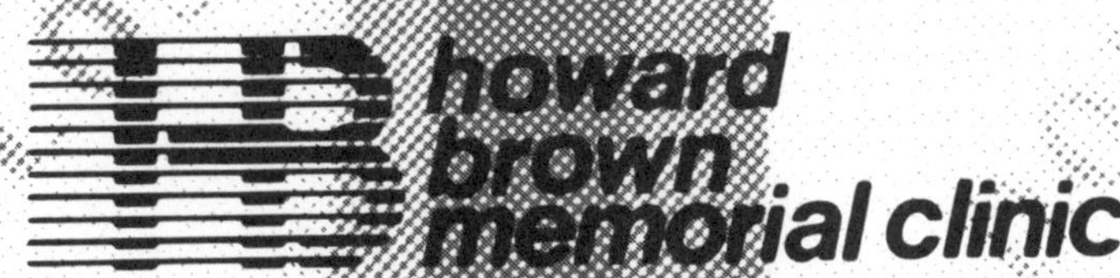

(312) 871-5777
ASK FOR SOCIAL SERVICES

Ask Marjorie Marginal

Cousins Cousins

I've recently met my cousin's lover and became attracted to him but because of loyalty to my cousin I've put my feelings aside. But now I find out that they only live together for financial reasons and they are both free to do as they please. Should I take a chance of destroying my relationship with my cousin or should I follow my loins?

— Moist Box

Dear Moist Box,

Your loins are longing for the beef! They wouldn't lead you wrong. Several points, however: how does Mr. Financial Reasons feel about you? Does he know how moist your box is? Why would your relationship with your "free to do as he pleases" cousin be endangered by your interest in his roommate? Girl, there seems to be some underlying issues here that have been left to stew too long! Get to cookin'!

Rudeness In Lieu of Manners

Unbeknownst to me, I recently (and quite accidentally) stumbled upon a rather notorious "tea room" on the campus of a large public university.

Imagine my shock and embarrassment! However, further surprises awaited me. Whilst using the facility properly (for which it was built), my eyes happened to glance over the commanding and overwhelmingly lewd graffiti on the walls —not to mention the grammatical, spelling, and syntax errors!

Quel surpris! Lo and behold, the name and telephone number, and in excruciatingly descriptive detail, the preferences of a tres cher ami of mine (one with whom I practically grew up!) were scrawled in her own distinctive, unmistakeably horrid penmanship (in elementary school, she received a "D").

Gentle Ms. Marginal, her curriculum vitae (as it were) was simply a fabrication of her twisted fantasies! Not only were her descriptions of herself outright lies, but what she claims to be able to do are beyond her uninspired and dull grasp.

Pity the poor sucker (pun intended) who, upon phoning her with dreams of debauchery, actually encounters her physically! I shudder to think of it! Also, what if someone connects me to such a low, base practice as to which my dear friend has sunk? We all know, la cage aux folles! How can I refute such pernicious and unfounded slander?

Thank you very much for handling this too distressing dilemma for me...I am sure you will give me clear wisdom to help me hold my head up in such a trying time.

— Truth In Advertising

Yo, Margie! I hear you the "Answer Bitch."

My problem is this nosy ho. I caught the bitch in my favorite bathroom cock-blockin' for points. Bitch pretendin' to pee, when she really tryin' to suck up all the dick.

I walks in, but I quick-like peep the ho. I jumps back so she can't see me. (She one of those talk-talk girls— always running off at the mouth when she should be tryin to get her mouth stuffed with some yummy dick!) Don't you hate it when you at yo favorite bookstore, bathhouse,or bathroom and these sissies want to hold an afternoon tea?

Anyways, I knew it was she cause she went to grade school with me and she always thought she better than everybody. One of them bitches always correctin' somebody. Well, the bitch had the nerve to pulls out this big ass red marker and start correctin' my shit on the wall and shit, like I'm stoopid or somethin'. She even crossed out my phone number from the message I wrote.

Madge, how can I get back my favorite bathroom from this snotty, overbearing busybody? How can I stop this ho from coverin' up my writin' and my number? What the fuck she doin' at my school seein' as how she so hi and mighty and only attended private schools? Marge, help!

— A Friend In Need

Dear Needy Friend and Truth in Advertising,

Tea of this sort isn't just for breakfast anymore. Let's agree that some groundrules need to be established. And, quite naturally, I'm the "Answer Bitch" to set them(that's M-A-R-J-O-R-I-E)!

First and foremost, true ladies never, EVER, edit material that's unsolicited. Secondly, get with it, girl! When in Rome, do as the Romans...If you're slummin' at a public school in the public tea room, show your privates and keep it private!

Tea room etiquette demands that we all play as equals; i.e., ain't nobody cruisin' the tea room better than anybody else that's crusin' there. As for truth in advertising, we all would hope to fuffill our fantasies while remaining well-grounded in reality. Nobody wants to buy a lemon, as when yours truly recently responded to an ad from a "chunky, outdoorsman" and was appalled to find a prudish, bookish school marm who was a sister, not a mister! Make lemonade? Pucker up!

The bigger question is why you two, who so clearly have so much in common (a common history, common habits) can't work together for each other's welfare and happiness? Next time out, she could act as look-out while you're busy having trade and you could school her on the fine art of taking high tea.

THING

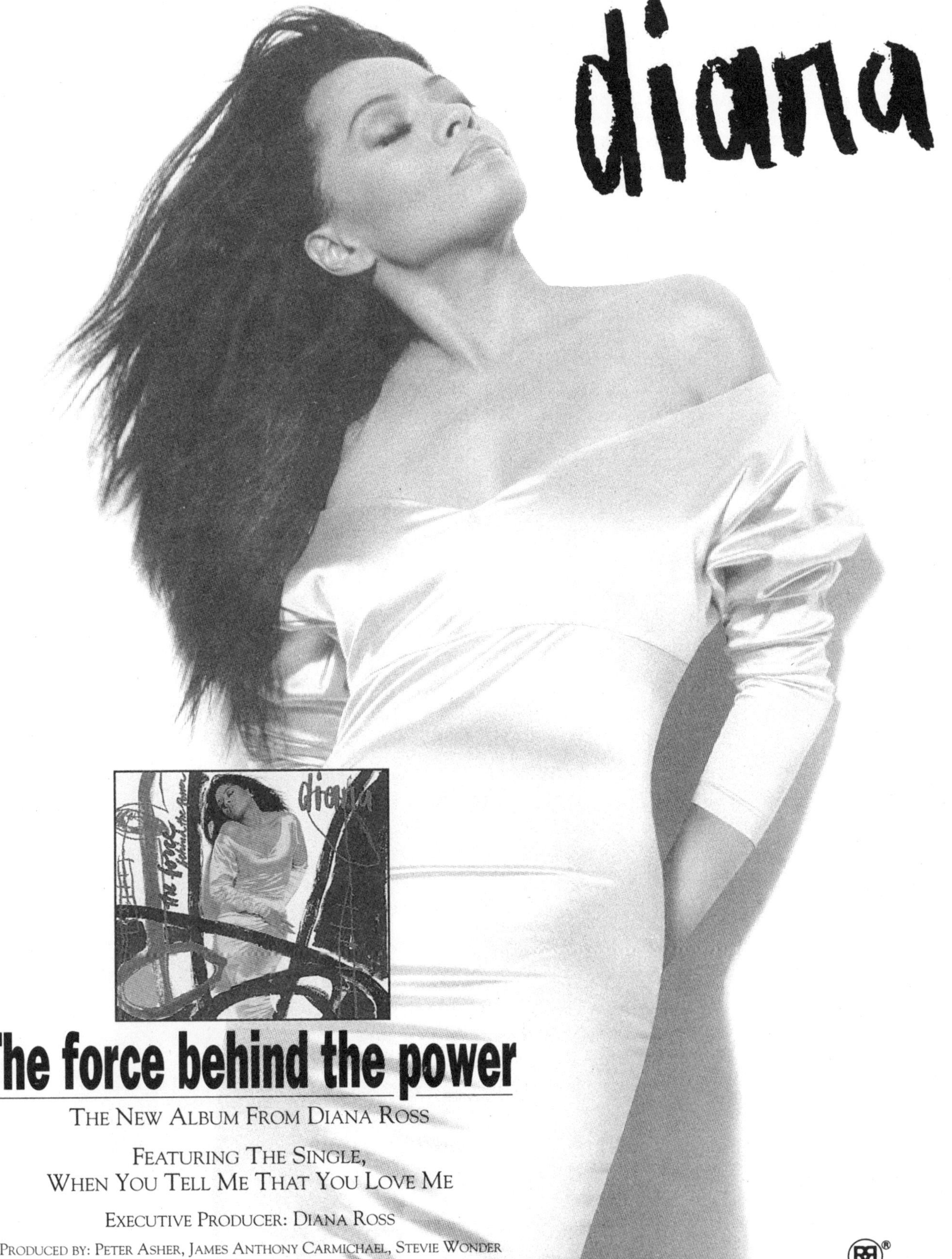

© 1991 Motown Record Company, L.P.
diana
The force behind the power
THE NEW ALBUM FROM DIANA ROSS
FEATURING THE SINGLE,
WHEN YOU TELL ME THAT YOU LOVE ME
EXECUTIVE PRODUCER: DIANA ROSS
PRODUCED BY: PETER ASHER, JAMES ANTHONY CARMICHAEL, STEVIE WONDER
Trademark Of Image Equity Management Inc

ACT LIKE YOU KNOW !

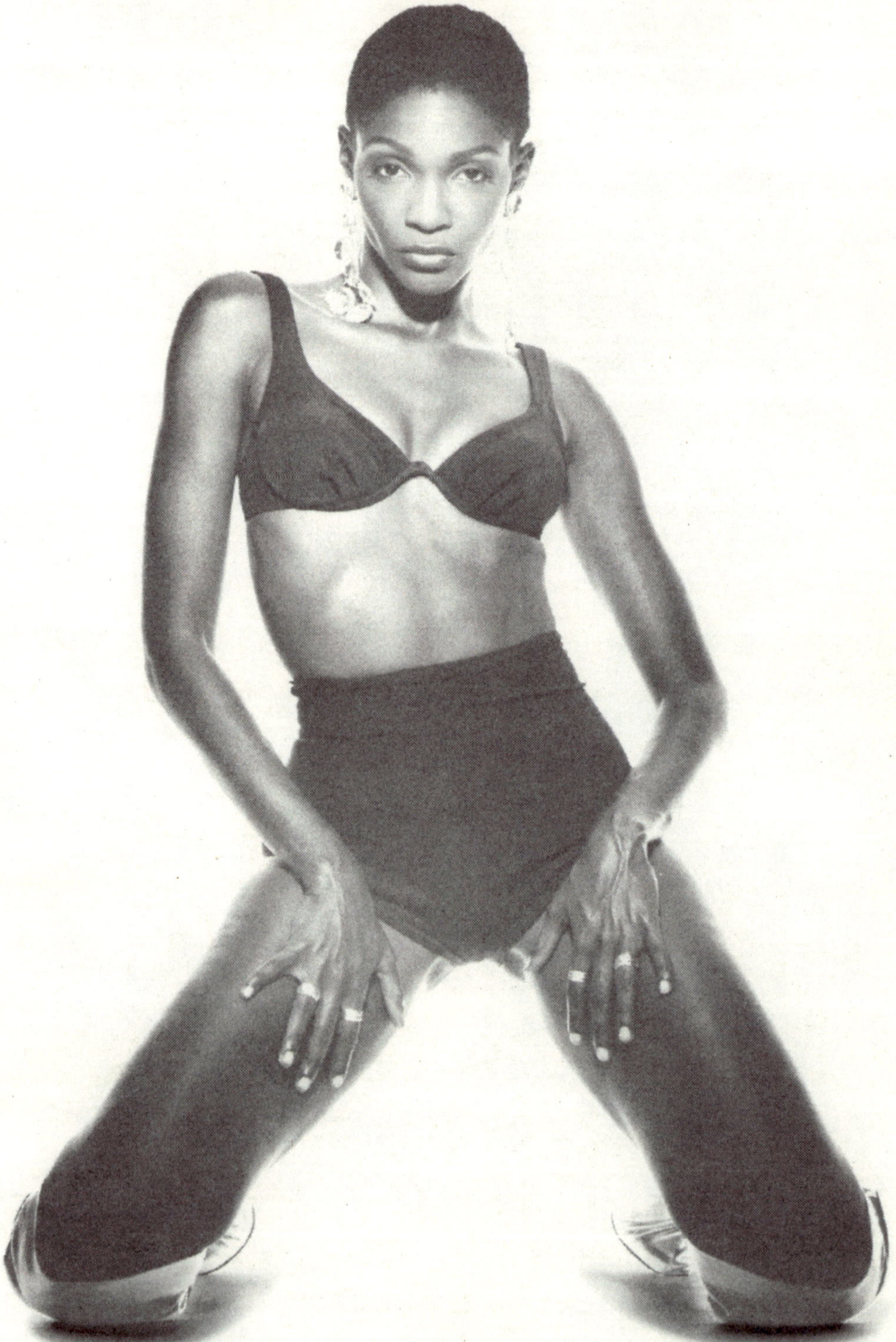

ALMIGHTY R S O C R E W • COLDCUT • DADDY-O • DE LA SOUL
DIGITAL UNDERGROUND • 808 STATE • GOLD MONEY • GROOVE GARDEN
INFORMATION SOCIETY • J.C. LODGE • LFO • MELLO-T • NAUGHTY BY NATURE
PARIS • PRINCE RAKEEM • QUEEN LATIFAH • STETSASONIC • TKA

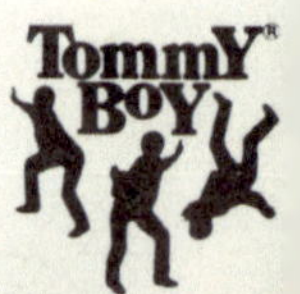

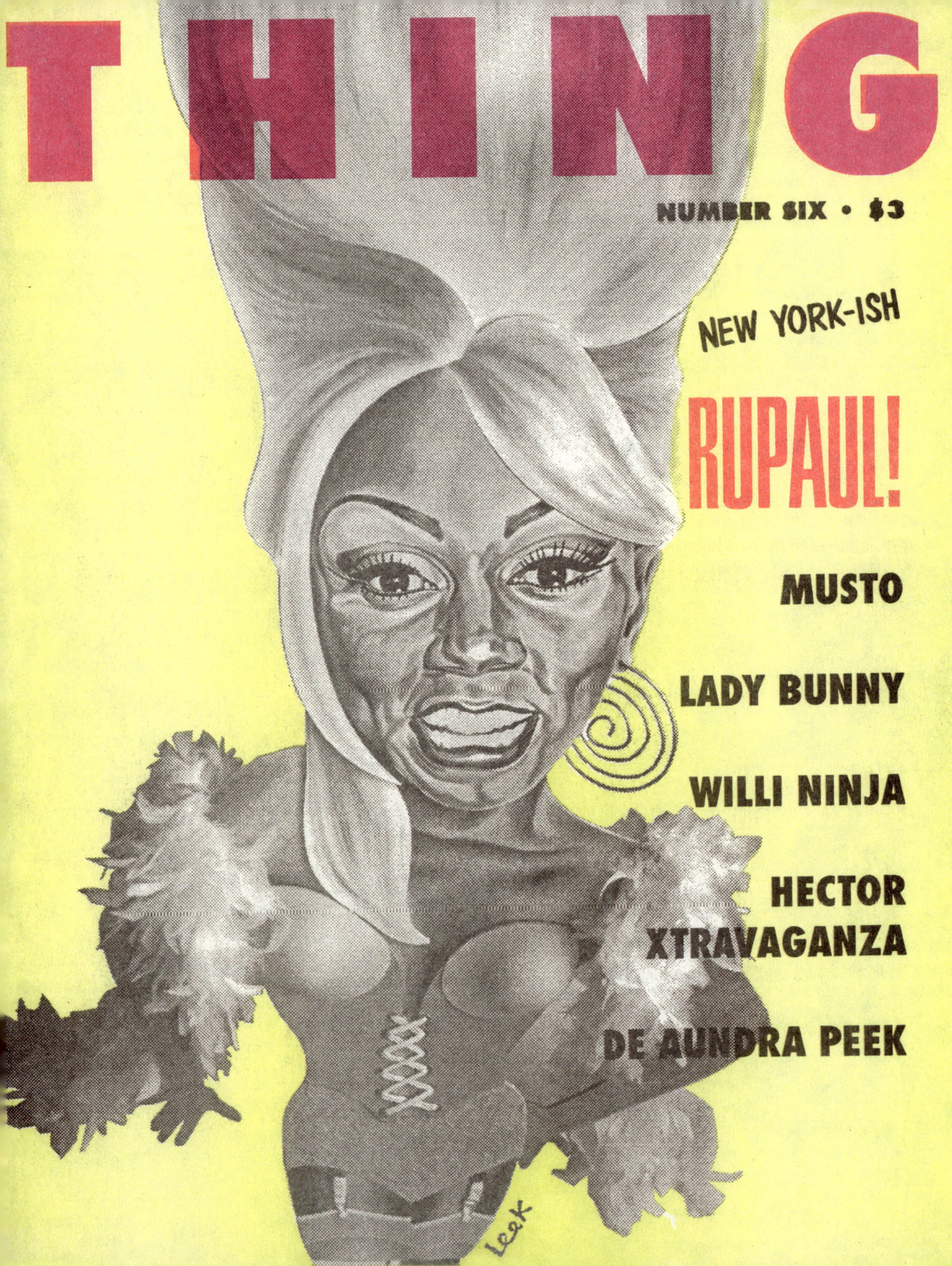

THING
NUMBER SIX • $3
NEW YORK-ISH
RUPAUL!
MUSTO
LADY BUNNY
WILLI NINJA
HECTOR XTRAVAGANZA
DE AUNDRA PEEK
leek

just right

SOUL II SOUL

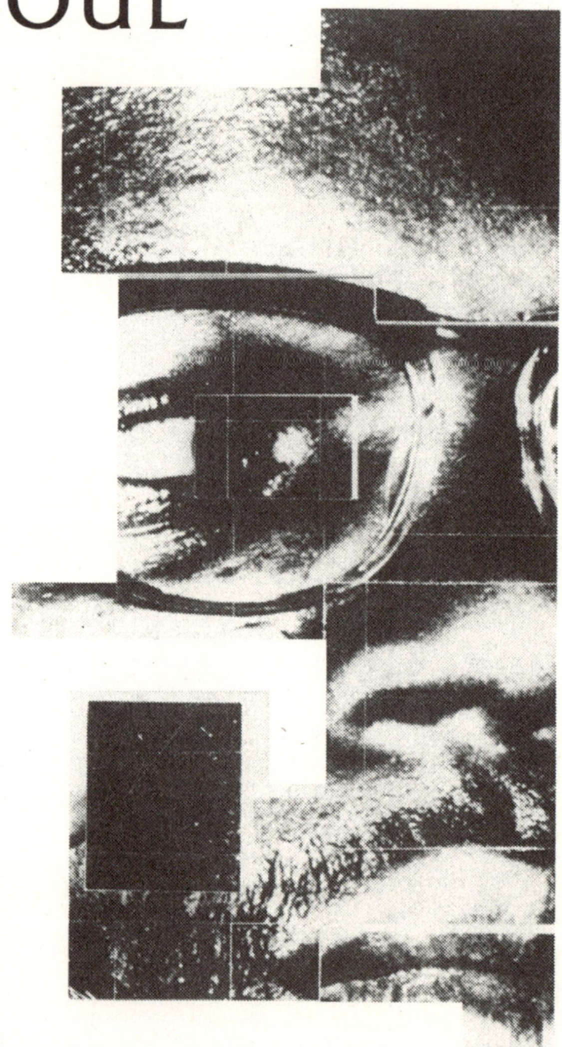
just right

is the new album

from innovator

jazzie b and the soul II soul

groove factory

featuring

"joy."

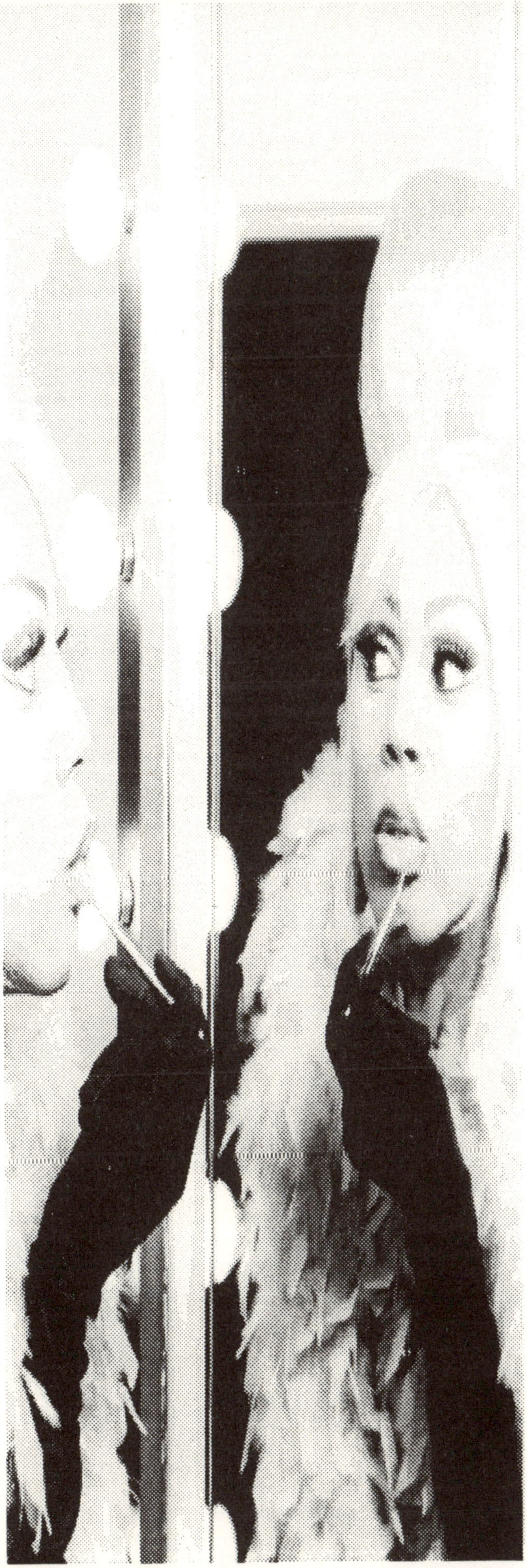

contents

EVERY **THING** TO GO!

APPLESAUCE — THE BIG APPLE SHITS!

DEPARTMENTS

• •

ON THE COVER: Lee Kay's Bubblehead Por-trit of RuPaul, from a photo by Renaldi & Zechman
THIS PAGE: Behind the scenes with RuPaul. Photo: Renaldi & Zechman

THING

THING
She Knows Who She Is

NUMBER SIX • SUMMER 92

PUBLISHER/EDITOR Robert Ford
CONTRIBUTING EDITOR Trent Adkins
ADVERTISING Terry Martin, Sylvia Michaels
ADMINISTRATIVE ASSISTANT Duane Baskins
GRAPHIC SERVICES Simone Bouyer
DESKTOP PUBLISHING International Media Associates
ACCOUNTING NIA Accounting Services

CONTRIBUTORS

Aaron Avant Garde, Bunny & Pussy, Scott Free, Chuck Gonzales, Essex Hemphill, Julian, Lee Kay, Keith Kotick, Steve Lafreniere, Terry Martin, DeAundra Peek, Rachel Pepper, Renaldi & Zechman, Lawrence Warren, Stephen Winter

Thing is published quarterly. Thing encourages unsolicited submissions, only those with a SASE will be returned. Editorial inclusion casts no aspersions on one's racial and sexual categorization (Things know who they are.) Opinions expressed are those of individual contributors and do not always reflect those of Thing. © 1992 THING

THING PUBLISHING

2151 W. Divison
Chicago Illinois USA 60622-3056
VOICE (312) 227-1780
FAX (312) 227-1886

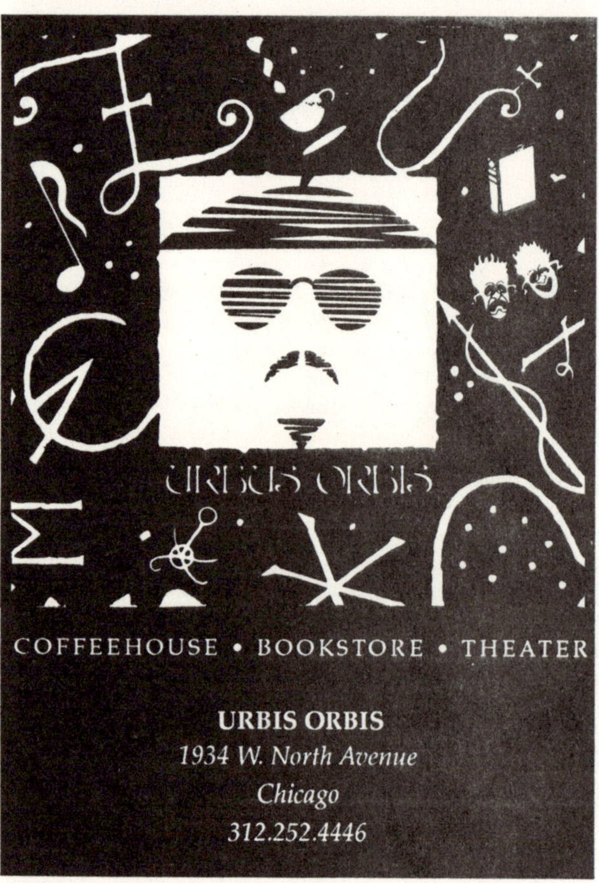

OUT NOW.

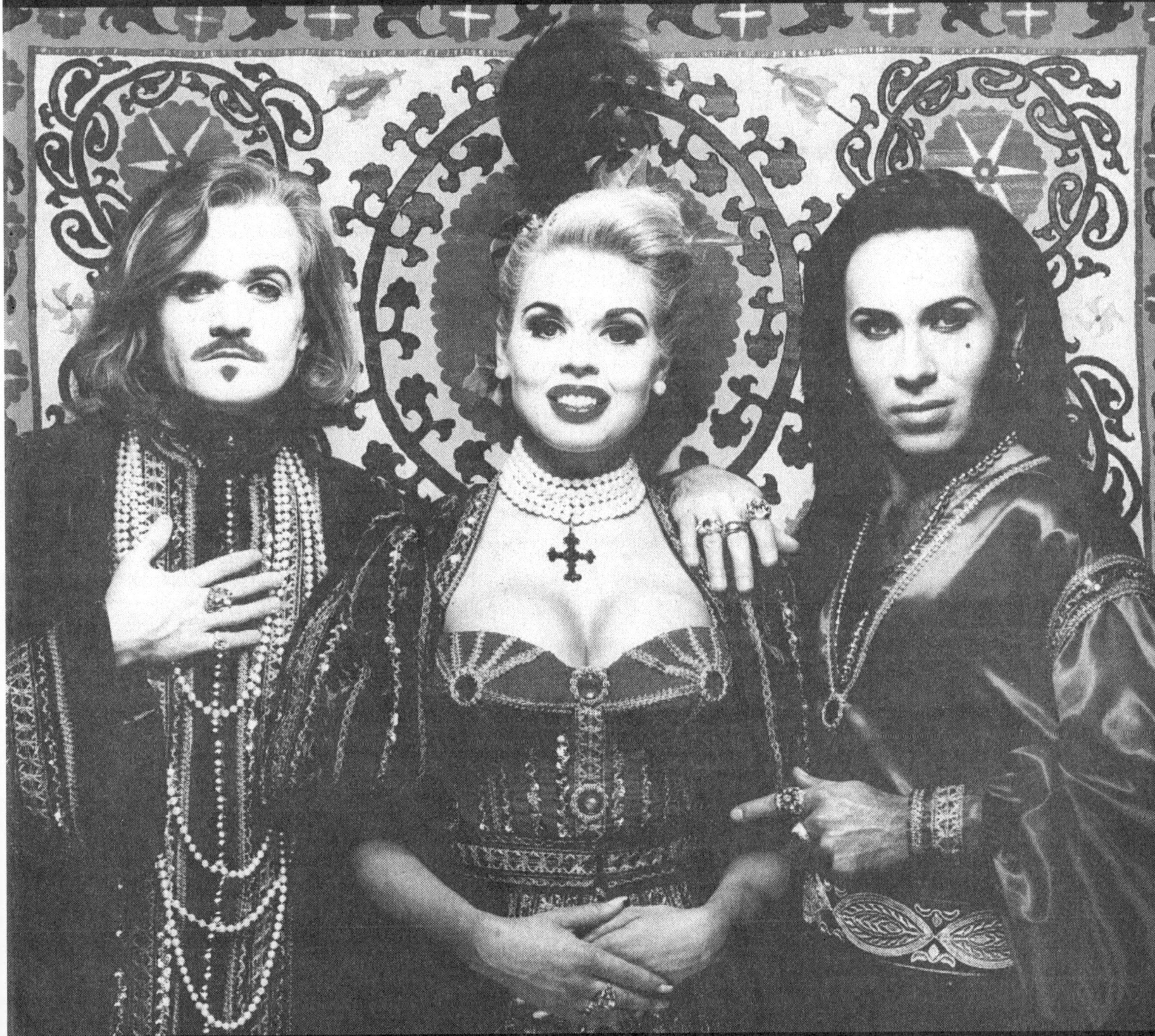

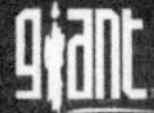

Army of Lovers

MASSIVE LUXURY OVERDOSE
The new album

Featuring "CRUCIFIED"

MONDO MAXI SINGLE:
available on vinyl (12") and compact disc (somewhat smaller but lasts longer) with remixes by DNA

Album available on Giant Cassettes and Compact Discs. ©1992 Giant Records

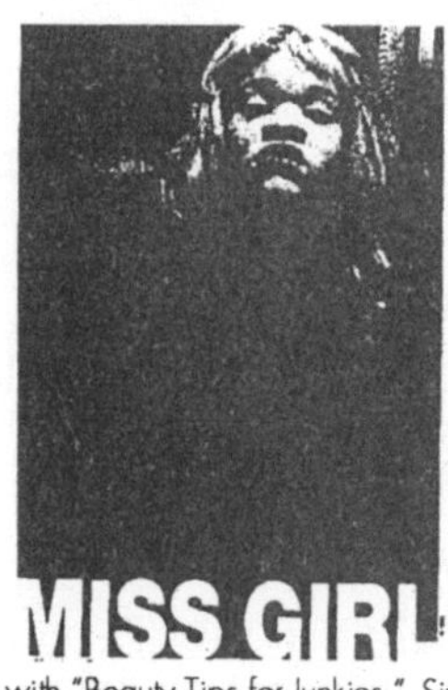

Los Angeles was the sight of **SPEW 2,** the second occasional meeting of the underground queer press and their fans. Best of the fest: *Ben Is Dead*'s Glamour issue with "Beauty Tips for Junkies," *Sin Brothers'* TRADE skullcaps, and Lyle Ashton Harris' flawless "Miss Girl" t-shirts (pictured). Worst idea: MASK (Mothers Against Serial Killers) ghoulish t-shirts of Jeffrey Dahmer. The next SPEW might be in Frisco, headed by A Different Light's Rachel Pepper, or Toronto, Canada headed by?

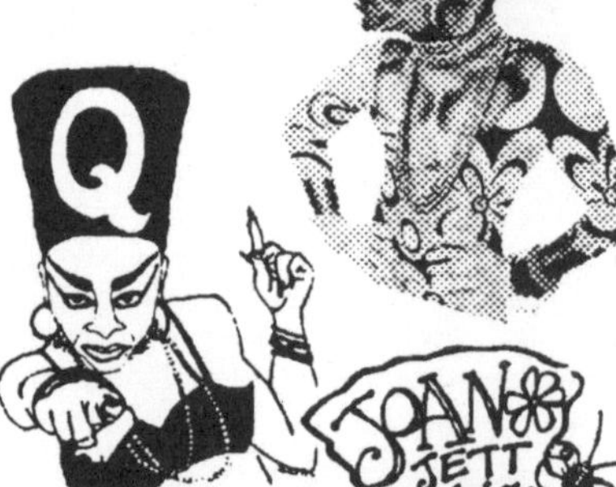

Go'on Ms. President Thing Girl! Quite unlike the average American, but very much like your average brilliant publicity whore, Ms. **Joan Jett Blakk** moves with a quickness into super real superstardom. This body builder and drag performance artist first became a Chicago mayoral candidate and is now a presidential hopeful. Photo-op or bust, Blakk continues a shameless affair with the local paparazzi (several *Nightlines* covers and counting). But what's *really* fresh are some artists' renderings. Or, like they say, you ain't really famous until somebody draws you. Local doodlebugging includes (clockwise) Tamara Fraser, Lee Kay's Bubblehead Por-trit ©, and illustrator Chuck Gonzales' rendering for *Gag*. Manhattan's Chip Wass and Michael Economy can't be far behind!.

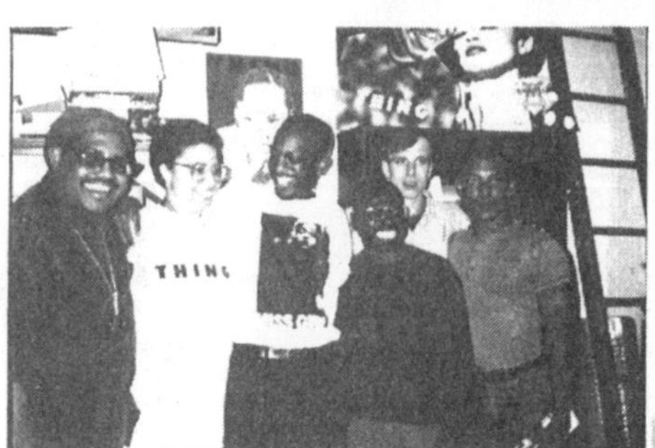

"Yaaaaay!!" Georgia's peach, **DeAundra Peek,** brings her double-wide mobile home-spun disco show to Chicago's Hothouse June 13th in a benefit for Illinois senatorial candidate Carol Moseley Braun. Info: (312) 489-2490.

"We'll do brunch!" Award-winning video maker **Marlon Riggs** was here for the Chicago premiere of his newest work, "Color Adjustments," at Randoph Street Gallery, and to accept some fancy award at the Chicago Hilton and Towers. The *Thing* offices were the sight of a co-hosted brunch with the Chicago-based group, Women in the Director's Chair. At left, L to R: Lawrence D. Warren, financial consultant Stephanie Coleman, Robert Ford, Marlon Riggs, ad sales director Terry Martin and longtime Riggs' friend Elija Ward. Photo Duane Baskins.

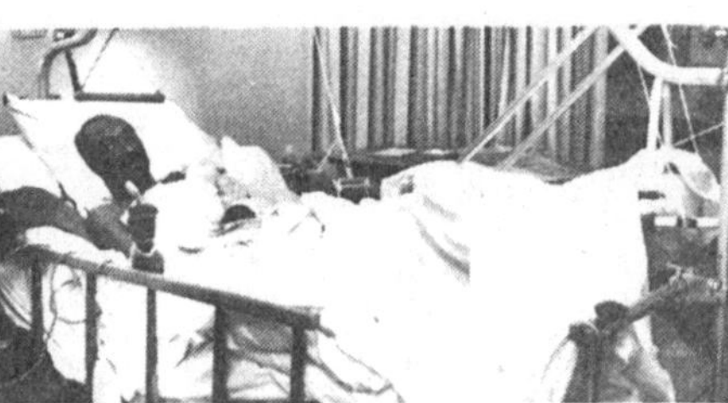

Alan Bell (above), publisher of *BLK*, the national black and gay newsmagazine, was a near casualty when his car was struck head-on this past April. He has several weeks in traction to look forward to, and months of physical therapy as well. *BLK*, which had just gone monthly, will suspend publication until a new editor can be found. Send all correspondence to: *BLK*, box 83912, Los Angeles, CA 90083. Photo Bruce Hunt.

Black To The Future...**Mother Superior** jumped the gun when she gave this issue of *Thing* a glowing review in her "Nasty Habits" *Windy City Times* column May 14. The "hot off the presses" *Thing #6* that she raved about was nowhere near the presses when she ran a mock-up of the Lee Kay cover and a blurb about how hot and hip it is (hence the eleventh hour copy you're now reading). Talk about your postmodern kind of review! Still, we're glad she loved us, even sight-unseen.

Thing's first big fundraiser, the **Lovely** party, was lovely indeed. Held this past Valentines Day, we improved our cash flow and had a good time to boot! Thanks to all who donated their energies; particularly DJs Freddie Bain, Mark Farina, Spencer Kincy, and Derrick Carter. Our next fundraising event will be an evening with Essex Hemphill Saturday, June 20th at the Bop Shop, 1807 W. Division. Call us at (312) 227-1780 for more info.

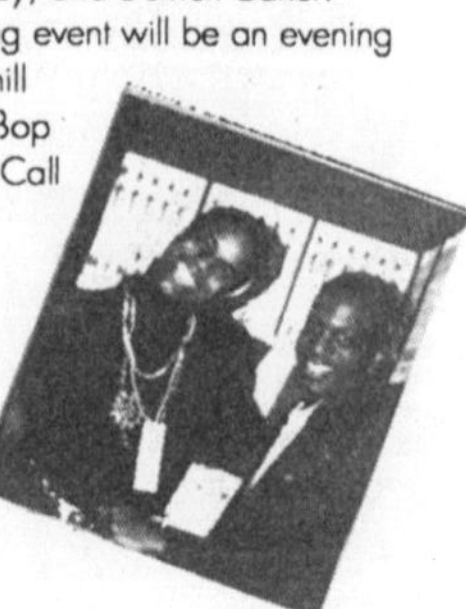

ABOVE detail from the "appropriated" Lovely invite **RIGHT** "All I want is a booth somewhere." Trent and Robert man the door at Lovely held at Rudely Elegant Theatre in the Layla Marmalade Room.

MADONNA'S ROOM? Buried among all the recent **Madonna** news about her mega-millions deal with Time/Warner was the chip that her new production company has the film rights to **James Baldwin**'s black queer opus Giovanni's Room! First she vogues, then she poses as house mother, now she's **Carl Van Vechten.** What's next, a remake of "Tongues Untied" starring Madonna? **RAVING MAD** Excuse me, can we stop RAVEing now? If we see one more invite that looks like a fifty pound box of laundry soap we're gonna lose it! PURE TECHNO GROOVES and JIVE FRESH and LIFE and all those records you don't know the names of. Yuck! It may have been cute for a minute, but MTV has had a RAVE...isn't that a big clue that its over? And what the hell are Smart Drinks, anyway? It's time to find a new hook. **de FLUX** Faithful readers will note that the new La Lounge de Lux was given a very decent review in the pages of *Gag* Magazine. Well, things have certainly changed since then. We've found one of the hosts, Mr. **Michael Blatter,** to be insufferably insensitive, since he was quite obvious in pandering to his straight white friends. Upon noticing that they'd all left around 2am, he decided that the party would be over for the few blacks and gays who remained, even though the place was jumpin'. It would seem that if he doesn't care about these people, then he ought not have **Gidget St. Clair, Andy Substance, Derrick Carter, Mark Farina,** and Co. co-hosting the party. The invite said 'til 4am and that's how long it should've gone. Adding insult to injury was witnessing Mr. Blatter stand idly by as a glass was broken in the middle of the floor, and he failed to alert wait staff to clean it up. Does he care that some jig-a-boo or fag might slip and fall, cutting themselves seriously enough to warrant a lawsuit? We guess not! People are more than happy to support the *other* hosts, but we smell a Blatter boycott in the offing. This kaflama recalls Kaboom's and Shelter's attitudes that often conspicuously discriminate along lines of race and sexual preference. Unnecessary!

sex, lies, & audiotape

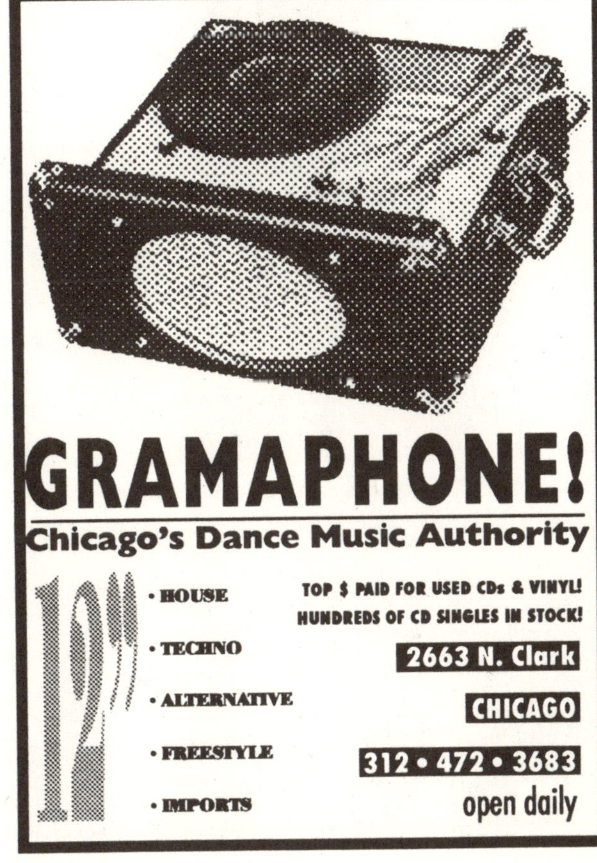

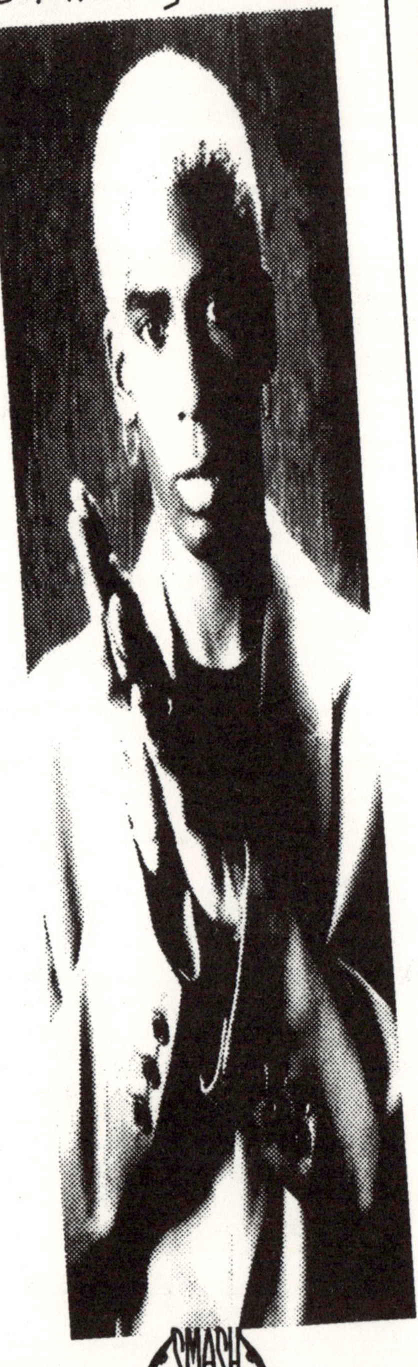

JAMIE PRINCIPLE
The Midnight Hour
SMASH RECORDS

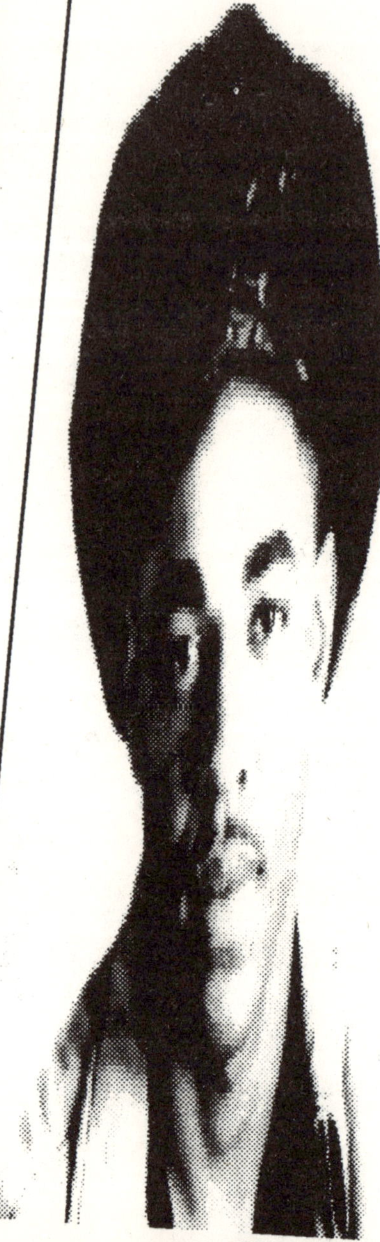

PM
DAWN
"Of The Heart, Of The Soul, & Of The Cross: The Utopian Experience"
GEE STREET
M-DOC
The Universal Poet
SMASH RECORDS

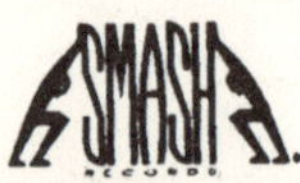

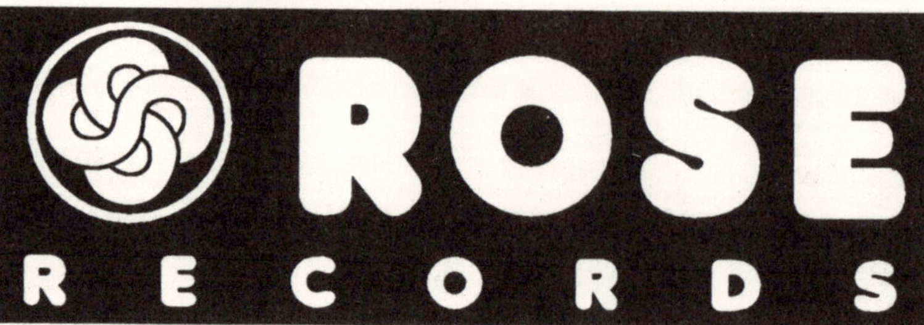

ROSE RECORDS
15% OFF THE REGULAR PRICE
when you mention this ad through the month of June

Derrick "The Maestro" Carter
TOP TEN
1. **Helpless** Urbanized *Maxi*
2. **Joy** Soul II Soul *Virgin*
3. **Back to Basics** Simulcast *111 East*
4. **Truth Will Set You Free** Peace Time *RCA*
5. **I Promise** Mark Rogers *Free Town*
6. **Roots & Culture** Peter Panic *Bumble Beat*
7. **Shoo Be Doo** Bas Noir *Atlantic LP cut*
8. **Get Your Act Together** (UK remix) B.D.P. *Classic Club*
9. **All I Want** Richard Rogers *Sam*
10. **Club Lonely** Lil' Louis *Epic*
PICKS
Beat Honey Pascal's Bongo Massive *Tomato*
Too Many Things Robert Owens *Demo*
Hey Fellas Simone *Strictly Rhythm*

Bill Coleman
TOP TEN "Sanity Preserved" (in no particular order)
1. **Wish** The Cure *Elektra*
2. **Diva** Annie Lennox *Arista*
3. **Introduction** Mr. Fingers *MCA*
4. **ah...** Bas Noir *Atlantic*
5. **Not Gonna Change** Swing Out Sister *Fontana*
6. **Ingenue** k.d. lang *Sire*
7. **24 Years Of Hunger** EG & Alice *WEA U.K.*
8. any new 12" touched by Todd Terry or Roger S.
9. multiple video showings of "The 10th Victim" & "Cleopatra Jones & the Casino of Gold"
10. **Live In Montreux** Dee Dee Bridgewater *Polydor France*

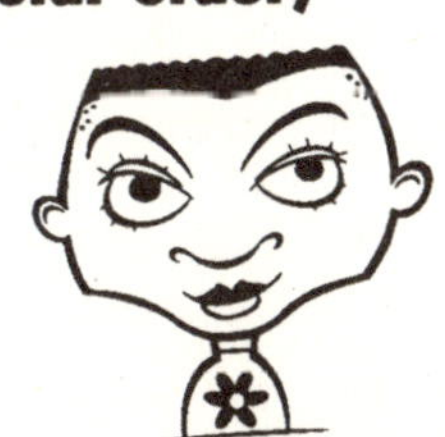

Illustration Chip Wass

Pure Mark Farina
TOP TEN
1. **Dead End Alley** Mr. Fingers *MCA*
2. **Club Lonely** Lil Louis *Epic*
3. **I'm In Heaven** Pearl Necklace *Mirage*
4. **Shoo Be Doo** Bas Noir *Atlantic LP cut*
5. **Let's Get Intimate** (Jamie mix) Body 2 Body *ID*
6. **Bad Bad Boys** Midi, Maxi, Effi *Columbia*
7. **Get Your Act Together** B.O.P. *Classic Club*
8. **Free** Bass Foundation *Magnet*
9. **Relics** Various *Transmat U.K.*
10. **As One** Robert Owens *Massive B*

Jazzie B is **Soul II Soul**. The sound system. The ever-evolving revolving groove factory. The conscience and concept behind the sound that changed the face and voice of pop music with the multi-platinum debut album *Keep On Movin'* in 1989. Soul II Soul defined it's very own musical genre. Almost everyone doing dance records tried to follow their lead; Madonna, Lisa Stansfield, George Michael, just to name a few. After a somewhat less successful sophomore effort (stateside anyway, the record was very well received worldwide) entitled *Volume II 1990 A New Decade* , Funki Dred designer, d.j., and record producer extraodinaire Jazzie B and the Soul II Soul posse are back at it with the release of **Volume III Just Right** (Virgin). Equipped with a brand new roster of guest musicians and vocalists, Jazzie B takes complete control over the production duties (no help from Nellee Hooper on this one), and delivers their most diverse and dynamic effort to date. This release combines 70's-influenced strings, crisp cool horns, reggae ragamuffin rhythms, and a lineup of vocal talent that's absolutely fierce. "Joy," the first single, features the soulful and sanctifying vocal stylings of Richie Stephens. Overflowing with optimism, the finely crafted melody and irresistible hook keep you singing along long after the song is gone. The 12" remixes from Tony Humphries should help break this in the clubs, but my favorite is still The Brand New Heavies mix.

A lot of other songs stand out on this record: "Take Me Higher" brings back Caron Wheeler's amazing vocal talent and the trademark string and rhythm arrangements that made "Back To Life" and "Keep on Movin'" club and radio anthems. "Just Right" debuts the breathtaking voice of Rick Clarke and at three minutes is way too short. Expect some re-working and a 12" to follow? "Future," the beautiful duet with Kofi and Bazil Meade has the potential to be a huge radio success. But the real gem here is "Move Me No Mountain," with lush strings, jazzy keyboards, poppin' bass and steppin' rhythms, and a vocal arrangement that smokes. Kofi's vocals are sensual and sweet; they soar and stretch out past all the soundalikes that seem to be dominating the scene of late (was that Ce Ce, Jomanda, or Kym Sims?)

The best thing about this record is that you can actually listen to it at home. So sit back, relax and enjoy, or get up off your butt and dance. What is Soul II Soul? A band that actually lives up to the hype. Very rare these days. Just right, indeed.

— *Terry Martin*

JUICE

dumb disco

Certainly, disco lyrics have never been known for their deep meaning or anything. But there are a few all-time favorite tunes whose lyrics defy interpretation. For example:

1 Black Box "Everybody, Everybody" These dumb lyrics were written by Italians who obviously had no idea what they were saying. *You won't belong to me, I let you down/ I walk around and see your night skyline/ I feel the light but you don't want to stay/ So lonely now, just let me on the town/Celebrate.* "Stairway To Heaven" should make such sense.

2 Crystal Waters "Makin Happy" *She screams A-ooo-wa/and sounds just like a mouse* is where the silliness starts. But nothing tops the imaginative chorus: *Makin happy, makin happy, happy, happy, happy.* Watsamatter, run out of rhymes? How bout Nappy, Snappy, Slappy, or Crappy?

3 Inner City "Good Life" Another no-frills chorus: *Good Life/Good Life/Good Life/Good Life/Good Life/Good Life/Good Life... Good Luck!*

4 Donna Summer "MacArthur's Park" Not always a disco record, the over-the-top fourteen minute "suite" treatment makes the "cake out in the rain" line sound even sillier. Thank God they'll never have that recipe again!

5 Right Said Fred "I'm Too Sexy" Yeah, right. This is the ultimate novelty record; worth a yuck or two when you first heard it, growing more and more tedious with each repeated listen. You're probably already too sexy for this song, anyway.

6 Desiya "Coming On Strong" *Boyy-ee Boyy-ee!.* The most repetitive song of recent memory, it's an object lesson in making a mountain of a molehill. Two twelve-inch singles, eight mixes, and almost NO lyrics to speak of: *play your funky funky song/on/on/on/on/on/on and on and on and on. Boyy-ee Boyy-ee!*

7 Chas. Brack "Wouldn't It Be Fun To Work In A Bakery?" Don't go looking for this one: it's a legend in the mind of Chas. Brack, inspired by an insipid bakery worker: *Wouldn't it be fun to work in a bakery?/NO/ (BOOMBOOMBOOMBOOM dooo-dooo-doo-dooo-dooo.)* Oh, well, guess you had to be there.

DJ Psycho Bitch
TOP TEN
1. **Ave Maria** Noys
2. **My 1st Fantastic F.F.** Jam & Spoon
3. **Drill** Komakino
4. **The Ballet** J'n'J
5. **Moody** Bomb the Bass
6. **Can You Feel It** Chez Damier
7. **Get Down, Get Down** D.D. Rave
8. **Rave the Planet** World Volume 3
9. **Revival Shadows** Public Ambient
10. **Auto Shutter** Plexus
PICK HIT
Dueling Techno Noys

Freddie Bain
TOP TEN
1. **Free Your Mind** Ira Levi *Strictly Rhythm*
2. **Nothing Can Stop Us** Saint Etienne *Warner Brothers*
3. **Black Ice Vol.1** (EP) *Velvet City*
4. **Gettin' Started** Pascal's Bongo Massive *Tomato*
5. **Club Lonely** Lil' Louis *Epic*
6. **Love Is the Master of Disguise** Eve Gallagher *More Protein*
7. **We Need Music** Keys & Tronics Ensemble *Irma*
8. **...ahh** Bas Noir *Atlantic LP*
9. **All I Want** Richard Rogers *Sam*
10. **My Face** Club Culture *X Energy*
PICK
Helpless Urbanized *Maxi*

Mystic Bill
TOP TEN
1. **Rave Off** Tribal Spirit *Division*
2. **You Can't Go Wrong** D.D.S. *Aztonk*
3. **Never Get Enough (Sunday Mix)** Omniverse *BVZ*
4. **Detroit Techno Soul** Eddie Santonio & Art Forest *M.I.D.*
5. **Drum Attack** Jambo *US Import*
6. **Monkey Wah** (instrumental) Radical Rob *R&S*
7. **Timbav** Party Atmosphere *Star Tracks*
8. **Black Magic Woman "92"** (instrumental) J&B Orchestra *Disco Magic*
9. **Ain't No Doubt** Elixir Vitae *Total Music Records*
10. **Emotion** Rhythm Section *RSR*
PICKS
Aiiia N2U *Mirage Promo*
Black Magic Karla St. James (Karr G. & Mystic Bill Mix) *Fly Records*
Shangrila On Dope I.D.F. (Karr G. & Mystic Bill Mix) *Tape*

DEEE-LITE

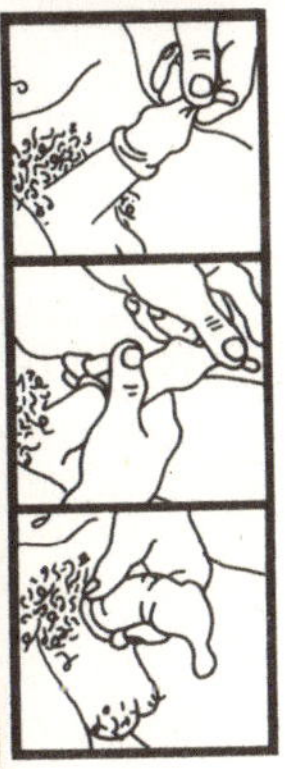

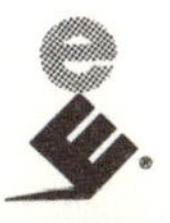

Elektra

LET'S FACE IT!
IT'S A
PRO-CHOICE
SINGLE!

HEAR   Shocking Groovelicity!

Deee-Lite

PRESENTS

THE NEW
SINGLE
"RUNAWAY"

WITH

"RUBBER
LOVER"

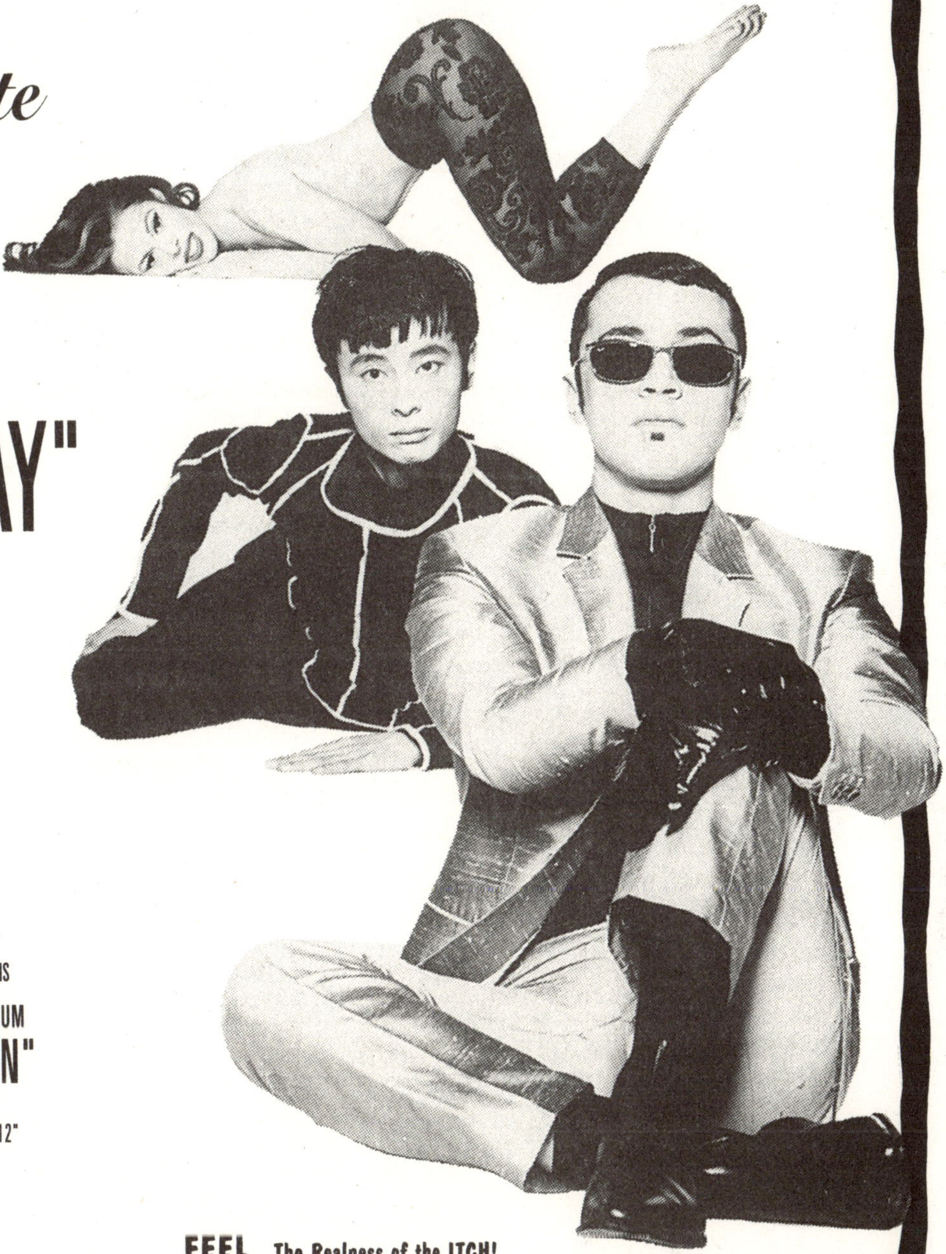

PRODUCED BY Deee-Lite
FOR SAMPLADELIC PRODUCTIONS
FROM THE UPCOMING ALBUM
"INFINITY WITHIN"
AVAILABLE ON
CD SINGLE, CASSETTE SINGLE, AND 12"

FEEL   The Realness of the ITCH!

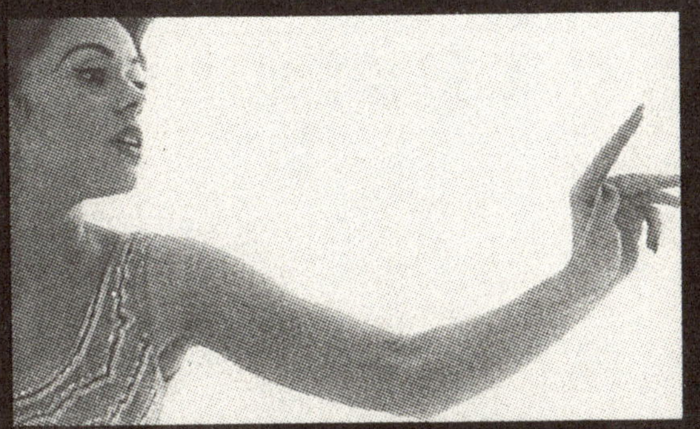

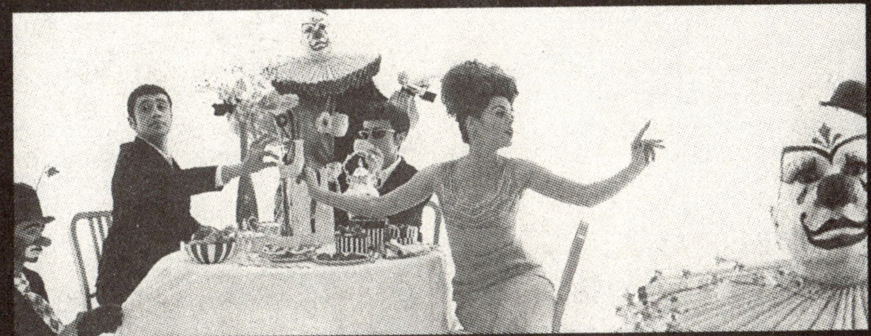

MANAGEMENT: GARY KURFIRST/OVERLAND PRODUCTIONS AND BILL COLEMAN/PEACE BISQUIT PRODUCTIONS   ART DIRECTION: MIKE MILLS AND LADY KIER   © 1992 ELEKTRA ENTERTAINMENT, A DIVISION OF WARNER COMMUNICATIONS, INC. A TIME WARNER COMPANY

Turn The Beat Around

1) Disco singer responsible for "Work That Body" and "When You Touch Me."
- **A.** Linda Clifford
- **B.** Tanna Gardner
- **C.** Vicki Sue Robinson
- **D.** Karen Young

2) "House Music" was NOT invented by...
- **A.** Frankie Knuckles
- **B.** Michael Connolly
- **C.** Larry Levan
- **D.** Farley Keith
- **E.** Ron Hardy

3) Which singer weighs the least?
- **A.** Martha Wash
- **B.** Darryl Pandy
- **C.** Loleatta Holloway
- **D.** Jocelyn Brown

4) Match the club to the city.
- **A.** Paradise Garage
- **B.** The Warehouse
- **C.** Zanzibar
- **D.** The Clubhouse
- **1.** Chicago
- **2.** New Jersey
- **3.** New York
- **4.** Washington, D.C.

5) Which singer is the worst ?
- **A.** Samantha Fox
- **B.** Madonna
- **C.** Stacy Q
- **D.** Crystal Waters

6) Match the tunes with their BPM range.
- **A.** "Back To Life"
- **B.** "Lets Go Dancing"
- **C.** "Lovin is Really My Game"
- **D.** "Over Like A Fat Rat"
- **E.** "High Energy"
- **1.** 140 ish
- **2.** 111 ish
- **3.** 120 ish
- **4.** 100 ish
- **5.** 130 ish

7) You're in the booth and you have to pee and get a drink. Which record is long enough?
- **A.** "Too Hot for Love"
- **B.** "Street Life"
- **C.** "E2 E4"
- **D.** "Souvenirs"

8) One of the first 12" singles was Le Pamplemousse's one and only hit. This song helped spur what dance craze?
- **A.** The Spank
- **B.** The Hustle
- **C.** The Popcorn
- **D.** The Bus Stop

9) Which producer isn't gay?
- **A.** Paul Jabara
- **B.** David Cole
- **C.** Bob Esty
- **D.** None of the above

10) Luther Vandross sang for two of these groups.
- **A.** Change
- **B.** Kleer
- **C.** Chic
- **D.** Klique

11) Former Chic girl Norma Jean Wright had a moderate mid 80's hit with this song.
- **A.** "Shoot Me With Your Love"
- **B.** "Shot In the Dark"
- **C.** "Hit Me With Your Best Shot"
- **D.** "Hit Me With Your Rhythm Stick"
- **E.** "Hot Shot"

12) Which ISN'T a disco record?
- **A.** "Sex Shooter"
- **B.** "I Want Your Sex"
- **C.** "Sex"
- **D.** "Sex and the Single Girl"

- **E.** "Sexy"
- **F.** "I'm Too Sexy"
- **G.** "Sexy Dancer"

13) Which of these songs was the most overplayed?
- **A.** "Let No Man Put Asunder"
- **B.** "Tainted Love/Where Did Our Love Go"
- **C.** "Situation"
- **D.** "It's Raining Men"

14) Find the real fish.
- **A.** Candy J
- **B.** Katrin Quinol
- **C.** Amanda Lear
- **D.** Stephanie Mills

15) Who DIDN'T make a disco record?
- **A.** Liza Minnelli
- **B.** Dolly Parton
- **C.** Janis Ian
- **D.** Janis Joplin
- **E.** Eartha Kitt
- **F.** Ethel Merman

16) What group recorded the seventies fag and dyke anthem "We Are Family?"
- **A.** The Richie Family
- **B.** Sister Sledge
- **C.** The Brothers Johnson
- **D.** The Pointer Sisters

17) Which female vocalist performed with Dr. Buzzard's Original Savanah Band?
- **A.** Fonda Rae
- **B.** Corey Daye
- **C.** Martha Raye
- **D.** Tia Monae

ANSWERS: 1) B 2) B or D 3) hard to tell, ain't it? 4) A/3, B/1, C/1, D/2, E/5 5) D 6) A/4, B/3, C/1, D/2, E/5 7) they're all long enough 8) A 9) B or D (our guess is D) 10) A&C 11) B 12) D 13) it all depends on which you're the most sick of 14) D 15) D 16) B 17) B

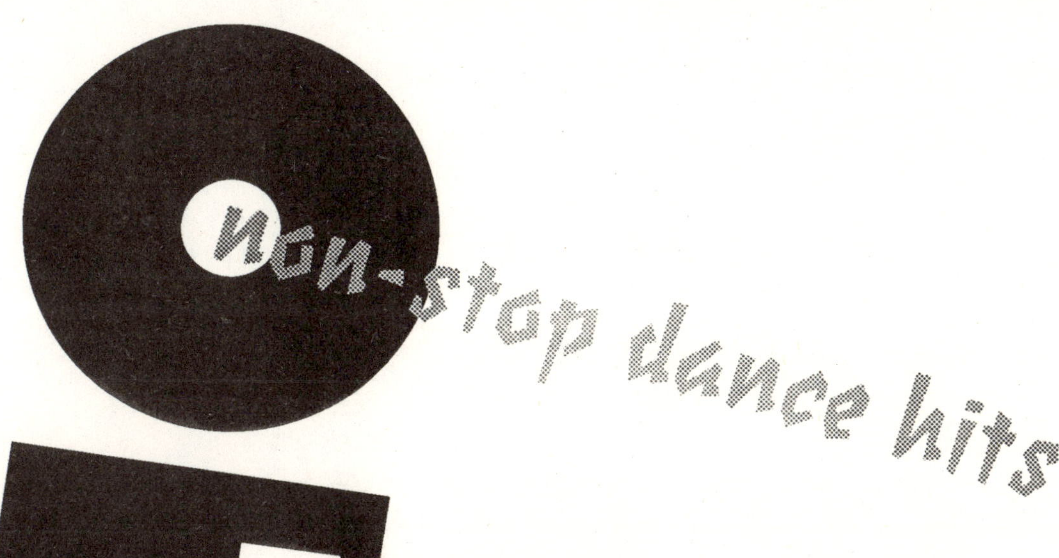

non-stop dance hits
MAURICE JOSHUA
featuring
CHANTAY SAVAGE
"I Gotta Hold On U"
ID 1011
Maurice

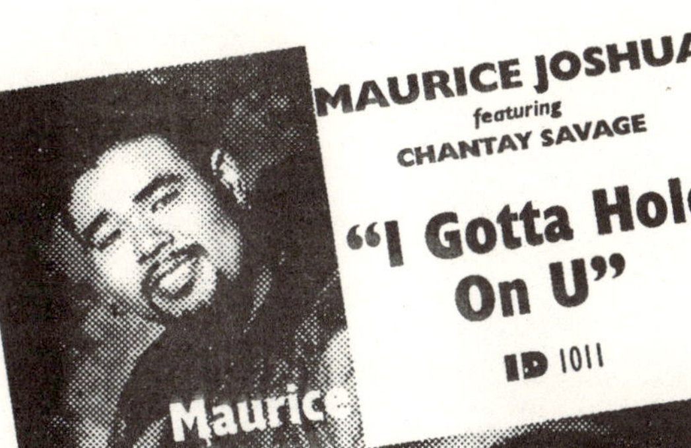

BODY 2 BODY
featuring
DONELL RUSH
CHANTAY SAVAGE
"Let's Get Intimate"
ID 1012
Chantay

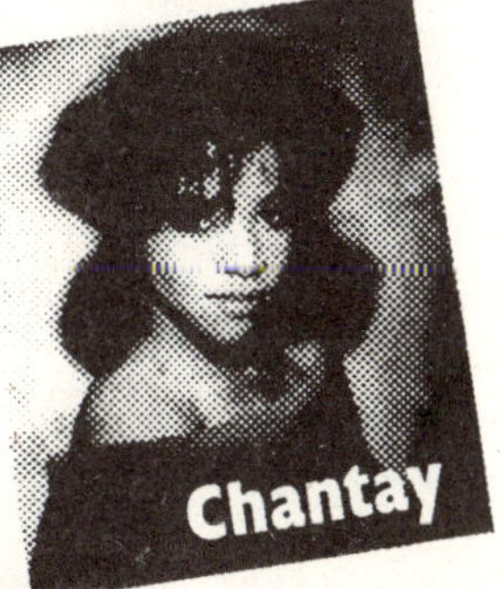

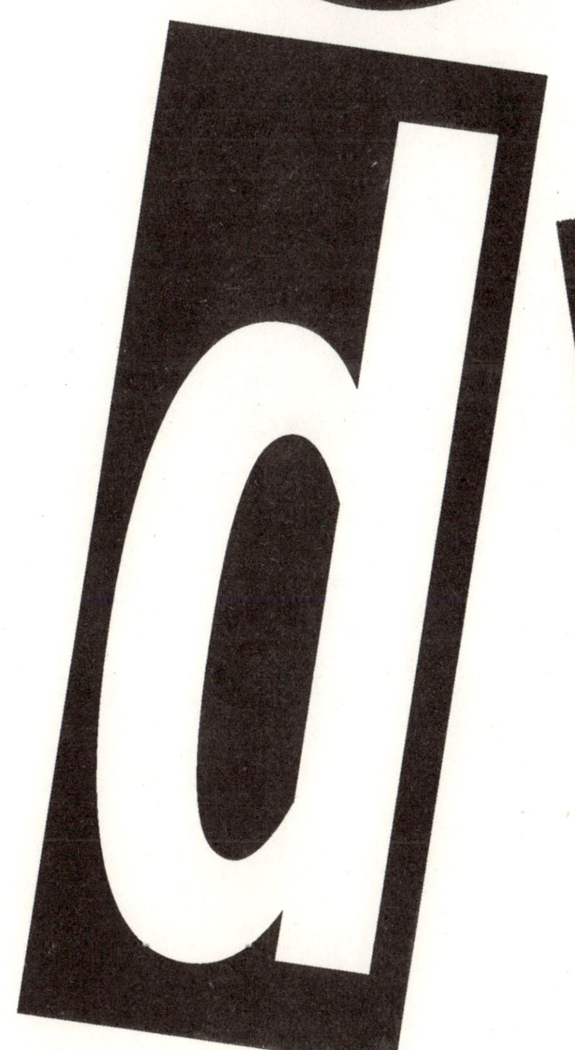

d
records
DONELL RUSH
"Symphony"
ID 1013
Produced by
STEVE "SILK" HURLEY
Donell
STN
"Hail To The Queen"
ID 1014
STN
SEX TRIP NETWERK
the independent label with the major label sound!

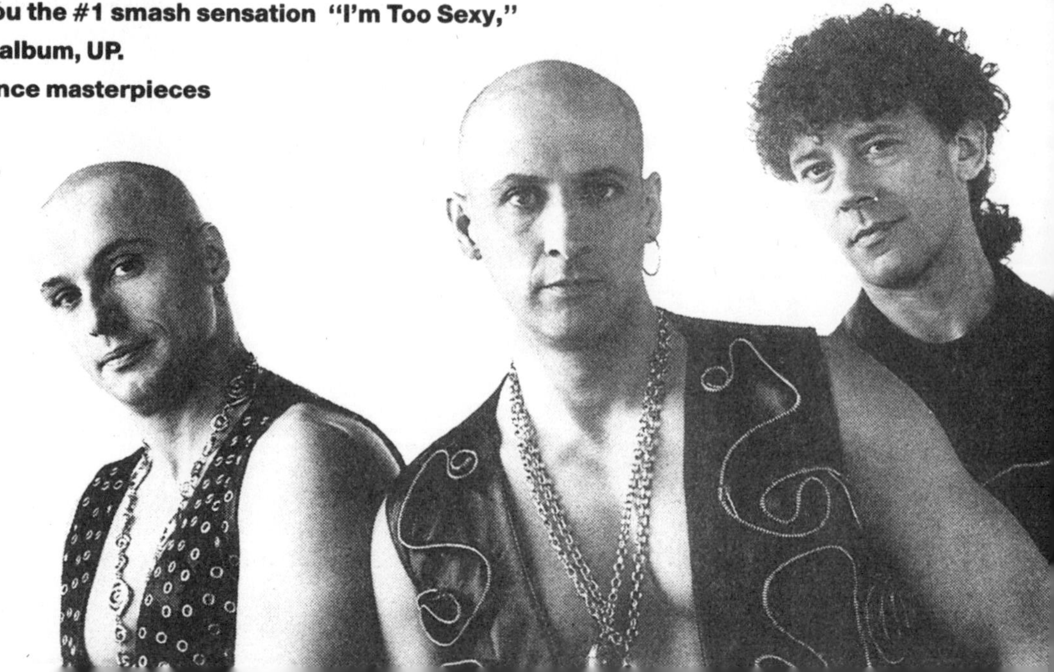

SINK YOUR TEETH INTO
MORE PROTEIN'S CLOSET CLASSICS VOLUME 1
THE ULTIMATE DANCE COLLECTION.

A savory sampling of 11 satisfying tracks
from the ultra-hip UK dance label founded by Boy George.
Featuring tasty turntable tidbits from
Eve Gallagher, MC Kinky, E-Zee Possee, Jesus Loves You, and more...

FIERCE!

M P

AVAILABLE. AT TOWER RECORDS
© 1992 Charisma Records America, Inc.

GET UP WITH RIGHT SAID FRED!

The hit team that brought you the #1 smash sensation "I'm Too Sexy,"
return with their first full-length album, UP.
Featuring ten non-stop dance masterpieces
designed to make you get UP,
and shake your little tush.

charisma

RIGHT SAID FRED UP

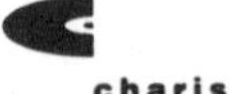

ON THE MARK

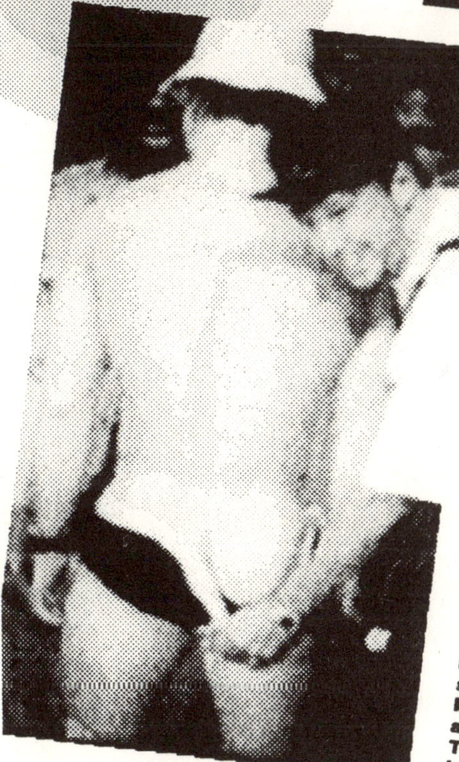

BULLSEYE: Donnie Wahlberg plays crack dealer on Marky Mark's pay-per-view video special, "Live In Yo Face."

by Robert Ford

You know the Marky story by now: even-younger brother of teen dream Donnie Wahlberg (of former teen dreams New Kids On The Block) breaks out as bad boy rap artist cum Soloflex ad. Marky's sexuality seems almost natural: his jacket slides off as easily as Gypsy Rose Lee's dress, revealing a body with every muscle pumped and what must be zero body fat. His randy demeanor and perfect pecs make Marky Mark the first male sex-kitten of the 90's; Madonna with a dick. Marky seems delightfully comfortable acknowledging his queer male fans, giving a pro-gay interview to the <u>Bay Area Reporter</u> and posing for a sexy Bruce Weber photospread in <u>Interview</u>.

It's impossible not to look at the Marky madness and think of Elvis (or the Stones or even Vanilla Ice), taking black music to white people with a sneer and a wiggle. But here in the multi-culti 90's, Marky has his shit down. He's surrounded by black rappers, dancers, and musicians (though the band sometimes sounds like it's being led by Paul Schaffer), and can ape the language remarkably well. Marky almost seems like he's black; all that's missing is the blackface. The "white nigger" stance makes him both sexy (you know what they say about black men) and saleable to the mass market — ultimately he's more Wally Cleaver than L.L. Cool J.

Marky Mark's "Live In Yo Face" April pay-per-view cable TV concert was right up there with a Chippendale's revue for cheap, safe beefcake (or in this case chicken-cake) sexuality. Here's a teen idol who's not afraid of getting his fans horny. These pre-pubescent fans know where their pubes are. Instead of the demure homemade signs that usually appear at these concerts (WE LOVE YOU, DONNIE), Marky inspires signs that read FUCK ME MARKY and STRAP A SADDLE ON AND RIDE ME LIKE A HORSE. Indeed. (If I were there, I could have carried one that read BURY YOUR ACNE SCARRED FACE IN THE PILLOW AND STICK YOUR BUTT UP IN THE AIR, MARKY). The concert ends with older brother Donnie coming on stage for the big encore (Marky Mark and the Funky

Bunch's first big hit, "Good Vibrations"). Marky's humpy chest glistening, he nonchalantly unhooks his b-boy belt and drops his slouchy jeans to let us look at his Calvins. With Marky's back to the audience, Donnie sneaks up and pulls his brother's briefs down to reveal the crack of his ass for a millisecond, inspiring homoerotic fantasies of what happened those late nights after Mr. and Mrs. Wahlberg had gone to bed. (He doesn't seem like a bottom, but you never know...)

Interscope's newly released home video "Music For the People" is culled from a world tour; clips of Marky in hotel rooms, on the streets, and on stage. The tape is leaden with stoopid-def backstage hi-jinks that are more stoopid than def, mostly padding to make the three MTV-overplayed videoclips worth a 19.95 list price. But for diehard fans, "Music For the People" is the ultimate Markyfest. Marky in baggy denim. Marky in Addidas spandex biker shorts. Marky in Public Enemy drag. Shaggy Marky and Marky in military buzzcut. Marky sneers, scowls, and smirks. This tape carries a parental advisory label and is indeed racier than the cable special. He sheepishly tells a reporter that he's a virgin, but hopes to remedy that soon. In boxer shorts, he leads the audience in a chant: "Everybody say 'Safe Sex'". And when asked how his larger than life stardom feels, he replys "Fat...as fat as my dick." In fact, on stage he says he just likes to "pull my penis around and have a good time." I, for one, would like to really see that.

Of course, the downside of the teen idol thing is that stardom is fleeting: just ask the Bay City Rollers, Duran Duran, or Shaun Cassidy. What will Marky do when he gets too old to rap? He could hire Pia Zadora's vocal coach and turn into Tom Jones in a few years. Or maybe star in some action/adventure flicks ("New Jack-Off City" anybody?). At the tender age of twenty, it's hard to imagine a future for this kid. But at least he's almost reached the age of consent.

T.A.'s top ten films

TOPKAPI Few things beat a good caper film and this one wins hands down with the fabulous Melina Mercouri as the beauty and brains behind a scheme to heist priceless jewels from an antique statue housed in a heavily guarded museum during Carnivale! And John Cassavettes is sexy,too. God, you want them to get away with this.

UNDERGROUND USA Independent director Eric Mitchell did this satire of the downtown art/club scene in N.Y.C. circa early eighties. Contains scenes shot at the Mudd Club, the most Godawful art opening and a Dianne Brill-ish girl-of-the-moment celebutante so at rock bottom you have to laugh to keep from crying.

SPIRITS OF THE DEAD Give me a good horror flick and I'm happy as a clam. Give me a *trilogy* of horror stories and I'm good to go. All three of these stories are well executed, all adaptations of Edgar Allan Poe tales. All three share the theme of impending death and irreversible fates for their respective protagonists. The first is directed by Roger Vadim of Barbarella fame and stars Jane Fonda as a tormented Countess in medieval Italy who watches the details of her demise unfold as a portrait tapestry of herself is completed. (Fonda's outfits are to die; one fabulous fur cape after another and the unbelievable close-ups of Jane Fonda at twenty-something are quite amusing.) The second is directed by Francois Truffaut, a chilling and effective treatment about a man who clairvoyantly witnesses his own death over and over until he finally completes it. The third, Fedrico Fellini's piece, Toby Dammit, is my favorite. Glamorous and very frightening, set sometime in the '60s, and tells the story of an english actor (quite in a state of decline) who flies to Rome to accept a prestigious award and meet his death. Dark and fairly gruesome with all the Fellini excesses; lots of film within a film mise en scene, cameras, fashion and mysterious and beautiful women.

BREAKFAST AT TIFFANY'S A young and gorgeous Audrey Hepburn is the main reason to see this film, a must for fashion mavens of any age. She looks fab in every shot. Kids take note: Hepburn as Holly Golightly remarkably works a cocktail *wardrobe* out of just a few pieces and proves two things :1) a little black dress goes a long way and, 2) you ain't got to be rich to have style, style, style!

AUNTIE MAME I'm sorry, there was absolutely no need for Lucille Ball to do a remake of the original Auntie Mame with Rosalind Russell. You get to see the fabulous Beekman Place go from look to look through the years as the eccentric and terribly fashionable Mame Burnside carries on and on. Quite the feel-good movie.

THE MACK Perhaps more elements of blaxploitation than Shaft and Superfly combined. And the soulful Willie Hutch score (including Brothers Gonna Work It Out) is now a classic.

WEST SIDE STORY The dance at the gym. The rooftop sequence. The color. The Jets and Sharks in tighter pants. The Puerto Ricanos. The tragic ending. Be still my heart!

WHAT A WAY TO GO Shirley MacLaine goes through money, husbands, and outfits in this movie the way some of us go through you-know-what. Thing gets beat and more beat and you live to see her next mourning dress.

THE SWINGER One of those corny sixties movies about good girls vs bad girls. Ann-Margret's out to pull off a promotional stunt that proves she's wilder than wild and bad bad bad! The beatnik orgy scene is the highlight with her beat rather Pucci-esque, literally body painting a canvas.

CARMEN JONES You've never seen so many beautiful black people on the screen looking so... gorgeous! Pearl Bailey, Diahann Carroll, Harry Belafonte, Brock Peters _and_ Dorothy Danridge! Based on the original opera Carmen, this mid-'50's update follows a woman who spurns one lover for another and suffers grave consequences for the mistake. Everybody looks wonderful in this. Very postmodernly, however, all the the singing is dubbed — with the exception of Pearl Bailey and Diahann Carroll.

16

THING

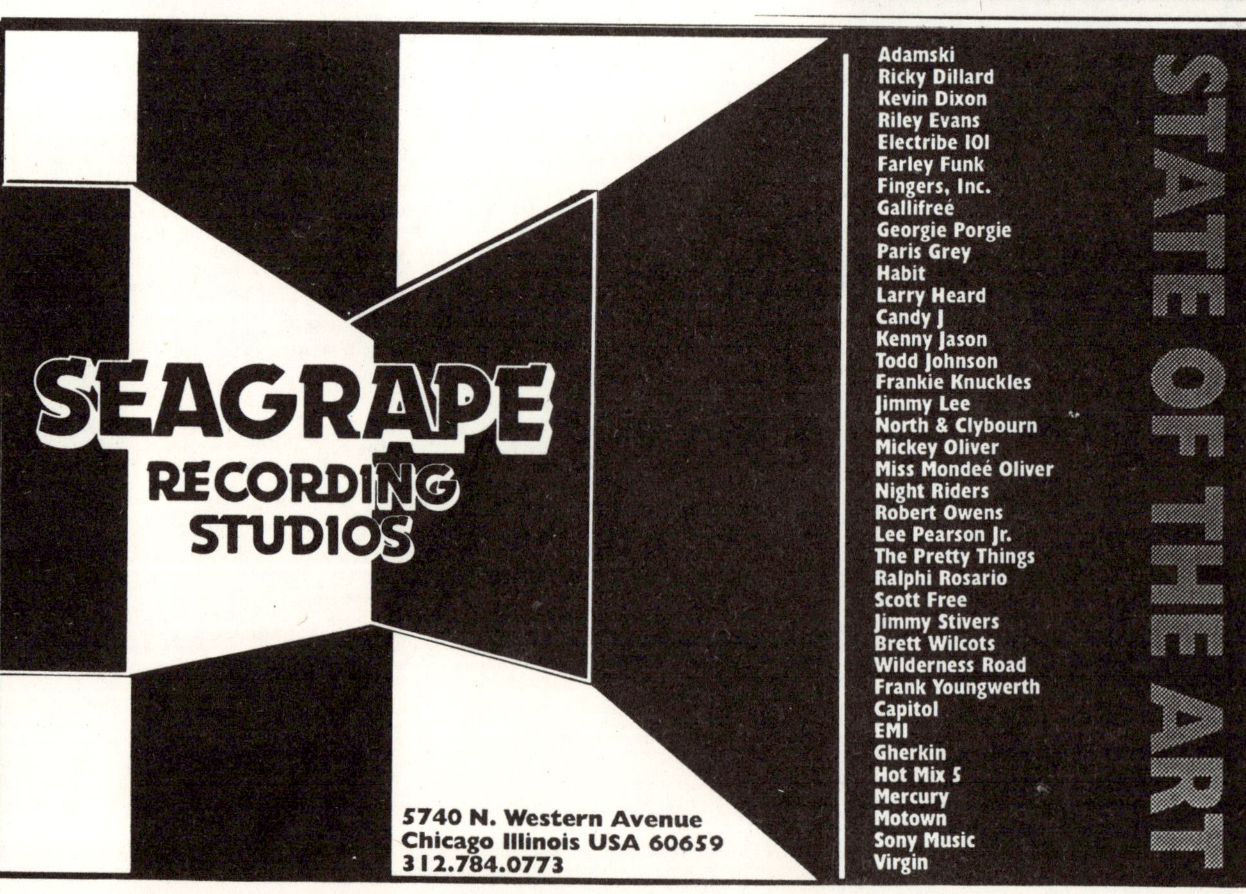

YOUNG SOUL REBELS

Isaac Julien is the Black gay British filmmaker who in 1989 produced the marvelous film "Looking For Langston," which imaginatively discussed the rich emotional and sensual life of Langston Hughes. It was a relief to anyone starved for positive, rich images of Black gay life. When news hit that Julien had completed his first feature film "Young Soul Rebels," I was delighted and eagerly awaited its release.

However I found "Young Soul Rebels" to be bland, boring and thoroughly predictable. "Young Soul Rebels" fails on several counts.

BY STEPHEN WINTER

The film is set in 1977, the time of the Queen's Silver Jubilee in England, but except for some cheap sight gags and a excuse for a riot, there is no apparent reason for the film to be set fourteen years ago. Julien tries to explore the differences in the punk, skinhead and soul movements of the time, but fails to convey any real social insights. A great deal of time is spent touching upon social/political conflicts; gay vs. straight; Black vs. white; Capitalist vs. anarchist; but not one idea is fully developed beyond brief yelling matches or some lame wry jokes. Julien touches upon controversy then veers into idiocy.

It isn't unreasonable to expect "Young Soul Rebels" to be a representation of gay Black life. Isaac Julien is a gay Black artist who has delved deeply into gay Black life in his previous work. Then why is Caz, the gay Black character, regulated to the back of this movie's bus? Instead of dealing with Caz's relationships, sexuality, politics or goals, we are treated to scene after dreary scene featuring motormouth Chris.

Chris and Tracy often kiss lovingly; Caz and Billibud kiss twice and never directly to the camera. Chris' relationship with Tracy is underlined by their radio star ambitions, while Caz doesn't seem to want Billibud for any other reason than to sex down a white boy. And speaking of sex, although the Chris and Tracy sex scene was badly done, it came early in the film and had lots of build up. We had to wait until the last reel to see Caz get any booty, and when he does, it is the most un-sensual and unexciting pre-ejaculation sequence I have ever seen.

The relationship between Caz and Billibud is made all the less believable by not addressing the homophobia that is inherent in the punk scene, especially in the 1970's. The idea that Billibud is a happy, well adjusted gay punk rocker is utopian at best and boring at worst. I have no idea why Julien didn't explore this obvious point; does he not possess the scope?

Maybe not. "Looking For Langston" was one of the strongest, lushest and most romantic films dealing with Black gay life, and it was also quite experimental. Maybe Isaac Julien's strength is with the abstract presentation of ideas based on political or social icons like Langston Hughes which can fall back into legend rather than reality. When faced with a story that demands a conventional narrative with real characters and a real plot, Julien is lost.

Hopefully, he will return to experimental films and again produce the dreamy images that he excels at.

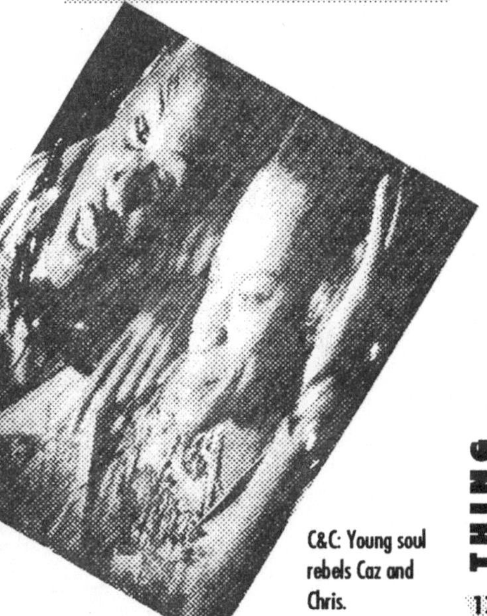

C&C: Young soul rebels Caz and Chris.

17

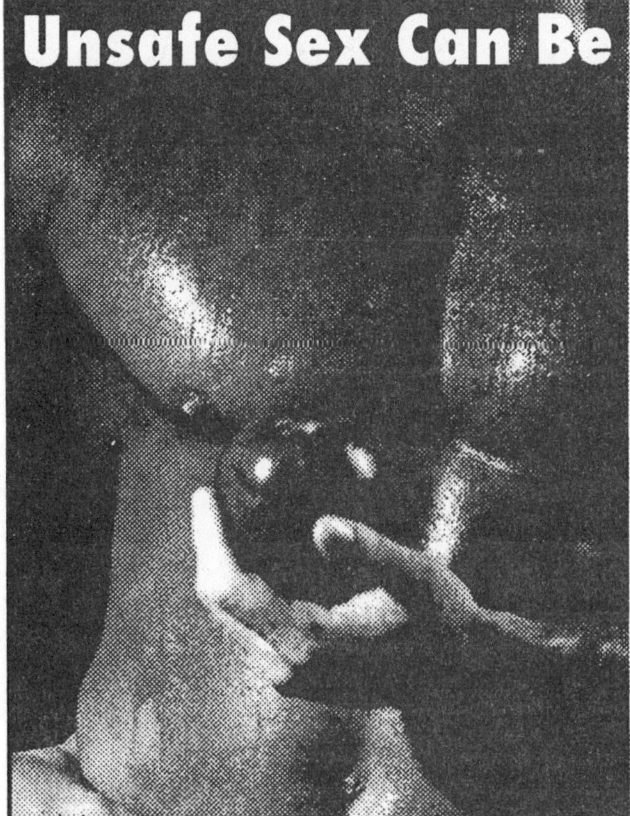

Unsafe Sex Can Be A Great Temptation

Talking about sex can help you make appropriate decisions

Join other people in our community for a free, one-time, confidential get-together. We'll talk about safer sex, HIV testing, fun with condoms, and other AIDS related issues of health and well being.

Don't Be Too Sexy To Get The Facts
Call and reserve a space in our next discussion group

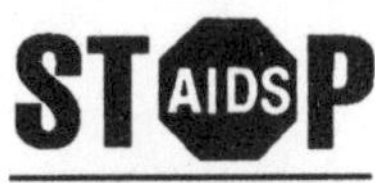

CHICAGO
AFRICAN AMERICAN PROGRAM

There's strength in our numbers

752-STOP
South Side

871-3300
North Side

A Multi-Cultural, Multi-Lingual Community Response
Un programa educacional de prevención de SIDA multi-cultural y bilingüe

PHOTO Rick Miracle

EVERY THING to GO!

MEGA ZINES

MAGS WE'RE BIG ON

ROBERT FORD
zine publisher (Thing)

Gag magazine is the latest fagzine out of Chicago, a dishy little club rag that manages to have some brains as well. Smartly designed by desktop design wiz Malone, the premiere issue featured an interview with door diva Byrd Bardot, a fashion spread with Giggles, and some rants against Calvin Klein, AZT, and Alyn Toler ("Girlfriend needs to be re-potted"). Lots of anonymous tales of nightlife kaflama, things that you'll gag over. Smarter than Project X, it makes the club scene fun to read about even if you stay home.

1153 N. Dearborn Chicago IL 60610 or (312) 248-4542

Gag magazine number one

STEVE LAFRENIERE
zine publisher (TGOC)

For me, the find of SPEW 2 was 19-year-old Brian Baltin's **Intent To Kill**. A 56-page xeroxed paean to the editor's obsessions (musical, cinematic, phenomenological), it's got the eccentric glimmer of connois-seurship with none of the fixedness of "sensibility." There's fragrant stuff here on subjects as far-flung as Swedish actress/filmmaker Mai Zetterling, Coil's John Gosling and Kim Novak's weirdly incandescent part in "Bell, Book, and Candle." Also, useful lists of recommended book and film titles. But maybe the best things about Intent To Kill are three stories by Baltin himself, as crepus-cular as they are utterly unlike anything being done by his contemporaries. To quote the editor's own intro, "It's just all illimitably sublime."

Brian Baltin, 2035 N. Rodney Drive #4, Los Angeles CA 90027 • $5/issue

RACHEL PEPPER
zine publisher (Cunt/Queer City)
zine buyer for A Different Light San Francisco

While I love just about every 'zine that crosses my path, what has tickled my fancy the most these days is the whole new wave of comic book style 'zines appearing in print. Perhaps my favorite is **HotHead Paisan**, drawn by Dianne DiMasse and produced with her partner Stacy Sheehan. Subtitled "The Homocidal Lesbian Terrorist", HotHead is a finely drawn cartoon series about a dangerous but loveable little dyke with a fiery tem-per and a mission to attack misogyny wherever it rears its ugly little head. Not for those who were offended by "Thelma & Louise." Or maybe, I should say, especially for them.

Giant Ass Publishing, box 214, New Haven CT 06502 • $3/issue

LARRY WARREN
zine contributor (Thing)

It's a bird, it's a plane, it's **Dragnett**, "The Feminist Militant Drag Queen Super Hero Comic Book with a Mission." This campy (what else?) comic book is a dish full of dirt, fun, and meaning. Produced by Hedda Lettuce for Lettuce Entertain You Comics, it chronicles the lives, loves, and battles of super-human- dragpower-embodied heroines Hedda Lettuce, Miss Understood, Glenda Orgasm, and Brenda Sexual whose mission is to rid the world of homophobia and to enlighten/educate the people. Great drawing, brilliant storylines, and a powerful message combine to make this a must-read for the unashamedly politically correct. I now include in my prayers a "land where drag queens can roam free of violence, hatred, and bigotry and where they can perform their lip-synch acts tension-free."

Hedda Lettuce, 46 E. 3rd ST #7, New York NY 10003 • $2/issue

a panel from Dragazine

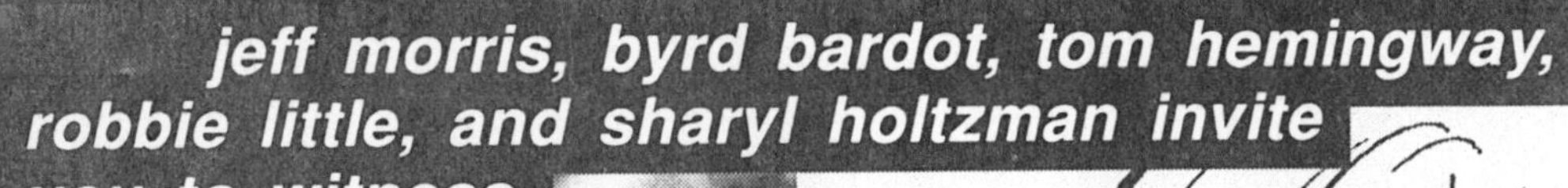

jeff morris, byrd bardot, tom hemingway,
robbie little, and sharyl holtzman invite
you to witness

thrust
a sunday spectacle

thrust dj ralphi rosario grooves you
into a sexy sweat

introducing miss kitty's
smart drinks available at fine clubs
in nyc, london, and tokyo

8pm, deep inside the riviera theatre
at 4746 north racine, five dollar cover

a gay managed and operated event

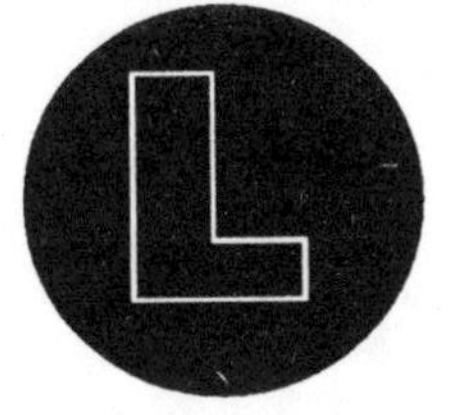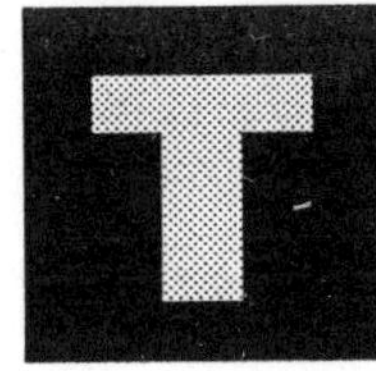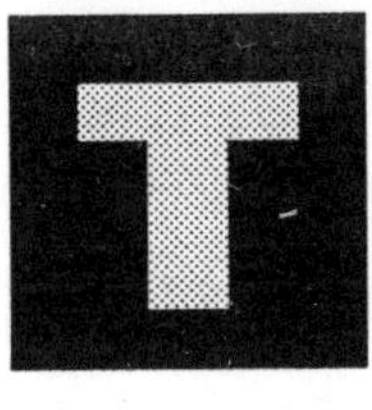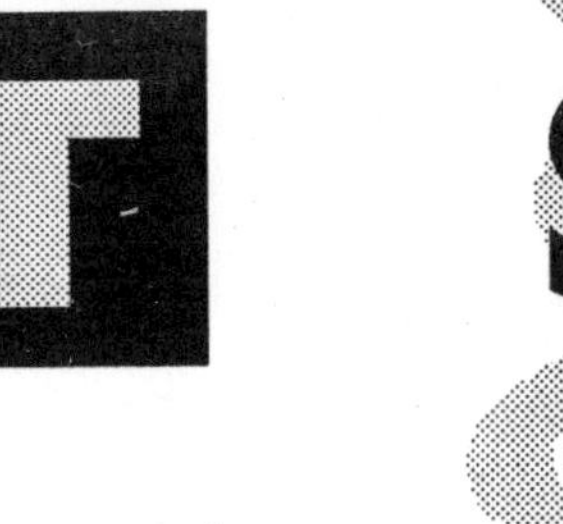

Perfect Casting
Audrey Hepburn in
The Jacquline de
Ribes Story.
Jacquline de Ribes in
The Audrey Hepburn
Story.

...Shoulda Been a Drag Queen
Grace Jones
Ultra Naté
Adeva
Stephanie Mills
Diana Ross
Eartha Kitt
Patti LaBelle
Tamara Dobson
Lady Miss Kier
Annie Lennox
Bette Midler

Oh,no!
"No, I can't front you."
"No, you can't come in."
"No way José."
"No, I don't think so."
"No, none for me, thanks."
"No, I've never tried that."
"No, I haven't had any work done."
"No, these are Payless."
"No, I've never done him."
"No, it ain't."
"No, don't be like that."
"No, I don't."
"No, sorry."

Fucking Like Bunnies
Jessica Rabbit
The Lady Bunny
The Goddess Bunny
Pussy Dujour
Pussy Galore
Bunny and Pussy
Pussy Washington
Justine and the Pussy
cats from Outerspace
Pussy Plantain
Pussy Du Jour
Octopussy
Pumpkinhead

Stay In!
Ashford and Simpson
k.d. lang
Olivia Newton-John
Merv Griffin
Billy Preston
Randy Travis
Richard Gere
Stedman Graham
Sherman Helmsley
David Cole
Arsenio Hall
Michael Feinstein
Michael Jackson
Whitney Houston
Magic Johnson
Carl Lewis
Luther Vandross
Richard Chamberlin
Tom Sellek
Jason Priestly

Family Feud
Mother Father Sister
Brother (MFSB)
Steak Daddy
Soror
Sustah Gurl
Big Sista
Big Daddy
Big Mama
Mama's Baby
Frat Bro
Bro Ham
Brother Man
Pops
Moms
My Cousin
Yarborough, Peoples
and Folks

Type Talk
Steve Lafreniere
Steve Marton
Kim Lovely
Arlene Ayalin
Craig Siegle
Brian Matthews

Cynthia P. Caster
Chuck Gonzales
Eric Kozoil
Roger Noel
Byrd Bardot
Tom E.
Malone
Arlis Ball
Simone Bouyer
Jeff Morris

Artists IN
Keith Haring
Jean Michael
Basquiat
Lee Kay
Tina Chow
Rick Tuttle
David Hockney
Simone Bouyer
James Battle
Warhol

No, no, no !
Sharon Stone
Michael Douglas
Joan Van Aark

Did you say...
sex?
records?
money?
drinks?
drugs?
rally?
all expenses paid?

Smut
ass
asshole
balls
basket
bird
box
buns
cakes
cookies
cock
cream
cum
cunt
clit
dick
fuck

groin
hole
meat
manhole
boy pussy
pearl
pookipsie
poontang
pussy
schlong
slit
snatch
tits

Ringin' It
Ma Bell
Patti LaBelle
Belle of the Ball
Southern Belle
Belle du Jour
Bela Lugosi
Bel-Tone
Clara Bell
Aunt Blue Bell
Bells of St. Mary
Belladonna
Cioa Bella!
Bellissimo
Bell Epoch
Vanessa Bell
Armstrong
Bell, Book and Candle

Pardon My French
En Vogue
Bas Noir
Cherchez Le Femme
Sassy Fitzpatrick
France Joli
Plastic Bertrand

Dinosaur DJs
Ralphi Rosario
Joe LoPresti
Turtle
Frankie Knuckles
André Hatchett
Jeff Davis
Joe Shanahan
Larry Brewer
Fred Hands
Larry Levan
Joe Smooth
Peter Lewecki

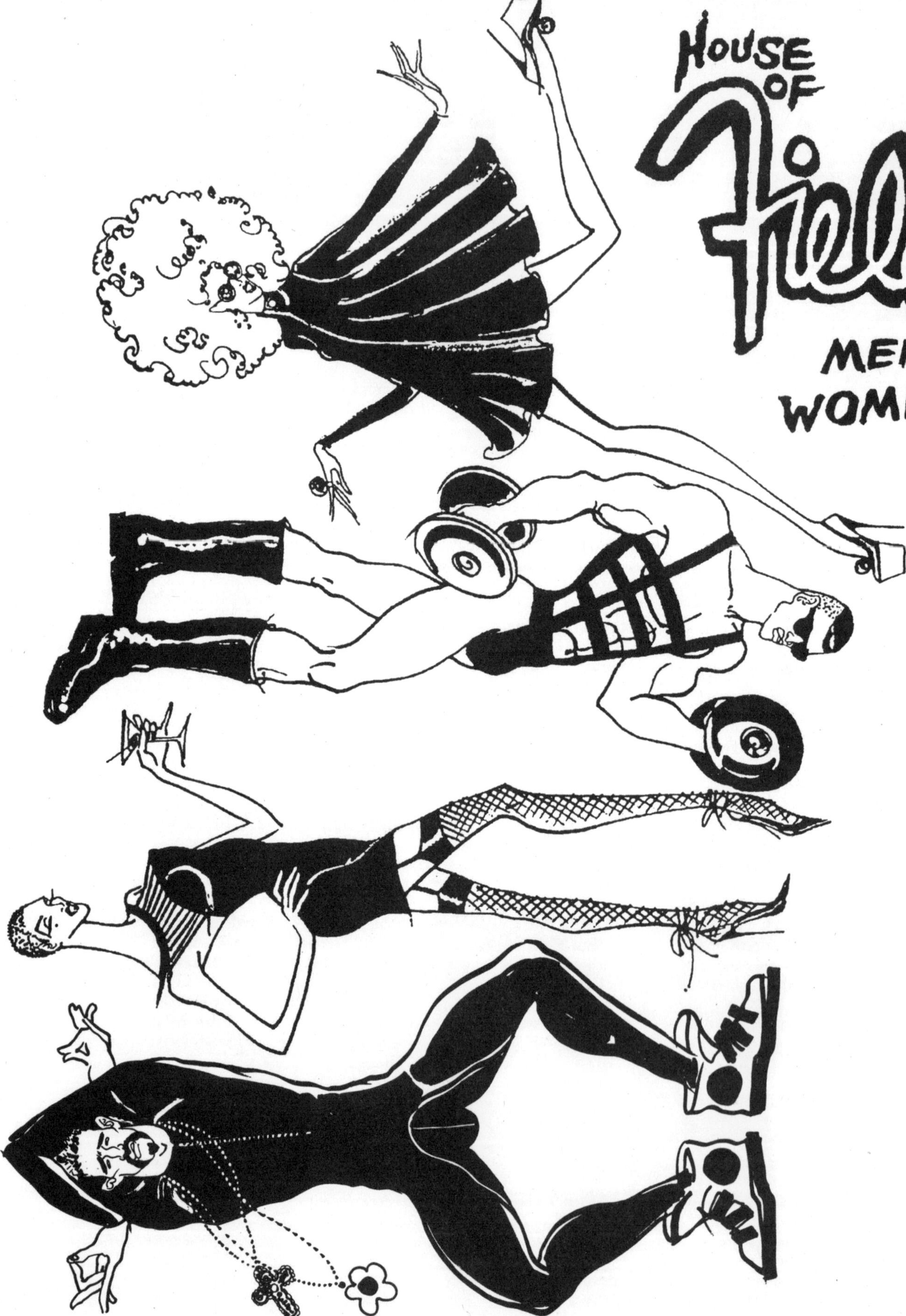

HOUSE OF
Field
MEN
WOMEN
Illustrations by Steven Broadway
AVAILABLE @ 99th FLOOR · 3406 N. HALSTED · CHICAGO 60657 · 312/348-7781

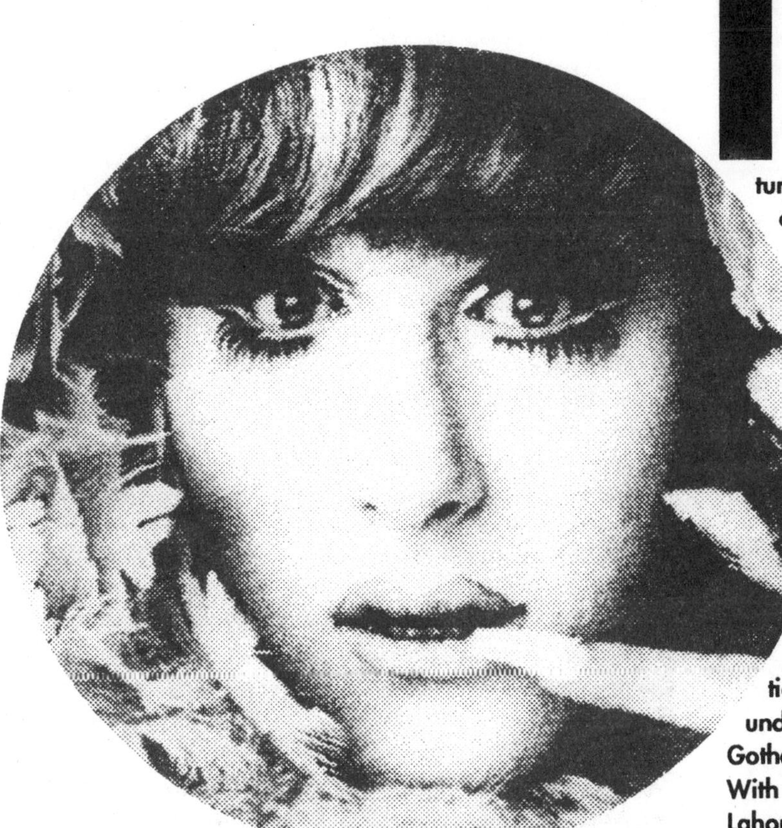

the LADY BUNNY

It's hard to be out and about in New York City these days and not know of The Lady Bunny. In no less than the nine years she's moved from Atlanta, Georgia to live in NYC, she has inviolably become an indispensible fixture within the city's downtown club and entertainment circuit. Diplomat, organizer, mother, girlfriend, sister, dancer, singer, fashion plate, hostess and beauty, hers is the charm capable of seducing a crowd or the sole admirer. She's the force behind the power of Wigstock, NYC's annual multi cultural, multisexual celebration of dragdom. Already seven years running it has fast become an institution among the youth and underground movements in Gotham and across the nation. With RuPaul, Deee-Lite, Larry Tee, Lahoma Van Zandt, Mona Foot, and Barbara Patterson Lloyd, Wigstock continues to feature some of the best in camp and cult entertainment. Last year's festival drew an estimated ten thousand spectators to Union Square Park. During a visit to NYC for the festival in '91, I met Bunny at the ShaSha Cafe in the Village. Later, I learned this would be cause for speculation from some who wondered, "What does Lady Bunny have to do with a black and gay magazine?"

by Trent Adkins

TA: What were you listening to just now on your headset?

LB: Oh, the latest stuff. You know, "Makin' Happy" and whatever. I have this friend that does these for me. I don't buy records; I get tapes.

I just like whatever, you know the stuff you hear out at the clubs. I like soul music mostly. I'm a big soul music fan from way back. I love Motown and all of that stuff, too. But I get enough of the Motown stuff not to have to go out and buy it. I am a *huge* Diana Ross fan! I've loved Diana throughout the years. Throughout the years!

TA: You poor thing! Really, what did you think of *Working Overtime*? We voted it that year's most embarrassing comeback.

LB: Oh, I loved *Working Overtime*! I actually love every track on that album!

TA: Gee, you're a true diehard! You and B-Boy. Y'all *love* the girl. Oh, she only has jillions of adoring fans!

LB: I am! I truly am! Actually, my all-time favorite Diana Ross song is "Work That Body"! So that shows how tired I am! (screams and laughs)

TA: Yeah, I'll concede "Work That Body" and "The Boss" were two of her best efforts. Frankie (Knuckles) used to play the sickest mixes of the Boss at the Warehouse and I remember "Work That Body" fiercely premiering at the Powerplant.

LB: Really! Oh, I love her! *The Boss* is my favorite album! I love it!

TA: Let's talk about the festival. When was the original idea for Wigstock? How long ago did you first do it?

LB: Seven years ago. It's very much a group idea, actually, between several people hanging out at the Pyramid one night, boozin'. And after the Pyramid closed, me, Wendy Wild, Brian Butterick who was and still is one of the managers at the Pyramid, and several members of this group, straight guys, a group called the Fleshtones, got together. They're kind of like a rock group that's popular around college music circles. We were just clowning around on the bandshell in Tompkins Square Park, late, late at night. We did it there for the first six years. But they were more into the rock and roll scene and so they wanted to combine drag and rock and roll and

have some kind of festival.

TA: Had you intended Wigstock to be annual?

LB: Well, it probably would've died there but I took the initiative and found out that it was very easy to get a park permit, which is like a fifty dollar application fee, and a five dollar Amplification of Sound fee from the police department. The police have always been very helpful with Wigstock. And usually the Parks Department is very helpful. I mean, I've never encountered any opposition from them because of the content or tone of the event. The very gay *tone* of the event! (Laughs all around.) Well, I hate to say 'gay event' because then it's too limiting. I mean, ninety percent of the performers are gay and probably seventy-five percent, or more, of the crowd is gay but everybody is welcomed there. It's not exclusively gay. It really bugs me to see some gay groups passing out flyers that say 'I Hate Straights.' I was at the Pyramid one Sunday night, and they're sort of catering to, or are pretending to cater to, a gay crowd. I'm not trying to read them, but they're trying to appeal to the militant East Village faggot who's in ACT UP, and who wears military boots, people with bald heads, and they're trying to get a hard, cruisey atmosphere and they call the night 'FUCK.' And so the MC got on the mike one night and said, in a voice that I've heard guys use when they're trying to sound more butch on the phone sex line...

TA: Ooh...!

LB: (Intoning a phony deep voice), "Wekome to FUCK! FUCK is queer! If there's any straight couples here, please refrain from making out on the dancefloor!" And that got a really big cheer from the audience! And I just thought it was so silly. I thought, how can you be at odds with ninety percent of the people on the face of the earth. I mean, if it wasn't for straight people makin' out... how the fuck do you think your gay ass got here, honey?! (Screams and laughs all around)

TA: Wigstock looks expensive, how do you pay for everything?

LB: Yeah, it's expensive even though we do it as inexpensively as possible. It was a lot more expensive this year. We have great sponsors. Limelight and Crowbar have been just great. The others were Creative Time and MAC Cosmetics and Coffee Shop. Plus we sold ads in the program and we held a lot of benefits at Channel 69 and at the Bank and at Sugar Reef Restaurant. We solicited private donations. I even sent a letter to Madonna, thinking that

she might want a tax write-off, but I don't think she got the letter. I tried faxing it to her publicist, but at least now she knows of the event and maybe next year... we'll see. We approached Absolut, but we're a little bit wackier than Gay Pride Day and they did not take the nibble even though Benjamin Lui, was helping us contact them.

TA: I remember him as Ming Vauze. I saw him backstage looking marvelous. What's he up to lately?

LB: Right now he's launching Donna Karan's menswear line at Barney's. He's really helpful, he's a real mover and shaker and is very well connected in the PR world and knows how things should be done. Basically, it's Scott Lifshutz and I who organize the whole thing, but Benjamin and Bobby Miller, who is my hairdresser, helped out with ad sales and everything.

TA: More about Benjamin, though. How'd you meet each other?

LB: Well, you know he was Andy Warhol's personal assistant for quite a while and he invited me to dinner with him and Andy and several friends for one of Benjamin's birthday parties and I came in drag and Andy Warhol kept taking all these photographs of me, and I was loving it! And somebody later said to me; Andy often takes out his camera with no film in it! Aaaahhh!! And that was probably one of those nights! But it was workin' for me, honey! I was posin' up a storm! I'm not sure how we first met. I've just always seen him out and stuff. He actually performed the first couple of years at Wigstock and he doesn't seem to actively pursue performing. He's got a sick sense of humor, kinda twisted. He'll do a lip sync number where it's really more jangling loud bracelets than knowing the words to the song. Sick stuff like that. But he's been such a big help with everything.

TA: Bunny, who influences your look? You look so great all the time. I think it's a real soft look.

LB: Haaaa! God, I always say, "Get a lot on!" I love Barbara Eden to death! Love, love, love her! I love Charo and I love the Gabor sisters, especially Zsa Zsa, she's so compelling. I mean, you just can't take your eyes off of her. I loved that whole police assault thing, that was so genius; an older has-been running around with an open flask and then smacking a police officer. I'm sure it was all invented by her publicist. I hope it was. I just love looking at her on the screen with all that white hair and the whittled down nose and the silicone cheeks and the slanted eye make-up, I just think that's it! I love that she sees herself as this...this...thing! Still. I think whether I like it or not, there's probably a little tinge of Mrs. Roper in me, you know from "Three's Company." (Laughs)

TA: How'd you come to hosting the parties at Limelight?

LB: Well, they'd wanted me to be more involved with the parties and actively promote the club. It's basically straight and there are a few club kids that I host the parties with and the boys love us to death. You know, we tell them, "You boys just get sexier every week!" And they love it. Here's these teenaged body builders, and a lot of them have never seen drag before, and I much prefer that over a club like Edelweiss where you sit around and judge how far along girls are with their hormones! We don't play any games with them like they're used to the straight girls doing with them, we just come right out and let them know, "Hey, lets do it, honey!" And the next thing you know you've got those condoms out and... haaaaa! But I love it because the boys in there are the ones who would kill you on the street for looking at them but here they are surrounding you telling you that they get the "tingle" with you that they don't get with a real girl. And all these gorgeous boys looming around me discussing the "tingle!" Honey, talking to me about the "tingle!" Honey, Miss Thing is feeling the "tingle" herself! ▼

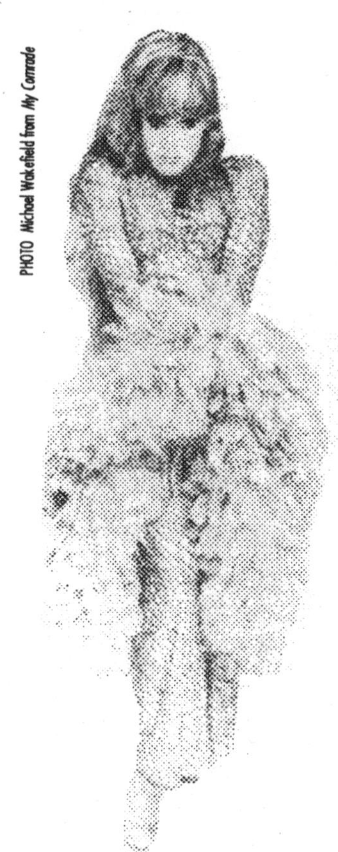

Honey, Miss Thing is feeling the "tingle" herself!

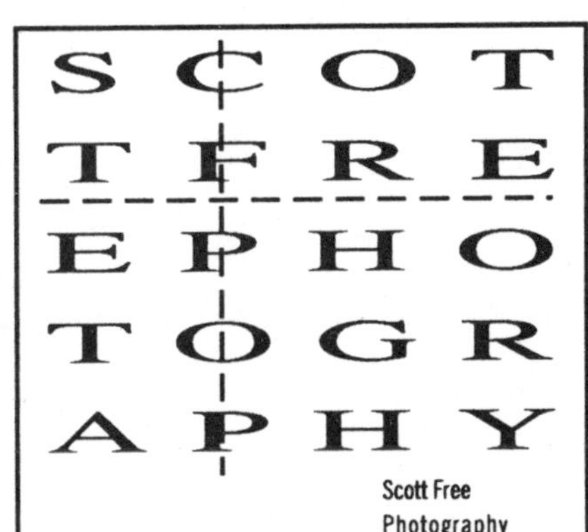

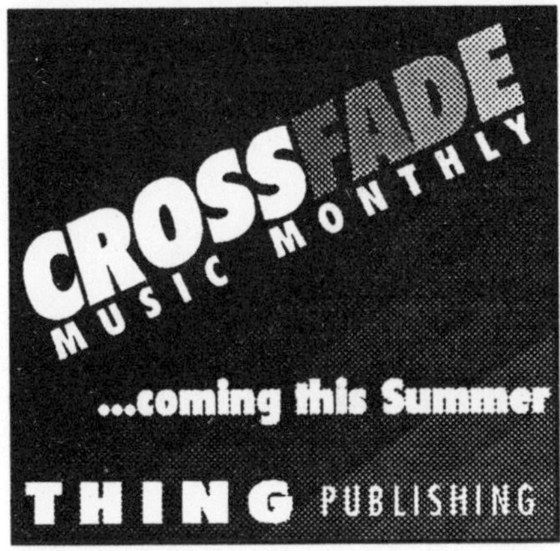

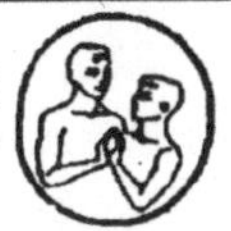

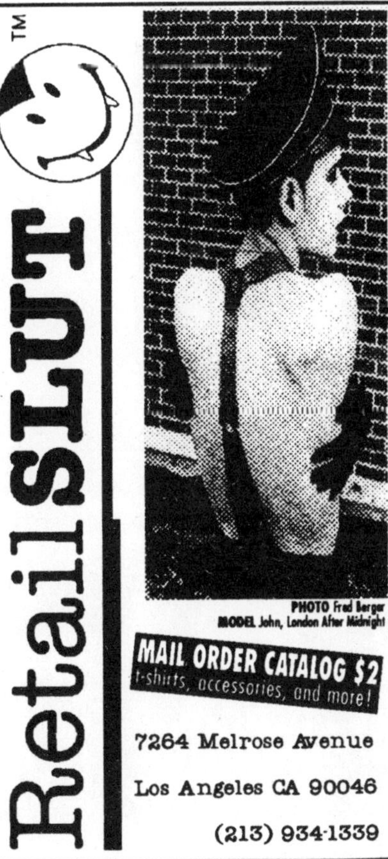

RUPAUL

RuPaul is our beloved space-goddess of the '90s. She's hot, she's tall, she knows how to do runway and she's causing quite a stir. Her forthcoming album is *The Return of Starbooty*, with tracks "Free Your Mind" and "Everybody Say Love."

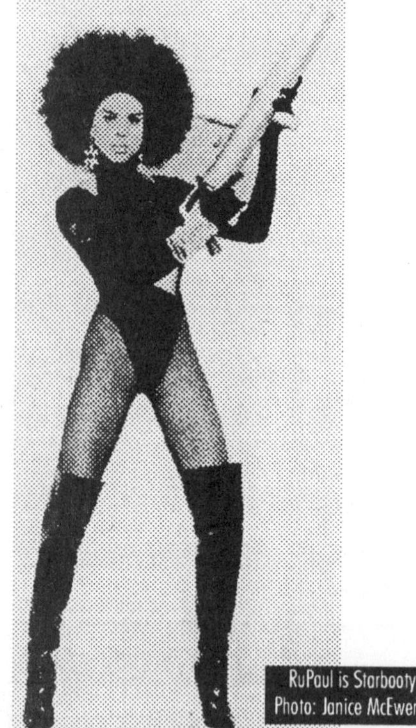

RuPaul is Starbooty.
Photo: Janice McEwen

by Skinny Vinny

Skinny Vinny: I once saw a fanzine of yours called *New York is a Big Fat Greasy Ho.*

RuPaul: I learned early on that there were very few black effeminate performers and that even if my products weren't going to be published, I was still going to write them. Looking back, it's kind of scary because I was so revealing. I revealed everything in those books.

SV: I thought they were great because clearly here was someone who had no problems getting their vision out to many people.

You must have had a heavy first impression of New York.

R: Well, I'm from San Diego. I didn't leave until I was fifteen years old and went to Atlanta. I'd never really been to a real city and there in Atlanta I was born again. In San Diego I lived in a mind ghetto where no one expected anything of me. Any individuality was squelched. My only refuge was pot, which saved my life. There I met show business. Atlanta was like a college for me until I came up here to the big city. Atlanta is a mystical place. There is more racism outside of the South than inside the South. The North has "invisible"

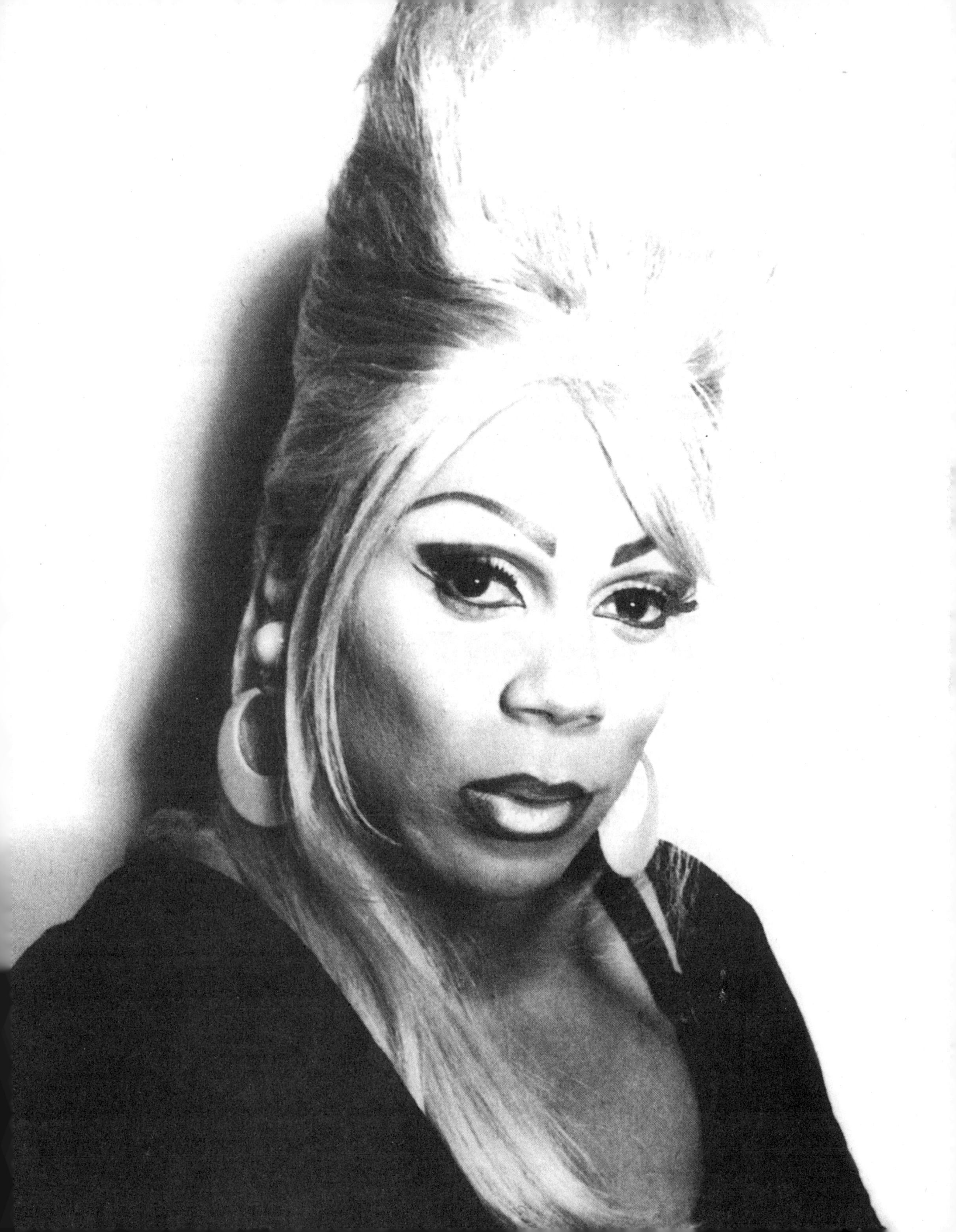

prejudice.

SV: What about racism and RuPaul?

R: It hurts. People put others down to try to feel better themselves. Also, it's the Dorothy thing; it was within herself all along. It's not something you'll find on a drugstore shelf, or from going out and having all these one night stands. I hope that the world, with the millennium coming, will have people look within to spirituality.

SV: You've always seemed to me like a breath of fresh air among a cabal of bitchy queens. How do you do it?

R: I've been positive, and it is hard among so much negativity, but I stay positive. Negativity is not my way of doing magic. What you believe comes true. You can change your destiny by changing your thoughts. I've always believed I was a star, I just had to show people that I was.

SV: And that you have done. Tell me, what's it like being on stage and doing the big festivals?

R: My biggest ambition now is to go to Japan. With the reincarnation of Starbooty here in the '90s, I decided I'd do more legs, bigger hair; you know, turn the volume up on everything I'd touched on before.

SV: I saw Starbooty, I loved it and was in shock that there was a videographer out there somewhere making such a creative and bodacious video, but I must admit my favorite point of Starbooty was at the end when you, a black drag queen, look head-on into the camera and say with all the conviction in the world: "I am Starbooty and I'm here to rid the neighborhood of drugs. Me and the U.S. Government." And you have your big gun, giving costume changes. Tell us about Starbooty, The Movie.

R: There are actually three of them in existence now. They are by John Witherspoon. They're cult underground videos. The album is the soundtrack to "Starbooty III." Before, Starbooty had been more goody-two-shoes, but this Starbooty is bigger and more sassy. This Starbooty will eat fried chicken and call someone a motherfucker. I'm just pumping it up because when I did the single, I went out as an astronaut in a catsuit. While I'm on stage, I astralproject to the back of the room saying "What does this audience want to see me do? What do I want to see me do? Well, they want to see me with the longest legs, the biggest hair and the skimpiest outfits. Then I come back onto the stage and I do it.

SV: I've felt it's easy to know what you like to see onstage, but then, when you're up there, it's not so obvious.

R: So, I've slowed down. I've relaxed. I do the runway part and draw the whole thing out because these are parts the audiences love.

SV: What's it like when you're not on stage dealing with those people who aren't familiar with your persona? You know, the day-to-day going to the corner store folks.

R: I'm alone. I love feminine energy and it scares me that I like to be alone so much. I do a TV show that broadcasts in the U.K. called "Best of Manhattan Cable" which takes a lot of time. I get fan letters from England and my friends say, "you're such a star over here." And I've never ever been there.

SV: What do you do on the show?

R: Special features. I did one on hookers on 14th Street. I went out with the girls and posed as one of them. Then I ask one what she thinks of my outfit and she smiles and says "Bitch, I think you're going to pull $7000.00 tonight, cunt!!!" I did another feature on the new black Barbie, which is the new African-American Barbie, Shawnee. I dressed as a guy and interviewed a psychologist from Mattell, some kids at Toys R Us, then, during the interview I have a flashback, a dream sequence, and I say: "Hmmm, I feel like Shawnee myself," and poof! I'm Starbooty.

SV: So you work on the show days?

R: The show is in reruns. Now we're working on a new show called "Ring My Bell."

SV: Is that cable, too?

"They want to see me with the LONGEST legs, the **BIGGEST** hair and the skimpiest outfits. Then I come back onto the stage and I do it!"

R: No, it's a network. They've just started getting cable there. They shot a pilot and it got picked up. Another pilot we shot called "Real People" that we're shopping to MTV etc. It's a drag queen asking real people questions that make them seem fabulous. It's a talk show.

SV: Oh God, Princess Di is going to watch you!

R: (Laughs) I'm accessible as a black woman. Our society doesn't know what to do with a black man. I've had to concentrate myself, but I'm very powerful and I'm not giving shade. It's all a positive love thing. A drag queen has more of a sense of humor, a TV takes it more seriously. But, as I say, 'You're born naked, all the rest is drag.' I'm showing people that I love myself and that is the RuPaul message. Love is wild. ▼

PHOTOS Renaldi & Zechman

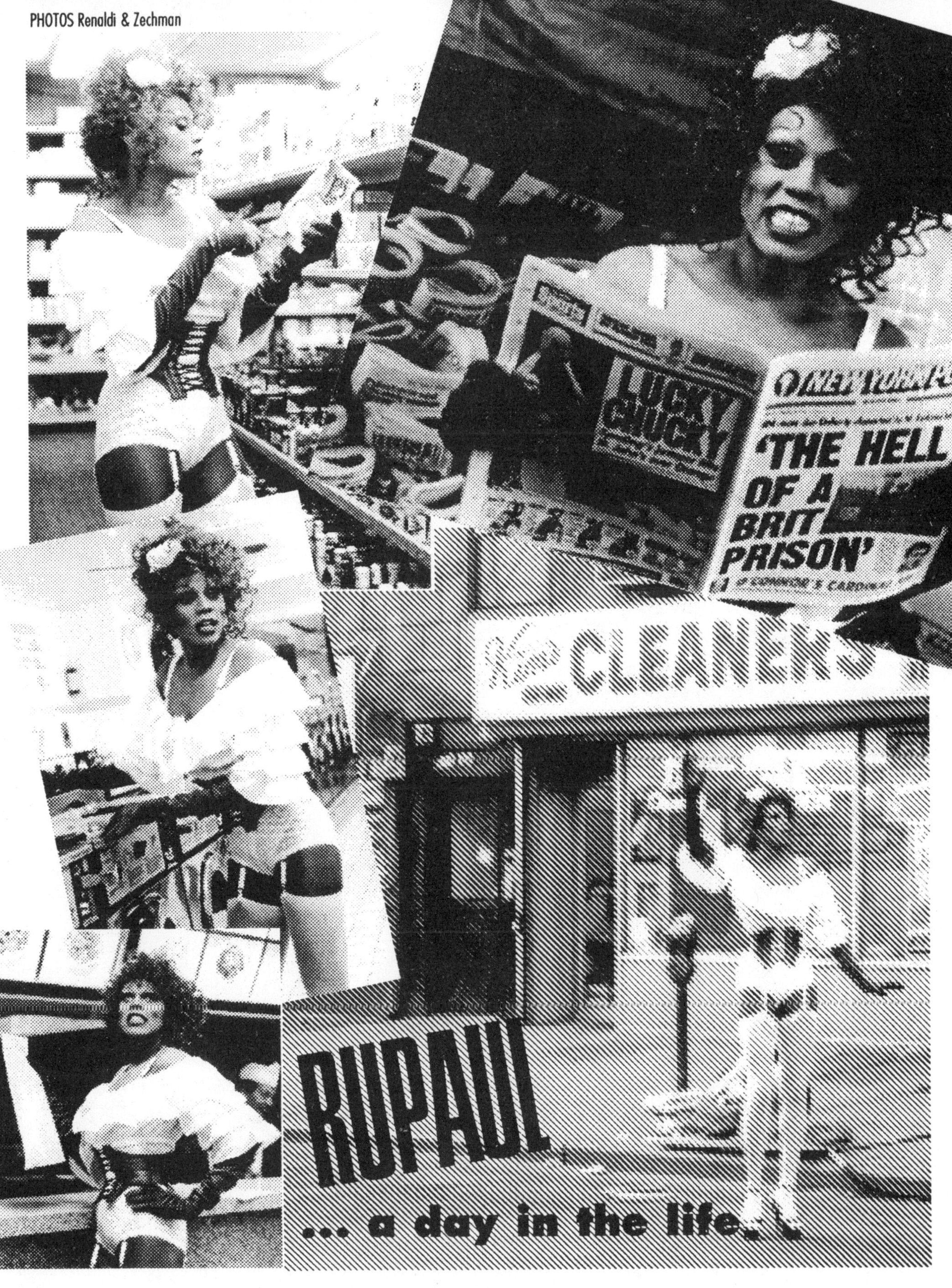

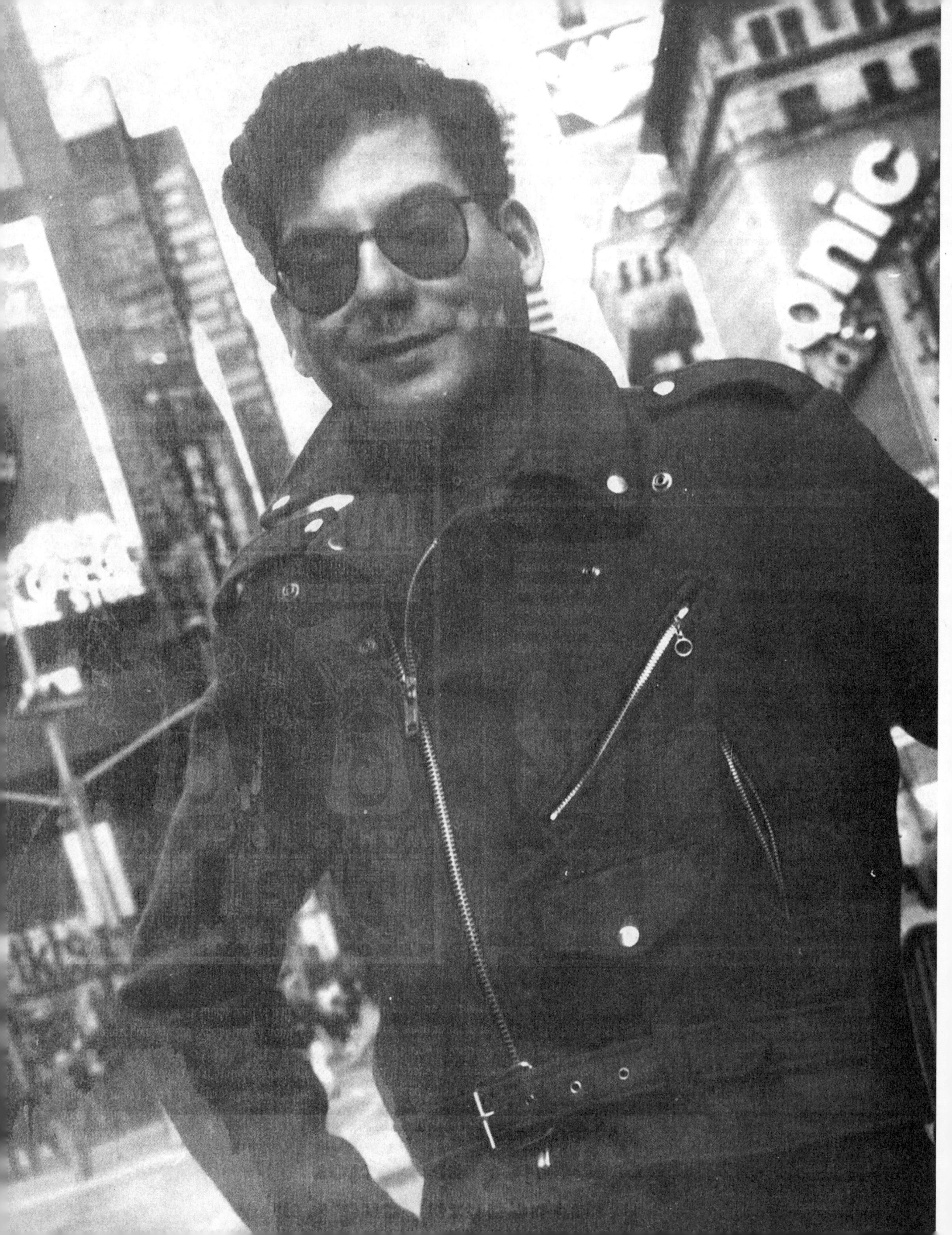

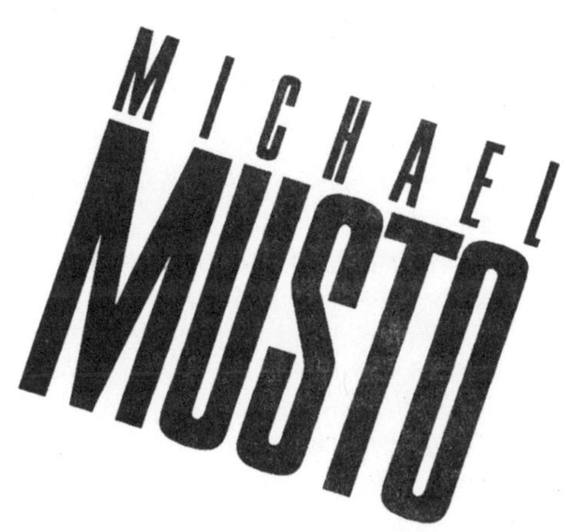

As an openly queer, no-holds-barred columnist for the *Village Voice*, Michael Musto seems to have found his niche in the drama that is New York City's nightlife and entertainment spheres. Reading any of his contributions to mags like *Vanity Fair, Penthouse Forum* and *Interview*, or his books "Downtown" and "Manhattan on the Rocks," it's apparent that despite the ingratiating schmooziness that's show biz, he don't kiss ass gratuitously; he kisses ass because it tastes good. I jumped at the chance to meet with him at his place after I recovered from the shock of simply finding him in the Manhattan Directory and answering the phone with, "Yes, this is Michael Musto. What kind of magazine is it? Ok, I'm free tomorrow." During my visit, he slurped what appeared to be ramen straight from the pot and I thought, "If only other legen-

Michael Musto: I followed Arthur Bell who did the column for thirteen years. He died of diabetes.

Trent Adkins: And you've been slowly but surely, since you've began doing the *Village Voice* column, developing it much in the way that he had? I mean, he's influenced you?

MM: In a way, but very much in my own way. A lot of people liked him a lot better... a lot of people didn't like him at all, so...

TA: Did the Voice find it necessary to have a gay columnist doing events and people? Did they choose you for being an openly gay writer?

MM: I don't know if they were specifically looking for that. I know they saw a lot of different applicants, some of whom were gay, some of whom weren't. But, when I started the column I wasn't that into gay politics. I was very open about that to the publisher at the time, David Shneiderman, and he said that's ok, we're not looking for another Arthur Bell, we want you to be yourself and take the ball and run with it. And that was the most liberating thing a columnist could hear is that this is your space and you're free to go wild with it.

TA: Do you ever get the desired results from angry things you've said in your column? Like, that thing with the Amaretto campaign where you let them have it because they rejected running an 'Amaretto di Musto' ad because you appeared too gay in your press kit.

MM: I try. I really try to shake people up and try to change the unfair things. Unfortunately, nothing

came of the Amaretto thing, they completely cowarded and sort of hoped it would just go away. I was very disappointed that GLAAD (Gay and Lesbian Alliance Against Defamation) did not rally to my support. I solicited them to help me and to do this big media campaign. I thought it was super fucked up because they got behind Greg Luganis, who's never admitted to being gay, when he was dropped off the Wheaties box. GLAAD rallied behind him as this big appalling thing, Wheaties against the gay community, and I thought, 'OK, it's because he's a major celebrity, even though he's not openly gay, they can support him.' I really could have used their help. I really think they (GLAAD) could have made a world of difference with the Amaretto thing and they didn't. They just refused to.

TA: Who else did you solicit to help you?

MM: It was before Queer Nation had been founded. Later they tried to help. ACT UP was strictly trying to address AIDS issues so it really wasn't in their arena.

TA: What do you think of Queer Nation, anyway? They're getting a lot of criticism from everywhere that they're ineffective and too militant, as bad to work with as the organizations they splintered from in protest. It's different from city to city. How do you perceive Queer Nation here?

MM: Well, it is different from city to city as well as from action to action. Each thing they do has different impacts. On a whole I think they're great. It does shake people up. Anything that startles peo-

ple is gonna make them change. That Amaretto column that I wrote did not invoke any immediate change. It's still gonna make people think and maybe it'll make that ad company think, well, maybe we should have more openly gay people in our campaigns. I've noticed lately there are a few more gays visible in advertising, and maybe that article had a tiny bit to do with it. Absolut is still running the Keith Haring after he died of AIDS. To me that shows a certain enlightenment and a refusal to be dictated by prejudice which in the case of Amaretto is truly disgusting because they want to bill themselves as a counterculture campaign. "These are people who are on the cutting edge." And of course at least three of the people are lesbian and gay but they got by, they played the game.

TA: How do you feel about your own celebrity? Do you think people are celebrating you for what you want to be celebrated for?

MM: I think any journalist has a very languished celebrity. Most of it is fall-out from the people you cover, I mean, you cover famous people so some of

it rubs off on you. But if you get too pleased with yourself as a celebrity you're just going to lose

track of what you're doing in the first place which is supposed to be reporting. On the other hand I love notoriety and I just promote myself like crazy. It's totally shameless, I'm very blatant about going after publicity and trying to make a name for myself. I have big birthday parties. Last year I had Mrs. Fletcher come out and do her big line, "I've fallen and I can't get up!" I had Sukreet Gabel sing at one of my parties. Then there are times where it

THING

PHOTO Renaldi & Zechman

kinda backfires. I don't know if you saw that piece in the *Chicago Tribune*...

TA: Yeah, I saw it.

MM: He compared me to Marcello Mastriani in "La Dolce Vita!"

TA: I think he confused it. It's actually kind of typical of the psuedo-hip reporting by the mainstream press in Chicago. I didn't think that was an accurate depiction of you really.

MM: The column name is based on "La Dolce Gilda," a short that Gilda Radner did on Saturday Night Live, which was a parody of "La Dolce Vita,' and also the quote he took about the movie is that Marcello sees his life as worthless in the decaying society of Rome and he can't change. So, I wrote the guy a letter, John Anderson, saying that I do not see my life as worthless and I really resent that and I listed all the things that I've done and how I have changed and how I love what I do. Of course, then he wrote me back saying, "Oh, I think you shape an entire community..." and all this bullshit that he neglected to put in the article.

TA: Do you think people misunder-

ILLUSTRATION Lee Kay

stand your zaniness for unprofessionalism?

MM: Well, when I was wearing the dresses, the hooped skirts and stuff, in a way that can feed into people's misconceptions and they don't take you as seriously as a journalist. A lot of people are always surprised, "Oh, he flounces around in feathered boas and yet he's obviously a responsible journalist. Like, my editors at the *Village Voice* were always amazed, like, "Oh, he's really professional and he's a perfectionist." Because I go down to every word and I want to constantly rephrase it 'til I think it's right. But sometimes the public image you present is very important to how people perceive you. So, now suddenly I've appeared in magazines in suits and things which is also ridiculous. And suddenly you get some respectful publicity based totally on image. So, to constantly tweak them, every once in awhile I'll show up looking... I'm not throwing anything out.

TA: Are you working on any plays right now?

MM: I'm working on a

movie right now that the Limelight is producing. Peter Gatien, the owner of the Limelight, is producing a documentary version of the the club kids. I just got the contracts today. I'm not sure I should be talking about this.

TA: So you'll be doing the screenplay?

MM: Yeah, I'm gonna write the screenplay. I guess it'll be like the club kid version of "Paris is Burning."

TA: What about these club kids? To what do you attribute their origins and their direction? Some people say they'll mutate into this or that...

MM: Well, they're already mutations. I always alternate between thinking they're really fabulous and fresh and energetic to thinking they're Satan itself. I think it came from a general disillusionment of young people in this city and in this country with the state of the country with all the problems coming down with AIDS and homelessness, things that make New York a bleak place to live sometimes. Just their total boredom and frustration with being told not to do drugs or have sex and a total lack of ambition in life other than a desire to become famous for any reason. That's all they can think of; "I want to be famous." They don't know why they want to be famous. That's probably what has created it.

TA: Are any of them really talented though?

MM: Some of them are. I think Ernie Glam is a really talented designer. And for what he does, Michael Alig is very talented He created this whole movement and he comes up with all these party ideas and puts it together. To me, nightlife is art and he's one of the best practitioners of it. But I think too many of them are just interested in escaping into the night and doing drugs and dressing up. I don't make any judgment on that. I think when you're young that's your time to sow your wild oats and they have every right to do it. I just wish more of them had more direction. When I first started the column everyone on the scene had some viable talent, and it was very exciting. Ann Magnuson and Keith Haring and all these people were starting out. John Sex..... God, two of those three are dead now!

TA: Uh-Hum.

MM: It seemed then that everyone had a purpose, everyone had a reason for being in the clubs. This is where it all came together. All different kinds of people went to clubs, not just club kid; editors, art dealers, and everybody came there for inspiration. This was around the mid eighties during the time of the Palladium and Area. Now, it just seems like only club kids go out and they just want to lose themselves and have fun. Which is fine. ▼

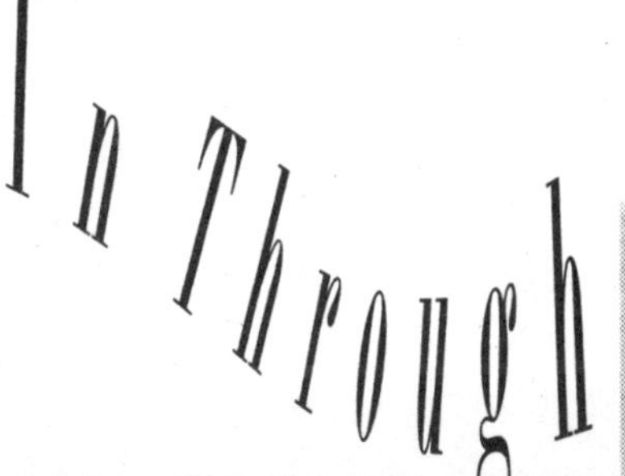

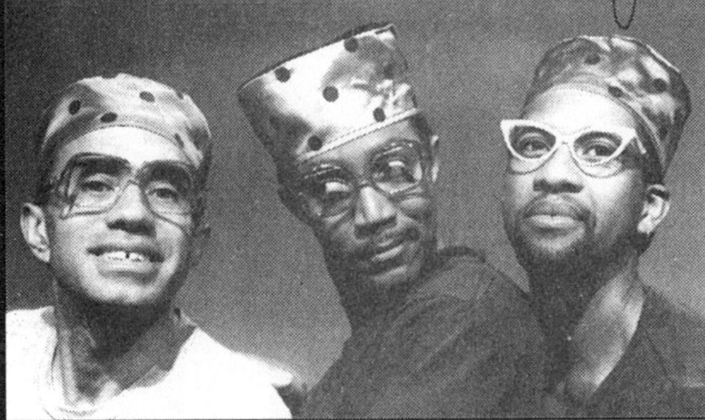

May 22 – June 14

Third Annual Series of Performance & Multi Media Art by Bisexuals, Lesbians & Gays

May 22/23	Chicago Performs
May 29	Cecilia Dougherty *Coal Miner's Granddaughter*
May 30	Who's Zoomin' Who: Lesbians on Tape
June 5/6	*Lisa Kron All My Hopes & Dreams*
June 12-14	Pomo Afro Homos *Fierce Love: Stories from Black Gay Life*
June 13	Pomo Afro Homos Workshop

For information and reservations call 312.666.7737

WILLI NINJA

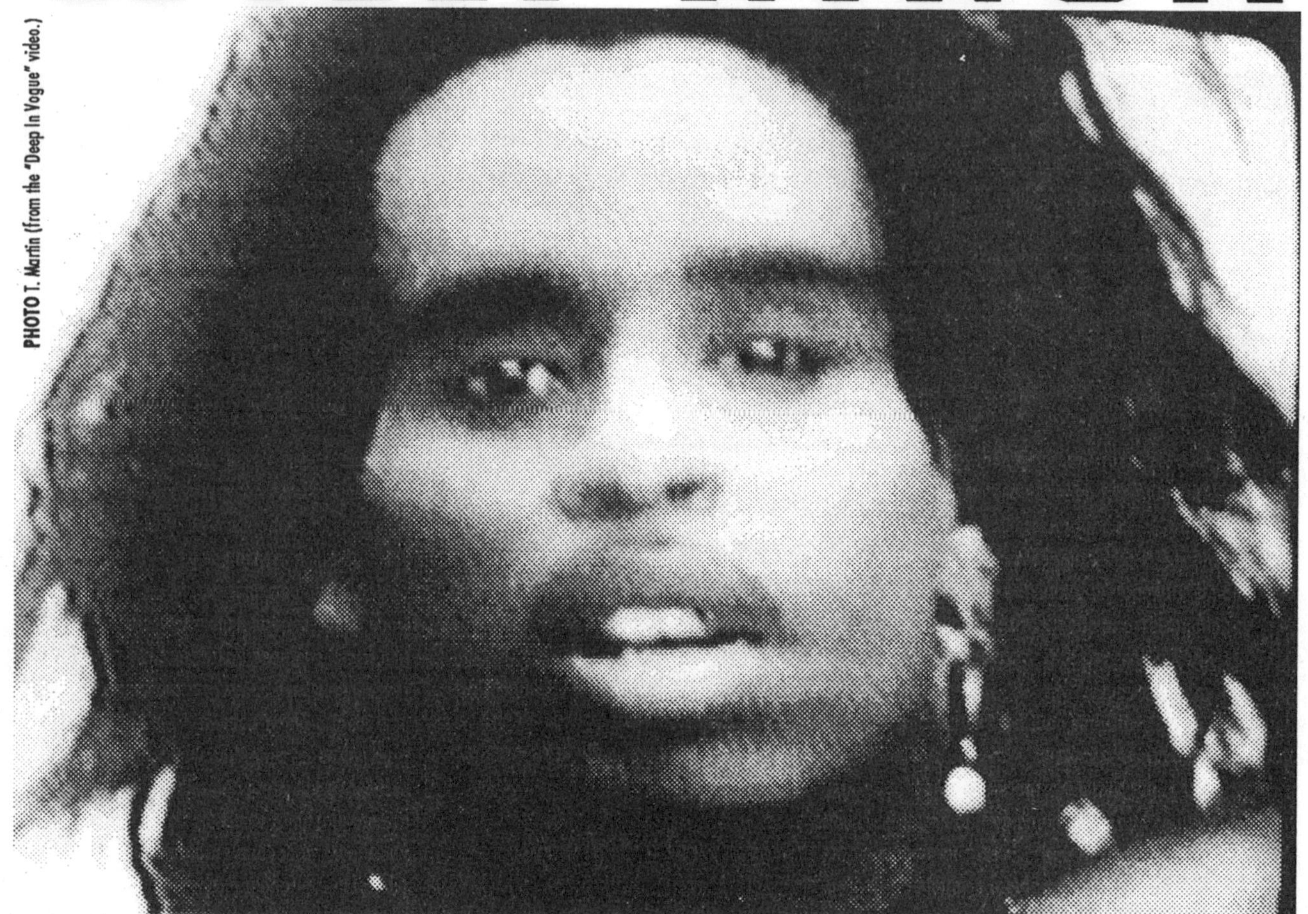

THING 34

Willi Ninja was born to dance. With no formal training, he has honed a whole new creative dance language: vogueing.   Malcolm McLaren captured him for the definitive "Deep in Vogue" video, and suddenly vogueing was "crossing over." His sense of style and movement made him a hot commodity as a fashion runway choreographer, and brought him work in the music video industry as well.

I caught wind that he was in Chicago for a few days doing a corporate trade show, and tracked him down. The only time for an interview would be at the crack of dawn, in the dressing room while the girls finished hair and makeup. Without the aid of caffeine I made the early call. My fears of meeting a "fierce ruling diva" ended when I met Willi. Truly friendly and down to earth, in a model-model world, Willi has his head on straight.

Robert Ford: Let's start with one of those questions you've probably answered a million times: how do you give the history of vogueing?

Willi Ninja: Not a million, about four million five hundred times...As you know, the dance started in the black drag balls in Harlem. It progressed literally, I'd say, from the hand movements the drag queens used to do with the "La Cage Aux Folles" look; big feathered fandance moves. And because there were a lot of them that didn't want to get up in drag. A lot of the boys that didn't want to go up in drag wanted stuff to do for themselves, categories they could compete in and win. I'm not sure who created or invented it, but it goes back to the early seventies. The moves progressed from that fandancing; also out of the fashion magazines. Making the moves a little more drastic and to the beat. Old school was a lot of hand movement, hardcore, quick hand movements and a lot of poses to the beat of the music. And as the years progressed, they just kept going on and on, adapting and adding new things. It's basically your challenge dance. Kind of like what breaking was for the homeboys, vogueing was for the gay population. Instead of fighting, you took it out on the dance floor. It has that meaning, too. But it is right now, as far as I'm concerned, a major art form created by the black and latin gay community. It should be seen as that, and not just taken as "oh, let mo throw a little shade here and there." A lot of people, even in the gay community, see the shady side of it, not the art form side of it.

RF: Do you see it gaining more respect as an art form?

WN: Yeah, it's gaining a lot of respect. PBS has aired different programs with it, "House of Tress", "Everybody Dance Now". It's getting respect in the dance world, as an art form. Which is good. A lot of professional dancers feel that there's no technique. As a friend of mine said, "there is technique in a dance if they've studied it and do it to perfection. So that's their technique. There's technique in freestyle and hip-hop, whatever." Just like in ballet, just like in jazz. So give us our due. For me, it is an art form. It is a dance.

RF: Have you studied dance?

WN: No, no formal training. My formal training was watching PBS, my mother taking me to the Apollo, being fascinated by music and dance. That was my teacher, and a teacher only corrects what's already inside of you. You don't have to have one person standing there yelling at you to be your teacher. If you have an adaptable mind, anything can be your teacher.

RF: Are you in touch with the New York ball scene much at all?

WN: Not really. When I am, I go in as a judge. My competition days are looong gone! I'm supposed to — if I'm in town in July — judge the Chanel ball, because they're starting theirs up again. I do like to go back to say "hey, I didn't forget." To help other people get out and try to further their careers as well. It's hard sometimes when you're trying to keep yourself floating, and you want to keep yourself in the eye, but you can't help nobody else if you can't help yourself.

RF: Have you seen that scene change much over the years? Has it grown any?

WN: It's grown as far as new ideas and concepts because now it's multiracial, almost. Now, some heterosexuals taking part. And I also see it getting kind of evil, because the new kids that are coming in are again taking the wrong idea; taking the bad instead of the good

RF: What did you think of Jenny's film, and the aftermath.

WN: The aftermath? I didn't even know that there was going to be any aftermath. It was just a pure fluke.

I enjoyed the film. I thought it was well done. It kinda educated people. It's like one section, not the whole, one small section of the black and latin gay community in New York, not the whole. A lot of people take the wrong thing and think that it's like the whole and it's not. That's what I try to do on a lot of the interviews and stuff is correct that. But it's just an education showing what happens when people have two things going against them: color and sexual preference. No, three things, excuse me: for a lot of them low income. They have to come up with new ideas and concepts to create their own life...

RF: ...create their own social order.

WN: Yeah, you're gonna create your own social world because you have no chance of being successful in the real world. Some of them do, but it's such a small number in that community. It's unreal! And what I find also is lot of middle class black gays (or some of the rich ones) like, "Ugh! How could they! Why don't they do this for themselves and get their

lives together!" So I say, "But darling, where were you? What kind of a neighborhood did you come from and what kind of education did you have because of your money? Give these kids their due. It might not be your cup of tea but at least they did something that kept them out of trouble for a little while. Gave them some way to let loose their energies and frustrations. You have the chance to go on; give these kids their chance to do something for themselves." We've got to stick together, not fight each other.

RF: There are so many factions in the gay community

WN:...Too many damn factions as far as I'm concerned.

RF: Those people who want a "straight-acting/straight appearing" slide into the mainstream thing and they don't want drag queens and leather queens to be visible.

WN: Darling no. Catch it: you're being hated, not because you're feminine, not because you're a drag queen, not because you're a leather queen, not because you're macho: you're being hated because you like another man, and you are a man. When you get that in your head, darling you better stop hating that next person that's in the same boat that you are. If you're hating that next person, what gives you the right to get something better than that person? You're doing the same thing that the heterosexual world is doing to you. My point of view of those people: they're full of s-h-i-t. Capital S-H-I-T with an exclamation point! You can quote me on that.

RF: Have you sensed a prejudice against voguers, that people expect them to all be boosters or shady...

WN: You saw in the film where I stressed "I have the receipts, I bought this!" I wanted to let them know that I'm not one of those people. They assume that all of us are. It's a hateful thing, because certainly not all of us are. You have Juan from the House of Adonis who dances with C&C, he's never lifted or done drugs in his life. You have Lance Adonis who's now in Disneyworld as a Disney character. You have Kevin from the house of Magnifique, working with Crystal Waters. There's a lot of children out there that work. From House of Africa there's a makeup artist in Europe. A lot of us have gone on and done well. And we have to keep this positive image out there, because they're assuming it's like, "watch them." ▼

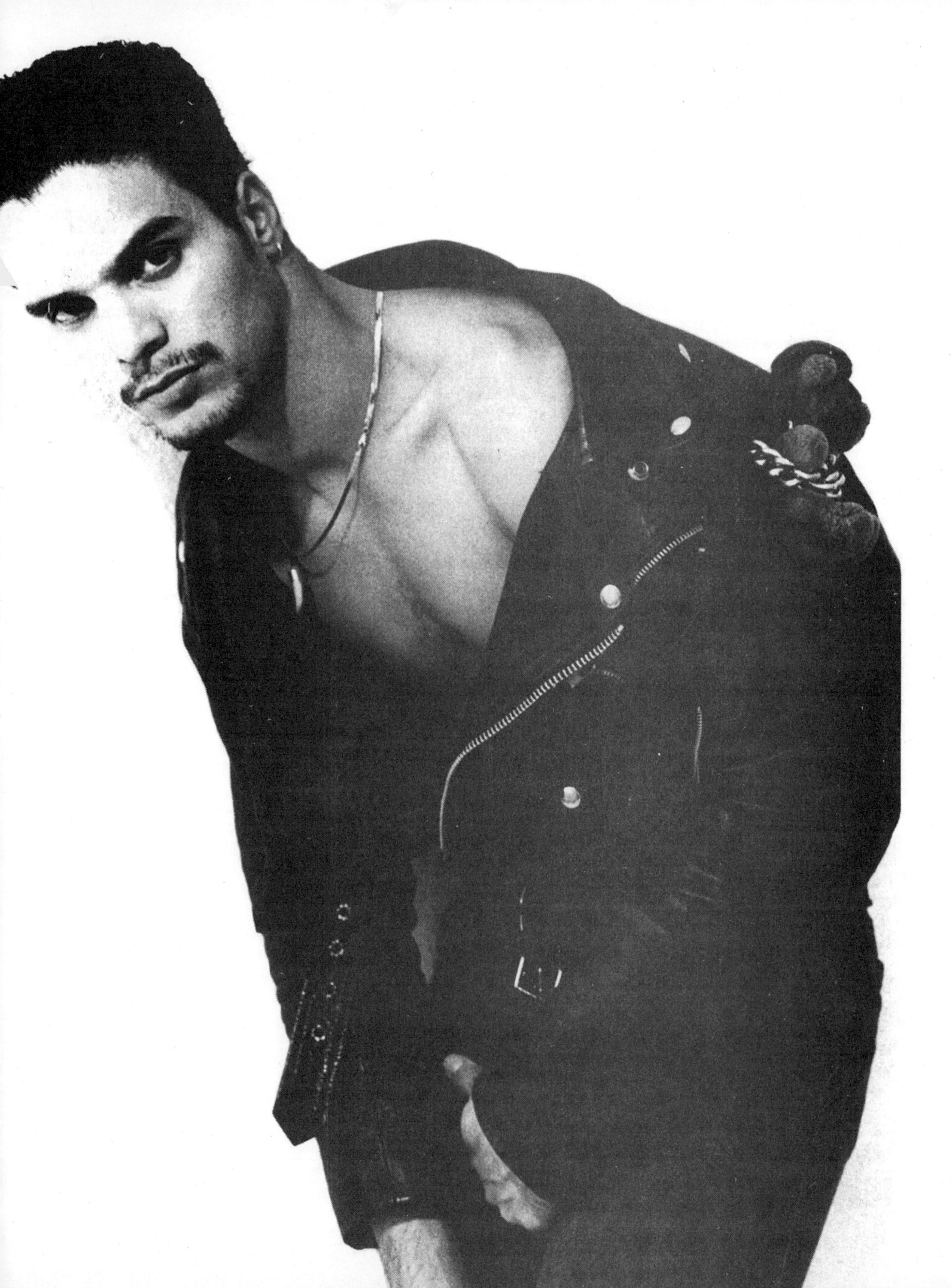

He had come to Chicago with the Carmen Xtravaganza entourage for the Miss Continental USA pageant in 1991. It was my first chance to really hang out with people from New York, and it sparked a desire to one day visit the city (this after I'd heard only the bad and the ugly). My newfound interest in the world of balls and vogueing was treated to lots of firsthand information, which later proved useful, once I finally made it to the east coast and walked my first ball (and no, I didn't get a trophy). Having already made friends with Hector, I had a familiar face to look forward to, and was greeted with the most heartfelt welcomes (all New Yorkers aren't assholes). Our exchanges have continued to the present, so that when Hector arrived for a visit in Chicago this past January, he didn't hesitate to look me up. At the *Thing* office, he was introduced to Trent (who immediately lost control of his juice flow), and with Leona's home delivery on the table, we delved into much cuisine, conversation and kee-kee...

Aaron Avant Garde: Pretend that I'm dumb and explain what this Xtravaganza stuff is all about. Is that your real last name?

Hector Xtravaganza: It can be, I've had it for ten years.

A: Where does it come from?

H: The House of Xtravaganza. I've been a Ganza for ten years now, but I've been walking balls for twelve...

A: Anyone familiar with "Paris is Burning" gets the flavor of what he's talking about.

H: Yeah, they know more or less what's going on with the Ganzas.

A: So you were one of their original members?

H: Since day one. We started off with about ten members, and I was like ... the third one...

A: How old were you then?

H: Let's not get personal.

A: Oh, she's not giving out ages... she's twenty plus! (kee-kee)

H: Before we started the House of Xtravaganza it started all with the black kids (I'm half black and half hispanic, for the record). They never wanted a Hispanic or white boy to enter their balls...

A: Oh, we get the real dirt now...

H: Yes this is the true dirt. I'm talking twelve years of history here.

A: So the Hispanics were the next to try and move in?

H: Well, I went to one, and I loved it, the way everyone was competing, and I said, "I could do that".

Every time I walked these balls and snatched a trophy, I always had to fight my way out, always...

A: Out of the building?

H: Literally, yes. Because the black kids weren't going for it. So I would get my trophy, and before I'd get to the door, I'd have only the top of it. I never left with a whole trophy...

A: OK, a hood ornament! (kee-kee)

H: Very that. They didn't want us in their houses, you know, Hispanics...

A: That's why you guys started a Latin house...

H: No. We didn't start just as a Latin house, because we have black kids in our house. It's just mostly Latin. And the name is very Latin, you know, *Xtrrrravagaaaanzaa.*

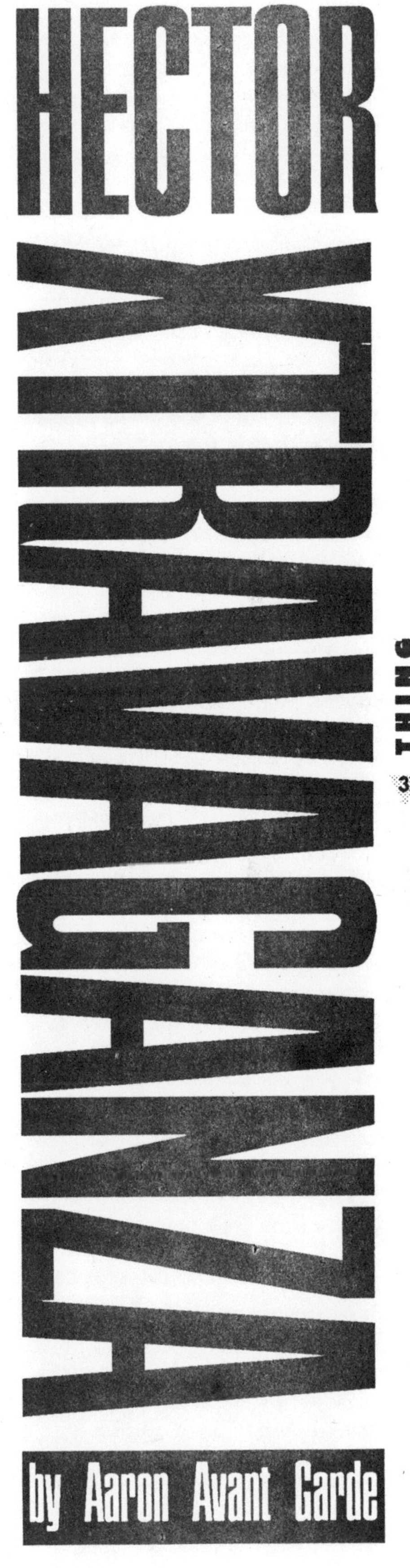

A: All right for "south of the border"...

H: You see? International! So, fighting our way out , we just decided to start our own house. And here I was in Georgia now (I used to go to Georgia every summer). Father Hector founded the house, and then he called me and said, "come on down, you're in the House of Xtravagaaaanza!" Now when we started walking the balls, it was much easier, because we had our own house . At our first ball, we came home with thirty-eight trophies out of fifty- eight . And at the next ball, it was about forty out of fifty...

A: Can you tie in the breakdancing craze with this somewhere? 'Cause I've read somewhere that people know vogueing has been around since before breaking...

H: Vogueing has been around for about three and a half decades, about thirty-five years.

A: I saw a special on PBS, where this breaker was saying that you really can't separate all those dances, like breaking , vogueing, pop locking...

H: I think with breakdancing and vogueing, there still is a big difference. Breaking, you're just throwing yourself all over the floor, but with vogueing you start from the top and work your way down, you know, and you "grace" the floor. On top, you use your arm's control, and you work your way down into dips, flips and splits, and so forth, but you 'grace' the floor. The floor can be yours, if you want it.

A: Let me stop you for a second. So, are you a native New Yorker?

H: No, I was born in Puerto Rico, but at the age of two months, I moved to Georgia. So for the first seven years of my life, I was with my father's side of the family, which is the black side...

A: So you lived in Georgia and you visited New York in the summers?

H: No. I lived in Georgia , then I moved to N Y . So every summer I started going back and forth.

A: But you were in Georgia when they "drafted" you?

H: Yeah, exactly. It was fun, I tell ya, and for ten years of my life I've been Hector Xtravaganza, and I'm well respected as Hector Xtravaganza.

A: Would you say that you guys are pretty much like family?

H: We started off as a family, a group, y'know what I'm saying? We were always together,

always meeting. We never had to say, "let's meet here", or whatever...we just knew. Like at the beach, we had our spot. If we knew we were going, we just met there. And in Central Park, same thing. Wherever, we always knew where we were going to be. At the clubs, we were always together, always.

Trent Adkins: What clubs did you go to?

H: Oh, the Sound Factory, now. First it was Crisco's...

T: Who's spinning now? Frankie's not anymore, right?

H: No. David Depino Xtravaganza. I follow him wherever he goes.

A: I thought Junior Vasquez was back there ...

H: He comes and goes. They fire him , then they hire him, then they fire him, then they hire him...

A: Ooh...! Dirt, dirt, dirt!

H: It's the truth!

A: Yeah, David Depino was punking us silly at Trax...

H: That's my baby. Wherever he goes, I'm there, always. The Xtravaganzas always follow him. He moved to Florida, and we went down there to party with him. Then he missed us, so he just moved back to New York. There's nothing like New York... except Chicago.

T: Are there any other clubs that you go to?

H: I go to Sound Factory, Trax , and then the Shelter... the best sound system in NYC.

**A: That's the New York Shelter...
T: Not to be confused with Chicago's Shelter...**

H: Well, I'm going to the Shelter tonight, so I'll let you know the difference... Oh! And then they have the boys... real boys... I always have a fab time at the Shelter... and just the system... the system is wonderful! It takes control of you.

T: Who's spinning there regularly?

H: I'm not sure...

A: I heard Larry Levan was there.

H: No, chile..!

T: Did you ever go to Zanzibar in New Jersey?

H: No, but a friend of mine manages it , and he keeps telling me to go, but I don't, because he's living for me and shit. So, I stay away.

T: I want to know, between the balls and stuff, what kind of work

are you busying yourselves with. When the movie "Paris Is Burning" hit, did you get a lot of offers?**

H: No. I don't like the movie at all, and if you want to talk dirt about the movie...

A: Yes! All the behind-the-scenes stuff!

H: Ask the questions, and you shall get it.

T: What don't you like about it ?

H: It just makes homosexuals look like wannabes, like we do nothing but steal, we don't have a home... when they were interviewing the young kid...

T: Those two little guys?

H: Yeah... it's two o'clock in the morning, what are you doing here?..." Oh, my mother's this, or I don't have a ... you know, she's gone, he's gone..." but there's *reasons* why those kids are out there. I became a runaway because my ma didn't accept the fact that I am what I am. My mother was very much, "I'd rather you be a hoodlum"...

A: No!

H: Yeah! Than be gay.

T: When did you come out to her?

H: When I was twelve.

T: So do you think these are the sentiments felt by a lot of people that were in the movie?

H: When Jenny (Livingston) first started, she said it was a school project. And the black kids accepted her, because it was a school project. For a white girl to be in Harlem, it wasn't easy. They let her bring in her cameras, and the project turned out to be a movie, and the whole bit. I didn't sign a release form, and a majority of these kids didn't. And Paris herself, the founder of "Paris is Burning," she's been using that for many years.

A: Every time she throws a ball, she uses that title?

H: Exactly. And now Jenny took it over. Paris is suing Jenny, and Pepper is, and I think Octavia is going to be suing her, also.

T: Did she interview you?

H: She wanted to, but I asked my mother what I should do. She said to be careful, because I don't know what she may use it for. And in the credits, they have my real name there. They don't have me down as Hector Xtravaganza. And you never know what may come out of this. I may make a record , you know what I'm saying, and do a video with a girl, and then someone like Arsenio will come out of the woodwork and say, "Weren't you in that gay movie? That drag, gay movie?".

T: Well, how do you feel about that? Do you think that being openly gay or identified is going to be limiting yourself from certain job opportunities?

H: I do. There are certain things I say no to just because of this fuckin' movie.

T: A lot of people criticize the film as being exploitative... I mean, in a lot of ways, the film transcended what a typi-cal movie like that would do. And you know, more white people saw that movie than black peo-ple, much less gay. The majority of people that saw that movie were straight white people, and like... middle aged.

H: Straight white people, that were doing nothing but laughing; everything was funny to them. I can't say that that's the true ball world. Just like in the straight world, there's a fuck-up, and then there's someone that's doing good. It's the same thing in the gay world. They show this one in the streets, but they don't show why he's stealing. Honestly, when I was younger, I was thirteen or fourteen, I was a shoplifter. But the only reason I did was because my mother, when she found out I

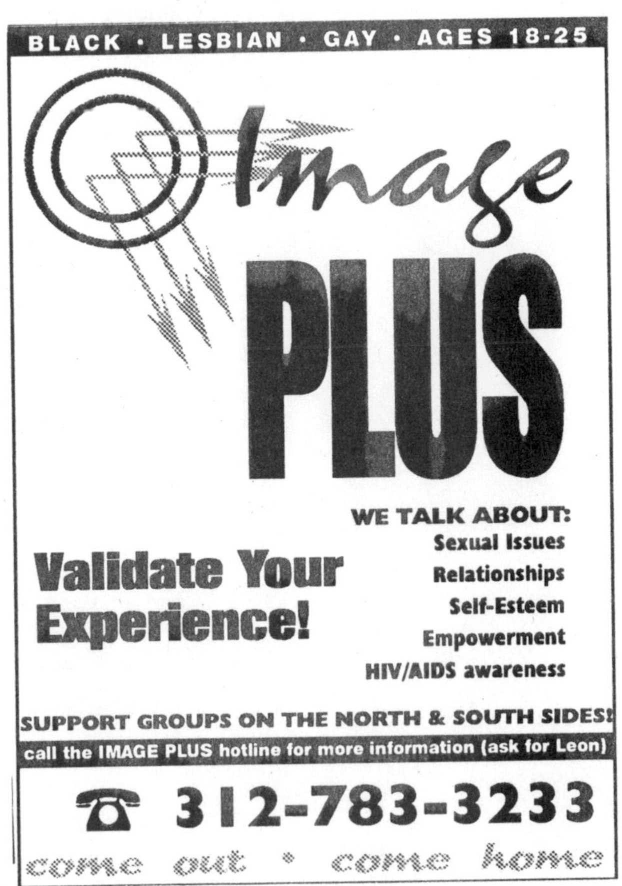

was gay, she didn't want to give me anything. So I always went for the thing's I needed. If I needed a pair of shoes to go to school, it wasn't just to go hang out. My mother never gave me the money I asked for. So then I went out and stole it. I'm the

baby out of twelve—that's eleven boys and one girl—and I was always getting seconds.

A: We hear you're a designer.

H: Yes, I make my own madness.

T: So what do you want to do career-wise? Are you going to be an entrepreneur, star model, actor...?

H: I feel like modeling and dancing don't last forever. So while you've got it, use and abuse it. So far, I've been to Osaka and Tokyo, Japan, doing runway and dancing in videos and performing. As far as designing, it can go as far as you want it to go. Right now I'm working on another project that has to do with "Paris is Burning," but I don't want to count my chickens before they're hatched.

A: Is it going to be another film?

H: I don't want to say, but this magazine will be the first to hear about it. ▼

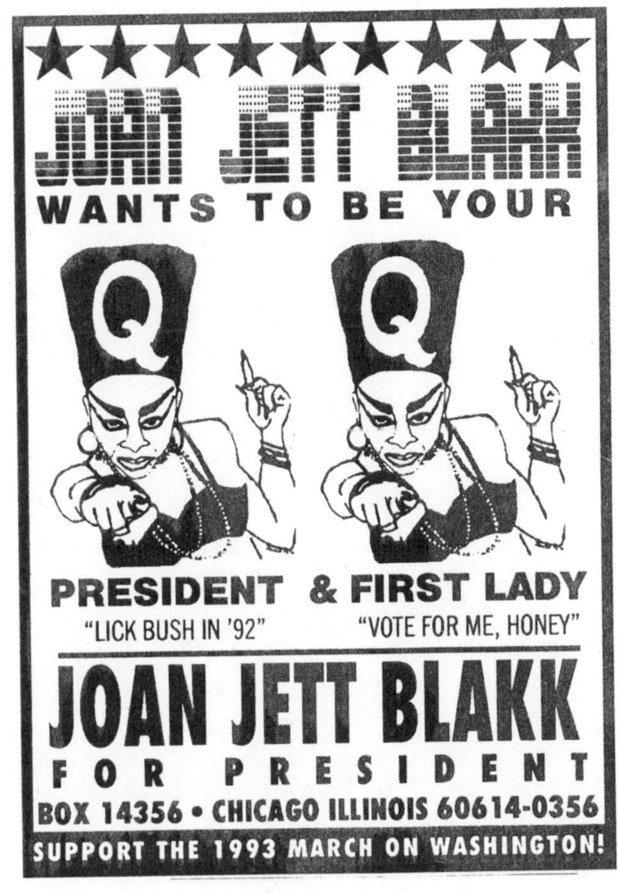

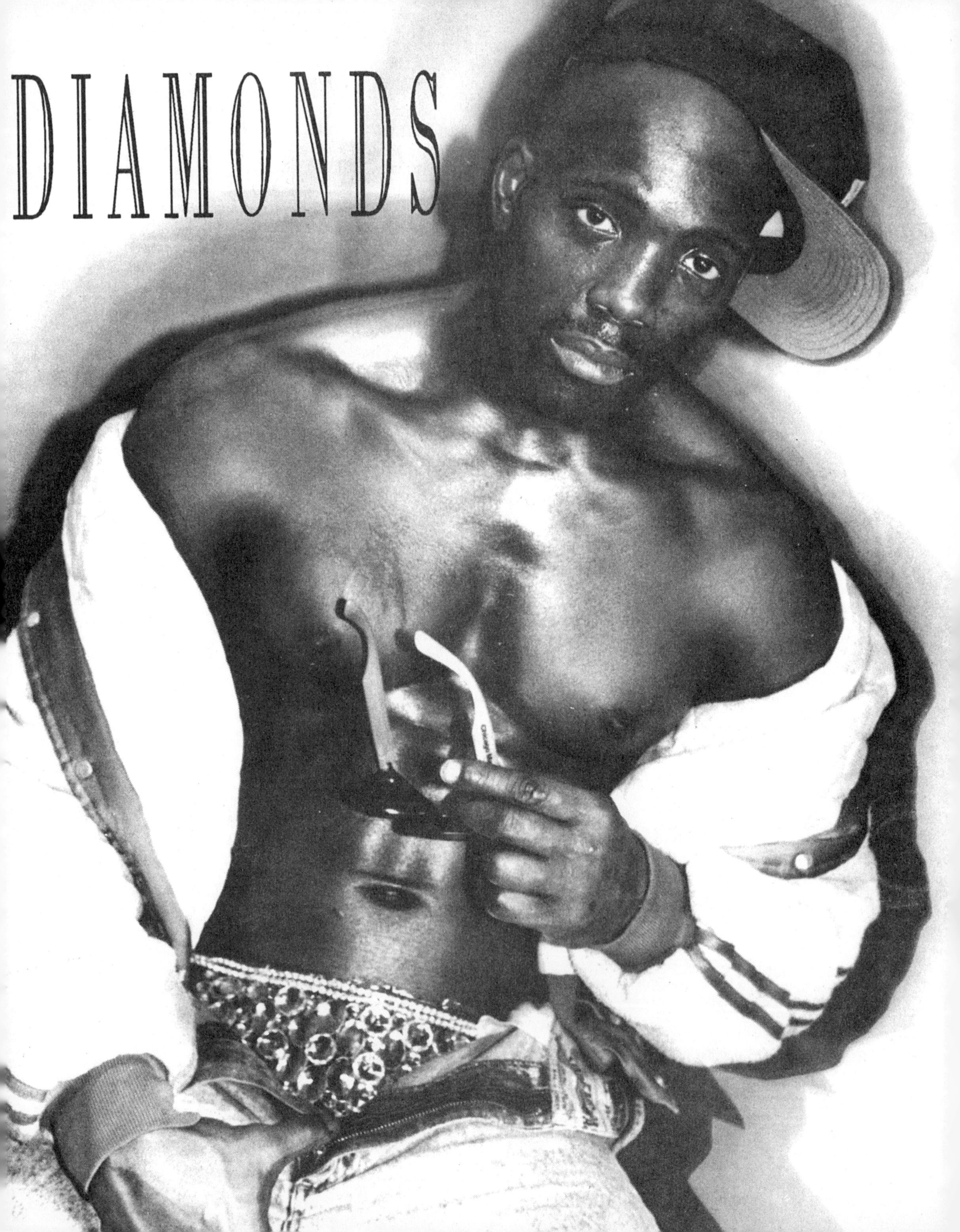
DIAMONDS

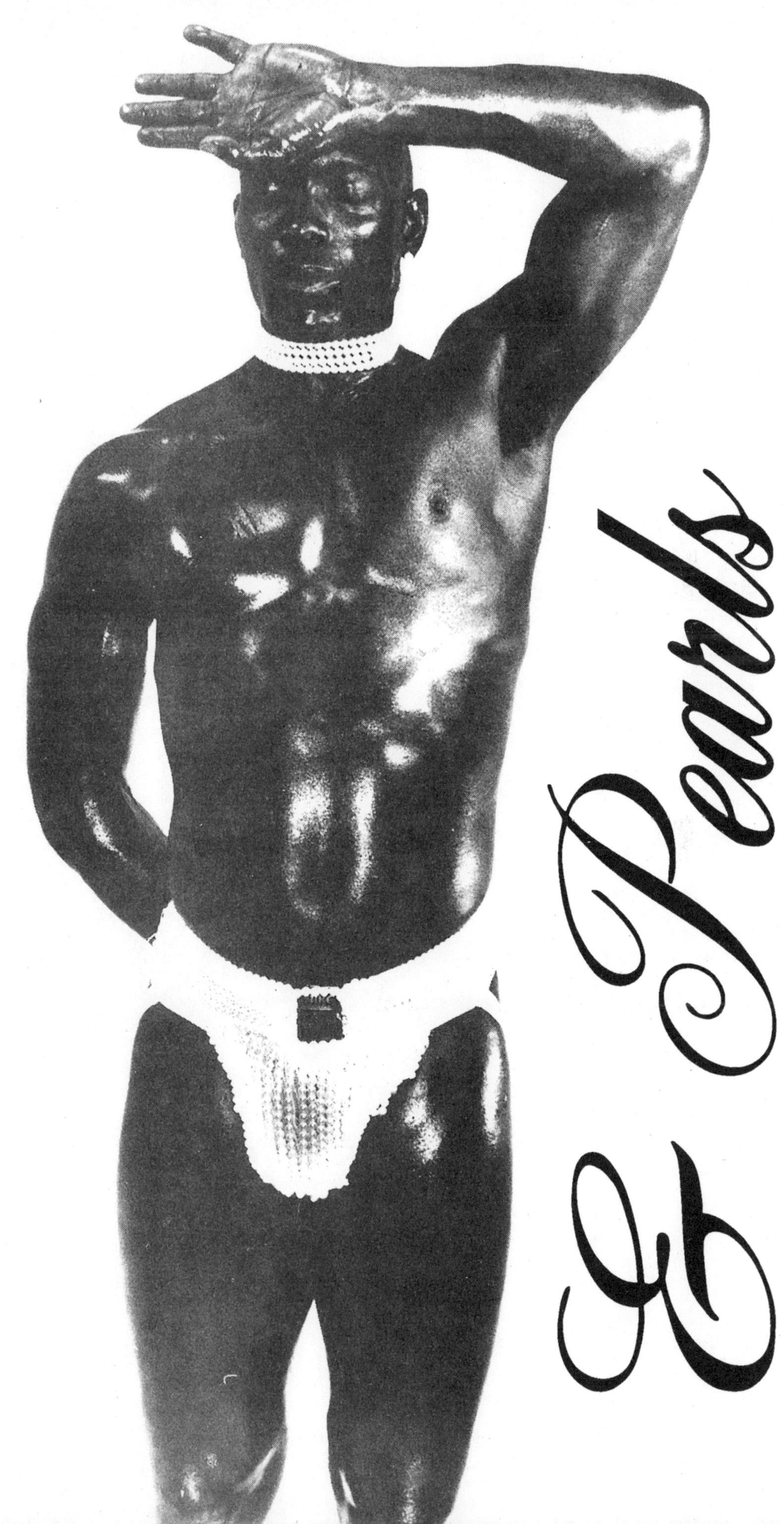
Pearls

Photos & Styling SCOTT FREE

Model JEFFREY PHILLIPS

LEAD THE WAY

Set the pace for the 3rd Annual AIDS Walk...

Organize a Walk Team at your company and get this year's walk off to a brisk start.

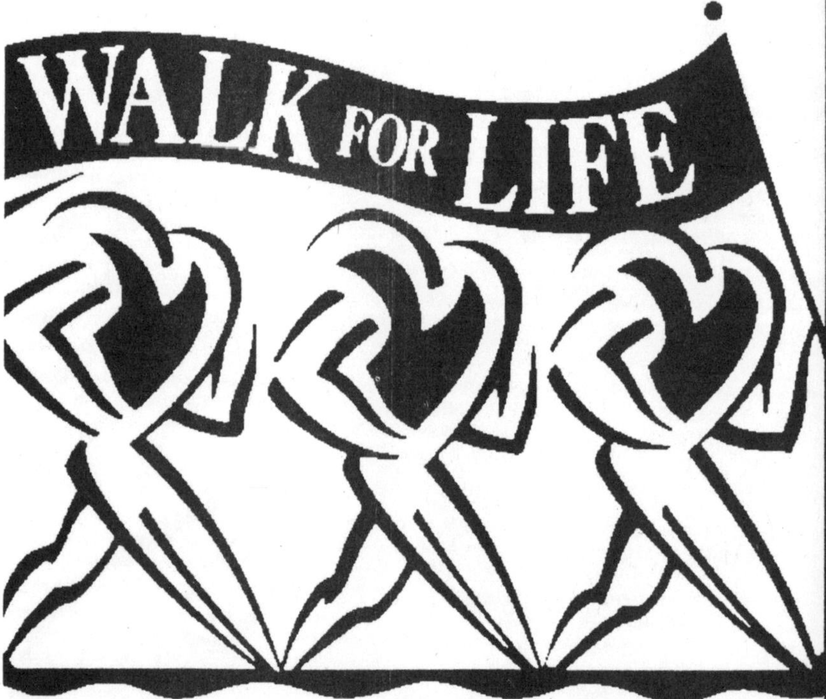

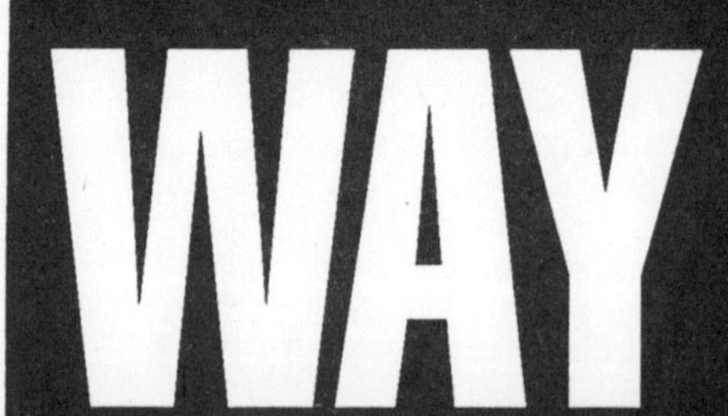

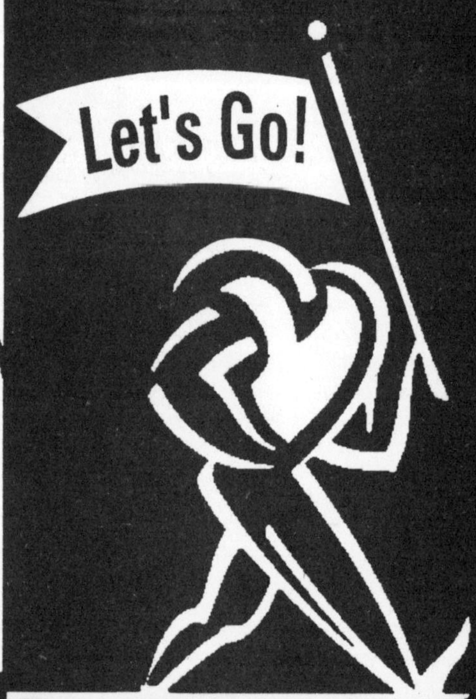

Walking as a Team in 1992

Yes, I want to help organize a Walk Team at my company. Please send me the Walk Team Captains kit.

Name: ____

Address:____

City: ___________________ State: _________ Zip: ___________

Company Name: _______________________________________

Phone: (day) ___________________ (evening) ________________

To get the new Team Captains Kit, which includes dozens of ideas that companies have successfully used to build Walk Teams send in this coupon to: AIDS Walk Chicago, 4753 N. Broadway, Chicago, IL 60640, call 334-0448 or fax this coupon to 271-6398.

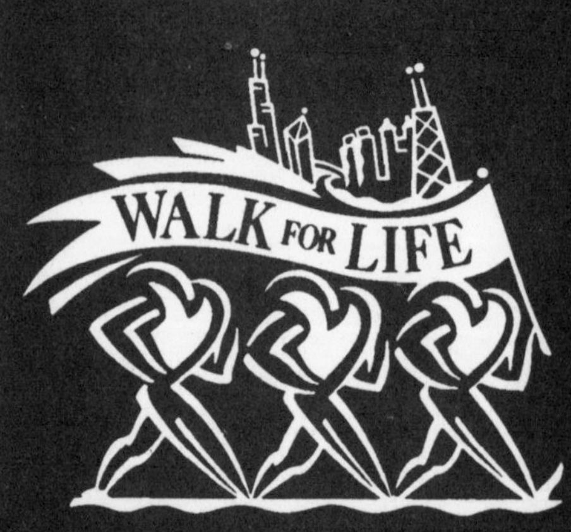

"THE WHOLE WORLD CAN KISS MY ASS TONIGHT!"

Lauren tried to decide exactly when to put the bullet through Cleveland's heart as she sat at the bar, one hand wrapped around the frosty glass holding her fast-disappearing vodka on the rocks, the other cradling the gun in her purse on her lap. Whitney Houston bellowed the chorus of her new hit, doing her own background vocals, declaring again and again and again:

I'm your baby tonight

Lauren wished the deejay would play something else because it seemed as if he had been mixing and remixing that song forever. She had at first been afraid to venture into this low-down neighborhood that showed up regularly in the newspapers as reporters tallied the body count from the shootings and stabbings and the occasional overdose. But she had chuckled (well, almost chuckled) when she reminded herself that she was carrying a gun. She had slipped it out of her brother-in-law's secret hiding place while visiting her sis-

ter's house a few days ago. That's when she had finally made up her mind about what to do about Cleveland.

As she watched the gay men and drag queens jockeying for space to express themselves on the tiny dance floor of LeBaron's, she wondered if she should wait until she caught Cleveland embracing some female wannabe and then shoot him. Or what if he fell into the arms of that rough-looking guy in the hooded sweatshirt, baggy jeans, and backward baseball cap in the corner? Or should she go up behind Cleveland as he danced, tap him on the shoulder, pull the gun from her purse, curse him, then kill him? And what if someone tried to stop her? Kill them too, she quickly decided.

Miss Latasha heard the thumping of the bass eight feet away from LeBaron's door, and when she put one of her black velvet pumps through the door, the bouncer said, "Hi, Tasha," and smiled at her as he did every Friday night. She knew he was shocked

by

julian

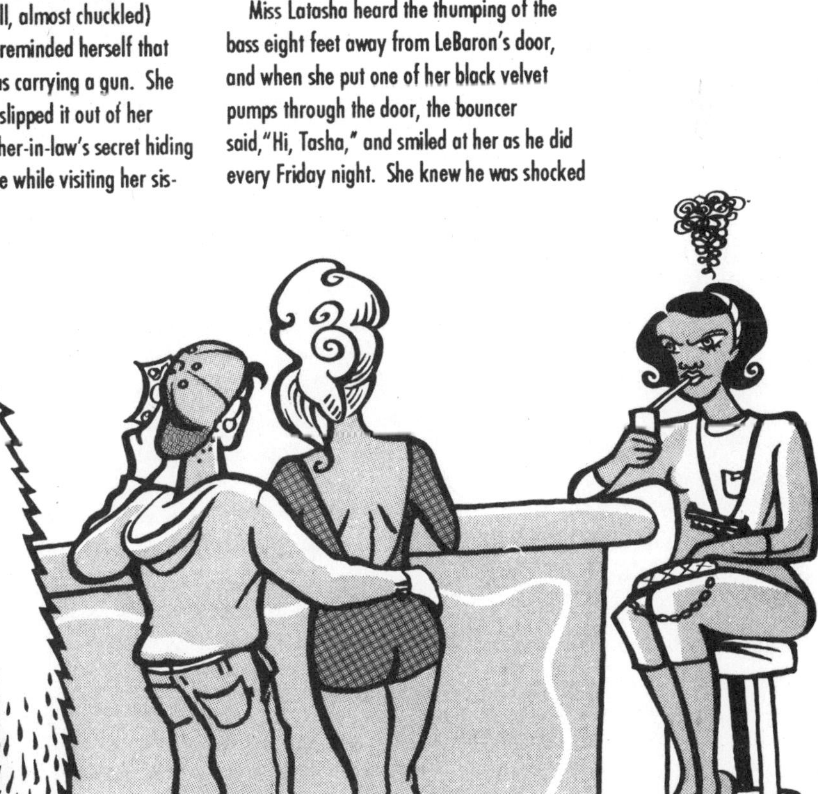

"THE WHOLE WORLD CAN KISS MY ASS TONIGHT!"

to see how toned down she looked tonight. No Diana Ross mane of hair cascading down her back, no sprayed-on-looking dress.

Instead she wore a simple black dress — above the knee to show off her well-toned legs (from lots of basketball and track in high school), black stockings, heels. Yes, her back was out — and a beautiful one it was, too. Smooth and brown, no pimples, ever. Her hair greased and pulled back into a French roll, a rhinestone comb holding it in place. Fake diamonds in the shape of starfish on her ears because —toned down or not — she was still MISS LATASHA. She had been coming to LeBaron's since 1975, when she used to stuff socks or toilet tissue in her bras for breasts. Now she had real ones (well, okay, fake "real ones"). Beautiful, centerfold breasts. And the beard which she used to cover up with layers of makeup was gone forever ("When are you going to get electrocuted, " an older drag queen had asked years ago). And most people had forgotten that her name had once been Leonard. Even her mother called her Latasha now. And her fans put a big, fat MISS in front of it.

As she made her way across the barroom, she deliberately zigzagged the dance floor where the lights were brightest when they flashed, and where all eyes would see her, removing her fake fur coat and slinging it over her shoulder, the whiteness of it accented by her lovely brown color.

"Hi, baby," she smiled to someone who called out to her as she dodged dancers on the dance floor : head high, lips perpetually moist and kissy.

Her best girlfriends were sitting at a table beside the dance floor, glammed up as usual, right by the floor-to-ceiling mirror: Hettie in a big wig with bangs (the Patti Labelle look); Arroya in a red leather miniskirt, white stockings on her thick golden legs, wearing her hair in a ponytail (from the neck up looking like Billie Holiday on her "Lady in Satin" album cover); Emma in a bustier showing off her made-to-order titties.

Latasha hugged a young queen named Rhonda, just a kid that she had recently taken under her wing. It was then that she noticed the woman at the bar who seemed to be staring at her. Latasha

looked away as one of her gentleman friends — a construction worker type in corduroys, light tan workboots, a cap and turtleneck — lit her cigarette. After Latasha lifted her head and smiled at him, she looked across the room again. That confirmed it. The woman was looking at her. Well, at least it looked like a woman.

Lauren looked away this time because even in a place like this, normal manners dictated that you not stare at people, no matter how incredible they look. She wondered (with a chilling laugh that no one heard because of the pounding of the music) if she were the only biological woman in this place. But no, there was that foursome of lesbians at the end of the bar kissing, caressing and "baby"-ing each other ("Here's your drink, baby. Let me have one of them cigarettes, baby.") She didn't know what would be worse — to be approached by one of them or by a man who thought she was a man pretending to be a woman. Or would they think she was a man turned into a woman to a man turned into a man with breasts and a dick? The thought of all those configurations was enough to make her order another drink.

Why would a man want another man? Why would a man want a man who looked like a woman instead of wanting a real woman? Why would a man want a "woman" who had once been a man? Why would a man want a man who looked like a woman but had a penis and breasts? And when you just looked at one of those "things", how could you tell what they had cut off or added anyway? These people were just real fucked-up, she concluded. She felt a wave of revulsion at the mental pictures she'd created of the various anatomical arrangements she imagined herself surrounded by, and felt quite nauseous. But the thought of going into the ladies' room — what did that sign mean in a place like this, anyway? — forced the bile back down her throat, which she touched lightly with the fingers of her gun-free hand.

Lauren pretended not to look at the "thing" in

the black dress again, but she had to admit that s/he did look very, very smart. She glanced toward the door once more in search of Cleveland, the offender. The freak. While turning back, she noted that Miss Black Dress was now on the dance floor. Her long white fingernails were dramatically highlighted against her skin as she placed her fingers on her thighs, balanced on killer heels that looked as if she had climbed a ladder and jumped into them (an expression Lauren's mother used to describe women who wore nosebleed heels) and worked her shoulders to the music, tilting her head in various directions in time to the beat.

The man who had lit Latasha's cigarette so attentively danced with her in the same way, never taking his eyes off her as he squinted at her through the smoke of the cigarette that dangled from his lips. The crowd bubbled up around them in an angry-looking boil of men and "near misses"

continued on page 53

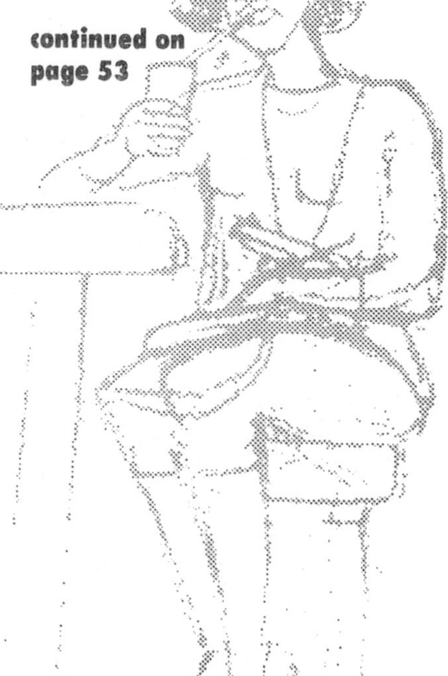

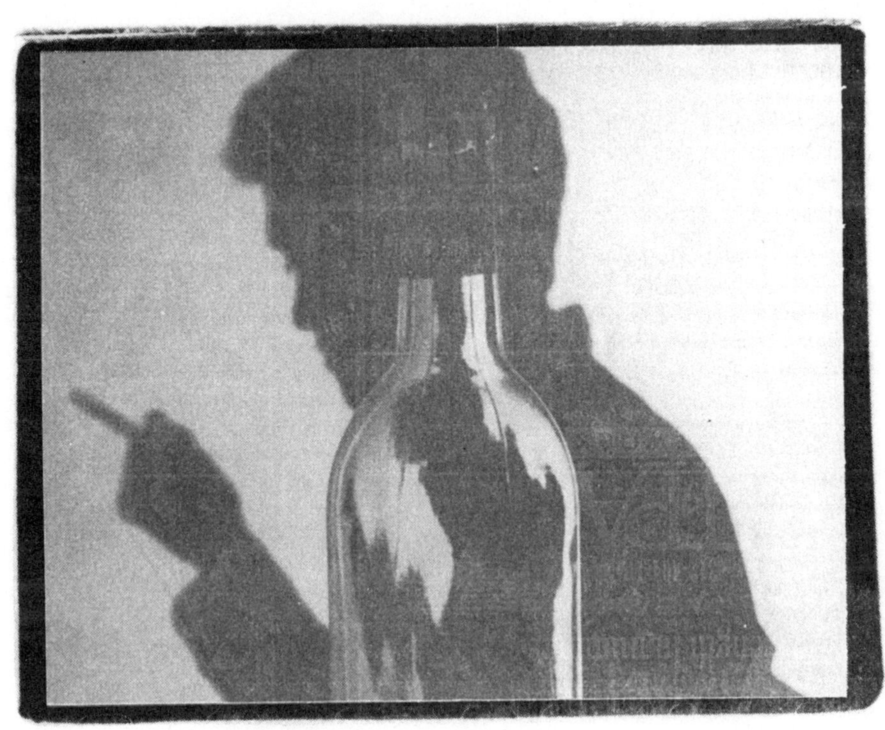

LSD,

XTC,

COKE,

even LITE

The beat goes on... names and games change...

and another morning after starts as the sun sets.

Howard Brown Memorial Clinic now offers

professionally-staffed alcohol and substance

abuse programs specifically for the gay/lesbian/

bisexual community.

For more information call 312.871.5777 and take the

first step toward regaining control over your life.

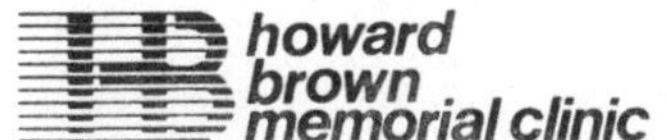

Lately, what with the price of paté, there just hasn't been enough trickling down into our purses for us to be able to toddle out to lunch, so we've been forced to wag on the wire. At first, we relished the respite from the teeming millions of cut and uncut fans. The leisure hours not spent troweling Erase over our stretchmarks (Pussy). Or trying to convince ourselves that widewale cords and chukka boots make us look exactly like we did in college (Buns).

Still, it only took a week before our touch-tone trashfests failed to thrill, and we were longing to be chomping the chow at some chic charcuterie... the obsequious waitstaff hovering around like a swarm of nellie gnats...our indiscreet lunchmates spilling the beans about their bare-assed exploits with the usual *bonhommie*, unaware that we'd soon savage them in print.

Sadly, in our fiscal rut, a regal repast was not to be. Still, we yearned to find someplace—anyplace—where we could make public spectacles of ourselves, just like old times, while perhaps harvesting a few stray tales to share with other needy friends. And so, broken and bitter, we stole from our holes and headed upward and outward into the lower depths of mainstream culture.

Slipping stealthily into a vinyl booth in some nameless FAMILY restaurant, we scanned the room to get our bearings. Rudely confronted by a cacophonous pack of whining brats, the stench of spilt milk, the drone of parents cooing at their young, we must have said something clever, but unkind. Because the next thing we heard was "Fucking queers!" And, suddenly we understood precisely what had brought the world to its present, precipitous decline.

★★★

Let this column be a warning to those who still contend that our current state of demise is a result of free enterprise run amok. As we see it, we're not witnessing the last, choking gasp of rampant capitalism, so much as the nascent breath of rampant...heterocentrism.

Oh, that we could go back in time, before the deification of the American Family. Before the emergence of the hysterical middle class, when—in certain circles—homos were held in high esteem. Back then, rich folks made the money and hired smartassed sissies to teach them how to use it. As High Priests of High Culture, we were given carte blanche to shape respectable society. Living off largesse, we amused, advised, composed, wrote, designed, danced and otherwise flourished.

Our patrons were not bound by the tyranny of bourgeois values, in commerce or in love. And, as for their sexuality, if, sometimes, by the fourth or fifth martini, the lines between their world and ours became, well, blurred, we didn't mind. And, besides, there was no one to pass judgment.

Television changed all that. Antennas sprouted on rooftops from coast to coast and suddenly the general public had a window on the wealthy. The two worlds collided with deadly force when Jack and Jackie invited the populace into their royal home. The populace recoiled in horror at the wanton display of sophistication and good taste, but before the First Couple could atone for their cultural excesses, they took their fateful trip to Dallas. And, thus came the waning of the Age of Elegance and the demise of the Dandy Demimonde.

With the nation tuned in, the mansion set could no longer live according to their own tastes. With illiteracy and apathy no longer sufficient barriers between them and the great unwashed, businessmen, clergymen and presidents alike were forced to do something they'd never done before: play to the gallery. High culture didn't count for shit.

And so began an endless procession of Tele-Monarchs, doing backflips for the camera, to appease the folks at home. After Camelot came the Texas Twostep. And, after that, the Cloth Coat. And, after that, Valium

THING

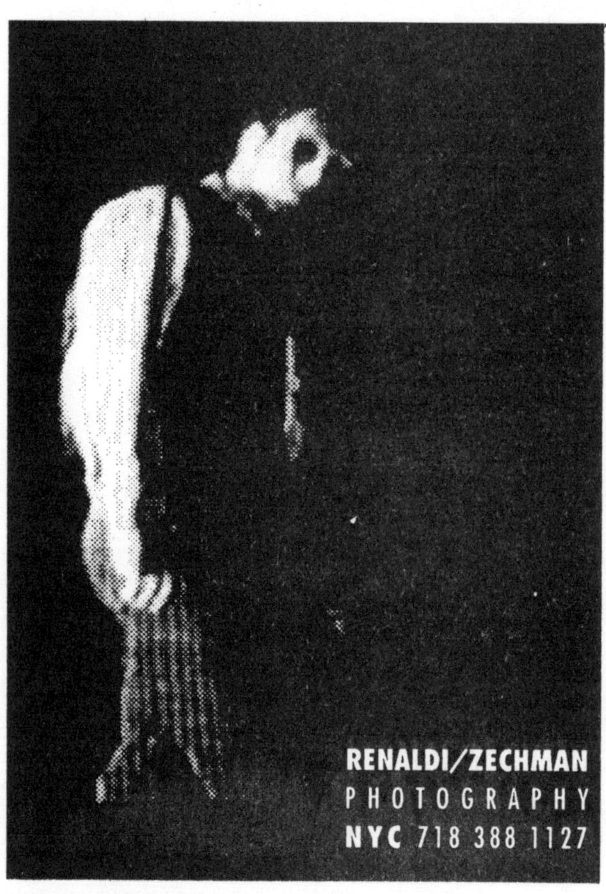

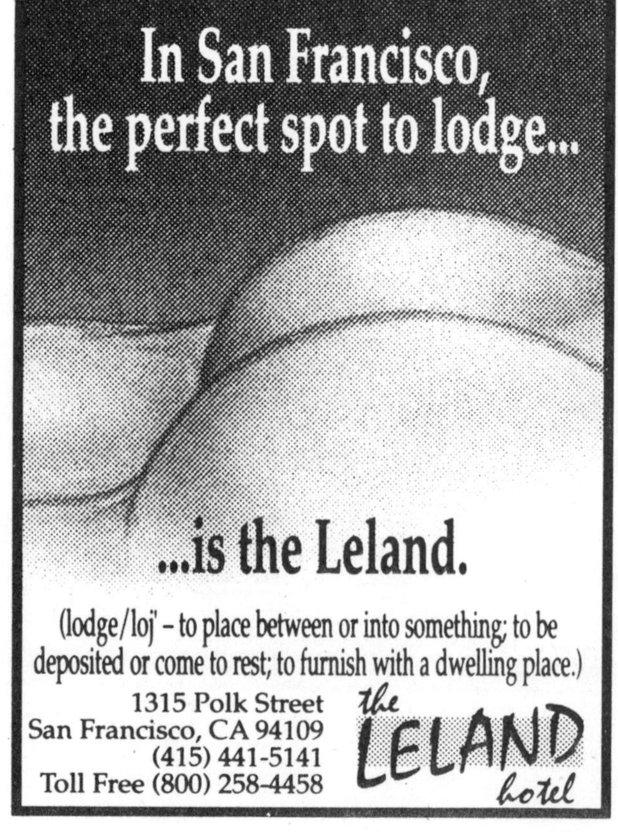

Vale. And, after that, Piety and Peanuts. And, then, with the Dawning of ReageanBush, the viewers got exactly what they'd asked for, and the transformation of effete intellectual snobs into anti-intellectual rubes began its final, fatal stage.

After all those years spent on the backlot, under lights, in front of the cameras, the Hollywood homeboy was a master of media manipulation. As he smiled and waved and waxed nostalgic about the tidy picket fences of his youth, and sang his hymns to Home and Hearth, regular Joes smiled and waved back and bought into the ultimate deception—signing up to fight in the great smoke-screen wars on Drugs, Free Speech, Sex and Civil Rights—while Ron's cronies robbed our country blind.

Warmed by the glow of burning books, the Volksbund demanded an encore. And they get a stellar performance from a wealthy CIA spook, masquerading as a Shriner from Des Moines. He tossed the Bill of Rights into the bonfire and the weenie roast began.

Now, with the blessing of this Everyman from Maine, the Tyranny of Family Values has metastasized into every fiber of the American body politic. Average American Families have converged into a veritable lynchmob. And, while they are encouraged to direct their venom at po' folks like us, their own demise is being hastened by the Bushmen they feel speak only for them.

★★★

And that's where we come in...or fade out, as the case may be. At first, being down on our heels made it difficult for us to lunch in the style to which we'd grown accustomed. Now, we've realized we cannot lunch at all. It's far too late to ply our public with chronicles about the sexual stunts of the dearly departed. We must step off of the sidelines and into the skirmish—whatever the hell that means. Not that we won't tell a tall tale or two if hard pressed. But, while our other *oeuvres* were naught but an array of anthropological appetizers, we now feel that, in light of the current political and social climate, we must give our readers something more substantial to chew on.

Bon Appétit!

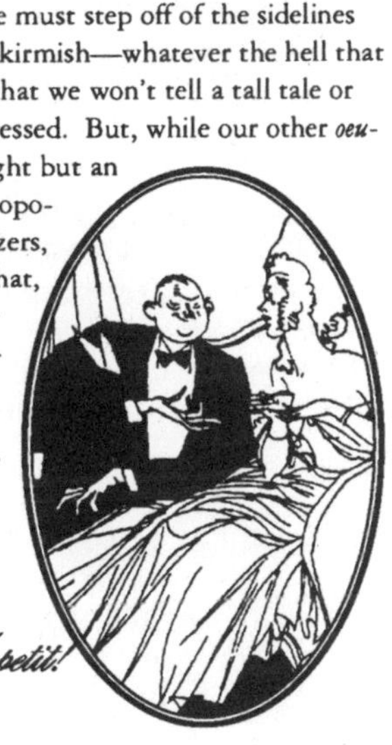

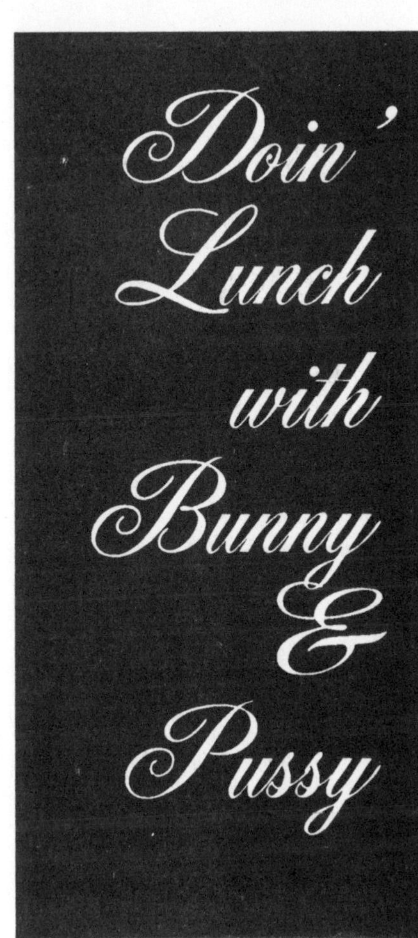

47

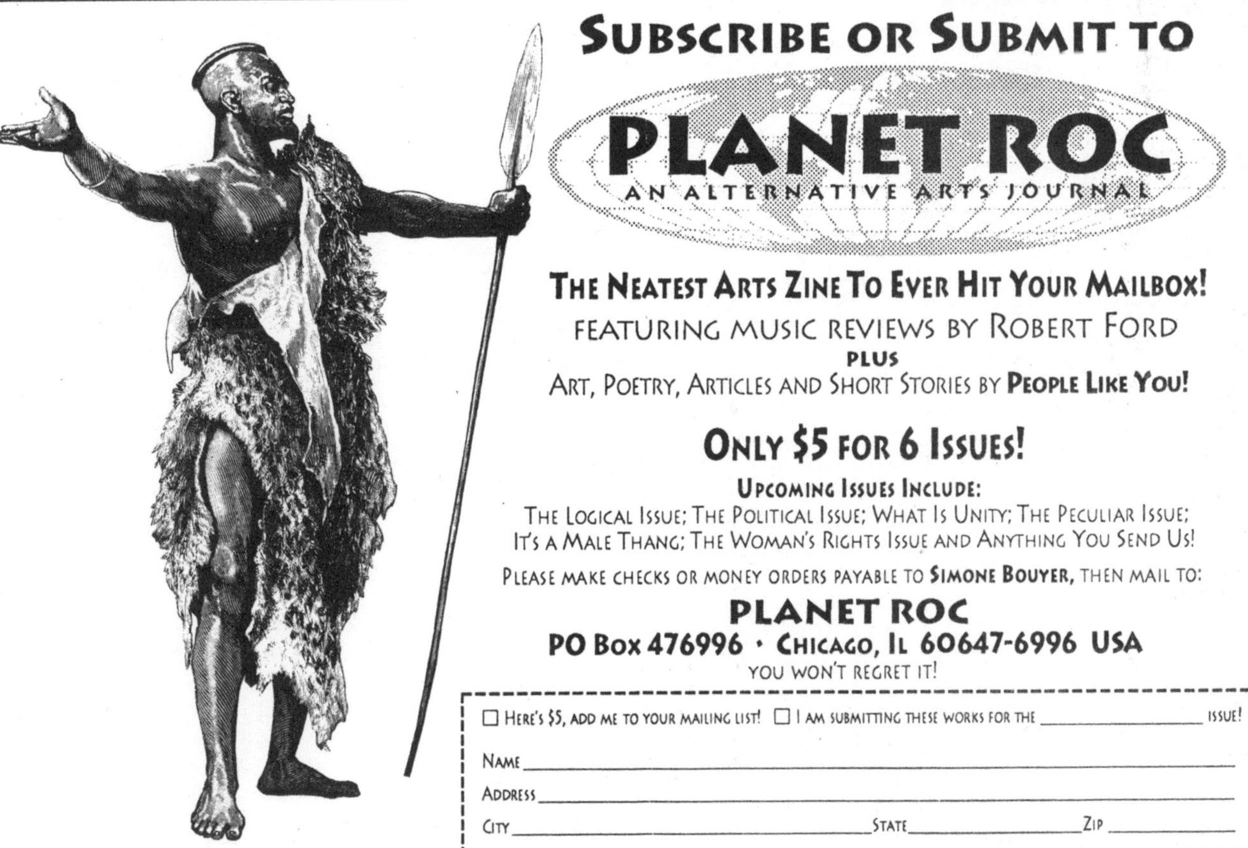

TEE

By T.Adkins

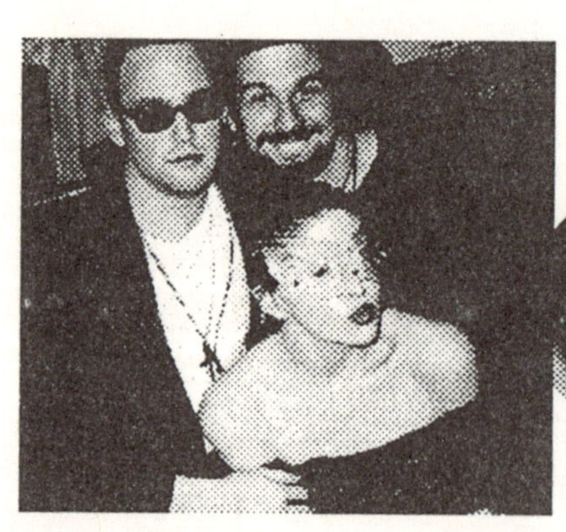

For a time now, hardcore Chicago nightcrawlers have been speculating about the development of the "afterhours," a party that gathers after the club closes. It's an idea that goes way back with certain clubgoers who, in the old days, say the late '70s, used to dash out of Carol's Speakeasy at 5am and hit it over to the Warehouse, where the party was just gettin' started. Other afterhours haunts were 161 West, The Powerplant, and Medusa's. Lately however, with more restrictive cabaret and bar licensing laws, too few places exist where children can cavort and carry-on into the wee small hours. Enter enterprising hosts and hostesses who take it upon themselves (and sometimes their unknowing roommates) and say, "OK, let's all go to my place!" And (as you might imagine) there are problems inherent with this type of hospitality. It can get real messy, real fast. For instance, what's to keep the entire club from coming over when you only want a few people? Or, how do you keep folks from getting out of hand or making a mess and trashing the joint? Bringing us to an important point: you can just about get away with *anything* as long as you're smart, discreet, considerate. Loud, obnoxious, and rowdy asses ain't welcome since nobody wants trouble with the neighbors or the police. Like, recently when some not too bright kids couldn't get into a host's building and, instead of waiting for someone to come along who knew the correct bell number, asininely decided to ring *every bell in the fucking building!* Of course, the neighbors complained and threatened to call Vera! How to do it right? Our trusty Afterhours Guide.

1 Know your host/hostess. Hardly anyone is willing to host a house full of strangers but most people always welcome into their home or apartment folks they know, love, trust. The booster and mopping quotient is super high when you don't know a soul, but they know the Estee Lauder products in your john cabinet and the designer labels in your closet. If you overhear or someone asks you, 'Who's place is this, anyway?' regard said person with suspicion and seriously consider asking them out. "Need a taxi?"

2 Know your place, don't be a hanger-on. If you ain't invited, don't think crashing is going to remedy your plight. Chances are, if no one's asked you, you ain't welcomed. You don't want to go someplace where you aren't welcomed, do you?! (She knows all about this.)

3 Pitch in on the clean-up. Put litter in its place. When friends come over, they usually don't spill beer or vodka and fail to wipe up. If the host has to do all the dirty work how often do you think he/she will be willing to have a soiree? Emptying an ash tray here and there and properly disposing of empties won't kill you and is bound to make a favorable impression on the host, increasing your likelihood of being asked back. Do your friends come over and piss on the upholstery, buy lunch on the carpeting once a week or monthly?

4 Contribute! Since they usually occur rather spontaneously at bars' closing and the same time liquor stores are closing as well, it becomes kinda important as to where the party favors are coming from. Bring your own shit is a fair policy. Nobody wants moochers and leeches at the party to suck up all the goodies after they haven't contributed shit to the kitty. The best afterhours happen when everybody pitches in. Assume it's pay your own way and you'll be fine.

5 Don't come to the party looking for trade. If getting fucked is that important to you, you should work the trade at the club where you have better odds.

Afterhours are strictly for hangin' out and gettin' full with friends—NOT cruising. Now, if a couple of *friends* want to drop in, get full, and hit it to do the nasty, that's totally different.

6 Be an asskickin' host. Honey, put your foot down! If you don't know somebody or don't want them in your bricks.... kick them the fuck out! Or kindly ask them to leave. Don't feel bad. You're only insulting and inconveniencing your guests by allowing *hustler types,* for example, to work the root on everybody.

7 Forewarn your roommate(s)! Maybe it wouldn't bother you to wake up to a house full of folks but I'd be pissed as hell to wake up to or walk into to such a scene, totally by surprise. Think of your guest: it doesn't feel right to have one roomie saying, "Come on in, chile!" and the other going, "What the hell are all these people doing here? I have to work in the morning!!"

8 Practice moderation. Know your limits, puh-leeze! With most substances, there's only so much you can do before you're no longer high but sick to your stomach. It's true with booze, Carol, Tina, Mary, X, A, K. Even pot gives you a headache after so much. Where's even the kid who can hold his/her own after munching too many shrooms? The next day, if you find yourself making excuses that begin with, "About last night...I'm sorry... I had little bit too much to drink, and I..." Please! Forget it!

9 Remember your home training. Ever-gracious hostess and racy revealer Wendy Quinn said it best, "A little common courtesy goes a long way." I don't know what your people been tellin' you but it's not all about you! If'n it is, have an afterhours by your damned self.

10 Don't tempt fate. Clean up behind yourself. Don't go tossin' your empty pony packs just any where. You never know who's coming in behind you lookin' for evidence. If you want to get busted, just say so.

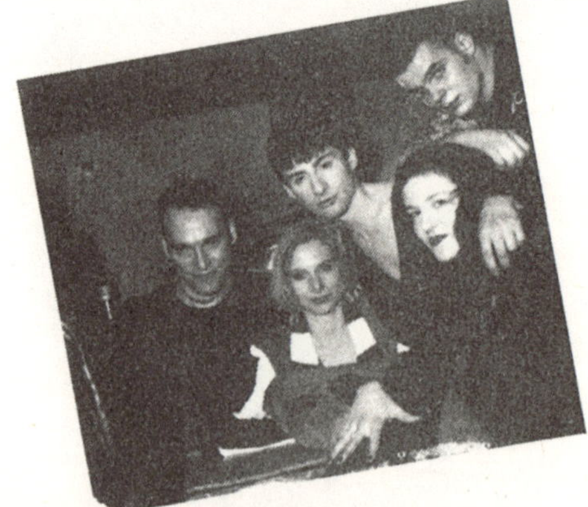

ABOVE L to R *White Shoulders: Andy Substance, Arleen and Billy (Mystic Bill) Torres in the Paramount Room at Shelter for Project X. I'm Gonna Get U Sucka! Rick Davis styles a gangsta lean at the Quench opening. HE GIVES GOOD HEAD!: Keoki and Freddie Bain in the booth at Cheeks.*

BELOW *Good enough to eat: (L to R) Michael Meza, Marsha, Chris (Pancake) Parlot, Arleen, and Yummy Mark at Neo. Photo, Al Carter*

Best Pre-Afterhours Hook-Up	NOT
Thursday Night Berlin	Tuesday Night Berlin
Sunday Night Cairo	Monday Night Cairo
Wednesday Night Quench	Friday Night Shelter
Saturday Night Cheeks	Saturday Night Vortex
Saturday Night Red Dog	Saturday Night Neo
Monday Night Neo	Wednesday Night Tom Tom
Tuesday Night Danny's	Monday Night Smart Bar

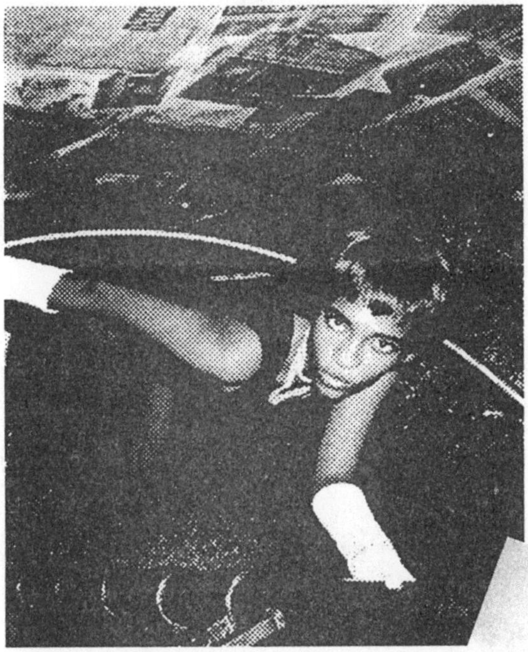

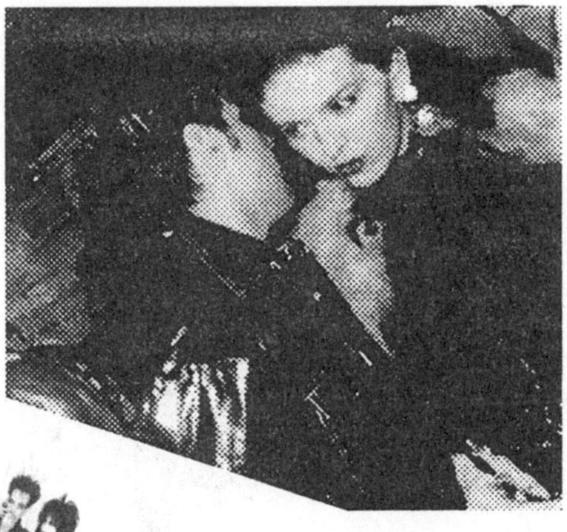

THING

49

Where's the Party?
(Things you hear at the Afterhours)

"Bumpage."

"I slept all day."

"Work today?"

"She ain't puttin' nothin' up her nose and the only thing she's poppin' is her kootchie!"

"Kooky boots."

"Is this cereal?"

"Who's tape *is* this?"

"New shoes?"

"Were you at the club?"

"See ya!"

"Stop it, g'on!"

"Are you driving?"

"Where do we go from here?"

"Wanna do a bump?"

"Oh, she's sick!"

"Call me a cab."

"Tacos anyone?"

"Fierce boots."

"I didn't see you at the club."

"How'd you get here?"

"Hey!"

"Really!"

"Is that Vodka?"

"Uhm, uhm, uhm... chile!"

"Hi, baby! How ya doin'?"

"Which is mine?"

"Oh, just do it!"

"Is Miss Carol here?"

"Uugghh!"

"Oh, no!"

"Fine!"

"Got any Advil?"

"Hi Mary!"

"Bye Mary!"

"Nice place."

"Well, maybe a small one."

"Please!"

"Okay!"

"I'm totally X-ing!"

"Who you gonna call?"

"Did you have a good time tonight?"

"The post-afterhours."

"Smoke?"

"Twist my arm, okay?"

"I'm *so* tired."

"Are you in line?"

"Are there any mixers?"

"Are the Davids coming?"

"This is kinda cute."

"Teddy's. Family only."

"Did you work tonight?"

"Did you make that?"

"Loved it."

"She would want to get away from here and leave folks alone."

"Did you like that?"

"Well, maybe a tiny one."

"Would you like something?"

"Can I do another one?"

"Is he holding?"

"Ooh, lovely!"

"I'm full."

"I haven't slept in days."

"Do you need something?"

"She's in the bathroom."

"I'm hungry."

"Nope."

"Probably in the bathroom."

"That's really cute."

"You can't get something for nothing."

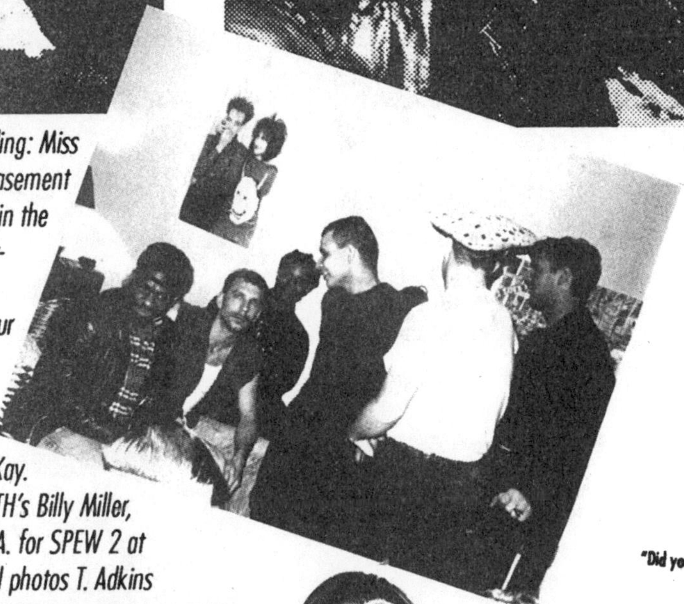

Best-Afterhours	NOT	Best Pre-Afterhour Activity	Best post-Afterhour Activity
Jim's and George's	The Project X Canal St. Outlaw Party	Shower	Bathing/Swimming/Whirl Pool
1466	The Vault	Disco Nap	Sleeping 8 to 10 hours
Aqua Neta's	Life (They die too early)	Sex	Sex
MayDay's	Michael Whatshisname	Dinner and cocktails	Tea and Crumpets
Teddy's	Substance Headquarters		

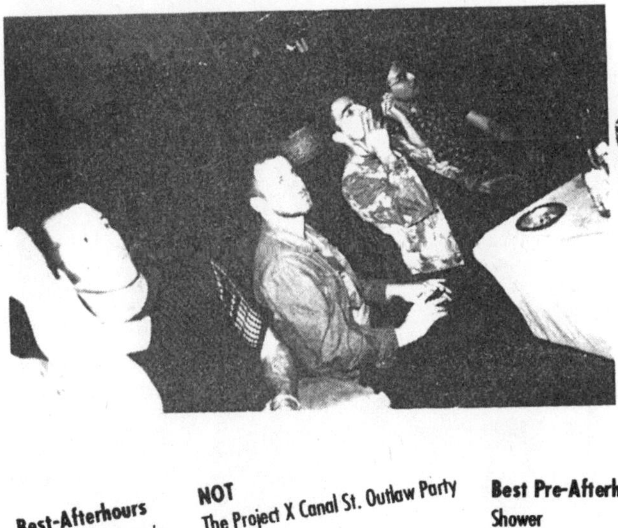

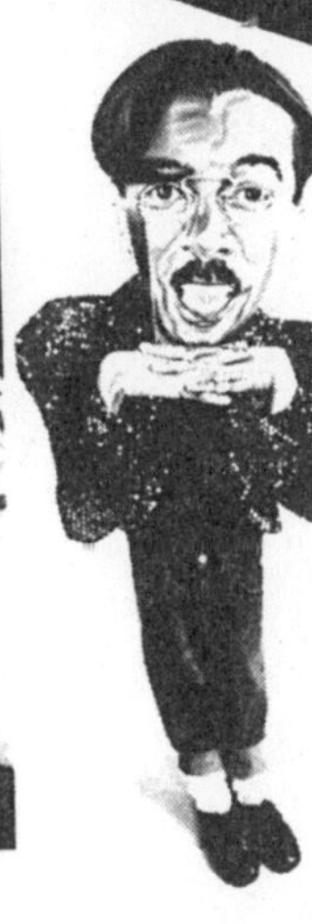

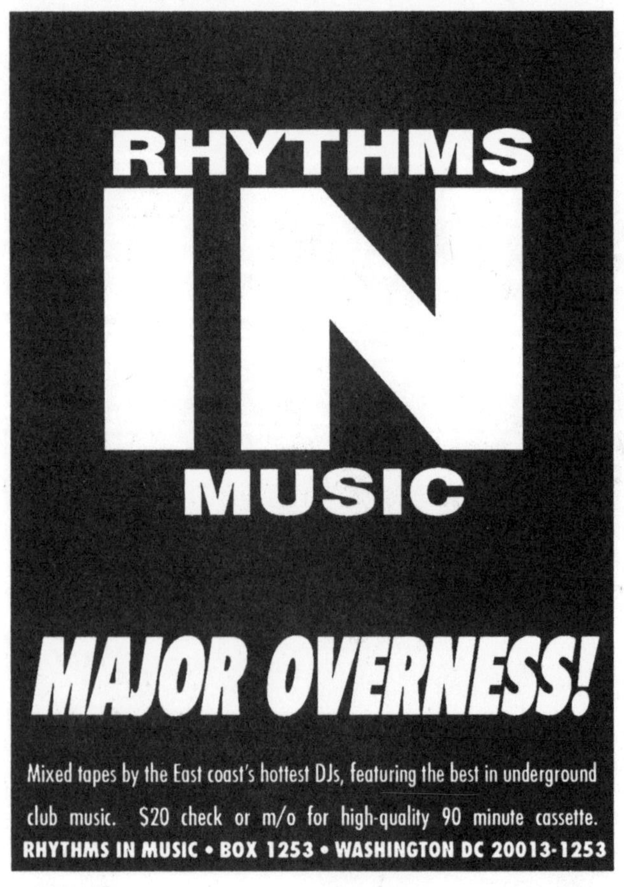
RHYTHMS
IN
MUSIC
MAJOR OVERNESS!
Mixed tapes by the East coast's hottest DJs, featuring the best in underground club music. $20 check or m/o for high-quality 90 minute cassette.
RHYTHMS IN MUSIC • BOX 1253 • WASHINGTON DC 20013-1253

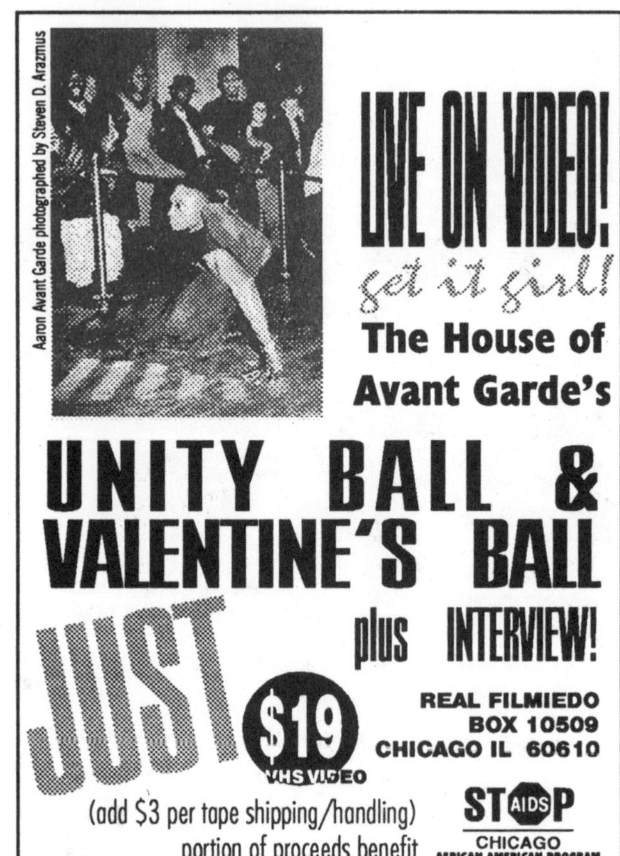
Aaron Avant Garde photographed by Steven D. Arazmus
LIVE ON VIDEO!
get it girl!
The House of Avant Garde's
UNITY BALL & VALENTINE'S BALL
JUST
plus INTERVIEW!
$19
VHS VIDEO
REAL FILMIEDO
BOX 10509
CHICAGO IL 60610
(add $3 per tape shipping/handling)
portion of proceeds benefit
STOP AIDS
CHICAGO
AFRICAN AMERICAN PROGRAM

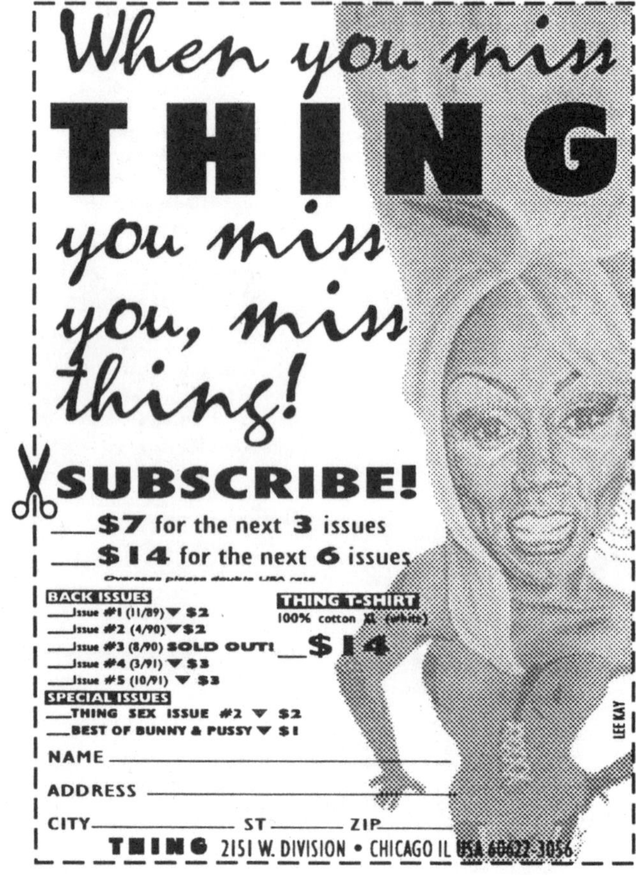
When you miss
THING
you miss
you, miss
thing!
SUBSCRIBE!
____$7 for the next 3 issues
____$14 for the next 6 issues
Overseas please double USA rate
BACK ISSUES
____Issue #1 (11/89) ▼ $2
____Issue #2 (4/90) ▼ $2
____Issue #3 (8/90) SOLD OUT!
____Issue #4 (3/91) ▼ $3
____Issue #5 (10/91) ▼ $3
SPECIAL ISSUES
____THING SEX ISSUE #2 ▼ $2
____BEST OF BUNNY & PUSSY ▼ $1
THING T-SHIRT
100% cotton XL (white)
____$14
NAME _______________________
ADDRESS ____________________
CITY __________ ST ____ ZIP ____
THING 2151 W. DIVISION • CHICAGO IL USA 60622-3056
LEE KAY

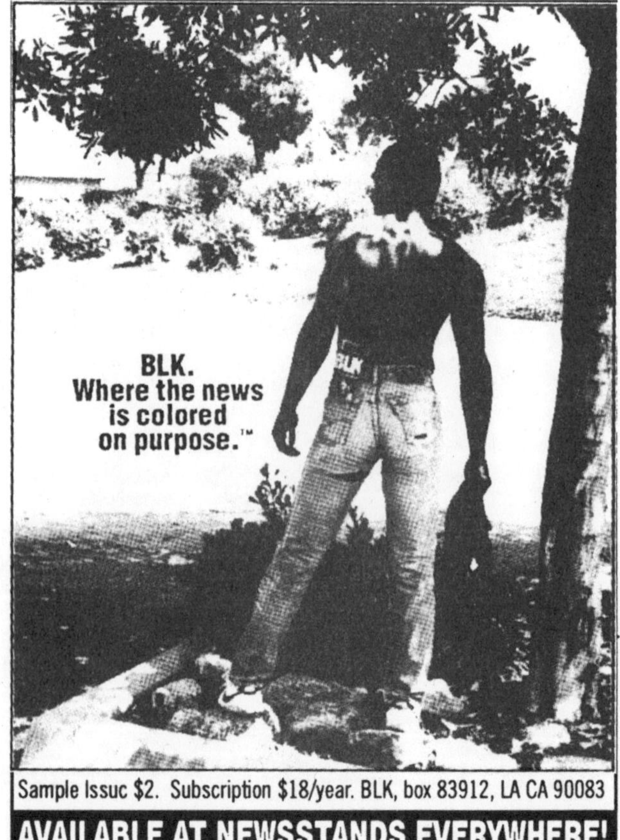
BLK.
Where the news
is colored
on purpose.™
Sample Issue $2. Subscription $18/year. BLK, box 83912, LA CA 90083
AVAILABLE AT NEWSSTANDS EVERYWHERE!

DeAUNDRA'S DIXIE DIARY

by DeAundra Peek

Hey y'all, this here's DeAundra Peek. Looka here y'all, I am soooooooo happy to be writin' this here Saga Of The South, which is my homeland, for y'all in *Thing*!

I had a big 'ol mess of fun at the SPEW 2 festival out in sprawlin big'n'wide Los Angeles, where I done met up with all them sweethearts from *Thing*, and now here I am! In case y'all don't know me, and to them that I ain't met yet, "Hey Y'all!" I am the star of my own TV show in Atlanta, Georgia USA called "DeAundra's Nitetime Soireé Partie". My show is on TV in New York and Minneapolis too y'all, makin' me and my co-stars **Duffy Odum** and **Candy Suntop** famous all over. I am about sixteen years old, I have natural blonde hair, and I am the youngest in a long line of natural-born God-given talented sisters, but ain't none a one of them has got their own TV show like me. That's on account they's all so much older and sorrier than me, and besides, y'all know that to get ahead in this here world y'all has got to be sweet and give love to get love.

Down at Odum's All Double Wide Mobile Homes Court we are all still buzzin' about our recent visit by our lil' homechild Mr. **RuPaul Charles**! Y'all know RuPaul done come from Atlanta? Me and my sorry sisters done taught him everything he knows about make-up, and he looks real pretty now that he's done fixed himself up and got that big hi-style recording contract on Tommy Boy. **Betty Jack De Vine**, y'all she's in the Senior Socialists for Peace, said she hadn't had so much fun since all a them holiday parties down at the community room at Odum's. Then, a couple of weeks later, we celebrated the release of my brand new video album "Meet Me At Odum's" on Funtone USA Records at Velvet, our favorite world-class club in downtown Atlanta. I am tellin y'all, them DeAundra look-a-like contestants even mixed me up!!

The Public Access Channel 12 that I'm on in Atlanta is about to get a new show y'all, called "Arbiters of Style". It's produced by youthful, smart, stylish and of color **Eugene Howard** and stylish, smart, and what they call "not of color" **Bill Curtis**. I am so excited to see the interview they did with **Miss Tula**, that real pretty model/book author, and they's supposed to have one with **Pebbles** comin' up!

Recently we were bein' taped for British Channel 4 by them **Pop Tarts**, **Randy** and **Fenton**, from the World of Wonder. They are makin' a new show called "Made In the USA" and asked us all to be in the pilot episode. Mr. **Larry Tee** came down from New York city and did a hi-fancy show at Velvet, shakin' that place down with them funky songs he made up himself. We had so much fun tapin' at famous Atlanta landmarks like the Jackson Street Bridge, The MLK Jr. Center and outside of that old-timey, privately owned cemetery which I ain't allowed to name on account a cause Miss **Margaret Mitchell** herself is buried there.

I am hereby officially sayin' a special "buy-bye darlin'" to **Lurleen Wallis**, who is runnin' off to Japan to be a spokesmodel for Fuji Sportswear and Feed and Seed, look for her on the blimp real soon. Miss **Judy LaGrange**, world famous psychic, has done predicted nothing but success for Lurleen.

I know y'all been waitin for this, it's the Vienner Sausage recipe, yeaaaaaa!

Twice Baked & Fried Vienners

1 can Hy Grade Vienner Sausages, imitation if possible
1 spray can Hy-Grade Cheese Whip
1 pack O' Boisies
1 jar Miracle Whip Lite Spread
1 blender

Take your vienners and split 'em down the middle after microwavin' for 5 minutes on high. Scoop out the insides and mash up in a bowl with some of the cheese whip and O'Boisies. Stuff that in the vienner shells and microwave on high for 4 minutes more, or till hot lookin'. In the blender, puree for 4 minutes the rest of the O'Boisies and the Miracle Whip Lite. Coat vienners and fry till done. Serve on a stick.

"THE WHOLE WORLD CAN KISS MY ASS TONIGHT!"

continued from page 44 — Lauren's new term for the drags. It looked celebratory, like a cleansing ritual. Like something that had to be done... a rite.

As Latasha danced with Bobby, she was careful not to wiggle her hips too much so that her already-short dress would not ride up in an unladylike fashion. She was saving her best dance move for the song's climax. That's when most of the dancers would do their most dramatic, soul-releasing moves — hands thrown in the air — front, back, above, sudden crouches that led to leaps on one foot, hops and spins; mad dashes across the dance floor; a sudden drop to the floor and then a slippery slide across the tiles; a jump into the arms of a partner. None of that for Miss Latasha. No, not tonight. She planned to get very still when the song peaked. Maybe lift one arm slowly above her head, look up at it, follow it down with her head, then one quick turn on one foot till she faced Bobby again.

Lauren was watching Miss Black Dress when Cleveland walked into the club, but she did not see him until the fourth time Diana Ross did her screams in "The Boss". The deejay played the screams over and over and over , with Ross screaming and singing:

> Whoo-hoo-hoo-hoo-hoo-hoo-hoo-huh-huh!
> Oww!
> Whoo-hoo-hoo-hoo-hoo-hoo-hoo-huh-huh!
> Love taught me,
> Taught me,
> Taught me!
> I was so sure
> so sure,
> but lo-o-ove taught me who was,
> who was the boss!

Lauren saw that the near misses were all on their feet now, like they had heard the national anthem, and looked at themselves in the full-length mirror, some lip-syncing and some singing along with Ross, hands moving, arms waving, vogueing, Ross-ing. She wondered what they saw in the mirror: a successful charade? A woman?

Cleveland. It was like watching a movie when she saw him standing beside Miss Black Dress on the dance floor, pausing to kiss her on the cheek. And she could have sworn his lips formed the words,"hey, baby," just like he always said to her when he came to her apartment. He kept moving, his coat in his hand, toward the seats lining the walls of the club. A man of about his height but a little stockier stood up and embraced him. They embraced each other. They sat there in the corner, arms around each other. Then Cleveland leaned over and pressed his juicy lips against the man's, whose lips reached out in response. Then Cleveland's lips headed for the man's ear — he did not see Lauren who had gotten up from her barstool and walked dazedly toward them — and he whispered to the man he loved, (with his nose touching the man's ear) the last words anyone would ever hear him say:

"I feel so good, the whole world can kiss my ass tonight!" ▼

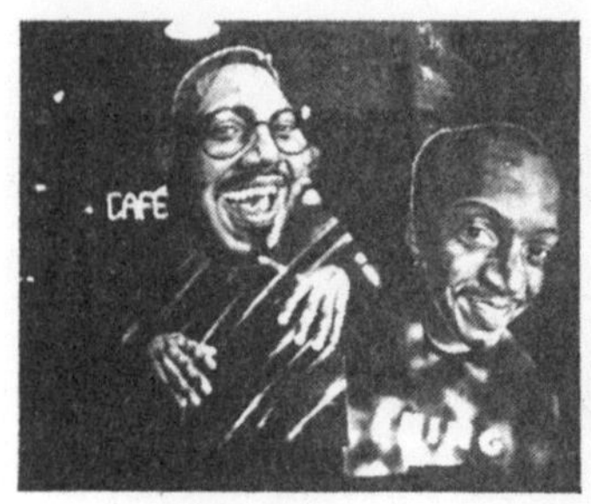

LEE KAY

Known to gay Chicago for his ever-changing installations at Roscoe's Cafe, Lee is an "architect" by day. His "bubblehead por-trits" are freestanding foamcore illustrations that bestow instant bigger-than-life star status to cult figures of the Bette Davis, RuPaul, Joan Jett Blakk and Roderick Conrad variety. Above: Lee's take on Thing's LDW and RF in the window at Roscoe's Cafe. Photo Duane Baskins.

RENALDI/ZECHMAN

Rich and Eric have a summer home on Fire Island and throw fabulous parties where many sexy boys attend to their every whim. Rich likes disco and Eric likes showtunes and hot fudge sundaes. They have the world's largest collection of Judy Garland memorabilia and love the photographs of Herb Ritts. Success has not spoiled them yet.

CHUCK GONZALES

Yummy Chuck Gonzales, as he is often referred to by *Thing* editors, is a local graphic design artist and freelance writer. His work for a long time was enjoyed commercially and is now becoming more and more visible among the circle of underground artists here in Chicago and elsewhere. Gonzales also contributes to *Gag* magazine.

SKINNY VINNY

A native Chicagoan, eons ago, Skinny Vinny travelled to Europe and came back a born-again diva. Since then, he's been residing in New York City where he's become a fixture on the East Village scene and the number one RuPaul Charles fan.

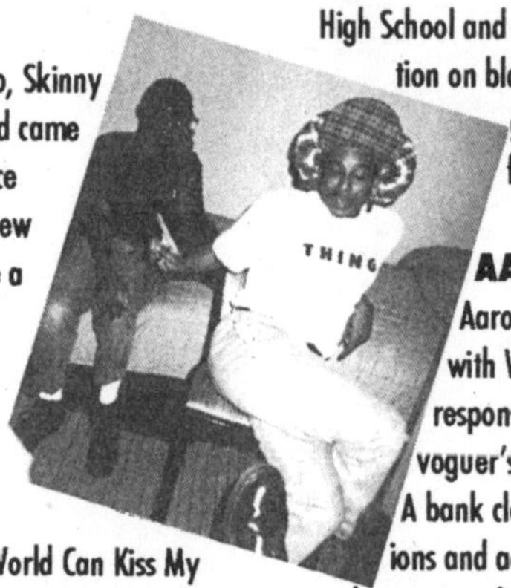

JULIAN

The short story "The Whole World Can Kiss My Ass Tonight" is from *Spade*, a self-published collection of poetry and prose by Larry Ferguson and Julian. Copies are available for seven dollars: send money orders payable to A. J. Johnson, Box 91076, Washington DC 20090-1076.

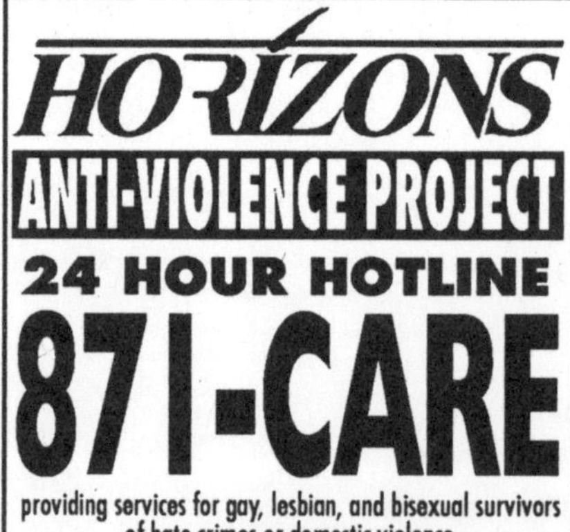

STEPHEN WINTER

Stephen is a recent graduate of the School of the Art Institute's film program. He is currently teaching film aesthetics to students at Chicago's Metro High School and completing his first film, a meditation on black gay male identity. He begins graduate film studies at NYU in the fall.

AARON AVANT GARDE

Aaron Pierre Brown Avant Garde, along with Wardell Ford Avant Garde, is responsible for founding the city's first voguer's house, the House of Avant Garde. A bank clerk by day, he also designs fashions and accessories, edits the Avant Gardian, and organizes the House's monthly balls. And he's a DJ, too Left: Aaron's gagging at Willi Ninja servin' it. Photo Kenny Avant Garde.

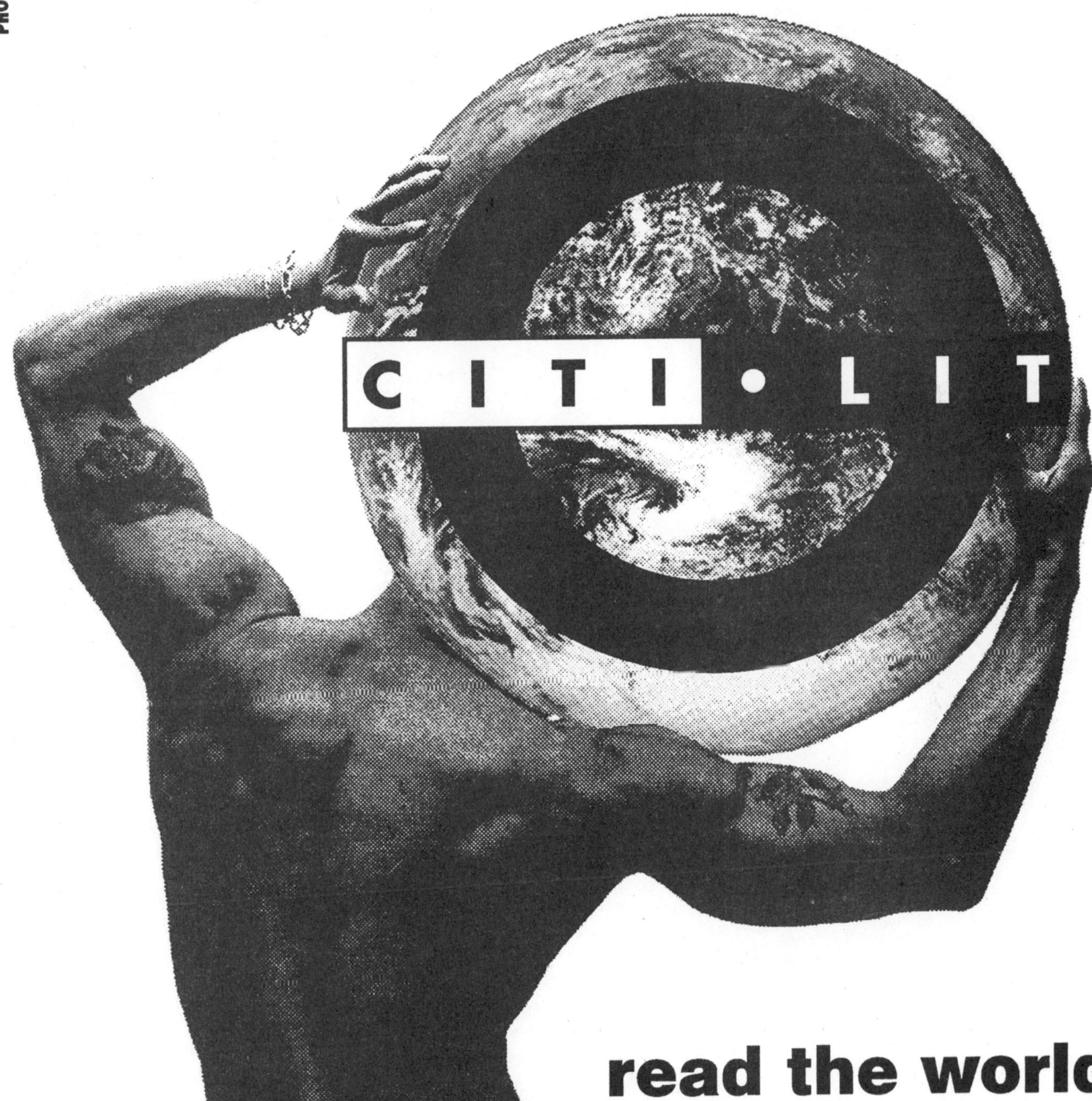

PHOTO Diana Solis MODEL Byron
CITI·LIT
read the world.
FRESH MAGS • USED BOOKS • 1570 1/2 N. DAMEN • CHICAGO

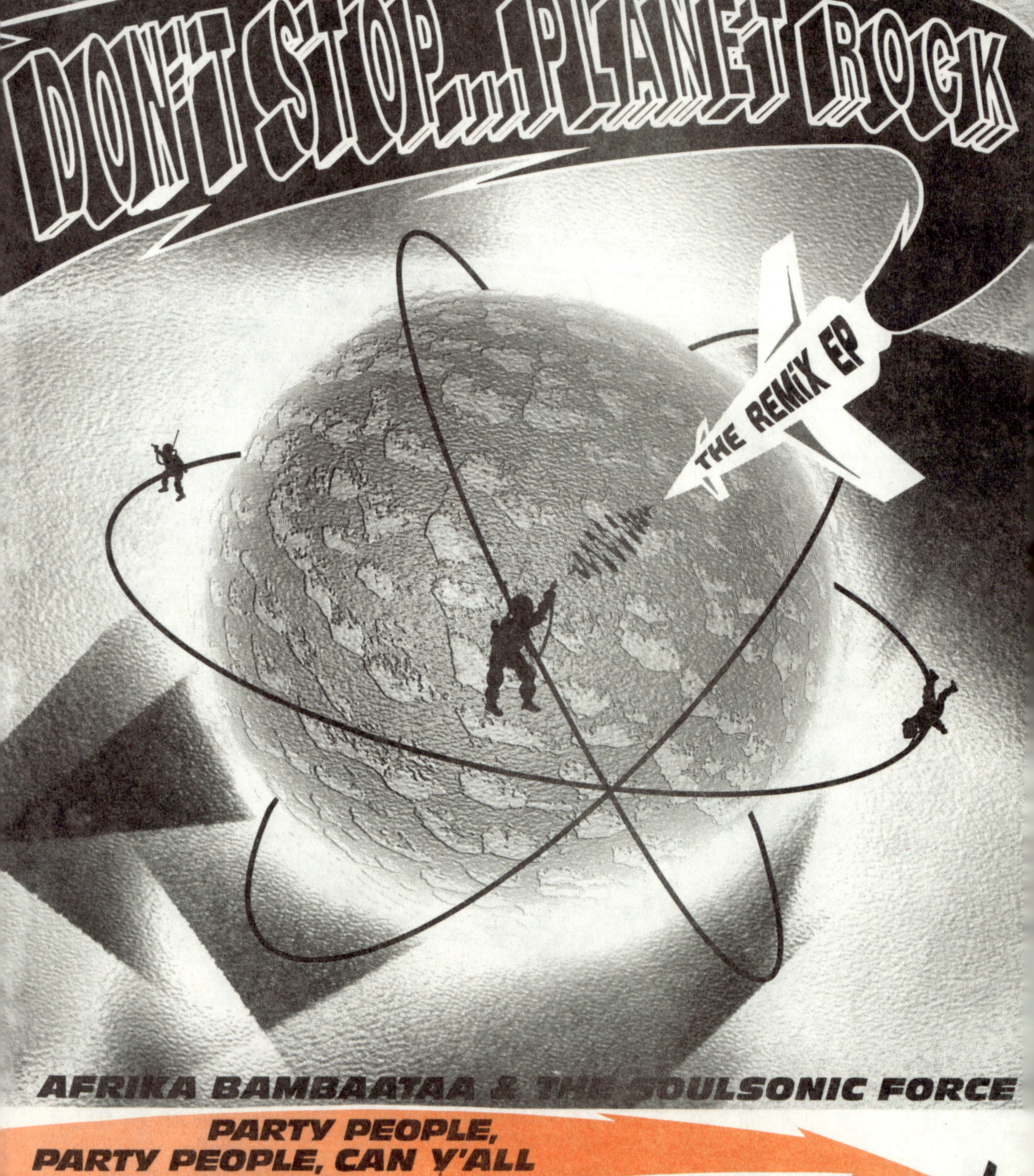

DON'T STOP...PLANET ROCK
THE REMIX EP
AFRIKA BAMBAATAA & THE SOULSONIC FORCE
PARTY PEOPLE, PARTY PEOPLE, CAN Y'ALL GET FUNKY?
THE RECORD THAT ROCKED THE UNIVERSE TEN YEARS AGO IS BACK.
PLANET ROCK/THE REMIX EP FEATURES A GROUP OF GLOBAL REMIXES BY
ERIC KUPPER & MOHAMMED MORRETTA, 808 STATE, DJ MAGIC MIKE, LFO, AND ELEKTRIC MUSIC ALONG WITH
THE ORIGINAL VERSION. REALLY FRESH.
Tommy Boy

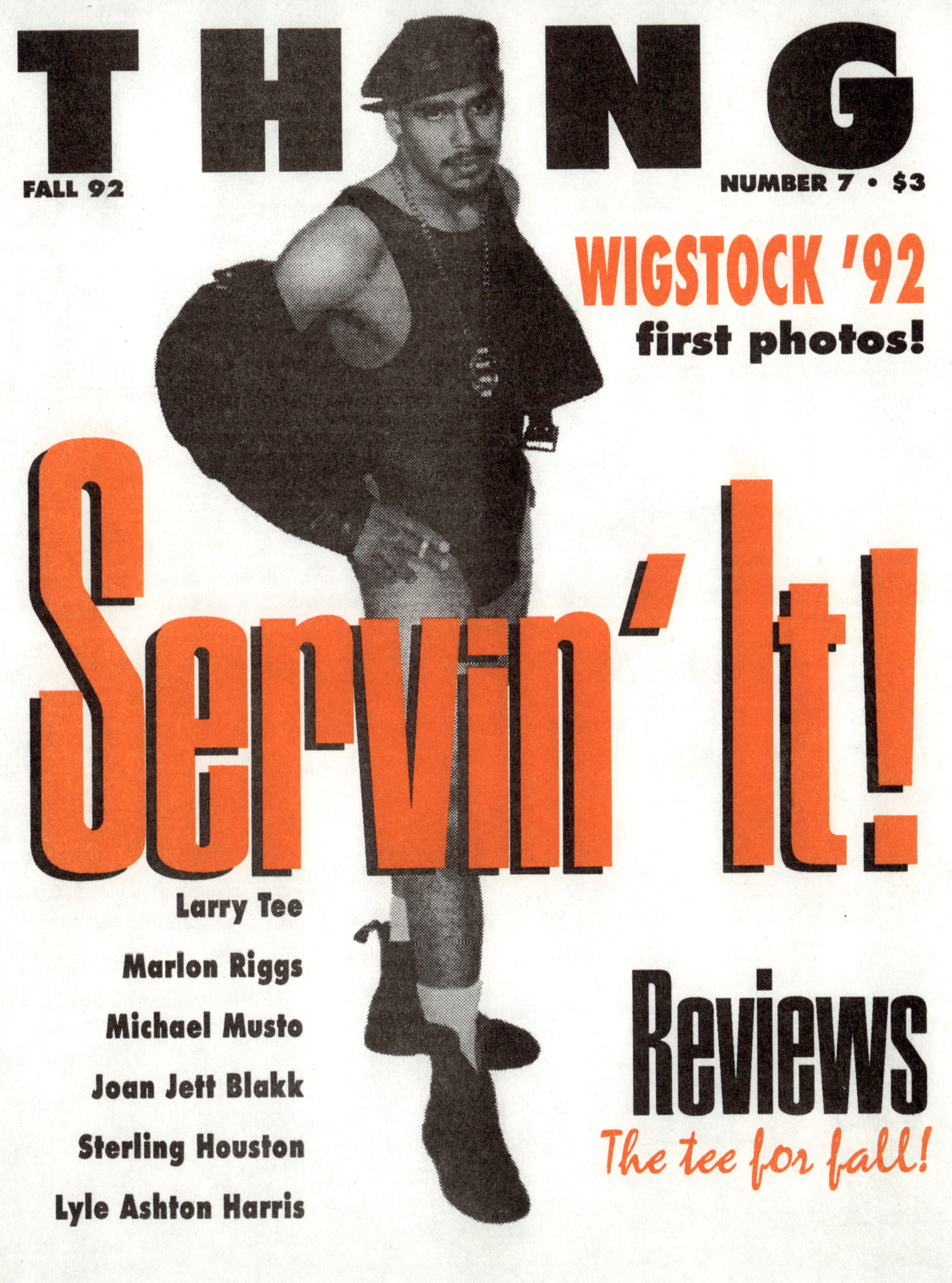

THING
FALL 92
NUMBER 7 • $3
WIGSTOCK '92
first photos!
Servin' It!
Larry Tee
Marlon Riggs
Michael Musto
Joan Jett Blakk
Sterling Houston
Lyle Ashton Harris
Reviews
The tee for fall!

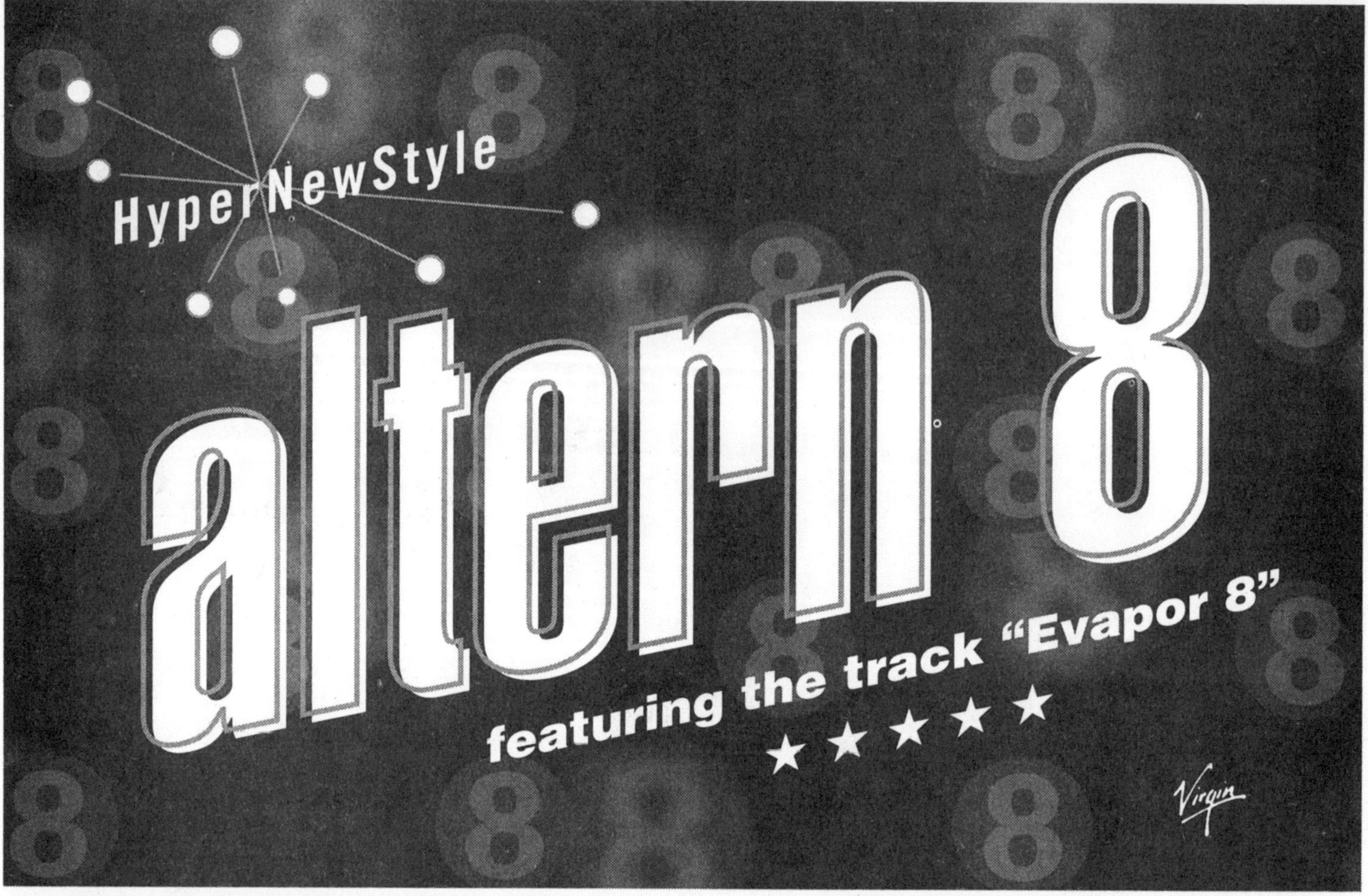

HyperNewStyle
altern 8
featuring the track "Evapor 8"
Virgin

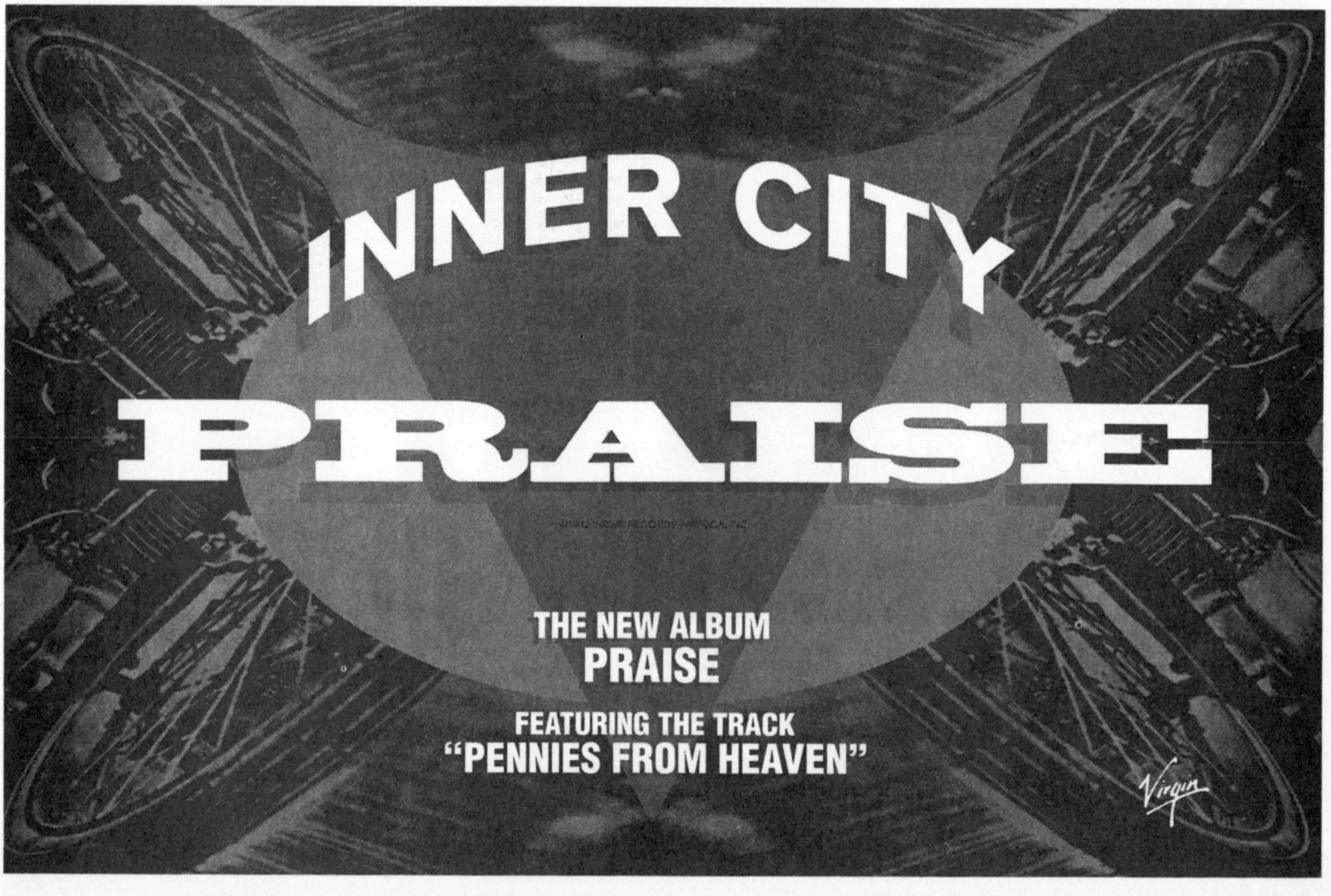

INNER CITY
PRAISE
THE NEW ALBUM
PRAISE
FEATURING THE TRACK
"PENNIES FROM HEAVEN"
Virgin

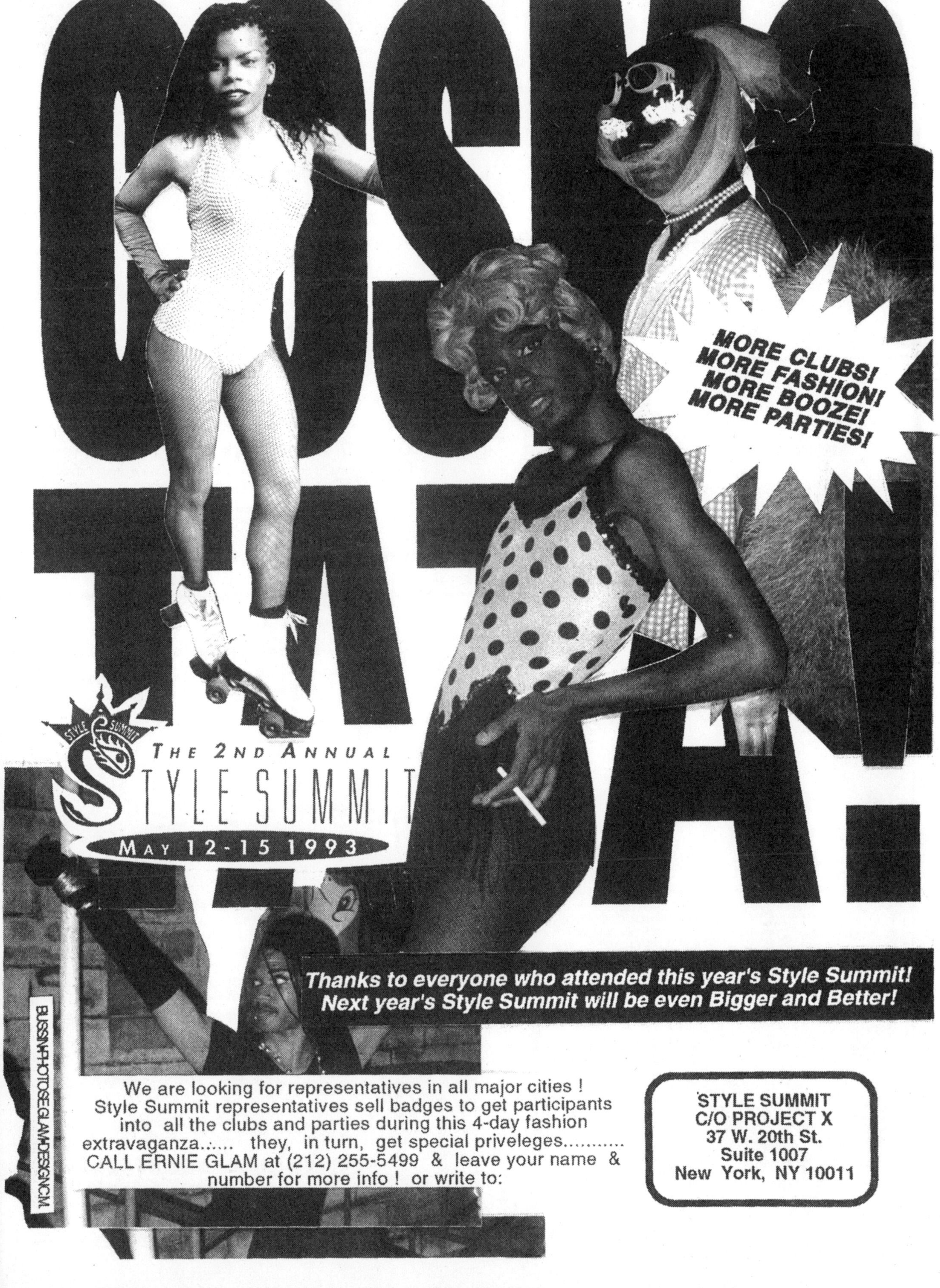

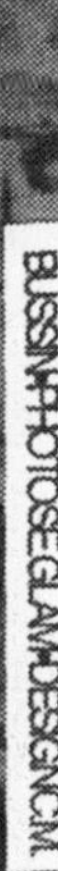

THE 2ND ANNUAL
STYLE SUMMIT
MAY 12 - 15 1993

Thanks to everyone who attended this year's Style Summit!
Next year's Style Summit will be even Bigger and Better!

We are looking for representatives in all major cities !
Style Summit representatives sell badges to get participants
into all the clubs and parties during this 4-day fashion
extravaganza...…..   they, in turn, get special priveleges..........
CALL ERNIE GLAM at (212) 255-5499 & leave your name &
number for more info ! or write to:

STYLE SUMMIT
C/O PROJECT X
37 W. 20th St.
Suite 1007
New York, NY 10011

COMING OUT

is a life long commitment to telling the truth about our lives.

COMING OUT

is also the key to the empowerment of our community, the only way we'll ever get proper AIDS funding, and the best way to put an end to discrimination.

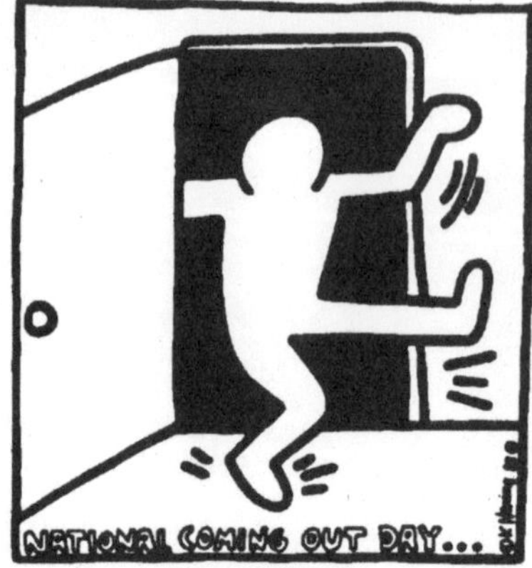

Please give generously to the most effective campaign our community will ever wage.

NATIONAL COMING OUT DAY-OCTOBER II

PO BOX 8270, SANTA FE , NM 87504-8270/505-982-2558

YOUR CONTRIBUTION IS TAX DEDUCTIBLE

THING

She Knows Who She Is

NUMBER SEVEN • FALL 92

PUBLISHER/ART DIRECTION
Robert Ford

EDITORS
Trent Adkins, Robert Ford, Terry Martin

ADVERTISING
Terry Martin, Sylvia Michaels

EDITORIAL ASSISTANCE
Duane Baskins, Ohmi Daniels, Steve Lafreniere, Karen Spies

GRAPHIC SERVICES
Simone Bouyer

DESKTOP PUBLISHING
International Media Associates

THING (ISSN 1064-9727) is published quarterly by Thing Publishing. Opinions expressed are those of individual contributors and do not always reflect those of Thing Publishing.
© 1992 THING

THING PUBLISHING

2151 W. DIVISION
CHICAGO, ILLINOIS USA 60622-3056
VOICE (312) 227-1780
FAX (312) 227-1886

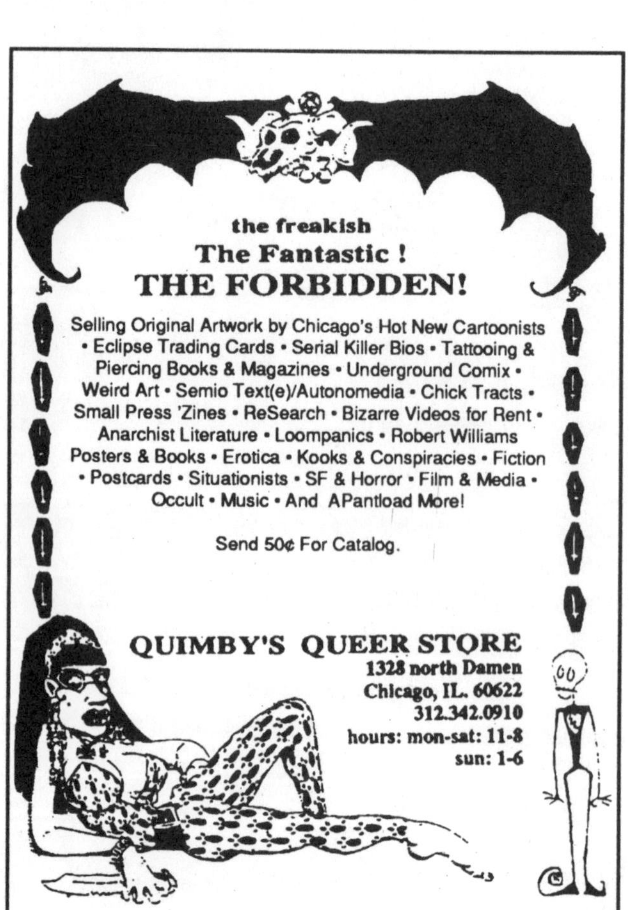

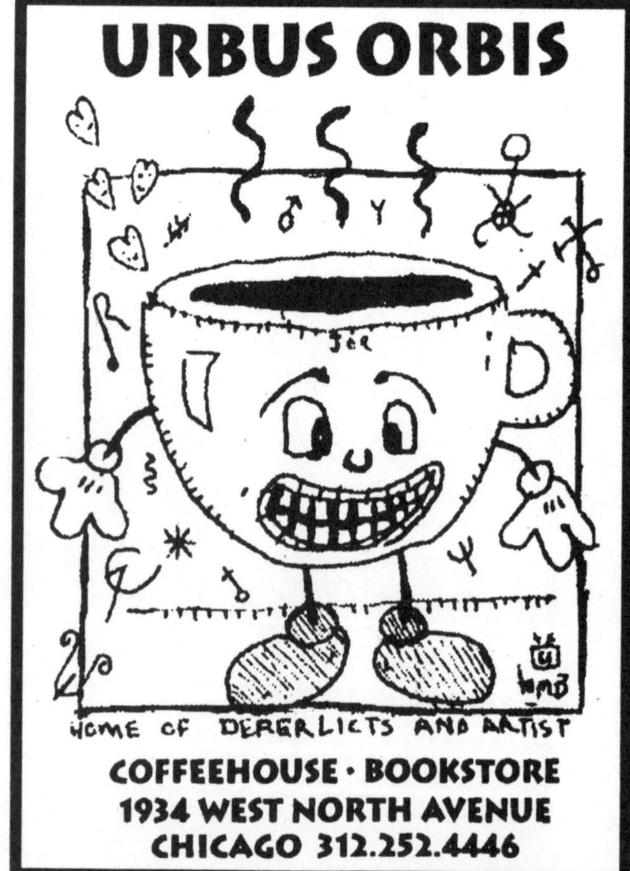

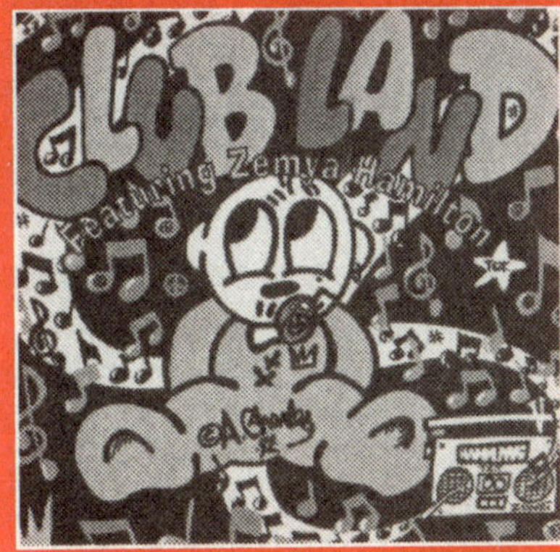

CLUB LAND

featuring Zemya Hamilton

Catch the scorching new single
"HYPNOTIZED"
from Clubland's self-titled debut album

"With great vocals, well-written songs and great hooks, Clubland defines the perfect pop house group." — Streetsound

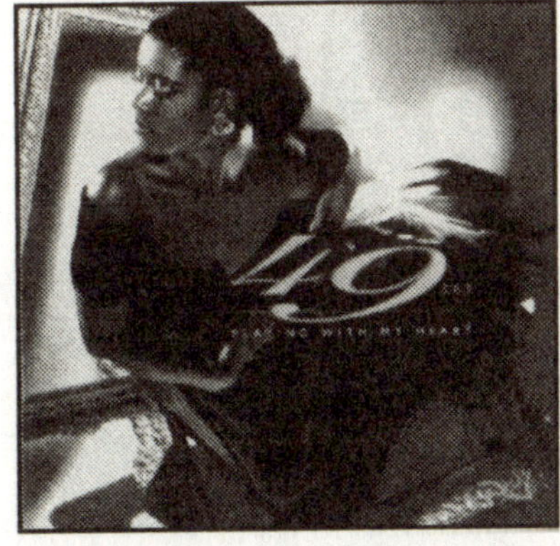

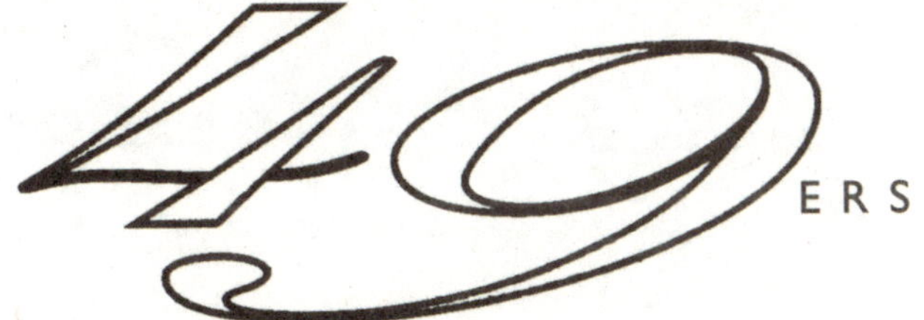

Prepare to hear
"THE MESSAGE"
featuring
Masters at Work
remixes

And don't miss the 49ers' fab new album, *Playing With My Heart.* Italian house never sounded better!

A blazing new talent returns with
"WÉ-WÉ"
featuring mixes by John Robinson and Edgewise

angēlique
kidjo

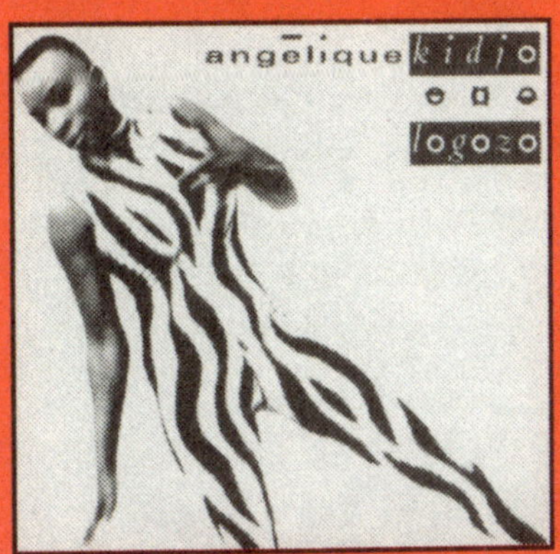

From the Mango Records album *Logozo*

The follow-up to the underground club smash "BATONGA"

TOO FIERCE!

Slammin' club sounds, exclusively on

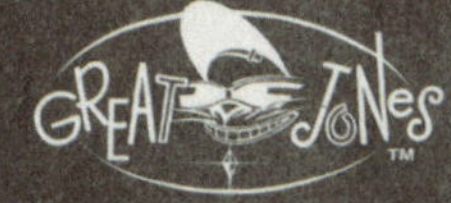

GREAT MUSIC FOR A GREAT CAUSE.

"Red Hot + Dance." The new album and home video dedicated to raising money for AIDS research and relief.

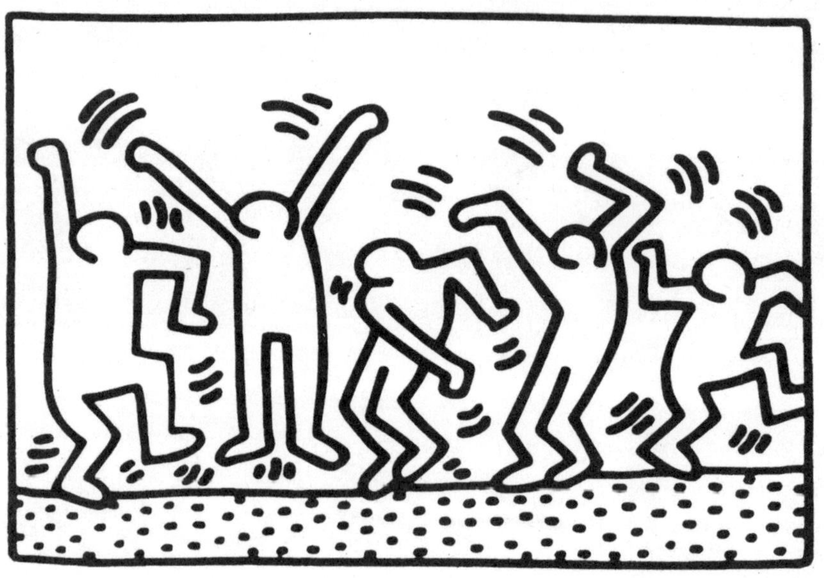

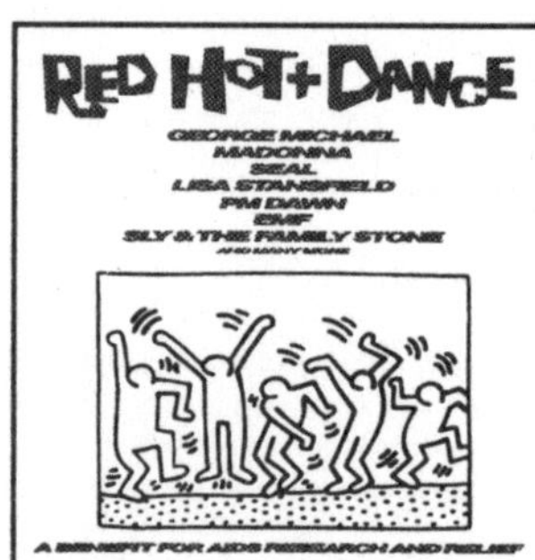

The new Album, CD, or Cassette.

Featuring 3 previously-unreleased tracks from **George Michael** you can't find anywhere else: the smash <u>Too Funky</u>, <u>Do You Really Want To Know</u>, and <u>Happy</u>. Plus hot new dance remixes of smash hits from **Madonna, P.M. Dawn, Crystal Waters, EMF, Young Disciples, Sabrina Johnston, Lisa Stansfield, Seal, Sly & The Family Stone,** and **tomandandy.** Featuring today's hottest remixers/producers—David Morales, Joey Negro, Nellee Hooper, Sly & Robbie, Brian Eno, and more.

The new Home Video.

Featuring live performances by **C+C Music Factory, EMF, P.M. Dawn, Lisa Stansfield, Crystal Waters, Seal,** and many more, combined with interviews and celebrity appearances into a mesmerizing spectacle. Also includes the bonus video of **George Michael's** <u>Too Funky</u>, and exclusive behind-the-scenes footage from the <u>Too Funky</u> filming.

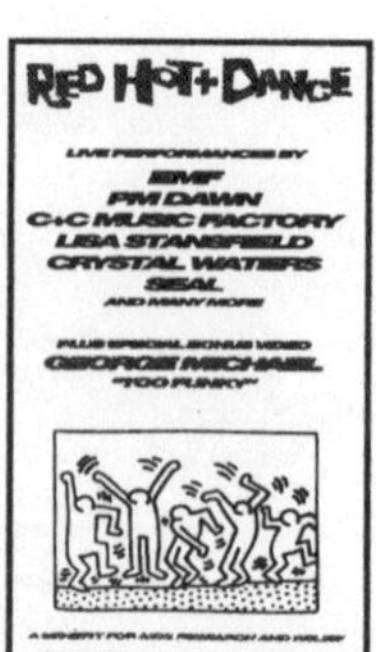

RED HOT + DANCE A step in the right direction.

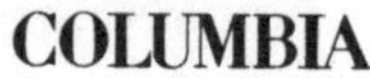

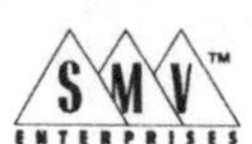

THING

SHE KNOWS WHO SHE IS • FALL 92

contents

EVERYTHING TO GO!

FEATURES

THE BACK

COVER & THIS PAGE: Lemuel photographed by T. Adkins

every THING to GO!

Wigstock 92!

PHOTOS: Robert Ford & Terry Martin

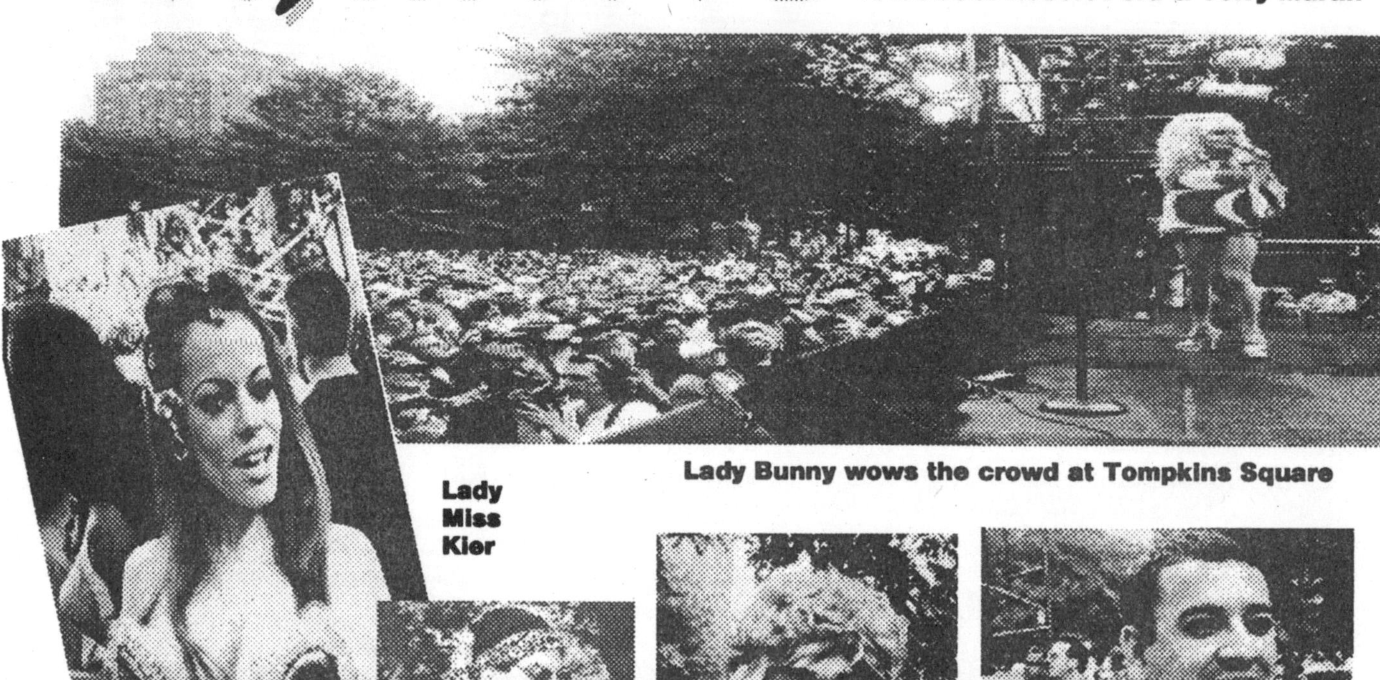

Lady Bunny wows the crowd at Tompkins Square

Lady Miss Kier

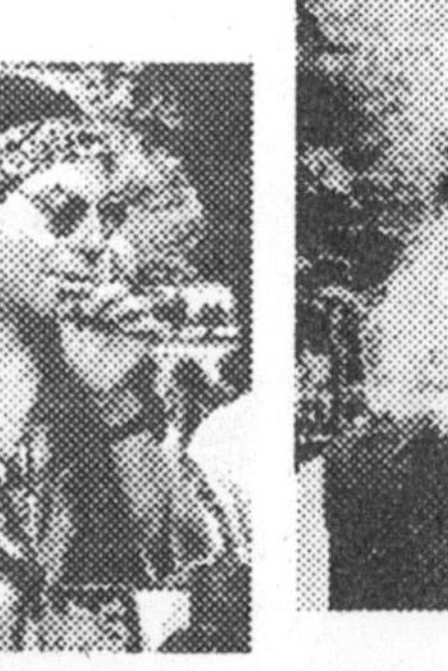

Michael Musto

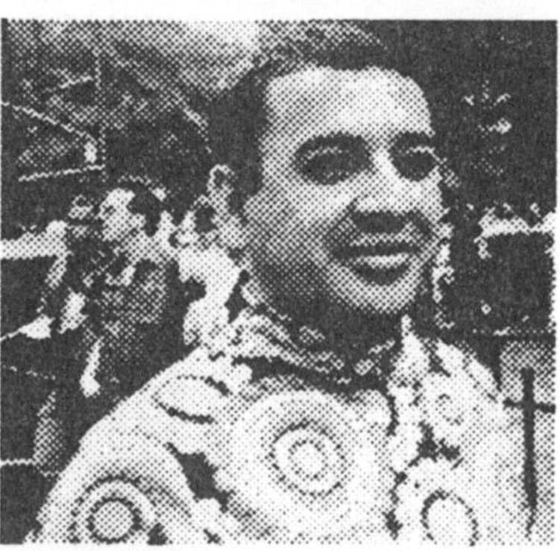

Skinny Vinny   Homoture's Fluffy Boy

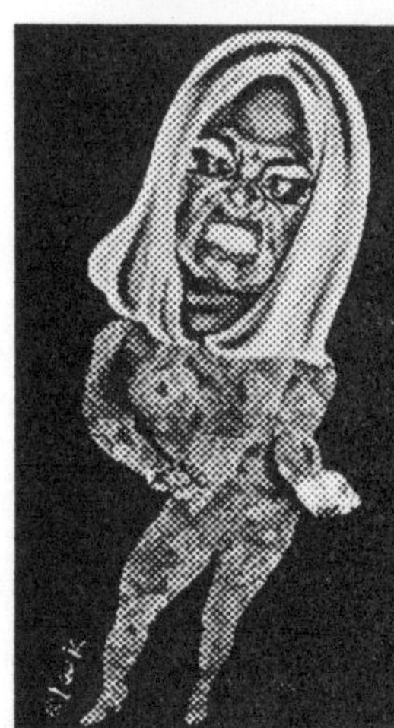

Girl, but LEE KAY gets around! His quest to bubblehead every queer celebrity under the sun continues with the almost-as-large-as-life Mona Foot. "She's almost as big as I am" says the 5'8" artist. He took snapshots of her this past summer at the queer Carol Mosley Braun benefit and the next thing you know, there's Mona in the window at Roscoe's! At this rate, we'll be seeing the entire cast of Wigstock, en masse peering onto Halsted Street in no time! (We can dream.)

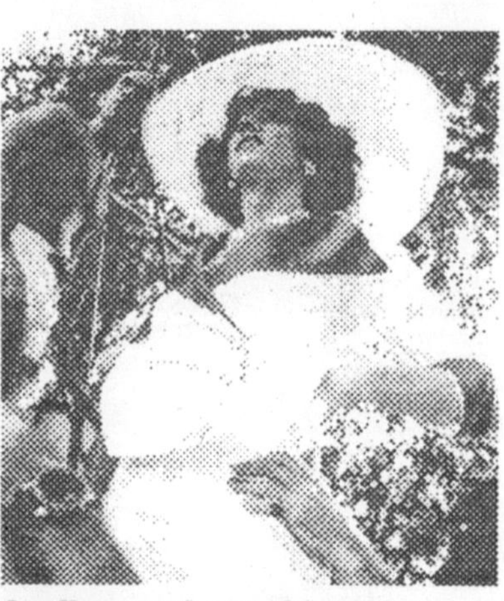

Ladies and gentlemen, Lypsinka!

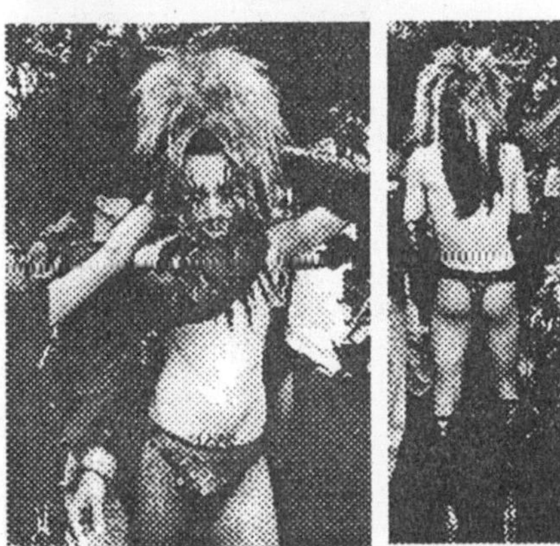

SUPERMODEL: RuPaul!

Front & Back: JoJo Field.

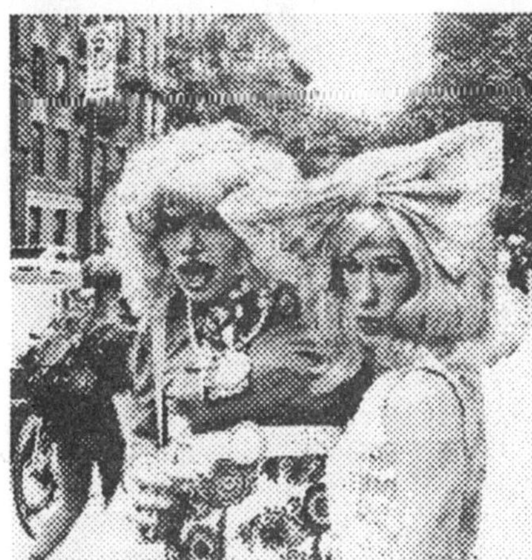

Yaaaaaay! DeAundra Peek and Daisy Chain.

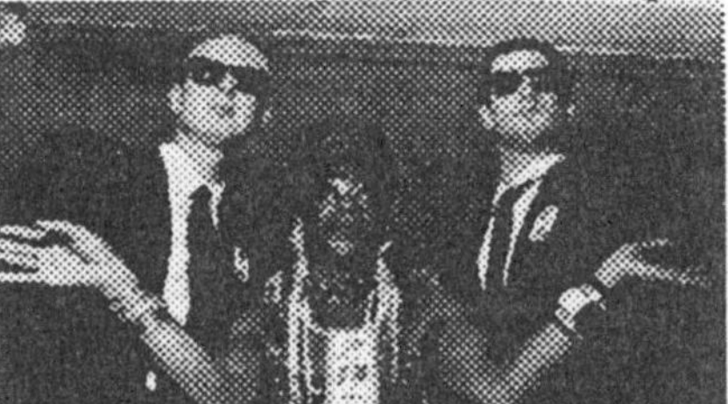

VOTE
baby, vote!

Hello, this is Joan Jett Blakk writing to you from my vacation home in Kenny-fag-port. I'm taking a small but much needed break from the campaign to cool my (high) heels and do some serious inhaling. Whilst I'm being so introspective, I feel it's time to remind everyone how important it is to vote. Now, I know already what some of you are thinking, you're thinking how you really don't want to throw your vote away to some drag queen who has no chance in hell of winning and that's all well and good 'cause this ain't the place to ask for votes, anyway. What I'm talking about is using that ballot thing to get some sort of a voice heard. Even a protest vote is a vote none the less. We certainly can't let those big fucks in Washington think we don't exist. I don't know if you remember, but Reagan was elected in 1984 with something like 38% of the vote and he called that a mandate! (The only Mandate I know about is the porn rag. Yum!) That's redick you less. Where was everybody else. All those folks were somewhere, honey, but not in the voting booth. Or maybe they were in there but they were doin' something else. (Can you say "wanking" boys and girls?) Anyway, we need to take this government on on all fronts. We need to be out in the streets protesting every stupid decision they make, we need to be out and open about who we are to with everyone, we need to hold hands in public. More PDA on the CTA! We need to trust each other even if we don't agree on certain issues. We need to tell each other when that shirt absolutely does not go with those pants. And we need to get out and vote, I mean, it's not the only way we can take over the country and get it on a more glamorous track, but it's one sure way. And I'm all for leaving no precious stone unturned in our fight for freedom and decent government!

Love you, mean it! Later, lunch!
Joan Jett Blakk,
Presidential Candidate

In our "ain't I a woman?" category, kudos to Natalie Hutchison and Mary Morten, co-directors and producers of the NIA project. The project, a thirty minute video, presents and documents the lives and voices of African-American lesbians. NIA (Swahili for purpose) directly confronts those, in both the African-American and lesbian communities, who would deny or belittle

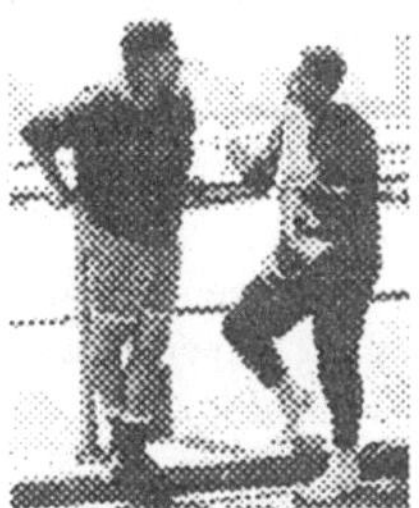

Natalie Hutchison (R) and Mary Morten, of the NIA project.

our existence. Clips from the work-in-progress presented this summer at the Randolph Street Gallery and Cafe Voltaire received enthusiastic acclaim. The project has received several grants, but individual donations (time, energy and talent) are enthusiastically welcomed. To learn more about the NIA project and upcoming events, contact Mary or Natalie at 312.728.9877.

Yes, dyke dreams really do come true. The Lesbian Community

DYKES
charge!

Cancer Project and Lesbian Chicago are now sharing a space and creating a safe place for lesbians to celebrate. Pat Parker Place, named after one of the most renowned poet activists of the African-American-lesbian community, is located at 1902 W. Montrose Avenue in Chicago. This space symbolizes the coming together of multi-ethnic lesbian communities. Lesbian Chicago offers free space to any lesbian group. Currently, Lesbian Chicago's meeting facilities are used for support,

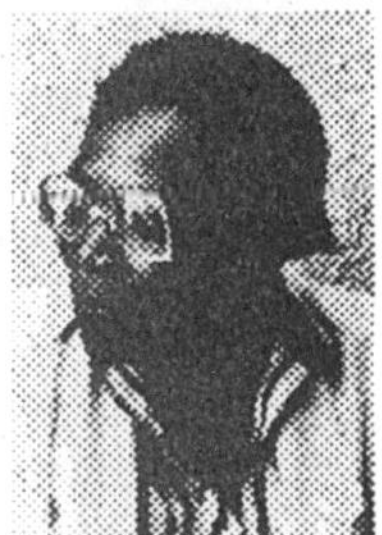

Pat Parker.

rap, and discussion groups. In the future, LC can provide space for classes, workshops, or rehearsals. For further information or to offer your talents to Pat Parker Place, contact: Valerie Lopez - Lesbian Chicago at 312.784.6037 or Mary McCauley II - LCCP at 312.561.4662

by shari james

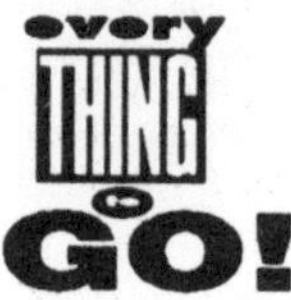

sex LIES & audiotape

TANGLED: What local label went through eleventh hour art kaflama 'cause their new boy disco star was a wee bit too queeny looking in the image?.... **FASTER PUSSYCAT, KILL! KILL!:** What

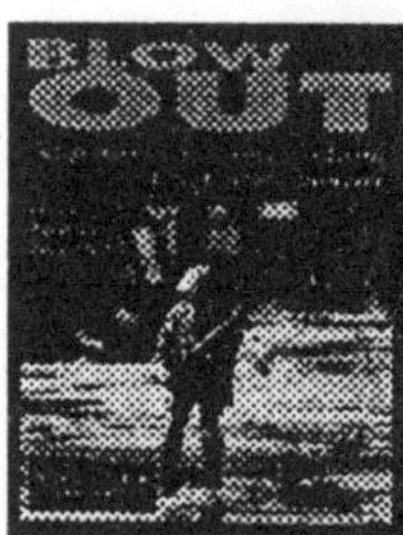

local celeb let one publisher have it (in stereo) at the Wednesday night one word fag bar? Disagreement is fine, but drama is so unnecessary!...

GIMME SHELTER!

What white whiz-kid thought up this tacky Shelter invite playing on all-too-recent LA riot imagery? Not a good look, especially for a club whose door-people lose the guest list when a party of black fags arrive (Ultra Naté plus

QUASHED Speaking of the unnecessary, what could be less erotic than that same party's safe sex spectacle? Prissy posing and oh-so-chic underwear aim for Weber but land somewhere below International Male. And ATTITUDE doing! What's so sexy about an aloof, pouty narcissist shaking it at you? Get dressed and quit ringin'! **OFF THE RECORD:** during a certain celebrity House interview, it was let slip that this season's read-you-for-points intro (Miss Thing, there is no guest list tonight!!) is based on a true story at NYC's Pyramid club. They told girlfriend! **SUF-FRAGETTE**

CITY Miss Joan, honey, sit down. Everybody loves you, which is why nobody has the nerve to tell you directly. But the musical act is tired! And the bruised-black lipliner has got to go, too. Girlfriend makes for many squirming fags and dykes when she's on the bill. Take a hint from RuPaul and Mona Foot: pump up the glamour and make it funky. **HOUSE MUZAK ALL NIGHT LONG** Has anybody noticed how, er, sappy some Frankie Knuckles mixes are? The lavish keyboards, the lush legacy of the strings...one expects Dinah Shore or the Lenon Sisters to come in with the chorus. We never thought we'd live long enough to see Frankie become the Percy Faith of House Music. The Nestea spot cinched it. We await the Lawrence Welk's Greatest Hits with Extra Production by Frankie Knuckles or Authur Fiedler conducting the Whistle Song and other National House Anthems. (And while we're at it, Larry Heard gets kinda Mantovanni-ish after too long, too.) **MERCY!** Some local clubowners, graduates of the BMCS school no doubt, make working for them a chore. Nobody likes getting dicked with no grease after standing on their dogs for hours bumpin' disco tunes. And the promised drink tickets and red carpet treatment? Please!! How much did you spend at the bar?

Miss Club Ownerness is grand enough to call you from her car phone at 7am but somehow can't manage to take your calls about your money. Hmmm...**WE WANT PUSSY!**

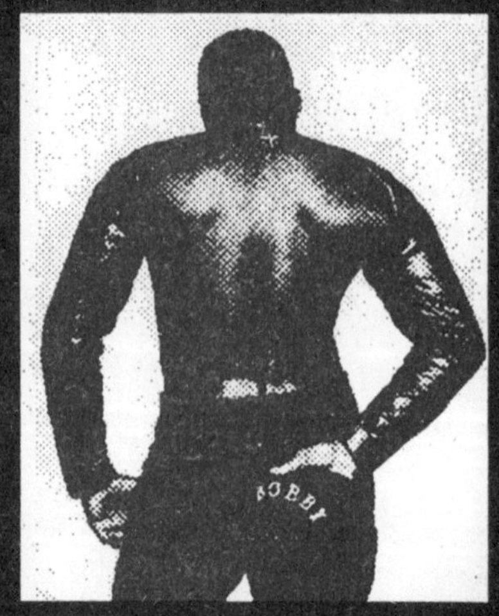

The Missing Pussy. Careful readers will note that the pair of anonymous naughties known as Bunny and Pussy aren't the duo any longer. What happened that we aren't hearing from Pussy now? Did they part amicably? Fans of Pussy needn't worry. We've heard that there's a forthcoming Pussy Talks with Sandra Bernhard and a piece with artist Diamanda Galas that's been a year (two?) in the making. **ON THE RIVIERA**... We hope that the Riv has hosted their last "gay night" and will have no need to advertise in this rag. Expenses incurred by certain ex-employees on their way to Betty Ford for advertising their failed Thrust Sundays have yet to be paid. Phone calls resulted in a round of passing the buck. We finally tracked down a bookkeeper who suggested we be inconvenienced to brave it into Uptown for cash, then boofed us by being "fired" moments before our scheduled arrival. Do we have time for this mess? I DON'T THINK SO! **BROKE?** A certain high profile clinic has no money for a (cheap) *Thing* ad this time; must be 'cause those weekly *Windy City* ads cost so much!

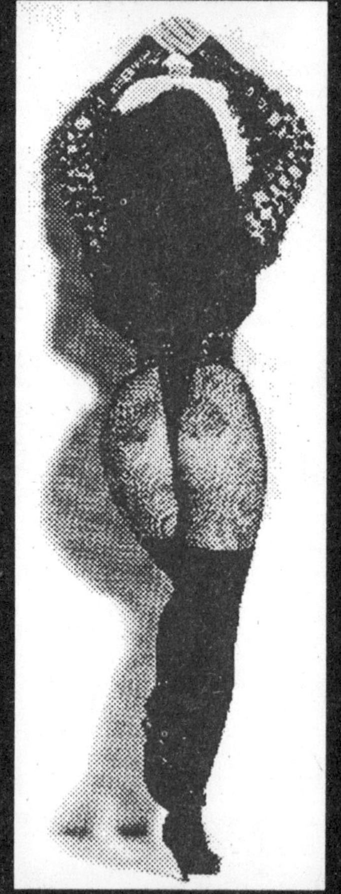

BABY'S GOT BACK: The rock and roll butt has been a popular icon since way before Springsteen, witness these recent celebrity rumps. Mr Whitney Houston gives us the Banjie Realness Booty, while Cher shares her penchant for tatoos and fishnets. Let's hope this trend doesn't catch on with Luther Vandross or Carnie Wilson!

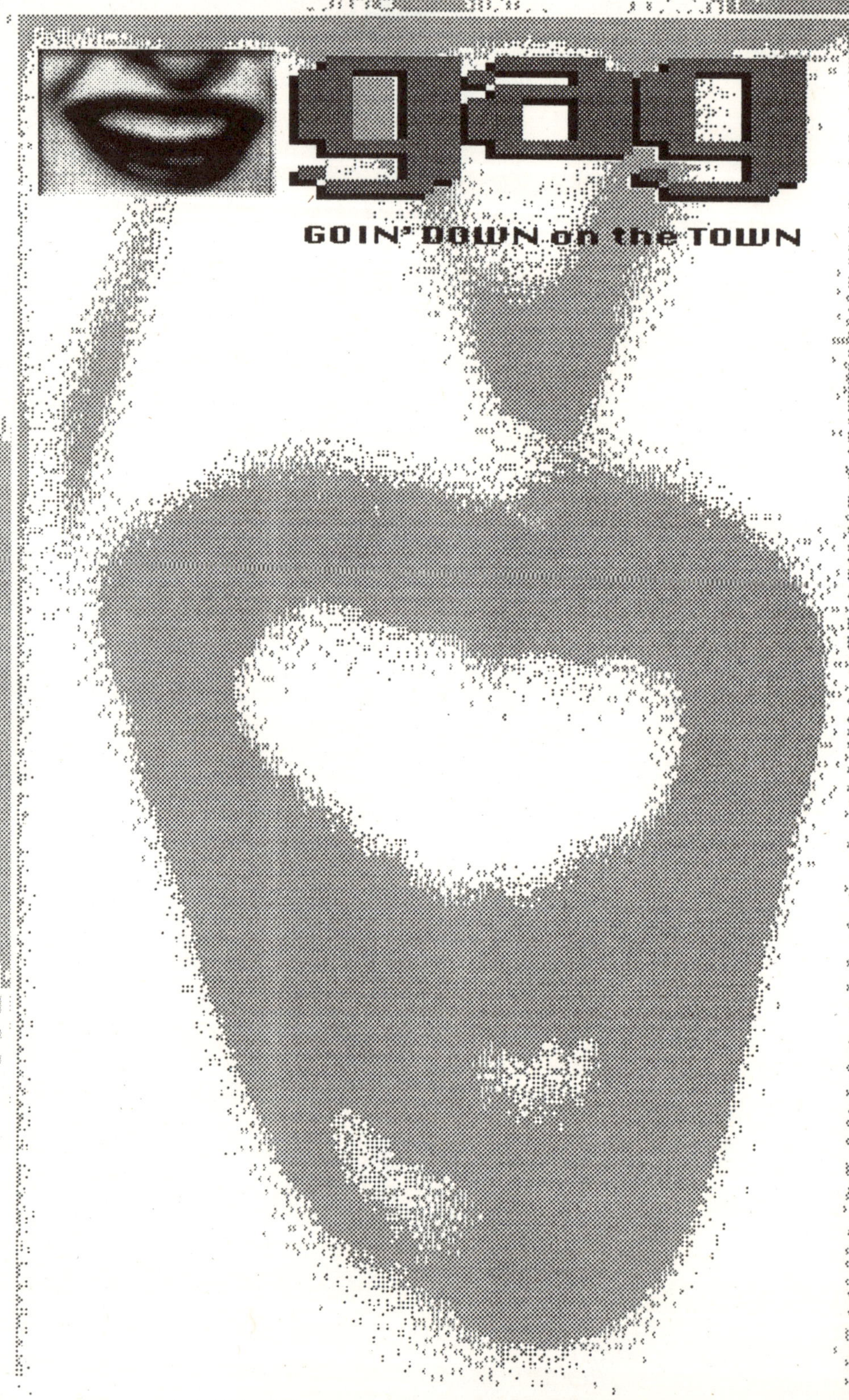
gag
GOIN' DOWN on the TOWN
1153 n dearborn # 203 chicago 60610

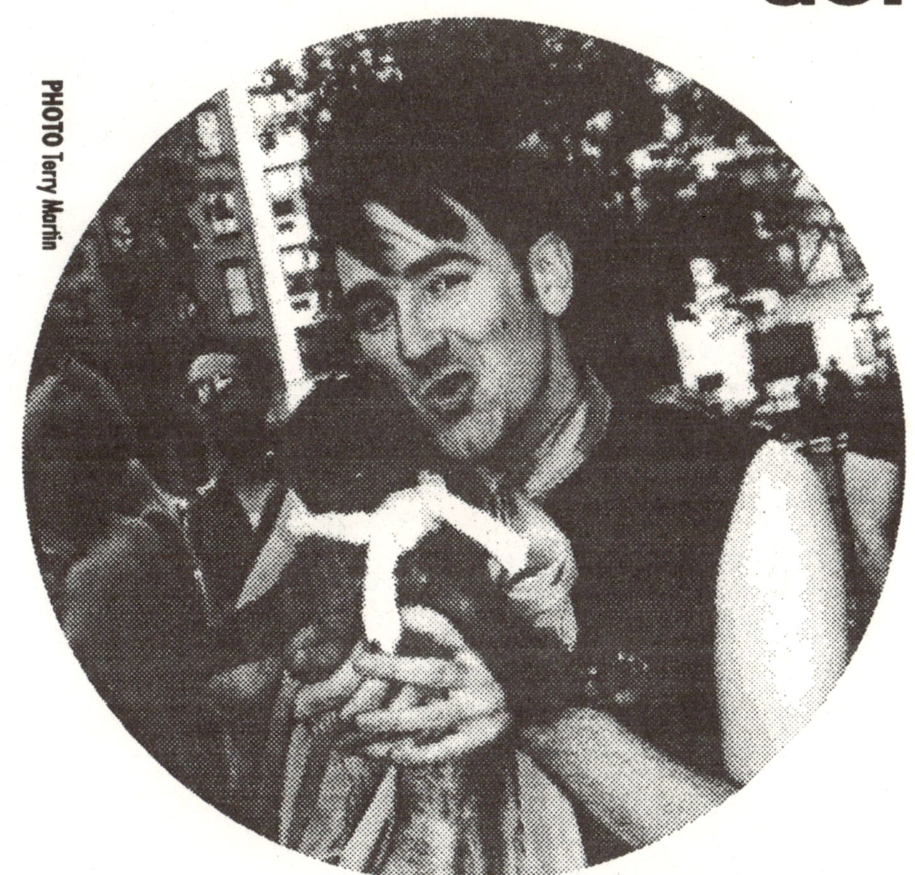

to **TEE: TA talks to LARRY TEE**

The first time I met Larry Tee, Lady Bunny cohort, Love Machine host, and former leader of the band The Now Explosion, he was with his perennial sidekick, wild-woman Lahoma Van Zandt and a friend at the Sound Factory in New York. They'd just closed the Roxy where Larry was spinning with Frankie Knuckles. I recognized the infamous pair right away: There was Larry Tee with that mod hair, too hip and too suave, and Lahoma looking even better than her photos in her trademark red spandex minidress and fuck-me stiletto mules. I'd become a fan through their many records, performances at Wigstock, their coverage in *My Comrade*, and through their roles in the films of John Witherspoon and Dick Richards. Larry and I met again in Chicago when he was brought here for the opening of Quench. Now, I'm returning a call to his apartment in the West Village to talk about his upcoming projects. And, to cull beauty tips. ▶▶ ▶▶ ▶▶

Trent: Larry?
Larry Tee: Yeah, who is this?
T: Trenton.
L: Hey, Trent! How are you?
T: Fine. How are you?
L: I'm doin' alright.
T: Are you screening your calls? I guess you should, you're such a big star. Anybody could be calling you.
L: No, no, no, not at all. Actually, I have a lovely, luxurious three-story apartment I lucked into and it took me awhile to get downstairs. I thought I heard somebody asking for DeAundra Peek.
T: No. I thought I heard DeAundra's voice when the machine went, "Leave a message-Yaaaaay!"
L: Oh, that's LaHoma on my machine. And of course, LaHoma was just down in Atlanta with DeAundra...
T: I know those DeAundra-isms can rub off on a girl rather quickly.
L: I'll tell you, right now, down in Atlanta, there's three Larry Tees and about six LaHomas! They've just... spawned! It's gotten so that LaHoma doesn't bring her new wigs because this one girl clocks the wigs and then gets 'em!
T: Imitation is the truest form of flattery. How are things in New York?
L: Oh, it's really hot in the city right now. It's awful.
T: Speaking of LaHoma, who's that gorgeous new girl in your group?
L: The new girl is Mihoko. She's from Nagasaki and she is gorgeous! She's absolutely out of her mind! Which is great, 'cause you need that with our burlesque style of cheap-pull-out-the-flash-light-then-use-the-toilet-paper way of performing. It's all very entertaining. She just loves a good cheap over-accessorized outfit and loves hamming it up. She's the door person at Disco 2000 and she was the VIP door girl at Palace de Beauté when we were doing that at the Underground.
T: I saw that piece with you and Joey Arias in *Paper* and you were talking about your new single "Come Fly With Me" which I saw you perform here at Shelter in Chicago. Is that out yet?

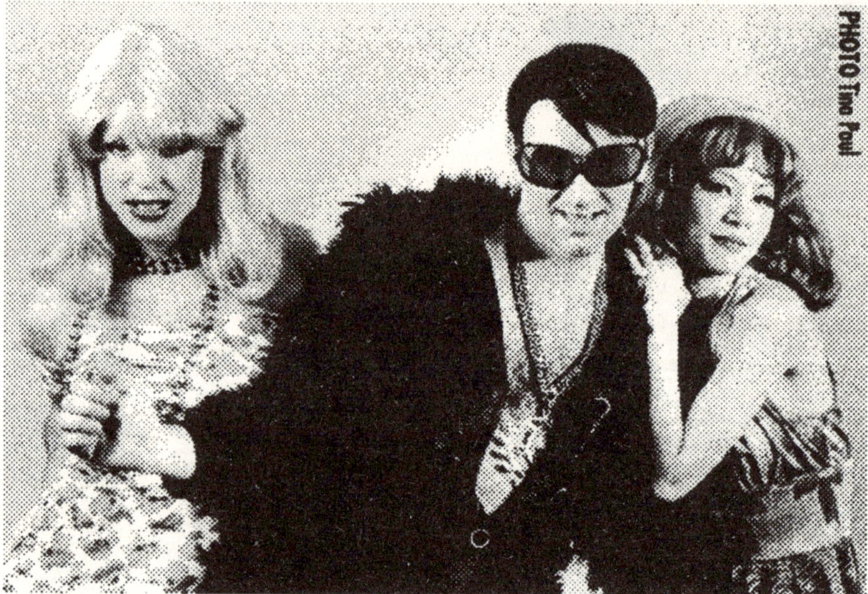

(L to R) La Homa, Larry Tee, and Mihoko.

L: Yeah, I did that there with those two adorable kids...
T: That was Marky (de Sade) and Jahnne (Vavoom).
L: Yeah, they were so sweet. Tell them I say hello. The "Come Fly With Me" video is already out on RockAmerica. There's a club there in Chicago that's playing it.
T: Berlin maybe?
L- No, although I should get one over there, too.
T: Vortex?
L: Yeah, it's at Vortex and I here they're dancing around to it there and stuff. Some friends of mine from Miami were really shocked when they heard people singing along to it.. you know, "Let's get high..." It gets to the point. I mean, what do people want to hear? "Let's do it." "Let's get high." It's one of the first things I want to hear. The single will be out on Funtone in September. I just finished a new track with RuPaul. We had been kind of strained for a while.
T: Really?
L- Yeah, well, you know Ru's cyclical and will be kind of on the hot side for a while and then not. And I'm always definitely on the not phase for about a good year and a half, but I went over and heard some of the Ru stuff and thought maybe if I submitted a song they might use it. So, I got out my rottenest idea book and thought, "Well, she needs a song about a supermodel, she's such a supermodel herself." 'Cause she's definitely serving that supermodel thing and plus I thought it would be a good point

of reference on a record so people would go, "Oh, I get it!" It's tongue in cheek and it's got a good beat and a sense of humour and plus it'll be fun to watch her perform it. I've been told she screamed when she heard the idea. I think it might get on the album. I think it may be the first single.
T: Hey, how's Bunny and everybody?
L: Oh, she's great. She just got back from doing a benefit out in San Francisco with Deee-Lite. She's doin' great, gettin' ready for Wigstock and everything.
T: Are you still doing Roxy with Frankie (Knuckles)?
L: No. It was getting down to once every two weeks, once every three weeks, and basically I can earn more money without doing it. There basically wasn't any money in it anymore. I'd done two years there.
T: Do you think you'll be doing anymore clubs there?
L: Well, certainly not in the middle of July. But certainly in the fall I think I'll crank up something new. I'm doing Electric Burlesque on Tuesday nights at Wonder Bar. Basically it's a large steak house with a big dancefloor and the crowd is really wild. Last week we had Grace Jones down there. She came to see her brother Chris do a number, kind of a Robert Owens/Mr. Fingers house type jam. He did a little nudie thing at the end that I could have lived without, though.
T: Hey, Larry got any beauty

tips? I'm compiling tips for a Beauty Book of the Stars.

L: You know, I don't think my beauty tips would work on anybody else. I never use soap on my Goddamned body! I let the water do its job. I *will* touch up the pits. I don't use make-up, so my tender eye tissue isn't being yanked and pulled. Poor LaHoma! She's my roommate and I get to see the damage on her from all the make-up and liquor so I steer clear of those two things. I'm not really into the sun. I don't tan. I'm such a shamelessly white thing. God, when I go out on the beach, kids run! swear to God! I look like a white shark that... honestly! That's my beauty regimen. Plus I don't like sweating. Which is why you'll rarely see me out cuttin' a rug on the dancefloor. I hate to sound like a puss. I will sweat. Sometimes I gotta stomp.

T: Do you have a favorite record right now?

L: I do love that "There's Some Whores in This House" track. Have you heard that one? It's just wicked. It's one of those records you can "stamp" your feet to. It's a very Sound Factory record. At like, eleven o'clock in the morning.

T: So where do you hang out when you're not working?

L: Well, like I say, I do love the Sound Factory. That's one place you can be sure to find me, 'cause I think it's the best, most unique nightclub on the planet. At least to my eyes. I'm sure there's better, but I like the way Junior (Vasquez) takes things down to the beat. You know he just kind of de-sembles beats, he's got his own thing and I just love to dance to it.

T: Where are you getting the inspiration for the stuff that you write and produce?

L: I like to dredge out sounds from old records or feelings from old records and then kind of take it from there. I think snatches of sounds off of old records can get really wicked and unusual. I love warped sounding stuff.

T: So, you're talking about sampling?

L- Sampling definitely. Sample a good sound. Put a layer or two of something funky on it... it gives people a reference and it's new, too. And of course, sometimes I don't sample at all. I mean I might sample drum sounds or something but not anything major.

T- How's your love life?

L- Great! Actually, it's kind of hard to have any love life during the summer.

Especially when you don't have air-conditioning.

T: I've never had that problem. Did you shop in Chicago while you were here?

L-Yes! The thrift stores there are the best! I got wonderful things. I got a feathered jacket! Like, real pimp wear for five dollars! I went around with Michael Mangiaforte. In New York you wouldn't be able to find it and if you did, it wouldn't be five dollars. When you talk to Michael Mangiaforte or anybody that has a club in Chicago, tell them, "What are you waiting for?! We want more Larry Tee!"

T: See! Thanks Larry.

L: Bye!

LARRY TEE'S TOP TEN

Whores In The House Frank Ski (Deco Clubtrax)

Some Lovin Liberty City (Murk)

Jump Around House Of Pain (Tommy Boy)

Rhythm Is A Dancer (Tee's Mix) Snap (Arista)

Masterblaster Joint Venture (Strictly Rhythm)

My Piece Of Heaven Ten City (East West)

Get With You Lidell Townsell (Mercury)

Oh Oh Why Rhythm Masters (Cutting Traxx)

Together Interceptor (Murk)

Para Los Rumberos Tito Puente (Elektra)

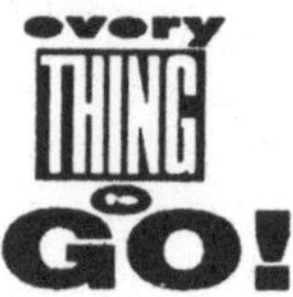

OSCAR MC MILLIAN

Ten City My Piece Of Heaven (East West)
Joint Venture Master Blaster (Strictly Rhythm)
Lil' Louis Saved My Life (Epic)
House Of Gypsies Somba (Freeze)
Scottie Deep Fathoms (Aztonk)
C&C Music Factory Keep It Coming (Columbia)
Vanessa Williams Work To Do (Wing)
Jimmy Polo Express Yourself (RCA Import)
Nu Shooz Time Will Tell (Atlantic)
Axxis All I'm Asking (One)

MIKE WINSTON

Lil' Louis Saved My Life (Epic)
Vanessa Williams Work To Do (Wing)
Club Ice Manhasset (MCA)
Terri Land Cherchez Le Femme (Alexia)
Roberta Gilliam Take Me (Emotive)
Nu Shooz Time Will Tell (Atlantic)
Michael Watford Closer To You (Tape)
Martha Wash Carry On (Tape)
Erb The Weekend (Clubhouse)
Tracie Davis We Can Make It (Relativity)

MIKE PRATA

The Wishdokta Mental Eclipse (White Label EP)
Nebula II Flatliner (RX) (J4m)
Underground Resistance The Seawolf (U.R.)
Frequency Systematic Imput (Lower East Side)
Sykosis 451 The Race To Space (Infra Sonic EP)
Trancesetters None Of The Above (First Impression)
Precious & Project Acid Cagliostro (Music Man)
The Enigmatist Get Stoopid (Bizzare)
Nino The Gun (Production House)
Flag Wonderful Day (Jumpin & Pumpin)

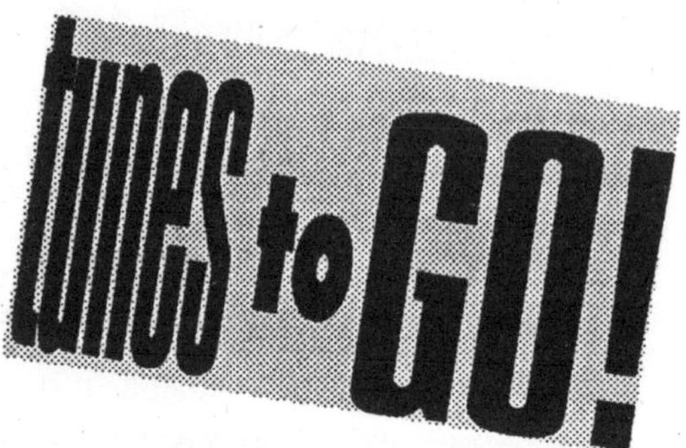

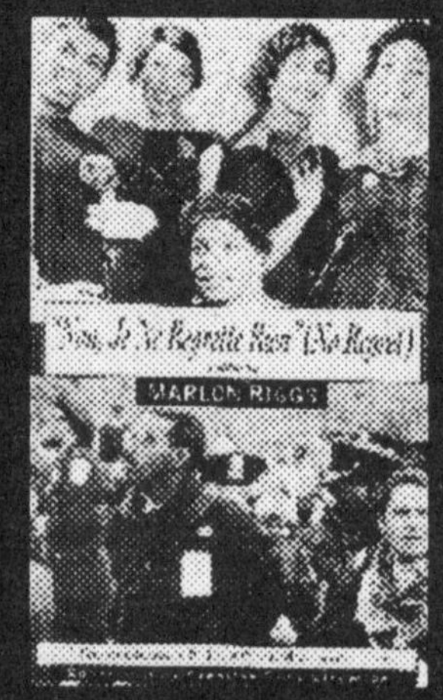

VIDEO REVIEW

"'Non, Je Ne Regrette Rien' (No Regret)" is the latest video release by Marlon Riggs, whose ground-breaking work "Tongues Untied" provided the first video document of black queer identity in America. The thirty-minute video was commissioned by the Fear of Disclosure project, a New York-based organization headed by Jonathan Lee. Fear of Disclosure began two years ago to distribute the video from which the project borrows its title, a collaboration between Phil Zwickler and artist David Wojnarowicz (both of whom have since died of AIDS). The Fear of Disclosure project documents the new social phenomenon of "coming out" as HIV positive through videos, reflecting the diverse communities which HIV impacts. The project also produced Marina Alvarez and Ellen Spiro's "(In)Visible Women" about Latino women and AIDS. New videos are in the works focusing on teenagers and Asian Americans.

"No Regret" looks at the issues around black gay men disclosing and accepting their HIV+ status. Five black gay men, from different eras and cultures, speak candidly and eloquently about living with HIV and being black and out. Riggs' relies on an unobtrusive style that seldom distracts us from the sheer power of the speakers' words. "No Regret" (the French title is a quote from Josephine Baker) covers a thorny and tangled group of topics with remarkable clarity. Sex, love, longing, desire, community, and family are discussed by this varied group. AIDS and the black church, issues of aging, eroticizing safer sex, and the impact of social class and politics are all touched upon. Among the subjects are Haitian born poet Assoto Saint, the late writer and activist Donald Woods, and National Task Force on AIDS Prevention director Reggie Williams.

"No Regret" premiered at the New Festival in New York this past June. The Chicago premiere is scheduled for December of this year, when Fear of Disclosure will host a series of screenings with the Film Center at the School of the Art Institute. Fear of Disclosure is working with distributors Frameline and Video Data Bank to coordinate community-based national screenings. Film festival entries and a PBS broadcast are also part of the plan to bring "No Regret" to a broader audience. For more information, contact Fear of Disclosure at (212) 923-1289.

— Robert Ford

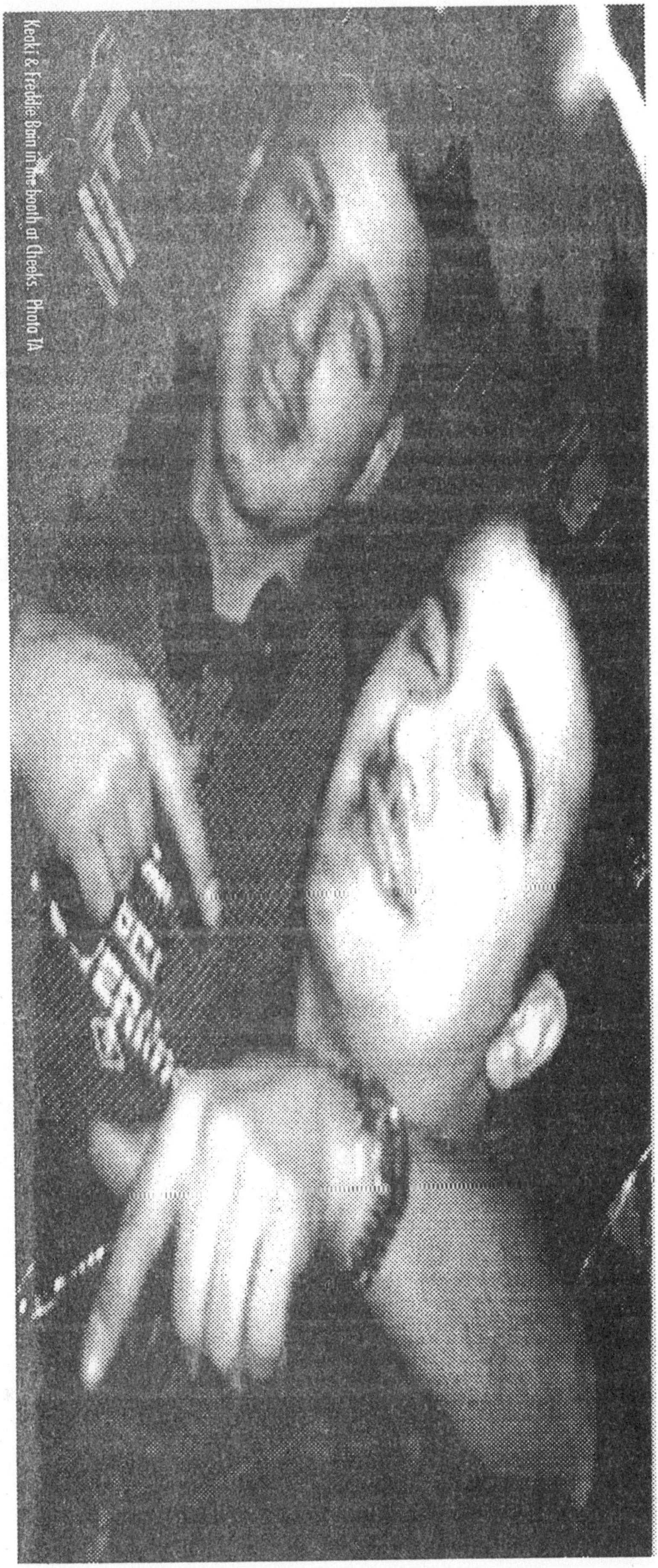

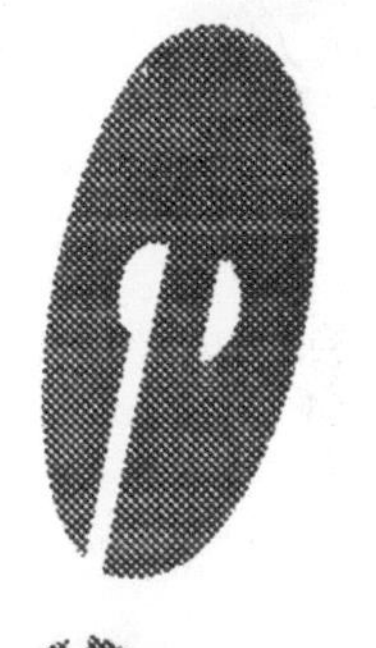
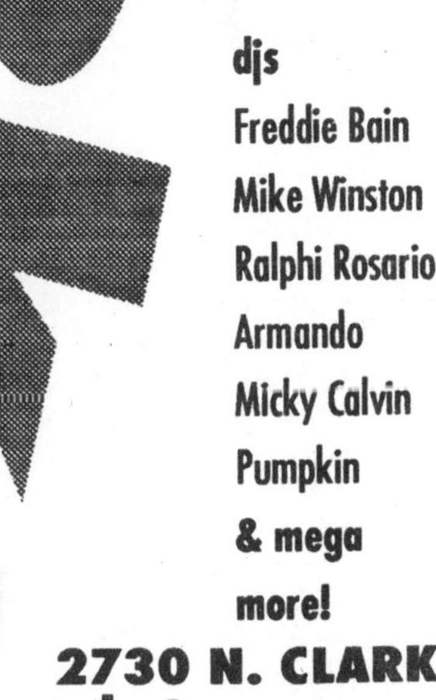

LOW trade!
FIERCE crowd!
GLAM drag!
CRUTE cocktails!
SICK beats!
OVAH ness!
CHEEKS
djs
Freddie Bain
Mike Winston
Ralphi Rosario
Armando
Micky Calvin
Pumpkin
& mega
more!
2730 N. CLARK chicago
THURSDAY Mercy! 11P-4A $2
FRIDAY Serious Dance Mob 12A-4A $2
SATURDAY C-MEN @ Cheeks 12A-5A $3
Kenki & Freddie Bain in the booth at Cheeks. Photo TA

REVIEWS

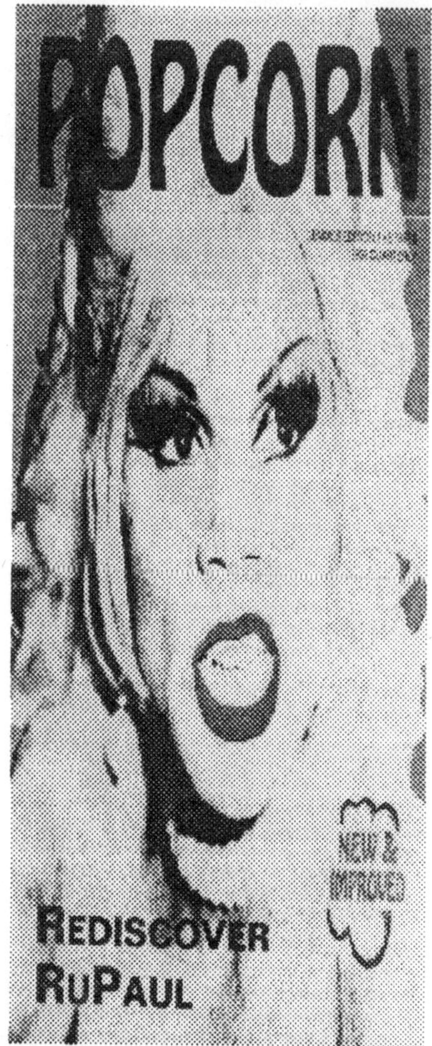

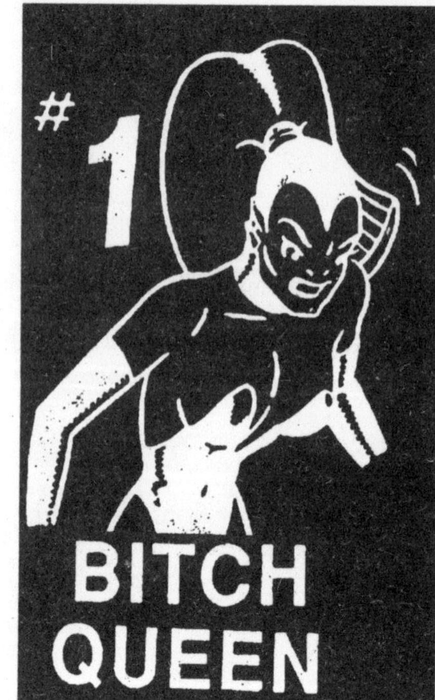

Many years ago, before *Thing* magazine, before *Think Ink* magazine, before *Planet Roc*, there was the idea for a music magazine to record and promote all the DJ drama that is the stay of our club-going, disco dancing lives in Chicago. We were gonna call it *BPM*. Now, *finally*, there is *Crossfade*, covering as much of the Chicago underground (and other) dance music scene as possible. Terry Martin's baby. I never thought I'd live to see it! Now *Thing* doesn't have to pass as "Chicago's coolest hip hop paper!" 2151 W. Division/Chicago IL 60622

— **Trent Adkins**

Hey kool girlz who want to do it for themselves... *Bitch Queen*'ll show you how, and then some. It'll leave you wondering what to make of Mz. Michelle who puts out (ahem) the first issue of her zine (methinks she's another bichick, but Fire Chick does have a bias, of course.) There are great blood and guts directions on how to fake a hemorrhage to get a free abortion. (Especially useful in years to come.) Good chick positive interview with a Guerrilla Girl. The whole zine is very — fuck "asking" —fuck just "taking back" — this is more like "attack!" *Bitch Queen* has a pro sex worker piece, reprints galore on many issues political with regards to women, queers and racism. You can read where to spit some venom at Nike for a particularly condescending and sexist ad campaign they wrought and thrust into our world. If that sounds too PC for your tastes, look and slobber over some cute spanky bondage -girl graphics, or turn to the page where she says that mace and whistles are ladylike wimp shit for stopping rapists — more of that age old argument that makes girlz take the nice way, the non-violent way, to stop a fucker — *Bitch Queen* wants you packin" a pistol, a shotgun, or a 38 special. Hail the Bitch girlz, she knows what she wants. Send it to her — she's begging for submission(s). (Fire Chick tends to have a one track mind.) box 1443/Boston MA 02117

— **Fire Chick**

Much like its food namesake, *Popcorn* magazine is light and fluffy, crunchy and delightfully habit forming. Atlanta has long been a mecca of entertainment and personalities with inimitably authentic Southern charm. Here's the news of all the southern belles and bellettes that follow Lady Bunny, RuPaul, Lurleen Wallis, Daisy Chain, Larry Tee, The American Music Show and Funtone Records, The Pop Tarts, Mr. Chuck, DeAundra Peek and the gang and on and on. And right now, it's the only place where you'll find the genius Betty Jack DeVine, *Popcorn*'s resident columnist and fabulous Thing-about-the-globe. Did she ever write a society column for The *County Herald*? 325 Edgewood/Atlanta GA 31312

— **Trent Adkins**

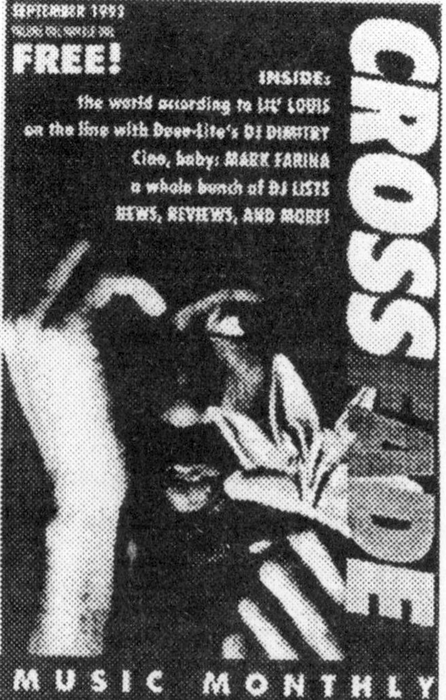

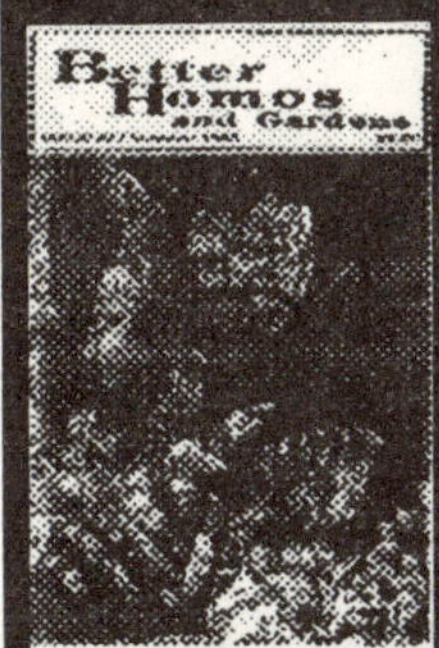

BETTER HOMOS AND GARDENS
EDITOR: Dan Levy
ADDRESS: 8283 1/4B Santa Monica Blvd. West Hollywood, CA 90046
"This is only my 2nd printing so it's all still new to me. I am also a performance artist and I attack this work in the same way, anything goes, especially things that I don't think should go, or things that I don't feel very secure about its those things I know need to get said, written, expressed. Always challenge the thought of what is right or wrong, good or bad, artistic or not, and mostly that I have the human right to explore and put it out there. It's cool to get things in the mail from perfect strangers Like this zine show!"

FERTILE LA TOYAH JACKSON MAGAZINE
EDITOR: Ms. Vaginal Davis
ADDRESS: 7850 Sunset Blvd. Penthouse Suite 110, Los Angeles, CA 90046
"Being in the zine business has taken its toll. My zine has an international following, and has become way too much for one person to handle. I've decided to stop publishing in order to concentrate on my live performances and underground film work. As the grande old matriarch of the homo core and queer zine movement, having been published in one form or another since the early 1980's I feel its time to retire gracefully."

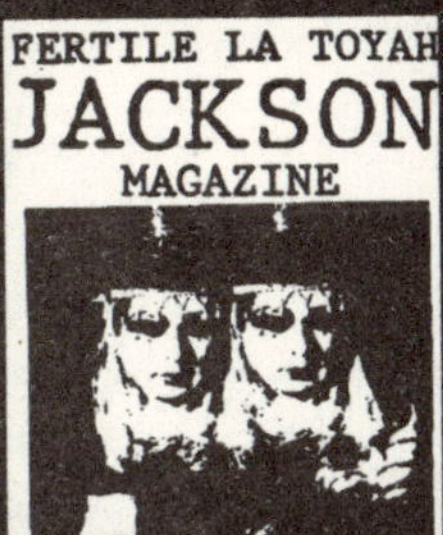

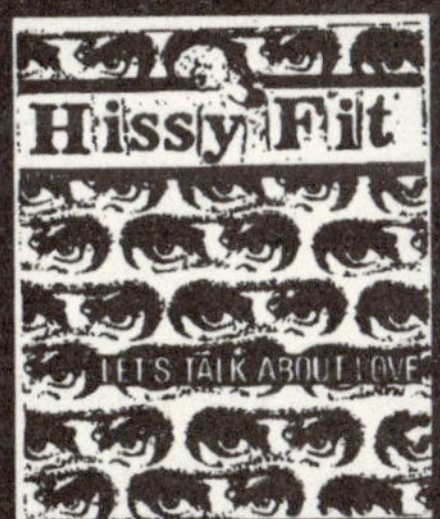

HISSY FIT
EDITORS: Paul LeRoy Gehres & Ed Oh
ADDRESS: 64 St. Marks Place NO.20, NYC 10003
"Networking is Fab! We love networking because it makes us even more famous."

ZACK
EDITOR: Rick Castro
ADDRESS: 1312 N. Stanley, Los Angeles, CA 90046
"Zack is published whenever I'm obsessed with some hot new thang! So that may be once a week or once a year. Title of magazine subject to change depending on who I'm obsessed with."

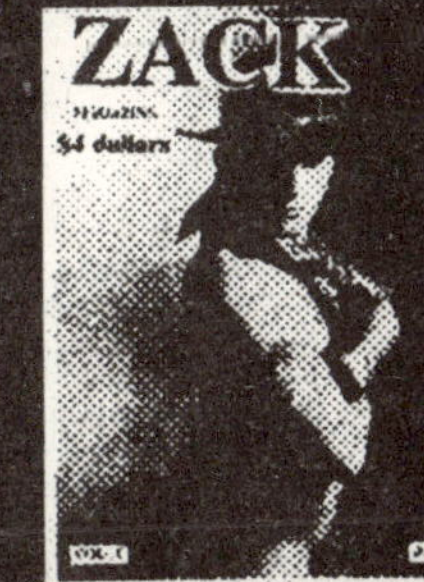

HOT LIP
EDITRIXES: Anonymous
ADDRESS: Box 2614, 211 East Ohio, Chicago, IL 60611
"We, the editrixes of HOP LIP, started publishing in the summer of 1991, as a lark. We thought it would be cool dyke fun. And it has been. One of the unanticipated results has been the mail we get from all over the place, requesting copies of our zine. It comes on postcards, the backs of napkins, ACT UP flyers every kind of scrap paper you can imagine. Sometimes we get offerings in return, buttons, plastic coins, poems. Usually the mail includes a single dollar bill, as payment. We don't know how all these people have heard about our zine, we think others in the zine pipeline are listing us, or talking about us, or something. That's all part of the fun."

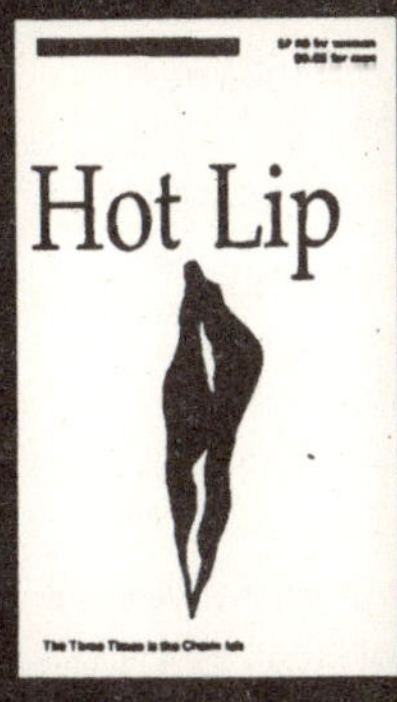

publisher's clearinghouse

Zinesters who are up on their history claim that the first zine was a science fiction fanzine published in the 1930's called *The Comet.* It came about in much the same way as zines do today—by people who didn't feel that the larger magazines were addressing their particular concerns or areas of interest. During the 70's & 80's this amateur underground activity was given a big shot in the arm with the introduction of accessible and cheap photocopying machines. Now anyone could be a publisher and their views and opinions were free to circle the globe.

These statements have been selected from some of the queer zines submitted to an international zine show that the *Aggressive School of Cultural Workers-Iowa Chapter* is organizing in Iowa City. The show was planned to coincide with the *Decentralized Worldwide Networker Congress 1992,* a call for alternative cultural producers to meet and network, within and between other communities, to strengthen the bonds between them and to plan alternative cultural strategies for the coming decade.

As part of the call for submissions for the show, editors were asked to submit a short statement on their "...thoughts/views, and experiences of zines and networking." It's been surprising how many people have put pen to paper to describe their experiences of doing zines, the statements succinctly encompass the range of responses received from other editors coming out of very different communities and concerns.

As of late July the show consists of about 200 zines from 14 different countries. The submission deadline was September 1st, but we'll accept zines throughout the length of the show. The show will be open each Saturday during September from 10:00AM–6:00PM at *Subspace.* If you are unable to attend at these times feel free to call us at (319) 351-3035 and alternative arrangements for you to view the show can be organized. If you are interested in receiving a copy of the catalogue for the show drop us a line and we'll contact you when it's available.

SUBSPACE • 221 W. BENTON • IOWA CITY IA 52246
— Stephen Perkins

reads:

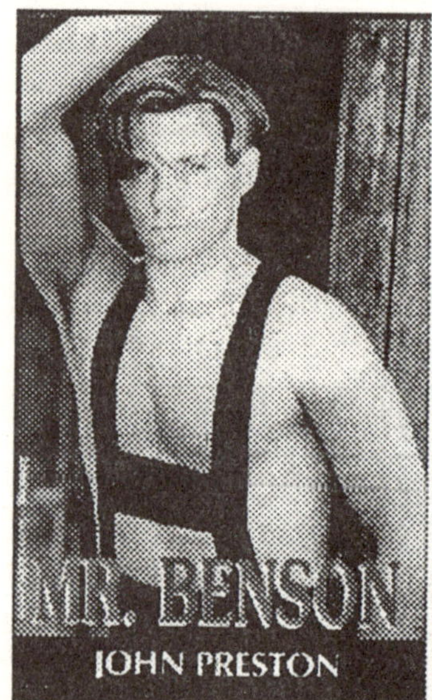

John Preston
Mr. Benson
(Badboy)

As a book of 'stroke fiction', *Mr. Benson* rates four stars: that is to say, I got off four times while reading it, and it probably would've been higher if I hadn't been pushed by a deadline. But-at the risk of sounding like a legal beagle defending a possibly pornographic novel—this book is clearly more than 'just' a stroke book. Oh, don't get me wrong: there's nothing wrong with being 'just' a stroke book; writing good prurient fiction is an art in itself, worthy of praise: the world needs more of it I'm just saying that there is another level to *Mr. Benson* (as there is to all good erotica, whether or not you choose to explore it).

That's the quality that always piques my interest in 'erotic fiction' (which, for brevity, henceforth will be called 'porn'): in amongst the dreck, occasionally you will encounter an author who takes his porn seriously, who knows that he's reaching a larger audience than Jonathan Katz can ever hope for, and who therefore provides his readers (who may, remember, be closeted small-town queers with little other gay-life contact) with positive role-models of how gay men can, and should, behave towards each other. An author who broadens the spectrum of possibilities available to his readers. Like I say, there aren't many of these authors around. When I encounter one, I try to find out more about him. John Preston is one.

Preston says that the first chapter of *Mr. Benson* was the first fiction he ever wrote-and would've been first-published, too, except that *Franny, the Queen of Provincetown* was rushed into print by Alyson, while Drummer took its sweet time about putting out *Mr. B.* How much of *Mr. B.* is real, how much is fiction:? You may be sure there are similarities between the author and the character, but the penthouse on Fifth Avenue isn't one of them. Preston has lived around the country, including NYC, but since his jobs have always been in gay publishing, you can assume that he's never been rich. I think we can safely say that Preston treats *Mr. B.* as an altar ego.

It's time to clarify something: I don't know John Preston. Oh, I've corresponded with him, off and on, for upwards of six years; I've met him several times; and he's done his best to teach me the art of getting published, for which I am grateful. He's even included me in one of his anthologies.

But every time I think I 'know' the man, some new fact pops up, which usually makes me shake my head and say 'Huh? I didn't know he did that!'-usually, in stark admiration. For a brief list of credits: co-founder of Gay House, Inc. (the first lesbian & gay community center in the United States, in Minneapolis); editor of The *Advocate* in the late 70's; author of at least eighteen books of fiction and non-fiction (several others don't appear on his resume because they're under another name), and editor of five more-two of which are now Book-of-the-Month club titles. That gives you some idea of where he's coming from. How does *Mr. Benson* fit into all this? After all, it's hard-core S&M porn, not the sort of thing that PC gay activists are 'supposed' to be writing. All the more reason, says he: "Porn keeps me honest." Writing fiction keeps you honest? Well, yes. It keeps you in touch with your own fantasies. Especially porn-fiction. When you've just written a brilliant porn story, incorporating all your deepest and darkest fantasies, and an admiring reader asks you at OutWrite "Where did you ever come up with that outrageous scene with the two leather studs & the dalmatian in the elevator?"—well, you can't very well claim that you got it out of a newspaper report.

But you wanted a review of *Mr. Benson*. OK, in the briefest possible terms: Jamie, a '70's NYC clone (and bear in mind, this was written in the seventies!), in his search for love in all the wrong places, meets Mr. Aristotle Benson, the ultimate top, who teaches Jamie that he belongs at his Master's feet. (No, this is not a Southern Baptist tract, although there are similarities.) Along the way, there is quite a bit of sex, some violence, several whippings and rapes and other scenes which may or may not be politically correct but which are indubitably essential to the story; and there is a "happy ending" worth of a Barbara Cartland novel. There is a pointed disdain for anything non-S&M: the 'clone' scene is raked over the coals more than once, and the New Jersey jokes get real old after a while. Don't buy it if you're expecting 'great' writing. It's good writing, and it succeeds in its goals, both primary (to get you off-assuming you're not completely turned off by kinky sex) and secondary (to educate & enlighten readers about the S&M scene—both those readers who are in the scene and the curious-but-uninitiated); but I don't think it was ever intended to join the Classics of World Literature on the dust-covered upper shelf.

Which brings us, oddly enough, to the subject of advertising - specifically, to a truth that ad execs have been cynically aware of for decades: sex sells. Think about it: which category do you refer to more often, your porn shelf or your CWL shelf? Which is closer to your heart: brain or gonads? I don't mean these questions to be rhetorical - I'm sure it differs from person to person - but for me, the porn shelf is far more effective in changing my personal outlook on life. Porn is site-specific: it goes directly to the spot where it can be more effective in changing your self-image, to wit, your libido. Show me a man whose libido is in constant contact with his brain — a man who spends time actively questioning and examining what turns him on— and I'll show you a man with a positive self-image, a man who values himself. And that's where a book like *Mr. Benson* comes in handy. You may not get off on all the sexual shenanigans performed in it - the branding scene, in particular, is liable to leave many of you squeamish, and the 'peg-boy' scene (where two boys are forced to sit on progressively larger sizes of dildoes) did very little for me. But there is no doubt that it explores the 'outer limits' for most of us. And that's an extremely healthy thing to do.

I have my problems with the essential thesis of *Mr. Benson* — that it is possible for a man to relinquish all responsibility, to commit himself to the ownership of a master — but whether or not it's true is irrelevant. It's hot, and it's thought-provoking. That's enough

— Scott "Spunk" O'Hara

> **excerpt:**
> "Mr. Benson doesn't believe in preliminaries. I didn't know that as I went through all my moves. I really did think I was dynamite in those days. I flashed my smile and showed my teeth. I made sure I stood so my ass stuck out. I made sure my jacket was open so he could see my chest and stomach through my T-shirt. Mr. Benson never blinked an eye. He never turned away. He just stood still and aloof.
>
> He was dressed in heavy black boots, button-fly jeans, a washed-out Levi's shirt and old, greasy leather jacket. The jeans weren't all that tight but I could see a huge cock hanging down one side and the keys didn't look make-believe. His hair was jet black and his mustached face was rough-skinned and tanned. I was so turned on to him I could feel my dick drip. I was getting hard and was sure he'd notice. I didn't know that Mr. Benson doesn't even bother with boys' cocks. He couldn't care less."

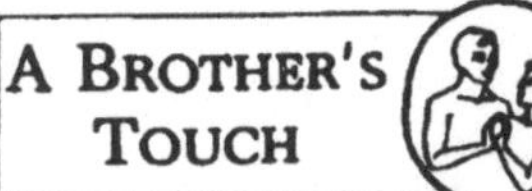

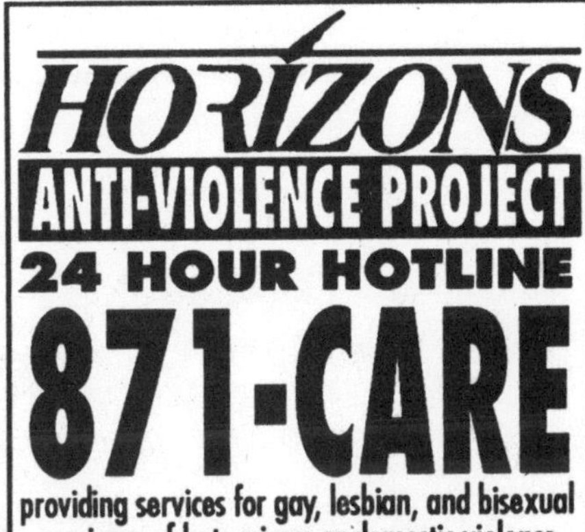

The two William H. Johnson shows draw well-deserved attention to this accomplished American painter. Born in 1901 in Florence, South Carolina to a mother who worked as a domestic, Johnson left for Harlem at seventeen and attended the National Academy of Design. He won several awards, but his instructor, Charles W. Hawthorne, hoping to expand the talented black pupil's opportunities raised funds for him to study in Paris. Johnson lived there for three years exploring the emerging modernist and expressionist styles.

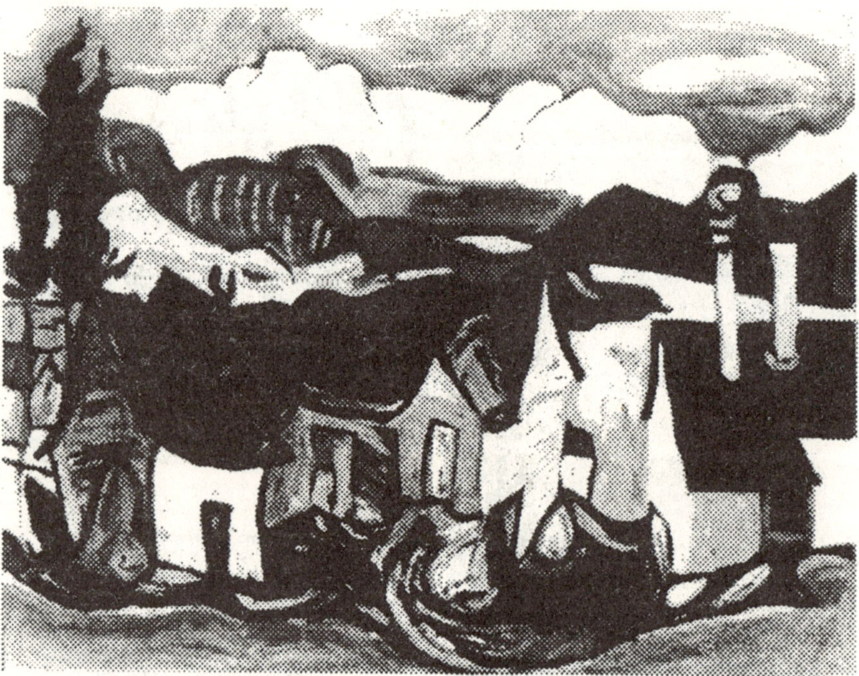

William H. Johnson "Chalet In The Mountains" (1938)

William H. Johnson
Studio Museum
(July 15-September 20, 1992)
Homecoming:
William H. Johnson
& Afro-America
Whitney Museum
(July 15-October 25, 1992)

Earlier works at the Studio Museum in Harlem reflect Johnson's ability to appreciate and master the European aesthetic. Paintings such as "Cagnes-sur-Mer" (ca. 1926-28) and "Street In France" (ca. 1928-30) contain the abstracted forms, attention to sunlight and energetic brushstrokes that were gaining popularity at the time and were typical of European artists such as Chaim Soutine. The Harlem show also includes three telling paintings dated 1930, which was the time Johnson returned to Florence, South Carolina for a year and painted his surroundings. The result: a very interesting blend of black and American subject matter employing modern European techniques and painting sensibilities. A favorite of mine is "Girl In A Green Dress" (1930). The sympathetic portrait of this peanut-butter colored thin black girl with large uncertain eyes that echo nothingness and the hollow darkness around her stops one. Her neck and collar bones have tension and the elongation of the entire figure recall French modernist Modigliani.

The Harlem show picks up on Johnson's return to Europe and to landscapes and still lifes, but chronicles his development as a painter emphasizing color and shape and mood over realistic picture. "Chalet In The Mountains" (ca. 1938) with its bright blues and yellows and bubbling landscape that makes little distinction between the sky and ground sets the stage for what is now the hallmark of Johnson's career, astute use of reverberating color, flat planar depiction of subjects with heavy black outlines and harrowing histories of black Americans and black spirituality.

The Whitney show focuses on Johnson's work between 1938 and 1946. Here one sees the incredible treasure Johnson recorded, not only of black experience in the rural south and the urban north, but of World Wars I & II. "Chain Gang" (ca. 1939) artistically is a wonder. Rhythm repeats throughout the interlocking bodies of brown prisoners and their black and white horizontal stripes. "Climbing Jacob's Ladder" (ca. 1944) also gives another key aspect of Johnson's work, besides reclamation of African primitiveness which was in vogue not only in popular culture (á la Josephine Baker earlier) but in avant-garde art as well (á la Picasso). Johnson paints the black saints, as well as Jesus, black. In other paintings as well, angels and other biblical characters are black. Not a traditional idea at the time. History proves Johnson to be not only a black painter who could imitate white European painters, but an American painter who contributed to the modern American aesthetic and an excellent purveyor of American black experience and American history as well.

— Tod Roulette

Following its presentation at the Whitney, Homecoming will travel to the Addison Gallery of American Art in Andover, Massachusetts (January 15-March 12, 1993); The Greenvliile County Museum in Greenvliile, South Carolina (April 13, - June 20, 1993), and the Amon Carter Museum in Fort Worth, Texas (October 16, 1993-January 4, 1994)

theater

Playwright Sterling Houston was "just a baby" when he left San Antonio to study theater in Los Angeles at the beginning of the 60's. He then headed for New York's experimental theater scene and joined forces with "cultural ecologist", playwright, and actor Charles Ludlam, performing and writing with the now-legendary Ridiculous Theater Company. In 1969, he moved to San Francisco and was the lead singer with punk trendsetters the Fleshtones until 1974. From there, Sterling worked with a number of progressive theater companies throughout the country as a performer, writer, and creative consultant. Based once again in San Antonio, he is the resident playwright at the Jump Start performance company. His latest play, Womandingo, is an uproarious and biting farce that re-tells the myths of lust and power in the Antebellum south. Loosely based on the 1957 pulp novel Mandingo (and subsequent 70's blaxploitation film), Womandingo adds the twist of gender and race-reversing each role. The silent black stud Mandingo is played by a white woman, while Southern Belles are cast with black male actors. The play won the Festival of Emerging American Theater FEAT award in its first performance in San Antonio, and will receive its Chicago premiere with the City Lit theater.

Robert Ford: How did the collaboration with Arnie Aprill at City Lit come about?
Sterling Houston: It came about through a really shared sensibility we had. We both enjoy outrageous humor, especially paired with political consciousness and outrage over social conditions. We both liked farce as a way of dealing with issues that are so extremely painful and ingrained that people have stopped hearing them when you talk about them. There's a mass turning off to talking about race, around gay community and AIDS issues. We found that this was an ideal way to make statements about those things, as well as create a very theatrical event in order to do that.

RF: The premise of it sounds pretty outrageous.
SH: It is. It's very funny and its disturbing in a really good way. It's like something your mother told you never to do and you do it. And it's like "ooh, I'm doin' it."

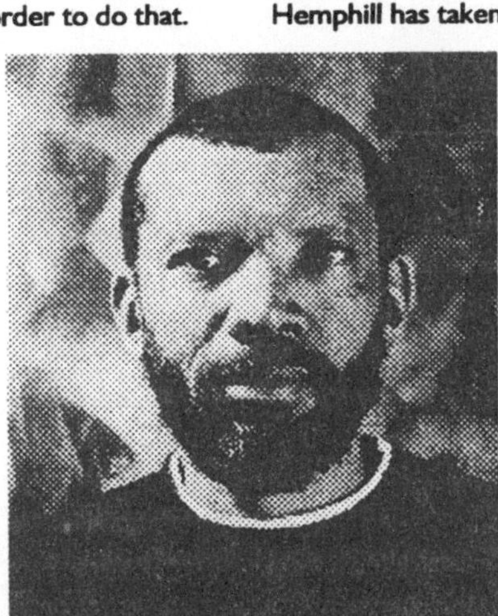

Sterling Houston

RF: Do you encounter a lot of homophobia from the black theater community?
SH: Actually, less than I expected to. The way the homophobia manifests itself is through silence. It just isn't talked about. I did a family memory piece called Driving Wheel. A lot of family histories, a lot of stories. And there's a character in it that's based on me, a talented black teenager coming out at sixteen. The play wasn't about that, but those issues were talked about. And only one review mentioned it. Although I get great, enthusiastic response, no one thanked me for making that boy queer the way he knew he was. I wrote to BLK when I was so angry about the exclusion of Pomo Afro Homos from the black theater festival last year, but I don't think that it ran. And on that same subject, I have felt excluded by my peers, the gay African American community. It's only been recently that I've been noticed, though I've been trying to be noticed for years. I have started to get some interest from the black gay literary scene. Essex Hemphill has taken an interest in my stuff. I just talked to Colin Robinson from Other Countries about working together.

RF: What part of the change in the story is the most subversive; the race switching or the gender switching?
SH: That's a good question. It's hard to value one over the other, because they both have the same effect; that is to really call attention to the construct of the role, whether its a sexual role or a racial one. There's no way to ignore what is being said by the characters apart from who is saying it. We're so used to having a certain person say certain things to us, and suddenly when that's reversed, when the opposite person is saying that to us, what is being said really comes out in big bold letters, and we really are able to look at it for what it really is, which is absurd, and outrageously cruel, and sexist and racist.
There's many very sexual overtones, as there were in the original book and film, to this young white man buying this beautiful black man as his slave, to do whatever he wants him to do. So when women play the role, its very clear that we're talking on more than one level. One actress in Chicago playing a role, when she got it, it almost brought her to tears, the anger that was pent up, and never really allowed to be expressed. When you step into the body of a big black man you can say pretty much anything about your oppression, and she had no trouble touching bases with that.

RF: You've performed in Womandingo yourself, right?
SH: I played the Scarlett Dred character in the first production.

RF: That's the role that Joan Jett Blakk is going to play in Chicago?
SH: Yes. It's funny the way this all evolved. When I started working on the piece, I really didn't know who Joan Jett Blakk was other than she was a highly political drag queen activist. I hadn't seen a picture or anything. When I was in Chicago this past summer finishing up the piece, I met Terrence and talked to him. I actually wrote the ending for Joan Jett Blakk. I had Scarlet become the rebel leader. Making a not too subtle point about how the real leadership is overlooked in this country by shutting out certain voices.

City Lit Theater's production of Womandingo is at the Victory Garden Theater, 2257 N. Lincoln in Chicago, now through November 8th. For reservations phone (312) 871-3000. Group sales contact Jeffrey Overas at Audience Projects (312) 929-TIXX.

lists

By The Numbers
Channel 69
Rocket 69
Jackie 60
Disco 2000
Car 54 where are you
77 Sunset Strip
Butterfield 8
Pennsylvania 6-5000
Route 66
Highway 69
96 Tears
101 Dalmations
808 State
Club 161 West
Bicardi 151
Virginia Slims 100
99 Luftbaloons
12 Angry Men
3 Men and a Baby
2 to tango
1000 Homo DJS
Chicago 7
49ers
76ers
76 Trombones
12 days of Christmas
40 days and 40 night
Around the world in 80 days
99 bottles of beer on the wall
50 ways to leave your lover
10 cents a dance
dime a dozen
one monkey don't stop no show

March Of The Falsettos
Sylvester
Byron Burke
Byron Stingley
Eddie Kendricks
Little Anthony
Johnny Mathis
Smokey Robinson
Frankie Valli
Klaus Nomi
Nina Hagen
Julee Cruise
the Gibb brothers

Dog Whistle
Mariah Carey
Minnie Ripperton
Deniece Williams
Blossom Dearie

Black Black People
Bootsy Collins
James Brown
Eunice Johnson

Black White People
Bryant Gumbel
Lavar Burton
Sammy Davis Jr.
John Johnson
Linda Johnson Rice
Arsenio Hall
Arthur Ashe

White Black People
Teena Marie
Lisa Stansfield
Marky Mark
Tom Jones
Vanilla Ice

White White People
Bill Clinton
Doris Day
Olivia Newton John
Pat Buckley
Pat Boone
Pat Buchanan
Cheryl Tiegs
Christie Brinkley
Claudia Schiffer

Q
Quartz
QW
NYQ
Queer National
Queen Bee
Quality Time
Quark Express
Quench
GQ
Compound Q
Quit it
Querelle

Homegrown House
London Broil
Cymbals & Instruments
Master C&J
Kym Sims
Darryl Pandy
Kim Mazelle
Cat Glover
Chante Savage
Liz Torres
Ten City
Paris Grey
Shawn Christopler

What's in a name?
Nnenna Freelon
Ceybil Jeffries
Jackée
Siedah Garrett
Bern'nadette Sta'nis
Melis'sa Morgan

Bury The Hatchet
Joe Shannahan/Rachel Cain
La Vicomtess Larvetta Larvon/Mrs. Marvin Lewis
Diana Ross/Mary Wilson
Beth Meyerson/Sukreet Gabel
Jean Smart/Delta Burke
Clarence Thomas/Anita Hill
Robin Givens/Mike Tyson
Joan Crawford/Christina Crawford
Joan Crawford/Bette Davis
Sonny/Cher
Johnny Carson/Joan Rivers
Jay Leno/Arsenio Hall

Oops, Upside Your Head

 BY MARC LOVELESS

Hate motivated anti-lesbian and -gay bias crimes have steadily increased over the past ten years. In some areas anti-lesbian and -gay violence has risen annually by as much as 100 to 200 percent, leaving the National Gay and Lesbian Task Force and local activist groups such as Horizons to conclude that anti-lesbian and -gay related crimes have reached epidemic proportions. In 1990, Congress passed and the President signed into effect the Hate Crimes Statistics Act. This act, sponsored in the House by Congressman John Conyer of Michigan and in the Senate by Senator Paul Simon of Illinois, is an attempt for law enforcement agencies to begin research on the type and number of hate crimes being committed. The first report due from the Federal Bureau of Investigation (FBI) is to be published this spring.

The issue of violence toward lesbians and gays is a major concern in the black lesbian and gay community. While much attention has been given to the events on the racially mixed north side of Chicago, activists and service deliverers are meeting to strategize on ways to confront incidents of violence to black lesbians and gays on the predominantly black south side of town.

In the book, "Violence Against Lesbians and Gay Men", author Gary David Comstock reviews and analyzes survey data collected over the past ten years which report incidents of violence against lesbians and gays. The Comstock studies indicate that although the frequency of violence towards black lesbians and gays is consistent with the general lesbian and gay community, the severity of the crimes reported is greater. For instance, a significant number of incidents in the general lesbian and gay population involve verbal assault, while black lesbians and gays experience more instances of physical assault. According to the Comstock study, black lesbians and gays have a higher likelihood of becoming victims of sexual assault, physical assault, homicide or criminal damage to property than their white counterparts.

Black lesbians and gays experience the threat of violence at a greater rate than their straight counterparts. According to Comstock, the increased threat of violence that black lesbians and gays face is consistent with the experiences of lesbian and gay Latinos/Latinas and Asian Pacific Islanders.

Reporting incidents of violence may be difficult for black lesbians and gays, but it is necessary. The most effective way to confront violence is simply to report it. The case of Jeffery Dahmer exemplifies the importance of reporting crimes and participating in the criminal justice system. Had his last intended victim been satisfied with only escaping, and had he not notified officials of his abuse, Dahmer may not have been stopped.

If you are the survivor of an anti-lesbian or gay-related crime and you do not report the incident, you are giving the perpetrator the incentive to re-attack you or someone else in the future. These offenders must be stopped. The most effective way to stop them is to report the crime and cooperate with law enforcement officials concerning the incident.

In Cook County, State's Attorney Jack O'Malley recently started a new program to help make it easier for lesbians and gay victims to come forward. Special services are now offered by the State's Attorney's Victim-Witness Assistance unit geared specifically toward the needs of lesbian and gay victims and witnesses. The goal of the program is to make testifying as simple and easy as possible by lending emotional support, guidance and financial assistance to gay and lesbian crime victims and witnesses.

Illinois' Hate Crimes Law allows perpetrators to be criminally charged for committing crimes motivated by hate of lesbians and gays. This law comes with mandatory sentencing; the first crime is to be charged as a misdemeanor. Second and subsequent crimes may be charged as felonies. In severe felony cases, such as murder, aggravated battery or sexual assault, the motive of hate is presented as sentencing to encourage stiffer penalties.

It is important that we look out for ourselves by looking out for each other. The laws that we live under guarantee our rights as individuals, to live our lives free from the threat of violence.

If the HIV/AIDS crisis has taught us anything it has taught us that we can organize, work together, and begin to take steps to change problem situations. Our success in addressing the AIDS issue shows that we can confront tough issues, such as violence and crimes toward the black lesbian and gay community, and make a difference.

My own recent encounter with urban violence happened in broad daylight, ironically just after having met with Marc Loveless about his anti-violence article for Thing. This was not what legalese would term a "hate crime." Indeed, my attackers cooed "yo, homie" to me as if their menacing intent weren't clearer than their words. An ill-chosen shortcut through the courtyard behind the local hoodlum high school was my mistake.

Not surprisingly, I stumbled the two blocks back home without a single stranger in the street offering help of any kind. (The Pink Angels, Guardian Angels, and Chicago police must have all been otherwise occupied.) I did report the incident, though almost 24 hours after it happened. A humpy Hispanic cop politely took the report, and even tried to tactfully ascertain if it were a hate crime. I knew even as I made my report that my assailants would never be caught. Even I couldn't identify them if pressed to. But I figured that I should at least make the bleak urban violence statistics a bit more accurate. I was let off easy, in retrospect. My swelling dissipated within a week and no cast was required on my broken nose.

Had this been a fag bashing, I could blame homophobia. Had they been rednecks, racism would be an obvious motive. I was never called a faggot or homo by the "brothers" as they blackened my eyes and busted my nose, but the blows hurt just as much. This was "black-on-black-crime;" motivated more out of a need to try to snatch power not afforded to them (or me) by society than for the measly dollar they finally got. Yet, in a way, it most certainly was a fag-bashing. I'm sure a sixth sense alerted them to my lack of swaggering machismo, making me the perfect target for their attack. It's a more insidious kind of homo-hate, really. They didn't feel compelled to attack verbally because by them it was simply understood. Being a sissy meant that I was prime to be messed with. And I became a prime example that their assertion was true.

I find now that my skin and bones are healed, something else definitely is not. The sight of boyz in the hood (many of whom I suspect are not too terribly unlike me save their heterosexuality, X baseball caps, gold chains, and Bulls jerseys) makes my kinky hair stand on end now. It's a gut-level response that is certainly politically incorrect, but I can't help it. I feel almost ashamed that fear would lead me to grasp on to the same assumptions that fuel white racists, but to me they do all look alike. And to them, because of my refusal to buy into the gangsta drag that is de rigeur for young black men, I look like as good a target for their petty thievery and violence as any white yuppie scum. Since that fateful day a few weeks ago, I tread nervously when I share the sidewalk with them. It shouldn't have to be like that, but it is. And as much as I would like to end this column with a neat and upbeat rejoinder, I'm afraid that I don't have one. And that's the saddest part about this whole despicable mess.

— Robert Ford

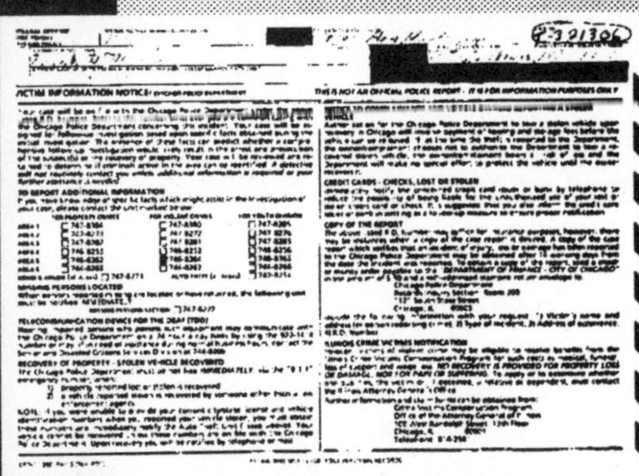

EXHIBIT A
post-attack
paperwork

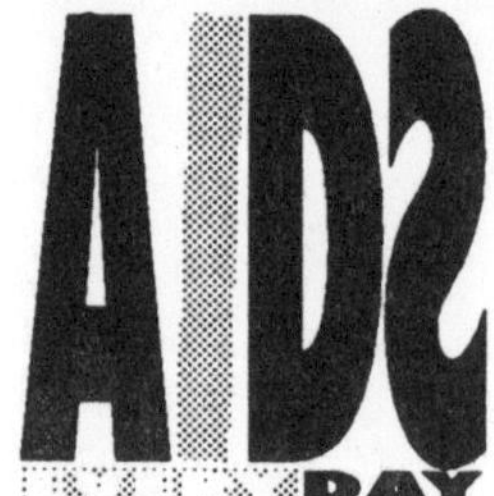

FUCKING FAGGOT

madrid st. angelo

Turning back the clock in his heart, James remembered an earlier day—an earlier night actually. His recollection tossed about on a sea of pseudo-celluloidal turbulence, the tears swelled in his eyes and his cock began to stiffen. Where was I then, he thought? Of course, New York, the lower East side. Trees all around, cool crisp winter air chilling his bones. And yes, coming back to him now, the really warm fire burning in his throat. Ahhh! the soothing, rough massage he'd grown accustomed to in his youth. He was an excellent head giver. This one flashback tormented him from time to time and now on the eve of his twenty-eighth birthday he found it impossible to escape himself having ever been thirteen years old, young, naive, so trusting and afraid. Hungry for maturity, starving for affection, and so intent on surviving what he foresaw as many lonely days and nights ahead.

Somewhere between college and his joining the volunteer squad at the Gay Men's Health Crisis, he'd awakened to a call within the gay black community, the call which would become his life's blood pulse. But even now as the shouts of protesters demanding a cure rang through the streets another voice echoed in the memory of his mind, "deeper you fucking faggot, suck me deeper".

No, no escape from the memory. Even though the moment had passed he longed for its return. There was a distinctness in that first face fuck. It was then—as confusing as it was—that he realized he loved, wanted, needed, desired and must have cock in order to remain mobile, functioning and worthy of self-redemption.

Flashback again.

Taking his walk on the wild side he thought, I will never be the same and I never was like any of them straight boys anyway. These thoughts reminding him of the lower East side too.

Trembling now in present phase he touched his tight cocoa stomach. Skin soft, the little hairs he had on his belly, moist. Now the tears falling gently and somewhere in between wanting to wipe his eyes or lay back and let the rain come down he determined to just stay still, controlled.

Fucking controlled. "Never more than I can handle", his life motto, although at this stage in the game he'd handled quite a bit already.

Jumping quickly off his bed he retrieved a book of poetry from within his dresser drawer, it's title; "Once Only the Most Daring", he turned to page 22 and ready softy to himself:

In this world of dead end streets
we seek to find a haven (colorless)
and never return to cloudy days
of ghosts and tears and heaven.

Boys we've loved and touched remind us
of our quest for love to find us
waiting
wanting

and breathing.

"Cheer up James baby," concluding his moments' reflection, "there's a party going on downstairs and you're the reason for it". So downstairs he went.

And now before him a cake with twenty-eight candles blaring—how'd they all fit?—beneath the light of the chandelier. And the man by his side, his right now other half, brother, lover, saying, "blow 'em out baby". Funny, James thinking, tonight I'll be sucking his cock and he'll be saying , "deeper baby, take me deeper".

Fifteen years ago his first taste of the devil pole and now with so much having passed and with so much presently being different ... Not a Goddamned thing had changed. The man by his side as white as the first man back in the park.

Closing his eyes he blew out the candles, wishing for the unwelcome touch of a strangers' hand behind his head, and the stranger's husky voice spewing the word f-a-g-g-o-t.

Opening his eyes he sighed knowing deep within him...time was up. No longer could he be a white man's man. And no longer would his deep throat utter yes.

—present phase end—

well but worried

Timothy G. Murphy

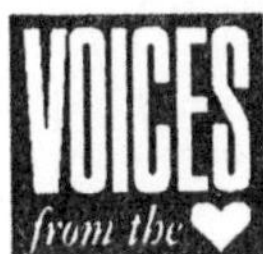

I'm HIV negative (I've gotten tested five times) but I'm a mess. I worry about HIV every time I have sex or every time I think about having it.

My HIV worries are like Queen Victoria sitting stiff and rigid on her throne and banging everyone's wrist with a ruler saying "No! No! No! You musn't have sex because of HIV. HIV remember child! HIV! Don't you forget about that now. I'm going to tell you all about it all the time — from now on — 24 hours a day, seven days a week!"

"Yeah! Yeah! Yeah! I hear you. What do want me to do. Just shut myself up in my room and watch home shopping and Mister Ed reruns the rest of my life?"

"That's better than letting the HIV boogie monster get you child. He's big and snarly and he's got big fangs and a lot of bad breath."

"OK, mama, so I'll stay at home and play cards with you. Does that satisfy you? Does anything satisfy you?"

"That does, son. It's very responsible of you to give up your sex life for me. I don't want to ever have to explain that you're not feeling to my bridge club on Wednesday night."

"Yeah, mama. I hear you."

So I sit at home now with mama and play cards and eat peanuts along with swallowing down my dreams of a sexual oasis and watch Geraldo and Oprah and think about the day when the Surgeon General announces the end of the epidemic with both a successful cure and a truly effective vaccine.

I'm just thinking of the day when I can do whatever I want with whoever I want anytime of the day or night or week or year.

But for now, at least the next few years, that doesn't look like its going to happen.

So what do I do now? Go and find myself another gay man and hope that he don't have it? I could get him tested five times like I did, but what if he fools around on me and the condoms don't work and something leaks and then I get infected or I infect him because none of my five tests detected the virus, but I still ended up having it anyway. Or what about the new mystery virus that may not exist and which they're not able to test for anyway? Why is all of this such an ordeal?

I think its because I watch too much HIV TV, that's it! And I read too many newspapers! Everyday I get bombarded with articles and stories and news flashes and exclusives on new drugs that probably don't work, but might work a little, and since there's so little else available that AZT or ddI or ddC or Compound Q and all of the other new drugs they develop every week of the year and answer for me seems just to wait and do nothing until the end of the epidemic is here.

All of a sudden I say good God! That isn't the answer is it? There has to be something else I can do than just sit at home and stare at the walls and the television and my mother sitting across from me looking just as scared and worried about this thing as I am.

I call the local AIDS volunteer office and ask stupidly whether they need any help down there assuming immediately that they don't need help because I assume they already have a lot of other volunteers who are ten times less worried about HIV and AIDS than I am. Who needs a nut case like me as a volunteer?

They say they do need someone once a week to read to a 35 year old man named Benjamin who lives on the South Side and who has lost much of his vision due to an opportunistic infection that may or may not be able to be treated with a new drug therapy they are developing.

I say yes I will help them out and I go to Benjamin's house and his mother opens the door and she takes me to his chair in the living room. As I begin to read him the first sentences of the Victorian novel he had started to read before he had started to read before he got sick I feel my fear and hopelesness disappear as I see that he is not afraid or hopeless.

I suddenly wonder for a moment who of the two of us is helping who.

My mother is very proud now that her son is helping those people who are in need.

VOICES FROM THE HEART is an ongoing column compiled by Michael Norman Haynes from STOP AIDS CHICAGO. Mail your stories c/o Thing magazine or contact Haynes direct at (312) 752-STOP for more information.

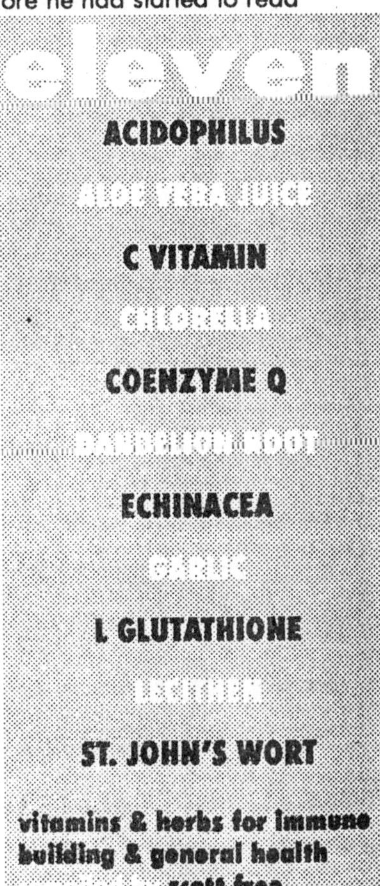

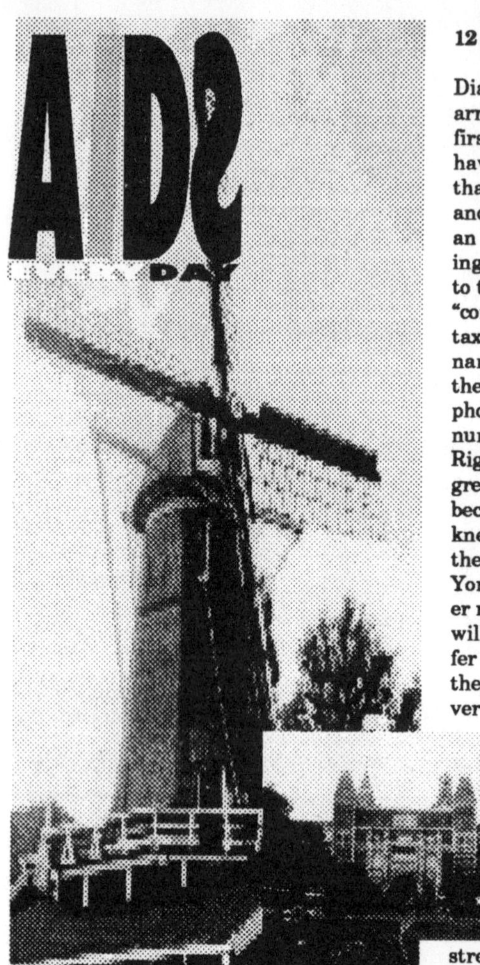

12 July 1992

It was as traumatic as I feared. Kat Diaz was nowhere to be found when I arrived on her doorstep this morning. At first I thought that the taxi driver may have let me off at the wrong address but that turned out not to be the case as per another taxi driver. After waiting for over an hour, getting even more weary and feeling the call of my bladder, I decided to go to the ACT UP/Amsterdam office to find "community" accommodations. Only the taxi driver couldn't make out the street name. Aldyn, it turns out, had mutilated the street name. I finally got to a pay phone, not that it did me any service. Five numbers and no answer at any of them. Right now, Chicago is sounding like a great place to be. Amazing how fond you become of "home" at moments like these. I knew I was fast falling apart so I called the hotel number given to ACT UP New York (I should have realized what I consider reasonable and what New Yorkers are willing to pay can and most often does differ considerably.) The plus here is yes they had rooms available and yes the driver knew where it was located. One hundred Forty Gilders! That is a lot for a person on a fixed income and no credit card in a foreign country. After I woke from my nap I took a walk, meanwhile ACT UP Amsterdam had called with rather complicated instructions on how to get to their offices and the correct spelling of the street name. I decided upon just getting a room at the Hotel Wilhelmina (just down the street-if only I had known) for the two remaining days until Michael arrives.

The people I met on my walk today were friendly. They sounded German but it's hard to tell. I an trying not to commit cultural faux pas. However, in my haste to make my flight I left my guide/info book at home. Thank the Goddess I read it several times before I left so I know the difference between service and tip.

13 July

I got some flowers. They brighten up my even smaller room at the Wilhelmina. No television in this room, no phone and no bathroom. I am a bit worried about the size of the double that Michael and I are to share. I might try to find us an apartment.

I love walking around Amsterdam. I didn't realize how far I had walked before until I took the tram back to where I first got off. Tomorrow I'll buy film so I can start taking photographs.

I forgot to bring my watch or a clock, but if movement around the hotel is any indication, it's still early. My neighbors are very lively; first I thought that they were having a party but then I realized that they're just having very loud sex.

14 July

Found my way to the neurology symposium today with just a few directions from the receptionist at the medical center and a desk clerk.

This conference is a big chi-chi affair. They give us lunch everyday and Thursday night there's a dinner cruise. That'll help me stay on the budget.

15 July

I moved into the double today. It's very nice. Large and airy. I bought some potted plants and will get cut flowers tomorrow. Michael is here here and I feel better. Not because I was afraid to be on my own but because it's always easier sharing the load and hotel bill with someone else.

16 July

I took Michael on the Neurology Dinner Boatride. It was a free dinner, what the heck. He had fun or least he said he did. Those neurologists really can party! One woman was heard over the PA system requesting in no uncertain terms M.C. Hammer. And this was after we'd docked. I took Michael to the red light district then promptly got us lost. The only reason that this was mildly disconcerting is because we'd heard the trams stopped running at 12am. They do not. The trams stop running at 12:20/12:30 so we just made it. I actually got us found by knowing what street I wanted, instead of only knowing the tram number.

17 July

It's about to begin. They arrived in ones, twos, threes, fives and more. By planes most but by train some. ACT UP/Paris being one by train. This is actually the part I like best, seeing folks I haven't seen in a while. Mike Shriver and Laura Thomas from ACT UP/San Francisco are two such people. Actually, I enjoy all of the ACT UP-ers.

I ate dinner with two guys from the neurology symposium, one from Edinburgh and the other from Bedsty in Brooklyn. It was a pleasant evening (actually I should say night because we didn't meet for dinner until 8:30pm and I didn't return to the hotel until after 12:30 am.) Poor Michael was left sitting on the steps waiting for me as the office closed down at 10:00pm.

I'm really tired tonight. I think my body's finally acclimating. Usually at this hour I'm more wired than a jumping bean.

18 July

I got up, ate breakfast, went to register for the conference. Went to a five hour ACT UP world meeting. Painted coffins. Ate dinner then went out to a bar, too

tired to stay. Walked home and now I'm in bed. It's 3:30 am on Sunday.

Araun is here. This is a surprise. He has lost so much weight...but not from illness. "You look great," I said. "I know," he replied. Jon Hammond from Philly is also here as well as Keith from New York City. The meeting was a bit rough because, try as we might, the Americans couldn't stop thinking of AIDS in terms of the USA which irked Europeans to no end.

Backing up a bit... the Conference Center looks like what I imagine the political conventions to look like. Tall, airy storerooms littered by signs, booths and security guards. You must wear your badge at all times and you must carry a second special pass with you as to prove that the first badge is really you. Activists are upset because the conference bags were given by Abbott Labs (Boo! Hiss!) and don't say AIDS on the front. There are no fountains in the medical Academy buildings. The conference check-in clerk suggested I get a drink of water from the bathroom. I declined.

Today's a busy day. I have the Women and HIV meeting to attend, the first demos began and tonight is the first night of the Global Meetings.

Days In Amsterdam
Saundra Johnson

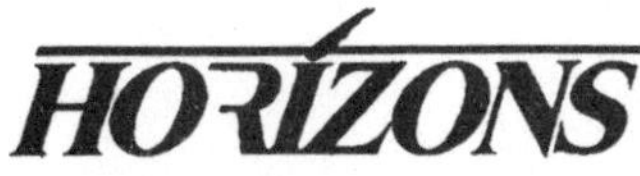

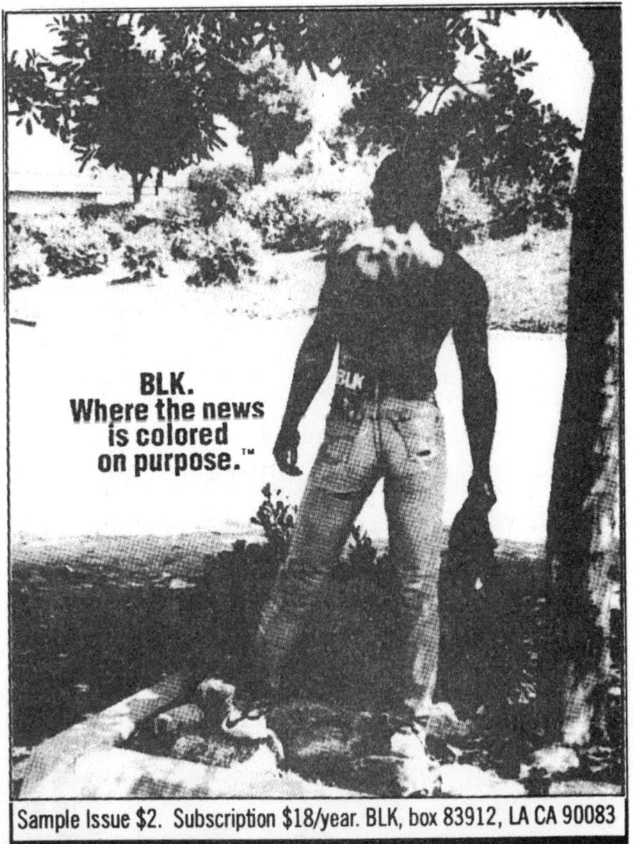

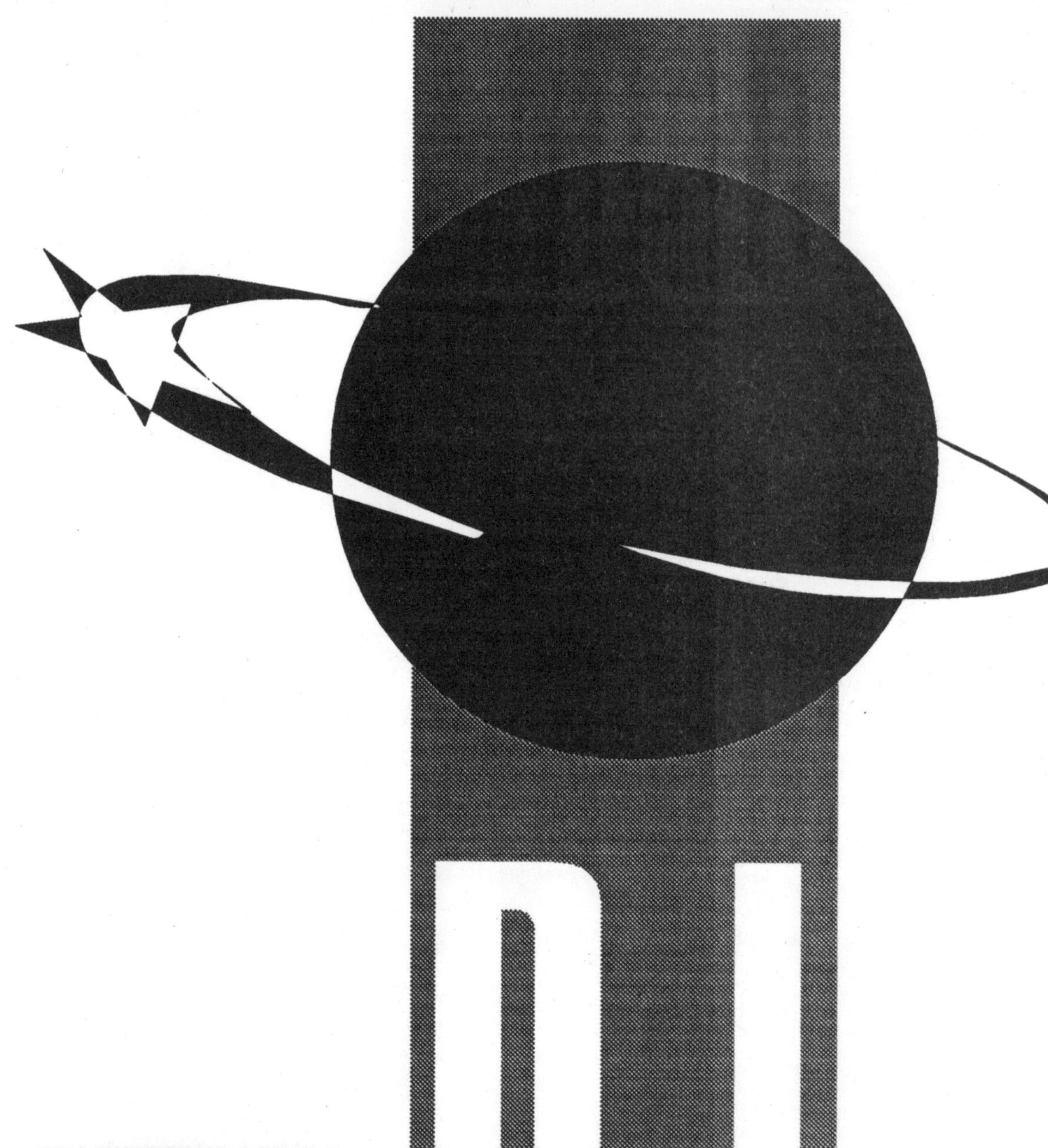

DJ WORLD

THE PRINCIPLE THEORY
featuring COCO COCKTAIL
"Bitch"
Produced, arranged, and
written by Jamie Principle
DJW 108

UNDERWORLD SOCIETY
"Possessed"
Produced, arranged, and
written by Jamie Principle
DJW 107

World Operations
André Halmon

VOICE
1.708.387.7100

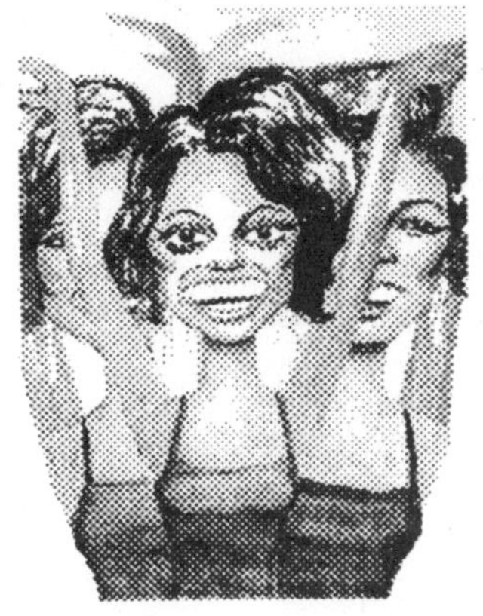
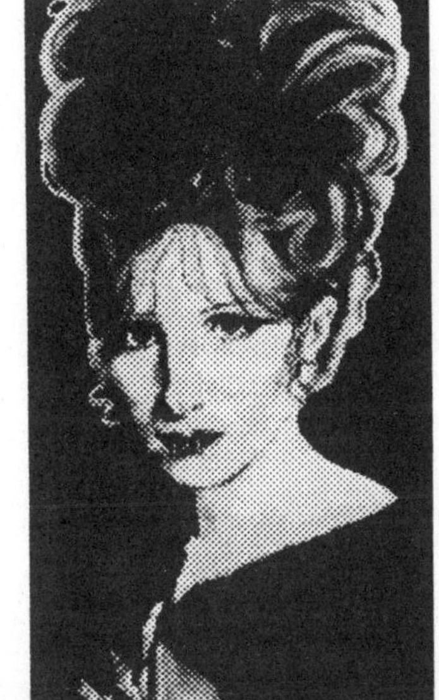

M U S T O
counts to ten

TOP TEN DIVAS OF ALL TIME

1. DIANA ROSS
Call her Mahog. Call her whatever. She is it—accept no substitutes.

2. BARBARA STREISAND
Not for any of her movies, just one song she recorded, "He Touched Me."

3. AGNES MOOREHEAD
Scary, brilliant, bewitching, a thinking man's diva. She comes to mind whenever I ask for "more head."

4. DIVINE
Beauty and the Beast all in one big barrel of fun, a camp goddess whose girth and mirth will never be surpassed.

5. CATHERINE THE GREAT
Defined horse dick for all time.

6. PAM GRIER
Blaxploitation diva who would never relax her hair or her body.

7. DIANA SCARWID
Underrated cult actress, from "Mommie Dearest" to "Brenda Starr." Give her a lifetime achievement award, already.

8. JOAN CRAWFORD
Wore her lipstick three inches beyond her lips but who was going to argue? Every inch a star.

9. DIANNE LADD
A character actress who gets better and better, just like fine wine.

10. MRS. BEASLEY
Buffy's doll from "Family Affair," she published her own cookbook and way outlived Buffy

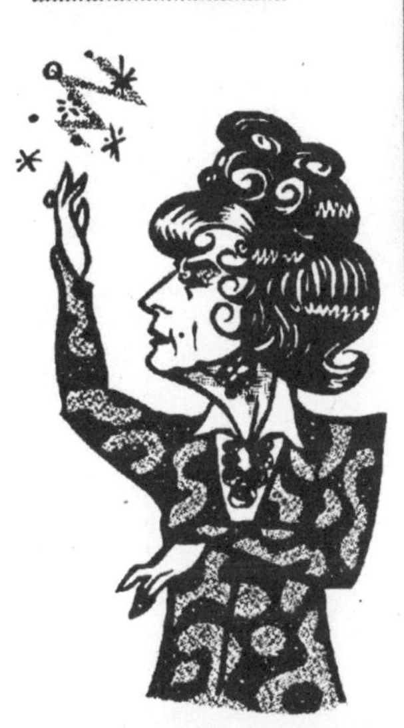
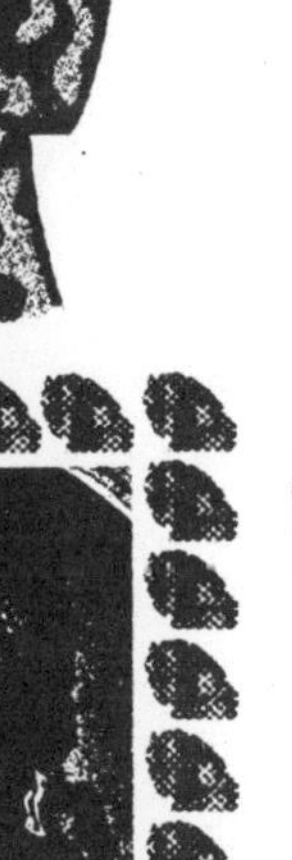
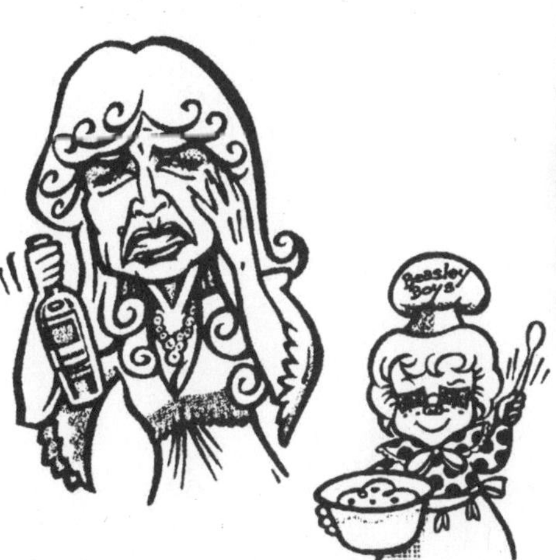
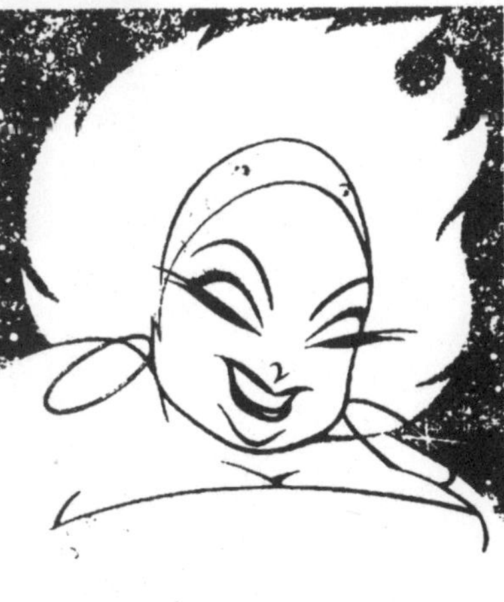

ILLUSTRATIONS OTIS F. RICHARDSON *Diana Ross* LEE KAY *Barbara Streisand, Michael Musto* MICHAEL ECONOMY *Divine, Joan Crawford* CHIP WASS *Pam Grier* MICHAEL HYACINTH *Catherine the Great* CHUCK GONZALES *Agnes Moorehead, Dianne Ladd, Mrs. Beasley.*

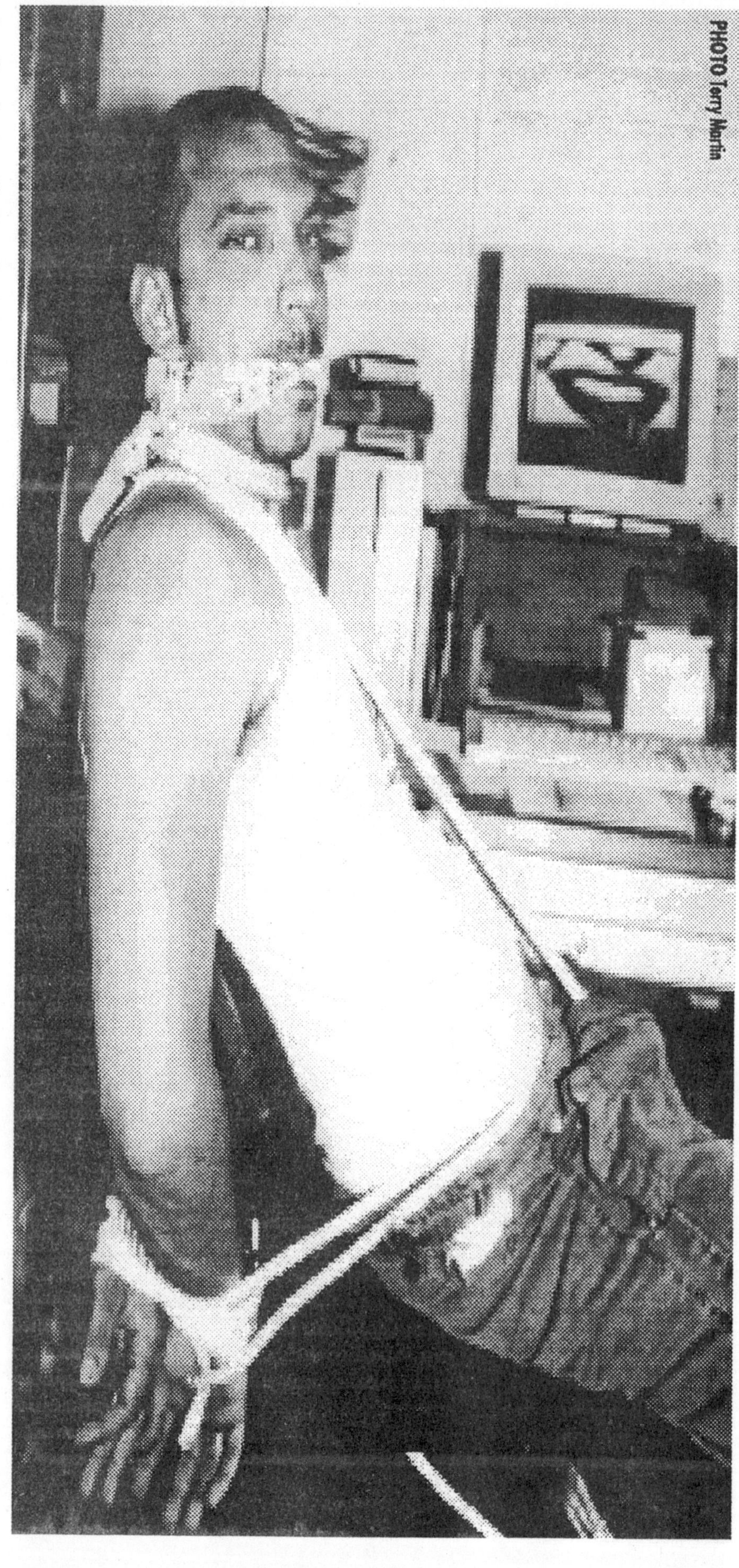

G_ag_ magazine came for Chicago's gay press with a vengeance, setting a new standard of hipness for local bar rags. _Gag_ gained instant notoriety for its wholly unapologetic approach to dish and dirt. But careful readers will note that's its a lot more than that, too. With activist graphics, celebrity interviews, and honest (if not scholarly) criticism by some of the city's most noteworthy art fags, _Gag_ rises above being merely a trash fest. Having more in common with the zines than with mainstream press, _Gag_ has managed to be the best of both worlds; a sense of humor and irreverence to rival _Bimbox_ combined with a monthly publication schedule, impeccable art direction, and full page ads from real advertisers. _Gag_ is born of the mind of Malone, who escaped from a childhood in Normal, Illinois to a career in advertising world. Finding agency life less exciting than it appeared in Bewitched (or thirtysomething), Malone hopped off the corporate treadmill and launched Propago, which is basically his Mac, visual sense, and talent for combining them into stunning advertising campaigns for a wide variety of clients. As an independent publisher, ad department worker, and fag myself, I was curious to compare notes with him. Once his wrists were free and the bandanna was removed from his mouth, we conversed over cappuccino at a trendy new coffee shop (which used to be one of the city's most notorious hustler bars). He decided not to press charges. I think he kinda liked the bondage stuff.

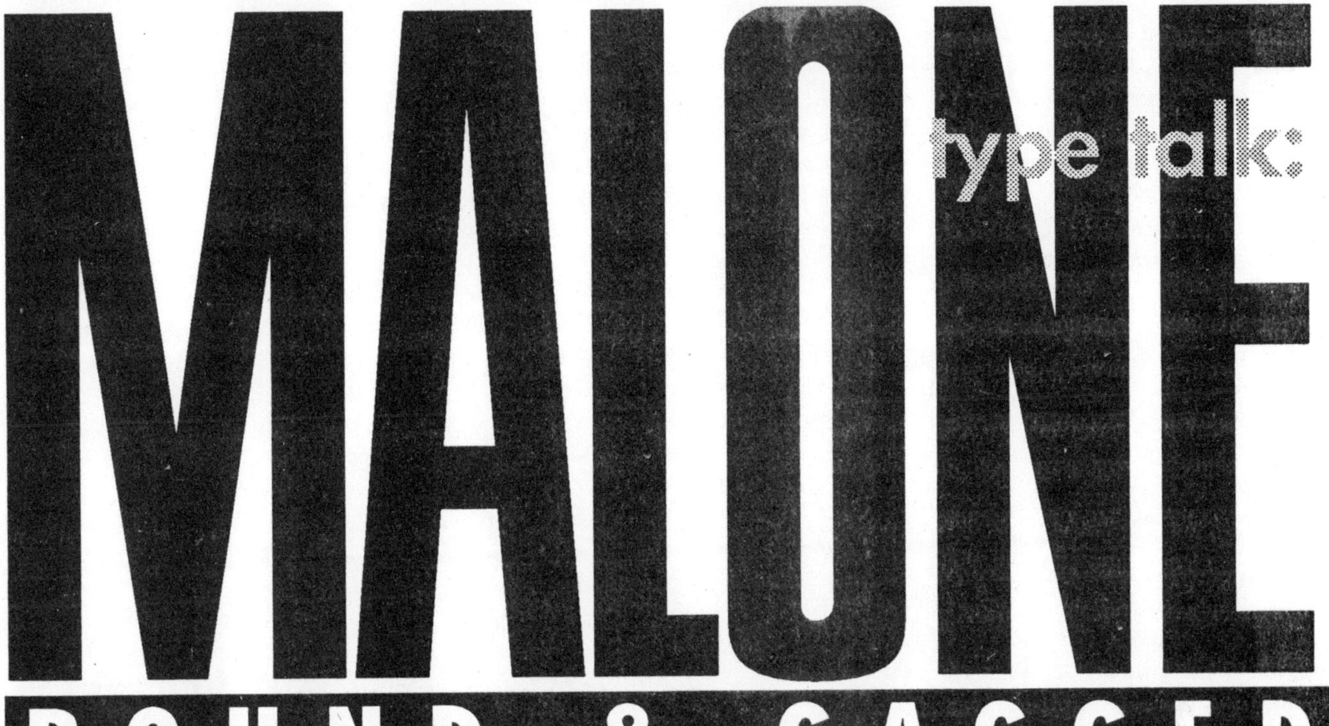

Robert Ford: What software do you use?
Malone: Oh, everything. As far as Macintosh Compatible, I use Pagemaker, Photoshop or Digital Darkroom for photo enhancement, Microsoft Word, even though I really don't know how to use it. And Freehand.

RF: Do you use Quark?
M: No I have it, I've never just sat down to learn it. Everyone's told me I should.

RF: Yeah, I switched to Quark for the last issue of *Thing*... and I don't know, some stuff about Pagemaker I like better, Some stuff about Quark I like better.
M: I kept hoping that Pagemaker was going to catch up with Quark with each new version. I've been using Pagemaker for three years; it's very hard to stop. That's the bitch about learning a new program, you need a good month of solid intense training on it to feel comfortable with it.

RF: I never had the patience to sit down with the manuals and stuff. I've never done a tutorial, where you make a little postage stamp with grapes on it.
M: What's funny is that you see somebody else's work in the general public and here they have almost the same graphics or something. That's the con to all of this "desktop" thing; it gives everyone license to be an art director, and you see so much schlock out there now, simply because someone can do it without paying someone else to do it, but with no regard to the actual design of the piece and the target of the piece.

RF: That's what's behind the 'zine movement, though. That kind of technology has become accessible, and people that nor- mally wouldn't publish are publishing, but then the flip side of that is there's a lot of bad publishing.
M: But not necessarily. A lot of my favorite zines are design-wise kind of atrocious from the traditional design school. Like *Agony*, I love that! Even though it's not much to look at, it definitely has a style and it's gonna mark a period of design history.

RF: Do you follow much of the zine stuff at all? Did you go to Spew?
M: No. I feel like I'm an outcast from all of that. I've been reading a lot more zines since I started *Gag* to see what everyone else is doing. I was a fan before I started *Gag*. But I'm not into organized anything. I feel like an outsider with all the zine kids. And I really don't feel I need to be a part of it either. If they have a Spew 3, I don't know if I'll attend.

RF: I hear rumor that Glenda Orgasm is doing one in New York.
M: Oh really? I might go to that. If it's in New York!

RF: Where do you go out?
M: The circuit.

RF: A better question might be where don't you like to go?
M: Well, I don't like doing Halsted street because it's just so predictable. One of them comes up with a mailbox contest and then it's something they all have. There's nothing creative. No originality at the Halsted street bars. In New York, when you go out there's always a production. The Sound Factory has dancers and light shows. You can walk anywhere and there's something going on. Entertainment's being provided either by the clubs or just the club kids. Here, there seems to

be so little theatre, at least on Halsted street. There's no fag theatre. It's the street theatre that I really thrive on. Chicago can't support that kind of venue as much as New York can. Sound Factory can get how many people on a given night? Here you pretty much have your core kids and the rest is filler. I don't like to believe that. I think that this town can really do something. It's getting to the point now where you can go out any night of the week and something is going on. But there's so much wasted talent here. Oscar McMillian should be spinning twice, three times a week.

RF: Do you think people misunderstand what you're trying to do with *Gag*? How would you describe the editorial stance?

M: Editorial stance... I really don't know. I'm not really a "publisher", I'm a designer. I don't know all the things, if I call myself a publisher, I'm supposed to do cause I've never done that. We really just put together stuff that we think will interest people. It's very camp, gay humor. But that hasn't been done, at least in Chicago. Yeah, I think a lot of people *do* misunderstand it. But I really don't want to have to put a page inside *Gag* that says "this is what *Gag* is about." I don't think the tone of *Gag* is really that vicious. It's not intended to be, and I don't think it is. Some things we probably shouldn't say. No, I'm not even going to say that.

RF: The whole point of the underground press is to get away from the "should" word.

M: Right. Someone left a message on the *Gag* line a couple of weeks ago saying" you call yourselves journalists, but...." and he goes on to list

something that we did, I don't remember what it was. But the fact is we've never called ourselves journalists. We've never referred to ourselves as that once. Because we're not. And we think that's kind of flip. Even though we're putting out a published piece, none of us are publishers or journalists. Most of the people that write for *Gag* aren't professional writers or anything. Like I tell contributors' it's not how you write, just write, get it down. Just write how you speak. Because that's what I want *Gag* to be, the voice of these boys.

RF: Is that a conscious thing not to caption the pictures?

M: Our first printing was 3,000 copies. So I thought of the 3,000 people who see this book, everyone's gonna know who everyone is. But then after that issue, everyone said "caption those photos." And I thought, "why?" It opens discussion. You're more apt to remember who it is if somebody tells you as opposed to reading it.

RF: It plays into the allure of the Inside Joke.

M: If you can read this, you know who that is. Trent offered to come over and caption them all sometime!

RF: What *Gag* item has gotten you in the most hot water?

M: I hear people say "well, so-and-so's really pissed about this" but I don't hear from them directly.

RF: Have you heard from Calvin Klein's lawyers?

M: I'm sure his lawyers know it's true!

RF: Do you think he's seen it?

M: Oh, we sent him copies. Care of Calvin Klein Industries. It never mentions him by name, so legally they can't call us on anything. But it is sick that.. how many fags own ten pairs of Calvin Klein underwear? I know that he gives back a lot through charity and whatever, but when you're that big of a fag it's like "oh, come on" I'm not trying to out him or anything. How could I?

RF: Do you think that queer celebrities have a responsibility to be out?

M: No. Unless they're doing something to harm the community or society. Or they're agreeing with some bent right-wing politician. If they're being hypocritical, absolutely. The same with politicians. When they're being hypocritical on an issue and you know they're a fag, call them on it! As fags we have to respect the right of privacy because that's what we hold up all the time to these right wing religious groups.

RF: That works both ways.

M: Just to point out a celebrity and say that they're a fag, I don't see what good that really does. I can see how someone in Des Moines, Iowa might think "well, so-and-so's a fag, and he doesn't look like a fag, so maybe all fags aren't like that". We can do that without outing celebrities. Most fags aren't the stereotype. But stereotypes of people exist because they *do* exist. Anyone that looks at someone that is the stereotype of a fag and says" you shouldn't be like that; you give us straight acting and appearing fags a bad rep" is such a slap in the face to everyone involved. How can you say something like that? That really means that they hate being a fag, they want fags to be more like them, conforming to straight society's values of what a man acts or looks like. But everyone mind-fucks all of these issues. Everyone wants to be either politically

"If your **ass** is exposed, we're gonna call you on it."

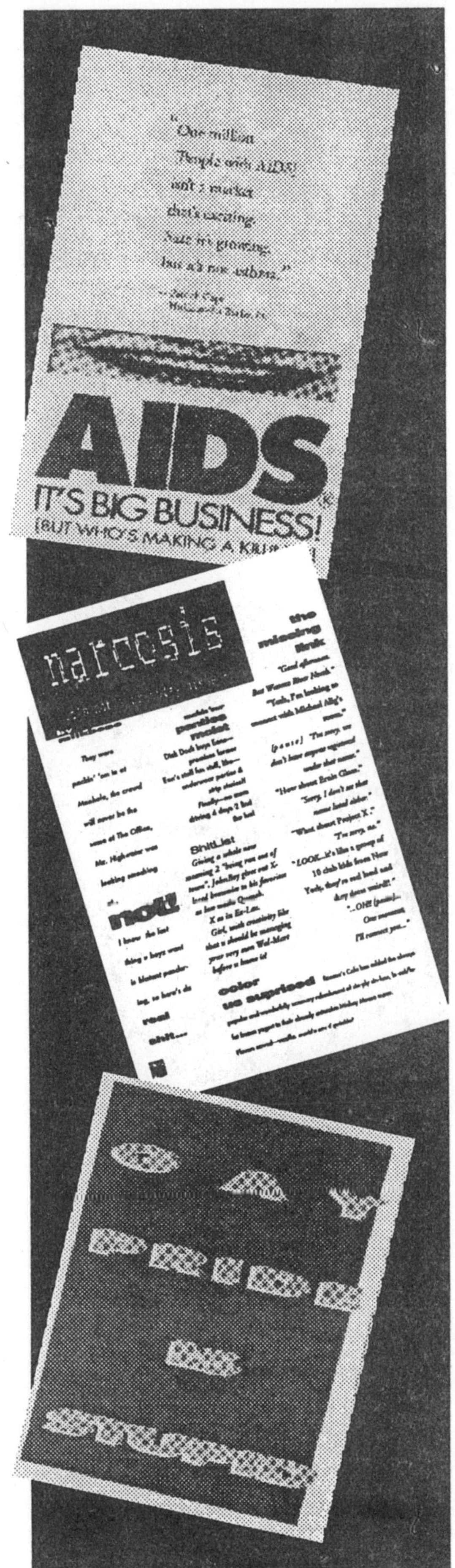

correct or politically incorrect. I think that if less time went into focusing on that kind of stuff, and more into where we're going as a union of people-gay,straight,black white,etc.

RF: People put emphasis on superficial issues because they're easier to deal with.

M: 'Cause there's really no right or wrong.

RF: What are your plans for *Gag?*

M: I have no plans for it really. I'm constantly getting advice on what I should do with it, but you know in your gut what's right and what's not. It could be a great ride for me and a bunch of fags to take.

RF: Have you gotten any response from the local gay press?

M: No, not really.

RF: There was a mention in John Henri-Damski's column. He did a column on pride day having outlived it's usefulness, and mentions the *Gag* "Gay Pride Is Stupid" page.

M: The parade is such a cliche now. Especially this year's theme; "Pride=Power". Pride does *not* equal power. What equals power is registering faggots to vote. That's where our power is . And in order to break the cliché, you have to make fun of it. Really shock people into thinking of it in a different way. That was the point behind "Gay Pride Is Stupid." How many people actually take pride in their sexuality? Whether they're straight or gay. To me it's always seemed so ironic.

RF: Do you get more dirt now because you have a magazine?

M: Actually I get a lot less now. A lot of people think "well I could give him some dirt on that person, but then that person could give him some dirt on me." So it's difficult now to get dirt. I really have to dig for it. I think *Gag* has to keep people on their toes. If your ass is exposed, we're gonna call you on it. Up until this point,no gay magazine ever said anything bad about anybody. Sure, Rick Karlin may have a snide quip about someone, but he never really called them on it. So people start to do something , they think,"ok is this politically correct?" Not politically correct but is this...cool? "Should I be doing this?" Everything we say generally has been said by other fags out there, we're just putting it in print.

RF: I think people overreact sometimes when it is in print.

M: Like I was telling you before,I just get so tired of people reading me personally wherever I go. Or anyone else that's involved with *Gag*. They make a beeline for us and say,"How could you have printed that?" When the majority of the time I personally didn't write it. I can say 99..maybe I should say 95...no 99 percent of the stuff that's written in *Gag* is true. I will not purposefully print anything that I know is false. There's so much stuff out there that someone has to cover that the major presses don't cover. And the stuff that being gay is so much a part of. All the campiness,all the dishing,all the "she said this" and "she did this." That's all gay culture, I think that we should really explore that.

RF: I can remember as a kid reading "The Boys in the Band" and getting really depressed thinking "oh my God, is this all I have to look forward to?" A bunch of bitchy queens just reading each other....

M: Un-hunh! A lot of times *Gag*'s done in such a faggy way that it can't help but be humorous. A lot of people that are really pissed at *Gag* because they were dished or one of their friends was dished... two months,three months, a year down the road, they look back on it and think that it's funny. If you personally are attacked it's going to sting a little. I'm not trying to win a popularity contest, otherwise I never would have started *Gag*. **THING**

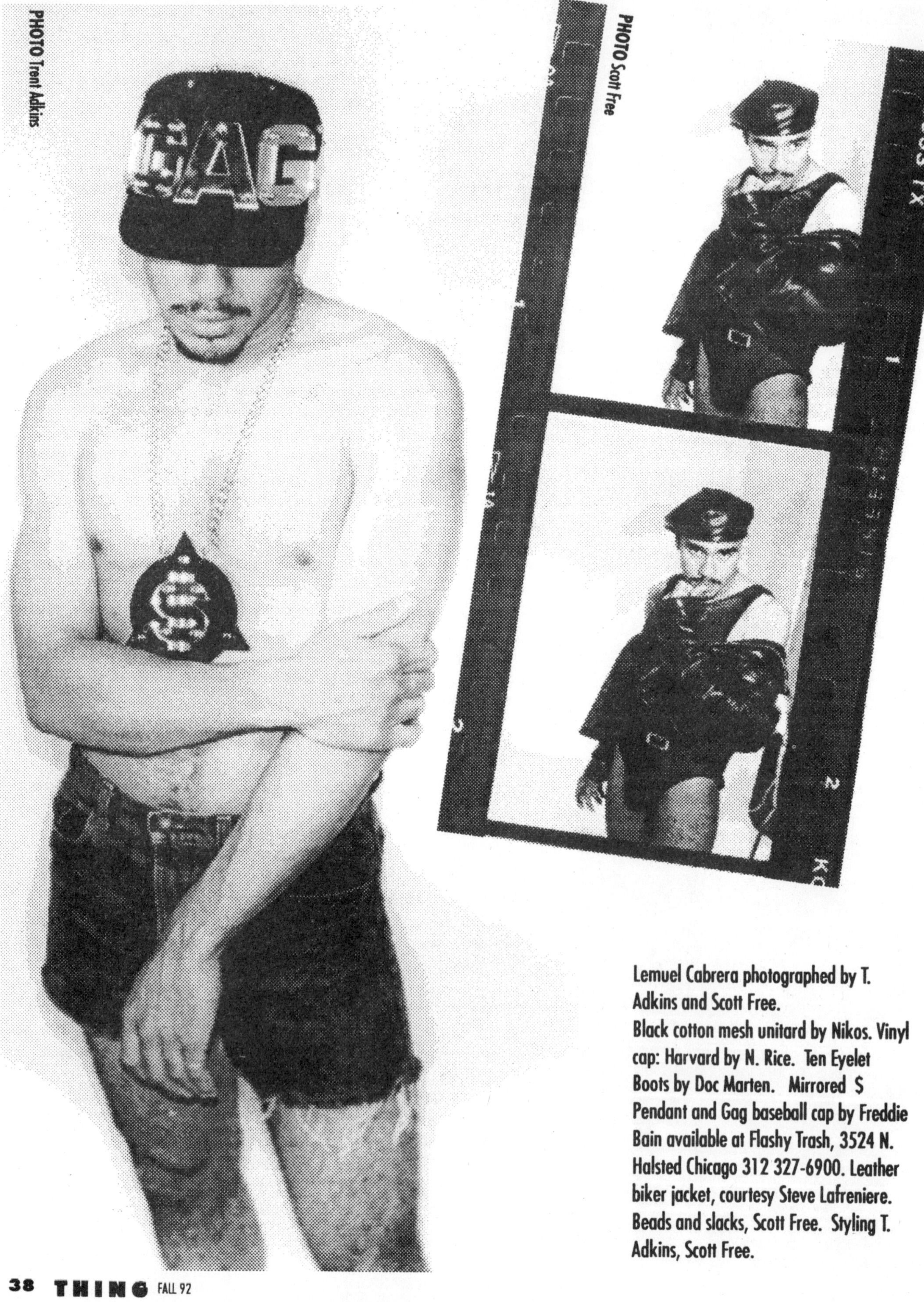

Lemuel Cabrera photographed by T. Adkins and Scott Free.
Black cotton mesh unitard by Nikos. Vinyl cap: Harvard by N. Rice. Ten Eyelet Boots by Doc Marten. Mirrored $ Pendant and Gag baseball cap by Freddie Bain available at Flashy Trash, 3524 N. Halsted Chicago 312 327-6900. Leather biker jacket, courtesy Steve Lafreniere. Beads and slacks, Scott Free. Styling T. Adkins, Scott Free.

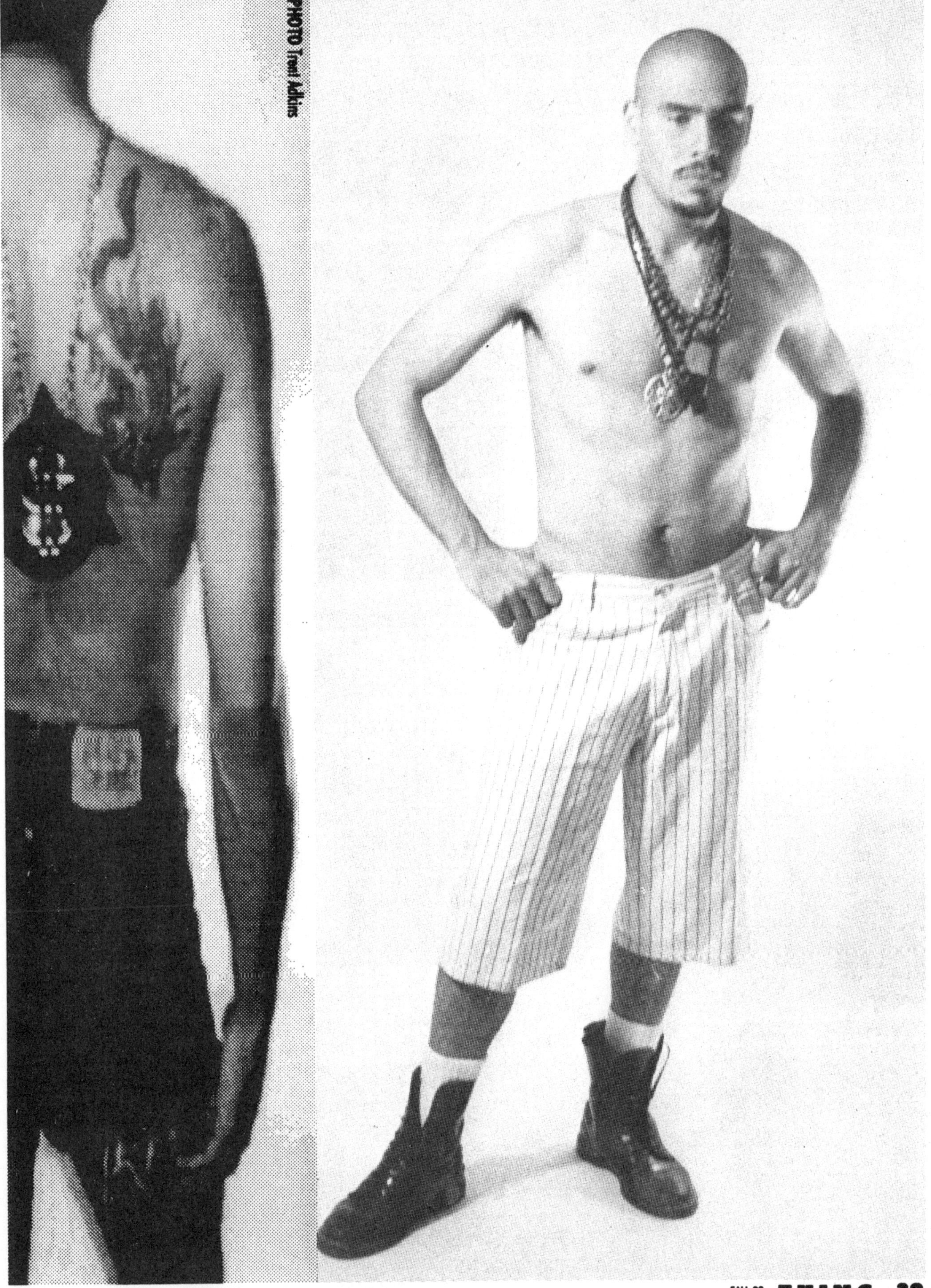
PHOTO Scott Free
PHOTO Trent Adkins

letter to the DEAD

PHOTO Lyle Ashton Harris

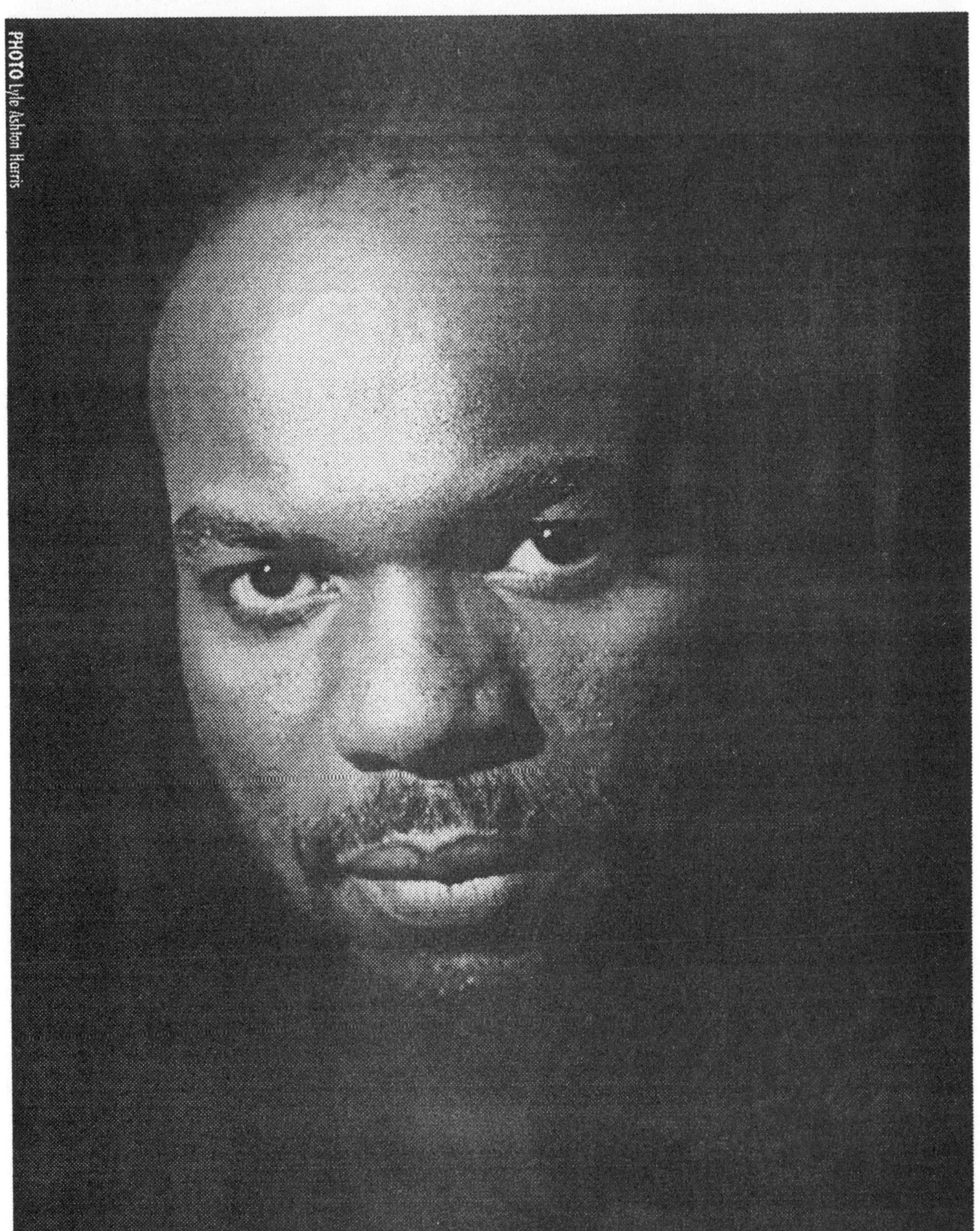

MARLON RIGGS

Dear comrades, lovers, girlfriends, family:

Ｆor what seemed the thousandth time I watched *Tongues Untied* a few days ago, this time of all places in Clemson, South Carolina. In a room filled with whites, in a small college town much like that room, I watched the screen and your image flicker by. How strange it was, in so alien an environment, to see you there, larger than life, singing, living, still. I listened close to the music of your voice—how much you remind me of voices centuries past—your raw-edged tenor blending rhythms and inflections descended from slaves into a hymn, a doo-wop declaration of freedom.

I listened and remembered: on the night of the San Francisco premier less than two years ago, you rested in a public hospital bed, laid low by pneumocystis. Remember? I dedicated the premier to you and your quick recovery. And when I saw you days later, your pride and glee were immediately self-evident. So clearly you spoke, so confident you seemed. Alone, you raised from the bed, and went to the bathroom. I watched and I thought, I too have been here, though for different reasons, and I know what effort—what will—so simple the task of rising to urinate requires.

I left you that day, both of us radiantly optimistic about your imminent return home. Two weeks later I was shocked by the news that you had returned to intensive care. Relapse. At your bedside I watched you struggle for each, single, irregular breath—each breath a battle between your will and the respirator. A friend lightly clasped your bloated hand. Your eyes flickered, your lips barely moved, I watched your face. Friends bent close to hear you, to decipher your mumbled whisper. But no one understood, and so, as tactile communication, they continued to hold your hand. I watched your face. "You're hurting him," I said. "Holding his hand hurts." The friend released his grasp, and your face, ashy, drawn, immediately relaxed.

Within your face I saw my own. Odd. I was not afraid. I studied you as I might study a mirror, witnessed the reflection of my own probable future, my not too dissimilar past. How close I, too, had come to being killed, not by the pneumonia, but by the most lethal accomplice: silence.

"Do you think I'm going to make it?" you asked us, eyes closed, barely a whisper. We looked at one another. No one spoke. Then the man who had once been your lover and had struggled to remain your friend, answered: "They're trying a new drug. But you have to rest. You have to stop fighting the respirator. Let it breathe for you. Rest so the drug can start to work."

The drug didn't work. Nor the respirator. You died the next day. And in my mind's eye I continually watch your face, study the slow drain of life from your dark-brown skin, your eyes, your chapped lips. I often see you as some superimposed photograph, you as you lay dying in the hospital that day, and you up on the screen, standing upright, tuxedoed, finger-snapping, smoothly defiant in your harmonizing doo-wop that "we come out tonight."

Tell me, Gene, how is it that you could come through so much—through alcoholism, financial dependency, racial self-hatred, internalized homophobia, neglected hypertension—tell me how you managed to master each of these demons yet would not—could not contend with that most insidious foe: the silence that shields us from the reality that we are risk, that our bodies might be sites of impending catastrophe. Did you believe, as so many of us still do, that black people "don't get it?"

Girlfriend, I remember when years ago I called one of the city's AIDS hotlines, and asked how KS looked on dark skin. You see I'd suddenly discovered a big blemish on my calf: it was not purple, it was not pink—such were the descriptions in all the information packets of the time—it was flat, round and pitch-black. Panicked, I nervously awaited an answer to my call: at the other end of the line, a woman told me that she had no information on the color of KS on dark skin, but I wasn't to worry, because—quote—"we don't get it".

I hung up, relieved, suspicious, confused. I went to the dermatologist. Two weeks I waited for the skin test result. The doctor called: "a mole," he said. Relieved I laughed. "But", he added, "moles don't usually grow that fast. This is unusual. Have you taken the test—to be sure?" "No," I curtly answered. That kind of certainty, then, was not what I was seeking.

How many of us have chosen this retreat—choose it still? Didn't you say, dear Chris, that the black community would pay dearly for denial? I heard you, but did I listen? We are sitting, the two of us, alone in your home (your lover Phil, of course, is away on some Task Force trip), and we are talking more honestly than we ever have. Sex, love, death, disease, denial: our final conversation, remember? "Black gay men," you said, "have fooled themselves into believing they are immune. The black community will pay a price." Coming from a whiteboy, I thought your words a little harsh. But you explained that AIDS can have a liberating effect on the tongue, lets you lash it like a whip, and get away with it. And I thought to myself: hmmmm, let's store that thought—just in case.

But that "just in case," I now know, was—as far as I was concerned—remote, theoretical. I heard you, Chris, but your message, I felt confident, was not meant for me. And the degree to which I embraced it, was out of ideological and political, not personal, necessity.

Ｏh, don't read me, girlfriend. You know I'm not the only one, though I should have known better. I should have had some sense knocked into me by the sight of gym buddy Alfredo—or should I say, gym bunny?—now, girlfriends, don't read me for being "sacrilegious." If you can't dish with the dead, then what's left? (Besides, you ain't gon' tell nobody no way!) Yes, should have known better when I saw the peculiar rash on Alfredo's brown, muscled back, a light-colored rash which spread to his chest, his arms, his face. Should have realized something was up when his weight went suddenly down. I watched him drop as many pounds as he once pressed. I watched, while like some sick solitary elephant that wanders off from the herd to die, Alfredo quietly disappeared from the clubs, the gym, disappeared into the shadows and silence of his apartment. When did you die, girlfriend? Even now, I don't think anybody knows, you did it so—discreetly.

Yes, Chris, I hear you: and we are paying a devastating price for such "discretion."

Remember? Ed, the first lover of my first and only lover. Melvin, the second lover of my first and only lover. Both Ed and Melvin, dead: why you two didn't awaken me to the possibility that black men do "get it," and that I might be the third in this succession of dying, dead lovers—why your deaths did not end this determined denial on my part is now no mystery to me. Denial runs deep, binds and burdens not just the solitary individual but the herd, the family, the race. Our silence about AIDS was a quintessential "black thang," but we refused to understand.

Funny. How crisis has a way of either deepening or disrupting our delusions. Were you watching, Lewayne, when the German doctors told me that both of my kidneys had ceased to function, and that I was HIV positive, to boot? Stunned, inert, silent, yet alert, I lay in that German hospital bed, my inner eyes, at last, beginning to open. Did you see what I see, Lewayne —

Lewayne, spitting image of myself, in height, head shape, and complexion, Lewayne, whose mother/father/family declined to visit you during your worsening illness, whose family effectively disowned you and wondered aloud wether you "deserved" to die; Lewayne, the first black man I knew to join this long, solemn procession: did you see, Lewayne, how quickly, quietly, my delusions of immunity disintegrated? Were you watching, girlfriend? Did you nod and sigh; "it's about time!"

Sweet Lewayne, who lost first sight, then life, to the raging virus, were you nonetheless my witness? Did you see over the ensuing months of my recuperation what happened to my kidneys, my sight, my tongue? How slowly, gradually, my kidneys once again started to work, how slowly, gradually I began to see the consequences of silence, and how as a consequence of this insight, my tongue unhinged from the roof of my mouth, dislodged from the back of my throat, slipped— free. And in the hospital, like some exuberant runaway escaped from slavery, I sang aloud, with all my might:

> Oh Freedom!
> Oh Freedom!
> Oh Freedom over me!
> And before I'd be slave
> I'd be buried in my grave
> and go home, yes! I'd go home
> and be free!

Surely, I thought some nurse would have rushed to the door and hushed me, or some less polite fellow patient simply demanded that I shut up all that noise. But no one came and no one protested, so from my hospital bed I continued to sing, with all my might:

> I shall not
> I shall not be moved
> I shall not
> I shall not be moved
> Just like a tree
> that's standing by the water

> Oh I shall not be moved!

Did you hear me, Harriet?
Did you hear my voice drop to a quieter song sung just for you—the song of someone escaped from captivity yet uncertain of his way:

> I don't believe
> you brought me this far
> just to leave me
> Oh, my God!
> I don't believe
> she brought me this far
> just to leave me

Did you hear, Harriet, the trembling trepidation in my voice (trembling which even now in remembering threatens to repossess me)? And didn't you, like the good shepherd that you are/have always been, didn't you come—and take my hand?

Beneath the continuous blare of Geraldo and Joan and Oprah and Donahue, The Young and The Restless, and All My oh-so-tedious Children, I heard you, Harriet, paid strict attention to your silent command: stand up and walk! It was then, my dear doo-wopping Gene, that I discovered what effort—what will—it required to rise from my sickbed to urinate. What pleasure to stand and pee!

Remember, Harriet?—remember how while my lover, mother, grandmother, friends, walked me through the hospital hallways with IV in tow, you walked with me, also, lightly holding my hand. And when we had escaped out of the woods, you pressed me on till we reached a river and you said simply, silently, with your eyes: wade in the water, child, if you want to get to the other side.

How many runaways had you so commanded? How many hung back and clung in fear to what they felt they knew, sought refuge in the woods, thick silence, darkest night? How many thought they could escape by becoming invisible? But didn't you know, Harriet, that slavery is never escaped as long as the master controls your mind. And don't you now see —

Our silence about AIDS was a quintessential "black thang" but we refused to understand.

oh I know you do!— the chilling parallel between the means by which we were held captive in your time, and the methods of our enslavement today. Don't you see the chains, my Harriet, sweet Moses, the chains not so much of steel and the law, but more insidious: the invisible chains, linked over centuries, of silence and shame. In this latest crisis, our new master is the virus; his overseer — silence; and his whip — shame.

How deeply were you scarred, dear Gene? Oh I know you sang Harriet's songs of freedom but when she led you to the water, why didn't you wade? What invisible chains bound your feet, your mind? Were they the same as mine? Was the stigma of this virus so powerful in your mind, as it was in my own, that you, too, sought refuge in pretense, denial? Did you somehow ignore, as did I, how quietly, one by one, your friends and comrades and lovers were stolen away? Did you, too, think that silence and invisibility were adequate cover?

Delusion, my child, Harriet's gaze reminded me. The master knows well the woods. Stalks best in darkness. Covets silence. Lays the most deadly traps within the most seductive shadows. Looks like you gotta wade, Harriet's eyes said to me, if you want to get to the other side.

Were you watching, Chris, when I stepped into the deep? I who have never learned to swim and was certain I would drown. Chilly, troubled waters

> ## "Black gay men have fooled themselves into believing they are immune. The black community will pay a price."

swept over my feet, rose gushingly to my ankles, my hips, waist, chest, then my neck. Troubled, angry waters whipped and tore at me, brutally washed away decades of deep-layered shame, washed away the denial, the fear, the stigma; cracked and splintered the master's lock and chain.

Before I knew it I was naked and trembling — and free. And that's when I began to sing, from the hospital bed, and I know I sang off-key but the quality of the song didn't matter as much as the affirming act of singing:

I woke up this morning with my mind
staying on freedom.
I woke up this morning with my mind
staying on freedom.
I woke up this morning with my mind
staying on freedom.
Hallelu—hallelu—hallelujah!

And then from somewhere nearby I heard another voice join in the refrain.

Come on and walk, walk!
Come on and walk, walk!
Come on and walk, walk!

I turned and looked and there stood Brother Baldwin, old bug-eyed Jimmy with the biggest smile, and he hugged my shoulder and turned me slightly, nodding at another figure nearby, and my mouth nearly dropped: there was Martin walking alongside Sojourner who held the hand of Ella Baker who walked alongside Langston who held the hand of Joe Beam, and in front of and behind them countless, countless, radiant, singing faces. In the hospital I shouted, with all my might, and nobody hushed me:

Ain't gonna let nobody turn me around
turn me around!
turn me aroun!
Ain't gonna let nobody turn me around!
I'm gonna keep on a-walking
Keep on a-talking
Marching up to Freedom Land.

WE ARE WADING THROUGH WATERS, deep, angry, cleansing waters, releasing fear and shame and enslaving silence in our wake. And I remember the shock of seeing you, Bayard, in all your naked nobility; wading with the rest of us; shouting us on. Oh what it meant to me to learn the full truth of your life, to see my first shining example of a black gay man like myself so committed to everybody's freedom.. How it hurt me, Bayard, to learn how they drummed you out of the movement because of your love, your life; how our most eminent black leaders threatened you, and the movement, by slurring your life, your love. (Adam Clayton Powell, Junior, I'm talking about you — and you should be ashamed. I hope these waters wash some of the dirt caked deep in your hide!)

I thank you, Bayard, for offering me a vision of what it might be like, on the other side. And I thank you, Jimmy, for so courageously claiming and revealing the full expanse of your identity and demanding that all of us do the same. And I thank you…No, girlfriend, I'm not going to go on like some droning starlet at the Academy Awards. But—Joe, I have to acknowledge you, Joseph Beam: for your life, and death, offer telling testament to how even when breaking public silence, private ones remain and these, too, can kill. Joe, you wrestled with clever demons—shame, rage, invisibility, self-hatred—and you prevailed, except with this one wily beast: silence. You should not have died alone, your illness kept secret. There is no shame to this disease, I have learned, and hence no need for secrets.

To each of you, to Harriet, my sweet Moses, especially, I thank you for having led me from the forest to the river and commanded me to wade. Repayment, my dear dead beloved, to any one of you, to all of you, for this singular act of liberation is impossible. But what I have learned from you I now pass on. As Harriet walked with me, I now walk with others. And as Harriet held my hand, we must hold each other's. As Jimmy, while abandoning the church never left the pulpit, so too each of us must be a witness. I've learned this, Chris, my blunt-speaking prophet, learned it the hard way, at the cutting edge of life, where death and I tangled with each other. And even now, as the virus continues its course through my veins, I know nonetheless I will reach the other side, one way or another.

Dear comrades, lovers, girlfriends, family: bless you for the blessings you've given me. I know but one way to redeem the precious gift of your lives, your deaths, and that is through living testaments, old and new, to all we have been and might become. For I know that through such testaments we are forever fortified: through such testaments we will keep on walking and keep on talking till we get to the other side. **THING**

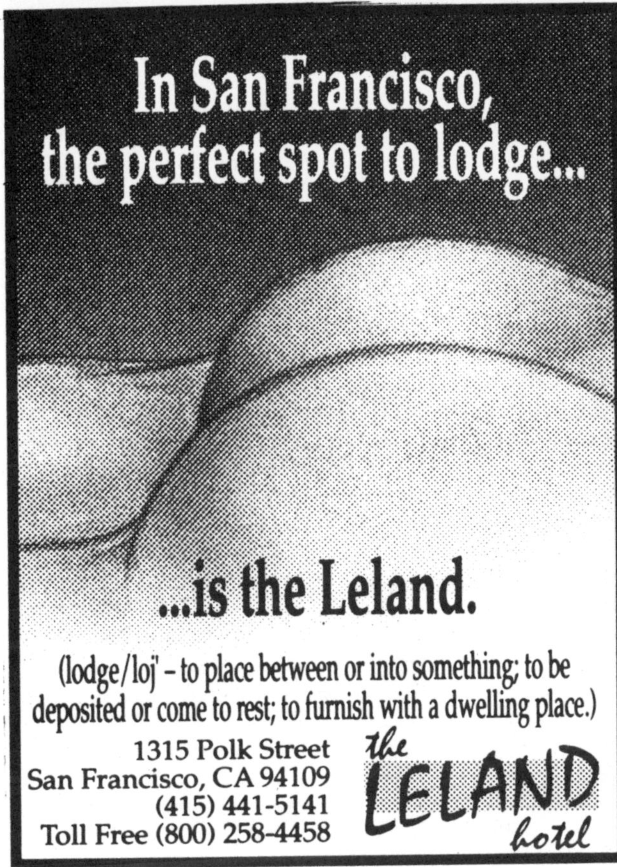

Living With HIV As A Young Adult Is Hard. But You're Not Alone.

Let's face it, your twenties can be rough years, and living with HIV makes them rougher. Finishing college, finding a job, getting insurance, or coming out can seem overwhelming for young adults when the burden of HIV is added. Many people in their twenties feel alone in their fight against HIV. It doesn't have to be that way.

We're TPA 20s--a free, peer support group sponsored by Test Positive Aware Network and designed specifically for young adults with HIV. Our aim is to help ourselves by sharing our problems and perspectives, confronting issues unique to our age group. We meet every first and third Sunday at 7 p.m. We're casual and friendly, and confidentiality is strictly maintained. To find out more about TPA 20s call 312-404-TPAN.

TPA Twenties

Strength in numbers.

312-404-TPAN

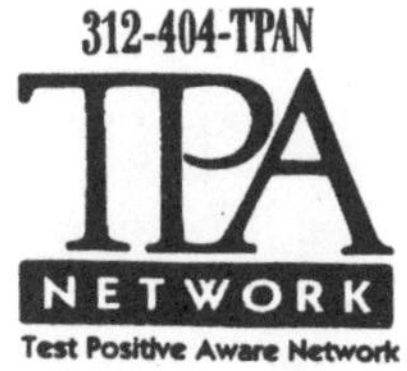

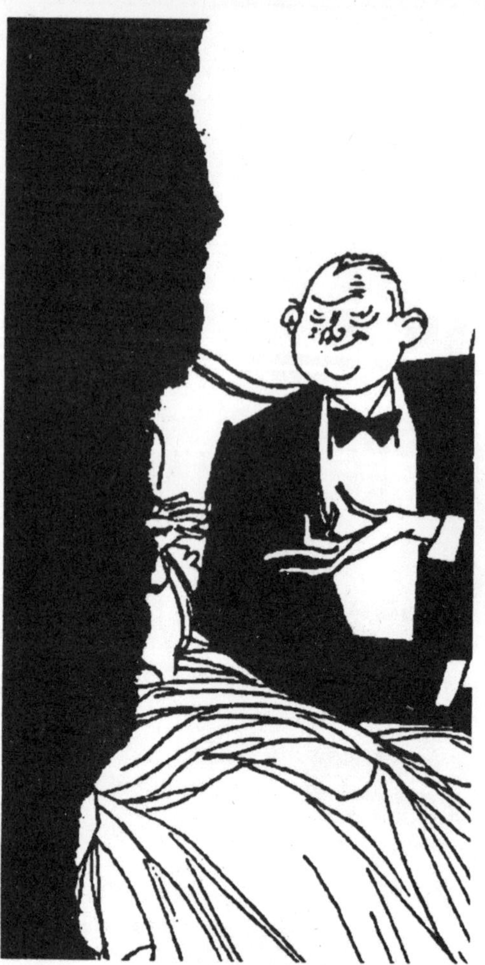

I called a friend in L.A. the other day. I knew he worked in that new-ish central city area that had been evacuated during the riots and I was curious to know how he'd fared. The discomfort he suffered was mostly psychological, as he'd returned from lunch unaware of the events unfolding and found his office building completely emptied.

I myself was rather surprised at the targets of the violence, and wondered why no one in the media had popped what I thought was a pertinent question: "Don't they sell maps to the stars' homes on the street corners of Hollywood anymore?" I realize there were levels of tension that demanded release, but after about five minutes of random violence, I would have thought someone would have conjured the notion to head for the HILLS and torch a few mansions (after a proper looting of gowns and jewels). After all, Fredrick's of Hollywood is hardly what one would call a heavy hitter in the class struggle.

Speaking of social unrest, as a minority in the minority of my ghetto, I was recently called a "white asshole" by some not-so-youthful Latino youths who hang out in front of my house. Now I can legitimately be called many things, like "commie pinko fruit" for starters, but I must confess that "white asshole" is a title I don't feel I can rightfully accept. "White" is relative in concept at best; that I am light-hued reflects only my father's side of the gene pool; my brother resembles my Spanish Creole Madre and has been called a "spic" in many of the more refined areas of the country. "Asshole" has always struck me as a term of endearment in the boudoir. "Bitch" I find socially correct and "White Bitch" as a pet name would do just fine. "Fairy" or "faggot" both could apply, though "cocksucker" has always been a bit graphic for my taste. And "Drag Queen" only works after 10:00 AM. Anything else becomes too literary for mere street confrontation.

The above incident has, however, given me cause for alarm. Having witnessed a rather frightening amount of violence the last few years, I've begun to fear the misplaced anger of the masses in their quest for equality and justice. When the "REVOLUTION" comes to my block, will they accept my Xeroxed maps to the North Shore and Hinsdale, or burn my humble cottage, cheering the demise of an enemy of the people, as rhinestones go pop in the flames.

★ ★ ★

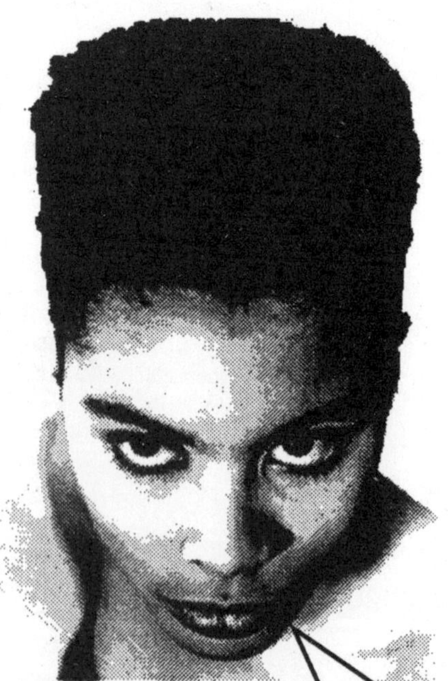

Political musings aside, I did hear a marvelous story from Gigi about a buddy of hers who was dumped by a fellow (for a fish!) and decided to get even. G's friend, six-foot-two and butch as nails, dolled himself up in heavy drag and waited for his ex-lover's new fiancee outside her place of work. When the unsuspecting bride-to-be exited, she was set upon and beaten to a pulp by this creature (who being indescribable was, hence, unapprehendable). Methinks the guy over-reacted. Six days after the honeymoon he would have gotten back his man though not on a permanent basis. (If those real women out there knew what hubby was really up to when he says he's going out for a pack of "smokes"...)

More from the married set: an ex-Marine construction worker took up both transvestism and cruising in the forest preserves. (When 200 pounds of rippling muscle-in-a-sun-dress asks if you like what you see, you'd be well advised to drop to all fours and respond in the affirmative.) Major Dad used to hide his "girl suit" in the back of his pick-up truck until his wife discovered his cache. He claimed sexual fidelity, and insisted the apparel had been found on the roadside and brought back for her. While the bimbo bought the story (further proof that heterosex-

uality is a drug that dims the mind) hubster realized he needed an alternative armoire. His fellatio friends were more than happy to hold on to an outfit or two, but balked at giving him a key (lest they be forced to explain such an apparition to a younger or more sensitive guest).

His solution was to stow some of his gear in the woods. A shallow indentation in the dirt by some trees, a pile of dead leaves, a few rocks, and it would be hidden from all but the eyes of the most experienced serial killer. Easy. Too easy. He appeared, fuming, one afternoon at the home of a sympathetic friend waving a tattered Cinch-Sack above his head, shrieking "Goddamned raccoons ate my high heels!"

That particular forest yields other examples of life in the raw. Our same Marine made the acquaintance of another married gentleman, who enjoyed bondage au natural. He wanted to be tied to wood—favoring deciduous trees— and fucked, preferably by "new friends".

On meeting our serviceman in a slip, he invited him back to his place as the wife and kids were off visiting granny for the day. He'd rigged his garage in anticipation of just such an occasion: hooks in the wall, plenty of

rope, and a couple of thick leather restraints. In an instant the Marine had a fresh coat of lip gloss and the nature lover was firmly secured to a beam. No sooner had the first lick occurred when the automatic garage door opened, allowing the earlier-than-expected wife and kids to view the tableau vivant. Mr. Few and Proud sprinted off down the driveway in his new pumps, leaving Daddy all trussed-up and dangling, shouting "Call 911! That son-of-a-bitch got away with my wallet!"

★★★

Oh, by the way, Pussy and I have not lunched of late, largely as a result of her latest excursion into the world of the svelte. As she eats only for sustenance, those unsightly saddle bags are now unsightly empty saddle bags and I fear that, at the rate she's going, the poor dear will soon be nothing more than hips and eye-makeup. Not a pleasant sight for a weak stomach. Anyway, I'm sure she'll be back, though I'm not counting the seconds. After all, I've lived my entire life without pussy. And so, I hope, have you.

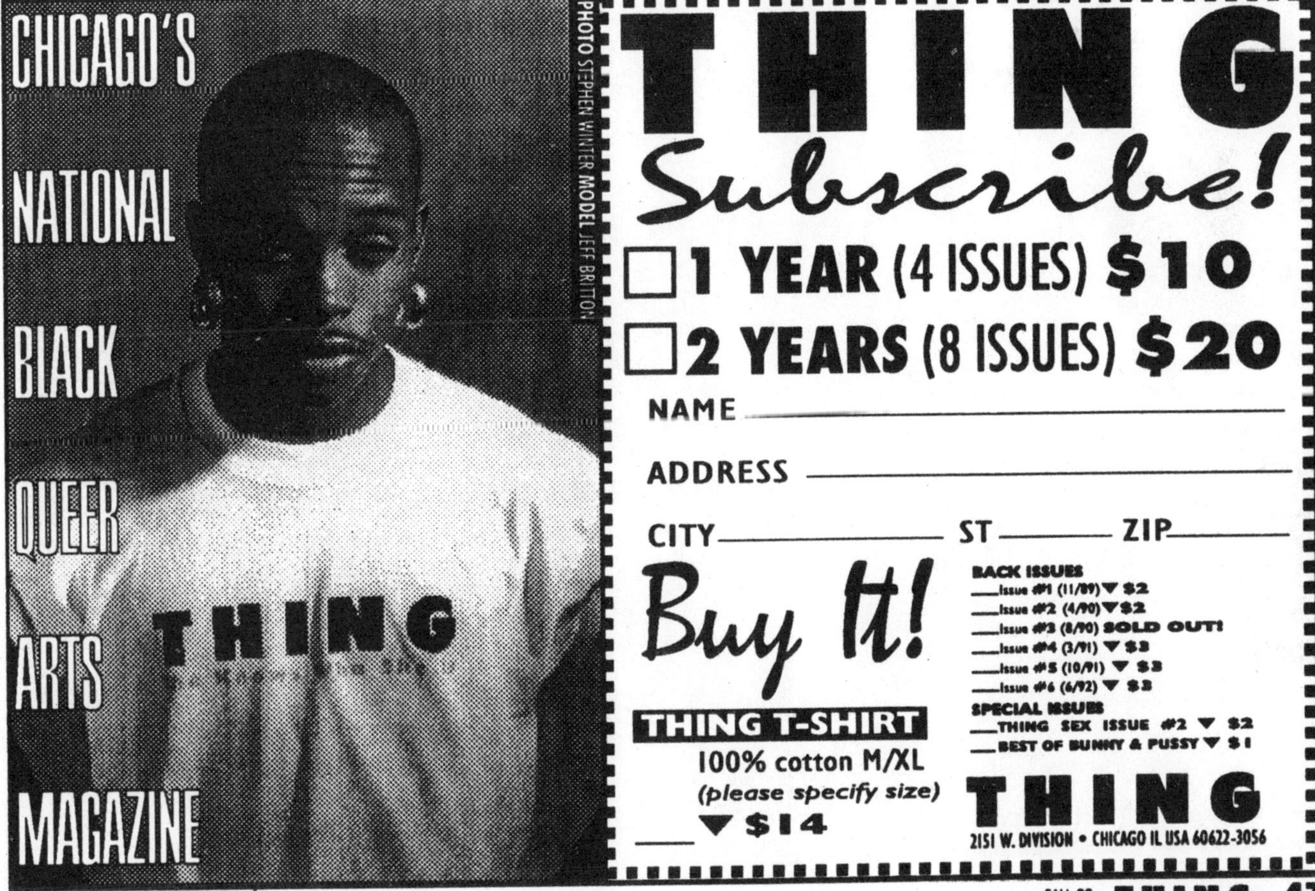

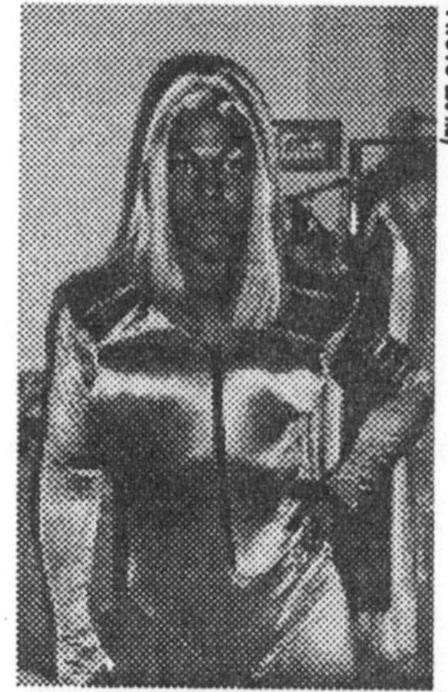

Mona Foot backstage at Hothouse for the Carol Moseley Braun benefit.

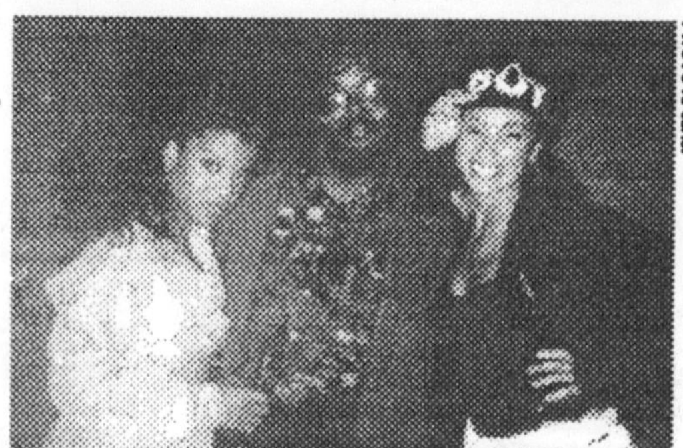

Chantay Savage, Savage Mann, and Julie Brown at Chantay's birthday party at the China Club Chicago.

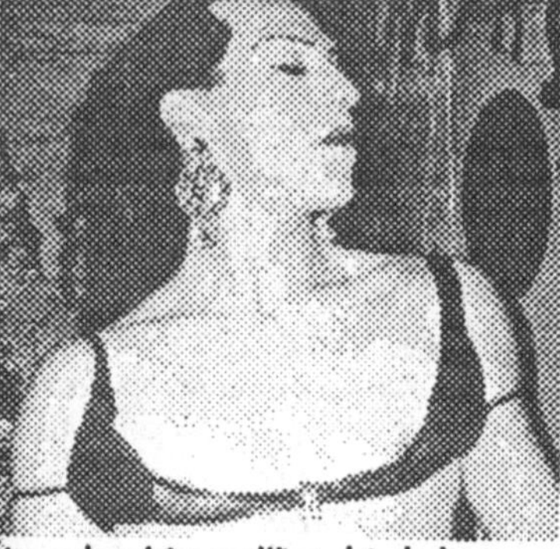

Joey Arias, pre-Wigstock in the basement at FUCK, Pyramid NYC.

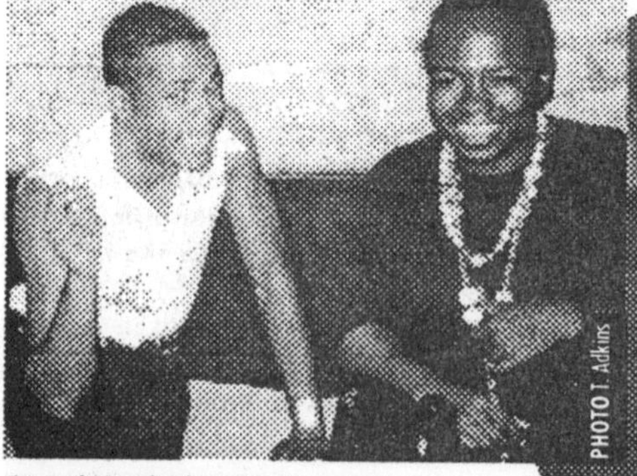

Eric and Miss Claude at Cairo.

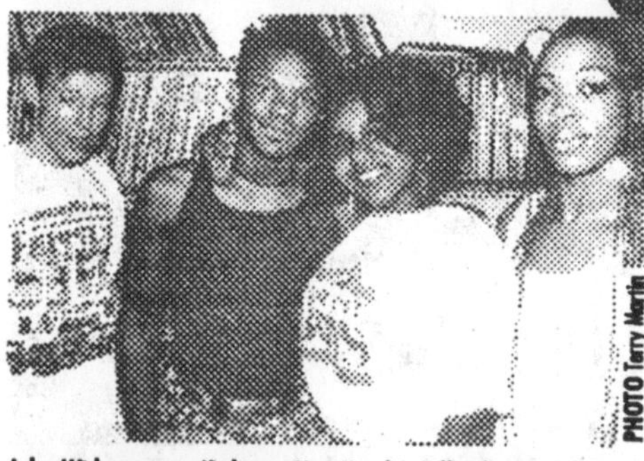

John Witherspoon (Lahoma Van Zandt), Bill Coleman, Ultra Naté, and Miss Reneé at the Maxi Records post-Wigstock party.

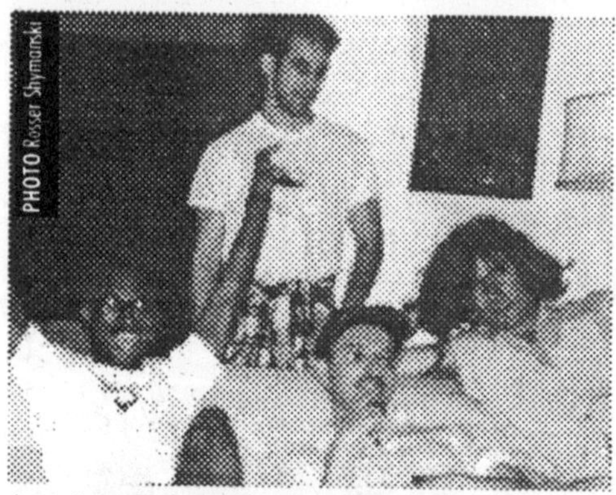

Aaron Avant Garde, Mark Fraitas (standing), Steve Lafreniere, John Volkening at Steve's party for Rosser Shymanski

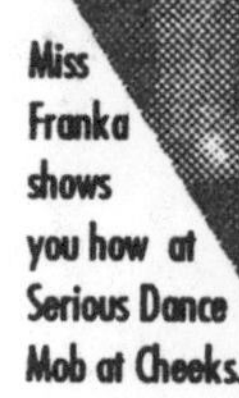

Miss Franka shows you how at Serious Dance Mob at Cheeks.

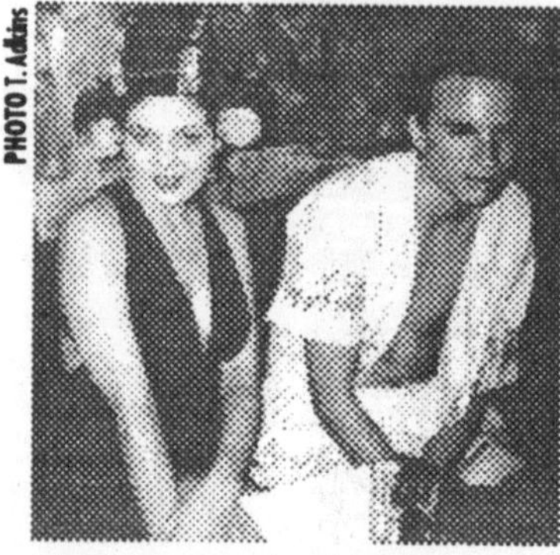

Jahnne Vavoom and friend at Cairo.

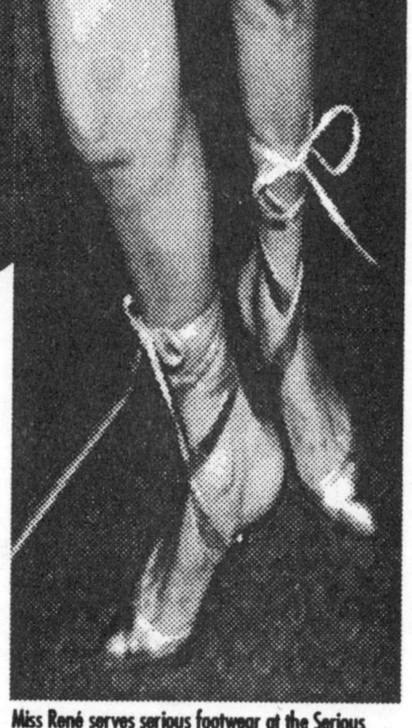

Miss René serves serious footwear at the Serious Dance Mob.

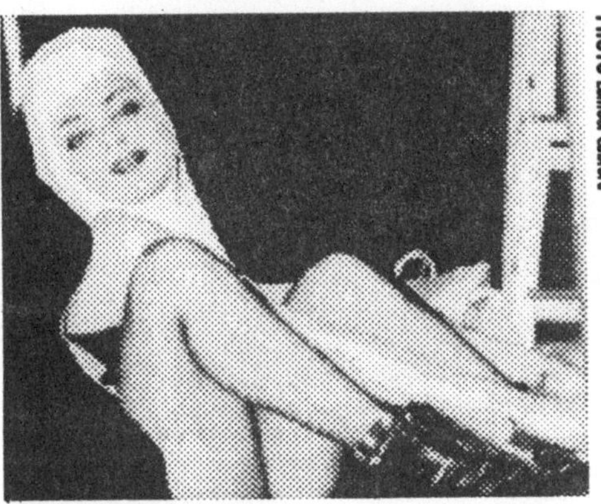

Jahnne as Sister Holy Roller (or some such) for Pope John Boy's party at Shelter.

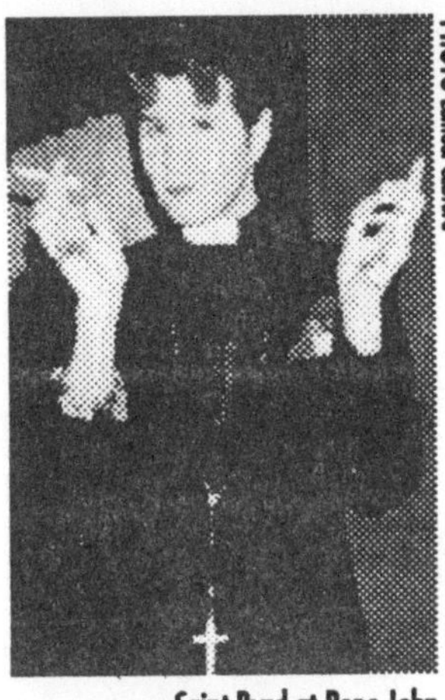

Saint Byrd at Pope John Boy's party.

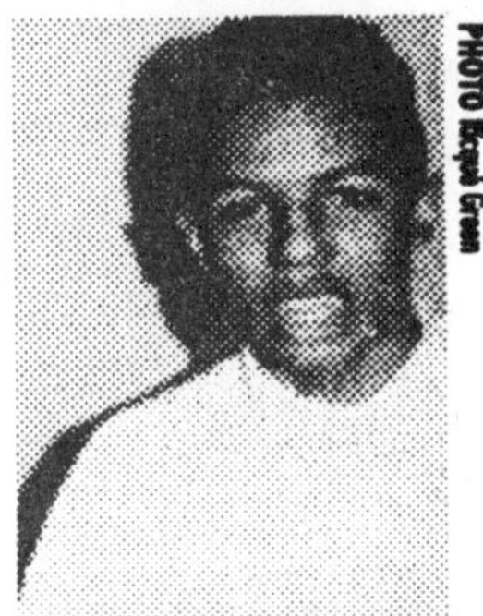

John Jourdan Young 1964-1992

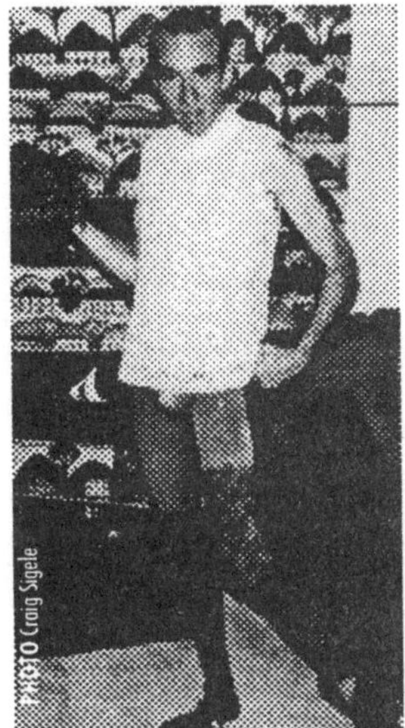

Who me?: Steve Marton readies for Wigstock at designer Jackie Rodgers' apartment.

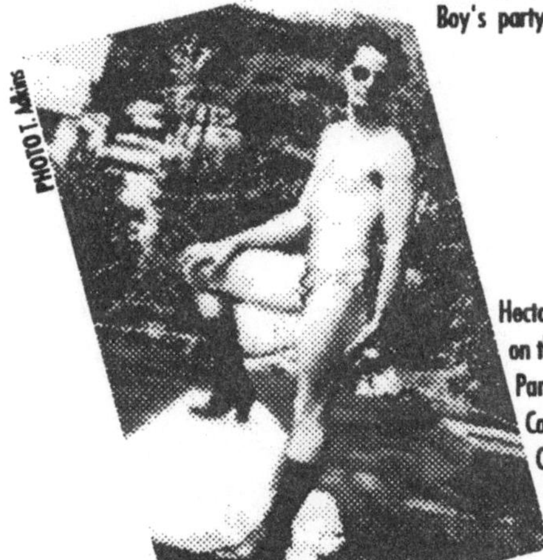

Hector Xtravaganza on the roof at Paradise Compound, Chicago.

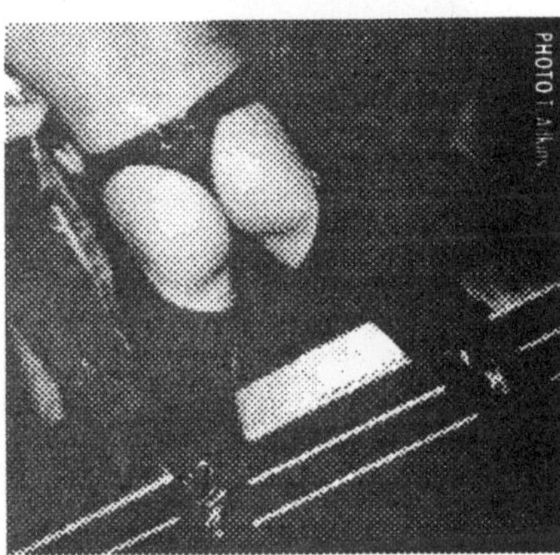

More cheeks at Cheeks: Rod Sanchez shakes it at the Saturday night C-Men party.

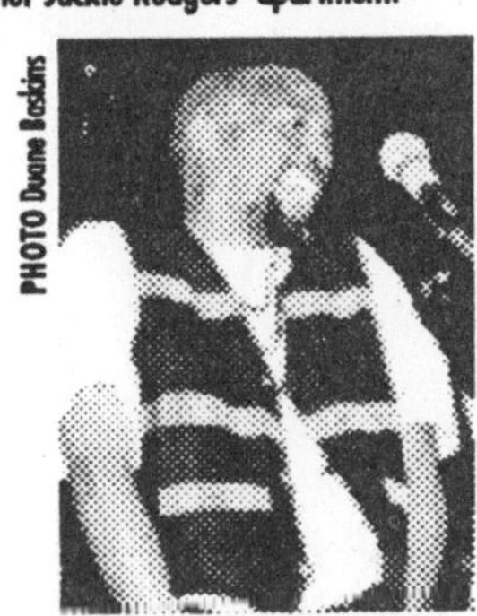

Essex Hemphill at the Bop Shop, Chicago.

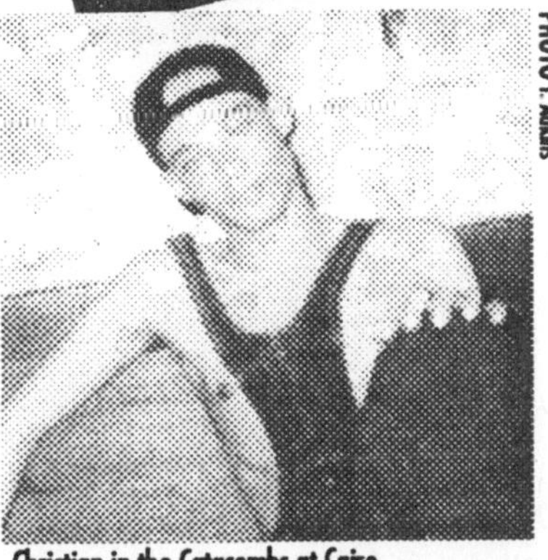

Christian in the Catacombs at Cairo.

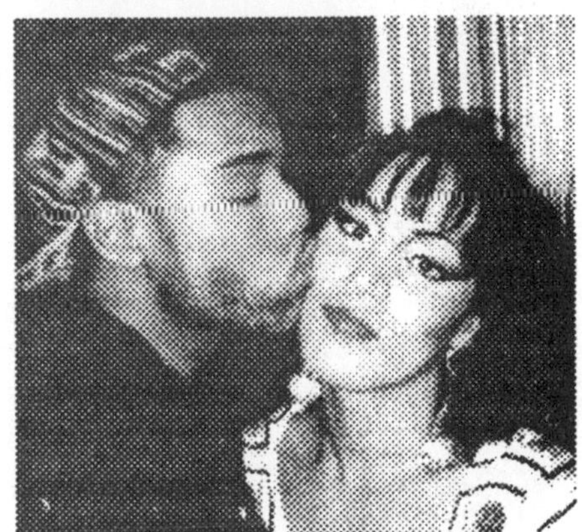

Trent and Christine at C-Men.

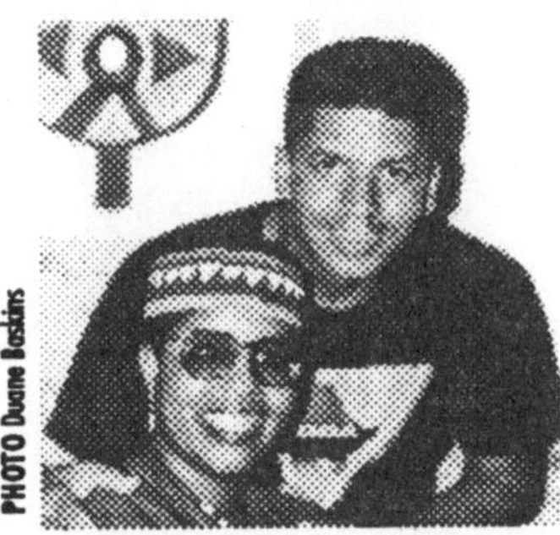

Writers Donna Rose and Alan Miller at the Parker Mansion.

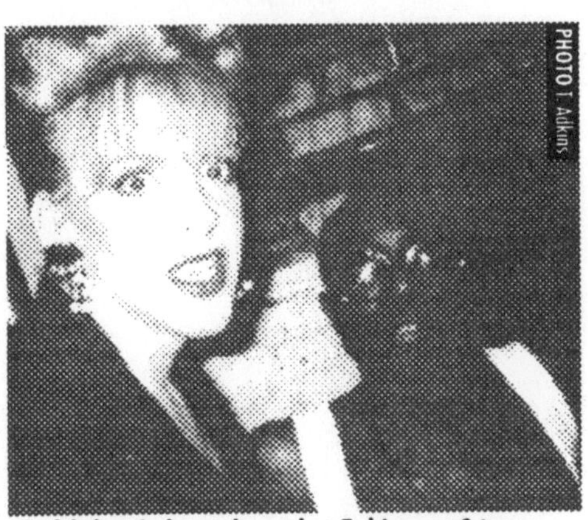

The fabulous Godiva and super-host Ted Jones at Cairo.

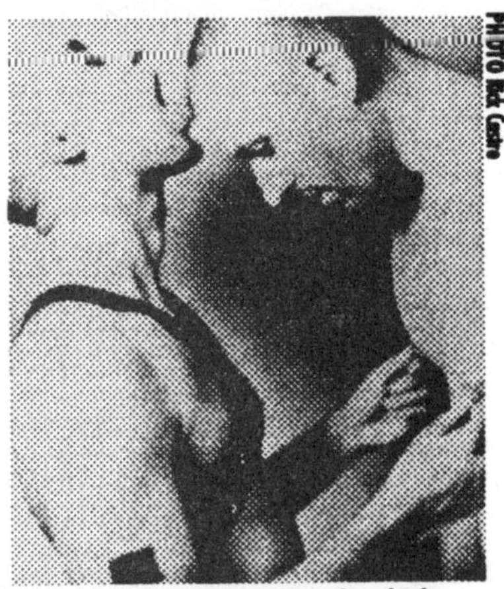

Lick it!: Sexy show-offs Gerald Paoli and John Volkening in a Rick Castro photo for The Advocate.

A workshop about love, truth and being powerful in life...

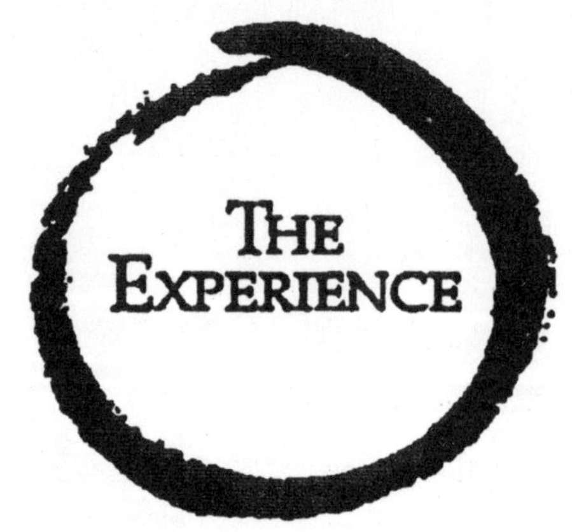

Life can be powerful

and empowering. Each experience is an opportunity to learn, grow and expand. With the normal stress we all face daily, it's far too easy to forget. The Experience is an opportunity to remember. In it you will learn, or recall, how to approach life as an exciting adventure, producing the results you want while enjoying the process.

The purpose of The Experience

is to support the participants to live truthfully, powerfully, lovingly, and with integrity. It provides you with a means to discover and experience your own power and the choices that are always available to you. You *can* have the life you choose! The Experience offers you tools for reaching your goals.

You will meet many new

and interesting people. Your relationships are a major focus of The Experience. You will learn how to enhance the quality of all types of relationships so that they are based on communication, love and intimacy.

No matter how well

you function today, you probably approach life with many self-imposed limitations. During the workshop, you will be able to see your life, and the many options it affords you, from a broader perspective.

The Experience is an investment in a vision of who you can be.

For Local workshop information, please contact:

Washington D.C.
Oct. 23-24-25, 1992
202/389-0403

Seattle
Oct. 23-24-25, 1992
206/624-4944

Dallas
Nov. 6-7-8, 1992
214/350-9390

Phoenix
Nov. 13-14-15, 1992
602/420-5469

Chicago
Nov. 20-21-22, 1992
708/439-8715

Atlanta
Jan. 29-30-31, 1993
404/365-0317

Los Angeles
Feb. 5-6-7, 1993
213/848-9571

Denver
Feb. 19-20-21, 1993
303/757-7763

Fort Lauderdale
Feb. 26-27-28, 1993
407/395-3804

All dates are subject to change.

THE EXPERIENCE NATIONAL OFFICE
3133 MAPLE DRIVE, SUITE 110 • ATLANTA, GEORGIA 30305
(800) 966-3896 • (404) 365-0317

DeAUNDRA'S DIXIE DIARY

Hey, y'all! This here's **DeAundra Peek** comin' to y'all all the way from Atlanta, Georgia USA! Right now, I'd like to extend my real special personal super-thanks an' WHATEVER to all a my sweetheart friends in Chicago who done showed me such a good time when I was there recently! Seein all them Vienner Beef factories all over the place really made me feel at home, and shoppin' on Maxwell

Mr. Lee Kay's bubble head.

Street was just like the Palmetto Mini Mall's Great Tire Fire Summer Sale. I guess it's time to move along, y,all...

Mr. **RuPaul Charles** done come through Atlanta at downtown clubdream Velvet, an' he done tore the house up! "Supermodel," his brand new single on Tommy Boy, is gonna come out "real soon" accordin' to Mr. RuPaul, and y'all know that means we don't know when, but we wish it was yesterday! Y'all, inside sources done said that Mr. RuPaul was wearin' a $1,000 wig, and sittin in a convertible in the big ole' Lesbian & Gay pride parade in New York City. Keep y'all's ears pealed for the song "Foxy Lady" with the special guest vocal by none other than **LaWanda Page**!

A commitment to L-O-V-E is what fuels artists **Ed Woodham, Wayne Sizemore**, and **Bill Morhar** on with their current Atlanta Children's Mural Project. Tandemized with the non-profit art/education group The Study Hall, they has got 35 kids aged 4-9 from the Inner City Black Youth program, an' they's all workin' together to expand each other's imaginations. "Raising and keeping self-esteem with these kids is great, we all work as a team to reach a goal. It gives all of us, kids, artists, everyone involved, a real sense of accomplishment," saided Woodham. Look for them to take it on tour real soon!

I am so happy to report about the three hi-style artist renderinisims of me that has done shown up in the last couple of months! In Chicago y'all has got 2: First off, that spectacular bubblehead por-trit by Mr. **Lee Kay**. He's that famous artist done paintin's of celeberties like **Tina Turner**, RuPaul, **Michael Musto**, **Joan Jett Blakk**, an' now me, DeAundra Peek! Also, Chicago has that talented **Chuck Gonzales**, the darlin' who done the drawin' a me on the poster for the **Carol Mosley Braun** benefit show from June! An' y'all, in Atlanta we has got Mr. **Terry Hardy's** big ole' paintin' of DeAundra as depicted on the Midway at South Fulton County Fair, Remember y'all, support y'all's homeartists!

Y'all know that the Black National Arts Festival was here in Atlanta recently, well, did y'all know that there was a few openly gay artists in it too? That's right, there was **Christial Walker**, a photographer who uses some kinda what they call "manipulation" to make new types a images outta regular ones, like addin' captions an' glitter an' stuff. There was poet **Alan Miller**, who does Japanese haiku-type writin' to express himself. Mr. **Freddie Styles** was the curator in the Invitational Exhibition. I am real happy to see that some kinda respect done been propped on them.

Bill Curtis, that multi-talentological co-producer of cable access hit "Arbiters of Style" done took a trip with his art partner **Robert Hamilton** to the big-time SIGGRAPH computer convention at hi-style confrence McCormick Place. Their stunnin' computer art portraiture was seen by 40,00 people that week ! Them boys even met up with Chicago socialites Mr. **Steve Lafreniere** and Mr. **Trent Adkins**, an' later on they went to a hi-fufi party at the Red Lacquer Room in the Palmer House Hilton & Arms. They had almost as much fun in Chicago as I did!

An' y'all, if somehow I could get a message through to them's that passed on, they's three sweethearts I'd call to Heaven an' say "Hey!" to; Glorious entertainment legend **Mickey Day**, who was sooooo funny an' an inspiration to all a us; Mr. **Melvin G. Ross**, a member an' leader of just about every rights-type group y'all can think of, includin' BWMT, AID/Atlanta, an' the National Coalition of Black Lesbians an' Gay Men; an' dancer/entertainer Miss **Erica Adams**, whose shows done thrilled people all over the South. I know in my heart they is all havin' fun wherever they are!

Just been announced y'all is real excitin' news that my new TV show, "DeAundra's Teenage Music Club," is gonna be included in the upcomin' Image Regional Lesbian & Gay Film Festival in Atlanta! An' the ratin's crew done told me that my new single, "Losin' My Vienners" is the top requested video on my TV show 4 weeks runnin'!

Them **Pop Tarts** in New York City is releasin' a brand-new album on Funtone USA Records called "Gagging on the Lovely Extravaganza" this fall. They has done honored me by includin' a sample of me, DeAundra Peek, singin' "ooh, la la la la la la la" (from my world popular version of **Dee-Lite**'s "What Is Love") in their new song called "Wig Out" — which also has Mr RuPaul singin' some stuff on it too!

TEAM ODUM'S UPDATE: Seems like Odum's All Double Wide Mobile Homes Court just can't lose, leastways not with **Duffy Odum** on Team Odum's! Y'all ain't gonna believe this, but he has done won all 16 competitions against the Del Vista Ray Mar Mobile Homes Park Team. Sometimes it was close, like the time **Dora Tennellie Stubbs** nearly beat him at vienner can rollin', or when he got lost an' we found him at Rango Fain's Snack Shed havin' a Vienner Pita Wrap an'a couple a packs a O'Boisies.

Meanwhile, in Japan, **Lurleen Wallis** has done gone an' become one a the top weather girls in the nation on the new game show "Wather Or Not" where Lurleen gets to blindfold contestants and then, like , spray 'em down with water so's they can guess if it's real rain or not—them Japanese! One time, she got herself locked in the typhoon Simulation Booth for a couple of hours, an' was she real glad to see all them firemen when they got her out!

Speakin' a Eleganza, they has done added two new members to the cast of the zaniest live glamour stage show! Wish a warm welcome to **Barbie-Q** an' **Scintilla Vortex**! Together with Miss **Trina Saxxon** and Kinky Kooky Krunchy Kung Fu **Clive Jackson** they bring they's every Friday night show at the Heretic all the charm that platform pumps an' 7" pile red shag carpetin' can pull outta Conyers, Georgia!

Y'all, it's time for me to run on now, I has got a whole mess a special appearances to make a course. Here's the vienner sausage recipe y'all been waitin' on all summer long! I love y'all!

VIENNERS GAZPATCHO SOUP, LITE

2 Cans Hy-Grade Vienners
  -Imitation Style
1 Squeeze Bottle, Hy-Grade Ketchup-Lite
1 Cup Imitation Freeze-Dried Pre- Fried Green Pepper Chips
  (Optional)
1 Cup Imitation Freeze-Dried Powdered Onion Shreds
1/2 Cup Hy-Grade Refined & Skimmed Corn Oil
6 Part-Time Plastic Ice Cubes
1 Cup Chunked Dry White Bread
1 Blender

Open your vienner cans, drain juice into the blender. Mix in the squeeze ketchup-lite, puree on high for 2 minutes, or till mixed. In a mixin' bowl, put all the imitation freeze-dried ingredients an' pour the blenderized mixture over that, soak till soft. Fold in the oil, makin' sure not to stir too fast or it'll chunk-up when you add the plastic ice cubes to cool it down. Add your chopped vienners, let marionate for awhile. Serve with the white bread chunks on top.

(snaps)

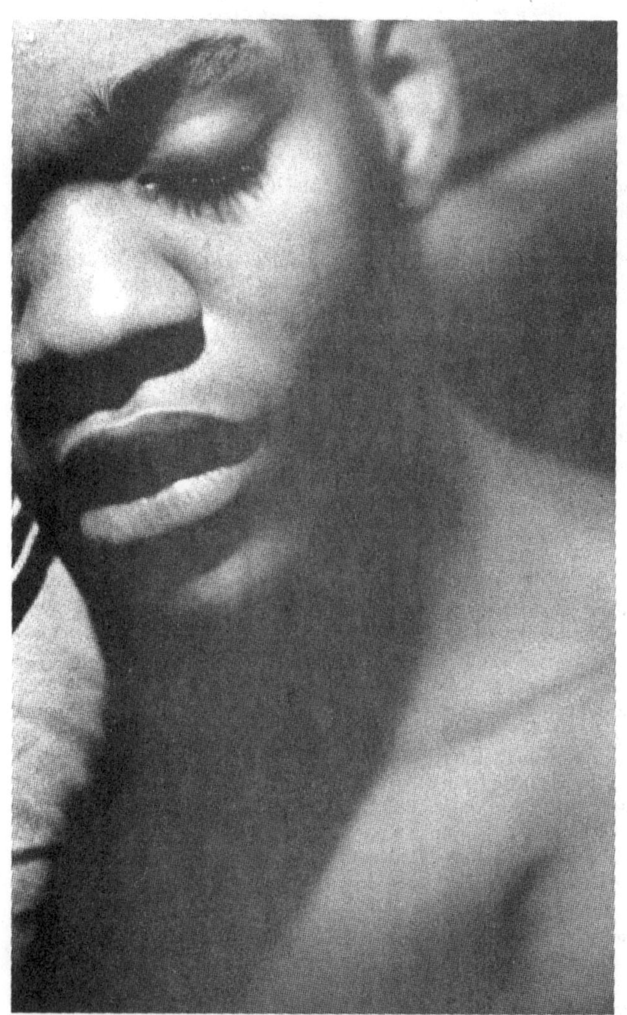 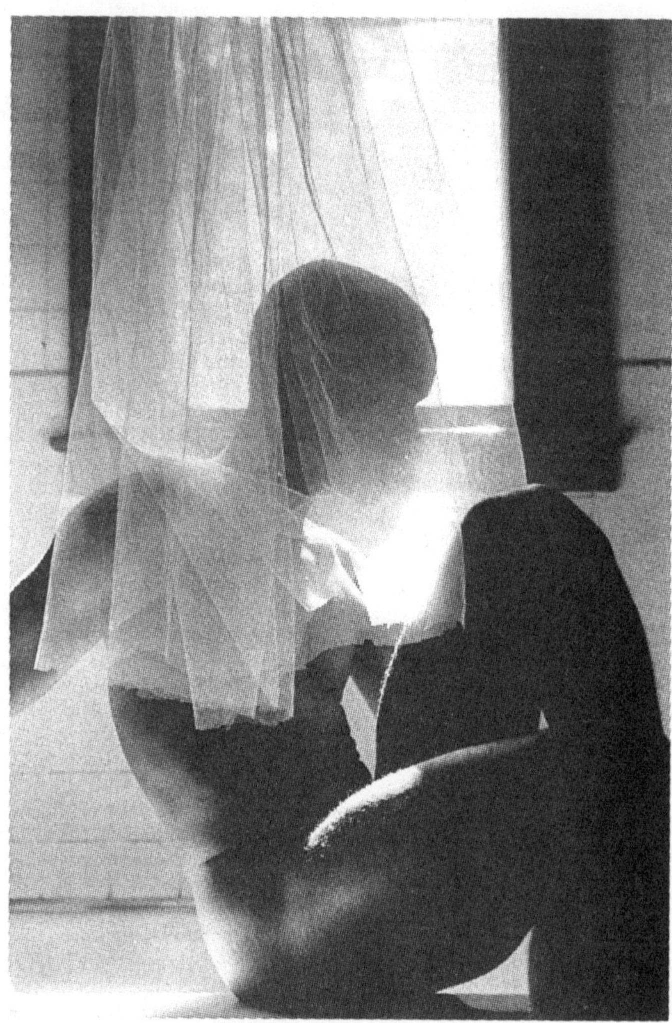

above
LYLE ASHTON HARRIS
(l) Untitled (r) Maine #1 1990

right
SCOTT FREE
untitled 1992

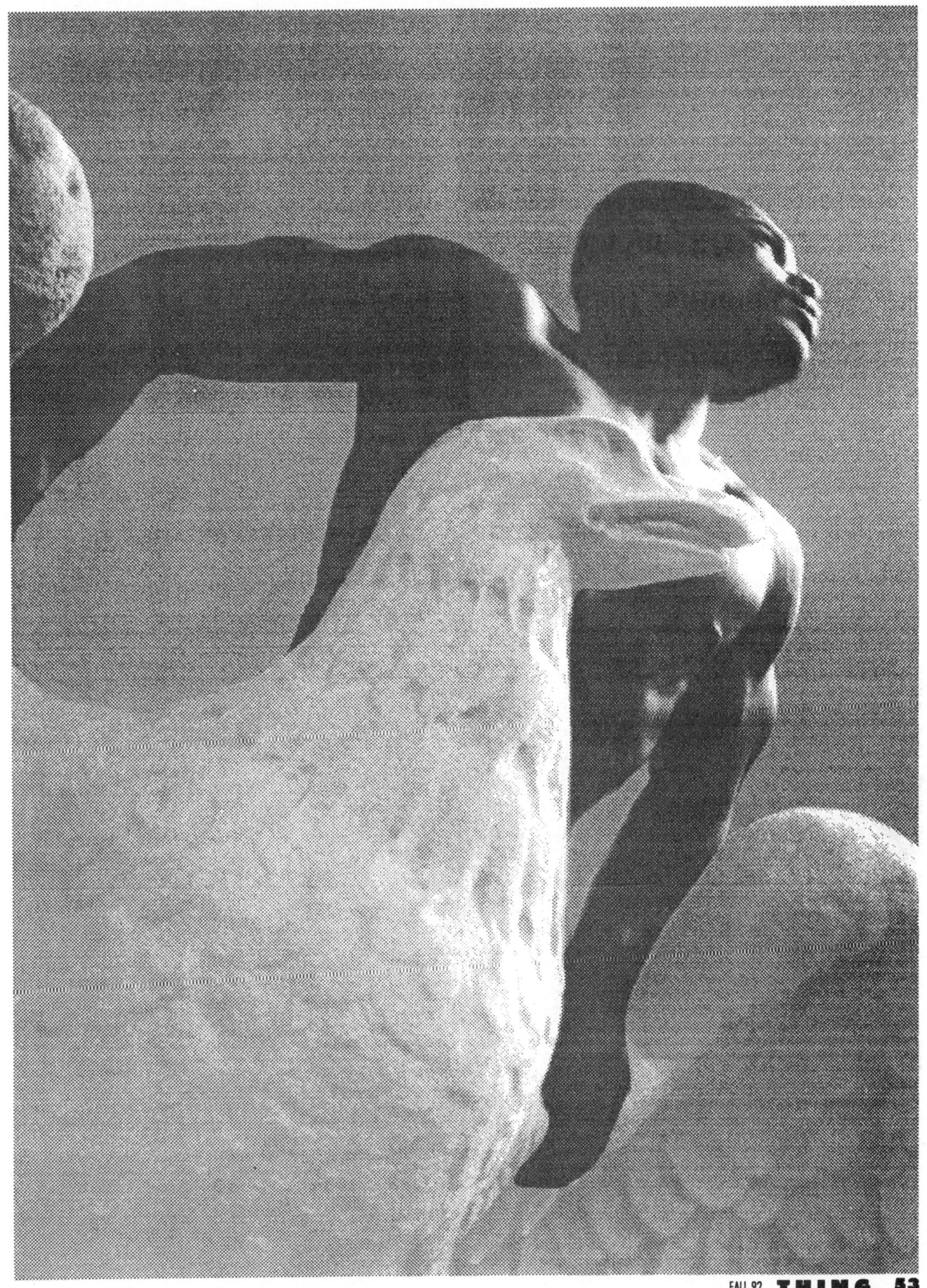

SCOTT "Spunk" O' HARA's porn career began when he won a big dick contest and a spread in *Drummer* magazine. *Diseased Pariah News* carries his "How I Got AIDS" column, and he's been interviewed in *Thrust* and written for *Advocate Men*. He can be seen fellating his own eleven-inch member in the film "Head Over Heels." Currently, Scott spends most of his time on his small farm in Wisconsin. Above: Spunky's self-portrait.

MARC LOVELESS was founder of Michigan's Lesbian and Gay Anti-Violence Project and is currently the Lesbian and Gay Victim Liason with the Illinois State Attorney's Victim Witness Assistance Division. (Whew!) An Aries, he says he's single and looking. Spot him in his signature red socks.

We can't tell you who **FIRE CHICK** really is, but her "boss" is fascist and repressive, somewhat of a "raisinhead."

The fabulous **TINA PAUL** has been photographing the celebrity/nightlife circuit in New York for years now. Paul's subjects are usually of the underground variety however her work is seen in many mainstream publications like *Interview* and *Vanity Fair*.

LEMUEL CABRERA is a local model/celebutante, often seen modeling fashions at Shelter, Chicago. His warm, friendly demeanor and handsome visage often prompts the query from queer boys; "is he gay?" Left: Lemuel photographed by Scott Free.

Lesbian literati **SHARI JAMES** left Chicago for a job with Yale University Press a few years ago. She was one of the earliest *Think Ink*-ers, and helped us "concretize" our vision of a magazine. Once again a Chicagoan, she can be found working at Barbara's Bookstore on Broadway, or attending classes at the U of C in Hyde Park.

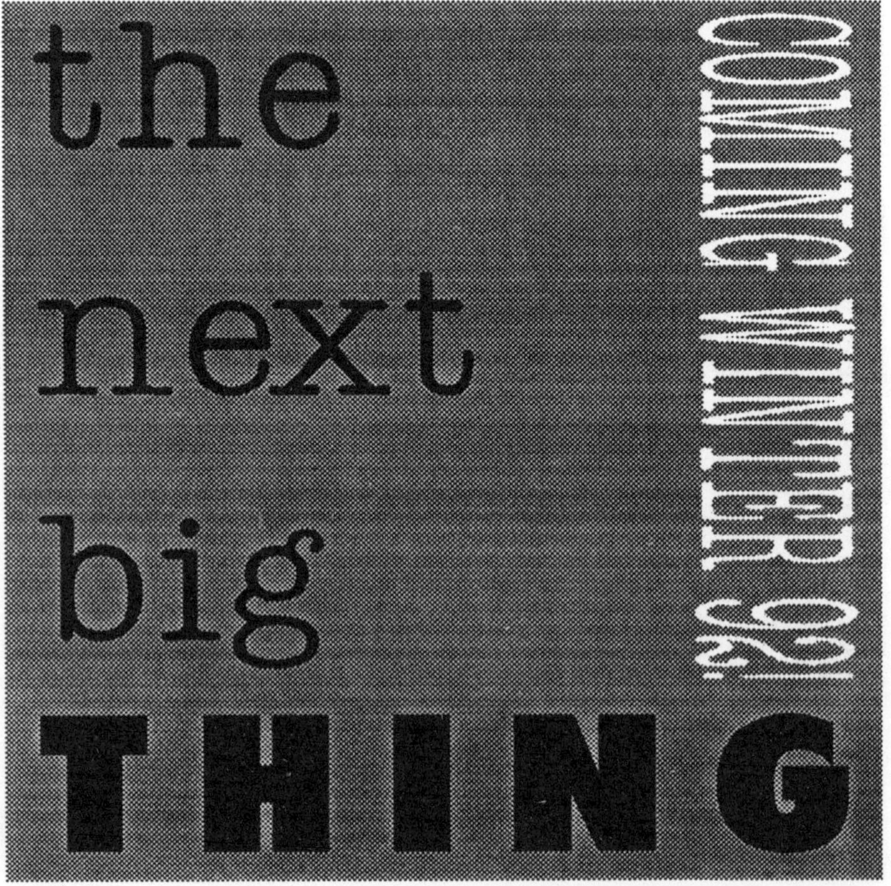

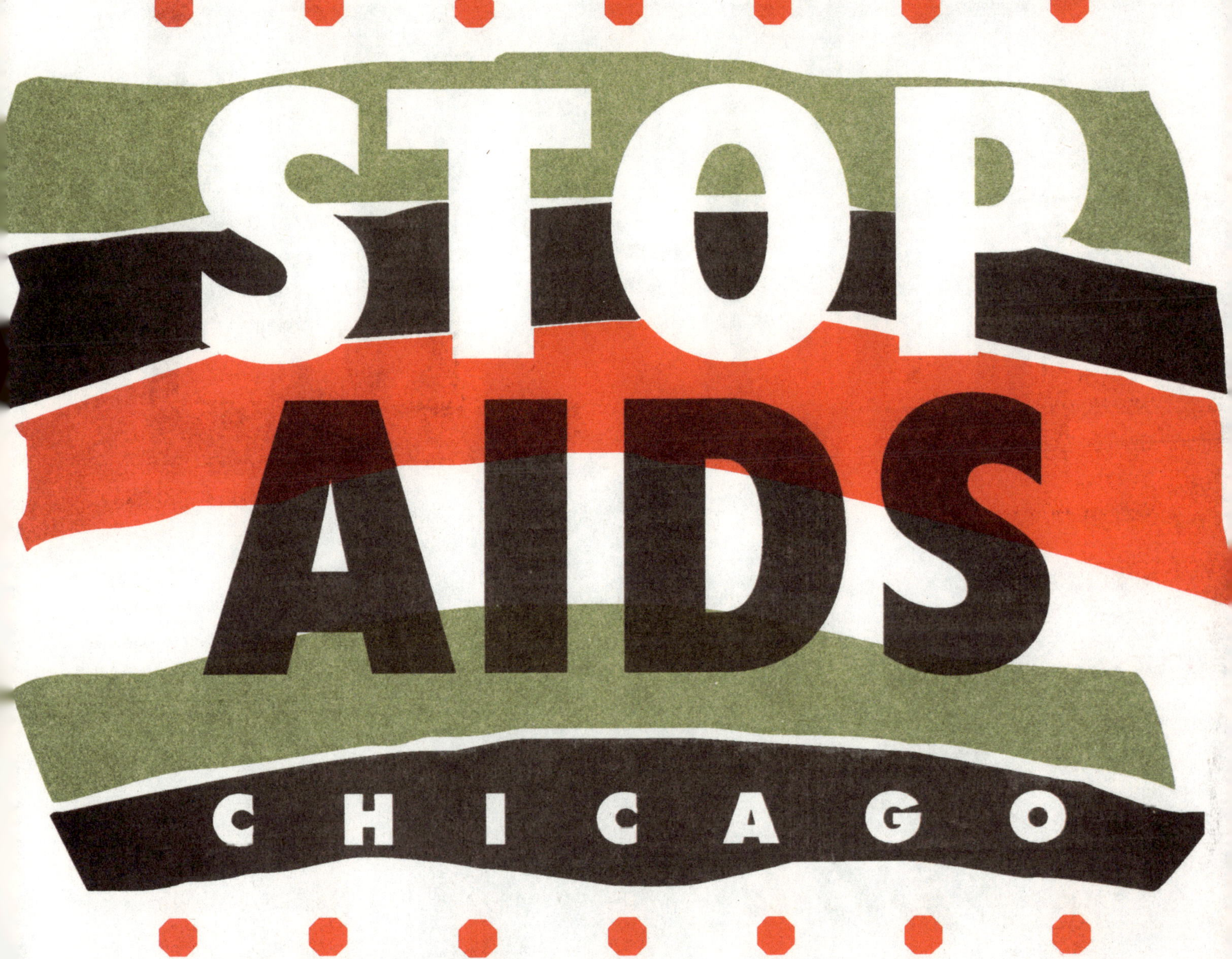
STOP
AIDS
CHICAGO
Communities of Color
working together
312-752-STOP   OR   312-871-3300

RUP★AUL

fall 1992 issue
you better work,
Bitch!

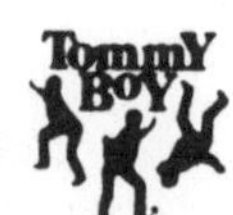

TommY BoY

COMING SOON FROM

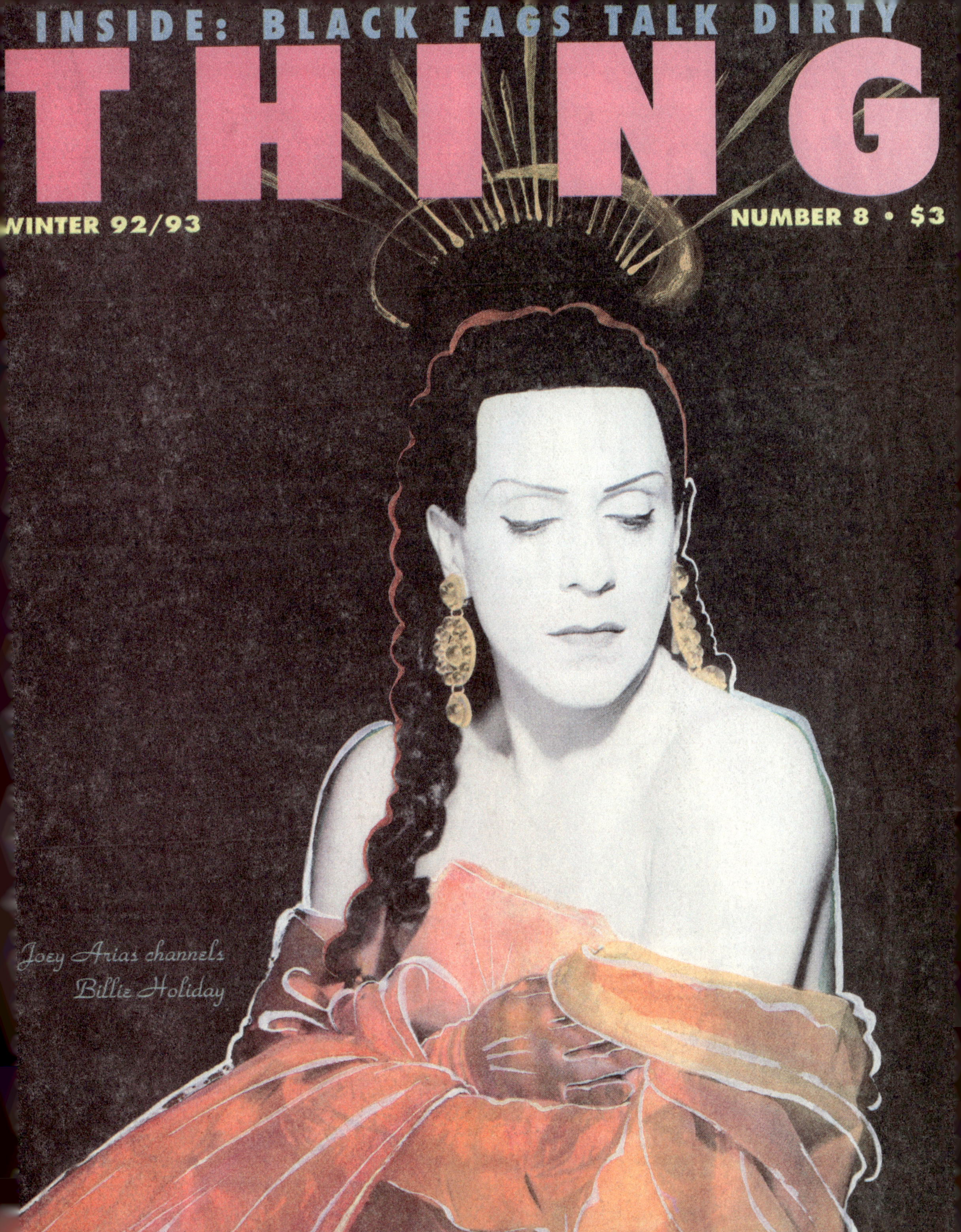

INSIDE: BLACK FAGS TALK DIRTY
THING
WINTER 92/93
NUMBER 8 • $3
Joey Arias channels
Billie Holiday

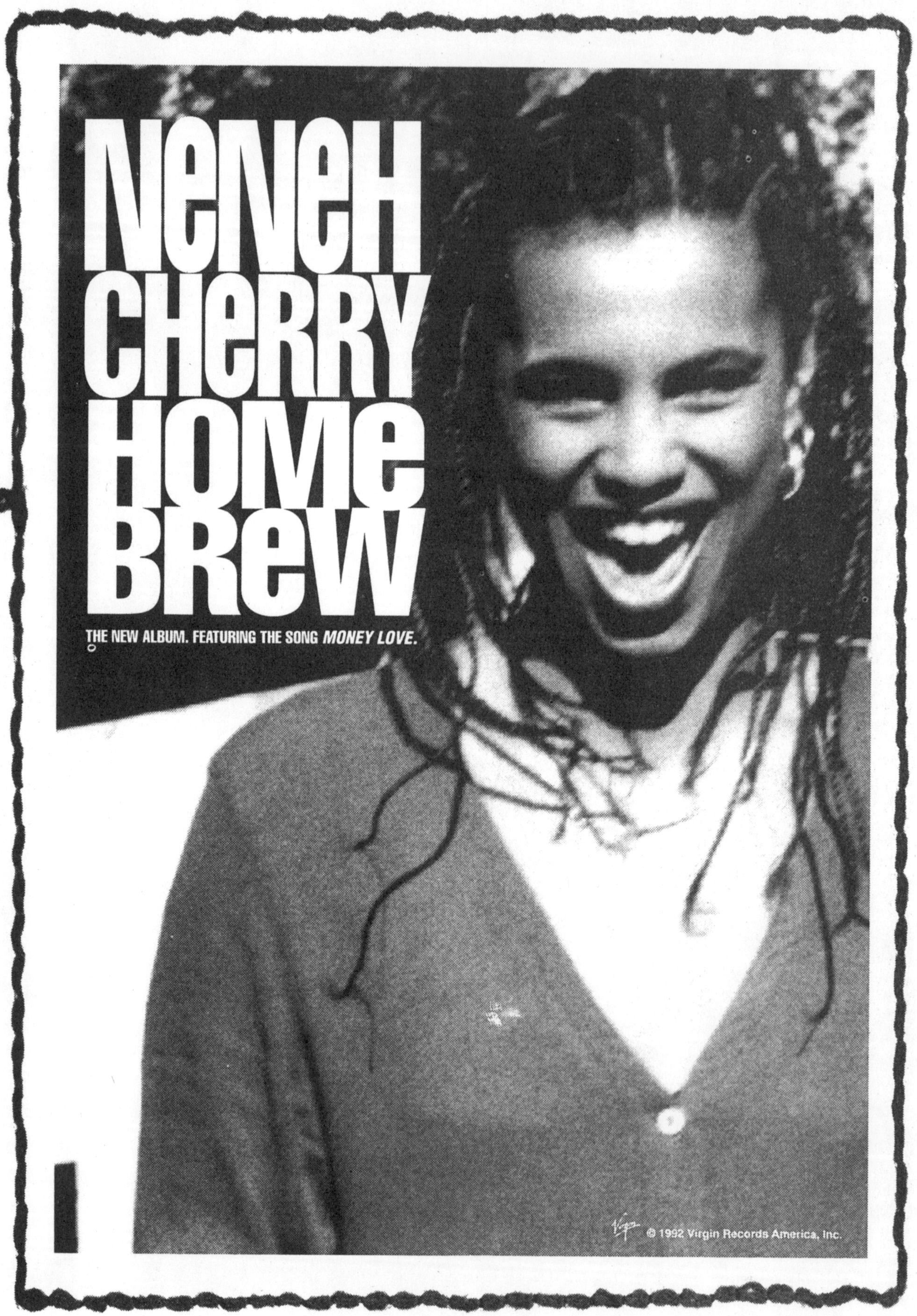

NENEH
CHERRY
HOME
BREW
THE NEW ALBUM. FEATURING THE SONG MONEY LOVE.
© 1992 Virgin Records America, Inc.

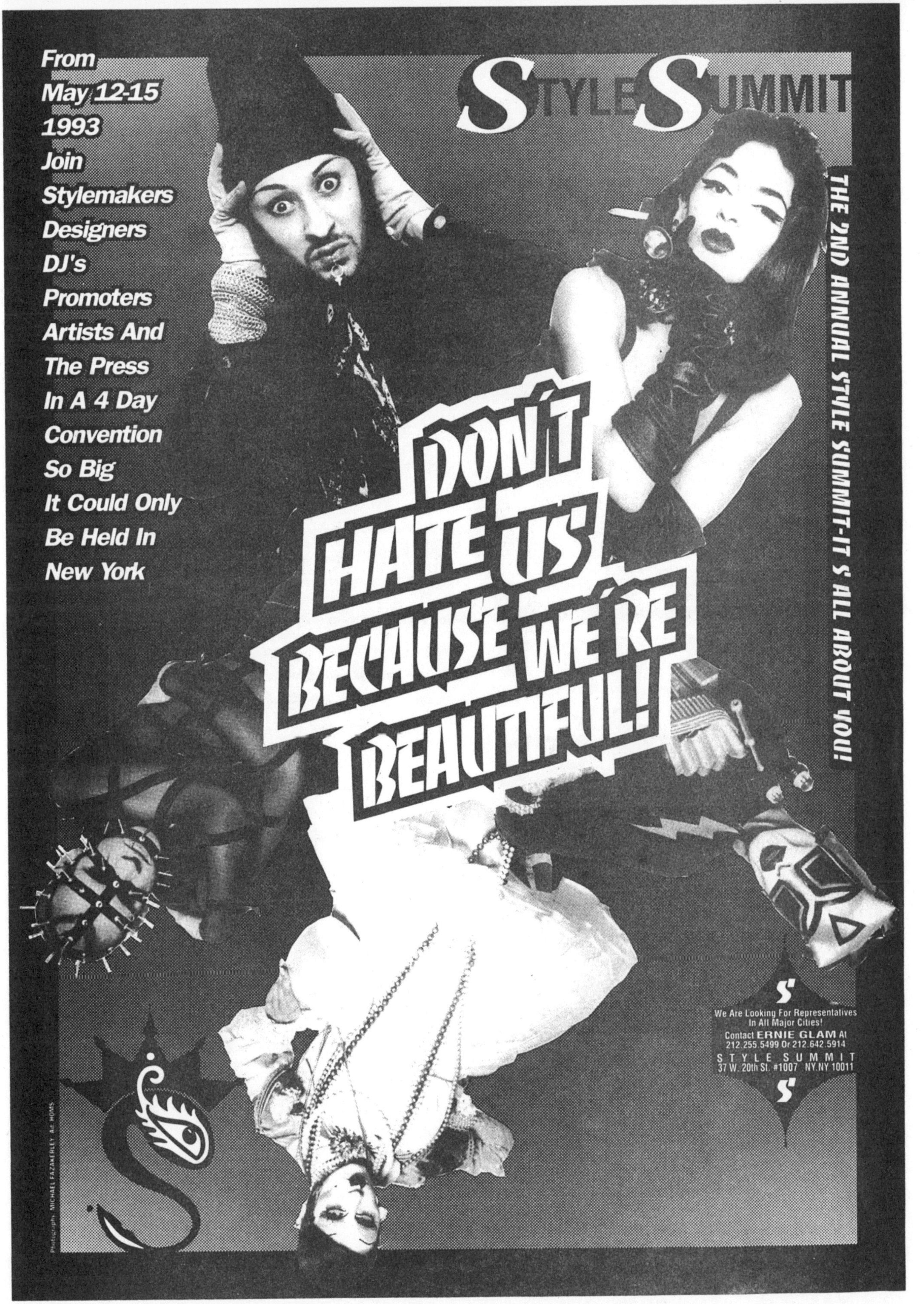

From
May 12-15
1993
Join
Stylemakers
Designers
DJ's
Promoters
Artists And
The Press
In A 4 Day
Convention
So Big
It Could Only
Be Held In
New York

STYLE SUMMIT

THE 2ND ANNUAL STYLE SUMMIT-IT S' ALL ABOUT YOU!

DON'T HATE US BECAUSE WE'RE BEAUTIFUL!

We Are Looking For Representatives
In All Major Cities!
Contact ERNIE GLAM At
212.255.5499 Or 212.642.5914
STYLE SUMMIT
37 W. 20th St. #1007 NY. NY 10011

Photographs: MICHAEL FAZAKERLEY At: HOSS

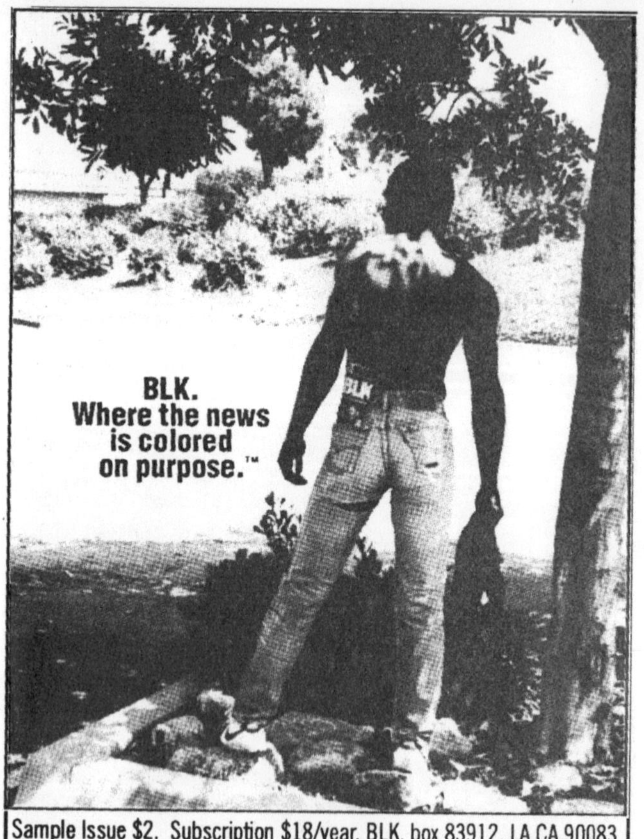

THING

NUMBER EIGHT • WINTER 92/93

PUBLISHER/ART DIRECTION
Robert Ford
EDITORS
Trent Adkins, Robert Ford, Terry Martin
ADVERTISING
Terry Martin, Sylvia Michaels
EDITORIAL ASSISTANCE
Duane Baskins, Omie Daniels, Steve Lafreniere
GRAPHIC SERVICES
Simone Bouyer
DESKTOP PUBLISHING
International Media Associates

THING (ISSN 1064-9727) is published quarterly by Thing Publishing. Opinions expressed are those of individual contributors and do not always reflect those of Thing Publishing.
© 1992 THING

THING PUBLISHING
2151 W. DIVISION
CHICAGO, ILLINOIS USA 60622-3056
VOICE (312) 227-1780
FAX (312) 227-1886

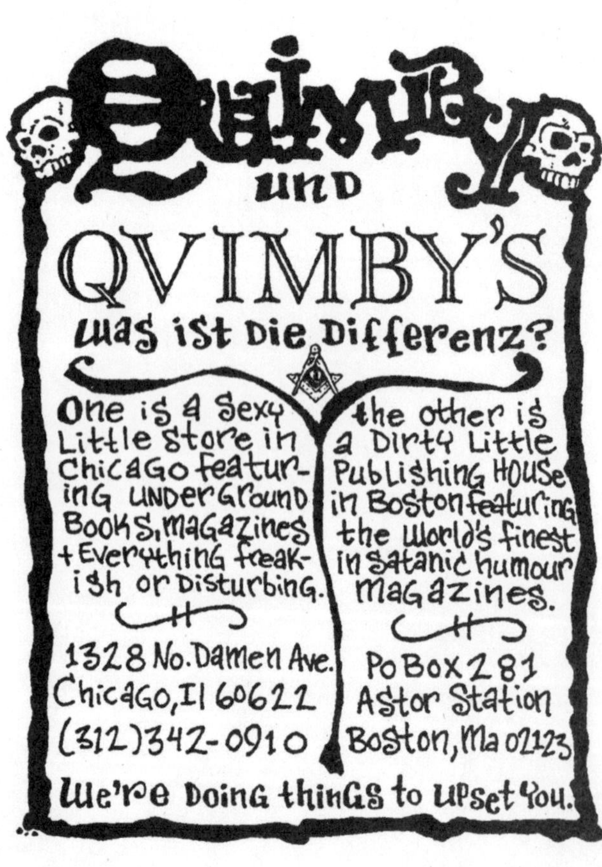

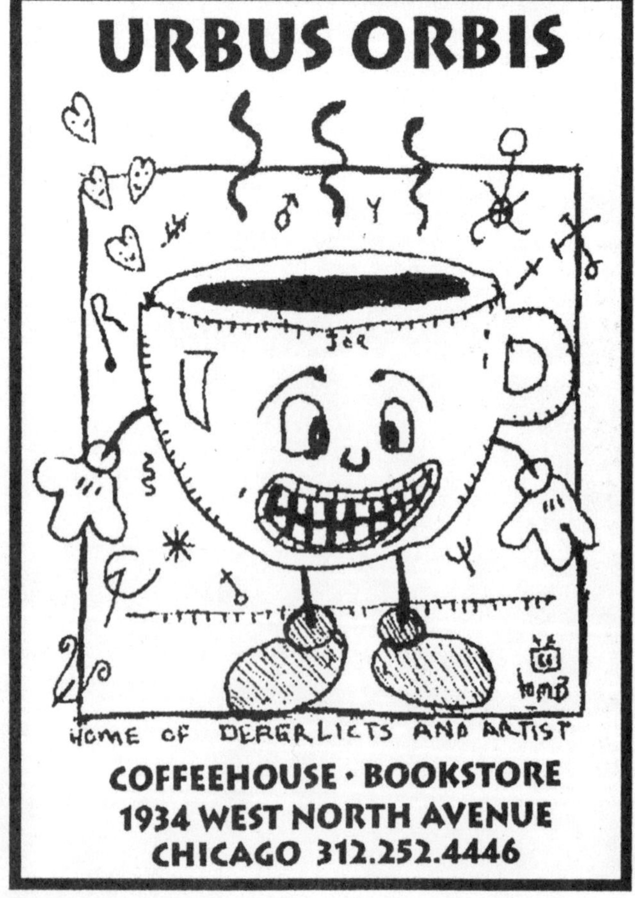

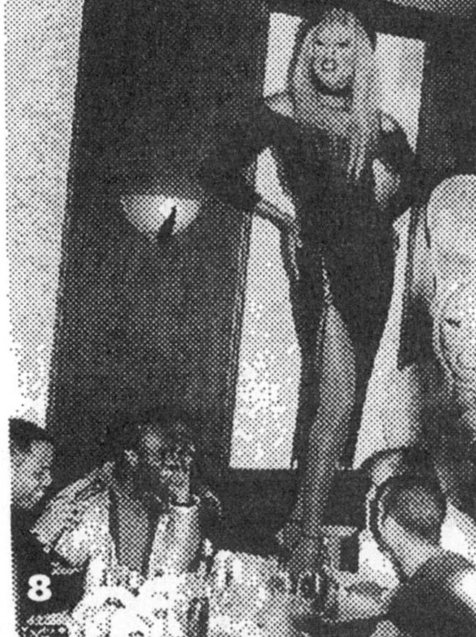

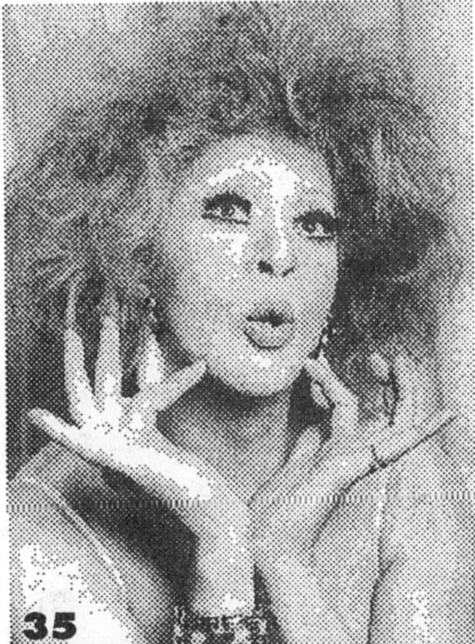

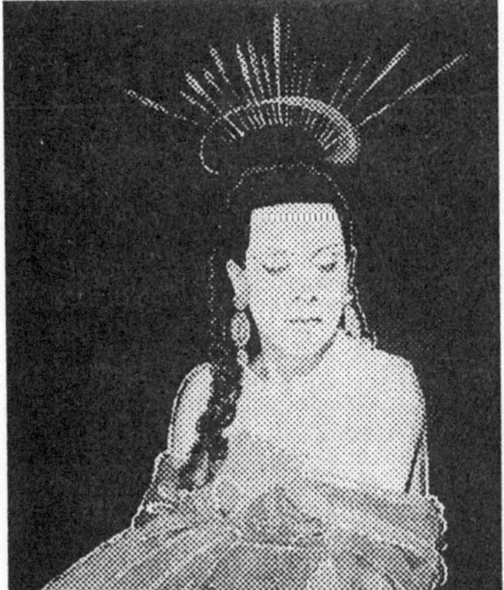

COVER : Joey Arias photographed by Len Prince. Colored by Ruben Toledo.

THING

SHE KNOWS WHO SHE IS • WINTER 92/93

contents

EVERYTHING TO GO!

FEATURES

THE BACK

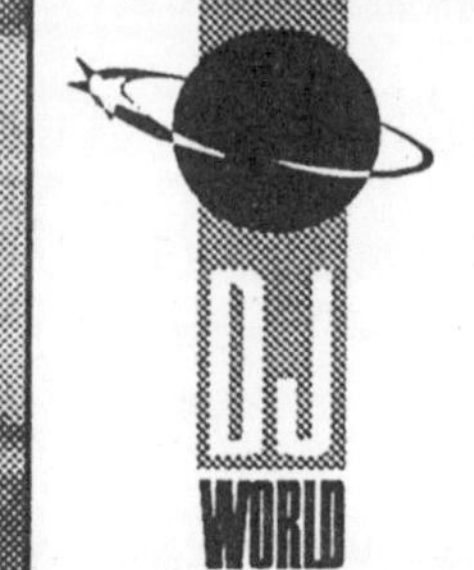

GET DOWN WITH THE SOUND.

I WANT SOME TRADE

Bernard's Amazing Disco Band

DJW 109

Bardot FEVER

Ralphi Rosario featuring Byrd Bardot

DJW 110

DJ WORLD

at a record store on your planet
INFO (708) 387 7100

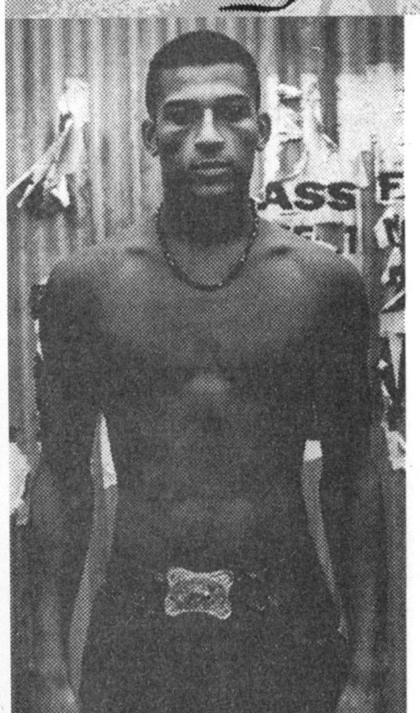

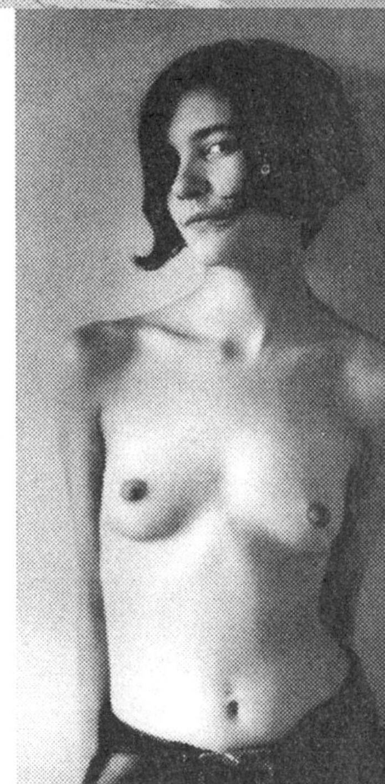

Consider This

A Pow Wow Records Dancefloor Collective

Includes:

"Change For The Better" LOVE TEMPO

"Woman In The Shadows" BASSCUT

"Saxy" HOUSEBOY

"Bambi" HAJIME TACHIBANA

"I Believe In You"
WILBUR FEATURING DEE DEE BRAVE

and the CD/cassette & 12" single

"I'll Be There" 2 INTENSE

Pow Wow Records
1776 Broadway, 12th Floor
New York, NY 10019
212-245-3010
212-956-2326 fax

Executive Producer:
Bill Coleman
for Peace Bisquit
Productions

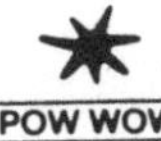

POW WOW

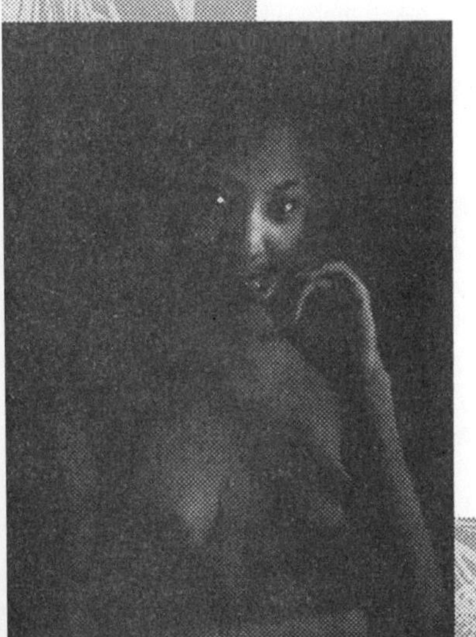

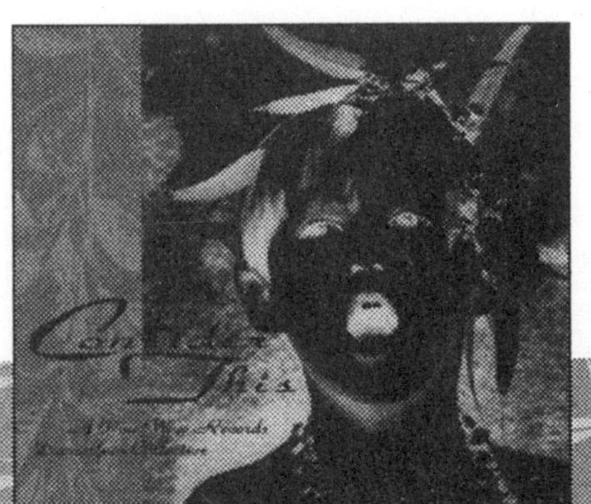

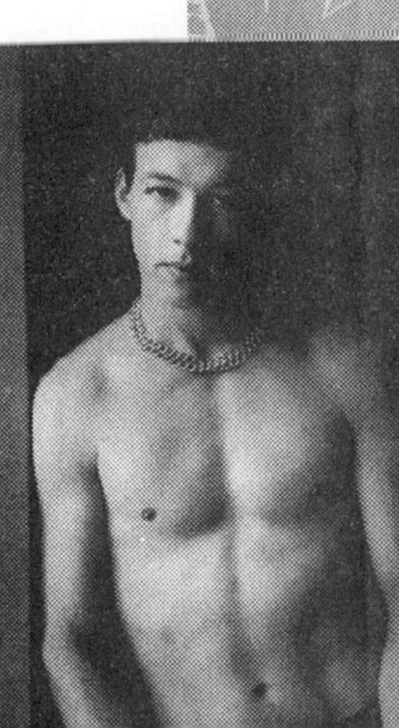

every THING to GO!

YOU BETTER WORK!

The fabulous **RuPaul Charles** made a show at La Locanda restaurant just before his performance at Quench November 18th & 19th. November 17th was not only the release date for "Supermodel/House of Love" but was Ru's birthday, too. In the preceding week our dreams were filled with buxom cocoa skinned starlets of amazonian stature. Ru arrived fashionably late. "Sorry I'm late," he pleaded, "but if I don't freshen up after a while, I turn into a big 'ol greasy man!" No matter, he got there just in time to rescue us from gagging to death on the dirt soul singer **Candy J** kept dishing. Promoter/publisher **Steve Lafreniere**, publisher **Robert Ford**, *Crossfade* editor **Terry Martin**, artist/writer **Jack (Hi-Fi) Walls**, photographer/producer **Scott Free**, fashion photographer **Scott Erik**, *Gag* publisher **Malone**, promoter Michael Mangiaforte, stylist/writer/performer **Michael Hyacinth**, artist **Lee Kay** (who came with the RuPaul bubble-head which graced the cover of *Thing* #6 in tow), and Tommy Boy's **Tammy Pisdell-Coleman**. It was cute. The food and service were fab and we even got Ru to stand atop the tables for photos!

During his visit, Ru was quite forthcoming with interesting little ditties about himself and his self-imaging as a belting blond sex goddess. "I get carried away talking about **Mathu** and **Zaldy** or (World of Wonder's) **Randy** and **Fenton**. I get really excited because they're so talented! I find it very sexy when people are talented like that." or "My head is taped in that picture. It's there just to give me a little lift here." or "I couldn't believe it when I got my first push-up bra. I was poking myself in the chest: I have real cleavage!" or "That outfit I'm wearing in the Supermodel poster with the fitted bodice is very painful. There's a fierce foundation underneath it. It took two people to get me into that piece!" and "I would love to do a movie for seven million dollars! I'm sure it would make at least twenty." Responding to the comment that the Supermodel video is particularly "black fag" he says, "Oh, it's a very black thing. Plus, we wanted the video to have that see-again-and-again quality. We just sat down and did a story board first and sketched the whole thing out. Randy edited the final version while I was away. I had total confidence in him doing a good job. He knows me and what I like and I gagged when I saw it for the first time! He's a genius!" We are gagging on the glamour. The fabu duds are by Mathu and Zaldy, **Mizrahi**, **Betsy Johnson**, **Todd Oldham** and **Anna Sui**. In short, he's beat to within an inch of his life! Hair up to there and *face*.

About his voice, RuPaul says "I like the cheap mikes better than the expensive ones because I have a very deep voice and the cheap ones emphasize the high end of my voice better." This from the performer *Gay Chicago*'s **Rick Carlin** foolishly referred to as a "diva wannabe" (!) But as you're reading this, it ain't **Madonna** nor **Grace Jones** who's making "You better work, bitch!" a household word; its RuPaul! **TA**

Top to bottom: playing like the paparazzi are a problem; with Steve Lafreniere's gift of Champale and Hi-Fi's "Blonde Bombshell" script for consideration; (l to r) Robert Ford, Terry Martin, Malone and Trent with Ru.

WATCH OUT!
events to watch for in the new year

Black Men's Exchange (BMX) is a group dedicated to challenging black homophobia in order to overcome the problems faced by all oppressed African-Americans. Their national cultural gathering and retreat takes place February 4-7, 1993. INFO: (916) 487-0439.

Long Beach, California is the site of the **6th National Black Gay and Lesbian Conference**, February 11-15 1993. Scheduled speakers include Essex Hemphill, Randall Keenan, and Tera Bates. INFO: (213) 666-5495.

A million queer activists on Capitol Hill is the goal of the **1993 March On Washington for Lesbian, Gay, & Bi Equal Rights & Liberation**, scheduled for April 25th. INFO: (505) 892-2558.

Club kids who aren't clueless should flock to the Project X **Style Summit**, four big nights of drugs, booze, music, and fashion happening at clubs (and certainly an outlaw location or two) May 12-15, 1993. INFO: (212) 255-5499.

What hath Steve (TGOC) Lafreniere wrought? The original Spew held here in Chicago in 1991 already spawned Spew 2 in LA in 1992. Now, just when you thought it was safe to go back into the water, **Spew 3** is being (dis)organized in Toronto, Canada (arguably the birthplace of homocore). May 15 & 16, 1992. INFO: box 504, Wellesley Street East, Toronto, Canada M4Y 1H4.

June 26, 1993 is the twenty-fourth anniversary of the Stonewall rebellion, which happened after Judy Garland's death in 1969 when the cops decided to raid The Stonewall Inn on Christopher Street in New York's Greenwich Village. To mark the twenty-fifth anniversary of this event, the **International March on the United Nations to Affirm The Human Rights of Lesbian and Gay People** is scheduled on this date in 1994. INFO: (718) 499-8984.

For those ignorant of the cultural significance of Aqua Net, Labor Day (the first Monday in September) is just another holiday. The glamour-influenced, however, have come to recognize the date as that of **Wigstock**, Scott Lifshutz & Lady Bunny's now-legendary day of peace and pumps in New York's Tompkins Square Park.

October 11, 1993 is **National Coming Out Day**. This public awareness campaign headed by Lynn Sheppod encourages people to live honestly being out. INFO:

December 1, 1993 is **Day Without Art** and **World AIDS Day**.

JANUARY
10 Sal Mineo
22 Martin Luther King, Jr.

FEBRUARY
1 Langston Hughes
8 James Dean

MARCH
25 Aretha Franklin
26 Diana Ross

APRIL
7 Billie Holiday
16 Dusty Springfield

MAY
29 Liberace
31 Walt Whitman

JUNE
1 Marilyn Monroe
30 Flo Ballard

JULY
11 Jack Wrangler

AUGUST
2 James Baldwin
6 Isaac Hayes
16 Madonna
18 Nona Hendryx

SEPTEMBER
5 Freddie Mercury

OCTOBER
3 Gore Vidal
16 Oscar Wilde
19 Divine

NOVEMBER
17 RuPaul

DECEMBER
25 Little Richard

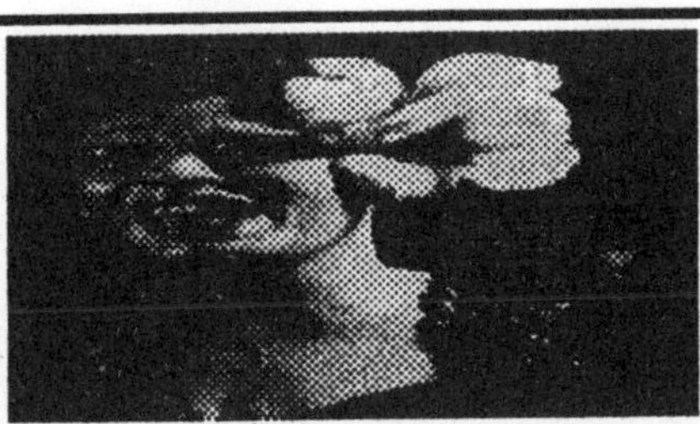

HOLIDAY LIST: our tribute to Ms. Holiday would be incomplete without a rundown of essential Lady Day recordings. Top five, in no particular order:
Songs For Distingué Lovers (Verve 815-055)
Lady In Autumn: Best of the Verve Years (Verve 849-434)
The Legacy 1933-1958 (Columbia/Legacy 47724)
The Complete Decca Recordings (GRP/Decca 601)
The Complete Billie Holiday on Verve 1945-1959 (Verve 513-859)

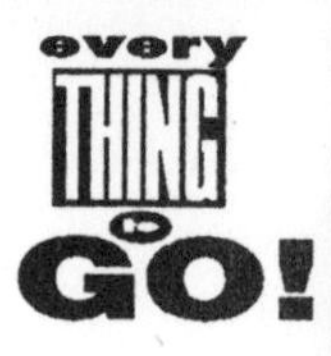

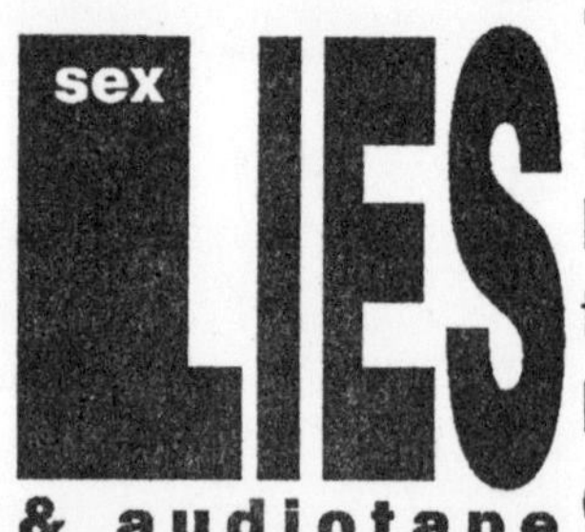

THREE'S COMPANY A publishing mogul and a party promoter had tongues wagging with their tug of war over a certain barely-legal club cutie. Ma Bell was the big winner as phone lines melted with the lava-like drama of this one. **DETAILS, DETAILS** An oft-blonde supermodel was stuck in town with no return ticket, having to dig into her mad money to make it home. How'd that happen? Seems that more than one party was asleep at the wheel. **SOME THINGS THEY NEVER CHANGE** Well, she finally stopped hiding behind that "baby in Michigan" line and admitted that she was a queen. As if we thought those feet and hands were the result of "big bones." But one question remains: does she still tuck?

BROTHER, CAN YOU SPARE A DIME? The black-on-black economic tip is definitely doin' the right thing, but *intent* of support (read: unpaid invoices) don't really do your homies much good. Especially when your ads show up (prepaid, no doubt) in *white* owned papers in the meantime. You don't support your community when you place an order; you support them when you pay the bill.

PUSSY GALORE Bunny no longer has to lunch alone, thanks to the return of the now-svelte Pussy. Last issue deadline, she was way too busy putting the finishing touches on a newly-published manuscript (something to do with Elvis impersonators). But according to the ever-informative Buns, her real distraction was the re-kindling of her Sapphistic tendencies. It seems that dumping a boyfriend, finding a girlfriend, and finishing a book left little time to dish dirt over patty melts. **BY ANY MEANS NECESSARY** Off the record, the owner of a newly (re)opened dance club expressed reluctance to hire one of this town's finest DJs to spin there. The reason: he might attract "too many black people." Never mind that thing was not above making fat bank off of Frankie Knuckles and his black fans during his heyday a decade ago. Question: just how many black people are too many black people? Five hundred? Fifty? Three? Tell you what, just keep running the place the way you're running it and I bet you won't get *any* of those pesky black people in there! (The good news: at least we won't be seeing a Malcolm X theme party there anytime soon.)

WHAT'S IN A NAME? There seems to be an increasing trend of using folks' names on a plugger when they ain't even been invited, much less agreed to host said night. We were even a victim of it, suddenly finding *Thing* among the hosts of a certain door diva's birthday bash a few months back. Good thing we showed up; otherwise we might have been accused of being shady!

ERB
WANTS YOU TO ENJOY

the WEEKEND

Produced & Mixed by Ron Trent & Braxton Holmes for Clubhouse Productions

Co-Produced by Big Ed of the Blak Beat Niks Executive producers Hula & K. Fingers of Da Posse

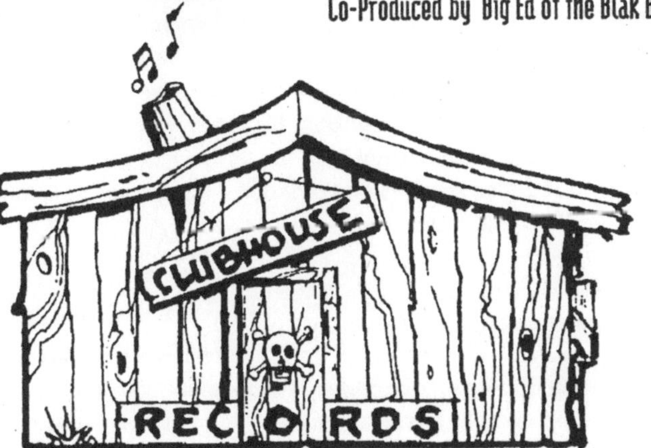

"A MIND SHATTERING EXPERIENCE"
COME JOIN THE CLUB

COMING SOON FROM CLUBHOUSE:

SCARLETT
"Thanx"

JUICE
"Take It Off"

NATURE LOVE
"Feels Right"

BLAK BEAT NIKS
"Blak Beat
Nik Theme"

DISTRIBUTED BY EMOTIVE RECORDS (212) 645-7330

FOR PRODUCTION, REMIX, & ARTIST INFORMATION CONTACT BRAXTON HOLMES (708) 331-2409

LARRY FLICK

Urbanized Helpless (Maxi)
Tyrell Corporation The Bottle (Cooltempo)
Angelique Kidjo Batonga (Great Jones)
Ten City My Peace Of Heaven (East West)
Clubland Set Me Free (Great Jones)
The Aloof On A Mission (Cowboy)
Sly & Lovechild Spirit of Destiny (Volante)
Mr. Fingers Closer (MCA)
The Daou Surrender Yourself (Columbia)
Kathy Sledge Take Me Back To Love Again (Epic)

MICHAEL PAOLETTA

Bas Noir Ah...Bas Noir (Atlantic LP)
Praise Easy Way Out (Giant/WB)
Leviticus feat. Victor Cook Life Story (Hogland)
Grace Under Pressure Make My Day (ARS UK)
Various Consider This (Pow Wow LP)
Dina Carrol Ain't No Man (A&M UK)
System 7 feat. Ultra Naté Altitude (Ten UK)
Nu Colors Tears (Polydor)
Karen Anderson Thank You (Nott-Us)
Lisa Stansfield Set Your Loving Free (Arista)

FREDDIE BAIN

Melis'sa Morgan Still In Love With You (Elektra)
Soulution Feels So Right (Illegal)
Funky Green Dogs Reach For Me (Murk)
Maurice Joshua I Gotta Hold on U (ID)
Chocolate Fudge Stomp E.P. (Azuli)
Urbanized Helpless (Maxi)
Classic Man Love (Nervous)
Tito Puente Para Los Rumberos (Elektra)
Scottie Deep Fathoms (Aztonik)
Soul Verité Chain Me To The Beat (Maxi)

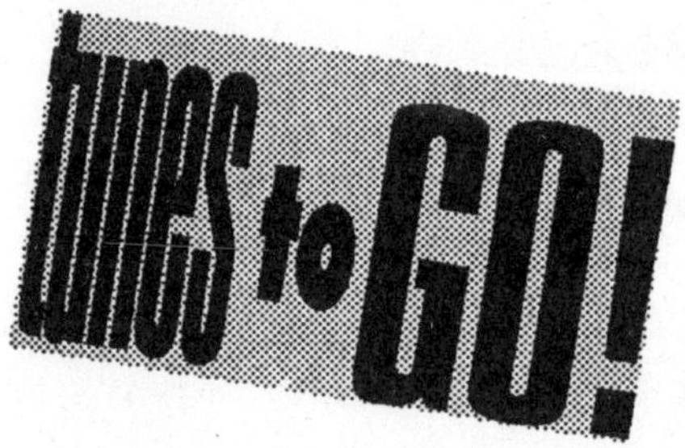

Larry Flick's 5 New Year wishes

When I was asked to list my wishes for the new year, my head spun...a new car?...gobs of cash?...five hours alone with a bound and nude Mel Gibson?...the possibilities seemed endless. And then I focused on dance music and its current state. My wishes became clear, and somehow one easily begat the other.

VISION

Not only in the sense of creative expression among artists, writers, and producers, but also in the capability to see beyond your own backyard. All too often, we forget that the world of dance music is vast and varied. Just because your record works the folks at the Sound Factory in New York or at the Warehouse in Chicago does not mean that it's a hit everywhere, or that people in other pockets of the world will get it. Conversely, just because you're over something does not mean it's truly over.

RESPECT

Recognize the differences in folks and the music that moves them. Then, try to respect them for their perspectives—no matter how tragic you think they are. No doubt, someone else in the world thinks you're a mess based on your point of view.

LOVE

We're all in this field because of an alleged love of dance music and it's culture—and yet negativity prevails. Who's dogging who in the name of money and status today? Sure, we all need and desire both. But don't loose that passion and love of music—the day you do, you're through.

UNITY

People in the music mainstream would love for the fags, dykes, and assorted weirdos of the dance music world to go away for good. They're trying to prove our lack of commercial viability. And even though they're wrong, they may win by default. We need to come together, get over the petty differences, and show them that dance music is one of the last havens for true creativity and freedom of expression.

HEALTH

Our community is dying at an astonishing rate. AIDS is ravaging the dance music world, taking away our pioneers as well as young hopefuls. Although we're helpless on a basic level, there's no need to increase our chances of illness. Take care of your body, as well as the bodies of those you love. Stay strong, and be strong for those who need you.

Five wishes never seemed so basic, and yet so impossible. Think about it.

Larry Flick is the dance music editor of Billboard *magazine.*

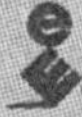

She made
the blues rock for
THE FIRST TIME.

She changed
rock 'n' roll for
ALL TIME.

But she's been
saving herself for
THE RIGHT TIME

ETTA
JAMES
THE
RIGHT
TIME

Produced by Jerry Wexler,
recorded in Muscle Shoals and featuring
some of soul music's greatest session
players, The Right Time is the new album
from 1993 Rock 'n' Roll Hall of Fame
inductee Etta James.

Elektra

On Elektra Compact Discs
and Cassettes
©1992 Elektra Entertainment, a division of Warner
Communications Inc. A Time Warner Company.

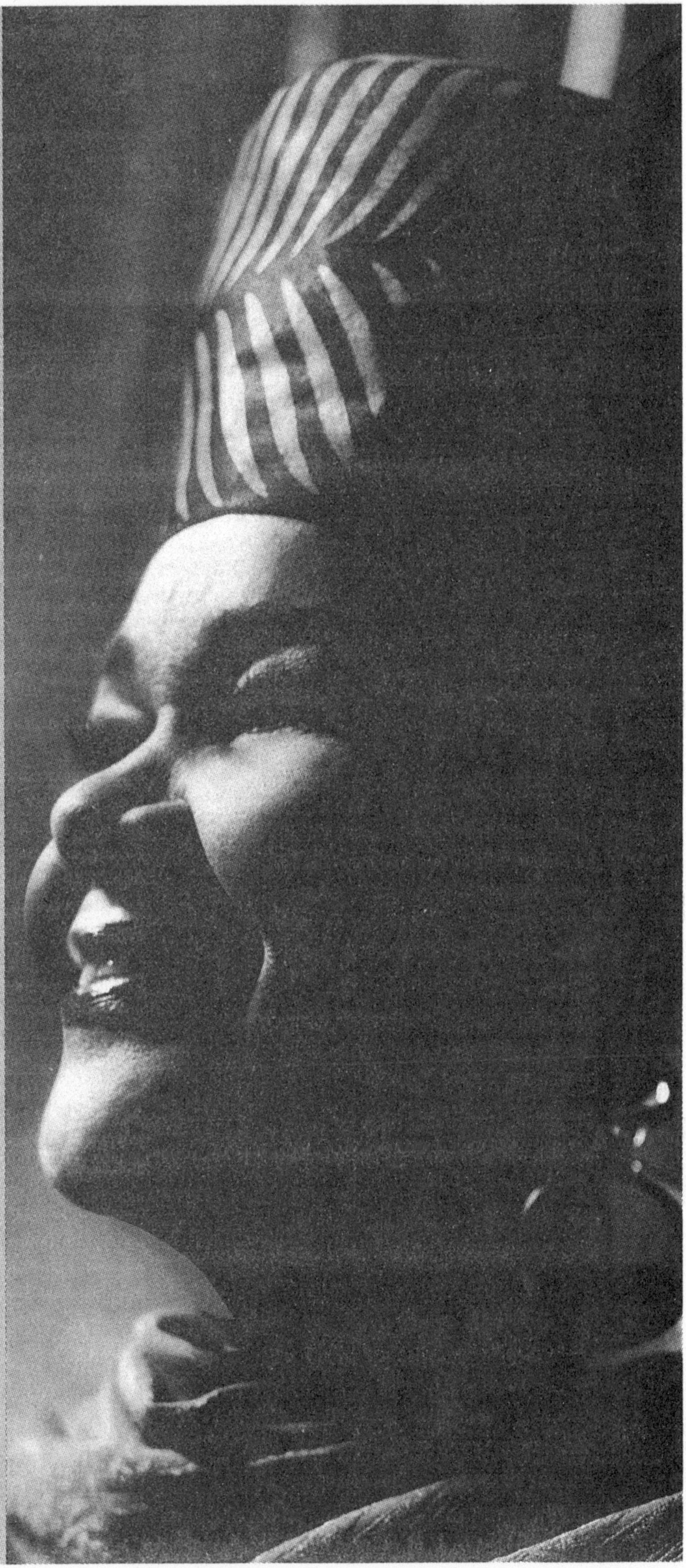

WHERE ARE OUR NITRATE KISSES?

GABRIEL GOMEZ **on New York & Chicago's queer film fests**

Lately, queers are all over TV, from the high school student on "One Life To Live", to the "Men On..." skits from "In Living Color" to Sandra Bernhard dating Morgan Fairchild on "Roseanne". Even drag queens have made inroads since "Paris Is Burning". Lypsinka is Sandra's talk show sidekick on HBO while RuPaul is well on her way to becoming a pop star with her own video, "Supermodel". But some things are still scarce even at the movies, like a real kiss between two men.

That's why the **6th New York Lesbian and Gay Experimental Film Festival** (September 10-20. 1992), or its more established cousin the **Chicago 12th Annual Lesbian and Gay International Film Festival** (November 6-16, 1992) are so important. Both show things you won't see at the local cineplex or even on Public TV. At festivals there is no fear of Jesse Helms or Tipper Gore scrutinizing everything you see. But even on the festival circuit there are limits. Time constraints, money, diverse interests all play a part as programmers try to squeeze into two weeks what should be available year round. Finding all elements of queer communities in one festival becomes an impossible task. Still you take what you can get, and very often that means some audiences are more equal than others.

Among the most popular screenings in Chicago (which means good box office) was a program called **All American Boys**, which included **An All American Story**. It's about a poor (in spirit that is) Stanford alum (or is it Yale?) who faces the trauma of coming out to his old classmates, but not to fear: mom still loves him. For pure nostalgia from white middle class suburbia, there was **The Disco Years**. Plenty of disco helps soothe the pain of a high school student whose mom is pretty unsympathetic to his burgeoning queer life and his sad discovery that love doesn't last forever. It would make a great after school special. Finally, **The Dead Boys Club** reveals how the past AIDS generation is haunted by their queer forbears, to have more sex, because it seems present day

guppettes in the making never quite get over their fear of sex in the era of AIDS.

New York's experimental focus means it can target overlooked audiences. The program "Fire!" featured the work of artists from the African Diaspora. Dawn Suggs' video, **I Never Danced the Way Girls Were Supposed To** replaces myths with the realities of African-American lesbian life. The sex between these women, that is black lesbian sex, is both erotic and everyday. They shut off the camera just as their play heats up. After all, if you don't know what black lesbians do you need a lot more than a 'how to' video.

Black Body, a video by Thomas Allen Harris, also confronts the perception of the black, queer body by posing the question, "How can I love you when I cannot love myself?" At once despised and desired, the body and bodies in question inspire contradictory impulses, from the sexual to the violent. While Vejan Smith's video **Mother's Hands** reveals a mother who, not only bakes and cleans for her family, but is also the source of physical and sexual abuse. Coming to terms with these contradictory recollections, telling the story, is a first step toward ending a cycle of domestic violence. Family values is definitely a concept that needs to be examined carefully.

Interracial sexualities are but one part of the historic development of the African Diaspora explored in this program. Carlo Carmona's **Slap Rap (1992)** and Dunye's **The Potluck and The Passion** show Asians, European descended Americans and African Americans who want each other despite the divisions that shape their lives. In "Slap Rap" sexual attraction is a bridge across the gap between a Buddhist African-American and an Asian evangelical Christian. While in Dunye's tape, sexual attraction leads one's character along the historic path of European domination. But the African-American lesbian she desires finds the strength to dump her when she meets a new friend in pride, another black lesbian. **Rage and Desire** by Jamaican film maker Ruppert Gabriel, examines the work and life of Nigerian photographer Rotimi Fani-Kayode, who died of AIDS in1989. Fani-Kayode's suffering from HIV related illnesses contrasts with an upbeat ending where his work continues to flourish under the supervision of his white, British, male lover.

The program "No Regrets" was the Chicago fest answer to multi-culturalism with; **Double the Trouble Twice the Fun** by Pratiba Parmar, about a disabled Indian gay man, **A Prayer Before Birth** about a black British dyke with MS, and Two Spirit People where Native Americans discuss queer sexualities within their own traditions. Marlon Riggs' tape **Non Je Ne Regrette Rien (No Regrets)** depicts African-American PWAs who really don't regret a thing as they struggle with HIV while maintaining their dignity and pride. On a separate program, **Party Safe! With Diana and Bambi** shows how the African-American women of Diana's Hair Ego spread their safer sex parties throughout the country, proving that even if black women's sexuality is not at the center of the universe, maybe for our own good, it ought to be.

Activism was well represented in New York by the likes of DIVA TV's **Target Bush**. From demos at the Bush summer home in Kennebunkport, to Houston's 1992 Republican Convention it carries a clear message "become an AIDS activist." **Can't Take That Away From Me** a video by Kevin Adams documents Paul Broussard's death from a brutal, anti-gay hate crime on July 4, 1991 in Houston. The case got police away from Dunkin Donuts long enough to organize a sting operation which uncovered (surprise), surprise) widespread bashing. This tape played in both fests, winning in Chicago the title of best experimental.

Stigmata: The Transfigured Body, by Leslie Asako Gladsjo also won as best documentary in Chicago and played in New York. It examines lesbians who pierce, tattoo, scar, and brand for serious fun. Both festivals favored **The Allure Of Fringe Erotics**, which was also the title of a panel in Chicago. **Skull Fuck** by Joe Kelly and Danny Fass, breached sexual frontiers in both towns, straining the body and credibility to inaugurate a new sex sensation. Radical desire has a few limits. Are you ready to skull fuck? New York pushed this radical desire thing with "Our Fanzine Friends" a collection centered on fetishes. John O'Shea's pop video, **No Money, No Honey**, stars Glen Meadmore and blacktress Vaginal Creme Davis where an undervalued, unknown drag queen becomes a star of the small screen. Harry Hay (the original radical faerie) appears as both old lech and gender fuck girl. They sing, "No I don't care that you're horny, cause you can't afford me." **Public Beard**, Annie Staley's super 8 film, puts body hair and masculinity into perspective. It's amazing what a close, shave, and a little glue can do for a woman. While Emily Nahmanso's Super 8 work, **Spring Break**, proves it; suburbia is scary. **Equal Rights for Unborn Drag Queens** by Sexual Orgasm Productions documents the conversion of drag queen talk show hostesses, Glenda Orgasm and Brenda Sexual, to charismatic Christianity. Pat Robertson and friends appear to be responsible for this sad, strange turn of events. Brenda finds that she needs *another* hole in her body for his second coming.

In Chicago drag queens took over "The Late Show: Queer TV." **Theo and Thea** is a long running Dutch TV show, and covering queers in one episode is no big deal for them. Their queer cave man is an imaginative addition to gay history, get it, even primitives don't mind queers. Deaundra Peek's **Hi Class Hall O Fame Theater** shows how classy underfunded drag queens manage to cover the world on cable from Atlanta. Another drag queen stars in **Fontavella's Box** which played in both cities. The imaginative costumes in this film could be the clubwear inspiration for the rest of the 1990's. If you weren't sure, Jerry Tartaglia's **Holy Mary** from the New York fest makes clear that the holiest of 'Marys,' the pope, is just another drag queen. Will he make it to Wigstock '93

do you think?

Chicago concentrated on feature films, after all, they had the Music Box and its amazing organ at their disposal. They took the opportunity to repeat a number of past successes like **Friends Forever**, the story of a cute little blond Danish school boy who discovers not just love but the fun of being poked by a dark, curly-haired soccer player in the briefest of running shorts, or that indeed, **Oranges are Not the Only Fruit**, there are also red-haired, Brit, born-again Christian dyke fruits. **I'll Love You Forever...Tonight** is a new film that started with poolside boys, but quickly degenerated into meaningful discussion on the morality of tricking. Anyway, it's a great title. **Twin Bracelets** shows how lesbian love between Chinese peasants works—very nicely for a while anyway and no they don't take very long to get right to it. Versace stole the idea of contrasting prints from them but they still do it better. There is more than nostalgia to all these old films as **The Wild Wild World of Jayne Mansfield** proves. She's past her prime in this soft-core porn travelogue which ends with a surprisingly candid look at the auto wreck where Jane died. And is that her mutilated body alongside her crushed and dearly loved Chihuahua? Poor, poor, Jane.

Brit stuff was everywhere in Chicago despite Clause 28 (which prohibits local governments from promoting homosexuality). Somehow they manage to fund queer work and show it on NATIONAL TELEVISION! **Portrait of A Marriage**, a costume drama about the author Vita Sackville-West, was just on our Public Television, but you needed to see it at the festival because a good 30 minutes were just too much education for the American public.

Back in the USA, **Changing Our Minds** is the story of Evelyn Hooker, who got the American Psychiatric Association to rescind its definition of homosexuality as an illness. Barbara Hammer's **Nitrate Kisses** includes the recollections of a dyke who was imprisoned by the Nazis, something many would like to forget. But her recovery of lost queer stories, with real sex scenes, makes it clear—queers can't forget and our fight is *not* over. **Where Are We?** confirms what my mother has always told me: "Beware the South." But even there queer soldiers find fun and good make-up. Just to put things in perspective **Kiev Blue** documents blue (queer) life in the Ukraine before homosex was decriminalized. But one of the characters wonders how can it be legal in Ukraine when it remains illegal here in 25 states? These four new American works deserve major release, or, at the very least, a spot on our homophobic public television stations. But since every single appearance of any queer at either place is still the cause of controversy, a steady stream of good queer stuff will only be found at festivals. Changing minds back in the USA will only happen when we get out of the place censorship has made for us. Today, everyone knows the price of silence. At least in our communities.

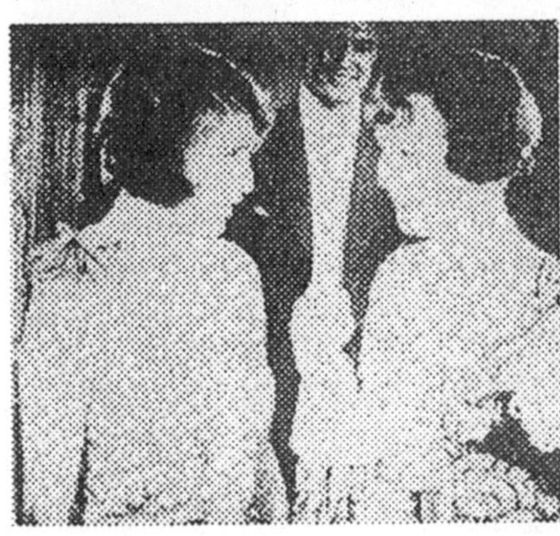

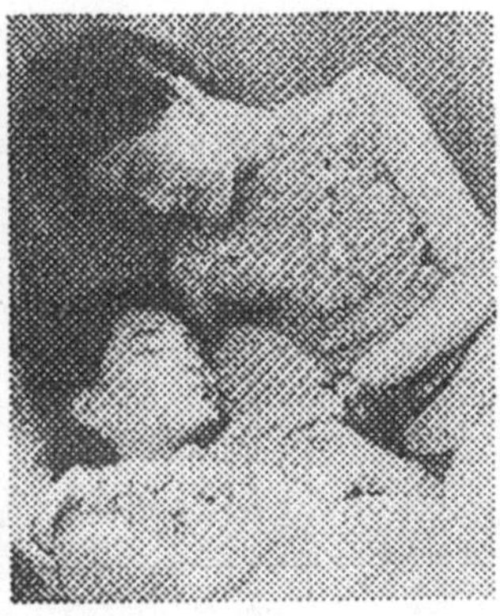

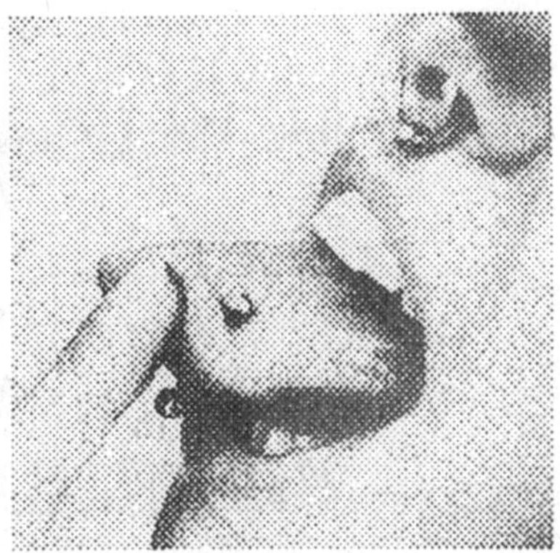

L to R: "Nitrate Kisses", "Twin Bracelets", and "Stigmata: The Transfigured Body".

HOWARD BROWN HEALTH CENTER

Celebrating 18 years of serving
Chicago's Gay and Lesbian community

AIDS Research
AIDS Education
Social Services to PWAs\HIV
HIV Positive Support Groups
HIV Antibody Testing & Counseling
Sexually Transmitted Disease Testing & Treatment
Women's Program
Nutrition Consultation
General Counseling

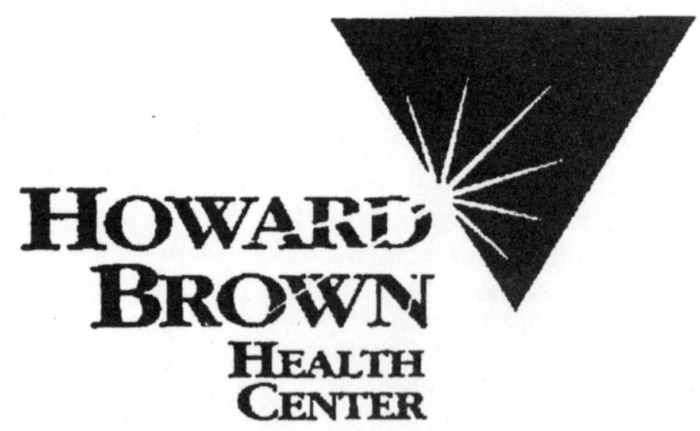

945 West George St., Chicago, IL 60657
(312) 871-5777

Brown Elephant Resale Shop, 3641 N. Halsted, Chicago (312) 549-3549
all proceeds benefit Howard Brown Health Center

Roy Gonsalves
Perversion
(Renaissance Press)

There are many voices speaking, singing and shouting the black gay experience in America today. But few ring as bold, funny, daring and honest as Roy Gonsalves.

In his latest book of prose and poems, *Perversion*, Gonsalves is not afraid to confront the realities and complexities that many times come with being black, gay and male in the 90's. Here addiction, AIDS, racism and homophobia walk hand in hand with unabashed sexuality, recovery, passion and spiritual redemption.

Gonsalves invites us to view the world from his eyes, and the landscape is quite scary. Through Obsession, Indiscretion, and Confession (three chapters in his book) the narrator inhabits a world where he is sexually abused because of his skin color ("Caricature"), drugs and alcohol destroy with finality ("Hell", "Fermented Dreams") and love, if he's lucky to find it, becomes an emotional battlefield ("HIV in G Minor", "Truth vs Romance"). Yet for all the horror that surrounds the author, he refuses to succumb to despair. Throughout the book are persistent, almost defiant, songs of survival and healing. For example, with every "The Exploiter":

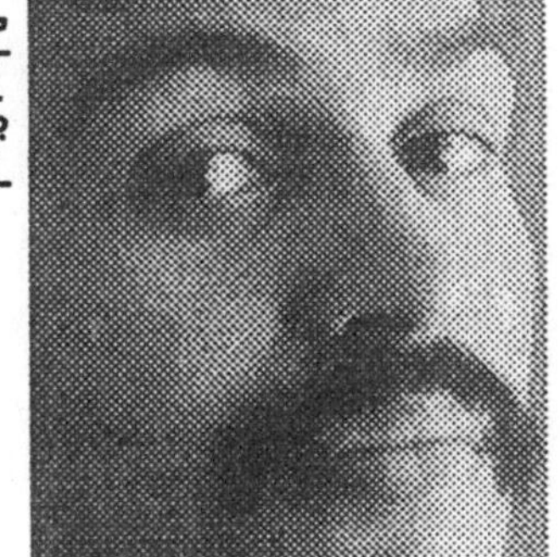

author Roy Gonsalves

He uses men of color
for toilets
Does not flush
When he is through
But goes home
To croissants
With pale hands
That massage his ego
And prays
He won't turn black

there is an affirming "Negritudy Booty":

I want Black hands all over me
Big lips on my mouth
Black English whispered in my ear
A big round ass rubbing up against my thighs
And plenty of rhythm
To put me to sleep.

And it is definitely Gonsalves' poetry, with his wry humor, frankness, down and dirty sexuality, and sensitivity, that carries this collection. Unfortunately, while his prose "Robert", "Bruce", and "The Diary of Calvin Jones" deals quite honestly with many of the same themes as in the poems, one comes away feeling that they are not complete, that the author has not told us the whole story. In addition, perhaps in an effort to stick to a formula, his prose loses much of the rhythm and punch that his shorter poems pack. The whole collection, however, unfolds into a kaleidoscope of situations and emotions most readers will find shocking, thought-provoking and amazing.

This is a must-read book for anyone who wants literature that challenges, not coddles. Gonsalves' final poem, "Remembrance", asks the reader to "sew one of my poems with red thread and remember me." *Perversion* guarantees that you will not forget Roy Gonsalves any time soon.

— Rodney McCoy, Jr.

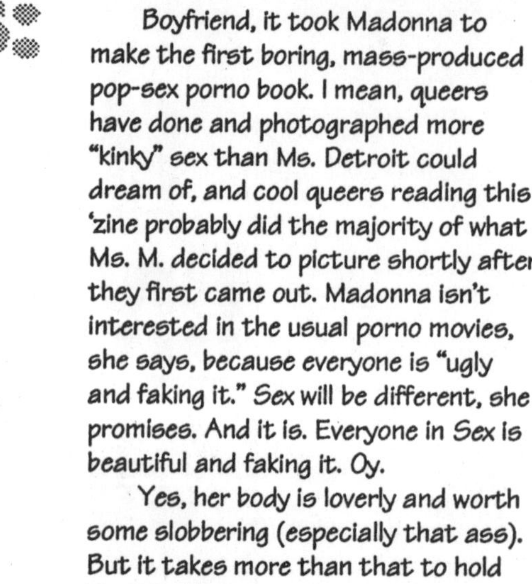

Boyfriend, it took Madonna to make the first boring, mass-produced pop-sex porno book. I mean, queers have done and photographed more "kinky" sex than Ms. Detroit could dream of, and cool queers reading this 'zine probably did the majority of what Ms. M. decided to picture shortly after they first came out. Madonna isn't interested in the usual porno movies, she says, because everyone is "ugly and faking it." Sex will be different, she promises. And it is. Everyone in Sex is beautiful and faking it. Oy.

Yes, her body is loverly and worth some slobbering (especially that ass). But it takes more than that to hold Fire Chick's interest over so many pages. O, look at her simulate sex with scary punk lesbians. O, look at her simulate sex with a dog. O, look at her simulate sex with a leather boy. O, look at her simulate sex with "exotic" white people of undeterminable gender. O, look at her simulate sex with beautiful black models in a swimming pool. O, look at her simulate sex with expensive clothes on. O look at her stand naked in a pizza parlor, see her stand naked on the street, see her lay naked in the park, watch her swim naked in a pool, see her stand naked a window. O, wake me up in the morning hon.

Go back to bed you self-absorbed naughty girly. Sex looks like a typical fashion-photo shoot. Steven Meisel knows beautiful lines, beautiful faces and camera angles, but he doesn't know a hot fuck, and he doesn't capture souls. The sex here is just another prop in his arsenal—fake as the glued-on sesame seeds on the bun in a McDonalds ad.

Butt most of all, what disappointed Fire Chick was the lack of pussy. There is no sex in Sex. O, Madonna talks a good talk—some of the only stimulation you can get is found in the text—but she shows nary a pussy. What a little cunt tease. For someone who pretends to have no hang-ups,

that's pretty lame. Some pubic hair, but no pink. We get 1 fag dick, not even an excited fag dick; it just hangs there in stasis. And lots of Madonna's tits. Good tits, but boring over so many pages. It's like, "I paid good money for these, don't you like them?" Reminiscent of Edie Sedgewick bouncing her tits around in "Ciao Manhattan." And it isn't like she didn't already show us her faboo knockers in her self-styled movie about her self on her tour singing her songs fighting her boyfriends throwing her tantrums projecting her latest persona promoting her album.

Sex is like fucking a Barbie doll (which was one of Fire Chick's favorite sex toys when she was younger)—pretty plastic. Madonna seems to have these half-baked ideas in her head—hey, punky lesbians looking dangerous with knives will sell—and once she gets down with the chicks she seems to be at a loss for what they should all do. No one gets cut—not even the chicks into cutting. And Madonna claims to have been shocked by a dyke's labia ring? Give it a rest boyfriend. It's not like we don't all know you've been around. Was that reaction calculated to distance you from being too much "that way" so that Ms. Suburban Hausfrau can identify (and buy)? (And she doesn't let us see the damned ring, either.)

What does Sex have then my dear babies? There are poses; not pussies; not passion. Each page is a pose, and when you turn the page, another pose pops up at the same emotional level but dressed in different clothes. Sometimes Meisel gets creative. He puts multiple exposures on the page. Ooo. We all get to see the way someone's head tilts or smile changes; or, he cuts the photos into odd shapes. Wow—Fire Chick was SO excited that she couldn't finish her Ho Hos.

After a few dozen pages, Fire Chick was actually and truly bored. No,

fire chick reads Sex

she is not saying this to be cool. Fire Chick actually liked that short and sexy "Justify My Love" video that was banned from MTV. The book is like the new album—it feels overproduced and strains desperately to be shocking. Once in awhile she hits it; there are some decent poses, but—like they say to a virgin—Madonna, relax, we'd both enjoy it more.

There is text. Some of it is in girl-ish curlie-cue handwriting. How "reveal-ing." And, unfortunately, homophobic. Dita is her "character", who states that she will "*teach you how to fuck.*" Madonna is sure to warn us that none of what we read or see is true, she made it all up. Whew. That must be of comfort to Mr. and Mrs. Breeder. Dita writes to her boyfriend in a series of "letters" about pussy juice, and licking her girlfriend-lover Ingrid (only because she misses her boyfreind's dick—must reassure those het boys). She acts all turned on by thoughts of group sex fantasies with her boyfriend (two girls, one boy, three girls, one boy, you get the picture) and tells him how hot she felt when she saw him with his hand down another girl's pants at a party. Then, the final "letter" finds her boyfriend getting sucked off by anoth-er boy when Dita sneaks in to his house uninvited. Dita is so shocked she runs out. (Any respectable bi-chick would have joined in the fun, or at least been turned on by the scene and stayed to watch.) Dita says to him in her last letter that they should spend some time apart because she has dis-covered his secret, and she says, "*Is that what you did on those fishing trips? I didn't know Ben was holding your rod for you. Did you catch any-thing?* [AIDS phobia too Ms. M? That's right, reassure your public that they only need worry about AIDS when it comes to male-to-male sex—right?] . . .*As for me, I think I'm gonna be sick. Next time you want some pussy, just look in the mirror.*"

That last jab of homophobia lets her hetero boy and girl fans know that Madonna may suck pussy to turn on her boys—typical breederboy fantasy fodder—but when it comes to true homogirl feelings or boy homo-sex, well, that is truly disgusting. The line Madonna draws in her "no-holds-barred" fan-tasy world is typical hetero crap, dressed up in leather and posed with a few queers to make it look "radical." But be sure that her vast pop audience will all know in the end, that for her, real homosex and certainly real homo love, make her sick. Her real feelings? Or Dita's calculation for mass appeal? Such dis-claimers make Sex safe for the suburban mid-dle-america crowd. They can pick up this book and have all their fears and fantasies con-firmed, not challenged, while feeling o-so-liber-al, open-minded and outrageous at the same time. Fire Chick might cream over thoughts of Madonna's tongue lapping at her shaved cunt, fucking Madonna in her tender ass with her 10" strap-on, and pissing into Madonna's open and lovely lips, but, of course, none of this is true, I made it all up.

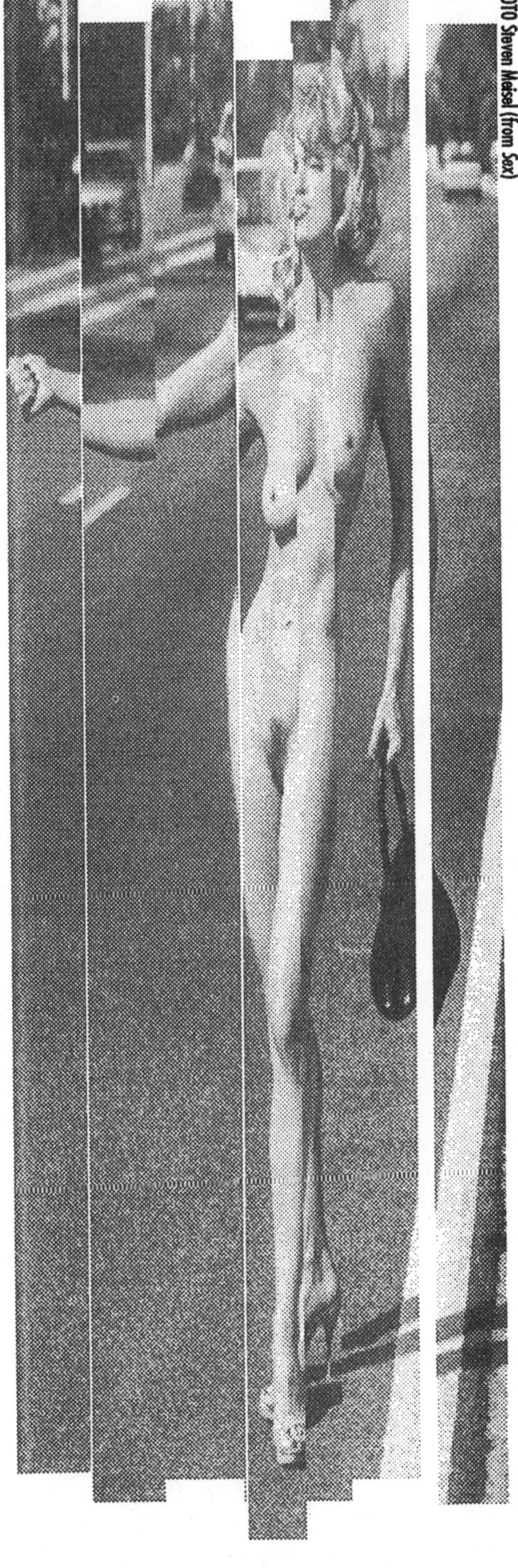

JEAN-MICHEL BASQUIAT
Whitney Museum of American Art

The '80s were heady times. I, like other art fags and dykes, was practically raised on the glamorous money-soaked environment of the art world. Even in Kansas. It was a time of overnight art stars: Keith Haring, Mark Kostabi, Kenny Scharf and parties with the ubiquitous Warhol. And there was a black artist commanding blue chip prices along with the rest: Jean-Michel Basquiat. Even his name was glamorous. His packaged street image was in truth much different from the middleclass privileged youth he had as a son of a Haitian accountant father and a Puerto Rican mother. He was very influenced by the newly emerging rap and hip hop and began, like Haring, doing his primitivist paintings on walls visible in the downtown art mecca, Soho. "SAMO" was his early signature which stood for same old shit and a reference to the racist character, Sambo. SAMO was followed by the symbol of copyrighting—a circled C. Basquiat was ambitious and savvy.

Layers of paint, text or both cover the surface of his works and give meaning to visually enticing work. He was able to manipulate and move from one code to another; Greek and historical mythology, pop culture and black experiences, using a grab bag of cultural references and languages: Gray's Anatomy, Universal Sign, Hatram, English, Spanish, Italian. French, German, racist ideology is turned on its head, processed and regurgitated as hip, disturbing, funny and poignant tales. One of my favorite pieces is "Untitled, Detail of Maid from Olympia" (1982). It is a perfect contemporary response to the exclusionary and racist art history canon. By focusing on the subservient black subject of a revered painting, Basquiat loudly questions culture. His method is not unlike the Deee-Lite rap sample from "Planet Earth" which says..."...take the children that live among us teach them the truth about Chistopher Columbus." I'm not surprised that his various dealers reportedly asked him to deliver simple images and messages. One would assume, less antagonistic.

Basquiat's seemingly simple words on paper and canvas are full of subtle double meanings and are very effective. The kindergarten or idiot savant chicken scratch of phrases like: "Aaron"—which refers to Negro baseball great Hank Aaron followed by a copyright symbol, perhaps seals blacks' right to claim him as well as Basquiat. The crown he draws over the name is the highest in Basquiat's lexicon. "No mundane options" (1981) states black people's experience as well as Basquiat's in white culture. His mad, wild, grimacing figures tend to look like tortured cartoon characters or black caricatures, half machine, half human, missing teeth, hair, limbs and smiles. None of them are just one color or even two. The colors are always mixed, one on top of another. "Molasses" (1983) is an adult cartoon where a headless bandit dog and hybrid rabbit are being sent to jail driven by a uniformed brown man who is hitting himself in the head with a hammer. Basquiat gives priority to the once only permissible black icons, athletes and musicians. They are blacks who not only excelled but transformed their craft given the tiny space allowed them, not unlike Basquiat himself.

Dead of a drug overdose at the age of 28 in 1988 and leaving a huge amount of work, both drawings and paintings, Basquiat is one figure from the '80's we are not soon to forget. The many well-endowed museums throughout the country who passed on the opportunity to host the Jean-Michel retrospective made a grave mistake.

— Todd Roulette

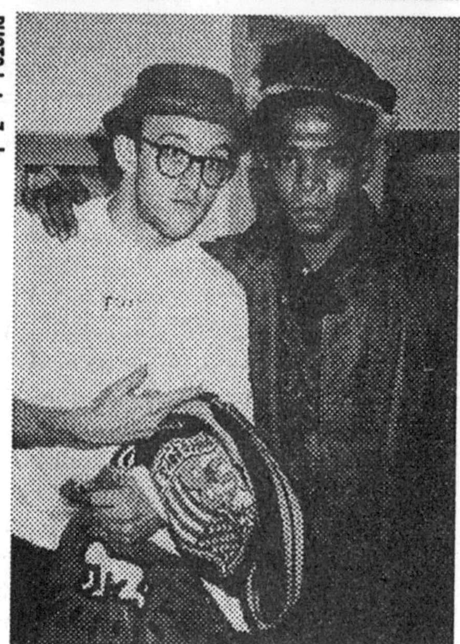

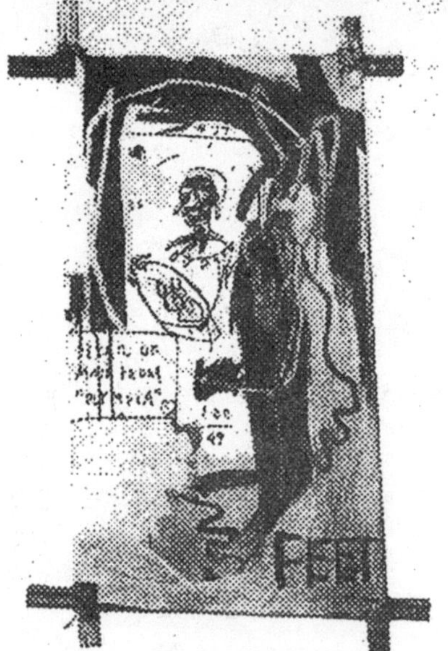

Top to Bottom: Basquiat by James Van Der Zee; Keith Haring with Jean-Michel; "Untitled (Detail of Maid from Olympia)".

The exhibition will travel to: 1.The Mevil Collection, Houston March 11 - May 9, 1993 2. Des Moines Art Center, Iowa May 22 - August 15, 1993 3. Montgomery Museum of Fine Arts, Alabama November 18, 1993 - January 9, 1994. "Jean-Michel Basquiat" The Whitney New York City October 23, 1992 - February 14, 1993

PRIVATE/PUBLIC
SAIC Betty Rymer Gallery/Gallery 2

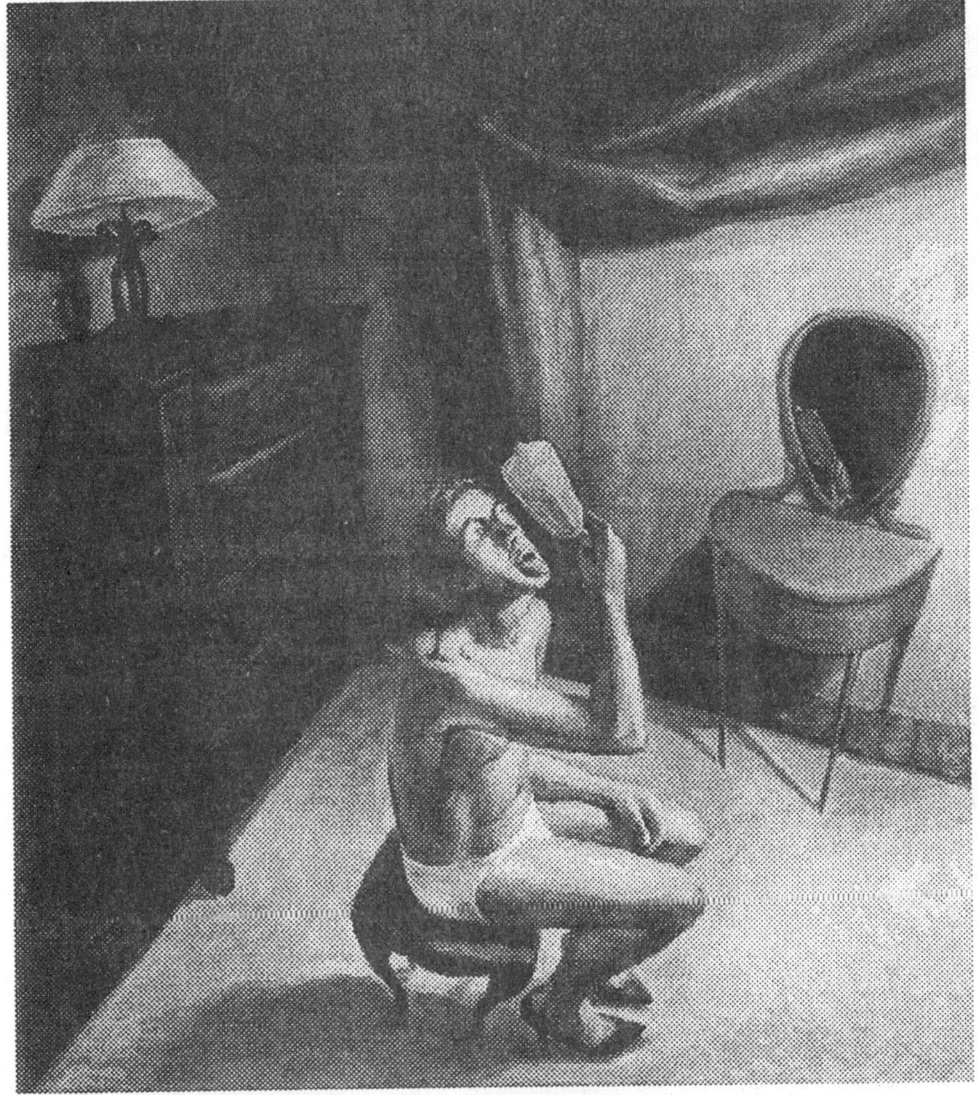

Hugh Steers, *Throat* **(1992)**

Assoto Saint, in Marlon Riggs' "Non, Je Ne Regrette Rien (No Regret)", says that he is not sorry for anything he did in his youth. He is not sorry for his backroom dalliances, nor his love affairs in Africa and Europe. He is not sorry for his homosexuality nor his enjoyment of homo sex. "No Regret" focuses on Saint and four other African/Caribbean American Homosexual men discussing their HIV status and how they have taken a seemingly despairing situation and turned into a condition that is empowering.

This piece was part of a larger show, *Private/Public*, the first national exhibition of works by artists who have AIDS or who are HIV positive. Shown at the Betty Rymer Gallery and The School of The Art Institute of Chicago's Gallery 2, there were also various workshops and symposia addressing issues of AIDS and representation in the arts.

The intentions of the curators was to create a forum for education as well as provide a safe space to show the diversity of work being produced by HIV impacted artists. In a pamphlet from the Rymer Gallery, the curators say that the work presented was made with hate, anger, and metaphorical implications of murder. "These artists are fighting an infection that manifests itself both physically and socially." For the most part, I found the work to be predictable and pedestrian—images of syringes, skeletons, and blood.

Fortunately, there were some pieces in particular that vitalized the show for me. Robert Blanchon's "Untitled (Protection)" (1992) for example. The installation is of written correspondence between the artist and his mother. In his letter, Blanchon apologizes for his parents inability to come to terms with his sexual orientation and in an attempt to keep communication lines open (and maintain dignity) divulges his HIV diagnoses. In her 16-page reply, his mother tells him that accepting God in his life will give him peace of mind. This piece very effectively demonstrates the exhibition's purpose - to make the private public (or the personal political?).

Hugh Steers painting "Throat" (1992) was both imaginative and sobering. A man sits in the center of his bedroom wearing black pumps and holding a hand mirror to his mouth. It's as if he is wondering if the sores in his mouth are from some accident he had eating tortilla chips or is it candiasis? How often have you found yourself in this paranoic dilemma?

Also, Richard Elovich's performance, "Someone Else From Queens Is Queer", effectively gave a face to a statistic by confronting the audience with his characters' first homosexual experience (with a man whose dick was bigger than anything human, no less) and hypodermic drug use.

Unfortunately, *Private/Public* didn't represent HIV/AIDS statistics with its participants. The curators realized this and as a remedy, documentation of artwork by artists living with HIV was accepted throughout the exhibition time, to be housed in SAIC's John M. Flaxman Library.

— Walter Youngblood

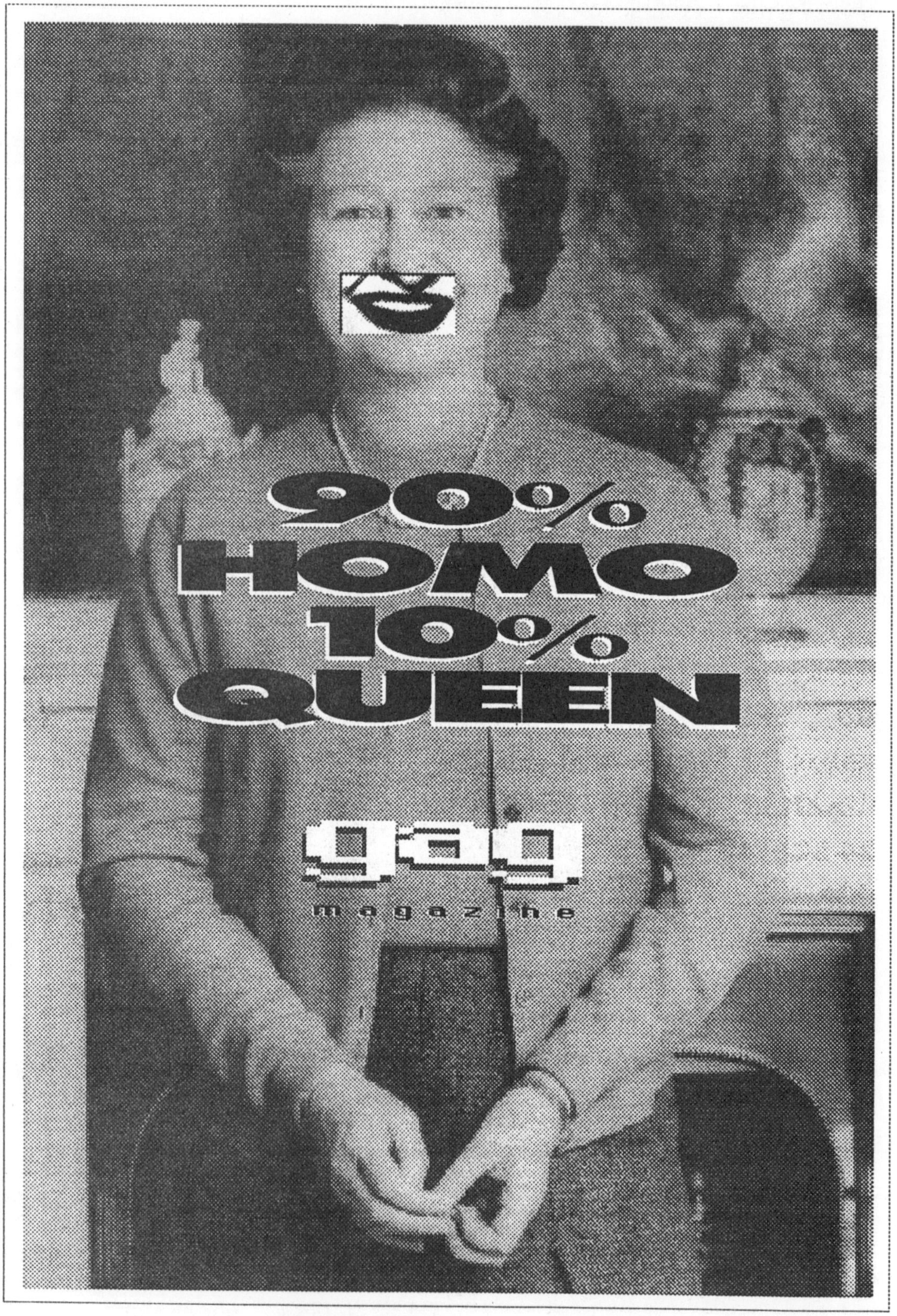

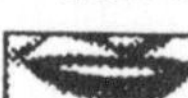
90%
HOMO
10%
QUEEN
gag
magazine
sample issue $3 2: gag 1153 n dearborn #203 chicago, Il 60610
free all over homoland-chicago

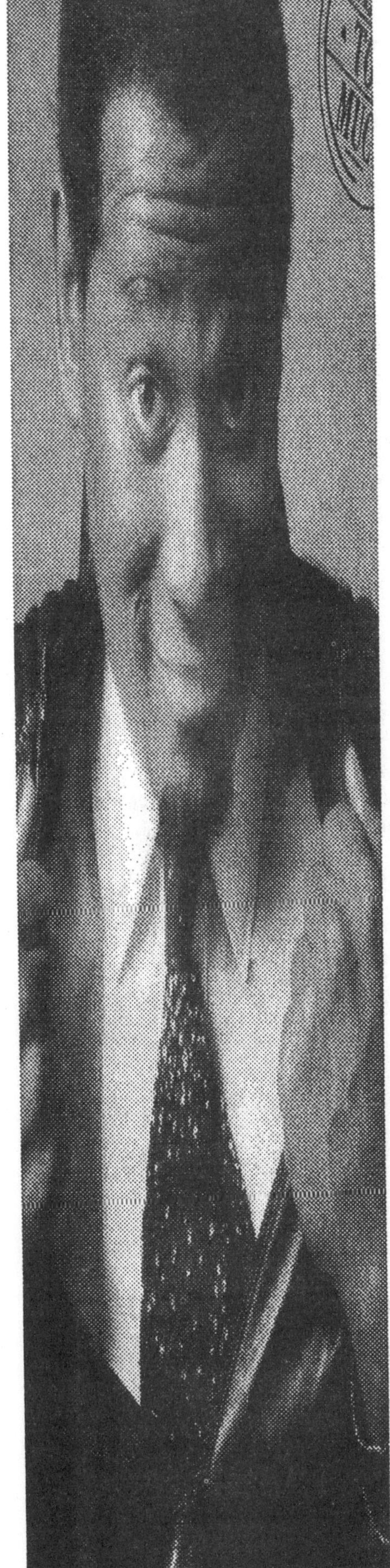

MUST🌐
counts to ten
10 FAVORITE ALBUMS OF ALL TIME

1. LOU REED "BERLIN"
So depressing it makes me feel better about myself.

2. DAVID BOWIE "LOW"
"Always Crashing In The Same Car" is my kind of dance song.

3. BARBRA STREISAND "GREATEST HITS"
Why? Because I'm gay.

4. CAROLE KING "TAPESTRY"
Before I realized that life is a cabaret, I was sure that life was a tapestry. Carole told me.

5. LUTHER VANDROSS "NEVER TOO MUCH"
His first album, when he was fatter and fiercer.

6. DIANA ROSS & THE SUPREMES "LOVE CHILD"
Gloomy, urban angst, Motown style. Diana's "Berlin".

7. DIANA ROSS & THE SUPREMES "SING & PERFORM 'FUNNY GIRL'"
I can't even describe this one. I'm just glad I own it.

8. NATALIE COLE "INSEPARABLE"
Fresh and forceful. Before her father died, I think, so she only sang duets with herself.

9. "BEST OF THE HUES CORPORATION"
For the millions of psychos who mistakenly feel that "Rock The Boat" was their only good song.

10. BROADWAY CAST "DREAMGIRLS"
Why? Because I'm gay.

NUMBER FIVE: Luther Vandross
from the *Never Too Much* cover.

ATLANTIC BEACH HOTEL

On the beach

DECK BAR
Tropical Specialties

SANDY BEACH TERRACE
Restaurant

Singles Available from $60!

ATLANTIC BEACH HOTEL
SAN JUAN
Puerto Rico
(809) 721-6900

lists

What's In A Name? Part II
Celine Dion
Cindy Herron
Soon Yi Farrow Previn
Emily Hadad
Organa Deluxe
La Palace de Beauté
Scyntilla Vortex
Pussy du Jour
RuPaul Charles

The Green Room
Bob Mould
Hilton Als
Monica Lynch
Diamanda Galas
Sandra Bernhard
Eartha Kitt
Erasure

Your Host for the House Hayride
Downtown Julie Brown
Christine (Racy Beats) Johnson
Holly Robinson
Nia Peebles
Pebbles
Neneh Cherry
Tyler Collins
Jasmine Guy
Debbie Allen

Got It Goin' On
Bill Coleman
Larry Flick
Lee Kay
RuPaul
Gregory Victorraine
Rosser Shymanski
Lady Bunny
Scott Lifshutz
Len Prince
David Lee Jones
Judy Weinstein
Ralphi Rosario

Behind The Scenes
Towa Towa Tei
David Geffen
George Wayne
Monica Lynch
Connie Varvitsiosis
André Halmon
John Epperson
Nasham Wooden

Pardon My French Part II
Chateau Marmont
Qui Monseur
Fu Toi

Oops!
William Burroughs
Claudine Longet
Lizzie Borden
Cheryl Ladd
Ted Kennedy
John Hinkley Jr.
Claus Von Bulow
Christian Brando
Le Nancy

BMCS
Medusa's
Cheeks
Shelter
Quench
Vortex
Clubhouse
Rivieria

Whatever Happened To...
Fay Wray
Carrie Snodgrass
Joey Heatherton
Yvonne Gage
Jill Dietz
Andrea True
Vickie Sue Robinson

Dearly Departed
Audre Lorde
Valentino
Robert Stern
Donald Redrick
Professor Eddie Lusk
Tom Rubnitz
Bob Caviano
Paul Jabara
W. Delon Strode
Scott McPherson
Donald Woods

Over The Top
Quincy Jones' *Messaiah*
Erasure's *Abba-esque*
Liza Minnelli *Live at Radio City*
Xaveria Gold's
Gonna Get Back to You
Whitney Houston's
I Will Always Love You

Voodoo Soul
Massive Attack
Brand New Heavies
Soul II Soul
D-Influence
YoYo Honey

Blue Bloods
Queen Samantha
Queen Latifah
Queen Esther
Queen Bee
Reavis Royalty

Sister Act
Dee Dee Warwick
Lorna Luft
Reebie Jackson
Blanche and Jane Hudson
Margaux Hemingway
Mackenzie Phillips
Warren Beatty
Nancy Sinatra
Sarah Gilbert
Roslyn Kind
Joan Fontaine
Gurlene and Gurlette Hussy

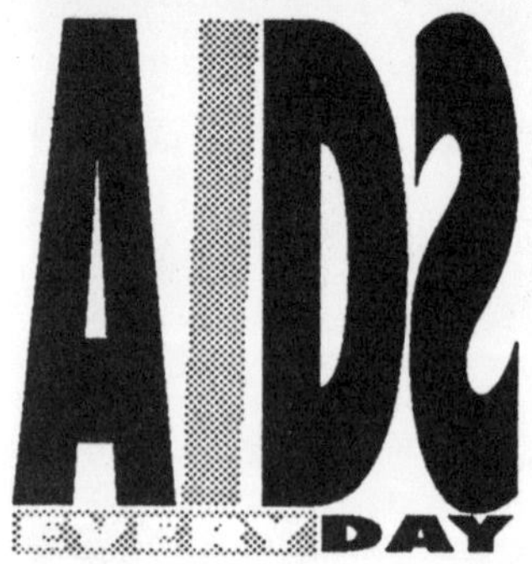

roy gonsalves

Bruce is a Teddy bear
In a man's body
He is Africa
A wild dance
And a good cry
Bruce has guns going off
In his head
That he could not stop

Bruce is tastier than Hershey's chocolate and sweeter than Domino's cane. His mother put him in the streets when he was thirteen because he was gay. As a child, he played James Brown on the stereo and danced to the beat, pretending he was a star. Bruce and his brother screamed and cried while holding each other when their father and mother drank and fought. He played with lots of Teddy bears and with the boy down the street. They kissed each other's nipples and hugged in his friend's bedroom when no one was home. One day he was forced by a strange man to eat his banana. The man tried to pee on him, but he ran away as fast as he could. Then his stepbrother started staying over and they began to fool around at night when everyone was asleep. He took care of the house and his little brother, but went too far when he started taking care of his mother and began pouring her liquor down the sink. When the cops brought him to the group home in Queens, Bruce met Mother Rose, a gay counselor, who took him under his wing. Even when the boys in the home broke the eye on Bruce's Teddy bear and he came after them with a spiked belt and a mop stick, Mother Rose defended him.

At college Bruce became the dorm mother. Many of the students came by to eat macaroni and cheese with pork chops. He went to fraternity parties where the booze flowed like it did at his mother's house. Bruce was the campus prima donna of dance. His movements made him the envy of the dance club and eventually their president. He danced with the grace of Judith Jamison and the finesse of Alvin Ailey. Even the straight guys in the fraternity loved him and admired the way he was proud, despite, they said, "being gay and black."

I met him when he was in college. I was lonely because I resorted to quick sex. It hurt less than getting emotionally involved. At the time I was working as a counselor at a high school in Brooklyn and feeling something was missing. Although I was handsome and well built, I didn't have anyone to save my love for like Whitney Houston did in her song. In fact, on any number of occasions I could be seen in public with some outrageous silk frock that I had made and called, "Notice-Me-Wear," because I was single and available. However, I was not going to throw my heart to the dogs for dinner. I was, in fact, still in recovery from two ex-lovers who had eaten my aorta for kicks. I was a cautious creature and put people into four categories: friends, tricks, business associates, and potential lovers. Dancing was my thing. I also liked to paint, sew, write poems, and could talk you to death on a slow day; could not sit still to save my life and was partial to roaming dark places and meeting invisible men who I never knew let alone saw again. I prayed two times a day and recently prayed for a man.

One night I was on a mission. I shaved the hairs carefully from my face, making waves like a whale in my hair with the curl activator and comb. Afterwards, I put on my silk suit, polished my black boots and sashayed down to Tracks Disco.

The people were all dressed in their best jeans, jewels, and gowns. Clothes pulled and tucked, hair teased with curls determined to impress any man, woman, dyke, queen or child. There were some hungry folks in the house and I was one of them. Starved of love by too many one night stands and dead end streets. I had sewn my wild oats into a quilt in memory of my departure. Even after four lovers who turned from chocolate kisses into bitter cough drops, I still had plenty of love to give.

I walked near the dance floor feeling lovely, like it was all about me. "It's Not Over" was playing wildly. Red lights were doing relevés and pliés against the walls. Ebony sculptures were possessed on the dance floor as if they were dancing for the spirits in a ceremony in Ghana. Trying to maintain my composure, I leaned against the wall, because I was too embarrassed to dance alone.

Bruce was on my right dancing himself into a grave. He was acting nonchalant. We snuck glances at each other, trying to be cool. I hoped he would ask me to dance, but he kept on dancing by himself. Finally, the music took control over my legs and lips and I asked him to dance. He looked so naive in his T-shirt and torn cutoff jeans, with his dancer calves extending to his black ankle boots.

We started off dancing cool, not extending our elbows above our shoulders; but as time wore on I was spinning like a top and he had pressed the button. We were the only ones who existed that night. By the end of the evening I had poked my finger through the tear in his pants and he had stuck his tongue in my ear. He was dignified when I asked him to come home with me. He said, "I never go home with anyone on the first night."

bruce

The first time he spent the night in my house we cuddled and fell asleep holding each other. The morning after, I told him I was HIV-positive and sexually compulsive. When I said this, he did not flinch, grab his clothes and run for the door. I was so relieved when he asked intelligent questions about what it meant. I explained carefully that it didn't mean I was going to die tomorrow and that I wasn't a danger to him as long as we practiced safe sex. I told him that I attended meetings that helped me deal with being sexually compulsive, because it was an addiction that could only be arrested with help. After we ate breakfast by candlelight, Bruce rubbed against me. If I had been a piece of paper I would have burned to death. He laid next to me like I was a big tit woman without a bra and he was a wet T-shirt. It was as if we had been lovers in another lifetime and had missed each other for a thousand years.

Even after I told him I had sex three times with someone else after I met him, he did not run away like I had the plague. I felt ten feet lower than dirt. So when he came over that weekend, hurt, I ran a hot tub of water with bubble bath, rose petals, lit several white candles, played Anita Baker and poured water on him like he was King Solomon and I was an insignificant slave. While he was bathing I ran to the store and bought a bouquet of long stemmed red roses, a package of strawberries and whipped cream. I pretended he was a work of art that I was sculpting. Scattering the petals of one of the roses over him while he laid in the tub, I used my hand to spread whipped cream on his chest and crotch. Then I fed him strawberries and ate the whipped cream from his body using my tongue to emphasize the points I wanted to make. When he smiled like he'd hit lotto, I know I had cleansed the cobwebs from his heart.

Bruce is a Teddy bear
Who fights Black revolutions
With his poems
And argues with the T.V.
He is the color of butternut
With a face like a Nigerian mask
Whose hair is fuzzy and soft
Like his heart.

What I love most about Bruce is that he tries anything once. I remember once we did paintings on the floor using our hands and feet. Then there was the time we took a bubble bath together and I decided we should paint fluorescent pink and orange on each other

to get in touch with our ancestors. He looked like a warrior about to go to battle. He cleansed me of thousands of dirty hands. When I got out of that tub I was the one who was conquered.

Three weeks ago I got a call from Dr. Schwartz recommending that I take AZT, because my T-cells went down to 115. Bruce cried all week secretly and was afraid to show he was scared he might have it too. He tried to explain that he had a lot on his mind and didn't feel like hugging when I needed desperately to be held. I decided to take the train to Boston to visit my mother. I never said anything, but I knew he wanted to run being so young. I wanted to run too, not from him, but from myself and the fear of death that smelled in the air like onions about to make you cry.

On the way to Penn Station, I bought two dozen roses for my mother. After sitting in the train for ten minutes the conductor asked me, "They're for my mother, I don't see her often," I explained. However, inside I felt I had let her down by being HIV-positive. My stomach felt sick from AZT, but the fear diminished the further I got from New York. When I arrived no one acted strange toward me. It was nice to know they still loved me and that I had someplace to go if I became too sick.

As I looked out the window, riding back to New York, the naked trees danced near the lake. The possibility that he would not be there when I got home was scaring me to death. I did not want to even consider it, because I had given myself completely to Bruce. He was my beloved. If he left me I would jump off the Brooklyn Bridge.

As I ran up the stairs at Lafayette station in Brooklyn, fear played hopscotch on the pit of my stomach. I felt weak when I opened the door to our apartment. I smelled smoke. The lights were off. A pan was on the stove burning profusely. I turned it off. It was charred linguine for dinner. Bless his heart. He forgot to turn off the stove he was so worried about me. I put the pan in the sink and ran water in it. There was a note on the table that said, "Welcome Home Baby."

Bruce is a Teddy bear
In a man's body
I told him my secrets
Bruce never yelled them back
But hugged me
Like Teddy never could.

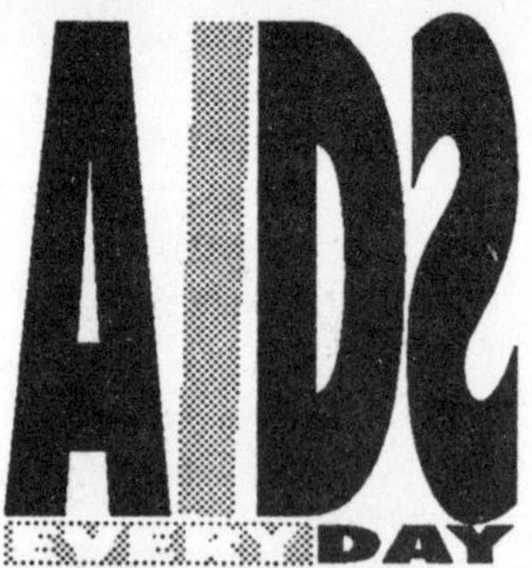

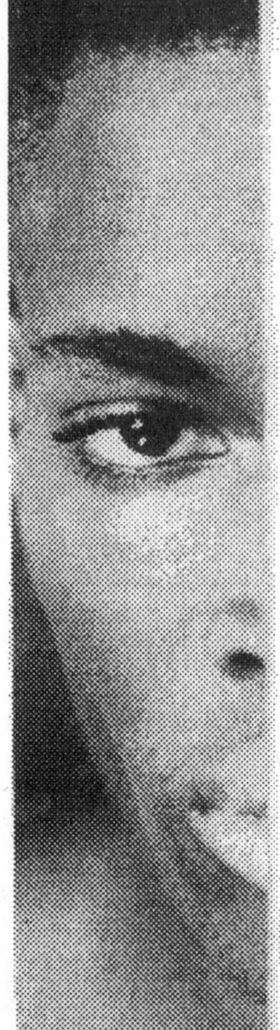

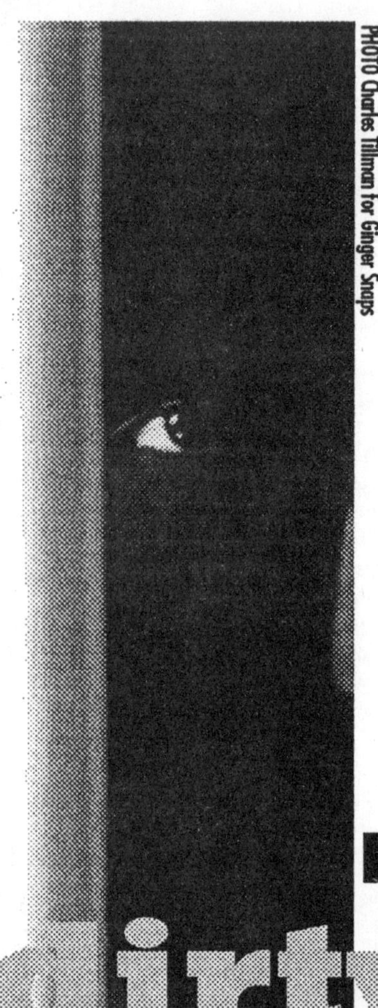

gay male community.

However, the heterogeneous nature of the community suggests that gay men may not exactly share one common language, even though engaging in similar behaviors. Bell and Weinberg (1978) found that the African-American gay men in their San Franciso-based study had ready sexual, but not social, access to the larger, generally White gay male community. Social isolation itself produces language differentiation. In addition, language is a primary means of indicating ethnic group membership either to signal similarity or to establish differentiation in interaction with another. Thus, we might expect that Black gay men have somewhat different words for describing behaviors targeted by "safer sex" interventions. To the extent that such language differences exist, the impact of public health messages may be impaired. For African-American men, this would be particularly unfortunate given their disproportionate risk for HIV infection.

Insofar as language is public while sexual behavior and feelings are often private, a schema for translating the private into the public in a safe manner is an important issue in an oppressed population. This allows for communication in public without fear of reprisal. Several studies suggest that gay men use coded terminology to a greater extent than heterosexual men and or lesbian women.

Drake (1980) notes slang is a socially important group phenomenon related to group identity,

dirty TALK

the different ways black & white gay men talk about sex

While gay men's language has been of interest in the fields of linguistics and literature for several decades, it was not until the AIDS epidemic that "gayspeak" acquired considerable attention from behavioral sex researchers. This health threat necessitated rapid development of public health interventions targeting specific sexual behavioral changes in the gay male population. Previous research had found that the most effective messages for producing health-related behavior change were those that were both in the language of the target population and delivered by credible sources.

For gay men, this has meant the extensive formulation of "safer sex" interventions in which low risk sexual behaviors are promoted using vernacular common to the

used to express both alienation, encoding a disdain for the existing social order and social distance or solidarity, on an interpersonal dimension. The area of sexuality, a prime concern of society, is one of the richest semantic fields for slang. Black gay men, quite aware of the legacy of physical and psychological intimidation by societal institutions, prejudices against both homosexuality and the Black community, and the overall lack of discourse on sexuality in the Black community, have developed even more refined methods of communicating with other Black gay men.

We present here some of the sexually-related termiof party." The latter phrase could also be used in a broader context to indicate refusal of sexual activities in general, or refusal of a particular person. Black gay men who engaged in both anal receptive and anal insertive intercourse were referred to as "flipflops" or "pancakes."

Food-based slang was frequent in describing oral-anal contact. References to eating chocolate chip cookies, peanut butter, tossing salad or eating at Joe's were common substitutes for licking and/or sucking the anus. In gay vernacular, "eating out" and "cleaning one's kitchen" serve the same purpose, obtusely describing a behavior that is frequently referred to as rimming in sex surveys. "Round the world" was a term used at times by our sample for oral sex from head to toe.

Sexual Body Parts

Important to the assessment of HIV-related sexual activity is some knowledge of terms used for different body parts. Slang for the anus and penis were invoked most often (see Table 2). Some terms are best understood within context. For example, "salami" is used to indicate a large penis. When paired with "boola" it refers to the large penis of an obviously heterosexual inner city lower class Black male. Referring to the penis by given names seemed fairly common among our participants, with "George" and "Herman" having the most recognition among the men. "Boygina" and "bogina" to refer to the anus are combinations of the words "boy" and "vagina". This same construction is seen in the word "boogina" which combines booty (the anus) and vagina. The "taint" is the erogenous zone between the scrotum and the anus. Its name comes from the fact that "it ain't the balls and it ain't the asshole, its the 't'aint."

---

types of HIV related behavior

DEEP KISSING
Gay Vernacular: French kissing, Tonguing, Suck face
Black Gay Vernacular: Tonguing, swapping spit, checking out his tonsils, giving a tonsillectomy (NY)

MASTURBATION
Gay Vernacular: Jerk(ed) off, Jack(ed) off, stroking, beat off, whack off, circle jerk, meatbeater, hand job
Black Gay Vernacular: jacked off, play with stuff, pumping, choke your bishop, chokin' the chicken, beat your meat, hand job,

FROTTAGE
Gay Vernacular: body rubbing, bump and grind, humping, dry humping
Black Gay Vernacular: slit fucking between thighs, college style, dry fuck, slick leggin'

ANAL INTERCOURSE
Gay Vernacular: butt fucking, heels on the ceiling, lay pipe, top/bottom man, bang, Greek, poke
Black Gay Vernacular: fucked you in your butt, did butt sex, worked your box, laying some pipe, drill/drilling, freak/freaking, George, George-ing, Legs up/legs reaching for heaven, Heels on the ceiling/put your pumps up, pumping/pump butt, serving, poke, doin' the do, getting done, boneing, getting your life, knockin' boots

ORAL/ANAL CONTACT
Gay Vernacular: rimming, eat out, eating ass, cleaning your/my kitchen
Black Gay Vernacular: tossing salad, tossing cookies, eating chocolate chip cookies, I like peanut butter, eatin' at Joe's

MANUAL ANAL INTERCOURSE
Gay Vernacular: Fisting, handballing, finger fucking
Black Gay Vernacular: Fingering, finger fucking

---

nology used by Black gay men in the United States. The purpose is to highlight both similarities and differences from White gay men in the hopes of developing better "safer sex" message for this population.

HIV-Related Sexual Behaviors

In Table 1, we present technical terminology for several HIV risk-related sexual behaviors and the vernacular common among gay men as drawn from "gay language dictionaries." We also list the phrases employed by some Black gay men to describe these behaviors. As can be seen, some terms overlap both the Black and White gay communities, while others may be used rarely, if at all, outside of the Black community. For the men in our focus groups, technical terms ranged in levels of familiarity. Both "frottage" and "fellatio" were least understood unless paired with gay vernacular.

Terms for anal intercourse elicited the most responses. While we listed several terms given for anal sex, many men also reported highly developed encoding of the behavior in language that would only be understood by in-group members. For one respondent this included describing the desire for anal sex as "My refrigerator is empty and I need something in it." He also described some risks of anal sex by commenting "If you play in someone's backyard you're bound to get paint on it (or get dirty)." Indication of disinterest in anal intercourse could easily be accomplished without direct discussion through phrases such as "the bakery is closed" or "It ain't that kind

---

terminology of sexual body parts

ANUS, RECTUM, BUTTOCKS
Gay Vernacular: ass, asshole, box, pussy, butt, rear, cupcakes, cakes, buns
Black Gay Vernacular: manhole, box, pussy, boy pussy, punk pussy, boygina, bogina, cupcakes, cakes, buns

PENIS
Gay Vernacular: dick, tool, shaft, rod, thing, piece, dong, meat
Black Gay Vernacular: pole, fishing pole, meat, sausage, salami, boola, Junior, Uncle Willie, Spermin' Herman, Hermy, George, piece, dong, ding-dong, sweet daddy, birdy, rod, trade

SCROTUM
Gay Vernacular: basket
Black Gay Vernacular: basket

CROTCH
Gay Vernacular: stuff, sack, bag, ball bag
Black Gay Vernacular: team

ZONE BETWEEN SCROTUM & ANUS
Gay Vernacular: taint, tumbutt
Black Gay Vernacular: taint

NIPPLES
Gay Vernacular: tits, titties, points
Black Gay Vernacular: tits, titties, ninnies

Terminology for sexual partners

In Table 3 we present a nonexhaustive list of terms used to describe sexual partners/objects. Some of these are common gay vernacular; some seem specific to Black gay men. A major term for describing a sexual partner was "trade." In contrast, White gay men seem to prefer "trick." What we quickly learned was that the term "trade," referring to a sexual partner of low status with an implied impermanent status, has infinite and essential modifiers. The level of commitment or familiarity within a sexual liaison considered "trade" cannot be determined by the use of the word alone. But when modified, the nature of the relationship is more clearly delineated. For example, in "rough" or "hamburger" trade there is little or no emotional attachment. Their sexual encounter would largely be without any continuing emotional commitment beyond the time of the sexual act. Other modifiers imply a regularity of contact, still outside the realm of a committed relationship, such as "weekend trade."

How trade is used will often be a function of the geographic area in which the term is used, the age of the persons involved, the level of comfort with gay-identification, and the extent to which the person with whom trade is being discussed is a part of the in-group of Black gay men. Trade therefore can be used to objectify a sexual partner (e.g., "my weekend trade is on his way over") or as an indication of behavioral activity as in "having trade," "doing trade" or "being trade" (e.g., "I was doing trade when the phone rang.")

A word analogous in complexity is "queen." The word's traditional meaning implies an effeminate man. But, again, modifiers further refine its nuances. There are different types of queens such as "Butch Queen," "Femme Queen," or "Drag Queen." Butch queens are characterized as rough looking ("...the kind that fought better than truck drivers and swished better than Mae West"). At first glance, butch queens give the appearance that they would never be the passive partner in anal sex, but in private they will. As in "trade," variations in its use allow description of behavior, e.g. "being a queen, looking like a queen," or "acting like a queen." "Acting like a queen" can refer to either a heterosexual or gay individual. In the popular television show "In Living Color," the Wayman brothers "act like queens" with their two snaps routine. "Acting like a queen" can be a way of merely identifying that a person is acting gay behaviorally without necessary denoting the person is gay. On the other hand, calling someone a queen whose gay identity is hidden is a way of letting them or others know that the information is not as hidden as assumed.

Discussion

Much of the vernacular used for sexual behavior, body parts, and sexual partners expressed by our African-American participants are shared with the larger gay community. However, differences in some terms, more or less emphasis on others, and differential preferences in terms for particular situations suggest that, like the heterogeneous nature of the gay male community, language varies, too. While this may be fairly obvious, the implications are potentially quite important. For example, during the conduct of our initial groups, participants who had taken part in other HIV-related studies revealed that in spite of indigenous interviewers conducting the interviews, they could tell by the language used that materials were written by someone not familiar with their culture. This may bias research findings in unpredictable ways. Knowledge of language and the way it functions in the communication system of Black gay men will aid us in designing instruments to meaningfully tap into their world of sexuality.

Differences in language patterns may reflect differences in cognitive structures. The language used in the asking of questions will influence the organization of internal cognitive concepts and thereby influence the answer given. In asking Black gay men about their sexual behavior, language that helps cognitively and affectively to transport them to an internal state of recall that best matches the actual context will be most helpful in the goal of changing that behavior. Our ability to design effective HIV prevention strategies for Black gay men will be a direct function of our level of understanding of sexual practices.

Black gay language reflects Black language in general in that it is not only language but style. Black language has been characterized as "dynamic, demonstrative and emotionally intense". We were unable here to provide for the voice inflections, speech rhythms, tonal patterns or non-verbal behaviors that accompany some of the vernacular. It is also within these parameters that Black gay men are able to define themselves. Both the words and the style of Black gay language, like Black dialect, reflects a way of looking at life, a point of view, a culture.

In using the terminology presented here for the conduct of HIV-related research, it is important to remember that linguistic and cognitive processes are embedded in a context. In assessing the sexual behavior of Black gay men, the asking of the questions that embody their vernacular must also be asked from a framework of their experience. Using appropriate vernacular for sexual body parts or sexual behaviors, while a step in the right direction, may not elicit the full range of sexual behaviors without, for example, knowing something about difference categories of partners in which to assess the activities. The more accurately the questions are framed, the greater the likelihood that the answers will be truthful and reflective of diverse experiences. Our interest here was not merely in acquiring the proper terminology in order to speak "Black gayspeak" but also to demonstrate the importance of context to that terminology. This is a critical point if your goal is the assessment of sexual behavior for the purposes of bringing about behavior change.

It is also important to note that not all Black gay men speak in the terms that we have presented. Some use none of our terms while others may range from using them in very specific contexts to broader applications. We make no claims to have covered all the terms used by Black gay men. We are sure that networks were biased by the urbanicity of the investigators. Yet, we reached a diverse group of Black gay men in our efforts to understand the role of language in sexual behavior and found much consensus. This is of significance as it evidences lines of cultural transmission of the usage of the terminology presented in our study across various African-American gay male communities throughout the United States.

Research and report by Vickie M. Mays, Ph.D. (University of California, Los Angeles), Susan D. Cochran, Ph.D. (California State University, Northridge), George Bellinger Jr. (Minority Task Force on AIDS, NY), Robert G. Smith, Nancy Henley, Ph.D., Marlon Daniels, Thomas Tibbits, Gregory D. Victorianne, Olu Kwasi Osei, Darryl K. Birt (University of California, Los Angeles). The authors would like to thank all of the men who participated in this study. Special thanks to Vinsonm Roberts, R.N., Tony T. Goree, Raymond Drake, and Lyle Ashton Harris, MFA. This report originally appeared in its complete version in The Journal of Sex Research (August 1992)

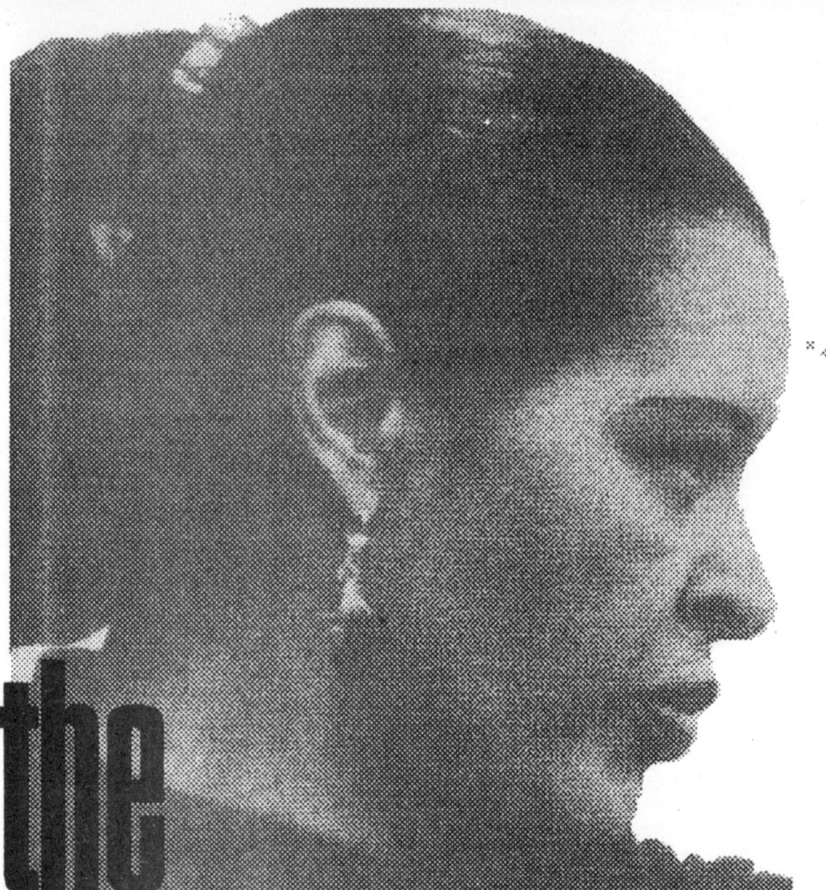

the
HOLIDAY

When he's not giving you rock-and-roll as subversive sex goddess Justine, or engaging in a little repartee with the famous to fill his chit-chat column in *Paper*, Joey Arias channels Billie Holiday. Equal parts send-up and spiritualism, he sings with his own voice and you'd swear that he's lip synching. He's been around the world with his act and is booked well into the new year. Ensconced in a suite at Hollywood's Chateau Marmont on the afternoon of his big gig at Atlas (Mo was rumored to have reserved a large table), he spent a few minutes on the phone to chat with us about his life and Billie's.

RF: Are you looking to doing a lot more bookings like this? Taking the show on the road?
JA: Yeah, the show is on the road. I've been doing this performance for four years, but then it kind of dropped for a bit. I got more back into a pop/dance thing. I'm still into dance (music) because I like dancing. But then all of a sudden, everyone wants Billie again, especially now since I'm doing it in drag. It's becoming more acceptable. People are looking at it as a new art form. It's not all about imitating Judy Garland. Even though I'm channeling the feeling of Billie Holiday, I'm not Billie Holiday. Billie Holiday was and always will be the great legend. I'm just channeling a feeling. And it really is a sensibility that's really magical.

RF: How did the Suzanne Barstch hookup come about?
JA: I was... starving! I had been involved with a management company that was trying to push me as a straight pop artist, which is not really what I'm all about. And I was losing the sensitivity of where I was coming from. And Suzanne had these once a month gigs and she asked if I'd like to carry on with her and I said yeah.

RF: How has response to the show been?
JA: Well, people want to see it! I've performed for Giorgio Armani, I've done it for Thierry Mugler, I've done it for Gaultier, and they love it! I did Carnegie Hall last year.

RF: As Billie?
JA: "Joey Arias Channels Billie Holiday." But I didn't do the visual form. I was pretty much in a straight suit, and worked it that way.

RF: Who showed up for the Carnegie Hall show?
JA: Oh, it was genius. Deee-Lite was there, Deborah Harry, Suzanne Barstch and company, business people, like really straight executives that were blown away. Actually, I was in this beautifully hand-tailored suit, real '30s looking. Not drag. But now it's really focused on a certain look.

RF: Is it different doing Billie as a boy?

Does it feel different to you?

JA: No. To tell you the truth, for me it's the same. I'm almost out of my body when I'm doing this. It's the people that are watching me that are telling me "Oh, hon, you should do it more in drag, this is the way it really works." I'm just taking the cues from my friends. Suzanne Barstch, who has reinvented the meaning of drag and has also made it mainstream, she's like "Darling, I vant you to do drrrrag!" And I'm like, *alright*!

RF: Is there a clear distinction to you between old school and new school drag?

JA: Yeah, definitely. Well, just getting up and miming the record, well...that's the old school. The old school is about imitating. The new drag is about creating a whole new caricature and being who you are. Look at Sister Dimension. She's not imitating Barbara Streisand, she actually is creating something from the universe. Drag has taken on different facets and gone beyond.

RF: What I was struck by when you channel Billie is that visually it is such an uncanny sort of resemblance.

JA: I think it's similar to someone who owns a dog, and they start to look like their dog. I'm doing so much Billie these days, more than ever now. I wasn't expecting that to happen, but it is, actually.

RF: How did your appreciation for Billie start? Was it through the movie, or were you familiar with her as a singer first?

JA: As a child, my parents played jazz and rhythm and blues music. And when I saw the movie *Lady Sings The Blues*, I thought it was a sham. They just took excerpts of her life and made it look really horrible. And her heroin overdoses weren't the really big part of her. She did that for a couple of years of her life. Her thing was more like pot and drinking and cocaine. That was more her story.

RF: I always heard the rumor that she was sleeping with Hazel Scott, the pianist.

JA: Yeah, but we'll never know.

RF: Are you with a live band for this

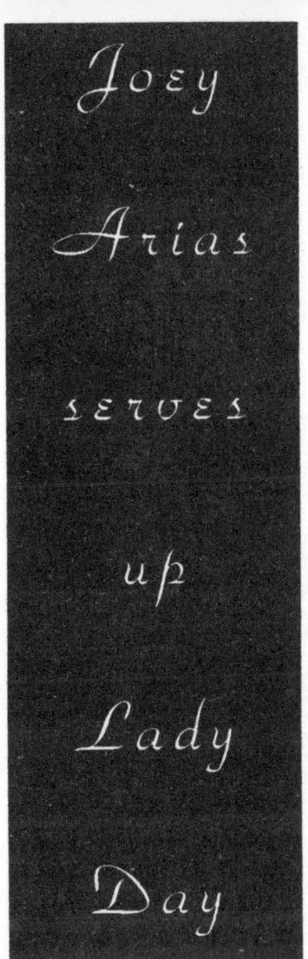

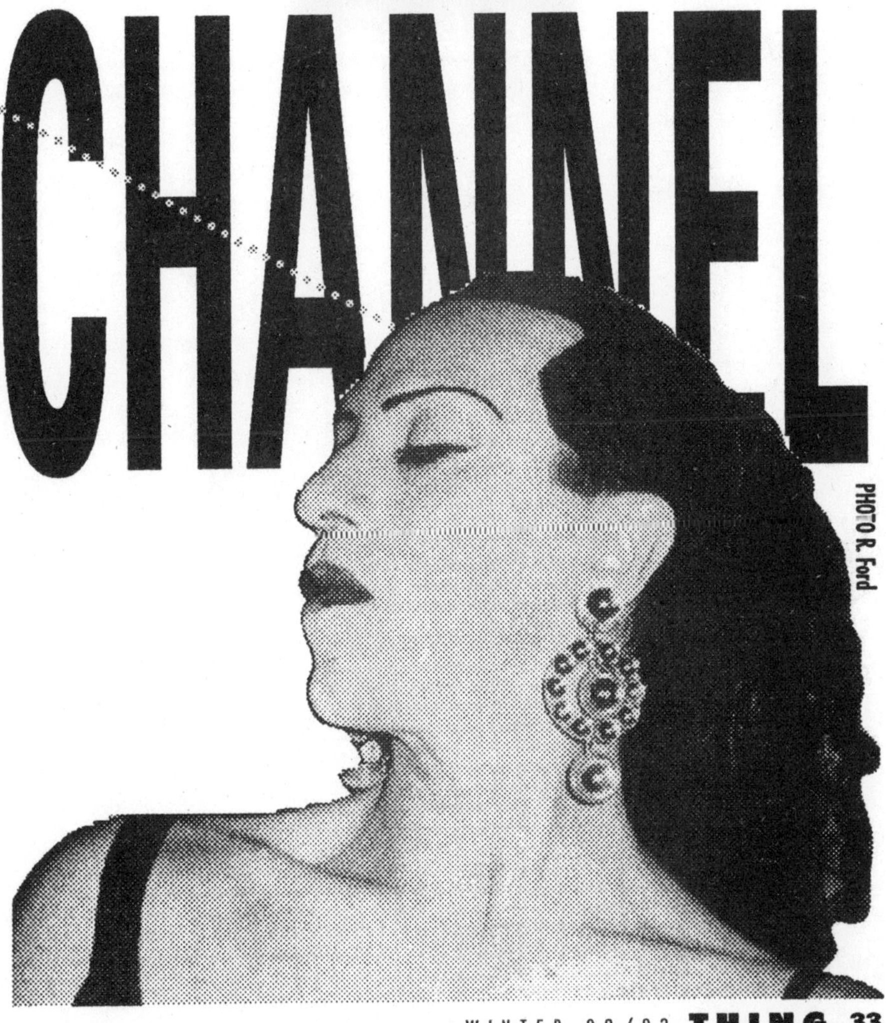

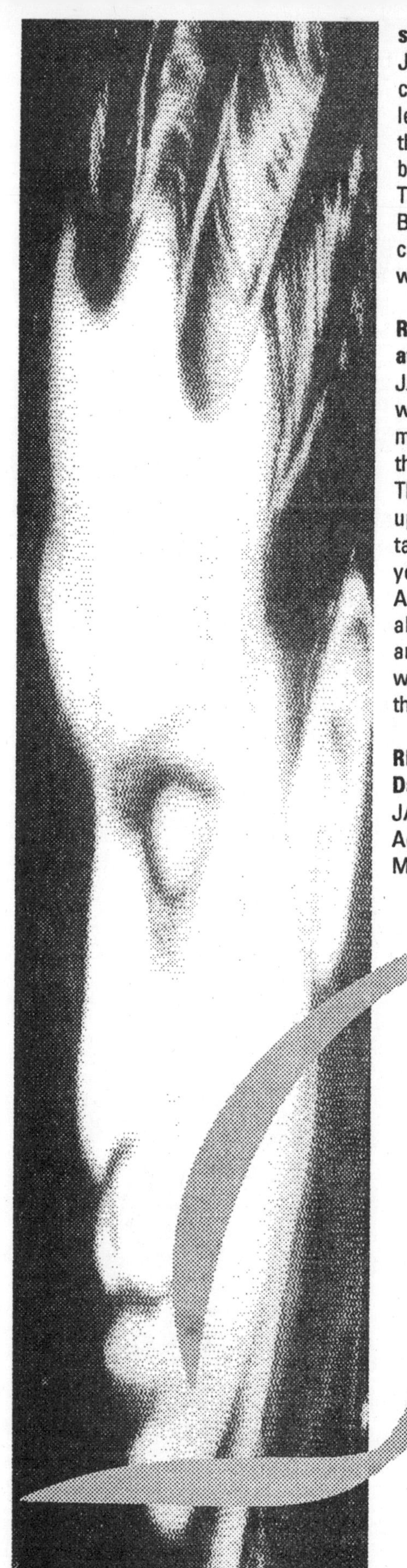

show?

JA: . There are two bands. The east coast band is a bunch of perfect college white guys, these jazz freaks, and then the west coast version has great black guys. It's amazing. They're...beyond hip. Whenever I do Billie, it's always live. Except for this cover of Madonna's Holiday, which I do with a tape.

RF: I saw you do that at the FUCK party at Pyramid before Wigstock.

JA: I was thinking of bringing the tape with me tonight and just blowing their minds. Work bitch, work! She knows the song; when she was doing "Speed-The-Plow" on Broadway we were upstairs in her dressing room and we talked a little bit and she goes, "I know you do my song, and mine's better." And I said it's not about being better, its about who has style. She looked at me and laughed and I'm like [shade]. This will be interesting to see her tonight; this time I'll be performing.

RF: Did you first know her in her Danceteria days?

JA: Oh, yeah. That whole mad scene. Actually I was with this band called Mann Parrish...

RF: I remember them! "Hip-Hop Be-Bop" and all of that.

JA: Yeah that was me.

RF: And the soundtrack to that porno movie "Heatstroke"

JA: Oh, you know all this shit already. I never got credit. Everybody got screwed in the deal.

RF: Are there any musicians around that you'd like to work with?

JA: Let's see...I want to work with a lot of the new jazz musicians. Actually, I think it would be hysterical to work with Harry Connick, Jr.

RF: Oh, he wouldn't have it!

JA: Of course, he wouldn't have it!

RF: From what I understand, he's horribly homophobic.

JA: I think it would be great to blow peoples minds by having that happen. There's so many people to think of who I'd really like to work with.

RF: Do you have a great nostalgia for the 40s and 50s?

JA: Yes, definitely. That's why I'm doin' it, to keep that feeling alive. I heard an interview with Billie and they asked her how she felt about young singers coming up wanting to sound like her and she said "It'd be nice to hear somebody want to be like me." And I thought to myself she probably never thought there'd be a man doing it. When you get reincarnated, you don't have to come back in a lady's body again. You could come back as a flower, whatever.

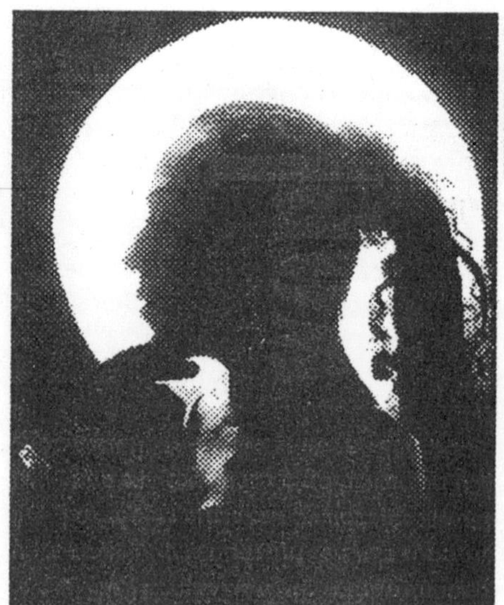

I'm almost out of my body when I'm doing this

LIVIN' LARGE: DORIAN COREY

BY AARON ENIGMA

A: So, what are you doing with yourself these days?

D: Still trying to keep soul and body together, and doing a little part-time work down at Sally's. A few nights a week at the club, that's all I really care to do right now. I like sticking close to home — or running to mad parties like Madonna's.

A: You went to the *Sex* kickoff party?

D: Yes. I was the only drag queen in there — other than a couple that were dancing for entertainment.

A: So give me some dirt!

D: Oh, it was a fabulous party — unlike the papers said. It was quite lovely. Seeing all the celebrities there, like Spike Lee and Naomi Campbell, Ashford and Simpson, Grace Jones.

A: Oooh no!

D: I asked Grace Jones to come back to the club with me after the party was over but she said she was getting back to bed. Her feet were killing her, she had been dancing crazy all night. The life of the party. All of a sudden when I ask her to come somewhere — "I'm tired." I said "Okay, Grace!"
But it was a fab party, very nice. Madonna made a showing around the place for about a ,minute and then disappeared, so I can't tell you what she did the rest of the evening. I've got a feeling that there was a VIP room inside the VIP room.

A: Yeah, they were crackin' me up the other day on the news — Madonna, Madonna, Madonna. "Oh, this book is so shocking"

D: And would you believe they interviewed me for that book! That's when I first met Madonna. But evidently I wasn't quite what she was looking for.

A: So they did an interview and photos, too?

D: Yeah. It was an office full of people. You'd take a photograph, then you'd meet her. She'd ask you questions then say they'd get in touch with you. One of those sort of things. I think in my case, she wanted a drag queen — she'd seen the movie and talked to me about Jenny and everything, but I think when she saw me in person she suddenly realized how much taller I appear in person than on the screen.

A: Oh!

D: On the screen I look lusciously average.

A: You sorta looked on the tall side when I saw you on Phil Donahue.

D: Without the first high heel, I'm 6'1". With heels, 6'4", 6'5", so you see how much I overpowered her.

A: Oh she wasn't going for that!

D: I don't think she could find a photograph compatible.

A: How has the gay community changed since the Stonewall days? Did you play any part in Stonewall at all?

D: Well, contrary to rumor, I was around then but Stonewall was like…I mostly relegated myself to uptown where we were living (I was still working with the live show) and then going out of the city. Stonewall was part of the gay scene in the Village, and I wasn't really down to full-fledged running the clubs then. Stonewall is what they hold up as the first stance for drag queens, but it didn't necessarily have that effect they say it had on Harlem, you see what I mean?

A: Un-huh.

D: It was a whole different area, a different format and climate, so the white children downtown and the black children uptown were going through the exact same thing.

A: So would you say that something equivalent to Stonewall happened at some point?

D: Stonewall was a cataclysmic scene that erupted. Uptown, the police would raid a straight club just as fast as they would raid a gay club. Racial color was more important than whether you sere straight or gay. We were fighting for gay rights in our own way, not on the same level, because we didn't have the same problems.

A: You were fighting more the racial thing.

D: Right. Back in those days, you'd find the drag queens poppin' into any ol' damn club — whether it was straight or gay. You just went where the action and fun was. It wasn't that you were relegated into your own little private set of clubs. The gay clubs didn't come until later. At that time, there weren't any gay clubs in Harlem. Maybe one or two bars, but no big thing. You weren't everywhere.

A: So do you think that the racism or the homophobia has gotten better or worse?

D: I think it's gotten worse, because it got in the open, and once you lay something in the open, everybody's gonna try and step on it. When the closet doors were shut, drag queens, of course, were out there anyways. We never had a closet. Let's face it, when you put a dress on and hit the world, you're declaring what you are.

A: Yeah, you're very visible.

D: So there's no question of coming out of the closet. Now that everything's out… Things are bad, especially here in New York. They're going to come to a head! You can't ram so much change down people's throats without them gagging.

A: Since the drag queens have been the most visible, what do you think about the attitude toward them then and now?

D: It's according to where you go, what

part of New York. Once you get down into midtown the attitudes are different because they've been there so long, they're part of the scene. When you get in the outskirts, you'll have this bash thing and whatnot. You've always had bashing among the drag queens, but it was never an item. They'd just say, "they dressed like that, they deserved it"

A: But most of the drag queens knew how to defend themselves, too.
D: That's right. These children that are supposedly straight looking, they're the ones getting bashed, so now they're protesting. The girls were always getting their asses kicked. It's just a thing of who you are and what you are.

A: You hardly ever hear too much of a drag queen getting beat up — even here— they'll turn into a man in a minute and whup yo' ass.
D: That's cause they're crazy. When one of them gets murdered, because of the lifestyle, that ripples through the community, because we know each other. It doesn't make the papers, it's just an item.

A: What future plans do you have?
D: Oh gee, nothing really special that I know of. Things with me usually just pop up at the drop of a hat. One day I'm doing nothing, and the next I'm booked to go to Las Vegas.

A: So you do work outside of New York?
D: Oh yeah, I'll work anywhere.

A: So, you've done Las Vegas?
D: Yeah, and Boston, Philly, Washington...oh yes, Cleveland (so many times), all over Ohio. I started out touring with a show.

A: You haven't been to Chicago?
D: We never got to Chicago.

A: Oooh I hate it! I mean you did Ohio...
D: I've done Detroit, I've just never gotten to Chicago.

A: In Cleveland what was that crowd like? Cause that's still pretty much in the midwest.

D: That was quite some years ago, about twenty-five. It was midwestern then too, but not really as bad as you think. At that time I was just working with a black review, and therefore I was working black clubs. So when you're working in the black neighborhoods, towns are always hotter. It doesn't matter how seedy, rundown, or country or western a town is. Get to the black neighborhoods and the soul music is poppin' — it's just that way.

A: Anything else lined up for the future?
D: You know my dear sister Pepper Labeija?

A: Yes.
D: Well, Pepper and a fabulous singer from the days of the Jewel Box named Carol are putting together a show in January at the Apollo theater.

A: I heard about that at the Paris ball this year. Pepper was a judge and she made an announcement about it. She was saying how they wanted to show that there's a lot of talent in the gay community. What is the House of Corey doing right now?
D: Barely hanging together — I have the most absentee house in the world. I've got one member in... well, in pretty good standing...in Jersey who's giving an affair in January. Most of the girls in my house are theatrical, so they're out working the clubs.

A: What's going on with the *Paris Is Burning* scandal? I know a lot of people were trying to sue Jenny Livingston.
D: Well, I believe all those lawsuits have evaporated, faded away, or just been given up 'cause I don't know of anyone that's still trying.

A: How do you feel about the movie? Do you feel it was exploitative?
D: No, not really. Everything's exploitation one way or another. The movie was an enlightenment. It really made the balls more famous, it made all those people much more well known. It made them seem more a part of the community. Someone else just had the clever idea to do it.

A: What was your part in Wigstock?
D: I always go to participate — you know, just to make a showing...'cause I

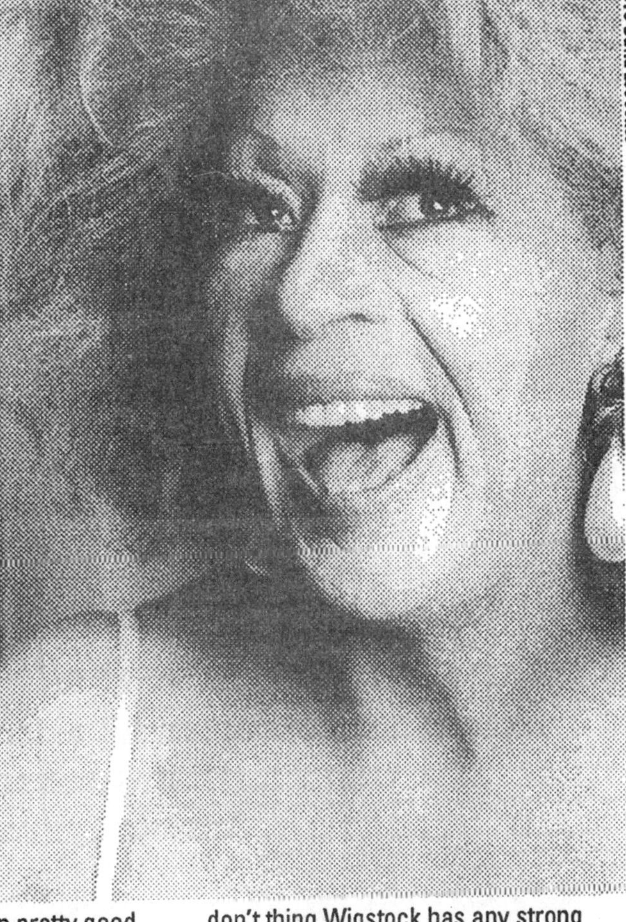

don't thing Wigstock has any strong meaning other than a chance for all these mad people to get together in the park and show their unity. There's no deep dark political thing; I think its more of a case of making yourself known and felt by the rest of the public.

A: Let your hair down.
D: Or up!

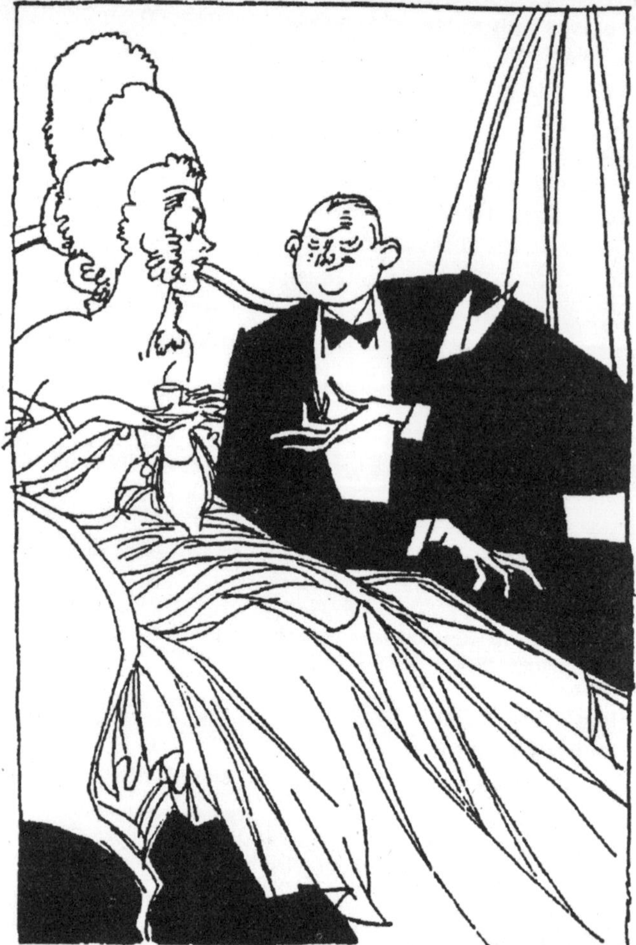

Gigi filled us in about an astounding ritual that goes on in the suburbs. It seems some randy Realtors use display model homes for after hours' queer klatches. Gigi was invited to one by a Saudi salesman and, although he was the star of the show—leaving luxurious skid marks in the breakfast nook—he also managed to take time out to make conversation with an obviously married attendee. Dicksucking Daddy regaled Gigi with tales of life as Good Neighbor Sam, boasting that, in addition to the usual Little League coaching and PTA duties, he also shoveled driveways in the winter months for everyone on his block—except, of course, the homos who lived three bi-levels down.

Did our Gigi waste him with a withering retort? No siree Bob. After all, he was hung like a horse and worked construction—so a girl must hold her

HIV or AIDS CONCERNED?

Chicago Department of Health AIDS Prevention Program offers:

- **Free Counseling and Testing**
- **Confidential Counseling and Testing**
- **Anonomyous Counseling and Testing**

Schedule an appointment at one of eight convenient locations

LAKEVIEW 2861 N. Clark/744-8829

ENGELWOOD 641 W. 63rd/747-0282

NEAR SOUTH SIDE 1306 S. Michigan/747-0103

UPTOWN 845 W. Wilson/744-7533

WEST TOWN 2418 W. Division/744-5464

ROSELAND 200 E. 115th/747-2818

NEAR WEST SIDE 2160 W. Ogden/746-6965

LOWER WEST SIDE 1713 S. Ashland/746-5157

Health Educators and AIDS resources and education also available

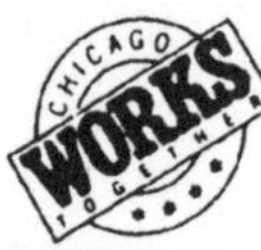

For further information contact:
Office of AIDS Prevention/Chicago Department of Public Health
Room 233, Daley Center, 50 W.Washington, Chicago Illinois 60602 (312) 744-4312

tongue. While we certainly understand the need for casual yet careful sex in this day and age, we were shocked by our friend's reluctance to call a spade a spade...and to allow himself to be thrust into a position far more humiliating than anything he does to get his rocks off. Although, in some ways, Gigi's attitude mimics the behavior of a bitter small-town spinster slut, he will never be accepted as the bitter Malltown homo-spinster slut. He's just your garden variety queer. And he should have recognized he was tossing his tush around on enemy turf.

Which brings us to the latest foray into the land of homosexual self-hatred...the military. Why on earth would any son of Sodom want to be a soldier? If the uniform is the hot button then a job as a bellhop can achieve the same result and you'll be providing a useful service and getting paid for it. But while service to a company has its benefits, service to this country is, at best, misadvised. While this country dislikes little yellow people and little brown people and wants to run roughshod over their world to make it safe for Coca-Cola, it positively HATES homos. Even if you could muster support for such an absurd foreign policy, you would do better to espouse your ignorance in the comfort of your own home because your own domestic policy could get you drummed out of the Marine Corps faster than you could say "Over There", with a capital D for dick-sucking on your permanent record and a complete loss of health benefits, pensions, and other promised perks. (Though they've always been willing to drag any old fruit off the streets in times of national emergency to use as cannon fodder.) Face it fruits, if you are in the services you are a tool of a society that hates you.

A word to the WACS. We suspect most of you diesel dykes enlist for the same reasons that many straight women go to college—to find a mate. Why buy into the male hierarchy of death and destruction when you can do just as well driving a UPS truck? Even in times of limited options, there are options.

This society is in no short supply of heteros willing to defend its genocidal policies in places like Cambodia...and Colorado. It has been a blessing that, even in these jingo- ridden, war-mongering times, no matter how carried away we've gotten with the picturesque distant bloodletting or how many red, white and blue festoons we've flung at our Fourth of July parties, we have not been given entree into Uncle Sam's death squads. And that is just as it should be. Join us in calling for a reaffirmation of the Ban on Buggers in the Barracks. It can only save us from ourselves.

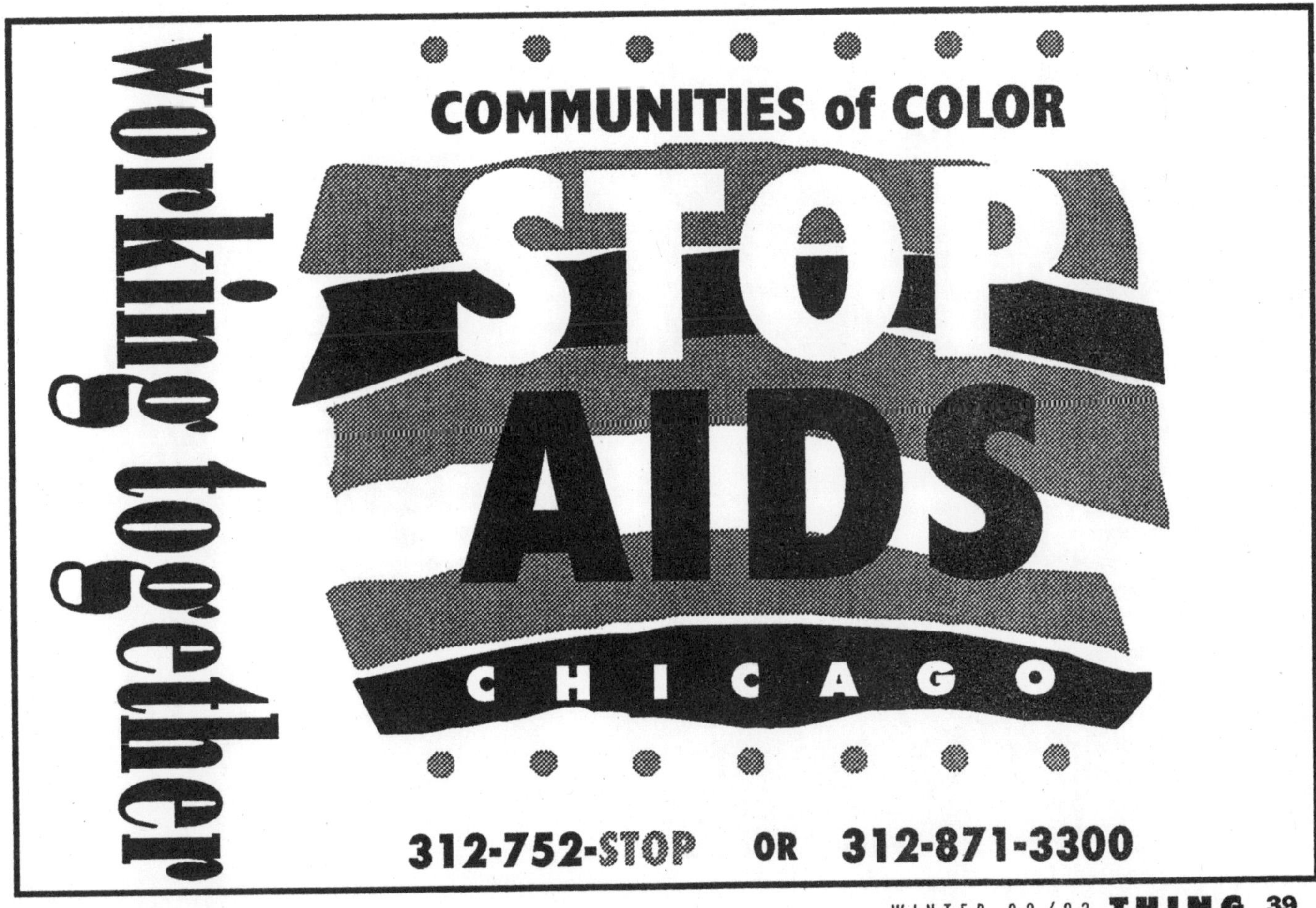

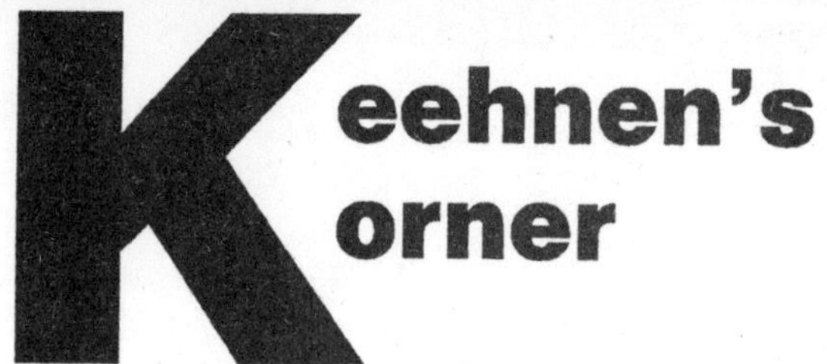Keehnen's Korner

by owen keehnen

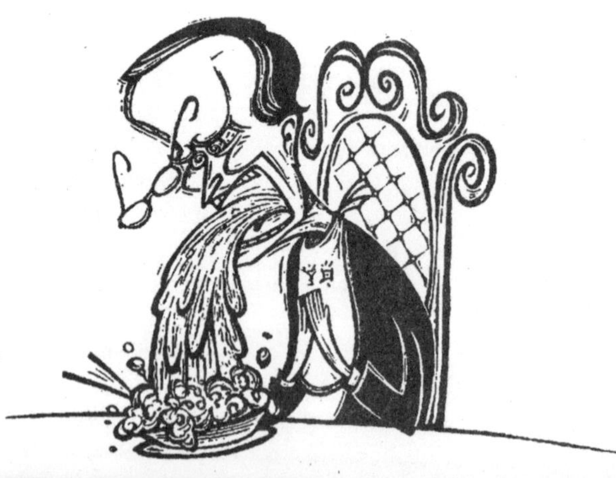

A Peek Inside My George Bush Scrapbook

On January 9, 1992; the day George Bush vomited, puked, barfed, blew-chow, purged the squirrel, tickled the nanny, freed the demon, summoned the earl, and then contorted his already contorted features as he collapsed from the big palace chair at a sumptuous looking state dinner in Tokyo, was also the 79th birthday of shriveled and also-publicly-humiliated former Republican President Richard M. Nixon.

Bush was 67 at the time of his 1/9/92 regurgitation, which would have been 84 candles for feisty feminist Simone de Beauvoir, the exact age as feisty octogenarian Katharine Hepburn at the time of Bush's 'touch of intestinal flu'. Ironically, Hepburn won an Oscar in 1967 for her role in the film 'Guess Who's Coming To Dinner' (not to be confused with 'Guess Who's Coughing Up Dinner'). The film brought Hepburn her second Academy Award and was also the final movie of her wizened, cantankerous, and two-time-Oscar-winning lover Spencer Tracy who died of a heart attack in 1967 at the age of 67. Believe it or barf!

I hate how incredibly boring the Academy Awards can be especially when there is so much potential. Those plastic acceptance speeches are the worst. I wish once someone would get behind the podium at The Dorothy Chandler Pavillion and say something truly startling like, "I hate my kids and my wife is an asshole." Or, "The entire cast and crew of this film, excluding myself, were a bunch of Class-A fuckers." Nielsen ratings would go through the roof if only Meryl Streep held her Oscar triumphantly over her head and shouted, "I had to fuck a lot of people to win this award, so imagine who Sally Field has had to fuck to win twice." I'd like a big scary-haired Cher say something like, "I'm surprised this is my first award. I should have won for both 'Silkwood' and 'Mask'. I wish Jessica Tandy would wrap one of her gnarled hands around the statuette and snarl, "So you pity me because I'm old, do you? Well, Hume and I think you're all full of shit and that's why we avoided Hollywood for years." I want to see Robert Wagner pass-out behind the podium and wake up screaming that he has seen the ghost of his beloved Natalie. I want 'Entertainment Tonight' to speculate on just who is on what drug and I want Leeza Gibbons to cover the event on crack. I want to hear Kevin Costner slur and I want to hear him refer to his wife as his "fuck squaw". I want to see Kim Basinger wander aimlessly about the stage. I want Spike Lee to win the Best Director Oscar but I want someone to tie his hightop shoelaces together the moment before his name is announced and I want his goateed face to fall directly into the crotch of Dina Merrill. I want a hidden microphone to catch the slurp slurp kissing sounds of Jaime Lee Curtis and her girlfriend during a commercial break from Kraft. I want to see Miss Lillian Gish booed from the stage. I want to see Charlton Heston deep throat his 'Ben Hur' statuette while being whipped by two representatives from the accounting firm of Price Waterhouse and I want it accompanied by Liza doing a rap medley. I want the head of Michael Landon to miraculously sprout from the forehead of Amy Irving a moment before she announces the winner for best special effects. I want to see Bob Hope embalmed on stage. I don't want Hollywood Babylon, I want Hollywood Armageddon.

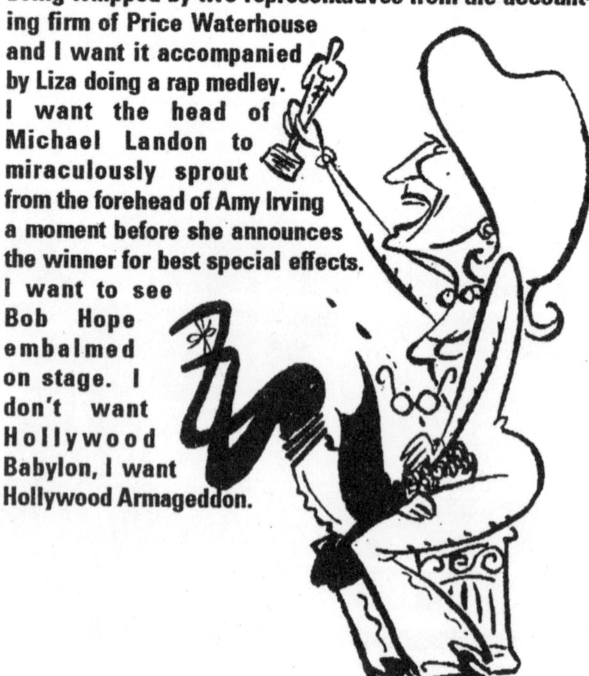

OSCAR WILD!

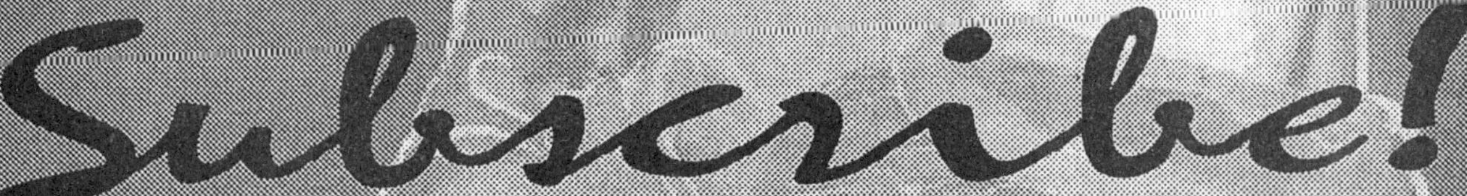

don't
miss
an
issue
of

THING

Subscribe!

□ 1 YEAR (4 ISSUES) $10
□ 2 YEARS (8 ISSUES) $20
□ THING TEE SHIRT $14
(M/XL ONLY)

NAME
ADDRESS
CITY   ST   ZIP

THING
2151 W. DIVISION • CHICAGO IL USA 60622-3056

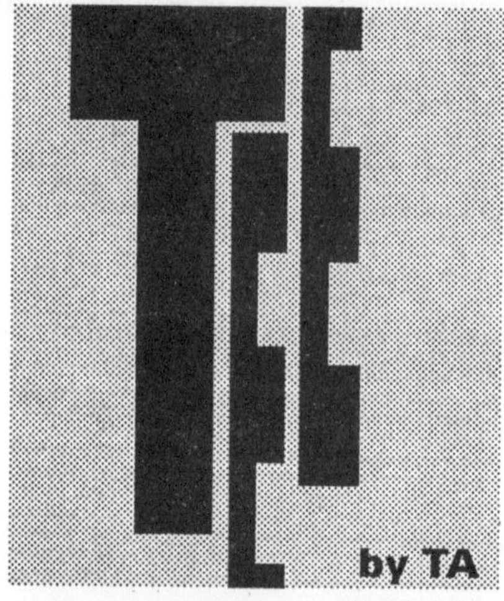

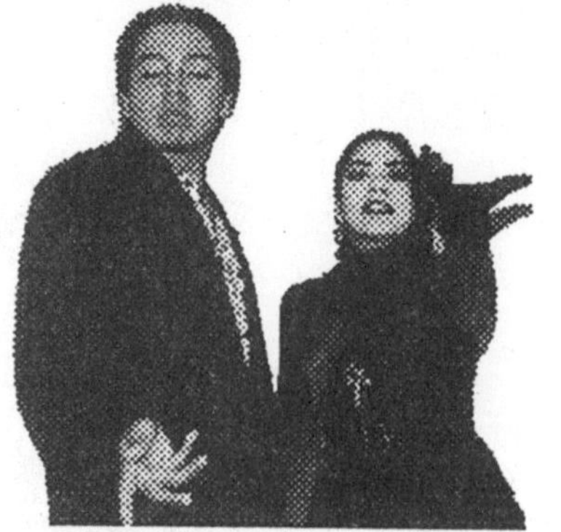

Santa Fé's **Virgil Ortiz** and pal **Dow-Sah** before ...

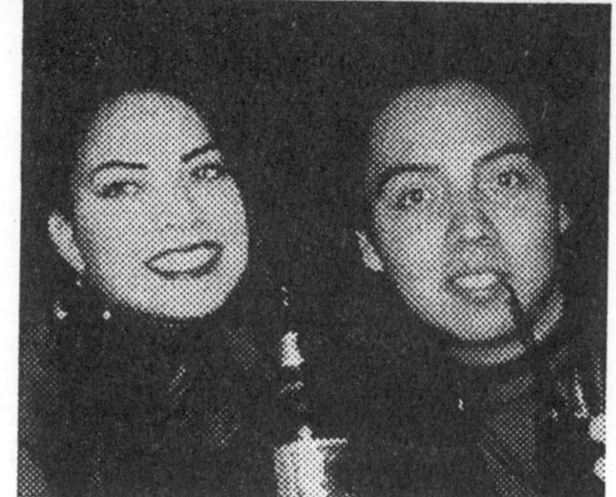

...and later at Quench.

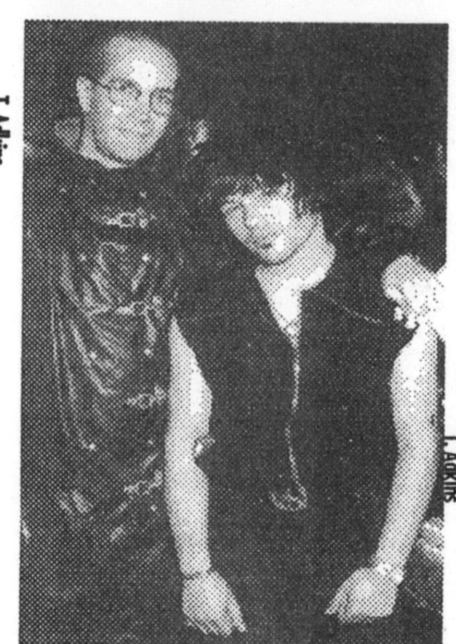

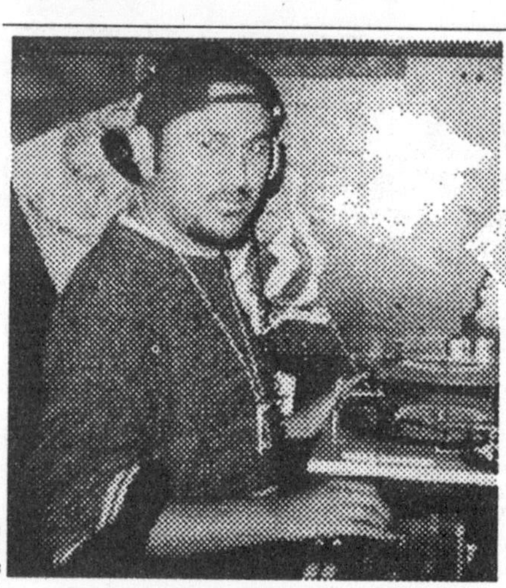

Everybody loves Cheeks' DJ **Pumpkin.**

Dave and **Chino,** The Atomic Kids in the Atomic Playpen at Sunday Night Cairo.

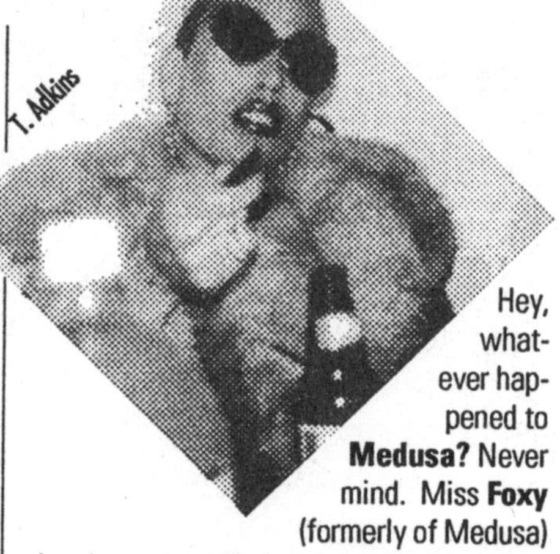

Hey, whatever happened to **Medusa?** Never mind. Miss **Foxy** (formerly of Medusa) has just opened her own namesake club at the old Eons, in a partnership with designer **Tom Hemingway** and their longtime pal **Blue**, also formerly of Medusa.

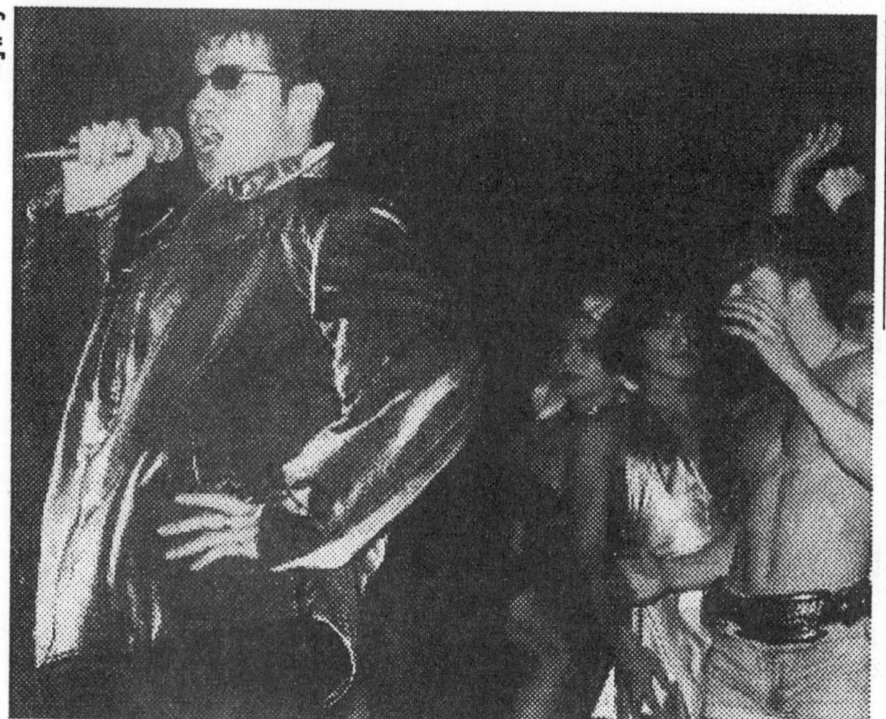

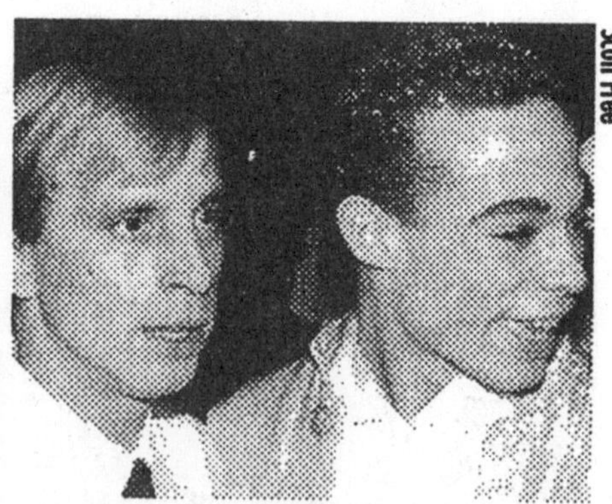

Who would open for **RuPaul** performing at Quench and the following Thursday night at Shelter? Why, our own Mr. **Byrd Bardøt** and DJ/Producer Mr. **Ralphi Rosario**, of course. The release of their new single, "Bardøt Fever" (and it is), is an example of what we're talking about when we say working the club. Here's Byrd on stage giving 'til it hurts during the Quench show, a plethora of club kids on board. Above: **Terry Martin** and **Christian** in the crowd.

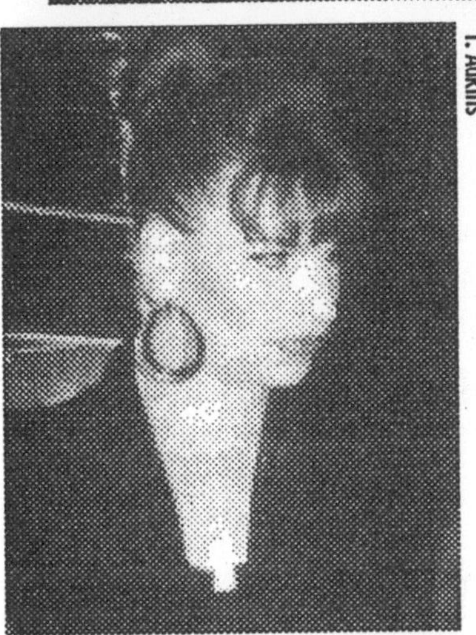

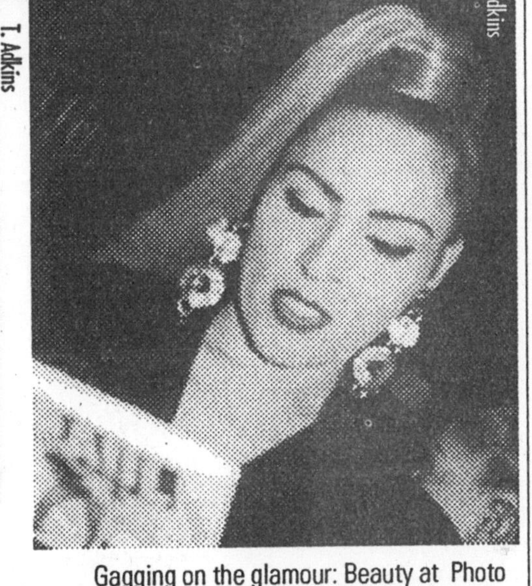

Miss Kitty of Kitty's International and Ellise Venus Amiro at Cheeks for Photo Party One.

The beautiful Misty Diamond at Cheeks.

Gagging on the glamour: Beauty at Photo Party One. P.S. Girl, let us hear from you!

"Well, alright!" The Lady Belle performing at Cheeks takes Patti to a whole new level of ultra glitzy gospelly glamour.

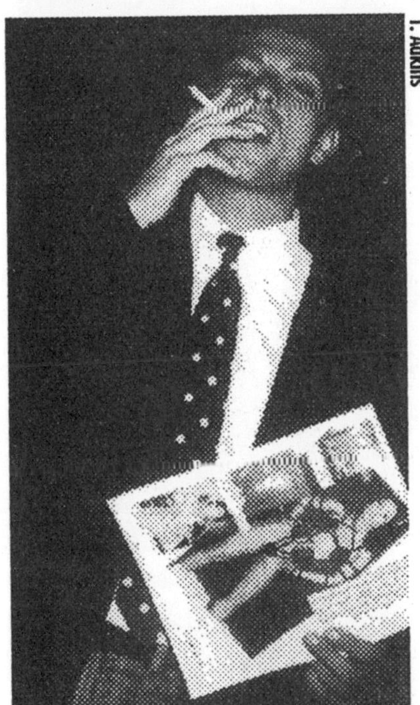

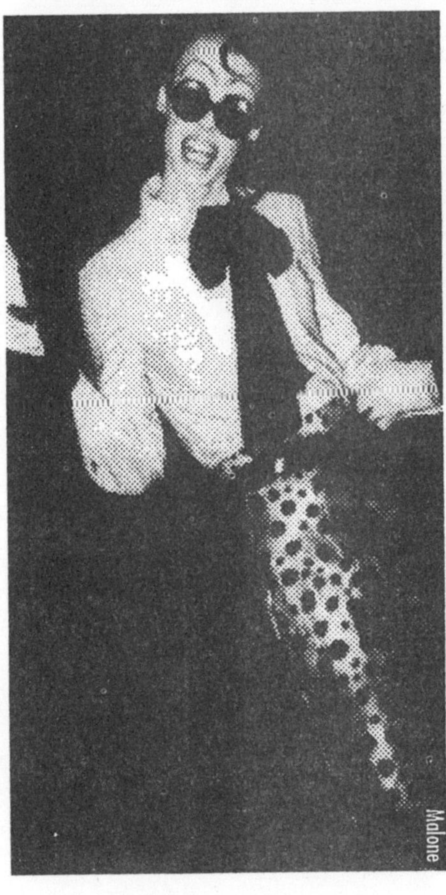

Say Cheese! The recent opening of the new Crobar nightclub was in many ways the same 'ol idea of downtown industrial. Some special attendees made it fun. Debonair Duffen (above) and (right) new club kid on the block, the amazing T. J. Mozerella.

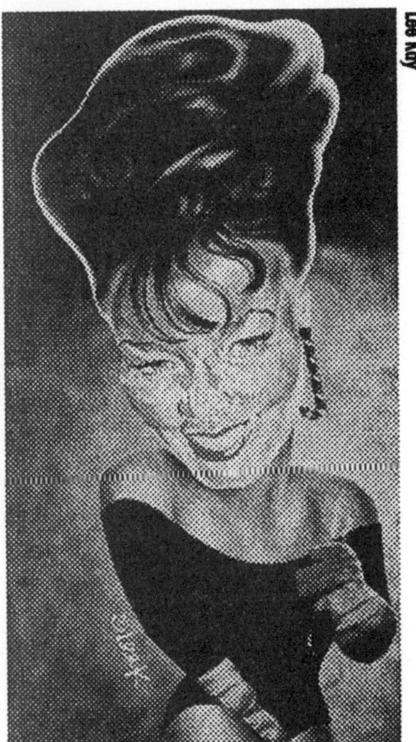

"Ain't she sweet?!" Look who was the recent subject of yet another queer underground Lee Kay bubblehead por-trit: singer Candy J, aka Sweet Pussy Pauline.

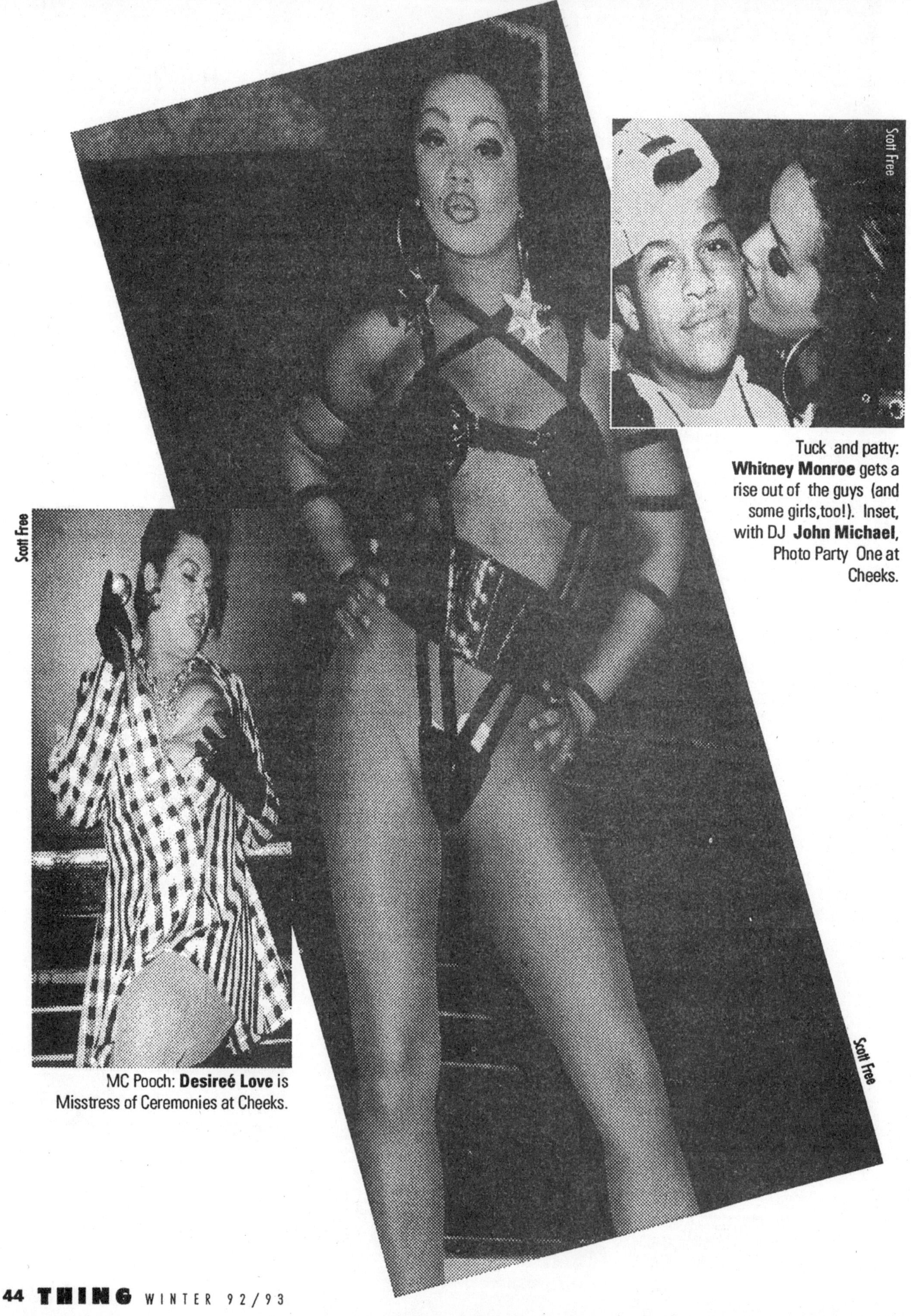

Tuck and patty: **Whitney Monroe** gets a rise out of the guys (and some girls,too!). Inset, with DJ **John Michael**, Photo Party One at Cheeks.

MC Pooch: **Desireé Love** is Misstress of Ceremonies at Cheeks.

DeAUNDRA'S DIXIE DIARY

Hey Y'all. Wow, has we been hoppin' down here in Atlanta, y'all! I has been goin' to all sorts a holiday trailer parties an' bake offs an' vienner pulls—eatin' myself into a state I'm scared I'm gonna take to a seize! Don't tell nobody this, but I had to go to **Maxine Odum**'s the other day so she could spray on some of that fabric stretcher stuff to make my dress fit!

Y'all, things is really goin' nuts at Popcorn, the weekly party at our downtown Atlanta club called Velvet. **Mr. Chuck**, "the host with the most" keeps bringin' 'em in. **Miss Scyntilla Vortex** had a dynamite hi-fashion show there recently that sent all a us gaggin' an' tellin' him that I need Miss Scyntilla to design a whole new wardrobe for my "DeAundra With a 'D'" World Tour that we got planned comin' up soon.

Talented Atlanta performance artist **Terrence Jackson** wowed everybody at the 800 East Performance & Art Emporium with his piece called "The Recognition Scene." It's all about this child who finds himself, an' calls everybody else onto the shag carpet so they can find theyselves too. Talk about powerful, Mr. Jackson sure does a good job makin' people think about what it's like bein' black an' gay an' feelin' some kinda outcastness. I bet there's a bunch a y'all done felt that same way sometimes!

Ever since his birthday done come with the release of his CD single "Supermodel" on Tommy Boy Records, **Mr. RuPaul Charles** is busier than **Duffy Odum** with a case a vienners! He has done been to Boston, Chicago (where I heard he done *worked*), Los Angeles, an' the moon! **Mr. Floyd Martin** with ACT-UP called me the other day sayin' he saw RuPaul on the BET Network breakin' some ground and sashayin' right to the top of the charts! An' look out for them kids on MTV's "Grind" show wettin' they's lips over the video, too. Even "Entertainment Tonight" is gettin' into the act by playin' the B side, "House of Love", durin' their hi-fashion segments.

Team Odum's Update: Ever since **Candi Suntop** sprained her thumb tryin' to get vienner cans open two at a time durin' the competition with Team Del Vista Ray Mar, things has done been in a slump. For example, last week we was havin' the Security Ditch Jumpathon, an' **Bud "Beebo" Lowery** slipped on the grease drain ramp from the back of Rango Frain's Snack Shed an' had to quit on account a cause them judges thought he was tryin' to cheat by slidin' under the finish ribbon.

Everybody down at Odum's would like to welcome **President Bill Clinton** to the White House! Bein' sixteen an' all, I ain't old enough to vote yet, but we did have a Look-A-Like contest at the Community Room an' I voted in that for my sorry sister **Sultra** on account a she wore her hair just like **Miss Hillary** does.

Y'all, another portrait a me has just surfaced again, it's by **Miss Quinn**, a leather jacket wearin' lesbian who can really draw! This one was a part a the float by our weekly gay paper *Southern Voice* that I rode on in the 1992 Lesbian & Gay Pride Parade last summer! Them Voicers had been holdin' on to the 8'x5' thing ever since then, an' **Lake Clare Parker Butler** got her road crew to tow it down to Odum's so's we can use it on my TV show set as a stand-in!

At Odum's we always celebrate the holidays with a special recipe my MeeMaw makes every year, an' here it is so y'all can enjoy it too!

Holiday Vienner Popcorn Balls

Ingredients
1 Quart Hy-Grade Corn Syrup Lite
3 Cans Hy-Grade Vienners, drained
3 Packs Hy-Grade Popcorn
   (Microwave style)
2 Mini-tubs Country Crock Churn Style
   (Lite)
1 Pack Food Coloring
   (Imitation Style)
1 Ball of String

How to Make It
Pour your corn syrup lite in a pan an' boil it up good, reduce to a simmer. In the microwave, pop all a the popcorn an' then add that to the simmerin' syrup. Quick-like, before that cools, add the vienners (chopped into bite-sized bits) and the tubs of Country Crock Churn Style an' mix well. Pour in food colorin' of your choice, or mix 'em for a real special holiday treat. Mash one end of a piece of string into a balled up mess a' this, an' hang it on your tree or from your stove!

BY DEAUNDRA PEEK

The portraits of New York photographer **LEN PRINCE** often grace the pages of *Paper*. Above: Len's photo of a Holiday-inspired Debi Mazar.

OWEN KEEHNEN is a Chicagoan with a quick wit and unusual sense of humor. He writes for zines he likes in his spare time, and is a frequent contributor to *Holy Titclamps* and *Spew*.

CHARLES TILLMAN lives in Brooklyn, where he runs Ginger Snaps Photos, specializing in "hot, fierce, African-American male photography."

ROY GONSALVES is the founder of the *Pyramid Periodical*, and part of New York's black and gay writing collective Other Countries.

We asked photographer Mark Contratto to shoot Dorian Corey to accompany the interview in this issue; he had been recommended to us by Tommy Boy's art director Erwin Gorostiza, for whom he shot RuPaul (he even has a cameo in the video). As it turned out, Mark was too busy with the likes of Marky Mark and Neneh Cherry to fit it in. But rather than boofing us, he graciously

sent his assistant **DAVID LEE JONES** to get the shots we needed. Thanks, guys!

A former Chicagoan and early Thing supporter and contributor, **TODD ROULETTE** now resides in New York. His writings have appeared in *Paper*, *Fad*, and the now defunct *QW*. Todd has just been named art editor of the Los Angeles based *BLK* magazine.

"Yummy" **CHUCK GONZALES**' bio has already appeared in *Thing* (issue #6), but this seemed like a good place to drop a blurb about his new contract with Chicago-based gay greeting card house Through Our Eyes. They've hired Chuck, Will Northerner, and Dwight Okita among others to develop new cards. Look for them in a queer store near you in 1993.

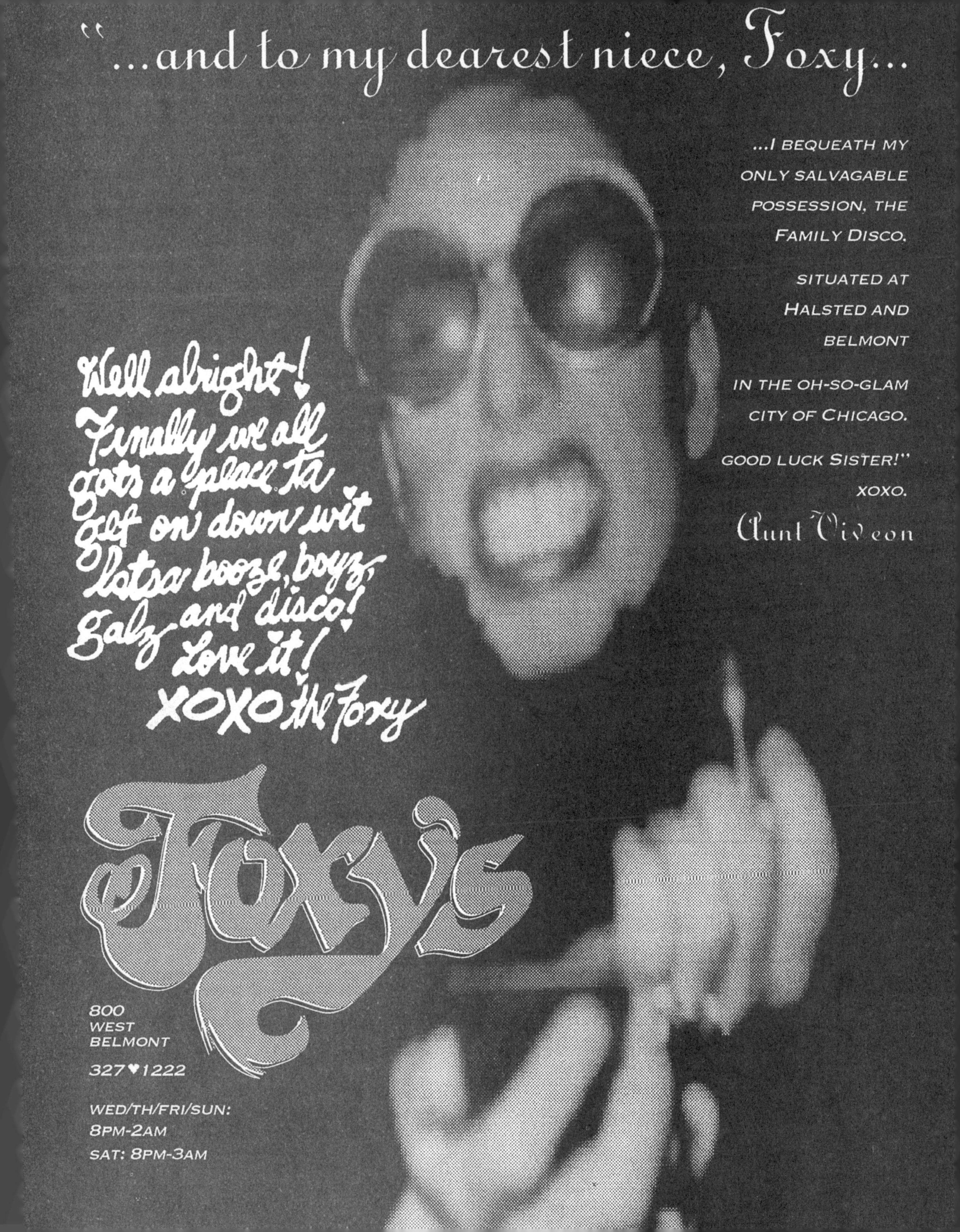

"...and to my dearest niece, Foxy...

...I BEQUEATH MY ONLY SALVAGABLE POSSESSION, THE FAMILY DISCO.

SITUATED AT HALSTED AND BELMONT

IN THE OH-SO-GLAM CITY OF CHICAGO.

GOOD LUCK SISTER!"

XOXO.

Aunt Vixeon

Well alright! Finally we all gots a place ta get on down wit lotsa booze, boyz, galz, and disco! Love it! XOXO the Foxy

Foxy's

800 WEST BELMONT

327♥1222

WED/TH/FRI/SUN: 8PM-2AM

SAT: 8PM-3AM

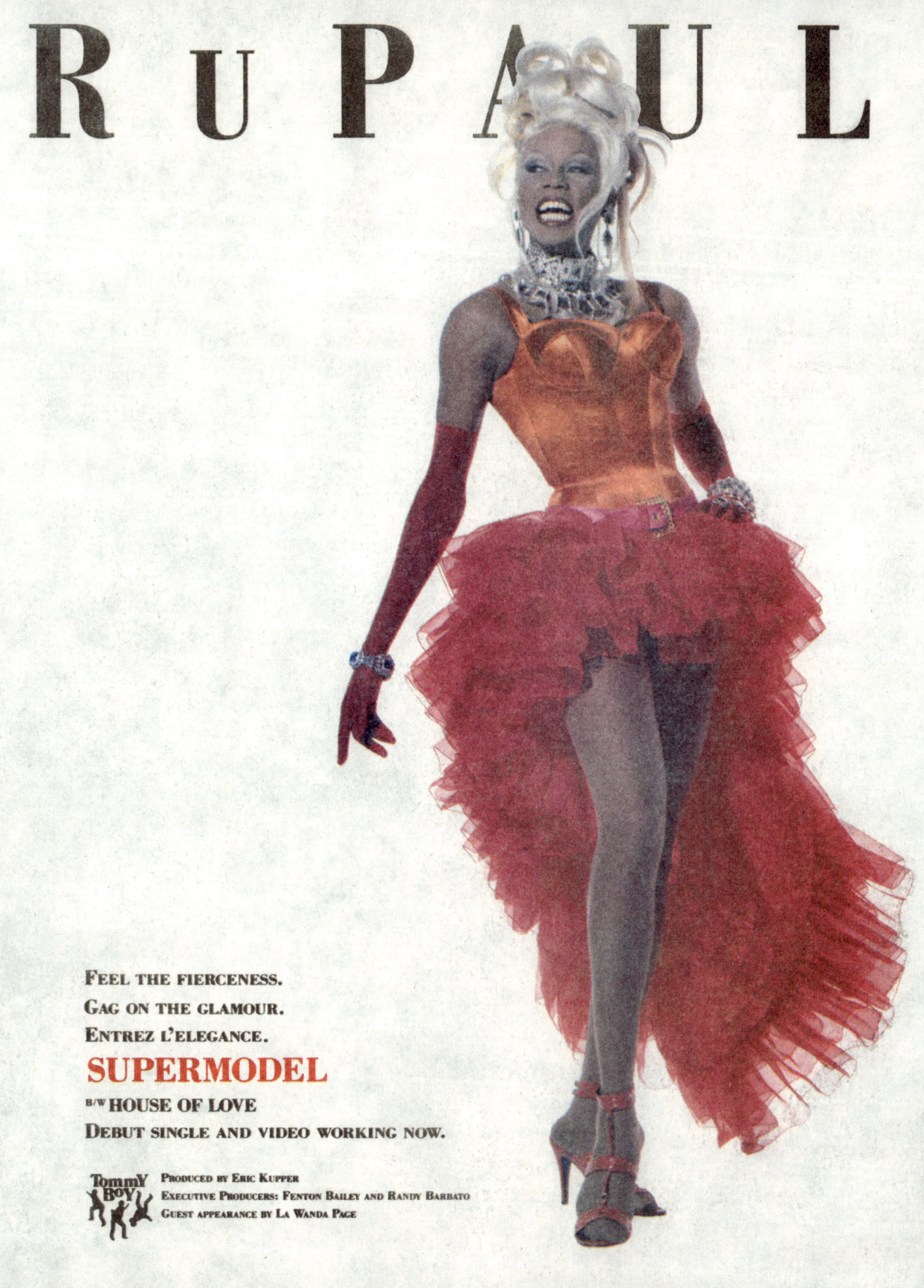

RuPAUL

FEEL THE FIERCENESS.
GAG ON THE GLAMOUR.
ENTREZ L'ELEGANCE.
SUPERMODEL
B/W HOUSE OF LOVE
DEBUT SINGLE AND VIDEO WORKING NOW.

TommY BOY

PRODUCED BY ERIC KUPPER
EXECUTIVE PRODUCERS: FENTON BAILEY AND RANDY BARBATO
GUEST APPEARANCE BY LA WANDA PAGE

THING

SPRING 93

NUMBER 9 • $3

GO
girls!

MARTHA
WASH

THE
FABULOUS
POP
TARTS

MISS
CANDY J

the
Beloved

conscience

FEATURING
"SWEET HARMONY"
"CELEBRATE YOUR LIFE"
"1000 YEARS FROM TODAY"
AND "OUTERSPACE
GIRL"

PRODUCED BY: JON & HELENA MARSH
MANAGEMENT: PEACE BISCUIT,
NYC & CMO, LONDON

THE
ATLANTIC
GROUP
© 1993 ATLANTIC RECORDING CORP. A TIME WARNER COMPANY

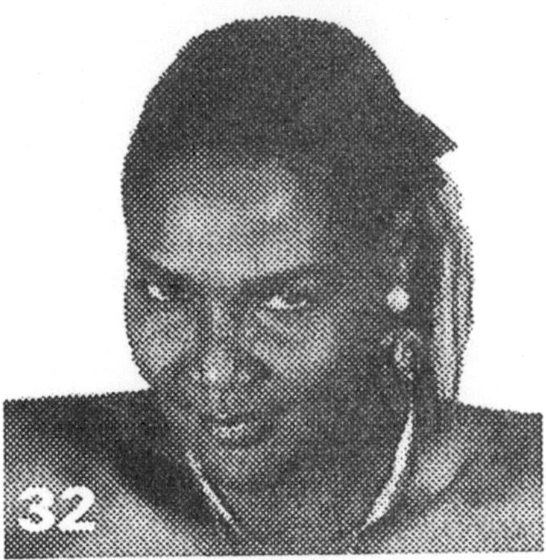

32

28

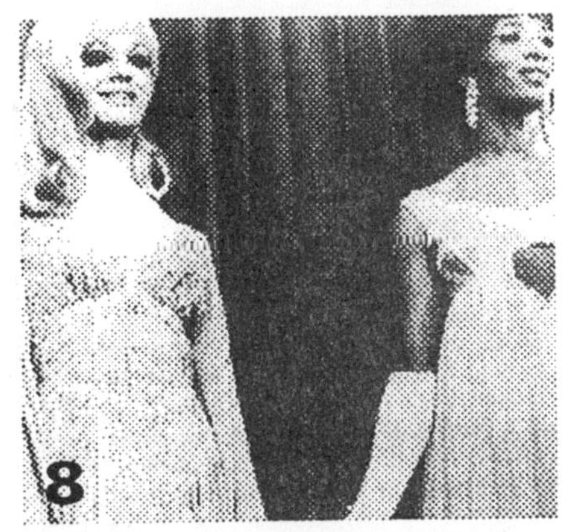

8

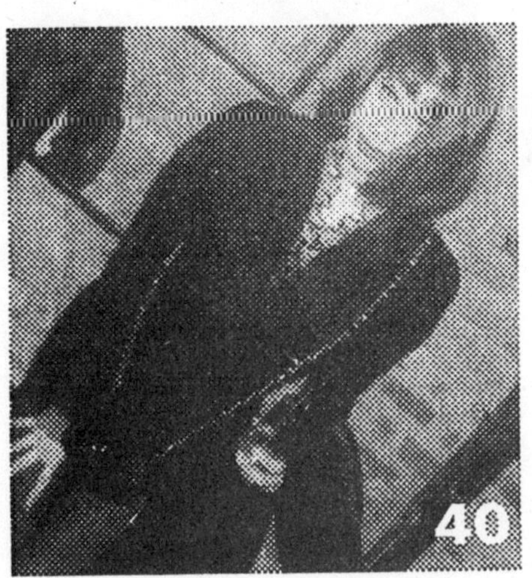

40

THING

SHE KNOWS WHO SHE IS • SPRING 93

contents

ON THE COVER Martha Wash photographed by Dan DuVerney. Makeup: Marcus Geeter.

TOP TO BOTTOM: Candy J/ Scott Free, Pop Tarts logo/Michael Economy, *The Queen*/Courtesy Lewis Allen, Lisa Patterson/T. Adkins.

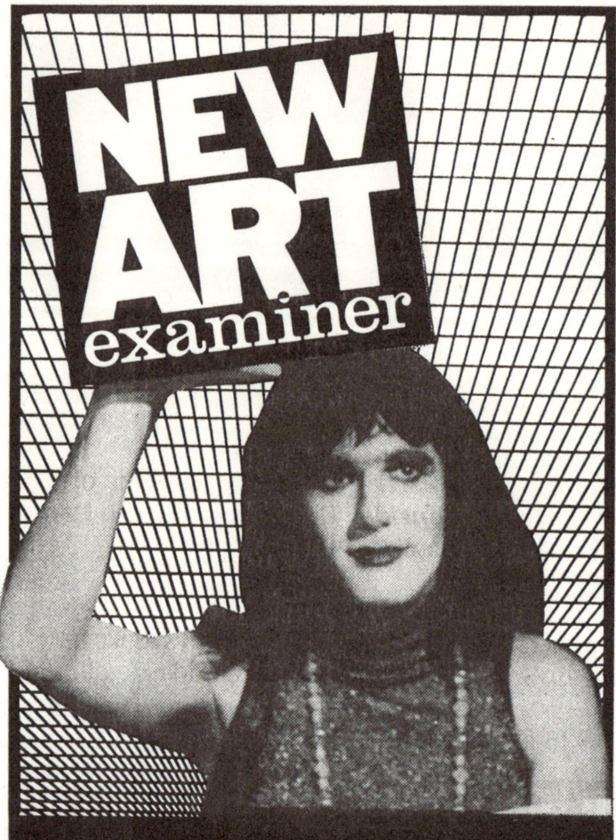

"Another weakness of American art magazines is a related subsevience to special interest groups, notably feminsts, militant blacks and homo-sexuals. *New Art Examiner*, for instance, one of the more radical of the magazines I examined, seems to make a point of giving space to extremists."

—Paul Johnson, *Modern Painters*, Volume 2, no. 2 (Summer 1989), pp. 127-128

NEW ART EXAMINER
The Independent Voice of the Visual Arts

One Year (10 issues) $35

Send check or money order to:
New Art Examiner
1255 South Wabash 4th Floor Chicago, Illinois 60605

THING

She Knows Who She Is

NUMBER NINE • SPRING 93

PUBLISHER/ART DIRECTION
Robert Ford
CONTRIBUTING EDITORS
Trent Adkins, Terry Martin, Dan Wang, LeRoy Whitfield
ADVERTISING
Matt Armendariz, Terry Martin, Sylvia Michaels, Jeffrey Overas
EDITORIAL ASSISTANCE
Duane Baskins, Omie Daniels, Steve Lafreniere, Dan Robinson
GRAPHIC SERVICES
Simone Bouyer

THING (ISSN 1064-9727) is published quarterly by Thing Publishing. Opinions expressed are those of individual contributors and do not always reflect those of Thing Publishing.
© 1993 THING

THING PUBLISHING

2151 W. DIVISION
CHICAGO, ILLINOIS USA 60622-3056
VOICE (312) 227-1780
FAX (312) 227-1789

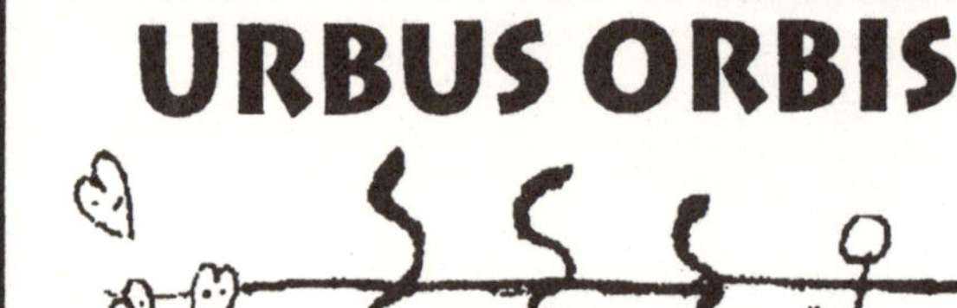

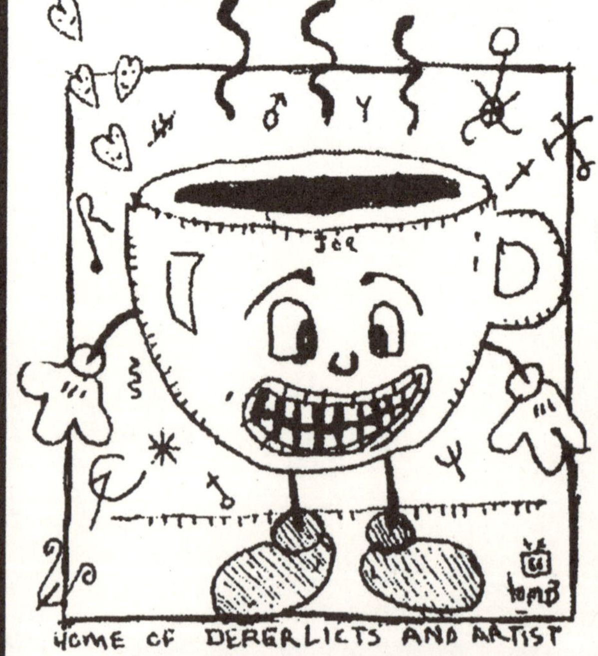

COFFEEHOUSE • BOOKSTORE
1934 WEST NORTH AVENUE
CHICAGO 312.252.4446

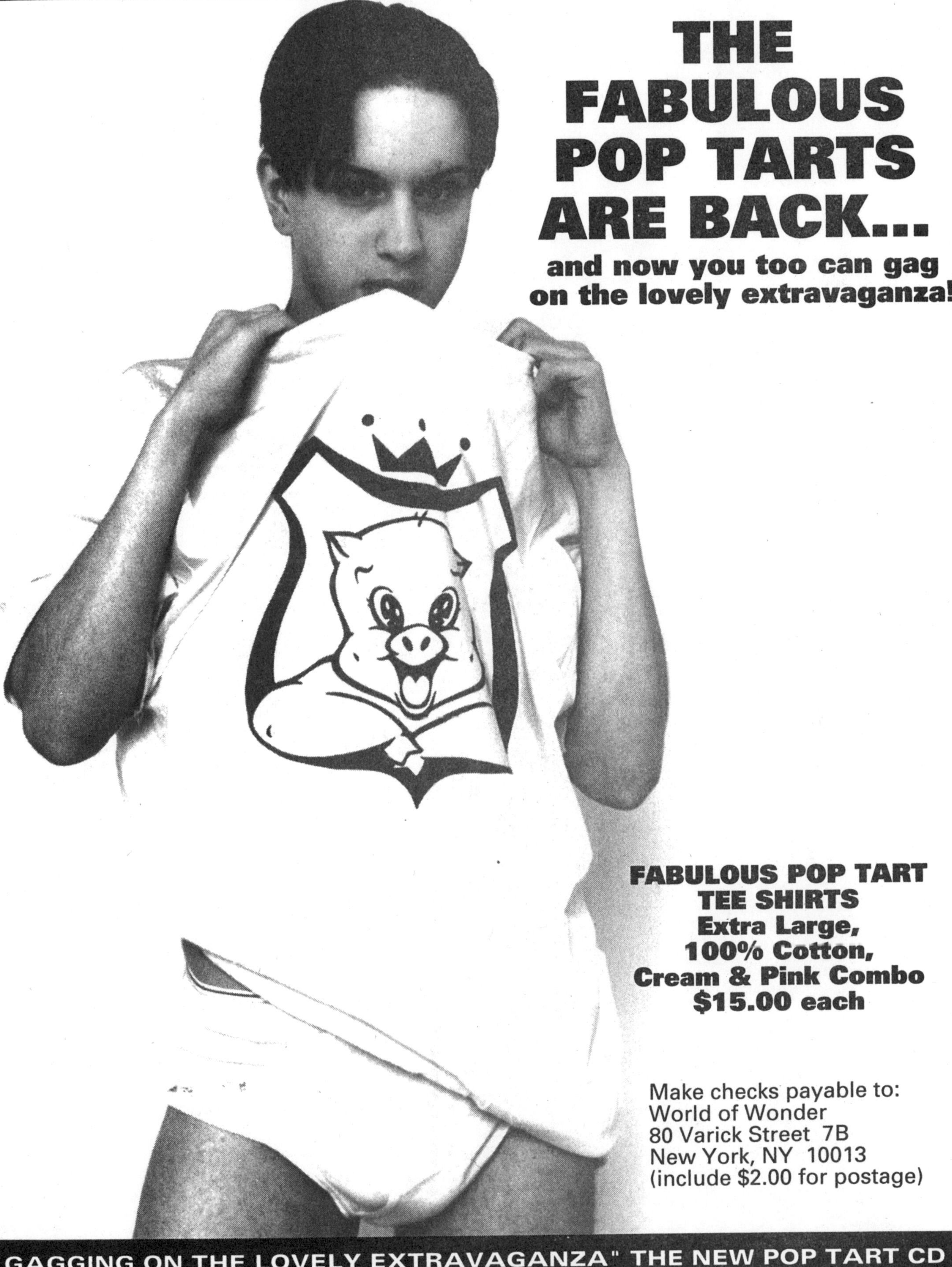

THE
FABULOUS
POP TARTS
ARE BACK...
and now you too can gag
on the lovely extravaganza!

FABULOUS POP TART
TEE SHIRTS
Extra Large,
100% Cotton,
Cream & Pink Combo
$15.00 each

Make checks payable to:
World of Wonder
80 Varick Street 7B
New York, NY 10013
(include $2.00 for postage)

"GAGGING ON THE LOVELY EXTRAVAGANZA" THE NEW POP TART CD
COMING SOON TO A RECORD STORE NEAR YOU

every THING to GO!

Consider This
Various Artists

(Pow Wow)

Consider This, the new compilation from New York's Pow Wow Records, is very refreshing not just for its sickening mixes of knockout dance cuts but for its brilliance in marketing as well. This is a compilation that will set well with professional DJs, House enthusiasts and even the general record buying public. It's pure genius to release these gems as long-playing record, CD, cassette, and 12-inch singles. This way, you get to actually play with the tunes and enjoy them to the utmost. Examining the CD, I was alarmed to see that one track, "I'll Be There" by 2 Intense, was not on the vinyl LP. And neither was "Change for the Better" by Love Tempo. "Oh, well," I thought, "here we go again with some of the best songs on the CD not available on vinyl so you can't mix them!" And whadda ya know...there's a 12-inch of "I'll Be There"! Go crazy with Basscut's "Woman in the Shadows"; trés bumpy bass and jazzé as all get-out. Elisa Burchette's soulful wailing and scatting sounds lovely. "I Believe In You", with vocalist Dee Dee Brave's odd Crystal Waters-esque warblings, thumps and bumps through some of the best changes and breaks. Monster mixer and producer Roger S. is killin' 'em with "I Can Feel It" by Tripp. But, of course, the new hit on this collection that *everybody* loves is "Breathless", Ultrabase's smooth and easy up-tempo Acid Jazz stylee that features producer Marcus Sherard's and Ananda's spacey whispers and chirps. Great horns and strings mix with fabulous percussion here. Producer and Pow Wow hooker-upper Bill Coleman even makes an appearance, co-producing with Pal Joey on the bumpy runway flavored hit "No Guilt". With the bouncy funk that this one renders, it's no surprise to find it co-written by Ultra Naté and J. Longo and co-engineered by the Basement Boys. All selections are dance gold. Thanks Bill.

— Trent Adkins

INSET One of the sexy graphics from *Consider This*

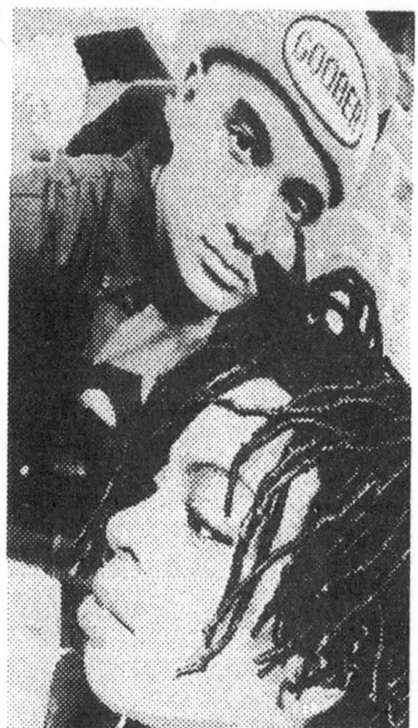

LEARN IT: Uncanny Alliance's Brimsley Evans and E.V. Miss Teak

Latest in a long line of whack disco tunes that owe much of their quirky personality to black fag slang is Uncanny Alliance's dance-floor hit "I Got My Education." A more venomous take on Crystal Waters' "Gypsy Woman (She's Homeless)," it's really a sly commentary on privileged folks who are impatient with the inability of the disadvantaged to somehow "get it together." And it's truly funny; the over-the-top rhymes about Miss Thing who had to pawn her

(photo credit: Annalisa Pessin*)*

uncanny disco
UNCANNY ALLIANCE serves the children a real education

diamond ring 'cause Burger King wasn't hiring are given flawless diva deadpan by vocalist E.V. Miss Teak's knowing delivery. She met fellow Queens borough resident Brimsley Evans at Manhattan's legendary Paradise Garage, grooving to the vibes of the late Larry Levan. A few years later, they decided to team up musically and formed their uncanny alliance, creating something that producer/lyricist/writer/vocalist Evans describes as "retro-nouveau-banjie-funk." Their first project, "I Got My Education," made it onto the dance floor first by way of cassette tapes given to influential New York jocks like David Depino, Junior Vasquez, Frankie Knuckles, and David Morales. Demand for the instantly hummable tune caused a bootleg version to make it to vinyl before theirs did. Their response: to do an even fiercer "bootleggers response" version complete with extended a capella intro featuring Miss Teak reading the culprits. *This is the real thing, bitch!* The entire Uncanny saga was snapped up by A&M records, who commissioned remixes by Mark Kitchen and Masters at Work and issued both a commercial 12" and a DJ-only double 12" with extra mixes. Chances are if A&M moves a lot of the single, an album won't be too far off. It'll be fun to hear Miss Teak and Brimsley let loose with some more fresh ideas.

— Robert Ford

FROM

frankie

Don't bother figuring out the bloody dripping head on the flyer, but Frankie was back in town, playing the Riv for valentine's day, and we were on the guest list (courtesy Maurice Joshua). The sound system was up and running by 10:30, and by around10:45 DJ Terry Hunter had the crowd itching to dance— with only 3 hours to party, you'd imagine that girls would have hit the floor sooner. But no! And the sound system had yet to be fine tuned, so everyone stood around checking out the outfits until 11:15. The crowd was almost all black, but beyond that there was every type imaginable: plenty of beautiful women with their male dates in tow, well-coiffed and attired in all shapes and sizes— little crocheted tops, big flower prints, Karl Kani caps and leather trenchcoats; very little attitude, and many smiling with a look of genuine joy; young DJ/producer-types in homeboy drag, looking serious and talking in the bathroom about their latest project (not yet to be heard for several weeks); and a small but noticeable number of queens and gay boys— lithe, muscle-bound, silk-shirted, Latin-swishing and cowboy-hatted— who had come to show their loyalty and mark their presence.

Things began really taking off as the Maurice mix of Miss Wash slowed down to a reggae beat. Terry Hunter took a bow at 11:30 or so, and Frankie came on amidst cheers; this was another homecoming, done before but no less sincere, and everyone was there to enjoy the music. The first hour heated up with Salsoul Orchestra's "You're Just the Right Size", Ashford and Simpson's "Found a Cure", and the rhythms of David Josephs' "You Can't Hide", which, in the flash of one of those uh-oh-it's-time-to-cut-a-rug-y'all mix moments, turned into Dajae (instant one-hit-wonder-to-be?) belting Cajmere's new anthem: "I'm feeling so blue, oooh oooh ooh ooooooh..." The floor indeed brightened up, and Frankie followed with a slew of recent tunes such as Trey Lorenz's "Photograph of Mary", Debbie Gibson's "Losin' Myself",Whitney's cover of Chaka, Karen Pollock's "You Can't Touch Me" and Rheji Burrell's "Dance Lessons"; and before we knew it, Celine Dion was moving mountains and at least a couple of straight boys off the floor. (Says Trent: "you came all the way from New York just to play that?") Alas, for a fleeting moment, the tiny mirrored ball hanging half-way from the ceiling fulfilled its prophecy.

But it wasn't about canned vocals for all too long, and the mix became suddenly touching and magical again as, between the bass and the kick, we began hearing that famous falsetto: "I wanna rock with you, all night...." And it was understood that Frankie was offering a prayer for great suffering Michael, born only miles away from where we were all dancing; for even after witnessing La Jackson bare his poor, sick soul (not to mention his pigmentation disorder) to over a 100 million people this week, who'd forget the beautiful songs that he's given us?

By the time Alicia Meyers' "I Want To Thank You" came on, it was a regular church session in the corner. Did the bass blow out for a minute or two? It didn't matter, since die-hard club goers such as Ephram Walls knew all the lyrics anyhow and more than made up for the sound system's deficiencies. The straight boys of course were not singing along, but thank God some queen was.

At 1:45, as George Benson crooned what seemed like the eighth chorus over of "Give Me the Night", I looked up at Frankie's unique silhouette, the same face we've seen so many times looking down at the turntables, reading the grooves on the records— always so calm, in control, and so strangely *contemplative*. And before we knew it, everyone was clapping. Robert's earlier suggestion about a house opera seemed suddenly appropriate: we had imagined a sort of West Side Story with Liz Torres as Maria and Shep Pettibone as Tony, but if Frankie ever made a house drama, he'd have to get the Gandhi treatment.

— Daniel Wang

GANT JOHNSON
- Poop/Supper Club, (NYC)
- **Butch Quick** Higher (Strictly Rhythm)
- **Romeanthony** Falling From Grace (Azuli)
- **Alex Hope & Blaze** Saturdays (Easy Street)
- **Whirlpool feat. MT** Fly High (5th & Madison)
- **Monie Love** Born 2 B.R.E.E.D. (Macintosh & Hurley RXs) (WB)
- **Ru Paul** Supermodel (RXs) (Tommy Boy)
- **Salsoul Orchestra** You're Just The Right Size (Salsoul)
- **Diana Ross** The Boss (Ultamix)
- **Frontline Orch.** Don't Turn Your Back...(Larry Levan RX's) (RFC)
- **Skee W** Get That Down Pat (Dance Baby)
- **22 Large** Take Me Away (Vinylla)

SPENCER KINCY
- Foxy's, Red Dog (Chicago). Frankie Go, Disco Maxi (Italy)
- **D Pac** Wouldn't Lie
- **Exposure** DJ Philippe Party Claps
- **Kamar** I Need You (Madhouse)
- **Victor Simonelli/Sound Of One** I Know A Place (One EP)
- **Deacon** Will We Be Lovers
- **Masters At Work** The Buttdance (Cutting LP Track)
- **B-Classic** Remember (Big Beat)
- **Alex M** Lakeview Slang
- **Nick Scotti** Wake Up Everybody (Reprise)
- **Vision** Is This Real
- **Spencer Kincy** Temple (Show Ya Right EP)

EARL PLEASURE
- Crobar, Foxy's (Chicago)
- **Monie Love** Born 2 B.R.E.E.D. (Warner Bros.)
- **Nikki Scott** Wake Up Everybody (Reprise)
- **Jaydee** Plastic Dreams (RS)
- **Kamar** I Need You (Madhouse)
- **Utah Saints** What Can You Do For Me (FFRR/London)
- **Sima** Give You Myself (D Vision)
- **Umoja** Unity 1992 (Polydor UK)
- **Talizam** Only You (Cowboy)
- **Gloria Estafan** Go Away (Epic)
- **Robin S** Show Mo Love (Big Beat)

ROGER S.
- Producer (NYC)
- **Nu Solution featuring Tonya Wynne** I Need You (One)
- **Home Grown** How Does It Make You Feel? (Murk RXs) (Tomato)
- **Victor Simonelli/Sound Of One** I Know A Place (One EP)
- **Bjork** Viciously Happy (Elektra)
- **Masters At Work feat. India** Can't Get No Sleep (Cutting)
- **Tumbe** One (Murk RX's) (Irma)
- **Ralph Falcon** Every Now And Then (Miami Sound)
- **Los Santeras** Siesta Santera (Bumble Beats)
- **Annie Lennox** Love Bird (Todd Terry dubs) (Arista)
- **4 On The Floor** Your Mind Is So Crazy (RX's) (Nightclub)

RALPHI ROSARIO
- Crobar, Foxy's, Shelter (Chicago)
- **Night Movers** Di ba da (Import)
- **Jaydee** Plastic Dreams (RS)
- **Gloria Estafan** Go Away (EPIC)
- **Todd Edwards** PART 11 (111 East EP)
- **Utah Saints** What Can You Do For Me (RX's) (FFRR, London)
- **House Of Gypsies** I Like You (Freeze)
- **Grampa** She's Crazy (Movin)
- **Kamar** I Need You (Madhouse)
- **Ron Trent** Re-Altered States (Cajual EP)
- **Masters At Work feat. India** Get Mo Sleep (Cutting)

tunes to GO!

"for the text"

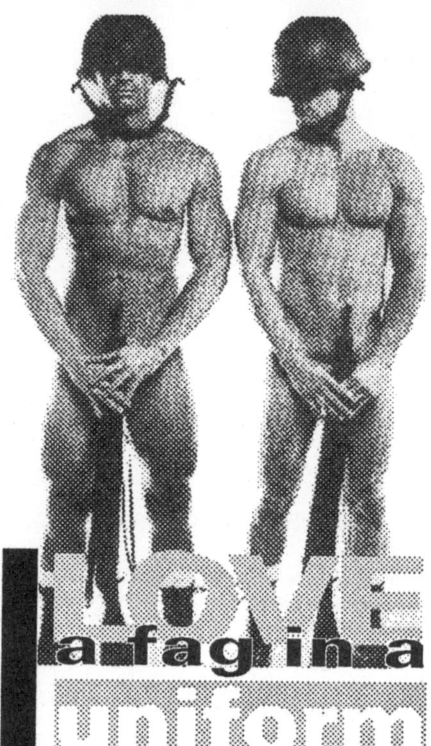

LOVE
a fag in a
uniform

We are not of the school of thought that asks why do gays and lesbians want to be in the military anyway. Why do black people want to sit at the front of the bus? Yes war is stupid, but military service offers benefits that are denied to those who are honest about who they love. Homophobia around this issue is so fierce that people are being bashed and killed for being homosexual as easily as folks were lynched for being black. At long last, we have a president with the balls to realize the great injustice of banning fags and dykes from the military. What can you do to show your support? Express yourself. 1-800-258-2222 is the number to call in support of lifting the ban. Ask the Western Union operator for #9355. Three letters are forwarded in your name to your congressional representative and state senators supporting an end to the ban on gays and lesbians in the armed services. It's well worth the $8.75 that will be billed to your phone. HOTLNE #9355 is the work of John Guggenmos, owner of D.C.'s Tracks nightclub. "It's critical (that) legislators know how we feel, especially when the congressional hearings on the ban start in March," Guggenmos says. And president Clinton needs the public's support. State representatives and Senators need to be deluged with letters against the ban. Currently, Congressional offices receive twice as much mail in support of the ban than they do demanding its lifting.
Research: Ed Bailey, Washington, D.C.

AT EASE!: The above graphic is by local photographer and writer, Genephyr Novak, someone with a unique idea about queer all her own. The image is available as a poster and on a white cotton T shirt (about $18.00) from Chicago's People Like Us Books (312) 248-6363, Women and Children First Bookstore (312) 769-9299, and Hardwear (312) 296-0801. Proceeds benefit the Chicago March on Washington.

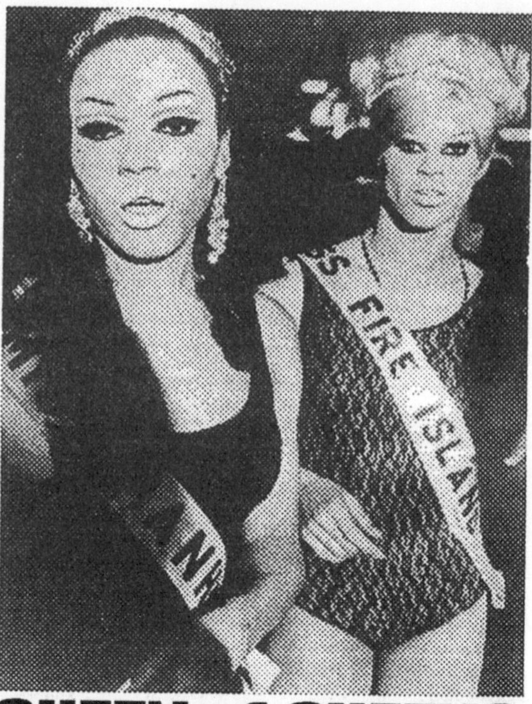

QUEEN of QUEENS

With the 1991 release of Jenny Livingston's *Paris is Burning*, art houses around the world were all abuzz over the phenomenon of the drag queen, intrigued by the serious female impersonators as well as the amateurs and hangers on. However, *Paris is Burning* wasn't the first of such documentaries chronicling sissy ball culture.

The 1968 documentary *The Queen* re-opened March 19, 1993 at New York's Film Forum. It depicts the preparations and judging of a transvestite pageant, and with categories like Bathing Suits, Evening Gowns and "the Transition" (or the tuck), it's obvious that the famed Love Ball wasn't the first downtown NYC drag pageant, either. Directed by Frank Simon, the film studies the Miss All-America Camp Beauty Pageant held at New York's Town Hall in February of 1967. Originally intended as a benefit for Muscular Dystrophy, Lady Bird Johnson, Bobby Kennedy and actor George Raft were all slated to chair the committee for the pageant but cancelled at the last minute. Too *outré* for even the sex-revolutionary sixties, it was widely rumored that the pageant would be raided by the FBI or CIA. (Rather ironic considering recent revelations concerning then FBI Director, J. Edgar "Mary" Hoover!). Andy Warhol and Edie Sedgewick did serve as judges, the film's producer Lewis Allen remembering Edie at the time living at the Chelsea ... "on her last leg." Harlowe, Miss Philadelphia, wins the title of Queen of Queens. She enjoys fifteen modest minutes of fame as a bit player opposite Orson Welles and as a model, posing with Rudi Gernreich's muse, Peggy Moffat. Writer Rona Jaffe, who later did a piece on the pageant for *Playboy*, and George Plimpton judged the categories, too. *The Queen* is a behind-the-scenes look at dragsters and the sixties' cult of the celebrity without being smaltzy or judgmental. It is entertaining as well as enlightening about the counterculture of Downtown New York in the late sixties and the gritty and glamorous world of trannies.

The film's 1968 release got press as diverse as *Variety*, Judith Crist for *New York* magazine, Chauncey Howell for *WWD*, *Cue* magazine's William Wolf and Kathleen Carroll for *The Daily News*. Writring for the *New York Times*, Renata Adler said, "...these gentlemen in bras, diaphanous gowns, lipstick, hairfalls and huffs ...one grows fond of all of them." Screened for the first time since its premiere twenty five years ago, *The Queen* will run at Chicago's Facets Multimedia, 1517 W. Fullerton, Friday, April 9 through Thursday, April 22. Phone (312) 281-4114 for info.

ABOVE The Peace and Love Ball: Misses Manhattan and Fire Island of 1967 tuck, strut, and fight for the title in *The Queen*.

green on THURSDAYS

Green On Thursdays is a documentary shot and produced in Chicago that focuses on Chicago's lesbian and gay anti-violence movement. The title is a reference to a practice of the 1800's, when gay men wore green ties to work on Thursdays in order to identify each other. Red Branch Productions collaborators Diedre Heaslip and Dean Bushala interview activists and hate crime victims (Trent Adkins, Steve Lafreniere, and Scout Weschler among them) drawing an urgent portrait of a community under siege and fighting back. The world premiere was at the Music Box theater this past winter. Its theatrical premiere is at Chicago's Facets Multimedia beginning April 23. A special screening with what promises to be a fiery panel discussion with the filmmakers, subjects of the film, and representatives from Chicago's police department and mayor's office is scheduled Sunday, April 25. Info:(312) 281-4114.

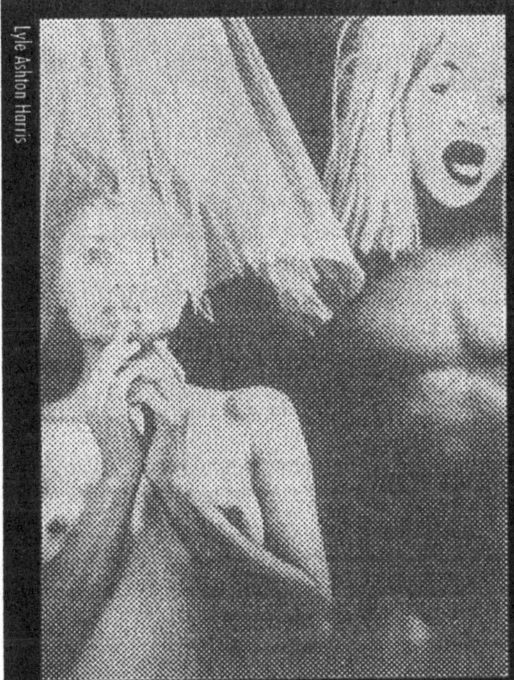

DRESS CODES

is the latest installation of the ongoing Currents series presented by Boston, Massachutses' Institute of Contemporary Art. *Dress Codes* features recent work by a diverse range of international artists who question the way gender, sexuality, identity, and power are defined through appearance. The curators have assembled a diverse range of artists from Chile, Canada, Belgium, and Japan, as well as from across the USA. Among the participants are artist and writer Lyle Ashton Harris, lesbian archivist Nina Levitt, and of course, the definitive post-modern drag icon RuPaul. An exhibition video program, various workshops (including one on becoming a "drag king" for women only) a reading room, and theater and film presentations are all part of the show. *Dress Codes* coincides with the annual ICA benefit, and this year's benefit "Suit Yourself" will be similarly dedicated to issues of crossdressing. The benefit is scheduled for May 15, 1993 at Boston's World Trade Center , and the show runs March 10 through May 30, 1993. Contact (617) 266-5152 for more information.

POP

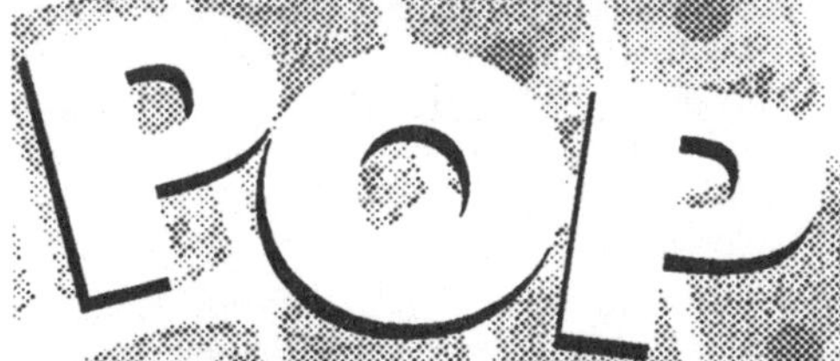

Postmodernism didn't start with as much of a bang as with a Pop. What we now take for granted as the blurred line between art and Madison Avenue was revolutionary when it first became evident to a group of artists working in that time: Roy Lichtenstein, Claus Oldenberg, and Andy Warhol among them. These works are the focus of **Hand Painted Pop: American Art in Transition 1955-62.** Sponsored by Philip Morris (celebrating 35 years of supporting the arts and lung cancer), the show opened at The Museum of Contemporary Art, Los Angeles last winter. It comes to Chicago's Museum of Contemporary Art April 3 through June 20, and then moves to the Whitney in New York July 16 through October 3.

lambda literati

The finalists of the fifth annual Lambda Literary Awards were announced March 1, 1993. This year finds many of the nominated books coming from "mainstream" publishers: Penguin USA leads the list with eight nominated titles, followed closely by St. Martin's Press with seven. Many of the categories had finalists selected from a much longer list of nominees. The five finalists in each of the fifteen categories are only representative of the boom in gay and lesbian publishing.

Among the nominees are Assotto Saint's new anthology of writings by gay men *Here to Dare* (Galiens), Dennis Cooper's collection of edgy queer writing *Discontents* (Amethyst), Randall Keenan's novel *Let The Dead Bury The Dead* (Harcourt Brace), and Essex Hemphill's collection of poetry and prose, *Ceremonies* (Plume). Nominated posthumously are poet Audre Lorde and artist and writer David Wojnarowicz.

The winners will be announced as part of the American Booksellers Association Convention, at a banquet held May 28, 1993.

Lambda nominee Essex Hemphill

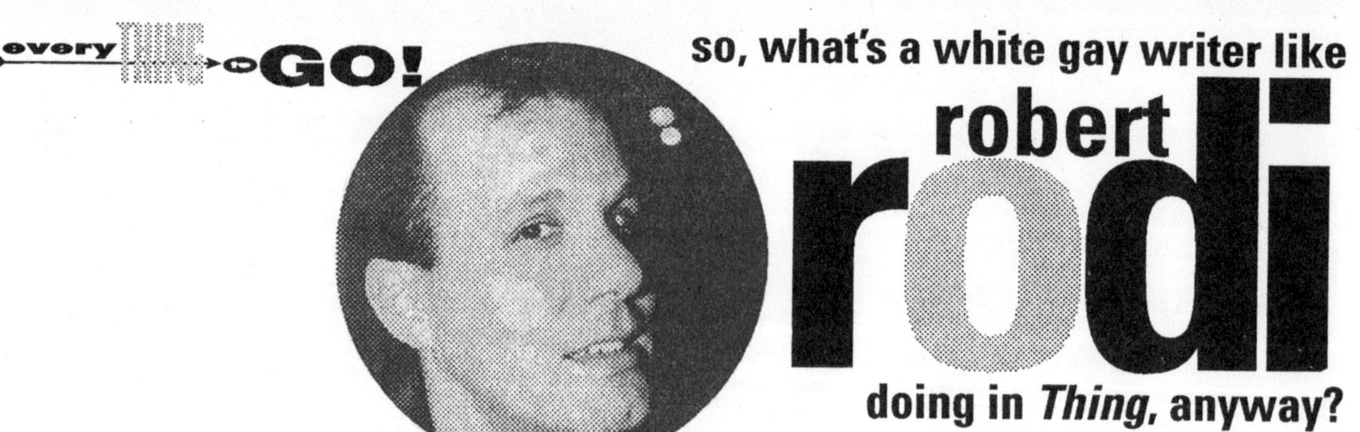

so, what's a white gay writer like
robert rodi
doing in *Thing*, anyway?
by LeRoy Whitfield

O.K. So I jump off the bus and run like hell to meet Robert. Don't want to miss him. Don't want to give a bad impression.

I pop in the Falcon Inn, a closet gay bar in the Hyde Park neighborhood on Chicago's South Side. A couple of brothers are watching the Bulls on the big screen, scoping the dim tavern on commercials.

I spot Robert right off. I had never seen him before but he is the only very white-looking, very white-acting white boy in this unofficially black bar. He is going from table to table asking the brothers "Um, are you from *Thing*?" The brothers stare at him like he's bugged. The scene is so fucking amusing that I just watch.

I'm, supposed to jaw-jack with Robert about *Closet Case*, his second novel that that focuses on a young, gay Chicago advertising executive's struggle with coming out on the job. As a young, openly gay Chicagoan employed at an advertising agency, Rob knows about this kind of thing.

LeRoy Whitfield: Robert? [He's out of breath.]
Robert Rodi: I was rushing. I just got here. I went past the bar at first. I went all the way under the viaduct before I realized I went too far and...This is a closet gay bar?
LW: Yeah.
RR: You would never think that just by looking at it.
LW: That's the point.
RR: Oh, right.
LW: Is *Closet Case* based loosely, or at all, on you?
RR: Well, certainly there are parts that are based on me...
LW: Which parts?
RR: I think mainly just the psychology, the thoughts that Lionel [the book's main character] has. The fact that he is excessively staying in the closet to make things easier for himself on the job, and at the same time he goes through hell everyday because he is always thinking 'Who knows, what are they [his co-workers] thinking?' and he's putting himself through just agony. That's kind of what I went through. None of the actual circumstances was part of what I went through but I think everyone has gone through this, being in the closet.
LW: You work at an ad agency?
RR: Yeah I do.
LW: So does Lionel.
RR: Yeah, he's an account executive, I'm a copywriter. I put him in an ad agency because that's the business I know. And I made him an account executive, because in that capacity he is responsible for going out and meeting clients all day long and representing the agency. I never meet clients. So there never would have been that

anxiety about my job as far as being closeted. My boss is who I deal with and not multi-billionaire clients. I just though it would be funnier to make him someone who had to schmooze on a daily basis and had to end up hiding that.
LW: Were you ever closeted at the job to begin with?
RR: Oh yeah, sure. I guess I have this different opinion about how you should handle yourself at a job. I don't think you should go in making a big huge theatrical announcement: 'I AM GAY,' because I think that invites a huge theatrical response. I usually just wait until people get to know me and then they just sort of find out naturally and if they find out naturally then they sort of take it naturally. I guess I was never really consciously closeted on this job I just didn't open up and announce that I was gay right away. But certainly by the time that I was on the Joan Rivers show I think everyone knew. Secrets are the only thing that get gossiped about in an office environment, once you're open; once they realize that this is not a vulnerability; once they realize that you're not hiding anything there's just no real gossip material there. So I think that's a good argument for coming out of the closet anyway 'cause it suddenly makes you boring. No one wants to talk about you anymore.
LW: Do you feel the need to declare, I mean I know what you were just saying about the theatrical announcement, but do you feel the need for people to know?
RR: Feel the *need* for people to know? I guess people with who I work pretty closely...um, yeah, I guess I do.
LW: Why?
RR: I don't know. I guess if I work with someone

pretty closely and like them. I mean part of working with someone closely is that you develop sort of a friendship. It's not like a real friendship in that you go out on ski weekends together or anything but I guess I would rather even that sort of relationship to be based on the truth. I mean the truth about me being a gay man. Plus, a lot of my social life has always revolved around the people that I work with. I throw parties with Jeffrey [his "spouse"] and I have them to the house. I guess I need to have everything above board there because I can't imagine having them to the house and hiding it like 'Oh yeah, he's my *roommate.'*
LW: Tell me about the Joan Rivers Show. I didn't see it.
RR: Well it was something. I mean she wanted to do a show on women whose best friends are gay men. Since I wrote the novel *Fag Hag* they called me up and wanted me to be on. The first half of the show they had these three women on- these three big bold women- and they had this shocking red hair- two of them had shocking red hair- and the third one should have. The four of them, Joan and the three women were having *the* best time. I mean blah, blah, blah, blah, blah. Then I came on and I had something to push, so it wasn't as many laughs with me. But later on people told me that they thought I did a pretty good job of bringing the tone down a little because they said that by the time those three women were finished talking about their gay friends, by the time Joan announced that there was a gay author coming out everyone expected me to come out there and go "Ohhhhhh you're faaaahhhhhbulous, girlfriend!" The fact that I was a little more serious they still thought it was

pretty good.

LW: Do you consider yourself a gay novelist?

RR: I don't know. Everyone asks me that. I prefer to think of myself as a novelist who writes about gay things. I think I just latched onto that because first of all its a commercial decision. Gay fiction is one of the easiest places to break into right now because its like a boom market. Gay people are buying books more than any other segment of the population. I think stories are important. Stories help you shape your identity. Gay people can't find stories about themselves anywhere except in books. You can't find them on TV or in movies, well, occasionally, but books are our real resource. But also I just feel strongly about making sure that the stories that I want to see are out there. I do basically comic stories. I think we all need a good laugh. I am more interesting. A lot of the gay fiction that I've read, I mean I don't want to put too many things down. I call it the navel-gazing school. I mean gay men who are obsessed with every feeling that wraps across their mind. I always think it is more interesting to look at the whole gay culture that's sprung up since the 70s that affects other groups in society, like women who fall in love with these characters and men who are on the fringe, half in and half out, and things like that. I want to make more comedy available too.

LW: Do you plan to tackle more serious social issues like the obvious, AIDS, or more serious dealings in the gay community?

RR: Well, I think I *do* tackle serious issues, I just do it in a comic manner. But I don't plan to tackle AIDS anytime soon. I always at least mention it. In the next novel one of the supporting characters is HIV-positive. But I am HIV-negative myself and so is Jeffrey and none of our close friends has dealt with this. So I think it would take a hell of a lot of nerve for me to to write an AIDS novel without first-hand experience. So unless and until I have first-hand experience with it I won't do anything with it. That's for other people.

LW: Because you don't have first-hand experience and no one around you is HIV-positive...

RR: That's not true, I have some good friends who are HIV-positive. They just haven't gotten sick yet. So eventually I will deal with it. I am just being hopeful when I say 'unless.' But I will eventually be dealing with that.

LW: Where do you plan to go? You got *Fag Hag* down and you've got *Closet Case* down. What are you working on?

RR: Well, I'm working on a third novel right now that is already under contract at Dutton. It should be out way in the future, like, May of 1994. Its another novel sort of about identity. Its about a cartoonist who works for a comic book company that has a comic book called "Princess Paragon" and its been running for 50 years and has gradually been selling less and less and less. So this high-powered cartoonist comes on board and tries to save the book by turning the character into a lesbian. So its about the repercussions that happen after that. It kind of deals with some dead serious things. Its kind of like my attack on corporate America and my satire of the '80s but instead of using an oil company, I'm using a comic book company.

LW: Lets play a game. Words and Phrases. I say something and say the first thing that comes to your mind. You know that game?

RR: Yes.

LW: Madonna

RR: Sex.

LW: Clinton.

RR: Gore.

LW: Gay.

RR: Uh, happy.

LW: Fag

RR: Hag.

LW: Robert Rodi.

RR: Uh, author.

LW: Genius.

RR: Einstein.

LW: The 90s

RR: Hope.

LW: Thank you.

RR: You're welcome. **THING**

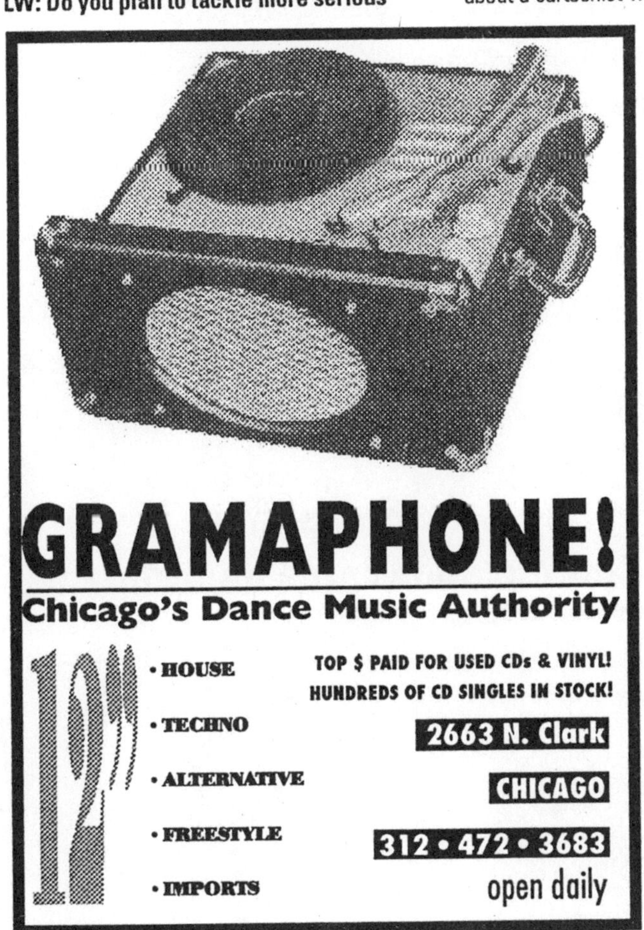

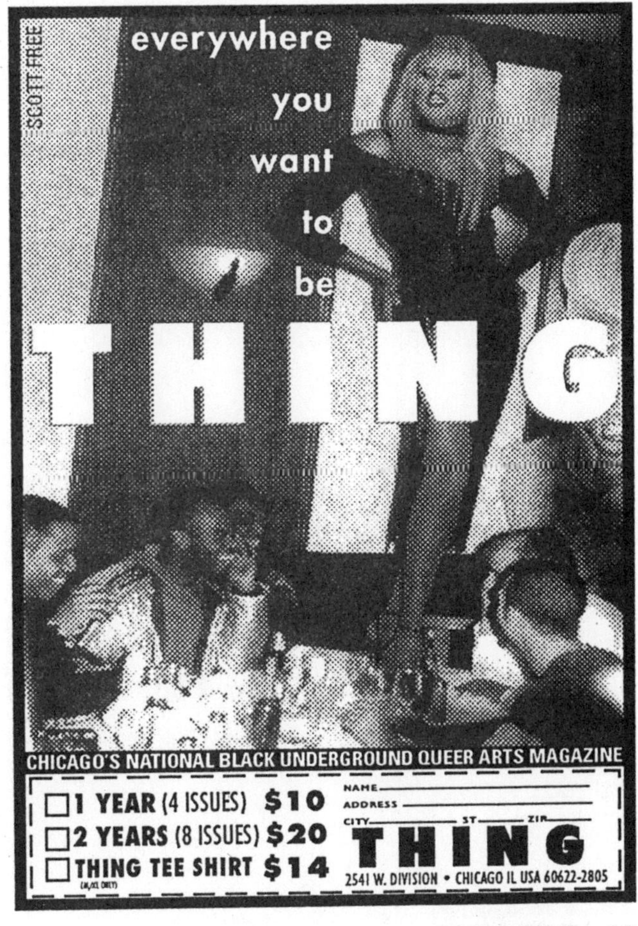

"you didn't hear it from me, but..."

AND A-ONE, AND A-TWO The first four of these dark parties featured some of Chicago's finest underground djs, their names prominently listed to attract fans of their musical skills, taste, and knowledge. The fifth one featured sound-waves by a white-bread party-promoter-cum-dj, making her disco debut. Now, we can't be too critical (not being brave enough to go and confirm our suspicions) but when the only thing one can say about the DJ is "I hear he's been practicing a lot"... thank you, I'll stay home with my Close n' Play!

SHAFTED The mom of a closet-case would-be fag turned out to be spoutin' mucho hot air about a law suit concerning her son's name (and almost a picture of his penis) gracing page three of a new queer black zine. As Sophie Tucker said: "fuck 'em if they can't take a joke".

A DOUBLE SCOOP OF FORMALDEHYDE IN A SUGAR CONE WITH SPRINKLES, PLEASE What fla-vor-of-the-month had the kids gagging in his posthumous appearance with a staple through his nipples? Personally, we've always preferred our trade to be breathing.

STILL THIRSTY Overheard at the packed and pumpin' New Years Eve afterhours when asked how the earlier midnight countdown party went: "Oh, it was great. What a great space. There was really a good vibe going on in there. (sheepishly) I would like to have seen a few hundred more *people* there, however..." Better luck next (life)time! And was anyone surprised that the only way they could top their first anniversary was by folding?

AND IN THIS CORNER Can we have a little less drama amongst the club tart royalty? That a round of he-say-she-say could turn into such a web of unnecessareness is bad enough, do we have to call Vera on each other's parties, too?

SOMEONE'S IN THE KITCHEN WITH DINAH Now we've seen everything: clueless white kids open a beanery with the idea of serving nouvelle soul food. In an arch setting with art-school-dropout caricatures of darkies on the wall and leopard print (read jungle) tablecloths, no less. With a soundtrack of predictable nostalgic r&b mixed by the ofay owner. Not to mention prices that most black folks in this city would roll their eyes at. And the darkest thing working or din-ing there (next to the obligatory busboy from the Zoe Baird Talent Agency) was your humble reporter, gagging on under-done collards. So, where's the restaurateur of color brave enough to open a diner called "Po' White Trash?"

PARLAY VOO FRANCAIS? Not only is her subscription way overpriced for a oh-so-slim black fag newsletter, what's with all the cutesy French department headings? Some sedit-ty folks think a cedilla is a substitute for elegance.

one picture is worth a thousand words department...

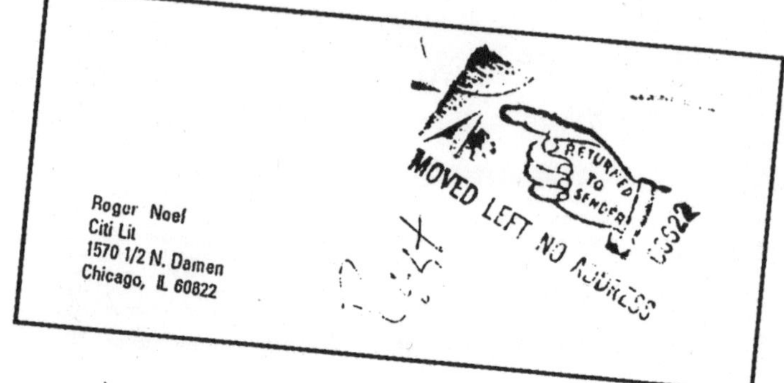

lists

The "N" word
Nigger
Niggah
Nigga's
Nigga
Nig
Negro
Negroe
Negroid
Negrewish (part black/part
Jewish, as in *Lisa Bonet and ugly ass
Lenny Kravitz are so Negrewish*)
Nighonk (a half white nigger)
NWA

Caucasian Persuasion
whitey
honky
Bobo and Mr. Charlie
Missy Ann
Mr. Establishment
white bread
peckerwood
cracker
Shannon Dougherty/Tori Spelling

Son Of Got It Goin' On
Jamoo
Mark Contratto
Maurice Joshua
Georgie Porgie
Reginald Thomas
Tom Hemingway
Chuck Gonzales

Dan I Am
Daniel Robinson
Daniel Wang
Dan Duverney
Diver Dan
Dan Rather
Danilo

Cancel my subscription
The Advocate
Genre
H.I.M.
10 Percent

Billy Club
Billy Name
Billy Beyond
Bill Coleman
Bill Stamets
Bill Anderson
Bill Clinton
Double Bill
Billy Miller
Billy Boy
Mystic Bill
Billy, Don't Be A Hero
Billy Joe McAllister
Mr. Bill

¡Aye!
Victor Hugo
Chi Chi Valenti
Chi Chi LaRue
Rudy De La Mor
Dorothy Malone
Delores Delgado
Ricky Ricardo
Coati Mundi
Fred Luna
Lupe Velez
Rita Moreno
Chita Rivera
Ricardo Montalban
Buster Poindexter
Charo

Pimp Shoes
Foti
Stacy Adams
Kham & Nates
Flagg Brothers
Fathers and Sons

Partners in style
Mathu & Zaldy
Dolce & Gabanna
Price & Walton
Warren Bennis/Susan Edwards
Hino & Malee

D Thing
Dee Dee Brave
Dee Dee Bridgewater
Dee Dee Warwick
Dee Dee Sharp Gamble
Ruby Dee
Kiki Dee
Sandra Dee
DiDi Seven
D cup
Deee-Lite
D-Influence
D Train
DeAundra Peek
D Mob
Defunkt
Debi Mazar

Lone Stars
Whitney Houston
Thelma Houston
Cissy Houston
Houston Person
Sterling Houston
Beauregard Houston-Montgomery
Stella Dallas
Tex Avery
Disco Tex and the Sex-O-Lettes
Laura Di San Antonio
Patti Austin
Sissy Hankshaw

Miss List
Miss Mary Mack
Miss Thing
Miss Honey
Miss Girl
Miss Lady
Little Missy
Miss Alana
Miss Brown To You
Swiss Miss
Miss America
Miss Universe
Miss Congeniality
Miss Continental
Miss Plus

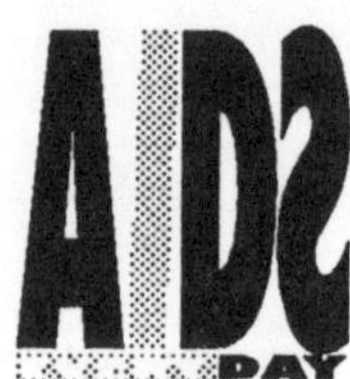

SINCE **D**ONALD **W**OODS' FUNERAL, I have taken steps to ensure that if I die a young man, my affairs will be handled proudly. I have spoken many times to my Mother about my death. She gets depressed when I bring up the subject. I wonder how she thinks I feel about the subject: after all it's my death we're talking about.

She asks me questions like: Why do I have to announce to the world that it was AIDS if that's what you die from? Why do I have to tell everybody if you died of AIDS, the only way you could have gotten HIV was through sex with another man? Why do I have to hang out the family linen?

Because, I tell her. I am an example. I must be the best example of a proud, Black, gay, HIV+ man that I can be. So that people in general recognize that any one of the above does not stop me from being a productive, loving human being. And more importantly, so that my young sister or brother who senses that he or she is homosexual will see from my example that living the life of an openly gay man has an up side, too. Many very up sides: My peers and I are getting shit done that will hopefully make it better for those of us who live as homosexuals in this puritanical, heterosexist nation.

But she doesn't get it. Not yet, anyway. She still thinks silence will protect her. I won't give up on her. She bore me and I want to bring her the recognition of my mortality and set her free of the fear. I may, however, need to disengage, detach, distance, divorce. She still feels she is somehow responsible. Still thinks that if I had told her earlier she could have helped. Still thinks that if she had done something differently I would have turned out "all right" - her words for heterosexual and happily married, well at least, married with children. Magical thinking doesn't work with sexual orientation either. I assure her that she could have raised me 50,000 different ways and I would be homosexual because that is just part of who I am.

She counters that homosexuality is not condoned by the Bible. I counter with, (Judeo-Christian) God didn't write the bible, man did and ask her if she has consulted other writings on homosexuality. She admits she hasn't. I point out that if she went to the library and read one book that alleged that Blacks were genetically inferior to Whites, she would be highly motivated to read a second opinion. That she would find a wide range of theories on racial equality or inequality. And that she would make her informed decision after reading several of the alternatives. Why can't she do the same regarding same sex orientation? Why can't she call P-FLAG (Parents and Friends of Lesbians and Gays) for some recommended reading?

She does not feel comfortable enough yet to do that.

I may be dead by the time you feel comfortable.

Yes, you may, she admits.

Her words slap me in the face and I tell her so just before I hang up the phone.

Mother, this is for you:

I agree that differences of opinion do not diminish the love between us. I know I can't compel you to do anything. Nor can you compel me. I cannot judge you. Nor you me. The only thing I owe you is to love you. My only responsibility is to tell you what I need, know that I won't always get what I ask and become willing to reduce or eliminate communication with you if I believe contact with you becomes detrimental to me.

I want you to be comfortable before you call P-FLAG but I am not sure that I have a lot of time for you to become willing to get comfortable.

What you seem insensitive to is the fact that I don't have a lot of time to dilly-dally around with theories of morality. I must deal in reality. I have huge doctor bills: $750 every three months just for basic doctor visits and blood tests, plus acupuncture, physical therapy, chiropractic and therapy, totalling another $900 per month and pharmaceutical, vitamin and herb therapy that costs about $300 per month. The total this year will run about $17,500.

The insurance company refuses to pay for vitamins, herb therapy, some of the blood work and some lab fees so, I don't get reimbursed for a lot of these expenses. Fortunately, most of my doctors will accept the assignment that my insurance company offers so I don't have to pay all the bills up front. Insurers drag their feet in making reimbursements and are trying to reject payments of T-cell blood tests which are essential for people living with HIV.

We who are infected did not invent this virus nor did we go out seeking it in some self-destructive behavior. We just got infected with it like a person gets infected with any other blood-borne or sexually transmitted disease. Insurers do not refuse payment of blood tests for syphilis, gonorrhea or the much more common herpes and NSU (non-specific urethritis), all sexually transmitted and at epidemic levels among heterosexuals as well as all other sexually active Americans. There is no cure for AIDS yet and you seem to think that I am trying to get attention, that I am just joking about being infected with HIV.

Being infected with HIV is incredibly stressful. I am a young man, at my prime and instead of having the chance to focus all of my energy on my contribution to humanity, I must put considerable effort into just staying alive. So you can perhaps understand how thoughtless it was for you to speak so off-handedly about my being dead before you are comfortable enough to call P-FLAG or deal with the reality rather than the morality of homosexuality.

What you don't seem to understand is that I blamed myself for being gay many, many times and for many, many years. As a child and adolescent, I thought everything that went wrong in our household was because of my secret sexual attraction to other boys and to men. I asked the God of my childhood to tell me what I had done wrong, what penance I could make so that I would be "normal." I asked Him, "Why me?"

And the answer I got to each question was: NOTHING. The answer I still get today, when I ask

SPIRITUAL REALITY & HIV

robert e. penn

these questions again, just to be sure, is: NOTHING. I hadn't awakened one morning and selfishly decided to be gay so that I wouldn't have to raise children or assume the other responsibilities of adulthood. I hadn't taken the easy or evil way out. I wasn't trying to hurt my family. I had done nothing wrong so there was no reparation possible or needed. I could do nothing to change. This is me as God/dess created me.

If you want to blame, blame the virus - human immunodeficiency virus. It is a human parasite which thrives in symbiosis with a specimen of genus homo sapiens but it is too stupid to recognize that when it grows aggressively, it kills its host and loses its nurturing environment.

I'm not in the hospital and I intend to keep it that way. I believe that unconditional support from my friends and family helps. I also believe that conditional love kills. I don't want people around me who think, "Too bad he chose the life of a homosexual. He would be well now if he hadn't, " or, "Such a waste of a good man." Those thoughts, no matter how well people think they conceal them, slip out and are noticeable, especially to small children, the very old and the ill. I would rather let go of people who offer only conditional love than die as a result of accepting their restrictions.

Are you going to wait until I'm dead to face reality? I humbly request that you not wait, that you risk a little discomfort this time for my sake because I am not afraid of dying, I am afraid of dying alone.

Mother, that is all for now.

IF AND WHEN **M**OTHER responds to me, I will know how to act. I will know whether to move closer or keep my distance. I will express my gratitude to the ancestors, grandfather rock, mother earth and the spirit that connects and holds us all if she moves closer and opens her heart to receive. And if she holds her ground, remaining afraid and unwilling, I will, must pray for her love to expand and again for me to accept her as she is.

I will not wave my mother off like some disinterested bystander or the malicious HIV negative gay men who won't date those of us who are HIV positive. After all, she is my flesh, this affects her world, too. But I will stay away from her if it is in my best interest. And this life-affirming action is so difficult to conceive of and implement because I am so accustomed to obeying her in spite of my needs, adapting, appearing straight and assimilating (ever assimilating, never assimilated) in the White mainstream culture, in order to survive in his homophobic, AIDS-phobic and racist environment known as the land of the free.

ON TRAFFIC MISDEMEANORS

Kevin Thaddeus Paulson

I BEGAN TO WRITE THIS ESSAY as an explanation to my lover, Brian, who is himself a dancer and artist. He respects that art requires sacrifice (such as selling furniture in order to afford dance class), but he doesn't understand my particular brand of sacrifice. And art.

I jaywalk.

Jaywalking is the political conjugation of dancing.

Many people regard jaywalking as a survivor skill inbred in native New Yorkers. But this opinion neglects style. Oh, I am not talking about those people who rush across one way streets without looking both ways. I am talking about people who can pause on Canal Street and light up a cigarette in the face of an oncoming M13 bus.

True jaywalking is not for convenience; it is subversive. True jaywalking is not for the purpose of getting somewhere on time.

I have jaywalked before mayors and bishops, presidential candidates, and television stars. I have jaywalked before more stretch limousines than the the average Hoosier sees in a lifetime. And I know that in jaywalking there is a passion and responsibility. Never expect to be the same person twice.

Participation in illegal pedestrian traffic changes us, enriches us. Jaywalking makes all persons equal. It allows the hero-

in addict with AIDS the opportunity to slow down, only if for a moment, the inexorable progress of the Exxon trucks. It ain't revenge, but it's close.

This is why I love New York City, the Grand Prix of Jaywalking. Here there is no respect left for the "Walk/Don't Walk" signs. Stop signs serve only as octagonal backdrops for graffiti. Survival is to the fittest, and the native New Yorker scoffs at the tourists who walk at the green, not in between.

My favorite place to jaywalk is the intersection of Broadway, Thirty-fourth Street and Sixth Avenue of the Americas. I was once told that this corner is the busiest in the world. If that isn't true, then it should be.

It is at this corner on a rainy August afternoon rush hour that I have single footedly brought down the island of Manhattan into gridlock. Presidential motorcades can do no better.

Any time that you prevent a taxi driver from picking up his intended fare, you get an extra ten points.

I have worried that jaywalking alone is not enough to separate me from an otherwise Middle Class Gay Lifestyle. But I use this misdemeanor as a spur to my other insurrections. Why, the FBI would never have thought of tapping my telephone until I helped organize ACT UP to jaywalk the FDA.

But jaywalking has its own rewards, as

well as its mysteries. I laugh at the policeman who glares at me, yet will never write a summons. There is no license plate to my rebellion. I ponder the pedestrians who gawk at me, shivering on their cold perch of curb. They see crossing the street as yet another obstacle in their gray pinstripe, "Gee, if-I-could-only-win-the-lotto lifestyles. They cannot see the adventure that breaking the law can be.

After all, why does the chicken cross the road?

I wonder most at drivers. As a vice-president of a major bank glares at me from behind a steering wheel of his tan Mercedes, does he stop to think that he is only being delayed from rushing out of the city that he rushed into a mere eleven hours earlier? Does he think of how silly this situation is that he who rules the lives of hundreds of workers is being forced to pause by my well-turned sneaker. I like to think that I make people take the time to smell the falafel.

But Brian asks, "Don't you watch where you're going?" Of course I do. I'm going forward. He is waiting. And even if he fills the Joyce Theatre for one of his performances, all of New York attends *my* dance.

Never expect to be the same person twice. Never look for your dreams where you last left them. On some morning you may realize that you are rushing to a job

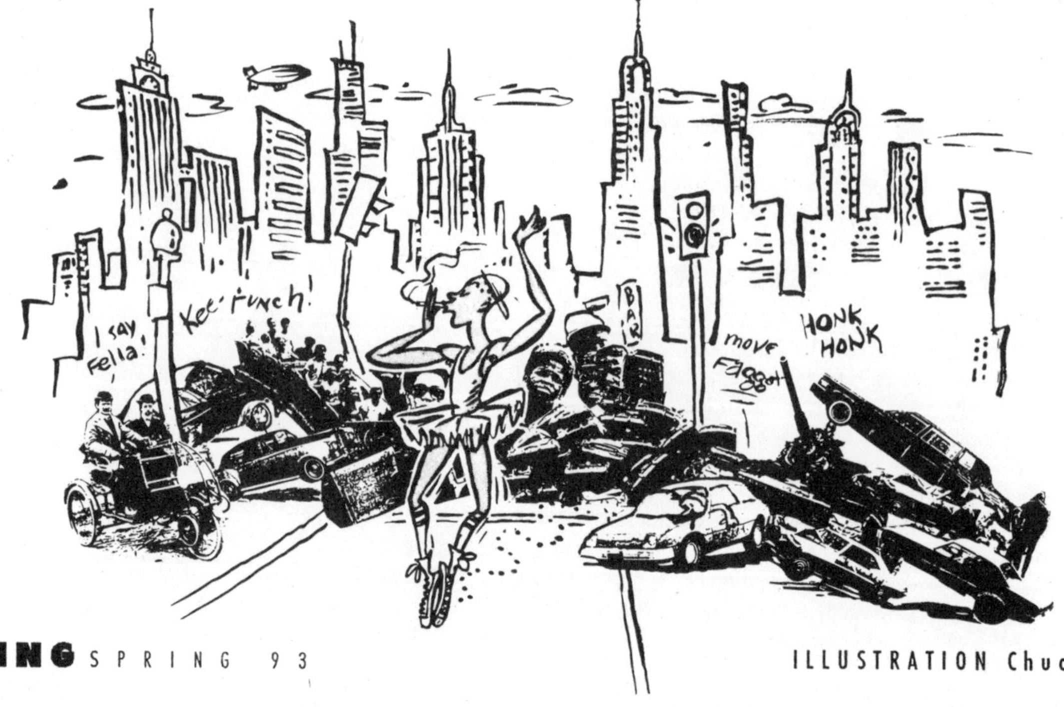

ILLUSTRATION Chuck Gonzales

which has no meaning for you. Only then can you become an urban guerrilla.

If a man does not keep pace with his companions, then perhaps he walks to the beat of a different stoplight.

Because jaywalking is an art, it is subject to no rules. But there are some pointers as a matter of good form:

1.Jaywalking is better on two-way streets than on one-way streets, and it is best on highways right before a three-day weekend.

2.Jaywalk in front of police cars whenever possible. This reminds officers inside that all rules are relative.

3.Jaywalk in front of funeral processions only when the deceased had voted for Ronald Reagan.

4. If you are having an argument with your lover, jaywalk when he starts to win.

5.If anyone tells you that jaywalking is stupid, tell them that so is giving advice to people who face down diesel truck drivers.

Remember that jaywalking is an extension of dance. It is a statement. It is dying stupidly for an ideal. Sort of like patriotism, only

Jaywalking is the

political conjugation

of dancing.

in reverse.

The most political act which I ever committed I did a few Octobers ago. As I was strolling down Fifth Avenue, I noticed a black limo pull up to the side of Saint Patrick's Cathedral. As I saw the man in glasses and a black dress enter the car, I new that my moment had come. I raced the car to the green-lit intersection and jumped in front of it. As the chauffeur/priest honked, I smiled slowly and genuflected. The light turned red. Maybe for just a moment I had slowed down the evil course of action of the evil Cardinal O'Connor.

MELODRAMATISTS INSIST ON running naked into the Cathedral or spitting up wafers with no flavor and less meaning. Why bother when one can beat him with his own lash?

I turned thirty a few months ago. My mother called then to say that I am now middle-aged as well as Middle Class. Yet I was content that at least I was not the person who she thought I would be. Nor am I any of the people who I imagined I would be. But I am happy. I have created, in concert with lover who does not understand jaywalking a home. I am the proud fairy godfather of a pride of Pekingeses.

I have learned not to expect to be the same person twice. Getting in touch with your smaller dreams in another kind of dance.

Life, like art, is subject only to the rules you make for it. So here are five rules:

Rule 1: Be happy where you are. Who knows if you would be happy where you really want to be?

Rule 2: Don't expect the unexpected, but carry your passport just in case.

Rule 3: Always take time to smell the falafel.

Rule 4: Never expect to be the same person twice. Do not wake up in the morning assuming that you are the same person you went to bed as. Dreams change you, even when you don't know what they are.

Rule 5: When in doubt, jaywalk.

THE QUEER MARCH ON WASHINGTON

activist GABRIEL GOMEZ on the history and hopes of the 1993 demonstration in DC

"WE MUST REALIZE if one of us is oppressed, we all are oppressed." This lofty statement is from the platform of the 1993 March on Washington for Lesbian, Gay and Bi Equal Rights and Liberation scheduled for Sunday, April 25. If it sounds a bit school-marmish, it may be because some of the people that this statement is targeted at don't quite believe it. Divisions within the Lesbian or Gay

equal rights in the tradition of the first great march on Washington where Dr. King took a moment to dream. Dreams may still be the only place to realize intangibles like equality and justice, but the march does offer a time and a place to bring those other bedroom activities out for good. And there could be a million queers there to help you do it.

We've been here twice before. In 1979 and in 1987 there were two sim-

question is will this translate into more people of color and women on the street? Whatever the crowd in D.C. looks like, it will see the same 50 % rule on race and gender parity governing both the morning and main stages. King is hopeful that this will ultimately mean change, noting that the last march helped spread ACT UPs throughout the country creating a national in-your-face kind of activism. Can the new face of the 1993 march generate a new body of queer activists that begins to resemble the actual variety of queer America?

It was this inclusiveness that led to a wide ranging platform of demands which scares some people. Fifty-three unofficial planks were leaked and caused a lot of pain because they seem to relegate white gay boys to a less prominent place than they are generally used to. The ultra-conservative gay organization The Log Cabin Club was so upset that they refused to come. But early signs of a right wing gay boycott of the march appear to have lost their momentum, due in part to the fact that seven official planks have replaced the scary unofficial 53. Also, a million queers in one town is bound to be too big a party to pass up, and you know how closet queens who made good money groveling to the Reagan/Bush nightmare can always be counted on for social occasions. Don't laugh if they show up on time though; remember we're being tolerant that weekend.

Scout Weschler, a National Co-chair based in D.C., acknowledged that some felt "that were not focused because we're not single focused." How can we be? There are already a number of events scheduled that are sure to separate the boy scouts from

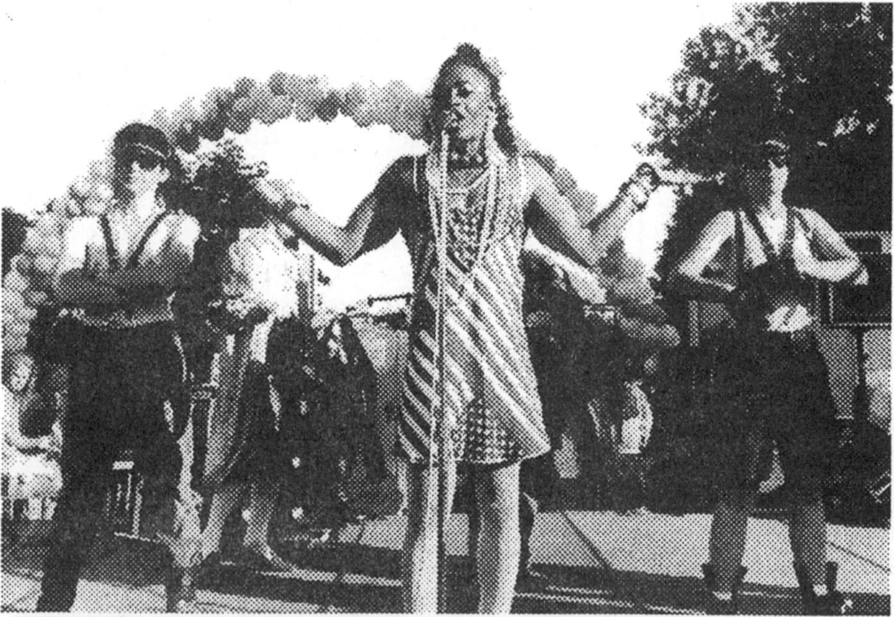

GET USED TO IT: Dyke activists Valerie Selinski and Scout Weschler flank Joan Jett Blakk as she encourages support for the 1993 March on Washington at Chicago's 1992 Pride rally

or bi community rest on who you are, or even who or what you do. There is no one community that holds everyone. The transgendered folks for example are not sitting this one out. But they are still waiting for the fourth such march to get their name into the official title. Among the organizers of the march there is no question that this demonstration is about

ilar marches, both overwhelmingly white and dominated by male issues. In '93 things are different. 50% of the representatives from the regions that administer the march at the grass roots levels are women and people of color. Tanya King, a representative from Northern California, found this already led to a feeling of empowerment in the planning stages. The

continued on page 22

THE QUEER MARCH ON WASHINGTON

sion of Lesbian, Gay, Bisexual, and Transgender studies in multicultural curricula. 5. We demand the right to reproductive freedom and choice, to control our own bodies, and an end to sexist discrimination. 6. We demand an end to racial and ethnic discrimination in all forms. 7. We demand an end to discrimination and violent oppression based on actual or perceived sexual orientation/identification, race religion, identity, sex, and gender expression, disability, age, class, AIDS/HIV infection.

continued from page 20

the leathermen. A park beautification is planned by the Forgotten Scouts for Friday the 23rd. They include bi's and lesbians in their invitation but it seems likely they will be stressing boy camaraderie. The following day a Queer Scout cookie sell-athon seems less gender specific. Everyone likes cookies. Imagine warming the heart of your favorite leather top with some freshly baked queer treats Saturday night at the S/M leather Fetish party and conference. (Hint: Scout Weschler despite her name is more likely to be there than at the park). Accommodating everyone isn't easy but its a job the organizers had to attempt.

SEVEN BASIC DEMANDS shape this event: 1. We demand the passage of a Lesbian, Gay, Bisexual, and Transgender Civil Rights bill and an end to discrimination by state and federal governments including the military; repeal of all sodomy laws and other laws that criminalize private sexual expression between consenting adults. 2. We demand massive increases in funding for AIDS education, research, and patient care; universal access to health care including alternative therapies; and an end to sexism in medical research and healthcare. 3. We demand legislation to prevent discrimination against Lesbians, Gays, Bisexuals, and Transgendered people in the areas of family diversity, custody, adoption and foster care and that the definition of family includes the full diversity of all family structures. 4. We demand full and equal inclusion of Lesbians, Gays, Bisexuals, and Transgendered people in the educational system, and inclu-

The breadth of all seven of these demands acknowledge what any decent queer knows; we are everywhere. The march platform is a practical solution. Queers can't be separated from their other community affiliations, their identities can't be fractured to emphasize only one element of their lives. White gay men have brought their concerns based in their realities to this movement. Its only fair that everyone else get equal time. And in D.C. quite a number of people will try.

BiNet USA, Old Lesbians Organizing for Change, the People of Color Lobby, Gay and Lesbian Elected Officials, the Gay and Lesbian Parent Association International, the Rainbow Alliance of the Deaf, AA & Al-Anon, Asian Pacifica Lesbians, the Gay and Lesbian Pilot's Association, Lesbian and Gay Union Members and the National Minority AIDS Council are all holding large national gatherings that weekend in D.C. But that's not all. Aside from still more meetings like the Transgender National Meeting on Saturday or the series of National Bear Gatherings there are the dances. Major women's dances will be held throughout the weekend and the two night Drag Show Extravaganza will surely hold plenty of interest for boys in frocks. On Sunday a big old Disco Dance and a few Divas Simply Singing (rumored to include Whitney, Dionne, and Patti) offer still more excuses to avoid that meeting or demo you ought to attend.

But seriously, the demos are the actual reason to go, and they happen during the day when you should be awake (or at the very least recovering.) On Thursday at 10 A.M. an AIDS Cure Now action will be held at the Health and Human Services building. The main event, THE MARCH, will assemble Sunday morning on Pennsylvania Avenue before noon and probably continue long after that. Avenues. Monday has two additional actions as well. The lifting of the military ban will be the rationale for an early morning officially sanctioned event at the ever-inviting Pentagon. That day at noon another demo at the Capitol building will be held on healthcare issues, specifically AIDS and breast cancer. Its unofficial though, because as Chicago representative Darrel Gordon says, some nervous queers are just a bit tense on the loss of focus, an issue that will probably seem a bit absurd under a disco ball just a few short hours before this action takes place.

ONE MILLION QUEERS is the hoped for attendance a figure that its assumed even *Time* and *Newsweek* will find impossible to ignore the way they did a half million in 1987. If nothing else no one will be able to ignore the increased visibility of women and people of color in leadership positions. Will slick Willie come? Will Hillary and Tipper, Al and Chelsea venture out on the front lawn to see just how queer this country is? No matter what happens or no matter how we see ourselves as different, I suspect the leaders of this country still consider us all one big perversion. With that in mind, find as many willing partners as you can and drag them down to the IRS on Saturday for the Wedding. Don't worry about commitment. As far as most of the rest of America is concerned, if it lasts a lifetime or just an afternoon you are still just queers. The difference is this time your union, whether deep and meaningful or just down and dirty, won't be out of place. **THING**

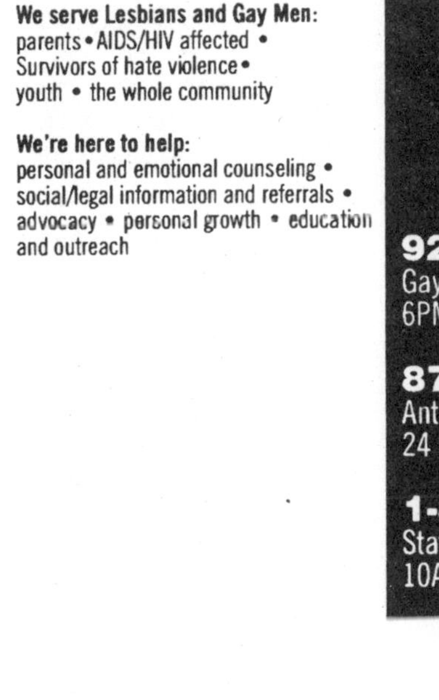

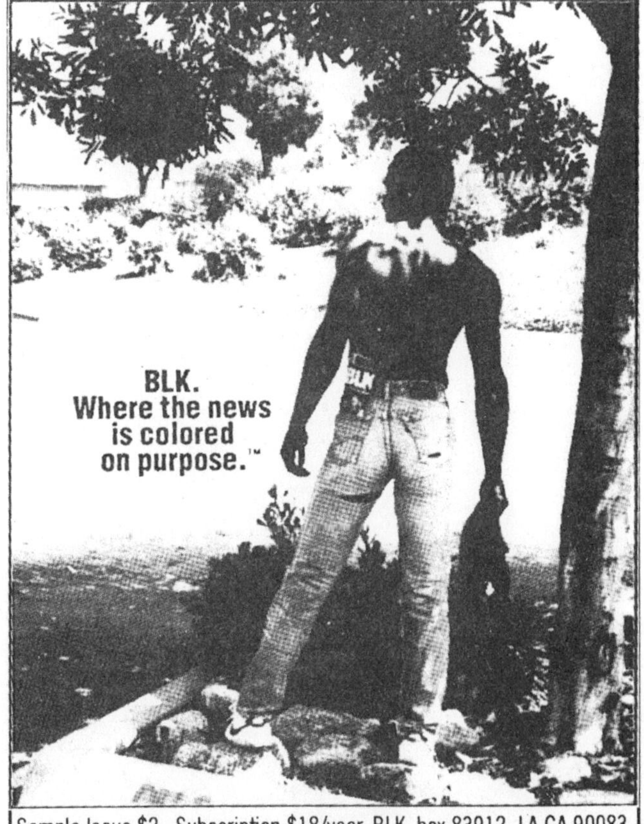

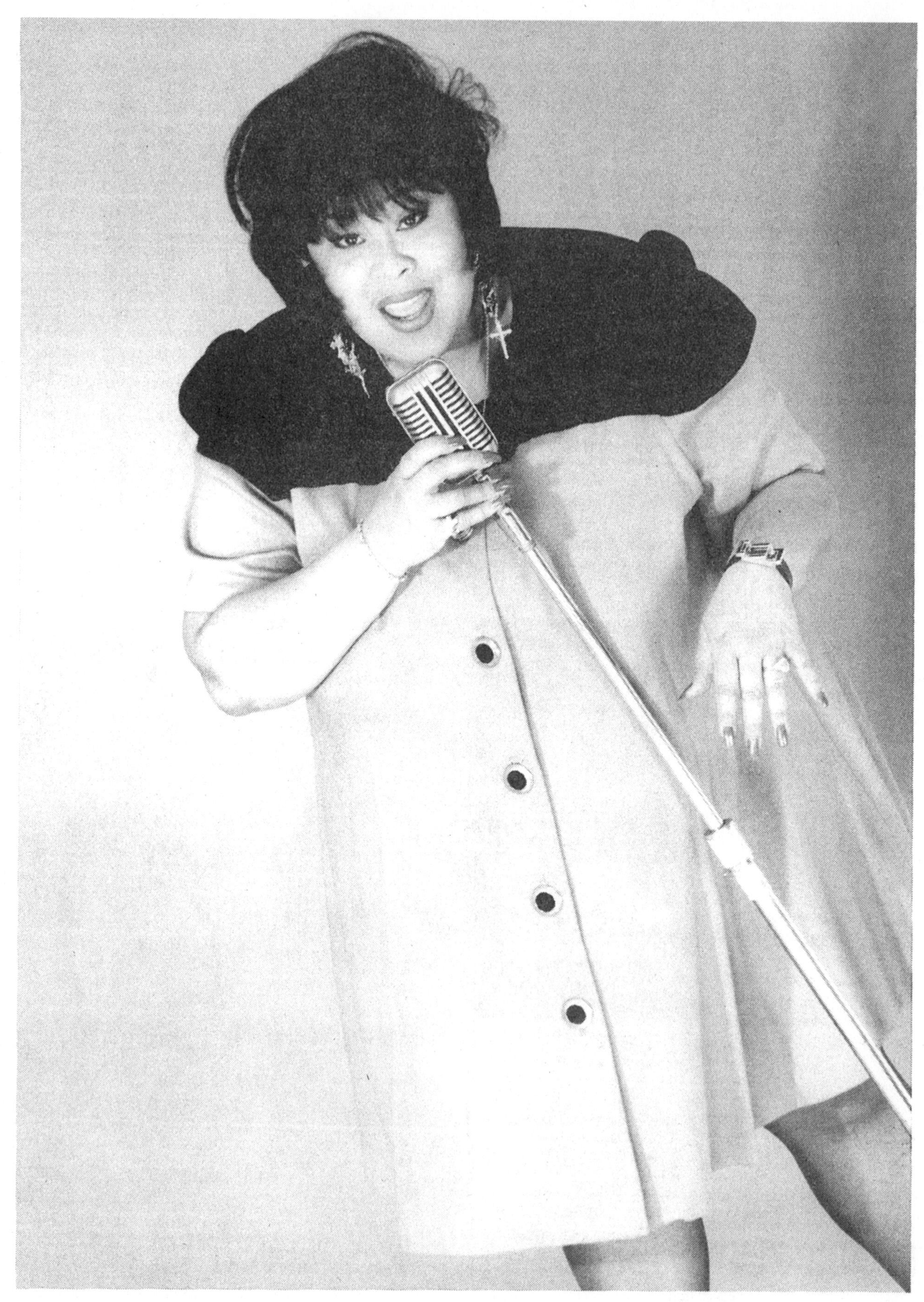

O U T I N T H E
WASH

Martha Wash finally gets the glass slipper. For too long, her stardom has been played out in the wings, first as a voice behind the goddess Sylvester, then as half of Two Tons O'Fun and The Weather Girls, two of disco's campier incarnations. When the MTV era hit, hers was one of the earliest scandals involving the games that were played with image manipulation. Black Box and C&C took her voice and hired models to lip synch. But shady music business trauma also turned out to be good press: RCA quickly won the bidding war, snapping her up for a long-overdue solo project. Her self-titled debut does not disappoint. Released just weeks ago, it has already spawned the house/disco anthem: "Carry On" Its hypnotic and sassy vamp provides a great canvas for her passionate disco gospel vocals.

Our fifteen minutes with Martha took place in Chicago on a recent press junket (doing WLUW, WGCI, B96, The Chicago Tribune, Jam Sessions, *and* a record release party!). And it was great to see her finally getting the major label treatment. An army of mink-clad promotion reps whisked her in from a block-long white limo for our photo shoot and interview, where it immediately became apparent that this diva was on no star trip. She's living large and loving it .

Robert Ford: Tell me a little bit about your musical background. I read somewhere that you had some opera training.

Martha Wash: When I was in high school I studied opera. My music teacher passed away, and when she did, I never went back into it. But I enjoyed it for the little time I studied.

RF: Was that before you started doing gospel music?

MW: I grew up singing gospel. Since about the age of two. My mother encouraged me to sing. She sang herself, so she sang in the church choir. She would bring me to church and growing up I was in the choir, and I used to play for the youth choir, and sang in the adult choir, so I've had experience.

RF: What was it like jumping from that gospel background to working with Sylvester? Was it a jolt?

MW: No, not at all. Its funny, because Sylvester came from a gospel background also. So it was really no strange thing. It was just going on to something else. And we sang gospel a lot. He loved to come up with old songs. We would sometimes sit and think of old, old, *old* gospel songs that you hardly ever hear about anymore. And we would just sit and sing and harmonize.

RF: Did any of your friends from the church criticize you for working in the disco industry?

MW: No. If they did, I didn't know about it. Not at all. My parents weren't thrilled. My mother especially was not thrilled. But she finally came around. She wanted me to continue singing gospel music. And I said "look, gospel music will never leave me because that's a part of me". We still do gospel in the shows. I'm just doing something else right now. So she came around, she even came to the show. There was no problem once she saw what I had to do, how I made my living. She became a big supporter.

RF: How did you first meet Sylvester? Was it an ad for an audition?

MW: I got a phone call for an audition. To do some recording as a background

T E X T
Robert Ford
P H O T O S
Dan DuVerney

singer. And when I went to the place where they were holding the audition, I didn't even know who it was for. And that's when I met Sylvester. And I sang a couple of songs for him, and he

asked "Do you know anybody else that's as large as you are that can sing?" and I said "yes." And I brought in Izora. And we went on from there.

RF: Did you know his music before you met him?

MW: Yes. It was a surprise, because I had only seen him once before. The first time I saw him he was the opening act for Billy Preston. In Berkley, California. When I saw him, it was like...well, what is he doing? I enjoyed it, but I wasn't quite ready for it. I came to see Billy Preston.

RF: Was he doing a big flamboyant act?

MW: Not really. I mean, he had his moments. He had the sequins and feathers and all this other kinda stuff. It wasn't drag. He had just come back from Europe. Previously, he had a band called Sylvester and the Hot Licks. They put out a few albums on the Blue Thumb label, years ago.

RF: They were doing Bessie Smith covers and that kind of thing, weren't they?

MW: Yeah, Sylvester loved the blues.

RF: Was the name Two Tons O' Fun Sylvester's idea?

MW: Well, that's been debated. It just kind of came into being. He had been Sylvester for a long, long time. And at first it was just Sylvester and background singers. And then it just kinda grew into Sylvester and Two Tons O' Fun.

RF: Sylvester was one of the first of the bigger celebrities to die from AIDS related causes. Did you see the influence of that in the music industry; did it cause people to become aware?

MW: No. Because it wasn't just Sylvester himself. There were too many other people. Not just in music but in the arts in general that were dying. Talented people. Just...gone. I did an interview with (*Billboard* dance editor) Larry Flick, and we were talking about some of the old DJs and things, and he made me stop and realize how many people I have known, from when I first started in this business with Sylvester up until now, who had passed. DJs, radio jocks, club owners, a lot of them are gone. And it was more than I had even thought.

RF: And when you multiply that by the people that you don't know...

MW: Exactly. At one point a few years ago I was getting a phone call just about every day, for a couple of weeks. Every day somebody had called to tell me of somebody who'd died of AIDS. And you get to a point where you say "I don't want to answer the phone. I don't want to know who it is." It's very depressing. Especially when its people you know and you cared about, and you worked with over the years. That's why I do my thing; donate my time and my services.

RF: I've seen where you've appeared at a number of AIDS fundraisers.

MW: When I have the time. Last year, in 92, I did more benefits in that one year than I ever had before. It's basically a continuation from doing them when the Weather Girls were together. It gets real hectic sometimes. I've done the danceathons from coast to coast. And the local benefits. I've done the AmFar things. I personally prefer the local ones as opposed to the national ones. I feel if you're going to raise the money in the area, keep it there. Because the money hopefully stays right there and is used right there. It's needed right then. I have nothing against research, that's fine. Millions are being spent on research, and in the meantime you've still got people right here in the community that need the help. I wish I didn't have to do it. But I have to. There have been too many

people that I know who have passed from AIDS. Not just celebrity people, but personal friends. Everyday, ordinary people. It's not a pleasant fact, but its here. And it seems like enough is not being done. You can research...honey, how long have they been trying to find a cure for cancer? In the meantime, the work still has to be done. A very grassroots type of thing. If you can get the community involved, it's better than waiting for the government to trickle down.

RF: Now, you probably are sick of talking about the whole Black Box/C&C Music Factory scandal...

MW: Um-humm! You're right.

RF: Did that experience make you more savvy in negotiating this label deal?

MW: I won't say that it made me more savvy in negotiating the deal. It's just given me more experience dealing with record companies. Being in this business, you have to experience stuff. You have to go through things. And it's not always pleasant. My thinking is: if you don't go through the bad, when the good comes you can hardly appreciate it. There's no good without the bad. You have to take them both. So I look at it as something that is negative, and trying to turn it into something positive.

RF: There's one other question about that whole controversy ...did you ever hear that Katrin Quinol was a drag queen?

MW: (*laughs*) That rumor went from the east coast to the west coast and all points in between. The first time I heard it I got hysterical. I laughed. I said "Okay! I've been reduced to a man dressed as a woman." I saw her once. And you know, I wasn't quite sure myself.

RF: I remember her from that "I Don't Know Anybody Else" video and she's got some big legs and hands for a girl.

MW: Alright! At first glance I thought she was a woman. She was supposed to be from Guadalupe, and she lived in Paris

RF: You do some jingle work too, right?

MW: Yes. I've done Dodge, Cheerios, Folgers coffee. I got a Kodak coming out soon. Coca-Cola.

RF: Is that stuff a lot different to record than "real songs"?

MW: It is. Because you have thirty seconds or sixty seconds to do it. I

think it's a good way to keep up with my chops. Being able to think quick and listen quick. Catch on quick and do it. And hope that it comes out fine.

RF: Do you ever want to produce?

MW: Yeah, I've thought about it. I'm not quite comfortable with it. Maybe later on. Maybe collaborating with somebody. My thing has always been in front of the microphone. The ones that can do both, and do it very well, I applaud them. I don't necessarily see it for me. Maybe I'm scared of it, I don't know.

RF: How did you hook up with the producers for this new project?

MW: Well, Eric Robinson wrote just about all the songs on the Two Tons album, so we went all the way back. He wrote "Just Us," "Earth Can Be Just Like Heaven," all those. He's been living in England for the last ten years. I called him and he sent me some songs. And I liked "Hold On". So he came over from England and we did both of those songs. Brian Alexander Morgan was called in by the a&r (artist and repertoire) director Kenny Ortiz to submit some songs. He produced five of the songs, and wrote three. Todd Terry produced three. Eric Beall and Steve Skinner produced two songs. That's a total of four producers. I didn't want to use a whole lot of producers. The songs that I picked, I liked how they sounded. I liked the lyrics and the music. And after I recorded all the songs, I thought it worked out very well. RCA wanted me to do the dance music, and I said "okay, fine. But I want to do the ballads" When I first heard "Now That You're Gone" thought it was perfect for the quiet storm stations. "Hold On (Part Two)" would work well on a gospel station. "Give It To You" and "Things We Do For Love" could go r&b or dance, depending on who mixes it. Because sometimes it's in the mix

RF: Do you have much of a hand in that, lining up the remixers?

MW: Nope. The next thing I know it's done. And I haven't always been thrilled with what I heard, but I'm dealin' with it.

RF: I just saw the videos for the first time last night, and they are both very good. Did you get involved with the concept or storyboards for them at all?

MW: Not really. Those two videos

were shot within two days of each other, and in the meantime I was on the road. So my manager and my designers got together with the video director and producer. One director was from England, the other was in Manhattan. It was crazy. Trying to shoot two videos in two days, it was kind of a nightmare. I had more fun with "Give It To You" than "Carry On".

RF: Were you prepared to walk onto the set with these half dressed humpy models?

MW: Well, when I looked at them, I thought "Oh Lord, bless their hearts!" They were in their undies. I said "let's try and get them some heaters or something", because it was cold in there. It was an old building in a park in New Jersey.

RF:And when were you shooting? In November?

MW: It was in October. It was cold and wet. Bad weather to be walking around in your underwear. They were good sports about being cold. And they enjoyed it too.

RF: How did you decide to do a reprise of "Just Us"?

MW: (laughs) Do you like it?

RF: Yes, I do.

MW: The a&r guy loved Two Tons O' Fun anyway. He thought it would be a good idea to take "Just Us", bring it up to a 90s feeling, with drum tracks and all this other kinda stuff, and see what happens. Well, it took me a while to get into it. He had Todd Terry just lay down some tracks. And I went in from there and I had to reprogram myself.

RF: The new version is a lot faster.

MW: It's a *whole* lot faster. A whole different kind of beat going on. Todd & I had to go back and forth over what to do where. I was surprised myself when it came out; it's not too bad!

RF: Did it feel funny to be doing that without Izora?

MW: Yes, it did.

RF: You could have called it "Just Me"

MW: (laughs) well, what can I tell you?

RF: Are you in touch with Izora at all?

MW: I haven't talked to her in quite a while. I've been on the road and trying to finish the album. That was a major effort. She's out on tour with the Weather Girls, and she's using her daughter. So it's both of them. And she's doing jingles here and there, so she's doing ok.

RF: Are you going to tour in support of this album?

MW: Yes, I'm planning to.

RF: Weren't you supposed to be here in Chicago about a year ago, a club date at Vortex?

MW: Oh, please! Oh honey, please! I don't even want to get into that. It's kinda strange how that whole situation happened. It was wrong. I don't like to say I'm coming and then not appear. Now there are those promoters that will tell the fans that the artist is coming and the artist don't know nothing about it. So let's leave it like that! But I came the following month to China Club and did my show. Chicago's been a good place as far as fan support over the years.

RF: A fan asked me to ask you if "Taking Away Your Space" would show up as part of your live show?

MW: I'm not going to say!

RF: It must be often requested.

MW: It is. And its nice to know that folks want to hear it. But let me put it like this: hopefully when they come to see the show, they'll like it. Right now I'm trying to schedule band rehearsals to get the show together, because I want to go out live.

RF: It must be harder to do track dates. And I would think that some of the clubs would rather bring you in with a tape than with a band.

MW: Tape is very constricting. You can't change and move and shuffle things around when you're working with a tape. In a live situation you can stop any time you want to. You can change it any time you want to. It's up to you. And touring with a band is part of a progression. I don't want to be considered just a dance artist. There's nothing wrong with it. Dance music, and doing the clubs and stuff, honey that's provided me and a whole lot of people a living. And I'm grateful for

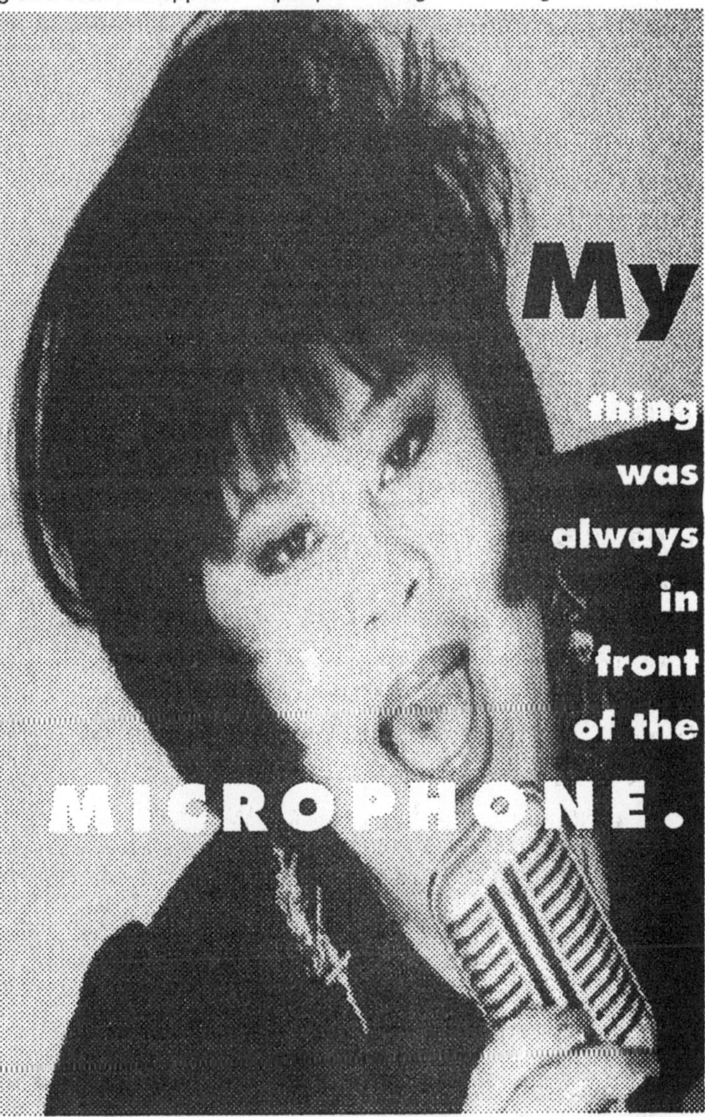

that. But, there is more. And that's what I'm striving for. I just hope that the album does well. It's getting a lot of support, and there are people waiting for it to come out. So I want to see multi-platinum. And I think there are enough fans out there.

RF: Do you feel like RCA is supporting you with this record?

MW: Let's put it this way: they're taking a chance on me and I'm taking a chance on them. Time will tell. I'm just keeping my fingers crossed. **THING**

GAGGING on the

Take any notions you may have of the word "busy" and throw them out the window because the Fabulous Pop Tarts and their production/management company World Of Wonder have redefined the term! Randy "Pop" Barbato and Fenton "Tart" Bailey are the Pop Tarts, and together they've created an entertainment dream producing albums, television shows, and managing the career of the Supermodel hisself, RuPaul. Trippin' out between Britain, Los Angeles and New York as they do, sometimes it's hard to pin down either one of these charming young men, but a couple of faxes and phone calls yielded lots of fun facts about plenty of their latest projects, including the forthcoming release of their newest album, *Gagging On The Lovely Extravaganza* on Atlanta's Funtone USA label.

Rosser: It's so great that you haven't even got the album out yet, and there it is written up in *Billboard* already!
Fenton: Well, the release date is still March 23rd because Dick (Richards, Funtone USA President) thought that would be a good day to release it on...
Randy: This record certainly was the most fun that we've had making, more than any other Pop Tart record. I mean, there's so many people on this record! It really excites me, because with each person there's like a host of other people who are in some way involved. Really, there are so many stars on that record. My favorite bits are everybody else's contributions. There are still parts that I listen to that just crack me up!

Fenton: The thing about *Gagging On The Lovely Extravaganza* is that we always, you know, having been previously signed to London Records, and having sort of experienced being part of the Polygram Group, it was really nice to leave all that behind. After the whole experience we were a bit iffy about the Pop Tarts. It was rather a traumatic episode, and so it was kind of nice to, to get it back to the level that we were comfortable with, pursuing it in the way that we felt was the right way to do it, you know, going with Funtone, talking to small magazines and stuff, and doing that sort of thing rather than doing this massive corporate thing, which didn't really suit the Pop Tarts because it's so quirky, it's so unto itself, it's...
Rosser: You wouldn't really want to say "inside joke"...
Fenton: I suppose it is sort of inside jokey isn't it?
Rosser: One of the things I love about it so much is that I laugh every time I listen to it, and I hear something new all the time!
Fenton: Well, hell, it's been four years in the making! I mean, some people write novels or build buildings in less time than four years, so there should be a lot in it!
Randy: My current rediscovery is "My Kitty Is A Martian", and you know we've had our cat for like 10 years, and we've always been teasing her, and we have been promising her we were going to make her a star, and we always though she had the potential, so we're happy to make her a part of the album. She wrote that song, incidentally. And you know, between you and me, she's been eating, she's let herself go somewhat, and she's a little jealous of RuPaul, 'cause Kitty was here waiting to be a superstar, and then along came RuPaul. You know, MTV's "The Grind" will come on, and everybody will gather around, and Kitty, she'll leave the room.
Fenton: We've got to get on with it and make a video for the first single, which will probably be the "Theme From Voyeurvision" the live telefantasy show that we wrote the theme song for. Jimmy Harry did the mix, and he wasn't mentioned in the *Billboard* piece, and in a way it's unfair because Jimmy Harry has really been the main producer on the album. I mean, he's done something to almost every single one of the tracks. So, if you can mention him...
Randy: Bill Coleman worked on "Voyeurvision" too. And Keoki, you know Keoki? He's doing a technomix, in fact I think he's doing that tonight! We're hoping that the video

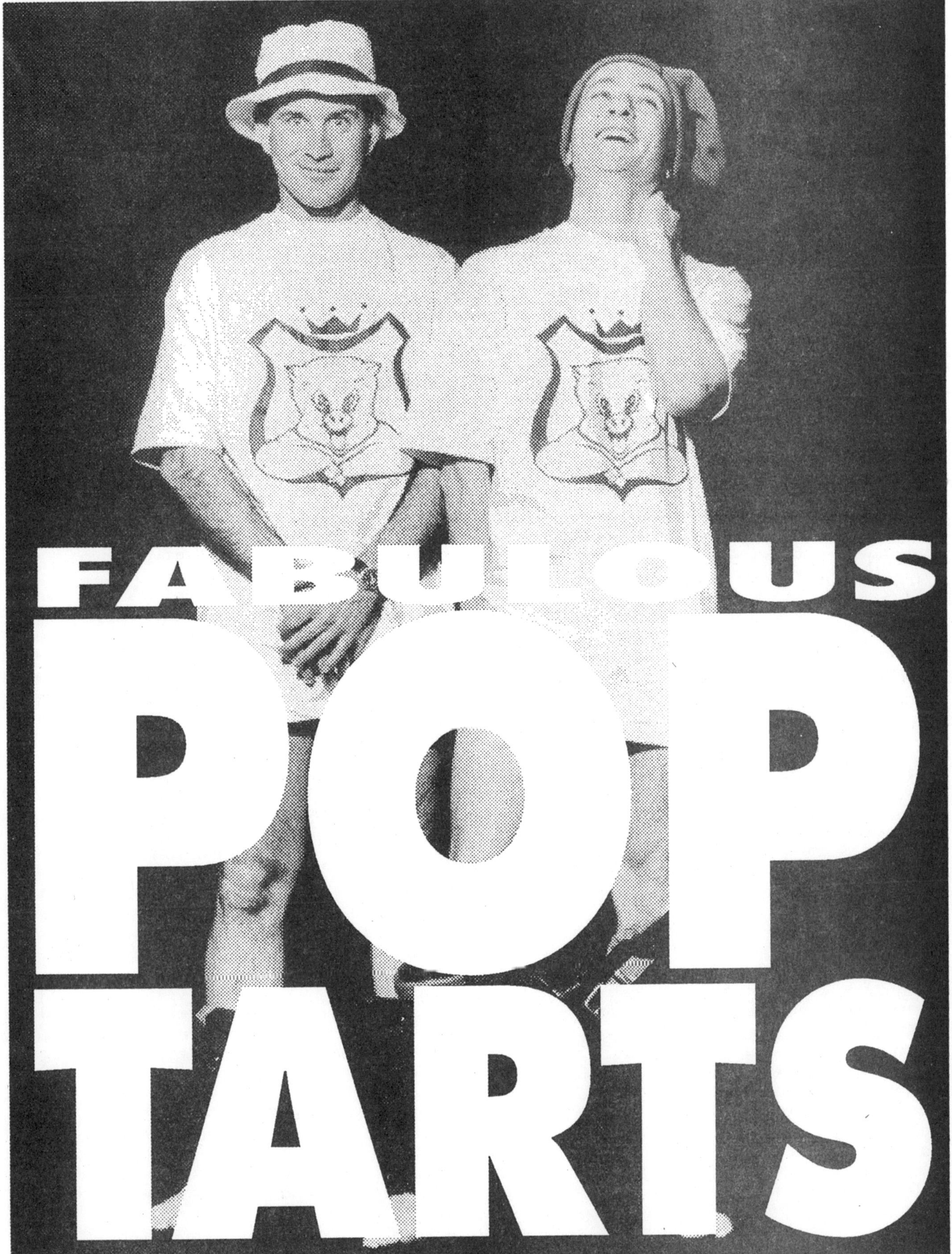
FABULOUS
POP
TARTS

will tie in a lot of the starts from public access across America, we want to include them in the video. Fenton and I will make sort of sparse appearances in the video. We have put out a call for two new Pop Tarts, but you know it's a demanding toll. People have been sending us their SAT scores, and their 8X10 glossies, and their used underwear... and based on that, hopefully we'll be able to make a decision.

Fenton: You know, I've always liked New Kids On The Block and the Monkees and bands like that, and I'm thinking, well, you know, it's hard to produce TV shows, and manage Ru and then kind of go out and do the clubs at night. I think there's younger, cuter people who could do it better, and who would look good in underwear!

Rosser: Getting back to Jimmy Harry, he's involved in something else with you?

Fenton: He co-wrote "Supermodel" and has produced a lot of the RuPaul stuff. He's got his own act too, called Whorgasm, which is just unbelievably frightening. It's kind of techno-grunge, Alice Cooper of the '90's. And we're looking after him, getting his solo career launched.

Randy: Whorgasm is like the antithesis of RuPaul. No one would ever make a connection between the two of them, yet they have so much in common. Whorgasm makes grunge look like bubblegum pop.

Rosser: Now, Jimmy Harry is the same one who did some of the great songs in "Shaggy Dog Animation" that played here in Atlanta with RuPaul in it a few years ago, right?

Fenton: Yes, he is.

Rosser: That show was really great. Well, it was so cool to see your article in *Billboard*, and then to flip the page and see RuPaul on the Dance Trax chart!

Fenton: Well, you know people in the music business have said, "Oh, you know drag queens are great, great novelty and all that..." But it's inevitable, and it's about time that it has happened.

Rosser: Well, RuPaul is perfect for it, he's so captivating.

Fenton: The very first time I saw RuPaul was at the New Music Seminar, and he was wearing those American football shoulder pads, a jock strap, and he was touting his Wee Wee Pole record. Well, the moment changed my life. He has always been the star he is today, it was just getting the rest of the world to recognize that.

Randy: Someone like RuPaul is kinda beyond, he's like he's someone who for the past 10 years has sacrificed his being for something much higher, and I know this sounds like, overly cosmic, but knowing Ru as I do—he's obviously become one of my best friends—well, his life has always been about sacrificing his being for a larger thing. It's beyond ego. I mean, he gets off on it, but it's totally beyond that. He's like this mega-celebrity superstar, he's product. Pure product.

Rosser: It must be a lot of fun to work with him.

Fenton: Yes it is, it is. He is so dedicated and hard working, he's just ready for it, you know. RuPaul is kind of the representative—there's so much downtown talent that similarly, until now, has gone unrecognized. You know, Deee-Lite did it too, there's only so much Coca-Cola people can drink, there's only so much CNN that people can take, and people are going to want different flavors and different things. It's

only a matter of time before the dam breaks and DeAundra Peek is number one on the dance charts too!

Rosser: Speaking of TV, you are working, eh?

Fenton: Three things that we're doing at the moment, one is a Valentine's Day special called "Love In The USA", which is like a special episode of "Made In The USA" and "Manhattan Cable", local cable, Public Access clips. It's kind of like the video equivalent of Madonna's *Sex* book. We did a story on the big porn convention in Las Vegas, a story on foot worshippers, and we're doing a story on lovers at sixty, sex over sixty to be precise. Married couples, over sixty, having sex.

Rosser: Oh my gosh.

Fenton: And they do it a lot!

Rosser: Ha ha ha ha. *Lets hope that's a prediction for our futures!*

Randy: We met lots of interesting people, including Russ Myers, and we did a story on the chapels out there and met a woman who owns 5 of them, they call her the "Chapel Queen of Vegas"—we're pushing a lot of buttons with it. And, we finished up a program called "Video World", and then there's the "L.A. Stories" project. All these things are on the party platforms that "everybody's a star", and the idea of access, you know, "you too can make your own program".

Fenton: What we did for "L.A. Stories" was find ten people who were involved in the riots, we've got a cop, a schoolteacher, gangleader, helicopter pilot, newspaper reporter, a Korean whose store was burned down, and a gynecological surgeon. All these different people and we've given them camcorders, and they've had these camcorders since September, and they've been making video diaries of their lives. What we're beginning to see, we're actually seeing into people's lives and we're seeing that people aren't cardboard cutouts, and that they are real people and that their lives are very complex, and it's sort of busting all the stereotypes. It's airing on the anniversary of the L.A. riots, on the BBC.

Rosser: So let me see, that's on the BBC...

Fenton: "Love In The USA" is going to be on Channel 4, in England, and "Video World" on Channel 4 too. We haven't got any TV shows in America yet.

Randy: You know, we're pretty much perceived as the purveyors of trash. World of Wonder, importing all of America's trash and kitsch. Of course, we don't agree with that. And I think that these other two programs will help us to legitimize us more...but of course both of them will have *lots* of trash.

Rosser: The kinds of things that people really want to see!

Randy: Exactly!

Rosser: Well, are you doing the music for these new shows as well?

Fenton: Yeah, we write the music for them too. In fact, some of the songs on the LP come from some of the TV shows.

Rosser: Like "Ring My Bell".

Fenton: It's one of my faves too, it's sort of, dunno, there's something about it.

Rosser: It has that sort of sixties hook with that tambourine sound in it, that shooka shooka sound jangling in there.

Fenton: Well, I don't even get to listen to it, we don't have a CD player! (*It had broken, they hadn't replaced it yet...*)

Rosser: Fenton, I'd like to ask you briefly about the book that you've written, which I have a press release about. It's called…

Fenton: *Fallen From Grace*. Actually, the book was written years ago, it came out in England a year ago. In fact, it was the first book on Michael Milken, came out before James Stewart's *Den of Thieves*, which was a big seller, but it's only just been published here in the States. Alan Dershowitz, the lawyer, wrote an introduction for it. It was when we first started managing RuPaul when I was writing it, when I was finishing it up. You know, after a time you can go long periods where there isn't much going on, and suddenly, everything happens all at once! And so for a time it was a bit touch and go—I thought I was going to lose my mind! Writing books is not recommended, it's too much hard work! Well, certainly writing factual books like that.

Rosser: All that research!

Fenton: Well, it may seem a bit obscure of a subject, or a bit off the track of the sort of things that we do, but it's actually what Milken was all about, it's sort of very much relevant to what we are trying to do, not that we are Michael Milken, we just don't have that great an interest in money, but, he was very much into getting other people's projects off the ground and stuff. He's kind of like the Andy Warhol of Wall Street.

Rosser: Any plans for vacation, travelling,

FENTON
RANDY

We have a call out
for two new Pop Tarts…

Younger, cuter
people…who would look
good in underwear.

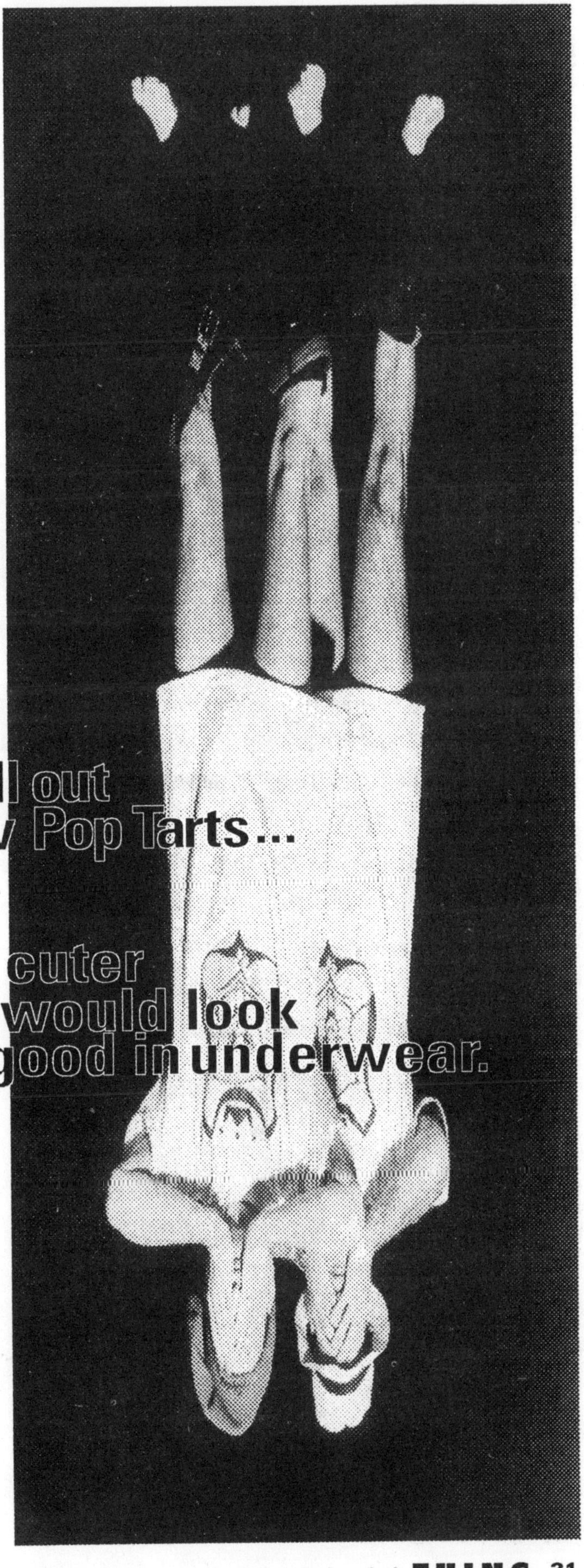

FUN?

Fenton: Fun? Well, it's all fun actually. It's hard to think about going on holiday, because in a way it is all a holiday. I've got to go to England next week, but not for very long. We'll have to make a movie with RuPaul.

Rosser: I was just talking about that with some people the other day!

Fenton: We are planning this year to make a feature film for theatre release on Wigstock. Because *Paris Is Burning* did so well, and there's so many people who'd like to go to Wigstock from all over America, but who can't get to New York on Labor Day. So you better…

Rosser: My bags are packed! My makeup's all put up and everything!

Fenton: You've got your medication… **THING**

Candy J

Somewhere just off-center of the borderlines that divide Chicago's social classes, there is a two-flat cobblestone building with Candice Jordan's name on one of the doorbells. Inside of her three bedroom flat, there is a music studio cluttered with keyboards, a computer she composes with, dozens of CDs, a mixing board, and flyers of past club dates. Her fans know Candice Jourdan by her many stage names; Candy J aka Sweet Pussy Pauline aka Hateful Head Helen, whose ribald triple-X rated rhythm tracks have become much-sampled underground hits. Today girlfriend is prepared to jaw-jack about her current projects and other disco drama.

LeRoy Whitfield: When did the persona of Candy J and Sweet Pussy Pauline all began?
Candy J: Child, I don't even know. About five years ago. I sold it from my house first. It was a joke, it was never supposed to come out. This DJ said 'Let me play that in the club.' I let him play it and everyone wanted a copy of it. Sold 137,000 copies.
LW: Really? And it's still selling, right?
CJ: Yes. And I own it. I have sued numerous people over it, including this. This is my newest little thing. *(She proudly hands me a copy of a 12" on Nervous Records, featuring uncredited samples of Sweet Pussy Pauline.)* I just sued them. You ever heard that? "One Leg on the Ceiling"?
LW: Um, no.
CJ: Ooooh, that's a fierce record, baby. I hated to have to do it. We reached a settlement so... I sued everybody, honey.
LW: That was my next question: Have you ever been burned in scandals over Sweet Pussy Pauline?
CJ: Oh, yes! The record came out in Italy and I didn't know nothing about it. What else? Yeah...I've sued a lot of people, honey.
LW: What is your favorite lawsuit story?
CJ: All of them, because they all made coins! *(laughs)* 2 Live Crew. Tony, Toni, Toné...Um...who else?
LW: 2 Live Crew?!
CJ: Yeah. Deee-Lite.
LW: Deee-Lite?!!
CJ: Yeah. Remember in their song *("Groove is in the Heart")* where it goes: *One, two, three- Brrrrrrrrr.*
LW: That was you?
CJ: Yup, that was out of my song. My name is on the album.
LW: And 2 Live Crew? Tell me about that.
CJ: Well I called them, honey, and told them that they had used my record without my permission. He said "So what are you saying? You're going to sue me?" I said "Yes." He said "Well, stand in line, bitch!!!" and hung up the phone. I reached a settlement with everybody.
LW: Sweet Pussy Pauline is a classic. You just finished Sweet Pussy Pauline II?
CJ: Yeah, its the new one that just came out about two weeks ago called

"The Walk" by Sweet Pussy Pauline. Its fierce! And I just got signed to Vinyl Solution in London for an album.
LW: Which is due out when?
CJ: Don't ask. Actually all of the music is finished.
LW: Who are your favorite singers?
CJ: Oh! You would be surprised. Phyllis Hyman. I love jazz. I sing jazz, honestly. But *(house and pop music)* seems to be keeping me in fierce coins, so I'm doing this.
LW: So would you ever do anything totally different like "Candy J Does a Revue" or "...a Tribute to..." You know, with a kind of jazzy appeal?
CJ: Larry Heard is doing a jazz song for me. It's real Sade, very Sade-like. Who else am I working with? Robert Owens. I'm doing something with him.
LW: Tell me about the single you are doing with Judy Tenuta.
CJ: Oh, do you want to hear it? Ain't nobody ever heard it. They just finished the video. Fabio is in it...Weird Al Yankovic is in it...I'll let you hear it.
LW: How did this deal come to pass?
CJ: Well, you know she's got a big gay following, so they asked me to do the music. It's kind of pop, though. Do you want me to call her?
LW: Uh, not right now. Where do you want to go with this record? Do you want it to stay underground or do you want it to hit Top 40?
CJ: This record? You tell me if you think it will hit Top 40. Maybe it will because of her. It's more underground than anything. *(She puts the tune on. Judy yodels "Attention....Calling all studs." I fall out laughing.)* What?
LW: I like her voice. You did the music for this?
CJ: Yeah.

LW: I finally see the connection.
CJ: Of what?
**LW: I think that Judy Tenuta is a persona. She's larger than life, she's in-your-face and you are

the same way.**
CJ: You think so?
LW: Yeah, I do. I mean, they're not the *same.*
CJ: Oh, you though it was going to be something nasty?
LW: No I didn't, but I see your personas: Sweet Pussy Pauline and Judy Tenuta as kind of in-your-face-entertainment. I mean, you're not on the same level, but I was really looking for a connection. At first, I thought you two really seemed like an unlikely music team.
CJ: I just do music. Sweet Pussy Pauline just happened to be my...I guess it is my biggest record. Is it? I'm supposed to have something on RuPaul's album. I was going to do a song for her.
But I do entirely different kinds of music than people know about. I am just doing something for Tracie Spencer. This will probably shock you. *(She puts another tape in. This time mellow R&B)* See I don't always sound nasty. I did the music and the background.
LW: When you bring out your record, do you think that people are going to expect you to be nasty or what are you going to present?
CJ: Well, no because you remember my other big record was "Some Things Never Change" on Hotmix 5 Records. That crossed over to radio. So, I mean, they know I can do that sort of stuff but everybody I guess just forgot that I do that. So my album is going to be strictly musical. I mean, I want to talk, but not necessarily nasty. Of course, there will be X-rated versions on the 12"s, but not on the album.
LW: There was a widespread rumor that you were pregnant. *(More gags)*
CJ: *(Acting)* Yes, well, I had an abortion. It was so painful. *(Laughs)* You're just saying that.
LW: No, no, no! I'm serious!
CJ: Really?
LW: What other rumors have you heard about yourself? I mean, you're at a point now where I'm sure they are circulating.
CJ: I've heard that I was a drag queen. Can you believe that? I didn't even know what it was at first. *(Me & Mark gag; Candy doesn't)*
LW: What others?

CJ: I read *(people)* pretty well, so people don't do that to me. Other than the rumors that started when I was on tour, saying my record must not be selling and I must not be doing that well, you know. But after recently purchasing my Benz, though, I think they'll get the message. But that's why I don't go out *(to nightclubs)* because it starts too many rumors. I just want to create music.

I just don't mix the two. You know, my personal life is my personal life. That's why I don't do interviews. Because, see, I remember I was in, um... what's the name of the fucking magazine? I was in all of them and they had rumors like that about me, and my agent told me that 'I don't think that should be a focal point *(of my career)*. *(Headlines read)* "Candy J: Is this the next Boy George"; "Candy J: Is he or she the future of dance music?" and I just kind of played it out. That's why I didn't tour Europe until this year. When I went over they it was like... I'm like all over MTV over there. But that never came up because I don't want that to be an issue. Like, if you come to my show and you think I'm a drag queen that's fine but you're going to have to pay 10 or 15 dollars to make that judgement.

LW: I heard that you worked successfully as a female car sales representative. *(Candy gags.)*
CJ: Yes, I used to be a broker. An auto broker. Oh, god! *(Gags again)* Who told you that?
LW: Robert. *(Ford,* **Thing** *publisher)* **You don't consider yourself a gay artist?**
CJ: No.
LW: What do you consider yourself?
CJ Just an artist, an entertainer. Have you ever seen one of my shows?
LW: No.
CJ: I'm just an entertainer. I don't think that my sexuality should be a focal point. Just my music. You will never ever hear me say that I'm a gay artist. I'm just the opposite of entertainers like RuPaul because her sexuality is the whole phenomenon.
LW: So you go a little more for realness?
CJ: Yeah. I'm just a girl making music the way I look at it.
LW: It seems that now, with the big RuPaul phenomenon, female impersonators are getting more attention. Do you see a new trend starting or a new level of respect on the horizon for female impersonators?
CJ: No. I do not think *(the hype)* is going to last. I mean, that's RuPaul. I think she's talented, but...
LW: Did you know her before she became RuPaul?
CJ: Yes. She came up to me in Atlanta and told me that she was going to be doing a record. That was about four years ago and I was like, okay.
LW: How big do you want to be? How far do you want to take this?
CJ: Well, they say I'm probably the most talked about underground artist. I want to cross over to radio, but I don't want to be like a Madonna. I don't think I'd be happy like that. As long as I can comfortably, consistently make $100,000 a year...
LW: Are you doing that?
CJ: Yeah, I've been making that for the last four years.
Mark E Mixx: Who did the tracks for "Let's Get Together"?
CJ: Me and a guy named Chuck Webb. I put that song out because I was trying to finish an album. It did alright in New York. I think it sold like 30,000 copies, which is okay for a dance record. That's kind of big for an independent label, that's what they think. But they didn't promote it and they didn't market it. But my biggest song- do you know what I'm known for in Europe? You will never guess.
MEM: Which one?
CJ: A song I did- you ever heard "Hurt Me, Hurt Me"? (She sings a bar)
MEM Oh, yeah. You did that one?
CJ: That song was massive in Europe. I thought that I was known for Sweet Pussy Pauline and "Some Things Never Change" and it was, like, huge. I didn't perform it on that tour because I didn't know it was so big. My agent told me that it didn't sell so he wouldn't have to pay me my royalties on it.
LW: Do you feel that you have a better grasp on your business affairs now than when you started?
CJ: Oh god, yes. I stopped and didn't put a record out for a year so I could learn all about the business. When I first started, my business managers told me that I was making $1,000 a show when it was really $2,000. I didn't find out until the next year when I went back to the club and they pulled out the contracts and said 'Okay, last year we gave you $2,000 so this year we'll give you $3,000.' I was like '$2,000?!' and that's how I found out he cheated me out of 30 grand. I had to stop. I learned the business, I learned the music- I went to school for music. I put myself together as a package. I am an act, not necessarily an artist. I guess RuPaul is an artist, but I'm more of an act because my shows are a little more dramatic. That's how I kept working without having to put out records, like a Grace Jones-type. I do 47 cities a year. I just added Europe this year.
MEM: Do you find that the crowd in Europe receives you differently than the crowd in the States?
CJ: No. When I first went over there they didn't know what to expect. I did this club called Sex, Café Du Paris, The Zap Club and Queer Nation. They were so crowded, I could barely even get in. They were screaming and hollering. I don't let people tape my shows, but I wish I had taped it. I was on this little bitty-ass stage, probably as big as this desk. I was, like "What is this?!" But it was just packed. I started singing, I did an a capella of "Love Sensation," and they just hollered! Adeva and Sybil told me that they wasn't like that, talkin' about they don't scream and holler like they do in the States. So, I'm going over there thinking that I'm going to have to really work. But, honey, they was jumpin' through the place! I went into the studio while I was over there with Frankie Fonsett, the guy who mixed Larry Heard's "Closer" and I got my record deal with Vinyl Solution for two albums and a production deal with Doc Records, who is, I think, distributed by CBS—again. But no, there is no difference between the crowds.
LW: Why did you say "again" like that? It sounds like you've had a bad experience with CBS.
CJ: I was offered a deal from CBS before and I turned it down because I didn't want to do any Sylvester stuff.
LW: You're from Detroit, why did you decide to make your base in Chicago versus other cities.
CJ: Because I have a house.
LW: Yeah, but you could have a house in Detroit.
CJ: I don't know. Because when I first came here, I came here to model and I wound up selling cars.
LW: Why not New York or L.A.?
CJ: I have an apartment in New York.
LW: Is there anything special

that is keeping you in Chicago?
CJ: The boys!
LW: As far as the lyrics for Sweet Pussy Pauline, do you do that freestyle or...
CJ: Freestyle. Everybody asks me that. But for $10,000, I bet you could come up with some lyrics real quick.
LW: Do you want to be taken seriously, I mean, as a serious performer? You said on your album there are going to be ballads and...
CJ: Yeah, its probably going to be one ballad but it is going to be leaning a little bit more toward underground dance because that's where my market is.
LW: How do your parents feel about what you are doing?
CJ: My father is a minister. When my mother head Sweet Pussy Pauline she was like, Candy, really. But they are really proud of me. "Some Things Never Change" was the number 2 radio record in Detroit for awhile. I perform there a lot. Sweet Pussy Pauline was big there, of course.
LW: Your father, as a minister, what did he think of the entire thing?
CJ: I bought him a car.
LW: You say you don't consider yourself to be a female impersonator, what do you consider yourself?
CJ: *(In her most feminine tone)* A woman. Why, what would make anyone think that I was gay or a drag queen? I don't under-stand. I mean, what is wrong with you, LeRoy?! *(We all gag. The phone rings. Its the famous accordion-playing love child/comedi-enne, [and Candy's neighbor] Judy Tenuta. She's on the speaker phone)* Hello?
Judy Tenuta: Hey, Candy.
CJ: Hhhhhiiiiiiiiiiii, Juudyyyyyyyy.
JT: I'm just calling you back because, um, you told me to.
CJ: I have some men here who would like to interview you for a magazine.
JT: Oh, yeah? What magazine?
CJ: *Thing.*
JT: *Thing*?! As in Miss Thing?
CJ: Yeah.
JT: Never heard of it.
CJ: I was going to bring them over.
JT: I can't do it tonight because I have a lot of stuff to do. I've got some heavy stuff on my mind too, Candy. Maybe a phone interview some other time. I'll send them a picture in the mail. Oh, oh, oh!! I just heard this new joke today Candy! Okay, there are two for-eign women at an airport. One of the women, who is at the airport to pick up her husband, sees that he has flowers when he gets off the plane. She turns to the other woman and says 'Oh no, he has flowers!' The other woman says 'Don't you like flowers?' and the other woman says 'Yes, but that means I have to keep my legs open for two weeks.' And the other woman says 'Why don't you just put them in a vase?' *(Nobody laughs, we all just look at each other)* Did you hear me 'Why don't you just put them in a vase?!' Hello?
CJ: Yeah, we're still here, girl. 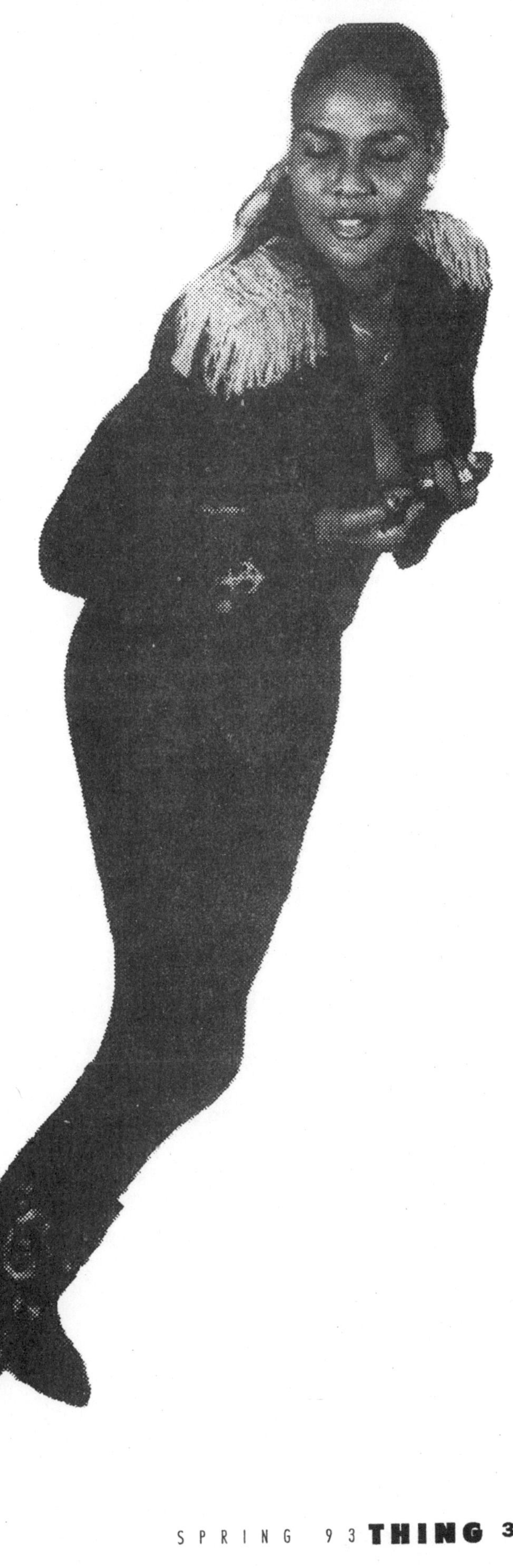

Bunny sans Pussy

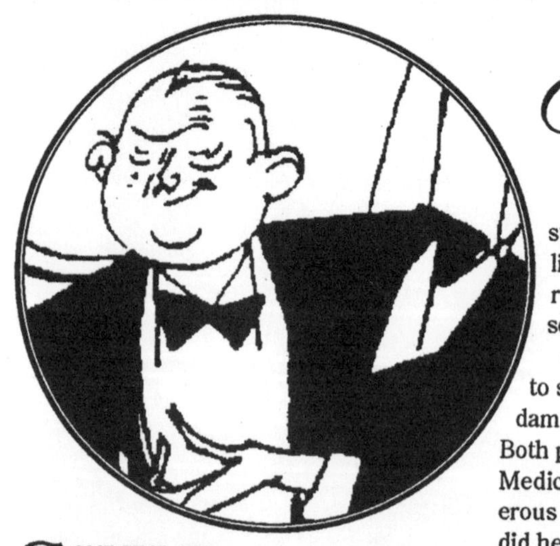

SOME TIME AGO I went with a friend to Florida where he was to have a short visit with his recently retired and transplanted Midwestern parents. After introductions and a bit of strained conversation, attention was turned to the perpetually-on television. There was some news item concerning some homeless single parent Latino physically challenged lesbians, or something like that, who were without welfare benefits and how something should be done to help them. My friend's father starts raving about those goddamned liberals and how they are going to ruin the country, giving it away, squandering it on the undeserving.

I found this to be a curious thing to say in light of the benefits the god-damned liberals had bestowed on them. Both parents received benefits from Medicare, Social Security, and a fairly generous pension through his union. What did he think, that the tooth fairy or, even less likely, the business establishment supplied these benefits that allowed him and his wife to live out their days in physical warmth and financial security rather than freezing their asses off in the rust belt working at minimum wage till death does its part? What makes these people think that their needs are greater or that they are more deserving of assistance from government then anyone else?

Let's consider what they actually need. They get money from several sources plus health care, they are in no jeopardy of losing either jobs or home. You would think that this would color favorably their views of the problems of the less fortunate. Of course there is the argument that they are indeed more deserving. Well, perhaps we should consider their contributions to the society, for instance, during wartime. I know that this particular WWII vet spent his time running rum back from Cuba at government expense. His wife showed solidarity with the grueling demands of total mobilization by keeping house.

Sometimes the Great Depression is mentioned as the hazing event that allows you into this special fraternity. Victims perhaps of casino-style fiscal policy but no more so than millions today. Is what we are talking about merely a case of Greedy Grannies or something more?

Thanks to unions, liberal Supreme Court justices, and humanitarian congressmen, a lot of those old shitbags have it all. And not only don't they want to give up any of it—which I can agree with to a point—but they don't want to see anyone else be helped by programs or policies that helped *them*, and this includes their immediate family. I have often thought that the bumper sticker "Ask me about my grandkids" should read " Send my kids to war but don't raise my taxes". America's health care system is in shambles, totally unavailable to large segments of society, but the golden years goldbrickers are sheltered. Higher taxes on gasoline could benefit society as a whole with road upkeep, public transit, etc., but when Gramps wants to get those extra trips to the mall without having to pay extra for his 9-mile-to-a-guzzling-gallon-yacht- sized car, his selfishness wins out.

B UT BUNNY, WHAT does this have to do with homosexuals? In case you hadn't noticed, the golden agers are part of the ultra-right coalition and this conservative movement has never been too keen on fairies. Homos are the only minority group left that you can discriminate against with impunity (not that a lynching of some big black buck at prime time wouldn't bring Superbowl-like ratings). I would say it has a lot to do with it.

Of course we must stop supporting groups that discriminate against us but ghetto-izing is not the answer, especially when the same oppressive institutions are supported just because they are in the neighborhood. The church of an organized religion is the same in Bensenville as it is in Andersonville. And do you really think that you can be all that you can be in the Army?

But Bunny, what does this have to do with the elderly? Dreams of dominance, fantasy, fear and free-floating resentment dance in the heads of all of us. The politics of exclusion are tempting. The elderly have reaped rewards from the system they seek to destroy, under the misguided sentiments and ill-informed assumptions promulgated by a fear-mongering ruling class and their Judeo-Christian lackeys. They have also been isolated by corporate strategies, and told that they need a selfish outlook to insure their golden years. The only thing to hope for is for it backfiring on the elderly so that they come to their senses and see how easily they have been manipulated. And as the rays of enlightened bliss shine down on this perfect world they realize that the strength of one minority lies in the strength of *all* minorities.

And would we be as kind if the ruby slippers were on the other foot? Perhaps it would be different but I wouldn't hold my breath. I personally have a lot of Pirate Jenny plowings walled up inside of me just itching to explode in a reign of terror. Maybe the hardest thing is just differentiating between the class struggle and P.M.S.

But in the meantime, gentle reader, what can we do? How can we encourage the elderly to see the path to the greater good? In what way can we influence this large block of voters to become more sensitive and responsive to the needs of others; to have them rekindle a concern for all humanity? PRAY. Pray for that magic moment when you find one of these reprehensible old vampires walking on a street (if any of them still walk). Pray you see them getting out of a large energy inefficient car with the Pat Robertson bumper sticker. Pray you see them try to cross a pot-holed street heading towards the far away WALK light that isn't working and pray that deregulated overloaded truck with a breaking distance of three light years is barreling down the street and pray that your laughing face is the last thing their subsidized uncataracted eyes ever see.

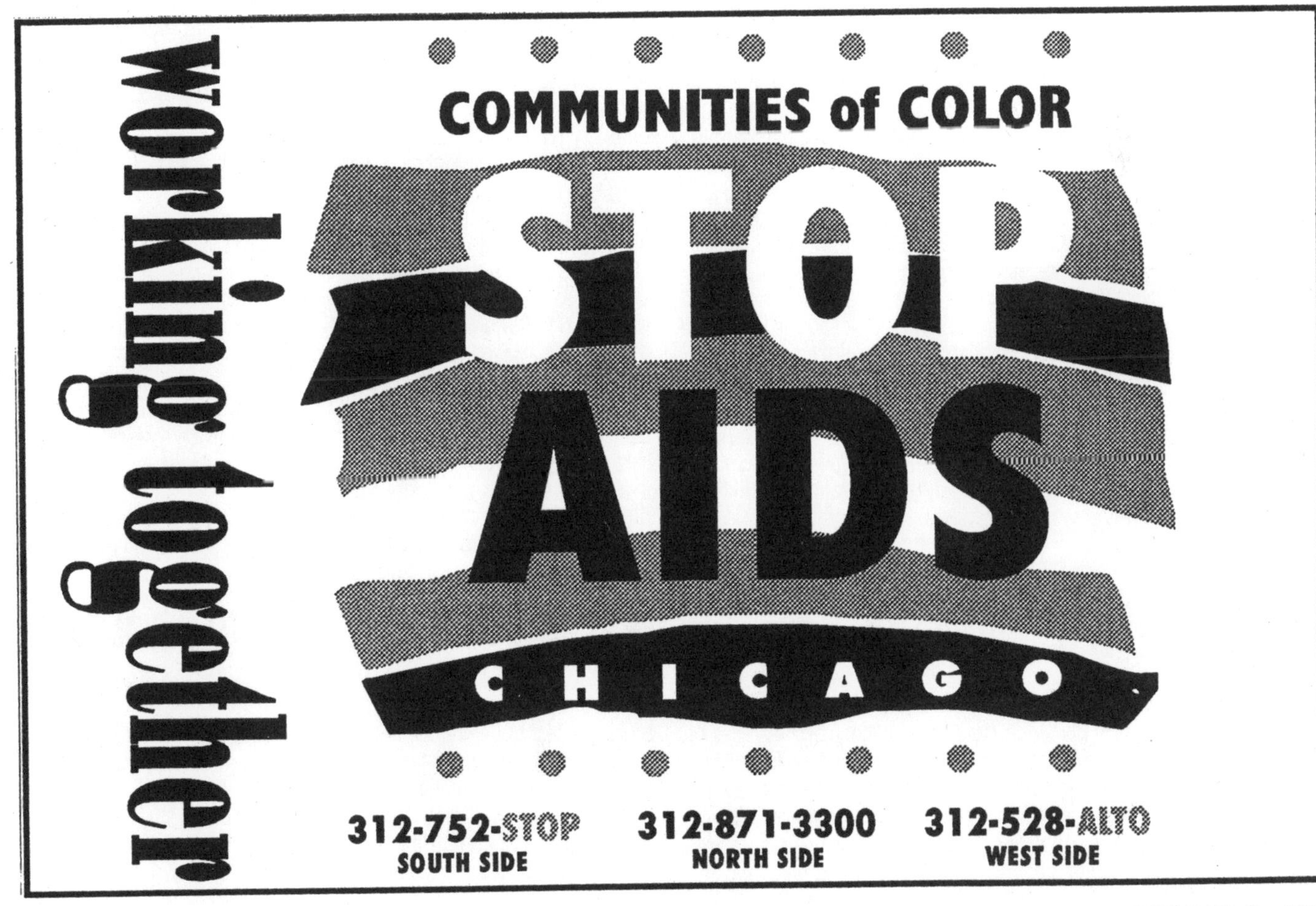

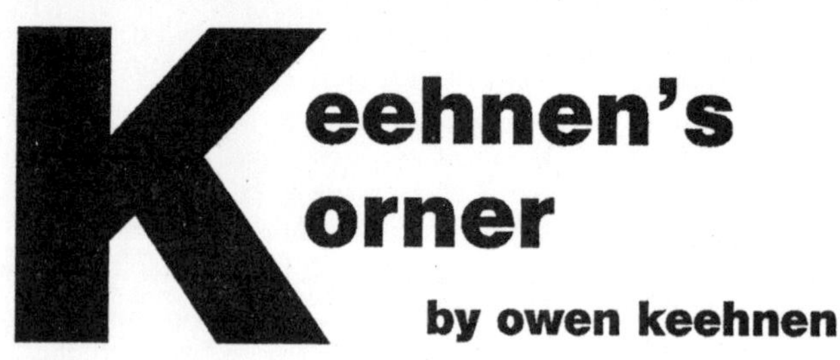

Keehnen's Korner

by owen keehnen

What do you do with a rotund, racist, sexist homophobe? In the case of current bigot du jour Rush Limbaugh, lots of things. In fact, here are 101 things you can do with and to him. **1.** Appoint him as Leona Helmsley's official valet when she is released from prison. **2.** Put Nair in his underwear. **3.** Pee in his custard pie. **4.** Use him for animal testing. **5.** Let him run his course like a bout of diarrhea. **6.** Shove an apple in his mouth and serve him to the homeless. **7.** Make him eat rancid roadkill. **8.** Have him loosen up by posing for photos with a bullwhip up his butt. **9.** Make him work as a roadie for Michael Bolton. **10.** Buy him a beer and have it served in a dribble glass. **11.** Use him for easy eye target practice for visually challenged gays and lesbians in the military. **12.** Make him write the official title of the 1993 March On Washington 500 times on the board after class. **13.** Make him over ala Marlene. **14.** Tickle him until he simultaneously farts and blows snot out his nose. **15.** Whisper to Sean Young that he is the reason she didn't get the Catwoman role. **16.** Chain him to a chair and make him watch continuous episodes of "BJ and the Bear." **17.** During an upcoming show, make him do an interpretive dance wearing only a black lace thong. **18.** Make him work the 'I Just Spotted Elvis' hotline during the full moon. **19.** Superglue diapers to all the windows of his house. **20.** Use him as a speed bump for riding lawnmowers. **21.** Let him age into compost. **22.** Handcuff Kathie Lee Gifford to his right hand and Jenny Jones to his left. **23.** Freely mix generous dosages of Rogaine to his Dristan Nasal Mist. **24.** Sick Kitty Kelly on him. **25.** Light a bag of dog poop, ring his doorbell, and run. **26.** Make him masturbate in front of a room full of people of nitrous oxide. **27.** Cover him in flour and make him a Pilsbury dough boy. **28.** Hire him as Shannon Doherty's chaperone. **29.** Turn him into a 'Home Shopping Network' junkie. **30.** Make him drink a big glass of hot dog water. **31.** Make him a volunteer in Pat Robertson's Castrations for Christ campaign. **32.** Introduce him to The Children of the Corn around harvest time. **33.** Lock him in a room full of mimes, and tell them that he is very sad and needs to be cheered up. **34.** Make him confess on the air that he is just a fatter, equally obnoxious version of Morton Downey Jr. **35.** Cajole a scout troop into tying him to a stake, using eight types of knots, and eating smores in front of him. **36.** Set him up on a date with Amy Fisher. **37.** Make him listen to frustrated poets ramble on about their need to create. **38.** Insert a microchip transmitter in his brain which constantly plays the Whitney Houston remake of 'I Will Always Love You'. **39.** Saw one of the heels off all his pumps the night of the big dance. **40.** Have him make a special guest appearance as a barrier on 'Roller Derby'. **41.** Sacrifice him to a volcano. **42.** Use him as the stunt double for Wile E. Coyote. **43.** Give him a pound of Ex-Lax lace fudge. **44.** Make him live as a woman for a day, as gay for a day, as African-American for a day, as a Jew for a day. **45.** Shave his head and make him tear up a picture of the Pope. **46.** Make him dedicate the rest of his life to creating pantyhose art. **47.** Use his head as a beehive. **48.** Force him to eat a freezer burned Oscar Meyer Variety Pack. **49.** Give him mandatory attendance season passes at The Anita Bryant Dinner Theater in Eureka Springs, Arkansas. **50.** Push him from a plane over Kennebunkport. **51.** Cover him with maple syrup, chocolate, nuts, and granola and promote him as the world's largest carmel ball. **52.** Use as the very first combination test crash dummy/inflatable impact bag. **53.** Offer him a seat in a chair with collapsible legs. **54.** Use him as a garbage disposal in a fish gutting factory. **55.** Use him as a fungus incubator. **56.** Hire Bryant Gumbel as the costar of his talk show. **57.** Remind him that since he brought it up, gluttony is also a cardinal sin. **58.** Remind him that since he brought it up, gluttony is also a cardinal sin. **59.** Have him walk around O'Hare Airport dressed as a nun and passing out condoms. **60.** Flatten him repeatedly with a steamroller, asphalt him, and use him as a playground for inner city kids. **61.** Make him eat a spoonful of ants. **62.** Let him pass like a kidney stone. **63.** Make him over ala Sylvester. **64.** Strip him, oil him, and have a 'Catch The Greased Pig' fund raiser. **65.** Hire him as 'An Outlet for Recovery Aggression' at The Betty Ford Clinic. **66.** Have him assume the tail position in a game of Crack The Whip with the U.S. Speed Skating team. **67.** Have him retrieve a penny from a light socket with his tongue. **68.** Hire Tammy Faye Bakker as his make-up girl. **69.** Make him polka at gunpoint. **70.** Slip a Whoopie Cushion and attached microphone onto his seat at a press conference. **71.** Call him repeatedly and ask if he has Janitor in a Drum or Prince Albert in a Can. **72.** Hire him as both dietician and public relations manager for Zsa Zsa. **73.** Replace his Lavoris Mouthwash with red food dye. **74.** Make him transcribe every episode of 'The Dukes of Hazzard.' **75.** Have him brainwashed to blurt either "Where's The Beef?", "I Can't Believe I Ate The Whole Thing!", or "Sit on it Potsie!" every fifteen minutes. **76.** Perform experimental dentistry on him. **77.** Raffle his ass to a chubby chaser on leather weekend. **78.** Have him be the official Sock It To Me Boy for the 'Laugh-In 25th Anniversary Special'. **79.** make him the new Empire Carpets spokesman. **80.** Feed him spoonful upon spoonful of yeast in a very dark and warm room. **81.** Make him get his daily straight razor shave in a moving car by trainees from barber colleges across the country. **82.** Make him work at a Chinese Restaurant as a singing fortune cookie. **83.** Send him somewhere far away for years of serious therapy. **84.** Have his crack dealer sell his story to 'The National Enquirer'. **85.** Quench him to death. **86.** Have him be the eye donor for The Royal Shakespearean Touring Company of 'King Lear'. **87.** Let trained seals cavort with him for a few hours at Disneyworld. **88.** Have plastic surgeons remove all his features and hair so his face resembles a newel post. **89.** Tape a picture of a cock to his back. **90.** Bleed him with river leeches. **91.** Have him go down on the digits of shrimp-master Fergie. **92.** Make him go door to door and apologize to everyone on the block for being a bigoted oaf and bully. **93.**

The Way Things Ought To Be

Repeatedly swathe his head with generous portions of Preparation H until it shrinks to the size of a cranberry. **94.** Make him lick dry ice. **95.** Have him depend upon the county health department for his medical needs. **96.** Register him as a vehicle in a demolition derby and have Phyllis Schafly ride on his shoulders. **97.** Put a clothespin on his tongue. **98.** Cover him with cheap plastic and make a bean bag chair. **99.** Make him say four 'Hail Marys' and give a $1,000 donation. **100.** Make him wear asbestos underwear. **101.** Or...simply turn him off.

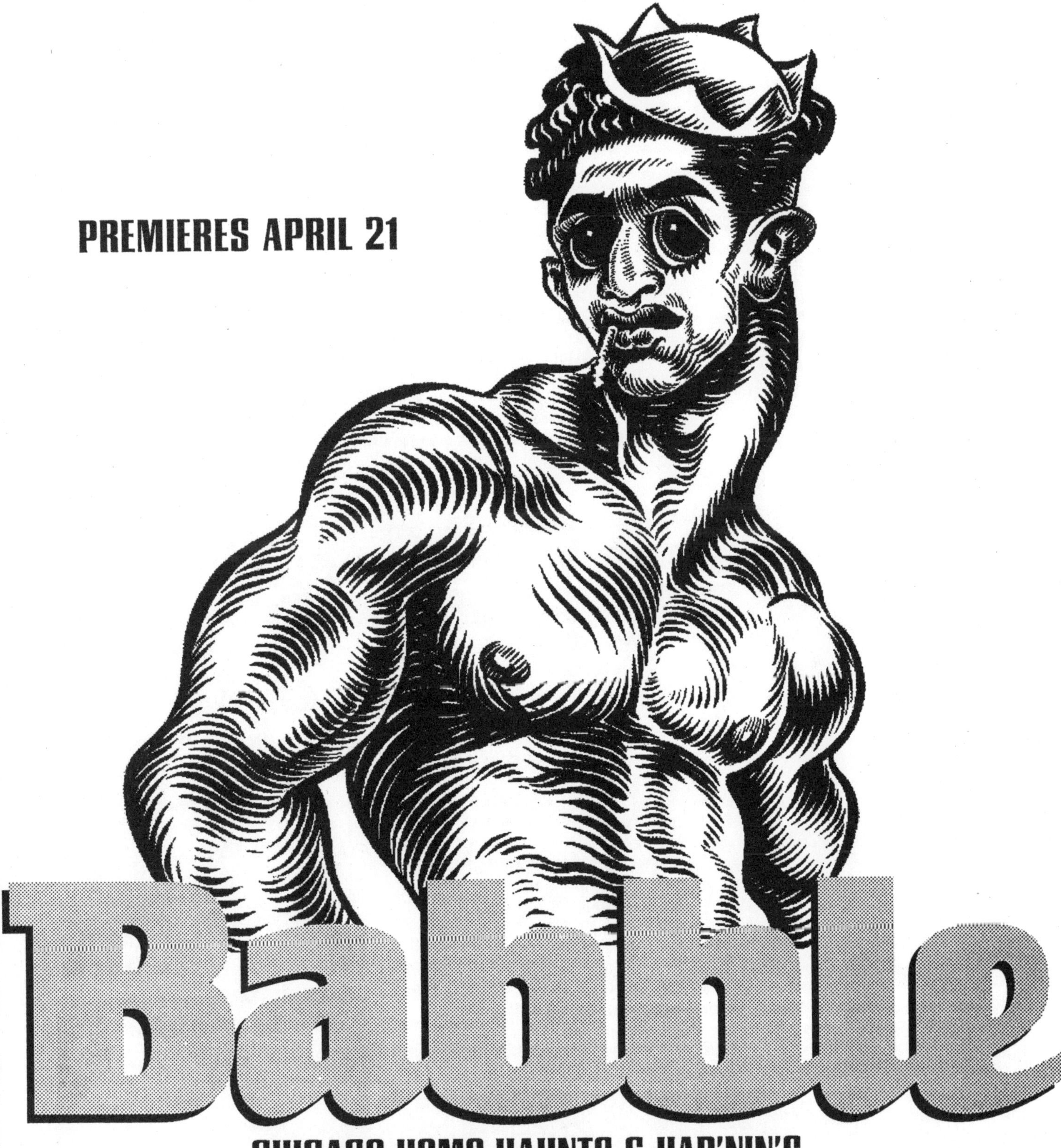

PREMIERES APRIL 21
Babble
CHICAGO HOMO HAUNTS & HAP'NIN'S

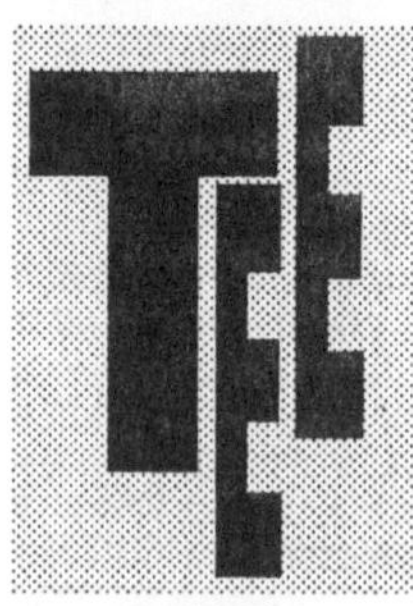

T. Adkins

Colorado, Not! Or "Put yo' money where yo' ass is!"

Thank the Goddess that Hollywood legend, Barbra Streisand, is givin' folks hell supporting a boycott of the state of Colorado. Amendment 2's passage with the November '92 elections.denies homosexuals equal protection under the law and is being attacked by opponents as unconstitutional and homophobic. Beloved Babs has gone on record saying that if a piece of legislation were passed in any state that discriminated against people of color "there would be no question about boycotting that state." How true. Gay, closeted, white, power-conscience Hollywood should all be behind the boycott. Instead, a great number of stars continue with vacations in Aspen, wimping out in defense of fags and dykes. So, thank the benevolent spirits that La Streisand can be vocal and angry and take a stand. The power of boycotting should never be underestimated. Money talks and bullshit walks. If all the people who spent their time and energy looting and burning L.A. (upset with the Rodney King verdict) would realize the power of their *dollars* and boycott a few major companies, (especially Hollywood releases like Batman Returns or products like Coca Cola, or McDonald's), — perhaps headway could be made in affecting change. Sure, it's not McDonald's or Coca Cola's fault that the California courts and national and local politics are sometimes tainted with prejudice and racism. Please. It isn't 'liberal' Aspen's fault that Amendment 2 passed; Aspen's voters were overwhelmingly against the measure. But it sure as hell would light a fire under the asses of the multi-billion dollar industries that employ tens of thousands of people and exert untold amounts of influence with law makers in Washington and state legislatures nationwide. If people said, "Look, this is an outrage! I refuse to give you my individual and collective support ($) and am committed to staying on your case (keeping my foot up your ass) until things change!" As long as people can run off to places like Aspen *escaping* from the reality of measures like Amendment 2, impervious to injustices and unfairnesses that affect a number of others and not themselves directly, shit will not change. And to see that the majority of Hollywood's elite could care less over this kind of blatant homophobia as law is enough to make a queen eschew every last major studio release forever. Because, as another legendary Tinseltown diva, Elizabeth Taylor, put it "...without homosexuals...there would *be* no Hollywood!"

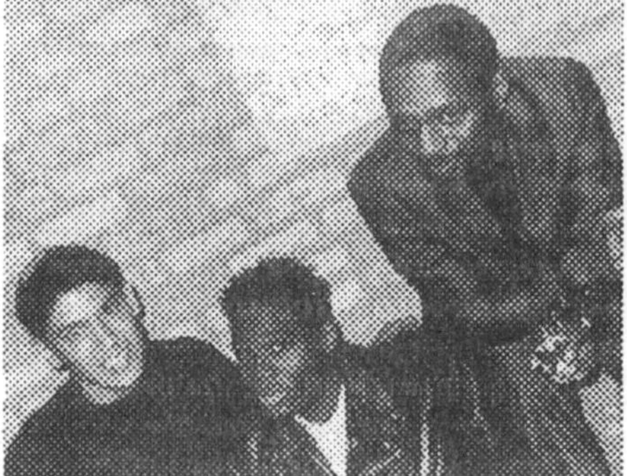

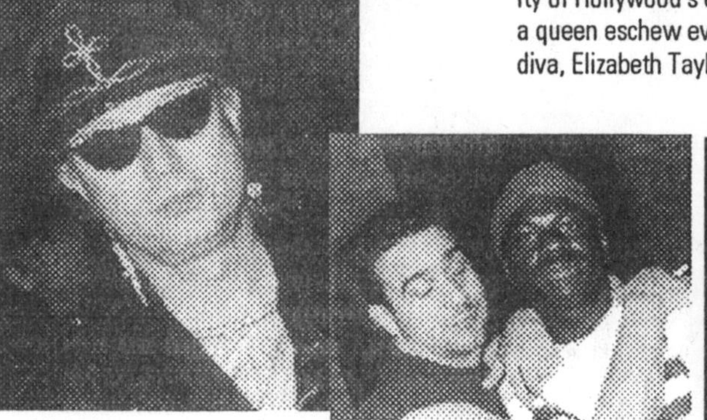

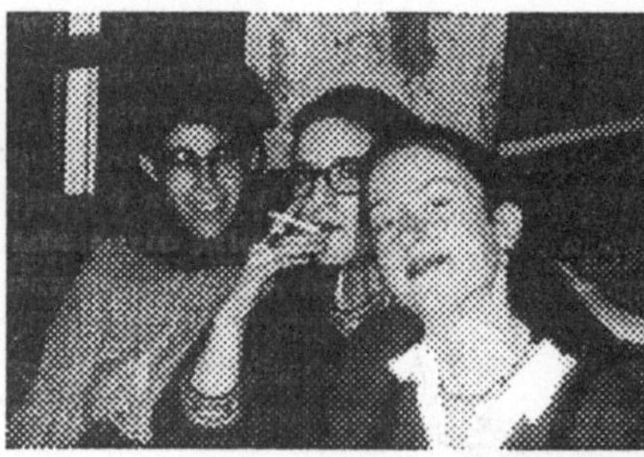

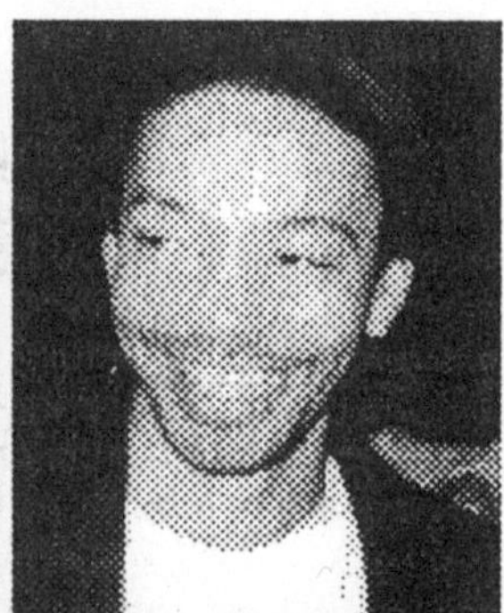

It Ain't Easy Bein' Cheesey!

Never let it be said that we don't like the folks who brought us *Gag* Magazine and the soon to debut *Babble*. We admire and appreciate their many efforts at pioneering alternative press here in Chicago and hosting some of the better parties. However, we must pull our weird sisters' coattails over the way some folks have let their "coolness" go to their heads. This was in full effect at the farewell to Gag party when a certain person assigned security duty had to front off certain others in a juvenile display of authority. It's truly late when the alternative underground mirrors the same kind of tired shit that's found in the mainstream clubs. While T. J. Mozzarella and friends sat chattering and ki-ki-ing in the stairwell, this reporter was rudely told to beat it, (obviously not fab enough to VIP with the big cheese). Mind you, everybody had been occasionally sitting there throughout the course of the evening. Should we have known not to be there? Couldn't we have been informed a little less dramatic and condescending manner, maybe? This drama was especially bothersome after the host had promised said reporter he was on the guest list, only to have to pay the five bucks upon entering, anyway. The Boys on Belmont ought to transcend Kaboom and Saturday night at Shelter, as far as these kinds of hassles go. If people who are on the guest list get such treatment, what happens to the paying Joes? Being made to feel the outsider is nothing new in playing the clique game. We just thought these kids were truly over the "We're *so* fabulous" mess. It's late.

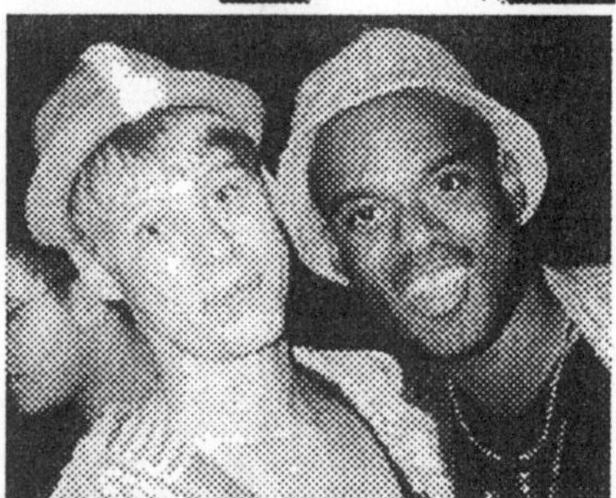

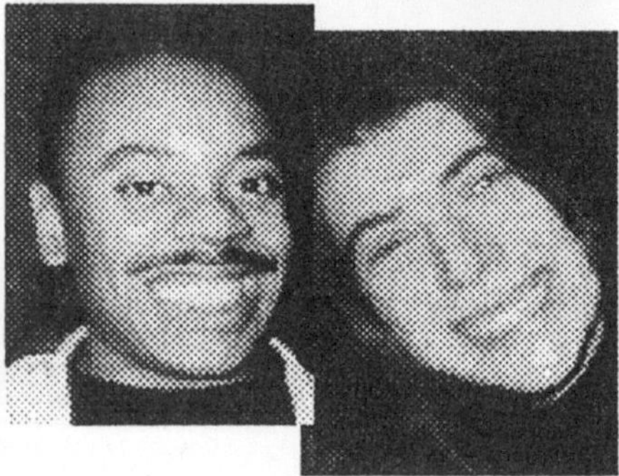

The opening of HiFi Bangalore's Boom Boom Room saw a big turnout of artists, writers, music mavens, and glamour bugs. Winding down; David Saucedo, Mayday Delish and HiFi Bangalore.Painter/performance artist, Lester Brodsky,aka, Leslie 2000. DJs Freddie Bain and Earl Pleasure. Debbie Gould, Shelley Schneider-Bellows and Pamela Hewett, Brian, Designer Chris Luker and his roomie Michael Hyacinth, aka, London Broil. The RuPaul Charles School of Pearly Whites; ID Records' director of World Operations, Andre Halmon, left, and Ever Productions' Patty Ryan, right.

FOXY'S: *Finally,* **Blue** and **Tom Hemingway** are doing their own club. Fortunately, Aunt Viveon's bequest of the family disco was entrusted to her beloved niece, fashion plate **Foxy.** Find **Aaron Enigma, Rodette, Steve Lafreniere, Steve** and **Craig, Brian Funk, Roberto Earl Pleasure, Ralphi Rosario, Miles Maeda, Andy Substance, Spencer Kincy,** DJ **Wess Kidd, Malone, Phil, Jack,** the **Louise**s **Joe Right, Lemuel, Terrence Smith, Marcus Sherard** and **Aisha Calloway, Chris, Terry Martin, Giggles** et al. The two rooms that were formerly sleepy Eons now "buzz." Great videos upfront. The dancefloor in back attracts a mixed and funky crowd of new and old music fans. **Freddie Bain**'s deep- mixes on Saturdays usually satisfies the crush of faithful dancers. Foxy's stage has seen **London Broil** and **Queerdonna. The Lady Bunny** performs April 8. *Foxy's 800 West Belmont 312 327-1222*

G.L.E.E. CLUB: New Sunday Night fag/dyke parties at Crobar is pulling all the people (plus) who frequented Cairo every Sunday. Crobar is managed by the folks who do KaBoom! Kaboom!'s Sunday night fag parties flopped because it was the most disconnected from the real gay community (anti gay and homophobic security, for instance). This time out, the management is much mo' fag-friendly. A lot of former Cairo staffers. Ace fag party promoter **Byron Dorsey** oversees the goings on. Music is by DJs **Ralphi Rosario** (formerly of Quench) and **TomE** with musical director **Terri Bristol.** The currently embroiled Mr. Windy City, **David Wilshire** and humpy **Pasta Joey** man the door. For all the state-of-the-artness of the sound system, (it's heavy duty) the music is sometimes too blaring. The bathrooms are the only place in the club where you can talk without losing your voice. Unless you're dancing, there's really not much else to do but stand around and watch the dancers and other spectators. Chicago's latest (downtown) version of H.I.M. The Nightclub. *Crobar 1543 North Kingsbury 312 243 2075*

CHEEKS: Even though this club boasts a stellar line-up of deep DJs, pesky little things (like a bad sound system and a booth that's several obstructive feet from the dance floor) make Cheeks an impossible challenge. You can hear **Braxton Holmes, Micky Oliver, Mike Winston, Bernard Badie,** all surely on the cutting edge of house now. Staff members **Patrick, Cocar, Tommy, Corky** and **David** and **DJ Pumpkin** are dears. The mirrors in back and the never ending parade of self-adoring dolls are a must-see; the place is notorious for its glamour wars. On a good night, Misses **René, Tanya,** and **Cynthia** work your nerves with the sickest 'ol cocktail ensembles. *Cheeks 2730 N. Clark 312 348-3400*

STOP 'n DRINK: This downtown hole-in-the-wall quickly replaced the legendary and infamous Rialto Tap. The trade and the tunes are just as rough and tough at Stop 'n Drink as the parties once were at the old Ritz on North State or 'ToTos.' Packed with African homeboys/girls, *Stop and Drink* is the place to go for all the New Yorkers and europeans who come to Chicago and want to see and hear "a Warehouse party." Also lovingly known as Stop 'n Stink, Stop 'n Think, and the Stop 'n Stab. *Stop 'n Drink 742 N. Clark 312 944-8233*

HI FI BANGALORE'S BOOM BOOM ROOM: Only recently opened at Red Dog and it's already *the* choice for real-life club tarts on Mondays. Artist and writer **Jack** (HiFi) **Walls** hosts. The two big rooms (one dancefloor and bar, the other lounge and bar) draw the city's most mixed crowd bi's, straights, DQs, northside fags, and the neighborhood mix of punks, bohos, and queers. Tres black and Latin. The deep underground is courtesy of **Freddie Bain** and **Orlando G.** They do an excellent mix of the old and new deep mix for an informed dance crowd. (These kids aren't just jumping up and down.) Opening night, the current Miss Continental, **MiMi Marks,** performed as Miss Pussy Dujour, giving face, hair and body as Deee-lite's *Pussycat Meow* bumped through the air. Also: Local drag legend **Aqua Neta, Cajmere** and **Dajae, Byrd Bardot.** Spot **Gina, Rodette, Clarence, MC Heather,** the **Steves,** the **Michaels,** the **Roberts,** Tom and Blue, the **Avant Gardes,** the **Enigmas, Louis, Sergio, Connie V.,** Spencer, Andy Substance, Foxy, **Jim** and **Hector,** the **Georges,** etc. *Red Dog 1958 W. North Avenue 312 278-5138*

BERLIN: A longtime viable alternative for straight kids bored with overly homogenized pop music and stuffy, narrow minded folks, also the choice of fags and dykes tired of the same 'ol same 'ol on Halsted St. Home of the Boys on Belmont. Tuesdays and Thursdays are official fag nights at Berlin. With an exceptionally good sound system, the selection of music is the better mix of rock, pop, disco, house, and techno. And good videos. The wait staff are super, and doorman **Stuart** has got to be the best anywhere. Frequent decor makeovers keep even the most jaded window dressers guessing what'll be next. Orientalia? Moulon Rouge? TV Land? Weimer cabaret? *Berlin 954 W. Belmont 312 348-4975*

BISTRO TOO: The Children continue to flock to the mega popular Thursday Dollar Night at ' the Bistros'. **TomE** swings with an emphasis on hip-hop and house that sends the young Black and Latino queer mix c-r-a-z-y! Drag Dolls, voguers, and homeboys are regular fixtures. At times, the dance floor literally heaves. *Bistro Too 5015 N. Clark 312 728-0050*

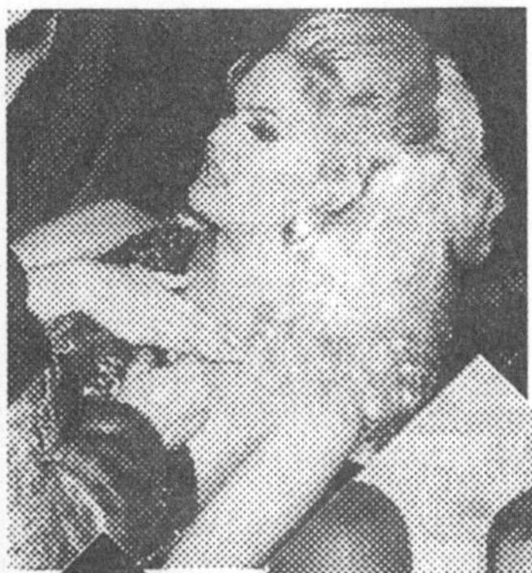

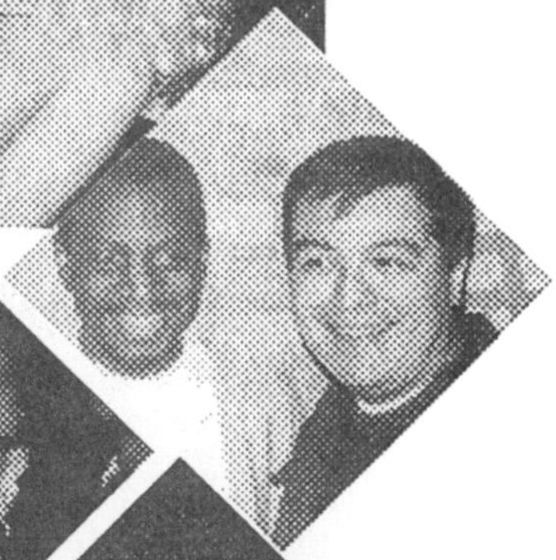

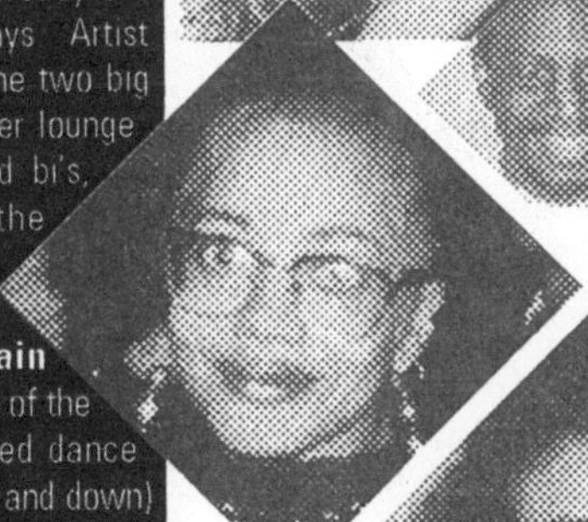

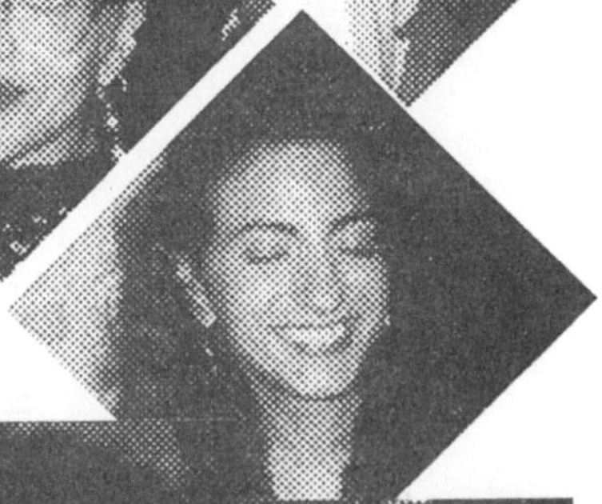

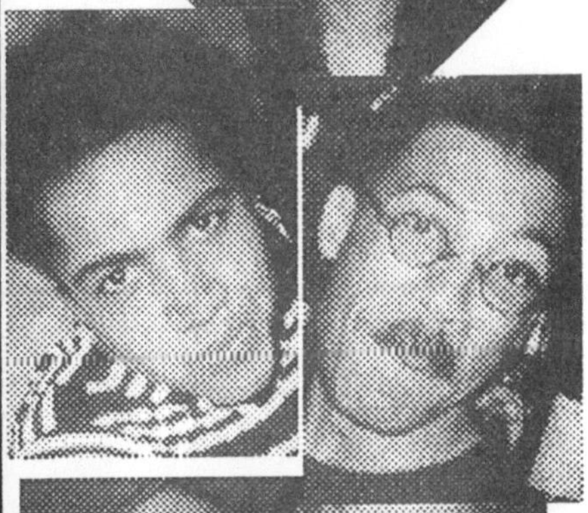

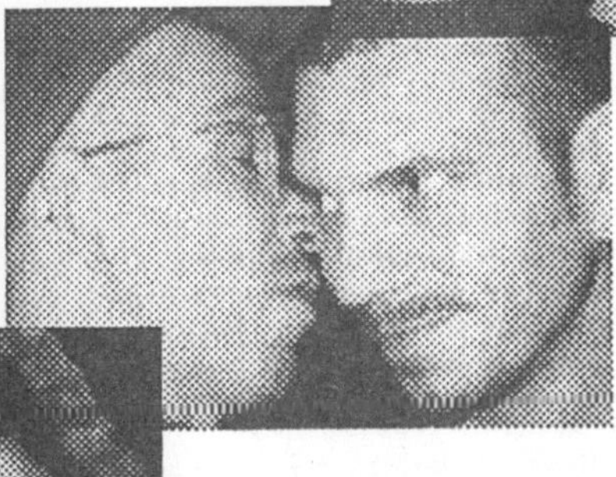

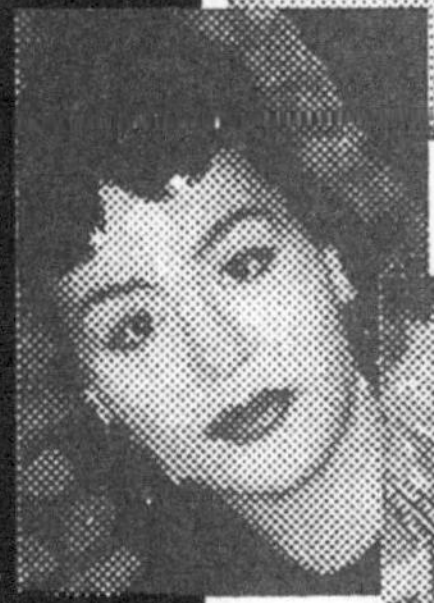

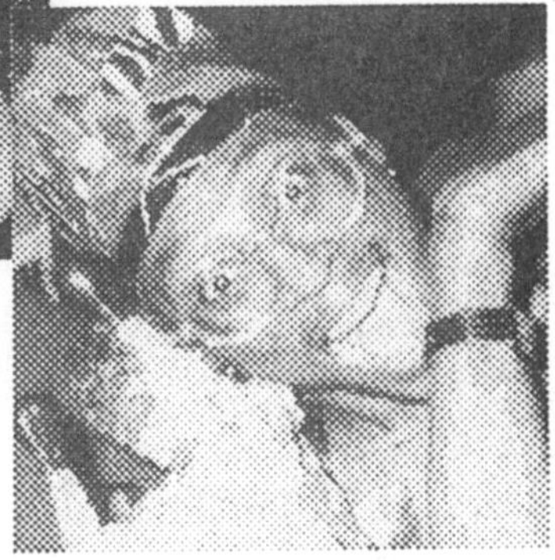

Some of everybody at The Boom Boom Room (from top): Mimi Marks as Pussy Dujour. Publisher's Ki-ki: Robert Ford and Élan magazine publisher, Jim Larralde. Painter Aisha Calloway. Neyda Martinez. Female preachin': MC Heather. Rodette. TGOC publisher and Fake producer, Steve Lafreniere and Babble mag's Malone. Voguer Plus: Fashion designer and CUT magazine publisher, Aaron Enigma, demonstrates "the gag!" Near right, Miss Gina. Photos T Adkins.

DeAUNDRA'S DIXIE DIARY

BY DEAUNDRA PEEK

Hey Y'all!! Here's to lookin' forward to a brand new world full a love since the inauguration of **President Bill Clinton**, signallin' that 1993 is definitely The Year Of Satisfaction, which is what everybody down here is callin' it.

I has got so much to tell y'all this time, you ain't gonna believe it! First off, **Mr. Richardson**, my producer, done told me that Miss **Phoebe Legere** had done gone in that real hi-style club called USA in New York recently an' she was wowed by seein' some a my very own videos right up there on them screens all over the club! Y'all watch out in Chicago for Miss Phoebe, on account a cause she's comin' there real soon for some kinda big ole' super-style art exhibit featurin' female wrestlers. Confidential to y'all, them ball peen hammer locks is her specialty...

Remember them days when your MeeMaw would surprise you with a fresh hot vienner pot pie right outta the microwave? Well, that was just about what it was like when I opened a package from my sweet friend **Fluffy Boy**, of *HOMOture* in San Francisco! He done sent me the 1993 *Girlfriend* calendar, an' y'all, I am the cover girl! I a course exploded, especially when I opened it to find **RuPaul, Joan Jett Blakk, Jerome Caja, Brie, Mr. Scott Free** (a nice boy who did have a show on TV in Atlanta before moving to California), an' a mess a other stars. Like vienner pot pie, they is goin' fast y'all!

Recently my TV show cohosts **Candy Suntop** and **Duffy Odum** an' me went on top 40 radio station WKLS 96 Rock's Wake Up show with their hosts **Christopher Rude, Radical Bradford,** and **The Family Jools**! We had so much fun cuttin' up with them nutty FM airmeisters, an' I even got to sing my big hit "Losin' My Vienners", (based on the **REM** song) which accordin' to Atlanta based *ETC.* magazine's **Jack Pelham,** had DOT officials wonderin' about traffic accidents. I am still tryin' to figure out what that means y'all, so if anybody knows please fill me in!

Special thanks goin' directly from me to **Rep. Cynthia McKinney** an' **Rep. John Lewis** for all a their work to unite this world. Both a them is workin' to take Georgia into the future beyond tomorrow's can a vienners!

Y'all, as a teen entertainer an' writer, it is important for me (an' all a us teens) to have big-time celebrity role models, so that's why I wanted to tell y'all about my friend Miss **Angie Bowie**'s new book *Backstage Passes*! It's a tell all y'all, an' media Angie an' media sources like **Pam Perry** an' **J. David Goldman** has said that Miss Angie an' cowriter **Patrick Carr** talk all about bein glitterin' glamourous sexual pharmeceuticals (whatever that means), all at the same time! Miss Angie signed my very own copy thinkin' a y'all too, sayin' "...all my love Miss Thing..."—aint' she the greatest?

Keepin' up with **Starbooty** these days is tough (talk about workin') but here's my official report so far: **RuPaul** has done been all over BET's "Video LP" show; on **Joan Rivers** with **Lady Bunny**, **Holly Woodlawn**, **John Epperson** (aka **Lypsinka**), **Miss Guy**, **Paris**, an' *Thing* cover girl **Joey Arias**; he's all that on MTV's "The Grind" show (which is hosted by **Eric**, who my cameraman **Stevetteridge** says is the cutest boy on TV next to Duffy Odum); featured in *Southbeach* magazine outta Miami; climbin' to the top a the *Billboard* Dance Trax Chart *an'* enterin' the Hot 100 Chart with a bullet—talk about gettin' it goin' on!! Just y'all wait till y'all hear my very own version of "Supermodel" from my latest TV series "DeAundra's Salon d'Odum's"! Starbooty himself said I could sing it!

Team Odum's Update: Competition is *fierce* a 'tween T.O.'s Captain Duffy Odum and **Sonya LaTrail Stubbs** of Team Del Vista Ray Mar. Last time, durin' the three-legged vienner toss, Sonya LaTrail missed Duffy an' flew into the security ditch out back, flinging them vienner cans all over Rango Fain's Snack Shed's parkin' lot. Luckily, **Nurse MacWorld** was there an got them splints on all them vienners so's they could finish playin', an' a course Team Odum's won, yeaaaaa!

Them boy's n' girls at **800 East** is at it again y'all, this time it's the 3rd Annual Super Style Show featurin' some a Atlanta's finest semi-undiscovered design talent! I's gonna be emceein' part a the show on Februrary 26th, presentin' stuff by **Bill Hallman, Nasreen Rahman, Wyatt,** an' **Shannon Dockery**.

An' for them that's been waitin' since last time, here's my special Vienner Sausage recipe.

Vienner Roll Ups

Ingredients
2 cans Hy-Grade Vienners (Imitation Style)
1 loaf white wheat bread
1/3 tub Country Crock Churn Style (lite, if available)
1 cup Miracle Whip Lite
2 packs Hy-Grade Saltine Crackers (no-salt type)
1 slab Velveeta Lite, grated
2 cans Hy-Grade Genuine Imitation Taco Paste
1 box toothpicks, party style

How To Make 'Em
Open your vienners, but don't eat em! Mash 'em up real good an' set aside. Spread Crock Churn Style on bread, cover that with a layer of Miracle Whip. Crunch up the saltines just itty sized, not dusty-like, sprinkle on bread, fork on mashed vienners. Generously add grated Velveeta Lite, then roll up bread an' seal tight with toothpicks to serve!

ILLUSTRATION Lee Kay PHOTO Thairin

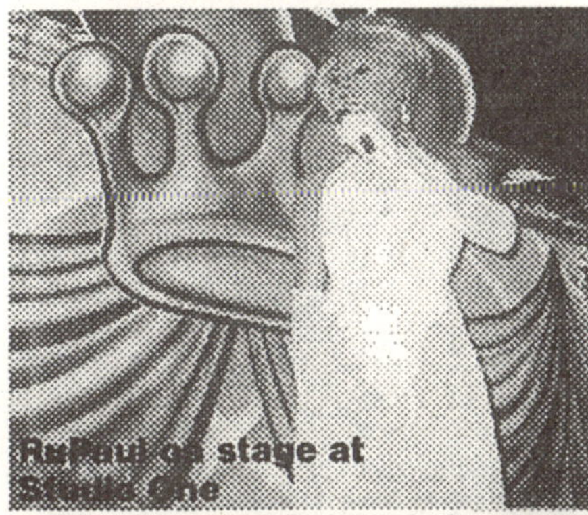

Big, Blonde, and Beautiful: The Lovely Miss Carol

RuPaul on stage at Studio One

RUPAUL'S FAVES!

FAVE MOVIE "The Wizard of Oz."
FAVE ACTOR Matthew Modine "honey he is fine!"
FAVE DREAM COME TRUE to have own tv variety show that is a mixture of Wheel of Fortune, the Cher Show, Saturday Night Live, and the Home Shopping Club.
FAVE COMIC LaWanda Page "Aunt Ester, honey."
FAVE MODEL Christy Turlington.
FAVE SINGER "Luthah!" Mr. Vandross.
FAVE PERSON TO GIVE A MAKEOVER TO Whitney Houston "She has so much to work with and doesn't do anything with it."
FAVE DIVAS Diana Ross and Cher.
FAVE CEREAL Captain Crunch with Crunchberries.
FAVE PERSON TO BE A HAIRDRESSER FOR Diana Ross or Dolly Parton.

WEST HOLLYWOOD— Me and my trusty sidekick **Joeseffee** bopped around WeHo (short for West Hollywood: cause everyone in this city is ho-ish so we be ho's!). We bopped on over to Revolver and didn't see **Madonna** or **Sandra Bernhard** in their usual hangout, so I posed for a pix and went out to catch some of the nightlife. Soon, I saw Miss Chak, Chak, Chak, Chak, **Chaka Khan** boppin' around WeHo sportin' purple hair and on the arm of a white man! My goodness gracious! There goes the neighborhood! Otherwise it was a typical WeHo week.

Mr. **RuPaul Charles** visited us a few weeks back. He gave a real swell interview for *BLK* magazine to yours truly, then performed at Studio One to a cheering crowd of gleeful fairies who clutched their tampons and begged for autographs. I was a bit peeved that security jumped my ass and tried to stop me from snapping pix of the tall bitch goddess diva girl thang! But I snapped a few for y'all! **Chi-Chi LaRue** put her big ass into Studio One long enough to wave to RuPaul and then split after the midnight show.

Tuesday night we bopped on into the Rage for "The **Lovely Carol** Show" at 9:15 pm. It was fly! Carol was lovely, big, blonde and beautiful as usual, just a small town gal from French Lick, Indiana with a dream and a craving for pop tarts. Carol threw shade at a sister girl who tried to sing **En Vogue**'s "Hold On" but had the tape playing while she sang along. The audience booed and Carol brought down the house singing along to "I'll Always Love You" with Miss **Whitney Houston**. We were surprised when **Diva** popped in to model her new ensemble. Diva is one of WeHo's classic drag queens. That night, she was wearing her **Liza Minnelli** wig but said she was doing **Michelle Lee** for us, so her and Lovely Carol made the classic Michelle "I look like a deer caught in the headlights of a car" Lee expression and we giggled like the gleeful fairies we're repudiated to be. Carol served snacks to the audience, handed out free t-shirts, and was presented with a Valentine's gift of chocolate covered cherries, a nude men calendar, and a condom.

Big Hair Day at the Rage was wild. The **Del Rubio Triplets** were the judges and may the biggest hair win!

Stay tuned for more fun and excitement, 'cause in the future you'll be meeting real life celebrities of WeHo including **The Goddess, The West Hollywood Cheerleaders, Suzy Q, DJ Johnny, the Campers, Erin Crystal, the West Hollywood Fag Hags, The Tyrant, Big Kenny, Evil Pete, That Dirty Al**, porno stars **Adrian** and **Antonio**, the fabulous go-go dancers at Studio One, and a lot of really nice people! Also, I'll be checking out the club scene at Arena (Thursdays are black night!), Spike, Probe, Meat, and every black fag's dream, the all-black, big, bad, beautiful 'Catch One.'

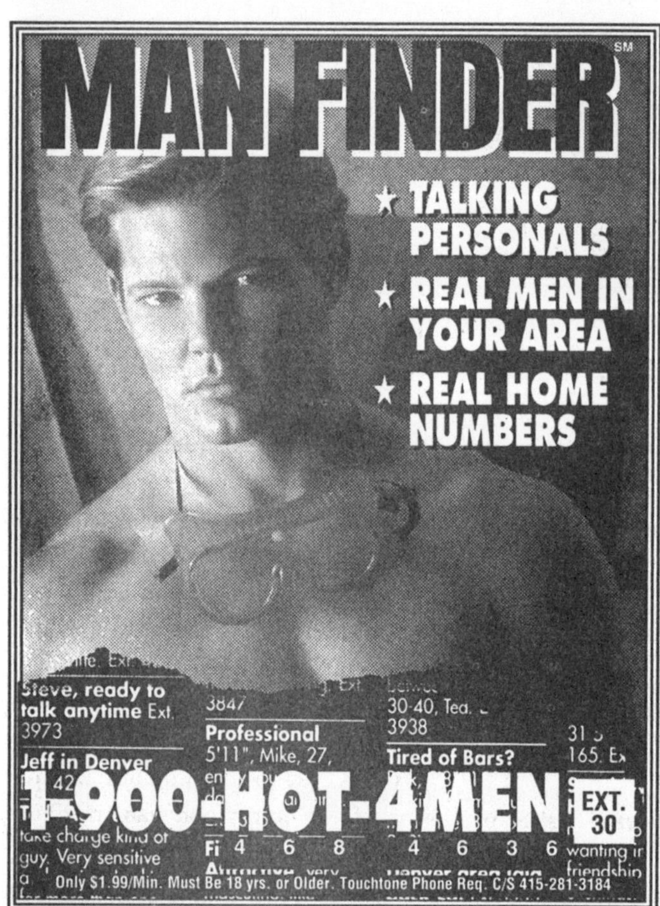

MAN FINDER
TALKING PERSONALS
REAL MEN IN YOUR AREA
REAL HOME NUMBERS
Steve, ready to talk anytime Ext. 3973
Jeff in Denver
Professional 5'11", Mike, 27,
Tired of Bars?
30-40, Tea.
1-900-HOT-4MEN EXT. 30
Only $1.99/Min. Must Be 18 yrs. or Older. Touchtone Phone Req. C/S 415-281-3184

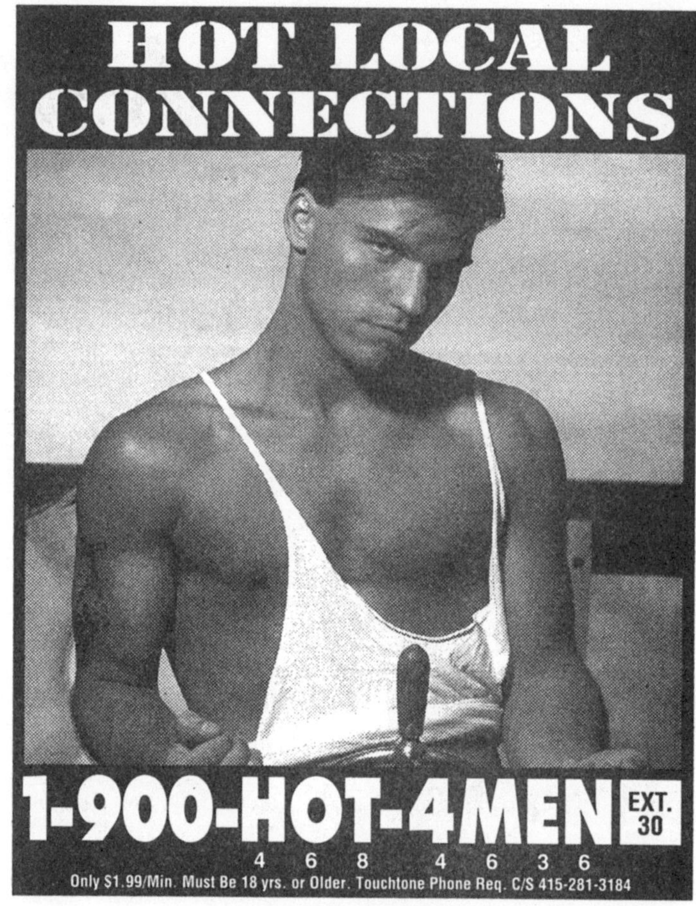

HOT LOCAL CONNECTIONS
1-900-HOT-4MEN EXT. 30
4 6 8 4 6 3 6
Only $1.99/Min. Must Be 18 yrs. or Older. Touchtone Phone Req. C/S 415-281-3184

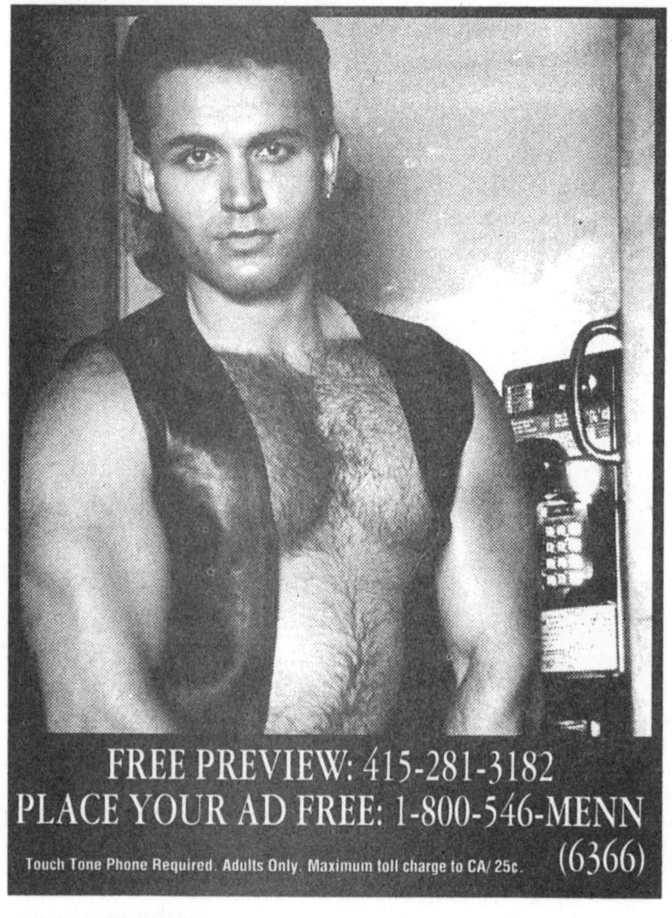

FREE PREVIEW: 415-281-3182
PLACE YOUR AD FREE: 1-800-546-MENN
(6366)
Touch Tone Phone Required. Adults Only. Maximum toll charge to CA/ 25c.

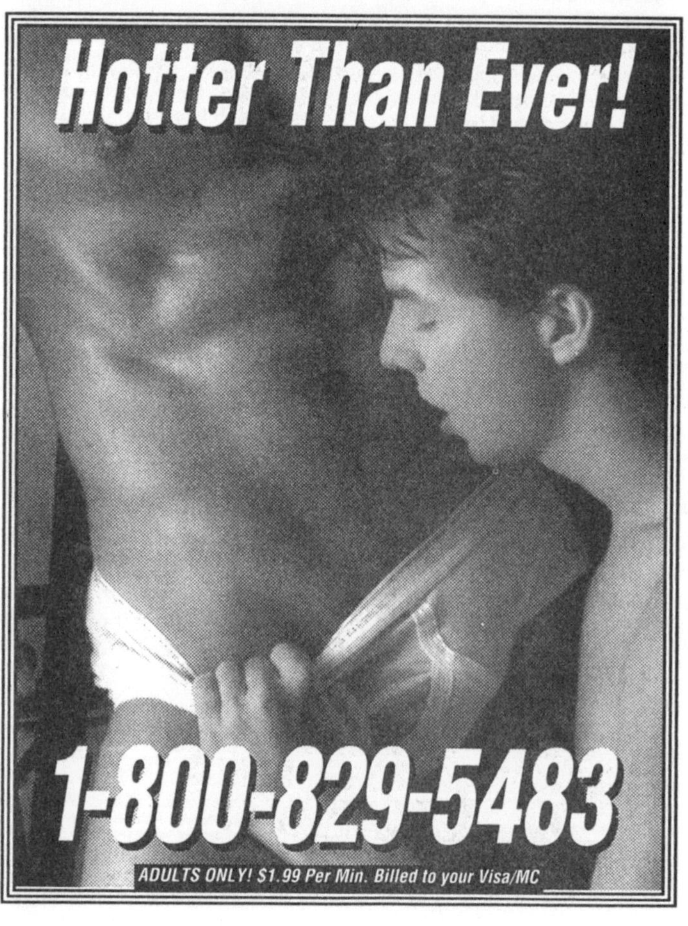

Hotter Than Ever!
1-800-829-5483
ADULTS ONLY! $1.99 Per Min. Billed to your Visa/MC

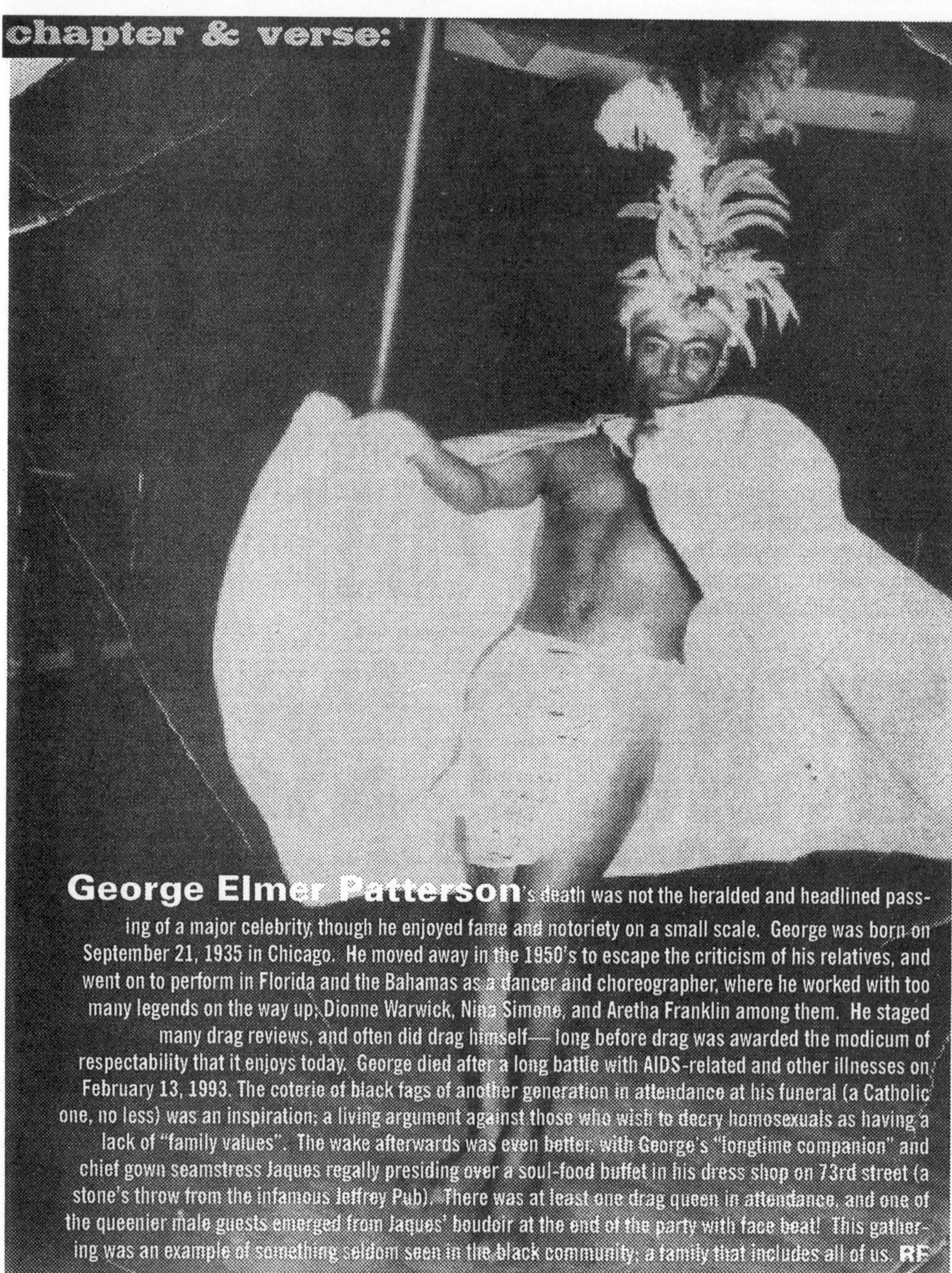

George Elmer Patterson's death was not the heralded and headlined passing of a major celebrity, though he enjoyed fame and notoriety on a small scale. George was born on September 21, 1935 in Chicago. He moved away in the 1950's to escape the criticism of his relatives, and went on to perform in Florida and the Bahamas as a dancer and choreographer, where he worked with too many legends on the way up; Dionne Warwick, Nina Simone, and Aretha Franklin among them. He staged many drag reviews, and often did drag himself— long before drag was awarded the modicum of respectability that it enjoys today. George died after a long battle with AIDS-related and other illnesses on February 13, 1993. The coterie of black fags of another generation in attendance at his funeral (a Catholic one, no less) was an inspiration; a living argument against those who wish to decry homosexuals as having a lack of "family values". The wake afterwards was even better, with George's "longtime companion" and chief gown seamstress Jaques regally presiding over a soul-food buffet in his dress shop on 73rd street (a stone's throw from the infamous Jeffrey Pub). There was at least one drag queen in attendance, and one of the queenier male guests emerged from Jaques' boudoir at the end of the party with face beat! This gathering was an example of something seldom seen in the black community; a family that includes all of us. **RF**

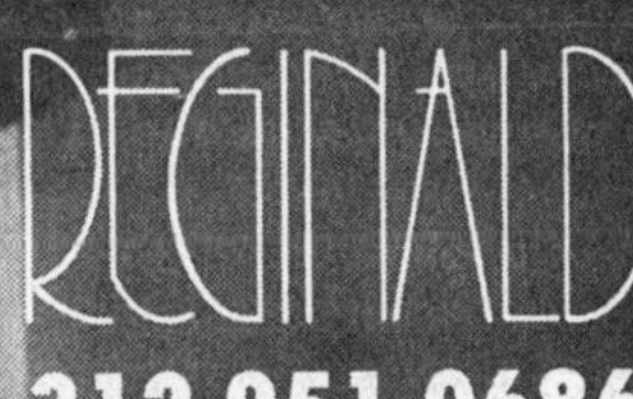
REGINALD
312 951 0686

LADY BUNNY

la grande mee-maw du wigstock...
one very special show at
foxy's
thursday, april 8th
800 west belmont   ☎ 327-1222

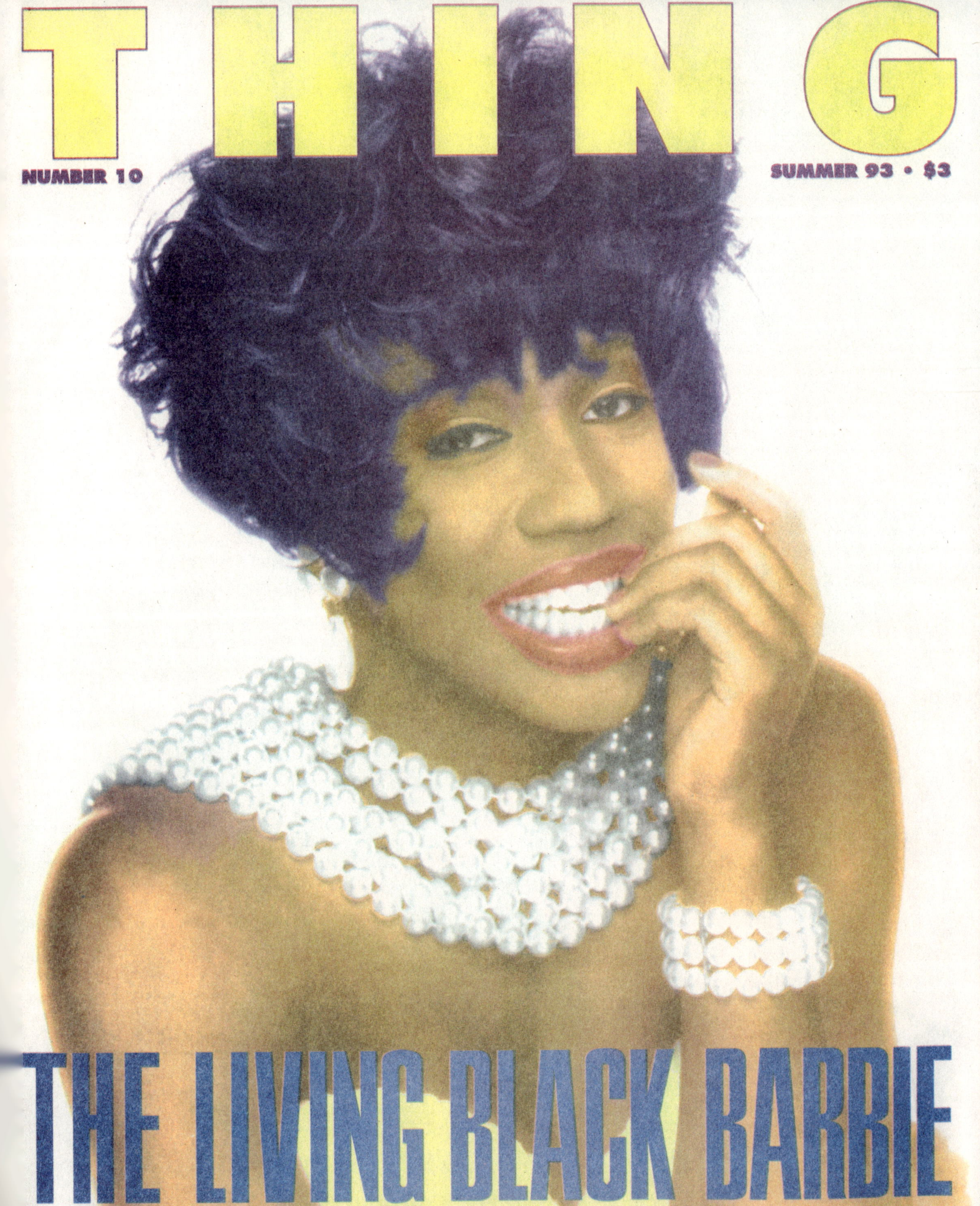

THIN G
NUMBER 10
SUMMER 93 • $3
THE LIVING BLACK BARBIE
Beauty tips from West Hollywood's most glamorous drag queens

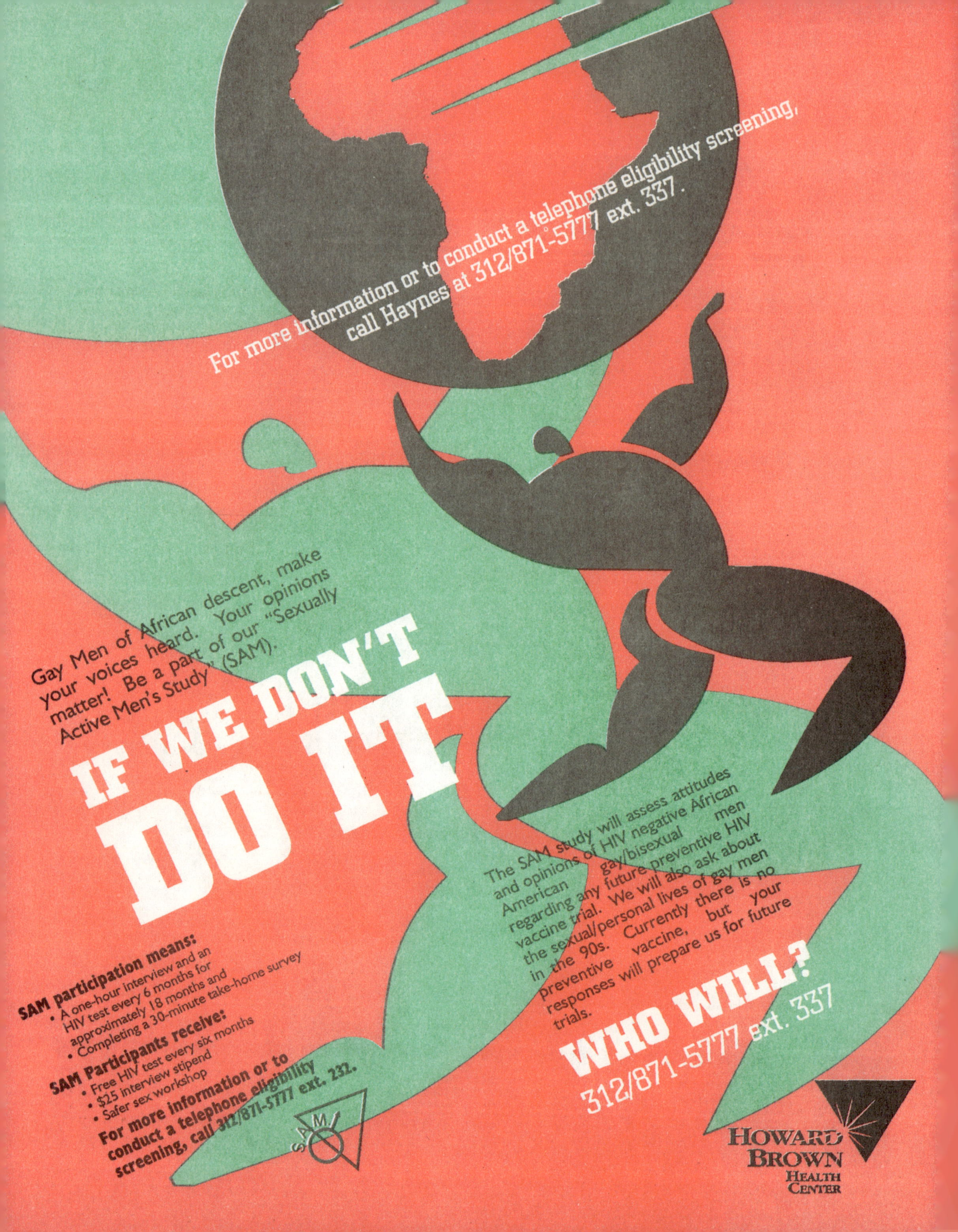

For more information or to conduct a telephone eligibility screening, call Haynes at 312/871-5777 ext. 337.

Gay Men of African descent, make your voices heard. Your opinions matter! Be a part of our "Sexually Active Men's Study" (SAM).

IF WE DON'T DO IT

The SAM study will assess attitudes and opinions of HIV negative African American gay/bisexual men regarding any future preventive HIV vaccine trial. We will also ask about the sexual/personal lives of gay men in the 90s. Currently there is no preventive vaccine, but your responses will prepare us for future trials.

SAM participation means:
• A one-hour interview and an HIV test every 6 months for approximately 18 months and
• Completing a 30-minute take-home survey

SAM Participants receive:
• Free HIV test every six months
• $25 interview stipend
• Safer sex workshop

For more information or to conduct a telephone eligibility screening, call 312/871-5777 ext. 232.

WHO WILL?
312/871-5777 ext. 337

HOWARD BROWN HEALTH CENTER

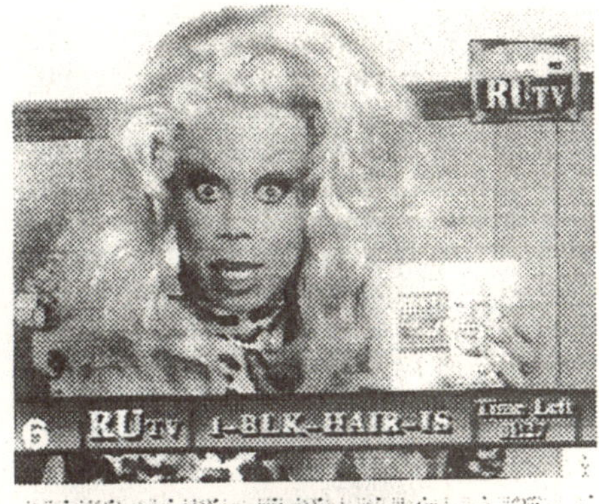

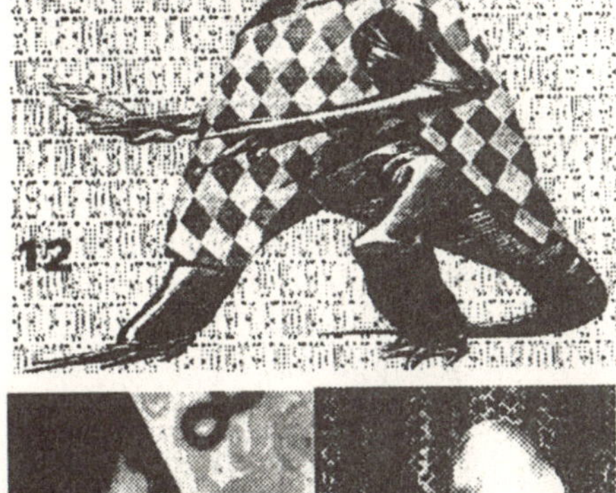

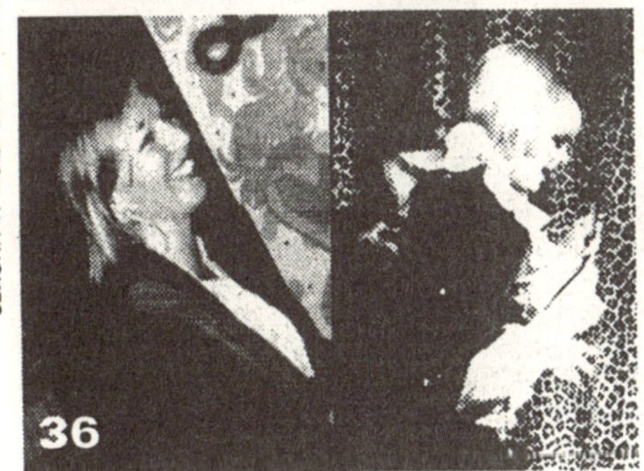

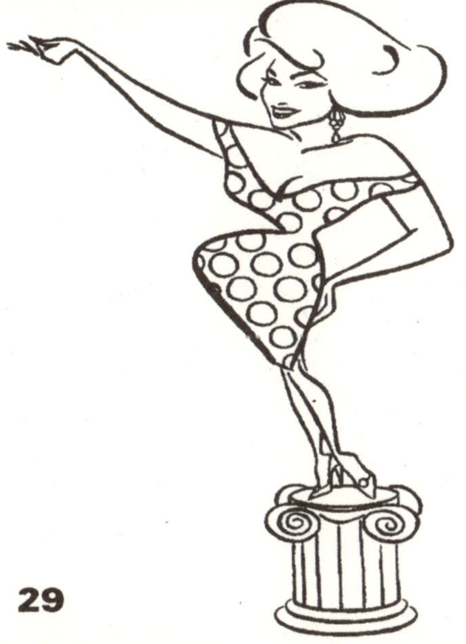

contents

NUMBER TEN • SUMMER 93

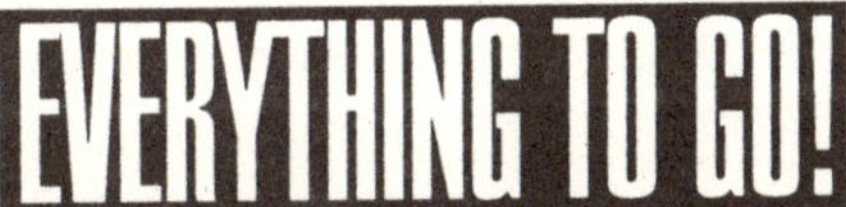

EVERYTHING TO GO!

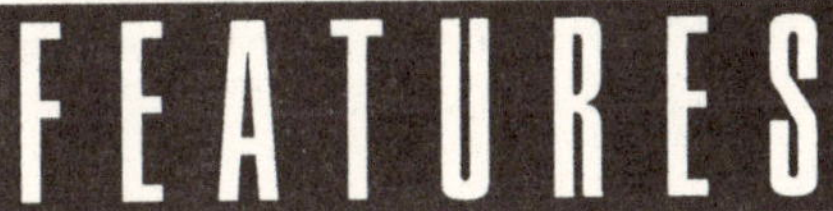

FEATURES

THE BACK

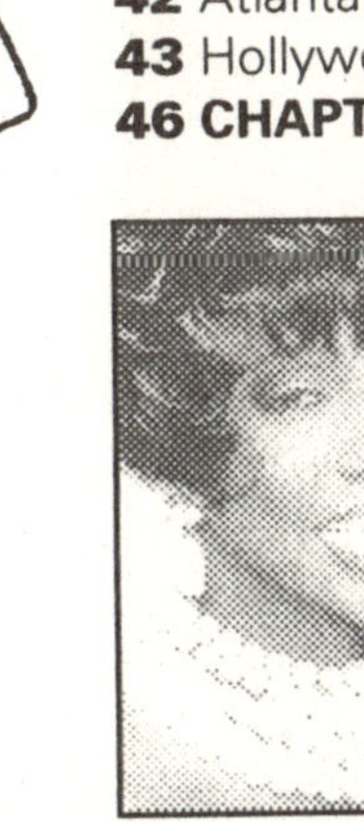

ON THE COVER: "Clutch your pearls!" It's Jazzmun, the living black Barbie. Photo by Hollywood Models. Styling Johanna. Digital coloring by Simone Bouyer.

THING SHE KNOWS WHO SHE IS PUBLISHER/ART DIRECTION Robert Ford EDITORS Trent Adkins, Robert Ford CORRESPONDENTS Aaron Enigma, Scott Free, Jamoo, Owen Keehnen, Terry Martin, DeAundra Peek, Todd Roulette, Les/Linda Simpson, Dan Wang ADVERTISING Terry Martin, Sylvia Michaels, Jeffrey Overas EDITORIAL ASSISTANCE Duane Baskins, Dan Robinson, L.D. Warren GRAPHIC SERVICES Simone Bouyer THING (ISSN 1064-9727) is published quarterly by Thing Publishing. Opinions are those of individual contributors and do not always reflect those of Thing Publishing. © 1993 THING
THING PUBLISHING 2541W. DIVISION STREET CHICAGO ILLINOIS USA 60622-2805 VOICE (312) 227-1780 FAX (312) 227-1789

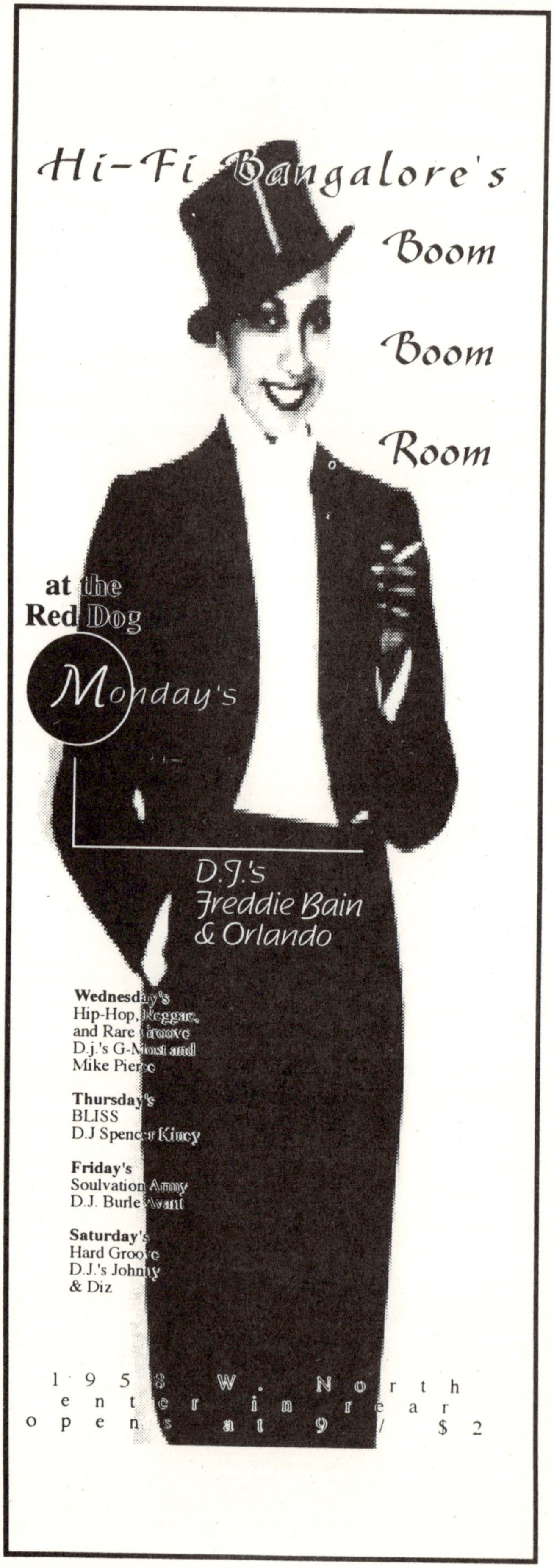

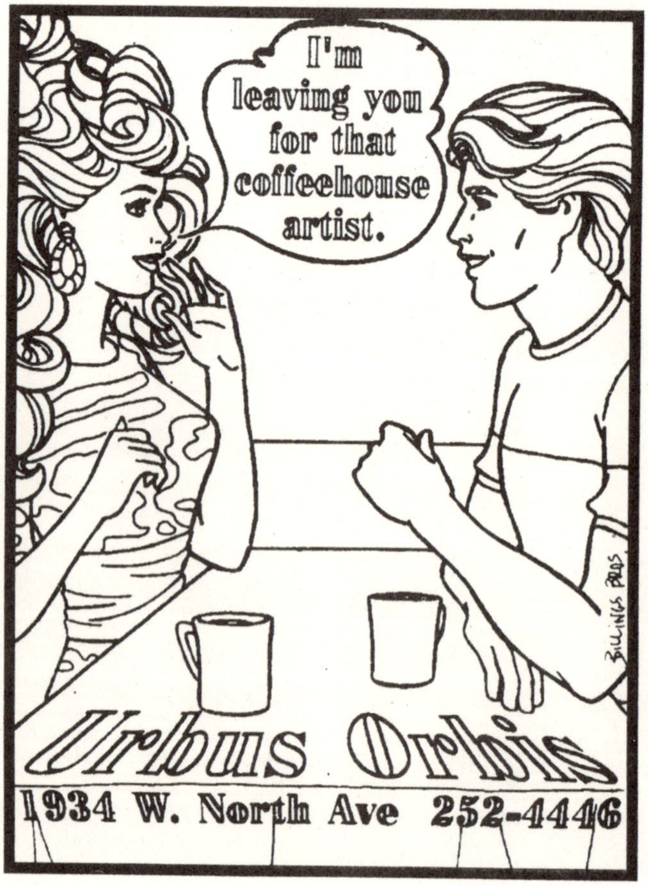

every THING to GO!
HOMOPHILE NEWS

Famous black gay thespians **Pomo Afro Homos** have been denied entry into the 1993 National Black Theater festival in August. Their award-winning theater pieces *Fierce Love* and *Dark Fruit* have been performed around the world to rave reviews, but their application to participate in the largest black theater festival in the nation was greeted with silence by festival director **Larry Leon Hamlin**. "To the best of our knowledge the Festival has never presented work about the black gay experience" notes Pomo Afro Homo's **Brian Freeman**. "Does the Festival believe that gay issues are irrelevant to African Americans?" Freeman urges their homophobia be challenged through a letter writing campaign. Write: The National Black Theater Festival, 610 Coliseum Drive, Winston-Salem NC, 27106.

Shouts out to **Earnest Hite** on being honored with a Stonewall award for his work in the community. The no-strings-attached award is given annually to men and women across the country devoted to gay and lesbian community work. Earnest and his partner, **Leon White**, run Image Plus, a gay youth program for African Americans. Among other things, the grant allowed Image Plus to enter the computer age, which in turn will make their outreach more effective.

Activist Earnest Hite.

Hung, literate, and cornfed **Scott O'Hara's** *Steam* is a slick and timely quarterly national listings and review guide for public man-to-man sex. With design know-how provided by *Diseased Pariah News'* desktop whiz **Beowoulf Thorne**, it's packed with tips on where to get off around the world. Those who prefer the more public of the venues listed (tearooms, parks, and the like) might also want to pick up *The Little Black Book* from Lambda Legal Defense. Co-authored by attorney **Evan Wolfson** and former *Outweek* editor **Gabriel Rotello**, the booklet offers tips for differentiating being cruised from a set-up, and offers advice on how to deal with a sex offense arrest. Available free from Lambda Legal Defense, either by single copy or in bulk to community outreach groups. Write: Steam c/o PDA Press, Route 2, Box 1215, Cazendovia WI 53925; Lambda Legal Defense, 666 Broadway #1200, New York NY 10012.

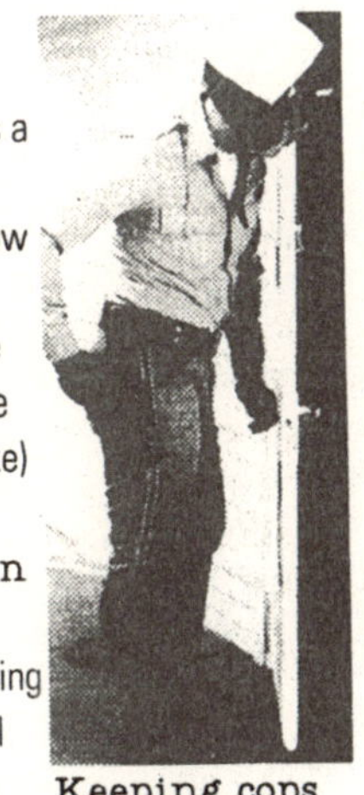

Keeping cops out of your sex life.

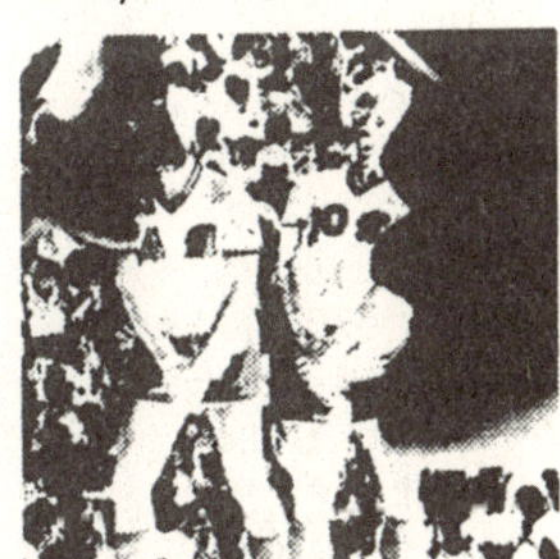

BLK's east-coast correspondent **Eric Washington** makes his *Village Voice* debut in the June 29th "Queer Issue" with a thoughtful and well-researched piece on black homophobia. The usually all-breeder *Details* gets very homo-friendly in their July 93 music issue. Frankie Goes To Hollywood's **Holly Johnson** writes about his life as an HIV+ pop star; comeback queen **Boy George** talks about being a fag in the music biz; **Flotilla DeBarge**, **Varla**, and **Joey Arias** as Justine pop up in the fashion layout with RHCP's **Anthony Kiedis**; and **Tom Jones** shows off his basket and still-humpy thighs (Ooooh, daddy!). And dig up the May 17, 1993 edition of *The New Yorker* for **Henry Louis Gates, Jr.**'s insightful and timely "Blacklash?".

A relaxed Holly Johnson.

The National Association of Men Of All Colors Together hosts its thirteenth annual national convention in Chicago, July 13-17, 1993. Keynote speaker is **Dr. Manning Marable**, whose topic is "Racism, Sexism, Homophobia: Obstacles to Progress." Musician/photographer **Scott Free** has put together a host of concurrent cultural events, including an art exhibition, video screening, and party at Trade and Flavor with world-class voguer **Aaron Enigma** and NYC transplant **London Broil**. For more information call (800) NA4-BWMT ext. 193.

Christopher Simons'"Approach Avoidance", from the MACT art event.

History in the making: Poet and writer **Essex Hemphill** and writer/photographer/producer **Ron Simmons** are looking for black, gay men sixty years of age and older to be interviewed for a documentary book project. "The Evidence Of Being" seeks to uncover and document a generation of black gay men. This important project will provide the world a glimpse into what it was like living doubly oppressed sixty years ago. Write: The Evidence of Being, box 48100, Washington DC 20002.

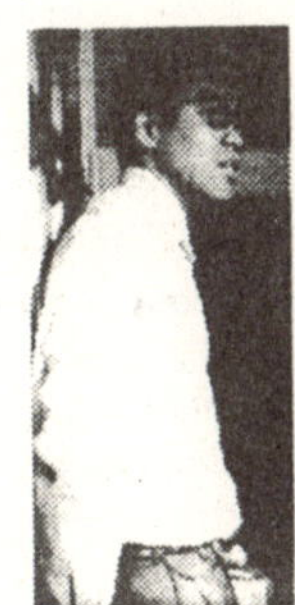

Billy Who?: from "Billy Turner's Secret."

New York's Village East theater hosts the opening of Frameline distributors' feature-length program of short works by homo filmmakers. *Boys Shorts: The New Queer Cinema* includes **Marlon Riggs'** seldom-screened "Anthem," and **Michael Mayson's** "Billy Turner's Secret," which focuses on homophobia in the black and Latino hood. The program opens in New York July 21, 1993 and will travel to film venues across the country. For more info, call Frameline at (415) 703-8650.

Yes, Louie Vega in Chicago — complete with bowler hat and two crates of records. But let it be said beforehand, in spite of the recent plethora of M.A.W. dubs, that this man is the real deal: Louie came from a jazz-playing family, innovated

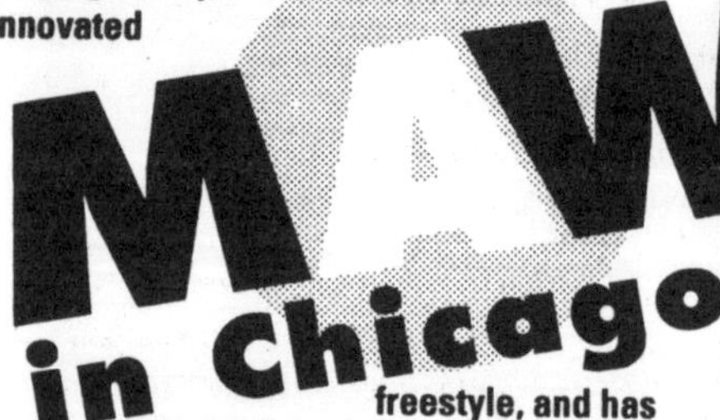

M.A.W.
in Chicago:

freestyle, and has been steeped in club music since its earliest days. In New York, on a Wednesday night at the Sound Factory Bar, I witnessed him keep an impossibly demanding crowd of serious dancers spinning in circles on the floor (literally) until 6 am with seamless mixes of such favorites as "The Poem," "Hot Shot," and the vibes break in the middle of "Free Man." I wasn't going to miss this show for anything, even considering the Shelter crowd on a Saturday night — but then again, that's why *you* didn't go, isn't it?

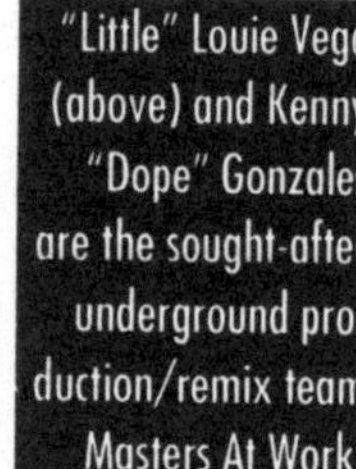

"Little" Louie Vega (above) and Kenny "Dope" Gonzales are the sought-after underground production/remix team Masters At Work.

To my surprise, however, there wasn't even much of a line at the door. The place began filling at around midnight; racially, it was in fact more diverse than any given night out at a gay bar, but you could literally count the queens on two hands here. Maurice Joshua of course was running around in his S.I.N. cap, and local talents such as Ron Trent, Mystic Bill and Lil' John Coleman all put in an appearance.

From 11:30 and on, it was the standard fare: "I Wanna Give You Devotion," "In the Mix," "Understand This Groove," "Brighter Days," "Photograph of Mary," "Sound Design," "Samba," "Nightcrawler," "I'll Be Your Friend," "Zig Zag," "Generate Power." Girlies in club outfits shaking away, white guys swaying with beer in hand: no high jinks, save a true lost child with a tropical bandanna on his head working away like a Soul Train.

People cheered when Louie came on at 1:00, but they obviously didn't seem to have any idea of who he was. It is notable that he kicked off on the original sax mix of Lil' Louis' "I Called You," and after that he played a good, continuous 45-minute set of mostly unrecognizable new records

and a few of his own commercial remixes. He even did a clever mix of the "Brighter Days" acapella over the dubs, but the furious moments were no doubt India (Louie's wife) scatting away on "Can't Get No Sleep."

In any case, Maurice presented Johnny D., also of New York, at about 1:45, and the music became much more obvious: Black Trax 3, the M.A.W. dub of Tito Puente's "Ran Kan Kan", a Nervous cut by Kenny Dope, Aly-us' "Follow Me" and "Club Lonely" (both the originals in full-length) of all things, and Todd Terry's beautiful "Makossa," the subtleties of which were all but lost on the Shelter's blaring sound system.

What You
Probably
Didn't Miss

Fortunately, however, Louie returned at 2:30 with some crazy beats, and then a long and rather bizarre remix of "Let No Man Put Asunder" that moved everyone onto the floor: the verses were all rearranged, the bassline would kick in now and then, and not ONCE did it ever say "it's not over between you and me"! The crowd had gotten slightly thinner, but people were really jumping now: slowly came Sinnamon's "I Need You Now" — that a capella for a full minute or so — then suddenly "uno dos tres quatro," the kick drums, and the next thing you knew it was Philly time with the full instrumental bootleg of "Love Is the Message". (Where was Aaron Enigma?) Yes, we've all heard it before, but the way he dropped it did feel like the sky coming down. Those saxes never sounded so good, but if automatic reaction to MFSB could be a measure of the real children in the house, there were none tonight. Back to the Paradise Garage: "Once in a Lifetime," "Touch and Go" (see Louie's Strictly dub of the organ), "Love Thang," the latter halves of "Running Away" and "My Love Is Free, " and then — gag — Dayjee's "Plastic Dreams," laid coolly and whimsically over with the dub of "I'm Every Woman." There was not much to be heard after that except some track with a sample from "Master Blaster" and a variation on the "doo doo doo's" of "Time Warp," which was the beginning of the end of Louie's set; so when he put his last record away and "Beat That Bitch With a Bat" came on, we knew it was time to leave.

Overall rating of the evening: a curiosity to satisfy, but if you weren't there, reading this page should just about make up for this relatively minor loss.

— Daniel Wang

tunes

RuPaul
<u>Supermodel Of the World</u> *Tommy Boy*

After years of paying dues in the netherworld, RuPaul Charles has finally arrived, smack-dab in the face of the mainstream. His debut album, "Supermodel of the World" could be a start on a voyage of longevity- he already has the gimmick, but it'll take more than that to stay on top. As a first attempt, the project is happy, optimistic and upbeat, but slightly vanilla. The music is the best thing to be noted about the album, while work in the area of vocal arrangement is needed on some tunes so that melody and music are not quite so interchangeable.

The first release, "Supermodel," is enjoying its limelight (with a techno/tribal remix that fills dancefloors), ushering in the RuPaul experi-

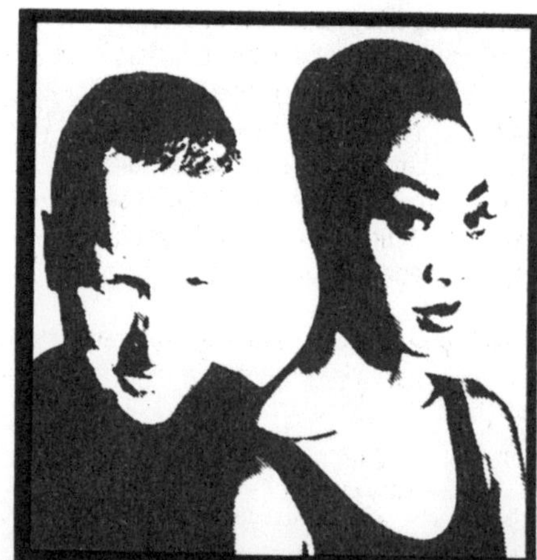

When last we heard from the team of Elisa Burchette and Hienrich Zwalen, known as Basscut, they'd just released their first CD The Art Of War. At that time, their single from the CD, "I'm Not In Love", was stormin' dancefloors nation wide but especially received a work out in east coast clubs in New York and Baltimore. Now they return with remixes of "Woman In The Shadows (The Only One)", the second single from the Consider This compilation. With five mixes and executive production work by Bill Coleman, we predict another dance storm by these two for this summer. It's jazzy and sophisticated and sure to get your butt movin' and your toes tappin' "Woman In The Shadows" is available on Pow Wow Records. —TA

to **GO!**

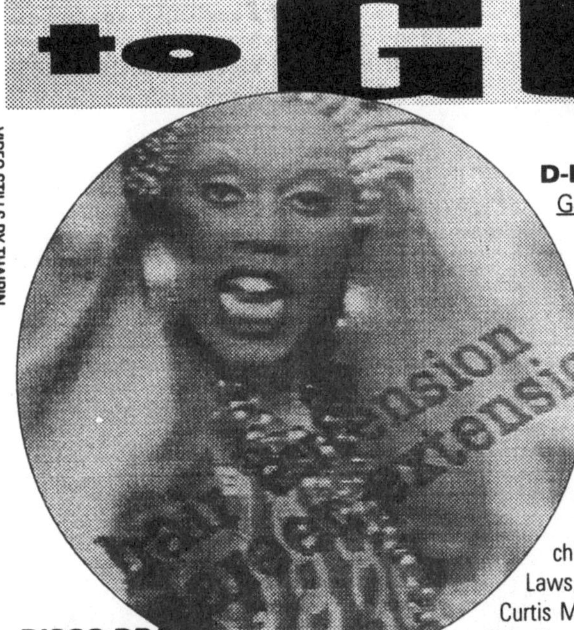

DISCO DRAG
Miss RuPaul

ence. The best song though is "House of Love." Ru's vocals are put to their best use over instrumentation that shows substance. "Back to my Roots," the second single, is of a more novel flavor, but shouts out a clear tribute to the versatility of African American hair(nuked or natural) as well as to the people who've found success "workin' it." Murk boy Oscar G.'s dope dub is sure to be pumpin' the wheels of steel (ooh-ooh, Tamba!)

My other favorites are "Stinky-Dinky," a seventies throw-back to the Ohio Players sound (think "Rollercoaster"), and "Everybody Dance," a cover of the popular Chic classic (not a noticeable improvement, but a good execution nonetheless). A novelty tune, "A Shade Shady" is a definite ballroom/runway must (as long as it doesn't get worn out... like "Supermodel"). "Miss Lady DJ' is pretty much a "filler," but it could grow on you. It definitely sheds light on how women continue to successfully infiltrate yet another male dominated arena: the turntables. Ironically enough, it's being touted by a drag queen.

The album has a lazy side, where it seems an onslaught of ad libs hides the lack of lyrics (like in "Free Your Mind") and vocals that seem a tad lackadaisical ("Ain't Nobody's Business"). I don't too much care for the corny law and order references on the grinder "Prisoner of Love," and "Supernatural" lacks the sensuality it strives to exude. Overall though, I'd say it's a start to success with staying power.
★★★ **Aaron Enigma**

D-Influence
Good 4 We *EastWest*

Good 4 We is the title of the new CD from D-Influence, the very funky group of young and racially mixed musicians that hail from the U.K. . And it's good for us that these people have a fabulous CD to get your blood moving on and off the dancefloor with some very slick and pared down instrumentations and fiercely soulful vocalizing.

This is p-a-r-t-a-y music for the children weaned on Hubert and Ronnie Laws, Earth Wind and Fire, Quincy Jones, Curtis Mayfield, The Crusaders, Donald Byrd and The Blackbirds, Bobby Humphrey, et. al. It's gritty R&B along the lines of the new school of Brand New Heavies, 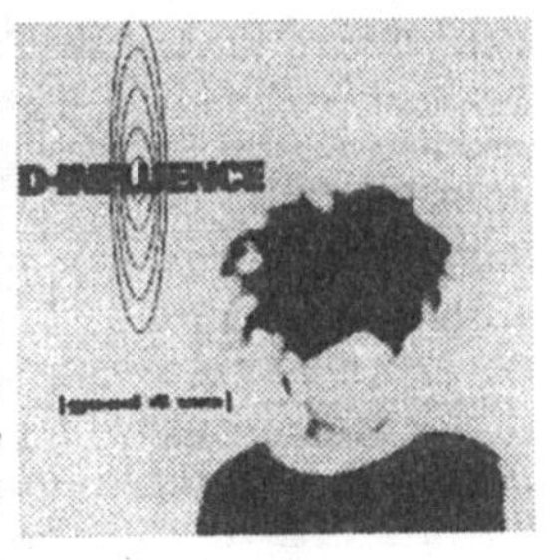 Massive Attack, De La Soul, Soul II Soul and Caron Wheeler. A very refined and meaningful use of samples and dance-jazz rhythms. Absolutely no filler.
★★★★ **Trent Adkins**

Caron Wheeler
Beach Of the War Goddess *EMI*

Background: Former Soul II Soul vocalist (handled leads on the essential singles "Keep On Movin'" and "Back To Life"). Her first solo outing was 1991's critically acclaimed *U.K. Blak* Been keepin' us wanting more since the Jam and Lewis-penned "I Adore You" popped up on the *Mo' Money* soundtrack last year.

Beach of The War Goddess gives us what we were waiting for. Caron's looking great; svelte and assured, with the tallest dreds yet. The liner notes read like a book, and include a booklist of suggested reading (a mix of Afro-feminist, political, and wholistic health titles). And of course there is the music; striking a graceful balance between serious synth funk and the whole mess of afro-cuban rhythms out there. Highlights include "Wonder" with Soul II Soul's Jazzie B. guesting and a searing

cover of Jimi Hendrix's "Wind Cries Mary." Caron makes multi-platinum Janet look like a poseur with her rhythm nation psychobabble and Sengalese braid extensions. Ms. Wheeler's afrocentric chill-pill is the perfect funk for thinking black groovesters this summer.
★★★★ **Robert Ford**

The D.A.M. Project
Stop, Look & Listen/I Can't Stop *Thumpin!*

This second release for Emotive Records new sub-label Thumpin!, "Stop, Look , and Listen", is a fresh and fierce 121 BPM deep underground club stormer, perfect for summer programming: cool and crisp with plenty of heat to get your dancefloor pumpin', thumpin' and sweatin! Freddie Bain is gonna love this record. Go on and work it, girlfriend.
★★★★ **Terry Martin**

Ethyl Meatplow
Happy Days, Sweetheart *Dali*

L.A queer friendly goth/grunge/punk/industrial /thrash/metal trio Ethyl Meatplow's long player *Happy Days, Sweetheart* is an, er, acquired taste. Some really humorous samples and twisted juxtapositions make their pointedly difficult brand of rock and roll worth listening to. There are two first singles to serve as introduction. "Devil's Johnson" is a catchy ditty about getting strung out on crack, with a video featuring the briefest glimpses of demented blactress Vaginal Creme Davis aimed at MTV. For adults 21 and over there's "Queenie," featuring MK mixes for the house crowd. Mistress Carla's deadpan, anguished vocals sound great over the smooth and funky synth track. And the hook is the perfect trashy refrain for a bar full of sweaty, drunk fags and dykes: "fucking bitch whore fucking dead queenie dead"
★★★★ **RF**

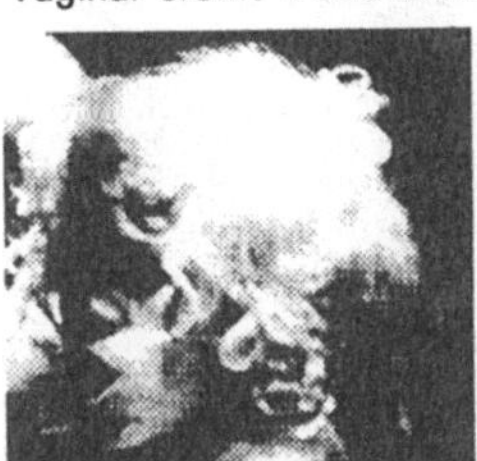

YES, MS. DAVIS: Vag's Meatplow cameo.

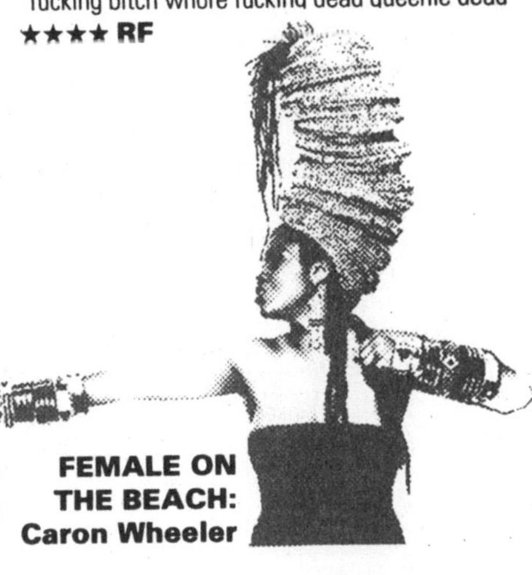

FEMALE ON THE BEACH: Caron Wheeler

B.O.P

The Underground *Strictly Rhythm*

This shit is dope! Strictly has forged a rep as stellar as West End or Prelude for serving up serious underground grooves. *The Underground* EP should prove to be another monster hit for this prolific NYC indie. All six tracks were produced written and mixed by the team B.O.P (Shank Thompson and Paul Scott). Every song on here could easily be a single, though the club-length timings and well-engineered pressing make this workable for any jock (I bet the CD sounds even better). And these aren't just jack beats either. Most feature down and gritty male vocals, and Valerie Higginbottom tears up the lead on the corny but cute "Sneakin' Around." "Get Up Out Of Your Seat" is one of the most intelligent sample tracks around, taking key elements of Made In U.S.A.'s hard-to-find seventies classic "Melodies" ("c'mon, where's the rest of the tape?") and working them for the nineties.
★★★ **RF**

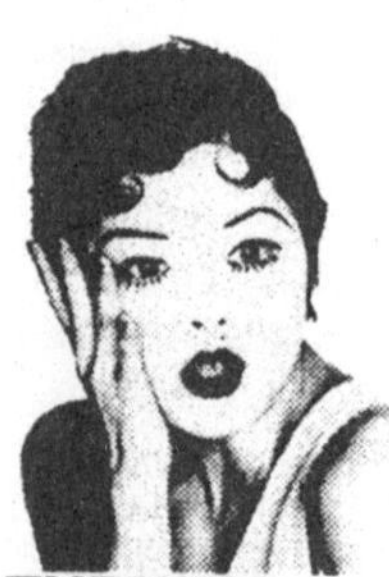

TURNING JAPANESE: Nokko

Nokko

I Will Catch U *Epic*

Deee-lite's soft spoken synth whiz, Jungle DJ Towa Towa Tei steps out on his own as a producer with this delightful new song. Lead vocalist Nokko has Japanese good looks to spare, and oddly enough sounds like forgotten August Darnell protege Christina. Remixed by the kids at San Francisco's 3rd Floor Productions, skip the tribal acid mess and go straight to the Deep Hump mix. And watch for the Nokko album, *Call Me Nightlife*.
★★★ **RF**

Taylor Dayne

Can't Get Enough Of Your Love *Arista*
Kind of like a bargain-basement cross between Barbra Streisand and Vickie Sue Robinson, Taylor Dayne is that nice little Jewish girl with the overdeveloped lung capacity. Her latest single is a LOUDLY sung cover of Barry White's smooth seventies classic "Can't Get Enough Of Your Love." A graceless and perfunctory C&C mix *almost* drowns out Taylor's strident, brassy vocals. And why go and ruin such a gorgeous song? Cover versions should take the listener somewhere new and unexpected, not send them screaming into the night. From Taylor's forthcoming opus *Soul Dancing*, coming soon to a cut-out bin near you.
★ **RF**

ALL THE KIDS' DISCO

Long before the term "house" became a catch phrase for all r&b underground disco, the genre of music was pretty strictly the turf of gay black men. Indie labels like Salsoul, Prelude, and West End cranked out tunes to satisfy the children at the Paradise Garage in New York, the Warehouse in Chicago, the Clubhouse in DC, and hundreds of other lesser-known clubs across the country. But while these records often boasted a decidedly gay aesthetic (fag hag big mama wailing vocals, campy tales of unrequited love and broken hearts, and fierce beats and sickening breaks), little of the music truly celebrated its sissyness. A few early exceptions include Mr. Melba Moore's early stab at gay club acceptability, "Miss Thing" (Epic, 1979). Kenton Nix's "Chillin Out" by Inez Brooks (West End, 1981), was an almost unplayable slow bump-and-grind predecessor to "Heartbeat." Its only redeeming quality is a break where Miss Brooks "reads" the "ladies" of her audience, and goes on to talk about how her boyfriend is "working her last nerve!"

Barbara Mason's "Another Man" (West End, 1983), a follow up to her "She's Got The Papers, But I Got The Man," addresses its gay audience more directly with the funny but homophopic tale of a woman spurned for another man. She suspects that he is wearing her sexy dresses, and notices when walking with him that "he was switching more than I was." Then she catches him holding hands on Market Street. The clincher is that she sums up the experience as "such a waste." Rumor has it that there's an Andy Warhol directed video for this one.

"Jump Back" by Dhar Braxton (Sleeping Bag, 1986) boasted one of the first mixes by C&C's Robert Clivilles, and was a pretty sizeable hit. DJs in the life of course first worked the a capella, where Miss Braxton walks with tens across the board as banjie girl realness letting her messy boyfriend have it. But again it was a bearded hit, with the reading being done by a straight woman, not a queen.

Ironically, it was cultural rapist Malcolm McLaren's ill-conceived *Waltz Darling* project that gave the children their voice. The single "Deep In Vogue" (Epic, 1989) took banal lyrics about "throwing shade," samples of Willi Ninja, and the bassline from "Love Is The Message" and made them into a irresistible lo-cal confection. From that point, a new trend was born. Spurred on by a cultural climate which is rebounding from Ronnie and Nancy's eighties into Bill and Hillary's nineties, fag boy disco has truly come out of the closet.

Witness RuPaul's crossover dream "Supermodel" (Tommy Boy, 1992), which took a drag queen's demanding cry for fierceness (WORK!) and married it to a frothy pop radio song, producing this past spring's most annoyingly hooky hit. Jack And Jill's "Work It Girlfriend" (Strictly Rhythm, 1992) is a DJ's delight; four entirely different intros, each more over the top than the last. (My favorite: "One queen asked me, 'you think you're fierce'? I said 'of course'. She said 'Miss Thing, all queens think they're fierce'. I said 'all Queens and me!'") But the new anthem promises to be Junior (Sound Factory) Vasquez's remix of "Get Huh" by The Ride featuring Roxy (Legal, 1993). Eight minutes

THE NEXT BIG MISS THINGS: Jose (r) and Luis serve it.

of a low house groove, with some shady, shady *shady* queen just going off. "Get huh! She's an onion-pussy bitch, I hate huh! That wig looks like a helmet. How dare she talk to me like that and she's standing by the stairs? I'll push her down backwards, I'll push her down backwards!" And in the true spirit of camp, her banter is full of pop cultural references: Bruce Lee, Ethel Merman, Deee-Lite, Don Knotts, Barbra Streisand's nose, and Mr. Snuffleupagus are among the icons that inspire thing's sickening similes. And queenspeak promises to further push into the mainstream with the upcoming Sire/Warner Brothers project from Madonna's Blond Ambition dancers Jose Gutierez and Luis Camacho. Another Junior Vasquez production, "The Queen's English" is real as ice water and twice as cold. The hook: *Vogue Miss Thing/You're so fierce*. There's a full-length album in the works, too. Finally, queer Latino pop stars! Don't be surprised if this becomes another crossover top 40 hit. (I hope they at least get a chance to break faces on "Soul Train".)

Like a voguer's ball, the dance music underground is wickedly competitive. Undoubtedly some child will document even more of our endless snap diva language and have us gagging on the dance floor.

— **Robert Ford**

Dynamic Duo

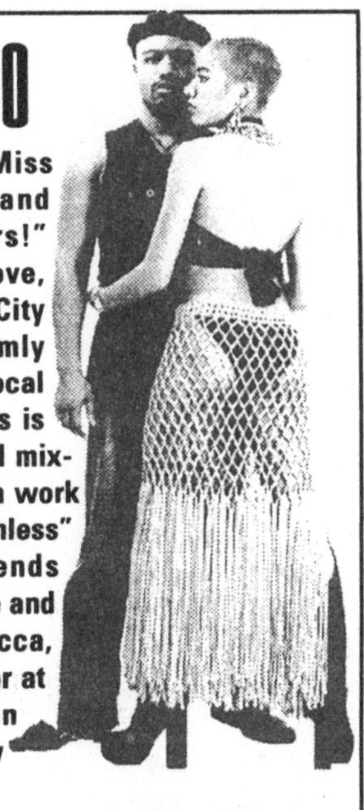

We knew something was up when Miss Giggles said, "First week in town and already she's doin' an afterhours!" Musician Marcus Sherrard and his love, artist Aisha Calloway, hit the Windy City just months ago but already have firmly planted themselves in the thick of the local party and entertainment circuit. Marcus is in and out of the studio engineering and mixing new material after completing such work as "Chain Me To The Beat" and "Breathless" on the *Consider This* CD. Aisha attends classes at the School of The Art Institute and bartends at the hot Halsted dance mecca, Foxy's. She is also a fashion contributor at the new weekly *Babble*, managing an occasional party at their cute Lakeview garden flat.— **TA**

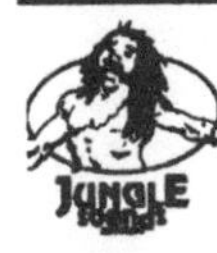
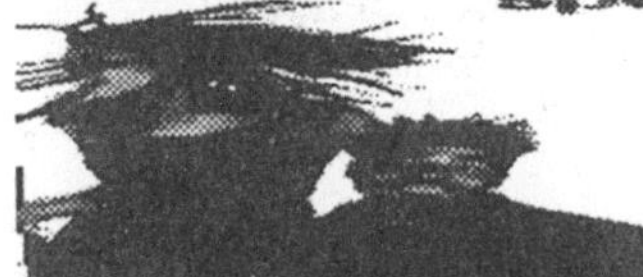
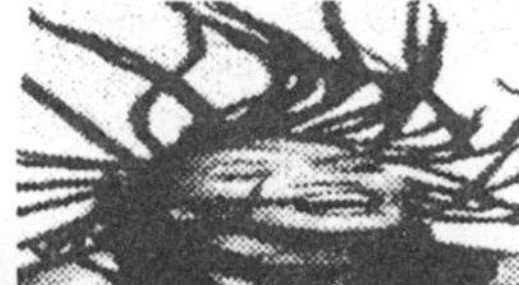
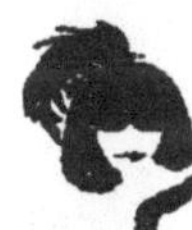
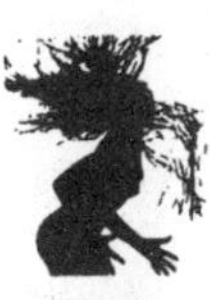
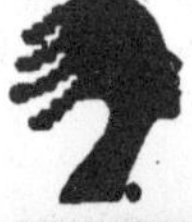

H O U S E   T H E   H A I R ?

As the fictitious RUtv tells in the "Back To My Roots" video, Black Hair Is. What it *is* exactly few could say. Versatile is one word that aptly describes its many styles and variations. It's also, for many black folks, often *the* object for personal self expression. Witness these logos and "hair treatments" from magazines to record sleeves. LEFT (from top) Jungle Sounds logo, Siedah Garrett's logo, Soul II Soul funki dred silhouette, *Essence* magazine logo. ABOVE: Reprise/Eternal recording artists Urban Speech (l), and anunidentified graphic from a local party plugger. — **TA**

MEMO TO THE MUSIC INDUSTRY:

Please spare us any more of the following:

120 BPM REMIXES OF 90 BPM RECORDS
If we want Janet Jackson to sound like a chip munk we'll pitch her up ourselves

DOUBLE PACK 12" RELEASES
Instead of umpteen lame mixes, how 'bout one really fierce one?

THE OBLIGATORY UNDERGROUND MIX
A few minor key synth farts does not constitute underground.

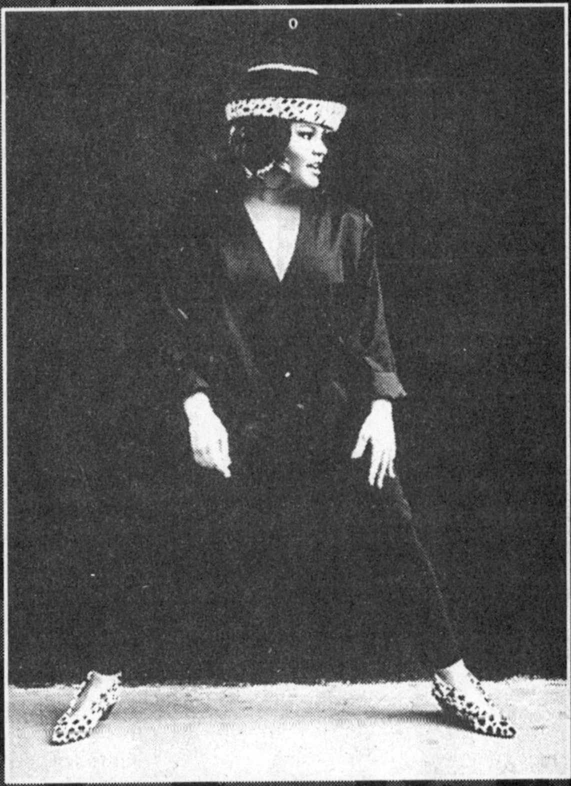

THE OBLIGATORY TECHNO MIX
If we wanted a Moby record, we would have BOUGHT a Moby record.

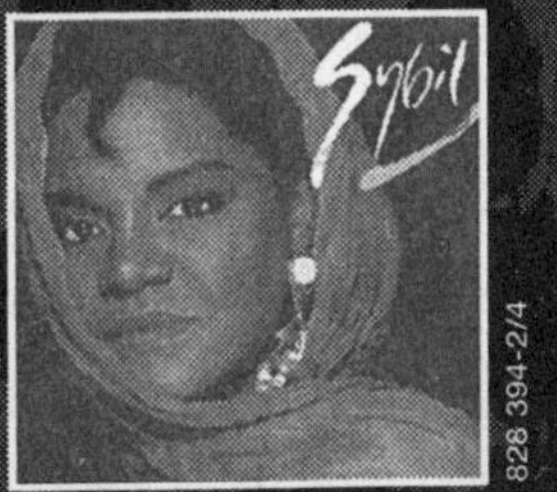

WHITE MALL HOUSE
Do we really need club music by Debbie Gibson and Celine Dion?

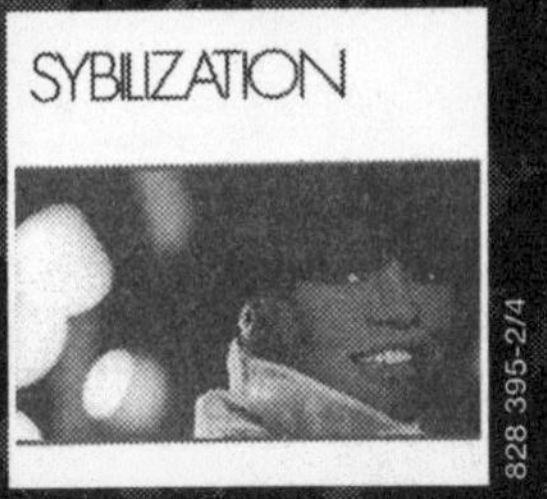

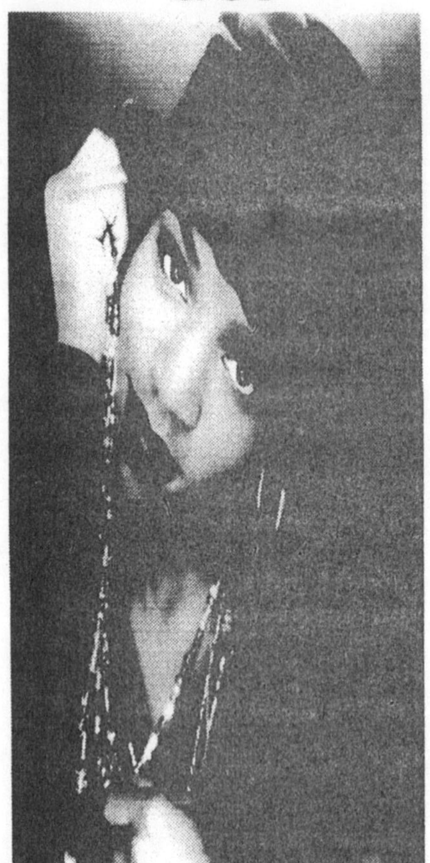

disco diva:
Chantay Savage
by robert ford

Was it really over a year ago that "I Gotta Hold On You" introduced house music devotees to the powerful voice of Chicago's Chantay Savage? Hers is the talent family: her father Frank taught blues great Albert King how to play the guitar, and her brother John "SavageMann" blows the sax for reggae combo Roots Rock Society. Chantay started singing in church, and she soon decided to make music her life, too. Follow-up singles from ID featuring Maurice Joshua, Steve Hurley, and Jamie Principle went on to equal dance floor success. Her current hit single, "If You Believe", in its 12" version is an extended piece of disco drama. The song starts with a reggae backbeat before soaring into a good old uptempo house stomper. "If You Believe" caught the ear of RCA records. Her debut album, *Here We Go*, is in stores now.

RF: How did you first stumble upon house music?

CS: In high school. It was the craze at the time. I had a lot of friends and we liked to go out and party. That's really what we were into. I was in a little dance troupe—some people still remember it, we were called Front Row— and we would go from party to party and dance and perform.

RF: Was that the whole high school "hotel party" circuit?

CS: Right.

RF: What djs were spinning that circuit?

CS: Back then? Farley (Keith), Steve Hurley, Andre Hatchett. And of course Frankie (Knuckles). I hung out at the Gallery. That was one of the best parties. Too bad it didn't last too long.

RF: How did you go from there to getting involved in making music?

CS: Once I got involved with ID. That's where the music began for me. I was already familiar with house music. I knew what we were looking for and I knew what I would want to hear in a club.

RF: Do you encounter a lot of sexism working in a mostly male dance music industry?

CS: Actually I never really got that from ID because I went in with some smarts about how things go. They knew that I could write, they knew that I could do vocal production. When you embark on a musical project with some kind of know-how, it diminishes the sexism.

RF: It makes them deal with you as a peer.

CS: Exactly. Sometimes I will notice it when I go somewhere else. But once the work begins, the sexism ends.

RF: Has it been a big adjustment to having to do all the other stuff involved in a music career— the video shoots and photo shoots and touring and all that stuff. It must be pretty hectic.

CS: It is pretty hectic. But you choose your career. It's going the way it should go. This is the career that I chose and a part of it is the video shoots and promo work. If I didn't have it, I'd be very concerned.

RF: Where have you played? I know

you've been on the road a lot. Have you been doing mostly showcase things and industry things?

CS: Yeah. I'm just getting off of the promo tour. Gosh, it ended Saturday. I was out for a month and I did practically the entire US. A lot of it the majority I'd say like sixty percent of it was radio stations, meetings, greeting you know dinners and stuff like that. The other forty was track dates. Some were different cities, different festivals a lot of stuff was sponsored by the radio station. ("If You Believe") is doing very well outside of Chicago.

RF: Why do you think this market hasn't responded to it as well as far as the radio response?

CS: Chicago's radio? I'm pretty sure it's a political thing. It's a political thing with radio. You know, they get very nervous about new artists . Some of the radio program directors like to follow other people's lead. See how it's playing in other cities and so forth and they do .. they go through those measures where as some PDs will just say hey, I like the song, I'll play it . Fortunately it has happened out where as Chicago is a little bit more conservative in choosing a song that they'll play.

RF: Right, they want to wait and see who else is playing it. Did you make a conscious decision not to do a "house" album?

CS: Yes and no. For me, I haven't really had the chance to reveal all of my musical influences to the public. All they've had a chance to hear is the house thing. Which is part of my past but by no means all that I have to offer. My roots are jazz, r&b, and blues. Which is where house music evolved from. To me, it's really a black thing. I remember early on, the vocals that you'd hear on house music would be almost like gospel vocals sung over tracks. The album gives me a chance to embark on other influences. Like "If You Believe" It's house-y, but it has a reggae influence. The song "Here we Go" has a jazz feel. Some of it has a little hip-hop overtone, and I like that, too.

RF: One of the factions within house has always seemed to be the gay house artists vs. the straight ones. Did you sense any of this at ID?

CS: Oh no. In fact, it was quite the contrary. ID always understood—and I agree—that the gay community supported house music more than any other community could. The music was so good that it drew everyone else. Anybody who had a problem admitting to that, its really their problem. Because they still ended up dancing to the music, and you still found them in the gay clubs, whether they tried to make excuses or do whatever they felt they had do do. The bottom line was the gay community was where house music was rampant. The gay community supports house music, really supports it, in terms of buying the music and supporting the artists.

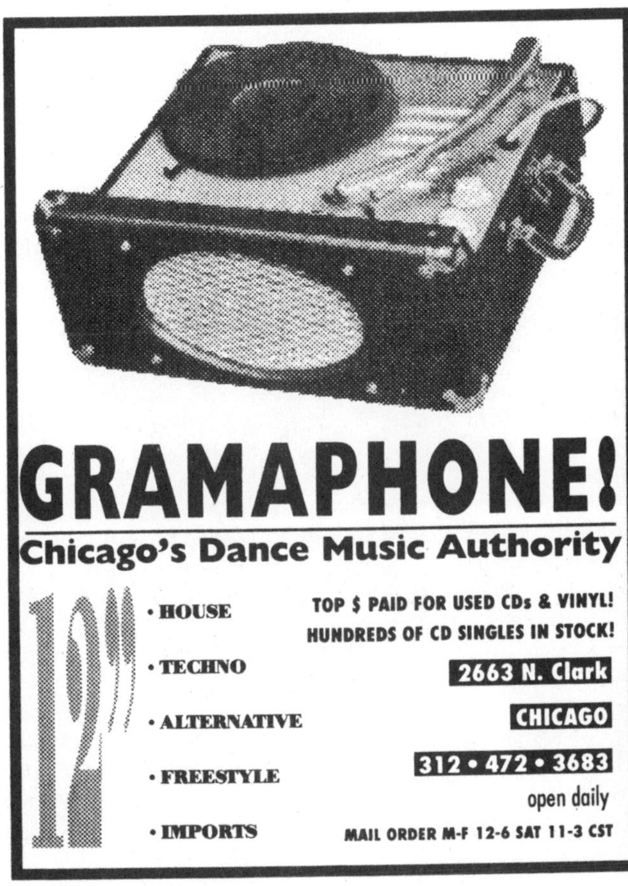

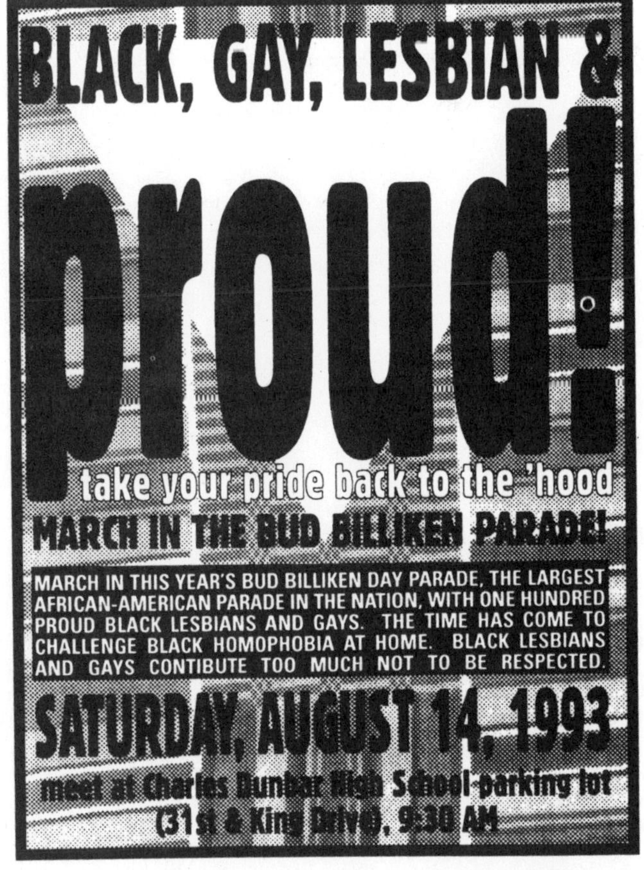

The Lizard Club
Steve Abbott
<u>Autonomedia</u>
160 pages $6.00

The best thing about the late author Steve Abbott's last book *The Lizard Club* is that it uses pop iconography and homocore references to illustrate a most unusual type of alien-ation and oth-erness: that of post-modern life as a lizard . It is never entirely clear if Lizard Club members are really lizards or just think they are. They live on the fringe of society while mingling in the

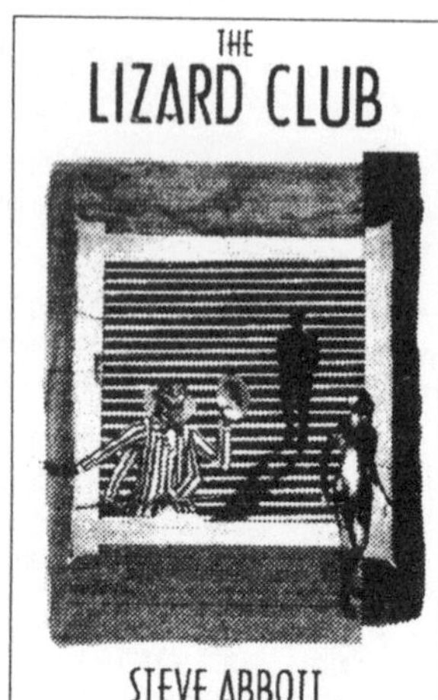

sometimes boring and humdrum workaday world (the main character is a marketing researcher). But Lizard Club members eat people and this poses such a problem for the protagonist that he joins a twelve step lizard rehab program. Funnier still, is how eating people is posed as an extension of carnal lust and fucking, making the practice of devouring humans whole seem understandable, rather like being a sexual pig. (Ever have a night when you just couldn't get enough?) The humor here is dark, rooted in ancient paganism as well as the contemporary rituals and sensibilities of fag/dyke queers, and not the ordinary lesbian/gay subculture. It's a good read and should have particular appeal for lovers of the macabre and homocore trivia.
Trent Adkins

Gone Tomorrow
Gary Indiana
<u>Pantheon</u>
244 pages $21.00

In Gary Indiana's new novel, *Gone Tomorrow*, the reader is engaged not unlike the gaper at the scene of a fatal crash: gasping in horror yet compelled to look on.

A variety of themes and issues in the story (political corruption, Fascist politics, sexual desire, torture, escapism, denial, s/m, suicide, murder, existentialism, etc.) come by way of characters whose experiences with art, fame and hedonism unfold in simple and real-life ways. Indiana wittily illustrates this story with prose that's economical but rich in color and mood.

In 1984 a group of actors and technicians assemble in the northern seaport of Cartagena, Colombia to shoot a feature length art film. We imagine director Paul Grosvenor as we'd imag-ine Bob Fosse or the German filmmaker, Rainer Werner Fassbinder, or Pasolini: filmmakers whose lives and legends themselves were the stuff of Fellini movies.

The characters seem as familiar as old friends, however eccentric. Valentina Vogel is Grosvenor's longtime film editor: beautiful, brooding, protective. Irma Irma is a cross-eyed (!) bombshell South American actress/seduc-tress. Michael Simard, (an obsession of the nar-rator), is the sexually ambiguous beautiful-beef-cake-boy-toy. Rich, ex-Nazi Carlotta Gavro, whose villa serves as guesthouse for a portion of the cast and crew, has a funny secret, too, regarding her son Alex, a has-been actor who is now seen on the late show... portraying Nazi officers in old war movies.

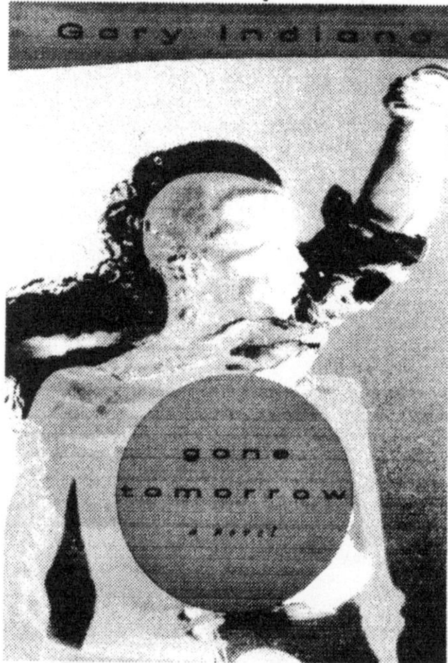

Fear and lust play significantly in *Gone Tomorrow*. That several of the major players are later stricken with AIDS is but the half of it. At the airport in Bogatá, the narrator witnesses a man brutally beaten by a soldier. "It was the kind of airport where inconvenient political types and luckless bystanders were sometimes mowed down in crossfire." This sense of peril is heightened by the presence of a grisly serial killer. Dubbed the Vampire of Cartagena, he/she preys nearly exclusively on tourists and is rumored to eat part(s) of his/her victims.

This heady mix of horror and glamour evokes images of a Warhol/Morrisey junket in South America with a Dracula/Manson type thrown in for good measure. Indeed, the narra-tor, (a smallish actor with effeminate manner-isms) sounds like an odd cross between Truman Capote and Bob Colacello. His sly observations and casual commentaries are introspective as well as being leveled at the other players. Because all of them are carrying-the-fuck-on posing, boozing, drugging, sexing and dying.
TA

Fragments That Remain
Steven Corbin
<u>Alyson</u>
320 pages $19.95

Fragments That Remain is the story of a African-American family living in modern day Harlem. Its central figure, Skylar Whyte, is a young, critically acclaimed movie actor— and is gay.

The Whytes as a family are by every defini-tion of the word dysfunctional. The father, Howard, is from an upper-middle class New Jersey family, poor of money but wealthy in love and family values. Howard uses his marriage to dark skinned Althea partially as a means of revenge for his mother's sudden and long-stand-ing lack of affection. The relationship sets the tone for the division that exists within the household especially after the birth of the first child, Skylar who is also dark skinned and the object of all of Althea's attention. Skylar and Althea both become the object of Howard's jeal-ousy driven violence. The addition of Kendall, the second and light-skinned son somewhat assuages Howard as he takes a liking to the boy and is determined to make him a replica of him-self, showering him with all his love and atten-tion. Despite the lack of paternal support, Skylar grows up to be self sufficient while Kendall falls victim to the indulgent and destructive habits of his father. Years later, Skylar is forced to face and reconcile a multitude of feelings towards his family when he learns his father is dying in the hospital.

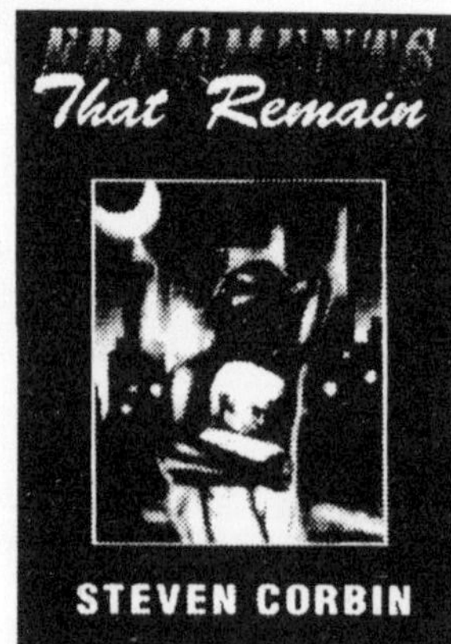

Skylar is super-sensitive to the discrimi-nations facing the two disen-franchised minority groups of which he is a member. The overt and sub-tle racism he experiences in his working sit-uation, i.e. white actors getting roles he would be perfect for, except for his skin color, as well as the violence and ignorance perpetrated on African-Americans and gays that is played out on the news eats at him like a cancer. It is a feeling not shared by his lover of four years Evan, a white, much sought-after model turned movie star. The non-involved, nonchalant attitude towards the plight of Blacks and Gays causes Skylar to question Evan's attraction to black men and his being able to "relate" to them. The racial slurs and the word racist are thrown around like frisbees and ultimately they form the wedge that drives them apart.

Although the writing style uses flashbacks and can sometimes be distracting in its erratic movements, Corbin tells the story in a manner that engrosses the reader. The detailed character development gives the reader a strong sense of the characters' identity, and their pain. I found myself getting extremely angry with the characters for their shortcomings, then empathizing when they are forced to expose the conditions of their personality defects. The plot is full of twists and turns and sometimes the familiar street you turn down does not lead you where you expect.

Overall, I think Corbin is to be commended for his insight and the approach by which he attempts to explain some of the causes of our own fragmented relationships. I hope that this can become a book people will read to learn how to start putting the pieces back together.
Sheldon Watson

quick reads:

WHAT'S WRONG WITH THIS PICTURE?: The idea of playing twenty questions with some of all-male porn's better known actors isn't altogether a bad one. That such a round-up would be conducted by someone from within the male video industry seems a smart bet, too, someone who'd understand the ridiculousness of the product as well as the necessity for these videos. It's interesting to learn that black super- stud Randy Cochran's mother actually encouraged his career, that he devoutly performs the Nicheren Shoshu Buddhist chant Nam-MyoHo-Renge-Kyo before shooting scenes. Why, then, is *Sorry I Asked: Intimate Interviews with Gay Porn's Rank and File* by Dave Kinnick (Badboy) lacking? *There are no pictures!* Time and money would have been well spent to include at least head shots (!) of these guys to accompany their interviews. As it is, we're stuck trying to guess, "So, whose ass is this?"— TA

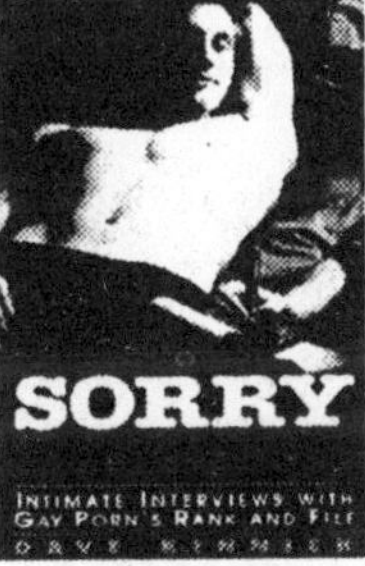

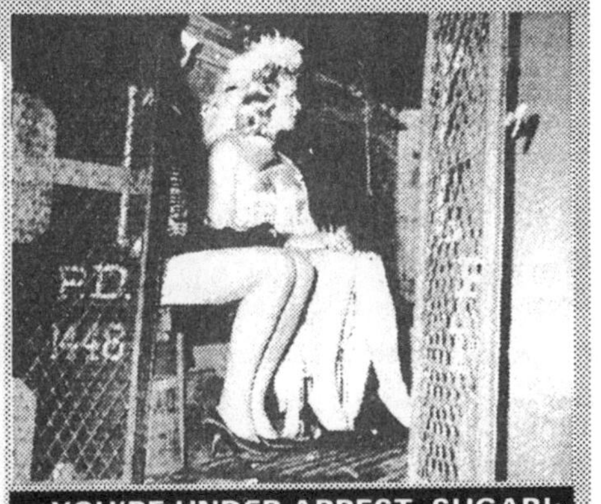

**YOU'RE UNDER ARREST, SUGAR!: This 1962 photo of queens in the paddy wagon after a police raid on the Artists' Exotic Carnival and Ball in New York is from Martin Duberman's definitive history of the early homophile movement, *Stonewall* (Dutton). The book chronicles the lives of six men and women from before that groundbreaking gay rebellion in 1969 to the first gay rights march in 1970, and is commendable for its care to record history including women and people of color. It also provides insight into the nascent Greenwich Village queer underground, and provides some juicy gossip as well.
— Robert Ford**

H.D. Motyl's
TOKEN OF LOVE

reviewed by **Jamika Ajalon**

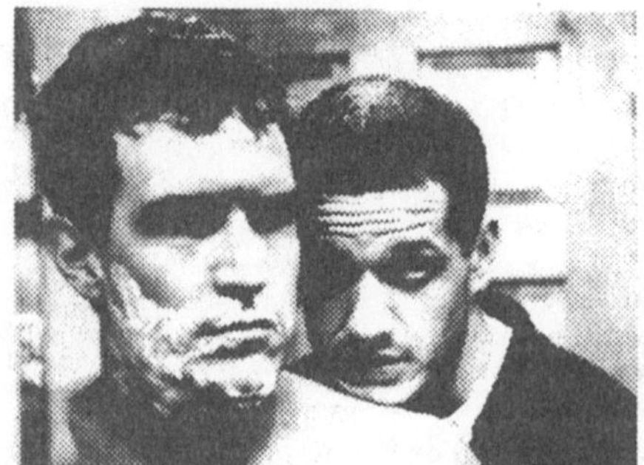

FIFTY WAYS TO LEAVE YOUR LOVER:
Bob Pries (l) and Kyle Hall in "Token."

Being the Black dyke that I am, I wasn't too terribly sure I would get too terribly excited about another white gay boy movie. There is not much worse than Pillsbury-doughboy fluff-n-stuff. H. D. Motyl's film "Token of Love", however, tickled my poetic sensibilities.

This thirty-minute drama plays on the psychological games when one is breaking up with her lover, but not in the way that may be expected.

The majority of the flick is set in Will's (played by Bob Pries) bathroom. While he's in the shower, his boyfriend Benjamin, (played by Kyle Hall), enters with a cup of tea and a lot on his mind.   As Will is shaving, Ben breaks the news. There is the familiar verbal combat; "....it's not you, let me explain..."   "…..I don't want to know" blah/ blah/ blah /blah

This scene is played out twice more, and intermixed with nostalgia (boys in bed, playfully erotic), and visual story-telling, (Ben preparing to break the news to Will). The style in which this story is told is complex and layered, as the viewer is not exactly sure what is actually happening and what is imagined.

With each scene in the bathroom, layers of truth (or lies?) are uncovered as Ben becomes more assertive and Will becomes more vulnerable.

The characters are believable. Both actors, Pries and Hall, deliver their dialogue with a realistic edge. It was never overly dramatic, except when Will has his dream monologue. This is probably more due to the script. During this bit I was hit with so many "waves" I was almost drowning in metaphors. I made it to shore alive, however, a little more at peace with both characters.

Poetic symbolic images are not only apparent in the script but also in the camera and editing style. The story moves along lyrically with a mixture of jump cuts and flash-backs which prolong and rip apart time.

Motyl's creative storytelling skills give a bit of flavor to what could have been another bland gay boy movie. The visually stimulating cinematography and unpredictable depiction of a cliched situation make this piece a worth-while view.

WHAT WE'RE WATCHING:

Frameline Distributors polled 200 lesbian and gay film and video makers, asking them to name their top ten. The resulting list of top vote-getters looks like this:

1. VERTIGO
Alfred Hitchcock, USA 1958
2. SUNSET BOULEVARD
Billy Wilder, USA 1950
3. THE TIMES OF HARVEY MILK
Robert Epstien, USA 1984
4. LA DOLCE VITA
Federico Fellini, Italy/France 1960
5. JEANNE DIELMAN
Chantal Ackerman, France 1975
6. CITIZEN KANE
Orson Wells, USA 1941
7. IMITATION OF LIFE
Douglas Sirk, USA 1959
8. THE WIZARD OF OZ
Victor Fleming, USA 1939
9. THELMA AND LOUISE
Ridley Scott, USA 1991
10. LAW OF DESIRE
Pedro Almodovar, Spain 1987

Of course, not every filmmakers' picks made the big list. John Water's included Warhol's *Chelsea Girls*, Russ Myer's *Faster Pussycat, Kill! Kill!*, and Liz Taylor's wicked performance in *Boom!* Barbara Hammer picked Maya Deren's experimental *Meshes Of The Afternoon* and Walt Disney's *Bambi*. And Gus Van Sant's cast votes for camp classic *Suddenly, Last Summer*, *Fellini's Roma*, and Kubrick's *A Clockwork Orange*.

on stage:

With the recent critical and box-office success-es of "Angels In America" and "Kiss Of The Spider Woman", the American theater has become an important medium of expression for gay and lesbian artists and concerns. Queer plays, performance groups and theater festivals have become increasingly popular across the country. Chicago is home to one of the more popular annual group of shows, Bailliwick's Pride Performance Series.

The current series features the Midwest premiere of "The Harvey Milk Show," a musical adaptation of the life and times of San Francisco's first openly gay city supervisor. The show portrays Milk's works of activism in the 1970's against Anita Bryant and the "moral majority,"and ends his homophobia-motivated murder by fellow supervisor Dan White. With a book by Dan Pruitt and music by Patrick Hutchinson, "Harvey Milk" won rave reviews in its world premiere in Atlanta last year.

Join *Thing* magazine for a special performance of "The Harvey Milk Show" at 7:30pm on Wednesday, July 28, 1993 at the Theater Building, 1225 W. Belmont. Tickets are just $10.50 (a $6.50 savings over the regular price), and a portion of the proceeds benefit *Thing* magazine. And join the staff of *Thing* and the cast of "The Harvey Milk Show" for cocktails at Foxy's (Halsted & Belmont) after the show. Your ticket stub is good for free admission to Foxy's and one well drink, wine, or beer that night. Reserve tickets by calling Ray Kasper at (312) 929-8499.

MUSTO

counts to ten

THE 10 BIGGEST QUEENS OF ALL TIME

1. Richard Simmons: Believes that you should only put things into your body that are good for you.

2. Paul Lynde: Did Poppers really kill him, or maybe his wrists flapped a little too hard.

3. Charles Nelson Reilly: He should have been in a big pink triangle instead of a Hollywood Square.

4. Dom DeLuise: That he's married with children is the only thing that differentiates him from the other people on this list.

5. Boy George: Remember when he claimed to be "bisexual"? And I'm Norman Schwartzkopf.

6. Liberace: Wait—Liberace was really gay? No! Noooooooooo!!!!!!

7. Jm. J. Bullock: The illegitimate spawn of Paul Lynde and Charles Nelson Reilly.

8. Franklin Pangborn: Old Hollywood's token queer, a character actor who out-flounced Ginger Rogers.

9. Elton John: His public coming out was the biggest shock since Jimmy Hoffa disappeared.

10. David Geffen: The music industry's reigning queen, his fling with Cher must have been as real as her current set of lips.

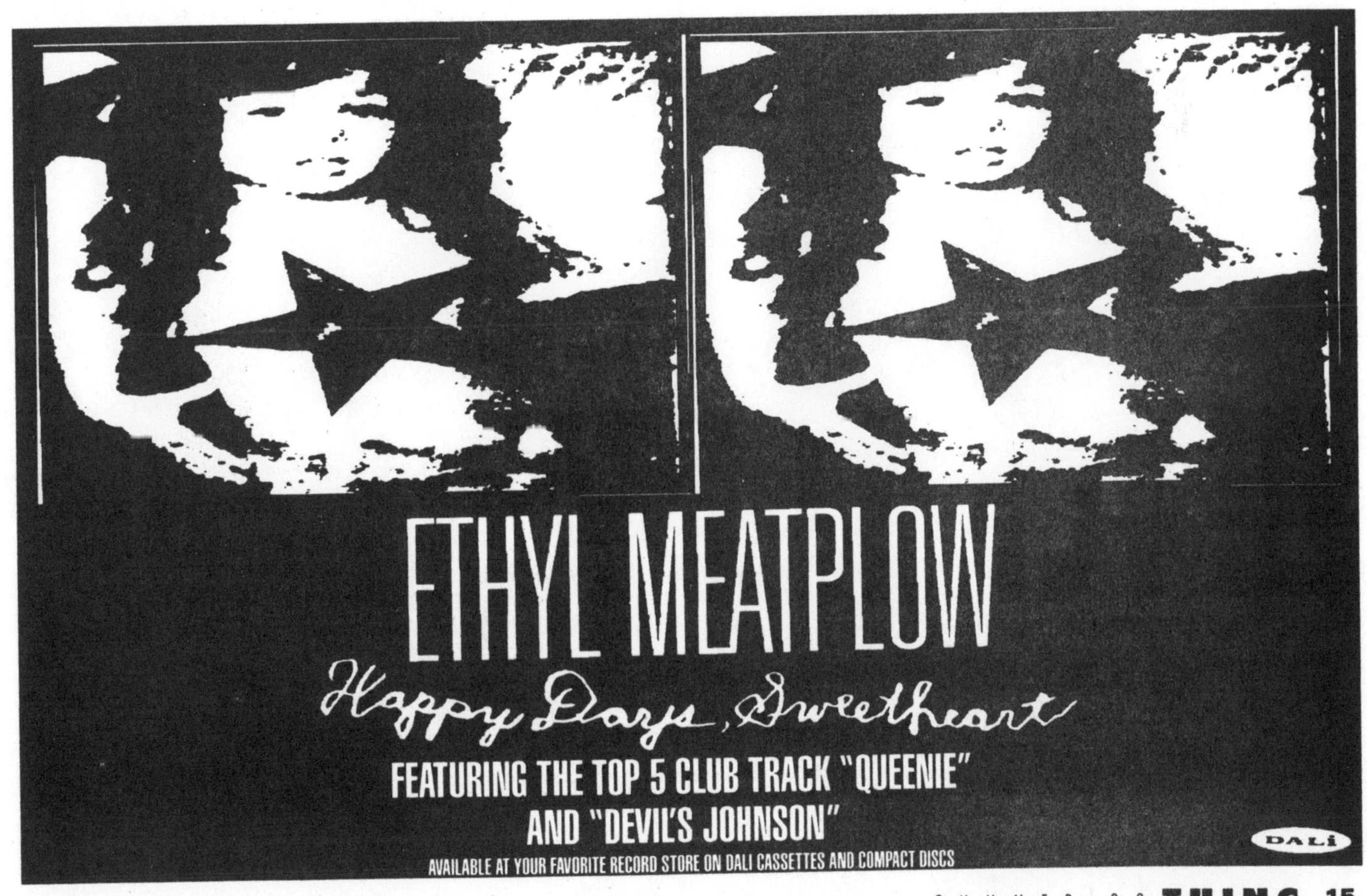

ATLANTIC BEACH HOTEL

On the beach

DECK BAR
Tropical Specialties

SANDY BEACH TERRACE
Restaurant

Singles Available from $60!

ATLANTIC BEACH HOTEL
SAN JUAN
Puerto Rico
(809) 721-6900

lists

Love, Peace and Hairgrease
Long Aid K7
Ultra Sheen
Afro Sheen
Nu Nile
All Ways
Dark and Lovely
Creme of Nature
Vitapoint
Optimum
Lady Bergamot
Royal Crown
Bone Straight
Dusharme
Sulphur 8
Palmer's Coconut
TCB
Pink Oil Moisturizer
Alberto V-05
Isoplus
Esirg Hairfood
Kemi Oyl
Hair Rep
B&B Super Gro
Dax

Back To My Roots
Bone Straight
Dark and Lovely
Creme of Nature
French Perm
Kiddie Perm
Get Smooth
Optimum
Revlon
African Pride
S Curl
Kemi
Glover's Mane
Bergamont

Word Up
Simiotexte
Grove Press
Farrar Strauss Giroux
Autonomedia
Alyson

Spell Check
RESPECT
IOU
Born to B.R.E.E.D.
Tell It Like It Ti Is
ABC

Got It Goin' On
Bobby Miller
Jack Walls
Frank Ceraolo
Tom Terrell
Tonya Reeves
Jim Fouratt
Haynes

Get A Clue
Victor Lee
Scott Erik
Camden Krass
Iaonnis Mookas
Memory Lane
Fluffy Boy
T.J. Mozarella
the Hughes twins
Buju Banton

Taylor Made
Taylor Mead
Taylor Dayne
Ann Taylor
The June Taylor Dancers
Elizabeth Taylor
Andy Taylor and Barney Fife
Johnnie Taylor
James Taylor

Hustles/Makin' A Livin'
Interview people who you never gave a damn about before
Film a underground documentary and sell it to a big distributor
Do artsy photographs of vacuous celebrities
Pose for a cereal box
Endorse a sneaker
Make hyper-minimalist couture at outrageous prices
License your name to pret-a-porter
Sign a white guy who can't rap
Sing backup for him
Lay down his break beats
Be an agent
Sell American style abroad
Play for a yuppie crowd at a big club on Saturday nights
Sing blues tunes at Carnegie Hall for middle-aged white people
Conduct the band on the Tonight Show
Write a sordid bestseller about your scene but change the names
Turn your adolescent/ghetto angst into a hit song
Do late night ads for the astrology hotline
Make boring disco records and sell them in $10 double-packs
Do a porno flick

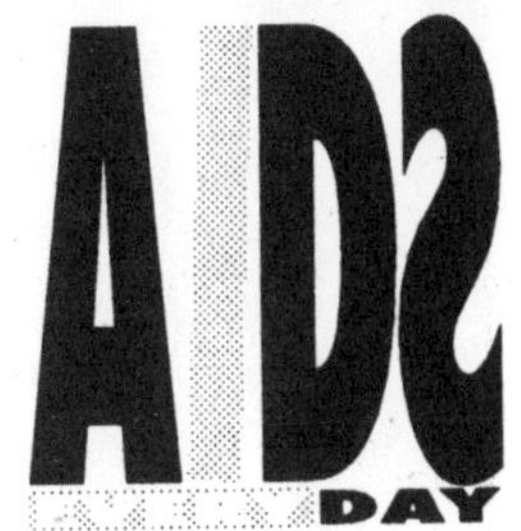

SPIRITUAL HEALING & HIV

I have often reacted strongly to the homo-phobic suggestion that I chose to be homo-sexual. I have insisted that there was no choice involved. I have retorted that I would never choose to be gay living in a country where being Black is already a significant dis-advantage, "Why would I choose to be gay?" I have thought a lot about it. Maybe I would have to be crazy, or at least compulsive, to choose a lifestyle against which the odds are so heavily stacked.

I have put it on the back burner and on the shelf. Invariably the concern returns to the forefront burner or falls at my feet from the shelf. And I must consider this dilemma again: I like a lot of people of all types. However, I am fulfilled by lesbians and gay men: socially, emotionally, spiritually, artistically, intellectu-ally and sexually. BUT the world, in general, remains hostile to us. Why?

Lo, and behold, in the shower one morning, the answer comes into me. I suddenly know for certain why I am gay. I know for certain why I am a Black homosexual male living in the racism-denying, misogynist, homo-hating, token-seeking American culture of the late twentieth century. It is beautifully simple: God made me a Black gay man so that the universe would be a better place in which to live.

BEFORE MY ARTICLE "Spiritual Reality and HIV" was published, in fact, before I even knew that it had been accepted for publication, I showed the text to a friend of mine. He is also a Black gay man who was raised by a family not dis-similar from my own. His

comment after reading the third paragraph was, "Your father was a 'race man,' right?"

Yes, my Father was. In the days between World War I and World War II, the few Black men who were fortunate enough to get an education were reminded constantly at their Black colleges that the future of the race depended upon their achievements. Each man was asked, no, told to be a Black Hercules: strong, untiring and above reproach, so that the race might advance against all the odds. The 'race man' was a strong and intelligent Black man, of the Renaissance variety, who was inculcated with the very highest stan-dards of leadership. Herculean Black men who would at all cost uphold the race.

Yes I am a 'race man.' And because my sexual ori-entation is sometimes ignored, suppressed or oppressed by Black people, myself included, I must be an 'orienta-tion man': I am an 'orientation race man.' I work hard. I persevere. I do what I need to do in order to uphold the people of color, orientation, HIV+ race. Not a race as in ethnology but a group that many would rather not acknowledge. I make every effort to be beyond reproach so that, when things are equal, I must be accepted and listened to, in a word: respected. I insist upon respect.

I DON'T REMEMBER my Father calling me a 'race man, jr.' but I got the message and I thank my ancestors for the power. I am standing on their shoulders and asking for the esteem due each and every one of us—in the warmth of daylight—to be myself: to be Black among White gays, to be gay among Blacks. To be a Black, gay, proud HIV+ man: me. Wherever, whenev-er.

And with that in mind, I wrote my mother demanding that she desist in telling me "that God didn't like homosexuals"—according to the bible that was written by men—and accept my reality.

R⊕BERT E. PENN

Well, the letter to my Mother worked. Though I had not written it with the expectation that it would, I wrote the letter for my sanity. Change usually takes a lot of time and I was not sure that my Mother was ready. My letter was blunt solely to describe as effectively as I could the lengths to which I was prepared to go in order to achieve that respect and acceptance that any person deserves, regardless of race, religion, gender, national origin, color, sexual orientation, ability, attitude, tone of voice, and so on. I sent the letter for my sanity.

Mother surprised me with the gift of listening. She heard in the letter what I had tried to explain on the telephone several times. Why now? I don't know and I'm definitely not complaining. She surprised me with an unscheduled visit to New York. During that day, she told me she had reached P–FLAG (Parents and Friends of Lesbians and Gays) in her city but the only meeting was at eight in the evening clear across town. I understood the time and place to be a real obstacle for a 72 year old woman who wears thick glasses. So I got her a telephone number of someone from P-FLAG in her town with whom she could discuss things over the telephone.

About a week after her visit, Mother gave me another gift: She wrote me that she had spoken with the P-FLAG person and enjoyed the conversation.

I thank whatever God/dess, Higher Power there is.

I congratulate my Mother! It must have been very difficult for her to make that call, to listen to another point of view. At least as difficult as it was for me to take a stand. She is so brave!

I WONDER NOW if I really needed to go to such an extreme form of communication—the angry letter—to pull her toward me, to share my reality more fully with her. I will never know.

I do know, however, that I may have to be just as firm again in the future. It was only one step. Should she slide back or sink into her fears again, I must be persistent, even vigilant.

I must speak out. We in the COLORlife, must speak out, inform both adversaries and friends alike whom they are dealing with so that we are taking whole: as fully integrated individuals. We are not 'as good as.' We are.

I am proud to be an orientation race man. I support others in their efforts to be yourself. My Mother responded to my strong statements. So will others. We can all be orientation people of color because God/dess made us so that the wold would be a more complete, healthy and interesting part of the universe. **THING**

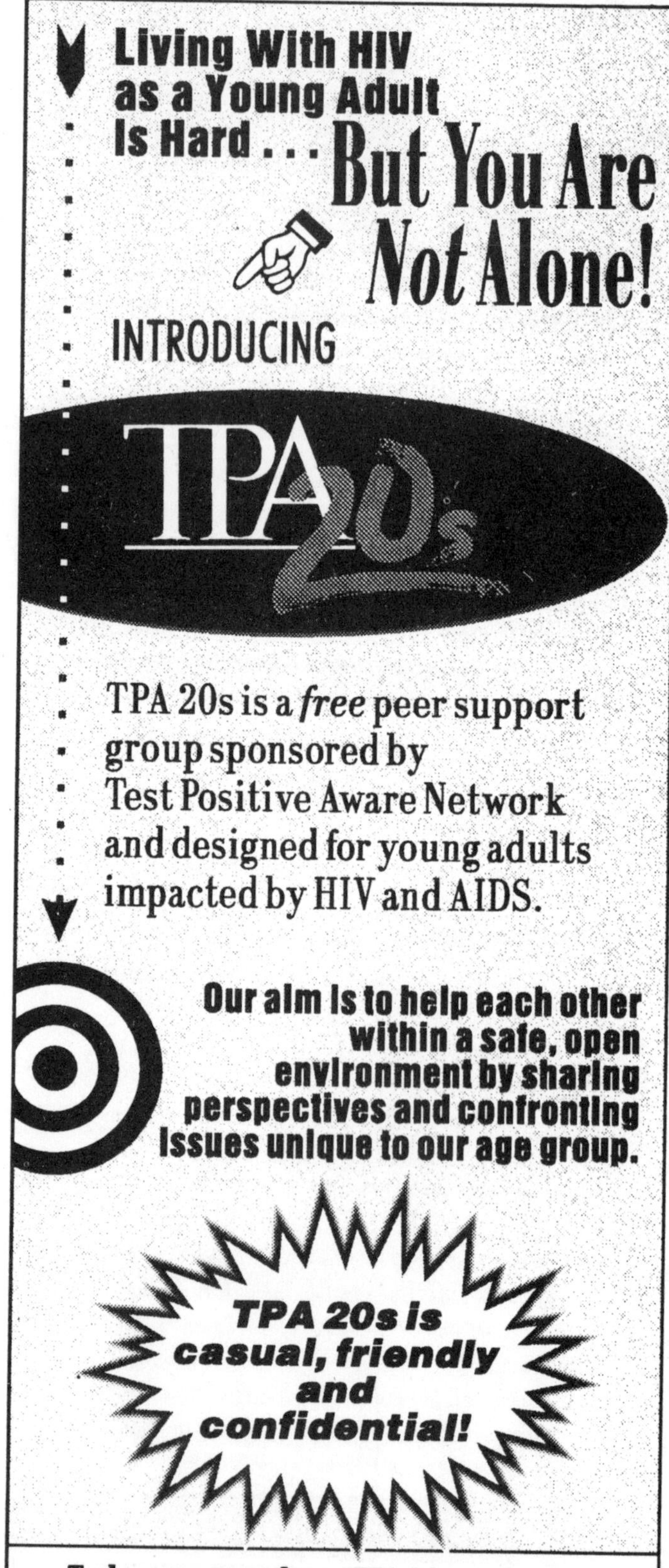

Little Boy Art Whore
TODD ROULETTE reports from the big march in D.C.

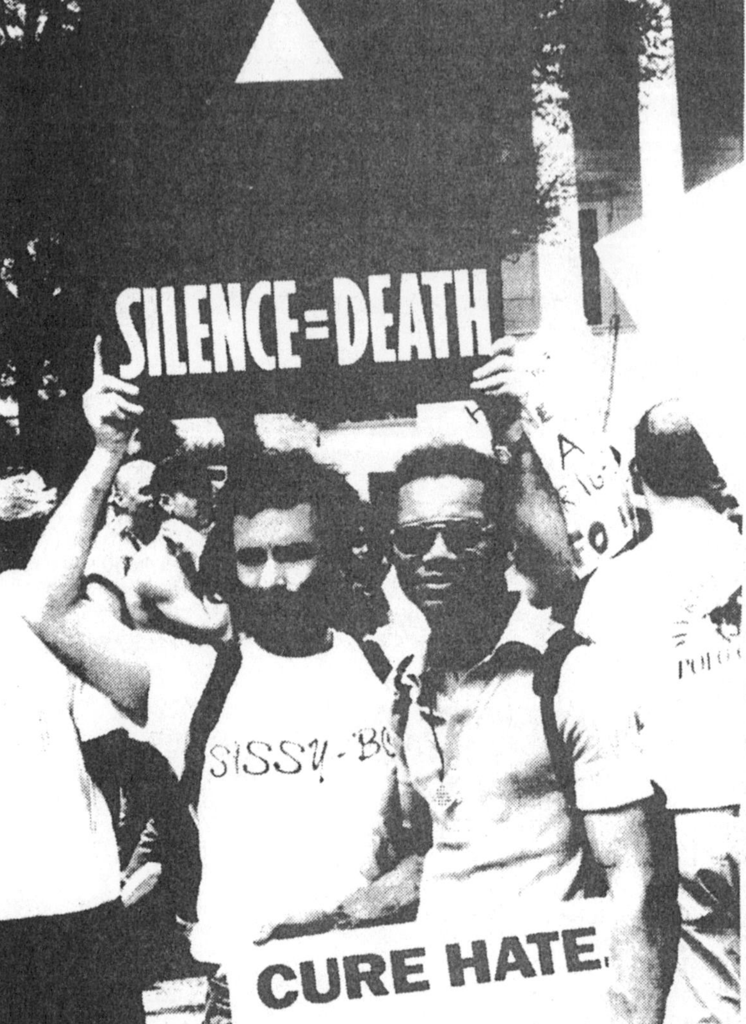

Cary CandyAss Leibowitz (l) and Todd Roulette

I SEEK GLAMOUR like a moth to a flame. But I am cheap. A friend came through Thursday night arranging for me to stay with his father's cousin, **Lucia**, an older woman, and I decided to take Peter Pan bus line instead of taking the train. Although I would have given my eye-teeth to have ridden with the cosmopolitan *Out* magazine on the X-2000. I also groveled for tickets that someone said I may have been able to get for a $1,000 benefit dinner and party. No luck. My grandmother always says do not trust anyone but Jesus. Well, one can always hope. Sharing the ride with me were boring gay men from Harvard and what I assumed was a black lesbian. We sat in the back of the bus. Just like the original 1966 Civil Rights March. I felt like we should have bonded, but I didn't want to force Afrocentricism. Suspicious, we looked at one another then pulled out reading material. I read my new *Allure* magazine and contemplated buying one of those new without-sun self-tanners by Clarins, Elizabeth Arden and Lancome. She read a cheap mystery paperback with a badly rendered cover picture.

FRIDAY EVENING

Later in the evening I attended a $75 benefit art opening for the Washington Project for the Arts, a non-profit art space. The group show was entitled *Beyond Loss: Art in the Age of AIDS*. I was able to get a complimentary ticket. The food was great. I walked around scouting out the crowd and noticed a number of good looking black men, well dressed and talking business it appeared. "Who are they?" I won-dered. City officials, non-profit arts administrators. Could they be gallery own-ers? I never found out and reserved my energy for flirt-ing with the cute, more bohemian black guys there (I counted nine). My friend the artist **Cary S. Leibowitz/CandyAss**, a quasi-international art star and I ate like pigs and watched **Degen Pener** and **Bob Morris**, both from the *New York Times* Style sec-tion, mingle. *Gay Cable News* interviewed artists **Anthony Viti** and **Oliver Herring**. Then we watched **Tim Miller**, a L.A. perfor-mance artist do his tongue-by-tongue description of two men having sex as he would perform it in the year 2000, the year he predicts the U.S. will inaugurate its first black lesbian president. I retired before the benefit after party to Lucia's home. She was a dream and had a nice posh place to boot.

SATURDAY MORNING

Lucia made me breakfast then I was off to DuPont Circle, the official hang-out place. It's funny how you don't notice how many white people there are when you are with them, but alone I couldn't help but notice. I went to all white schools I could deal, I reasoned. I filled out Lift the Ban mail-in cards and bought pink triangle temporary tattoos, T-shirts, postcards, and a sundry of other things. Outside a corner drug store I danced with two adorable Asian go-go boys from New York (who worked as realtors). We hooted and hollered at passers by. Saw three long lost friends from college and a number of checkerboard chicks (black men who date white men) and a number of hot black men mostly in groups, but many with white friends. Black lesbians seemed to be few and far between though I noticed the older ones. The com-

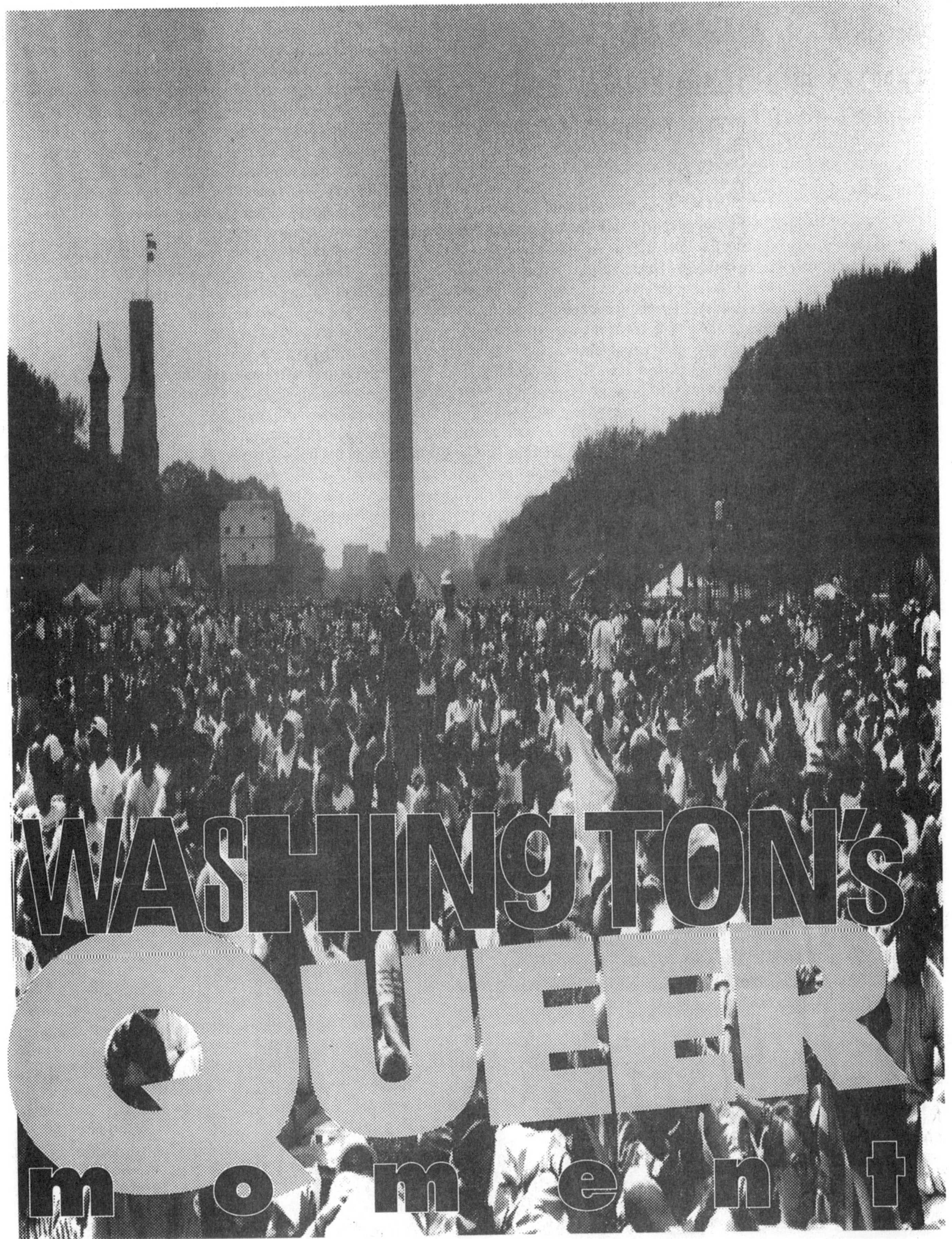

WASHINGTON'S
QUEER
moment

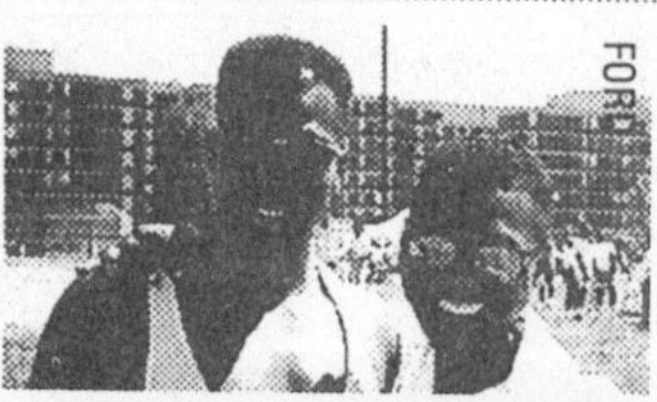

Los Angeles based *SBC*'s namesake Stanley Bennett Clay (r) with *SBC* DC correspondent Mark S. Johnson.

Not as widely reported on as the April's historic march, the third annual Black Lesbian and Gay Pride day in DC was the unofficial kick-off of summer for queers of color. All of black gay DC as well as kids from across the nation packed the capitol. A weekend full of events built up to the all-day festival, held the Sunday before Memorial day at Bannaker field. Friday night was a boat party with performers including the way overdone and over the top Lady Elegance, followed by late-night comradarie at Soul Brothers Pizza restaurant. A screening on Saturday afternoon featured a well-chosen program of short films and videos by black gay and lesbian filmmakers. Saturday night saw much club-hopping between DC's leading gay bars; mega-disco Tracks, the Back Door Pub, Nob Hill (touted as America's first black gay bar),The Hung Jury, Club G&G, and the Brass Rail. Die-hard club tarts jacked until sunrise at Blagden Alley Warehouse to the sounds of Basement Boy Teddy D and DJ Pope. Lasting into the early morning with a fierce mix of new music and classics, this party was truly reminiscent of the Warehouse, the Loft, Paradise Garage, and DC's own legendary Clubhouse. Sunday's big event at the field featured representation from a wide variety of black, lesbian, and gay groups and vendors. The crowd (estimated at over 3,000) was mostly black, but with enough Asians, Latinos, and whites to truly rate as multi-cultural. Also notable was the gender parity; lots of out and lovely women kept it from being another all-boy activity. With lots of fresh, tasty, and reasonably priced food and drink and plenty of information to peruse and merchandise to buy, the festival provided an opportunity for sun-drenched enlightenment and networking. After sundown, the clubs were hopping again, with a club crawl between Tradewinds, G&G, and the Hill competing with a special guest appearance by Chicago homegirl Xaviera "You Used To Hold Me/Gonna Get Back To You" Gold at Tracks. The weekend was a fun and unifying event, with something for almost everyone. (In fact, there were two commemorative t-shirts available; one dropping the "lesbian and gay" from the logo for brothers and sisters not quite "in the life"). Though plagued with the usual political intrigue that often accompanies a group endeavor, the volunteer staff did a remarkable job of organizing. And all net proceeds went back to the community as donations to black AIDS service providers in the DC area. For info on next year's celebration, contact (800) 497-0693. **—RF**

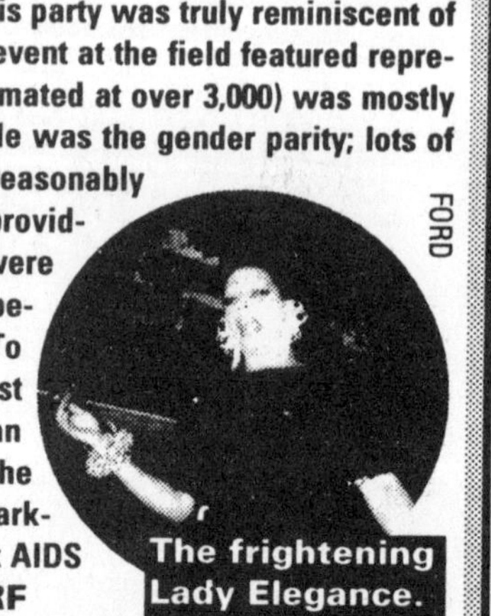

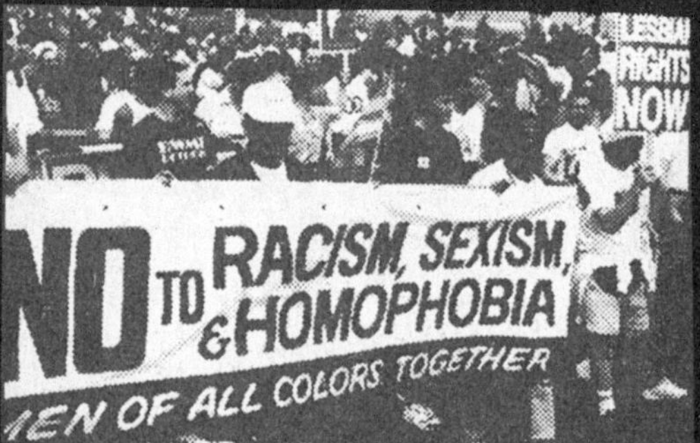

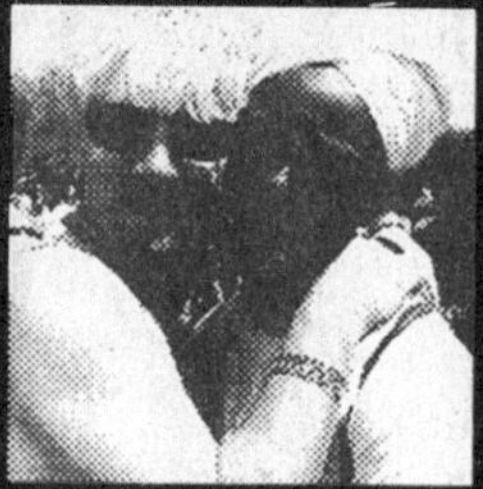

The frightening Lady Elegance.

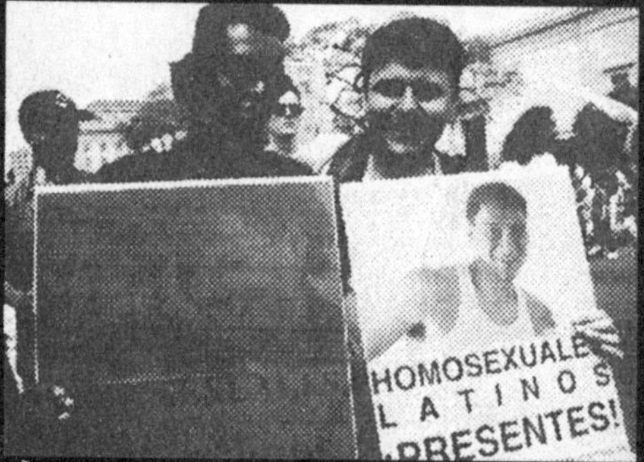

Clockwise froim above: Marchers carry Eduardo Aparicio's Latino activist posters; MACT contingent; Lady Bunny's wigmaster Bobby Miller with Afro-ditee; The Lady Bunny waiting in the wings at the Drag Show On The Mall; Larry Kramer; topless dykes; the Asian/Pacific Island group; Dorothy Hajdys carrying a photograph of her late son, murdered gay sailor Allen Schindler.

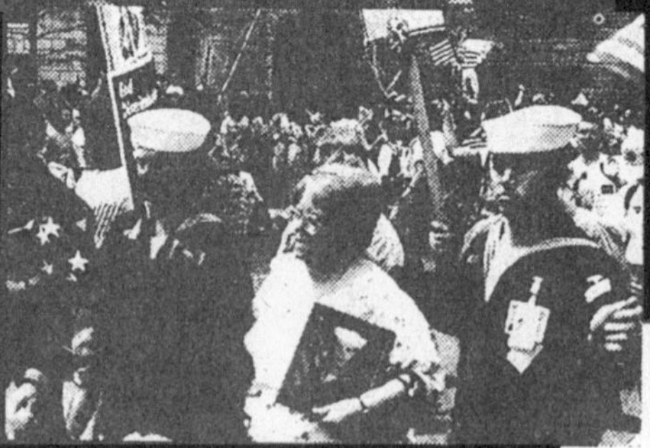

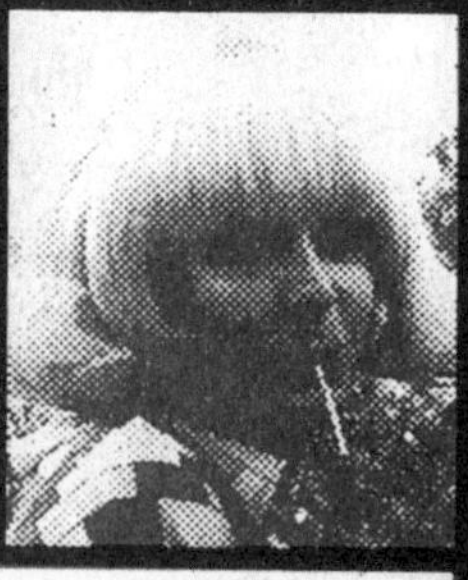

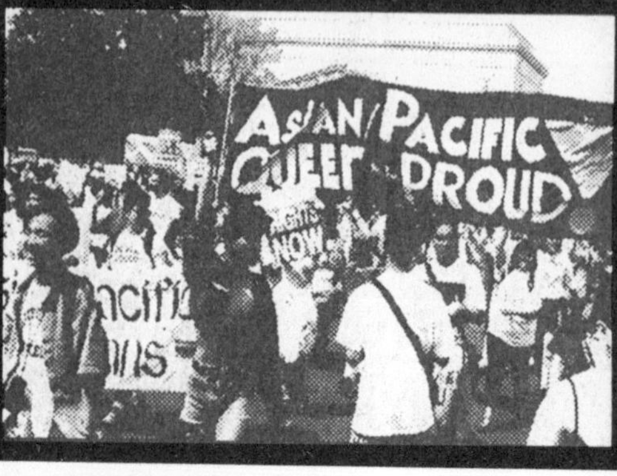

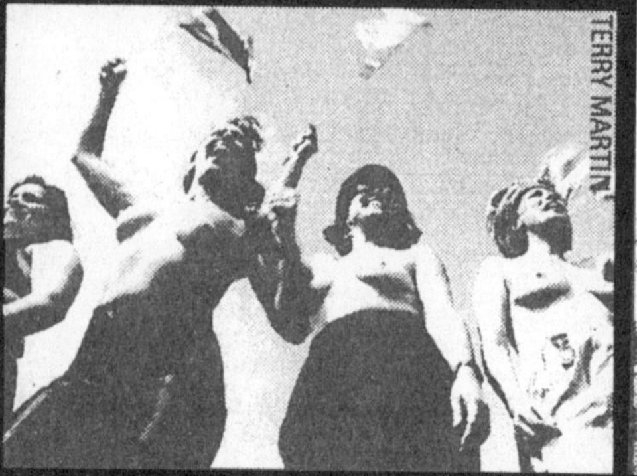

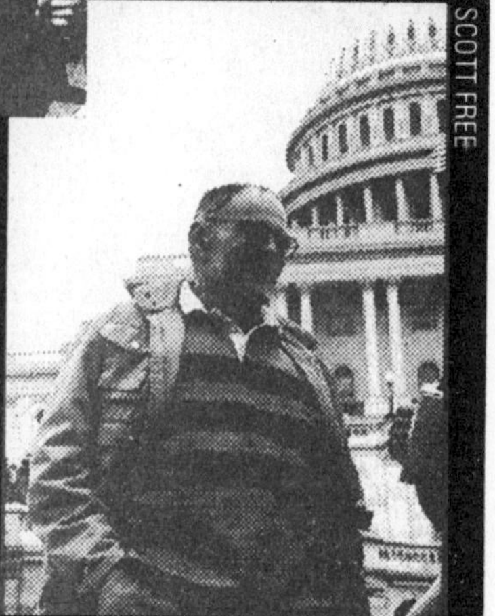

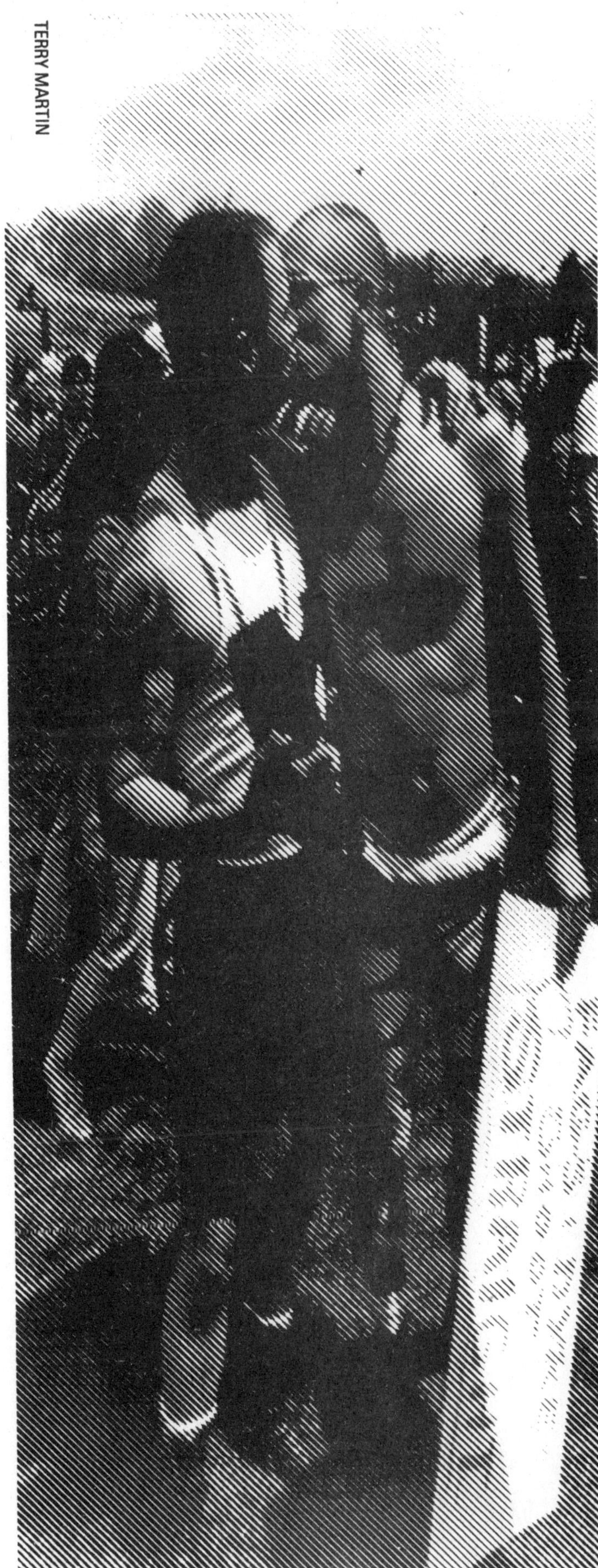

plicity of race, sex and socialization in this country is no joke. I'm afraid. There was a black focused conference going on Washington's predominantly black SouthWest side, but I didn't know how to get there or want to go by myself and didn't want to be politely turned down upon asking someone. I let it go.

SATURDAY EVENING

At the Blagden Art Warehouse, I wrestled in vain for a complimentary ticket of $10 to no avail. The price was worth it, I'm happy to say. **Carmen** and **Melena**, L.A. drag queens and performance artists were the hosts for the evening.

They began the night out by telling people of color to move to the first couple rows of seats. I was already in row two. They said it was important for people of color to be visible so everyone knows you are contributing your energy and money. Melena, swathed in patriotic spangle turban and dress, gave a chilling performance of monologue and operatic attack about having once been a straight white male. as a straight white male he was proud to sing the National Anthem for everyone that was just like himself. Now sent back to live as a black, gay male he cries when he hears it and screams when he sings it. Impressive.

Brian Freeman of PoMo Afro Homos reenacted dating a black gay man in San Francisco and read a to-the-point indictment (in the form of poetry) of **Larry Kramer**, GMHC, AME, and the First Baptist through Last Baptist response to the AIDS crisis and lack of attention to the concerns of black gay men. It was a reality check I needed and a voice I had been wanting to hear. After an unsuccessful attempt to locate the Drag on the Mall which promised to be an evening of vogueing and song on 15th street, I and a distant acquaintance walked around DuPont Circle.

He shocked me by disclosing his being HIV-positive and boyfriend problems. I listened sympathetically. I told him about my own living with HIV. He decided to turn in and I decided not to, there were too many boys out and it was too nice. I hopped into a corner store to get some Chocolate Chip Cookie Dough ice cream (Ben & Jerry's) and on my way out heard someone snarl, "You are just trash." Naturally I turned around. It was the ever attractive and smart **Tom Kalin**, *Swoon* filmmaker and his beau eating Famous Amos chocolate chips—small world. We watched the boys and I left them to circle the strip. At a stop light two really hip boys (Latin) in an open jeep motioned me over to them. I gave one of them a spoonful of ice cream and they asked me to get in.

Surprisingly, I said no thanks. They spun around the corner with tons-o-boys in the truck, waved and kept going. It was a gay boy's dream Daytona Beach Spring Break. Time now: 2am. I hopped in a cab.

SUNDAY MORNING

"Good Morning Sleeping Beauty" Lucia called to me. God I love this woman, I thought. I took a cab to the Corcoran Gallery to meet everyone and march with the Arts Coalition for the March on Washington. The crowd was huge, bigger than the estimated 300,000 easy. The New York art boys all showed up and a few dealers including **Bill Arning**, the director of New York's White Columns non-profit space, a doll. I was very happy. But then they were gone. CandyAss, me and friends got separated from them.

Before I knew it, a number of AIDS Coalition to Unleash Power (ACT UP) placards were being handed to me. This was not the Arts Coalition for the March on Washington (ACMOW). My spirits sank as everyone around me began to blow whistles and bang against their posters. I can't deal with this. I did my protesting in college. This is supposed to by my vacation. Reluctantly, I picked an appropriately sized and colored sign and took to the march.

There were a number of nice chants like *people of color under attack/what do we do/ACT UP, fight back.* I got it fast. Along the side was the twin art duo of **Thomas Harris** (filmmaker) and his brother, **Lyle Ashton Harris** (artist and drag personae). They waved and took my picture. Then in front of the White House people whispered "die-in, die-in." Instantly I felt transformed into one of those brave gay men on TV I would marvel at in high school. I was elated and edgy. I did not want to be arrested. Me and CandyAss laid down on the hot pavement my "Cure Hate, Stop AIDS, Homophobia Kills" sign across my chest. I stared up at the beautiful still sky with one bird swimming across it and thought last year someone I knew well was alive and now they are dead of AIDS. He was a real protester. I soaked in the sun and let go. My last die-in I was negative and this time I knew it could be my first and last March. When I saw the bible-bangers after getting up, I was ready. I held my "Cure Hate," like a shield against Goliath. Me, the former Holy Ghost choir boy turned Unitarian agnostic. We all shouted "Shame, Shame, Shame" as they quoted scriptures and held bad illustrations of Christ, hell and the Holy Bible. They needed a couple of lessons in tolerance and a good artist. I was so moved by my chance to condemn them my group walked on without me.

ON THE LAWN

Finally we all made it, somewhat intact. We swigged Evian and downed Haagen-Daaz bars and listened to Larry Kramer rant, **Cybil Shepard**, and others. But, the highlight for me was listening to the three speakers from the NAACP. My friends couldn't understand my enthusiasm as I leapt to my bare feet and yelled. I couldn't get over the NAACP's progressiveness.

HOMEWARD BOUND

Rode back to New York in a friend's Jeep Cherokee. I put the "Cure Hate" banner in the side window. The roads were full of people honking. At 9pm the off road (TacoTico) was full of fabulous queers. The locals were aghast. We stayed over outside Philadelphia in a hotel someone else paid for, thank God. Monday morning I ran in the door to show everyone my very noticeable tan—accomplished without a spray-on self-tanner—and they showed me the *New York Post.* CandyAss and me on the pavement in front of Bill and Hillary's. That "Cure Hate, Stop AIDS, Homophobia Kills" began as a bothersome accessory and ended up a proud coming of age symbol for me. The *Post* photo is simply a glamour bonus. **THING**

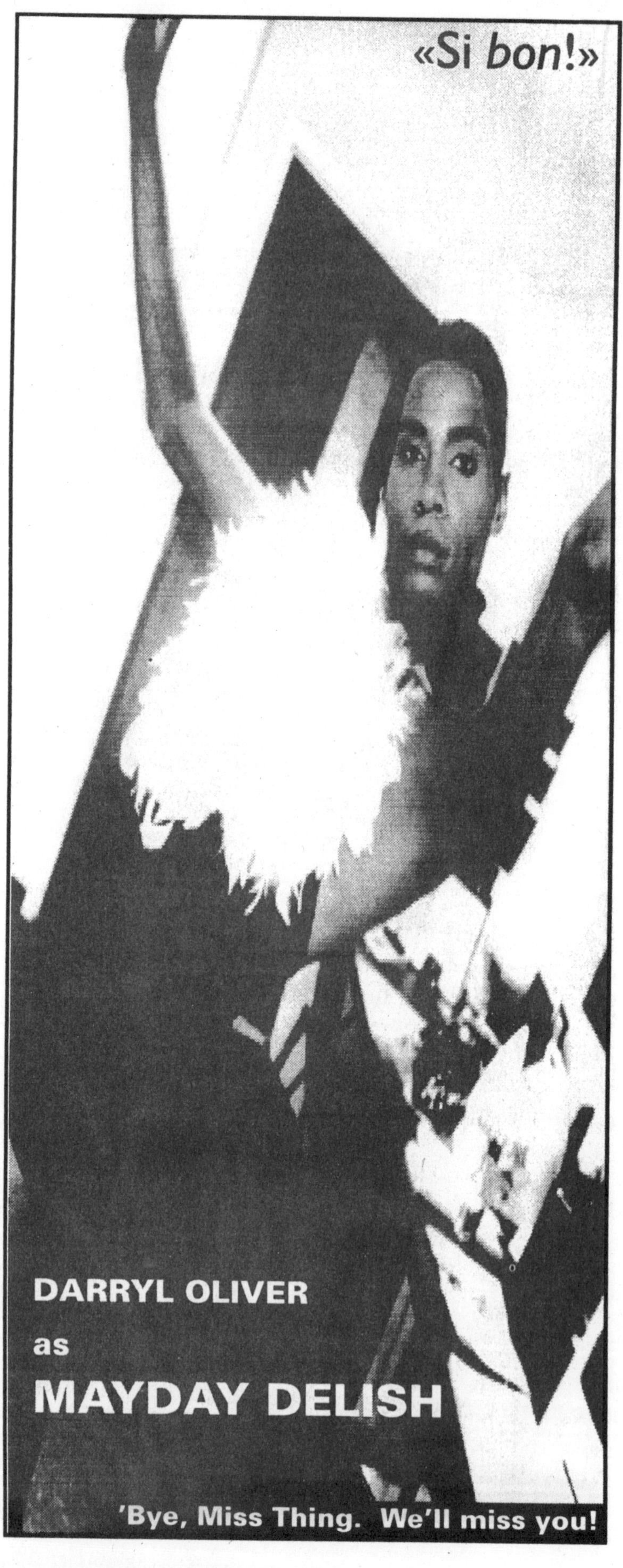

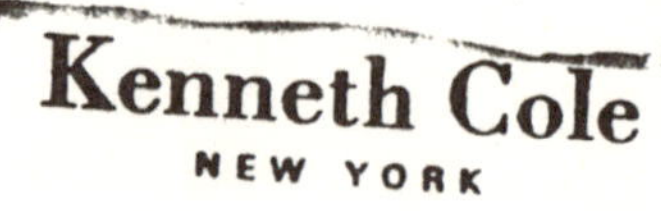

Kenneth Cole
NEW YORK

IN SUPPORT OF OUR NATION,
EVERYONE SHOULD HAVE THE
RIGHT TO BEAR ARMS—
BUT NOT BARE FEET.
— KENNETH COLE

new york   san francisco   amsterdam

CORPS ★ US ARMY RECRUITING
GAY RIGHTS NOW

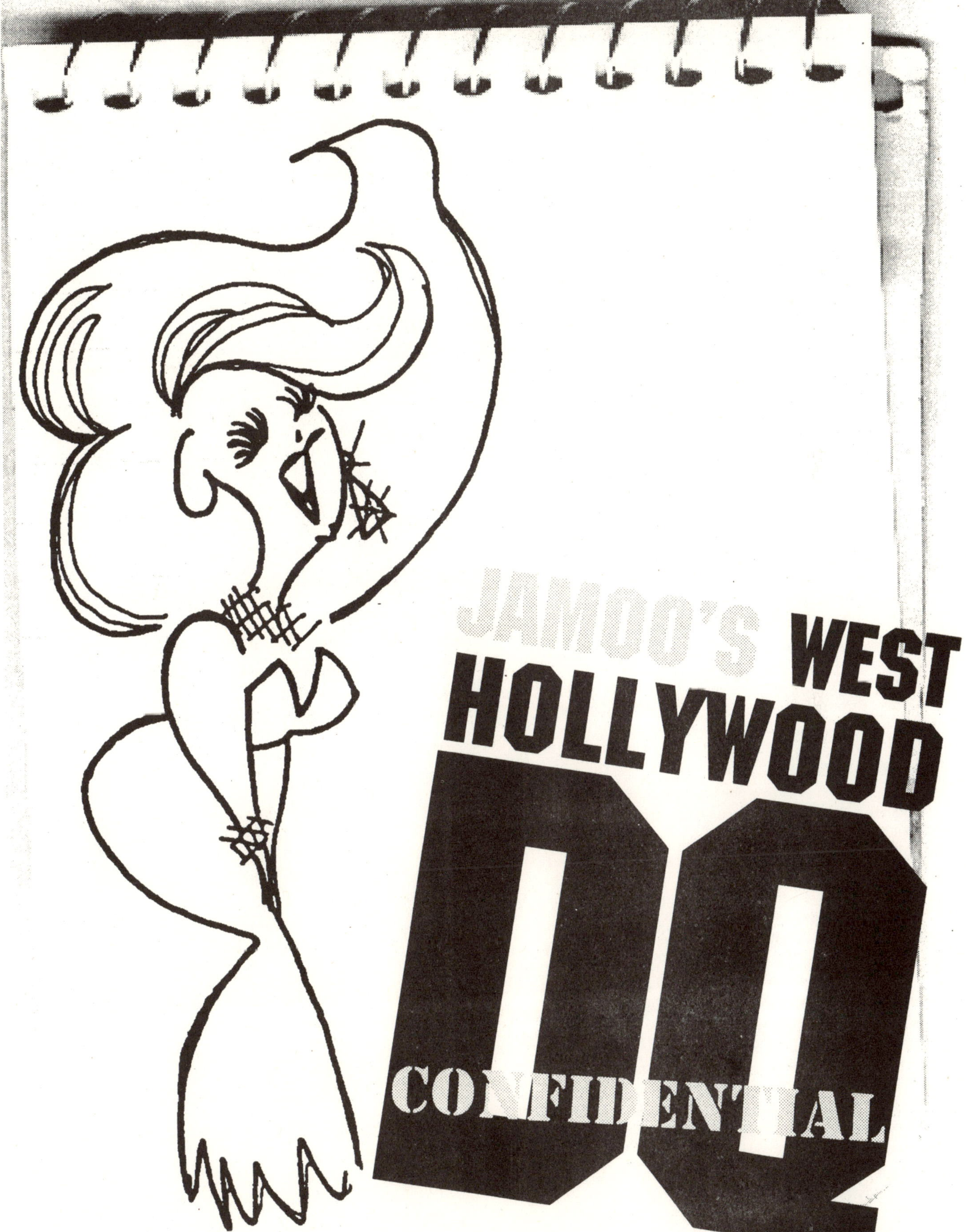

JAMOO'S WEST HOLLYWOOD CONFIDENTIAL

JAZZMUN

IS IT EASY BEING THE LIVING BLACK BARBIE?

Is anything easy? I don't think so. I have to wake up every morning and look at myself in the mirror and say "Girl you're made out of plastic, realize it! You're a phony black bitch and you know it." But you know, I get over it real fast and I wash my face with the best of cleansers and put on my moisturizer, and then I put on my make-up and I start my day. I walk down the street and all the guys in the cars honk at me and all the girls' claws grow outta nowhere and they wanna be me. So you think it about it, is it easy being you? But on a serious note, it is a lot of hard work. I do a lot of exercises, a lot of physical, rugged training with big, burly men who really work me over. So to answer your question, no!

HOW DID YOUR "LIPSTIK" CLUB NIGHT COME ABOUT?

Well, it was a concept I thought of cuz as we all know it's all about me. I was jobless and soon to be homeless and my Mercedes was going to be repossessed. I thought "What am I gonna do?" I knew Scott Forbes from a while back and I went to his office. He offered me Thursday nights, and it's been nothing but sold out crowds.

DESCRIBE HOW YOU'D KILL SHANNON DOUGHERTY.

I hate every single one of those motherfuckers on 90210. Where do they get off thinkin' they're in high school at the age of 24? And Shannon Dougherty, this little white bitch thinks she can go around and throw attitude wherever she goes. Does she know who I am? Honey, she needs blonde hair in order to be throwin' more attitude than I. I remember seeing her on Arsenio and she dogged her boyfriend . But you know what? I have him, I'm fucking him as you're sitting there contemplating your next gig which you're never gonna get, your career is over. Gurl you're through. Siddown, honey!

ARE YOU REALLY A VIRGIN?

I never been touched by the right man, so I guess I'm considered a virgin. Just 'cause I had men don't mean I _had_ men. As a matter of fact I was voted the Girl of Immaculate Conception because I'm the only girl besides Mary able to have a baby without a man actually physically inserting a cock inside of me.

IF YOU COULD BE IN ANY EPISODE OF GILLIGAN'S ISLAND, WHICH ONE WOULD IT BE AND WHO WOULD YOU PLAY?

What's Gilligan's Island? Honey, I'm black. I'm a black girl and I watch black shows. Ask me anything about Good Times or The Cosby Show and I be able to tell you. I'm a Cosby girl, honey. Definitely not Gilligan's Island. I don't understand how people can be stranded on one island for 20 years and not get off. They musta all been on crack or something.

IF WE CAUGHT YOUR BLACK ASS SHOPPING WHAT WOULD BE IN YOUR CART?

First and foremost toothpaste honey, 'cause nothing beats fresh breath. Then I get some toilet paper honey 'cause a smelly ass won't do. And Baby Wipes to wipe it so it'll be baby fresh. Then you'll find mascara, lipstick, and you might even find —I hate to tell you this—an enema, you never know. A girl's gotta be ready for that special day. Hairspray for my 25 wigs, bobby pins, and much, much junk food. I'm a junk food girl.

Her titties have no nipples and her pussy spells Mattel. She's JAZZMUN, the Living Black Barbie. This priceless drag bitch diva originated from San Diego county and relocated to Hollywood after an appearance on the now-defunct _Putting On The Hits_ in 1985. This creature soon joined the La Cage Aux Folles touring company in 1988 and toured 13 states. This black-ass goddess is hailed for her startling impersonations of Miss Ross, Whitney Houston, Grace Jones, Donna Summer, Sade, Karyn White, Mary J. Blige, Tina Turner, and Vanity. Many celebs have caught girlfriend's act, including Milton Berle, Paula Abdul, Dionne Warwick, Sally Struthers, Caesar Romero, John Stamos, and Grace Jones. Amazing Grace even gushed "Jazzmun is the best Grace ever!"

Jazzmun performed for Johnny Carson with Julian Viva (aka Viva Sex)! On the Byron Allen show Miss Jazz played Byron's date in a spoof of the Dating Game. She also bopped folks on Rick Dees' _Into The Night_, and played a go-go dancer on _thirtysomething_! Most recently this foodstamp lovin' chile was seen on Montel Williams as Whitney Houston. This fierce ruling ho from the projects is ready to serve the children and sell the garment, or as Jazzmun puts it "I've been everywhere, know everybody, done everything. It's all about me in '93!" You go gurl!!

IS IT EASY BEING GLAMOROUS?

Thanks for asking, Jamoo! You know, people often think that glamour is a snap. But I'm here to tell you that glamour is a twenty-three hour a day job! (I do take an hour for lunch.)

HOW DID "BIG HAIR DAY" COME ABOUT?

The first annual Big Hair Day in May of 1991 came about based on an item that appeared in my Carol-Gram calendar. A make-up artist named Steve Wanzell contacted me and we whipped it into a big event that took Los Angeles and —may I be so bold as to say— the world by storm. Every news agency in L.A. covered it, and CNN <u>Headline News</u> ran it every half-hour the next day! Through the publicity generated, the <u>London Observer</u> ran my picture and a blurb about it, and through that, England's number one TV show <u>The Word</u> sent a crew, and we beamed the second annual Big Hair Day LIVE to England. Oh, what a trans-Atlantic time we had!

IF YOU COULD BE BLACK WHO WOULD YOU WANT TO BE AND WHY? ARETHA FRANKLIN? PATTI LABELLE? MISS ROSS?

Ooooh! I would want to be a cross between the Queen of Soul, Miss Aretha, with hair like Miss Patti and the legs of the one and only Tina Turner. But I have to settle for just being Lutheran.

IF YOU COULD BE IN ANY EPISODE OF GILLIGAN'S ISLAND, WHICH ONE WOULD IT BE AND WHO WOULD YOU PLAY?

Well, I'd be Ginger Grant, which you might think of as not a stretch, but Ginger and Mary Ann could really do just about anything with coconuts! Besides, Ginger had better hair and I love the gold beaded gown she took on the "three hour tour." A true gal never travels without her beaded gown.

DO YOU DRINK COKE OR PEPSI?

If you must know, I drink Tab.

IF WE CAUGHT YOU OUT SHOPPING WHAT WOULD BE IN YOUR CART?

Several packs of Brown Sugar and Cinnamon Frosted Pop Tarts, a pound of Challenge butter, and a gallon of whole milk.

IF RUPAUL ASKED YOU TO HAVE LUNCH AT MCDONALDS, WHAT WOULD YOU WEAR AND WHAT WOULD YOU ORDER?

RuPaul is soooo glamourous there would be serious glamour rays going on and we might injure the other diners. The possibilities are mind boggling! But if we ate at McD's I'd probably have the salad, dressing on the side, and an iced tea... NOT! We probably wouldn't even get a chance to eat those greasy McChicken thing sandwiches with our large fries and (so-called) milk shakes that we ordered because we'd be girlfriend gabbing about much more important glamour issues like Aqua Net vs. White Rain, the best sized teasing comb for the most lift-and-separate, and oh so very much more! Oh, and I'd wear a simple day frock.

WHAT IS YOUR DREAM COME TRUE?

Eeeeeew! This is a toughie! I have so many dreams! I'd love to have a TV show, I'd love to find "Mr. Right." I'd love everyone in the world to operate from the same rules of etiquette, because if we did we could all live in harmony and life would be one big progressive cocktail party! Ah, a girl can dream, can't she?

She's big, she's blonde, she's beautiful. She's THE LOVELY CAROL, and "Caroliscious!" When this gal isn't busy performing and hosting parties and functions for fags you can find her hidden away in her little bungalow tucked under the "H" of the Hollywood sign where she spends her days eating Pop Tarts and playing with her toy poodles Fifi and Flipper. She's launched her own line of beauty products, "Carol's Lovely Bubbles", "Carol's Edible Cosmetiques", and "Constantly Carol Cologne". Appearances on *Entertainment Tonight*, MTV, E!, and *Growing Pains* have helped her star take off, but it was her role as a brain-eating zombie in *Return Of the Living Dead* that is most memorable. Carol was named "L.A.'s Best Diva" in L.A. Weekly's "Best of L.A. Issue." Carol is always willing to lend a hand to a good cause, like the Dance for Life AIDS benefit at Studio One which she kicked off. Fashion, big hair, and parties; is she a real woman or a fag trapped in a woman's body? You decide!

THE LOVELY CAROL

ERIN KRYSTLE

IS IT EASY BEING GLAMOROUS?

No, it isn't There is a lot of preparation involved in styling each look, from choice of outfit, accessories, hairstyle, appropriate and complimentary make-up, which all depends on the time of day, destination, and the occasion, whether it's for lunch, dinner, a movie, theater, clubbing, or performing. My main objective is to wear something very fashionable, that will bop with style. If everything is laid out and organized, I can get ready in 30-45 minutes; if I'm bopping an extravagant hairdo (I especially like updos), add another 15-30 minutes.

HOW DID "HUMAN SEXUALITY" COME ABOUT?

I have two separate careers as an entertainer. My female persona of Erin and my male persona of Eriq. People always tease me about how they never can expect to see me any certain way. Sometimes I'm female and other times I'm male. So I thought it would be interesting to sing a song that was sexually ambiguous and incorporated both Erin and Eriq's personalities, to make people think about the fine line between masculinity and femininity, and the presence of both gender traits in every one of us. When I perform "Human Sexuality" people will question wether I'm a woman or a man. I choose to express both of these traits in varying degrees and combinations of extremes and subtleties.

ERIN KRYSTLE was born deep in the heart of Texas. This talented chick began singing in gospel choirs and moved on to dancing in a go-go cage on Austin's legendary Sixth street. This petite powerhouse has appered in films such as Candyman, and has an extensive resume of commercials, videos, theater, and print work. Erin stands out as a true original because she is one of the few performers who is as comfortable out of drag as she is in it. Miss Thang is shoppin' and boppin' her demo tape around, so look for her on MTV and BET soon after you read this.

WHAT'S YOUR FAVE EPISODE OF GILLIGAN'S ISLAND?

When Mary Ann isn't Mary Ann anymore because she's Ginger, and Ginger isn't Ginger anymore because she's Mary Ann. It showed me that if someone like Mary Ann, who is considered to be a "Plain Jane" tomboy kinda girl, could transform into a glamorous woman with just make-up. a gorgeous gown, and a well-coiffed updo, so could I.

DO YOU DRINK COKE OR PEPSI?

I normally drink water, but I will drink Coke before Pepsi because it's the real thing, just like me and all my transgender sisters and brothers around the world.

IF WE CAUGHT YOU OUT SHOPPING WHAT WOULD BE IN YOUR CART?

Low-fat milk, whole-wheat bread with unbleached enriched flour or baguette de campange, smoked gouda cheese, pate, carrots, romaine or green leaf, blue cheese, honey dijon or caesar's dressing, fruit juice, red wine, coffee beans, chicken, turkey, tuna fish, Haagen-Dazs coffee ice cream bars with chocolate toffee crunch coating, and a jumbo jar of "hot" Pace picante from the city of my birth , San Antonio, where folks know what a picante should taste like. And tortilla chips.

IF RUPAUL ASKED YOU TO HAVE LUNCH AT MCDONALDS, WHAT WOULD YOU WEAR AND WHAT WOULD YOU ORDER?

I'd wear a simple red, nautical drop waist dress by Laura Ashley with layers of white cotton petticoats edged with eyelet, accessorized with pearl earrings, pearl necklace, white flats, and a simple white purse. Natural minimalistic makeup would be necessary, with softly curled bangs and high ponytail with a big white bow; and of course I'd eat fish...the fish sandwich that is.

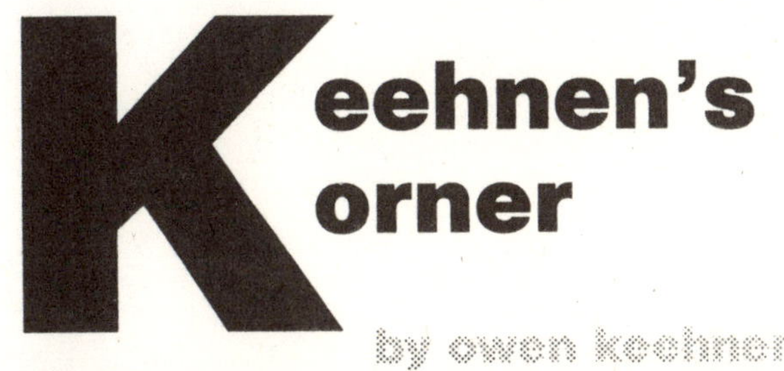

A Clint Confession

Well, since by his own admission he's now fashionable, who am I to resist…

As a teen I went to see movies all the time and quite often I went to the Times Theater in Rockford. I remember going to see 'The Eyes Of Laura Mars' and during the coming attractions I went down some winding stairs to the Men's Lounge and in the middle stall, the center of three there was something…It wasn't a glory hole, a huge penis etching, tearoom times, dried semen, or anything like that. But, scrawled on the back of the stall door in block letters was "Clint Eastwood will turn your dick Every Which Way But Loose." It was a clever tie-in for the previous Times feature and sort of a hot thought too. I'd seen the movie, which sucked and also spawned a sequel, a couple imitations, and the yahoo series 'BJ and the Bear.' However, Clint the man was definite fantasy material and had fine nasty potential. I remember him wearing a tight white t-shirt in his fight sequences.

I closed my eyes and imagined double Oscar winner Clint Eastwood turning my dick every which way but loose. He was wearing a five-day beard and his 'High Plains Drifter' poncho. He was jacking me off perfectly. He was playing misty for me. Clint was making my day.

Just about the time he took off his wide-brimmed hat so he could bend forward and do the unforgiven, I was hit by a pleasure/fantasy spasm. I kicked the back of the stall door with magnum force, startling the guy with one thigh propped upon the middle sink, stroking his basket, and watching me through the gap beside the stall door. Our eyes connected and in my mind I heard a bar of the theme from "The Good, The Bad, and the Ugly." I unlocked the door and opened it a crack. He stepped inside and unzipped his fly. We started at each other and each other's cocks as we jacked off into the toilet.

I kept thinking about that matinee through the Oscars this year.

---

by the CIA, studio insurance investigator, a hit man, The Kennedys or any of a string of jealous of sorry lovers. Early in the morning of August 5, 1963, Marilyn Monroe Mansfield. I drifted off to sleep and awoke a few hours later, still somewhat groggy and still a little intoxicated. I'm not even sure if this was real or not. It might all be a dream or a hallucination, but I don't think so. Anyway, when I awoke I saw Jayne Mansfield slitting the throat of a chicken with a sacrificial knife right there in her pink heart-shaped bed. She dripped the chicken blood onto her mammoth breasts and rolled one clockwise and the other counterclockwise, around and around. It was dizzying. Then she smacked them together three times

When I asked her what she was doing she laughed maniacally and her eyes rolled back until only the whites were showing. She said she possessed the power of Pazouzou, said something in fluent French, then uttered something in a strange tongue I'd never heard before. A thunderbolt cracked outside the window of the Pink Palace. Previously unobtrusive marble statues below in the garden appeared in the flashes like phantoms.

Suddenly, Jayne leapt up upon her knees on the bed and began bouncing, her pink polka-dot bow was askew, and her breasts were flying in all directions, and she was screaming "Marilyn!"

When she finally collapsed upon the bed I looked at her not-sucked-in-now belly and saw the mark of an upside

---

at the movies

"**It** was no suicide, no sir. I'll tell you that, and it wasn't accidental either. It was murder. The truth will shock and amaze you and ultimately make you nod in agreement. Marilyn wasn't killed was the victim of the dark demonic powers of Jayne Mansfield.

On that night, the night Marilyn died, I had just finished having sex with Jayne down crucifix pressed out upon her skin. Jayne's chalky strawlike hair lay loose upon the pink satin pillow, it splayed upward as though in her unconscious state she were descending into the very pit of hell itself. She was Satan's starlet. I hadn't the courage to come forward with the truth until now…and I'm very excited about the book."

FASHION

editorial

PHOTO/CONCEPT/CONSTRUCTION Scott Free
DESIGNS Calvin Klein, Marithé & François Girbaud
MODELS Matthew (Klein) Derek (Girbaud)

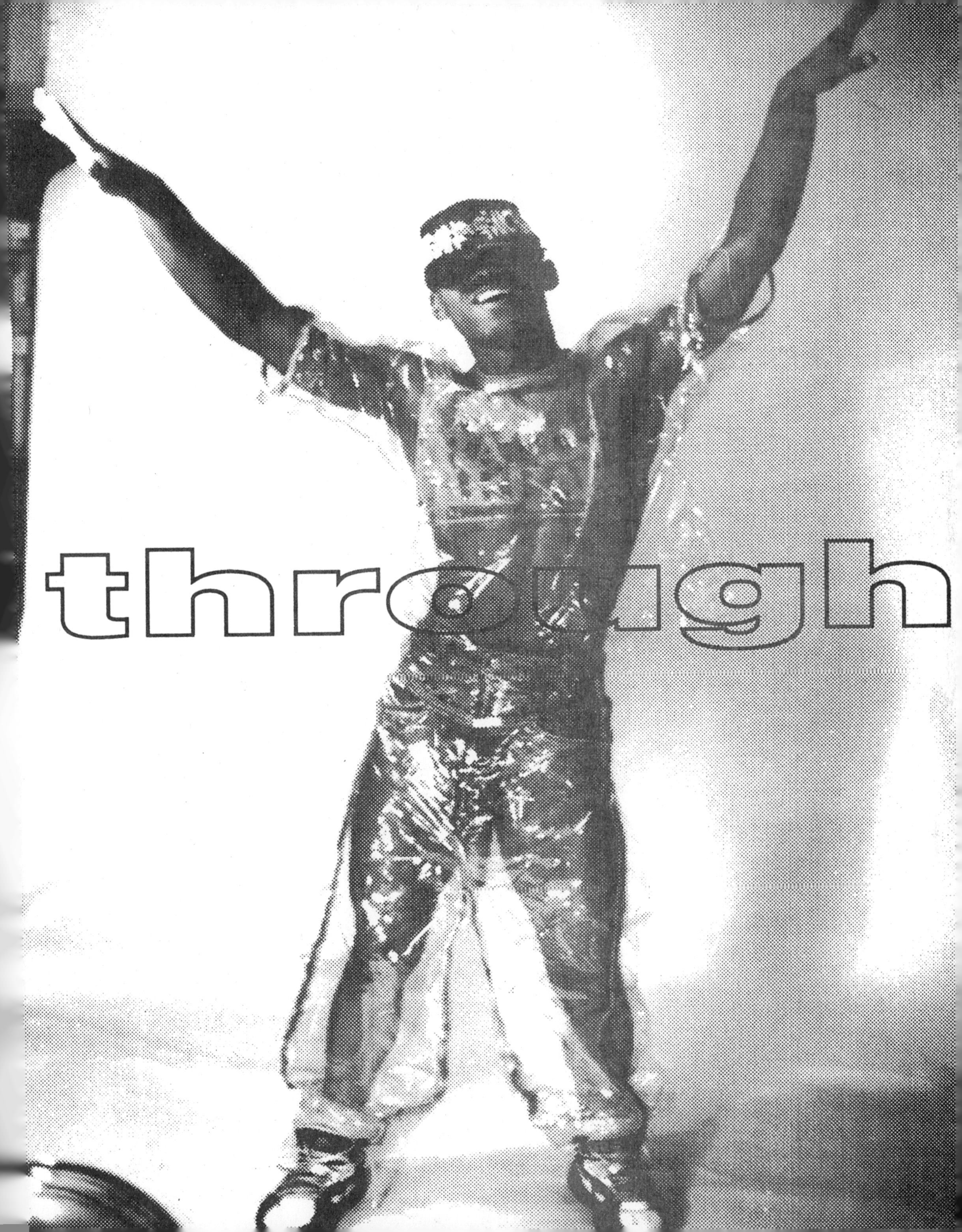
through

ALL PHOTOS TRENT ADKINS EXCEPT WHERE NOTED

TEE

Edited by T. Adkins.

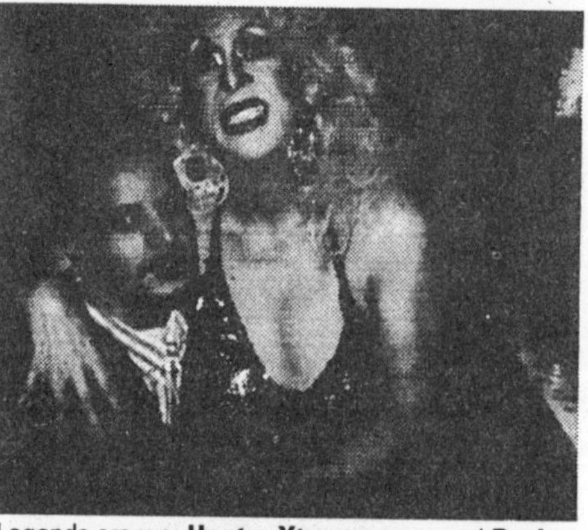

Legends are we: **Hector Xtravaganza** and **Dorian Corey** in the dressing room at Sally's, NYC.

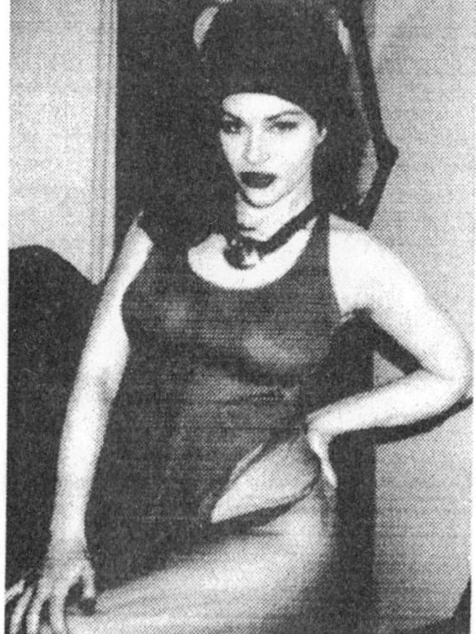

Thing afterhours: A rare late night out for Hair by Hare co-hort, Mademoiselle **Linda** aka **Diabla**.

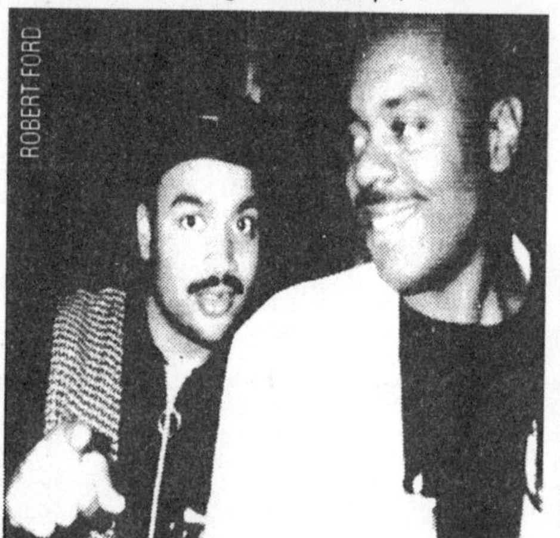

Producers **Steve "Silk" Hurley** and **André Halmon** at the Dome Room.

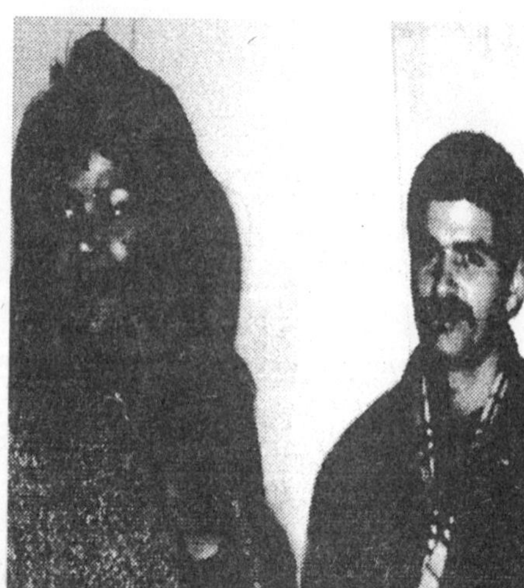

Singer **Candy J** and friend in the sound booth at Hothouse for the Spring Thing benefit party.

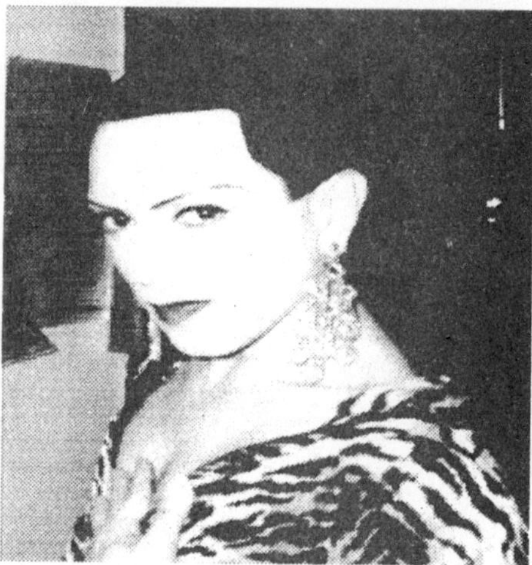

Following his channeling of Billie Holiday at Shelter's Paramount Room, New York City performer/singer/writer **Joey Arias** was guest of honor at an afterhours at the *Thing* offices. For us, it was immediately following the Spring Thing Hothouse bash with Candy J. "Thanks!"

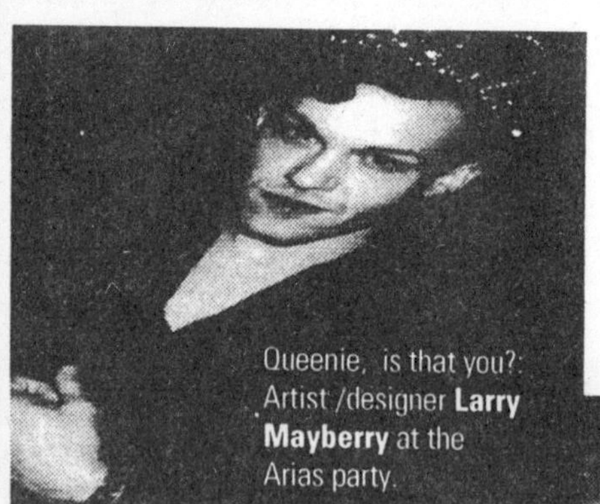

Andy Soma** and **Pat O'donell** the Arias afterhours.

Queenie, is that you?: Artist/designer **Larry Mayberry** at the Arias party.

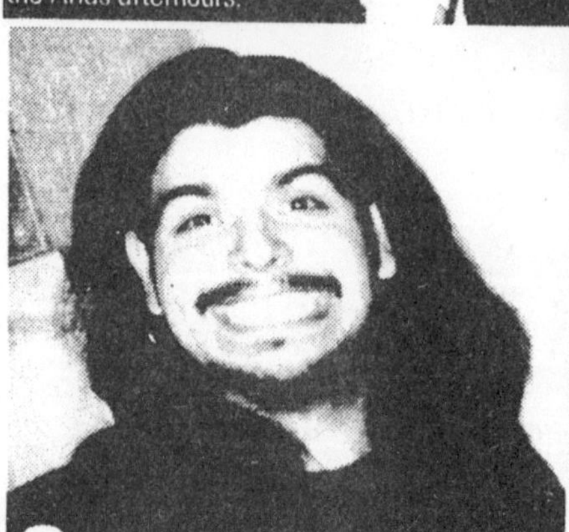

RuPaul Charles School of Smiley Face, Class of 93: **Dave J** at the Joey Arias party.

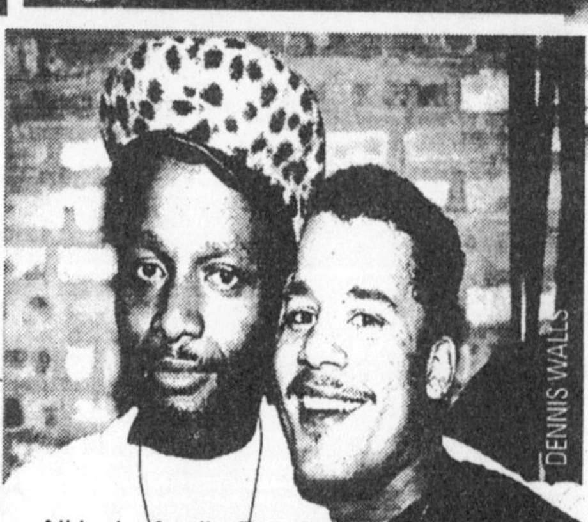

All in the family: Cousins HiFi and Bert Bangalore at the Boom Boom Room.

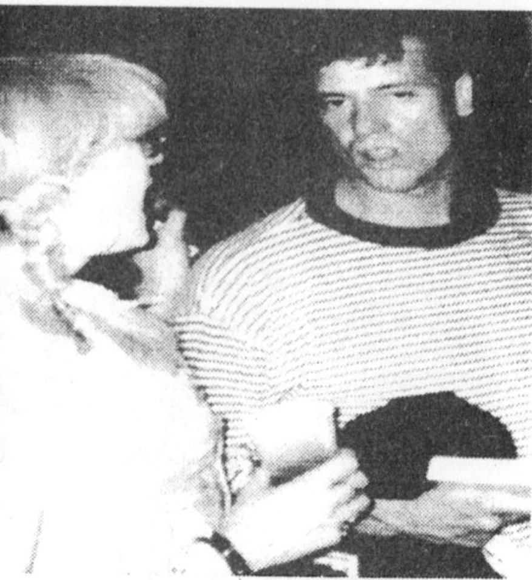

"Fon-fon-fon": **Tom Hemingway** and **Latrushka** at Seance.

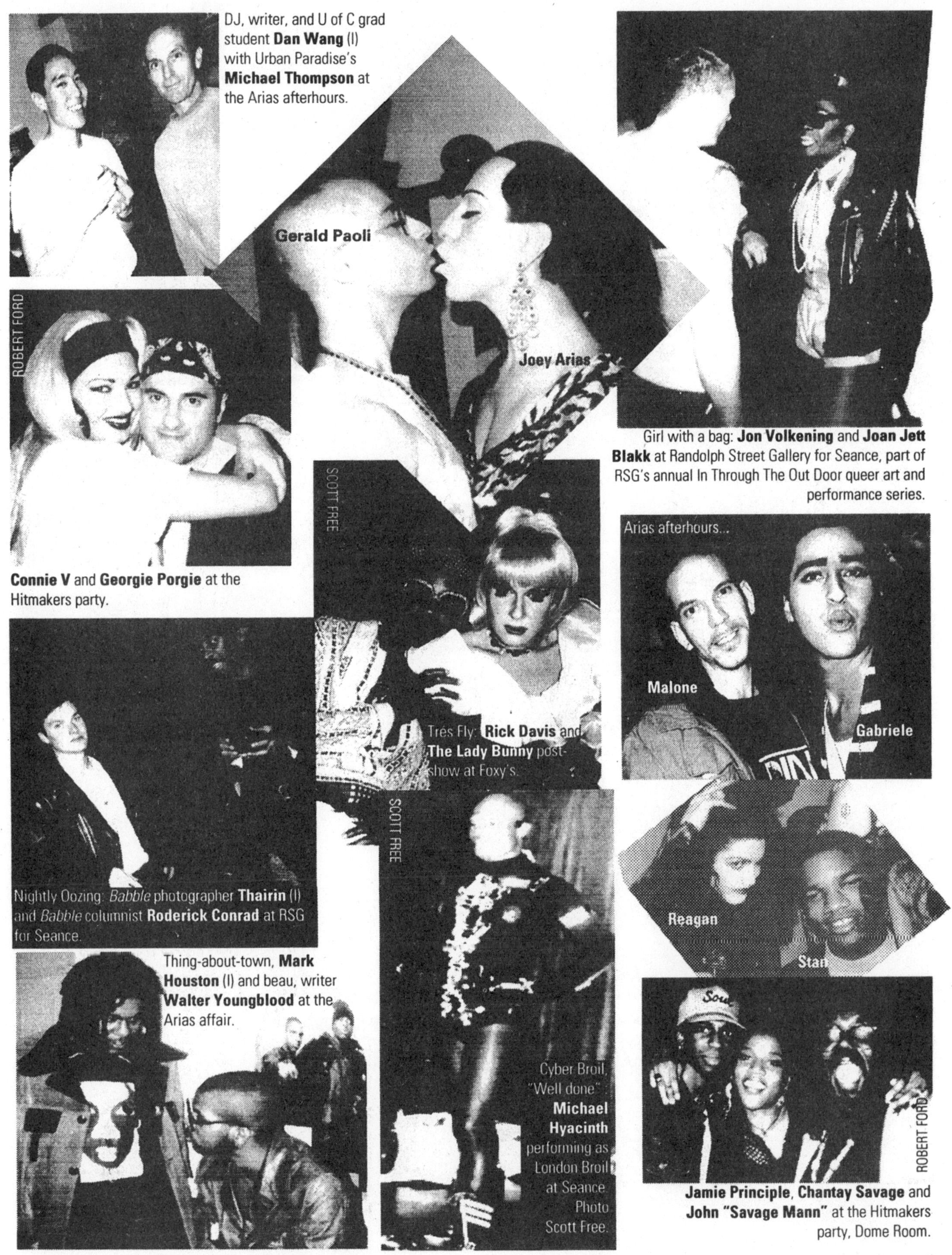

DJ, writer, and U of C grad student **Dan Wang** (l) with Urban Paradise's **Michael Thompson** at the Arias afterhours.

Connie V and **Georgie Porgie** at the Hitmakers party.

Nightly Oozing: *Babble* photographer **Thairin** (l) and *Babble* columnist **Roderick Conrad** at RSG for Seance.

Thing-about-town, **Mark Houston** (l) and beau, writer **Walter Youngblood** at the Arias affair.

Trés Fly: **Rick Davis** and **The Lady Bunny** post-show at Foxy's.

Cyber Broil, "Well done": **Michael Hyacinth** performing as London Broil at Seance. Photo Scott Free.

Girl with a bag: **Jon Volkening** and **Joan Jett Blakk** at Randolph Street Gallery for Seance, part of RSG's annual In Through The Out Door queer art and performance series.

Arias afterhours...

Jamie Principle, **Chantay Savage** and **John "Savage Mann"** at the Hitmakers party, Dome Room.

LIES

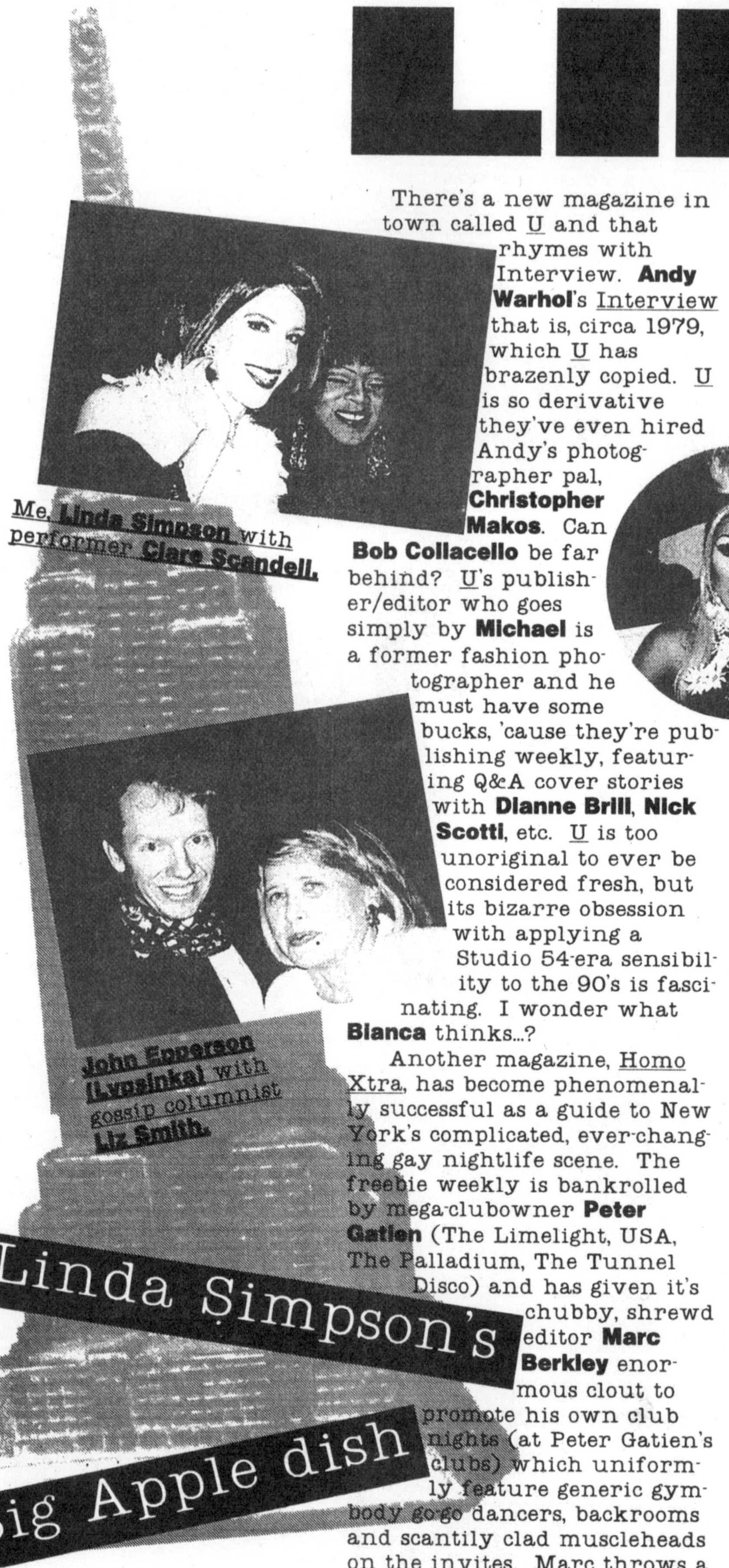

Me, **Linda Simpson** with performer **Clare Scandell**.

John Epperson (**Lypsinka**) with gossip columnist **Liz Smith**.

RuPaul at the Pyramid, pre-super-stardom.

There's a new magazine in town called <u>U</u> and that rhymes with Interview. **Andy Warhol**'s <u>Interview</u> that is, circa 1979, which <u>U</u> has brazenly copied. <u>U</u> is so derivative they've even hired Andy's photographer pal, **Christopher Makos**. Can **Bob Collacello** be far behind? <u>U</u>'s publisher/editor who goes simply by **Michael** is a former fashion photographer and he must have some bucks, 'cause they're publishing weekly, featuring Q&A cover stories with **Dianne Brill**, **Nick Scotti**, etc. <u>U</u> is too unoriginal to ever be considered fresh, but its bizarre obsession with applying a Studio 54-era sensibility to the 90's is fascinating. I wonder what **Bianca** thinks...?

Another magazine, <u>Homo Xtra</u>, has become phenomenally successful as a guide to New York's complicated, ever-changing gay nightlife scene. The freebie weekly is bankrolled by mega-clubowner **Peter Gatien** (The Limelight, USA, The Palladium, The Tunnel Disco) and has given it's chubby, shrewd editor **Marc Berkley** enormous clout to promote his own club nights (at Peter Gatien's clubs) which uniformly feature generic gym-body go-go dancers, backrooms and scantily clad muscleheads on the invites. Marc throws a drag queen on stage now and then, but his agenda isn't about promoting creativity or nurturing talent. It's about packing the joint with mainstream homos, and Marc is laughing all the way to the bank. <u>Homo Xtra</u> has set the pace for NY's night scene and its iron grip has been chilling.

Speaking of drag queens (weren't we?), **RuPaul**'s incredible jump from Avenue A to MTV has been intensely scrutinized by her downtown "sisters." **Lypsinka**, who used to be America's best known drag queen, professed (in <u>U</u> magazine!) her happiness at Ru's success, but suggested that RuPaul would make a better talk show host than a singer. Meow! And that from someone who only lip-syncs! The **Lady Bunny** and **Lahoma Van Zandt** used to be thisclose to Ru, but had a falling out and no longer speak to RuPaul, let alone congratulate her. As for Ru's other close friends... Well, I can't think of any, but Ru has always been a solo act-friendly and chatty, yet introspective and distant. Actually, success seems to have made her more at ease, although I know she's hungry for even greater heights. Listen, Ru and I are Scorpio queens, both born on November 17th, and my insights have astrological merit.

Ru is just one of a gaggle of black drag artists hot on the scene right now. There's **Donna Giles** who recently wowed 'em on **Montel Williams** with her incredible singing voice, and her **Joan Rivers**

Linda Simpson's
Big Apple dish

& New York garbage!

impersonation. **Afro-ditee**, who like me is originally from Minnesota, is the new Miss Boy Bar, which is very prestigious…I guess. Afro-ditee is very now, very hip, and in her $600 **Vivienne Westwood** platform shoes does a fierce **Sistah Souljah**. **Princess Diandra** and I recently appeared on "The **Jane Pratt** Show" (topic: drag), and Diandra upstaged us all by changing wigs during commercials. Diandra is always jetting off to Japan and Europe to perform her heavy-on-the-**Diana Ross** cabaret act, and she's the mother of the House of Ecstasy, whatever that means…

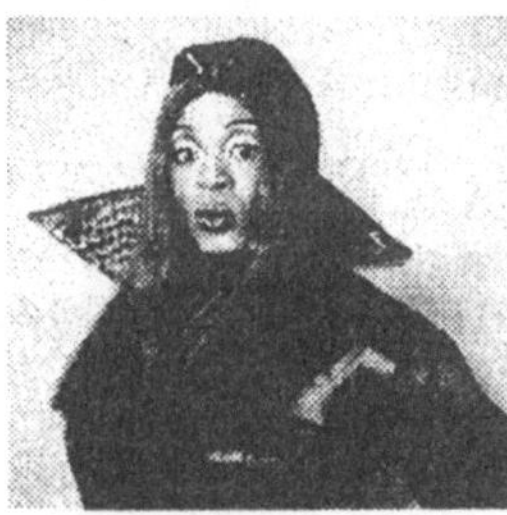

Downtown diva <u>**Mona Foot**</u>

Then there's **Desire, Baby Ru, Lola, Girlina, Ebony Jet, Mona Foot**, etc., etc. Everywhere you look there's some Nubian crossdresser, many of them experts in the kooky disco trend, "runway", which involves gliding across the dance floor like it's a high-fashion catwalk and you're Naomi Campbell but thirty times more flamboyant. It's a gas to watch and very gay.

One place they won't be doing runway or any type of dancing is "Poop", the Friday club night at The Supper Club. Immediately after being profiled in <u>Vanity Fair</u> it closed.

"I love it, it's hot and then it's gone!" shrieked ex-hostess The Lady Bunny. Poop was wildly uneven, but one night was a blast when **Cher** showed up with **Thierry Mugler**, his hunky date, and of all people, **Codie Ravioli**, a pre-op transsexual manager from The **Patricia Field** Boutique.

That's the great part about New York, you never know what type of crazy characters you're going to come in contact with. Like my Egyptian taxi driver the other night, **Ahmed**, who picked me up after my television show taping. Six-feet and muscular, Ahmed gave me a ride I'll never forget…

But I don't want this column to give the impression that life in New York is just about sex, drags and disco music. I dutifully voted in the school board elections (right wing fanatics were trying to take it over), drove down to DC for the Gay & Lesbian March, and I co-hosted New York's Gay Pride Rally. New York may be progressive, but many of its inhabitants are ignorant and homophobic, and the struggle to live a gay lifestyle in peace and harmony ain't always easy. Being glamorous is fabulous darling, so is gay liberation. Combining the two is truly divine, be it in New York, Chicago or Timbuktu. Take care. Love, Linda.

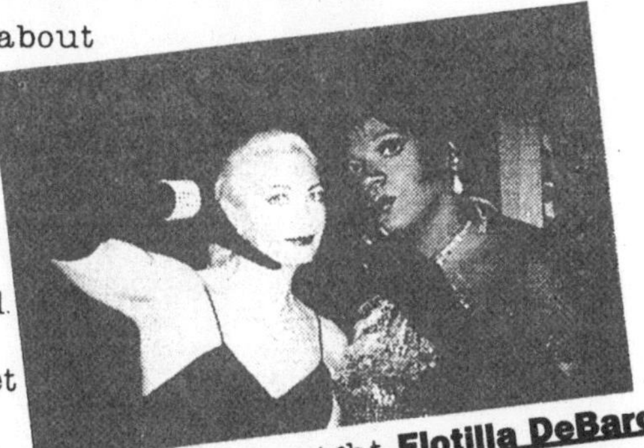

Go-go dancer <u>**Desire**</u> kisses an admirer.

Heavyweight <u>**Flotilla DeBarge**</u> (r) with <u>**Catherine Harkness**</u>.

Tabboo! (l) & <u>**Bunny**</u> at Poop.

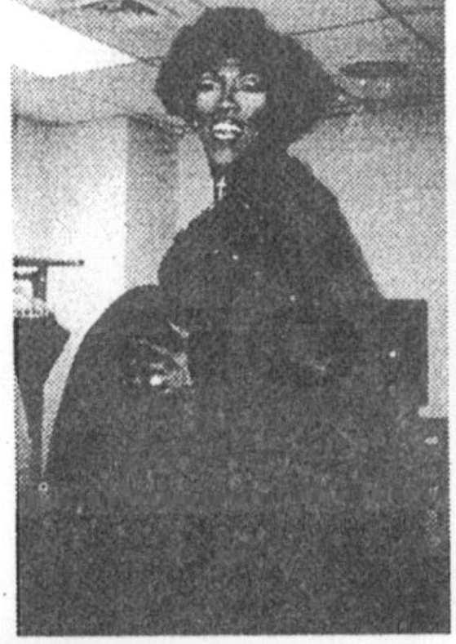

<u>**Princess Diandra**</u> as a pregnant <u>**Whitney Houston**</u> in the green room at "The Jane Pratt Show."

Linda Simpson is a drag queen club hostess, magazine publisher (MY COMRADE), and television personality ("Party Talk" on Manhattan Cable). "I may not be as well known as other local media hogs, er, stars, like Lady Bunny, Lypsinka and RuPaul, but the hip set knows me, and The New York Times called me a kind of mother superior of the downtown drag set. How's them credentials?"

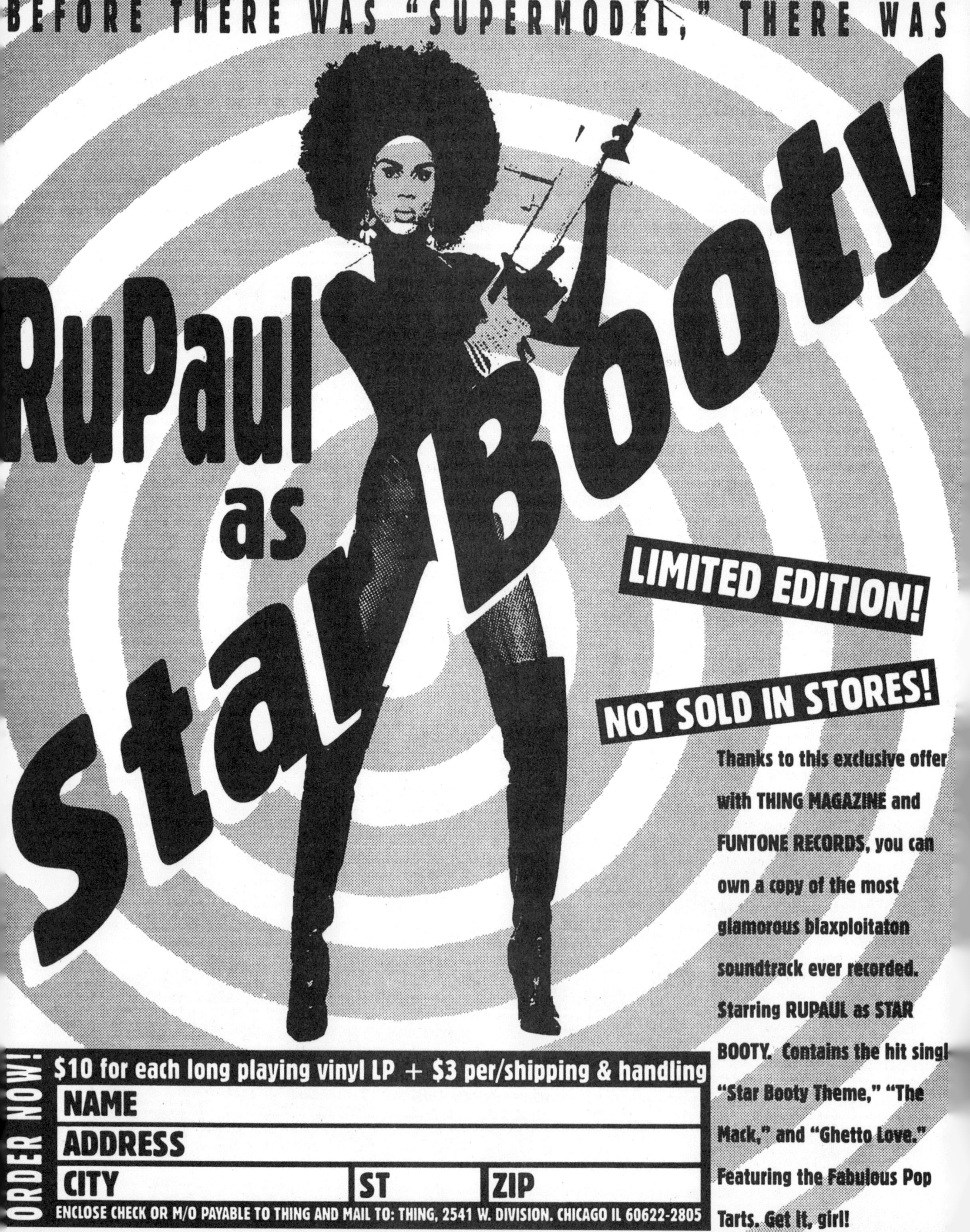

BEFORE THERE WAS "SUPERMODEL," THERE WAS
RuPaul as
Star Bbooty
LIMITED EDITION!
NOT SOLD IN STORES!
Thanks to this exclusive offer with THING MAGAZINE and FUNTONE RECORDS, you can own a copy of the most glamorous blaxploitaton soundtrack ever recorded. Starring RUPAUL as STAR BOOTY. Contains the hit singl "Star Booty Theme," "The Mack," and "Ghetto Love." Featuring the Fabulous Pop Tarts. Get it, girl!
ORDER NOW!
$10 for each long playing vinyl LP + $3 per/shipping & handling
NAME
ADDRESS
CITY
ST
ZIP
ENCLOSE CHECK OR M/O PAYABLE TO THING AND MAIL TO: THING, 2541 W. DIVISION. CHICAGO IL 60622-2805

DeAUNDRA'S DIXIE DIARY

BY DEAUNDRA PEEK

Can y'all believe it's summertime again? Wow, down at Odum's All Double Wide I has got all the ceilin' fans blowin' like crazy just to keep the dew from buildin' up on my forehead! Once again, I has got a ton a stuff to tell!

It is my pleasure to welcome into the world the lovely puppies that my producer **Mr. Richardson's** doggie **Miss Tina** done had recently! Little **Sashay** and **Shanté** are just about the cutest puppy supermodelettes y'all has ever done seen. Y'all should see it when they come a runnin' for the vienner tray!

Seems like comic books is the thing these days, for example they's **Mark Ewert's** book *Ruh Roh* outta Los Angeles that features a mess a folks from all over the place, an y'all, some a them drawin's in there is made for adults only…Look for it at some a what they call progressive booksellers. An' here in Atlanta, our very own **Clayboye** has done it again with his *Gladys' Alien Abduction*, about how some aliens done wignapped superstylist **Gladys Kravitz** lookin' for some glamour or they was gonna destroy all the popcorn on the earth! Gladys gives them plain little things some fierce workin' an' they end up gloriously gorgeous!

Speakin' a that, them 800 East artist has been at it again too! For three weeks in May, I done helped them out with their "Cartoon Show" in the Cartoon Cabaret where I was the pilot, takin' the audience on some kinda Magical Tornado Trailer Twistin' Twirlin' Tour, complete with acts like **Jackson, Miss Saasha, DisFuncsha, La Banana, Miss Shanti** (as a Smurf, can y'all believe that?), an' **Steve Flavet** from the famous band LMNOP doin' his own poetry!

I hope y'all is sittin' down for this one—that show "48 Hours" on CBS done called the other day wantin' us to send a mess a stuff to them so's they might show it! Last month, they exposed Atlanta's **Christian Borden** at that Club USA in New York City when a bunch a people went there for the Style Summit! Keep y'all's eyes peeled!

A course, I can't tell y'all nothin' about **RuPaul** that y'all don't already know on account a cause he has done gone an got so famous, but what I will tell y'all is that my very own authorized video version a "Supermodel" is makin' the rounds! Mr. Richardson done told me that President **Monica Lynch**, a Tommy Boy Records, has done seen it, an' he says everybody thinks it's so good it's gonna win a mess a Oscars! I know y'all has got RuPaul's album "Supermodel of the World" stuck in the stereo permanent like I do!

Get a load a this y'all, chantoise **Joey Arias** has done gone to Vienner, Austria (vienner sausage capitol a the world!) to be head model at **Thierry Mugler's** hi-style fashion show there! Joey's leadin' off tons a other models includin' bigger than life **Jeff Stryker** an' superstar **Brooke Shields**! Also in Vienner, Sweet-as-a-rock-candy **Barbara Spitz** is doin' the "Sound Of Music" there with a knock 'em dead show! Y'all know that Miss Barbara is one a them 2000 people done slept with Miss **Angie Bowie** (don't ask me about

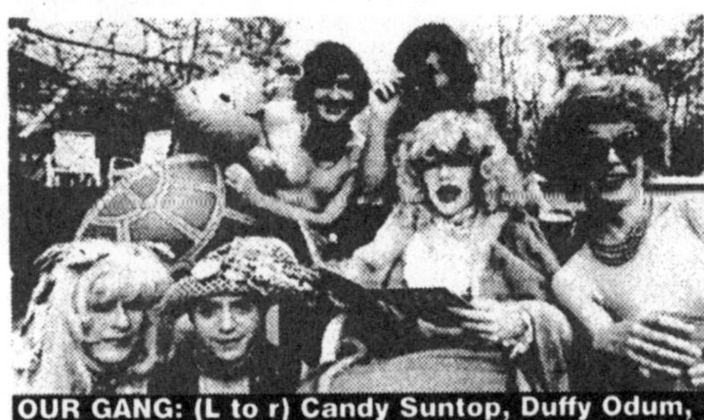

OUR GANG: (L to r) Candy Suntop, Duffy Odum, Dick Richards, Bud Bebo Lowry, me, and Betty Jack Devine. Photo by Mr. Chuck Morgan.

anythin' else they did…), as reported in Miss Angie's book *Backstage Passes*, which comes out in paperback in the fall!

I know y'all saw that story on them **Fabulous Pop Tarts** in the last issue a *Thing*, an' since then they has come out with the remixes a the TV show them "Voyeurvision" on a 12"! **Jimmy Harry**, DJ **Keoki**, an' **Bill Coleman** done 'em, an' they are slammin' everybody at Odum's All Double Wide Mobile Homes Court all over the place! They's 'sposed to be showin' some clips from the TV show in that new **Sharon Stone** movie *Sliver*.

Just about everybody done gone to the March On Washington, an' I'm callin' it "The Feelgood Event of the Century" on account a that's what it was! Y'all guess what, I done ran into none other than my sweet friend **Joan Jett Blakk** at the Washington Monument Drag Showcase! I had fun at the DC Arts Center bein' in a performance with part a the Atlanta Lesbian & Gay Arts Festival folks. Dr **Shirlene Holmes** play "A Lady And A Woman" done wore my hands out clappin'! My very special "Hey Darlin'" to the Funky Dread Sweetie Pie who said he reads this here column! All I can say is, I gave you my button, now write in darlin'!

And a course I was at Atlanta's Gay Pride celebration this year! Entertainment chairperson **Chris Hatcher** had me emceein' some parts a the fun! Chicago socialites **Steve Lafreniere, Jon Volkening**, an' **Gerald Paoli** done made a pilgrimage down here to celebrate with us! I love them boys.

ACT UP Atlanta's second annual WIGWOOD Festival Fundraiser was a blast! Spectacles was made by **Miss Shocka-Laka-Luv, Trina Saxxon, Barbie-Q, Mona Love, Col. Lonnie Fain, Betty Jack DeVine, Theodopolis, Onassis**, an' a mess a celebrities! I had a fit over the Wig Auction, where they done sold off one a RuPaul's tressettes! Special thanks to **Lady Bunny** for the inspiration, an' in lovin' memory a all them people who done passed on from AIDS.

Team Odum's Update: The Summer Community Room Competition left Team Del Vista Ray Mar out in the heat y'all, on account a cause they lost out in the Jello Siftin' Trials. I a course cheered when Duffy Odum won, as usual, but his stomach-ache later wasn't no fun.

Summer Savory Vienner B-B-Q Kabobs

Ingredients
3 cans Hy-Grade Vienners (Imitation style)
1 cup Hy-Grade Ketchip-Lite (Imitation style)

How To Make 'Em
Soak your vienners in the ketchup for a couple of hours, load 'em on the kabob skicks an' set in the sun over the parkin' lot for 20 minutes till hot.. This here is the simplest recipe I know, so's Y'all don't build up no sweat! Yeaaaaa!

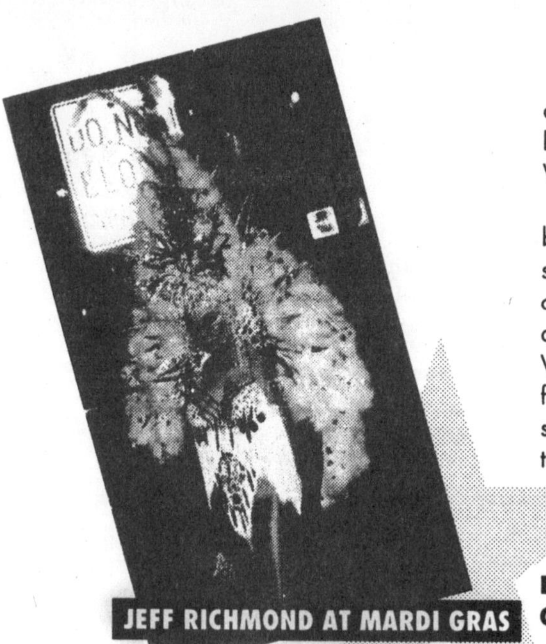

WEST HOLLYWOOD—Well my trusty sidekick (back stabbing, no-rent paying bitch) **Joeseffee** was incarcerated for being a ho in WeHo! No kidding, so I'm going at it alone these days here in my glamorous little suite tucked away up Hilldale St. right off Dicks St. (you know I live off dicks) in the heart of West Hollywood.

Madonna and her girlfriend **Ingrid** were at "Girl Bar" at Studio One twice in the last month. Madonna was resplendent in her gold tooth and was intently watching some lesbian go-go dancers wiggle their goodies. Meanwhile other celebrity fag hags have been flockin' to WeHo in great biblical numbers.

Shannon Dougherty was at Revolver. Sho' nuff she was! Shannon's biggest fan, a drag queen who's a dead ringer for her told me the whole story. Shannon locked herself in the at Revolver and wouldn't come out because she was so upset over maybe being written out of *90210*. So the drag queen went in an comforted her by saying "Shannon you're great, I love you! Look at me, I'm your biggest fan, I'm fucking **Brenda Walsh** *90210*!" So Shannon cheered up and took heart and got drunk in WeHo! The "I Hate Brenda" newsletter dedicated to the little tramp is selling really well here

at A Different Light, the fabulous gay bookstore smack-dab in the middle of WeHo!

Oscar night was FUN! After bopping on up to Sunset to watch the stars get outta their limos at Spago I came down to the club scene to get an earful. Van Go's Ear restaurant in Venice was the site of an Oscar bash for **Jaye Davidson**, who is still smarting over the loss of that golden tampon statuette. Celebs attending included **Mike Meyers**, **Sandra Bernhardt**, **Rosie** and **Tom Arnold**, **Jackee**, **Alec Baldwin**, **Kim Basinger** (slut!), **George Michael** (boy slut!), and a whole slew-o-drag queens!

I hate **Marcia Brady**! And so does everyone at Dragstrip 66. The "Night of a Zillion Jan's" party was a groovy success at the Strip. Queens galore flocked to the club dressed as **Jan** (second-to-the-eldest-but-older-than- the-youngest-one-in-curls) **Brady**. Swell prizes like "The Best of the Bradys" CD were given out featuring the smash hit of the 70s "It's a Sunshine Day!" And may the best Jan win (and she did; you go gurl! Kongrats!)

Sad to say the "Attack of the Living Dead Idols" party at Dragstrip 66 wasn't as successful but maybe those kids will come up with a better-themed party like a "I look like **Ginger Grant/Tina Louise**" party.

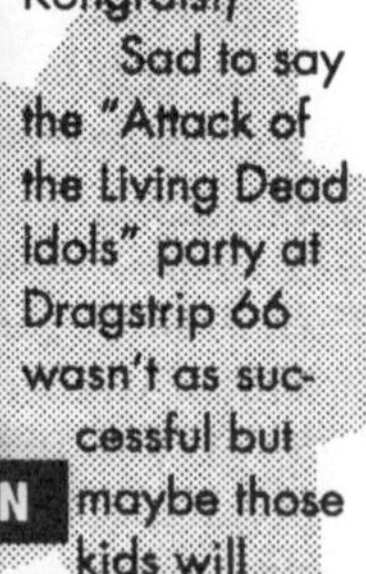

Club Fuck was busted, it's true, it's true! Cops and firemen frisked naked dancers and patron Fuckers a few weeks back. There goes the neighborhood! Rumor has it that porn star **Adrian** got caught with his teeny weeny exposed. Adrian was

doing his famous towel dance at MEAT (which he only gets $75 bucks a night for and puts all *that* money...well, never mind) when an audience member jerked his towel off. With his bare meat dangling, Adrian proceeded to jump off the stage and sock the fairy in his kisser!

Thursdays at Mickey's it's the "Calendar Man Contest", so I bopped in there with my fired **José** to check it out. Porn pup **Antonio** (star of "Viva Macho 2") was wiggling on the stage then proceeded to pull his undies down and show us his bare Black/Puerto Rican buns before turning around and even daring to flash his brown worm! I told him his

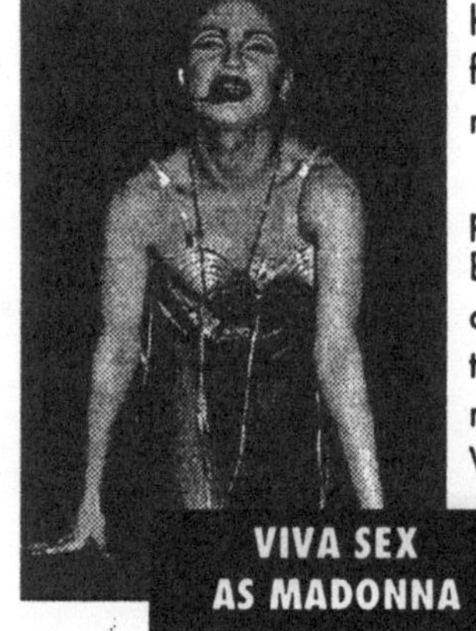

movie was good and he giggled like a gleeful pixie and thanked me.

New clubs are poppin' up like daisies. Better Days just started on Sundays at Peanuts, the best (scuzzy, scummy) lil' drag bar in WeHo. It was nothing but gay boys, queens, and lezzies, though, how disgusting!

Where to go on a Saturday night before heading to the big bad black Catch One? Well me an **Ron** bopped into Manhattan Coolers along with **The Goddess** (aka **Niagara Rane**) and her sidekick **Toe-Knee**. Oriental drag queens **Asia** and **Ming Vase** weren't there but my dear friend **Miz Ruthie** was hosting karoake. She was diva and she shined. The chile was decked out in wigs, go-go boots, hats, and mini-skirts along with gloves and plastic beads for accessories. She changed outfits twice and started the show off with "I Will Survive" followed by **Patsy Cline**'s "I Fall to Pieces". It was priceless and Ruthie was a most excellent hostess, serving us bar snacks, margaritas, and summer hummers with cute lil' purple plastic mermaids floating in the glasses.

Pia Zadora is a whore! Miss

Thing, her nanny, and her string-haired chilluns were sitting outside of "The Cultured Glass" slurping down yogurt when me and my pals **Travis** and **T-Mack** passed by. I waved and the bitch looked at me and *snarled*.

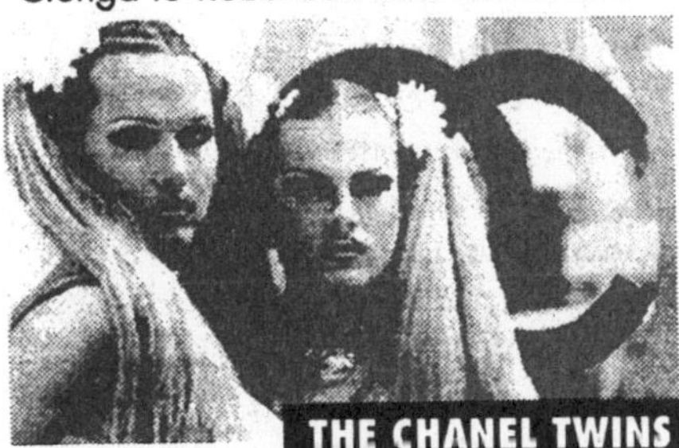
JAZZMUN'S BACK

So to that I say, be careful who you try an' dis, Missy, you stringy-haired, fake-tittied, lousy-actress, sunburned, fishy, no talent in yo' little pinky only claim to fame bein "Lonely Lady" ho! And your agent is getting a copy of *Thing* on his desk. Maybe you'll rejoice over yo' name being in print for the first time since you recorded "When the Rain Begins to Fall" with **Jermaine Jackson** over a fucking decade ago!

Mardi Gras in WeHo was fun! The streets were blocked off from La Cienga to Robertson and fairies flew

THE CHANEL TWINS

through the air with the greatest of ease. **Lovely Carol** held a kick-ass Mardi Gras show and cracked jokes about Fat Tuesday and her waistline. Eat all the Pop Tarts you want Miss Thang, we luv ya, honey! Beads were handed out a plenty and I danced the night away with my gorgeous boyfriend **Rafael**, licking the sweat off his hairy brown Puerto Rican body. I'm a ho and proud of it!

I bopped into Lipstix Thursday

and was lucky enough to sit by the infamous **Chanel Twins**, **Linda Evangelipstick** and **Christy Girlington**. They were very ladylike till **Jazzmun** started bumping pussies with them at which time they began screaming like teenage girls on their periods who just had a wet dream about **Luke Perry**. It was a madhouse, but the twin bitches worked the runway in their matching ensembles. (Shoes didn't match though; "queens on a budget" I say. As my white Texan daddy would say, "If ya cain't do somethin' right then don't do it at all!")

Jazzum bopped us all doin' Miss One (**Diana Ross**) "Muscles" while a big-dicked black stripper and a blonde white boy stripper felt the brown diva up and down while she gushed and giggled and forgot the words. I bopped in a week later and sat down with **Erin Krystle**'s boyfriend **Scott** who was escorting **Apollonia** to the show. I was a tad disappointed Apples didn't grace us with another live song like the previous week but she was decked to the max in black and lookin *fur-eee-us!* With her was the lovely and gentle Miss **Pebbles**. Pebbles serves you real fish. She was a real lady and bopped a tiger-striped cat-suit with her long tresses and fierce make-up. **Viva Sex** bopped 'em when she did "Like a Virgin" looking uncannily like Madonna herself. It was the "Truth or Dare" remix by the way. Then some little ethnic fairy named **Mario** had a birthday and Jazzmun called him up on stage to sing happy b-day an let him fondle the strippers while he giggled, gushed, an blushed like a whimsical lad, go figure!

Down to The Greenery to eat

and chat with the cute French waiter **Denis** (it ain't the same there no more though since cute Brazilian waiter **Marshall** moved to Texas as rumor has it) and who should be sittin' there with three fags but Miss "Young and Restless" herself **Heather Toms** (**Victor** and **Nikki**'s chile)! Heather was eatin' her anorexic ass off after partyin' at Mickey's.

The *Advocate*'s token Nigger-O-Color and half-white Jewboy **David Ehrenstein** bopped into the New Athletics Club to hang out on his off day and get some sun on his light-skinned ass. He tanned by the pool, ordered a tuna melt, and walked around with his belly a-bulgin' over his swimsuit like a cute pot-bellied piglet. His new book, *The Scorsese Picture*, is just ready to go! The Hollywood high-yella gossip hound promised more surprizes in his future *Advocate* column too!

ERIN KRYSTLE

Everyone's gossipin' out how the *Advocate* no longer provides coffee service 'cause they be too poor, and that budget cash spooge of 1.5 million ain't gettin' the job done. Looks like those snotty rich white gay thirtysomethings got what they deserved. It don't feel too nice being on foodstamps and welfare does it **John Knoebel**? The 10th floor on Hollywood Blvd. is shrinking as they scrambled to also cut dental benefits and cram their staff-o-fairies into half the space of the suite.

An ya'll wanted to vote for **Clinton**? Who by the way has a half black child from a female prostitute in Arkansas.

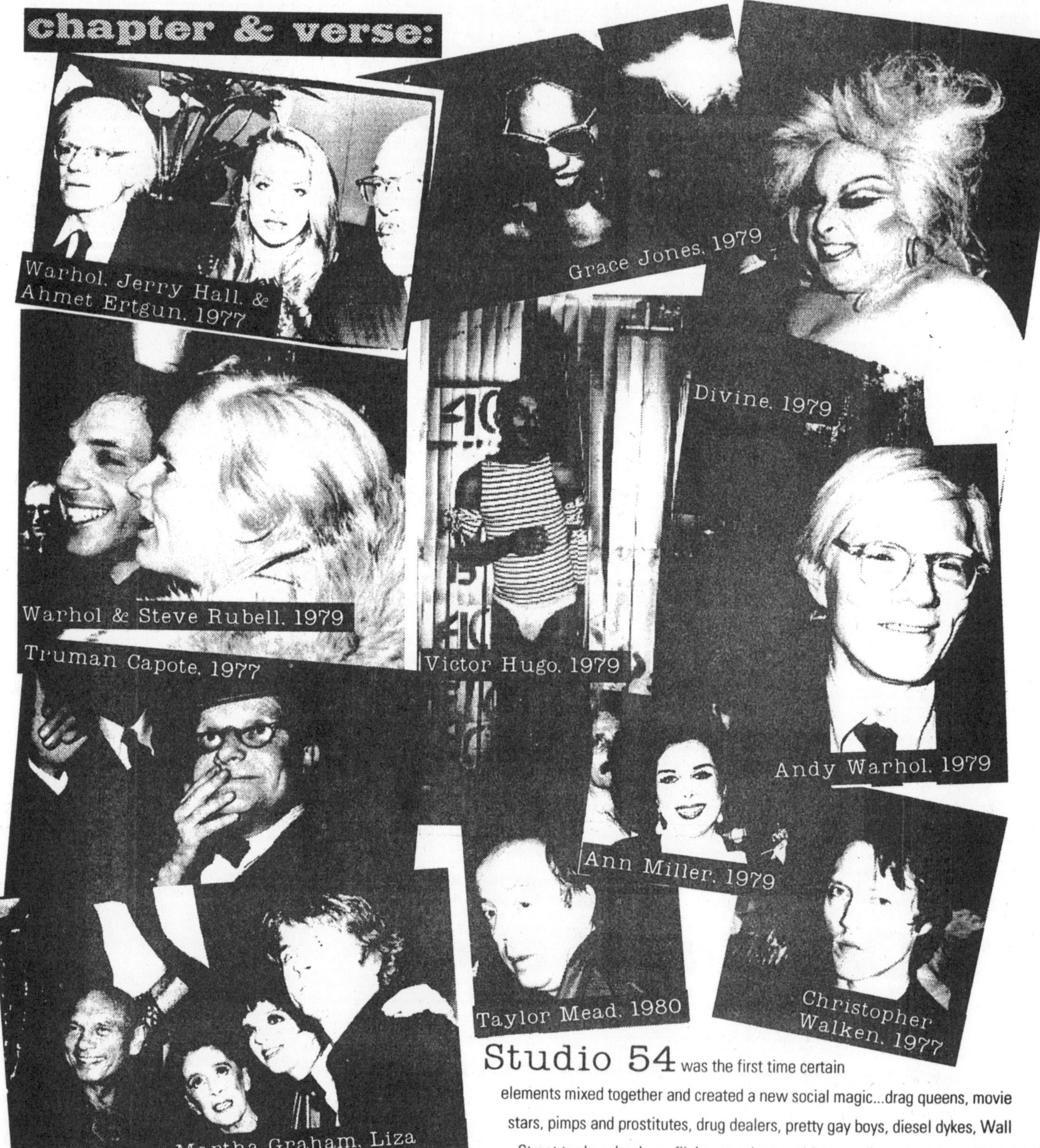

Studio 54 was the first time certain elements mixed together and created a new social magic...drag queens, movie stars, pimps and prostitutes, drug dealers, pretty gay boys, diesel dykes, Wall Street traders, bankers, flight attendants, athletes ,artists, musicians, black, white, yellow, red, brown, and lavender. Everybody but the Pope passed through those doors. These photos are just a sample of the daily fare to be found there. As house photographer, I was given carte blanche to shoot at will in ANY area of the club. These are a few of my favorite people from that time period. Even now when I look at these images, they send me reeling back to those crazy coked-out nights where those on the dance floor mimicked the moon with the spoon. Long live the daze of glory known as Studio 54... never before and never again.

--Bobby Miller

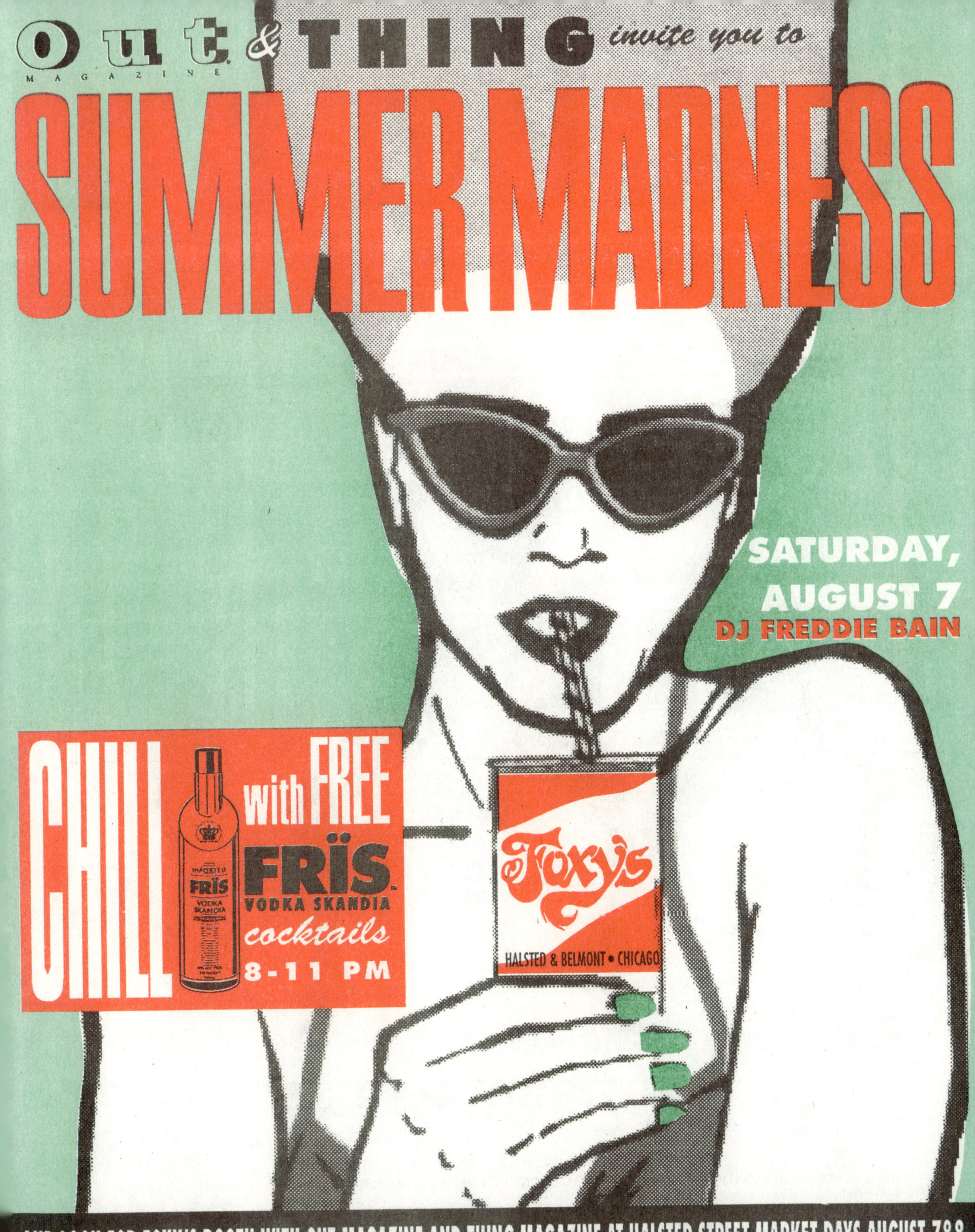

Out & THING invite you to
MAGAZINE
SUMMER MADNESS
SATURDAY, AUGUST 7
DJ FREDDIE BAIN
CHILL with FREE FRÏS VODKA SKANDIA cocktails 8-11 PM
IMPORTED FRÏS VODKA SKANDIA
Foxy's
HALSTED & BELMONT • CHICAGO
AND LOOK FOR FOXY'S BOOTH WITH OUT MAGAZINE AND THING MAGAZINE AT HALSTED STREET MARKET DAYS AUGUST 7&8.

RuPAUL
SUPERMODEL OF THE WORLD

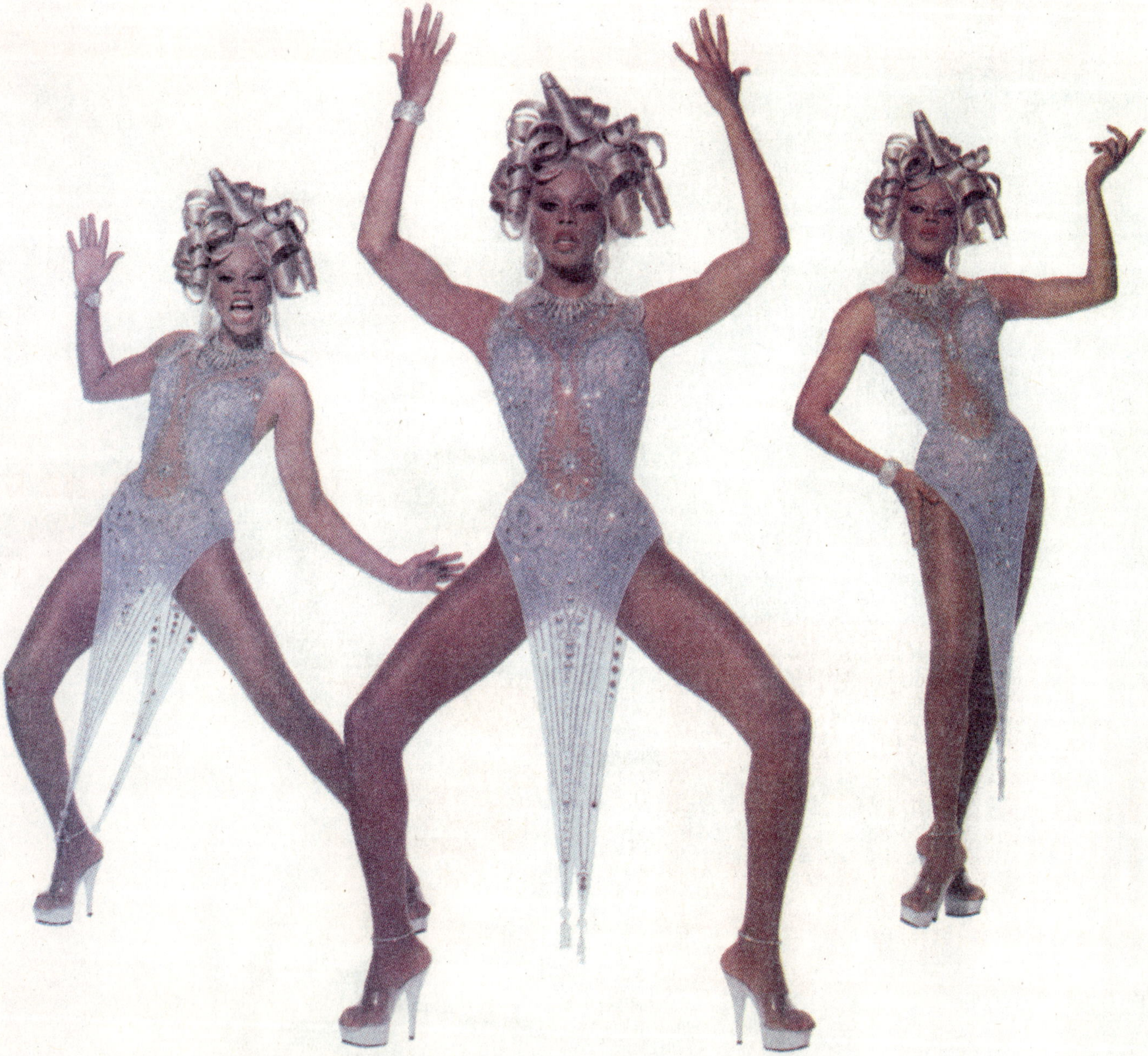

MANAGEMENT:

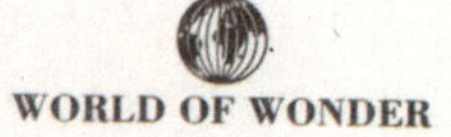

WORLD OF WONDER

THE DEBUT ALBUM. INCLUDES THE SINGLES
"SUPERMODEL (YOU BETTER WORK)" AND "BACK TO MY ROOTS".

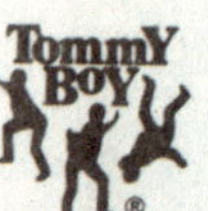

THING
© 2025 THING and Primary Information

ISBN: 979-8-9885736-4-7

THING was published between 1989 and 1993. The first two issues of the magazine were sized at 7 x 8.5 Inches, with all remaining issues sized at 8 x 11 inches. For the purposes of this publication, the first two issues have been scaled up to 8 x 11 inches to match the dimensions of the later issues.

Editors: Robert Ford, Trent D. Adkins, Lawrence Warren
Designer: Simone Bouyer
Managing Editors (2025): James Hoff and Sam Korman
Designer (2025): Rick Myers

Printed at Musumeci, Italy

Primary Information would like to thank Phil Aarons, Simone Bouyer, DeForrest Brown Jr., Stephanie Coleman, Ken Hare, Solveig Nelson, and Rachel Valinsky.

Primary Information is a 501(c)(3) non-profit organization that receives generous support through grants from the Michael Asher Foundation, Galerie Buchholz, the Patrick and Aimee Butler Family Foundation, The Cowles Charitable Trust, Empty Gallery, The Ford Foundation, The Fox Aarons Foundation, the Helen Frankenthaler Foundation, Furthermore: a program of the J. M. Kaplan Fund, the Graham Foundation for Advanced Studies in the Fine Arts, Greene Naftali, the Greenwich Collection Ltd, the John W. and Clara C. Higgins Foundation, Metabolic Studio, the New York City Department of Cultural Affairs in partnership with the City Council, the New York State Council on the Arts with the support of the Office of the Governor and the New York State Legislature, the Orbit Fund, the Robert Rauschenberg Foundation, the Stichting Egress Foundation, VIA Art Fund, The Jacques Louis Vidal Charitable Fund, The Andy Warhol Foundation for the Visual Arts, the Wilhelm Family Foundation, and individuals worldwide. Primary Information receives support from the Arison Arts Foundation, The Willem de Kooning Foundation, the Marian Goodman Foundation, the Henry Luce Foundation, the Mellon Foundation, and Teiger Foundation through the Coalition of Small Arts NYC.